CENGAGE ADVANTAGE: SOCIOLOGY

United States Map

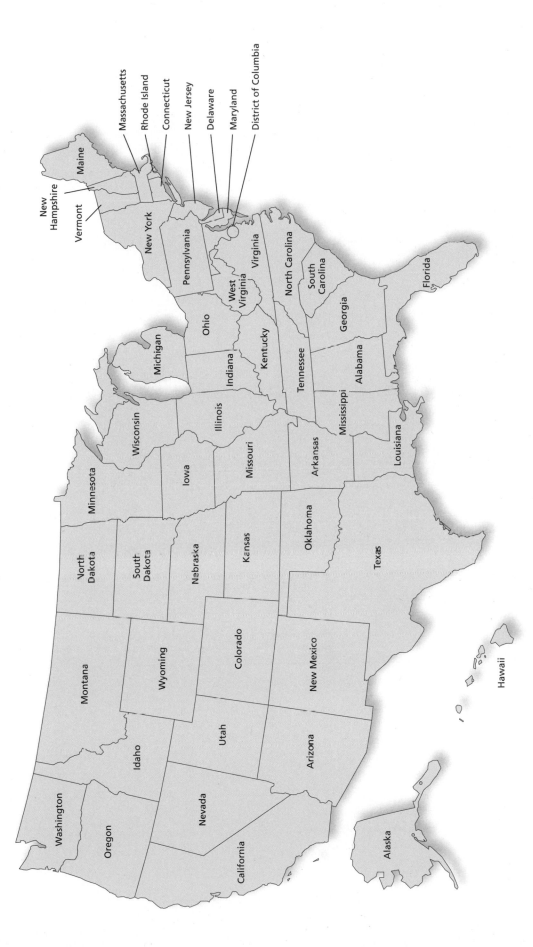

World Map

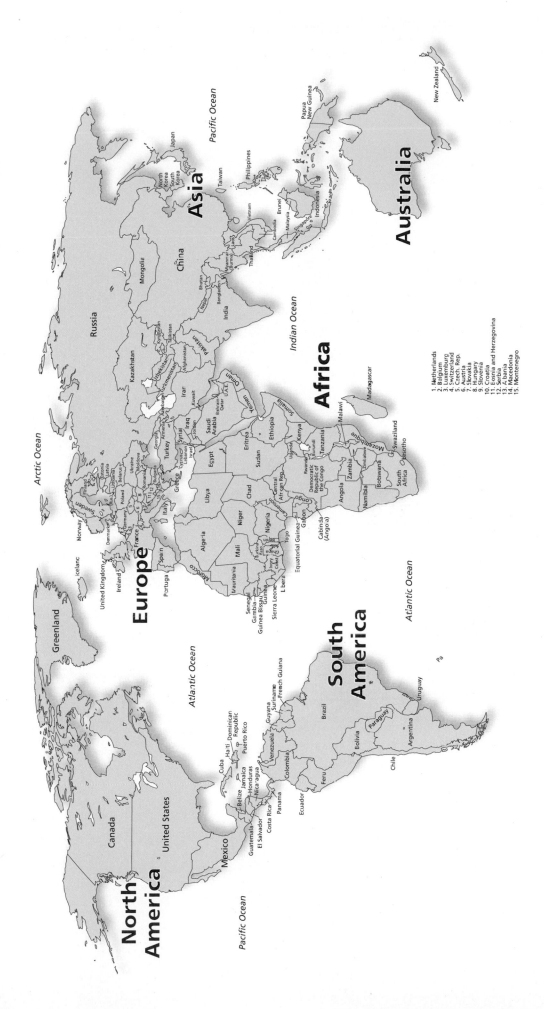

CENGAGE ADVANTAGE: SOCIOLOGY

ELEVENTH EDITION

Jon M. Shepard

Virginia Polytechnic Institute
and State University

WADSWORTH
CENGAGE Learning™

Australia • Brazil • Japan • Korea • Mexico • Singapore • Spain • United Kingdom • United States

Cengage Advantage: Sociology, 11ᵗʰ Edition
Jon M. Shepard

Acquiring Sponsoring Editor: Erin Mitchell

Development Editor: Liana Sarkisian

Assistant Editor: John Chell

Editorial Assistant: Mallory Ortberg

Media Editor: Melanie Cregger

Marketing Manager: Andrew Keay

Marketing Coordinator: Jack Ward

Marketing Communications Manager: Laura Localio

Design and Production Services: PreMediaGlobal

Art Director: Caryl Gorska

Manufacturing Planner: Judy Inouye

Rights Acquisitions Specialist: Tom McDonough

Photo Research: PreMediaGlobal

Text Research: PreMediaGlobal

Cover Designer: Caryl Gorska

Cover Image: Absodels/Getty Images

Compositor: PreMediaGlobal

For product information and technology assistance, contact us at
Cengage Learning Customer & Sales Support, 1-800-354-9706

For permission to use material from this text or product,
submit all requests online at **www.cengage.com/permissions**.
Further permissions questions can be emailed to
permissionrequest@cengage.com.

Library of Congress Control Number: 2011936339

ISBN-13: 978-1-111-82957-5

ISBN-10: 1-111-82957-8

Wadsworth, Cengage Learning
20 Davis Drive
Belmont, CA 94002-3098
USA

Cengage Learning is a leading provider of customized learning solutions with office locations around the globe, including Singapore, the United Kingdom, Australia, Mexico, Brazil, and Japan. Locate your local office at **www.cengage.com/region**

Cengage Learning products are represented in Canada by Nelson Education, Ltd.

To learn more about Wadsworth, Cengage Learning, visit **www.cengage.com**

Purchase any of our products at your local college store or at our preferred online store **www.cengagebrain.com.**

Instructors: Please visit **login.cengage.com** and log in to access instructor-specific resources.

Printed in Canada
1 2 3 4 5 6 7 15 14 13 12 11

For Jon

About the Author

While an undergraduate student, Jon Shepard
was inspired and nurtured by his sociology
professor, Richard Scudder. After graduating
from Michigan State University with a Ph.D. in
sociology, Shepard taught introductory sociology
and the sociology of organizations at the
University of Kentucky. For fourteen years, he
was Head of the Virginia Tech Department of
Management. He is the author of ten books and
more than forty professional journal articles.
He has received teaching awards, including the
University of Kentucky Great Teacher Award,
at both universities.

Contents in Brief

Contents

Boxes

Maps

World Maps

Preface

A Note to Students from the Author

The issues discussed in my freshman introductory sociology class were not the sort that I spent time thinking about: Is divorce more likely or less likely when people have the same social-class background? Are some races inferior to others? What is the social significance of Darwinism?

Suddenly, I began to see human behavior in a different light. I discovered that Richard Wright's classics, *Native Son* and *Black Boy*, are not merely stories about black youth but rather autobiographical reflections of the black experience in America. Prejudice and discrimination are not just characteristics of individuals; they are part of society as a whole. I learned that football, the game I was playing, is actually as much a business as a sport. It became apparent that the fraternity I was about to join was not only a brotherhood but also part of the campus social hierarchy.

I began to see social relationships as essential for human survival. And if the world is a stage and all its men and women merely players, these players generally deliver their lines and act out their parts as if they were rehearsed, and with a definite flair for mimicry. Yet, the action that sociologists label *social structure* depends less on the conscious learning of appropriate attitudes, beliefs, and behavior than on unreflective acceptance of our culture and society. In this sense, we are like puppets responding to tugs on the strings that bind us to essential social relationships—relationships in which people, I came to understand, do not usually behave randomly and do not always behave only as individuals. People often think, feel, and behave in rather predictable ways because of what they have been taught and because of the many social pressures to which they have been exposed. At the same time, however, individuals interacting with others create their own understandings of situations. In this sense, human beings are not like puppets, because they have the potential to buck tradition; they are active, thinking creatures even when they are conforming.

Society was demystified for me. I came to value sociology as a tool for understanding the world. In fact, this experience led me to major in sociology and subsequently to obtain my Ph.D. in the field. I have never regretted those choices.

You might not major in sociology. You can, however, enjoy this course and take lifelong benefits from the slant on social life that sociology provides.

A Note to Instructors from the Author

Several specific goals continue to energize me as we introduce the significance and excitement of sociology to students. First, sociology—with its perspectives, concepts, theories, and research findings—offers a window on the social forces that affect us all daily. This perspective is vital for students as they grapple to understand the social factors that promote patterned behavior in themselves and others. Second, the material must be readable and at the same time theoretically and empirically sound. Third, students deserve a textbook design that is dynamic and demonstrates, clearly, the application of a new perspective to their personal lives. Fourth, I want a presentation from which students can not only learn the basics of sociology, but can acquire the ability to pose their own questions about social life. Finally, the catalyst: stimulate students to become more active learners.

Unifying Themes and Features

Sociological Imagination

The study of sociology encourages critical thinking about conventional wisdom through the development of the sociological imagination—the mind-set that enables individuals to see the relationship between events in their personal lives and events in their society. To this end, each chapter opens with a question about some aspect of social life. The answer to each question contradicts a popular or commonsense belief. Sometimes the question will focus on a result that even sociologists doubted until a sufficient amount of convincing research was done. The correct answer is given at the beginning of the chapter and further elaboration of the explanation will be within the chapter itself. Topics covered include the following:

- Suicide (Chapter 1, "The Sociological Perspective")
- Television and violence (Chapter 4, "Socialization over the Life Course")
- Selfishness and human nature (Chapter 5, "Social Structure and Society")
- Date rape (Chapter 7, "Deviance and Social Control")
- Racial inequality (Chapter 9, "Inequalities of Race and Ethnicity")
- Gender income inequality (Chapter 10, "Inequalities of Gender")
- National health care (Chapter 15, "Health Care and Aging")
- Revolutions and social change (Chapter 18, "Social Change and Collective Behavior")

See Sociology in Your Life

A boxed feature called *See Sociology in Your Life* now appears in each chapter. This feature presents interesting, timely, and relevant examples intended to stimulate the sociological examination in students' personal lives. Here are some examples:

- "Should You Believe Everything You Read?" (Chapter 2, "Social Research")
- "Facebook and Personal Identity" (Chapter 4, "Socialization over the Life Course")
- "Privacy in a Digital World" (Chapter 6, "Groups and Organizations")
- "Cyber Criminals Want Your Identity" (Chapter 7, "Deviance")
- "Cyber Bullying and Stratification" (Chapter 8, "Social Stratification")
- "Spinning a Web of Hate" (Chapter 9, "Inequalities of Race and Ethnicity")
- "Gender-Based Hierarchy" (Chapter 10, "Inequalities of Gender")
- "Looking for Mr. or Ms. Right" (Chapter 11, "Family")
- "How to Avoid Bigotry in Sport" (Chapter 16, "Sport")
- "Terrorist Attacks and Disaster Myths" (Chapter 18, "Social Change and Collective Behavior")

Of course, opportunities to cultivate a sociological imagination permeate the entire text.

Consider This research

A second boxed feature within each chapter, entitled *Consider This Research*, presents the theory, methods, conclusions, and implications of significant sociological studies. This feature demonstrates the scientific method in social research.

Several criteria guided the selection of these research studies. Some studies, such as Emile Durkheim's work on the social antecedents of suicide, are sociological landmarks. Others, such as Philip Zimbardo's experiment involving a simulated prison and George Ritzer's analysis of the McDonaldization of higher education, reinforce a major point in a chapter. Still other studies illustrate the imaginative use of a major research method. Durkheim's application of existing sources in the study of suicide and Donna Eder's use of a variety of research methods in her study of popularity in middle school are examples.

Given these criteria, it is hardly surprising that many of the studies included are sociological "classics"; they have had a lasting influence on the field and are continuously cited by researchers. Like classics in all fields, these pieces of research generally have high interest value. They are innovative in approach and explore important topics in ingenious ways. If read carefully, these detailed accounts of significant sociological studies cannot fail to pique interest in social research and stimulate the sociological imagination. Here are some other examples:

- "Teenagers in a Cultural Bind" (Chapter 3, "Culture")
- "High School Reunions" (Chapter 4, "Socialization over the Life Course")
- "Adopting Statuses in a Simulated Prison" (Chapter 5, "Culture and Society")
- "Who's Popular, Who's Not" (Chapter 8, "Social Stratification")
- "No Shame in My Game" (Chapter 9, "Inequalities of Race and Ethnicity")
- "Men's Work, Women's Work" (Chapter 10, "Inequalities of Gender")
- "The McDonaldization of Higher Education" (Chapter 12, "Education")
- "Tough Guys, Wimps, and Weenies" (Chapter 16, "Sport")
- "Gang Violence" (Chapter 17, "Population and Urbanization")
- "The Withering of the American Dream?" (Chapter 18, "Social Change and Collective Behavior")

Accent on Theory

Each chapter contains a prominent section on the distinctive views of three major theoretical perspectives—functionalism, conflict theory, and symbolic interactionism. In each chapter a table, entitled "Focus on Theoretical Perspectives," presents succinct illustrations for the three theoretical perspectives. Two emerging social theories, feminist social theory and postmodernism, are introduced in Chapter 1.

Global Perspective

Never has the world been as interconnected as it is now. Gone are the comfort and simplicity of geographic isolation. Events in one nation can have repercussions for other nations. Thus, it is imperative that some sociological phenomena be viewed in a global frame. Consequently, this edition offers ample coverage of globalization, global crime and crime control, global terrorism, global inequality, global gender inequality, global ethnic diversity, global political and economic systems, world religions, global health care, and globalization and sport.

To this end, cross-cultural examples and research are throughout the text. This cross-cultural emphasis alerts students to our tendency to accept our own culture while rejecting others. By interacting mentally with other cultures within the context of sociological concepts, theories, and research findings, students are better able to apply the sociological perspective to their daily lives. This cross-cultural emphasis encourages in students a more self-conscious awareness of their own society and a better understanding of other cultures.

In each chapter, a world map feature, entitled *Think Globally*, displays a worldwide comparison of a particular social phenomenon. In addition, a U.S. map is included in each chapter. Each *Sociology Eyes America* permits a state and regional comparison of some aspect of American culture.

Critical Thinking

Intellectual historians trace critical thinking—questioning commonly held assumptions—to fifth-century-B.C. Greece, particularly to the Athenians (Brinton 1963). Full-fledged Western interest in critical analysis did not appear until the eighteenth century, the period known as the Enlightenment (Gay 1966). Respect for critical and reasoned analysis has been a key element of the Western world ever since.

Critical thinking is crucial for today's college students. First, the tradition of liberal education is the tradition of critical thought (Pelikan 1992). Second, as the nature of work continues to move from physical labor to cerebral activities, the facility for critical reasoning becomes an increasingly valuable asset on the job. Third, it doesn't take a rocket scientist to realize the need for critical thought among all American voters; behavior of our political leaders makes this point daily. Finally, but not least, critical thinking is vital in personal contexts such as family life, decision making, and personal enrichment.

Critical thinking is incorporated in this edition in three ways:

1. **The SQ3R method.** The promotion of critical thinking lies at the heart of the "question" step of the SQ3R method described in "A Text Message" prior to Chapter 1.

   Although gaining information is essential, we emphasize further interaction with the knowledge as it is being acquired. Following are some sample critical-thinking SQ3R questions:

   - If prisons do not rehabilitate, what are some alternatives?
   - Is the negative image of the poor in America accurate?
   - What is required to prove the existence of the power elite in American society?

2. **Critical-thinking questions.** Critical-thinking questions are liberally interspersed throughout each chapter. Questions follow the *Consider This Research* and *See Sociology in Your Life* features. A critical-thinking question is also included in each table, figure, and map. A set of four to six critical-thinking questions appears in the *Review Guide* at the end of each chapter. Consequently, a critical-thinking opportunity appears at least every few pages. These wide-ranging questions encourage students to think critically and creatively about the ideas within a

chapter. Sometimes students will apply these ideas to a particular aspect of society. At other times students will use sociological ideas to analyze and understand events and experiences in their own lives.

For example each *Consider This Research* closes with a series of critical-thinking questions under the heading, "Thinking About the Research." The subsequent questions follow a description of Stanley Milgram's study of group pressure and conformity:

- Discuss the ethical implications of Milgram's experiment.
- If the researcher had not been present as an authority figure during the experiment to approve the use of all shock levels, do you think group pressure would have been as effective? Explain.

3. **The sociological imagination.** It is easy to fall into a pattern of nonreflection about prevailing ideas that are passed from generation to generation. The feature *Using the Sociological Imagination*, described earlier, opens each chapter with a question designed to challenge some aspect of a social myth.

What Is New in the Eleventh Edition?

New topics include modernization, postmodernization, terrorism, cyberbullying, global crime and crime control, global and domestic ethnic diversity, Middle Easterners as a U.S. minority group, global gender inequality, global health care, world religions, disability, Obama health care reform, globalization and sport, the Tea Party, and social media and crowds. In the process of adding, revising, and expanding existing topics, over 30 new concepts and more than 400 new references have been added. In addition to twenty-eight new figures and tables, the most current information is added to other figures and tables.

Nearly all of the U.S. and world topical maps are either new (16) or updated (12). Ten of the world maps are new to this edition:

- Access to World Markets (Chapter 4, "Socialization")
- Relative Wealth of Nations (Chapter 8, "Social Stratification")
- Ethnic Diversity (Chapter 9, "Inequalities of Race and Ethnicity")
- Global Gender Gap Index Rankings (Chapter 10, "Inequalities of Gender")
- Gay Marriage (Chapter 11, "Family")
- Illiteracy Rates (Chapter 12, "Education")
- International Terrorist Incidents (Chapter 13, "Political and Economic Institutions")
- Religions of the World (Chapter 14, "Religion")
- Old-Age Dependency (Chapter 15, "Health Care and Aging")
- Political Violence (Chapter 18, "Social Change and Collective Behavior")

Six of the U.S. maps are new:

- Immigration to the United States (Chapter 3, "Culture")
- Employment/Population Rate by State (Chapter 5, "Social Structure")
- Percentage of Children in Single-Parent Families (Chapter 11, "Family")
- Importance of Religion in One's Life (Chapter 14, "Religion")
- Teen Birth Rate (Chapter 17, "Population and Urbanization")
- Children in Single-Parent Families (Chapter 18, "Social Change and Collective Behavior")

Sociology comprises eighteen chapters divided into five parts. The following thumbnail sketches of each chapter place the additions in the context of their appearance. New topics appear in bold typeface.

Part 1 contains chapters introducing the nature of sociological theory and inquiry. **Chapter 1** first covers the sociological perspective, its practical uses, and history. Three major sociological theories (functionalism, conflict theory, and symbolic interactionism) close the section. New material expands the presentation of two emerging social theories, feminist theory and postmodern theory. **Chapter 2** explores the major research methods used by sociologists. It concludes with an enhanced discussion of ethics in social research. The concept of ethnography is new to this edition.

Part 2 presents the foundations of social structure. **Chapter 3** promotes a broader understanding of the pivotal concept of culture. It expands the section on culture as a tool kit and broadens the concept of counterculture to include terrorism.

Chapter 4 focuses on socialization, the process of learning to participate in society through the acquisition of culture. Cyberbullying contains new information and early adulthood receives a new emphasis.

Chapter 5 examines the concept of social structure. It explains and illustrates the major sociological concepts underlying social structure. This chapter contains a new section on modernization and sociological theory with an expanded description of preindustrial society. **Chapter 6** distinguishes among various types of groups and the interactions within them. **Chapter 7** opens with the biological, psychological, and sociological explanations of deviance. The last half of the chapter focuses on global and domestic crime. The coverage of juvenile crime now includes race and gender. There are new sections on global terrorism, global crime, and global crime control.

Part 3 explores social inequality. **Chapter 8** takes up social stratification, one of the most integral areas of sociology. It incorporates new material on global poverty, including dependency theory. **Chapter 9** turns to the significance of race, ethnicity, prejudice, and discrimination in America. A new section covers global and domestic ethnic diversity. Middle Easterners are new to the coverage of U.S. ethnic groups and white ethnics have new coverage. New concepts include racial profiling, transnationals, and internal colonialism. **Chapter 10** concentrates on gender inequality. It now embodies a new section on global gender inequality and adds the chivalry hypothesis.

Part 4 covers basic social institutions. **Chapter 11** looks at the family. New to this edition is racial and ethnic group differences in family. **Chapter 12** turns to the organization of schools, the functions of education, educational inequality, and the transmission of culture in schools. New information on competitors of traditional public schools includes for-profit schools, homeschooling, and the concept of school choice. A new section on higher education entails state budgets and college costs, community colleges, distance learning, and for-profit colleges and universities.

Chapter 13 covers the political and economic institutions. This chapter includes a new section on terrorism. It has expanded coverage on multinational corporations and the nature of work in the contemporary American economy. **Chapter 14** delves into sociology's unique perspective on the institution of religion. New to the eleventh edition is coverage of world religions and Islamic fundamentalism. In addition, it introduces neo-paganism and the concept of ecclesia.

Chapter 15 is a combined chapter covering health care and the inequalities of age. Global health care, disability, and Obama health care reform are additions to this chapter. **Chapter 16** explores the institution of sport. Its major topics include the nature of sport, theoretical perspectives and sport, sport and social mobility, racial and ethnic inequality in sport, and gender inequality in sport. A new section on globalization and sport closes the chapter.

Part 5 turns to the topic of social change. **Chapter 17** contains the related topics of population and urbanization. **Chapter 18** combines the areas of social change and collective behavior. New to this chapter are the Tea Party as a social movement and social media and crowds.

Review Guide

The Review Guide at the end of each chapter begins with integrated goals and chapter summary. Next is a Concept Review of approximately 50 percent of the concepts introduced in each chapter. Students can test their grasp of key concepts by matching concepts with definitions. A Check Yourself review consists of a sample of questions taken directly from the Check Yourself questions appearing at the end of each major chapter section. In each chapter, a Graphic Review feature tests understanding of a particular table or figure in the chapter. Several Critical-Thinking Questions follow the

Concept Review. These broad questions provide practice for essay tests. An Answer Key closes each Review Guide.

Supplements for the Eleventh Edition

Supplements for the Instructor
Instructor's Edition of *Sociology: The Essentials*. An Instructor's Edition (IE) of this text containing several features useful to instructors is available. The IE contains a walk-through of the several themes and many features of *Sociology* along with a complete listing of available bundles for this text. To obtain a copy of the Instructor's Edition, contact your Cengage Sales Representative.

Instructor's Resource Manual with Test Bank. This manual offers the instructor brief chapter outlines, student learning objectives, detailed lecture outlines, and teaching suggestions to facilitate in-class discussion. American Sociological Association (ASA) recommendations are noted for each chapter and matched to the A-heads of the detailed outlines to help instructors streamline their teaching methods with the American Sociological Association. Innovative class activities and Internet activities are included for each chapter. The test bank has 180 new questions, which are noted, and each multiple-choice and true/false item has the question type (factual, applied, or conceptual) and corresponding learning objective indicated.

ExamView® Computerized Testing. Create, deliver, and customize tests and study guides (both print and online) in minutes with this easy-to-use assessment and tutorial system. ExamView offers both a Quick Test Wizard and an Online Test Wizard that guide you step-by-step through the process of creating tests. The test appears on screen exactly as it will print or display online. ExamView includes all new eleventh edition test bank questions. Using ExamView's complete word-processing capabilities, you can enter an unlimited number of new questions or edit existing questions included with ExamView.

PowerLecture™ with ExamView®: A 1-stop Microsoft® PowerPoint® Tool. PowerLecture instructor resources are a collection of book-specific lecture and class tools on either CD or DVD. The fastest and easiest way to build powerful, customized media-rich lectures, PowerLecture assets include chapter-specific PowerPoint presentations, ExamView test files, images, animations and video, instructor manuals, test banks, useful Web links and more. PowerLecture media-teaching tools are an effective way to enhance the educational experience.

Wadsworth's Introduction to Sociology 2007 Transparency Masters. A set of black-and-white transparency masters consisting of tables and figures from Wadsworth's introductory sociology texts is available to help prepare lecture presentations. It is free to qualified adopters.

Videos. Adopters of *Sociology* have several different video options available with the text.

Wadsworth's Lecture Launchers for Introductory Sociology. An exclusive offering jointly created by Wadsworth/Cengage Learning and Dallas TeleLearning, this video contains a collection of video highlights taken from the "Exploring Society: An Introduction to Sociology" Telecourse (formerly "The Sociological Imagination"). Each three- to six-minute-long video segment has been especially chosen to enhance and enliven class lectures and discussion of twenty key topics covered in any introductory sociology text. Accompanying the video is a brief written description of each clip, along with suggested discussion questions to help effectively incorporate the material into the classroom.

ABC® Videos (Introduction to Sociology Volumes I–IV). ABC Videos feature short, high-interest clips from current news events as well as historic raw footage going back forty years. Perfect for discussion starters or to enrich your lectures and spark interest in the material in the text, these brief videos provide students with a new lens through which to view the past and present, one that will greatly enhance their knowledge and understanding of significant events and open up to them new dimensions in learning. Clips are drawn from such programs as *World News Tonight, Good Morning America, This Week, PrimeTime Live, 20/20,* and *Nightline,* as well as numerous ABC News specials and material from the Associated Press Television News and British Movietone News collections.

Readers
***Classic Readings in Sociology*, Fourth Edition (edited by Eve L. Howard).** This series of classic articles written by key sociologists will complement any introductory sociology textbook. The reader serves as a touchstone for students: original works that teach the fundamental ideas of sociology.

***Understanding Society: An Introductory Reader*, Third Edition (edited by Margaret Andersen, University of Delaware, Kim Logio, St. Joseph's University, and Howard Taylor, Princeton University).** This reader includes articles with a variety of styles and perspectives, with a balance of the classic and contemporary. The editors selected readings that students will find accessible, yet intriguing, and have maximized the instructional value of each selection by prefacing each with an introduction and following each with discussion questions. The articles center on the following five themes: classical sociological theory, contemporary research, diversity, globalization, and application of the sociological perspective.

***Sociological Odyssey: Contemporary Readings in Introductory Sociology,* Third Edition (edited by Patricia A. Adler, University of Colorado and Peter Adler, University of Denver, Colorado).** This reader contains highly engaging, current articles that bring hot sociological topics to life for readers. Students enjoy the Adlers' balanced selection of timely readings, which cover issues and areas of interest to the general collegian, including male college cheerleaders, exploitation of immigrant laborers, teenage girls and cell phone usage, cyber romantic relationships, and cheating. In-depth introductions, explanation of theory, and discussion questions before each reading help guide students through the material.

***Sociological Footprints: Introductory Readings in Sociology,* Eleventh Edition (edited by Leonard Cargan, Wright State University and Jeanne H. Ballantine, Wright State University).** This anthology of seventy-six sociological studies provides a link between theoretical sociology and everyday life. *Sociological Footprints* offers classical, contemporary, popular, and multicultural articles in each chapter to show students a wide range of perspectives. Articles address today's most important social issues that are relevant to student's lives, social construction of sex, divorce trends, and American health care crisis. Each article is preceded by a short introductory essay, a series of guideline questions, and a list of glossary terms found in the article and therefore establish the student's reading of the article into a solid sociological framework.

Online Resources

Shepard, *Sociology*, Eleventh Edition Student Companion Website. *www.cengage.com/sociology/shepard/.* This Website, available to all students, provides useful learning resources for each chapter of the book:

- Practice quizzes
- Glossary
- Flash cards
- Crossword puzzles
- Web links
- Video exercises
- Learning modules
- Virtual explorations
- InfoTrac® College Edition with InfoMarks® exercises
- MicroCase exercises
- Map the stats exercises
- Animations

WebTutor™ ToolBox for WebCT® or Blackboard®. Preloaded with content and available free via access code when packaged with this text, WebTutor ToolBox pairs all the content of this text's rich Student Companion Website with all the sophisticated course management functionality of a WebCT or Blackboard product. You can assign materials (including online quizzes) and have the results flow automatically to your gradebook. ToolBox is ready to use as soon as you log on—or, you can customize its preloaded content by uploading images and other resources, adding Web links, or creating your own practice materials. Students have access only to student resources on the Student Companion Website. Instructors can enter a pincode for access to password-protected Instructor Resources.

InfoTrac® College Edition with InfoMarks®. With each purchase of a new copy of the text comes a free four-month pincode to InfoTrac College Edition, the online library that gives students anytime, anywhere access to reliable resources. This fully searchable database offers twenty years' worth of full-text articles from almost 5,000 diverse sources, such as academic journals, newsletters, and up-to-the-minute periodicals including *Time, Newsweek, Science, Forbes,* and *USA Today.* This incredible depth and breadth of material—available twenty-four hours a day from any computer with Internet access—makes conducting research so easy, your students will want to use it to enhance their work in every course. Through InfoTrac's InfoWrite, students now also have instant access to critical-thinking and paper writing tools. Both adopters and their students receive unlimited access for four months.

Acknowledgments

Once again, my wife, Kay Shepard, is my partner in pursuit of an improved text. She also knows how to make the train run on time. My secretary, Monica Gomez, consistently considers deadlines as targets met, a vital element in bringing all the pieces together. As development editor, Liana Sarkisian, stood ready to help at any time, and she did so repeatedly.

Several colleagues have provided thoughtful and helpful reviews for the eleventh edition. Many thanks to the following individuals: Dr. Annette Chamberlin, Virginia Western Community College; Laura Eells, McPherson College; Dr. David LoConto, Jacksonville State University; Dr. Patricia Masters, George Mason University; Dr. Sadie Pendaz, Normandale Community College; Dr. Isaac Sakyi-Addo, Calhoun Community College; Mike Schneider, Midland College; Nicole Stokes-DuPass, Union County College.

In addition to those individuals, the following colleagues have provided critiques of previous editions: G. William Anderson, Robert Anwyl, Paul J. Baker,

Melvin W. Barber, Michael G. Bisciglia, Jerry Bode, Patricia Bradley, Ruth Murray Brown, Brent Bruton, Victor Burke, Bruce Bylund, David Caddell, Albert Chabot, Reba Chaisson, Stephen Childs, William T. Chute, Carolie Coffey, Kenneth Colburn Jr., Jeremy Cook, William F. Coston, Jerome Crane, Ray Darville, Betty J. Daughenbaugh, Alline DeVore, Mary Van De-Walker, Mary Donahy, Susan B. Donohue, M. Gilbert Dunn, Lois Easterday, Mark G. Eckel, Irving Elan, Ralph England, K. Peter Etzkorn, Mark Evers, Susan Farrell, Joseph Faulkner, Kevin M. Fitzpatrick, John W. Fox, Jesse Frankel, Larry Frye, Pamela Gaiter, Roberta Goldberg, Michael Granata, Ramona Grimes, James W. Grimm, Laura Gruntmeir, Justine Gueno, Rebecca Guy, Penelope J. Hanke, Thomas Harlach, Cynthia Hawkins, Kenneth E. Hinze, Amy Holzgang, Carla Howery, Emmit Hunt, Keith Kerr, David H. Kessel, Gary Kiger, James A. Kitchens, Joseph Kotarba, Irving Krauss, Mark LaGory, Raymond P. LeBlanc, Jerry M. Lewis, Jieli Li, Roger Little, Richard Loper, Roy Lotz, Scott Magnuson-Martinson, Judy Maynard, Elaine McDuff, R. Lee McNair, Doris Miga, Alfredo Montalvo, Edward V. Morse, Charles Mulford, Bill Mullin, Daniel F. O'Connor, Jon Olson, Charles Osborn, Thomas R. Panko, Margaret Poloma, Roksana Rahman, Carol Axtell Ray, Deborah Richey, Larry Rosenberg, Ellen Rosengarten, William Roy, Josephine A. Ruggiero, Steven Schada, Paul M. Sharp, Edward Silva, James Skellinger, LaFleur Small, Robert P. Snow, Mary Steward, Ron Stewart, Robert F. Szafran, David Terry, Ralph Thomlinson, Marcella Thompson, Charles M. Tolbert, Deidre Tyler, David Waller, Carrol W. Waymon, Michael E. Weissbuch, Dorether M. Welch, Lois West, Carol S. Wharton, Douglas L. White, Paul Wozniak, David Zaret, and Wayne Zatopek.

A Text Message

u g2b crz 2 ms dis

Want to learn more and earn a better grade? This text is based on a proven method for student success called SQ3R. I know that looks like a Roman sign, but stay with me. The SQ3R method will help you identify the significant ideas, grasp these ideas more readily, remember the essential points, and be better prepared for exams. With this in mind, it is key for you to understand the five steps of SQ3R as they appear in this book. The following explains how the S in SQ3R refers to *survey*; the Q refers to question; and 3R refers to *read, recite,* and *review.*

S *Survey.* Before reading a chapter, read the outline and the goals at the beginning. Then read the integrated goals and summary at the end of the chapter in the *Review Guide.* This survey provides you a heads-up familiarity with the chapter content and takes only a few minutes.

Q *Question.* Subheadings throughout the text are phrased as questions that help you identify important issues. For example, instead of broad headings such as "Working Women," you are guided by more to-the-point questions such as "Have men and women reached financial equality?" and "How do American women fare globally?"

R1 *Read.* Of course, reading is involved in every assignment. As part of that reading, your comprehension increases immeasurably if, as you read, you focus on the answer to each subhead question.

R2 *Recite.* Following each major section is a feature called *Check Yourself.* Your response to these questions will be an indication of your comprehension: A hesitancy here reminds you to reexamine the material you just covered.

R3 *Review.* A *Review Guide* closes each chapter. Components of this guide include a Summary, a Concept Review, a Check Yourself Review, a Graphic Review, and Critical-Thinking Questions to help you prepare for an exam.

The SQ3R MENU below identifies each of the five steps of the SQ3R method. Beside each step is the symbol that will appear as a reminder at appropriate places throughout the text.

Notice that the Check Yourself feature appears at the end of each major section within a chapter. The Review Guide follows the entire chapter. Keep in mind that neither feature is a comprehensive exam. Rather, they are mini-tests designed to prevent false confidence, the problem we all have when we think we know something that we do not fully understand.

SQ3R as Expressed in This Text

SQ3R STEP	Symbol in Text	Location in Text
Survey	S	-Outline -Goals -Summary
Question	Q	-Subheading questions
Read	R1	-Assigned reading
Recite	R2	-Check Yourself
Review	R3	-Review Guide

CENGAGE ADVANTAGE: SOCIOLOGY

The Sociological Perspective

© Larry Harwood/Cengage Learning

S GOALS

- Illustrate the unique sociological perspective from both the micro and macro levels of analysis.
- Describe three uses of the sociological perspective.
- Distinguish sociology from other social sciences.
- Outline the contributions of the major pioneers of sociology.
- Summarize the development of sociology in the United States.
- Identify the three major theoretical perspectives in sociology today.
- Differentiate between two emerging theoretical perspectives.

1

USING THE SOCIOLOGICAL IMAGINATION

Why do people commit suicide? Answers immediately come to mind: prolonged illness, loss of a lover, public disgrace, depression, heavy financial loss. Each of these explanations assumes personal crisis as the sole motivation. Yet, suicide is affected not only by personal trauma but also by social forces. Specifically, sociologist Emile Durkheim revealed that suicide rate varies with social characteristics. Highly socially integrated people—married, females, Catholics—exhibit lower rates of suicide. More socially isolated persons—unmarried, males, Protestants—show higher suicide rates. After 100 years, research continues to support Durkheim's findings and conclusions.

Durkheim is one of the pioneers of sociology who will be profiled in this chapter. Before turning to these pioneers, however, we will discuss the unique sociological perspective that Durkheim identified and developed (R. A. Jones 2005).

The Sociological Perspective R1

Beyond Psychology: The Social Animal

A couple divorces because the love is gone; a student commits suicide because she is depressed. These explanations look at individual causes of behavior. At the psychological level, this makes perfect sense. Sociology, however, looks beyond individual factors to explain social behavior: A husband and wife are more likely to divorce when they are from different social classes; people with weak social bonds commit suicide more often. Social classes and social bonds are distinctly social, not individual, factors. Thus, the overarching objective of this book is to enable you to view yourself and your world from a sociological perspective, to move from the individual level to the group level in understanding social behavior.

The Importance of Perspective

Q Why begin your study of sociology with a discussion of perspective? We all interpret the happenings around us through our own perspective—our own particular point of view. It can hardly be any other way. For example, if, as an American, you were asked to observe a fish tank, what would you tend to describe? Because you have been raised in an individualistic and competitive culture, you are likely to notice which fish is the most

beautiful or which fish is the biggest. Coming from a more collectivist culture, a Chinese person is more likely to notice the context in which the fish swim. A Chinese person would more likely notice things like the cleanliness of the water in which the fish swim or the size of the fish tank relative to the number of fish in the tank. (See "Think Globally" 1.1 for another example of perspective mattering.)

Defining Sociology

Q At this point, how would you define sociology? As a novice to the field, you may at first view sociology as the study of human groups. As you progress, however, you will acquire a more precise understanding of **sociology** as the scientific study of social structure, which actually refers to patterns of social relationships. In the meantime, the first four chapters lay a foundation for Chapter 5 ("Social Structure and Society").

Until Chapter 5, then, your understanding of the concept of social structure will be understandably vague. For now it is sufficient for you to become familiar with two key aspects of the sociological perspective: (1) Individuals share patterns of behavior with others in their group or society and (2) sociologists can view social relationships from either of two separate levels of analysis: within a group or between groups.

The decision to attend college is not merely a choice made by an isolated individual. Social relationships, with teachers, parents, peers, and others, influence a person's decision to become a college student. Sociologists study these patterned social relationships referred to as *social structures*.

Pattie Steib/Used under license from Shutterstock

THINK GLOBALLY   1.1

A World Turned Upside Down

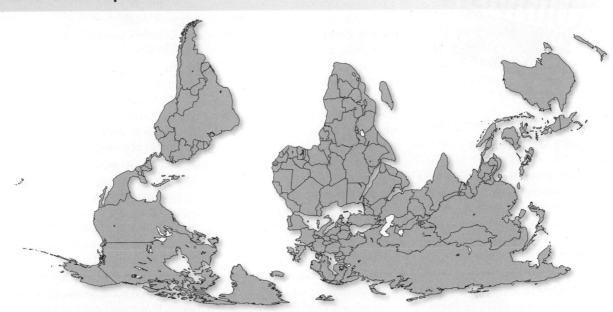

Without turning this map upside down, locate the United States. Do you find it more difficult than usual? Do you find this view of the world disorienting? Because you are so used to the conventional representation of the Earth, you may reject this worldview. So it is with any perspective.

In this book, you will be asked to abandon the typical American psychological perspective in favor of the sociological perspective.

1. How would you feel if this map were universally substituted for the one you know? Describe your feelings, and explain why you feel this way.

2. What does your reaction to this map tell you about the power of the perspective you bring to a situation?

Patterns of Behavior

Q What is an example of "patterned" social behavior? As you know, college students in a classroom do not all behave exactly alike. Some attempt to write down everything their professors say, some just listen to the lecture, some record the lecture, and others text their friends. Yet, if you visit almost any college or university, you will find patterned relationships. Professors lecture, students remain in their seats; professors give examinations, students take them. Although the individual characteristics of students and professors may vary from school to school, students and professors relate in similar patterned ways. It is the predictable, *recurrent* patterned interaction of people and the social structures created by such interaction that capture the attention of sociologists.

Q How does group behavior differ from individual behavior? Emile Durkheim (1966; originally published in 1895), a pioneering nineteenth-century sociologist, argued that we do not attempt to explain bronze in terms of its component parts (lead, copper, and tin). Instead, we consider bronze an alloy, a unique metal produced by the synthesis of several distinct metals. Even the consistency of bronze is not predictable from its components: bronze is hard, whereas lead, copper, and tin are soft and malleable. Durkheim reasoned that if a combination of certain metals produces a unique metal, some similar process might happen in groups of people. Indeed, people's behavior within a group setting cannot be predicted from the characteristics of individual group members. Something new is created when individuals come together as a collective. Sometimes the citizens of a city whose team has just won a major championship (e.g., World Series, Super Bowl) become unruly and frenetic, breaking windows, tearing down street signs, starting bonfires. College students on spring break in Florida repeatedly behave in ways they never would as individuals in their home communities. Whether because members value their group's ways or because they yield to social pressures of the moment, the behavior of a group cannot be predicted simply from knowledge about the individual members. A group is not equal to the sum of its parts any more than is bronze (see "Consider This Research").

Emile Durkheim—The Study of Suicide

Emile Durkheim, the first person to be formally recognized as a sociologist and the most scientific of the pioneers, conducted a study that stands as a research model for sociologists today. His investigation of suicide was, in fact, the first sociological study to use statistics. In *Suicide* (1964; originally published in 1897), Durkheim documented his contention that some aspects of social behavior—even something as allegedly individualistic as suicide—can be explained without reference to individuals.

Like all of Durkheim's work, his study of suicide is best considered within the context of his concern for social integration (R. Collins 1994; Pickering and Walford 2000). Durkheim wanted to see if suicide rates within a social entity (e.g., a group, an organization, or society) are related to the degree to which individuals are socially involved (integrated and regulated). In his study, Durkheim described three types of suicide: egoistic, altruistic, and anomic. He hypothesized that

egoistic suicide increases when individuals do not have sufficient social ties. Because single (never married) adults, for example, are not heavily involved with family life, they are more likely to commit suicide than are married adults. On the other hand, he predicted *altruistic suicide* as more likely to occur when social integration is extremely strong. The Al Qaeda agents who slammed jetliners into the World Trade Center and the Pentagon in 2001 are one example, as are suicide bombers. Altruistic suicide need not be this extreme, of course. Military personnel who lay down their lives for their country are another illustration.

Durkheim forecasted his third type of suicide—*anomic suicide*—to increase when existing social ties are broken. For example, suicide rates increase during economic depressions. People suddenly without jobs, or without hope of finding any, are more prone to kill themselves. Suicide may also increase during periods of prosperity. People may loosen their social ties by taking new jobs, moving to new communities, or finding new mates.

Using precollected data from government population reports of several countries (much of the data from the French government statistical office), Durkheim found strong support for his predictions. Suicide rates were, in fact, higher among unmarried than married people and among military personnel than civilians. They were also higher

among people involved in nationwide economic crises.

Durkheim's primary interest, however, was not in the empirical (observable) indicators he used, such as suicide rates among military personnel, married people, and so forth. Rather, Durkheim used the results of his study to support several of his broader contentions: (1) social behavior can be explained by social rather than psychological factors; (2) suicide is affected by the degree of integration and regulation within social entities; and (3) because society can be studied scientifically, sociology is worthy of recognition in the academic world (Ritzer 2008). Durkheim was successful on all three counts. If Auguste Comte told us that sociology *could* be a science, Durkheim showed us *how* it could be a science.

Evaluate the Research

1. Do you believe that Durkheim's study of suicide supported his idea that much of social behavior cannot be explained psychologically? Why or why not?
2. Which approach do you think Durkheim followed in his study of suicide: functionalist, conflict, or symbolic interactionist? Support your choice by relating his study to the assumptions of the perspective you chose.

Q How is conformity related to global group behavior? We live in groups ranging in size from a family to an entire society, and they all encourage conformity—conformity often promoted by social forces that individuals do not create and cannot control. American, Russian, and Chinese citizens, for instance, have distinctive eating habits, types of dress, religious beliefs, and attitudes toward family life. Groups of teenagers within a society tend to listen to the same music, dress alike, and follow similar dating customs.

Q Why is the existence of conformity important to sociology? Because a high degree of conformity within societies exists, similarities or patterns in social behavior exist. Sociologists can attempt to understand, explain, and predict the often invisible social processes that permit successive generations to live predictable and orderly lives without each generation creating its own new guidelines for social living. Because a particular generation is spared this trouble, its members usually fail to ask why things are the way they are, or why things are changing. Sociologists, in contrast, constantly wrestle with these questions.

Q But don't people, in turn, affect society? Yes. But, it is necessary to begin with the social emphasis because without some considerable degree of conformity, there can be no group life. Still, this necessary nonindividualistic emphasis should not obscure the effect that individuals can have on social structures. Individuals are active, thinking beings who do not always follow social scripts. The interplay between individuals and their social structures is a two-way street: people are affected by social structures, and people change their social structures. Consequently, you should not conclude that all human behavior in groups is determined by preexisting social structures. For example, historian Joyce Appleby (2001) documents how the first generation born after the American Revolution fashioned a national culture based on an interpretation of their parents' creation of a new nation.

In summary, the sociological perspective focuses on the group, examines patterns of behavior, isolates patterns of conformity, and recognizes the effects of people on society. Table 1.1 illustrates these unique aspects of the sociological perspective using suicide rates among Catholics and Protestants.

TABLE 1.1

WHAT SOCIOLOGISTS SEE AND HOW THEY STUDY SUICIDE: Comparing Protestants and Catholics

SOCIOLOGISTS FOCUS . . .	SOCIOLOGISTS MIGHT INVESTIGATE . . .
on the group, not the individual.	distinct characteristics of both Protestants and Catholics that affect their differential suicide rates.
on patterns of social behavior.	data to determine if Protestants and Catholics actually do consistently commit suicide at different rates.
on social forces that encourage conformity.	the ways that greater social integration among Catholics promotes a lower rate of suicide compared to more socially isolated Protestants.
on the effects people have on social structure.	the means that Protestants may use to lower their suicide rate, such as the promotion of social involvement through church activities.

Levels of Analysis: Microsociology and Macrosociology

Sociologists work from two distinct levels of analysis: They study the interaction of people "within" groups (*microsociology*) and they research the "intersection" of groups as a whole (*macrosociology*). *Macro* means "large"; *micro* means "small." Macro research focuses on entire groups. Microanalysis investigates the relationships within groups. Macro views from a distance, micro from close range (Helle and Eisentadt 1985a, 1985b; Scheff 1990; A. H. Hawley 1992).

Suppose for the moment that social structures are directly observable as tangible objects and that we are cruising at 20,000 feet at the controls of Sociologist One. On a clear day at this altitude we would be able to observe definite social structures, just as we can observe the lay of the land from an airplane. At 20,000 feet we will see no movement in the form of people interacting. We are at the macro level. Suppose we wish to get a closer look and start descending. As we descend, we will begin to see people interacting. When we focus on these relationships, we are at the micro level. Formal definitions of microsociology and macrosociology will make more sense against this general background.

Microsociology is concerned with the study of people as they interact in daily life. Consider the practice of knife fighting among street gangs. At the micro level, a sociologist attempts to explain participation in gang knife fighting based on the social relationships involved. For example, gang leaders, to validate their right to leadership, may feel that they must either fight members of their own gang who challenge their position or fight leaders of other gangs.

Macrosociology focuses on groups without regard to the interaction of the people within. Some sociologists examine entire societies (Tilly 1978, 1986; Wallerstein 1979, 1984; Skocpol 1985; Lenski 1988; Nolan and Lenski 2010). We will use the term *macrosociology* in referring to the study of societies as a whole as well as to the relationships between social structures within societies. For example, sociologists might study the patterned relationships between the defense industry and the federal government, or the effect of the economy on the stability of the family.

The macro and micro levels of analysis are complementary; their combined use tells us more about social behavior than either one alone (Alexander et al. 1987; Sawyer 2001). To understand gang warfare, a microsociologist would want to know about the social relationships involved—the relationships between gang leaders and followers or between gang members and police on the beat. To supplement this understanding of gangs obtained at the micro level, the macro level can be used to examine the larger social structures of which

gangs are a part. A macrosociologist might look for the aspects of a society or social structure that produce the poverty promoting delinquency in the first place—such as lack of education and joblessness.

Uses of the Sociological Perspective R1

Q Why study sociology? Each of the following three personal benefits of sociology involves critical thinking and analysis of social issues. First, the sociological perspective enables you to develop the *sociological imagination*. Second, sociological theory and research can be applied to important public issues. Third, the study of sociology can sharpen skills useful in many occupations.

The Sociological Imagination

Q What is the sociological imagination? Knowing how social forces affect our lives can help prevent us from being prisoners of those forces. C. Wright Mills called this personal use of sociology the **sociological imagination**—the set of mind that enables individuals to see the relationship between events in their personal lives and events in their society. The sociological imagination invites us to examine the intersection between personal biography and social influences. Events affecting us as individuals, Mills pointed out, are closely related to the ebb and flow of society (Mills and Etzioni 1999). Decisions, both minor and momentous, are not isolated, individual matters. Historically, for example, American society has shown a bias against childless marriages and only children. Couples without children have been considered selfish, and only children have often been labeled "spoiled" (Benokraitis 2010). These values date back to a time when there was a societal need for large families because of the high infant mortality rate and the need for labor on family farms. Only now, as the need for large families is disappearing, are we reading of the benefits of one-child families—to

the child, to the family, and to society. The sociological imagination enables us to understand the effects of such social forces on our lives. With this understanding, we are in a stronger position to make autonomous decisions rather than merely conform (Game and Metcalfe 1996; Peck and Hollingsworth 1996; K. T. Erikson 1997; Berger and Zijderveld 2009).

This broadened social awareness permits us to read the newspaper with a more complete understanding of the implications of social events. Instead of interpreting an editorial opposing welfare as merely a selfish expression, we might see the letter as a reflection of the importance Americans place on independence and self-help (A. M. Lee 1990; Straus 2002). The sociological imagination, then, opens our minds and expands our horizons. It enables us to question conventional wisdom and free (intellectually liberate) ourselves from unwanted social pressures to conform (Berger 1963, Berger and Luckmann,1967).

Q How will the debunking theme open our minds and stimulate our sociological imagination? Despite the availability of accurate information and explanations, people tend to cling to myths and false ideas about social life—impressions that are passed from generation to generation. Plato's "Allegory of the Cave" comes to mind. In *The Republic*, Plato describes a cave in which people have been chained, from childhood, so they cannot move. Forced to look only straight ahead, these prisoners cannot see behind them the blazing fire and a raised walkway in front of the fire. Men walk along the wall carrying all types of objects. The shadows on the wall in front of the prisoners, made by the walking men and the fire, are the only things the prisoners have ever seen. Their interpretations of these shadows constitute reality to them. Sociology attempts to replace common misconceptions about social life (shadows on the cave wall) with accurate information and explanations (Ruggiero 2001).

Because the task of sociology is to reveal the nature of human social behavior, it often opens our minds and leads us to question what we usually take for granted. What people take to be unassailable truth may, under

The sociological imagination allows us to see that joining a gang is a social act providing some young men and women with a sense of security and belonging they haven't found elsewhere.

scientific examination, be false. The sociological imagination, then, replaces common misconceptions about social life with accurate information and explanations.

Q **How does the sociological imagination expand our horizons and encourage intellectual liberation?** Like all liberal arts courses—anthropology, history, literature, and philosophy—sociology encourages intellectual liberation (Bierstedt 1963; Brouilette 1985). You can, for example, learn that among the Winnebago Indians of Wisconsin it was socially acceptable for parents to kill children who became too great a liability (Radin 1953). Among the Toda of southern India, female infants were frequently killed at birth; if twins of different sexes were born, the female was always killed (Murdock 1935). The Winnebago and Toda, like all humans, had been taught the ways of their group. Through the sociological imagination, you can become aware of the rationale for infanticide practiced by a society under extreme population pressure and living on the margin of subsistence.

Even more interestingly, sociology provides a window into our own social world, allowing us to see the many social forces that shape our lives. Sociology thus complements rather than replaces other ways of viewing human behavior. The more we seek to apply a range of different perspectives in attempting to interpret social forces and their meanings, the greater will be our understanding of our own behavior as well as the behavior of others. With such understanding comes the potential for greater personal freedom from social pressures. Consider divorce, for example. Social research reveals many factors in modern society that promote marital failure. Divorce is more likely to occur among couples who share particular characteristics: low levels of education, early marriages, premarital pregnancies, or living arrangements with parents. Awareness of the inevitable pressures of such marriages may convince couples under these circumstances either not to marry, or at least to anticipate and prepare more effectively for such problems. The successful application of the sociological imagination enables us to share Somerset Maugham's insight that "tradition is a guide and not a jailer."

Applied Sociology

Q **Do sociologists have a moral responsibility to speak against and attempt to change aspects of social life they believe to be wrong?** From the time it first appeared on the American academic scene in the late 1800s, sociology has steadily attempted to move from its origins as a social problem-solving discipline to a nonsocially involved science. During the intervening years, disagreement has periodically surfaced on the compatibility of these two viewpoints (A. M. Lee 1978; Weinstein 2000; Hamilton and Thompson 2002; Burawoy 2005; Phillips 2008; Steele and Price, 2008). Those arguing against the involvement of social scientists in the eradication of social ills view science as "value neutral"; that is, scientific research is supposed to discover what actually exists, with no room for personal value judgments as to what *ought* to exist. The idea of value neutrality has dominated sociological thought for years. And although the idea of science as a value-neutral enterprise remains strong among sociologists, those favoring the interjection of standards of good and bad are on the increase (J. Q. Wilson 1993; Bickman and Rog 1997). This issue has gained considerable prominence in the form of both **humanist sociology,** which places human needs and goals at the center (A. M. Lee 1978; Scimecca 1987; Giddens 1987), and **liberation sociology,** whose objective is to replace human oppression with greater democracy and social justice (Feagin 2001).

Q **Does sociological research influence public policies and programs?** Yes. Social scientists, for instance, contributed to the 1954 Supreme Court decision outlawing separate but equal schools for African Americans and

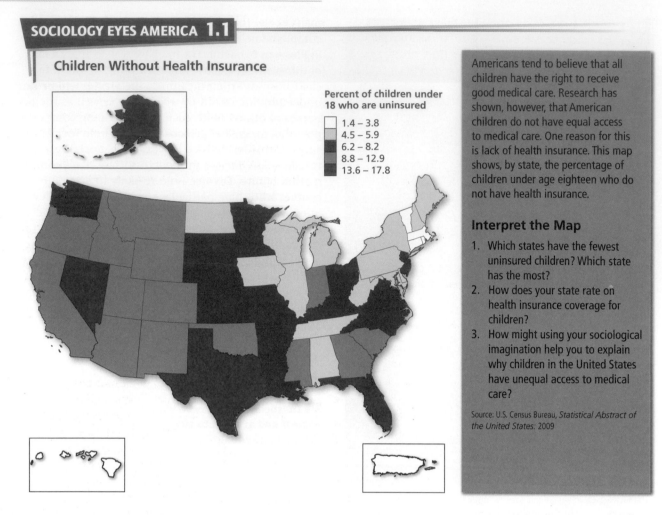

SOCIOLOGY EYES AMERICA 1.1

Children Without Health Insurance

Percent of children under 18 who are uninsured

- 1.4 – 3.8
- 4.5 – 5.9
- 6.2 – 8.2
- 8.8 – 12.9
- 13.6 – 17.8

Americans tend to believe that all children have the right to receive good medical care. Research has shown, however, that American children do not have equal access to medical care. One reason for this is lack of health insurance. This map shows, by state, the percentage of children under age eighteen who do not have health insurance.

Interpret the Map

1. Which states have the fewest uninsured children? Which state has the most?
2. How does your state rate on health insurance coverage for children?
3. How might using your sociological imagination help you to explain why children in the United States have unequal access to medical care?

Source: U.S. Census Bureau, *Statistical Abstract of the United States:* 2009

whites. This is one of the earliest examples of the U.S. court system accepting social science research as a basis for legal decisions. Subsequent research has explored a variety of related topics, including the effects of school quality on student performance, the impact of social environment on measured IQ, the influence of school desegregation on the performance of African American and white students, and the effects of busing when desegregating schools.

Knowledge, then, is a prerequisite to the creation of sound laws, and that is where sociology contributes. Before attempting to create any national policy regarding children's access to health care, for example, it is necessary to know the extent of the problem of inaccessibility (see "Sociology Eyes America 1.1"). The definition of family is another example. Traditionally, American culture limited marriage to the legal union of a man and a woman. Recent research tells us that Americans are increasingly adopting alternatives such as same-sex marriage, civil unions, and unmarried cohabitation as legitimate forms of family. What constitutes a legal family has policy implications affecting health insurance coverage, inheritance rights, child custody, and end-of-life decisions. Lawmakers considering these

legal questions will have to take into account research addressing the evolving definition of family (Powell et al. 2010).

Some sociologists advocate intervention beyond policy-related research. Following a long-neglected lead (Wirth 1931), **clinical sociology** (or "sociological practice") involves using sociological theories, principles, and research to diagnose and measure social intervention (Steele and Price 2008). Clinical sociologists provide help for individuals or serve as agents for change in organizations, communities, and even entire societies (Black 1984; Erickson and Simon 1998; Du Bois and Wright 2000; Koppel 2002; R. H. Hall and Tolbert 2008). Clinical sociologists may work as marriage and family therapists, might design intervention programs to reduce juvenile delinquency, or may redesign the social environment of cancer patients.

Sociology and Occupational Skills

Q How will the study of sociology contribute to the development of work skills? Most employers are interested in four types of skills: the ability to work well with others, the ability to write and speak fluently, the ability to solve problems, and the ability to analyze information. Because computers have revolutionized the office, information analysis skills are becoming much more important to managers in all types of organizations. In addition, the increasing complexity of work demands greater critical analysis and problem-solving skills. The levels of each of these skills can be improved through the broad liberal arts foundation of sociology (Billson and Huber 1993; Stephens 2002, American Sociological Association 2007; Ferrante 2009).

Q What about more specific preparation for employment?
In addition to general skills, specific sociology subfields offer preparation for fairly specialized jobs.
Consider these examples:

- Training in race relations is an asset for working in human resources (personnel) departments, hospitals, or day-care centers.

- Background in urban sociology can be put to good use in urban planning, law enforcement, and social work.
- Courses focusing on gender and race serve as valuable background for work in community planning, arbitration, and sexual harassment cases.
- Training in criminology is sought by agencies dealing with criminal justice, probation, and juvenile delinquency.
- Courses in social psychology are valuable for sales, marketing, and advertising, as well as for counseling.

These jobs only scratch the surface; students of sociology are prepared to pursue many other careers (see "See Sociology in Your Life"). Consider this selected list: manager, executive, college placement officer, community planner, employment counselor, foreign service worker, environmental specialist,

Job Opportunities in Sociology

In general, all employers are interested in four types of skills regardless of what specific career path you choose. These skills are:

- The ability to work with others.
- The ability to write and speak well.
- The ability to solve problems.
- The ability to analyze information.

Because computers have revolutionized the office, for example, information analysis skills are becoming much more important to managers in all types of organizations. The increasing complexity of work

demands greater critical thinking and problem-solving skills. Knowledge is of limited use if you can't convey what you know to others.

The study of sociology helps students develop these general skills, so it is a solid base for many career paths. For sociology majors, the following list of possibilities is only the beginning— many other paths are open to you.

- Social services—in rehabilitation, case management, group work with youth or the elderly, recreation, or administration.
- Community work—in fundraising for social service organizations, nonprofits, child-care or community development agencies, or environmental groups.
- Corrections—in probation, parole, or other criminal justice work.
- Business—in advertising, marketing and consumer research, insurance, real estate, personnel work, training, or sales.
- College settings—in admissions, alumni relations, or placement offices.

- Health services—in family planning, substance abuse, rehabilitation counseling, health planning, hospital admissions, and insurance companies.
- Publishing, journalism, and public relations—in writing, research, and editing.
- Government services—in federal, state, and local government jobs in such areas as transportation, housing, agriculture, and labor.
- Teaching—in elementary and secondary schools, in conjunction with appropriate teacher certification; also in universities, with research opportunities.

Think About It
1. Which of the career paths listed is most interesting to you? What is it about this area that you find interesting?
2. Evaluate your current strengths and weaknesses in the four primary skill areas.

Source: Adapted from *Careers in Sociology*, American Sociological Association, 2006.

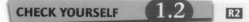

CHECK YOURSELF   1.2   R2

Uses of the Sociological Perspective

1. The _____ is the set of mind that enables individuals to see the relationship between events in their personal lives and events in their society.
2. Which of the following is *not* one of the uses of the sociological imagination?
   ____ a. seeing the interplay of self and society
   ____ b. creating new aspects of culture not thought of by others
   ____ c. questioning aspects of social life most people take for granted
   ____ d. understanding the social forces that shape daily life
3. _____ sociology places human needs and goals at its center.

Answers: 1. sociological imagination; 2. b; 3. Humanist

guidance counselor, health planner, journalist, labor relations specialist, marketing researcher, public relations supervisor, research analyst, writer, and editor (American Sociological Association, 2007).

The Social Sciences R1

Sociology and the Social Sciences

Your initial understanding of sociology includes its unique social-world focus and the uses of the distinctive sociological perspective. You can further clarify your grasp of sociology by distinguishing it from the other social sciences.

It was not until the nineteenth century that Auguste Comte coined the term *sociology*. Comte's ideas about sociology were embedded in his ideas about psychology, economics, and political theory. He viewed sociology as the one comprehensive social science.

Gradually, scholars developed the various social sciences to the point that they could be legitimately distinguished. Nevertheless, the social sciences have enough in common to overlap with one another at many points.

Q What is anthropology? Because anthropology investigates culture, it is the social science most closely related to sociology. Historically, anthropologists have concentrated on the study of "primitive" or nonliterate societies, whereas sociologists have focused on the modern, complex, industrial societies of Western civilization. Because anthropologists are interested primarily in small nonindustrial societies, they tend to study entire societies. Sociologists, on the other hand, investigate more limited aspects of modern societies, such as political revolutions or the status of women vis-à-vis men. Today some anthropologists have extended their studies to include research in modern, complex societies, examining, for instance, cultural characteristics of neighborhoods and communities.

Q What is psychology? Psychology focuses on the development and function of mental-emotional processes in human beings. Whereas sociology and anthropology concentrate on human groups, psychology takes as its domain the individual. Sociology and psychology have some common interest in an aspect of behavioral science called social psychology, a field that focuses on the interactions between individuals and groups. A social psychologist, for example, is interested in the ways in which groups promote conformity among their individual members.

Q What is economics? Economics is the study of the production, distribution, and consumption of goods and services. It deals with such matters as the impact of interest rates on the flow of money and the effects of taxation on consumption. Economics uses highly developed mathematical models to predict changes in economic indicators. Although these economic models are not always correct, they are sophisticated, and they give economists greater predictive power than that of most other social scientists. Sociology and economics merge in an area of study called economic sociology, which concentrates on the interrelationships between the economic and noneconomic aspects of social life. An economic sociologist, for example, would be interested in the relationship between the extent of industrialization in a particular society and the degree of workers' involvement in union activity.

Q What is political science? Political science studies the organization, administration, history, and theory of government. Political scientists are concerned, for example, with voting patterns and political party participation. In recent years, political science has moved beyond its earlier preoccupation with the workings of government toward the study of political behavior in its broadest sense. This trend has inevitably bound closer together the interests of political scientists and political sociologists. Both political scientists and political sociologists share an interest in the social interaction that occurs within the political institution as well as the interaction between the political institution and other institutions, including economic and educational institutions. Both disciplines conduct research on the location and use of power, the process of political socialization, the functioning of special interest groups, and the workings of political protest.

Q What is history? History examines past events in human societies. As a field of study, history is sharply divided into two camps (Landes and Tilly 1991). Humanistic historians believe that history cannot use the methods of the social sciences. They view any attempts at scientific generalization as the simplification of complex, unique human experiences rooted in specific times and places. Description, they argue, is the only legitimate function of the historian. Social scientific historians, in contrast, assume the existence of uniform, recurring patterns of human behavior that transcend time and place. The role of the historian, they contend, is to identify and verify these patterns. In recent years, the relationship between sociology and history has become more mutually beneficial. Sociology is currently more open to the use of historians' work in their attempts to document recurring patterns and provide explanations of historical reality; and more historians are now committed to the collection and analysis of primary sources with an eye to establishing recurrent and universal historical patterns.

Q How do various social sciences view the family? Here, by way of illustration, are distinctive social science approaches to the specific study of the family:

- *Sociologists.* Some sociologists investigating the family focus on the social causes of divorce. Factors thought to contribute to higher divorce rates in American society include early marriage, poor mate selection, economic prosperity, increased participation of women in the labor force, and the weakening of the stigma formerly associated with divorce (see Chapter 12, "Family").

- *Anthropologists.* An interest of some anthropological researchers is whether the nuclear family of married biological parents and their legitimate offspring exists universally in human societies. This topic can be studied by examining documented evidence on as many societies as possible and by attempting to find one or more societies where the nuclear family is not the norm (Leach 1982).

- *Psychologists.* Some psychologists are interested in studying familial retardation—cases of mental retardation that tend to appear in poor families with no known organic basis. Familial retardation is traced largely to an impoverished environment, including inferior nutrition and medical care and the relative absence of early emotional support and intellectual stimulation (Coon and Mitterer 2008).

- *Economists.* Economists use the family as the unit of analysis for the distribution of income. For example, currently, the bottom 60 percent of American families receive less than one-third of the nation's total income (Baumol and Blinder 2010).

- *Political scientists.* The relationship between voting and the family is a topic of research for political scientists. Political scientists have found, for example, that although voting on Election Day is done by private ballot, voting is primarily a group phenomenon. The family is the most important influence in forming political party identification and determining the voting behavior of its members. Political attitudes and behaviors are shaped, often unintentionally, by family members—who also exist in similar economic, religious, social class, and geographical environments (T. E. Patterson 2010).

- *Historians.* The relationship between slavery and the family has been the subject of research by historians. Using slavery in the United States as a case study, a controversial study by historian Henry Gutman (1983) presents evidence from twenty-one urban and rural communities in the South between

CHECK YOURSELF 1.3 R2

The Social Sciences
Match the following fields of study and aspects of family life.
_____ a. anthropology
_____ b. sociology
_____ c. history
_____ d. political science
_____ e. economics
_____ f. psychology

(1) distribution of income and the family
(2) effects of slavery on family stability
(3) relationship between voting and the family
(4) effects of early marriage on divorce
(5) link between early childhood emotional support and familial retardation
(6) universality of the nuclear family

Answers: a. (6); b. (4); c. (2); d. (3); e. (1); f. (5)

1865 and 1880 to challenge the long-standing assumption that slavery destroys the family structure. For example, Gutman concluded that most African American households during the slavery era had a father and mother present. In short, African American slave families tended to be stable and intact.

Founders of Sociology ▣R1

European Origins

Sociology is a relatively new science, emerging as a distinct area of study in the late nineteenth century (L. J. Ray 1999; J. H. Turner 2002a; Jones, Le Boutillier, and Bradbury, 2011). In fact, it is only during the past half century that sociology has taken its place as a legitimate social science. The origins of sociology, however, can be seen in the work of eighteenth-century philosopher Adam Smith. A man of the Scottish Enlightenment, Smith believed that humans possess a natural affection for others. This led him to seek hidden forces of social harmony to match unseen physical forces like gravity and magnetism. In Smith's desire to do for the understanding of social life what Newton had done for the physical world lay the seeds of modern social science (G. S. Wood 2003).

▣ Who wrote *The Wealth of Nations*, and what is the book's relevance to capitalism? Famous for his absent-mindedness, Scotsman Adam Smith (1723–1790), was revered by other Enlightenment scholars for his intellectual gifts and practical nature. Smith began as a moral philosopher at the University of Glasgow, spent years as a tutor to the stepson of one of the men whose tax policies provoked the American Revolution, and during his last years held the position of Commissioner of Customs for Scotland (Muller 1993).

The Smith influence is most often associated with economics. This is small wonder; Smith's most famous book, *The Wealth of Nations* (Smith and Cannan 2000; originally published in 1776), is considered foundational to capitalism. Even sociologists themselves, though, often fail to place him among the founders of their field, despite the reflection of his ideas by the founders of sociology in the nineteenth century.

▣ What were Smith's contributions to sociology? Smith made two major contributions to the development of sociology. First, he attributed much of human behavior to the influence of society. People learn honesty, for example, through participation in the family, church, community, and government. The roots of the human personality lie in our association with others.

In addition to emphasizing the sociological perspective, Smith laid the foundation for a sociological theory known as symbolic interactionism (discussed later in this chapter). He wanted to explain one's ability to follow society's rules. This ability, reasoned Smith, develops from the human need for the approval of others (Herman 2001). The concepts Smith used to express this idea in his second book, *The Theory of Moral Sentiments* (1976; originally published in 1759), inspired later sociologists to explore the relationship between human personality and society.

Smith thought like a sociologist and used a sociological perspective in his moral philosophy and economic analysis. The term *sociology*, however, had not yet been coined, and the field had not been established. Sociology was not formally introduced until the nineteenth century, some forty years after the death of Adam Smith.

▣ What was occurring in the nineteenth century that sparked the emergence of sociology? Nineteenth-century Europe was torn by social change and controversy. The old social order of the Middle Ages—based on social position, land ownership, church, kinship, community, and autocratic political leadership—was crumbling under the social and economic influences of the Industrial and French Revolutions. The move from farm to factory resulted in the loss of a stabilizing community. This social disharmony led Auguste Comte, Harriet Martineau, and other intellectuals to grapple with the restoration of community, social order, and predictability (Nisbet 1966; Mazlish 1993). Thus, in an important sense, the emergence of sociology as a distinct area of study was a conservative reaction to the social chaos of the nineteenth century. The central ideas of the major pioneers of sociology, all of whom were European, will shed further light on the origins of the field (J. A. Hughes, Martin, and Sharrock 1995; Camic 1998; Ritzer 2010a).

▣ How do you think Auguste Comte's personality might have contributed to his breakup with his mentor? Auguste Comte (1798–1857) was a Frenchman born to a government bureaucrat. A small child, often ill, Comte proved early on to be an excellent student, although he had difficulty balancing his genuine interest in school and his rebellious and stubborn nature. In fact, his protest against the examination procedures at the Ecole Polytechnique (of MIT stature) led to his dismissal. A year later, Comte became secretary to the famous philosopher Henri Saint-Simon. Most of Comte's significant ideas were reflected in the writings he and Saint-Simon composed together. Differences between Comte and his mentor slowly eroded their relationship, which finally ended in an argument over whose name was to appear on a publication.

Q What were Comte's major ideas? Comte is recognized as the father of sociology. The improvement of society was his main concern. If societies were to advance, Comte believed, social behavior had to be studied scientifically. Because no science of society existed, Comte attempted to create one himself and coined the term *sociology* to describe this science. Sociology, he asserted, should rely on **positivism**—the use of scientific observation and experimentation in the study of social behavior. When Comte wrote that sociology should rely on positivism, he meant that sociology should be a science based on knowledge of which we can be "positive," or sure. He also distinguished between **social statics,** the study of social stability and order, and **social dynamics,** the study of social change. This distinction between social stability and social change remains at the center of modern sociology.

As a result of his bitter breakup with Saint-Simon, Comte was almost prevented from writing his masterwork, *Positive Philosophy*. (It was in this work that Comte elucidated his principle of "cerebral hygiene." To prevent others from polluting his thoughts, Comte stopped reading.) After parting ways with Saint-Simon, Comte never found another well-paid position. He was forced to rely on intermittent activities—tutoring and testing in mathematics, for example. It was only after a few of his followers invited him to prepare some private lectures that Comte presented his ideas to the world.

Comte died before very many beyond his private circle came to appreciate his work. Later, European scholars recognized and widely adopted his belief that sociology could apply scientific procedures and promote social progress.

Q What motivated Harriet Martineau to begin a writing career? Harriet Martineau (1802–1876), an Englishwoman born into a solidly middle-class home, was self-reliant and strong willed. Her writing career, which included journalism and fiction as well as sociology, began in 1825 after the Martineau family textile mill was lost to a business depression (Webb 1960; Fletcher 1974; Pichanik 1980; Desmond and Moore 2009). Without family income, and with few immediate prospects for marriage following a broken engagement, Martineau sought a dependable source of income to support herself. She became a popular writer of celebrity stature, whose work outsold that of Charles Dickens.

Q What did Martineau contribute to the early development of sociology? Martineau, an important figure in the founding of sociology, is best known for her translation of Comte's *Positive Philosophy*. Done with Comte's approval, Martineau's translation remains the most readable. She also made original contributions in the areas of research methods, political economy,

Harriet Martineau (1802–1876) emphasized sociology as a science and introduced feminism. Her profound deafness prevented her from earning a living as a teacher so she became an author.

Mary Evans Picture Library/The Everett Collection

and feminist theory (Hill and Hoecker-Drysdale 2001; Lengermann and Niebrugge 2007).

Martineau's book *How to Observe Manners and Morals* (1838) was the first methodology book in sociology. In it she emphasized several crucial research principles: the use of a theoretical framework to guide social observation, the development of predetermined questions in gathering information, objectivity, and representative sampling (Lipset 1962).

Martineau followed these research methods while conducting a comparative study of European and American society. Although not as well known as Alexis de Tocqueville's *Democracy in America*, which was published at about the same time (originally published in 1835), Martineau's *Society in America* (1837) remains her most widely read book today. Martineau compared America favorably with England, but she believed that America had not lived up to its promise of democracy and freedom for all its people. Slavery and the domination of women, she wrote, revealed a significant gap between American ideals and social practices (Terry 1983).

In *Society in America,* then, Martineau established herself as a pioneering feminist theorist who, like other early feminists, saw a link between slavery and the oppression of women. Consequently, she was a strong and an outspoken supporter for the emancipation of both women and slaves.

Through her penetrating analysis of the subordination of American women, Martineau again stands as an important envoy of contemporary feminist theory. Doors to the economic institution, she observed, were closed to women. Martineau thus identified economic dependency as the linchpin of female subordination. The oppression of women, in short, was due to sociological forces; subordination of women was part of the structure of society.

Q Why did Herbert Spencer not attend Cambridge University, his father's alma mater? Herbert Spencer (1820–1903), the sole survivor of nine children, was born to an English schoolteacher. Due to Spencer's continual ill health, his father and uncle home schooled him, mostly in mathematics and the natural sciences. Because of his poor background in Latin, Greek, English, and history, Spencer did not feel qualified to enter Cambridge University, his father's alma mater. His subsequent career became a mixture of engineering, drafting, inventing, journalism, and writing.

Q How did Spencer view society? To explain social stability, Spencer offered an analogy based on biology. Like a human body, a society is composed of interrelated parts working together to promote its well-being and survival. People have brains, stomachs, nervous systems, and limbs. Societies have economies, religions, governments, and families. Just as the eyes and the heart make essential contributions to the functioning of the human body, legal and educational institutions are crucial for a society's functioning.

Q Why did Spencer oppose social reform? Spencer introduced a theory of social change called social Darwinism, based on Charles Darwin's theory of evolution. Spencer believed that evolutionary social change led to progress, provided that people did not interfere. If left alone, natural social selection would ensure the survival of the fittest. On these grounds, Spencer opposed social reform. The poor deserve to be poor, the rich to be rich. Society profits from allowing individuals to find their own social class level without outside help or hindrance. To interfere with poverty—or the result of any other natural process—is to harm society.

When Spencer visited America in 1882, he was warmly greeted, particularly by captains of industry. After all, his ideas of noninterference provided a moral justification for their economic practices, whether respectable or ruthless. Later, public support for government intervention increased, and Spencer's ideas began to slip out of fashion. He reportedly died with a sense of having failed.

Spencer's theories have crumbled over time. But he brought to the table for the science of sociology a discussion of the way societies are structured.

Q What were Karl Marx's basic commitments, and why, at one point, did he deny being a Marxist? The most influential of the nineteenth-century intellectuals was

Karl Marx (1818–1883) was a social scientist who underscored the importance of conflict in social change. Parts of his writings were later used a basis for communism.

the German scholar Karl Marx (1818–1883). Although he did not consider himself a sociologist (his doctorate was in philosophy), his ideas have had a significant influence in shaping the field. Marx was deeply troubled by the long hours, low pay, and harsh working conditions in the capitalist system of his day. Preferring social activism to the abstractness of philosophy, Marx was guided by his conviction that social scientists should seek to change the world rather than merely observe it. In part through long association with his friend and collaborator Friedrich Engels, the son of an industrialist, Marx's commitment to democracy and humanism was channeled toward a concern for the poverty and inequality suffered by the working class. Forced by political pressures, Marx moved from Germany to France and finally settled in London, where he devoted the remaining decades of his life to a systematic analysis of capitalism.

Unfortunately, in the minds of many today, Marxism is equated with communism. Although some of his writings were later used as a basis for communism, it is likely that he would be as discouraged with the practice of communism in the twentieth century as he was with the utopian communists of his time. In fact, at one point Marx was so unhappy with others' erroneous interpretations of his work that he disavowed being a Marxist himself.

Q What is the legacy of Marx? Herbert Spencer and Karl Marx had different conceptions of society and social change. Spencer depicted society as a set of interrelated parts that promoted its own welfare. Marx described society as a set of conflicting groups with different values and interests; the selfishness and ruthlessness of capitalists harmed society. Spencer saw progress coming only from noninterference with natural, evolutionary processes. Marx disagreed.

Marx did, however, believe in an unfolding, evolutionary pattern of social change. He envisioned a linear progression of modes of production from primitive communism through slavery, feudalism, capitalism, and communism. However, he was also convinced that the transformation from capitalism to a classless society could be accelerated through planned revolution. Although his political objective in interpreting capitalism was to hasten its fall through revolution, he believed that capitalism would eventually self-destruct anyway because of its inherent contradictions.

Although recognizing the presence of several social classes in nineteenth-century industrial society—farmers, servants, factory workers, craftspeople, owners of small businesses, moneyed capitalists—Marx predicted that ultimately all industrial societies would contain only two social classes: the **bourgeoisie,** those who owned the means for producing wealth in industrial society, and the **proletariat,** those who labored at subsistence wages for the bourgeoisie. For Marx, the key to the unfolding of history was **class conflict**—conflict between those controlling the means for producing wealth and those laboring for them. Just as slaves rebelled against slave owners and peasants revolted against the landed aristocracy, wage workers would overtake the capitalists. Out of this conflict would emerge a classless society—one without the exploitation of the powerless by the powerful.

Q Which capitalist institution did Marx consider primary? According to the principle of **economic determinism** (an idea often associated with Marx), the nature of a society is based on the society's economy. A society's economic structure determines its other systems: legal, religious, cultural, and political. Marx himself did not use the term *economic determinism.* The term was applied to his ideas by others—no doubt a consequence of his concentration on the economic institution as primary in capitalist society. Marx recognized that even in capitalist society economic and noneconomic institutions affect each other. Not only that, but he wrote that sometimes the economy "conditions" rather than "determines" the historical evolution of capitalist society.

Q Who was the first French sociologist, and what were some of his concerns? Emile Durkheim (1858–1917) was the son of a French rabbi. Durkheim originally intended to follow this family rabbinical tradition, but later experiences led him to become an agnostic, although he retained an intellectual interest in religion throughout his life. In fact, one of Durkheim's major concerns was social and moral order, an emphasis undoubtedly related to his upbringing in the home of a rabbi:

> From Judaic family training and an intimate environment Durkheim gained a deep and permanent concern for universal moral law and the problems of ethics, a concern that was not combined with any indulgent sense of humor. Indeed, he was eminently without humor and somewhat "heavy-handed." (Simpson 1963:1)

Durkheim was a brilliant student even during his early school years. In college, he was so intensely studious that his schoolmates nicknamed him "the metaphysician." He eventually became the first French academic sociologist.

Q What were Durkheim's foremost contributions? According to Durkheim, social order exists because of a broad consensus among members of a society. This consensus is especially characteristic of preindustrial, nonliterate, simple societies based on **mechanical solidarity**—social unity that comes from a consensus of values and beliefs, strong social pressures for conformity, and dependence on tradition and family. Witnessing the social upheaval brought on by industrial and democratic revolutions, Durkheim attempted to describe social order in complex, industrial society. In this modern, more complicated society, he contended, social order is based on **organic solidarity**—social unity based on a complex of highly specialized roles. These specialized roles render members of a society dependent on one another for goods and services.

Although Comte, Martineau, and other early sociologists emphasized the need to make sociology scientific, they did not have the necessary research tools. They did, however, influence later sociologists to develop more scientific methods: to replace armchair speculation with careful observation, to engage in the collection and classification of data, and to use data for formulating and testing social theories. Durkheim was one of the most prominent of these later sociologists. He first introduced the use of statistical techniques in his groundbreaking research on suicide. (See Using the Sociological Imagination, at the beginning of this chapter, and Consider This Research, later in the chapter.) In that study, Durkheim demonstrated that suicide involves more than an individual process. By revealing that suicide rates vary according to group characteristics—the suicide rate is lower among Catholics than Protestants and lower among married than single persons—Durkheim documented that human social behavior must be explained by social factors in addition to just psychological ones. In other words, Durkheim studied humans as members of groups not as individual physical objects.

Q Who wrote *The Protestant Ethic and the Spirit of Capitalism?* Max Weber (1864–1920) was the eldest son of a well-to-do German lawyer and politician. Weber's father was a man rooted in the pleasures of this world. His mother, in stark contrast, was a strongly devout Calvinist who rejected the pleasure seeking of her husband. While Weber's father was preoccupied with life on earth, Weber's mother concentrated on her future salvation. Weber was affected psychologically by the conflicting values of his parents. Even though he suffered a complete mental breakdown, he eventually recovered to do some of his best work. His mother's influence is clearly reflected in his work, especially in his regard for the sociology of religion and in one of his most famous books, *The Protestant Ethic and the Spirit of Capitalism* (Barbalet 2008; Ritzer 2011).

Max Weber's (1864–1920) model of a bureaucracy reflected greatly increased efficiency in business and government. Today, however, bureaucratic is often used as a synonym for unimaginative, plodding, or despotic.

The Art Archive/Culver Pictures/Picture Desk

Q How did Weber contribute to the development of sociology? As a university professor trained in law and economics, Weber wrote on a wide variety of topics, including the relationship between capitalism and Protestantism, the nature of power, the development and nature of bureaucracy, the religions of the world, and the nature of social classes. Thanks to the quality of Weber's work and the diversity of his interests, we can credit him with being the single most important influence on the development of sociological theory (Radkau 2009).

According to Weber, humans act on the basis of their own understanding of a situation. Consequently, sociologists must discover the personal meanings, values, beliefs, and attitudes that people bring to social situations. Understanding the subjective intentions of human social behavior could be accomplished through what Weber called the method of *verstehen*—understanding social behavior by putting oneself in the place of others. This empathetic perspective was apparently rooted in Weber's personal nature. According to Weber's wife, he "showed throughout his life an extraordinary appreciation for the problems other people faced and for the shades of mood and meaning that characterized their outlook on life" (Bendix 1962:8).

Because Weber and Marx were not intellectual contemporaries, and because Weber disagreed with Marx on many points, it is often said that Weber was debating with Marx's ghost (Wiley 1987). It was out of honest differences on issues, not disrespect, that Weber opposed some of Marx's ideas. Although Marx was, at times, openly political in advocating his ideas, Weber stressed objectivity. He strongly counseled sociologists to conduct **value-free research**—research in which personal biases are not allowed to affect the research process and its outcome. Marx saw religion as retarding social change, whereas Weber believed that religion could promote change. Also, whereas Marx emphasized the role of the economy in social stratification, Weber's analysis involved several dimensions.

One should not conclude from these differences, however, that Weber's approach to sociology was antagonistic to Marx's. Actually, Weber was the most prominent of the second-generation German scholars who were concerned with power and conflict in society. Although there are significant differences in detail, both Marx and Weber took the problems of capitalism as their unifying theme (R. Collins 1994).

One of Weber's most notable contributions is the identification of rationalization as a key influence in the transition from preindustrial society. **Rationalization**—the use of knowledge, reason, planning, and objectivity—in industrial society marked a change from the tradition, emotion, superstition, and personal relationships of preindustrial society. With rationalization, for example, businesses were to be run on proven economic principles rather than custom. One of the most familiar effects of rationalization is the expansion of bureaucracy as the dominant type of organization. According to Weber, rationalization, with its emphasis on social control, would ultimately imprison us all in an "iron cage," robbing us of our freedom, autonomy, and individuality.

Sociology in America

Although the early development of sociology occurred in Europe, the maturation of sociology has taken place primarily in the United States. Because sociology has become a science largely through the efforts of American sociologists, it is not surprising that worldwide most sociologists are American. Sociological writings in English are used by sociologists throughout the world, reflecting the tremendous global influence American sociologists have had since World War II. But, of course, American sociologists have been heavily influenced by the European originators of sociology. This is partly because early American sociologists had to rely on the writings of Smith, Comte, Martineau, Spencer, Marx, Durkheim, Weber, and others. Where would they have turned but to the existing body of literature published by the Europeans? There is, however, another reason for the strong European influence. Just as sociology in Europe was born during a time of rapid, disruptive change, sociology emerged in the United States during the period of rapid urbanization and industrialization following the Civil War. It is little wonder that Lester Ward (1841–1913), the founder of American sociology, picked up on Comte's conviction that sociology could promote social progress. Like Comte, Ward believed that sociological analysis could improve industrial, urban society.

Q Historically, how did American sociology develop? From its founding in 1892 to World War II, the first department of sociology at the University of Chicago stood at the forefront of American sociology. Housed at the University of Chicago have been a number of exceptional minds. George Herbert Mead, John Dewey, William I. Thomas, and Dorthony Swane Thomas pioneered the study of human nature and personality. Urban social problems such as prostitution, slums, and crime were studied extensively by Robert E. Park and Ernest Burgess. The study of social and cultural change was championed by William F. Ogburn. On the whole, the early Chicago School became closely linked with the idea of social reform. Emphasis on seeking solutions to problems of race, crime, and poverty continued at the University of Chicago after World War II with scholars such as Howard Becker, Joseph Gusfield, Herbert Blumer, David Riesman, and Erving Goffman (Abbott 1999).

Edith Abbott, Sophinista Breckenridge, Marion Talbott, and other female sociology researchers collaborated with the men at the Chicago School. They contributed to many studies of urban problems such as housing, child rearing, education, and poverty. Some of these women were professors in the Department of Sociology; others worked as university administrators (Deegan 1991, 2000). Many more women, having been denied university appointments, contributed to the development of social work rather than academic sociology.

After World War II, eastern universities such as Harvard and Columbia, midwestern universities such as Wisconsin and Michigan, and western universities such as Stanford and the University of California at Berkeley emerged as leading institutions fostering a diversity of sociological emphases. Sociologists such as George A. Lundberg underscored the application of the research methods of physical scientists; they wanted to make sociological research more sophisticated and scientific. Lundberg was known as a neo-positivist for his revival of Comte's scientific approach to sociology. A sociologist at Harvard, Talcott Parsons, returned to the development of general theories of society à la Weber, Durkheim, and other European scholars. Parsons was one of the leading proponents of functionalism (discussed later), which is one of several dominant theoretical perspectives in sociology today. Robert K. Merton, a Columbia University sociologist and a student of Parsons, advocated applying more specific theories, rather than general ones. Merton also stressed the importance of empirical research. By the 1970s, the number of practicing sociologists had grown dramatically. As a result, talented and influential sociologists were no longer located in only a few elite colleges and universities.

In their quest toward developing general sociological theories and establishing sociology as a science, sociologists between World War II and the 1960s had nearly lost sight of the idea that sociology could help solve social problems. Social reform emerged again during the turbulent 1960s and remains an important part of sociology today. "Humanist" sociologists, who owe much to sociologist C. Wright Mills, believe that sociology cannot be ethically neutral about important social issues. Rather, they argue, sociologists have an inherent obligation to question social arrangements and work for social transformation (A. M. Lee 1978; Scimecca 1987; Giddens 2000).

Neglected until recently, two early contributors, Jane Addams and W. E. B. Du Bois, were close friends and coworkers. Although neither was a researcher or scientist, both were concerned about applying sociology to social problems.

Q How did Jane Addams contribute to American sociology? Jane Addams was the best known and most influential of the early female sociologists in the United States

Library of Congress Prints and Photographs Division, Washington, D.C. [LC-USZ62-10598]

Humanist sociologists apply sociological theories and research findings to problems such as those that occupied Nobel Peace Prize winner Jane Addams—the urban poor in general and the plight of poor working women in particular.

(1860–1935). Although her mother died when she was two years old, Addams's father provided a loving and comfortable home for her and her eight brothers and sisters. In addition to the physical comforts he provided, her father set an example with his love of learning.

Addams was an excellent student. Her earlier education emphasized practical knowledge and the improvement of "the organizations of human society." She attended The Women's Medical College of Philadelphia but was compelled to drop out because of illness (Addams 1981; originally published in 1910).

Like other female sociologists of her time, Addams focused on developing further the sociological theories of pioneering sociologists such as Durkheim and Weber. She worked with sociologists of her generation to establish sociology as a respected academic discipline within the university. She made two other distinctive contributions. First, she rejected the prevailing view among her male colleagues that individuals are socially determined. In her mind, individuals have the will to guide their social behavior. Second, again going against the norm, she advocated applying sociological theory to social ills (Lengermann and Niebrugge 2007; T. O'Connell 2010).

During her childhood, Addams was exposed to many episodes of government corruption and to business practices that enriched owners and harmed workers. This was the beginning of her social conscience. While on one of her European trips, she saw the work being done to help the poor in London. With this example of social action and with her earlier exposure in the United States to corruption and exploitation, Addams began her life's work seeking social justice.

She cofounded Hull House in Chicago's slums. There, people who needed help—immigrants, the sick, the poor, the aged—could find some relief. Addams focused on the problems caused by the imbalance of power among the social classes. She invited sociologists from the University of Chicago to Hull House to witness firsthand the effects of the exploitation of the lower class. In addition to her work with the underclass, Addams was active in the women's suffrage and peace movements (Deegan 2000; Knight 2010).

Addams distanced herself from other sociologists of her day who feared that her social reform work would hamper ongoing efforts to establish sociology within the university. Consequently, the early histories of sociology either referred to her as a social worker or failed to recognize her at all.

Nevertheless, as a result of her tireless work for social reform, Addams was awarded the Nobel Peace Prize in 1931—the only sociologist to receive this honor. This is ironic in that Addams herself suffered a sort of class discrimination. She was not considered a sociologist during her lifetime, in part because she did not teach at a university. She was considered a social worker (a less prestigious career) because she was a woman and because she worked directly with the poor.

Q How did W. E. B. Du Bois contribute to an understanding of black communities? Together with other early African American sociologists, W. E. B. Du Bois (1868–1963), an African American educator and social activist, influenced the early development of sociology in the United States (Young and Deskins 2001). Although Du Bois's father was part white and part black (known then as a mulatto) and his mother was a direct descendant of a freedman Dutch slave, Du Bois was considered black by his associates. He attended an integrated high school in his native Great Barrington, Massachusetts, and was the first black to receive a diploma there. Du Bois earned a doctorate degree from Harvard University in 1895 and taught at a number of predominantly black universities during his career.

Du Bois learned firsthand about racial discrimination and segregation when he attended Fisk University in Nashville, Tennessee. From this experience and from teaching in rural, all-black schools around Nashville, Du Bois decided to fight what was then called "the Negro problem"—a racist policy based on the assumption that blacks were an inferior race. He did this by scientifically studying the social structure of black communities, first in Philadelphia and later in other places. In collaboration with Isabel Eaton, Du Bois published *The Philadelphia Negro,* a classic work on urban African Americans.

Besides contributing to the understanding of black communities, Du Bois worked for civil rights. He was the only black member of the Board of Directors of the National Association for the Advancement of Colored

Founders of Sociology

1. _____ is the idea that sociology should use observation and experimentation in the study of social life.
2. Which of the following sociologists contended that social change leads to progress, provided that people do not interfere?
   a. Durkheim b. Weber c. Martineau d. Spencer e. Marx f. Du Bois
3. According to the principle of _____ a society's economic system molds the society's legal system, religion, art, literature, political structure, and other social arrangements.
4. According to Durkheim, the United States is a social order based on _____ solidarity.
5. According to Weber, the method of _____ involves an attempt to understand the behavior of others by putting oneself mentally in their place.
6. Du Bois focused only on the American race question. T or F?

Answers: 1. Positivism; 2. d; 3. economic determinism; 4. organic; 5. verstehen; 6. F

People (NAACP) when it was founded in 1910, and he was the editor of its journal *Crisis* for the next twenty-four years.

Du Bois's concern for his race did not stop at the borders of the United States. He was also active in the Pan African movement, which was concerned with the rights of all African descendants, no matter where they lived. While continuing to document the experience and contributions of African people throughout the world, Du Bois died in the African country of Ghana, at the age of ninety-five (D. Lewis 1993, 2000).

Major Theoretical Perspectives R1

Theory and Perspective

Q Do scientific theories compete with each other? It is normal in science for competing, even conflicting, theories to exist simultaneously. This may be because of insufficient evidence to determine which theory is accurate. Or it may be that different theories explain different aspects of reality. This is true even for the "hard" sciences, such as modern physics. Einstein's theory of general relativity, for example, was inconsistent with the widely accepted Big Bang theory of the origin of the universe. And Einstein was deeply bothered by quantum theory, whose laws have become the foundation of modern developments in such fields as chemistry and molecular biology. Just as theories in physics oppose one another, several major theoretical perspectives compete in sociology. Each provides a particular perspective.

Q How does perspective affect perception? As implied earlier, a person's perspective draws attention to some things but blinds him or her to other possibilities. This fundamental power of perspective is graphically illustrated in drawings that psychologists often use to illustrate the concept of perception. One drawing in Figure 1.1 is a picture of an old woman—or is it?

W. E. B. DuBois (1868–1963) focused on the question of race inside and outside the United States.

The Art Archive/Culver Pictures/Picture Desk

FIGURE 1.1

The Importance of Perspectives

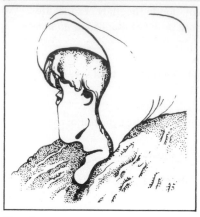

View I

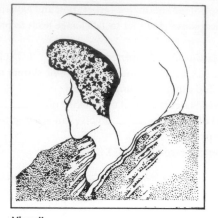

View II

View III

Our perception of things is heavily influenced by our perspective. Decide whether you want to look at View I or View II (cover the other view). After examining View I or View II, look at View III. If you decided to look at View I, you should see the old woman in View III. If you decided to look at View II, you should see the young woman in View III. Can you see both? Try it on your friends.

If you stare at the old woman long enough, she becomes a beautiful young woman with a feather boa around her neck. If you continue to look, the drawing returns to its original form. You cannot, however, see the old woman and the young woman at the same time.

Which image is real, the old woman or the young woman? It depends on your focus; your perspective influences what you see. So it is with any perspective. One perspective emphasizes certain aspects of an event; another perspective accents different aspects of the same event. When a perspective highlights certain parts of something, it necessarily places other parts in the background.

Sociology has three overarching theoretical perspectives: functionalism, conflict theory, and symbolic interactionism. Each of these perspectives provides a different slant on human social behavior (see Table 1.2). The exclusive use of any one of them prevents our seeing other aspects of social behavior, just as one cannot see the old woman and the young woman at the same time. All three perspectives together, however, allow us to see most of the important dimensions of social life that are of interest in sociology. These three perspectives can be placed within the context of macrosociology or microsociology. Functionalism and conflict theory are best viewed from the macro level, symbolic interactionism from the micro level.

Macrosociology: Functionalism

Functionalism emphasizes the contributions (functions) performed by each part of a society. For example, family, economy, and religion are all parts of a

society. The family contributes to society by providing for the reproduction and care of its new members. The economy contributes by dealing with the production, distribution, and consumption of goods and services. Religion contributes by emphasizing beliefs and practices related to sacred things. Functionalism focuses on social integration, stability, order, and cooperation.

Q Who were the originators? Among the major pioneers of this perspective was, of course, Herbert Spencer, who compared societies to living organisms. Although sociologists no longer use the organism metaphor, they still view society as a system of interrelated parts. Emile Durkheim, a contemporary of Spencer's, greatly contributed to the development of this theoretical perspective. Two of the strongest supporters of functionalism are American sociologists Talcott Parsons and Robert Merton.

Q What are the assumptions of functionalism? First, functionalists see the parts of a society as an integrated whole. A change in one part of a society leads to changes in other parts. A major change in the economy, for example, may change the family. This is precisely what happened as a result of the Industrial Revolution. Before the Industrial Revolution, when most people made their living by farming, the need for a large farm labor force was fulfilled by having many children. The need for a large family declined dramatically as industrialization substituted machines for manual labor. Smaller families, then, became the norm.

TABLE 1.2

FOCUS ON THEORETICAL PERSPECTIVES:
Assumptions of Functionalism, the Conflict Perspective, and Symbolic Interactionism

This table contains the major assumptions of the three major theoretical perspectives. Although the assumptions of functionalism and conflict theory are direct opposites, each focuses on the nature of society. Symbolic interactionism uniquely addresses interpersonal issues in sociology.

Functionalism	The Conflict Perspective	Symbolic Interactionism
1. A society is a relatively integrated whole. 2. A society tends to seek relative stability. 3. Most aspects of a society contribute to the society's well-being and survival. 4. A society rests on the consensus of its members.	1. A society experiences inconsistency and conflict everywhere. 2. A society is continually subjected to change. 3. A society involves the constraint and coercion of some members by others.	1. People's interpretations of symbols are based on the meanings they learn from others. 2. People base their interaction on their interpretations of symbols. 3. Because symbols permit people to have internal conversations, they can gear their interaction to the behavior they think others expect of them and they expect of others.

Source: The assumptions of functionalism and the conflict perspective are based on the work of Ralf Dahrendorf, "Toward a Theory of Social Conflict," *Journal of Conflict Resolution* 2 (June 1958):174. Adapted by permission of Sage Publications, Inc., © 1958.

Functionalists realize that societies are not perfectly integrated. Although the actual degree of integration varies, a certain degree of integration is necessary for the survival of the society.

Second, functionalists assume that societies tend to return to a state of stability after some upheaval has occurred. A society may change over time, but functionalists believe that it will return to a stable state by incorporating change in such a way that society will be similar to what it was before any change occurred.

The idea that a society changes yet maintains most of its original structure over time is referred to as **dynamic equilibrium**—a constantly changing balance among the parts. The student unrest on college and university campuses during the late 1960s is an illustration of dynamic equilibrium. The activities of student protestors did create some changes. The public no longer accepts all American wars as legitimate, universities are now more responsive to students' needs and goals, and the public is more aware of the importance of environmental protection. These changes, however, have not revolutionized American society. They have been absorbed into it, leaving it only somewhat different from the way it was before the student unrest. In fact, many of the student "radicals" are now part of the middle-class society they once rejected.

Third, most aspects of a society exist to promote the society's survival and welfare. It is for this reason that all complex societies have economies, families, governments, and religions. If these elements did not contribute to a society's well-being and survival, they would disappear.

According to Robert Merton (1996), **manifest functions** are intended and recognized at the time; **latent functions** are unintended and unrecognized until later. In 1696, Scotland's Parliament established free public schools in all parishes. These schools were to enable the young to read Holy Scripture. Unintended consequences included the establishment of education as a way of life for middle-class Scots and the intellectual flowering of the Scottish Enlightenment in the eighteenth century (Herman 2001). One of the manifest functions of secondary schools, for example, is teaching math skills. A latent (and positive) function of schools is the development of close friendships.

Not all elements of a society make a positive contribution. Those that have negative consequences result in **dysfunction.** Bureaucratic rules, for example, often result in rigidity and impersonality. If a secretary in your sociology department treats you like a "number" rather than an individual, you don't like the inflexibility and impersonality.

Finally, according to functionalism, there is—among most members of a society—a consensus on values. Most Americans, for example, agree on the desirability of democracy, success, and equal opportunity. This consensus of values, say the functionalists, accounts for the high degree of cooperation found in any society.

There are legitimate criticisms of the functionalist perspective: It tends to legitimize the status quo, and it neglects social change. Conflict theory, in contrast, takes social change as a focal point.

Macrosociology: Conflict Theory

Conflict theory emphasizes conflict, competition, change, and constraint within a society (Schellenberg 1982; Giddens 1979, 1987). Although this theoretical perspective was not very popular among most American sociologists until the 1960s, its roots go back as far as those of functionalism.

Q Who were the originators? Karl Marx, Max Weber, and Georg Simmel (1858–1918) are three German sociologists whose work underlies the conflict perspective. According to Marx, class conflict is inevitable in capitalist economies. Modern conflict advocates such as C. Wright Mills, Ralf Dahrendorf, and Randall Collins do not limit themselves to class conflict. They broaden Marx's insights to include conflict between any segments of a society, a point Weber had made much earlier (R. Collins 1994). For example, conflict exists between Republicans and Democrats, unions and management, industrialists and environmentalists.

Q How are the assumptions of conflict theory often the reverse of the functionalist perspective? Functionalism emphasizes a basic agreement on values within a society, concentrating on the ways people cooperate to reach common goals. Conflict theory, in contrast, focuses on the disagreements between various groups in a society or between societies. Groups and societies compete and conflict as they attempt to preserve and promote their own special values and interests.

Q How do conflict advocates view power? Because advocates of conflict theory see social living as a contest, their central question is, Who gets what? Their answer is: Those with the most **power**—the ability to control the behavior of others, even against their will—get the largest share of whatever is considered valuable in a society. Those with the most power have the most wealth, the most prestige, and the most privileges. Because some segments have more power than others, they are able to constrain the less powerful.

Wealthy and powerful corporations, for example, have long manipulated income tax laws (Ehrenreich 1994; Barlett and Steele 2002; Huffington 2004; Johnston 2005, 2007a, 2010; Kocienewski 2011). Taxes paid on income earned in a foreign country are not taxed again by the Internal Revenue Service (IRS). These foreign tax credits are fair until the tax loopholes used by corporations are considered. In the first place, U.S. corporations take foreign tax credits above what is needed to prevent double taxation. To compound the problem, some corporations claim tax credits for foreign income that is not taxable in the United States. Consequently, corporations use foreign tax credits to reduce their U.S. taxes on their U.S. income. General Electric paid no income tax to the IRS on profits of over $10 billion in 2009, receiving instead $1.1 billion tax benefit. Exxon Mobil paid $15 billion in income taxes in 2009, none of it going to the IRS (Censky 2010). Corporations continue to prevent changes in the tax code.

Taking advantage of tax code is not limited to corporations. Millions of Americans pay less than their fair share of taxes annually, including those taxpayers with incomes in excess of $200,000 who, in a given year, pay no federal income tax at all (Ehrenreich 1994; Lewis and Allison 2002). In addition, the U.S. tax code favors the rich. In 2007, the top 400 tax payers had an average income of almost $350 million. At the same time, their effective income tax rate fell to less than

How does this photo of a post-Katrina New Orleans neighborhood emphasize the conflict approach to studying society?

Mario Tamal/Getty Images

> **TABLE 1.3**
>
> **Average Income After Tax, 1979–2007 (in constant 2007 dollars, adjusted for changes in family size)**
>
> | Family Income Category | After-Tax Incomes | | |
> |---|---|---|---|
> | | 1979 | 2007 | % Change |
> | Lowest 20% | 15,306 | 17,700 | 14% |
> | Second 20% | 31,000 | 38,000 | 18% |
> | Middle 20% | 44,100 | 35,300 | 20% |
> | Fourth 20% | 57,700 | 77,700 | 26% |
> | Highest 20% | 108,170 | 198,300 | 45% |
> | Top 5% | 169,600 | 140,500 | 61% |
> | Top 10% | 346,600 | 1,319,710 | 74% |
>
> As this table reveals, people in certain income categories profited more between 1979 and 2007 than others. Relate these data to the conflict perspective.
>
> Sources: Congressional Budget Office, Effective Federal Tax Rates: 1979–2007, December 2007.

17 percent (Johnston 2010). Between 1979 and 2007, the lowest 20 percent family income category gained 14 percent in after-tax income, while the top 1 percent gained 74 percent (see Table 1.3). By 2010, the wealthiest 1 percent of Americans had received 53 percent of President Bush's 2001 individual tax cuts, totaling nearly $500 billion.

Originally, President Obama proposed to extend the Bush tax cuts, set to expire in 2010, to all but the richest 2 percent of Americans, individuals making more than $200,000 annually and families making more than $250,000. The Republicans, who won the House of Representatives and reduced the Democratic majority in the Senate in 2010, offered a different plan. Under the Republican proposal, low- and middle-income taxpayers would pay higher taxes, and the richest 1 percent would pay less. Moreover, the richest 1 percent of taxpayers would receive almost 35 percent of the total tax cuts in 2011. The Republicans blocked Obama's effort to end the tax cuts for the wealthiest Americans. A compromise extends the tax cuts for two additional years, along with a generous tax exemption for wealthy estates benefiting a relatively few super-rich Americans (Herszenhorn 2010; Herszenhorn and Hulse 2010).

Q **How does conflict theory explain social change?** Because many conflicting groups exist and the balance of power among these groups may shift, conflict theory assumes that social change is continual. For example, the women's movement is attempting to change the balance of power between men and women. As this movement progresses, we see larger numbers of women in occupations once limited to men. More women are either making or influencing decisions in business, politics, medicine, and law. Gender relations are changing

in other ways as well. More women are choosing to remain single, to marry later in life, and to have fewer children—or none. According to the conflict perspective, these changes are the result of increasing power among women.

Q **Which is the better perspective, functionalism or conflict theory?** There is no "better" theoretical perspective. Each perspective emphasizes certain aspects of social life. The advantages of one perspective highlight the disadvantages of the other. Functionalism explains much of the consensus, stability, and cooperation within a society. Conflict theory explains much of the constraint, conflict, and change.

Because each perspective has captured an essential facet of society's nature, their combination, or synthesis, is a reasonable next step. Some attempts to combine functionalism and conflict theory have already been made (Dahrendorf 1958b; van den Berghe 1963, 1978). One of the most promising is the attempt to specify the conditions under which conflict and cooperation occur. Gerhard Lenski (1984; Nolan and Lenski 2010) contends that people cooperate—even share the fruits of their labors—when scarcity threatens their survival. But conflict, competition, and constraint are likely to occur when there is more than enough for everyone. Thus, as a society moves from a subsistence economy to an affluent one, conflict, competition, and constraint increase. And the more a deprived group questions the legitimacy of its condition, the more likely it is to conflict with privileged groups (Coser 1998), as illustrated by the civil rights and women's movements.

Both functionalism and conflict theory deal with large social units and broad social processes—the state, the economy, evolution, and class conflict. At the close of the nineteenth century, some sociologists began to introduce a new focus on human social behavior. Instead of being preoccupied with larger structures per se (such as society and social class), they began to recognize the importance of microsociology, people's interactions within social structures.

Microsociology: Symbolic Interactionism

Q Who were the originators of symbolic interactionism, and what were they thinking? Max Weber and Georg Simmel were among the earliest contributors to the theoretical perspective of interactionism, which holds that groups exist only because their members influence one another's behavior. Later sociologists—namely, Charles Horton Cooley, George Herbert Mead, W. I. Thomas, Erving Goffman, Harold Garfinkel, and Herbert Blumer—expanded the insight of interactionism. They created symbolic interactionism, the most influential theoretical approach to interactionism.

Q What is symbolic interactionism? Symbolic interactionism targets a less abstract view of human social behavior than either functionalism or conflict theory. This perspective focuses on the actual interaction between people (Reynolds and Herman-Kinney 2003; Charon 2010).

Basic to the symbolic interactionist perspective is the concept of a symbol. A **symbol** is something chosen to represent something else. It may be an object, a word, a gesture, a facial expression, or a sound. A symbol is something that is observable, something concrete; but it may represent something that is not observable, something abstract. A frown can be a symbol of either

disapproval or concentration. Your school mascot, like the Hokie Bird of Virginia Tech, is a symbol of your college or university. More seriously, because African Americans were aware of past lynchings carried out by whites, blacks in 2007 took the sudden appearance of nooses across America as a symbol of hate (Fears 2007).

The meaning of a symbol is not determined by its own physical characteristics. Those who create and use the symbol assign a meaning to it. In 2007 presidential hopeful Mike Huckabee ran a televised political ad claiming to put politics aside momentarily to celebrate the birth of Christ. In the background of the talking head ad was a window pane, which appeared to form the shape of the Christian cross, thus using an object (window pane) to symbolize a central religious symbol. If people in a group do not share the same meaning for a given symbol, confusion results. For example, if some people interpret the red light of a traffic signal to mean "go," while others see the green light to mean "stop," chaos will result.

The importance of shared symbols is reflected in the formal definition of **symbolic interactionism:** the theoretical perspective that focuses on interaction among people—interaction based on mutually understood symbols.

Q What are the basic assumptions of symbolic interactionism? Herbert Blumer (1969a, 1969b), who coined the term *symbolic interactionism,* outlined three assumptions central to this perspective (see, again, Table 1.2). First, according to symbolic interactionism, we learn the meaning of a symbol from the way we see others reacting to it. For example, American musicians in Latin America soon learn that when audience

According to symbolic interactionism, social life can be likened to a theatrical performance. Don't we convey as much about ourselves in the way we dress as do the actors in this high school play?

Chris Ware/The Image Works

members whistle at the end of a performance, they are unhappy; their whistling is a symbol of disapproval, as is the symbol of booing in the United States.

Second, once we learn the meanings of these symbols, we base our behavior (interactions) on them. Now that the musicians have learned that whistling symbolizes a negative response, they will, if the crowd begins whistling, decide against an encore. This is opposite the response they would have in the United States, where whistling has a very different meaning.

Finally, symbols are central to interaction in yet another way. We use the meanings of symbols to imagine how others will respond to our behavior. Through this capability, we can have "internal conversations" with ourselves. These internal conversations enable us to visualize how others will respond to us before we act. This is crucial because we guide our interactions with people according to the behavior we think others expect of us and we expect of others. Meanwhile, these others are also having internal conversations. The interaction (acting on each other) that follows is therefore symbolic interaction.

Q **What approach has Erving Goffman added to developments in symbolic interactionism?** In an attempt to understand human interaction, Erving Goffman introduced **dramaturgy,** an approach that depicts human interaction as theatrical performance (Goffman 1961a, 1963, 1974, 1979, 1983; C. Lemert and Branaman 1997). Like actors on a stage, people (the performers) present themselves—by their dress, gestures, tone of voice—in such a way as to enhance their performance and create in others a favorable evaluation. Goffman labels this effort **presentation of self.** Through this kind of "impression management," we attempt to create a favorable evaluation of ourselves in the minds of others.

Think about your own impression management. Most students come to college concerned about acceptance by new peers. Consequently, you make decisions (consciously or not) about how you want others to view you. You may wear blue jeans and T-shirts; you may choose a preppie look. You may prominently display posters and magazines to present the desired image. You may leak appropriate personal information such as athletic, musical, or sexual prowess.

Performances, according to Goffman's theater analogy, may have a front and a back stage. College students may behave one way with dates and let down when alone with other campus classmates. Students may conduct themselves maturely when their parents are visiting campus, only to revert to old habits with their roommates. Managed behavior changes in various settings.

Goffman's theoretical approach stimulated further research. Dramaturgical symbolic interactionists have documented diverse arenas of American drama and ritual: social life, including singles bars; work, including nurses; athletics, including college football; politics, including effects of corruption; and religion, including the public's view of their social world (Deegan and Stein 1978; T. R. Young 1990; Hochschild 2003).

Although the feminist perspective grew most directly out of conflict theory, feminist sociologists use the micro perspective as well. They have done very important research within the tradition of symbolic interactionism (West and Zimmerman 1987; Gardner 1994).

Q **What are the limitations of symbolic interactionism?** By virtue of being a microsociological theoretical perspective, symbolic interactionism sometimes fails to take the larger social picture into account. Social interaction in everyday life is sometimes affected by societal forces beyond the control (or even awareness) of individuals. Anthony Giddens (1979, 2000), in his *structuration theory*, attempts to overcome this potential limitation. Although Giddens recognizes that social structures influence the individual—a central point of both functionalism and conflict theory—he emphasizes the effects individuals have on social structures. He looks at individual recognition of social forces and their subsequent actions based on this recognition. Despite the micro limitations, symbolic interactionism is one of the most influential theoretical perspectives in sociology today (Fine 1993).

Q **Each theoretical perspective seems lacking in some aspect. How, then, do these perspectives contribute to our study of sociology?** Because specific perspectives emphasize different aspects of social life, one perspective cannot be said to be inherently superior to the others. Each tells us something different about group life. All three perspectives could be used, for example, to better understand deviant behavior. Functionalism emphasizes integration, stability, and consensus, so it accents the negative consequences of deviance. It underscores the cost of crime to society and the threat to public safety. The conflict perspective views deviance quite differently. Because various groups compete to influence the passage and enforcement of legislation, those with political power tend to create and to enforce the laws. Consequently, those in power often classify those with little power, such as prostitutes and drug addicts as deviants. Interactionism focuses on the relationships within a group of deviants. It looks, for example, at the processes by which members of a drug-using group influence others to join them. It studies the ways drugs are bought from pushers, the methods for raising money to pay the pushers, and the ways people who use drugs interpret the user's activities.

CHECK YOURSELF 1.5 R2

Major Theoretical Perspectives

1. A _____ perspective is a set of assumptions accepted as true by its advocates.
2. Indicate whether the following statements represent functionalism (F), conflict theory (C), or symbolic interactionism (S).
   ____ a. Societies are in dynamic equilibrium.
   ____ b. Power is one of the most important elements in social life.
   ____ c. Religion helps hold a society together morally.
   ____ d. Symbols are crucial to social life.
   ____ e. A change in the economy leads to a change in the family structure.
   ____ f. People conduct themselves according to their subjective interpretations of reality.
   ____ g. Many elements of a society exist to benefit the powerful.
   ____ h. Different segments of a society compete to achieve their own self-interests rather than cooperate to benefit others.
   ____ i. Social life should be understood from the viewpoint of the individuals involved.
   ____ j. Most members of a society agree that democracy is desirable.
   ____ k. Social change is constantly occurring.
   ____ l. Conflict is harmful and disruptive to society.
3. According to the _____ approach, humans use impression management to control the attitudes and responses of others toward them.

Answers: 1. theoretical; 2. a. (F), b. (C), c. (F), d. (S), e. (F), f. (S), g. (C), h. (C), i. (S), j. (F), k. (C), l. (F); 3. dramaturgical

Two Emerging Social Theories R1

Feminist Social Theory

As in any social science, sociological theory continues to grow in new directions. Two emerging, yet not fully developed, theories are *feminist social theory and postmodern social theory*.

Q **What is feminist social theory?** Feminist social theory links the lives of women (and men) to the structure of gender relationships within society. Three frameworks within the broad umbrella of feminist theory can be isolated: *liberal feminism, radical feminism*, and *socialist feminism* (Freedman 2001; Andersen 2010). Each of these frameworks attempts to explain the relationship between gender, social class, and minority status.

Advocates of **liberal feminism** focus on equal opportunity for women and heightened public awareness of women's rights. Operating within the existing structure of society, liberal feminists look to legal and social change to rectify the abridgment of women's rights. If women are to receive the same treatment accorded men, Americans must alter long-standing laws, social policies, and social structures. Equal pay for equal work, abortion rights, and civil rights are among the issues uniting the liberal feminist perspective.

Liberal feminism attributes the subordination of women to unequal rights and to the ways in which males and females are taught by society to view themselves. **Radical feminism** traces the oppression of women to male-dominated societies. Males in patriarchal society use their power, prestige, and economic advantage to dominate females. Male-controlled institutions—family, religion, economy, education, government—define women as subordinate to men and, thus, ensure the perpetuation of female subordination. Radical feminists are especially interested in male supremacy and the ways men gain and maintain the power to control all social institutions (Crow 1998).

Q **What does socialist feminism add to radical feminism?** Socialist feminism, which is actually more radical than radical feminism, sees capitalism as the source of female oppression. This perspective of capitalism, however, goes beyond the Marxist interpretation. Socialist feminists contend that female oppression extends beyond women being the property of men in capitalist societies. Because female oppression exists in societies without a capitalist economic base, socialist feminists reason that more than capitalism is at work in female oppression. That something else is patriarchy. Patriarchy is the means for male domination of females in preindustrial and authoritarian societies (Khouri 2005). In capitalist society, the power relations of the class structure combine with the force of patriarchy to create and maintain male oppression of women.

Despite some significant differences in theoretical perspectives, the various feminist theorists share at least two common themes. First, they believe that sociology carries a bias from years of theory and research shared by white middle-class males from Western Europe and North America. Second, they believe that the nature of gender and gender relationships is sociological (rather than psychological), embedded in social structures.

Postmodern Social Theory

Q **What is postmodernism?** It is intellectually embarrassing to summarize postmodern social theory as if it is a single simple view shared by all postmodernists. However, even the lowest common denominator version of postmodern sociological theory is helpful.

The term *postmodern* obviously draws its meaning from its departure from modernism. Though the dates are somewhat arbitrary and controversial, **modernism** refers to broad changes beginning in the late nineteenth century and ending around World War II. Modernism is the culmination of the European Enlightenment characterized by a belief that humans are autonomous beings, that legitimate worldviews can be formed through reason, and that objective truth is knowable. Challenging these assumptions, **postmodernism** assumes that individuals are not autonomous, that reason is an unreliable way to interpret the world, and that we cannot discover ultimate truth (McCallum 1996). This definition obviously needs clarification.

According to postmodern theory, humans do not exist independently or think autonomously within the community to which they belong. Everything is culturally relative; there is no absolute truth. Even reason is unreliable because our culture influences our interpretation of truth. The postmodernism perspective is in stark contrast to the modernism approach where individuals using independent reason discover absolute truth (Baert and Da silvia 2010; Jones, Le Boutillier, and Bradbury 2011).

Q **Do postmodernists believe nothing is true?** Postmodernists do not deny that *some* things are true. In any community, capital punishment kills people, extreme subjugation of women stunts their personal development, and social inequality gives some people advantages over others. Postmodernists, though, are questioning those versions of belief systems such as socialism, capitalism, and communism that community members believe are superior to other belief systems because they are absolute "truth."

Q **What does postmodern theory tell us about the nature of society?** Still in its infancy, postmodernism is more an analysis of a social condition than a body of theory (Lyotard 1979; Ritzer 1998, 2008, 2011). Postmodernists believe that the pretense of objective truth is used by the powerful to legitimate and maintain power over others. By pretending the validity of some absolute truth, elites drown out the voices of dissenters; they dominate and marginalize the weak and disadvantaged. According to postmodernists, this occurs within a particular economic environment.

Q **In what economic environment did postmodernism emerge?** Postmodernism arose concurrently with the transition of Western society from industrialism to postindustrialism, after World War II. In **postindustrial society,** knowledge (information) and service organizations dislodge the production of goods as the major source of power and the prime mover of social life (Bell 1999). The preeminence of manufacturing is displaced by information industries such as Microsoft and Google and by service industries like health care and financial services.

Along with postindustrialization comes *globalization*. **Globalization** is the process by which increasingly permeable geographical boundaries lead different societies to share in common some economic, political, and social arrangements (Scott and Marshall 2009; Ritzer 2010). The process of globalization, then, promotes increased interaction and interdependence among societies around the world. We will return to this economic environment in Chapter 5 ("Social Structure and Society").

CHECK YOURSELF  **1.6**   **R2**

Emerging Theoretical Perspectives

1. Match the three feminist theoretical frameworks with the following words and phrases.

    ____ a. liberal feminism   (1) patriarchy

    ____ b. radical feminism   (2) capitalism and patriarchy

    ____ c. socialist feminism   (3) equality of opportunity

                                      (4) social and legal reform

2. The theoretical perspective that denies the existence of objective reality is called _____.

Answers: 1. a. (3), b. (1), c. (2); 2. postmodernism

On to Chapter 2

This chapter focused on the sociological perspective, with considerable emphasis on sociological theory.

Any science requires the empirical testing of its theories. The next chapter, "Social Research," focuses on that topic.

INTEGRATED GOALS AND SUMMARY

1. **Illustrate the unique sociological perspective from both the micro and macro levels of analysis.**
   - Sociology is the scientific study of social structure. It maintains a group rather than an individual focus. It emphasizes the patterned and recurrent social relationships between group members and uses social factors to explain human social behavior. Macrosociology and microsociology are levels of analysis crucial to understanding the sociological perspective.

2. **Describe three uses of the sociological perspective.**
   - Sociology benefits both the individual and the public. First, through the sociological imagination, individuals can better understand the relationship between what is happening in their personal lives and the social events occurring in their society. The sociological imagination promotes the questioning of conventional, and often misleading, ways of thinking, and it provides a vision of social life that extends far beyond the often narrow confines of one's limited personal experience. Second, sociological research contributes to public policies and programs. Third, sociology enhances the development of occupational skills.

3. **Distinguish sociology from other social sciences.**
   - It was not until the nineteenth century that the process of differentiating the various social sciences seriously began. Five of the major social sciences—anthropology, psychology, economics, political science, and history—are clearly distinguishable from sociology. Although each is a separate field in its own right, each shares some areas of interest with sociology.

4. **Outline the contributions of the major pioneers of sociology.**
   - Sociology is rather young. It was born out of the social upheaval created by the French and Industrial Revolutions. In an attempt to understand the social chaos of their time, early sociologists emphasized social stability and social change. Sociology received its start primarily from the writings of European scholars Adam Smith, Auguste Comte, Harriet Martineau, Herbert Spencer, Karl Marx, Emile Durkheim, and Max Weber.
   - Auguste Comte, the generally acknowledged father of sociology, believed that society could advance only if studied scientifically. Harriet Martineau contributed to research methods, political theory, and feminism. According to Herbert Spencer, social progress occurs only if people do not interfere with natural processes. Karl Marx argued that history unfolds according to the outcome of conflict between social classes. In capitalist societies, the conflict is between the ruling bourgeoisie and the ruled proletariat.
   - Emile Durkheim shared with the earlier pioneers a concern for social order. Two of his major contributions were the nonpsychological explanation of social life and the introduction of statistical techniques in social research. One of Max Weber's major contributions was also methodological. His method of *verstehen* assumed an understanding of human social behavior based on mentally putting oneself in the place of others. He also explored the process of rationalization as it existed in the transition from traditional to industrial society.

5. **Summarize the development of sociology in the United States.**
   - American sociology has been heavily influenced by the early European sociologists, in part because it, too, was born during a time of social upheaval (following the Civil War). From its founding in the 1800s to World War II, the hotbed of American sociology was the University of Chicago. After World War II, sociology departments in the East and Midwest rose to prominence.

6. **Identify the three major theoretical perspectives in sociology today.**
   - A theoretical perspective is a set of assumptions considered true by its advocates. Functionalism and conflict theory are the province of macrosociology. Symbolic interactionism is part of microsociology.
   - According to functionalism, a society is an integrated whole, seeks a dynamic equilibrium, is composed of elements promoting its well-being, and is based on the consensus of its members. The conflict perspective contradicts these assumptions. A society experiences conflict at all times, is constantly changing, and rests on the domination of some of its members by other members.
   - According to symbolic interactionism, people's interpretations of symbols are based on the meanings they learn from others. People base their interaction on their interpretations of symbols. Because symbols permit people to have internal conversations, they can gear their interaction to the behavior they think others expect of them and they expect of others.

7. **Differentiate two emerging theoretical perspectives.**
   - Feminist theory, a form of conflict theory, can be divided into three frameworks—liberal feminism, radical feminism, and socialist feminism. Although there are important differences among these theoretical frameworks, they each link the lives of women and men to the structure of gender relationships within society.
   - Postmodernism rejects the idea that humans are independent entities, that reason is a reliable way of thinking, and that objective truth can be ascertained.

CONCEPT REVIEW

____ a. economic determinism
____ b. mechanical solidarity
____ c. positivism
____ d. dynamic equilibrium
____ e. social structure
____ f. bourgeoisie

____ g. macrosociology
____ h. sociology
____ i. *verstehen*
____ j. symbol
____ k. latent function
____ l. conflict theory

____ m. presentation of self
____ n. social dynamics
____ o. theoretical perspective
____ p. postmodernism
____ q. radical feminism

1. a set of assumptions accepted as true by its advocates
2. the theoretical perspective that emphasizes conflict, competition, change, and constraint within a society
3. an unintended and unrecognized consequence of some element of a society
4. the ways people attempt to create a favorable evaluation of themselves in the minds of others
5. the study of social change
6. the method of understanding the behavior of others by putting oneself mentally in another's place
7. patterned, recurring social relationships
8. the scientific study of social structure
9. the use of observation, experimentation, and other methods of the physical sciences in the study of social life
10. something that stands for or represents something else
11. the idea that the nature of a society is based on the society's economy
12. social unity based on a consensus of values and norms, strong social pressure for conformity, and dependence on tradition and family
13. the assumption by functionalists that a society both changes and maintains most of its original structure over time
14. members of industrial society who own the means for producing wealth
15. the level of analysis that focuses on relationships between social structures without reference to the interaction of the people involved
16. the theoretical perspective that denies the existence of objective truth
17. the feminist social theory that traces the oppression of women to the fact that societies are dominated by men

CHECK YOURSELF REVIEW

1. Microsociology focuses on the relationships between social structures without reference to the interaction of the people involved. T or F?
2. W. E. B. Du Bois focused only on the American race question. T or F?
3. _____ explanations of group behavior are inadequate because human activities are influenced by social forces that individuals have not created and cannot control.
4. According to Durkheim, the United States is a social order based on _____ solidarity.
5. The _____ is the set of mind that enables individuals to see the relationship between events in their personal lives and events in their society.
6. A _____ perspective is a set of assumptions accepted as true by its advocates.
7. Match the following fields of study and aspects of family life.
   ____ a. anthropology
   ____ b. sociology
   ____ c. history
   ____ d. political science
   ____ e. economics
   ____ f. psychology
   (1) distribution of income and the family
   (2) effects of slavery on family stability
   (3) relationship between voting and the family
   (4) effects of early marriage on divorce
   (5) link between early childhood emotional support and familial retardation
   (6) universality of the nuclear family
8. Indicate whether the following statements represent functionalism (F), conflict theory (C), or symbolic interactionism (S).
   ____ a. Religion helps hold a society together morally.
   ____ b. Symbols are crucial to social life.
   ____ c. A change in the economy leads to a change in the family structure.
   ____ d. Many elements of a society exist to benefit the powerful.

____ e. Social life should be understood from the view-point of the individuals involved.

____ f. Social change is constantly occurring.

9. Match the three feminist theoretical frameworks with the words or phrases.

____ a. liberal feminism

____ b. radical feminism

____ c. socialist feminism

(1) Patriarchy

(2) capitalism and patriarchy

(3) equality of opportunity

10. Which of the following is not one of the uses of the sociological imagination?

a. seeing the interplay of self and society

b. capacity for creating new aspects of culture not thought of by others

c. ability to question aspects of social life most people take for granted

d. capability of understanding the social forces that shape daily life

11. Which of the following sociologists contended that social change leads to progress, provided that people do not interfere?

a. Durkheim

b. Weber

c. Martineau

d. Spencer

e. Marx

f. Du Bois

GRAPHIC REVIEW

Table 1.3 contains data on average income (after taxes) in America—by income category. Answering the following questions will test your understanding of this table.

1. What is the most important generalization you can make from the data?

_____

_____

_____

2. How would conflict theorists interpret the data?

_____

_____

_____

3. Would functionalists agree with the interpretation of conflict theorists? Why or why not?

_____

_____

_____

CRITICAL-THINKING QUESTIONS

1. Think of a recent time you conformed. Were you responding to group pressure? Explain.

_____

_____

2. Apply the sociological imagination to your college choice. Identify the social forces (e.g., family, friends, school, and the media) that you believe had the most influence on your decision.

_____

_____

3. Max Weber introduced the concept of *verstehen*. How would you use this approach to social research if you wanted to investigate the importance of money to your peers?

_____

_____

4. Think of an aspect of human social behavior (e.g., college sports or fraternities and sororities) that you would like to know more about. Which of the three theoretical perspectives would you use? Explain your choice.

_____

_____

5. Could any of your behavior over the past week be described by the dramaturgical perspective? Explain, using personal examples.

_____

_____

ANSWER KEY

Concept Review

a. 11
b. 12
c. 9
d. 13
e. 7
f. 14
g. 15
h. 8
i. 6
j. 10
k. 3
l. 2
m. 4
n. 5
o. 1
p. 16
q. 17

Check Yourself Review

1. F
2. F
3. Individualistic
4. organic
5. sociological
    imagination
6. theoretical
7. a. 6
    b. 4
    c. 2
    d. 3
    e. 1
    f. 5
8. a. F
    b. S
    c. F
    d. C
    e. S
    f. C
9. a. 3
    b. 1
    c. 2
10. b
11. d

2 Social Research

Spencer Grant/PhotoEdit

S GOALS

- Identify the major nonscientific sources of knowledge about society.
- Explain why science is a superior source of knowledge about society.
- Outline the steps sociologists use to guide their research.
- Discuss cause-and-effect concepts, and apply the concept of causation to the logic of science.

- Differentiate the major qualitative research methods used by sociologists.
- Describe the major qualitative research methods used by sociologists.
- Describe the role of ethics in research.
- State the importance of reliability, validity, and replication in social research.

USING THE
SOCIOLOGICAL
IMAGINATION

Does lower church attendance result in a rise in juvenile delinquency? The finding of a statistical link between church attendance and delinquency (delinquency increases as church attendance decreases) meets the test of common sense. We can easily speculate on why this would be the case. An observed relationship between these two events, however, does not necessarily mean that one causes the other. In fact, delinquency increases as church attendance decreases because of a third factor—age. Age is related to both delinquency and church attendance. Older adolescents not only go to church less often but are also more likely to be delinquents. The apparent relationship between church attendance and delinquency, then, is actually produced by a third factor—age—that affects both of the original two factors.

Mistaken ideas can survive when people rely on sources of knowledge not grounded in the use of reason and not stimulated by the search for truth. A major benefit of sociological research lies in its replacement of false beliefs with more accurate knowledge. Before we turn to the logic of scientific research and the methods of sociological research, it will be helpful to consider some sources of knowledge.

Sources of Knowledge About Society ☒

Nonscientific Sources of Knowledge

We all have a problem in assessing the truth of information we encounter. That problem is called "motivated reasoning": the tendency to accept less critical information that is consistent with ideas we already have and to reject information that contradicts our present beliefs. Recent research on the brain helps explain why this happens. When confronted with information we consider neutral, brain activity is centered in areas that control higher reasoning. Exposure to political information (about which we usually have strong feelings) triggers activity in areas of the brain involving emotion (McArdle 2008). Given the power of motivated reasoning in filtering information, we need to be aware of nonscientific sources of knowledge that tend to short-circuit reasoning power, leaving us prey to erroneous thinking. The rest of this chapter explores how science promotes the use of reasoning rather than emotion in evaluating information.

Q How do we know what we think we know? Four major nonscientific sources of knowledge are intuition, common sense, authority, and tradition. *Intuition* is quick and ready insight that is not based on rational thought. To intuit is to have the feeling of immediately understanding something because of insight from an unknown inner source. For example, the decision against dating a particular person because "it feels wrong" is a decision based on intuition.

Common sense refers to opinions that are widely held because they seem so obviously correct. The problem with commonsense ideas is that they are often wrong. Some people take as common sense, for example, that property values will decline when African Americans move into a white middle-class neighborhood. Others believe that men are superior to women. Yet, research supports neither of these ideas. As philosopher Alasdair MacIntyre writes, "Because common sense is never more than an inherited amalgam of past clarities and past confusions, the defenders of common sense are unlikely to enlighten us" (MacIntyre 1998:117).

An *authority* is someone who is supposed to have special knowledge that we do not have. A king believed to be ruling by divine right is an example of an authority. Reliance on authority is often appropriate. It is more reasonable to accept a doctor's diagnosis of an illness than to rely on information from a neighbor whose friend had the same symptoms (although even a single doctor's diagnosis should not be accepted uncritically). In other instances, however, authority can obscure the truth. Astrologers who advise people to guide their lives by the stars are an example of a misleading authority. Advocates of science and supporters of authority are currently debating an approach to teaching science: evolution versus intelligent design.

The fourth major nonscientific source of knowledge is *tradition*. Despite evidence to the contrary, it is traditional to believe that an only child will be self-centered and socially inept. In fact, to avoid these alleged personality traits, most Americans still wish to have two or more children (Sifford 1989). And barriers to equal opportunity for women persist in industrial societies despite evidence that traditional negative ideas about the capabilities of women are fallacious.

Nonscientific sources of knowledge often provide false or misleading information (Adler and Clark 2003), sometimes leading to completely opposite conclusions. One person's intuition tells him to buy oil stocks, whereas another person's intuition tells her to avoid all energy stocks. One person's commonsense conclusion may deem the feminist movement as harmful to the family, while it seems perfectly obvious to someone else that feminism promotes family values.

Intuition, common sense, authority, and tradition engender motivated reasoning because conceptions

When forming opinions about global warming, a majority of Americans rely on scientific sources. The protestors in this picture are concerned about the harm that will be done to the planet should we listen to those relying on nonscientific sources regarding climate change.

Jewel Samad/Getty Images

they generate are emotion-laden. Information from these sources of knowledge comes as pronouncements that attempt to deny any opportunity for falsification. Without choice there is room only for emotional thinking.

Science as a Source of Knowledge

Science is considered a superior source of knowledge. In part, this is because science is based on the principles of objectivity and verifiability.

Q What is objectivity? According to the principle of **objectivity**, scientists are expected to prevent their personal biases from influencing the interpretation of their results. A male, antifeminist biologist investigating aptitudes, for example, is supposed to guard against any unwarranted tendency to conclude that males make better scientists than females. Researchers must interpret their data solely on the basis of merit; the outcome they personally prefer is irrelevant. This is what Max Weber (1918–1946) meant by value-free research (see Chapter 1).

Can scientists really be objective? Sometimes, scientists unintentionally let their personal biases influence their work. For example, in the 1950s, pioneering sex researcher Alfred Kinsey revolutionized popular thinking about sex in America. He has been accused of being both a homosexual and a masochist, characteristics said to unduly influence his research. James H. Jones (1997) makes this charge and presents evidence that Kinsey was a man with an ideological agenda whose research methods undermine his claim to objectivity. Kinsey's generalizations about the American population were

based, according to Jones, on data gathered largely from volunteers, including disproportionate numbers of male prostitutes, gays, and prison inmates.

Q How can subjectivity be reduced? Scientists, then, cannot possibly be completely objective. But if subjectivity in research cannot be eliminated, it can be reduced. According to Zinn, the best approximation of objectivity exists when researchers strive for the truth and follow specific safeguards: continually reexamine their thinking, permit contradicting evidence to alter their view, and make public any evidence that runs counter to their view of the truth. If researchers are aware of their biases, they can consciously take their biases into account. They can be more careful in designing research instruments, selecting samples, choosing statistical techniques, and interpreting results. According

When investigating the cause of a murder, modern police have to be guided by the principle of multiple causation.

Robert Voets/CBS Photo Archive/Getty Images

Should You Believe Everything You Read?

It is sometimes said that we are living in the "age of instant information." One unfortunate side effect is the tendency for studies and research results to be reported in the media without background or explanation. There are, however, some easy steps you can follow that will make you a savvy consumer in the information marketplace.

BE SKEPTICAL. Be suspicious of what you read. The media sound-bite treatment tends to sensationalize and distort information. For example, the media may report that $500,000 was spent to find out that love keeps families together. In fact, this may have been only one small part of a larger research project. Moreover, chances are the media have oversimplified even this part of the researcher's conclusions.

CONSIDER THE SOURCE OF INFORMATION. The credibility of a study may be affected by who paid for the results. For example, you should know whether a study on the relationship between cancer and tobacco has been sponsored by the tobacco industry or by the American Cancer Society. Suppose that representatives of tobacco companies denied the existence of any research linking throat and mouth cancer with snuff dipping. Further suppose that an independent medical researcher concluded that putting a "pinch between your cheek and gum" has led to cancer in humans. The self-interest of the tobacco companies taints their objectivity.

At the very least, you want to know the source of information before making a judgment. This caution is especially relevant to Internet research. Because Internet information varies widely in its accuracy and reliability, sources must be evaluated with great care.

EVALUATE THE DATA YOU ARE GIVEN. In a series of books, sociologist Joel Best (Best 2001, 2004, 2008) develops the point that many statistics are flawed. This poses a serious problem in the consumption of information, he argues, because of the sanctity of numbers. Statistics that interest us are assumed to be factual or they wouldn't be made public. Actually, the numbers we read range from reasonably accurate to near fiction. Best offers a rule of thumb for evaluating statistics: Be wary of statistics presented without information about the methods that produced them. It ought to be possible to know the original source of a statistic so that an interested person could learn about the methods the researchers used to collect the data and the measurement choices they made. Of course, the general reader seldom makes such a detailed follow-up. Still, media sources can provide some information about the numbers they report such as the source of the data, the definition of terms, the number of people polled, and the phrasing of questions. The more information given, the more confidence we can have in our ability to assess the data reported. Be wary of numbers that are thrown out as naked "facts."

DO NOT MISTAKE CORRELATION FOR CAUSATION. Remember that a correlation between two variables does not mean that one caused the other. At one time, the percentage of Americans who smoked was increasing at the same time that life expectancy was increasing. Did this mean that smoking caused people to live longer? Actually, a third factor—improved health care—accounted for the change. Do not assume that two events are related causally just because they occur together.

Think About It

Bring to class an article reporting on a study. These articles can often be found in news magazines. Be prepared to explain how these three safeguards apply to the article's report.

---

to Swedish economist Gunnar Myrdal (1983), personal recognition of biases is insufficient; public exposure of them is essential. Personal values, Myrdal contends, should be explicitly stated, so that those who read a research report can be aware of the author's biases (see "See Sociology in Your Life").

Q What is verifiability? **Verifiability** means that a study can be repeated by other scientists. This is possible because scientists report in detail on their research methods. Verifiability is important because it exposes scientific work to critical analysis, retesting, and revision by colleagues. If researchers repeating a study produce results at odds with the original study, the original findings will be questioned. Under these circumstances,

erroneous theories, findings, and conclusions will not survive (Begley 1997).

A Model for Doing Research

In an effort to obtain accurate knowledge, social scientists use a research model known as the *scientific method*. This model follows several distinct steps: identifying a problem, reviewing the literature, formulating hypotheses, developing a research design, collecting data, analyzing data, and stating findings and conclusions (Schutt 2006; Blaikie 2009).

Sources of Knowledge About Society

1. Intuition is quick and ready insight based on rational thought. T or F?
2. The major problem with nonscientific sources of knowledge is that such sources often provide erroneous information. T or F?
3. Define objectivity and verifiability as used in science.
4. According to Gunnar Myrdal, it is enough that scientists themselves recognize their biases. T or F?

Answers: 1. F; 2. T; 3. Objectivity exists when an effort is made to prevent personal biases from distorting research. Verifiability means that any given piece of scientific research done by one scientist can be duplicated by other scientists; 4. F

Identifying the Problem

Researchers begin by choosing an object or a topic for investigation. A research question may be chosen for a variety of reasons—because it interests the researcher, addresses a social problem, tests a major theory, or responds to a government agency's needs.

Reviewing the Literature

Once the object of study has been identified, the researcher must examine the literature for relevant theories and previous research findings. For example, a sociologist investigating suicide will probably develop an approach that makes use of the classic study of suicide by Emile Durkheim as well as other studies on the topic.

Formulating Hypotheses

From a careful examination of relevant theory and previous research findings, a sociologist can state one or more **hypotheses**—tentative, testable statements of relationships among variables. These variables must be defined precisely enough to be measurable. One hypothesis might be, "the longer couples are married, the less likely they are to divorce." The independent variable (length of marriage) and the dependent variable (divorce) must be defined and measured. Scientists measure variables through the use of **operational definitions**—definitions of abstract concepts in terms of simpler, observable procedures. Divorce could be defined operationally as the legal termination of marriage. If so, the measurement of divorce would be qualitative—the couple is either legally married or not. Length of marriage could be measured quantitatively—the number of years a couple has been legally married.

Developing a Research Design

A research design describes the procedures the researcher will follow for collecting and analyzing data. Will the study be a survey or a case study? If it is a survey, will data be collected from a cross section of an entire population, as with the Harris and Gallup polls, or will a sample be selected from only one city? Will simple percentages or more sophisticated statistical methods be used? These and many other questions must be answered while the research design is being developed.

Prominent among these questions is the determination of the population and sample to be used in the study. A **population** consists of all those people with the characteristics a researcher wants to study. A population can be all college sophomores in the United States, all former drug addicts living in Connecticut, or all current inmates of the Ohio State Penitentiary. Most populations are too large and inaccessible to collect information on all members. For this reason, a sample is drawn. A **sample** is a limited number of cases drawn from the larger population. The sample must be selected carefully if it is to have the same basic characteristics as the population. If a sample is not representative of the population from which it is drawn, the survey findings cannot be used to make generalizations about the entire population (Winship and Mare 1992). The U.S. Census Bureau regularly uses sample surveys in its highly accurate work. The Gallup and Harris polls are also recognized as reliable sample indicators of national trends and public opinion.

Collecting Data

There are three basic ways of gathering data in sociological research: asking people questions, observing people's behavior, and analyzing existing materials and records. Sociologists studying the harmony in interracial marriages could question couples about their communication skills and compatibility. They could locate an organization with a large number of interracially married couples and observe couples' behavior. Or they could compare the divorce rate among interracially married couples with the divorce rate of the population as a whole.

Analyzing Data

Once the data are collected and classified, they can be analyzed to determine whether the hypotheses are supported. This is not as easy or automatic as it sounds, because results are not always obvious. Because the same data can be interpreted in several ways, judgments have to be made. Guarding against personal biases is especially important in this phase of research.

Stating Findings and Conclusions

After analyzing the data, a researcher is ready to state the conclusions of the study. It is during this phase that the methods are described and the hypotheses are formally accepted, rejected, or modified. The conclusions of the study are then related to the theory and research findings on which the hypotheses are based, and directions for further research are suggested. Depending on the findings, the original theory itself may have to be altered. Whether the statement of conclusions appears in a scientific journal, a book, or online, it includes a description of the methods used. By making the research procedures public, scientists make it possible for others to duplicate the research, conduct

a slightly different study, or proceed in a very different direction.

Using the Research Model

Realistically, do sociologists follow these steps? Some sociologists believe that this research model is too rigid to capture spontaneous, subjective, and changeable social behavior. They may prefer to discover their findings without preconceived ideas of outcome, without hypothesis-biased observations, and without an inflexible research design. Even though most sociologists do follow the model, they do not do so mechanically. They may conduct exploratory studies prior to stating hypotheses or before developing research designs. Or they may alter their hypotheses and research designs as their investigations proceed.

This does not mean that these steps can be ignored in conducting sociological research. Most sociologists more or less go through this process anyway. And all researchers, even those who say they do not follow this procedure, have the model in mind as they do their work. Moreover, research reports are evaluated by other sociologists with this method in mind. If researchers seriously violate the research process, their findings and conclusions may not be viewed as credible.

CHECK YOURSELF   2.2   R2

A Model for Social Research

Listed here are the steps in the research model. Following are some concrete examples related to the sociability of the only child. Indicate the appropriate example for each step number.

_E_ Step 1: identifying the problem
_a_ Step 2: reviewing the literature
_b_ Step 3: formulating hypotheses
_g_ Step 4: developing a research design
_c_ Step 5: collecting data
_f_ Step 6: analyzing data
_d_ Step 7: stating findings and conclusions

a. The researcher reads past theory and research on the sociability of only children.
b. From previous research and existing theory, the researcher states that only children appear to be more intelligent than children with siblings.
c. The researcher collects data on only children from a high school in a large city.
d. The researcher writes a report giving evidence that only children are more intelligent than children with brothers or sisters.
e. The researcher decides to study the intelligence level of only children.
f. The researcher classifies and processes the data collected to test a hypothesis.
g. The researcher decides on the data needed to test a hypothesis, the methods for data collection, and the techniques for data analysis.

Answers: Step 1: e; Step 2: a; Step 3: b; Step 4: g; Step 5: c; Step 6: f; Step 7: d

Causation and the Logic of Science 🔳

The Nature of Causation

Q **What is causation?** Scientists assume that an event occurs for a reason. According to the concept of **causation**, events occur in predictable, nonrandom ways, and one event leads to another. Why does this book remain stationary rather than rise slowly off your desk, go past your eyes, and rest against the ceiling? Why does a ball thrown into the air return to the ground? Why do the planets stay in orbit around the sun?

More than 2,000 years ago, Aristotle claimed that heavier objects fall faster than lighter ones. In the late 1500s, Galileo contended that all objects fall with the same acceleration (change of speed) unless slowed down by air resistance or some other force. But it was not until the late 1600s that Sir Isaac Newton developed the theory of gravity. We now know that objects fall because the Earth has a gravitational attraction for objects near it. The planets remain in orbit around the sun because of the gravitational force created by the sun.

Because scientists assume causation, one of their main goals is to discover cause-and-effect relationships. They attempt to discover the factors—there is usually more than one—that cause events to happen.

Q **Why multiple causation?** Leo Rosten, noted author and political scientist, once wrote, "If an explanation relies on a single cause, it is surely wrong." Events in the physical or social world are generally too complex to be explained by any single factor. For this reason, scientists rely on the principle of **multiple causation**, which states that an event occurs as a result of several factors operating in combination. What, for example, causes crime? Cesare Lombroso, a nineteenth-century Italian criminologist, believed that criminals inherited the predisposition to commit crimes and that certain physical traits (large jaws, receding foreheads) could identify these deviants. Modern criminologists reject Lombroso's (or anyone else's) one-factor explanation of crime. They cite numerous factors that contribute to crime, including drugs; excessive materialism; peer pressure; hopeless poverty in slums; and overly lax, overly strict, or erratic child-rearing practices. Each of these factors is a variable.

Because social life is very complex and individuals have freedom of choice, it is impossible to establish 100 percent causation. Consequently, social scientists rely on strong correlations. It is difficult, as well, to establish absolute truth in sociology because relationships between variables can change over time. For example, conservative ideas and memberships in the Republican Party may be strongly correlated during one historical period, but not another. At the time of the Civil War, the Republican Party was founded on very liberal ideas such as the abolition of slavery. Finally, a sociological finding does not apply to everyone in a group. The more people in a group to which the finding does apply, the stronger the correlation. Sociologists often must use qualifying statements in their conclusions, like "most" or "some" of the people with conservative ideas are Republicans. Some may be libertarian, some may be apolitical, and some may even be Democrats.

Causation and Variables

Q **How, in a research project, are variables related to causation?** A **variable** is a characteristic (e.g., age, education, or social class) that is subject to change. It occurs in different (varying) degrees. Some materials have greater density than others; some people have higher incomes than others; the average literacy rate is higher in developed countries than in developing ones. Each of these is a **quantitative variable**, a variable that can be measured and given a numerical value. Because differences can be measured numerically, individuals, groups, objects, or events can be pinpointed at some specific point along a continuum. In contrast, a **qualitative variable** consists of variation in kind rather than in number. It denotes differences in distinguishing characteristics of a category rather than differences in numerical degree. Sociologists often use sex, marital status, and group membership as qualitative variables. This is an either/or or yes/no variable: People are either male or female; they are either single or married; they are either Greek or they are not (See Table 2.1 and "Think Globally" 2.1 for other examples of quantitative and qualitative variables).

Once scientists identify the variables (qualitative or quantitative) to investigate, they define these variables as either independent or dependent. Variables that cause something to occur are **independent variables.** Variables in which a change (or effect) can be observed are **dependent variables.** Marital infidelity is an independent variable (although, of course, not the only one) that may cause the dependent variable of divorce. Poverty is one of several independent variables that can produce a change in the dependent variable of hunger. Whether a variable is dependent or independent varies with the context. Hunger may be a dependent variable in a study of poverty; it may be an independent variable in a study of crime (see Table 2.1).

An **intervening variable** influences the relationship between an independent variable and a dependent variable. A government support program, for example, may intervene between poverty and hunger. With a strong safety net, very poor parents and their children may experience no more hunger than working-class families. Poverty is the cause of hunger, but it does not have to be if there is government intervention in the

THINK GLOBALLY **2.1**

The Wired World

This map shows the number of Internet users as a percentage of total populations. These data constitute a quantitative variable.

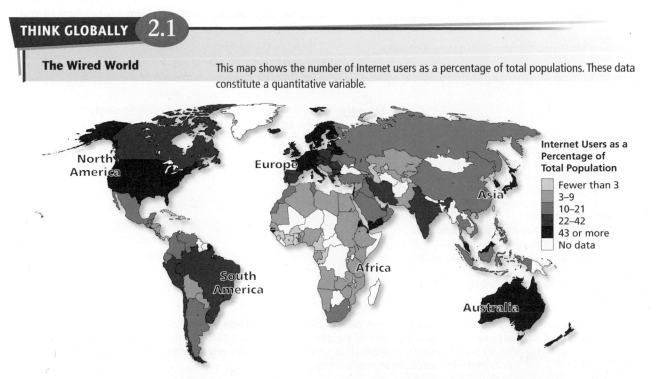

Internet Users as a
Percentage of
Total Population

- Fewer than 3
- 3–9
- 10–21
- 22–42
- 43 or more
- No data

Source: From John L. Allen and Christopher J. Sutton. *Student Atlas of World Politics.* 9th ed. (p. 120). Copyright © 2011 by The McGraw-Hill Companies. Reproduced by permission of McGraw-Hill Contemporary Learning Series.

Interpret the Map

1. Explain why the data in this map constitute a quantitative variable.

2. What would need to be done with the data to make them a qualitative variable?

3. If you were using Internet users as a percentage of the total population in research, would it likely be a dependent or an independent variable?

form of income and food. The poor *without* a safety net will experience more hunger; the poor *with* a safety net will not.

Q What is a correlation? After identifying which independent and dependent variables they will study, sociologists attempt to find out how the variables are related. They describe these relationships in terms of correlations. A **correlation** exists when a change in one variable is associated with a change (either positively or negatively) in the other.

A correlation may be positive or negative. A **positive correlation** exists if both the independent variable and the dependent variable change in the same direction. A positive correlation exists if we find that grades (dependent variable) improve as study time (independent variable) increases (see Figure 2.1). In a **negative correlation,** the variables change in opposite directions. For example, an increase in the independent variable is linked to a decrease in the dependent variable. A negative correlation exists if we find that grades (dependent variable) go down as time spent videogaming (independent variable) increases.

Q What are the criteria for establishing a causal relationship? Establishing causation is much more complicated than establishing a correlation between two variables. In a causal relationship, one variable actually causes the other to occur. Three standards are commonly used for establishing causality (Lazarsfeld 1955; Hirschi and Selvin 1973). These standards can be illustrated in the mistaken assumption that lower church attendance causes higher juvenile delinquency. (See Using the Sociological Imagination at the beginning of the chapter.)

1. *Two variables must be correlated.* Some researchers found that juvenile delinquency increases as church attendance declines (Stark, Kent, and Doyle 1982). Does this negative correlation mean that lower church attendance causes higher delinquency? To answer this question, the second criterion of causality must be met.

2. *All possible contaminating factors must be taken into account.* A major problem in establishing causality lies in the control of all relevant variables. Holding contaminating factors constant (ruling out their influence) is one of the greatest challenges in science.

TABLE 2.1

Forming Quantitative and Qualitative Variables

Please indicate whether you strongly agree, agree, disagree, or strongly disagree with each of the following statements:

	Strongly Agree	Agree	Disagree	Strongly Disagree
a. Most schoolteachers really know what they are talking about.	1	2	3	4
b. To get ahead in life, you have to get a good education.	1	2	3	4
c. My parents encouraged me to get a good education.	1	2	3	4
d. Children should not be allowed to quit school at sixteen.	1	2	3	4
e. Too little emphasis is put on education these days.	1	2	3	4
f. My parents think that going to college is essential.	1	2	3	4

These questions are designed to measure the value people place on education. The total score of this measure can range from 6 for those strongly agreeing with all six statements (highest value on education) to 24 for those strongly disagreeing with all six statements (lowest value on education). Like any quantitative variable, most actual scores will fall somewhere between these two extremes.

In your own words, describe your views on the importance of education.

_____

_____

_____

Answers to this question could be used by a sociologist to classify people into one of two categories: those who place a high value on education or those who place a low value on education.

Although all cause-and-effect relationships involve a correlation, the existence of a correlation does not necessarily indicate a causal relationship. Just because two events vary together (are correlated) does not mean that one causes the other. Two totally unrelated variables may have a high correlation. In fact, the correlation between lower church attendance and delinquency is known as a **spurious correlation**—an apparent relationship between two variables, which is actually produced by a third variable that affects both of the original two variables.

The negative relationship between church attendance and delinquency occurs because age is related to both church attendance and delinquency (older adolescents attend church less frequently, and older adolescents are also more likely to be delinquents). Thus, before we can predict that a causal relationship exists between church attendance and delinquency, we need to take into account all variables relevant to the relationship. In this instance, the age variable reveals that the

FIGURE 2.1

Positive and Negative Correlations

Examine the graphs below. Choose two examples of your own to illustrate a positive and a negative correlation. Briefly explain why you would expect the type of correlation in each case.

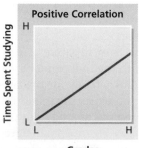

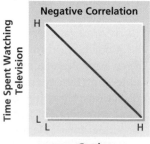

In a positive correlation, increases in one variable are associated with increases in the other. Grades (dependent variable) improve with time spent studying (independent variable).

In a negative correlation, increases in one variable are associated with decreases in the other. Grades (dependent variable) decrease as time spent watching television (independent variable) increases.

relationship between church attendance and delinquency is not a causal one. Church attendance is the contaminating factor here.

3. *A change in the independent variable must occur before a change in the dependent variable can occur.* The cause must occur before the effect. Does lack of church attendance precede delinquency, or vice versa? Logically, either one can precede the other, or they can occur simultaneously. Thus, even if the original correlation between church attendance and delinquency is maintained after holding age and other possible contaminating factors constant,

causality between these two variables still cannot be established. Why? Because it cannot be determined which occurred first.

The Experiment as a Model

An excellent way to illustrate causation is the experiment. Although used infrequently by sociologists, experiments provide insights into the nature of all scientific research because they are grounded in the concept of causation (K. Johnson 2008; see "Consider This Research" for a sociological experiment).

Marianne Bertrand and Sendhil Mullainathan— What's in a Name?

Social researchers infrequently use the experiment as a method of study. And when they do use the experimental method, it is usually a field or "natural" experiment—an experiment done outside the laboratory in the context of normal social life (Babbie 2010b). Marianne Bertrand and Sendhil Mullainathan (2002) conducted a field experiment on racial discrimination in the labor market.

Bertrand and Mullainathan began their research with the knowledge that racial inequality exists in the U.S. labor market. This chapter has documented the presence of this inequality. Using race as their experimental variable, the authors asked two research questions: (1) Do employers actively discriminate against African Americans in hiring by rejecting them in favor of whites who are only equally qualified and (2) does improving the credentials

of African Americans compared with whites overcome this discrimination? With their field experiment design, Bertrand and Mullainathan sent résumés in response to a series of Chicago and Boston help-wanted ads and used the rate of callback for interviews as the measure of success for each résumé. To manipulate the perception of race, the researchers randomly assigned half of the résumés very white-sounding names such as Emily Walsh or Brendan Baker. The other half of the résumés were randomly given very African American–sounding names like Lakisha Washington or Jamal Jones. The researchers responded to each employment ad by sending two higher-quality résumés (one with a white-sounding name, the other with an African American–sounding name) and two lower-quality résumés (one with a white-sounding name, one with an African American–sounding name). They responded to more than 1,300 ads for a wide variety of white-collar jobs, sending out almost 5,000 résumés.

Even though race was assigned randomly, callback rates for African Americans and whites were quite different. Applicants with white names received one callback for every ten or so résumés. Fifteen callbacks were required for résumés with African American names. In other words,

white names attracted 50 percent more callbacks than African American names. Because applicants' names were randomly assigned, the researchers could safely attribute the differential callback rate to racial discrimination.

Race, they found, also influenced the likelihood of higher-quality résumés being rewarded with invitations to interviews. Whites with better résumés received 30 percent more invitations to interviews than whites with lower-quality résumés. In contrast, African American applicants did not benefit from appearing better qualified. That is, African Americans saw little benefit from upgrading their credentials.

Bertrand and Mullainathan conclude that discrimination is an important reason for poor African American performance in the U.S. labor market. African Americans get fewer interview opportunities and are not highly rewarded for improving their observable qualifications. As long as these conditions exist, racial inequality will persist.

Evaluate the Research

1. Discuss the implications of these findings for African American incentives.
2. Relate this research to the tendency to blame the victim.
3. Identify some public policy implications of these findings.

In an attempt to eliminate all possible contaminating influences, an **experiment** takes place in a laboratory. By ruling out extraneous factors, a researcher can determine the effects (if any) of an independent variable on a dependent variable. According to the logic of experiments, if the dependent variable changes when the experimental (independent) variable is introduced but does not change when it is absent, the change must have been caused by the independent variable.

The basic ingredients of an experiment are a *pretest*, a *posttest*, an *experimental variable*, an *experimental group*, and a *control group*. Suppose a researcher wants to study, experimentally, the effects of providing information on drug use (the experimental, or independent, variable) on student attitudes toward drug use (the dependent variable). After selecting a class of eighth graders, the researcher could first measure the teenagers' attitudes toward drug use (pretest). Then, at a later time, the class might view a film demonstrating the harmful effects of drugs. After the movie, the students could again answer questions about their attitudes toward drug use (posttest). Any changes in their attitudes toward drug use that took place between the pretest and the posttest could be attributed to the experimental variable. Such a conclusion might be wrong, however, because the change could have been due to factors other than the experimental variable: A student in the school might have died from an overdose, a rock star might have publicly endorsed drug use, or a pusher might have begun selling drugs to the students.

The conventional method for controlling the influence of contaminating variables is to select a control group as well as an experimental group. In the preceding example, half of the eighth-grade class could have been assigned to the **experimental group,** the group exposed to the experimental variable, and half to the **control group,** the group not exposed to the experimental variable. Assuming that the members of each group had similar characteristics and that their experiences between the pretest and the posttest were the same, any difference in attitudes toward drug use between the two groups could reasonably be attributed to the students' exposure or lack of exposure to the film.

Q **How can a researcher make experimental and control groups comparable?** The standard way to make experimental and control groups comparable—except for exposure to the experimental variable—is through matching or randomization. In **matching**, participants in an experiment are matched in pairs according to all factors thought to affect the relationship being investigated. Members of each pair are then assigned to one group or the other. In **randomization**, which

The survey is the most widely used research method for collecting data in sociology. Surveys are best conducted in person, although use of the telephone is now widespread. An advantage of the survey is that it permits the gathering of information about a large number of people.

is preferable to matching, subjects are assigned to the experimental or control group on a random (chance) basis. Assignment to one group or the other can be determined by flipping a coin or by having subjects draw numbers from a container. Whether matching or randomization is used, the goal is the same—to form experimental and control groups that are alike with respect to all relevant characteristics except the experimental variable. If this requirement is met, any significant change in the experimental group, as compared to the control group, is attributed with considerable confidence to the experimental variable. That is, a causal link will have been established between the independent and dependent variables.

Quantitative Research Methods ▣

Because sociologists find it difficult to create experimental and control groups, they tend to rely more on other research methods, classified as either quantitative or qualitative. Quantitative research uses numerical data (see "Reading Tables and Graphs"). Qualitative research rests on descriptive data.

Quantitative research methods include survey research and precollected data. About 90 percent of the research published in major sociological journals is based on surveys, so this approach is discussed first.

CHECK YOURSELF **2.3** R2

Causation and the Logic of Science

1. Match the following concepts and statements.

   ___ a. causation
   ___ b. multiple causation
   ___ c. variable
   ___ d. quantitative variable
   ___ e. qualitative variable

   ___ f. independent variable
   ___ g. dependent variable
   ___ h. correlation
   ___ i. spurious correlation

   (1) something that occurs in varying degrees
   (2) the variable in which a change or an effect is observed
   (3) a change in one variable associated with a change in another variable
   (4) the idea that an event occurs as a result of several factors operating in combination
   (5) a factor that causes something to happen
   (6) the idea that the occurrence of one event leads to the occurrence of another event
   (7) a factor consisting of nonnumerical categories
   (8) when a relationship between two variables is actually the result of a third variable
   (9) a variable consisting of numerical units

2. An ___experiment___ attempts to eliminate all possible contaminating influences on the variables being studied.

3. The group in an experiment that is not exposed to the experimental variable is the ___control___ group.

Answers: 1. a. (6), b. (4), c. (1), d. (9), e. (7), f. (5), g. (2), h. (3), i. (8); 2. experiment; 3. control

Survey Research

The survey, in which people are asked to answer a series of questions, is the most widely used research method among sociologists. It is ideal for studying large numbers of people.

Q How are effective surveys conducted? In survey research, care must be taken in selecting respondents and in formulating the questions to be asked (Black 2001). Researchers describe the people surveyed based on populations and samples.

Q How are representative samples selected? A random sample is selected on the basis of chance so that each member of a population has an equal opportunity of being selected. A random sample can be selected by assigning each member of the population a number and then drawing numbers from a container after they have been thoroughly scrambled. An easier and more practical method, particularly with large samples, uses a table of random numbers in which numbers appear without pattern. After each member of the population has been assigned a number, the researcher begins with any number in the table and goes down the list until enough subjects have been selected.

If greater precision is desired, a **stratified random sample** can be drawn. With this method, the population is divided into categories such as sex, race, or age. Subjects are then selected randomly from each category. In this way, the proportion of persons in a given category reflects the population at large.

These employees of the U.S. Census Bureau are entering data from one of the government agency's many surveys. Researchers, private individuals, business organizations, and political leaders use these data as representative of the U.S. population.

Bob Daemmrich/The Image Works

READING TABLES AND GRAPHS

Tables and graphs present information concisely. They are chock-full of fascinating findings, which you can easily decode. Just follow the steps outlined here. The steps are keyed to Table 2.2 and Figure 2.2.

1. Begin by reading the title of the table or graph carefully; it will tell you what information is being presented. Table 2.2 shows median annual incomes in the United States by sex, race, and education.
2. Find out the source of the information. You will want to know whether the source is reliable and whether

its techniques for gathering and presenting data are sound. The figures originated from the U.S. Bureau of the Census, a highly trusted source.

3. Read any notes accompanying the table or graph. Not all tables and graphs have notes, but if notes are present, they offer further information about the data. The notes in Table 2.2 and in Figure 2.2 explain that all the data refer to the total money income of full-time and part-time workers, ages 25 and over, in a March 2003 survey.
4. Examine any footnotes. Footnotes in Table 2.2 and Figure 2.2 indicate that the data are categorized by the highest grade actually completed.

Although you may have assumed this, "years of schooling" could have referred to the total number of years in school, regardless of the grade level attained.

5. Look at the headings across the top and down the left-hand side of the table or graph. To observe any pattern in the data, it is usually necessary to keep both types of headings in mind. Table 2.2 and Figure 2.2 show the median annual income of African American and white males and females for several levels of education.
6. Find out what units are being used. Data can be expressed in percentages, hundreds, thousands, millions,

TABLE 2.2

Median Annual Income by Sex, Race, and Education

Examine the following data on median annual income by sex, race, and education. State the conclusions you can make from these data. Which findings most surprise you?

Median earnings in dollars as compared with education attainment*

Demographic Group	Less than High School	High School	Associate's Degree	Bachelor's Degree	Master's Degree
White males	$25,886	$38,214	$48,444	$73,477	$89,678
African American males	$19,705	$29,640	$38,921	$53,029	$63,801
White females	$15,278	$24,276	$33,223	$42,846	$54,532
African American females	$14,869	$24,724	$34,774	$41,560	$51,695

*Based on highest grade completed.

Note: These figures include the total money income of full-time and part-time workers, ages 18 and over, as of 2007.

Source: U.S. Census Bureau, *Statistical Abstract of the United States: 2010* (129th ed.), Washington, DC, 2009, p.149, Table 227.

Q How is information gathered in surveys? In surveys, information is obtained through either a questionnaire or an interview. A **questionnaire** is a written set of questions that survey participants answer by themselves. In an **interview**, a trained interviewer asks questions and records answers. Questionnaires or interviews may be composed of either closed-ended or open-ended questions (May 2001).

Closed-ended questions are those for which a limited, predetermined set of answers is possible—multiple-choice questions, for example. Because participants must choose from rigidly predetermined responses, closed-ended questions sometimes fail to elicit the participants' underlying attitudes and opinions. On the positive side, closed-ended questions make answers easier to quantify and compare. **Open-ended questions** ask the respondent to answer in his or her own words. Answers to open-ended questions, however, are not easy to quantify, and the interviewer may inadvertently change the meaning of the respondent's answers by rephrasing them.

billions, means, and so forth. In Table 2.2 and Figure 2.2, the units are dollars and years of schooling.

7. Check for trends in the data. For tables, look down the columns (vertically) and across the rows (horizontally) for the highest figures, lowest figures, trends, irregularities, and sudden shifts. If you read Table 2.2 vertically, you can see how income varies by race and sex within each level of education. If you read the table horizontally, you can see how income varies with educational attainment for white males, African American males, white females, and African American females. A major advantage of presenting these data as a graph (Figure 2.2) is that the sudden shifts, trends, irregularities, and extremes are easier to spot than they are in tables.

8. Draw conclusions from your own observations. Again, look at Table 2.2 and Figure 2.2. Although income tends to rise with educational level for both African Americans and whites, it increases much less for African American men and for women of both races than for white men. At each level of schooling, African American men earn less than white men. In fact, white male high school dropouts have incomes only $3,754 below African American male high school graduates; white male high school graduates earn only as much as African American males with an associate's degree. White women and African American women both appear to improve their earning power through high school and college education, but neither match white and black males comparably educated.

FIGURE 2.2

Median Annual Income by Gender, Race, and Education

Clearly, this table documents the income advantage that white males in the United States have over white females and African Americans of both sexes. Explain how this situation can be used to challenge the existence of a true meritocracy.

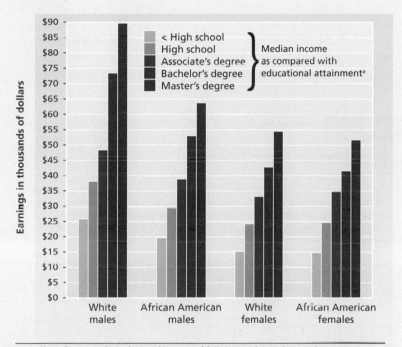

Note: These figures include the total income of full-time and part-time workers, ages 18 and over, as of 2007.

ᵃ In terms of highest degree completed

Source: U.S. Census Bureau, Statistical Abstract of the United States: 2010 (129th ed.), Washington, DC, 2009, p.149, Table 227.

Q What are the advantages and disadvantages of closed-ended survey research? Surveys based on closed-ended questions have the advantage of precision and comparability of responses. They permit the use of statistical techniques, a feature they have in common with experiments. Statistical techniques can be used because of still other advantages in survey research (see "Basic Statistical Measures"). For example, surveys permit the collection of large samples, which in turn permit more detailed analysis; surveys include a large number of variables; and surveys can involve quantified variables.

The survey research method has several disadvantages, however (Schuman 2002). (1) Due to the large samples usually involved, surveys are expensive. (2) Because survey questions are predetermined, interviewers cannot always include important unanticipated information, although they are encouraged to write such information in the margin or on the back of the interview form. (3) The response rate—particularly

BASIC STATISTICAL MEASURES

Statistics are methods used for tabulating, analyzing, and presenting quantitative data (Levin and Fox 2002). Sociologists, like all scientists, use statistical measures. The statistics you will encounter in this textbook and in the sources you are likely to read later, such as *The Wall Street Journal, Time, Newsweek,* and *The Economist,* are easily comprehended. Among the most basic statistical measures are averages (modes, means, medians) and correlations.

An *average* is a single number representing the distribution of several figures: Suppose the following annual salary figures were those of nine highly paid Major League Baseball players:

$3,300,000 (catcher)
$4,500,000 (first base)
$3,600,000 (second base)
$4,900,000 (starting pitcher)
$3,600,000 (third base)
$5,300,000 (left field)
$4,200,000 (center field)
$6,100,000 (right field)
$4,300,000 (shortstop)

There are three kinds of averages that can make these numerical values more meaningful (see Figure 2.3). Each gives a different picture.

The *mode*—in this case $3,600,000—is the number that occurs most frequently. The mode is appropriate only when the objective is

to indicate the most popular number. If a researcher were to rely on the mode alone, though, in a report of these Major League Baseball salaries, readers would be misled, because no mention is made of the wide range of salaries ($3,300,000 to $6,100,000).

The *mean* is the measure closest to the everyday meaning of the term *average*. It lies somewhere in the middle of a range. The mean of the salary figures listed earlier—$4,422,222—is calculated by adding all the salaries together ($39,800,000) and dividing by the number of salaries (9). The mean, unlike the mode, takes all of the figures into account, but it is

distorted by the extreme figure of $6,100,000. Although one player earns $6,100,000, most players make considerably less—the highest-paid player earns nearly twice as much as the lowest-paid player. The mean is distorted when there are extreme values at either the high or low end of a scale; it is more accurate when extremes are not widely separated.

The *median* is the number that divides a series of values in half; that is, half of the values lie above it, half below. In this example, the median is $4,300,000—half of the salaries are above $4,300,000, half are below. What is the advantage here? The median is not distorted by extremes.

FIGURE 2.3

Mode, Mean, and Median of Salaries

Suppose that you were negotiating your salary with a Major League Baseball team. Also suppose that your agent presented these average salaries as currently accurate with the news that management would give you only one chance to declare your bottom-line salary. Which type of average would you choose? Explain why.

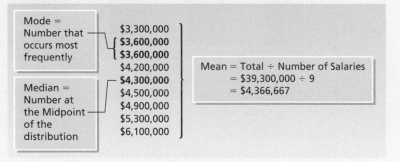

for mailed questionnaires—is often low. A respectable return rate is about 50 percent, although researchers make an effort to obtain a return rate of 80 percent or higher. Even in interviews, some people are not available and some refuse to answer the questions. Because nonresponses can make the sample unrepresentative, surveys may be biased. (4) The phrasing of survey questions may also introduce bias. For example, negatively phrased questions are more likely to receive a "no" answer than neutrally phrased questions. It is better to

ask, "Are you in favor of abortion?" than "You aren't in favor of abortion, are you?" Respondents also interpret the same question differently. If asked about the extent of their drug use, some respondents may include alcohol in their answers; others may not. (5) Surveys cannot probe deeply into the context of the social behavior being studied; they draw specific bits of information from respondents, but they cannot capture the total social situation. (6) Survey researchers must be on guard for the *Hawthorne effect*, when unintentional behavior on

Some aspects of social life, such as neighborhood youth gangs, are best studied in their natural setting. Why do you think this is so?

the part of researchers influences the results they obtain from those they are studying (Roethlisberger and Dickson 1964; originally published in 1939). As researchers and survey participants interact, participants detect cues regarding what the researchers are trying to find. The participants, depending on the circumstances, may attempt to please the researcher, frustrate the researcher's goals, or give "socially acceptable" answers.

Precollected Data

The use of previously collected information is a well-respected method of obtaining data. This is known as **secondary analysis.** In fact, the first sociologist to use statistics in a sociological study—Emile Durkheim—relied on precollected data (see "Sociology Eyes America" 2.1 and 2.2).

SOCIOLOGY EYES AMERICA **2.1**

Suicide Rates

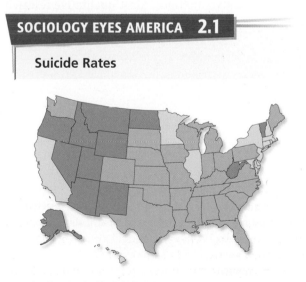

Deaths per 100,000 Population

☐ Above average: 14.4 or more
☐ Average: 10.5 to 14.3
☐ Below average: 10.4 or fewer

Source: *National Vital Statistics Reports,* from the Centers for Disease Control and Prevention, 2005.

SOCIOLOGY EYES AMERICA **2.2**

Population Density

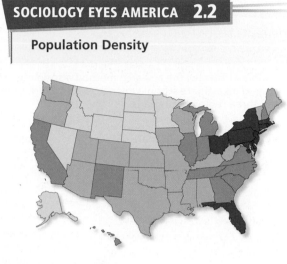

People per Square Mile

■ 1,000 or above
260–999
130–259

26–129
25 or below

Source: U.S. Census Bureau, *Statistical Abstract of the United States: 2004–2005*

Interpret the Map

1. Emile Durkheim hypothesized that one variable in the suicide rate is the degree to which the individual has group ties. One indication of group ties is population density. Based on Sociology Eyes America 2.2, where would you expect to find the highest suicide rates in the United States? Does Sociology Eyes America 2.1 agree with your hypothesis?

2. Durkheim used a research method known as secondary analysis. Explain what that means. Could he have used a better method? Why or why not?

3. Using what you have learned from Durkheim's research, formulate a hypothesis about mass suicide.

Q What are the major types of precollected data? The sources for precollected data are as varied as government reports, company records, voting records, prison records, and reports of research done by other social scientists. The U.S. Census Bureau is one of the most important sources of precollected data for sociologists. The Census Bureau collects information on the total population every ten years and conducts countless specific surveys each year. Consequently, detailed information exists on such topics as income, education, race, sex, age, marital status, occupation, death rates, and birth rates. Other government agencies also collect information. The U.S. Department of Labor regularly collects information on the nation's income and unemployment levels across a variety of jobs. The U.S. Department of Commerce issues monthly reports on various aspects of the economy.

TABLE 2.3

FOCUS ON THEORETICAL PERSPECTIVES:
Investigating School Violence and School Funding

This table illustrates the research method a sociologist of a particular theoretical persuasion would *most likely* choose to investigate school violence and school funding. Any of the three sociologists, of course, could use *any* of the three research methods.

Theoretical Perspective	Research Method	Approach to the Research Question
Functionalism	Survey	• A questionnaire on violence in high school is sent to a national, random sample of principals. The survey examines a possible relationship between incidence of school violence and level of school funding.
Conflict theory	Case study	• A particular high school with low funding is studied with respect to a relationship between school violence and school funding. Researchers interview administrators, teachers, and students.
Symbolic interactionism	Participant observation	• Concealing her identity, a researcher takes a temporary job at a high school with low funding. She attempts to covertly observe a possible link between school violence and school funding.

Q What are the advantages and disadvantages of precollected data? Precollected data can provide sociologists with inexpensive, quality information. Existing sources of information also permit the study of a topic over a long period of time. With census data, for example, we can begin in 1960, with the onset of the War on Poverty, and trace the changes in the relative income levels of African Americans and whites. Also, because others have collected the data, the researcher cannot influence the answers.

Because the information was collected for different purposes, there is also a downside to precollected data. The existing information may not exactly suit the current researcher's needs. In addition, the people who

originally collected the data may have been biased. Finally, sometimes precollected data are simply too old to be valid. (Table 2.3 associates a research method with a particular theoretical perspective.)

Qualitative Research Methods R1

Sometimes qualitative (nonquantitative) research methods can reveal aspects of social reality better than quantitative methods. Most qualitative research

CHECK YOURSELF **2.4** **R2**

Quantitative Research Methods
1. Match the following terms and statements:
   __2__ a. population
   __4__ b. representative sample
   __1__ c. random sample
   __3__ d. sample
   __5__ e. survey
   (1) selected on the basis of chance so that each member of a population has an equal opportunity of being selected
   (2) all those people with the characteristics the researcher wants to study within the context of a particular research question
   (3) a limited number of cases drawn from the larger population
   (4) a sample that has basically the same relevant characteristics as the population
   (5) the research method in which people are asked to answer a series of questions
2. Use of company records would be an example of using  precollected data.

Answers: 1. a. (2), b. (4), c. (1), d. (3), e. (5); 2. precollected

methods include field research and the subjective approach (Neuman 2005; Lincoln and Denzin 2005; Strauss and Corbin 2007).

Field Research

Q What is field research? Field research investigates aspects of social life that cannot be measured quantitatively and that are best understood within a natural setting. The world of prostitution, the inner workings of a Mafia family, and events during a riot are all topics best studied through field research.

Q What method of research do field researchers most often prefer? The most popular approach to field research is the case study—a thorough investigation of a single group, a single incident, or a single community. Case studies generally use one or more of three approaches: intensive observation, information obtained from informants, and informal interviews. To supplement these techniques, researchers may use newspaper files, formal interviews, official records, and surveys.

The case study method often assumes that the findings in one case can be generalized to similar situations. The conclusions of a study on drug use in Chicago, for example, should apply to other large cities as well. It is the researcher's responsibility to indicate factors that are unique and that would not apply to other situations. Researchers conducting case studies sometimes use the techniques of ethnography.

Q How is ethnology applied in field research? Ethnography, an approach to field work developed by social anthropologists, attempts a detailed and accurate description of a group's way of life (Babbie 2010a). Ethnographic studies typically make little or no claim of explanation. A thorough and accurate description is their principal aim. The study of an isolated, primitive tribe comes to mind as prototypically ethnographic research.

Ethnography, however, is not limited to distant, isolated villages. William Foote Whyte's study of an urban Italian neighborhood in the 1940s is a prominent example of ethnographic research. A key informant, named "Doc," permitted Whyte to observe the social life of these Italian immigrants. Whyte's book, *Street Corner Society*, presents an accurate and detailed description of life in this neighborhood, from its members' point of view (Whyte 1993).

An ethnographic researcher may or may not act as a member of the group being studied. When a researcher does act as a member of the group, this person is using the research technique of "participant observation."

Q What is participant observation? In participant observation, a researcher becomes a temporary member of the group being studied. Sociologists sometimes

reveal themselves as participant researchers, as Whyte did in Cornerville. So did Elliot Liebow when he studied two dozen disadvantaged African American men who hung around a particular corner in Washington, D.C. His study illustrates the open or covert approach to participant observation. Even though he was a white outsider, Liebow participated in the daily activities of the men: "The people I was observing knew that I was observing them, yet they allowed me to participate in their activities and take part in their lives to a degree that continues to surprise me" (Liebow 2003:253).

A researcher using a covert approach to participant observation joins a group without informing its members that he or she is a sociologist. A compelling account of covert participant observation appears in *Black Like Me*, a book written by John Howard Griffin (1961). Griffin, a white journalist, dyed his skin to study the life of African Americans in the South. Although he had previously visited the South as a white man, his experiences while posing as an African American were quite different. (See Table 2.4 for a summary of the advantages and disadvantages of various research methods.)

Q What are the advantages and disadvantages of field studies? Field studies can produce a depth and breadth of understanding unattainable with quantitative research methods. Uniquely, they can reveal insights into a social situation from the experiences of the people involved. Adaptability is another advantage. Even after a field study has begun, it is easily altered when new insights or oversights are discovered. (This is in contrast to survey research, where changes are not practical once research is in progress.) In addition, field studies are valuable where survey research would be either impossible or biased—as in a study of skid-row derelicts or organized crime. (Imagine studying a delinquent gang with a set of questions about their activities.) Because of these advantages, field studies may produce insights and explanations not likely to be unearthed through quantitative research.

Disadvantages do exist, however. The findings from one case may not be generalizable to similar situations. One mental hospital or community may be quite unlike any other mental hospital or community. If possible bias of the survey research sample is a major problem, so is the potential bias of the field researcher. In the absence of more precise measuring devices, the researcher often has to rely on personal judgment and interpretation. Because of personal blind spots or emotional attachment, the researcher may not accurately interpret his or her observations. Moreover, the lack of objectivity and standardized research procedures makes it difficult for another researcher to duplicate a field study. Because of these disadvantages, many sociologists regard the results of field studies as insights that must be investigated further with more precise quantitative methods (see Table 2.4).

TABLE 2.4

Research Methods: Advantages and Disadvantages

A summary of the advantages and disadvantages of several basic research methods is presented here. Suppose that you wished to do a study of the relationship between dating and self-esteem in high school. From the table, select the method that you think is best suited to your research. Explain the advantages and disadvantages of this method to your research.

Research Method	Definition	Advantages	Disadvantages
Quantitative Methods Survey research	People answer a series of questions, usually predetermined.	• Precision and comparability of answers. • Use of statistical techniques. • Information on large numbers of people. • Detailed analysis.	• Expensive due to large numbers. • Low response rate. • Phrasing of questions introduces bias in favor of certain answers. • Researchers' behavior can affect answers given.
Secondary analysis	Information gathered by one researcher is used by another researcher for a different purpose.	• Inexpensive. • Can study a topic over a long period of time. • Researchers' influence on subjects avoided.	• Information collected for a different reason may not suit another researcher's needs. • Original researcher may already have introduced biases. • Information may be outdated.
Experiment	Occurs in a laboratory setting with a minimum of contaminating influences.	• Can be replicated with precision. • Variables can be manipulated. • Can be relatively inexpensive. • Permits the establishment of causation (rather than just correlation).	• Laboratory environment is artificial. • Not suited to most sociological research. • Number of variables studied is limited.
Qualitative Methods Case study	Thoroughly investigates a small group, incident, or community.	• Provides depth of understanding from group members' viewpoint. • Unexpected discoveries and new insights can be incorporated into the research. • Permits the study of social behavior not feasible with quantitative methods.	• Difficult to generalize findings from one group to another group. • Presence of researcher can influence results. • Hard to duplicate. • Takes lots of time. • Difficult to be accepted as a group member (in case of participant observation).

The Subjective Approach

Q What is distinctive about the subjective approach? The subjective approach to research has a long and honorable place in sociology. Recall from Chapter 1 Max Weber's method of *verstehen,* in which the subjective intentions of people are discovered by imagining oneself in their place. The subjective approach, then, studies an aspect of human social behavior by ascertaining the interpretations of the participants themselves. A prominent example of the **subjective approach** is ethnomethodology, a development in microsociology that attempts to uncover taken-for-granted social routines.

Q How does ethnomethodology work? Ethnomethodology is the study of processes people develop and use in understanding the routine behaviors expected of themselves and others in everyday life. Ethnomethodologists assume that people share the meanings that underlie much of their everyday behavior. Through observing others and through a process of trial and error in social situations, people develop a sense of appropriate behavior. This understanding prevents them from making silly or serious social errors and saves them from having to continually decide the fitting behavior for particular situations. Predictable, patterned behavior is a result of this process (Livingston 1987; Atkinson 1988; Hilbert 1990; Pollner 1991).

Q **How can ethnomethodologists discover what is going on in the minds of individuals as they construct a mental sense of social reality?** Because they are not mind readers, ethnomethodologists have had to be inventive. Harold Garfinkel (1984) is a prominent advocate of ethnomethodology. He believes the best course to understanding people's construction of social reality is to deprive them momentarily of their mental maps of daily routines. If people are deprived of their definitions of expected behaviors, they reconstruct a coherent picture of social reality. Ethnomethodologists can learn by observing this process of reconstruction.

Garfinkel writes of situations that his students have created. Here the researchers can observe what people do when deprived of their taken-for-granted social routines. The following passage describes a situation in which an experimenter (E) is attempting to deprive a subject (S) of his sense of expected routine by asking for more detailed information than is normally required in everyday situations. In the context of watching television, the experimenter first asks, "How are you tired? Physically, mentally, or just bored?"

> S: I don't know, I guess physically, mainly.
> E: You mean that your muscles ache or your bones?
> S: I guess so. Don't be so technical.
> (After more watching)
> S: All these old movies have the same kind of old iron bedstead in them.
> E: What do you mean? Do you mean all old movies, or some of them, or just the ones you have seen?
> S: What's the matter with you? You know what I mean.
> E: I wish you would be more specific.
> S: You know what I mean! Drop dead! (Garfinkel 1984:43)

The researcher continues this type of conversation until the subject is disoriented and can no longer respond within a previously developed frame of reference. The researcher can then observe the subject's creation of a new definition for expected or "normal" social interaction.

Ethics in Social Research [R1]

The Issue of Ethics

Research is a distinctly human activity. Although there have been ethical principles for conducting research, such as objectivity and verifiability, there are researchers who have not honored these guidelines (Greenberg 2003; Chang 2002; Goodstein 2002; Spotts 2002).

Unfortunately, there is a long list of examples of ethical lapses in medical research. From 1932 to 1972, in what are known as the Tuskegee Syphilis Experiments, the Public Health Service of the U.S. government deliberately did not treat approximately 400 syphilitic African American sharecroppers and day laborers, so that biomedical researchers could study the full evolution of the disease (J. M. Jones 1993; Reverby, 2000). The Tuskegee Syphilis Experiments violated many of the rules of ethics by failing to inform the subjects of the nature of the research, and even lying to them about what was being done to them. Following the shock of the Tuskegee Syphilis Experiments, we learned that from the mid-1940s to 1974 American medical researchers experimented on prison inmates with chemical warfare agents and other poisonous chemicals (Hornblum 1998). In 2010, the United States publicly apologized for infecting nearly 700 Guatemalan prison inmates, mental patients, and soldiers with venereal diseases. American public health doctors conducted these experiments in the late 1940s to test the effectiveness of penicillin treatment (McNeil 2010). Federal investigators in the United States have documented more than ten years of fraud in some of the most important breast cancer research ever conducted

CHECK YOURSELF **2.5** [R2]

Qualitative Research Methods

1. Field studies are best suited for situations in which _quantitative_ measurement cannot be used.
2. A _case study_ is a thorough investigation of a small group, an incident, or a community.
3. In _participant_, a researcher becomes a member of the group being studied.
4. According to the _subjective_ approach, some aspect of social structure is best studied through an attempt to ascertain the interpretations of the participants themselves.
5. _____ is the study of the processes people develop and use in understanding the routine behaviors expected of themselves and others in everyday life.

Answers: 1. quantitative; 2. case study; 3. participant observation; 4. subjective; 5. Ethnomethodology

(Crewdson 1994). In a Cincinnati hospital, from 1960 to 1972, approximately 100 women and men with cancer were subjected to experimental radiation over their entire bodies in U.S. military–funded research on the effects of nuclear war. Twenty-one died within a month of exposure and nearly all of them died within months of this "therapy" (Stephens 2002).

Unfortunately there are many more recent examples. In 2006, the worldwide leading researcher of human cloning, South Korean Woo Suk Hwang, revealed that most—and perhaps all—of his stem cell cultures were fake. Scott Reuben, a prominent medical researcher on pain management, admitted in 2009 to fabricating much of the data in twenty-one of his journal articles written since 1996. During this period, Pfizer, the manufacturer of the painkilling drug he was investigating, underwrote Reuben's study. After physician Andrew Wakefield published a study linking autism to childhood vaccines, millions of parents avoided childhood vaccinations, which, of course, led to the return of several formerly conquered diseases, resulting in some deaths. Turns out, according to the *British Medical Journal*, Wakefield doctored the evidence in his article, thus committing "deliberate fraud" (Deer 2011).

Finally, one study found that between 2000 and 2008 almost 800 research papers were withdrawn from medical journals, 197 of which were retracted for using false data or for reporting only those results that supported the desired result (Steen 2010). Moreover, over half of these papers were written by authors who had written other fraudulent articles in the past.

While less dramatic, some social scientists have also been accused of ethical lapses. In 2001 three prominent historians (Stephen Ambrose, Doris Kearns Goodwin, and Joseph Ellis) faced charges of plagiarism, including in their writings the work of others without citation. Several other eminent social scientists placed subjects in stressful situations without informing them of the true nature of the experiments (Milgram 1963, 1965, 1974; Zimbardo, Anderson, and Kabat 1981).

Laud Humphreys (1979) studied homosexual activities in men's public bathrooms ("tearooms"). By acting as a lookout to warn the men of approaching police officers, he observed their activities closely. As participants left the tearooms, Humphreys recorded their license plate numbers to obtain their addresses for personal interviews. After waiting a year, Humphreys falsely presented himself as a survey researcher to obtain additional information.

Q Did Humphreys violate the code of ethics as a covert participant observer? Yes, Humphreys violated the privacy of these people. Most did not want their sexual activities known, and Humphreys did not give them the opportunity to refuse to participate in the study.

Humphreys also deceived the men by misrepresenting himself in both the tearooms and their homes. Finally, by recording his observations, Humphreys placed these people in jeopardy of public exposure, arrest, or loss of employment. (Actually, because of his precautions, none of the subjects were injured as a result of his research. In fact, to protect their identities, Humphreys even allowed himself to be arrested.)

As you might expect, these and other studies have created great interest in a code of ethics among sociologists. So, there is now, in fact, a formal code of ethics for professional sociologists (American Sociological Association 2011).

A Code of Ethics in Sociological Research

The formal code of ethics for sociologists covers important areas beyond research, including relationships with students, employees, and employers. In broad terms, the code is concerned with maximizing the benefits of sociology to society and minimizing the harm that sociological work might create. Of importance in the present context are the research-related aspects of the code.

Sociologists are committed to objectivity; the highest technical research standards; accurate reporting of their methods and findings; and protection of the rights, privacy, integrity, dignity, and autonomy of the subjects of their research. Because the first several topics have been covered earlier in this chapter, the focus in this section is on the rights, privacy, integrity, dignity, and autonomy of participants in sociological research.

Occasionally, adherence to the code presents a challenge to the researcher. Mario Brajuha, a graduate student at a major American university, kept detailed field notes while engaging in a participant observation study of restaurant work (Brajuha and Hallowell 1986). Because of suspected arson after a fire at the restaurant where he was employed as a waiter, his field notes became the object of interest by the police, the district attorney, the courts, and some suspects. By refusing to reveal the contents of his field notes, Brajuha protected the rights of those individuals described in his notes. He did so in the face of a subpoena; threats of imprisonment; and the specter of personal harm to himself, his wife, and his children. The case was finally dropped after two difficult years.

Q Do ethical concerns make research more difficult? Yes, but it is the researcher's responsibility to decide when a particular action crosses an ethical line—a decision not always easy to make, because moral lines are often blurred. Moreover, the researcher must balance the interests of those being studied against the need for accurate, updated data.

It is generally thought that using human corpses in automobile crash tests is unethical. Ethical standards also apply to potentially harmful social research utilizing live humans.

Michael Rosenfe d/Getty mages

Although Kai Erikson is one of the most sensitive and outspoken critics of disguised observation, he has defended it on grounds that it is—on occasion—the only way to obtain relevant information:

Some of the richest material in the social sciences has been gathered by sociologists who were true participants in the group under study but who did not announce to other members that they were employing this opportunity to collect research data. . . . It would be absurd, then,

to insist as a point of ethics that sociologists should always introduce themselves as investigators everywhere they go and should inform every person who figures in their thinking exactly what their research is about. (K. T. Erikson 1967:368)

Balance is the key. At the very least, researchers should protect their subjects—whether in experiments, surveys, or field studies—from social, financial, psychological, or legal damage (M. Hunt 1999).

CHECK YOURSELF 2.6 R2

Ethics in Social Research

1. Situations a, b, and c describe three research situations involving possible ethical violations (Babbie 2010a. Match each situation with the appropriate aspect of the social science code of ethics for research on human subjects.
   (1) concern for participants' privacy
   (2) avoidance of deception
   (3) obligation not to harm participants
   a. After a field study of deviant behavior during a riot, law enforcement officials demand that the researcher identify those people who were observed looting. Rather than risk arrest as an accomplice after the fact, the researcher complies.
   b. A research questionnaire is circulated among students as part of their university registration packet. Although students are not told they must complete the questionnaire, the hope is that they will believe they must, thus ensuring a higher completion rate.
   c. Researchers obtain a list of right-wing radicals they wish to study. They contact the radicals with the explanation that each has been selected "at random," from among the general population, to take a sampling of "public opinion."

Answers: 1. a. (3), b. (2), c. (1).

A Final Note ▣

Reliability, Validity, and Replication

Researchers can heed all the important research considerations discussed in this chapter and still not conduct a good study. They can be mindful of objectivity, sensitive to the criteria of causation, and careful in the selection of the most appropriate method (survey, precollected data, field study). Still, they may fail to produce knowledge superior to that yielded by intuition, common sense, authority, or tradition.

Q What additional measures must a researcher consider? Sociologists must pay careful attention to the quality of measurement (Babbie 2010b). Consequently, they must emphasize reliability and validity in the creation and evaluation of the measuring devices they use for the variables they wish to investigate.

Q What is meant by reliability? A measurement technique must yield consistent results on repeated applications—a requirement called **reliability.** Reliability is tested by repeated administration of a measurement technique, such as a questionnaire, to the same subjects to ascertain whether the same results occur each time. Suppose a researcher, after deciding to study satisfaction with day care among parents, designs a questionnaire. If, on repeated applications of the questionnaire to a sample of parents, the level of satisfaction remains consistent, then confidence in the reliability of the measurement device rises. Should, on the other hand, the level of satisfaction—from one administration of the questionnaire to the next—vary over a period of time, then we would doubt that satisfaction with child care is actually being measured.

The problem of reliability is likewise an issue in qualitative research. Suppose that our field researcher is also interested in satisfaction with day care among the children. If the level of satisfaction among the children seems different each day to the researcher, then doubt again starts to surface about the reliability of the measurement technique being used.

Even when a measurement technique is reliable, it still may not produce scientifically sound results. This is because a measurement technique must be not only reliable but also valid.

Q What is validity? Validity exists when a measurement technique actually measures what it is designed to measure. Thus, a technique intended to measure parental satisfaction with day care may yield consistent results on repeated applications to a sample of parents, but not actually be measuring satisfaction at all. The measurement device might be tapping parental need to view day care positively (to mask guilt feelings about permitting someone else to be the care provider during working hours). Children at a day-care center may appear satisfied to the visiting researcher because they are neglected during the day and welcome his or her attention, or because the day-care provider has coached them to appear satisfied. A measurement technique, in short, may be consistently measuring something very different from what it purports to measure.

Q How does replication contribute to the self-corrective nature of research? Replication—the duplication of the same study to ascertain its accuracy—is closely linked to both reliability and validity in that reliability and validity problems unknown to original researchers are likely to be revealed as subsequent social scientists repeat the research. It is partially through replication that scientific knowledge accumulates and changes over time.

A major goal of scientific research is to generate knowledge that is more reliable than can be obtained from such nonscientific sources as intuition, common sense, authority, and tradition. Through efforts to be objective and to make their research subject to replication by others, researchers attempt to portray reality as accurately as possible. The methods of research presented in this chapter are the specific tools sociologists use to create knowledge of social life that is as accurate as possible.

However, empirical results obtained through the use of research methods are not the final goal of science. As Gerhard Lenski has stated, "Science is more than

---

CHECK YOURSELF **2.7**

A Final Note

1. Match the concepts on the left side with the definitions on the right side.

   ___ a. reliability   (1) when a measurement technique yields consistent results on repeated applications

   ___ b. validity   (2) the duplication of the same study to ascertain its accuracy

   ___ c. replication   (3) when a measurement technique actually measures what it is designed to measure

Answers: 1. a. (1), b. (3), c. (2)

method: its ultimate aim is the development of a body of 'verified' general theory" (Lenski 1988:163). For this reason, there is constant interaction between sociological theory and research methods. Theory is used to develop hypotheses capable of being supported or falsified through testing. These results, in turn, may support existing theory, alter it, or lead to its ultimate rejection and the creation of a new theory. According to Lenski, divorced from research methods, "sociological theory has more in common with seminary instruction in theology and biblical studies" (1988:165) than it does with the natural sciences model that sociology is emulating.

Theory is trustworthy and useful only to the extent that it has been tested and found to be valid.

On to Chapter 3

Chapter 1 introduced you to the sociological perspective and defined sociology as the scientific study of social structure. The current chapter elaborated on the methods sociologists use to study social structure. The next five chapters explore the foundations of social structures, starting with culture.

S   INTEGRATED GOALS AND SUMMARY

1. **Identify the major nonscientific sources of knowledge about society.**
   - People tend to get information from such nonscientific sources as intuition, common sense, authority, and tradition. Generally speaking, these sources are inadequate for obtaining accurate knowledge about social life. The advantage of scientific knowledge is grounded in its objectivity and verifiability.
2. **Explain why science is a superior source of knowledge about society.**
   - Objectivity is the aim of social scientists. Subjectivity can be minimized if researchers make themselves aware of their biases and make their biases public when presenting their findings. Through verification of past research, scientists can expose erroneous theories, findings, and conclusions.
3. **Outline the steps sociologists use to guide their research.**
   - A research model involves several distinct steps: identifying the problem, reviewing the literature, formulating hypotheses, developing a research design, collecting data, analyzing data, and stating findings and conclusions. These steps form a model for scientific research.
4. **Discuss cause-and-effect concepts, and apply the concept of causation to the logic of science.**
   - The concept of causation—the idea that the occurrence of one event leads to the occurrence of another event—is central to science. All events have causes, and scientists attempt to discover the factors causing those events.
   - Three criteria must be met before a cause-and-effect relationship can be said to exist. First, two variables must be correlated. That is, change in the independent variable (the causal factor) must be associated with a change in the dependent variable (effect). Second, the correlation must not be spurious, that is, due to the effects of a third variable. Third, it must be shown that the independent variable always occurs before the dependent variable. Scientists think in terms of multiple causation because events are usually caused by several factors, not simply by a single factor.

5. **Differentiate the major qualitative research methods used by sociologists.**
   - The experiment is a good example of a research method that is based on the idea of causation. Sociologists, however, do not generally use the experimental research method because it is often impossible to control the relevant social variables.
   - Two major quantitative research methods are the survey and precollected data. Surveys can draw on large samples, are quantitative, include many variables, are relatively precise, and permit the comparison of responses. Researchers must take care to collect representative samples for their surveys. Precollected data permit high-quality research at reasonably low cost and reveal changes in variables over an extended period of time.
6. **Describe the major qualitative research methods used by sociologists.**
   - Field studies are best used when some aspect of social structure cannot be measured quantitatively, when interaction should be observed in a natural setting, and when in-depth analysis is needed. The case study is the popular approach to field research. Some sociologists have adopted a subjective approach in which emphasis is on ascertaining the subjective interpretations of the participants themselves.
7. **Describe the role of ethics in research.**
   - Researchers have an ethical obligation to protect participants' privacy and to avoid deceiving or harming participants. Preserving the rights of subjects is sometimes weighed against the value of the knowledge to be gained. While usually harmless, these compromises sometimes place the subjects in jeopardy.
8. **State the importance of reliability, validity, and replication in social research.**
   - Demands on researchers go even further. They must design measurement devices that give consistent results each time they are used (reliability), and measurement techniques must actually measure what they intend (validity).

CONCEPT REVIEW

Match the following concepts with the definitions below them.

____ a. participant observation
____ b. experiment
____ c. verifiability
____ d. subjective approach
____ e. experimental group

____ f. independent variable
____ g. objectivity
____ h. correlation
____ i. population
____ j. sample

____ k. field research
____ l. case study
____ m. survey
____ n. replication

1. the group in an experiment exposed to the experimental variable
2. a statistical measure in which a change in one variable is associated with a change in another variable
3. a research approach for studying aspects of social life that cannot be measured quantitatively and that are best understood within a natural setting
4. a thorough, recorded investigation of a small group, an incident, or a community
5. all those people with the characteristics a researcher wants to study within the context of a particular research question
6. the principle of science stating that scientists are expected to prevent their personal biases from influencing their results and their interpretation of the results

7. a variable that causes something to happen
8. the type of field research technique in which a researcher becomes a member of the group being studied
9. a principle of science by which any given piece of research can be duplicated (replicated) by other scientists
10. a research method in which people are asked to answer a series of questions
11. the duplication of the same study to ascertain its accuracy
12. a limited number of cases drawn from a population
13. laboratory research that attempts to eliminate all possible contaminating influences on the variables being studied
14. a research method in which the aim is to understand some aspect of social reality through the study of the interpretations of the participants themselves

CHECK YOURSELF REVIEW

1. The major problem with nonscientific sources of knowledge is that such sources often provide erroneous information. T or F?
2. According to Gunnar Myrdal, it is enough that scientists themselves recognize their biases. T or F?
3. The group in an experiment that is not exposed to the experimental variable is the _____ group.
4. Field studies are best suited for situations in which _____ measurement cannot be used.
5. In _____, a researcher becomes a member of the group being studied.
6. An _____ attempts to eliminate all possible contaminating influences on the variables being studied.
7. Use of company records would be an example of using _____ data.
8. According to the _____ approach, some aspects of social structure are best studied through an attempt to ascertain the interpretations of the participants themselves.
9. Listed here are the steps in the research model. Following are some concrete examples related to the sociability of the only child. Indicate the appropriate example for each step number.
   ____ Step 1: identifying the problem
   ____ Step 2: reviewing the literature
   ____ Step 3: formulating hypotheses
   ____ Step 4: developing a research design
   ____ Step 5: collecting data
   ____ Step 6: analyzing data
   ____ Step 7: stating findings and conclusions
   a. Read past theory and research on the sociability of only children.

   b. From previous research and existing theory, a researcher states that only children appear to be more intelligent than children with siblings.
   c. A researcher collects data on only children from a high school in a large city.
   d. A researcher writes a report giving evidence that only children are more intelligent than children with brothers or sisters.
   e. A researcher decides to study the intelligence level of only children.
   f. A researcher classifies and processes the data collected in order to test a hypothesis.
   g. A researcher decides on the data needed to test a hypothesis, the methods for data collection, and the techniques for data analysis.
10. Situations a, b, and c describe three research situations involving possible ethical violations (Babbie 2010a). Match each situation with the appropriate aspect of the social science code of ethics for research on human subjects.
    ____ a. After a field study of deviant behavior during a riot, law enforcement officials demand that the researcher identify those people who were observed looting. Rather than risk arrest as an accomplice after the fact, the researcher complies.
    ____ b. A research questionnaire is circulated among students as part of their university registration packet. Although students are not told they must complete the questionnaire, the hope is that they will believe they must, thus ensuring a higher completion rate.

_____ c. Researchers obtain a list of right-wing radicals
they wish to study. They contact the radicals
with the explanation that each has been selected
"at random," from among the general population, to take a sampling of "public opinion."

(1) concern for participants' privacy
(2) avoidance of deception
(3) obligation not to harm participants

GRAPHIC REVIEW

Table 2.2 displays the median annual income in the United States by sex, race, and education. Demonstrate your understanding
of the information in this table by answering the following questions.

1. What does this table tell us about the relationship among sex, race, and education in the United States?
_____
_____
_____

2. Identify the demographic group that enjoys the greatest economic benefits of education.
_____
_____
_____

3. Identify the demographic group that benefits the least, economically, from higher levels of education.
_____
_____
_____

CRITICAL-THINKING QUESTIONS

1. Suppose a noncollege friend insists that you are wasting
your time in college because the experience gained from
the "university of hard knocks" is all a person needs to
know the truth. What arguments would you use to defend science as a better source of knowledge?
_____

2. Suppose your sociology professor reports on his recent
study showing that men are generally better business
managers than women. If you are concerned about a possible lack of objectivity on his part, what questions could
you ask him to boost your confidence in his results?
_____

3. The experiment is the research model for investigating
causal relationships. What is there about the nature of

causation and the design of experiments that supports
this claim?
_____

4. Do you think that a selected sample of 3,000 individuals
could yield an accurate picture of the leisure habits of
Americans? Why or why not?
_____
_____

5. Pretend that you are a sociologist studying the relationship between the receipt of welfare payments and commitment to working. Describe the research method you
would use, and show why it is the most appropriate to
this topic.
_____
_____

ANSWER KEY

Concept Review

a. 8
b. 13
c. 9
d. 14
e. 1
f. 7
g. 6
h. 2
i. 5
j. 12
k. 3
l. 4
m. 10
n. 11

Check Yourself Review

1. T
2. F
3. control
4. quantitative
5. participant observation
6. experiment
7. precollected
8. subjective
9. Step 1: e

Step 2: a
Step 3: b
Step 4: g
Step 5: c
Step 6: f
Step 7: d
10. a. 3
    b. 2
    c. 1

3 Culture

© Louis-Laurent Grandadam/Getty Images

GOALS

- Identify the three major dimensions of culture.
- Describe and illustrate the interplay between language and culture.
- Discuss cultural diversity and its promotion within a society.
- Describe and illustrate the relationship between cultural diversity and ethnocentrism.

- Outline the advantages and disadvantages of ethnocentrism, and discuss the role of cultural relativism in combating ethnocentrism.
- Explain the existence of cultural similarities that are shared around the world.
- Explain the relationship between culture and heredity.

Does the existence of cultural diversity rule out cultural similarities? In other words, what, if anything, could the United States have in common with Afghanistan? What could we Americans have in common with a society that does not approve of women appearing in public with uncovered faces? What do we share with the citizens of Bhutan, who believe that gods assume human form to direct normal day-to-day affairs? How do we relate to the culture of Ingushetia, a republic inside Russia, where it is legal for men to have several wives—all at the same time?

Many Americans, in enthusiastic endorsement of multiculturalism, ignore the similarities among cultures. In reality, however, despite the surface differences, social scientists document a wide variety of "cultural universals" shared by all cultures. Like the United States, for instance, Iraq (or Bhutan or Nigeria) has families, schools, houses of worship, economics, and governments. Later in this chapter we elaborate on this evidence. First, however, we examine the nature of culture and society.

Coming from a different culture than that of other sunbathers doesn't prevent this Amish family from enjoying a day at the beach.

Dimensions of Culture R1

Culture and Society

Q What is the difference between culture and society?
Culture is a people's way of life that is passed from generation to generation. It consists of physical objects as well as patterns of thinking, feeling, and behaving. On the material side, American culture includes such physical objects as skyscrapers, fast-food restaurants, videogames, and cars. On the nonmaterial side, American culture includes various beliefs, rules, customs, a family system, and a capitalist economy. Although culture and society are tightly interwoven and cannot exist without each other, they are not identical. A **society** is a group of people living in a defined territory and participating in a common culture. Culture is that society's total way of life.

Q Why is culture important? Culture underlies human social behavior. What people do and don't do, what they like and dislike, what they believe and don't believe, and what they value and discount are all based, in large part, on culture. Culture provides the blueprints people in a society use to guide their relationships with others. It is from culture that teenage girls are stimulated to compete for positions on the women's basketball team, and it is from culture that teenage boys come to believe that "pumping iron" is a gateway to popularity.

Human social behavior, then, is based on culture. And because culture is not innate, man must learn human behavior. The concepts presented in this chapter help substantiate this point.

If you wanted to describe and analyze a culture, where would you begin? How would you classify the components of a people's way of life? The sociological classification system consists of three major dimensions of culture: the normative (standards for behavior), the cognitive (knowledge and beliefs), and the material (tangible objects). An elaboration of each dimension will help you better understand the nature of culture.

The Normative Dimension

The normative dimension of culture, which consists of the standards for appropriate behavior of a group or society, is heavily tied into functionalism with its emphasis on social integration, stability, and consensus. The most important aspects of the normative dimension are norms, sanctions, and values.

TABLE 3.1

Do's and Taboos Around the World

Bulgaria	• A nod means no, and a shake of the head from side to side means yes.
Great Britain	• Never touch the Queen, not even to gently guide her, and don't offer to shake her hand unless she extends her hand to you first.
Germany	• Shaking hands while your other hand is in your pocket is considered impolite.
Greece	• Unlike the British, the Greeks do not respect lines, or queues, in public places.
Italy	• Italians consider it unfeminine for a woman to pour wine.
Russia	• Whistling at public gatherings is a sign of disagreement and disapproval.
Turkey	• It is considered rude to cross your arms over your chest or to put your hands in your pockets while talking to someone.
Oman	• It is an insult to sit in such a way as to face your host with the soles of your shoes showing. Do not place your feet on a desk, table, or chair.
Iran	• Shaking hands with a child shows respect for his parents.
Saudi Arabia	• At political events, it is customary for men to greet elders and dignitaries by kissing their right front shoulder.
The People's Republic of China	• Some pushing and shoving in stores or when boarding public transportation is common and not considered rude.
India	• Since the head is considered a sacred part of the body in India, you should not pat children on the head or touch an older person's head.
Japan	• Women should avoid wearing high heels in order not to risk towering over Japanese counterparts.
South Korea	• Koreans, especially women, cover their mouths when laughing to avoid impolitely showing the inside of their mouths.

Source: Roger E. Axtell, *Do's and Taboos Around the World*, revised and expanded ed. (New York: Wiley, 2009).

Q **What are norms?** **Norms** are rules defining appropriate and inappropriate behavior (Hechter and Opp 2005). A Hindi peasant in India may be lying dead of starvation beside perfectly healthy and edible cattle, because in India cows are sacred. A Far Eastern woman may have her head severed for going to bed with a man before marriage. Each of these instances is a result of cultural norms—rules that specify ways of behaving for specific situations. Norms help explain why people in a society or group behave similarly in similar circumstances. (See Table 3.1.)

William Graham Sumner (1906), an early sociologist, wrote perceptively about norms. Anything, he stated, can be considered appropriate when norms exist that approve of it. This is because once norms are learned, members of a society use these norms to guide their social behavior. Norms are so ingrained that they guide our social behavior without our awareness. In fact, we may not even be consciously aware of a norm until it has been violated. For instance, we do not think about standing in line for concert tickets as a norm until someone attempts to step in front of us. Then it immediately registers. Taking one's turn in line is expected behavior, and cutting in line is violating that norm.

Norms vary widely from society to society. For example, infants in the United States typically sleep apart from their parents. Cross-cultural research, however, reveals that infants sleeping with their parents (particularly their mothers) is the common arrangement, a worldwide norm. Then look at the penal codes around the world. The United States has a much harsher record than is the norm in most cultures, with America holding 25 percent of all imprisoned citizens in the world. America's incarceration rate is six times higher than the median rate among all nations of the world (Haviland et al. 2001).

Norms range from relatively minor rules, such as applause after a performance, to extremely important ones, such as laws against stealing. Sumner identified three basic types of norms: folkways, mores, and laws. These three types of norms vary in their importance within a society, and their violation is tolerated to different degrees.

Q **What are folkways?** Rules that cover customary ways of thinking, feeling, and behaving but lack moral overtones are called **folkways.** For example, whether one uses a cell phone in a restaurant is not a moral issue; it qualifies as a folkway. Folkways in the United States include shaking hands when introduced and opening doors for older persons.

Because folkways are not considered vital to the welfare of the group, disapproval of violators is not very great. Those who consistently violate folkways—say, by persistently talking loudly in quiet places or wearing shorts with a suit coat and tie—may appear odd. We

In Japanese culture an emphasis on politeness enables people to learn to live harmoniously in close quarters.

may avoid these people, but we do not consider them wicked or immoral.

Some folkways are more important than others, and the social reaction to their violation is more intense. Failure to offer a woman a seat on a crowded bus draws little reaction, but obnoxious behavior at a party after excessive drinking may bring a severe negative response from others.

Q **What are mores?** **Mores** (pronounced MOR-ays; singular, *mos*) are norms of great moral significance. They are thought to be vital to the well-being of a society. Conformity to mores elicits significant social approval; violation of this type of norm evokes strong disapproval. For example, Americans subscribe to a long-standing mos requiring able-bodied men to work for a living. Able-bodied men who do not work are stigmatized (Waxman 1983).

Although conformity to folkways is generally a matter of personal choice, conformity to mores is a social requirement. As in the case of folkways, some mores are more vital to a society than others. Failure to stand while the national anthem is being played is not as serious a violation of American mores as using loud profanity during a worship service. Choosing, unnecessarily, to live on welfare is a more serious breach of appropriate conduct than either.

Some mores are more serious than others. A **taboo** is a mos so important that its violation is considered repugnant. Although definitions of incest vary from society to society, the incest taboo is generally regarded as the only taboo existing in all societies. Hindus in India have a taboo forbidding the killing of cows. While modern Saudi Arabia has lifted the taboo on women traveling abroad without a male companion, women are still forbidden to drive (Fattah 2007). Most cultures of the world share a taboo against the use of nuclear weapons.

Q **Is there always a hard line separating folkways and mores?** The distinction between mores and folkways is much more clear-cut in small, primitive societies. Not so much in large, modern ones. The former tend not to change; the latter are in constant flux. When in the context of change, the line between folkways and mores can become blurred. Consider premarital teenage sex among females. In 1950s America, the prohibition against female teenage sex before marriage was a hard and fast norm. Shame visited any female (and her family) who was even accused of premarital sex, let alone pregnant. Virginity before marriage signified good character. Today, while premarital sex among teenage girls is discouraged (and frowned on when done indiscriminately), the norm against it is much less strong. Americans are now much more tolerant of premarital sexual experimentation, even among teenagers. As Figure 3.1 shows, the premarital teenage sex rate in the United States has doubled between the 1950s and the early part of the twenty-first century (Risman and Schwartz 2002; "Teenage Sexual Activity" 2005; *World Almanac and Book of Facts* 2011).

Tellingly, the current debate between advocates of teenage sexual abstinence and advocates of public condom dispensation centers more on methods of birth control than sexual activity itself. The normative storm has moved from the prohibition against teenage sex to the prevention of pregnancy.

Other less serious norms change in importance as well. In the 1950s, only groups such as sailors, motorcycle gangs, and prostitutes publicly displayed tattoos. Any others sporting such designs were "deviants" and invited distrust, devaluation, and expressions of disgust. Tattoos somehow threatened the social order of most Americans. Today, you may see a tattoo on your girlfriend, one of your parents, your professor, or your favorite NFL player.

Q **How do laws differ from mores?** **Laws,** the third type of norm, are norms that are formally defined and enforced by officials. Folkways and mores emerge slowly

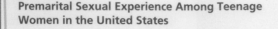

FIGURE 3.1

Premarital Sexual Experience Among Teenage
Women in the United States

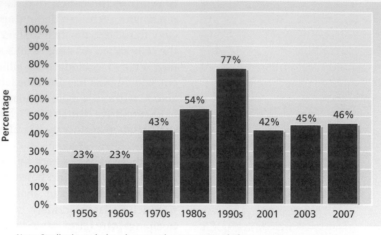

Note: Studies in each decade covered a two-year period.
Source: Based on Sandra L. Hofferth, John R. Kahn, and Wendy Baldwin, "Premarital
Sexual Activity Among U.S. Teenage Women over the Past Three Decades," *Family
Planning Perspectives* 19 (1987):49; Planned Parenthood Federation of America, Inc.
"Planned Parenthood Fact Sheet: Sexuality Education in the U.S";
www.ppfa.org/ppfa/sex-ed.html/ (June, 1995); and "Assessing Health Risk Behaviors
Among Young People," U.S. Department of Health and Human Services, Centers for
Disease Control and Prevention, 2002; Kaiser Family Foundation, January, 2005, *World
Almanac and Book of Facts 2010*, New York; World Almanac Education Group Inc., 2010,
P.171.

INTERNET LINK The Internet has an extensive list of sources
that pertain to premarital sexual activity. Several of these provide
useful data for the sociologist researching in this field. To begin, go
to Campaign for Our Children at www.cfoc.org/.

and are often unconsciously created, but laws are consciously created and enforced.

The Taliban militia in Afghanistan created a strict set of gender-apartheid laws. Women were not permitted to work outside the home, were banned from schools, and could go outside only if accompanied by a male relative.

Mores are an important source of laws, as was the case in many of the Taliban laws. At one time in human history, the norm against murder was not written down. But as civilization advanced, the norm prohibiting murder became formally defined and was enforced by public officials. But not all mores become laws. For example, it is not against the law to cheat on a college examination (although one can be expelled or otherwise punished). Nor have all laws been mores. For example, fines for overtime parking and laws against littering have never been mores.

Laws often remain on the books for a long time after the mores of a society have changed (Koon, Powell, and Schumaker 2002). It is illegal in Minnesota to hang male and female undergarments on the same clothesline; and card playing on trains is prohibited in New York. Mores and laws can also overlap. Although private citizens may show strong disapproval of a father who fails to support his children, public officials can do little unless the mother is willing to start legal action.

Because norms must be learned and accepted by individuals, conformity to them is not automatic. For this reason, groups must have some means for teaching norms and encouraging conformity to them. They do this, in part, through sanctions.

Q **How are norms enforced? Sanctions** are rewards and punishments used to encourage conformity to norms. They can be formal or informal. **Formal sanctions** are sanctions that may be given only by officially designated persons, such as judges and college professors. In 2009, a Syrian woman in Saudi Arabia was sentenced to forty lashes for conversing with two young men who were not her immediate relatives. The two men, said to be bringing her bread, were also sentenced to prison terms and lashes. Further, in 2009, a Somali man was stoned to death for adultery. His pregnant girlfriend was spared until after she had the child.

Formal sanctions can also be positive. Soldiers earn the Congressional Medal of Honor for heroism, and some students receive an A for academic performance.

Informal sanctions are sanctions that can be applied by most members of a group. They, too, can be positive or negative. Informal sanctions include thanking someone for pushing your car out of a snowbank or glaring harshly at someone who is cheating on a test.

Sanctions are not used randomly or without reason. Specific sanctions are associated with specific norms. Teenagers who violate their parents' curfew are not supposed to be beaten or locked in a closet. Instead, a society or group develops appropriate sanctions for following or failing to follow specific norms (A. V. Horwitz 1990).

Sanctions, most often, are not necessary. After we reach a certain age, most of us conform without the threat of sanctions. We may conform because we believe that the behavior expected of us is appropriate, because we wish to avoid guilty feelings, or because we fear social disapproval. In other words, if we have been properly socialized, we will mentally sanction ourselves before breaking a norm.

The severity of the sanction for a deviant act varies from one society to another and from one time to another. In 2010, an Iranian court sentenced a woman to be stoned to death for adultery. The court later rescinded the original punishment and sentenced her to be hanged instead. During the 1960s, possession of an ounce of marijuana could result in several years in prison. Today, possession of a small amount of marijuana in most states is a misdemeanor, and in several states it is equivalent to a minor traffic violation.

Sometimes, informal sanctions are illegally imposed. A soccer sportscaster was shot in the knees in Avellino, Italy, by irate fans. The rash of "dowry deaths" in India, not too long ago, is also an example of illegal sanctioning. Some mothers-in-law, upset over the small size of their sons' wives' dowry, poured gasoline over their daughters-in-law and threw matches on them.

So far, we have discussed norms and sanctions as aspects of normative culture. Although norms and sanctions are relatively specific and concrete, the next major component of the normative dimension of culture—values—is rather broad and abstract. Values are much more general than norms.

Q What are values? **Values** are broad cultural principles that most people in a society consider desirable. Values are so general that they do not specify precise ways of thinking, feeling, and behaving. Thus, different societies or different groups within the same society can have quite different norms based on the same value.

For instance, the value of freedom has been expressed differently in America and in the former Soviet Union. In the Soviet Union, as Robin Williams (1970) notes, freedom was expressed in the right to such things as employment, medical care, and education. Americans have different norms based on the value of freedom—the right to free speech and assembly, the right to engage in private enterprise, the right to a representative government, and the right to change where they live and work.

Q Why are values important? Values are important because they have a tremendous influence on human social behavior—mainly because norms are based on them. A society that values democracy will have norms ensuring personal freedom; a society that values humanitarianism will have norms providing for its most unfortunate members; a society that values hard work will have norms against laziness. Values are also important because they tend to permeate most aspects of daily life. In America, for example, the value of freedom affects more than a person's political life. It affects such diverse areas as relationships in the family, treatment within the legal system, the operation of organizations, and the choice of religious affiliation.

Q What are the basic values in American society? Any attempt to describe the basic values of American society is risky. Because America has so many diverse groups and because it is constantly changing, any one set of values is unlikely to receive unanimous support (Etzioni 2001). Despite these problems, Robin Williams (1970) has done an excellent job of outlining fifteen major values guiding the daily lives of most Americans. Whether or not his classification is complete, it provides

Joern Pollex/Staff/Getty Images Sport/Getty Images

The U.S. Women's World Cup team is defeating Japan to enter the 2011 finals. What cultural values do these women demonstrate?

a picture of the major values influencing Americans. These values include achievement and success, activity and work, humanitarianism, efficiency and practicality, progress, material comfort, equality, freedom, democracy, individuality, science and rationality, external conformity, group (racial, ethnic, religious) superiority, morality, and patriotism. Following is a sample of the values identified by Williams:

- *Achievement and success.* Americans emphasize achievement, especially in the world of work. Success is supposed to be based on effort and competition, and it is viewed as a reward for performance.
- *Activity and work.* We tend to stress action over inaction in almost all instances. For most Americans, continuous and regular work is an end in itself, advancement is to be based on merit rather than favoritism, and all citizens are supposed to have the opportunity to perform at their best.
- *Efficiency and practicality.* Americans pride themselves on getting things done by the most rational means. We search for better, faster ways of doing things, praise good workmanship, judge work performance by its practical consequences, and depend on science and technology.
- *Equality.* Americans advocate equality for all citizens. In interpersonal activities, we tend to treat one another as equals, to defend everyone's legal rights, and to favor equal opportunity for everyone.
- *Democracy.* Americans emphasize that all citizens are entitled to equal rights. All Americans should have equal rights and equal opportunity under the law, and power should not be concentrated in the hands of the elite.
- *Group superiority.* Despite their concern for equality of opportunity, Americans tend to place greater value on people of their own race, ethnic group, social class, or religious group.

These values, clearly, are interrelated. The values of achievement, success, activity, and work are related to the values of efficiency and practicality. Equally obvious is the conflict between some values: Americans value group superiority while stressing equality and democracy.

Q Are these values prominent in American society today? Williams identified fifteen major American values approximately forty years ago. Although most of these values have remained remarkably stable over the years, some have changed somewhat. For example, today there is less emphasis on group superiority than in the past, as can be seen in the apparent decline of openly racist attitudes and behavior (Farley and Haaga 1988; Rochon 1998). However, it is usually a case of norms and behavior, rather than underlying values, that change radically. In other words, it is probably because

The bride, groom, and guests march in a traditional wedding ceremony in Indonesia. What values are reflected in this event?

of civil rights laws that many Americans are now less likely to make overt racist statements and discriminate against minority members. They simply behave in a way that is consistent with changed norms. So, as yet, racism remains part of the fabric of American culture.

Likewise, the norms related to hard work and activity have changed. According to Lionel Lewis (1982), many Americans now work as hard at their leisure (e.g., long-distance running and mountain climbing) as they do at their jobs.

Williams's analysis of major American values remains basically sound today, but it is not surprising that some, quite validly, believe that his list is incomplete. George and Louise Spindler (1983), for example, wish to add optimism, honesty, and sociability to the list of major American values.

Although functionalism is the basis of the normative dimension of culture, symbolic interactionism is related to the cognitive and material dimensions. Be alert to these theoretical relationships.

The Cognitive Dimension

Q Why do cultural beliefs matter? **Cognition** is the process of thinking, knowing, or processing information. The cognitive dimension of culture, then, refers to its complex of ideas and knowledge. The most important aspect of the cognitive dimension of culture is **beliefs**—ideas concerning the nature of reality. Actually, beliefs are influential whether they are true or false. The Romans believed that Caesar Augustus was a god; the Tanala, a hill tribe of Madagascar, believed that the souls of their kings passed into snakes. On the American frontier, it was believed that a dog howling in the distance foretold a death in one's family, that anyone who brought a shovel into a cabin would carry out a coffin, and that a bird on one's windowsill or inside one's home meant sorrow in the future. While each of these beliefs is false, other beliefs—such as the belief that the human eye can distinguish more than 7 million colors or the belief that no life exists on Mars (Begley 1994)—are factually supported by evidence.

Regardless of their truth, beliefs are important, because people tend to base their behavior on what they believe. Beliefs are also important because people are very attached to them, sometimes in ways that seem bizarre to outsiders. After surrendering their property and families following a siege, members of a Chinese village fought to the death rather than cut off their ponytails (Lilla 2008).

Both the normative and cognitive dimensions are part of **nonmaterial culture**: the norms, values, and beliefs of a group of people. We now turn to "material" culture.

The Material Dimension

Q **How do a society's physical objects reflect its culture?** **Material culture** consists of the concrete, tangible objects within a culture—automobiles, basketballs, chairs, highways, birth-control pills, art, jeans. Artifacts, or physical objects, have no meaning or use apart from the meanings people give them. Consider newspaper and pepper as physical objects. Of course, each of these two things separately has some meaning for you, but can you think of a use for them in combination? Some midwives have used pepper and newspaper in a process known as nettling. An elderly medical doctor tells the story of his first encounter with nettling:

The ink of my medical license was hardly dry, and as I was soon to find out, my ears would not be dry for some time. I had never delivered a baby on my own and faced my maiden voyage with some fear.

Upon entering Mrs. Williamson's house, I found a local midwife and several neighbors busily at work preparing for the delivery. My fear caused me to move rather slowly and my happiness over my reprieve prompted me to tell the women that they were doing just fine and to proceed without my services.

Having gotten myself off the hook, I watched the ladies with a fascination that soon turned to horror.

At the height of Mrs. Williamson's labor pains, one of the neighbors rolled a piece of newspaper into a funnel shape. Holding the bottom end of the cone she poured a liberal amount of pepper into it. Her next move was to insert the sharp end of the cone into Mrs. Williamson's nose. With the cone in its "proper" place, the neighbor inhaled deeply and blew the pepper from the cone into the inner recesses of Mrs. Williamson's nose—if not her mind.

Suddenly alert, Mrs. Williamson's eyes widened as her senses rebelled against the pepper. With her mighty sneeze, I was introduced to nettling. The violence of that sneeze

reverberated through her body to force the baby from her womb in a skittering flight across the bed. An appropriately positioned assistant fielded the baby in midflight and only minor details of Orville's rite of birth remained.

Before this doctor was introduced to nettling, this particular combination of newspaper and pepper had no meaning for him. And until nettling was devised, the combination was without meaning for anyone, even though the separate physical objects existed as part of the culture.

Physical objects do not have the same meanings and uses in all societies. Although it is conventional to use a 747 jet for traveling, it is possible that a 747 downed in a remote jungle region of the world could be used as a place of worship, a storage bin, or a home. In the United States, out-of-service buses, trains, and trolley cars have been converted to restaurants.

Clearly, the cultural meaning of a physical object is not determined by the physical characteristics of the object. People use newspaper and pepper during childbirth or make a temple of a downed 747 jet because of cognitive and normative definitions. The meanings of physical objects are based on the beliefs, norms, and values people hold with regard to them. This is readily apparent when new meanings of a physical object are considered. At one time, only pianos and organs were used in church services; guitars, drums, and trumpets were not "holy" enough to accompany a choir. Yet, many churches today use these "worldly" instruments regularly in their worship activities. The instruments have not changed, but the cultural meanings placed on them have.

Ideal and Real Culture

There is sometimes a gap between cultural guidelines and actual behavior. This gap is captured in the concepts of ideal and real culture. **Ideal culture** refers to cultural guidelines publicly embraced by members of a society; these are the guidelines we *claim* to accept. **Real culture** refers to *actual* behavior patterns. Sometimes subterranean real cultural patterns are publicly denied because they conflict with the ideal culture. For example, one aspect of America's ideal culture is honesty. Yet, in real culture, some taxpayers annually violate both the letter and spirit of existing tax laws, some business people engage in dishonest business practices, and some college athletes do the "high $500" handshake (during which a team booster leaves illegal money in their palms). These are not isolated instances. Real culture often passes these patterns from generation to generation. Keep in mind that we are not referring to cases of individual deviance, such as people who murder, rape, and rob. These latter types of antisocial behavior violate even real culture.

Q **Does the fact that we sometimes ignore cultural guidelines make ideal culture meaningless?** Absolutely not. In an imperfect world, ideal culture provides high standards. These ideals are targets that most people attempt to reach most of the time. Otherwise, social chaos would prevail. Ideal culture also permits the detection of deviant behavior. We sanction individuals who deviate too far from the ideal cultural pattern. This helps preserve the ideal culture.

Culture as a Tool Kit

According to the dominant view, culture guides behavior by providing the values or ends toward which behavior is directed. Ann Swidler, a contemporary critic of the culture-as-a-way-of-life approach, thinks that culture should be viewed as a "'tool kit' of symbols, stories, rituals, and worldviews, which people may use in varying configurations to solve different kinds of problems" (Swidler 1986:273). In this view, culture provides a range of choices to be applied in defining and solving the problems of living. Because the content of any culture is not fully consistent, the "tools" that are chosen vary among individuals and situations. This view of culture is gaining visibility. Its eventual prominence in the sociological approach to culture remains to be seen (Hays 1994).

Q **How does culture as a tool kit work?** Let's take an example of something you have given serious thought to: love and marriage (Swidler 2003). Culture affects the way (strategy of action) one pursues the choice of a future marriage partner. At one end of the continuum, culture may permit a marriage partner chosen only by one's parents, as in traditional China, Korea, and Japan (Peoples and Bailey, 2009). On the other hand, American culture provides for considerable latitude in going about the choice of a mate. For your grandparents in the 1950s, a sequence of steps provided management for a couple's level of commitment. They could negotiate an increasing level of commitment by "going steady" and then becoming "pinned," ringed, and engaged.

CHECK YOURSELF **3.1** R2

Dimensions of Culture

1. _____ consists of all the material objects as well as the patterns of thinking, feeling, and behaving that are passed from generation to generation among members of a society.
2. A _____ is composed of a people living within defined territorial borders who share a common culture.
3. _____ are rules defining appropriate and inappropriate ways of behaving.
4. _____ are rewards and punishments used to encourage desired behavior.
5. Indicate whether the following are formal sanctions (F) or informal sanctions (I).
    _I_ a. A mother spanks her child.
    _F_ b. A professor fails a student for cheating on an exam.
    _F_ c. A jury sentences a person to life in prison for espionage.
    _I_ d. A husband separates from his wife after she has an affair.
6. _____ are broad cultural principles embodying ideas about what most people in a society consider desirable.
7. _____ are ideas concerning the nature of reality.
8. Indicate whether each of the following best reflects a belief (B), folkway (F), mos (M), law (L), or value (V).
    ____ a. conception that God exists
    ____ b. norm against cursing aloud in church
    ____ c. norm encouraging the eating of three meals daily
    ____ d. idea of progress
    ____ e. norm against burning a national flag
    ____ f. norm encouraging sleeping in a bed
    ____ g. norm prohibiting murder
    ____ h. norm against overtime parking
    ____ i. idea that the Earth's orbit is elliptical
    ____ j. idea of freedom
9. _____ culture consists of the concrete, tangible objects within a culture.
10. _____ culture refers to aspects of culture publicly embraced by members of a society.

Answers: 1. Culture; 2. society; 3. Norms; 4. Sanctions; 5. a. (I), b. (F), c. (F), d. (I); 6. Values; 7. Beliefs; 8. a. (B), b. (M), c. (F), d. (V), e. (M), f. (F), g. (L), h. (L), i. (B), j. (V); 9. Material; 10. Ideal

Couples could signal each other their level of commitment by advancing (or not) to the next stage. The choice not to advance while at a lower level of commitment made it easier to discontinue a relationship. And because these steps developed over a relatively long period, there was time to consider changes in one's strategy of action. Culture does not prescribe these well-defined sequential steps in the same way today, though some couples do construct a strategy for action around them. Modern couples now have additional resources for going about the selection of a marriage partner. For example, the decision to have a long-term sexual relationship with someone signals a level of commitment. Deciding to live together ratchets the level of commitment higher.

For today, then, as for yesterday, culture provides resources for a strategy of action in mate selection. But according to culture-as-a-tool-kit advocates, culture influences a strategy of action. An American today can choose which aspects of culture to use in advancing toward marriage. In addition to the more traditional way of showing increased commitment, couples today may choose to have a long-term sexual relationship or even to live together before marriage.

Q How is culture as a tool kit related to the sociological imagination? The sociological imagination allows us to see the relationship between events in our personal lives and events in our society. This knowledge, in turn, increases freedom from social forces if we so wish. The same potential liberating effect is present in the idea of culture as a tool kit. By understanding the influence of culture on the process of selecting a mate, for example, we can be freer to choose from the variety of available cultural resources as we create a strategy of action. For example, culture tells young people that the best way to break up is face to face (Gershon 2010). However, electronic media now provide other ways to end a relationship. Do you want to separate via text messaging? Are there socially acceptable ways to do that? The sociological imagination helps you examine such nontraditional alternatives.

Language and Culture R1

Culture is the social heritage of humans. This heritage is altered by each generation and must be learned by new members of society. Both the creation and the transmission of culture depend heavily on the human capacity to develop and use symbols, the most significant of which is language. The following discussion relies on concepts central to symbolic interactionism. Symbolic interactionism, you will recall, emphasizes our use of symbols in subjective interpretations of human social behavior.

Symbols, Language, and Culture

Q Once again, what are symbols? Symbols—things that stand for, or represent, something else—can range from physical objects to words, sounds, smells, and tastes. As you saw in Chapter 1, however, the meaning of a symbol is not dictated by its characteristics. There is nothing intrinsically good about the sound created by applause. In the United States, for example, applause warms the heart of an entertainer, a politician, or a professor, but in Latin America it symbolizes disapproval.

Of course, once meaning has been assigned to applause and we learn to associate it with approval or disapproval, it seems as though the appropriate meaning is determined by the applause itself. In the Islamic world, the required head scarf for women is a symbol of modesty. Americans see it as a symbol of male oppression. When an Iraqi man threw both of his shoes at President George Bush in 2008, he was throwing more than just the shoes on his feet. Throwing a shoe at someone in Iraq symbolizes extreme disrespect and contempt (Raghavan and Eggen 2008).

In Lewis Carroll's *Through the Looking Glass,* Humpty Dumpty says to Alice with some finality, "When I use a word, it means just what I choose it to mean—neither more nor less." So it is with symbols. Of course, the same word can symbolize very different things. Shortly after September 11, 2001, American teenagers appropriated newly current words for their own purposes. Ground-zero bedrooms were a total mess; mean teachers were terrorists; a disciplined student experienced a *jihad;* and out-of-style clothes were burqas (Wax 2002). Even the symbol "nine-eleven" was expanded from its conventional meanings as a numerical value and an emergency phone number to include the 2001 terrorist attacks in New York, Washington, and Pennsylvania. (See Table 3.2.)

Symbolic culture is not limited to vocal, written, or material symbols. **Gestures,** whether in the form of facial expression, body movement, or posture, also carry culturally defined and shared symbolic meanings (E. T. Hall 1976, 1979, 1990). Most Americans know that each gesture, whether it is shaking one's fist at another driver, forming a circle with one's forefinger and thumb, or extending one's thumb in the direction of traffic while walking along a highway, conveys a commonly held meaning to other Americans. Sometimes, though not frequently, gestures may change within a culture. For example, it used to be that men publicly holding hands could only suggest a homosexual relationship. Today, when NFL players hold hands in the huddle, it symbolizes team solidarity. And different gestures transmit different meanings in various cultures. Americans hold a thumb upright, either to signal strong approval or

TABLE 3.2

Symbols Created for Internet Communication

The symbols in the left column were created to stand for the symbols in the right column. Why are both columns called symbols?

:-)	Happy
;-)	Winking
:-(	Sad
:-D	Laughing
:-O	Surprised
:-@	Screaming
:-P	Tongue in cheek
R	Are
UOK?	Are you OK?
B	Be
B4	Before
BBL	Be back later
BRB	Be right back
BTW	By the way
XLNT	Excellent
4	For, Four
GR8	Great
L8R	Later
LOL	Laughing out loud
LUV	Love
NO1	No one
OIC	Oh, I see
PLS	Please
PCM	Please call me
C	See
THX	Thanks
TTUL	Talk to you later
2	Too, to, two
2DAY	Today
2MORO	Tomorrow
WAN2	Want to
?	What
U	You
YR	Your

to request a ride. The same gesture in Nigeria is taken as an insult (Axtell 2009).

Q **What is the relationship between language and culture?** Language frees humans from the limits of time and place. It enables us to generate new culture by providing a written and verbal foundation of past and present knowledge. Through language, elements of existing culture can be recombined to create something novel. It allows us to create culture. Only the years of scientific research recorded in books and scientific journals made the Human Genome Project possible.

Equipped with the symbols of language, humans can transmit their experiences, ideas, and knowledge to others. Although it may take some time and repetition, we can teach children the dangers of fire and heights without their being burned or toppling from stairs. This process of social learning, of course, applies to other cultural patterns as well, such as exhibiting patriotism, consuming food, or staying awake in class.

According to Edward Sapir (1929) and Benjamin Whorf (1956), language is our guide to reality; our view of the world depends on our particular language. Our perception of reality is at the mercy of the words and grammatical rules of our language. And because our perceptions are different, our worlds are different. This is known as the **hypothesis of linguistic relativity**. Subsequent research has discredited the extreme assertion of linguistic relativity that language entirely determines thinking. Studies do reveal, however, that language significantly shapes thought (Boroditsky 2001; Kenneally 2008; Lupyan 2008; Pinker 2007, 2008; Wade 2010).

Q **What can vocabulary reveal about a culture?** When something is important to a society, its language will contain many words to describe that entity. The Agta of the Philippines have thirty-one different verbs meaning to fish (M. Harris 1990). The importance of time in American culture is reflected in many words—*era, moment, interim, recurrent, century, afternoon, semester, eternal, annual, meanwhile regularly,* and *semester,* just to name a few. When something is unimportant to people, they may not even have a word for it. When Christian missionaries first went to Asia, they were dismayed because the Chinese language contained no word for—and therefore no concept of—sin. Other missionaries were no less dismayed to learn that Africans and Polynesians had no way to express the idea of a single, all-powerful God.

Language can also tell us the value a society or group places on something. Much of the hip-hop culture and the hip-hop music that embodies it reflect a general denigration of all women, especially black and Latino women. For example, hip-hop lyrics degrading women scream sexism and misogyny. Routine references to women (except one's momma) as "bitches" and "hos" reduce women to submissive sex objects to be used personally or sold to others.

CHECK YOURSELF 3.2 R2

Language and Culture

1. _____ are things that stand for, or represent, something else.
2. Because of _____, culture can be created and transmitted.
3. According to the hypothesis of linguistic relativity, words and the structure of a language cause people to live in a distinct world. T or F?
4. The language we learn determines forever how we see the world. T or F?

Answers: 1. Symbols; 2. language; 3. T; 4. F

Q Are people prisoners of their language? Linguist Guy Deutscher contends that the idea of a prison-house of language is a fundamental error of linguistic relativity. Actually, research reveals that people can reason logically and understand ideas present in other languages (Deutscher 2010). Thus, although behavior and conceptions of social reality are colored by language, it does not follow that people are trapped by it.

Cultural Diversity and Similarity R1

As you view cultural diversity and cultural similarities, you should be aware of the appropriate theories inherent in each discussion. Conflict theory, with its emphasis on inconsistency, conflict, and change, undergirds any discussion of cultural diversity, whereas functionalism is the basis for a sociological analysis of cultural similarity. Symbolic interactionism is intimately connected with the role of language in culture and with the cognitive and material dimensions of culture. (For other connections between culture and the theoretical perspectives, see Table 3.3.)

Cultural Diversity

In ancient Rome, adultery was an accepted practice among the upper classes, and divorce was granted upon agreement of the couple. In modern Italy, adultery is frowned on, and divorce has only recently been legalized. Some American married couples frown on open relationships, while others advertise their "swinging" behavior in newspapers and magazines. These examples reflect the almost endless cultural variations in the world. Not only do different societies have different beliefs, norms, values, and sanctions, but various groups within the same society have their own cultural patterns. Even in a simple society, cultural diversity makes it impossible for all members to participate in all aspects of culture. In modern societies,

TABLE 3.3

FOCUS ON THEORETICAL PERSPECTIVES: Culture

This table illustrates the unique slant that each of the three major theoretical perspectives takes on culture. Select a different aspect of culture for each perspective and make up your own table.

Theoretical Perspective	Aspect of Culture	Example
Functionalism	• The norm requiring students to listen to their teachers on request	• This norm promotes better education for everyone because of a lack of disorder.
Conflict theory	• Drug use by a member of a drug subculture	• Because of a lack of power, he or she is more likely to go to jail than an upper-class user.
Symbolic interactionism	• Confederate flag on the back window of a truck	• To the driver, the flag may be a symbol of cultural heritage; to an African American, it may represent slavery.

SOCIOLOGY EYES AMERICA 3.1

Immigration to the United States

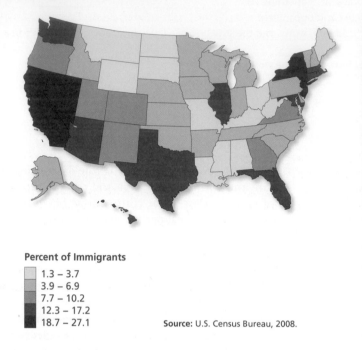

Percent of Immigrants

- 1.3 – 3.7
- 3.9 – 6.9
- 7.7 – 10.2
- 12.3 – 17.2
- 18.7 – 27.1

Source: U.S. Census Bureau, 2008.

The United States has long been the destination of immigrants from around the world. These immigrants have contributed to the nation's rich cultural diversity in a wide variety of ways. This map shows the percentage of immigrants who have come to the United States by state.

Interpret the Map

1. Which states had the most immigrants? Which states had the fewest?
2. About how many immigrants settled in your state?
3. Why would it be correct to say that the United States is a nation of immigrants?

cultural diversity is staggering. Given the biological similarity among humans, this diversity must be explained by nongenetic factors. (See "Sociology Eyes America" 3.1.)

Q How is cultural diversity promoted? Cultural diversity exists within all societies, due, in part, to the presence of social categories. A **social category** is a group of persons who share a social characteristic such as age, sex, or religion. Members of social categories are expected to participate in aspects of culture unique to them. A particular age, gender, or religion, for example, often has distinctive activities associated with it.

Cultural diversity also stems from the existence of groups—known as *subcultures* and *countercultures*—that are somewhat different from the larger culture. Although these groups do participate in the dominant culture—they may speak the language, work at regular jobs, eat and dress like most others, and attend recognized houses of worship—they also think, feel, and behave in ways that set them apart. Subcultures and countercultures are more prevalent in large, complex societies.

Q What is a subculture? A **subculture** is a group that is part of the dominant culture but differs from it in some important respects. By tradition, Americans like to see themselves as part of a large, single culture. This

view was fueled by the long-standing conception of the United States as a "melting pot" that absorbs peoples from around the world into "American" culture. This viewpoint minimized the presence of cultural diversity in the United States. Since the 1960s, there has been a movement toward an emphasis on the cultural uniqueness of subgroups. This movement, known as **multiculturalism,** accents the viewpoints, experiences, and contributions of minorities (women as well as ethnic and racial minorities). In fact, many scholars are concerned that the current emphasis on cultural differences is unduly fragmenting American society (Schlesinger 1998).

Sociologists have studied many subcultures, both before and after the rise of multiculturalism. Devotees of the Grateful Dead band—both live and participate in the dominant culture. "Deadheads," as they call themselves, subscribe to a subculture constructed around the band. They share a unique language, mode of dress (featuring tie-dyed clothing), and liberal attitudes toward drug use. Deadheads tend to have mainstream jobs and lives. For them, participation in the subculture revolves around hearing the band when it is close enough to attend. Many Deadheads, however, take off for months to follow the band on tour around the country (R. G. Adams 1995). Other subcultures in America are those formed by athletes, actors, and surfers, as well as by people in mental hospitals, convents, and universities. (For other excellent examples, see G. A. Fine 1996; Redhead 1997; Meuller 1999; Schaefer and Zellner 2011; also see "Consider This Research.")

Subcultures attempt to be different from the larger culture in particular ways, and consequently, substitute these ways for other generally accepted practices. Some subcultures not only want to be *different*, but they also make a show of their opposition *against* the larger culture. These groups are called "countercultures."

Q Is a counterculture a subculture? A **counterculture** is a subculture that deliberately and *consciously* opposes certain central aspects of the dominant culture. One

Jacquelynne Eccles— Teenagers in a Cultural Bind

Adolescence is often marked by drama and difficulty. Jacquelynne Eccles and colleagues (1993) investigated the experience of American teenagers entering a Midwestern junior high school and discovered that some teenage troubles are more than hormonal—they are cultural as well. The relationships among seventh graders, teachers, and parents are embedded in the normative and cognitive aspects of culture.

Eccles conducted a two-year study of students from twelve school districts in middle-class Michigan communities. She studied 1,500 early adolescents moving from sixth grade in an elementary school to seventh grade in a junior high school. Students filled out questionnaires at school in two consecutive years—the sixth and seventh grades. This procedure permitted Eccles to document changes the teenagers experienced after the first year of their transition.

The findings were not encouraging. The relationships between students and teachers deteriorated over the year, a deterioration Eccles found related to the culture of junior high school. At the very time when young adolescents especially need supportive relationships outside the home, personal and positive relationships with teachers fall victim to cultural and organizational changes in junior high school. There was increased grouping based on academic achievement and increased public evaluation comparing students with one another. This heightened emphasis on student ranking comes just when young adolescents are at the peak of concern about their status relative to their peers. In addition, in the junior high culture, the students experienced less opportunity to participate in classroom decision making. The resulting diminished school motivation and lessened academic self-confidence is as predictable as it is unfortunate. The culturally defined educational structure of junior high works directly against the fact that adolescents develop better in emotionally supportive environments.

Eccles's news was no better on the home front. In fact, the results in the family paralleled those reported for the school. Excessive parental control over teenagers went up at the same time school motivation and self-esteem of the junior high school students went down.

As a check on these general findings, Eccles compared students in more culturally supportive schools and families with those in less supportive ones. In both the school and the family settings, she found more positive results in culturally supportive environments. Students who were able to participate in school and family decision making showed higher levels of academic motivation and self-esteem than their peers with less opportunity to participate.

The solution, Eccles concludes, exists in a cultural change within both the schools and the family. Schools and the family need to develop balanced cultural expectations of young adolescents based on their developmental needs. At this age, young people have a growing need for autonomy. Neither cracking down on them nor relinquishing control strikes the proper balance. The task is for the family and the school to provide "an environment that changes in the right way and at the right pace" (Eccles et al. 1993:99).

Evaluate the Research

1. Do you recall your first year in junior high school? Analyze your experience based on the cultural definitions that existed in your school and home at the time.
2. Do adolescent students belong to a subculture? A counterculture? Explain.
3. Which of the three theoretical perspectives is most helpful in understanding the social relationships Eccles describes? Apply this perspective to explain her findings.

can understand counterculture only within the context of its underlying opposition to some aspect of the dominant culture (see "Consider This Research"). An example is the counterculture formed on American college and university campuses in the 1960s. What Edward Suchman (1968) called their "hang-loose" ethic rejected such central aspects of American culture as material success, achievement, hard work, efficiency, authority, premarital chastity, and the nuclear family.

Q **Do countercultures ever become violent?** Though violence is not a necessary part of being a counterculture, some countercultures contain elements that do resort to threats of violence and physical force. Prison countercultures engage in violence primarily within the confines of prison. Their targets are other inmates. But other countercultures may spawn violence against targets within the larger society. These countercultures can be thought of as having terrorist elements within them (O'Kane 2007; Law 2009; J. R. White 2009).

Terrorism is the illegal use of violence or threats of violence to intimidate a government, a group, or an individual in pursuit of a political, religious, economic, or social goal. The militia movement in the United States is based on political opposition. Members of the militia counterculture congregate in isolated compounds, sharing a way of life fashioned to resist the authority of the federal government. Fully armed, members of the militia organize their lives around a future violent revolution against their oppressor (Stern 1996; Ferber 1998). History tells us that even the most ferocious militia is not likely to engage in violence. The exceptions produced by the militia movement are, however, a real concern for U.S. law enforcement officials. Those most likely to take action sometimes call themselves three percenters because they believe the other 97 percent of the movement is all talk and no action. Many officials view the 1995 Oklahoma City federal building bombing that killed 168 people as either part of the militia movement or an outgrowth of it. McVeigh had been a member of several white-supremacist groups and militias before he and his friend, Terry Nichols, acted (Gellman 2010).

The skinheads, a neo-Nazi counterculture founded in the United States at the beginning of the 1980s, is a counterculture based on racial, ethnic, and sexual orientation intolerance. This intolerance appears in violent acts against gay men and lesbians, ethnic minorities (particularly Jews), and blacks. Skinheads see themselves as patriotic defenders of a belief in racial superiority and "sexual correctness" who have a right to use violence against their targets (Wooden 1995). A final example of terrorism by some members of a counterculture exists within the anti-abortion movement. Violence within the anti-abortion movement got its start in 1984 when Michael Bray led a small group of radicals in the burning of seven abortion

These skinheads are giving the Nazi salute during their training outside Moscow. Are they part of a subculture or a counterculture?

International terrorism grabbed America's attention following the attack on the World Trade Center. Less evident are the diverse forms of domestic terrorism.

clinics in the mid-Atlantic region. In 1993 another group within the anti-abortion movement led by Paul Hill began to target humans, killing seven doctors, nurses, and security guards at abortion clinics between 1993 and 1998 (Law 2009). In 2008, Dr. George Tiller, a Kansas City doctor who provided late-term abortions, was gunned down in his church by an anti-abortion radical. Dr. Tiller's murder followed a long period of harassment, including having his clinic bombed in 1985 and being shot in both arms in 1993.

Of course, not all members of militia, skinhead, and anti-abortion groups advocate violence or use physical force. The leaders of these countercultures may, however, express their opposition in such extreme terms that intimidation and violence seem justified to some radical members.

The preceding examples are of "homegrown" terrorists who commit acts of violence within their own society. International terrorism, such as Al Qaeda's airplane attacks on the World Trade Center and the Pentagon, will be discussed at several points throughout the book.

Q How do cultural differences affect attitudes toward others? People who spend most of their lives with others culturally similar to themselves—who hardly ever deal with people different from themselves—will almost inevitably use their own cultural standards to judge others. This tendency to judge others in relation to one's own cultural standards is referred to as **ethnocentrism.** The ethnocentric eye may see those who are different as inferior, ignorant, crazy, or immoral. We are shocked by the Yanomamö women of Venezuela and Brazil who measure the affection of their husbands by the number of beatings they are given (Chagnon 1997). Less exotic examples of ethnocentrism are plentiful—extreme nationalism being one. Members of all societies tend to offer themselves as exemplary models. The Olympic Games are much more than an arena for young men and women to engage in healthy and exuberant competition; they are also an expression of ethnocentrism.

Ethnocentrism also exists within societies. Members of country clubs, religious groups, and schools all over America typically feel that their particular ways are superior and that others should adopt them as well (see "Think Globally" 3.1). Regional rivalries in the United

THINK GLOBALLY 3.1

Global Tourism

Although people often want to observe and experience cultures different from their own, exposure to cultural diversity can be uncomfortable. Most international tourist travel occurs among countries sharing common cultural traditions and languages.

Source: From John L. Allen and Christopher J. Sutton. *Student Atlas of the World* 3rd ed. (p. 51). Copyright © 2009, National Geographic Society. Reprinted by permission.

Interpret the Map
1. Identify the world regions that receive the highest and lowest number of tourists.
2. Are there any reasons to believe that these travel patterns might change in the near future? If so, what factors might bring about this change?

These victims of genocide in West Darfur, Sudan, illustrate the disastrous consequences of extreme ethnocentrism.

States stimulate humor that often reflects an underlying ethnocentrism. Boston is said by some (mostly Bostonians) to be the hub of the universe. Some inhabitants of the Eastern seaboard believe that only a wasteland separates them from the Pacific Ocean, while some more enlightened Easterners are willing to concede the addition of California in describing all that is good in the United States. Of course, those in middle America feel that virtue resides with them.

Q Are there advantages of ethnocentrism? Up to this point, ethnocentrism has been portrayed as either politically incorrect or ridiculous. It may be both. But to some degree it is inevitable. And its inevitability is rooted partly in the advantages it offers to social life. Imagine the expense and effort required to create the integration, high morale, and loyalty that ethnocentrism provides a society or group. Few things draw people closer together than shared loyalty or a conviction that they are right and superior. Such commitment makes people feel good about themselves and their fellow group members. Fires of nationalism and patriotism are not fanned by declaring that your nation is slightly below average! Finally, ethnocentrism promotes social stability because people who are convinced that truth and beauty are theirs seldom entertain the need for change.

People are ethnocentric not simply because they recognize the benefits of ethnocentricity for social life. No. Ethnocentrism would be pervasive even if it did not offer these advantages. We are taught the rightness of our culture from a variety of sources (home, church, peers, schools, mass media), so it is only natural that this "rightness" becomes the yardstick for evaluating other cultures and how their members think, feel, and behave. Judgments of all kinds are nearly always alloyed with socially derived convictions regarding right and wrong. Ethnocentrism, then, is a predictable by-product of the transmission of culture.

Q What are the disadvantages of ethnocentrism? A price may be paid for the integration, morale, loyalty, and stability that ethnocentrism provides. Extreme ethnocentrism has ill effects within societies as well as between them. On the intrasocietal side, extreme ethnocentrism may create such a high degree of integration and stability that innovation is hampered. Societies whose members are too firmly convinced of their righteousness may choke off exploration for new solutions to persistent problems. Further, they may reject, without examination, solutions that might be gleaned from other societies. And if heightened ethnocentrism impedes both the internal creation of ideas and the external influence for solutions to long-standing problems, it may create an even greater disadvantage in facing the challenge of new problems and unfamiliar circumstances.

On the intersocietal front, social and political conflict is nearly always a result of extreme ethnocentrism. Global peace and welfare become secondary goals in a world in which ethnocentrism intensifies intersocietal conflicts based on power struggles for economic superiority and/or military supremacy.

We have already seen some of the negative consequences of ethnocentrism for a society. Ethnocentrism has harmful effects on individuals as well. **Culture shock**—the psychological and social stress we may experience when confronted with a radically different cultural environment—is one such negative consequence. Even cultural anthropologists, who are trained professionals, may experience culture shock (Chagnon 1997). If trained anthropologists can experience culture shock, it is easy to understand why immigrants are stunned by cultural practices foreign to their own. As a U.S. native, you might be surprised at the shocks, large and small, that internationals face in this country. When one newcomer was asked by a checkout clerk if he wished paper or plastic, he got very confused and upset. How could he choose paper or plastic when he thought payment required money? More seriously, imagine the difficulties of dating if you came from a culture in which interaction with the opposite sex among the young is limited to relatives (Pipher and Cohen 2002). You will probably better understand culture shock if you take an overseas job assignment (Wagster 1993).

Cultural Relativism

Ethnocentrism can injure others when we attempt to impose our ways of thinking, feeling, and behaving on them. Despite good intentions, outsiders have, in many instances, harmed members of other cultures.

Q **What can be done to reduce the negative personal effects of ethnocentrism?** Awareness of ethnocentrism and the harm it can cause is a necessary first step to its control. An important second step lies in a perspective known as **cultural relativism.** According to this perspective, we are not to view values, norms, beliefs, and attitudes as correct or incorrect, desirable or undesirable; we should view them within the total cultural framework of a people and evaluate them in relation to their place within the larger cultural context of which they are a part rather than according to some alleged universal standard that applies across all cultures. Cultural relativism gives us a unique window through which to observe cultural variations.

Offering one's mate for sexual activity with an overnight guest is not allowed in most societies. Hans Ruesch, in his novel *Top of the World* (1959), however, reveals a society in which this practice was not only acceptable but also expected. In traditional Eskimo society, it was a serious personal affront to the husband if a guest refused to "laugh" (have sexual intercourse) with his wife. Applying cultural relativism, you would ask how this norm fits with other aspects of Eskimo culture. Under conditions at that time, all Eskimo possessions were handmade, difficult to replace, subject to hard use, and easily destroyed. Within this cultural context, lending wives made sense, as Ernenek explains:

> *Anybody would much rather lend out his wife than something else. Lend out your sled and you'll get it back cracked, lend out your saw and some teeth will be missing, lend out your dogs and they'll come home crawling, tired—but no matter how often you lend out your wife she'll always stay like new.* (Ruesch 1959:88)

Ernenek is not an isolated example. Among the !Kung San, who live in southern Africa, a mother is morally bound to kill a child who is either deformed or one of a set of twins right after the birth. This is culturally very sensible given the mother's way of life. As a member of a hunting and gathering economy, a !Kung mother carries her infant wherever she goes until the child can walk, and she does this for some 5,000 miles.

A growing child who cannot learn to walk cannot be constantly carried past the first year or so. Since the !Kung mother also has to carry food, water, and possessions, she cannot carry twins. With survival of the group at stake, the !Kung see no immorality in their behavior toward twins and infants with little hope of survival (Wade 2010).

Q **So, according to cultural relativism nothing is ever wrong?** A good and troubling question. Many argue that it is a short step from accepting cultural relativism where norms are valid within a particular culture to accepting such norms as valid for anyone anywhere. That anything goes is the fear (Rosaldo 2010).

However, this concern is based on confusion between *cultural relativism*, which is a sociological term, and *ethical relativism*, which is a philosophical concept. According to **ethical relativism**, morality (right and wrong) depends on the norms of the group or society in which they exist. An ethical relativist sees no moral absolutes. Cultural relativism, in contrast, does not involve questions of morality. It focuses on what "is," not what "ought" to be. It is simply a tool to aid in understanding the ways of another society or group within the context of its surrounding culture. To understand Ernenek's behavior regarding wife sharing does not mean you have to forgive it or to agree with it. It just means you have to engage it intellectually (Rosaldo 2010).

Cultural relativism, then, does not require us to accept other cultural ways as our own, nor does it require engagement in alien cultural practices. But because it is impossible, as a cultural relativist, to view aspects of another person's culture ethnocentrically, cultural relativism removes barriers between ourselves and those who are culturally different; it is essentially an antidote to ethnocentrism.

Q **How can cultural relativism be used in everyday life?** Cultural relativism can help us adjust more easily when we are meeting new people or entering new situations. For example, your adjustment to a college roommate from another country, another region of the United States, or even another social class will be smoother if you attempt to understand your roommate from the viewpoint of his or her own cultural background. And if significant cultural differences exist between you and your spouse, cultural relativism can enhance your marital relationship. It is also useful at work, where you will need to cooperate with people from other cultural environments. And given the growing importance of America's international business ties, someday you may well be practicing cultural relativism with people from Japan, Germany, Egypt, or Saudi Arabia (see "Sociology in Your Life").

Cultural Relativism

Different behaviors, traditions, and expectations can often result in misunderstandings between people of different cultures. As just noted, learning to look at things from a point of view different from your own, and not making value judgments based on your beliefs and norms, is called cultural relativism. Having mutual respect and understanding for other cultures is sometimes more effective than modern technology and money in producing change and goodwill between nations.

Cultural relativism is illustrated in the true story of a young Peace Corps volunteer who was sent to a remote village to help build a well. The stream that was near the village was used for everything from watering goats to bathing to washing clothes to cooking and drinking. It was obvious that clean drinking water would benefit the village and improve health. Armed with plans, equipment, and budget and schedule, the hopeful volunteer arrived ready to begin.

At first, the village people were not very willing to help. After several weeks of lonely effort the volunteer met with the council to ask why nobody was helping her with this urgent project. "A well would be nice," the people agreed, "but what we really need is a good soccer field where we can play without getting hurt on the stones and uneven ground." So the volunteer agreed that some of the money and equipment could be used to build a good soccer field first.

After several weeks of effort, the soccer field was complete and a village soccer team was formed. Now work was able to start on the well, but once again the villagers seemed reluctant to help. Another council meeting was held, and the volunteer was told, "Ah yes, the well would be nice, but what we really need is a bridge across the stream so other villages can easily come to play soccer on our field." Since she couldn't dig the well alone, the volunteer agreed that some more time and money would be used to build a bridge. Unfortunately, the bridge proved to be more difficult than expected, and by the time it was complete, the budget and schedule were both used up.

The volunteer went back to the capital, disappointed and resentful that she had not been able to improve the village. Some weeks later, she was invited back by the villagers for a festival to celebrate the success of the soccer tournament they had arranged. When she arrived, she was astonished to find a new well in the very center of the village. She asked the village elders for an explanation.

"The soccer tournament is important to us," she was told, "because it gives us pride and importance and gives us a reason to meet with the people of the other villages. We really never wanted a well."

"Then why did you build it?" she asked.

"We didn't build it because we wanted it," was the answer. "We built it because YOU wanted it."

Think About It

1. What assumptions did the volunteer make about the needs of the villagers? What were the actual needs? Who was more right about what the villagers needed? Why?
2. Describe a recent time when you made assumptions that turned out to be culturally based.

Cultural Similarity

The world seems to display an overwhelming diversity of social and cultural behaviors. In Bulgaria, a nod means no and a shake of the head means yes. Upon entering a home in India, you may be adorned with a garland of flowers—which you should remove immediately as a sign of humility. It is not polite to accept food in Iran until your host has offered it to you a number of times. Despite these surface differences, sociologists and anthropologists have identified many behaviors that are shared by all cultures. For example, all societies have families, schools, houses of worship, economies, governments, and systems of prestige.

A poll compared Arabs (eight countries) and Americans with regard to the values they consider most important to be taught to their children (Zogby 2002). As Table 3.4 reveals, Arabs and Americans generally subscribe to common values. The same values (self-respect, good health and hygiene, responsibility) are among the top three for both Arabs and Americans. In fact, convergence is very high on five of the top six values. The biggest differences are on a couple of values lower on both lists. Americans place greater emphasis on teaching their children respect for authority. Arabs give the teaching of religious faith a more prominent place. For both, shared values focus on personal and family concerns rather than on external matters such as political issues.

George Murdock (1945) identified about seventy **cultural universals,** general cultural traits thought to exist in all known cultures. These universals included athletic sports, cooking, courtship, division of

TABLE 3.4

A Comparison of Values Among Arabs and Americans

This table contains a comparison of the ranking of values to be taught to children among Arabs and Americans. Do the data support the existence of cultural diversity or cultural similarity? Explain.

Value	Arab Rank	American Rank
Self-respect	1	2
Good health and hygiene	2	3
Responsibility	3	1
Respect for elders	4	5
Achieve a better life	5	8
Self-reliance	6	4
Religious faith	7	12
Serious work habits	8	6
Obedience	9	11
Creativity	10	9
Tolerance of others	11	10
Respect for authority	12	7

Source: James J. Zogby, *What Arabs Think: Values, Beliefs, and Concerns* (Utica, NY: Zogby International, 2002), 94.

labor, education, etiquette, funeral rites, family, government, hospitality, housing, incest taboos, inheritance rules, joking, language, law, medicine, marriage, mourning, music, obstetrics, property rights, religious rituals, sexual restrictions, status differences, and tool-making. When each of these universals is examined more closely, the similarity among cultures becomes even more apparent (see Figure 3.2).

FIGURE 3.2

Cultural Universals

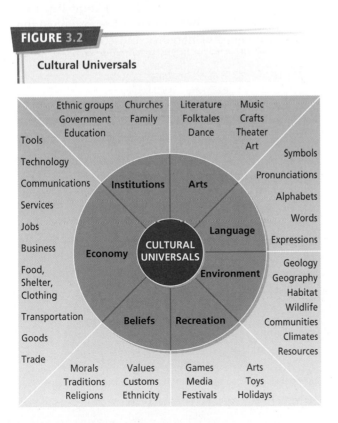

Q **How are cultural universals expressed?** Just because societies share a cultural universal does not mean that they express it in the same way. Usually, cultures develop different ways of demonstrating the same universal trait. These may be thought of as **cultural particulars.** The Manus of New Guinea, for example, place men completely in charge of child rearing. Among the Mbuti pygmies, the Lovedu of Africa, and Navajo and Iroquois Indians, men and women share equally in domestic and economic tasks (Little 1975).

Q **Why do cultural universals exist?** The biological similarities shared by all humans help to account for the presence of cultural universals. Because babies are born and need care, some type of family structure develops. Because nourishment is necessary, food preparation exists. Because people become ill, there is some sort of medical care. Because people die, there are funeral rites, mourning, and inheritance rules. So goes the list of human biological similarities and their influence on culture. A second source of cultural universals is the physical environment. For example, the awesomeness of nature and people's inability to explain physical phenomena—the eclipse of the sun, the creation of the universe—contributes to the development of religion. Because humans cannot survive in extreme climates without artificial protection, cultures create some form of housing. Conflicts often occur over natural territorial borders such as rivers and mountains, so groups establish provisions for maintaining order within as well as between societies.

Finally, cultural universals exist because societies face many of the same public issues. To survive, a society

CHECK YOURSELF   3.3   R2

Cultural Diversity and Similarity

1. Indicate which of the following are social categories (SC), subcultures (S), or countercultures (C).
    ____ a. Chinatown in New York City
    ____ b. motorcycle gang
    ____ c. Catholics
    ____ d. females
    ____ e. revolutionary political group
    ____ f. the superrich
2. The tendency to judge other societies or groups according to one's own cultural standards is known as _____.
3. The psychological and social stress one may experience when confronted with a radically different cultural environment is called _____.
4. _____ is the idea that any given aspect of a particular culture should be evaluated in terms of its place within the larger cultural context of which it is a part rather than in terms of some alleged universal standard that applies across all cultures.
5. _____ are general cultural traits thought to exist in all known cultures.
6. Which of the following is not one of the reasons that cultural universals exist?
    a. physical environment
    b. biological similarity of humans
    c. cultural predetermination
    d. problems of maintaining social life

Answers: 1. a. (S), b. (C), c. (S), d. (SC), e. (C), f. (SC); 2. ethnocentrism; 3. culture shock; 4. Cultural relativism; 5. Cultural universals; 6. c

prepares for certain social provisions: It socializes new members, produces and distributes goods and services, and devises means of dealing with the supernatural.

Culture, Society, and Heredity R1

Culture and Heredity

Q What is the relationship between culture and biology? Instincts are genetically inherited, complex patterns of behavior that always appear among members of a particular species under appropriate environmental conditions. Although nonhuman animals are heavily hardwired for action through instincts, human infants cannot go very far on the basis of their genetic heritage alone. They lack immediate and automatic solutions to the problems they face. Without instincts to determine the type of shelter to build, the type of food to eat, the time of year to have children, or the type of mating pattern to follow, humans create and learn their own ways of thinking, feeling, and behaving. That is, humans must rely on the culture they have created—even for such basic needs as eating and reproducing.

Q Is genetic heritage without influence on human behavior? Although humans lack instincts, they are nevertheless affected by their genetic nature. Research on twins reared together and apart has examined the relative influence of heredity and environment on

Studies of identical twins show that you inherit about half of your personality traits.

personality traits. It is estimated that about 50 percent of the diversity in measured personality characteristics is attributable to genetic heritage (Tellegen et al. 1993; Messner 1997).

In addition, humans have reflexes—simple, biologically inherited, automatic reactions to physical stimuli. A human baby, for example, cries when pinched; its eyes blink in response to a foreign particle; and the pupils of its eyes contract in bright light. Humans also have biologically inherited drives, or impulses, to reduce discomfort. They want to eat, drink, sleep, associate with others, and have sexual relations.

Genetically inherited personality traits, reflexes, and drives, however, do not "determine" human social behavior. If instincts controlled humans, we would all behave in the same way. Instead, culture channels the expression of these biological characteristics (Good et al. 1994). Most boys in traditional American culture, for example, are taught not to cry in response to pain, whereas boys in Jewish and Italian cultures learn to pay more attention to physical discomfort and express it more obviously (Zborowski 1952, 1969). To cite another example, humans have inherited the capacity for love. Awareness of this fact, however, does not allow us to predict the precise ways that different groups of people will express the ability to love. The people of one culture may believe that being one of several husbands is the most natural form of marriage, whereas members of another culture may endorse monogamous marriage.

Some social and biological scientists are challenging the traditional sociological perspective on human nature. Their divergent perspective is called *sociobiology*.

Sociobiology

Sociobiology is the study of the biological basis of human behavior. Sociobiologists argue that like physical characteristics, human social behavior is shaped through the evolutionary process. Thus, sociobiology is the application of Darwinian natural selection and modern genetics to human social behavior (Pinker 2003).

Q **How do sociobiologists view human behavior?** According to Darwin's theory of evolution, all organisms evolve through the process of natural selection. Those organisms best suited to an environment survive and reproduce themselves, and the rest perish. If human behavior is based on millions of years of evolution, say the sociobiologists, then most human behavior is basically self-protective (Dawkins 1990). Those behaviors that improve our chances for survival are genetically retained and reproduced. Parental affection and care, friendship, sexual reproduction, and the education of children must therefore be biologically based because they contribute to the survival of the human species.

Some sociobiologists even contend that there may be specific genes for such things as aggression, religion, homosexuality, group loyalty or altruism, the creation of hierarchies, and the incest taboo.

Sociobiologists believe that the sharp line usually drawn between human and nonhuman animals is inappropriate. DNA testing shows that humans and apes (chimpanzees, gorillas, orangutans, and gibbons) are more closely related than either are to monkeys. Moreover, the chimpanzees' closest relative is not the gorilla but humans; we differ in only 1.6 percent of our DNA (Diamond 1993, 1999).

Nonhuman animals learn and transmit their knowledge—as when a group of chimpanzees spontaneously begin to use long sticks to ferret ants from an anthill for a meal (De Waal 1999; Whiten et al. 1999). Many nonhuman animals, assert sociobiologists, exhibit intelligence of a kind formerly thought to be unique to humans, including use of language (Begley 1993; E. Linden 1993a; Fagot, Wasserman, and Young 2001; Hauser 2001). Researchers have observed chimps in the wild deliberately, consistently, and repeatedly using a tool as a weapon against one of their own kind (E. Linden 2002a, 2002b; Mercader et al. 2007). These findings tend to support pioneer sociobiologist Edward Wilson's (1978, 1986) contention that the study of human behavior must begin with the genetic heritage of humans.

Contemporary evolutionary social scientists report some aspects of social behavior they believe are genetically based. Women, it is reported, look for different characteristics in men they prefer to date and marry than men value in women (Buss, Malamuth, and Winstead 1998). And stepfathers are more likely to abuse their stepchildren than biological fathers their own offspring (Daly and Wilson 1997).

Q **What do the critics of sociobiology say?** Some critics of sociobiology fear that this perspective will be used as a justification to label specific races inferior; others fear that it will be used to argue for the superiority of the male (M. L. Andersen 2010). Still other critics fear that the sociobiological perspective will be used to bolster the assumption of innate human selfishness. Marxists object to sociobiology on the grounds that it justifies the existence of Western capitalism.

Critics join in common objection to a genetic explanation of human social behavior. There is, they contend, too much social diversity around the world for human behavior to be explained on strictly biological grounds (Parker and Easton 1998). The human brain and the unique human capacity for using language and creating social life have allowed humans to overcome any contribution to behavior that might come from their genes. Humans, liberated from the confines of their genes by a large, well-developed cerebral cortex—which permits,

CHECK YOURSELF **3.4** R2

Culture, Society, and Heredity

1. A genetically inherited, complex pattern of behavior that always appears among members of a particular species under appropriate environmental conditions is a(n)
   a. reflex.
   b. instinct.
   c. drive.
   d. need.

2. Scientists agree that humans have instincts for self-preservation, motherhood, and war. T or F?

3. Indicate which of the following are drives (D), which are reflexes (R), which are instincts (I), and which are human creations (H).
   ____ a. eye blinking in dust storm
   ____ b. need for sleep
   ____ c. reaction to a loud noise
   ____ d. socialism
   ____ e. sex
   ____ f. racial inequality

4. According to sociology, culture totally determines the nature of human behavior. T or F?

5. _____ is the study of the biological basis of human behavior.

6. Sociologists now agree that genetic heritage plays no part in the shaping and limiting of social life. T or F?

Answers: 1. b; 2. F; 3. a. (R), b. (D), c. (R), d. (H), e. (D), f. (H); 4. F; 5. Sociobiology; 6. F

among other things, abstract thinking—create and transmit a dazzling array of ways for thinking, feeling, and behaving. Nonhuman species, which either have no cerebral cortex or have an undeveloped one, behave as they do because of a strict genetic code. Birds do not walk south for the winter, salmon do not fly upstream, and lions do not prefer ferns to fresh meat. Critics believe that sociobiology should not sidetrack sociologists from their efforts to understand and explain human behavior from the sociological perspective. They agree with the nineteenth-century English philosopher John Stuart Mill: "Of all the vulgar modes of escaping from consideration of the effect of social and moral influence upon the human mind, the most vulgar is that of attributing the diversities of conduct and character to inherent natural differences" (Zinn 2003:33).

Since the early days of sociobiology, some common ground has emerged between sociologists and sociobiologists. An example of common ground appears in a study of liberal political ideology (Settle et al. 2010). These researchers found that people with a specific variant of a gene labeled DRDR are more likely to be politically liberal, providing they also had a number of friends while growing up. Those with this gene, the researchers contend, enjoy having different experiences and receive pleasure from novelty. As a result, they have friendships with people from different social, racial, religious, and sexual backgrounds. This exposure, in turn, makes them open to new and changing information and activities. This interaction,

then, of a genetic predisposition toward varied experiences combined with the experiences gained through a variety of adolescent friendships creates a more liberal perspective. Their research, the authors conclude, indicates the need to include both nature and nurture in research on political preferences.

Anthropologist Marvin Harris (1990) agrees that there is some biological continuity between human and nonhuman animals and that there is a basic human nature. Evolutionary psychologists and some sociologists now contend that human biology and the human capacity for creating a nearly infinite variety of ways for thinking, feeling, and behaving are two sides of the same coin. The genetic heritage of humans, they argue, shapes and limits human nature and social life. Consequently, they contend, sociologists should not overlook the complex relationship between genetic heritage and the human capacity for creating social life (Lopreato 1990; Weingart et al. 1997; Konner 1999; Pinker 2003; Ridley 2003; Shanahan, Bauldy, and Freeman 2010).

On to Chapter 4

This chapter introduced the concept of culture, the way of life learned by members of a society. Culture provides the *content* of what we learn as members of a society—norms, beliefs, values, and so forth. Chapter 4, "Socialization over the Life Course," illuminates *how* culture is learned.

S INTEGRATED GOALS AND SUMMARY

1. **Identify the three major dimensions of culture.**
   - Culture consists of all the material objects as well as the patterns of thinking, feeling, and behaving passed from generation to generation within a society. A society is a group of people living within defined territorial borders who share a culture.
   - The three broad categories of culture are the normative, cognitive, and material dimensions. The normative dimension of culture is composed of norms, sanctions, and values. Norms are rules defining appropriate and inappropriate ways of behaving. There are several types of norms. Folkways are not considered vital to a group and may be violated without significant consequences. When mores—norms considered essential—are violated, social disapproval is strong. Some norms become laws. Sanctions—positive and negative, formal and informal—are used to encourage conformity to norms. Values are broad cultural principles defining the desirable. Norms and values are not the same thing; the same value can be expressed through radically different norms. In complex societies, some values conflict.
   - Material culture is composed of the concrete, tangible aspects of a culture. Aspects of material culture—desks, trucks, cups, money—have no inherent meanings. Material objects have meanings only when people assign meanings to them.
   - Cultural guidelines and actual behavior do not always match. Sociologists distinguish between the cultural guidelines a society claims to accept (ideal culture) and the behavior patterns actually practiced (real culture).

2. **Describe and illustrate the interplay between language and culture.**
   - Language is an important aspect of the cognitive dimension of culture. Beliefs, another important aspect of the cognitive dimension, are ideas concerning the nature of reality. Whether or not they are actually true, beliefs have a great influence on the members of a society.
   - Because humans are capable of creating and communicating arbitrary symbols such as language, they have the ability to create and transmit culture. Gestures, such as facial expressions or body movements, also carry culturally defined and shared symbolic meanings. Language is also important because it organizes people's view of reality. According to the hypothesis of linguistic relativity, people actually live in different worlds because their languages make them aware of different aspects of their environment. People are not

forever trapped by their language, but they are limited by it unless they learn to see the world from another linguistic viewpoint.

3. **Discuss cultural diversity and its promotion within a society.**
   - Wide cultural variation exists from one society to another as well as within a single society. Because all humans are basically the same biologically, cultural diversity must be explained by nongenetic factors. Cultural diversity within societies is promoted by the existence of social categories, subcultures, and countercultures.

4. **Describe and illustrate the relationship between cultural diversity and ethnocentrism.**
   - Learning a culture results in strong attachment to a particular way of life. That way of life becomes the only way to view the world to those taught it. Cultural diversity, thus, naturally leads to competing worldviews. These competing worldviews promote ethnocentrism, the tendency to judge other cultures in relation to one's own culture.

5. **Outline the advantages and disadvantages of ethnocentrism and discuss the role of cultural relativism in combating ethnocentrism.**
   - Ethnocentrism has positive and negative consequences. On the positive side, ethnocentrism promotes a close bond between a culture and its members. On the other hand, ethnocentrism can hamper innovation and promote conflict between groups.

6. **Explain the existence of cultural similarities that are shared around the world.**
   - Some cultural universals are found in all societies. The expression in specific practices, however, varies widely from one society to another. Cultural universals exist because of the biological similarity of humans, common limitations of the physical environment, and the common problems of sustaining social life.

7. **Explain the relationship between culture and heredity.**
   - Contrary to popular belief, humans do not have instincts. Most behavior among nonhuman animals is instinctual, but human behavior is not the sole product of genetic heritage. Human behavior is learned. Even genetically inherited reflexes and drives do not determine how humans will behave, because people are heavily influenced by culture. Although culture does not determine human nature, it does significantly condition it. Sociobiologists are now arguing for recognition of the role of biology in human behavior.

CONCEPT REVIEW

Match the following concepts with the definitions listed below them.

_____ a. cultural universals
_____ b. sociobiology
_____ c. sanctions
_____ d. informal sanctions
_____ e. real culture
_____ f. cognition

_____ g. society
_____ h. cultural particulars
_____ i. laws
_____ j. taboos
_____ k. ethnocentrism
_____ l. mores

_____ m. subculture
_____ n. formal sanctions
_____ o. culture shock
_____ p. gestures

1. the study of the biological basis of human behavior
2. general cultural traits thought to exist in all known cultures
3. subterranean patterns for thinking, feeling, and behaving
4. rewards and punishments that may be applied by most members of a group
5. norms that are formally defined and enforced by designated persons
6. norms so strong that their violation is thought to be punishable by the group or society or even by some supernatural force
7. the widely varying, often distinctive ways societies demonstrate cultural universals
8. the psychological and social stress one may experience when confronted with a radically different cultural environment

9. the process of human thinking
10. norms of great moral significance, thought to be vital to the well-being of a society
11. rewards and punishments used to encourage desired behavior
12. a group of people who live within defined territorial borders and who share a common culture
13. rewards and punishments that may be given only by officially designated persons
14. the tendency to judge others in terms of one's own cultural standards
15. a group that is part of the dominant culture but differs from it in some important respects
16. facial expressions, posture, and body movements that carry culturally defined and shared symbolic meanings

CHECK YOURSELF REVIEW

1. According to the hypothesis of linguistic relativity, words and the structure of a language cause people to live in a distinct world. T or F?
2. Sociologists now agree that genetic heritage plays no part in the shaping and limiting of social life. T or F?
3. _____ consists of all the material objects as well as the patterns for thinking, feeling, and behaving that are passed from generation to generation among members of a society.
4. Because of _____, culture can be created and transmitted.
5. The tendency to judge other societies or groups according to one's own cultural standards is known as _____.
6. _____ is the idea that any given aspect of a particular culture should be evaluated in relation to its place within the larger cultural context of which it is a part rather than according to some alleged universal standard that applies across all cultures.
7. _____ are broad cultural principles embodying ideas about what most people in a society consider to be desirable.
8. Indicate whether these statements best reflect a belief (B), folkway (F), mos (M), law (L), or value (V).
_____ a. conception that God exists
_____ b. norm against cursing aloud in church

_____ c. norm encouraging the eating of three meals daily
_____ d. idea of progress
_____ e. norm against burning a national flag
_____ f. norm encouraging sleeping in a bed
_____ g. norm prohibiting murder
_____ h. norm against overtime parking
_____ i. idea that the Earth's orbit is elliptical
_____ j. idea of freedom
9. Indicate whether the following are formal sanctions (F) or informal sanctions (I).
_____ a. A mother spanks her child.
_____ b. A professor fails a student for cheating on an exam.
_____ c. A jury sentences a person to life in prison for espionage.
_____ d. A husband separates from his wife after she has an affair.
10. Indicate which of the following are social categories (SC), subcultures (S), or countercultures (C).
_____ a. Chinatown in New York City
_____ b. motorcycle gang
_____ c. Catholics
_____ d. females
_____ e. revolutionary political group
_____ f. the superrich

GRAPHIC REVIEW

The trend toward increased premarital sexual experience among teenage females in the United States is graphically illustrated in Figure 3.1. The following questions ask you to relate this trend to the normative dimension of culture.

1. During the 1950s, in the United States, what type of norm did the prohibition against premarital sex among teenage females represent?

_____

_____

_____

2. What type of norm regarding premarital sex among teenage females exists in America today?

_____

_____

3. Compare the types of formal and informal sanctions used to discourage premarital sexual activity among American female teenagers during the 1950s and today.

_____

_____

_____

_____

CRITICAL-THINKING QUESTIONS

1. Distinguish the normative, cognitive, and material aspects of culture. Cite illustrations to show an understanding of the differences.

_____

_____

2. The ability to use language is cited by sociologists as a characteristic separating humans from nonhuman animals. Discuss the relationship between language and culture. Provide examples.

_____

_____

3. Functionalists and conflict theorists would be expected to have different views of countercultures. Identify these differences, and defend the position

you prefer in relation to the theoretical perspective you support.

_____

_____

4. Discuss the relationship between cultural relativism and ethnocentrism. Give one or more examples to make the connection.

_____

_____

5. Sometimes you hear it said that people are just "naturally" selfish. Do you agree or disagree that humans are capable only of pursuing their own self-interest? Defend your position.

_____

_____

ANSWER KEY

Concept Review

a. 2
b. 1
c. 11
d. 4
e. 3
f. 9
g. 12
h. 7
i. 5
j. 6
k. 14
l. 10
m. 15
n. 13
o. 8
p. 16

Check Yourself Review

1. T
2. F
3. Culture
4. language
5. ethnocentrism
6. Cultural relativism
7. Values
8. a. B
   b. M
   c. F
   d. V
   e. M
   f. F
   g. L
   h. L
   i. B
   j. V
9. a. I
   b. F
   c. F
   d. I
10. a. S
    b. C
    c. SC
    d. SC
    e. C
    f. SC

4

Socialization

Ron Fehling/Masterfile

GOALS

- Discuss the contribution of socialization to the process of human development.
- Describe the contribution of symbolic interactionism to our understanding of socialization, including the concepts of the self, the looking-glass self, significant others, and role taking.
- Compare and contrast the theories of Freud, Erikson, and Piaget.

- Distinguish among the concepts of desocialization, resocialization, and anticipatory socialization.
- Better understand the socialization process of young people.
- Describe the stages of adult development.
- Discuss the unique demands of socialization encountered in late adulthood.
- Compare and contrast the application of functionalism and conflict theory to the socializing effects of mass media.

Does violence on television lead to real-life violent acts? Until fairly recently, Americans strongly disagreed about the spillover effect of television violence. Moreover, social scientists hesitated to claim a causal link between television violence and actual violence. No longer. After hundreds of studies, researchers now find common ground in citing the connection between televised aggression and personal aggressiveness.

This link between televised violence and real violence is another example of a culturally transmitted human social behavior. As humans learn the culture around them, they adopt certain patterns of behavior. This learning process begins at birth and continues into old age. It is called *socialization*.

The first section of this chapter documents the importance of socialization for human development. A discussion of theoretical perspectives, with an emphasis on symbolic interactionism, then follows. The next two sections portray socialization as it unfolds throughout the life cycle. This chapter closes with an examination of mass media in light of functionalism and conflict theory.

Social Participation or Social Deprivation

According to an enduring popular belief, human nature is spoiled by civilization. Society corrupts. Jean-Jacques Rousseau's "noble savage" has been a frequent theme in romantic novels. Underlying this idea is the belief in a fundamental human nature that exists prior to social contact. Whether this is true or not, the nature of humans is shaped by socialization. Human beings at birth are helpless and without knowledge of their society's ways of thinking, feeling, and behaving. If a human infant is to learn how to participate in social life, much cultural learning has to take place.

Nearly all the human social behavior we consider natural and normal is learned. How, for example, is one supposed to behave at a cocktail party? Certainly, an individual is expected to have a drink. But what will the drink be—white wine or sparkling water? Asking seriously for a Bloody Mary with fresh cow's blood would result in signs of disgust and social disapproval. Yet, in some African tribes, a glass of cow's blood would be relished (Douglas 1979). Children in some Palestinian

refugee camps aspire to becoming suicide bombers just as other children wish to be police officers or athletes (Miller and Penniman 2002).

One source of these aspirations is the family. Palestinian mothers have been observed celebrating their children's success in blowing up other children. Their infants are sometimes outfitted as suicide bombers (Will 2002). Preference for cow's blood or admiration for a suicide martyr is, like nearly all aspects of social life, acquired through **socialization**—the process of learning to participate in group life through the acquisition of culture.

Learning about the countless aspects of social life begins at birth and continues throughout life. For example, infants in most American homes are taught to eat certain foods, to sleep at certain times, and to smile at certain facial expressions. But socialization is not limited to the early years; it is a lifelong process enabling people to fit into all kinds of social groups. Socialization must occur if freshmen are to adjust to their new environment, if plebes are to survive at West Point, if presidents of the United States are to govern, and if nursing-home residents are to adapt to their unfamiliar setting. Would-be executives who prefer warm cow's blood to dry white wine will have to keep their tastes a secret or abandon their occupational aspirations.

Q How is socialization related to personality? Although socialization is a lifelong process, the most important learning occurs early in life. Childhood cases of extreme social isolation reveal that without early prolonged and intensive social contact, children do not learn such basics as walking, talking, and loving. Without socialization, a human infant cannot develop a **personality**—the relatively organized complex of attitudes, beliefs, values, and behaviors associated with an individual.

The Importance of Socialization

How can the effects of socialization be assessed? An accurate assessment of socialization would require an experiment comparing a control group of normally socialized infants with an experimental group of socially isolated infants. Assuming that these two groups of children were biologically the same, the differences between them at the end of the experimental period could be attributed to socialization. For obvious reasons, there is no such evidence on human infants. There has, however, been some experimental research with monkeys and some nonexperimental evidence from studies of socially isolated children.

Q How do monkeys react to social isolation? Experiments by Harry Harlow (Harlow and Zimmerman 1959; Harlow and Harlow 1962; Harlow 1967; Blum

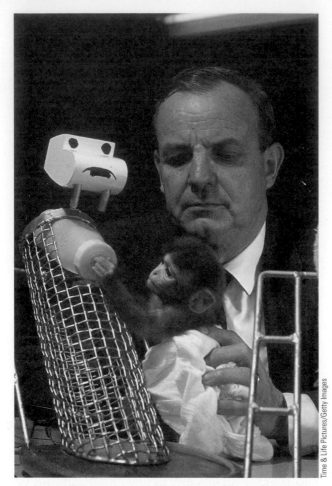

Monkeys fail to develop psychologically and socially when deprived of their mothers. Can we generalize from monkeys to human children?

Time & Life Pictures/Getty Images

2002) have shown the negative effects of social isolation among rhesus monkeys. In one experiment, infant monkeys were separated from their mothers at birth and were then exposed to two artificial mothers—wire dummies of the same approximate size and shape as real adult monkeys. One of the surrogate (substitute) mothers had an exposed wire body; the other was covered with soft terry cloth. Free to choose between them, the infant monkeys consistently spent more time with the soft, warm mother. Even when the exposed wire surrogate became the only source of food, the terry cloth mother remained their preference. Clearly, closeness and comfort were more important to these monkeys than food. When agitated by a mechanical toy bear or a rubber snake, these infant monkeys consistently ran to their cloth mothers for security and protection.

Apparently, infant monkeys need intimacy, warmth, physical contact, and comfort. Indeed, Harlow has shown that infant monkeys raised in isolation become distressed, apathetic, withdrawn, hostile adult animals. They never exhibit normal sexual patterns;

and as mothers, they either reject or ignore any babies they may have, sometimes even abusing them physically.

Q Can we generalize from monkeys to humans? Generalizing research findings from nonhumans to humans is risky, because people are not monkeys. Nevertheless, many experts on human development believe that a human infant's emotional need for affection, intimacy, and warmth—like Harlow's monkeys—is as important as the infant's physiological need for food, water, and physical protection. Babies denied close human contact usually have difficulty forming emotional ties with others. Touching, holding, stroking, and communicating appear to be essential to normal human development. Although Harlow's findings with monkeys cannot be applied directly to humans, similar findings on human children have given the research considerable credibility. According to a Lawrence Casler study (1965), for example, the developmental growth rate of institutionalized children can be improved by only twenty minutes of extra touching a day. Cases of socially isolated children provide additional support.

Social Isolation Among Humans

There is dramatic evidence that children deprived of social contact do not develop all of the characteristics associated with being human. Prominent among this evidence are cases of children who were deprived—both socially and emotionally. Fortunately, documentation includes observations of the changes that occurred when such unfortunate children were placed in an environment designed to socialize them. We will look at the histories of three children—Anna, Isabelle, and Genie—who were socially and emotionally neglected or abused (K. Davis 1947; Curtiss 1977; Pines 1981).

Q Who was Anna? Anna was the second child born to her unmarried mother. They lived with Anna's grandfather, who was incensed by the latest evidence that his daughter did not measure up to his strict moral code. Anna and her mother were forced to move out of the house. After several months of moving from one place to another, repeated failures at adoption, and no further alternatives, Anna and her mother returned to the grandfather's house. Anna's mother so feared that the sight of the child would anger her father that she confined Anna to an attic-like room on the second floor of their farmhouse. Anna was kept alive on milk alone until she was discovered at the age of five. Barely alive, she was extremely emaciated and undernourished. Her legs were skeleton-like, her stomach bloated. Apparently, Anna had seldom been moved from one position to another, and her clothes and bed were filthy. Positive emotional attention was unfamiliar to her. When she was found, Anna could exhibit no signs of intelligence, nor could she walk or talk.

During the first year and a half after being found, Anna was in a county home for children. Among other things, she learned to walk, understand simple commands, eat by herself, tend to personal neatness somewhat, and recall people she had seen. But her speech was that of a one-year-old. Anna was then transferred to a school for retarded children, where she made some further progress. But still, at the age of seven, her mental age was only nineteen months, and her social maturity was that of a two-year-old. A year later she could bounce and catch a ball, participate as a follower in group activities, eat normally (although with a spoon only), attend to her toilet needs, and dress herself (except for handling buttons and snaps). Significantly, she had acquired the speech level of a two-year-old. By the time of her death at age ten, Anna had made some additional progress. She could carry out instructions, identify a few colors, build with blocks, wash her hands, brush her teeth, and try to help other children. Her developing capacity for emotional attachment was reflected in the love she had developed for a doll.

Q Who was Isabelle? Nine months after Anna was found, Isabelle was discovered. She, too, was the child of a single mother and was kept in isolation for fear of social disapproval. Isabelle's mother, a deaf-mute since the age of two, stayed with the child in a dark room, secluded from the rest of the family. When found at the age of six and a half, Isabelle was physically ill from an inadequate diet and lack of sunshine. Her legs were so bowed that when she stood, the soles of her shoes rested against each other, and her walk was a skittering movement. Unable to talk except for a strange croaking sound, Isabelle communicated with her mother by means of gestures. Like an animal in the wild, she reacted with fear and hostility to strangers, especially men. Some of her actions were those of a six-month-old infant.

Isabelle's first IQ score was near the zero point, and her social maturity was at the level of a two-and-a-half-year-old. Despite the belief that Isabelle was feeble-minded, an intensive program of rehabilitation was begun. After a slow start, Isabelle progressed through the usual stages of learning and development, much like any normal child progressing from ages one to six. Although the pace was faster than normal, the stages of development were in their proper order. It took her only two years to acquire the skills mastered by a normal six-year-old. By the time she was eight and a half, Isabelle was on an educational par with children her age. By outward appearances, she was an intelligent, happy, energetic child. At age fourteen, she participated in all the school activities normal for other children in her grade. To Isabelle's good fortune, she, unlike Anna,

benefited from intensive instruction at the hands of trained professionals. Her ability to progress may also have been due to the presence of her mother during the period of isolation.

Q Who was Genie? A more recent case did not end as happily as Isabelle's. Genie, from the time she was nearly two, was kept isolated in a locked room by her father. When she was found, at the age of thirteen, much of her behavior was subhuman. Because Genie's father severely punished her for making any vocal sounds whatsoever, she was completely silent. In fact, she neither sobbed when she cried nor spoke when in a fit of rage. Because she had hardly ever worn clothing, Genie did not notice changes in temperature. Never having been given solid food, she could not chew. Because she had spent her entire life strapped in a potty chair, Genie could not stand erect, straighten her arms or legs, or run. Her social behavior was primitive. She blew her nose on whatever was handy or into the air when nothing was available. Without asking, she would take from people things that attracted her attention.

Attempts to socialize Genie over a four-year period were not successful. At the end of efforts to rehabilitate her, Genie could not read, could speak only in short phrases, and had just begun to control some of her feelings and behavior. Genie paid a high price—her full development as a human being—for the isolation, abuse, and lack of human warmth she experienced.

Anna, Isabelle, and Genie are the most fully documented cases of socially isolated children, but other cases continue to surface. For example, six-year-old Betty Topper was kept chained to a bedpost (by a two-foot-long chain and a harness normally used on horses) since she was a year old in a home littered with trash and debris. Early reports state that when found, thirty-pound Betty was covered with her own waste and could only make moaning sounds (McNary 1999). Happily, Betty showed some signs of improvement fairly quickly, gaining weight and giving her doctors high fives after only one month of care.

Q What other disruptions in social contact retard human development? The implication from case studies such as Anna, Isabelle, and Genie is unmistakable: The personal and social development associated with being human is acquired through intensive and prolonged social contact with others. But cases of extreme social isolation are not the only evidence for this generalization. Children can be affected adversely when the degree of contact with others is limited or when emotional attachments are not formed (Blum 2002; Gopnik 2009).

In pioneering research, René Spitz (1946a, 1946b) compared the infants in an orphanage with those in a women's prison nursery. After two years, some of the children in the orphanage were retarded, and all were psychologically and socially underdeveloped for their age. By the age of four, a third of them had died. No such problems were observed among the prison nursery infants. Not one of them died during this period, even though the physical environment was not as clean as that of the orphanage. Spitz traced the difference between the two groups of infants to the emotional, physical, and mental stimulation offered in each setting. In the prison nursery, the infants' mothers were with them for the first year of their lives. The mothers were not present in the foundling home, and the infant-nurse ratio there was seven or eight to one. They were isolated from the other children as well. Also, in contrast to the infants in the prison nursery, the infants in the orphanage lacked the stimulation normally provided by toys. Social isolation, then, need not be extreme—as it was for Anna, Isabelle, and Genie—to cripple social and personality development.

Further research supports Spitz's conclusions. William Goldfarb (1945), for example, investigated a group of children reared in an institutionalized infant home. He compared these children, who were in the infant home from shortly after birth to three years of age, with children who had spent nearly all their lives in foster homes. He found that the institutionalized children suffered personality defects from their early years of deprivation that persisted even after they were placed in foster homes. Compared with the children who had known only foster homes, the institutionalized children had lower IQ scores, were more emotionally and socially immature, had more difficulty caring about others, and were more passive and apathetic.

Lytt Gardner (1972) attributed a condition known as *deprivation dwarfism* to emotional deprivation. He conducted an intensive study of six "thin dwarfs"—children who were underweight and short for their age and who had retarded skeletal growth. Gardner found that these children had come from families missing the normal emotional attachment between parents and children. When such children were removed from their hostile family environments, they began to grow physically; on returning home, their growth was stunted once again. According to Gardner, deprivation dwarfism is a concrete example—an experiment of nature, so to speak—demonstrating "the delicacy, complexity and crucial importance of infant-parent interactions" (L. Gardner 1972).

In another study, some infants adopted from a Lebanese orphanage were compared with children who remained in the orphanage. Initially, all of these children existed in stark cribs, lying on their backs in a barren room. Human touch was limited to diaper changing. After one year, the children's intellectual, motor, and social development was on a six-month-old level. Those children left in the orphanage continued to be underdeveloped, whereas the adopted infants experience many developmental strides. In another orphanage study, some preschool-age children (average IQ 64) were placed in an institution for retarded adults, where each was "adopted" by an older woman and received much attention from patients and staff members. Children who remained in the orphanage (or another orphanage) lost an average of 20 IQ points over three years. An average gain of 28 points was experienced among the "adopted" orphans (Ornstein and Ehrlich 2000). A more recent study also documents the relationship between early childhood social contact and IQ (Carey 2007). In this study, children raised in orphanages scored an average IQ eight points below children placed in foster homes in their early years. Children reared from birth by their own biological parents scored, on average, 28 points above children from foster homes.

The process of socialization, then, permits us to develop the basic characteristics we associate with being human. It is also through socialization that we learn culture and learn to participate in society.

CHECK YOURSELF   4.1   R2

Social Participation or Social Deprivation

1. _____ is the process through which people learn to participate in group life through the acquisition of culture.
2. According to sociologists, no fundamental human nature exists prior to social contact. T or F?
3. Thanks to recent breakthroughs, research findings on the need of infant monkeys for warmth and affection can easily be applied to humans. T or F?
4. The cases of Anna, Isabelle, and Genie indicate that the personal and social development associated with being human is acquired through intensive and prolonged social contact with others. T or F?
5. Social isolation need not be extreme to damage social and personality development. T or F?

Answers: 1. Socialization; 2. T; 3. F; 4. T; 5. T

Theoretical Perspectives and Socialization ®

Functionalism, Conflict Theory, and Symbolic Interactionism

Q **How does each theoretical perspective view the socialization process?** Each of the three major theoretical perspectives sheds light on the processes of socialization, although the symbolic interactionist perspective facilitates a more complete view than the other two. The contribution of functionalism is more implied than explicit. That is, the very concept of socialization is based on the idea that people fit into groups by virtue of learning the culture of their society. People assume their place in society by learning and accepting what society expects of them. The process of socialization assumes continuity and stability—as does functionalism. In fact, if it were otherwise, the existence of society would not be possible (see Table 4.1).

The conflict perspective views socialization (the learning of roles and acceptance of statuses) as a way of perpetuating the status quo. When people are socialized to accept their family's social class, for example, they help perpetuate the existing class structure. People are socialized into accepting their social fate before they have enough self-awareness to realize what is happening. Once social class socialization has taken place, it is very difficult to overcome. Consequently, socialization maintains the social, political, and economic advantages of the higher social classes. People who do not challenge their lot in life can never mount a revolution against the class structure.

The contribution of symbolic interactionism to our understanding of the socialization process is more precise than either functionalism or conflict theory. Symbolic interactionism helps us appreciate the subtleties of socialization: the development of the self-concept, the role of symbols and language in interpreting the social environment, the process of learning and assuming roles, and the social antecedents of human nature (Hewitt 2002).

Symbolic Interactionism and Socialization

Charles Horton Cooley (1864–1929) and George Herbert Mead (1863–1931), the originators of symbolic interactionism, challenged the belief prominent in their day, that human nature is biologically determined. To them, like Adam Smith in the eighteenth century, human nature is a social product (Herman 2001).

Symbolic interactionism, when applied to socialization, involves a number of key concepts, including the self-concept, the looking-glass self, significant others, role taking (the imitation stage, the play stage, the game stage), and the generalized other.

Q **What is the looking-glass self?** From watching his own children at play, Cooley formulated insights about the development of the **self-concept**—an image of oneself as an entity separate from other people—that still stand today. Cooley and Schubert (1998) noted the many ways that children interpret the reactions of others toward them. From such insights, children learn to judge themselves in relation to how they imagine others will react to them. Thus, others serve as mirrors for the development of the self.

TABLE 4.1

FOCUS ON THEORETICAL PERSPECTIVES: Socialization

Each theoretical perspective has a unique view of the socialization process. This table identifies these views and illustrates the unique interpretation of each view with respect to the influence of the mass media on the socialization process.

Theoretical Perspective	View of Socialization	How the Media Influences Socialization
Functionalism	• Stresses how socialization contributes to a stable society	• Network television programs encourage social integration by exposing the entire society to shared beliefs, values, and norms.
Conflict theory	• Views socialization as a way for the powerful to keep things the same	• Newspaper owners and editors exercise power by setting the political agenda for a community.
Symbolic interactionism	• Holds that socialization is the major determinant of human nature	• Through words and pictures, children's books expose the young to the meaning of love, manners, and motherhood.

Others serve as mirrors for the development of our self-concepts. The looking-glass self is based on our perceptions of others' judgments of us. As these children play, they are building their self-concepts through imagining the judgments of the other.

Cooley termed this the **looking-glass self**—a self-concept based on our perception of others' judgments of us. We use others as mirrors reflecting back our imagined reactions of them to us. According to Cooley, the looking-glass self is the product of a three-stage process that is constantly taking place. First, we imagine how we appear to others. Next, we imagine the reaction of others to our imagined appearance. Finally, we evaluate ourselves according to how we imagine others have judged us. The result of this process is a positive or negative self-evaluation. Of course, this is not a conscious process, and in any given instance the three stages occur in rapid succession.

Suppose that you have a new professor you want to impress. To do so, you prepare especially well for the next day's class. As you participate in the class discussion the next day, you have an image of your performance (stage 1). After finishing your comments, you think your professor is disappointed (stage 2). Because you wished your professor to be impressed, you feel bad about yourself (stage 3).

Q How can the looking glass be distorted? Because the looking-glass self comes from our imagination, the mirrors we use may be distorted. The looking glass may not accurately reflect others' opinions of us. In the preceding example, your professor may have been so impressed that he could not show his genuine reaction. If so, you misread her lack of expression and silence. A child sent to his room for using obscene language may not know how difficult it was for his parents to conceal their amusement.

Although we may misinterpret others' perceptions of us, this does not diminish the effectiveness of the looking-glass process. Even though we incorrectly believe that a professor dislikes us, the consequences to us are just as real as if our interpretation were true. E. L. Quarantelli and Joseph Cooper (1966) found the self-concept of dental students to be nearer to the evaluations they *thought* their instructors had given them than to the evaluation their instructors had actually given them. Despite the possibility of distortion in the looking glass, the relationship between self and others is well established.

Q Can we go beyond the looking glass? Although not denying that our self-evaluations are heavily influenced by our perception of others' evaluations of us, Viktor Gecas and Michael Schwalbe (1983) believe that other factors also affect self-concept. They suggest going beyond the looking glass to consider other sources of influence on the development of self-concept.

According to Gecas and Schwalbe, the looking-glass self-orientation depicts human beings as oversocialized, passive conformists, with self-concepts based solely on the real or imagined opinions of others. (This is ironic, because Cooley and other symbolic interactionists view individuals as active and creative.) Gecas and Schwalbe argue that one's perception of control of his or her environment affects the self-concept as well. Individuals with power on the job, for example, tend to have higher self-esteem than powerless individuals (Kanter 1993). True, part of the response is due to social recognition (or lack of it) from others; part of this effect, however, is attributable to the presence or absence of control over one's fate. A feeling of self-efficacy, in short, contributes to self-esteem.

Q Are all people in our looking glass equally significant? No. As George Herbert Mead pointed out, some people are more important to us than others (G. H. Mead 1934). Those whose judgments are most important to our self-concept are called **significant others.** For a child, significant others are likely to include mother, father, grandparents, teachers, and playmates. Teenagers place heavy reliance on their peers. The variety of significant others is greater for adults, ranging from spouses, parents, and friends to spiritual leaders and employers.

Q **What is role taking?** Because humans have language and the capacity for thinking, we can carry on silent conversations. That is, we can think something to ourselves and respond internally to it. This facility is crucial for anticipating the behavior of others. Through internal conversation, we can imagine the thoughts, emotions, and behavior of others. This ability enables us to engage in **role taking**—the process that allows us to take the viewpoint of another individual and then respond to ourselves from that imagined viewpoint.

Role taking is a cognitive process that permits us to play out scenes in our mind and anticipate what others will say or do. Thus, we avoid a trial-and-error method, which would be necessary if we could not mentally anticipate the behavior of others. If, for example, you wanted to ask your employer for a raise, and if you could not mentally put yourself in your boss's place, you would have no idea of the objections that she might raise. But by role taking her reaction, you can be ready to justify your request.

Q **How does the ability for role taking develop?** According to Mead, the ability for role taking is the product of a three-stage process: the imitation stage, the play stage, and the game stage. In the **imitation stage,** which begins around age one and a half to two years, the child imitates (without understanding) the physical and verbal behavior of a significant other. This is the first step in developing the capacity for role taking. At about the age of three or four, a young child can be seen playing at being mother, father, police officer, teacher, or astronaut. This play involves acting and thinking as a child imagines another person would. This is what Mead called the **play stage**—the stage during which children take on roles of others one at a time.

The third phase in the development of role taking Mead labeled the **game stage,** the stage in which children learn to engage in more sophisticated role taking. After a few years in the play stage, children are able to consider the roles of several people simultaneously. Games they play involve several participants, and there are specific rules designed to ensure that the behavior of the participants fits together. All participants in a game must know what they are supposed to do and what is expected of others in the game. Imagine the confusion in a baseball game if young first-base players have not yet mastered the idea that the ball hit to a teammate infielder will usually be thrown to them. In the play stage, a child may pretend to be a first-base player one moment and pretend to be a base runner the next. In the game stage, however, first-base players who drop their glove and run to second base when an opposition player hits the ball will not remain in the game for very long. It is during the game stage that children learn to gear their behavior to the norms of the group.

Q **When do we start acting out of principle?** During the game stage, a child's self-concept, attitudes, beliefs, and values gradually come to depend less on individuals and more on generalized referents. Being an honest person is no longer merely a matter of pleasing significant others such as one's mother, father, or minister. Rather, it begins to seem wrong *in principle* to be dishonest. As this change takes place, a **generalized other**—an integrated conception of the norms, values, and beliefs of one's community or society—emerges.

Q **What is the self?** According to Mead, the self is composed of two analytically separable parts: the "me" and the "I." The **"me"** is the part of the self formed through socialization. Because it is socially derived, the "me" accounts for predictability and conformity. Yet, much human behavior is spontaneous and unpredictable. An angry brother may, for example, spontaneously and unaccountably yell hurtful words at a sister he loves. Afterward, his reaction may be, "I don't know what came over me. How could I do that to a person I care for?" To account for this spontaneous and unpredictable part of the self, Mead wrote of another dimension of the self—the **"I."**

The "I" doesn't operate just in extreme situations of rage or excitement but interacts constantly with the

---

CHECK YOURSELF   4.2   R2

Theoretical Perspectives and Socialization

1. In its approach to socialization, _____ emphasizes social interaction based on symbols.
2. According to the looking-glass process, our _____ is based on how we think others judge the way we look and act.
3. Those individuals whose judgments of us are the most important to our self-concept are _____.
4. _____ is the process of mentally assuming the viewpoint of another individual and then responding to oneself from that imagined viewpoint.
5. According to George Herbert Mead, children learn to take on the roles of individuals, one at a time, during the _____ stage.
6. In Mead's theory of the self, the _____ is the unsocialized side, and the _____ is the socialized side.

Answers: 1. symbolic interactionism; 2. self-concept; 3. significant others; 4. Role taking; 5. play; 6. "I," "me"

"me" as we conduct ourselves in social situations. According to Mead, the first reaction of the self comes from the "I"; but before we act, the initial impulse is directed in socially acceptable channels by the "me." Thus, the "I" normally takes the "me" into account before acting. However, the uniqueness and unpredictability of much human behavior demonstrates that the "me" does not always control the innovative, unpredictable dimension of the self.

Psychology and Life Course Theories ®

Because socialization involves our entire life course and because the development of human personality is part of that life course, we will veer temporarily from sociology and present several psychologically oriented life course theories. The theories range from the psychoanalytic theory of Sigmund Freud to the psychosocial perspective of Erik Erikson and the cognitive perspective of Jean Piaget.

A Psychoanalytic Perspective

Aside from his theories of the unconscious, Sigmund Freud's (1856–1939) greatest contribution was his work regarding the influence of early childhood experiences on personality development. Experiences within the family during the first few years of life, Freud contended, largely shape future psychological and social functioning.

Q What is the composition of the human personality? According to Freud, the personality has three parts: the id, the ego, and the superego. The *id* is made up of biologically inherited urges, impulses, and desires. It is selfish, irrational, impulsive, antisocial, and unconscious. The id operates on the pleasure principle—the principle of having whatever feels good. Newborn infants are said to be totally controlled by the id; they want their every desire fulfilled without delay. Very early in life, members of society—usually parents—interfere with the pleasure of infants. Infants gradually learn to wait until it is time to eat, to control their bowels and bladder, and to hold their temper. In many ways, they must face the fact that others are not around merely to satisfy their impulses.

To cope with this denial of pleasure, children begin to develop an *ego*—the conscious, rational part of the personality that thinks, plans, and decides. The ego is ruled by the reality principle, which allows us to delay action until a time when the gratification of our desires is more likely. Thus, the ego mediates between the biological, unconscious impulses of the id and the

denying social environment. But the ego is not itself sufficient to control the id. Nor need it be.

At about four or five years of age, the *superego*—roughly the conscience—begins to develop. It contains all the "right" and "wrong" ideas that we have learned from those close to us, particularly our parents. By incorporating their ideals into our personality, we develop what may be thought of as an internal parent. Parents are no longer the only source of punishment for wrongdoing; we punish ourselves through guilt feelings. At the same time, we feel good about ourselves when we live up to the standards contained in our superego. Through this internal monitoring system, we learn to channel our behavior in socially acceptable ways and to repress socially undesirable thoughts and actions.

Q What is the relationship among the id, the ego, and the superego? Freud did not see the id, ego, and superego as separate regions of the brain or as little people battling and negotiating inside our heads. Rather, he saw them as separate, interacting, and conflicting processes within the mind. The id demands satisfaction; the superego prohibits it. The ego supplies rational information in this conflict; it attempts to gain satisfaction within the limits set by the superego and the social environment. The following example, although an oversimplification, should clarify the relationship among these three parts of the personality:

Let's say you are sexually attracted to an acquaintance. The id clamors for immediate satisfaction of its sexual desires, but is opposed by the superego (which finds the very thought of sexual behavior shocking). The id says, "Go for it!" The superego icily replies, "Never even think that again!" And what does the ego say? The ego says, "I have a plan!" (Coon and Mitterer 2008:369)

If the ego has difficulty controlling the id, then some sexually related experience—sexual intercourse, masturbation, even rape—may follow. Should the superego be dominant, sexual desires may be sublimated into other activities, such as working, dancing, studying, or stamp collecting. If the ego is not overwhelmed by the id or superego, it will encourage more socially acceptable behavior, such as dating or marriage.

Psychosocial Development

Psychoanalyst Erik Erikson (1902–1994) extended the human development research of his mentor, Sigmund Freud. Like his teacher, Erikson (1973) emphasized the role of the ego as the mediator between the individual and society and wrote of "crises" accompanying each stage in human development. Erikson, however, differed from Freud in his underlying assumptions and in his specific ideas on the relationship between self and socialization. To Freud, the human personality is almost totally determined in early childhood. Erikson, in contrast, believed that personality may change at any time in life. Whereas Freud attributed most human behavior to universal instincts, Erikson emphasized cultural variations. Although Freud contended that parents are the most influential forces in personality development, Erikson considered the impact of peers, friends, and spouses to be significant as well.

According to Erikson, all individuals pass through a series of eight developmental stages from infancy to old age. Each of these developmental stages involves a psychosocial crisis or developmental task (see Table 4.2). Personal identity is firmly established or impaired, depending on how successfully an individual handles each turning point. The effects of successfully or unsuccessfully meeting these crises are cumulative: Successful management of a crisis at an earlier stage increases the chances of mastering later developmental tasks; those who fall behind in one stage will have increasingly greater difficulty in the following stages. Those individuals whose egos adequately meet the psychosocial crisis at each developmental stage are the most mature and the happiest and have the most stable personal identities.

Several additional points about Erikson's eight stages of psychosocial development should be kept in mind. First, Erikson does not use the word *crisis* to mean a threat or catastrophe. Rather, it is a turning point, a crucial period during which growth or maladjustment may occur, depending on how the crisis is handled. Second, although the way a crisis in one developmental period is handled affects the management of later crises, no crisis is necessarily solved permanently. Thus, a sense of trust developed early in life may, because of social experiences, turn to distrust later; and a sense of self-doubt may, through relationships with others, later change to self-confidence. Third, as already implied, each crisis must be solved via interaction with others, and characteristics developed at earlier stages of development (trust, autonomy, industry, and so forth) require the support of others if they are to be maintained. Fourth, each crisis is solved within a particular social setting—family group, school, peer group, neighborhood, or workplace.

Cognitive Development

Jean Piaget (1896–1980) was concerned primarily with the development of intelligence, or cognitive abilities—thinking, knowing, perceiving, judging, and reasoning. According to Piaget (1981; Piaget and Inhelder 1973; Piaget and Valsiner 1999), children gradually develop cognitive abilities through interaction with their social setting—through the process of socialization. Piaget contended that children are not merely passive recipients of social stimuli; they are actively engaged in interpreting their environment as they attempt to adjust to it. Cognitive ability, in Piaget's theory, advances in stages. Learning to solve problems in one stage must precede problem solving at later stages. Piaget isolated four stages of cognitive development: the sensorimotor stage, the preoperational stage, the concrete operational stage, and the formal operational stage.

Q **What cognitive development occurs in the sensorimotor stage?** The *sensorimotor stage,* where the basis for thought is laid, begins at birth and lasts until the age

TABLE 4.2

Erik Erikson's Stages of Psychosocial Development

Examine Erik Erikson's eight stages of psychosocial development. Do any or all of these stages ring true in your life? Explain.

Theoretical Perspective	Crisis	Favorable Outcome
1. First year of life	• Trust versus mistrust	• Faith in the environment and in others
2. Ages two to three	• Autonomy versus shame and doubt	• Feelings of self-control and adequacy
3. Ages four to five	• Initiative versus guilt	• Ability to begin one's own activities
4. Ages six to twelve	• Industry versus inferiority	• Confidence in productive skills; learning how to work
5. Adolescence (ages twelve to eighteen)	• Identity versus role confusion	• Integrated image of oneself as a unique person
6. Early adulthood (ages eighteen to thirty-five)	• Intimacy versus isolation	• Ability to form bonds of love and friendship with others
7. Middle adulthood (ages thirty-five to sixty)	• Generativity versus stagnation	• Concern for family, society, and future generations
8. Late adulthood (over age sixty)	• Integrity versus despair	• Sense of dignity and fulfillment; willingness to face death

During Piaget's sensorimotor stage of development, children are learning to coordinate their bodily movements. Learning to walk is one way children learn to use their senses—touching, hearing, seeing, and feeling.

of eighteen months to two years. It is called the sensorimotor stage precisely because most of its activities are associated with learning to coordinate body movements with information obtained through the senses—touching, hearing, seeing, feeling. Only gradually do children come to realize that they are an object separate from other things. Initially, they do not realize that they can cause things to happen. A baby shaking bells on its crib does not realize who has caused the sound.

One of the most significant developments during this stage is the development of a sense of "object permanence"—a sense that objects exist even when they cannot be seen. Once this level of thought is reached, a child will, for example, pursue a ball that has rolled under a bed. Later a child can anticipate the reappearance of an object. Instead of looking into the entrance of a tunnel after an electric train has entered, a child will watch for the train's reappearance at the other end of the tunnel. During this stage, children come to see their world as an understandable and predictable place.

Q How do children think during the preoperational stage? Between the ages of two and seven, during the *preoperational stage,* children learn to think symbolically and to use language. Initially, they have difficulty

distinguishing between what they call something (a symbol) and the object itself; an object and the symbol used to represent it are the same to them. If you throw away a milk carton that has been used as a child's toy truck, you will have a difficult time convincing the child that it was only a milk carton.

Another dominant characteristic of children during the preoperational stage is self-centeredness. Children's extreme egocentrism is clearly reflected in their inability to see things from others' points of view. Many children believe that the sun and the moon follow them when they are taking a walk. In one type of experiment, children have been placed opposite adults with a two-sided mirror between them. When asked what the adults see in their side of the mirror, the children answer "me!"

In the preoperational stage, thoughts and operations are not reversible. Consider this conversation researcher John Phillips (1975) had with a four-year-old boy:

"Do you have a brother?"
"Yes."
"What's his name?"
"Jim."
"Does Jim have a brother?"
"No."

Q What about the stage of concrete operations? Increasing abstractness dominates the stage of *concrete operations,* which spans the ages of seven to eleven. A child begins to think logically about time, quantity, and space; handle arithmetic operations; and sort items into logical categories. In addition, children can reverse thoughts and operations during this stage. The reversibility of thought allows an older child to recognize that A-B-C is the reverse of C-B-A and to recognize that if he has a brother, then his brother also has one. A certain degree of abstract thinking is reflected in the children's ability to imagine themselves in the place of others and to gear their behavior to others.

Despite the movement toward abstract thinking that occurs during the stage of concrete operations, the child continues to have difficulty if concrete objects are not involved. Logical thinking is tied to action, to the observation or manipulation of concrete symbols and objects. For example, children at this stage of development can master the concept of the conservation of quantity by watching someone pour liquids into different-sized glasses. In the preoperational stage, if children see water poured from a slender glass into a wide glass, they assume that the wider glass has less water in it because the level of the water appears to be lower. During the stage of concrete operations, however, children come to realize that the amount of water

CHECK YOURSELF **4.3** R2

Psychology and Life Course Theories

1. Listed here are the three major parts of the personality according to Freud. Match these parts with the examples.

    ___ a. id

    ___ b. ego

    ___ c. superego

    (1) A student decides not to cheat on an examination because the professor seems to be watching the class closely.

    (2) A student does not cheat on an examination because she feels too guilty about it.

    (3) A man kills his girlfriend in a fit of jealous rage.

2. The major role of the _____ in Freud's theory of the personality is to mediate between innate impulses and the conscience.

3. Whereas Freud believed that the human personality is almost totally determined in early childhood, Erikson held that personality can change _____.

4. According to Erikson, the successful management of a psychosocial crisis at an earlier stage increases the chances of mastering later crises. This means that the effects of success or lack of success at earlier crisis points are _____.

5. Match Jean Piaget's stages of cognitive growth with the statements below them.

    ___ a. sensorimotor stage

    ___ b. concrete operational stage

    ___ c. formal operational stage

    ___ d. preoperational stage

    (1) A child thinks without the aid of concrete objects and manipulations.

    (2) A child recognizes that 3 + 2 is the same as 2 + 3.

    (3) A child learns that a cat that runs under a couch still exists.

    (4) A child believes that a box is a spaceship.

6. The ability to imagine oneself in the place of others develops during the stage of _____.

Answers: 1. a. (3), b. (1), c. (2); 2. ego; 3. at any time; 4. cumulative; 5. a. (3), b. (2), c. (1), d. (4); 6. concrete operations

---

is the same in both glasses. They could not grasp this idea without an understanding of concrete operations. But it is only in the next stage that complete abstract thought becomes possible.

Q **What is unique about thinking in the stage of formal operations?** A fundamental change in cognitive ability begins to occur some time after the age of eleven. Children learn to think without the aid of concrete objects and manipulations; they can begin to think in terms of abstract ideas and principles. Gradually, the adolescent can reason about hypothetical matters. For example, if you ask younger children, "What would life be like if people had wings?" they would say something like "That's silly" or "People don't have wings." But during the stage of formal operations, children become willing to speculate on such matters. Children also learn during the *formal operations* stage to consider relationships that are logical, even if they are ridiculous. If younger children are asked to complete the sentence "If day is dark, night is _____," they will argue that day is not dark. Older children will answer that night is light. It is during this stage, then, that the capacity for adult thinking develops.

Socialization and the Life Course R1

Desocialization, Resocialization, and Anticipatory Socialization

Over our life course, we abandon old ways of life, adopt new ways, and prepare for transitions from one period of life to another. *Desocialization, resocialization,* and *anticipatory socialization,* concepts that describe these processes, are associated with symbolic interactionism (Lachman et al. 1994; Lachman and James 1997). Erving Goffman's work on "total institutions" provides an excellent, albeit extreme, illustration of these concepts.

In *Asylums,* Goffman (1961b) writes about places such as mental hospitals and prisons as **total institutions**—places in which residents are separated from the rest of society. These residents are controlled and manipulated by those in charge, the purpose being to change the residents. The first step toward change is **desocialization**—the process of relinquishing old norms, values, attitudes, and behaviors. In extreme situations, such as mental hospitals and prisons, desocialization involves an attempt to obliterate the resident's old self-concept. Along with the self-concept go the norms, values, attitudes, and behaviors associated with the personal identity the resident had upon entering the institution. This is accomplished in many ways. Replacing personal possessions with standard-issue items promotes sameness among the residents. It deprives them of the personal effects (long hair, hair brushes, baseball caps, T-shirts) that identify them as unique individuals. Serial numbers and the loss of privacy also contribute to the breakdown of past identity.

Once the self-concept has been fractured, **resocialization**—the process of learning to adopt new norms, values, attitudes, and behaviors—can begin. The staff, using an elaborate system of rewards and punishments, attempts to instill a new self-concept in the residents. Rewards for conformity to these new identities include extra food or special periods of privacy. Punishments for nonconformity involve loss of special privileges, physical punishment, or physical isolation.

Less extreme cases include basic training in the U.S. Marine Corps and the plebe (freshman) year at the U.S. Military Academy. In even less extreme form, these concepts illuminate changes in our normal life course. Desocialization and resocialization occur as a child makes the transition into the adolescent subculture, when young adults begin their occupational careers, and as the elderly move into retirement or widowhood.

This soldier in training is now part of a total institution. This drill sergeant is tearing down his previous self-concept so that a new one appropriate to combat can be developed.

(See "Sociology Eyes America" for other examples of desocialization and resocialization.)

Q **Can socialization begin prior to joining a group?** **Anticipatory socialization**—the process of preparing oneself for learning new norms, values, attitudes, and behaviors—does not generally occur in the extreme

SOCIOLOGY EYES AMERICA 4.1

U.S. Rates of Imprisonment

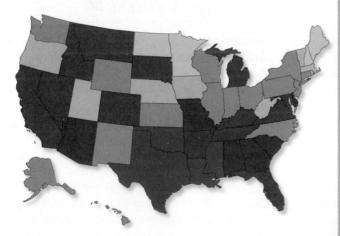

Rates of Imprisonment

- 600 or more
- 500–599
- 400–499
- 300–399
- 200–299
- 199 or less

Source: U.S. Department of Justice, Bureau of Justice Statistics, 2009.

The United States has one of the highest rates of imprisonment in the industrialized world. Justice officials worry that some prisons function as "schools for crime." If prisons do first desocialize and then resocialize inmates toward criminal identity, then the U.S. prison system is unintentionally increasing the criminal portion of the population. This map shows the number of prisoners with sentences of more than one year per 100,000 U.S. residents.

Interpret the Map

1. Where does your state rank in terms of imprisonment rate? Can you relate the extent of imprisonment in your state to the nature of the socialization that occurs in your state?

2. Do the states adjoining your state have imprisonment rates that are similar or dissimilar to your state? Does it matter in terms of socialization?

social settings represented by total institutions. This is because anticipatory socialization involves voluntary change. Teenagers, because they want to resemble those their own age, may willingly abandon many of the norms, values, attitudes, and behaviors learned previously. Consequently, preteens begin very early to observe the ways of teenagers, their new **reference group**—a group used to evaluate oneself and from which to acquire attitudes, values, beliefs, and norms. University seniors, normally seen on campus only in jeans and oversized sweatshirts, suddenly, as graduation nears, are wearing tailored suits and more serious expressions. Initiating their transition into the business world, they are meeting with company recruiters as well as talking with friends who are recent graduates. By anticipating the new environment they are about to enter, graduating seniors are, in effect, preparing themselves for the resocialization they know awaits them (Atchley and Barush 2004).

Q Are these life stages culturally universal? Stages of the life course as we know them did not exist in previous societies. There was no thought of "childhood" or "midlife" crisis in preindustrial society; people did not live that long. Even as late as 1900, life expectancy in the United States was only 49–50 years (Atchley 2001).

Socialization of the Young

Q What are the major effects of the family? The child's first exposure to the world occurs within the family. Being dependent and highly impressionable, the child is virtually defenseless during the first few years of life. Through close interaction with a small number of people—none of whom the child has selected—the child learns to think and speak; internalizes norms, beliefs, and values; forms some basic attitudes; develops a capacity (or incapacity) for intimate and personal relationships; and acquires a self-image. By the time the child develops some independence and judgment, the family has accomplished considerable socialization. Development does not end at age five, but the family has firmly established a foundation for later development (Santrock 2008).

The impact of the family reaches far beyond its direct effects on the personal and social development of the child. Our family's social class significantly affects how others treat us and what we think of ourselves. Our family of birth largely determines our place in society. Jean Evans offers an illustration of this in the case of Johnny Rocco, a twenty-year-old living in a city slum:

Johnny hadn't been running the streets long when the knowledge was borne in on him that being a Rocco made him "something special"; the reputation of the notorious Roccos, known to neighbors, schools, police, and welfare agencies as "chiselers, thieves, and trouble-makers" preceded him. The cop on the beat, Johnny says, always had some cynical smart crack to make. . . . Certain children were not permitted to play with him. Wherever he went—on the streets, in the neighborhood, settlement house, at the welfare agency's penny milk station, at school, where other Roccos had been before him—he recognized himself by a gesture, an oblique remark, a wrong laugh.
(J. Evans 1954:11)

The effects of social class usually extend into adulthood. For example, in a major study of occupational attainment, Peter Blau and Otis Duncan make this observation about the relationship between one's family and subsequent work life:

The family into which a man is born exerts a profound influence on his career, because his occupational life is conditioned by his education, and his education depends to a considerable extent on his family. (Blau and Duncan 1967:330)

Q What about school? In school, children are under the care and supervision of adults who are not relatives. The first year of school involves a transition from an environment saturated with personal relationships to an impersonal environment. Rewards and punishments are based on performance rather than affection. Although a mother may cherish any picture that her child creates, a teacher evaluates his or her students by more objective standards and informs those who are not meeting these standards. Slowly, children are socialized to be less dependent emotionally on their parents. In addition, the school links children to the broader society. It creates feelings of loyalty and allegiance to something beyond the children's families.

Further underlying the formal studies of the school is the **hidden curriculum**—the subterranean informal and unofficial aspects of culture that children are taught as preparation for life in the larger society. The hidden curriculum teaches children discipline, order, cooperation, and conformity—characteristics thought to be needed for success in modern bureaucratic society, whether the child becomes a doctor, college president, secretary, assembly-line worker, or professional athlete.

Q Is socialization in the public school always functional? Not according to educational critic John Holt (1995a). Life in schools, for example, is run by the clock. Whether or not a student understands a current project, and whether or not the child is ready to switch to a different subject, a bell signals that all children must move to the next scheduled event. Getting through a predetermined set of activities within a given time period often becomes more important than learning. And there are rules and

In addition to teaching academic subjects, schools offer a "hidden curriculum"—informal and unofficial aspects of culture taught to prepare children for life in the larger society. The children in this photograph are learning the values of order and waiting in turn.

regulations, Holt says, to cover almost all activities—how to dress, how to wear one's hair, which side of the hall to walk on, when to speak in class. Teachers reward children with praise and acceptance when they recite the "right" answers, behave "properly," or exhibit "desirable" attitudes.

Q How do peer groups contribute to socialization? The **peer group**—composed of individuals roughly the same age with similar interests—is the only agent of socialization that is not controlled primarily by adults. Children usually belong to several peer groups. A child may belong to groups composed of neighborhood children, schoolmates, service club members, and religiously affiliated friends.

In the family and at school, children are subordinated to adults, but through the peer group, young people have an opportunity to engage in give-and-take relationships and to experience conflict, competition, and cooperation. The peer group also gives children experience in self-direction: They begin to make their own decisions; experiment with new ways of thinking, feeling, and behaving; and participate in activities that involve self-expression (see "See Sociology in Your Life").

The peer group further promotes independence from adults by introducing the child to a social milieu that is often in conflict with the adult world. Children learn to be different from their parents in ways that contribute to the development of self-sufficiency.

The capacity for intimacy is enhanced because the peer group provides an opportunity for children to develop close ties with friends outside the family, including members of the opposite sex. While children are making close friends with a few individuals, they are also learning to get along with large numbers of people, many of whom are quite different from themselves. This helps develop the social flexibility needed in a mobile, rapidly changing society.

The rise of formal education has contributed immensely to the emergence of a peer world that is not only separate from adults but also beyond their control. Because young people in school are isolated from adult society for most of their preadult lives, they learn to depend on one another for much of their social life (*The State of Our Nation's Youth* 2001).

Q Who has more influence on young people—friends or family? An important factor contributing to the dependence of adolescents on each other is the distribution of the population in advanced industrial societies. Most Americans now live in either urban or suburban areas. In addition to the prevalence of the dual-employed family in American society, both parents may commute many miles to work. If so, they spend much of their time away from home. Consequently, once children reach the upper levels of grade school, they may be spending more time with their peers than they do with their parents.

Urie Bronfenbrenner (1970) notes that peer groups fill the vacuum created in the lives of children who receive an insufficient amount of attention from their parents. And according to Judith Harris (1998), peers are more important than parents in socializing children. Even though most sociologists do not agree with this author's extreme conclusion, they do believe that the peer group is having an increasing effect on social development.

Facebook and Identity Theft

Almost three quarters of online teens in America use social network sites (Lenhart et al. 2010). Facebook alone has some 500 million accounts, which is approximately 1 of every 14 persons in the world. Since its launching in 2004, Facebook has been a presence for today's college students, and promises to be even more influential in the future. Consequently, its place in the socialization of America's youth merits examination.

As just discussed, Erik Erikson depicted personality development as the result of working through a series of successive crises throughout life. If successful in meeting these crises, a teenager learns trust, self-control,

self-confidence, and independence. At adolescence, the development of personal identity moves from the family to the outside world. By age eleven or twelve, a preteen spends about 40 percent of her time with friends. Teens set out to find their place with peers.

It is true: It is important that teens present themselves to others in face-to-face interaction. However, Facebook can be an important vehicle for identity development because it provides a unique place to present oneself to others: Here is what I look like; these are the things I like and dislike; this is what I value. Because writing requires a fuller picture of one's identity, Facebook is a unique venue for a more detailed and comprehensive self-portrait to present to peers.

Communication via Facebook provides what seems to be a safe place to try out things one might not risk in person. This guarantees feedback often missed in face-to-face interaction.

Another use of Facebook in identity formation is the creation of a shadow Web page, a Web page under a fake name. A shadow Web page may

contain information about an individual that is considered off-limits to friends. Rosen suggests that a shadow Web site may be an aid in handling Erikson's adolescent crisis of identity versus role confusion:

> *Consider, for example, the teen who is struggling with her sexuality, political views, or any other topic that might cause distress or embarrassment among her friends if posted on her [public] Web page. The shadow page allows free expression . . . and the possibility of experimentation without embarrassment or consequences.* (Rosen 2007:79)

While Facebook can serve these functions, it can also have dysfunctions. Cyber bullying and sexual abuse are just two examples.

Think About It

1. Does your experience approximate the description just given? Explain. What about your friends?
2. Do you think that the dysfunctions associated with Facebook outweigh the benefits? Develop your answer.

Q **What role do the mass media play in socializing youth?** **Mass media** are means of communication designed to reach the general population, and sociologists agree they are a powerful socializing agency. A primary function of the mass media is informing children about their culture. From the mass media—television, radio, newspapers, magazines, movies, books, the Internet, tapes, and disks—children learn the behavior expected of individuals in various social statuses of their own culture (Riesman 2001). Although these popular images may be distorted (detective and police work are not as exciting and glamorous as depicted) or stereotyped, the media display role models for children to imitate (Cavender and Fishman 1998). The media often present characters in such simple, one-sided forms that it is easy to recognize behavior suitable for men, women, heroes, and villains. Learning these role models helps to integrate the young into society. Mass media also offer children ideas (sometimes real, sometimes idealized) about values in their society: achievement and success, activity and work, democracy, and equality.

Sex and aggression are also important aspects of American culture. Mass media play a role in socializing youth about both of these behaviors, sometimes in very negative ways.

Q **What role does television play in the promotion of violent and sexual behavior?** The only activity that American children engage in more than watching television is sleeping. About ninety-eight percent of all households in the United States have at least one television set; the average number of sets in a household is 2.8; nearly three-quarters have three or more television sets. The average U.S. household watches about six hours daily. At 65, the average American will have spent nine years in front of a television. Any medium with which so many people spend this much time must contribute significantly to the socialization process (see Thinking Globally).

By the time an average American child completes elementary school, he or she will have seen 8,000 murders. At age eighteen, that same average child will

By the end of elementary school the average American child will have viewed 200,000 violent acts. What is the relationship between media violence and real-life violence?

must converge, as they did [at Columbine]. . . . *But just as every cigarette increases the chance that someday you will get lung cancer, every exposure to violence increases the chances that some day a child will behave more violently than they would otherwise.* (To Establish Justice . . ., 1999: vi)

Of course, extreme violence is more likely to surface among individuals with multiple risk factors. Those most likely to be involved in violent behavior not only watch media violence, they may also be gang members, substance abusers, or extremely poor people.

Teenagers who watch a significant amount of television containing sexual content (flirting behavior, sex scenes, and discussions of sex) have a much higher probability of becoming pregnant or of impregnating a partner, according to Anita Chandra and her colleagues (Chandra et al. 2008). Their research tracked 700 twelve-to-seventeen-year-olds for three years. The first of its kind, this study found a direct relationship between watching sexually charged content on television and teenage pregnancy. Teens who viewed the most televised sexual programming were twice as likely to be involved in a pregnancy as peers with the lowest exposure.

The newer forms of mass media also have effects on teenage behavior. Some of these effects are negative, while other effects, contrary to popular adult thinking, may be positive.

Q What are some of the effects of the new technology? Video games are played in 90 percent of American homes with young children, with an average playing time of up to thirteen hours a week (Martin and Oppenheim 2007). Craig Anderson and his colleagues (2008) tested whether frequent exposure to violent video games promotes physical aggression over time. They researched both high violence (United States) and low violence (Japan) cultures. The results of their study were consistent with earlier experimental and cross-sectional research: Playing violent video games is a significant risk factor associated with later physical aggression.

The Anderson study seems to confirm video gaming as a lone wolf, violent, and antisocial activity. Some of it certainly is, but apparently not all of it. According to a study of 1,102 youth ages twelve to seventeen, the average teen plays many different kinds of games and most often plays them with family and friends both online and offline (Lenhart et al. 2008). Focusing on the connection between gaming and civic experiences among teens, these researchers found that teens have numerous experiences playing video games that involve dimensions of civic and political life, such as thinking about moral and ethical issues and making decisions about city and community affairs. What's more,

have witnessed 200,000 violent acts. As noted in "Using the Sociological Imagination" at the beginning of this chapter, social scientists have, in the past, been reluctant to recognize a causal connection between media violence and real-life violence. However, after hundreds of studies involving more than 10,000 children, most now conclude that watching aggressive behavior on television significantly increases aggression (Strasburger 1995; Dudley 1999; Anderson and Bushman 2002; Carter and Weaver 2003).

Researchers now generally agree that at times the effect of television is direct, concrete, and dramatic. At least twenty-nine Americans, for example, shot themselves while imitating the Russian roulette scene from *The Deer Hunter.* A sixteen-year-old murdered his mother to kick off an intended killing spree modeled by the *Scream* movies. Would-be copycats followed the massacre at Virginia Tech, just on the basis of the news reports. Television's effects, though, are usually more hidden, subtle, and long term:

[N]ot every child who watches a lot of violence or plays a lot of violent games will grow up to be violent. Other forces

Edouard Berne/Getty Images

THINK GLOBALLY 4.1

Access to World Markets This map singles out the relatively few high-income countries that dominate the world markets. It also shows relative distance of countries from world markets.

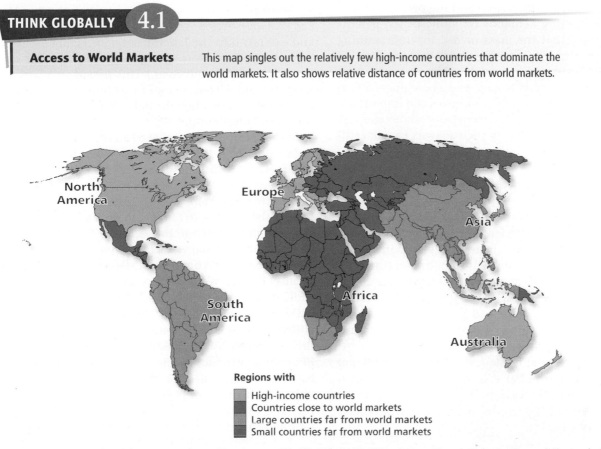

Regions with

- High-income countries
- Countries close to world markets
- Large countries far from world markets
- Small countries far from world markets

Source: International Bank for Reconstruction and Development / The World Bank: *World Development Report: Reshaping Economic Geography* (p. 272). Copyright © 2009. Reproduced by permission.

Interpret the Map

1. Discuss how the mass media might function differently in terms of socialization within countries close to world markets and countries distant from world markets.

2. Compare the relative role of school, peergroup, and family as agents of socialization in countries near to and far from world markets.

---

the researchers report, teens with civic gaming experiences are more likely to be civically engaged offline, going online for information about current events, trying to convince others how to vote, and raising money for charity. According to these results, video gaming has the potential to socialize youth for civic activities (Kahne, Middaugh, and Evans 2008).

Social networking, shared video gaming, and texting, now pervasive among the young, offer new avenues of communication, friendship development, and self-expression. To explore this area of socialization, Mizuko Ito and his colleagues (Ito et al. 2008) conducted a three-year ethnographic study of youth engagement with the new media, conducting interviews with and observations of 800 youth and young adults. The digital world, they conclude, offers opportunities for youth to learn more about their culture. Most use online networks to develop friendships that were initially formed in school, sports, church, or other local activities. Some use the online media to pursue special

interests, thus often finding new peers outside their local community-based boundaries.

Q Are there other agents of socialization during childhood and adolescence? The family, school, peer group, and mass media are the major agents of socialization during childhood and adolescence, but they are not the only ones. Although religion does not have the same degree of influence in all societies, it can affect the moral outlook of young people, even in secular societies such as the United States. Athletic and academic teams teach young children to compete, cooperate, follow rules, make friends, and handle disagreeable peer relationships. Other potentially significant agents of socialization are youth organizations such as the Cub Scouts, Girl Scouts, and YMCA.

Q Do these agents of socialization ever conflict? Yes. In complex societies, conflict between agents of socialization is inevitable. Some families work at cross purposes with the schools; the church and the peer group may place conflicting demands on adolescents; parents may believe that the mass media are undermining the values they are teaching their children. Conflict may even occur within a single agent of socialization. One of a child's parents may emphasize materialism, whereas the other parent minimizes the importance of possessions. Little League baseball coaches may talk of fair play but encourage their players to win at all costs.

Early and Middle Adulthood Socialization

Although indispensable, childhood and adolescent socialization are not sufficient for the demands of adult life. If adults are to participate successfully in society, they must continue to undergo socialization (Lachman et al. 1994; Lachman and James 1997; Santrock 2008). And with the extension of the life span, the elderly confront new situations and roles as well (Clausen 1986; Hogan and Astone 1986; Atchley and Barush 2004; Hillier and Barrow 2011).

There are several models of adult developmental stages (van Gennep 1960; E. H. Erikson 1982; Neugarten 1968; R. Gould 1975; Levinson 1978, 1986). Despite differences in detail, it is possible to paint a general portrait of adult socialization.

Q What are the stages of development in adulthood?
Early adulthood begins toward the end of the teen years and extends into the late thirties. (See Figure 4.1 for a graphic presentation of one model of the stages of development in adulthood.) This period involves a move beyond adolescence and a preliminary step into adulthood; it ends when the individual has made a life within the adult world.

Moving from adolescence to adulthood has never been easy, but it is occurring later than in the past. Robin Henig (2010) points out that in 1960, about three-quarters of American men and women had completed the major steps to adulthood by age 30. They had finished school, left home, secured a job, married, and brought children in the world. In 2000, less than half of thirty-year-old women and one-third of thirty-year-old men had completed these steps. Sociologist Michael Kimmel writes of "guyland"—a stage between adolescence and adulthood in which guys congregate with other guys, delaying "the demands of parents, girlfriends, jobs, kids, and the other nuisances of adult life" (Kimmel 2008:4). Rather than enter the early phase of adulthood, young men in "guyland" move back home after college or live in group apartments in large cities with other guys from their dorm or fraternity. After graduation, they take a series of dead-end jobs and spend huge amounts of time playing video

FIGURE 4.1

Developmental Periods in the Eras of Early and Middle Adulthood

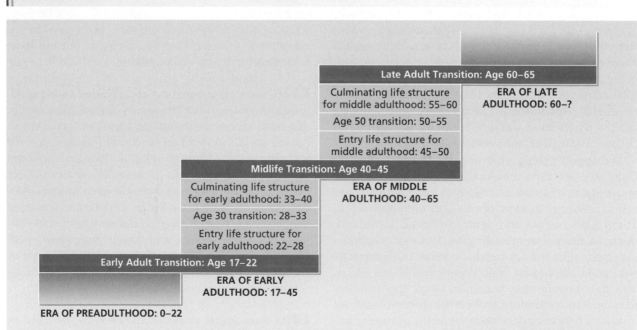

Source: From *The Seasons of a Man's Life* by Daniel J. Levinson et al. Copyright © 1978 by Daniel J. Levinson. Reprinted by permission of Alfred A. Knopf, a division of Random House, Inc.

games, drinking, gambling, and watching sports. The current recession, with its high unemployment, adds to the complexity of lifestyles. In a 2010 national survey, 85 percent of college seniors stated their intention to move back home with their parents from graduation.

When the move to early adulthood does occur, young people forge a temporary link between themselves and the adult world that involves, among other things, choosing an initial occupation and establishing a new family through marriage. Toward the end of the twenties and early thirties, some of the earlier provisional choices may be reevaluated. Marriages may be in jeopardy, divorce may be a possibility, and extramarital affairs are not uncommon. Between ages thirty and forty, a settling-down period tends to occur, during which adults, more conscious of their mortality, attempt to make a place in life for themselves and their families. Central to this period is an interest in achieving occupational success, contributing to society, and establishing a solid family life.

Next comes the transition from early to *middle adulthood*. This is the period when new questions about one's place in the world may arise. Adults may wonder what they have done with their lives and what they wish to do with the rest of their working years. Sometime during the forties, choices are made either to continue the path already taken or to establish a somewhat different life. In the case of the latter, a number of things may occur, including such drastic steps as an occupational change, a divorce, an extramarital affair, or a move to a new community. Typically, more subtle changes take place. For example, family life improves or deteriorates, work becomes more important, or thoughts turn toward retirement. Between the midforties and retirement age, adults complete the tasks of middle adulthood. Acceptance of one's level of occupational achievement occurs. Emphasis on success is replaced by concern with personal relationships and the "small pleasures of life," including children and grandchildren. (See Consider This Research for another example of experiences during adulthood.)

Q Does this model apply to both men and women? Research supporting the preceding model is primarily based on the male experience. Because insufficient research has been done on females, it remains to be seen how well these developmental stages fit women. Preliminary work, however, indicates that the model is less applicable to women than to men. Women have unique socialization experiences (Rosenfeld and Stark 1987).

Q What are some of the socialization experiences unique to women? In early adulthood, women may experience conflict between the ideal wife-mother model they learned as children and the modern roles they may

now value. Men often reinforce the traditional female domestic roles by expecting their mates, who have demanding jobs outside the home, to perform most of the household work (Pendleton, Poloma, and Garland 1980; Skinner 1983; Hochschild 2001; Hochschild and Machung 2003). Many women now experience added pressure in a society that expects more of them than it does of men.

For women who spend most of their adult lives as full-time wives and mothers, middle adulthood presents some special problems. Those women who have based their identity and self-worth on their home, husbands, and children may experience a void when grown children don't require as much attention and husbands at the peak of their careers are preoccupied with work. Also, economically dependent women who experience the death of a husband or a divorce may experience multiple shocks—declining level of living, breaking into the job market, returning to school.

Although signs of early aging—such as wrinkles, weight gains, and loss of body shape—come to men as well as women, it is females who feel the greatest negative repercussions. This is in large part due to the double standard of aging. Many of the characteristics associated with masculinity—aggressiveness, competitiveness, ambitiousness, and decisiveness—are heightened by physical maturity. In contrast, traditionally held images of femininity are diminished in midlife.

The current generation of more highly educated and occupationally successful young women will be in a much stronger position to handle the social and economic difficulties of middle adulthood. Actually, some evidence indicates that women in middle adulthood are faring better than the popular image suggests, despite the continuing pay gap between men and women (Isaacs 2007b). The loss of family responsibilities is opening new doors of opportunity for many women at the midpoint of their lives (Kendall 2010). Many women in midlife are initially entering the labor force, resuming earlier careers, or pursuing higher education.

Late Adulthood Socialization

Q What are the major demands of late adulthood? Length of life is closely linked with the economic base of a society. A study of the Bushmen, a hunting and gathering people, shows that 40 percent of them die before the age of fifteen. Even a century ago, the life expectancy of most people did not exceed thirty-five to forty years. In modern societies, adults can now expect to live beyond seventy. This longer life span exposes aging people to demands unique in human history. The major challenge in American society during *late adulthood* is the withdrawal from participation in certain major aspects of social life (Mitford 1998; Cavanaugh and Blanchard-Fields 2001;

Keiko Ikeda—High School Reunions

If you asked most Americans to talk about their experience at a recent high school reunion, what would they say? "It was great seeing old friends." "I was curious about how things turned out for people I loved and hated as a teenager." "I plan to get together with some old friends in the near future." High school reunions are generally thought to be playful amusement, a time to recapture fond memories of youth.

One researcher wished to investigate the meaning of high school reunions. Keiko Ikeda (1998) studied eight reunions in the American Midwest. He observed these reunions armed with a camera, tape recorder, and notebook. After each reunion, he conducted in-depth, life-story interviews with samples of participants.

Like all in-depth observational studies, the results are too complex and varied for comprehensive reporting. One aspect of Ikeda's study, however, reveals the cultural nature

of high school reunions. He compared several reunions of one high school— tenth, fifteenth, twentieth, thirtieth, fortieth, and fiftieth. Ikeda focused on the relative emphasis on the past and the present. As you can see from the following passage, the past becomes more important as age increases:

In the earlier reunions (the tenth and fifteenth years), a concern with relative status and a sense of competitiveness is expressed, often blatantly, through award-giving ceremonies. . . . The hall was decorated in the school colors, and images of the high school mascot were present, but beyond this no high school memorabilia were displayed. The music, too, was current, and not the rock 'n' roll of the late sixties and early seventies.

The twentieth-year reunion of the Class of '62 is typical of a transitional phase in which elements from the past begin to assume an important role. The past is expressed in high school memorabilia . . . in . . . films and slides taken during high school, and in . . . high school anecdotes that are playfully interwoven throughout the ceremonial events.

In the thirtieth-year reunion of the Class of '52, the past firmly occupied center stage. A carefully crafted, chronological narrative of

the senior year, entitled "The Way We Were," was read, in which major class activities were recalled month by month. . . .

In the fiftieth-year reunion, we find a dramatic disappearance of all ritual activities. According to the president of the Class of '32, his class had held reunions every ten years since graduation, and in earlier ceremonies they had given awards, but this time, "none of the folks in the reunion committee felt like doing that kind of thing." It seemed that attendees at the fiftieth-year reunion, for the most part, had risen above concerns of past and present and were content to celebrate together the simple fact that they all still had the vigor to attend a reunion.

Source: Keiko Ikeda, *A Room Full of Mirrors* (Stanford, CA: Stanford University Press, 1998), 143–145.

Evaluate the Research

1. Ask several adults to describe the activities at one or more high school reunions they have attended. Compare their descriptions with Ikeda's findings.
2. Suppose you had a class assignment to study an upcoming reunion at your school. Select a research question you would want to ask. Identify the research methods you would use.

Benokraitis 2010). Roles are lost because statuses are lost. Two of the most important lost statuses are those of worker and spouse. One cannot act like a worker if no coworker or bosses are present; one cannot act like a wife if no husband exists.

Older people are expected to retire from work. There are many cues: Workmates begin to encourage retirement; a high level of job performance is no longer expected; deserved promotions are given to younger people; rewards for work diminish; duties are fewer;

demotions occur; retraining programs are not made available. Moreover, retirement is considered by most people to be the right thing to do.

Although older workers are expected to retire, they receive little preparation for this stage of life (Seale 1998). They are simply cut off at an arbitrary age— to be creative and active or to stagnate and be passive. They are forced to assume what has been called a "roleless status" (Shanas 1980; Hooyman and Kiyak 2007). The transition from work to retirement may carry negative consequences for social identity and self-esteem:

> *An individual may intellectually apprehend the processes of compulsory retirement policies and yet be emotionally unable to accept them as beyond control. If the older worker incorporates the negative societal stereotypes, a gradual shift in self-image will occur, one that is difficult to overcome in the retirement years. When the negative appraisal summarized in "We see you as a bumbling old fool" becomes internalized to "I am a bumbling old fool," a downward spiral is set in motion that is difficult to break.*
> (Hendricks and Hendricks 1987:332)

In addition, most older people face the loss of a spouse. There is little or no preparation for single life after the death of one's mate, and very few single people sixty-five and older remarry, particularly women. Nevertheless, there is intense socialization immediately following the death of a wife or husband. Though people often expect the widowed to resume activities and establish independence, there are helpful members of the community—doctors, social workers, friends, spiritual leaders, relatives—available during the mourning period. This is particularly important in a society where the elderly frequently live alone rather than with relatives. Like retirement, there is scant cultural definition of roles for a widowed person. Widowhood is another roleless status.

An increasingly significant proportion of Americans live into retirement years. While not all older people adjust well to separation from meaningful work roles, this couple appears to be adapting nicely to the role requirements of late adulthood.

Ben Blankenburg/iStockphoto.com

Q **Why, then, do aging adults tend to be well adjusted?** Gerontologists have long puzzled over the consistent research revealing a large majority of aging adults adjusting relatively well in a youth-oriented society—even one that pushes them aside. To solve this puzzle, noted gerontologist Robert Atchley and Amanda Barusch (2004) studied 1,271 residents of a small Midwest town of 25,000 over a twenty-year period. In the process, he developed **continuity theory:** Most aging people maintain consistency with their past lives and use their life experiences to intentionally continue developing in self-determined channels. Because change and continuity are not mutually exclusive, Atchley contends, details can change as long as basic life themes and patterns are maintained. Moreover, adaptation via continuity can vary from one area of a person's life to another. Atchley found that the highest degree of continuity occurs in people's values, beliefs, and ideas, followed by continuity in social relationships. Not surprisingly, given their changes in status (retirement, widowhood, health), aging people tend to be less successful in maintaining continuity in activities.

There are, in fact, some signs of continuity. For example, about three-quarters of baby boomers intend to continue working after retirement, building lives around both work and leisure (M. Freedman 2007). And in 2007 the U.S. Census Bureau reported that Americans over fifty years of age remarry at a rate similar to the population as a whole (55.8 percent for males; 43.5 percent for females).

Q **How do older people face death?** Americans are not very well socialized when it comes to handling death (Moller 1995a, 1995b). Death is simply not a subject very much discussed in the United States. Americans do not even die. They "pass on," "go to their just reward," "go to a better world," "leave us," "buy the farm," or just "go." In fact, sixty-six euphemisms for dying have been identified (DeSpelder and Strickland 1991). Americans do not like to talk about death, particularly to the dying. Relatives often attempt to keep the dying person from knowing that he or she is dying, and dying people sometimes keep their own prognosis secret (Atchley 2001; Leming and Dickinson 2002). Consequently, dying Americans do not know how to fulfill the status of a dying person. The status of a dying person is, like retirement and widowhood, a status almost devoid of roles. Dying Americans face conflicting advice. One person may advise a dying person to accept death after a long and fruitful life. Another person may offer Dylan Thomas's advice:

> *Do not go gentle into that good night,*
> *Old age should burn and rave at close of day;*
> *Rage, rage against the dying of the light.*
> (D. Jones 1971:207. By Dylan Thomas from *The Poems of Dylan Thomas*, copyright © 1952 by Dylan Thomas. Reprinted by permission of New Directions Publishing Corp.)

Death is handled differently in other cultures (Kübler-Ross 2008; Seale 1998). Among Alaskan Indians, the dying participate in the timing of and planning for their own death. According to Lois Grace, a deacon of the Kawaiahao Church in Hawaii, the Hawaiian people believe that death is a constant companion, whether they are hunting, partying, or staying at home. When someone dies, a big luau among friends and relatives follows a wailing procession. Children are prominently included in the funeral so that they can learn early that death is a part of life. Among the Japanese, death is not something to fear. A dead person "goes to the pure land, the other shore, a place often described as beautifully decorated pools and silver, gold and *lapis lazuli*" (Kübler-Ross 2009:30). Memorial services held by ministers are more for the family than for the deceased.

Partly because of the gradual aging of the American population, death and dying are now topics of greater interest to researchers. Consequently, we are beginning to learn how dying people face death. We know, for example, that people are more accepting of death if they are permitted to talk openly and freely about it (Martocchio 1985; Sanders 1992). Those in **hospices**—organizations that provide support for the dying and their families—appear to be better prepared for death in part because they can share their feelings with others who are dying (Mor et al. 1988; DeSpelder and Strickland 1991).

Elisabeth Kübler-Ross (2008) identified five stages of the terminally ill. In the first stage, *denial and isolation,* there is a refusal to accept the fact that one is going to die; some individuals even attempt to convince themselves that they have been suddenly cured. In the second stage, *anger* is the dominant emotion. After the dying person has accepted the fact that this is actually happening to him or her, the reaction becomes "Why me?" Patients in this stage may express anger in various ways. The third stage involves *bargaining.* Most bargains are made with God and involve asking for more time. Postponement is the basis of bargaining: "If only I could see my son married" or "If only I could see my grandchild born." The fourth stage, *depression,* begins when the terminally ill patient can no longer deny the reality of dying. The predominant emotion during this stage is a deep sense of loss for oneself and for one's family. In the *acceptance,* or last, phase, the dying person is able to think about death with a degree of quiet expectation. Although this is not a happy stage, it is, as one patient expressed it to Kübler-Ross, a time for "the final rest before the long journey."

Whether these five stages apply to cultures other than the United States has yet to be determined. And as some sociologists have pointed out, even for American society, these stages are not necessarily followed in all cases. People may move back and forth among the stages and may exhibit characteristics of more than one stage at the same time. It is dangerous to view these stages in the dying process as an inevitable progression.

The Sociology of the Life Course

Let's look at some qualifications to this description of early, middle, and late adulthood. First, as you have already seen, the model of early and middle adulthood is based primarily on samples of males. Second, although this model may describe a general pattern, not all people go through each of these stages. Some individuals handle developmental tasks in unique ways, and some skip periods of growth and change. Third, the ages given for each period are only approximate; individuals may enter stages at different ages. Although these qualifications do nothing to diminish the value of examining adulthood from a developmental perspective, they do alert us to the existence of sociological factors that differentially affect the socialization experiences of both women and men. Thus, complete reliance on this model for predicting what will happen to people and how they will behave masks variations traceable to sociological factors (Rossi 1974; George 1993). The model omits, for example, important social influences of gender, social class, race, and ethnicity. For purposes of illustration, let's consider the effects of gender and social class on retirement and widowhood, the two major late adulthood adjustments.

Q How does social class influence retirement? **Social class** refers to a segment of a population whose members have a relatively similar share of society's desirable goods and who share attitudes, values, norms, and an identifiable lifestyle. (Social class is explored in detail in Chapter 8, "Social Stratification.") Two desirables associated with social class are economic resources and occupational status. Each of these sociological factors affects the experience of retirement.

Financial security is one of the most important determinants of satisfaction among retirees (Atchley and Miller 1983; Calasanti 1988). Occupational status also ranks high as a predictor of satisfaction in retirement. First, retirees who held higher-status jobs are generally more financially secure than those with lower-status jobs. Second, higher-status occupations have other characteristics promoting better adjustment to retirement. For example, higher-status occupations involve more interpersonal contact and greater participation in a variety of structured activities. The social skills and the more positive attitudes toward group activities can be transferred into more satisfying nonwork retirement activities (Kohn and Schooler 1983). Consequently, these people experience less social isolation and loneliness.

CHECK YOURSELF **4.4** R2

Socialization and the Life Course

1. The informal and unofficial things that are taught to children in school to prepare them for life in the larger society are called the _____.
2. The _____ provides children with needed experiences they are unlikely to obtain within the family.
3. Because there is almost no cultural definition of what retired and widowed persons should do, they are in what has been called a _____ status.
4. Match the following stages of dying with the accompanying statements.
   ____ a. denial and isolation
   ____ b. anger
   ____ c. bargaining
   ____ d. depression
   ____ e. acceptance
   (1) "Why me?"
   (2) "What will Martha do without me?"
   (3) "I would be fine if I could just see Julia graduate."
   (4) "I am going to be fine, you'll see; just leave me alone for a while."
   (5) "My marriage has been a good one. There is little left for me to do."

Answers: 1. hidden curriculum; 2. peer group; 3. roleless; 4. a. (4), b. (1), c. (3), d. (2), e. (5)

Q How do gender differences affect widowhood? Widowhood negatively influences the quality of life of both elderly men and elderly women. Gender, however, appears to exercise differential effects. The major sociological factors associated with gender are the degree of financial security (gender and social class interact) and the extent of social involvement.

Adjustment to widowhood appears to be related to financial resources (Brubaker 1991). And older widows are usually at a disadvantage financially, especially if they have been economically dependent on their husband and are not covered by their husband's pension plan (Choi 1992). The situation is even worse for economically dependent women who are under sixty years of age, because they do not qualify for Social Security benefits. Even if they qualify for Social Security benefits, they live well below the poverty line (Watterson 1990). Thus, poverty or near poverty is the fate of a substantial proportion of widows in the United States (S. Thomas 1994).

Although women are at a disadvantage in adjusting to widowhood financially, they benefit from their greater capabilities for emotional expression and for attaining and maintaining a network of social support involving friends, relatives, and other widows. Widowers, on the other hand, are more socially isolated, have more difficulty displaying grief, express greater loneliness, and recover more slowly from the loss of their spouse (T. B. Anderson 1984; J. K. Burgess 1988; C. Morgan 1989).

Socialization and the Mass Media: Functionalist and Conflict Theories R1

Because the mass media are playing an increasingly important role in the socialization process, additional coverage will apply the functionalist and conflict theories. Socialization through the family, schools, and religion is covered later in separate chapters.

Functions of the Mass Media

A major challenge in identifying the functions of the mass media is the separation of their unique functions from those of other institutions that use the mass media for their own purposes. However, some successful attempts isolate the societal functions of the mass media (Lasswell 1948; C. R. Wright 1960; McQuail 1987).

Q What are the functions of the mass media? The media have consequences for societies, groups, and individuals. We focus here only on societal consequences:

1. *The mass media provide valuable information regarding events inside and outside a society.* The mass media deliver warnings of natural disasters or military invasions. They also provide data regarding political candidates, stock market trends, or consumer

products. In addition, by publicizing information about deviant behavior, the media enhance social control.

2. *The mass media promote social continuity and integration.* The mass media expose an entire population to the society's dominant beliefs, values, and norms. The media socialize the young, continue its process of socialization into adulthood, and transmit new cultural developments to the population.

3. *The mass media provide entertainment.* By providing amusement, diversion, and relaxation, the media contribute to the reduction of social tension. People are better able to perform their social functions, and society is more stable.

4. *The mass media explain and interpret meanings of events and information.* This process tends to support established cultural forms and to enhance the building of consensus among members of a society. Obviously, the media are involved in the process of socialization as they attempt to translate meanings of events and information for the population.

5. *The mass media can help mobilize society.* The mass media can galvanize a society for war, motivate great numbers of people to join a humanitarian movement, or move citizens to protest government policies.

The functions just outlined are positive ones. Functional analysis, as you know, also identifies negative consequences.

Q **So, what are some samplings of the dysfunctions?** The media may foster panic while delivering information; increase social conformity; legitimate the status quo and impede social change while promoting social continuity and integration; divert the public from serious long-term social issues through a constant menu of trivial entertainment and short-term emphasis; shape public views through editorializing as they "interpret" the meanings of events and information; and create violence via public mobilization (Rosenwein 2000).

A relatively recent, more personal, dysfunction of mass media is cyber victimization (Marcum 2009). Bullying, of course, is not new. Electronic media, on the other hand, have introduced a new dimension to bullying, one potentially much more damaging to young people than traditional face-to-face bullying. **Cyber bullying** is bullying through electronic media such as e-mail, instant messaging, chat rooms, web sites, and cellular phones (Kowalski, Limber, and Agatston 2008). Two unique features make cyber victimization especially dangerous. First, anyone can do it. It doesn't

The mass media serve several functions in modern American society. How does the *Daily Show* with Jon Stewart comply with these functions?

require the strength or courage of a personal confrontation. Someone willing to terrorize another person needs only a cell phone or computer. Second, the bully never goes away. A schoolyard bully doesn't go home with you; but, a cyber bully may be waiting in your home when you arrive, anticipating your reaction to carefully planted virtual blows.

Conflict Theory and the Media

As you have come to expect, conflict theory underscores more fundamental drawbacks to mass media. In this section we examine the mass media from the conflict perspective, beginning with the neo-Marxian model and concluding with the power elite model.

Q **What is the Marxian view of American media?** Marxists see the ruling class as monopolizing the media. This monopoly earns a profit for them and bolsters their power, but in the process, workers are exploited by being paid less than they deserve, consumers are overcharged, and the ruling class receives excessive profits. They view the media as necessary to disseminate the **ideology** of the ruling class (i.e., the set of ideas they use to justify and defend their interests and actions) and to reduce the impact of competing ideas. By controlling the marketplace of ideas, the ruling class can dilute the development of class consciousness and subsequent political action on the part of the workers. The media, then, are seen as a tool of manipulation by which the ruling class maintains its power.

There is a non-Marxian theory that also sees a few elite individuals in control of American society and, of course, in control of the mass media. This is the theory of the **power elite**—a unified coalition of top military, corporate, and government leaders (the executive branch in particular). Chapter 14 ("Political and Economic Institutions") will cover the power elite theory in greater depth. For now, we will concentrate on this theory as it applies to the mass media.

Q **Do members of the power elite control the mass media?** Thomas Dye (2001) explores three lines of indirect evidence: the organizational concentration of the media, the agenda-setting power of the media, and the media's ability to socialize the population.

The mass media are increasingly becoming concentrated in fewer corporate hands. Likening the mass media to a near totalitarian state, Ben Bagdikian (2004) documents the decline, since 1983, in the number of corporations controlling most of America's print publications, television, radio, and movies—from fifty to five. Despite the growth of cable television, American television is still controlled primarily by four major networks: the American Broadcasting Companies (ABC), Columbia Broadcasting System (CBS), the National Broadcasting Company (NBC), and the Fox Network. Most of America's local television stations must affiliate with one of these four networks because they cannot afford to produce all of their own programming. Each of the networks is permitted to own local stations, a combination that covers more than one-third of households in the United States. Some ground has been lost to cable television—more than 90 percent of all households in the United States who own a television are cable subscribers. The four networks maintain almost 40 percent of all television viewing. Moreover, all four networks are now part of larger corporations, a move that greatly magnifies their power. ABC, for example, is now part of The Walt Disney Company, a corporation that owns, in addition to its famous movie studio and theme parks, the ABC television network; eight television stations; six radio networks; nineteen radio stations; four daily and thirty-five weekly newspapers; numerous magazine and book publications; and such cable television holdings as ESPN (an all-sports network), the Arts and Entertainment Network, and Lifetime Cable Network (*Directory of Corporate Affiliations 2010*).

Of the four networks, Fox is the only one located outside the United States. News Corp. Ltd, an Australian-based corporation, owns numerous Fox Television stations, Fox News Radio, HarperCollins Publishers, the *Wall Street Journal*, *TV Guide*, the *Boston Herald*, News American Publishing Company, the *New York Post*, News Ltd. of Australia, and Twentieth Century-Fox Film Corporation (*Directory of Corporate Affiliations* 2010). News Corp. Ltd.'s principal activities are the printing and publishing of newspapers, magazines, and books; commercial printing; television broadcasting; film production and distribution; and motion picture studio operations.

Newspapers and radio stations receive most of their national and international news from two wire services: the Associated Press (AP) and United Press International (UPI). Newspaper ownership is increasingly becoming monopolized as major newspaper chains absorb local papers. The New York Times Company owns not only the *New York Times* but also many other daily newspapers along with radio and television stations. Consider the concentration of power created by the merger of TimeWarner and AOL:

> When AOL took over TimeWarner, it also took over: Warner Brothers Pictures, Morgan Creek, New Regency, Warner Brothers Animation, a partial stake in Savoy Pictures, Little Brown & Co., Bullfinch, Back Bay, Time-Life Books, Oxmoor House, Sunset Books, Warner Books, the Book-of-the-Month Club, Warner/Chappel Music, Atlantic Records, Warner Audio Books, Elektra, Warner Brothers Records, Time-Life Music, Columbia House, a 40 percent stake in Seattle's Sub-Pop records, Time magazine, Fortune, Life, Sports Illustrated, Vibe, People, Entertainment Weekly, Money, In Style, Martha Stewart Living, Sunset, Asia Week, Parenting, Weight Watchers, Cooking Light, DC Comics, 49 percent of the Six Flags theme parks, Movie World and Warner Brothers parks, HBO, Cinemax, Warner Brothers Television, partial ownership of Comedy Central, E!, Black Entertainment Television, Court TV, the Sega channel, the Home Shopping Network, Turner Broadcasting, the Atlanta Braves and Atlanta Hawks, World Championship Wrestling, Hanna-Barbera Cartoons, New Line Cinema, Fine Line Cinema, Turner Classic Movies, Turner Pictures, Castle Rock productions, CNN, CNN Headline News, CNN International, CNN/SI, CNNN Airport Network, CNNfi, CNN radio, TNT, WTBS, and the Cartoon Network. (Alterman 2003:22–23).

Similar lists can be made for each of the other four media giants (*Directory of Corporate Affiliations* 2010). In 1996, the federal government loosened regulations on radio station ownership. Scooping up hundreds of local stations, six chains broadcasted to 42 percent of the national radio audience (Fonda 2003). The Federal Communications Commission (FCC) in 2003 attempted but failed to loosen media ownership restrictions, eliminating the long-standing ban on the cross-ownership of newspapers, television stations, and radio stations in the same cities. The commission ruling, rejected by a federal appeals court, would also have permitted television broadcast networks to own more stations at the local and national level, up to 45 percent of the national audience (Ahrens 2003). Continuing its effort to loosen the law, the FCC voted in 2007 to permit broadcasters, in the nation's twenty largest markets, to also own a newspaper.

Advocates of the power elite model underscore the ability of the media to set a political agenda. Through agenda setting, the media select for the public which issues are important for consideration (R. H. Turner and Killian 1987). The media can create, publicize, and dramatize an issue to the point that it becomes a topic for debate among both political leaders and the public. Or the media can downplay an issue or an event so that it disappears from public view. Although agenda setting is not accomplished only in the television arena, television is the most powerful force: "TV is the Great Legitimator. TV confers reality. Nothing happens in America, practically everyone seems to agree, until it happens on television" (W. A. Henry 1981:134). Not only can the media attempt to tell us *what* to think, as the functionalists suggest; they are also said to be extremely successful in determining what we think *about*.

Conflict theorists also underscore the media's role in socializing the population. It is through television (and increasingly the Internet) that most Americans stay in touch with affairs in this country as well as events in the rest of the world. Because television is the most widely shared experience in the United States, it has the dominant role in portraying what media consider to be the most important beliefs, norms, attitudes, and values for people to hold. Through entertainment programming, news coverage, and advertising, television is constantly exposing Americans to a particular view of the most desirable and appropriate ways to think, feel, and behave.

The foregoing analysis does not prove that the mass media primarily serve the interests of the elite. It does, however, suggest the potential for the media to be doing so. Conflict theorists, of course, contend that this potential is being realized.

On to Chapter 5

Sociology was defined in Chapter 1 as the scientific study of social structure. At that time, we deferred a discussion of social structure because the foundation of any social structure is its culture and the socialization of its members into that culture. Now, having covered culture in Chapter 3 and the process of socialization in this chapter, we are in a position to clarify the nature of social structure. The conceptional relationships among culture, socialization, and social structure will come together for you in the next chapter.

CHECK YOURSELF **4.5** R2

Socialization and the Mass Media

1. The _____ are those means of communication that reach large audiences without any personal interaction between the senders and the receivers of messages.
2. Which of the following was *not* discussed in the text as a function of the mass media?
   a. provision of information
   b. creation of consensus
   c. mobilization of society
   d. promotion of social discontinuity and disintegration
3. Which of the following was *not* presented as indirect evidence for the power elite model of the mass media?
   a. foreign infiltration into the media industry
   b. organizational concentration of the media industry
   c. agenda setting
   d. socialization of the population

Answers: 1. mass media; 2. d; 3. a

S INTEGRATED GOALS AND SUMMARY

1. **Discuss the contribution of socialization to the process of human development.**
   - Socialization, the process of learning to participate in group life through the acquisition of culture, is one of the most important social processes in human society. Without it, we would not be able to participate in group life and would not develop many of the characteristics we associate with being human. Evidence of the importance of socialization has been shown in studies of isolated monkeys and children. Socially isolated primates—including humans—do not develop as we would expect.

2. **Describe the contribution of symbolic interactionism to our understanding of socialization, including the concepts of the self, the looking-glass self, significant others, and role taking.**
   - Several major theories emphasize the importance of socialization for human development. Although functionalism and conflict theory bear on the socialization process, the most fully developed sociological approach to socialization comes from symbolic interactionism. Key concepts include the self-concept; the looking-glass self; significant others; role taking; the imitation, play, and game stages; and the generalized other.

3. **Compare and contrast the life course theories of Freud, Erikson, and Piaget.**
   - Several major life course theories emphasize the importance of socialization for human development from a psychological viewpoint. Sigmund Freud accentuated the interaction between the biological nature of human beings and the social environment. Erik Erikson, a student of Freud's, described a series of developmental stages that occur from infancy to old age. Each of these developmental stages is accompanied by a psychosocial crisis, or developmental task. In Erikson's view, socialization and personality development are not confined to childhood; they are lifelong processes. According to Jean Piaget, the ability to think, know, and reason develops through interaction with others. If we are to mature cognitively, Piaget contends, each of us must pass through four identifiable stages in the proper developmental sequence.

4. **Distinguish among the concepts of desocialization, resocialization, and anticipatory socialization.**
   - Symbolic interactionism contributes to our understanding of socialization as a lifelong process. The concepts of total institutions, desocialization, resocialization, anticipatory socialization, and the reference group are particularly important in this regard.

5. **Better understand the socialization process of young people.**
   - During childhood and adolescence, the family, school, peer group, and mass media are the major agencies of socialization. The family makes a tremendous impression on the child both because it is the first agency of socialization and because the child is dependent and highly impressionable.
   - The school is generally the first agency of socialization that is controlled by nonrelatives. In school, children are exposed to new standards of performance applied to everyone, are encouraged to develop loyalties beyond their own families, and are prepared in a number of ways for adult life. In addition, by exposing children to such skills as reading and writing and such subject matter as mathematics and English, schools train children to be disciplined, orderly, cooperative, and conforming.
   - The peer group is the first agency of socialization that is not controlled by adults and consequently provides young people with experiences they cannot easily obtain elsewhere. In peer groups, young people learn to deal with others as equals, gain experience in self-direction, establish some degree of independence from their parents and other adults, develop close relationships with friends of their own choosing, and learn to associate with various types of people.
   - Specific effects of the mass media are difficult to document. Still, we know that television, radio, newspapers, and other mass media play a significant part in the socialization process by introducing children to various aspects of their culture.

6. **Describe the stages of adult development.**
   - Socialization in infancy, childhood, and adolescence makes a profound contribution to personality development and one's ability to participate in social life. There is, however, an increasing recognition that socialization continues throughout life, even into old age. There is much interest now in viewing adulthood from a developmental perspective.

7. **Discuss the unique demands of socialization encountered in late adulthood.**
   - The extension of life expectancy through medical science has created problems of adjustment unparalleled in human history. At an arbitrary age, most older workers are deprived of a meaningful work life. They are forced to retire whether or not they are yet productive. Despite these changes, aging adults tend to be psychologically well adjusted. However, just as there is little preparation for retirement, there is hardly any prior socialization for losing a mate. Like retirement, widowhood is a roleless status. Nor are Americans well socialized to face the prospect of their own death. Despite this relative lack of socialization, Americans tend to go through several stages in the process of dying.

8. Compare and contrast the application of functionalism and conflict theory to the socializing effects of mass media.
   - The mass media encompass those means of communication that reach large audiences without any personal interaction between the senders and the receivers of messages. The major forms of mass communication are television, radio, newspapers, magazines, movies, books, tapes, disks, and now the Internet.
   - Although the functions of the media are intertwined with other institutions, it is possible to isolate their major functions. The media provide information, promote social continuity and integration, supply entertainment, explain and interpret events and information, and can mobilize the society when necessary. Some negative consequences, or dysfunctions, are also associated with the mass media.
   - Both the neo-Marxist and power elite views have been applied to the mass media. Proponents of the power elite model point to the concentration of power in the media, the agenda-setting power of the media, and the media's ability to socialize the population as at least indirect evidence of a ruling class in America.

CONCEPT REVIEW

Match the following concepts with the definitions listed below them.

____ a. significant others
____ b. ideology
____ c. looking-glass self
____ d. personality
____ e. total institution
____ f. anticipatory socialization
____ g. resocialization
____ h. hospices
____ i. social class
____ j. peer group
____ k. "I"
____ l. reference group

1. the process of preparing oneself for learning new norms, values, attitudes, and behaviors
2. organizations designed to provide support for the dying and their families
3. the spontaneous and unpredictable part of the self
4. the set of ideas used to justify and defend the interests of those in power in a society
5. one's self-concept based on perceptions of others' judgments
6. a group composed of individuals of roughly the same age and interests
7. a relatively organized complex of attitudes, beliefs, values, and behaviors associated with an individual
8. a group we use to evaluate ourselves and to acquire attitudes, beliefs, values, and norms
9. the process of learning to adopt new norms, values, attitudes, and behaviors
10. those persons whose judgments are the most important to an individual's self-concept
11. a segment of the population whose members have a relatively similar share of the desirable things and who share attitudes, values, norms, and an identifiable lifestyle
12. a place in which residents separated from the rest of society are controlled and manipulated by those in charge

CHECK YOURSELF REVIEW

1. According to sociologists, no fundamental human nature exists prior to social contact. T or F?
2. Thanks to recent breakthroughs, research findings on the need of infant monkeys for warmth and affection can easily be applied to humans. T or F?
3. In its approach to socialization, _____ emphasizes social interaction based on symbols.
4. According to the looking-glass process, our _____ is based on how we think others judge the way we look and act.
5. Whereas Freud believed that the human personality is almost totally determined in early childhood, Erikson held that personality can change _____.
6. According to Erikson, the successful management of a psychosocial crisis at an earlier stage increases the chances for mastering later crises. This means that the effects of success or lack of success at earlier crisis points are _____.
7. The informal and unofficial things that are taught to children in school to prepare them for life in the larger society are called the _____.
8. Because there is almost no cultural definition of what retired and widowed persons should do, they are in what has been called a _____ status.
9. Match Jean Piaget's stages of cognitive growth with the statements.
   ____ a. sensorimotor stage
   ____ b. concrete operational stage
   ____ c. formal operational stage
   ____ d. preoperational stage
   (1) A child thinks without the aid of concrete objects and manipulations.
   (2) A child recognizes that 3 + 2 is the same as 2 + 3.
   (3) A child learns that a cat that runs under a couch still exists.
   (4) A child believes that a box is a spaceship.

10. Match the following stages of dying with the accompanying statements.
    ___ a. denial and isolation
    ___ b. anger
    ___ c. bargaining
    ___ d. depression
    ___ e. acceptance

(1) "Why me?"
(2) "What will Martha do without me?"
(3) "I would be fine if I could just see Julia graduate."
(4) "I am going to be fine, you'll see; just leave me alone for a while."
(5) "My marriage has been a good one. There is little left for me to do."

GRAPHIC REVIEW

"Sociology Eyes America" 4.1 shows the rate of imprisonment by state.

1. Why was a rate used as the measure rather than the total number of inmates?

_____

_____

2. Why would a high number like 100,000 U.S. residents be used in the calculation?

_____

_____

_____

CRITICAL-THINKING QUESTIONS

1. Defend the proposition that human nature is more a matter of nurture than nature. Cite evidence in your argument.

_____

2. What do you think is the greatest contribution that symbolic interactionism has made to our understanding of the socialization process? Why?

_____

3. You are now a college student. Have you undergone (or are you currently undergoing) desocialization, resocialization, or anticipatory socialization? Provide examples from your own experience.

_____

_____

4. Evaluate the statement that socialization ends after childhood. Be specific in your line of argument.

_____

5. Discuss the pros and cons of the mass media from the viewpoint of sociologists. Use specifics in developing your thoughts.

_____

_____

ANSWER KEY

Concept Review
a. 11
b. 5
c. 6
d. 8
e. 13
f. 1
g. 10
h. 3
i. 12
j. 7
k. 4
l. 9

Check Yourself Review
1. T
2. F
3. symbolic interactionism
4. self-concept
5. at any time
6. cumulative
7. hidden curriculum
8. roleless
9. a. 3
   b. 2
   c. 1
   d. 4
10. a. 4
    b. 1
    c. 3
    d. 2
    e. 5

5 Social Structure and Society

Allstar Picture Library/Alamy

S GOALS

- Explain what sociologists mean by social structure.
- Distinguish between role and status.
- Discuss the relationship between role performance, role conflict, and role strain.
- Define the concept of society, and the relationship between means of subsistence and the structure of society.

- Compare and contrast preindustrial, industrial, and postindustrial societies.
- Delineate the unique perspectives functionalism, conflict theory, and post-modern theory have on modernization.

114

USING THE SOCIOLOGICAL IMAGINATION

Are humans genetically self-ish? Many would say that, by their very nature, people are basically selfish. Evidence indicates otherwise. If humans, as a species, shared the trait of selfishness, we would not expect to find a society populated by cooperative members. Yet, the economic relationships in hunting and gathering societies are grounded in the practice of sharing. Lacking a conception of private property or ownership, members of hunting and gathering societies view even thrift as an indication of selfishness. If genetically programmed to be selfish, these people could not exist without a sense of personal ownership. They would be incapable of such communal concern.

Members of hunting and gathering societies, like members of most groups, know what is expected of them and what they can expect from others, and they engage in the same basic social patterns time after time. All groups have patterned and predictable social relationships that are passed from generation to generation. These patterned social relationships are referred to as *social structure*, which is the basic subject matter of sociology.

Social Structure and Status 🄡

Your understanding of sociology as the study of social structure will jell in this chapter. You learned in Chapter 3 that culture shapes human social behavior—that in the absence of biological preprogramming, culture has to provide the raw material for thinking, feeling, and behaving. Without culture, humans would have no blueprint for social living. This chapter will lead you through a set of sociological concepts that demonstrate the flow between culture and social structure.

In *As You Like It*, William Shakespeare wrote:

All the world's a stage. And all the men and women merely players; They have their exits and their entrances; And one man in his time plays many parts.

All members of a group have parts they are expected to play. Students are expected to attend class, listen to the instructor, fulfill class requirements, and take examinations. Professors are expected to teach class, make assignments, and grade examinations. On any American college campus, you will find similar relationships between students and faculty members. Here,

each student–faculty interaction is orderly and predictable. If, however, you found yourself in a class where students shouted the professor down, the custodian presented lessons, and the students did all the teaching, you would miss the presence of structure. Without the order and predictability you expected, you would become apprehensive about the educational process in general and about relating to those unfamiliar professors. To fit in, you would need awareness of the underlying social structure.

Fortunately, we are usually spared such confusion because groups are relatively predictable. Upon entering a new group, we bring knowledge of the ways people normally relate to one another. In other words, in our minds, we carry a social map for various group situations. We have mental images—however unconscious and hazy—of the group structure in which we want to participate. This awareness permits us to engage in patterned social relationships within groups, without personal embarrassment or social disruption. This underlying pattern of social relationships is called **social structure.**

The mental maps of social structure are not part of our genetic heritage; they must be learned from others. In the process, we learn statuses and roles—major elements of social structure.

Q **What do sociologists mean by status?** People may refer to themselves as students, doctors, welders, secretaries, mothers, or sons. Each of these labels refers to a **status**—a position a person occupies within a social structure. Status helps us define who and what we are in relation to others within the same social structure. We acquire some social statuses at birth. For example, a newly born female instantly becomes a child and a daughter. From then on, she assumes an increasingly larger number and variety of statuses.

Q **How do people acquire social statuses?** There are two basic types of social statuses—ascribed and achieved statuses. An **ascribed status** is neither earned nor chosen; it is assigned to us. At birth, an infant is either a male or a female. Except in instances of sex-change operations, we cannot select our gender. Age is another prominent example of an ascribed social status. In some societies, religion and social class are ascribed by the family of birth. If you were born into a lower-class home in India, for example, you would not be permitted to rise to a higher social class.

An **achieved status** is earned or chosen because people have some degree of control and choice. In most modern societies, for example, an individual can decide to become a spouse or a parent. Occupations are also achieved statuses in modern societies; people have latitude to choose their work. Plumber, electrician, sales representative, nurse, executive, lawyer, and doctor are achieved statuses.

Sociologists are interested in the relationships among social statuses. A sociologist investigating college athletics, for example, may focus on the status of the athlete in relation to the statuses of teammate, coach, parent, and professor (see Figure 5.1).

Q **What is a status set?** In addition to these relationships, an athlete will occupy various other statuses that may be totally unrelated to that of athletics. A **status set** is all of the statuses that an individual occupies at any particular time. One athlete may be an architect major, an artist, and a church choir member; another may be a service club leader, a motivational speaker, and a mother. Each of these statuses is part of another network of statuses. Assume, for example, that in addition to being an athlete, an individual is a part-time jazz musician. In this status, she would interact with the statuses of nightclub owner, dancer, and fellow musician, among others.

Q **Are all of a person's statuses equal?** Some statuses are more important than others. **Master statuses** are important because they influence most other aspects of a person's life. Master statuses may be achieved or ascribed. In industrial societies, occupations—achieved for the most part—are master statuses. Our occupation strongly influences such matters as where we live, how well we live, and how long we live. "Criminal" can be an achieved master status because its effects permeate the rest of that person's life.

Eileen M. Collins, commander of the 2005 space shuttle *Discovery*, was the first woman to command a U.S. space shuttle. Her master status of astronaut is achieved; her master status of woman is ascribed.

FIGURE 5.1

The Interrelationships of Social Statuses

Social statuses cannot exist in isolation. For example, without other statuses (parent, administrator, referee), the status of college athlete would have no meaning. All statuses, then, are interrelated with other statuses.

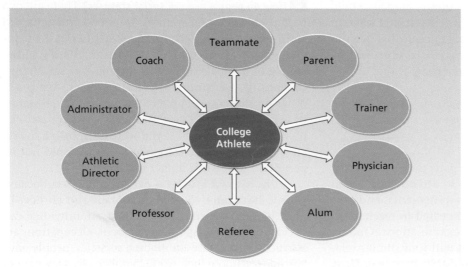

Social Structure and Status

1. _____ refers to the patterned relationships among individuals and groups.
2. A _____ is a position a person occupies within a group.
3. Match the type of status with the examples that best illustrate it.
    ____ a. ascribed status
    ____ b. achieved status
    ____ c. master status
    ____ d. status set
    (1) basketball coach, mother, author, daughter, professor
    (2) occupation, gender, race, ethnicity
    (3) president of the United States
    (4) sex

Answers: 1. Social structure; 2. status; 3. a. (4), b. (3), c. (2), d. (1)

Ascribed master statuses are no less important to a person's life than achieved master statuses. A person who acquires an immunity deficiency through a blood transfusion in a hospital becomes an AIDS victim who will likely suffer prejudice and discrimination in employment, housing, and social relationships. The physically handicapped often have similar experiences.

Age, gender, race, and ethnicity are also ascribed master statuses because they significantly affect the likelihood of achieving other social statuses. Age categories, gender, and various racial and ethnic minorities do not normally constitute social classes because all social classes contain males, females, young people, retired persons, racial categories, and ethnic people. But these statuses are especially influential in social class placement because they affect other social statuses that a person may occupy. When will the United States have a female president? Would you let a nineteen-year-old or a ninety-year-old handle your case in court—or remove your appendix?

Social statuses are similar to the parts performers play on the stage. Prostitute, pimp, police officer, and judge are parts that individuals play in real life. The behavior of an individual depends largely on the part, or status, that individual holds. This is because parts in real life are based on culturally defined roles.

Social Structure and Roles R1

Roles

What are roles? **Roles** are the culturally defined rights and obligations attached to a status; they indicate the behavior expected of an individual holding that particular status. Any status carries with it a variety of roles. For example, the roles of a modern doctor include

keeping abreast of new medical developments, scheduling office appointments, diagnosing illnesses, and prescribing treatment.

Roles can be thought of as the glue that holds a network of social statuses together; the roles of one status are matched with those of other statuses through rights and obligations. **Rights** inform individuals of behavior they can expect from others. **Obligations** inform individuals of the behavior others expect from them. The rights of one status correspond to the obligations of another. Doctors, for example, are obligated to diagnose their patients' illnesses. Correspondingly, patients have the right to expect a diagnosis. Patients have an obligation to keep their office appointments, and doctors have a right to expect that they will do so.

To continue the stage metaphor, roles are the script that indicates to the actors (status holders) what beliefs, feelings, and actions are expected of them (see Table 5.1). Just as a playwright or screenwriter specifies the content of a performer's part, culture determines the parts played in real life. Mothers, for instance, follow dissimilar maternal "scripts" in different cultures. Most American mothers tend to emphasize independence more than most German mothers do.

As noted in Chapter 1, Erving Goffman, with his dramaturgical approach, deserves the most credit for developing the analogy between the stage and social life. In a sense, Goffman's life's work was devoted to the distinction between culturally prescribed roles and the fulfillment of those roles.

Role Performance and Social Interaction

How is role performance tied to social interaction? Statuses and roles provide the basis for group life. But roles are activated only when people in statuses engage in role performance. This occurs through the process of social interaction.

Role performance is the actual conduct, or behavior, activating a role. Although some role performance can occur in isolation, as when a student studies alone for an examination, most of it involves social interaction. **Social interaction** is the process of two or more persons influencing each other's behavior. For example, before two boys begin to fight, they have probably gone through a process of insult, counter-insult, and challenge. Fortunately, most social interaction is not as negative and violent, but the same process of influence and reaction is involved (Turner 2002c).

Not all social interaction follows expected role performance. Spectators at a professional golf tournament are not supposed to cheer bad shots or boo good ones. When some American fans at the 1999 Ryder Cup competition did both, they insulted European players and fans.

If statuses are analogous to the parts of a play and roles are the script, then social interaction represents the way actors respond to cues given by other actors, and role performance is the actual performance. Table 5.1 illustrates this metaphor.

Relationship Between Culture and Social Structure

Q **What is the relationship between culture and social structure?** Figure 5.2 outlines the links that connect culture and social structure. Starting at the top of this figure, the first major bond between culture and social structure is the concept of *role*—culturally defined rights and obligations attached to a social status. The second link is a *status*—a position that a person occupies within a group. It is through the roles attached to

---

TABLE 5.1

The Stage Analogy

This table draws an analogy between rehearsed behavior on the stage and real social behavior. In your own words, describe the parallel between the sociological concepts on the right and the stage terms on the left.

Stage	Social Life
Parts	Statuses
Script (lines)	Roles
Cues	Social interaction
Actual performances	Role performance

---

each status that culture enters the picture. The manner in which roles are actually carried out *is role performance,* the third link in the conceptual chain. Role performance occurs through *social interaction.* This is the fourth link between culture and social structure. Social interaction based on roles is observable as patterned relationships, which constitute social structure. In turn, an existing social structure affects the creation of—and changes in—culture. (Note the two-headed arrow in Figure 5.2.)

Q **Are all these terms necessary?** Concepts are necessary for sociology, as they are for physics. Both sociologists and physicists deal with abstractions, with unobservable phenomena whose existence must be assumed from the observation of things that can be seen. Before 1970, physicists had never directly observed individual atoms. Instead, they used indirect methods, such as

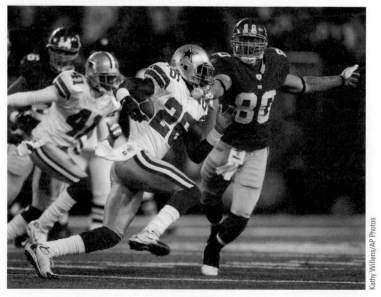

Each of these Dallas Cowboys and New York Giants professional football players have particular roles and statuses on their teams.

Kathy Willens/AP Photos

FIGURE 5.2

The Links Between Culture and Social Structure

Sociologists concentrate on the study of social structure. They have developed a set of concepts and a conception of their relationship in order to understand the basic nature of social structure.

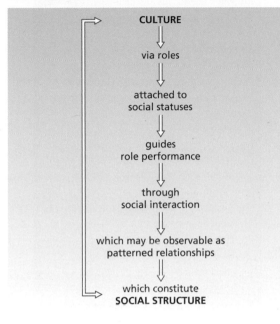

CULTURE

⇓

via roles

⇓

attached to
social statuses

⇓

guides
role performance

⇓

through
social interaction

⇓

which may be observable as
patterned relationships

⇓

which constitute
SOCIAL STRUCTURE

The process of role selection prior to behavior occurs in nearly all instances of social interaction. The range of acceptable responses does have limits. This is especially so in jobs at fast-food restaurants where almost all behavior is rigidly programmed.

photographs of X rays beamed at a small crystal of rock salt, to infer the existence of atoms. Just as physicists have used indirect methods, sociologists use the observation of patterned relationships (something concrete) to infer the existence of social structure (something abstract). If the concepts and relationships outlined in Figure 5.2 were not known, it would be as difficult for sociologists to establish the existence of social structure as it would have been for the ancient Greeks to document the existence of atoms. Concepts and their relationships are necessary building blocks for any area of scientific study.

Q **To what degree is social interaction "playacting"?** Although the stage metaphor is a valid one, there is danger in taking it literally. First, "delivery of the lines" in life is not the conscious process practiced by stage performers. Most real-life role performance occurs without much forethought because we act in ways that have been unconsciously adopted through observation, imitation, and socialization.

Second, there is more of a discrepancy between roles and role performance in real life than between a stage script and its performance. Although performers may sometimes ad-lib, change lines to suit themselves, or introduce a little "business," overall

they adhere to the script. Differences between a role and role performance in real life are neither as easy to detect nor as easy to control as departures from a script.

Keep in mind, however, that the range of acceptable responses is not limitless. Only certain responses are considered culturally legitimate. It is not an appropriate response for the professor to bodily eject the student from her office, and the student would be foolish to pound the professor's desk in protest.

Role Conflict and Role Strain

The existence of statuses and roles permits social life to be predictable, orderly, and recurrent. At the same time, each person holds many statuses, and each status involves many roles. This diversity invites conflict and strain.

SOCIOLOGY EYES AMERICA 5.1

Employment/Population Ratio by State

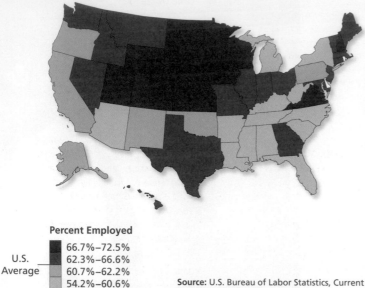

Percent Employed

U.S. Average

■	66.7%–72.5%
■	62.3%–66.6%
■	60.7%–62.2%
■	54.2%–60.6%

Source: U.S. Bureau of Labor Statistics, Current Population Survey, Geographic Profile of Employment and Unemployment U.S. Census Bureau, Statistical Abstract of the United States: 2010 – Table Number 580 <http://www.census.gov/compendia/statab>

For many Americans, occupation serves as their primary master status. Americans tend to define themselves and be defined by what they do for a living. Employment allows people to fulfill their role expectations as earner, which can also affect the performance of spousal and parental roles. This map shows the percentage of each state's civilian labor force, aged 16 and older, that is employed.

Interpret the Map

1. Which states had the highest employment rates in 2004? Which states had the lowest rates?
2. About what percentage of the civilian labor force in your state was employed in 2004?
3. How can employment (or lack of it) affect the performance of spousal and parental roles?

Q **What is the difference between role conflict and role strain?** **Role conflict** occurs when the performance of a role in one status clashes with that in another status. College students who hold the statuses of student and employee often find it difficult to balance study and work demands.

Because groups and subcultures have unique role prescriptions, they also exhibit unique role conflicts. As young, affluent, successful individuals, athletes attract a large number of "friends." Because the athletes pay all the bills, these friends often evolve into employees paid to do certain functions for the athletes. Role conflict for athletes inevitably flows from the mixing of business and personal relationships.

Moreover, the transitions in our life often introduce further role conflicts. For example, upon marriage we take on the role of husband or wife without abandoning the role of son or daughter. The added demands of being a "good" spouse may clash with the demands of being a "good" son or daughter.

Role strain occurs when some of the roles of a single status clash. College basketball coaches, for example, recruit for the next season while attempting to win games in the current season. University professors teach classes, spend time with students, and publish their research findings. Each of these roles is time consuming, and the fulfillment of one role may interfere with the performance of others. If expectations for you as a college student pressure you to perform well academically, join a fraternity or sorority, pursue a sport, date, and participate in other college activities, you will probably experience some degree of role strain.

How can role conflict and role strain be managed? Role conflict and strain may lead to discomfort and confusion. To reduce anxiety and have smoother relationships with others, we often solve role dilemmas by setting priorities. When roles clash, we decide which role is more important to us and act accordingly. A student who misses work frequently because of school requirements can eliminate the role conflict by quitting work and assigning priority to school. If he or she remains in both statuses, he or she can reduce work hours or cut down on extracurricular school activities. A university professor may decide to emphasize either teaching or research. By ranking incompatible roles based on their importance, we reduce role conflict and strain.

We can also segregate roles. This is especially effective for reducing the negative effects of conflicting roles. An organized crime member may reduce role conflict by segregating his criminal activities from his role as a loving father. A college coach experiencing

CONSIDER THIS... RESEARCH

Philip Zimbardo— Adopting Statuses in a Simulated Prison

Did the behavior of American soldiers at Abu Ghraib prison in Iraq surprise you? Well, it didn't surprise Philip Zimbardo, professor emeritus at Stanford University. He has seen "good" people do "bad" things before—in a college psychology laboratory! Zimbardo designed an experiment to observe the behavior of people without record of crime or violence in a mock "prison." He was amazed at the rapidity with which statuses were adopted and roles fulfilled by "liberal" college students randomly assigned to play prisoners and guards. This experiment reveals the ease with which people can be socialized to statuses and roles when they find themselves in a social structure that warrants it. Zimbardo's own words describe the design and results of this experiment (Zimbardo 2008).

> In an attempt to understand just what it means . . . to be a prisoner or a prison guard, Craig Haney, Curt Banks, Dave Jaffe and I created our own prison. We carefully screened over 70 volunteers who answered an ad in a Palo Alto city newspaper and ended up with about two dozen young men who were selected to be part of this study. They were mature, emotionally stable, normal, intelligent

college students from middle-class homes. . . . They appeared to represent the cream of the crop of this generation. None had any criminal record. . . .

Half were arbitrarily designated as prisoners by a flip of a coin, the others as guards. These were the roles they were to play in our simulated prison. The guards . . . made up their own formal rules for maintaining law, order and respect, and were generally free to improvise new ones during their eight-hour, three-man shifts. The prisoners were unexpectedly picked up at their homes by a city policeman in a squad car, searched, handcuffed, fingerprinted, booked at the Palo Alto station house and taken blindfolded to our jail. There they were stripped, deloused, put into a uniform, given a number and put into a cell with two other prisoners where they expected to live for the next two weeks. . . .

At the end of only six days we had to close down our mock prison because what we saw was frightening. It was no longer apparent to most of the subjects (or to us) where reality ended and their roles began. The majority had indeed become prisoners or guards, no longer able to clearly differentiate between role playing and self. There were dramatic changes in virtually every aspect of their behavior, thinking, and feeling. . . . We were horrified because we saw some boys (guards) treat others as if they were despicable animals, taking pleasure in cruelty, while other boys (prisoners) became servile, dehumanized robots who thought only of escape, of their own individual survival and of their mounting hatred for the guards. We had to release three prisoners in the first four days because they had such acute situational traumatic reactions as hysterical

crying, confusion in thinking, and severe depression. Others begged to be paroled, and all but three were willing to forfeit all the money they had earned [$15 per day] if they could be paroled. By then (the fifth day) they had been so programmed to think of themselves as prisoners that when their request for parole was denied they returned docilely to their cells. . . .

About a third of the guards became tyrannical in their arbitrary use of power, in enjoying their control over other people. They were corrupted by the power of their roles and became quite inventive in their techniques of breaking the spirit of the prisoners and making them feel they were worthless. . . . By the end of the week the experiment had become a reality.

Source: Published by permission of Transaction, Inc., from *Society*, vol. 9, no. 6. Copyright © 1972 by Transaction, Inc.

Evaluate the Research

1. If you were asked to discuss Zimbardo's experiment within the context of one of the three major theoretical perspectives, which would you choose? Why?
2. One of Zimbardo's conclusions, not stated in the preceding account, is that the brutal behavior found in real-life prisons is not due to the antisocial characteristics or personality defects of guards and prisoners. Can you argue, sociologically, that he is right in this conclusion? How?
3. There was some controversy over the ethics of this experiment. Do you think this experiment could be carried out today under the sociological code of ethics discussed in Chapter 2? Why or why not?

the role strain associated with coaching and recruiting may, for example, assign the recruiting to his or her assistant, at least until the season ends.

Q **Can conformity to roles ever be complete?** No. Complete conformity to all roles is impossible. This poses

no problem as long as role performance occurs within accepted limits. Professors at research-oriented universities may be permitted to emphasize teaching over research. Coaches may accent fair play, character building, and scholarship. But professors at research universities who do too little publishing or coaches

CHECK YOURSELF 5.2 R2

Social Structure and Roles

1. _____ are culturally defined rights and obligations attached to statuses.
2. The rights of one social status correspond to the _____ of another one.
3. _____ occurs when the performance of a role in one status clashes with the performance of a role in another status.
4. _____ occurs when the roles of a single status are inconsistent.
5. Match the following concepts with the examples listed beside them.

   ____ a. role   (1) A mother is expected to take care of her children.
   ____ b. role performance   (2) A husband and wife discuss disciplining one of their children.
   ____ c. social interaction   (3) A university president hands out diplomas at a graduation ceremony.

6. Which of the following is *not* one of the differences between the stage and social life?
   a. There is considerably more discrepancy between roles and role performance in social life than between a stage script and its performance.
   b. Unlike the stage, there are no cues and responses in real life.
   c. Role performance in real life is not the conscious process that actors go through on the stage.
   d. In social life, the cues and responses are not as programmed and predictable as on the stage.

Answers: 1. Roles; 2. obligations; 3. Role conflict; 4. Role strain; 5. a. (1), b. (3), c. (2); 6. b

Reducing Conflict in Two-Career Families

Families with two working adults have special strains. While in 1960, less than 20 percent of married women with young children worked outside of the home, by 2004, the figure was about 65 percent. This increase has resulted in added role conflict for women. In a two-career family, the woman is more likely to suffer from conflict because she is still generally expected to balance her traditional homemaker roles with her career roles. The women are not the only ones who suffer, however. The effects of this conflict are felt by husbands and children as well. Because you will likely be faced with the stress associated with dual-career families, you would be wise to learn now some techniques for reducing role conflict.

1. **Focus on the positive.** Conflict can be reduced when couples define their situation positively. If both partners are working from choice rather than necessity, it can be helpful to begin each day remembering some of the reasons why they first made the choice for both to work. These reasons might include additional income or personal satisfaction.
2. **Put family needs first.** Role conflict can be most effectively managed when family roles are placed ahead of working roles. When a baby-sitter fails to show up, when a child is sick, or when a parent–teacher conference is called, one of the parents can place these demands above work-related demands. Placing a higher priority on family needs will help keep the family support structure intact.
3. **Assume one role at a time.** Conflict can be reduced if a person focuses on only one role at a time. Leaving job-related problems at work and family issues at home is often difficult but is very effective in reducing role conflict.
4. **Find the compromise balance.** Although many men take active roles in child care today, in order to meet family obligations, women still make the most compromises in their careers. With the increasing number of women in better-paying professional careers, we should expect more equality in career compromises between husbands and wives.

Think About It

Identify three ways that you believe would help reduce role conflict in a dual-career family. Provide specific examples not given in the text.

TABLE 5.2

FOCUS ON THEORETICAL PERSPECTIVES: Illustrating Social Structure Concepts

This table illustrates how each theoretical perspective might view a major concept. The concepts could be switched to any other theoretical perspective and illustrated from that perspective. Associate each concept with a different theoretical perspective and provide your own example.

Theoretical Perspective	Social Structure Concept	Example
Functionalism	Role	• Social integration is promoted by culturally defined rights and obligations honored by group members.
Conflict theory	Ascribed master status	• Ascribed master statuses such as gender and race empower some to subjugate others.
Symbolic interactionism	Social interaction	• Roles are carried out by individuals based on the symbols and meanings they share.

who win too few games usually will not be rewarded for very long. At some point, they will have exceeded the acceptable limits for deviation from expected role performance.

Theoretical Perspectives and Social Structure

If you stop to think about it for a moment, you will realize that the concepts of role, social status, and patterned relationships reflect the concerns of functionalism with stability, order, and consensus (see Table 5.2). The concepts of role behavior and social interaction have the strong flavor of symbolic interactionism. Also present in the study of social structure, but not as apparent, are the ideas of conflict theory. To illustrate conflict, consider the struggles between street gangs and law enforcement officials and the clashes between teenagers and their parents. To illustrate change, consider women's more prominent role in sports and the economy, and ponder the effects of globalization on your career choices.

In as much as you now have a grasp on the concept of social structure, you can explore the specific social structures with which the rest of the text is concerned. The first social structure we will examine is society.

Society **R1**

A society is the largest and most self-sufficient social structure in existence. As you may recall from Chapter 3, a **society** is composed of a people living within defined territorial borders, sharing a common

culture. Theoretically, a society is independent of all outsiders. It contains enough smaller social structures—family, economy, government, religion—to meet most of the needs of its members. As you will see, preindustrial societies met these criteria; they truly could be independent and self-sufficient. But modern societies, although capable of caring for most members' needs, must have political, military, economic, cultural, and technological ties with other societies. In fact, as we move toward a global society, the fate of all people becomes linked.

Anthropologists and sociologists have classified societies in various ways. Because all societies must fulfill the need for food, one classification system (the one we use in this chapter) is based on the way subsistence is addressed. This classification system is based on the evolution from the four types of preindustrial societies (hunting and gathering, horticultural, pastoral, and agricultural societies) to industrial societies and finally to postindustrial societies (Haviland et al. 2011). A society's solution to the subsistence problem is clearly reflected in its culture and social structures (see Table 5.3).

Preindustrial Societies

Q What is unique about a hunting and gathering society? The **hunting and gathering society** survives by hunting animals and gathering edible foods such as wild fruits and vegetables. This is the oldest solution to the subsistence problem. In fact, it was only about 9,000 years ago that other methods of solving the subsistence problem emerged.

Although not all hunting and gathering societies are identical, they do share some basic features (Beals,

TABLE 5.3

Comparison of Major Types of Society

Carefully examine this comparison of major types of society. Choose one type of society and explain why the nature of its culture and social structure fits with its means of subsistence and technological base.

Type of Society	Time of Origin	Means of Subsistence	Technological Base	Culture and Social Structure
Hunting and Gathering	First type of society to emerge among humans	Hunting animals and gathering edible foods in nature	Simple handmade tools	Small nomadic bands based on kinship and cooperation; common ownership of property; scant division of labor along sex and age lines within families
Horticultural	About 9,000 years ago	Domesticating plants	Slightly more advanced handmade tools (digging sticks, hoes, spades)	Less nomadic living in more permanent settlements; bands organized around families; more conflict among bands; neglible division of labor based on sex and age
Pastoral	About 9.000 years ago	Domesticating animals (goats, sheep, cattle)	Handmade horticultural tools; meat-cutting tools; knowledge in such areas as grazing land, carrying capacity, breeding, size and composition of herds, weather, water supply	Live in long-term villages; some trade emerges; women remain at home while males attend herds; greater economic surplus leads to more complex division of labor; greater competition over surplus
Agricultural	About 5,000–6,000 years ago	Permanent land cultivation and harnessing of animal energy	Plow and animal energy	Increased productivity releases people from land; more complex division of labor branching outside economic roles; establishment of smaller cities; emergence of separate political, economic, and religious institutions; state replaces family as prime mover; appearance of distinct social classes; emergence of trade and money economy
Industrial	About 250 years ago	Application of science and technology to production	Power-driven machines	Economy shifts from subsistence to an open market due to greater food surplus; growth of large cities; importance of kinship declines; education moves out of homes and increases in importance; women become less subordinate to husbands; influence of religion less pervasive; social institutions become more complex, specialized, and independent; social relationships more impersonal
Postindustrial	Around 1970	Development of service industries	Intellectual	Greater social instability in the form of divorce, crime, and rapid social change; less social and cultural consensus; reduced gender inequality; individualism increases; urban population moves out of large cities

Hoijer, and Beals 1977; Service 1979). Hunting and gathering societies are usually nomadic; that is, they must move from place to place as the food supply and seasons change. Because nomads must carry their possessions with them, they accumulate few material goods. Hunting and gathering societies also tend to be very small—usually fewer than fifty people—with members scattered over a wide area. Because the family is the only institution in hunting and gathering societies, it tends to all the needs of its members. On a day-to-day basis, association is typically limited to the immediate family. In fact, these societies are organized either as self-sufficient family groups or as loose combinations of families or bands. Thus, hunting and gathering societies are tied together by kinship. Most members are related by blood or marriage, although marriage is usually limited to those outside the family or band.

Q Cooperation or competition? Which is more valued in preindustrial society? Economic relationships within hunting and gathering societies are based on cooperation—members sharing their surplus with other members. Most members of this type of society are kin, and sharing takes place without the expectation of reciprocation. Members of hunting and gathering societies seem simply to give things to one another. In fact, the scarcer something is, the more freely it is shared. Generosity and hospitality are valued; thrift is considered a reflection of selfishness. Because the obligation to share goods is one of the most binding aspects of their culture, members of hunting and gathering societies have little or no conception of private property or ownership.

Without a sense of private ownership and with few possessions for anyone to own, hunting and gathering societies have no social classes, no rich or poor. These societies also lack status differences based on political authority because they have no political institutions; there is no one to organize and control activities. According to E. Adamson Hoebel, when the Inuits wanted to settle disputes, they had dueling songs. The people involved in the dispute prepared and sang songs to express their sides of the issue. Their families, as choruses, accompanied them. Those listening to the duel applauded their choice for the victor (Hoebel 1983).

The egalitarianism of hunter gathers is not just a preference; it is so central that challenges to it are quickly defeated. When powerful individuals attempt to elevate themselves above the group, coalitions form to place them back with everyone else. Sanctions against upstarts range from mild to deadly:

> *Others in the group will mock them or ignore their orders. If they persist, they will be shunned or even evicted from the group. If they are too intimidating, they will be killed. To avoid blood feuds, the group that has decided to eliminate a domineering leader will often assign one of his own relatives to kill him.* (Wade 2010:46)

The division of labor in hunting and gathering societies is limited to the sex and age distinctions found in most families. Men and women are assigned separate tasks, and certain tasks are given to the old, the young, and young adults. This scant division of labor exists because there are no institutions beyond the family. Also, more leisure time is available in hunting and gathering societies than in any other. Today, few true hunting and gathering societies remain other than the Khoi-San (Bushmen) in southern Africa, the Kaska Indians in Canada, and the Yanomamö of Brazil.

Q What is a horticultural society? According to archaeological evidence, **horticultural societies** solved the subsistence problem primarily through the domestication of plants. This type of society came into being

Judging from this photograph, to what type of society do these Thailand rice farmers belong?

Digitalpress/Dreamstime LLC

about 9,000 years ago. The transition from hunting and gathering to horticultural societies was not abrupt. It occurred over several centuries. In fact, some hunters and gatherers in the Middle East were harvesting wild grains with stone sickles 10,000 years ago, and early horticultural societies also hunted and gathered (Nolan and Lenski 2010).

The shift from hunting and gathering to horticulture leads to more permanent settlements. Subsistence no longer requires people to move frequently in order to take advantage of available food. Instead, people can work a land area for extended periods of time before moving on to more fertile soil. This relative stability in simple horticultural societies—and particularly in the permanent settlements in the Middle East and southeastern Europe—permits the growth of large societies with greater population densities.

The family is even more basic to social life in horticultural societies than in hunting and gathering societies. In hunting and gathering societies, the survival of the band usually has uppermost priority. In horticultural societies, primary emphasis is on providing for household members. This is because producing food in horticultural societies can be accomplished through the labor of family members. With the labor necessary for survival, households can be more self-sufficient and independent: "The family is to the . . . [horticultural] economy as the manor to medieval European economy, or the industrial corporation to modern capitalism: each of these is the central production-institution of its time" (Sahlins 1968:75).

While hunters and gatherers seldom engage in interband raids, there is considerable intervillage conflict in horticultural societies. Much of the fighting, however, resembles modern contact sports more than warfare. Satisfaction is often gained more from defeating the enemy in games than from killing him. Although conflict does sometimes lead to battle and death, religious beliefs and rituals keep slaughter within bounds (Plog and Bates 1990). Still, Napoleon Chagnon (1997) estimates that at least 24 percent of all male deaths among the Yanomamö (South American preindustrial people) are due to warfare—a figure consistent with those for other tribes that constantly feud with their neighbors.

Q **How is the subsistence problem addressed in pastoral societies?** Most horticultural societies keep domesticated animals such as pigs and chickens. They do not, however, depend economically on the products of these animals the way *pastoralists* (herders) do. In **pastoral societies,** food is obtained primarily by raising and caring for domesticated animals. For the most part, these are gregarious (herd) animals such as cattle, camels, goats, and sheep, all of which provide

both milk and meat. Because food grains are needed to supplement the food obtained from animals, pastoralists must also either cultivate some land or trade with people who do (Peoples and Bailey 2009; Nanda and Warms 2011; Bailey and Peoples 2011).

There is more physical mobility in pastoral societies than in those based more fully on the cultivation of land, although the degree of mobility may vary greatly. Permanent (or at least long-term) villages can be maintained if, as seasons change, herd animals are simply moved to different pastures within a given area. In such societies, the women remain at home while the men take the herds to different pastures. A permanent village, however, cannot exist if, as the weather changes, an entire population moves with the herd (nomads).

Because both horticultural and pastoral societies can produce a surplus of food, they usher in important social changes unknown in hunting and gathering societies. With a surplus food supply, some members of the community are free to create a more complex division of labor. People can become political and religious leaders or makers of surplus goods such as pottery, spears, and clothing. Because nonedible goods are available, an incentive to trade with other peoples emerges.

The creation of a surplus also permits the development of social inequality, although it is limited by the size and dependability of the surplus. Even a relatively small surplus, however, means that some families (or villages or clans) can, for the first time, rise above others. Houses and storage facilities for the surplus goods become personal rather than group property. The introduction of personal property ownership enables some people to gain more wealth than others, with an accompanying increase in social prestige. The egalitarianism among hunters and gatherers is gradually replaced by a hierarchical society. This transition does not occur easily. Within horticultural societies, people

This farmer lives in an agricultural society. How does his society differ technologically from a horticultural society?

can react strongly to the disruption in social harmony caused by these new wealth and status inequalities. Among the Tsembaga of Central New Guinea, a man whose animals and gardens do especially well may be betrayed to an enemy (Wade 2010). Competition over resources can take the form of warfare, which in turn leads to the emergence of political leaders or possibly the creation of slavery.

Q **What are the characteristics of an agricultural society?** The transition from horticultural to **agricultural society** was made possible largely through the invention of the plow (Nolan and Lenski 2010). The longer the horticulturalists worked the soil with their digging sticks, hoes, and spades, the greater their disadvantage. With these crude implements, horticulturalists could not control the weeds, and they could not dig deeply enough to reach the soil's nutrients, which recede farther below the root line each year of cultivation. The plow, which appeared about 5,000 to 6,000 years ago, did not solve these problems completely, but it was effective enough to permit the permanent cultivation of land. The plow not only controlled the weeds but also turned the weeds into fertilizer by burying them under the soil. By digging more deeply into the ground, the plow was able to reach nutrient-rich dirt that had sunk below root level. The result was more productivity—more food per unit of land.

Moreover, the plow permits a shift from human to animal energy. Only humans can use a hoe or spade, but oxen can pull a plow. Using draft animals also increases productivity because larger areas can be cultivated with fewer people. As a result, more people are released from the land. This, then, frees those people to engage in noneconomic activities such as formal education, concerts, and political rallies. This leads, in turn, to other significant changes: the introduction of occupations not directly tied to farming (such as politician, blacksmith, and haberdasher); the establishment of cities; the development of more complex economic specialization; and the emergence of separate political, economic, and religious institutions.

Although family ties remain important, the state replaces the kinship group as the guiding force for agricultural societies. Advanced agricultural societies are monarchical, headed by a king or an emperor who desires as much control as possible. Distinct social classes appear for the first time. Wealth and power are based on land ownership, which is controlled by the governing elite. While the elite enjoy the benefits of the economic surplus, the peasants do most of the work.

Urban merchants hold less prestige than the governing class. They are better off than the peasants; but they, too, work hard for their living. An economy, based on trade and a monetary system, begins to emerge as an identifiable institution. The agricultural economy develops two basic sectors: a rural, agricultural sector and an urban, commercial sector. Institutional specialization is reflected in the increasing separation of the political and religious elite. Although rulers are often believed to be divinely chosen, few of them double as religious leaders.

Industrial Societies

The Industrial Revolution was "a kind of discontinuous leap in human history; a leap as important as that which had lifted the first . . . [horticultural] settlements above the earlier hunting communities" (Milberg and Heilbroner 2007:102). The Industrial Revolution created **industrial society**—a society whose subsistence is based primarily on the application of science and technology to the production of goods and services.

Q **What happens to societies as new technologies appear?** Alberto Martinelli and Neil Smelser (1990) have identified some basic structural changes that occur in societies shifting from an agricultural to an industrial economic base. Industrialism brings with it a change away from simple, traditional technology (plows, hammers, harnesses) toward the application of scientific knowledge (see "Think Globally 5.1"). With this change comes the discovery and adoption of new, complex technological devices. Early examples of industrial technology include the steam engine and the use of electrical power in manufacturing. More recent technological developments include nuclear energy, aerospace-related inventions, the computer, and nanotechnology. These technological devices are used in factories and in agriculture.

In industrial societies, then, the trend is away from human and animal power toward power-driven machines. With this mechanization, the shift is away from subsistence farming toward the selling of agricultural goods on the open market. Farmers are able to produce a surplus sufficient to support themselves and many others. This food surplus supports urbanization, the movement of people from farms and villages to gigantic urban concentrations. Thus, industrial society is also an urban society, with vast concentrations of people located in and around many urban centers. In fact, about half of the world's population now lives in cities. And the world's urban population is expected to grow by 72 percent (to almost 5 billion). By 2030, half of the world's population will, for the first time, live in cities (United Nations 2007; World Population Data Sheet 2010).

THINK GLOBALLY 5.1

Extent of Agricultural Production

As societies move from the preindustrial to the postindustrial stage, fewer people are required to raise food to feed the population. This map shows the percentage of each country's total GDP value added from agricultural products, an indirect measure of the proportion of each country's population involved in the production of agricultural products.

Percentage of Total GDP Value Added from Agriculture

- Less than 3%
- 3%–7%
- 8%–14%
- 15%–24%
- 25% or more
- No data

Source: From John L. Allen and Christopher J. Sutton, *Student Atlas of World Politics*, 9th ed. (p. 124). New York: Copyright © 2011 by The McGraw-Hill Companies. Reproduced by permission of McGraw-Hill Contemporary Learning Series.

Interpret the Map

1. After examining this map, what generalizations about types of societies around the world would you make? Explain.

2. Which countries do you think could be ready to move from one type of society to another? Be specific about countries and types of societies.

3. What parts of the world are the least likely to change in the near future? Explain your answer.

Q What happens when structural differentiation develops? The concept of structural differentiation also helps to describe industrial society. **Structural differentiation** occurs when a single social structure divides into two or more social structures. Under the new circumstances, these new separate social structures operate more efficiently than the one alone. Under the domestic form of production, for example, the family performs a variety of economic roles. In the change from domestic to factory production, economic activities are moved from the family to the factory. Because economic and familial functions are now two separate institutions, their activities become increasingly segregated.

Other kinds of changes occur through structural differentiation. The education of the young moves from the home to the school. Because an industrial society requires an educated labor force, education is extended from the elite to the masses. Kinship declines in importance as the immediate family begins to separate socially and physically from the extended family. Personal choice and love replace arranged marriages. Women, through their entrance into the workforce, become less subordinate to their husbands. Religion no longer pervades all aspects of social life as various institutions—political, economic, familial, educational—become more and more independent of religious influence. Individual mobility increases dramatically, and social class is based more on occupational achievement than on the social class of one's parents.

Because the United States has long been an industrial society, we accept its characteristics as a given. The effects of industrialization are easier to observe in societies currently moving from an agricultural to an industrial economic base. For example, Vietnam and Malaysia, two countries currently undergoing industrialization, are experiencing these kinds of changes at the beginning of the twenty-first century (Phu 1998; S. Singh 1998).

Q How do preindustrial and industrial societies differ?
Ferdinand Tönnies, Emile Durkheim, and Robert Redfield were three early sociologists who, each with his own unique approach, compared preindustrial and industrial societies. Contemporary sociologists generally agree that each of these three men was successful at isolating central features differentiating the two types of societies.

Ferdinand Tönnies (1957; originally published in 1887), an early German sociologist, distinguished between **gemeinschaft** (German for "community") and **gesellschaft** (German for "society"). The former—closely approximating preindustrial society—is based on tradition, kinship, and intimate social relationships. The latter—representing industrial society—is characterized by weak family ties, competition, and less personal social relationships.

Shortly after Tönnies formulated his distinction, Emile Durkheim (1997; originally published in 1893) made a similar observation. He distinguished the two types of societies by the nature of their social solidarity—the degree to which a society is unified.

Social solidarity, Durkheim contended, is predicated on a society's division of labor. In societies in which the division of labor is simple—in which most people are doing the same type of work—**mechanical solidarity** is the foundation for social unity. A society based on mechanical solidarity achieves social unity through a consensus of beliefs, values, and norms; strong social pressures for conformity; and dependence on tradition and family. In this type of society, which is best observed in small, nonliterate societies, people tend to behave, think, and feel in much the same ways; to place the group above the individual; and to emphasize tradition and family.

Modern industrial societies, in contrast, involve a very complex and differentiated division of labor. Because people perform very specialized jobs, they are dependent on others and must cooperate with them. Whereas farmers in a simple society are largely self-sufficient, members of an industrial society depend on a variety of people to fulfill their needs—barbers, bakers, manufacturers, and other suppliers of services. This modern industrial society is based on **organic solidarity.** It achieves social unity through a complex of specialized statuses that forces interdependence among members of a society. Dependence and need for cooperation replace the homogeneity of beliefs, values, and norms characteristic of simpler societies. The term *organic solidarity* is based on an analogy with biological organisms. If a biological organism composed of highly specialized parts is to survive, its parts must work together. Similarly, the parts of a society based on organic solidarity must cooperate if the society is to survive.

In this same vein, anthropologist Robert Redfield (1941) distinguished between a folk society and an urban society. A **folk society** rests on tradition, cultural and social consensus, family, personal ties, little division of labor, and an emphasis on the sacred. In an **urban society,** social relationships are impersonal and contractual; the importance of the family declines; cultural and social consensus diminishes; economic specialization becomes even more complex; and secular concerns outweigh sacred ones.

Postindustrial Society

Some societies, including the United States, have passed beyond industrial society into **postindustrial society.** The postindustrial economic base is grounded more in service industries than in manufacturing industries and relies on expertise in production, consumption, and government (Kumar 2004).

Q What are the major features of postindustrial society?
Daniel Bell (1999) identifies five major features of postindustrial society:

1. *For the first time, the majority of the labor force is employed in services rather than in agriculture or manufacturing.* Today, the United States is the only country in the world in which more than half of all employment is in services—trade, finance, transportation, health, recreation, research, and government. In fact, more than 75 percent of all employed workers in the United States are in service jobs.
2. *White-collar employment replaces much blue-collar work.* The shift to a service economy in postindustrial society—with an emphasis on office work—leads to a preponderance of white-collar workers. They outnumbered blue-collar workers in the United States for the first time in the mid-1950s, and the gap is still increasing. The most rapid growth among white-collar workers has been in professional and technical employment.
3. *Theoretical knowledge is the key organizing feature.* In postindustrial society, knowledge is used for the creation of innovations as well as for the formulation of government policy (computers permit economic forecasting so that various economic theories can be tested). As theoretical knowledge becomes more important, so do educational and research institutions.
4. *Through new means of technological forecasting, society can plan and control technological change.* In industrial society, technological change is uncontrolled. That is, the effects of a technological innovation are not assessed before its introduction. The pesticide DDT was introduced as a benefit to agriculture before its harm to living things had been determined. The internal combustion engine contributes to our affluence and economic growth

Industrial society addressed the problem of subsistence primarily through the application of science and technology to the production of goods and services. Assembly line workers are common in industrial society.

John A. Rizzo/Getty Images

but contaminates the environment. On the other hand, technology is more intensely scrutinized in postindustrial society. In the race to provide the automobile industry a lighter and cheaper metal, the aluminum industry claimed that a one-ton increase of aluminum in place of steel would reduce carbon dioxide pollution by twenty tons over the life of an average car. A scientific study successfully challenged this claim, showing that it would take thirty-two to thirty-eight years of driving aluminum-intensive vehicles to offset the pollution released by the production of aluminum required to build those vehicles (Chamberlain 1999). Technological assessment in postindustrial society will permit us to consider the effects—good and bad—of an innovation before it is introduced.

5. *Intellectual technology dominates human affairs.* A new intellectual technology dominates in postindustrial society, much as production technology dominated industrial society for the past 150 years. With "intellectual technology," mathematical-type problem-solving rules can, in many cases, replace

CHECK YOURSELF 5.3 R2

Society

1. A _____ is the largest and most self-sufficient group in existence.
2. The _____ society is the oldest known solution to the subsistence problem.
3. The _____ society solved the subsistence problem primarily through the domestication of plants.
4. The transition from horticultural to agricultural society was made possible largely through the invention of the _____.
5. _____ occurs when one social structure divides into two or more social structures that operate more successfully separately than the one alone would under the new circumstances.
6. A society based on _____ solidarity achieves social unity through a complex of highly specialized roles that makes members of a society dependent on one another.
7. Which of the following is *not* one of the major features of postindustrial society?
   a. emphasis on theoretical knowledge
   b. employment of the majority of the labor force in service industries
   c. reliance on intellectual technology
   d. increased dependence on skilled blue-collar workers
   e. shift toward the employment of white-collar workers

Answers: 1. society; 2. hunting and gathering; 3. horticultural; 4. plow; 5. Structural differentiation; 6. organic; 7. d

human judgment. With computers, it is possible to consider, simultaneously, a large number of interacting variables. This capability allows us to manage the large-scale organizations that prevail in postindustrial society. Intellectual technology enables complex organizations—including government at national, state, and local levels—to set rational goals and to identify a means for reaching them.

These, then, are some of the most general features of postindustrial society. These features center primarily on technological and economic matters. The broader process of *modernization* encompasses these modifications as well as other societal changes. We will examine these additional alterations within the context of functionalism.

Modernization and the Theoretical Perspectives ▣

Functionalism and Modernization

Modernization entails the broader social changes—there are a host of them—that accompany economic development based on industrialization. According to **modernization theory,** the changes associated with modernization are the result of an evolutionary process by which societies become increasingly complex. It follows, then, that the trend toward modernization

is one of the most significant trends in human history (Haferkamp and Smelser 1992; Chase-Dunn 1999; Fukuyama 1999, 2000; Giddens 2002).

As a part of functionalism, modernization theory sees the changes in social structure as result of adaptation. In this case, adaptation occurs as a response to economic development.

Q **What are some of the broader societal changes associated with modernization?** Some significant demographic alterations accompany modernization. Population growth occurs as the death rate declines and life expectancy increases. Between the thirteenth and seventeenth centuries, for example, Europe had a life expectancy as low as twenty years; by 1930, life expectancy had increased to more than sixty years and now stands at seventy-six years (*World Population Data Sheet* 2010). The population moves from rural to urban areas. Whereas most members of traditional societies work the land, most members of modern societies live and work in towns and cities, where industry and jobs are located.

Modernization alters stratification structures as well. Traditional society is characterized by a bipolar stratification structure—the wealthy at one end, the poor masses at the other. Modernization brings an expansion of the middle and upper classes. As more emphasis is placed on personal effort and achievement, social mobility increases and inequality generally declines.

Occupational knowledge in an industrial society, like the knowledge needed by these science technicians, cannot be learned in the home. What does this mean for education in an industrial society?

Laurence Gough/Used under license from Shutterstock.

As the role of the state expands, modernization transforms the political institution. It becomes more centralized and more involved in social and economic affairs. At the same time, modernization promotes political democracy, even though the extent of democratization varies considerably from society to society. Although political power is not equalized as a result of modernization—there is always a powerful elite—power is more widely dispersed.

Modernization transfers education from the family to a formal system of education. Education is no longer designed just for the privileged few but for the entire society; primary education, in fact, is intended for all members of a modernizing society. A literate population is absolutely necessary to create a workforce suitable for an industrialized economy.

Modernization also affects family life. The nuclear family replaces the extended family. Because the economy ceases to be based on a familial division of labor, people must move to cities to work. Extended family ties can be obliterated; they simply become much harder to maintain, and much of their intimacy can be lost. With modernization, other institutions adopt functions formerly of the family's domain. For example, government assumes more responsibility for the elderly, schools take care of children's educational needs, and the mass media provide entertainment.

Q **Given these changes, do all modernizing societies become alike?** This question is debated among scholars (M. C. Waters 2001; Eitzen and Zinn 2009; Eitzen and Atalay 2010; Lemert et al. 2010). Advocates of the pattern of **convergence** foresee the development of social and cultural similarity among modernizing nations. They contend that as societies adopt the newest technological arrangements, they tend to develop social and cultural commonalities. This is said to occur because a particular technology carries in its wake a particular occupational structure, which in turn exercises similar wide-ranging effects on various social structures and social relationships. The necessity for an industrializing society to develop an educated populace is another major unifying force. Other pressures for uniformity include the enlarged role of government, the influence of multinational corporations within modernizing countries, and the accelerated growth of large-scale organizations (Inkeles 1998). This, say those who see a convergence among modernizing societies, leads to the creation of a **global culture:** a homogenized way of life spread across the globe.

Movement toward a global culture, for example, can be read into the television coverage of the 2000-millennium celebrations. Never before had the world shared in New Year's celebrations from Australia west to Hawaii. This international exposure—fueled by the almost universal adoption of computer technology and the commonly shared telecommunications technology—may foretell increased cross-cultural influence in the twenty-first century.

Will globalization lead to the creation of a global culture shared by all highly developed countries? Or will new technology simply be incorporated into the existing cultures of countries undergoing globalization?

Rolf Bruderer/Blend Images/Jupiter Images

Supporters of the pattern of **divergence,** on the other hand, do not see social and cultural homogeneity as an inevitable result of modernization; they do not envision the emergence of a global culture. Rather, they see the persistence of cultural differences among modernizing societies as a result of intervening idiosyncratic social and cultural forces in the move toward modernization. Advocates of divergence offer as evidence less developed countries that are now undergoing modernization along lines somewhat different from the path taken by Western societies (Guillen 2003, 2010).

Q **Where does this leave us with respect to the creation of a global culture?** As in most complex debates, there may be a middle ground that is closer to the truth. This middle ground may be found in distinguishing between "globalization" and "global culture." **Globalization** is the process by which increasingly permeable geographical boundaries lead different societies to share in common some economic, political, and social arrangements. But, rather than creating a homogenized worldwide way of life, a global culture, modernization and globalization may provide some common social arrangements that are incorporated into different societies in unique ways consistent with their preexisting cultures. If so, then social and cultural elements of traditional societies would not completely vanish under the influence of modernization and globalization; traditional elements may blend with the new (Mazaar 1999; Pieterse 2009). Changes in the family during modernization, for example, depend in part on the type of traditional family a society has. Some traditional family structures are more compatible with modernization than others are. To cite another example, democratization usually accompanies modernization, but its extent and form may vary due to the specific social and cultural traditions of a society. Although modern Japan is more democratic than it was in premodern times, it is less democratic than most Western societies. And although the Soviet Communist Party leaders voted overwhelmingly in July 1991 to endorse the principle of private property, freedom of religion, and a pluralistic political system, serious political opposition has since arisen. The lack of democratic progress is obvious when Russian President Vladimir Putin can choose the next president of Russia by simply endorsing his protégé, Dimitri Medvedev. Even before the 2008 election, Putin was labeled "the older czar" and Medvedev "the younger czar" (Schwirtz 2007).

Conflict Theory and Modernization

World-system theory sees persistent social and cultural diversity among modernizing nations. It is one specific interpretation of conflict theory (Chase-Dunn and Hall 1997; Chase-Dunn 1999; Kardulias 1999; Guillen 2003, 2010).

Q **What is world-system theory?** According to **world-system theory,** the pattern of a nation's development hinges on its place in the world economy. The world economy is divided into segments: core and peripheral nations, such as Burma and Kenya. Core nations, such as the United States, dominate the world economy, which leads to their control and exploitation of the rest of the world. To benefit themselves, core nations take unfair advantage of the cheap labor and natural resources of peripheral or less developed nations (Wallerstein 1979, 2001, 2003a, 2003b, 2004).

Q **What are the consequences of the world-system arrangement?** As a result of this world-system arrangement, the standard of living is much higher in core nations, whose skilled workers operate in a free labor market. Workers in peripheral nations provide unskilled, coerced labor and suffer a low standard of living. Peripheral nations do not develop as much as they could if they were not dominated and exploited by the core nations. In fact, world-system advocates contend, this deterrent to peripheral national development is the prime perpetuating impetus for the existing arrangement. Consequently, the economic, social, and cultural gap between core and peripheral nations is increasing (Rossides 1997; Wallerstein 2000; R. H. Robbins 2004; Stiglitz 2003, 2007).

According to many advocates of globalization, free markets promote democracy, prosperity, and peace (Mandelbaum 2004b; T. Friedman 2000, 2007). Free markets are said to promote enfranchisement of the masses, increase economic equality, and reduce conflict within and between societies. Looking at Russia and developing countries in Latin America, Africa, and Asia, Amy Chua (2004) questions this happy mix assumed by globalists. Conceding that free markets promote democracy, the results, Chua argues, do not include increased economic equality and reduced conflict. Instead, the introduction of the free market in a developing country creates a new class of extremely rich elites who tend to belong to the same minority group. This "market-dominant minority" is subsequently subjected to ethnic hatred and violence from the recently enfranchised majority. The majority government uses its newly acquired political freedom and power to wreak revenge on the politically weaker minority elites and confiscate or destroy their property. In Indonesia, to cite one of Chua's cases, the suppressed Muslim majority unleashed a vicious attack against the economically dominant ethnic Chinese, looting their businesses,

Modernization and the Theoretical Perspectives

1. _____ is a process involving all those social and cultural changes accompanying economic development.
2. Which of the following is *not* one of the major consequences of modernization discussed in the text?
   a. social and cultural convergence of modernizing countries
   b. increased urbanization
   c. greater equality
   d. more political democracy
   e. widespread development of the nuclear family
3. According to _____ theory, the pattern of a nation's development largely depends on the nation's location in the world economy.
4. World-system theory would predict a (convergence/divergence) between core and peripheral nations.

Answers: 1. Modernization; 2. a; 3. World-system; 4. divergence

breaking their store windows, and raping their women. Because Chua is going against the more conventional view, she is certain to be challenged by globalists. The same is true for Naomi Klein, who argues that Milton Friedman's free market movement (see M. Friedman 2002) has failed to deliver on its promise of a peaceful, prosperous global world. Rather, she argues, this movement's brand of capitalism has taken advantage of crises brought on by war to enrich those already rich and powerful (Klein 2007).

Postmodernism and Modernization

In Chapter 1, postmodernism was described as more of an analysis of a social condition than a body of theory. That social condition is one in which modernity is glorified for its freedom and affluence, while its virtues are used to mask the negative realities associated with empire building, oppression, and exploitation. Postmodernism, then, contains within it a critique of modernism (and globalization) on the grounds that its benefits are enjoyed by some to the detriment of others (Lemert 2005; Eitzen and Zinn 2009; Eitzen and Atalay 2010; Lemert etal. 2010).

For that reason, postmodernism questions the key assumptions of modernism. Postmodernism emphasizes the domination of the weak by the strong, which reduces human autonomy. Postmodernism points out that dependence on reason has produced many horrific consequences such as the creation of nuclear weapons and global warming. Finally, postmodernism questions the existence of ultimate truth on which everyone can agree because the powerful always have a version of the "truth" they impose on others.

Q Is there any evidence to support the postmodernist critique? There are two kinds of evidence that could point to some validity to the postmodernist critique of modernism. One kind of evidence is indirect; the other is direct. Indirect evidence comes from the promoters of modernism who spend a lot of time and energy on the plights of less affluent countries that postmodernists contend are being exploited. The World Bank and the United Nations, for example, continuously express concern for poverty in less developed countries (*World Development Report* 2000/2001, 2003, 2006, 2008; The *Millennium Development Goals Report* 2010). Whether these groups are sincerely interested in reducing poverty (as the modernists say) or simply using their efforts to cover up the ills of modernization (as the postmodernists claim), it is obvious that massive poverty in less developed countries does exist. And the very presence of social ills like poverty in poor countries constitutes direct evidence for the postmodernist critique. This direct evidence will be discussed further in Chapter 8 ("Social Stratification"), under the heading of global poverty.

On to Chapter 6

The nature of social structure should now be more obvious to you. And it needs to be because the remainder of this text is about social structures. This chapter introduced you to the concept of society as a social structure and also discussed the even broader social structures created when societies influence each other in the process of globalization. In Chapter 6, we will cover groups and organizations, two other types of social structure that exist both within and between societies.

S INTEGRATED GOALS AND SUMMARY

1. **Explain what sociologists mean by social structure.**
   - Relationships among individuals are patterned. This underlying pattern of social relationships is called *social structure*. Social scientists have developed the concepts of status, role, role performance, and social interaction to explain the existence of social structure.
2. **Distinguish between role and status.**
   - A status is a position that a person occupies within a social structure. Individuals occupying interrelated statuses usually behave toward one another in orderly and predictable ways. Some statuses are ascribed, or assigned, to people; other statuses are achieved, or earned. Still other statuses (master statuses) are so significant that they affect most other aspects of a person's life.
   - Roles—the glue that binds a network of social statuses—are the culturally defined rights and obligations attached to social statuses. Rights inform one person of the behavior that can be expected from another person; obligations inform individuals of the behavior that others expect from them. The rights of one status correspond to the obligations of another status.
3. **Discuss the relationship between role performance, role conflict, and role strain.**
   - Role performance occurs when roles are put into action. Role performance takes place through social interaction. Role conflict occurs when the performance of a role in one status clashes with the performance of a role in another status. Role strain occurs when the roles of a single position are inconsistent. Role conflict and role strain, which may lead to discomfort and confusion, can be reduced by setting priorities and segregating roles. Because of role conflict and role strain, an individual's conformity to all roles is impossible. This does not cause a problem so long as roles are carried out within certain tolerance limits.
4. **Define the concept of society and the relationship between means of subsistence and the structure of society.**
   - A society is composed of a people living within defined territorial borders, sharing a common culture. The way

a society solves the problem of subsistence heavily influences the society's culture and social structures. Historically, societies have become larger and more complex as the means for solving subsistence problems have improved. The major types of societies are hunting and gathering, horticultural, pastoral, agricultural, industrial, and postindustrial.

5. **Compare and contrast preindustrial, industrial, and postindustrial societies.**
   - Although both the horticultural and agricultural revolutions brought significant change, the greatest transformation came with the Industrial Revolution. The leap from preindustrial to industrial society was so great that many scholars have been able to isolate the basic characteristics distinguishing these two types of societies.
   - Postindustrial society is on the rise. This type of society has a predominately white-collar labor force with the following features: concentration in service industries, base of technical knowledge, reliance on technical forecasting, and dependence on computer technology.
6. **Delineate the unique perspectives functionalism, conflict theory, and postmodern theory have on modernization.**
   - Modernization entails the broader social changes associated with industrialization. Functionalism, conflict theory, and postmodern theory express different views of these changes. Functionalism concentrates on alterations in population, stratification, politics, education, and the family. Of particular interest to functionalists is the idea of a global culture.
   - Conflict theory, likewise, responds to globalization. World-systems theory, for example, examines the emergence of a two-tiered world economy, composed of more developed (core) nations and less developed (peripheral) nations. Postmodernists also emphasize inequality. They underscore the empire building, oppression, and exploitation that develop via modernization and globalization.

CONCEPT REVIEW

Match the following concepts with the definitions listed below them.

____ a. society
____ b. urban society
____ c. industrial society
____ d. organic solidarity
____ e. achieved status

____ f. rights
____ g. hunting and gathering society
____ h. social structure
____ i. role strain
____ j. master status

____ k. structural differentiation
____ l. gesellschaft
____ m. folk society
____ n. role performance
____ o. modernization theory

1. a slot within a social structure occupied because of an individual's efforts

2. a society that solves the subsistence problem through hunting animals and gathering edible fruits and vegetables

3. roles informing individuals of the behavior that can be expected from others

4. when one social structure divides into two or more social structures that operate more successfully separately than the one alone would under the new circumstances

5. a society based on tradition, cultural and social consensus, family, personal ties, little division of labor, and an emphasis on the sacred

6. the actual conduct involved in putting roles into action

7. occurs when the roles of a single status are inconsistent with one another

8. patterned recurring social relationships among individuals and groups

9. people who live within defined territorial borders, sharing a common culture

10. a status that affects most other aspects of a person's life

11. Tönnies's term for the type of society characterized by weak family ties, competition, and impersonal social relationships

12. a society whose subsistence is based primarily on the application of science and technology to the production of goods and services

13. social unity based on a complex of highly specialized statuses that makes members of a society dependent on one another

14. a society in which social relationships are impersonal and contractual, kinship is deemphasized, cultural and social consensus are not complete, the division of labor is complex, and secular concerns outweigh sacred ones

15. proposes that change associated with modernization are the result of an evolutionary process by which societies become increasingly complex

CHECK YOURSELF REVIEW

1. _____ refers to the patterned relationships among individuals and groups.

2. _____ are culturally defined rights and obligations attached to statuses.

3. The rights of one social status correspond to the _____ of another one.

4. _____ occurs when the roles of a single status are inconsistent.

5. A _____ is the largest and most self-sufficient group in existence.

6. The transition from horticultural to agricultural society was made possible largely through the invention of the _____.

7. A society based on _____ solidarity achieves social unity through a complex of highly specialized roles that makes members of a society dependent on one another.

8. _____ is a process involving all these social and cultural changes accompanying economic development.

9. Which of the following is *not* one of the differences between the stage and social life?

   a. There is considerably more discrepancy between roles and role performance in social life than between a stage script and its performance.

   b. Unlike the stage, there are no cues and responses in real life.

   c. Role performance in real life is not the conscious process that actors go through on the stage.

   d. In social life, the cues and responses are not as programmed and predictable as on the stage.

10. Which of the following is *not* one of the major features of postindustrial society?

    a. emphasis on theoretical knowledge

    b. employment of the majority of the labor force in service industries

    c. reliance on intellectual technology

    d. increased dependence on skilled blue-collar workers

    e. shift toward the employment of white-collar workers

11. Match the type of status with the examples that best illustrate it.

    ____ a. ascribed status

    ____ b. achieved status

    ____ c. master status

    ____ d. status set

    ____ e. role

    ____ f. role performance

    ____ g. social interaction

    (1) basketball coach, mother, author, daughter, professor

    (2) occupation, gender, race, ethnicity

    (3) president of the United States

    (4) sex

    (5) a husband and wife discuss disciplining one of their children

    (6) a university president hands out diplomas at a graduation ceremony

    (7) a mother is expected to take care of her children

CRITICAL-THINKING QUESTIONS

1. Suppose that a college friend of yours wants to know the meaning of the term *social structure*. Use the stage analogy to develop an understandable answer. Use examples.

_____

_____

2. Have you experienced role conflict or role strain lately? If so, describe the situation. If not, explain why you have been immune to role conflict and role strain, making clear the meaning of the concepts.

_____

_____

3. Discuss some of the basic distinguishing features of preindustrial and industrial societies. Illustrate your answer.

_____

4. In what ways will your work life be different in a postindustrial society than in an industrial society?

_____

_____

REVIEW GUIDE

ANSWER KEY

Concept Review

a. 9
b. 14
c. 12
d. 13
e. 1
f. 3
g. 2
h. 8
i. 7
j. 10
k. 4
l. 11
m. 5
n. 6
o. 15

Check Yourself Review

1. Social structure
2. Roles
3. obligations
4. Role strain
5. society
6. plow
7. organic
8. e
9. b
10. d
11. a. 4
    b. 3
    c. 2
    d. 1
    e. 7
    f. 6
    g. 5

6 Groups and Organizations

AP Photo/Pablo Martinez Monsivais

S GOALS

- Define the concept of the group, and differentiate it from social categories and social aggregates.
- Outline the basic characteristics of primary and secondary groups.
- State the functions of primary groups.
- Differentiate between in-groups and out-groups.
- Discuss the idea of a social network.
- Describe the five major types of social interaction.
- Elaborate on the existence of cooperation and conflict in groups.

- Discuss the nature of group processes: task accomplishment, leadership styles, and decision making.
- Define the concept of formal organization, and identify the major characteristics of bureaucracy.
- Discuss the advantages and disadvantages of bureaucracy.
- Distinguish between formal and informal organization.
- Describe the iron law of oligarchy, and demonstrate its importance with examples.
- Discuss prejudice and discrimination in organizations.

Most people assume that conflict should be avoided because it is disruptive and interferes with group effectiveness. Conflict does have some negative consequences. Not as well known, however, are some social benefits of conflict. Giving full consideration to the different opinions in a group, for example, can prevent a group from being a victim of the self-deceptive belief that the majority is right. In other words, openness to disagreement and conflict can prevent groupthink.

The space shuttle *Challenger* is an excellent example of a disastrous decision that was based on conformity to group ideas. The *Challenger* was launched from Kennedy Space Center on January 28, 1986. Just over a minute after the launch, the *Challenger* disintegrated, and in the instant of explosion, took the lives of all seven astronauts on board.

As is true for all space mission personnel, the *Challenger* team was composed of a number of specialists. The engineers on the team had recommended against takeoff that morning because crucial parts had never been tested at so low a temperature. As victims of groupthink, the NASA leaders screened out this opposition; they acted as if the engineers lacked the intelligence and courage to make the "right" decision. The leaders downgraded the opinions of the engineers and convinced most of the group that the decision, except for the engineers, was unanimous. By avoiding consideration of a dissenting view, the majority lost the shuttle's passengers and harmed NASA's long-term objectives (Moorhead, Ference, and Neck 1991).

Concept of the Group **R1**

Due in no small part to socialization, Americans generally think in individualistic terms. This individualistic orientation is often a stumbling block to those first introduced to the concept of the group. Perhaps it will ease the transition into thinking about groups (rather than individuals) if we begin by focusing on what is thought of as an individualistic activity—but in fact is a group endeavor. Art is a likely candidate for this purpose.

Think of painting and you are likely to have images of Rembrandt, Renoir, or Picasso. The art of dance will call to mind Nureyev, Baryshnikov, or Savion Glover.

It may be Gershwin, Sondheim, or Webber who comes to the fore when the subject of musical achievement on Broadway is the topic. In short, when we think of art, we think of individual artists. Without denigrating the talent, hard work, and achievements of individual artists whose works are precious to us, Howard Becker wants to underscore the fact that even such an allegedly individualistic pursuit as art "involves the joint activity of a number, often a large number of people" (Becker 1982:1).

Becker begins his book *Art Worlds* with this story told by Anthony Trollope, the famous nineteenth-century English novelist:

It was my practice to be at my table every morning at 5:30 a.m.; and it was also my practice to allow myself no mercy. An old groom, whose business it was to call me, and to whom I paid £5 a year extra for the duty, allowed himself no mercy. During all those years at Waltham Cross he was never once late with the coffee which it was his duty to bring me. I do not know that I ought not to feel that I owe more to him than to any one else for the success I have had. By beginning at that hour I could complete my literary work before I dressed for breakfast. (Becker 1982:1)

Trollope's groom is one member of the complex network of social relationships that permitted this artist to accomplish his work. Moreover, the activities of both Trollope and his groom had to mesh with those of many other people (printers, publishers, and editors, to mention only a few) if the literary works of this Victorian writer were ever to become available to the public. Some of these relationships were personal and face-to-face; others were not. This chapter elaborates on the variety of group relationships and the contexts in which they appear throughout social life.

A **group** is composed of people who are in contact with one another; share some ways of thinking, feeling, and behaving; take one another's behavior into account; and have one or more interests or goals in common. Because of their characteristics, groups play an important role in the lives of their participants as well as influence the societies in which they exist.

Types of Groups **R1**

Categories, Aggregates, and Groups

A group should be distinguished from a **social category**—people who share a social characteristic. A taxpayer, a woman, and a college graduate each belong to a social category. A group is also sometimes confused with a **social aggregate**—people who happen to be at the same place at the same time, such as students waiting in line for concert tickets. Although neither categories nor aggregates are groups, some of their members may form groups. Victims of a disaster (an aggregate)—such as residents of a town devastated by a tornado—may work together to cope with the emergency. Citizens of a state (a social category) may band together in an organized tax revolt. These people may form a group if they begin to interact regularly; share ways of thinking, feeling, and behaving; take one another's behavior into account; and have some common goals.

Primary Groups

Primary and secondary groups are two principal types of groups (see Table 6.1). At the extremes, the characteristics of these two types of groups—and the relationships that occur within them—are opposites. But most groups sit at different points along a continuum from primary to secondary.

Q **Why is a primary group described as tightly integrated?** A **primary group** is composed of people who are emotionally close, know one another well, and seek one another's company. The members of a primary group have a "we" feeling and enjoy being together. These groups are characterized by relationships that are intimate, personal, caring, and fulfilling.

Charles Horton Cooley, one of the founders of symbolic interactionism, coined the term *primary group*. Primary groups are the most important setting for socialization. The family, neighborhood, and childhood play groups, Cooley observed, are primary because they are the first groups an infant experiences. People, of course, participate in primary groups throughout life. Close friends in high school and college, neighbors

People in primary groups are emotionally close, know one another well, enjoy one another's company, and share a feeling of "we-ness." The family is the most important primary group to which we belong.

Andresr/Used under license from Shutterstock

who keep an eye on one another's children, and friends who meet weekly for golf are examples of primary groups.

Q **What conditions promote the development of primary groups?** A number of conditions favor the development of primary groups and **primary relationships.** Although primary relationships may occur in their absence, the likelihood of having a primary relationship is increased if these conditions exist.

- *Small group size.* It is difficult for the members of large groups to spend enough time together to develop close emotional ties; the chances of knowing everyone fairly well are far greater in small groups. Thus, members of a bridge foursome are more likely to develop primary relationships than are members

TABLE 6.1

Characteristics of Primary and Secondary Groups

You belong to both primary and secondary groups. Select one of each, and describe your experience with the functions it is supposed to perform.

	Nature or Relationship	Function	Examples
Primary Group	• Close and continuous social interaction	• Provides emotional support • Contributes to socialization process • Promotes conformity and social control	• Family • Soldiers in combat • Street gang
Secondary Group	• Impersonal social interaction	• Aids achievement of group goals	• Aerobics class • NFL football team • Telecommunications law firm

of a metropolitan chamber of commerce, even when both groups meet regularly.

- *Face-to-face contact.* People have maintained primary relationships despite separation by war, prison, or residential changes and have even established long-distance primary relationships through e-mail or telephone conversations, but primary relationships occur more easily when interaction is face-to-face. People who can see one another and who can experience such nonverbal communication as facial expressions, tone of voice, and touch are much more likely to develop close ties.
- *Continuous contact.* The probability of developing a primary relationship also increases with prolonged contact. Intimacy rarely develops in a short period of time. In spite of reported love at first sight, most of us require repeated social contact for development of a primary relationship.
- *Proper social environment.* The development of primary relationships is also affected by the social environment in which interaction occurs. If individuals are expected to relate to one another strictly on the basis of status or role, primary relationships are unlikely to develop. Total personalities are usually not considered, and personal concern for one another does not seem appropriate. Lawyers who see judges in court face-to-face, in the presence of a small number of people, over a long period of time are nevertheless unlikely to develop primary relationships with them. Forming primary relationships when unequal statuses are involved is always difficult. This is the reason primary relationships do not usually develop between students and professors, bosses and employees, or judges and lawyers.

Q **What are the functions of primary groups?** First, primary groups provide emotional support through caring, personal, and intimate relationships. During World War II, the German army refused to disintegrate despite years of being outnumbered, undersupplied, and outfought. These conditions should have led to desertion and surrender, but they did not. According to Edward Shils and Morris Janowitz (1948), strong primary relationships within German combat units accounted for the Germans' stability and resilience against overwhelming odds. Although social cohesion developed among American soldiers during the Korean conflict, it was not the same as during World War II. Because of special combat conditions and a personnel rotation system, "the basic unit of cohesion was a two-man relationship rather than one that followed squad or platoon boundaries" (Janowitz 1974:109).

Second, primary groups contribute to the socialization process. For infants, the family is the primary group that provides the emotional support necessary for the development of both an integrated personality and a sense of self. The family also conveys information about culture so that children learn to participate in social life. In addition, primary groups promote adult socialization as individuals adjust to new and changing social environments—as they enter college, take new jobs, change social classes, marry, and retire. Primary groups make these adjustments less painful because membership in them helps people fit into new social situations. Frequent interaction with people who demonstrate genuine concern for others aids adjustment to a new social setting.

Finally, primary groups promote conformity and contribute to social control. The stability and perpetuation of a society depend on the members' acceptance of the society's norms and values. Unless most of the members of a society support the norms and values, that society cannot continue to exist in its present form. Primary groups teach new members the norms and values of the group and provide the pressure to conform. William F. Whyte's (1993) study of an Italian slum gang illustrates social control within primary groups. Whyte found that rank within this gang determined how well the members performed in sports. Bowling scores of gang members, for instance, corresponded with status in the gang—the higher the rank, the higher the score. If a lower-ranked member began to bowl better than those above him, the others used verbal remarks— "You're bowling over your head" or "How lucky can you get?"—to remind him that he was stepping out of line.

Secondary Groups

Q **Why is a secondary group not an end in itself?** A **secondary group** exists to accomplish a specific purpose. Unlike a primary group, a secondary group is impersonal and goal oriented; it involves only a segment of its members' lives. Work groups, volunteer groups formed during disasters, and environmental organizations are all examples of secondary groups. The relationships of the group members are **secondary relationships**— impersonal interactions involving only limited parts of their personality. Interactions between salespersons and customers, employers and workers, and dentists and patients are secondary relationships.

Secondary relationships are not necessarily unpleasant. But the purpose of the group is to accomplish a task, not to enrich friendships. In fact, if friendship becomes more important than the task, a secondary group may become ineffective. If the members of a college basketball team become more interested in the emotional relationships among themselves or with their coach than in playing their best basketball, their play on the court could suffer.

These Goth teenagers gathered in a Swedish park are clearly a group. Are they an in-group or an out-group?

Ladi Kim/Alamy Limited

Q Do secondary groups ever include primary relationships? Although primary relationships are more likely to occur in primary groups and secondary relationships in secondary groups, there are a number of exceptions. Many secondary groups are settings for primary relationships. Members of a work group may relate to one another in a manner that is personal, demonstrate genuine concern for one another as total personalities, and have relationships that are fulfilling in themselves. Similarly, members of a primary group occasionally engage in secondary interaction. One family member may, for example, lend money to another member of the family at a given interest rate with a specific repayment schedule.

Reference Groups

Q How do we use groups as a point of reference? We use certain groups to evaluate ourselves and to acquire attitudes, values, beliefs, and norms. Groups used in this way are called **reference groups**. Reference groups may include families, teachers, college classmates, student government leaders, college Greek organizations, rock groups, or professional football squads.

Reference groups influence self-esteem and behavior. Say, for instance, that because of the imagined reaction by reference groups (such as parents and teachers), a student is motivated to study. The resulting grade point average creates a sense of accomplishment and boosted self-esteem.

You may have a reference group without being a member; you may only aspire to be a member. For example, you need not be a member of a ballet troupe to view dancers as a reference group. You need only assess yourself in terms of their standards and subscribe to their beliefs, values, and norms. Junior high school girls, for example, may imitate high school girls' leadership style or athletic interests. Junior high school boys may copy high school boys' taste in clothing and music.

Reference groups need not be positive. Observing the behavior of a group you dislike may reinforce a preference for contrary ways of acting, feeling, and behaving. For example, a violent gang may provide a blueprint for behavior to avoid.

In-Groups and Out-Groups

Q How is social life an interplay between in-groups and out-groups? In-groups and out-groups can exist only in relation to each other; one is the flip side of the other. An **in-group** encourages intense identification and loyalty. The level of identification and loyalty is sufficiently compelling that members tend to exclude others. An **out-group** is a group toward which in-group members feel opposition and competition. It is from membership in these groups that people divide into "we" and "they."

Q Where are these groups found? In-groups and out-groups develop in virtually every social arena—for example, college Greek organizations, athletic teams, political parties, racially or ethnically divided neighborhoods, and countries at war. Because of different tastes, perspectives, and values, everyone prefers some groups over others. And by virtue of being in some groups, you are out of others. As a college student, you can easily identify many of the in-groups and out-groups in your social landscape. For example, jocks and cheerleaders are in-groups for some, out-groups for others. Phi Beta Kappa is an in-group for its members and an out-group for students uninterested in academics. At Columbine High School, students knew about a number of cliques beyond the publicized jocks and cheerleaders—preppies, stoners, gangbangers, skaters, nerds. Different schools have variations of these in- and out-groups. At Austin High School in Texas, "kickers" wear oversized belt buckles, large hats, and cowboy boots. California schools have surfer cliques (A. Cohen 1999). A "we" versus "they" mentality can even develop between generations. Baby boomers (Americans born between 1945 and 1964), for instance, are accused of bashing Generation X (America's twenty-somethings) as unambitious complainers who want the good life handed to them (Giles 1994).

The formation of in-groups and out-groups depends on the establishment and protection of group boundaries. If nothing distinguishes "us" from "them," then there can be no "ins" and "outs." Group boundaries remind in-group members that movement over the line places them on the outside. To the outsiders, group boundaries form an entrance barrier (Hogg and Abrams 2001).

Q **How are group boundaries maintained?** Maintaining something as important as group boundaries requires commitment from the group members. Unfortunately, this may involve clashes with outsiders. Skinheads (neo-Nazis) periodically attack Jews or destroy their property. Members of an urban gang may injure or kill a member of another gang who has entered their territory. Boundaries are also maintained through group symbols. Symbols may be as benign as a right-to-life bumper sticker or as intentionally threatening as having one's head shaved. Groups also may adopt certain words and rituals (handshake, high five) to demarcate themselves. These are easily recognized at a social club initiation ceremony.

As this description of group boundaries suggests, in-group and out-group relationships can have serious consequences. Let's consider some of these repercussions.

Q **What is the sociological importance of in-groups and out-groups?** Membership in an in-group has both positive and negative aspects. Those on the inside may benefit from heightened self-esteem and a sense of social identity. However, in-group members may foster an inflated sense of their own worth while promoting an unrealistically negative view of others. Alison Gopnik states it this way:

> When you divide people into arbitrary groups the "in-group" will start to dehumanize and dislike the "out-group." Give a bunch of undergraduates red feathers and blue feathers to wear, and very quickly the red feathers will start to prefer the company of other red feathers, and decide that the blue feathers just aren't their type. You don't need a long history of conflict or oppression to hate another group. Just giving them a different name is enough. (Gopnik 2009:218)

This distortion of reality, which in-groups often deliberately create, is self-deluding. If such self-delusion becomes central to the identity of in-group members, psychological and social development is retarded. Moreover, some members may be personally damaged, not realizing the false basis for their self-esteem.

Harm is not confined to in-group members. In fact, out-group members experience many more negative effects. The increase in self-esteem enjoyed by in-group members can come at the expense of outsiders. Even more serious is the physical damage that may be done by extremist groups such as neo-Nazis or certain religious factions willing to kill others in the name of their deity (O'Brien and Palmer 1993). Historically, racial or ethnic majorities have viewed minorities as outsiders—effectively denying them everything from a sense of worth to equal opportunity (Schaefer 2010). Males have been accused of using a similar pattern of dominance against females (Andersen 2010).

In-group/out-group relationships, of course, generally do not take such extreme forms. Spirited competition among sororities and friendly athletic rivalries are more typical expressions of these groups. The relative harmlessness of most cases, however, should not mask the potentially serious consequences of in-groups and out-groups, consequences related to conflict, power, and self-respect.

Social Networks

Q **What are social networks?** As individuals and as members of primary and secondary groups, we interact with many people. All of a person's social relationships constitute his or her **social network**—a web of social relationships that joins a person to other people and groups. This total set of social relationships—this social network—includes family members, colleagues, classmates, physicians, church members, close friends, car mechanics, and store clerks. Social networks tie us to hundreds or thousands of people within our community, throughout the country, and even around the world (Doreian and Stokman 1997; Bruggeman 2008).

The Internet is expanding the amount of interaction and the flow of information within networks. Before the Internet, for example, environmental activists across the United States had to depend on slower, more cumbersome means of communication, such as the print media, the telephone, and letter writing. Through Facebook and twitter, for example, environmental organizations can supply almost unlimited information to anyone with access to the Web. For example, volunteers can now easily recruit others to join them in addressing the Chesapeake Bay's environmental problems. Protests in various regions of the country can be organized very quickly, and feedback among network members can be instantaneous.

This increased ease, speed, and frequency of social contact can promote a sense of membership in a particular network. Whereas opponents to gun control were once largely unaware of one another, they may now feel part of a nationwide social network.

Q Are social networks groups? Although a person's social network includes groups, it is not a group per se. A social network lacks the boundaries of a group, and it does not necessarily involve close or continuous interaction. Because many of the relationships are sporadic and indirect, not all participants experience a feeling of membership. Although a social network does not preclude close ties—like those of college alums who maintain contact via Facebook and twitter—most ties in a social network are secondary in nature.

Q How strong are the ties in a social network? Social relationships within a network involve both strong and weak ties (Granovetter 1973; L. C. Freeman 1992). Strong ties exist in primary relationships, such as those with one's parents or spouse. These ties are emotionally close and intimate and are based on a genuine concern for the other person(s). Weak ties, most often found in secondary relationships, include salespersons, distant relatives, and most coworkers. These ties are more impersonal and goal oriented (Mizruchi and Stearns 2001).

The number and type of strong ties are heavily influenced by level of education. More highly educated people have a larger number of strong ties, a greater variety of strong ties, and more strong ties outside the family. Not unexpectedly, older people have fewer strong ties;

CHECK YOURSELF 6.1 R2

Concept of the Group and Types of Groups

1. A _____ is composed of several people who are in contact with one another; share some ways of thinking, feeling, and behaving; take one another's behavior into account; and have one or more interests in common.

2. A _____ group is composed of people who are emotionally close, who know one another well, who seek one another's company because they enjoy being together, and who have a "we" feeling.

3. Listed here are some examples of primary and secondary relationships. Indicate which examples are most likely to be primary relationships (P) and which are most likely to be secondary relationships (S).
   ___ a. a marine recruit and his drill instructor at boot camp
   ___ b. a married couple
   ___ c. a manager and his professional baseball team
   ___ d. professors and students
   ___ e. car salespersons and their prospective customers

4. Which of the following is *not* a condition that promotes the development of primary groups?
   ___ a. small group size
   ___ b. face-to-face contact
   ___ c. continuous contact
   ___ d. interaction on the basis of status or role

5. Match the following terms and statements:
   ___ a. group   (1) skinheads
   ___ b. in-group   (2) spectators at a Fourth of July fireworks display
   ___ c. social aggregate   (3) orchid growers
   ___ d. social category   (4) teenage subculture
   ___ e. reference group   (5) members of a regular Saturday night poker game

6. A _____ is a web of social relationships that joins a person directly to other people and groups and, through those individuals and groups, indirectly to additional parties.

Answers: 1. group; 2. primary; 3. a. (S), b. (P), c. (S), d. (S), e. (S); 4. d.; 5. a. (5), b. (1), c. (2), d. (3), e. (4); 6. social network

and outside the home, urban dwellers have more strong ties than do rural residents. Although women have as many strong ties as men, more of these ties are within the family (C. S. Fischer 1982; Marsden 1987).

Q **What are the functions of social networks?** Social networks serve several important functions. First, networks provide a sense of belonging (Putnam 2001). Second, they furnish support in the form of help and advice. Third, networks are a useful tool for those entering the labor market. Getting to know relevant people is often useful to one's career (Putnam 1996; Petersen, Saporta, and Seidel 2000). Finally, networks can bring people together who have not been in contact for a while or who otherwise would never meet. Facebook helps locate past schoolmates, old friends, or even past loves. Online dating Websites like Match.com and eHarmony connect one to a pool of dating possibilities otherwise unavailable.

The use of networks to locate new places of employment deserves special attention because of gender differences. Although the social networks of American females and males are equally extensive, men are more enmeshed in "good-old-boy networks" containing many higher-status contacts (Lin, Ensel, and Vaughn 1981). In the past, women tended to have more ties with family members and fewer higher-status ties. This situation is changing, however, as gender inequality diminishes in the United States and as more women are seeing networks as a pathway to higher status and more powerful positions.

Social Interaction in Groups **R1**

Social interaction is crucial to groups. Robert Nisbet (1970) describes five types of social interaction basic to group life: cooperation, conflict, social exchange, coercion, and conformity (see Table 6.2).

Cooperation

Q **What is cooperation, and when are people most likely to cooperate? Cooperation** is a form of interaction in which individuals or groups combine their efforts to reach some common goal. Cooperation usually occurs when reaching a goal depends on united resources and efforts. The survivors of a plane crash in a snow-covered mountain range must cooperate to survive. Victims of floods, mudslides, tornadoes, droughts, or famines must help one another to survive their crisis. This is not to say that cooperation exists only during emergencies. Children who agree to a set of rules for a game, couples who agree to share household duties, students who march in support of a community project, and groups who organize to prevent a major power-line installation are cooperating. Indeed, without some degree of cooperation, social life could not exist.

San Diego State and Brigham Young University, shown here, were two of more than sixty teams in the 2011 NCAA tournament. What forms of social interactions are involved within and between these teams?

TABLE 6.2

Illustrating Types of Social Interaction

A type of social interaction is illustrated from the viewpoint of a particular theoretical perspective. Each interaction can be viewed from either of the other two perspectives. Associate a type of social interaction with a different theoretical perspective, and make up your own example.

Theoretical Perspective	Type of Social Interaction	Example
Functionalism	Conformity	• Team integration is promoted when basketball players accept their roles on the floor.
Conflict theory	Coercion	• Conflict in prisons is kept in check by the superior power of the guards.
Symbolic interactionism	Social exchange	• Two college students may work together in preparing for an exam because passing a course carries the same symbolic value for each of them.

Conflict

Q What is conflict, and are all consequences negative?
Individuals or groups who work together to obtain certain benefits are cooperating. Those who work against one another for a larger share of the rewards are in **conflict.** In conflict, defeating the opponent is considered essential. In fact, defeating the opponent may become more important than achieving the goal and may bring more joy than winning the prize.

As pointed out earlier in "Using the Sociological Imagination," conflict is usually considered a disruptive form of interaction—one to be minimized or eliminated. A cooperative, peaceful society is assumed to be better than one in conflict. Although conflict does have some undesirable consequences, it can also be socially beneficial.

According to Georg Simmel (1858–1918), a major benefit of conflict is the promotion of cooperation and unity *within* opposing groups. Although conflict may lead to the separation of groups, it can strengthen relationships within groups. Thus, the Revolutionary War drew American colonists together even though it brought them into conflict with the British. Similarly, a labor union becomes more integrated during the process of collective bargaining. And police officers who attempt to stop a husband from physically abusing his wife may find themselves under attack by both mates. According to historian Stephen Oates (1977), the "outside meddling" of Stephen Douglas and other Democrats united the Illinois Republican party and secured the U.S. Senate nomination for Abraham Lincoln. The threat of an impeachment trial of President Clinton united the Democratic party during the 1998 congressional elections. And the events of 9/11 unified Americans with increased levels of patriotism.

Another positive consequence of conflict is the rejuvenation of norms and values. Equality of opportunity, freedom, and democracy have always been important values to Americans. But until the nonviolent civil rights demonstrations, the urban violence in large northern cities, and the abuse experienced by civil rights supporters, as well as the poverty, inequality, and lack of opportunity among America's minorities were largely invisible to white society. Once these problems were forcibly called to the public's attention, actions were taken to reaffirm these basic values. Among these actions were Lyndon Johnson's War on Poverty, the Civil Rights Act of 1964, the Equal Employment Opportunity Act of 1972, and affirmative action programs (Fineman 1992).

Conflict may also be beneficial when it challenges norms, beliefs, and values. Domestic opposition to the Vietnam War in the 1960s—which tragically involved unparalleled conflict and violence on college and university campuses—ended the military draft, brought into question the legitimacy of political and military intervention in other countries, enlarged the American value of patriotism to include opposition to certain wars, and encouraged higher education to be more responsive to students' needs. These events did alter some norms, beliefs, and values—a lesson not lost on African Americans during the 1992 riots in Los Angeles.

A study by Douglas Maynard (1985) concludes that conflict can have benefits even for young children. In a study of first-grade children, Maynard observed a sense of social structure emerging from disputes and arguments. Authority and friendship patterns were also the product of social conflict.

Social Exchange

Q What is the nature of a social exchange relationship?
In *The Nicomachean Ethics*, Aristotle observed:

> All men, or most men, wish what is noble but choose what is profitable; and while it is noble to render a service not with an eye to receiving one in return, it is profitable to receive one. One ought, therefore, if one can, to return the equivalent of services received, and to do so willingly.

In this passage, Aristotle touches on **social exchange,** a type of social interaction in which one person voluntarily does something for another, expecting a reward

Supporters greet President-elect Barack Obama after his 2008 Democratic nomination victory. Is social interaction between Obama and his supporters an example of cooperation or exchange?

Ryan Anson/AFP/Getty Images

in return. If one person helps a friend paint his or her room, expecting that some equivalent help will be returned, the relationship is one of exchange. In an exchange relationship, it is the benefit derived rather than the relationship itself that is central. An individual who does something for someone else obligates that person. This obligation can be repaid only by a return favor. Thus, the basis of an exchange relationship is reciprocity, the idea that you should do for others as they have done for you (P. M. Blau 1986).

Exchange relationships are not always exploitative; many exchange relationships are based on trust, gratitude, and affection. You may help someone move out of a dormitory into an apartment because he or she has been friendly to you. You may expect some response—help when you move, or maybe just an expression of appreciation. We usually do anticipate some response even though we may be unaware of it.

Q **What is the difference between cooperation and exchange?** Although both cooperation and social exchange involve working together, there is a significant difference between these two types of interaction. In cooperation, individuals or groups work together to achieve a shared goal. Reaching this goal, however, may or may not benefit those who are cooperating. And although individuals or groups may profit from cooperating, that is not their main objective. For example, a group may work to build and maintain an adequate supply of blood for a local blood bank without thought of personal benefit. If, however, the primary objective of the group is to guarantee blood availability for its own members, then it has an exchange relationship with the blood bank. In cooperation, the question is, How can we reach our goal? In exchange relationships, the implied question is, What's in it for me?

Coercion

Q **In what way is coercion an involuntary interaction?** In **coercion**, an individual or a group compels others to behave in certain ways. The central element is domination. In a sense, coercion is an unequal exchange: Because of superior power, someone can get something from someone else without repaying. Domination may occur through physical force, such as imprisonment, torture, or death. But coercion is generally expressed more subtly through social pressure—ridicule, rejection, ostracism, withdrawal of love, denial of recognition. Coercion is a part of many social relationships. Parents may coerce children with a curfew; employers may coerce employees with dismissal; professors may coerce students to study via the threat of a test. Obviously, conflict theory underlies this type of social interaction.

Conformity

Q **Do most people conform to group pressures?** **Conformity** is behavior matching group expectations. When we conform, we adapt our behavior to fit the behavior of those around us. While some people are more likely to conform than others are, most people conform to the expectations of some group most of the time. Social life—with all its uniformity, predictability, and orderliness—simply could not exist without this type of social interaction. Without conformity, there could be no universities, governments, or places of worship; without conformity, there could be no culture or social structures (see "Consider This Research").

The Business of Groups

Nineteenth-century social philosopher Georg Simmel was one of the first to recognize the importance of groups for society. But, he argued, group members face a dilemma. Belonging to a group requires that members submit to social control, losing some personal freedom in the process. If these people remain outside the group, however, they lose such possible benefits of membership as economic security and social acceptance (Simmel 1964; originally published in 1908). For this reason, most groups encounter both cooperation and conflict. Because these pressures can interfere with the smooth functioning of the groups, social scientists have devoted considerable attention to task accomplishment within groups, various leadership styles for groups, and group decision making.

Q **What is the nature of task accomplishment within groups?** Most groups are designed to accomplish certain tasks, which can range from planning leisure activities to manufacturing a product. At the same time, members of groups have self-images and desires that do not necessarily mesh with the goals of the group as a whole. Beginning with Robert Bales (1950), social scientists have tried to understand the ways in which task accomplishment within groups could expedite both the achievement of the group's goals and the needs of individual group members.

When Bales developed a scheme, called *interaction process analysis*, he identified two basic problems that any social system must address. First, the group must solve *instrumental problems*. These are the issues that directly relate to achieving the goals of the group. A group trying to elect a political candidate must find solutions regarding fund-raising, advertising, arrangements for speeches and rallies, charges from the opposing candidate, and so on. Second, a group faces *social-emotional problems*. These challenges are the problems that involve individual satisfaction, disagreements, and other related matters that inevitably

Stanley Milgram—Group Pressure and Conformity

Can a group move a normally nonviolent person to physically and severely punish a victim? As incredible as this may sound, researcher Stanley Milgram (1964) revealed this as a possibility.

As noted in the text, Solomon Asch (1955) demonstrated that group pressure can influence people to such an extent that they will deny their true sense perceptions. Specifically, they can be pressured to match up uneven lines—lines they originally perceived as different lengths. Milgram wanted to know if group pressure could have the same effect on behavior. Can group pressure cause people to treat others in ways they otherwise would not?

To test this question, Milgram could have chosen a behavior relatively easy to induce, such as sharing food with a stranger or doing minor damage to someone else's property. Instead, Milgram asked research participants to administer increasingly higher electric shocks to people who appeared to be in pain. And these research participants were people just like you and me!

Milgram placed eighty males in an experimental situation in which a team of three individuals (one naive subject who did not know the nature of the experiment and two "confederates" who did know the nature of the experiment) tested a fourth person (another confederate in the experiment) on a learning task. Each mistake by the fourth party brought an apparent electric shock from the

naive subject. The two confederate "testers" (participants cooperating with Milgram) on each team suggested increasingly higher shock levels for successive mistakes made by the "learner" (the confederate in the electric chair). The researcher recorded the degree to which the team's naive member resisted or went along with group pressure to increase the voltage levels.

After explaining to the naive tester that the experiment was investigating the effects of punishment (electric shocks) on memory, the researcher strapped the learner into an electric-chair apparatus in full view of the other three team members. These three were seated in front of a large shock generator whose switches were labeled from 15 to 450 volts in 15-volt increments. The lowest-level group of switches was labeled "Slight Shock"; the highest-level group of switches read "Danger: Severe Shock."

The naive subject controlled the maximum shock that could be administered. He could keep the shock level at 15 volts throughout or increase the shock level in line with the group's recommendation. It was his decision.

The learner in the electric chair not only answered questions; as the shocks became stronger, he grunted, protested, and finally demanded that the experiment stop. Each of these complaints was actually prerecorded and played in coordination with a given shock level. No discomfort was indicated until a 75-volt shock was administered. At 120 volts, the learner shouted that the shocks were becoming painful. Groans followed a 135-volt shock, and at 150 volts, the learner cried out to be released from the experiment, complaining of a heart condition. At 180 volts, the learner cried out, "I can't stand the pain," and 285 volts was followed by an agonized scream. From 300 to 450 volts, the victim continuously shouted desperately that he would no longer answer questions.

Milgram first needed to know how far the naive subject would go in administering shocks *without* group influence. To accomplish this, an identical experiment was run minus the two confederates in the punishing group. Response to group pressure was measured by the difference in the naive subject's behavior in the two situations.

Group pressure heavily affected the level of shock administered by the naive subject. That is, the average shock level in the three-person situation was significantly higher than in the one-person situation. Perhaps most interesting are the results on *maximum* shock levels. When alone, only two naive subjects went beyond the point where the learner first vehemently protested. Under group pressure, twenty-seven of the naive subjects went beyond this point. Nineteen of the naive subjects went above 255 volts ("Intense Shock"), and ten went into the group of voltages labeled "Danger: Severe Shock." Seven even reached 450 volts (the highest shock level possible).

The research by Milgram and Asch reveals the power of group pressure to create conformity in thought and behavior. Although conformity must occur to a degree for social structure and society to exist, many scholars worry about the extent to which social pressure can determine how humans think and act.

Evaluate the Research

1. Discuss the ethical implications of Milgram's experiment. (You may want to refer to Chapter 2 for pointers about ethics in social research.)
2. If the researcher had not been present as an authority figure during the experiment to approve the use of all shock levels, do you think group pressure would have been as effective? Explain.

arise whenever individuals try to coordinate their activities.

A number of laboratory studies conducted by Bales and his associates have further indicated the significance of both instrumental and social-emotional processes, as Stephen Wilson notes:

> . . . if the group is going to do its job, (1) task-oriented interaction must be high; (2) more answers must be given than questions asked; (3) there must be more interaction contributing to the solidarity of the group (positive social-emotional) than detracting from solidarity (negative social-emotional). In other words, there must be, as Bales's theory suggests, some degree of balance to keep the individuals together as a group. (S. Wilson 1978:66–67)

Q What is the nature of leadership in groups? It was once believed that leaders are born and that people have to possess certain traits to be effective as leaders. It is now known that no leadership trait is absolutely necessary for effective leadership, but Ralph Stogdill suggests that successful leaders are likely to have the following combination of traits:

> The leader is characterized by a strong drive for responsibility and task completion, vigor and persistence in pursuit of goals, venturesomeness and originality in problem solving, drive to exercise initiative in social situations, self-confidence and sense of personal identity, willingness to accept consequences of decision and action, readiness to absorb interpersonal stress, willingness to tolerate frustration and delay, ability to influence other persons' behavior, and capacity to structure social interaction systems to the purpose at hand. (Stogdill 1974:81)

Because such traits must further develop into action, considerable research focuses on leadership behavior. Studies by Rensis Likert (1961, 1967) emphasize the importance of supportive behavior, in which leaders try to provide direction in a way that maintains others' sense of personal worth and importance. Similarly, Ralph White and Ronald Lippitt (1960) found that democratic leaders (who try to build consensus about decisions) are more effective than authoritarian ones (who give orders without considering the preferences of group members). Both, however, were more effective than laissez-faire leaders (who make little or no attempt to organize group activities). Subsequent studies suggest that appropriate leadership behavior depends on the situation presented by the group to be led. Fred Fiedler (1967), for example, argues that leaders should be more authoritarian if they face a situation in which they have very high or very low amounts of control. In intermediate situations, leaders should be more democratic and concerned with the quality of human relationships.

If Fiedler's theory is correct, the popular leader of an infantry platoon (high control) or the disliked supervisor of an ineffective work crew (low control) should be more authoritarian than the well-liked director of a research team facing an unstructured task (intermediate control). Fiedler's theory has been criticized on several grounds, but it is an indication of the increasing tendency for social scientists to understand leadership in its situational context (Ashour 1973; Schriesheim and Kerr 1977).

Q Can groups make better decisions than individuals? We use groups in many settings to solve a variety of problems. In some situations, group decisions are superior to the decisions made by individuals. For example, researchers find that groups are useful for solving intellectual tasks because they allow people to hear several points of view and provide a setting in which the merits of various ideas can be discussed (H. H. Kelley and Thibaut 1969).

However, group pressure can also harm the quality of decisions by leading to excessive conformity and loss of individuality. The Spanish writer José Rodó writes that "every society to which you remain bound robs you of a part of your essence and replaces it with a speck of the gigantic personality which is its own."

These business people are in the process of making a decision. Name one possible positive consequence and one negative consequence of group decision making.

Actually, the same thing could be said of each group to which an individual is strongly committed. For the sake of group membership, we may relinquish part of our individuality and independence.

The tendency to conform to group pressure is dramatically illustrated in a classic experiment by Solomon Asch (1955) in which many participants publicly denied their own senses in order not to deviate from majority opinion. Asch assembled numerous small groups of male college students, ostensibly for experiments in visual judgment. He asked the groups to compare the length of lines printed on two cards (see Figure 6.1). One card showed a single vertical line, which was to be used as a standard for comparison with three lines of different lengths on a second card. Each participant was asked to identify the line on the second card that matched in length one of the lines on the first card. In each group, all but one of the subjects were instructed by Asch to choose a line that obviously did not match. The naive subject—the only member of each group unaware of the real nature of the experiment—was forced either to select the line he actually thought matched the standard line or to yield to the unanimous opinion of the group. In earlier tests of individuals in isolation, Asch had found that the error rate in matching the lines was only 1 percent. Under group pressure, however, the naive subjects went along with the majority's wrong opinion over one-third of the time. If this large proportion of naive subjects yielded to group pressure in a group of strangers, it is not difficult to imagine the conformity in groups to which people are emotionally committed (Myers 2001).

Q How does *groupthink* discourage alternative points of view? Irving Janis (2006) argues that many group decisions are likely to be the product of **groupthink**, a

FIGURE 6.1

Cards for Asch's Experiments

Which of the lines on card A matches the line on card B? You must be thinking, "What a no-brainer." You may be surprised to learn that in a group setting, many people associated the other two lines in card A with the line on card B. Read about Asch's experiment in the text.

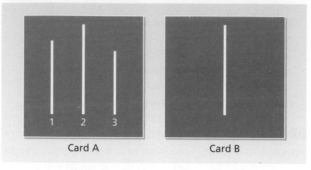

Card A   Card B

situation in which pressures toward uniformity discourage members of the group from expressing their reservations about group decisions. During the Kennedy administration, for example, a decision to launch the ill-fated Bay of Pigs invasion against Cuba was made only because several top advisers to the president failed to reveal their reservations about the plan. Another example of groupthink is said to be found in the George W. Bush administration's buildup to the invasion of Iraq in 2003. The small number of designers of this plan is accused of selecting only intelligence that could lead to allegations of the presence of weapons of mass destruction, as well as the presence of Al Qaeda in Saddam Hussein's Iraq. This would convince those who did not share their convictions that war was necessary (Heilbrunn 2008; Kaplan 2008; Weisberg 2008). Such

CHECK YOURSELF   6.2   R2

Social Interaction in Groups

1. Match the following types of social interaction with the examples beside them:
   _4_ a. cooperation   (1) paid blood donors
   _3_ b. conflict   (2) students doing what a professor assigns
   _1_ c. social exchange   (3) Saddam Hussein invading Kuwait
   _5_ d. coercion   (4) flood victims helping each other
   _2_ e. conformity   (5) employees forced to work overtime or be fired

2. According to Robert Bales, interaction within groups must be designed to solve both _____ problems and _____ problems.

3. Social scientists agree that leaders must have certain traits if they are to be effective. T or F?

4. Solomon Asch's experiment demonstrates the positive consequences of group pressure. T or F?

5. A situation in which pressures toward uniformity discourage members of a group from expressing their reservations about group decisions is called _____.

Answers: 1. a. (4), b. (3), c. (1), d. (5), e. (2); 2. instrumental, social-emotional; 3. F; 4. F; 5. groupthink

hesitancy to destroy the illusion of "assumed consensus" often leads to group decisions that have not been subjected to critical evaluation. Research indicates that groupthink can be avoided only when leaders or group members make a conscious effort to see that all group members participate actively and that points of disagreement and conflict are tolerated.

We have been viewing groups as relatively small social units. Now, we turn to larger social units known as formal organizations. It will become evident that groups are very much a part of any formal organization.

Formal Organizations 🔳

Even in the early 1900s, Charles Horton Cooley (1902) foresaw a shift from primary groups toward secondary groups. Until the 1930s, most Americans lived on farms or in small towns and villages. Nearly all of their daily lives were spent in primary groups—families, neighborhoods, and churches. As industrialization and urbanization advanced, however, Americans became more enmeshed in secondary groups. Born in hospitals, educated in large schools, employed by huge corporations, regulated by government agencies, cared for in nursing homes, and buried by funeral establishments, Americans—like members of other industrialized societies—find themselves within secondary groups known as *formal organizations*. This major change accompanies the transition from preindustrial to industrial society. The trend is continuing. Citizens of modern societies are highly dependent on large organizations—both business and nonbusiness.

Understanding the nature of organizations is essential to comprehending industrial and postindustrial society (Blau and Meyer 1987; Pfeffer 1997; Hodson and Sullivan 2008; Kramer 2010; Lune 2010).

Theoretical Perspectives and Formal Organizations

Although it is not always explicit, functionalism and conflict theory are intimately involved in the sociological study of formal organizations. Bureaucracy, for example, with its emphasis on structure, stability, rules, and hierarchy, is based squarely on functionalism. When sociologists examine the dynamics of organizations, they don't abandon functionalism, but conflict theory does play a predominant role.

The Structure of Formal Organizations

A **formal organization** is deliberately created to achieve one or more goals. Examples of formal organizations are high schools, colleges, corporations, government agencies, and hospitals.

Q **How are formal organizations and bureaucracies related?** Most formal organizations today are **bureaucracies**—formal organizations based on rationality and efficiency. Although bureaucracies are popularly thought of as monuments to inefficiency, they prove to be an efficient form of organization for industrial society. Despite his deep concern about its negative consequences, Max Weber, who first analyzed the nature of bureaucracy, wrote of its efficiency.

These impatient bank customers are clearly experiencing the effects of formal organizational structure. Do you think most organizations are bureaucratic in nature?

Randy Faris/Corbis Super RF/Alamy Limited

Q What are the major characteristics of bureaucracy?
From a study of history and an observation of events of his day, Max Weber sketched the basic organizational principles that were being developed to promote rational and efficient administration. Weber identified the following characteristics of a bureaucracy:

- *The organization has a division of labor based on the principle of specialization.* In a bureaucracy, each person is responsible for certain functions or tasks. (See Figure 6.2 for an organizational chart outlining the division of labor in a modern university.) A specialized division of labor improves organizational performance because an individual can become an expert in a limited area of organizational activity.
- *The organization has a hierarchy of authority.* To clarify the concept of authority, it is necessary to distinguish it from power. **Power** is to the ability to control the behavior of others, even against their will. **Authority** is the exercise of legitimate power—power that produces compliance because those subjected to it believe that obedience is the proper response. Bureaucratic organizations tend to have a pyramidal shape. The greatest amount of authority is concentrated in the few positions at

the top, with decreasing amounts in the expanding number of lower positions (see Figure 6.2). Organizational effectiveness and efficiency are enhanced by a hierarchy that can coordinate the many statuses involved in a highly specialized organization.

- *Organizational affairs are based on a system of rules and procedures.* Rules and procedures guide the performance of work and provide a framework for decision making. They stabilize the organization because they coordinate activities and cover most situations.
- *Members of the organization maintain written records of their organizational activities.* These records of work and activities are kept in files. This organizational "memory" is essential to smooth functioning, stability, and continuity.
- *Statuses in the organization—especially managerial ones—are considered full-time jobs.* Bureaucratic statuses are not considered avocational. This increases the commitment of the organization's members and demands their full attention.
- *Relationships within the organization are impersonal, devoid of favoritism.* For example, personnel are selected on the basis of technical and

FIGURE 6.2

University Organization Chart

Each organizational position and department within a bureaucracy has certain tasks associated with it. The connecting lines indicate who reports to whom and who has authority over whom.

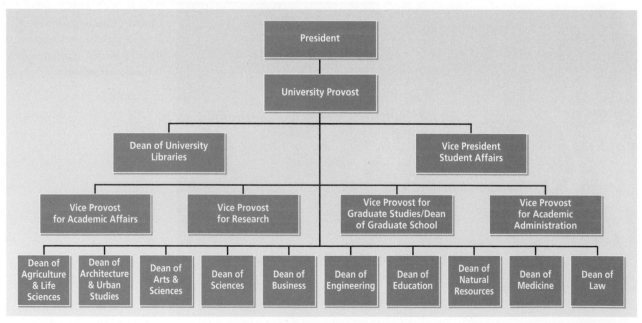

professional qualifications and promoted on the basis of merit. Similarly, relationships with clients are conducted without regard to personal considerations. The norms prohibiting the influence of favoritism and personal relationships in organizational activities are intended to ensure equal treatment for those who work in the organization as well as for those who are served by it.

- *Employees of bureaucratic organizations do not own their positions.* Bureaucratic positions cannot be sold or inherited. This allows organizations to fill positions with the most qualified people. Those in bureaucratic positions are held responsible for their use of equipment and facilities.

For Weber, bureaucratic organization involved a set of strategies that would promote order in human relationships. Weber believed that the achievement of order would be increasingly difficult in societies undergoing industrialization. (See "Sociology Eyes America.") In preindustrial societies, activities in one aspect of life were related to activities in every other aspect. As societies modernized, people's activities became less closely related, and traditional systems of norms and values began to weaken. As Kenneth Thompson (1980) indicates, Weber saw bureaucracy—with its hierarchy of authority, system of rules and procedures, and inherent safeguards—as a way to maintain control in an increasingly complex society.

Q **Do modern organizations practice these characteristics of bureaucracy?** In his formulation of bureaucratic characteristics, Weber used the **ideal-type method**. This method isolates, to the point of exaggeration, the most basic characteristics of some social entity. It involves the construction of a *pure* type. Because real life is seldom as pure as an abstract description, social entities do not have all the characteristics of an ideal type to the maximum degree. Universities, for example, are less bureaucratic than business firms, in part because universities employ large numbers of professionals whose quality of work is adversely affected by a bureaucratic environment (Litwak 1961).

Practically speaking, then, the characteristics of bureaucracy are best thought of as a series of continua; various organizations emphasize each characteristic of bureaucracy to different degrees. In fact, some units within an organization may be more bureaucratic than others (R. H. Hall 1962). In a university, for example, the president's office is much more bureaucratic than an academic department of philosophy or biology. The more closely an organization is based on the characteristics identified by Weber, the more bureaucratic it is.

SOCIOLOGY EYES AMERICA 6.1

Membership in Labor Unions

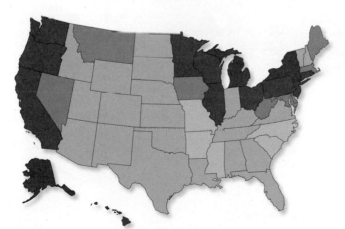

Union Membership Rates (2009)

20% or above
15.0%–19.9%
10.0%–14.9%
5.0%–9.9%
4.9% or below

Source: U.S. Department of Labor, Bureau of Labor Statistics, 2009.

Labor unions, organizations created by workers to improve working conditions, are bureaucracies. They have a division of labor, a hierarchy of authority, a system of rules and procedures, written records, and promotion based on merit within the organization. This map shows the percentage of employed workers in each state who are members of labor unions.

Interpret the Map

1. Which states had the highest union membership rates in 2009? Which states had the lowest rates?
2. Why do you think it is that not all workers are members of labor unions?

Advantages of Bureaucracy

Q **What are the advantages of bureaucracy?** Citing the advantages of bureaucracy, Weber wrote:

> *The decisive reason for the advance of bureaucratic organization has always been its purely technical superiority over any other form of organization. The fully developed bureaucratic mechanism compares with other organizations exactly as does the machine with the nonmechanical modes of production.* (Gerth and Mills 1958:214)

Weber's model of bureaucracy was formulated in response to the inadequacies of earlier organization forms. In monarchies, for example, positions were appointed on the basis of favoritism and politics. Administrators had little or no training for the work they were doing. Because these officials were wealthy, administration was only an avocation. And because high positions were politically based, power could be lost overnight. Moreover, when a king or queen was replaced, the entire leadership structure changed drastically.

As Weber correctly saw, earlier types of organizational structure were out of step with the rise of the capitalist market economy, which required steadiness, precision, continuity, speed, efficiency, and minimum cost—advantages bureaucracy could offer. **Rationalism**—the solution of problems on the basis of logic, data, and planning rather than tradition and superstition—was on the rise, and the characteristics of bureaucracy were consistent with this sweeping trend. (See "Think Globally 6.1.")

As strange as it might sound, bureaucracy is designed to protect individuals. Without rules, procedures, and the norm of impersonal treatment (which everyone hates), decision making would be arbitrary. It might sound great, for example, to abolish final exams; but then grading might not be as objective. This, of course, is not to say that most professors in a nonbureaucratic setting would be abusive or that favoritism does not occur in bureaucratic organizations. Nevertheless, formally established rules and procedures and the norm of impersonality ensure an important degree of equal treatment.

THINK GLOBALLY **6.1**

Human Development

Each year, the United Nations ranks the countries of the world in terms of their human development. The human development index (HDI) is based on each country's life expectancy, educational attainment, and adjusted real income. This map shows how the world's countries ranked on the HDI in 2010.

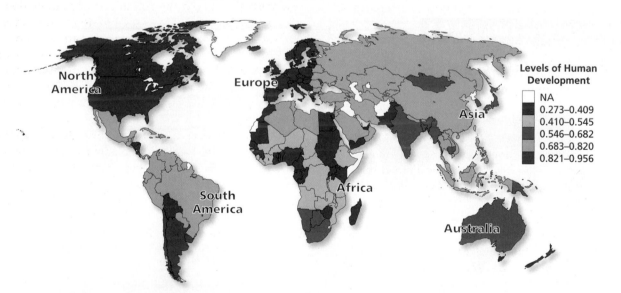

Levels of Human Development

- NA
- 0.273–0.409
- 0.410–0.545
- 0.546–0.682
- 0.683–0.820
- 0.821–0.956

Source: United Nations Development Programme, *Human Development Report 2010*.

Interpret the Map

Support or refute the following statement: "To achieve a high ranking on the HDI, a country must have well-established and stable bureaucracies in the areas of health care, education, and the economy."

A famous account of the benefits of specialization is found in Adam Smith's *The Wealth of Nations.* Published in 1776, this book attempts to answer the question: What is the source of wealth in a society? For centuries, the mercantilists found wealth in the gold and silver in the royal treasury. Smith, expressing the new economic thought of the French physiocrats, gives a different answer: The wealth of nations resides in the productive power of labor, power that is best promoted by the division of labor. Smith illustrates with a description of a pin factory, citing the benefits that come when "one man draws out the wire, another straightens it, a third cuts it, a fourth points it, a fifth grinds it at the top for receiving the head" (A. Smith 1965:4/1776). By this process, Smith notes, ten men working in the factory can make 48,000 pins daily, whereas a man working alone could make only 20 or so pins. Recognizing pin making as a "trifling" example, Smith emphasizes that the division of labor is readily applicable to any type of "art and manufacture."

Disadvantages of Bureaucracy

Q **What are the disadvantages of bureaucracy?** Although Weber praised bureaucracy as the most efficient type of organization, he expressed concern that the formal rationality of bureaucracy would lead to socially undesirable outcomes. ("See Sociology in Your Life" highlights undesirable consequences of bureaucracy in a digital world.) For one thing, Weber noted that bureaucracy represented "the concentration of the material means of management in the hands of the master" (Gerth and Mills 1958:221). This leads to concerns about the person who controls bureaucratic organizations. In the words of Charles Perrow, one of the foremost contemporary scholars of organizations:

At present, without huge, disruptive, and perilous changes, we cannot survive without large organizations. Organizations mobilize social resources for ends that are often essential and even desirable. But organizations also concentrate those resources in the hands of a few who are prone to use them for ends we do not approve of, for ends we may not even be aware of, and, more frightening still, for ends we are led to accept because we are not in a position to conceive alternative ones. The investigation of these fearful possibilities has too long been left to writers, journalists, and radical political leaders. It is time that organizational theorists began to use their expertise to uncover the true nature of bureaucracy. This will require a better understanding both of the virtues of bureaucracy and its largely unexplored dangers. (Perrow 1986:6)

Weber himself raised the specter of what he called the *iron cage of rationality.* He feared the likelihood of rationality spreading to all aspects of social life, creating a dehumanizing social environment and entrapping everyone. George Ritzer (1998, 2009, 2011) refers to the "McDonaldization of society" as a metaphor to express Weber's iron cage of rationality. McDonald's, Ritzer argues, is the epitome of rationalism in organizations. On the dehumanizing effects of extreme rationality, Ritzer writes:

. . . fast-food restaurants are . . . often dehumanizing settings in which to eat or work. Customers lining up for a burger or waiting in the drive-through line, and workers preparing the food often feel as though they are part of an assembly line. Hardly amenable to eating, assembly lines have been shown to be inhuman settings in which to work. (Ritzer 2004:17)

It is the McDonaldization of everything from lube jobs to medicine that Ritzer believes threatens modern society with Weber's iron-cage nightmare. If the nightmare is still there when we awaken, then the rational has become irrational (Alfino, Caputo, and Wynyard 1998).

Although Weber was deeply concerned about the societal implications of bureaucracy, others have focused on bureaucracy's internal inefficiencies (Hummel 1987; Leibenstein 1987). The famous Parkinson's law, named after C. Northcote Parkinson (1993), states that work always expands to fill the time available for its completion. According to this principle, there is often little relationship between the amount of work to be done and the size of the staff assigned to do it. Thus, even when there is more staff than needed to do a given amount of work, those assigned to do the work will always find plenty to do, and their supervisors may even feel that additional help is needed. Parkinson's law is obviously intended to portray wastefulness in bureaucracies.

It is important to note that Parkinson's law applies to the bureaucratic form. The blame for wastefulness in bureaucracy lies not with lazy individuals but with the way this type of organization grows. According to Parkinson, the phenomenon he describes exists because bureaucrats want to multiply the number of people under them in the hierarchy and because bureaucrats spend much of their time creating work for one another.

In addition, although promotion on the basis of merit is supposed to decrease favoritism and increase efficiency, it may also have some drawbacks. Those selected for promotion in an organization are, if the system is based on merit, those who are doing their present jobs well. As long as they continue to do well in their new jobs, these people are likely to continue to be promoted. The problem, according

Privacy in a Digital World

In *The Unwanted Gaze*, Jeffrey Rosen (2000) attempts to document the destruction of privacy in the United States. He examines the legal, technological, and social changes eroding control over personal information. Because even deleted e-mail, for example, can be retrieved by others, a record of private self-disclosures exists permanently. Private preferences, tastes, and tendencies are revealed on every Website we hit. During the impeachment of President Clinton, prosecutors legally gained access to Monica Lewinsky's bookstore purchases and unsent love letters on her own computer.

If Monica Lewinsky's loss of privacy is shocking to you, consider workplace vulnerability. Probably more than three-fourths of the

Fortune 1,000 companies now have employee-monitoring software, and many of these firms keep their monitoring practices secret. More and more corporations are firing employees who violate prohibitions against the personal use or abuse of telecommunications technology. E-mailing a friend or coworker a heated threat to file a discrimination suit against the company for failing to promote you could result in termination even if you later deleted it (Faltermayer 2000). Business ethicist Laura Hartman offers this sobering picture:

A multitude of basic and inexpensive computer monitoring products allows managers to track web use, to observe downloaded files, to filter sites, to restrict your access to certain sites, and to know how much time you have spent on various sites. These include products such as WebSense, Net Access Manager, WebTrack and Internet Watchdog.

One particular firm, SpyShop.com, claims to service one-third of the Fortune 500 firms. This firm sells items such as a truth-telling device that links to a telephone. You are told that you can interview a job candidate on the phone and the device identifies those who lie. Another firm, Omnitracks, sells a satellite that fastens to the top or inside of a truck. The product allows trucking firms to locate trucks at all times. If a driver veers off the highway to get flowers for her or his partner on Valentine's Day, the firm will know what happened.

SpyZone.com sells an executive investigator kit that includes the truth phone I mentioned earlier, as well as a pocket recording pen. Other outlets sell pinhole lens camera pens, microphones that fit in your pocket. The motto of one firm is "In God we trust. All others we monitor." That firm offers a beeper buster: a computer program that monitors calls placed to beepers within a certain vicinity. A screen on your computer will show you all the numbers so that you can determine whether the individual is being distracted during working hours. (Hartman 2000:12)

Think About It

To what extent do employees have a right to privacy in the workplace? Analyze workplace privacy from a functionalist, conflict, and symbolic interactionist perspective.

---

to Laurence Peter and Raymond Hull (1996), is that people are promoted until they find themselves in jobs that are beyond their capabilities. Thus, according to the Peter Principle, employees in a bureaucratic hierarchy tend to rise to their level of incompetence. Organization members who have reached their level of incompetence shift their concern from performing competent work to sustaining organization values. They also begin to evaluate subordinates on the basis of promptness, courtesy, and cooperativeness rather than competence.

In *The Organization Man*, William H. Whyte (1972; Whyte and Nocera 2002) maintains that organizations have become so influential that they shape our nature. Organizations, Whyte argues, reward people who are good team players and who can sell their personalities

and promote the organization at the same time. "Organization men and women" sell themselves, adjust to different social environments, remain flexible, remain uncommitted to any set of values, and adjust their personalities to the people and groups around them.

These popular ideas about bureaucracy have gained wide acceptance, even though Parkinson's law and the Peter Principle were both satirically written. It is not that these ideas are necessarily wrong; we simply cannot evaluate their validity at this time because they defy scientific study. There are, however, other negative consequences of bureaucracy that are more widely recognized by social scientists. Among these are goal displacement and trained incapacity.

Eating fast food seems like a harmless activity (fat content aside). However, many sociologists think the rationality and standardization undergirding fast-food industry promote dehumanization. Do you?

Q What is goal displacement? When organizational rules and regulations become more important than organizational goals, **goal displacement** occurs (Merton 1968). Professors who emphasize grades more than learning are practicing goal displacement. Social workers who become more concerned with eligibility requirements than with delivering services are engaging in goal displacement.

Q What is trained incapacity? According to Thorstein Veblen (1933), **trained incapacity** exists when previous training prevents someone from adapting to new situations. Trained incapacity involves tunnel vision, inflexibility, and inability to change. The crew of the USS *Vincennes*, on July 3, 1988, mistook an Iranian passenger airliner for an Iranian F-14 jet fighter heading their way. Instead of destroying a menacing military plane, the *Vincennes* crew killed all of the nearly 300 civilian passengers on a regularly scheduled flight over the Persian Gulf. This tragic accident occurred because the *Vincennes* was created to operate on the open sea, not on a small body of water with all sorts of air and water vehicles constantly coming into its radar sights. Instead of identifying the passenger airliner for what it was, the crew acted on the basis of its prior training and did what it thought was necessary for self-protection. The crew's training resulted in a tragedy, essentially preventing the crew from adapting to the new environment. The crew's incapacity stemmed from its training.

Q Do alternatives to bureaucracy exist? Weber developed his theory of bureaucracy for the organizations that were in the changing society in which he lived. During the 1960s, some sociologists began to see bureaucracy as an outmoded organizational form. Warren Bennis (1965), for example, contended that bureaucracy

was no longer able to deal with the individual goals of employees and the increasing rates of social change. He therefore predicted that bureaucracies would be replaced by **organic-adaptive systems**—organizations based on rapid response to change rather than on the continuing implementation of established administrative principles:

> The key word will be "temporary"; there will be adaptive, rapidly changing temporary systems. These will be "task forces" organized around problems-to-be-solved. The problems will be solved by groups of relative strangers who represent a set of diverse professional skills. The group . . . will evolve in response to the problem rather than to programmed role expectations. The "executive" thus becomes coordinator or "linking pin" between various task forces. . . . People will be differentiated not vertically, according to rank and role, but flexibly and functionally according to skill and professional training. (Bennis 1965:31–35)

Bureaucracy, of course, has not disappeared, and Bennis (1979) has qualified some of his earlier predictions. Increasing numbers of organization researchers would agree, however, that bureaucracy is best suited for relatively stable, predictable situations. In situations characterized by rapid change and uncertainty, other forms of organization are likely to emerge (Mintzberg 1979). Such attempts to relate the structure of organizations to the situations they face have been labeled the *contingency* approach to organization theory (Burns and Stalker 1966; P. R. Lawrence and Lorsch 1967; Shepard and Hougland 1978). Although some have criticized aspects of the contingency approach (Pennings 1975; Pfeffer 1978), it is a useful corrective to the traditional assumption that there exists "one best way" to organize.

A strong advocate of alternatives to the bureaucratic form of organization, Joyce Rothschild (1979, 1986) studied cooperative organizations—organizations intended to be on the other end of the spectrum. Co-operative organizations, owned and managed by their employees, are characterized by full membership participation, minimization of rules, promotion of primary social relationships, hiring and promotion based on intimate ties and shared values, elimination of status differences, and a deemphasis on job specialization.

In 2008, two life-long high-tech entrepreneurs published a controversial book on alternatives to bureaucracy. Based on their experience in the current business environment, Ori Brafman and Rod Beckstrom (2008) distinguish between centralized (bureaucratic) organizations and decentralized (nonbureaucratic) organizations, using the analogy of the starfish and the spider. If you cut off a spider's head, it dies; if you cut off a starfish's leg, it grows a new one, and if large enough, that leg can create a brand new starfish. This is because the spider's life is controlled by its brain, while the major organs of a starfish are replicated throughout each arm.

Similarly, decentralized organizations, such as the Internet or Al-Queda, are composed of many smaller units able to operate, grow, and multiply independently of one another. Bureaucratic organizations, such as the spider, are centrally controlled so that destruction of an important part of an organization can destroy or seriously damage the whole thing. Starfish can adapt to changing circumstances; spiders cannot. This basic approach will remind you of Warren Bennis's "organic-adaptive systems" described earlier.

Although some analysts contend that nonbureaucratic forms of organizations are best suited to new business technologies and the future environmental context (Drucker 1988; T. Peters 1988; Mazaar 1999), most scholars agree that bureaucracy will remain the dominant organizational form. This does not mean, however, that some organizations cannot be non-bureaucratically structured. It is just that such organizations will be few in number. Nonbureaucratic organizational principles are most useful as a supplement to bureaucratic organization, as in research laboratories or in organizational work teams (S. P. Robbins 1990).

Q **What are some of the differences among formal organizations?** Sociologists, such as Amitai Etzioni (1975), have attempted to take differences in formal organizations into account by classifying organizations into categories. Some organizations, such as spiritual groups, political parties, universities, and service clubs, are joined because people want to join; they are joined because of personal interest or emotional commitment. Because members are free to join or not, these are voluntary organizations. Etzioni refers to them as *normative organizations* because shared understandings provide an important basis for coordination of members' activities. Organizations that people are forced to join are *coercive organizations*. Examples include prisons, custodial mental hospitals, concentration camps, forced-labor camps, elementary schools, and military systems using the draft. Other organizations are *utilitarian organizations*; people join them because of the benefits they derive from membership. Work organizations, including factories, offices, and professional firms, are examples of utilitarian organizations. Utilitarian organizations fall somewhere between the first two types. People are not forced to work (it is not a coercive organization), and yet they must work to be self-supportive (it is not a voluntary organization). Thus, utilitarian organizations are neither entirely voluntary nor entirely coercive; they have some elements of both.

Whereas Etzioni classified organizations according to the motivation for membership, Peter Blau

CHECK YOURSELF 6.3 R2

Formal Organizations
1. A formal organization is _____.
2. The ability to control the behavior of others even against their will is _____.
3. Which of the following has *not* been seen as an advantage of bureaucracy?
   ____ a. its avoidance of the use of inappropriate criteria in hiring employees
   ____ b. its use of rules to provide definite guidelines for behavior within the organization
   ____ c. its success in hiding the true nature of authority relationships
   ____ d. its encouragement of administrative competence in managers
4. Social workers who become more concerned with eligibility requirements than with delivering services to their low-income clients are engaging in _____.

Answers: 1. a group that has been deliberately and consciously created for the achievement of one or more specific goals; 2. power; 3. c; 4. goal displacement

and Richard Scott (1982) categorized organizations according to the recipients receiving the most benefit. In *mutual-benefit organizations* (political parties, professional associations, labor unions, social clubs), the prime beneficiary is the membership. These organizations exist to promote the interests of those who belong to them. *Business organizations*, on the other hand, are expected to serve the interests of their owners. Because these organizations are profit oriented, they emphasize maximum gain at the least cost. The prime beneficiary of a *service organization* is the organization's clients. The goal of social work agencies, schools, and hospitals is to aid those people who qualify for their services. *Commonwealth organizations* (the military, the Department of State, police and fire departments, the Environmental Protection Agency) are intended to serve the general public.

Dynamics of Formal Organizations R1

The discussion thus far describes the basic formal framework of organizations. But organizations also have dynamic processes (R. H. Hall and Tolbert 2008). This section is concerned with the informal groups within formal organizations as well as the tendency toward a concentration of power at the top.

Informal Organization

Bureaucracies are designed to act as secondary groups governed by the hierarchy of authority, by rules and procedures, and by impersonality. But, as anyone who has worked in a bureaucratic organization observes, there are primary relationships as well. Primary relationships emerge as part of the **informal organization**—a group (within a formal organization) guided by unofficial norms, rituals, and sentiments that are not part of the formal organization. Based on common interests and personal relationships, informal groups usually form spontaneously.

Q **When was informal organization first recognized?** The existence of informal organization within bureaucracies was first documented in the mid-1920s, when a group of Harvard researchers were studying the Hawthorne plant of the Western Electric Company in Chicago. In a study of fourteen male operators in the Bank Wiring Observation Room, F. J. Roethlisberger and William Dickson (1964; originally published in 1939) observed that work activities and job relationships were based on norms and social sanctions of that particular group of male operators. Group norms prohibited "rate busting" (doing too much work), "chiseling" (doing too

little work), and "squealing" (telling group secrets to supervisors). Conformity to these norms was maintained through ridicule, sarcasm, criticism, hostility, and "binging" (hitting deviants on the arm). The group also had its own unique stratification structure, with soldermen at the bottom, wiremen in the middle, and inspectors at the top.

The Need for Informal Organization

Q **Why does informal organization exist?** Informal groups spontaneously develop to meet needs that the formal organization ignores. Whereas modern organizations are designed to be impersonal, informal groups offer personal affection, support, and humor. In addition to humanizing the formal organization, informal organization is a means of protection. Informal organization encourages conformity, and the resulting solidarity protects group members from maltreatment by those outside the group.

Q **How does informal organization affect the formal organization?** Early studies, starting with the Bank Wiring Observation Room, concluded that informal organization resulted in behavior counterproductive to the organization's goals. In the Hawthorne study, for example, workers enforced the informal norm of producing an average of two units a day. Workers who turned out more than two units per day were forced by the group to stop exceeding the informal production quota.

Later research revealed beneficial consequences as well. Among carpenters and bricklayers, Raymond Van Zelst (1952) found, for example, that establishing work groups on the basis of friendship patterns increased workers' job satisfaction; decreased friction and anxiety among work partners; and created a friendly, cooperative atmosphere—all of which contributed to lower turnover and higher productivity.

Joseph Bensman and Israel Gerver (1963) described the use of an illegal tool in an airplane factory. This tool, called a tap, is used to thread nuts so they will fit with wing bolts that are slightly out of alignment. Otherwise, the defect would have to be reported. The tap is outlawed—its use can lead to dismissal—because a tapped nut does not have proper holding power under flight conditions. However, use of the tap was tolerated by management as long as it was handled discreetly. In fact, without its use, the productivity of the plant would have suffered. Thus, the use of the tap was controlled informally by supervisors, inspectors, and workers themselves. In short, to avoid detection by Air Force inspectors, supervisors and workers evolved an informal organization complete with norms and sanctions for the systematic use of an illegal device. The formal organization considered itself to have benefited from this informal subterfuge. (Of course, the same could not be said for the passengers who traveled in the planes.)

The Role of Power in Formal Organizations

The word *organization* itself implies power. A hierarchy of authority is an expression of power distribution—in decreasing amounts from top to bottom. And organizations are political in more subtle ways. Every organization has people whose interests and goals conflict. Many preferences of top executives are not shared by wage workers; the outlooks of sales managers are often at odds with the views of production managers. Because a rational choice between all these conflicting views often requires more information than decision makers can assemble, decision making is usually political. Those with the most power usually get their way (Cyert and March 1963; H. A. Simon 1976; Pfeffer 1981).

Achievement of organizational goals requires the exercise of power. Although the employment of a power advantage is beneficial in organizations, power may be monopolized by individuals for their own limited purposes. This tendency is articulated in the *iron law of oligarchy* (Michels 1949; originally published in 1911).

Q How does the pyramidal shape of bureaucratic organizations promote the iron law of oligarchy? According to the **iron law of oligarchy** formulated by German sociologist Robert Michels, power tends to become increasingly concentrated in the hands of a few members of any organization. Michels observed that even in organizations intended to be democratic, leaders eventually gain control and other members become virtually powerless. In fact, he concluded that this increased concentration of power occurs because those in power want to remain in power:

> It is organization which gives birth to the dominion of the elected over the electors, of the mandatories over the mandators, of the delegates over the delegators. Who says organization, says oligarchy. (Michels 1949:401)

Politics in the United States is a prime example of Michels's principle. Voter apathy is reflected in low voter turnout for elections at all levels of government. Because so few are involved in the political process, those who are politically active gain an inordinate amount of power. The same thing occurs in organizations such as labor unions. Membership passivity over an extended period of time permits those at the top to consolidate power. Leaders stay in power by building a loyal staff, controlling communications, and marshalling resources (money, jobs, favors).

Q Why does organization lead to oligarchy? According to Michels, three organizational factors encourage oligarchy. First, members of organizations need to delegate decision making to a hierarchy of authority. Even in highly democratic organizations, such as the socialist parties of Europe, it is necessary for the masses to delegate much of the decision making to a few leaders. *Delegation* means creating a hierarchy of authority.

Second, the advantages held by leaders at the top of the hierarchy allow them to consolidate their power. They are able to monopolize power because of their social and political skills, and once in power, they use these skills to strengthen their positions. Moreover, merely by doing their jobs, leaders of the organization gain special knowledge not available to the membership. They can create a staff that is loyal to them; they can control the channels of communication; they can use organizational resources to increase their power.

Third, oligarchy in organizations is encouraged by the characteristics of the followers. The membership tends to defer to the greater skills possessed by their leaders. The nonelites believe that their leaders are more articulate and are doing a better job than they could do. In addition, the masses are passive, even indifferent; they do not want to spend a lot of time in organizational activities. The general membership may, in fact, feel grateful to those at the top for the leadership they are providing.

Q What are the consequences of oligarchy? Democratic organizations—the type of organization in which oligarchy presents the greatest problem—suffer from this tendency toward oligarchy, contended Michels, as those in power come to care more about perpetuating their power than about organizational goals. Oligarchic leaders become excessively careful and conservative as the maintenance of their positions becomes more important to them than considering the interests of the membership. As a result, the desires of the membership may be sacrificed.

Q Must oligarchy always develop? Research documents the iron law of oligarchy in a variety of organizations, including political parties, legislatures, religious organizations, labor unions, and the American Sociological Association. There is, however, opposition to oligarchy in organizations; otherwise, all organizations would be oligarchic. According to Alvin Gouldner, if there is an iron law of oligarchy, there must also be an iron law of democracy: "If oligarchical waves repeatedly wash away the bridges of democracy, this eternal recurrence can happen only because men doggedly rebuilt them after each inundation" (Gouldner 1955:506). Sentiment from the masses is continuously bubbling up to depose oligarchic leaders in democratic organizations. The survival of democracy in the face of oligarchy can be seen in the democratic removal of entrenched labor leaders and politicians. Although the odds against turning out entrenched leaders are high, it happens often enough to remind us that oligarchy does not completely destroy democracy. Moreover, if they are to remain in power, oligarchic leaders have to pay attention to the desires of their followers. Although mere responsiveness to the membership may not be the ideal form of democracy, its presence indicates that even oligarchic leaders often do not have a totally free hand to do as they please (Sayles and Strauss 1967; Voss and Sherman 2000).

Other research concludes that concentration of power does not inevitably lead to an abandonment of the organization's goals for the selfish benefit of the leaders. Research on the policies of churches toward civil rights and on other controversial issues led James Wood to note that "many organizations exist precisely to foster values that are precarious when left to individuals" (J. R. Wood 1981:101). He found that such values can most effectively be implemented when leaders have a strong organizational base of support. Given a choice between the leaders' personal benefits and the maintenance of the organization's values, the leaders often choose to maintain the organization's values.

Joyce Rothschild and J. Allen Whitt (1987) also question the alleged inevitable connection between organization and oligarchy. They challenge the iron law of oligarchy through an investigation of cooperatives—organizations owned and operated by the workers themselves. Although not all cooperatives prosper or even survive, Rothschild and Whitt maintain that the very existence and persistence of cooperatives contradict the assumption that organization leads to oligarchy.

Race, Ethnicity, Gender, and Social Class in Organizations

By the nature of organizations, power is concentrated in relatively few positions at the top. Mirroring the broader society, top positions in the hierarchy of organizations are held by white men from higher social classes. Consequently, minorities, women, and lower-class members are subject to the same patterns of prejudice and discrimination they experience in their nonwork lives (D. T. Miller 1999). The term

Women do not have a voice among these high-level business executives. Why do you think societal gender inequality is still pretty consistently reproduced in organizations?

glass ceiling reflects the fact that few women and minorities get promoted to the more powerful (higher) positions.

Q **How does the treatment of minorities mirror society?** One of the most graphic reflections of inequality in organizations is found in the secretly taped meetings of Texaco's upper managers in 1996. The racial discrimination suit filed by Texaco's African American employees was settled in their favor for $115 million shortly after the content of these tapes hit the mass media. Texaco could hardly deny reparations for company racism when it became public knowledge that one top executive used the "N" word and another joked that "black jelly beans were stuck to the bottom of the bag" (Solomon 1996).

Much more systematic evidence of inequality exists. Even among employees with identical education, white men receive disproportionately more promotions than African Americans, Latinos, and Native Americans. It works the same way with dismissal: The federal government (the environment most favorable to minorities) discharges African American employees at a rate double that of whites (Zwerling and Silver 1992; DeWitt 1995). These and other studies provide convincing evidence of prejudice and discrimination against minorities in organizations (Feagin 1991; Cose 1995; see Chapter 9).

Q Is societal gender inequality reproduced in organizations? Yes it is. Like racial and ethnic minorities, women receive fewer promotions than white men, even when they have the same level of education. This occurs, in part, because women are judged by higher criteria than men. Women, too, are more likely to be let go than men (White and Althauser 1984; Aldrich 1999; H. Smith 1999).

Sociologist Rosabeth Moss Kanter (1993) conducted a classic study of gender inequality in organizations. Because men overwhelmingly outnumber women in the upper ranks of organizations, Kanter found that even successful women find themselves in a minority status. Successful women in male peer groups become symbols of what-women-can-do. On the one hand, this makes them highly visible in an environment in which success depends on visibility. On the other hand, they sometimes feel the loneliness of being different from the other group members, having to sacrifice their privacy and anonymity. Because of their visibility, the few women in the upper ranks feel extra pressure to avoid making mistakes. Even those women who experience little or no discrimination feel they have to work harder than the average man.

Another indicator of gender inequality is **sexual harassment**—the use of one's superior power in making unwelcome sexual advances. Sexual harassment has been documented in nearly all types of organizations, including the military, the government, corporations, factories, and universities (Lott 1994). More will be said about this topic in Chapter 10, which explores gender inequality in American society.

Q How is social class perpetuated in organizations? Organizations perpetuate social class levels through the placement of working-class people in low-paying, temporary, and dead-end jobs. Members of the upper and middle classes enter higher-level jobs with higher salaries and wages and greater opportunities for advancement. And this cannot be entirely explained by social class differences in education. Persons from upper-class families tend to receive more favorable treatment than do lower-class persons with comparable educational credentials (Blau and Meyer 1987). Educational qualifications are often overshadowed by stereotypes associated with class differences in speech, dress, and behavior. Employees from lower-class backgrounds are more likely to be denied promotion, to receive lower pay raises, and to be dismissed than their higher-class coworkers who display proper "manners" and dress more stylishly.

Racial, ethnic, gender, and social class inequalities are mirrored in organizations. Not only do organizations reflect societal inequalities—they perpetuate them.

Organizations and Their Environments

The **organizational environment** consists of all the forces outside an organization that exert an actual or potential influence on the organization. An organization's environment includes the general technological, economic, political, cultural, and related conditions in which the organization operates (W. R. Scott 1992; DiMaggio 2001). Interest in environments has increased in part because of the growing realization that organizations can survive only to the extent that they can generate enough support among environmental actors to continue receiving needed resources (in the form of money, new members, or whatever). It is equally true, however, that many organizations have sufficient resources to exert significant influence on their environments (Florida and Kenney 1991). Whether they are influencing outside actors or are the recipients of influence, organizations are frequently involved in interorganizational relationships.

Q Do organizations themselves interact? An **interorganizational relationship** is a pattern of interaction among authorized representatives of two or more formally independent organizations. Interorganizational relationships develop for many reasons, but most researchers agree that a need for resources possessed by other organizations and an awareness of the availability of those resources in the other organizations contribute to the formation of interorganizational relationships (Hougland and Sutton 1978; Alter and Hage 1992).

Although organizations become involved in interorganizational relationships because they need outside resources, all parties are concerned that the interests of their own organizations be protected. As Figure 6.3 shows, although the police must interact with fourteen other organizations in the area of problem youth, only three of these relationships are regularly cooperative. Six of the relationships, including those with important organizations such as the juvenile court and the detention center, are regularly marked by conflict (R. H. Hall and Tolbert 2008).

On to Chapter 7

Society was the first major type of social structure covered in this text (Chapter 5 "Social Structure and Society"). In the present chapter we explored groups and organizations, two additional types of social structure. Your understanding of social structure to this point is largely one of order and conformity. Chapter 7 reveals disorder and nonconformity in its presentation of deviance and the need for social control in social structures.

FIGURE 6.3

Patterns of Cooperation and Conflict in Interorganizational Relationships Involving the Police

This figure illustrates the nature of interorganizational relationships. Even when the police need the help of other organizations to reach their goals, only three of their fourteen interorganizational relationships are cooperative.

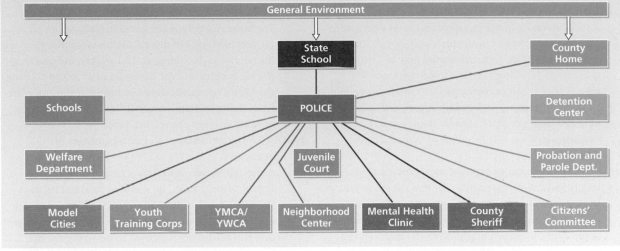

■ Cooperative   ■ Conflictual   ■ Neutral

Source: Richard H. Hall, *Organizations*, 7th ed (p. 225). Copyright ©1999 by Pearson Prentice Hall. Reprinted by permission.

CHECK YOURSELF  **6.4** **R2**

Dynamics of Formal Organizations

1. A group in which personal relationships are guided by rules, rituals, sentiments, and traditions not provided for by the formal organization is known as a(n) _____ organization.
2. The effects of informal organization on the formal organization are almost always negative. T or F?
3. The theory known as the _____ emphasizes the danger of power becoming concentrated in the hands of a few members of any organized group.
4. Cooperative patterns tend to dominate in interorganizational analysis. T or F?

Answers: 1. informal; 2. F; 3. iron law of oligarchy; 4. F

S **INTEGRATED GOALS AND SUMMARY**

1. **Define the concept of the group, and differentiate it from social categories and social aggregates.**
   - Group members interact, share culture, consider one another's behavior, and have some common interests and goals. Groups are sometimes confused with social categories and social aggregates.
2. **Outline the basic characteristics of primary and secondary groups.**
   - A primary group is composed of individuals who know one another well, interact informally, and like being together. A secondary group is goal oriented, and its members interact without personal or emotional involvement. Likewise, a primary relationship is intimate and personal, whereas a secondary relationship is impersonal.

- Primary groups are more likely to develop when a relatively small number of people are involved, when interaction is face-to-face, when people are in contact over a long period of time, and when the social environment is appropriate. Primary groups are formed in part because of the emotional support and sense of belonging they provide. This type of group serves society by aiding in the socialization process and by helping to maintain social control.

3. **State the functions of primary groups.**
   - We use reference groups to evaluate ourselves and to acquire attitudes, values, beliefs, and norms. Reference groups may be those we merely aspire to join, or even those we use as negative role models.

4. **Differentiate between in-groups and out-groups.**
   - Intense feelings of identification and loyalty envelop in-groups. The feelings often involve opposition, antagonism, and competition toward out-groups. Efforts must be made to maintain group boundaries, the consequences of which have significant social implications.

5. **Discuss the idea of a social network.**
   - A social network (not a group per se) links a person with a wide variety of individuals and groups. The social relationships that are formed may be "strong" (parents and children) or "weak" (distant relatives, members of a college class). Social networks provide a sense of belonging and social support and help in the job market. More women are now using networking, once the sole province of men, for career advancement.

6. **Describe the five major types of social interaction.**
   - Five types of social interaction are basic to group life. In cooperation, individuals or groups combine their efforts to reach some common goal. When individuals or groups work against one another to obtain a larger share of the valuables, they are in conflict. In conflict, defeating one's adversary is thought to be necessary. Social exchange is a form of interaction in which one person voluntarily does something for another person with the expectation that a reward will follow. Coercion exists when one person or group is forced to behave according to another person's or group's demands. When a person behaves as others expect, conformity occurs.

7. **Elaborate on the existence of cooperation and conflict in groups.**
   - Most groups experience both cooperation and conflict. This is partly because groups satisfy some personal needs, such as social acceptance, while thwarting others, such as personal freedom. Social scientists have been very interested in the ways in which interaction within groups can achieve group goals while fulfilling the needs of individual group members.

8. **Discuss the nature of group processes: task accomplishment, leadership styles, and decision making.**
   - Moving beyond the trait theory of leadership, social scientists focus on appropriate leadership behavior. More recently, studies of leadership suggest that appropriate leadership behavior depends on the situation a leader faces.
   - In some situations, group decision making has been shown to be superior to individual decision making. Intellectual tasks, for example, are better handled through groups. On the other hand, group pressure may damage the quality of decision making because of the excessive conformity of group members.

Many group decisions are reached in situations in which group members are discouraged from expressing their reservations. At the extreme, this is called groupthink.

9. **Define the concept of formal organization, and identify the major characteristics of bureaucracy.**
   - A formal organization—the epitome of a secondary group—is deliberately created to achieve some goal. There are many types of formal organizations in modern society, but most share one feature—they are bureaucratic. According to Max Weber, bureaucracy is the most efficient type of formal organization. Using the ideal-type method, Weber outlined the characteristics that give bureaucracy its technical superiority over other types of organizations.

10. **Discuss the advantages and disadvantages of bureaucracy.**
    - Although Weber saw bureaucracy as an efficient organizational form, he was well aware of its negative side. When rules and regulations become more important than organizational goals (as they often do), those who are supposed to be served by the bureaucracy suffer. Adherence to rules and regulations may also make bureaucrats overly conservative; such people learn their jobs so well that they cannot adapt to changing times and circumstances. Such problems have led researchers to examine alternatives to bureaucracy. Although most social scientists agree that bureaucracy is appropriate for many situations, contingency theorists suggest that other types of organizations may fit particular circumstances.

11. **Distinguish between formal and informal organization.**
    - The existence of primary groups and primary relationships within formal organizations has received considerable attention. These informal groups can either help or hinder the achievement of formal organizational goals, depending on the circumstances.

12. **Describe the iron law of oligarchy, and demonstrate its importance with examples.**
    - The exercise of power in organizations is receiving increasing attention. Power can benefit organizations by facilitating change and adapting to changing conditions, but power can also be used for the benefit of a small, unrepresentative group within the organization. The applicability of the iron law of oligarchy to modern organizations is a continuing source of debate among sociologists.

13. **Discuss prejudice and discrimination in organizations.**
    - Minorities, women, and lower social classes suffer from power differentials in organizations. For this reason, organizations serve to perpetuate the inequality that exists in the broader society.

CONCEPT REVIEW

Match the following concepts with the definitions listed below them.

____ a. social exchange
____ b. rationalism
____ c. ideal-type method
____ d. bureaucracy
____ e. out-group

____ f. iron law of oligarchy
____ g. organizational environment
____ h. group
____ i. conflict
____ j. secondary group

____ k. formal organization
____ l. primary relationship
____ m. social category
____ n. conformity
____ o. in-group

1. a type of formal organization based on rationality and efficiency
2. occurs when individuals or groups work against one another to obtain a larger share of the limited valuables in a society
3. a type of social interaction in which an individual behaves toward others in ways expected by the group
4. a social structure deliberately created for the achievement of one or more specific goals
5. several people who are in contact with one another; share some ways of thinking, feeling, and behaving; take one another's behavior into account; and have one or more interests or goals in common
6. a method that involves isolating the most basic characteristics of some social entity
7. a group toward which one feels intense identification and loyalty

8. the principle stating that power tends to become concentrated in the hands of a few members of any social structure
9. all the forces outside the organization that exert an actual or potential influence on the organization
10. a group toward which one feels opposition, antagonism, and competition
11. a relationship that is intimate, personal, based on a genuine concern for another's total personality, and fulfilling in itself
12. the solution of problems on the basis of logic, data, and planning rather than tradition and superstition
13. a group that is impersonal and task oriented and involves only a segment of the lives and personalities of its members
14. a number of persons who share a social characteristic
15. when one person voluntarily does something for another, expecting a reward in return

CHECK YOURSELF REVIEW

1. Social scientists agree that leaders must have certain traits if they are to be effective. T or F?
2. The effects of informal organization on the formal organization are almost always negative. T or F?
3. A _____ is a web of social relationships that joins a person directly to other people and groups and, through those individuals and groups, indirectly to additional parties.
4. Social workers who become more concerned with eligibility requirements than with delivering services to their low-income clients are engaging in _____.
5. Which of the following is *not* a condition that promotes the development of primary groups?
   a. small group size
   b. face-to-face contact
   c. continuous contact
   d. interaction on the basis of status or role
6. Which of the following has *not* been seen as an advantage of bureaucracy?
   a. its avoidance of the use of inappropriate criteria in hiring employees
   b. its use of rules to provide definite guidelines for behavior within the organization

   c. its success in hiding the true nature of authority relationships
   d. its encouragement of administrative competence in managers
7. Listed here are some examples of primary and secondary relationships. Indicate which examples are most likely to be primary relationships (P) and which are most likely to be secondary relationships (S).
   ____ a. a marine recruit and his drill instructor at boot camp
   ____ b. a married couple
   ____ c. a manager and his professional baseball team
   ____ d. professors and students
   ____ e. car salespersons and their prospective customers
8. Match the following terms and statements.
   ____ a. group
   ____ b. in-group
   ____ c. social aggregate
   ____ d. social category
   ____ e. reference group
   (1) skinheads
   (2) spectators at a Fourth of July fireworks display
   (3) orchid growers
   (4) teenage subculture
   (5) members of a regular Saturday night poker game

CRITICAL-THINKING QUESTIONS

1. Identify one of your primary groups. Discuss the three functions of primary groups using your own experience to illustrate.

_____

_____

2. Think of a club you belong to on campus or a club you joined as a high school student. Was this a primary or secondary group? Support your answer with the use of sociological concepts and actual experiences.

_____

_____

3. Recall an in-group in which you are (or were) a member. Discuss the consequences this group had for others. Defend the right of this group to exist on sociological grounds.

_____

_____

4. Think of an example of groupthink at your school. Analyze this situation in relation to positive or negative consequences.

_____

_____

5. Most Americans think of bureaucracies in a very negative way. Develop an argument you could use the next time someone endorses the prevailing view of bureaucracy in your presence.

_____

_____

6. Analyze your school as a bureaucracy. Give an example of the following characteristics of bureaucracy: (a) a system of rules and procedures and (b) impersonality and impartiality. Discuss a positive and negative consequence of each characteristic.

_____

_____

ANSWER KEY

Concept Review

a. 15
b. 12
c. 6
d. 1
e. 10
f. 8
g. 9
h. 5
i. 2
j. 13
k. 4
l. 11
m. 14
n. 3
o. 7

Check Yourself Review

1. F
2. F
3. T
4. social network
5. goal displacement
6. d
7. c
8. a. S
   b. P
   c. S
   d. S
   e. S
9. a. 5
   b. 1
   c. 2
   d. 3
   e. 4

Deviance and Social Control

AP Photo/Chris Pizzello

S GOALS

- Define deviance, and explain its relative nature.
- Define social control, and identify the major types of social control.
- Describe the biological and psychological explanations of deviance.
- Discuss the positive and negative consequences of deviance.
- Differentiate the major functional theories of deviance.

- Compare and contrast cultural transmission theory and labeling theory.
- Discuss the conflict theory view of deviance.
- Compare crime in the United States and the world.
- Discuss the nature of global terrorism.
- Compare and contrast crime control domestically and globally.

How often is rape committed by a stranger? Unfortunately, many young people today know someone who has been raped. When women find themselves outdoors and alone, they are often fearful of possible surprise attacks by dangerous strangers. This is a genuine concern, and women are smart to be cautious; yet, more than 80 percent of reported rapes in the United States are committed by individuals who are known to their victims. Experts use the terms *date rape* and *acquaintance* rape to describe this reality.

As date or acquaintance rape illustrates, deviant behavior may involve perversion. Deviance, however, is not limited to "nuts, sluts, and perverts" (Liazos 1972). **Deviance** is *any* behavior that departs from societal or group norms. It can range from criminal behavior (recognized by almost all members of a society as deviant) to wearing heavy makeup (considered deviant by some religious groups).

Deviance and Social Control [R1]

The Nature of Deviance

Without conformity and predictability in human behavior, society could not exist. Order and stability are the cornerstones of social life. All the same, we know that social life includes people who breach norms. Some people violate norms by robbing banks, assaulting others, or committing murder. Some incidents of less severe deviance are high profile because they involve a prominent public figure. Tiger Woods's serial marital infidelity would probably have gone unnoticed (except to family and friends) were he an average professional golfer. If he had been a private citizen, Congressman Christopher Lee's posting on the Internet of a photo of his naked upper body would not have made the national headlines. Had Brett Favre not been an iconic NFL quarterback, the photograph he sent of his naked lower body to a young woman would have remained a private affair. Figure 7.1 illustrates the frequency of two types of juvenile deviance.

Most behavior tends to fall within a normal range of social expectations. *Deviance,* behavior outside this range, may be either *positive* (overconforming) or *negative* (underconforming).

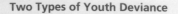

FIGURE 7.1

Two Types of Youth Deviance

What does the graph indicate about the trend in youth violence?

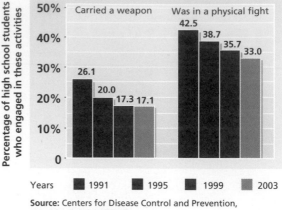

Source: Centers for Disease Control and Prevention, "Healthy Youth!" (2004).

Q What is the distinction between positive and negative deviance? **Negative deviance** involves behavior that underconforms to accepted norms. Negative deviants reject the norms, misinterpret the norms, or are unaware of the norms. This is the kind of behavior popularly associated with the idea of deviance. There is, however, another type of deviance. **Positive deviance** encompasses behavior that overconforms to social expectations (Heckert 2003). Positive deviants conform to norms in an unbalanced way. Underlying this type of deviance is an idealization of group norms that leads people to extremes of perfectionism. In its own way, positive deviance can be as disruptive and hard to manage as negative deviance. Few people find a society characterized by slavish and unchallenged conformity any more desirable than a disorderly and unpredictable society.

This more complete picture of the nature of deviance is illustrated in Figure 7.2. Think about the norms related to personal appearance in American society. For example, the mass media are constantly telling young people that thin is good and fat is bad. Negative deviants will miss the mark on the obese side. Positive deviants may push themselves to the point of anorexia. Most young people will weigh somewhere between these two extremes.

Q How is identifying deviance a challenge? Deviance is a matter of social definition. In a diverse society like the United States, it is often difficult to agree on what does and does not constitute deviance. Jerry Simmons asked a sample of respondents to list categories or types of persons they considered deviant:

The sheer range of responses predictably included homosexuals, prostitutes, drug addicts, radicals, and criminals. But it

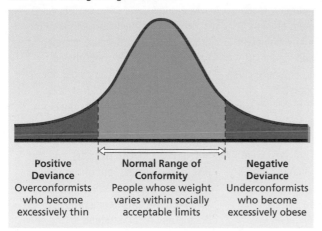

FIGURE 7.2

The Distribution of Deviance Relative to the Norm of Leanness

Most people conform to norms within a socially acceptable range. Only at the extremes of this normal range of behavior does deviance appear. We are accustomed to talking about negative deviance, behavior that involves underconformity. We are much less aware of positive deviance, or overconforming behavior. Leanness as the desirable standard for physical appearance is illustrated in this figure. Think of another example that exists among college students.

Positive Deviance	Normal Range of Conformity	Negative Deviance
Overconformists who become excessively thin	People whose weight varies within socially acceptable limits	Underconformists who become excessively obese

Source: Adapted from Jay J. Coakley, *Sport in Society*, 10th ed. (Boston, WBC/McGraw-Hill, 2009).

also included liars, career women, Democrats, reckless drivers, atheists, Christians, suburbanites, the retired, young folks, card players, bearded men, artists, pacifists, priests, prudes, hippies, straights, girls who wear makeup, the President of the United States, conservatives, integrationists, executives, divorcees, perverts, motorcycle gangs, smart-alec students, know-it-all professors, modern people, and Americans. (Simmons 1969:3)

To this list, Leslie Lampert would add obese people. For a week she wore a "fat suit," adding 150 pounds to her normal body weight, to experience firsthand what it feels like to be an overweight woman in American society. According to Lampert, American "society not only hates fat people, it feels entitled to participate in a prejudice that at many levels parallels racism and religious bigotry" (Lampert 1993:154).

Q **Why do sociologists limit their study of deviance?** Because minor instances of behavior that some might consider deviant occur frequently in modern societies, sociologists generally reserve the term *deviance* for violations of *significant* social norms. Significant norms are those that are highly important either to most members of a society or to the members with the most power. For sociologists, then, a **deviant** is a person who violates one or more of society's most highly valued norms (Tepperman 2009).

Public reactions to deviants are usually negative and involve attempts to change or control the deviant

behavior. As scientists, sociologists, however, do not make such value judgments. To them, deviant behavior is neither good nor bad; it is simply behavior that violates social norms and draws a negative response from others.

Conditions Affecting Definitions of Deviance

Identifying deviance is clearly a relative matter. Insight into the relativity of deviance began early in the history of sociology. According to William Graham Sumner, norms determine whether behavior is deviant or normal (Sumner 1906). Because norms vary from group to group, society to society, and time to time, the behavior considered to be deviant varies. Emile Durkheim contended that no behavior is deviant in itself, because deviance is a matter of social definition.

According to Sumner, Durkheim, and many other sociologists, the deviance label depends on three circumstances: the social status and power of the individuals involved, the social context in which the behavior occurs, and the historical period in which the behavior takes place.

Actresses Mary-Kate Olsen and Ashley Olsen are famous anorexics. How would you explain to your parents that their behavior is "positive"?

Kevin Winter/Getty Images

William Chambliss— Saints and Roughnecks

William Chambliss (1973), over a two-year period, observed the behavior of two teenage gangs at Hanibal High School. In addition to gang activity, Chambliss documented the responses of parents, teachers, and police to the delinquent behavior.

The Saints—eight children of white, stable, upper-middle-class parents—were pre-college, good students, and active in school affairs. The Roughnecks—six young men from lower-class white families—were poor students.

Both gangs engaged in similar amounts of delinquency. Yet, the Saints were slated for bright futures, while the Roughnecks were on track to dead-end lives. That was the picture held by parents, teachers, and law enforcement officials. And that was the way events actually turned out.

Why? The answer makes Chambliss's study sociologically fascinating. Deviance is relative to social class; it may be *primary* or *secondary*.

Hanibal townspeople simply never recognized the Saints' behavior as delinquent. When caught stealing or driving drunk, the Saints were seen as good boys "playing pranks" or "sowing wild oats." How else, parents, teachers, and law enforcement officials asked themselves, could you explain such behavior from well-mannered, well-dressed teenagers with nice cars and money in their pockets?

No such benefit of the doubt was extended to Roughnecks caught in the same acts. When these badly dressed, rude, not-so-rich boys were caught by the police stealing property or drinking excessively, they were seen as heading for trouble.

The Roughnecks engaged in secondary deviance—their delinquency evolved into a lifestyle and permeated their personal identities. Others responded to them as deviants, and they gradually incorporated this labeling into their self-definitions. The more they saw themselves as deviants, the more time they spent in deviant activities. Two of the boys dropped

out of high school: one sentenced to thirty years for murder, the other sentenced for life on a murder conviction. Another Roughneck finished high school and become a gambler. There was scant information on a fourth Roughneck: He was "driving a truck up north." Two went to college on athletic scholarships and turned their lives around.

In contrast, the Saints engaged in primary deviance. Because, claimed Chambliss, they were not labeled, the Saints' acts of deviance did not come to dominate their lifestyle or self-image. In fact, seven of the eight Saints attended college right after high school. Five of these graduated in four years, one in six years, and the last in seven years. Four of the college graduates went to graduate school. Among these four were a lawyer, a doctor, and a PhD student.

Evaluate the Research

1. From your understanding of Chambliss's study, is deviance socially created? Explain.
2. Which of the three major theoretical perspectives best explains Chambliss's findings? Support your choice.

Q **How do social status and power influence the definition of deviance?** Researcher William Chambliss (1973) demonstrated the importance of social status and power in defining deviance. As a participant observer, Chambliss watched two teenage gangs for two years at Hanibal High School. While at Hanibal High, Chambliss observed the school and nonschool activities of the two gangs: the Saints, a gang of eight upper-middle-class white boys, and the Roughnecks, a gang of six lower-class white students. Although the Roughnecks and the Saints engaged in many of the same types of deviant behavior, the Roughnecks were judged by community members as worthless kids who were poor students, heavy drinkers, and violent individuals. Why, Chambliss asked, "did the community, the school, and the police react to the Saints as though they were good, upstanding, nondelinquent youths with bright futures but react to the Roughnecks as though they were tough, young criminals, who were headed for trouble?" (Chambliss 1973:28). The different treatment of these two gangs seemed to be traceable to their social class backgrounds. Lower-class people are more likely to be labeled deviants than are middle- or upper-class individuals, even when they behave in similar ways. (See "Consider This Research" for more detail.)

Of course, high status does not always protect those who engage in deviant behavior. Bernie Madoff, whose financial Ponzi scheme cost trusting investors some $65 billion, was sentenced in 2009 to 150 years in prison, the maximum penalty allowed (Taibbi 2011). And charges of child sexual abuse by Catholic priests have been very costly to the Catholic church. In addition to a damaged reputation resulting from a storm of highly negative media coverage, the Catholic church is faced with declining parishioner financial contributions and payments of some $100 million in settlements agreements.

Q How do definitions of deviance vary with social context? Behavior can be considered conforming or deviant only within a particular social context; behavior considered deviant in one society may be acceptable and even encouraged in others. Suppose a group of people believe that gods live in rocks and trees and that these spirits are capable of granting them favors: power over their enemies, the ability to heal the sick, and the foresight to predict the future. Among the traditional Alaskan Eskimo, such people would be awarded high social status and deference. But in a highly industrialized society, members of such a group would be considered strange and deviant.

Deviance is also relative from group to group within the same society. Conformity to the norms of one group may earn intense disapproval from another. Teenagers, for example, are usually torn between conforming to the demands of their peers and meeting the expectations of their parents.

The possibility of being considered deviant from at least one group's point of view is likely in a society as complex as modern America. For instance, deviance can even vary within a geographical area. In Florida, it is illegal to play casino games on land. Three miles offshore in international waters, it is acceptable to play slot machines, cards, and other games of chance.

Q How do definitions of deviance vary over time? Societal approaches to cigarettes and drugs illustrate the variations of labeling over time. Gerald Markle and Ronald Troyer (1988), who studied the changing definition of cigarette smoking in American society, found that definitions of smoking have varied considerably. The definition of smoking was quite negative during the early 1900s, when smoking was banned by fourteen states. It became positive during the 1950s when advertising began to depict smoking as glamorous and sophisticated. Today, smoking is prohibited in places as diverse as restaurants, government buildings, corporate offices, airplanes, elevators, physicians' offices, and university buildings. By 2008, fourteen states had statewide smoking bans covering bars (whether they serve food or not), casinos, restaurants, and workplaces. Twenty states had less comprehensive statewide bans. Only sixteen states had no statewide smoking prohibitions.

Like the United States, Europe has traditionally taken a strong stance against drug use. There is now a movement toward liberalization. While only a few countries favor legalizing hard drugs, several are less militantly opposed. As part of this shift from a war on drugs to an

Definitions of deviance change from time to time. Although same-sex marriage is still viewed by many Americans as a form of deviance, prohibitions have loosened to the point that many gays, such as this California couple in 2008, are willing to legally acknowledge their living relationship.

informal truce, some countries are tolerating marijuana use, and even the user of heroin or other hard drugs is less likely to be criminalized. Germany now authorizes local governments to permit citizen possession of drugs for "personal use." In the Netherlands, drug use is now considered a public health issue rather than a criminal matter. Portugal has decriminalized the use of all previously banned narcotics from marijuana to crack cocaine. Even though the 2002 Nevada ballot initiative to legalize possession of up to three ounces of marijuana failed, its very presence reflects growing support for the legalization of marijuana in the United States (Hawkins 2002; J. Stein 2002). Since 1996, fifteen states have legalized medical marijuana use. Actually, almost half of Americans now favor legalizing marijuana, up from 12 percent in 1970.

There are even signs of some loosening of laws on crack cocaine. Extremely harsh penalties for possession of crack cocaine were enacted during the 1980s' "tough on crime" era. For example, crack offenders spend more time in prison than people convicted of manslaughter. One mother was condemned to 24 years in jail at the age of 72 for refusing to testify against her son. Possession of 100 times more powder cocaine is required for the same sentence involving crack offenders. In 2007, the U.S. Supreme Court voted 7–2 to unbind federal

CHECK YOURSELF **7.1** **R2**

Deviance and Social Control

1. _____ is behavior that violates norms.
2. A major problem that sociologists have in defining deviance is its _____.
3. _____ is the means for promoting conformity to a group's or society's rules.

Answers: 1. Deviance; 2. relativity; 3. Social control

district judges from the prior commission guidelines that created the large discrepancy in punishments given to crack and powder cocaine offenders. A day later, the U.S. Sentencing Commission voted unanimously to give incarcerated crack cocaine offenders an opportunity to reduce their sentences to a level comparable to powder cocaine offenders (Fears 2007).

Forms of Social Control

Human behavior is predictable most of the time. We generally know what to expect from others and what others expect of us. You know by now: This is no accident. Just as laws of physics help us predict the actions of the physical world around us, social and cultural mechanisms promote order, stability, and predictability in social life. We feel confident that drivers will not drive on the wrong side of the road, waiters will not pour wine over our heads, and strangers will not expect us to accept them as overnight guests. Without **social control**—means for promoting conformity to norms—social life would be capricious, even chaotic. There are two broad types of social control: internal control, which lies within the individual, and external control, which exists outside the individual.

Q What is the distinction between internal and external social control? Internal social control is self-imposed and is acquired during the socialization process. For example, most people most of the time refrain from stealing, not just because they fear arrest or lack the opportunity to steal, but because they consider theft to be wrong. The norm against stealing has become a part of the individual. This is known as the *internalization* of social norms.

Unfortunately for society, the internalization of norms is not complete in all societies or groups. If it were, we would have no deviance at all. Because the process of socialization does not ensure the conformity of all people all of the time, external social control must also be present.

External social control is based on sanctions—rewards and punishments—designed to encourage desired behavior. Positive sanctions, such as awards, salary increases, and smiles of approval, are used to encourage conformity. Negative sanctions, such as fines,

imprisonment, and ridicule, are intended to stop socially unacceptable behavior. Sanctions may be formal or informal. Ridicule and gossip are examples of informal sanctions; imprisonment, capital punishment, exile, and honorary titles are formal sanctions.

Biological and Psychological Explanations of Deviance **R1**

Many sociologists, despite the rise of sociobiology, remain skeptical of biological explanations of human behavior. The search for some biological foundation for deviance, however, has a long history and is still occurring.

Search for a Biological Basis for Deviance

Q What are some biological explanations of deviance? One of the earliest proponents of biological causes of deviance was Cesare Lombroso (1918), an Italian physician who saw a relationship between physical traits and crime. Lombroso believed that criminals were accidents of nature, throwbacks to an earlier stage of human evolutionary development. American psychologist William Sheldon (1949), a direct intellectual heir of Lombroso, identified three basic types of body shape: endomorphs (soft and round), mesomorphs (muscular and hard), and ectomorphs (lean and fragile). Sheldon concluded that criminals were more likely to be mesomorphs.

The theories of Lombroso and Sheldon are not generally considered valid today, but the search for a connection between physical characteristics and deviant behavior continues. Contemporary research in this area is much more sophisticated methodologically than the work of Lombroso and Sheldon (Rowe 1983, 1986; Mednick, Gabrieli, and Hutchings 1984; Brunner et al. 1993; Rafter 2008; Walsh and Beaver 2009). The most influential contemporary attempt to establish a link between biology and criminal behavior appears in a book entitled *Crime and Human Nature*, by James Q. Wilson and Richard Herrnstein (1985). The authors argue that Lombroso was thinking in the right direction. Although criminals are not born, the authors

Because of its hurtful nature, gossip can be a very effective informal sanction.

contend that many people are born with "constitutional factors"—personality, intelligence, anatomy—that predispose them to serious criminal behavior. Wilson and Herrnstein point to research on twins and adopted children. Criminality is said to be more common among identical twins than among fraternal twins. This is taken to be important because identical twins are the same genetically, whereas fraternal twins are only as genetically similar as brothers and sisters. Sons of chronic offenders raised in noncriminal homes are reported to have a three times greater probability of following a life of crime than sons of nonoffenders who have been adopted by law-abiding parents. Wilson and Herrnstein are careful to point out that they are referring only to genetic predispositions toward criminal behavior. People with these biological predispositions do not necessarily become criminals; these predispositions may be offset by socialization in an emotionally supportive environment, such as the family.

Q How do sociologists evaluate biological explanations of deviance? Sociologists generally have not placed much stock in biological explanations of deviance. There are five main reasons for this.

1. Biological theories ignore the fact that deviance is more widely distributed throughout society than are the hereditary and other physical abnormalities that are supposedly the causes of deviance.
2. Biological theories almost totally discount the influence of social, economic, and cultural factors. These theories fail to explain how a person can have a genetic predisposition for something that is relative.
3. Early biological theories of deviance were based on methodologically weak research.

4. There are ideological problems and controversial implications inherent in the biological approach. Forced sterilization of "defectives" and related eugenic strategies for reducing crime have created a storm of protests.
5. Finally, biological factors are more often invoked to explain the deviance of armed robbers, murderers, and heroin addicts than, say, the crimes of corporate executives, government officials, and other high-status persons (Empey 1982).

Personality as the Source of Deviance

Q What common focus do psychological theories of deviance share? As varied as they are, psychological explanations of deviance all locate the origin of criminality in the individual personality (J. Hagan 1994). This is to be expected because psychology, as discussed in Chapter 1, concentrates on the development and functioning of mental-emotional processes in human beings. More specifically, psychological theories of deviance take for granted the existence of a "criminal personality": a pathological personality with measurable characteristics that distinguish criminals from noncriminals. Pathological personality traits may be either inherited (and therefore related to biological explanations of deviance) or socially acquired (Raine 1993).

Although Sigmund Freud did not attempt to explore the origins of deviance, his biologically based instinctual approach to human personality lends itself to such exploration. Psychologists who have adapted Freud's theories to the study of deviance believe that deviance is due to unconscious personality conflicts created in infancy and early childhood. For example, criminality is said to be the result of biologically based desires beyond the control of a defective ego and superego. Other psychological explanations of crime are based on the identification of specific personality traits. Delinquents are said to be more aggressive, hostile, rebellious, or extroverted than nondelinquents (Glueck and Glueck 1950; Eysenck 1977). Some advocates of the psychological search for the criminal personality contend that criminals are born rather than made, an approach closely akin to biological explanations of deviance (Yochelson and Samenow 1994).

Q What is the sociological critique of psychological theories of deviance? Psychological theories fall short of a thorough grasp of deviance. First, they often ignore social, economic, and cultural factors shown by sociological research to affect the likelihood, frequency, and types of deviance. Second, psychological theories focus on deviance such as murder, rape, and drug addiction with relatively little to say about such deviance as white-collar crime. Third, psychological theories tend

How did the Reverend King's philosophy of nonviolence, which, however, encouraged the breaking of laws, benefit American society?

AP Images

to view deviance as the result of physical or psychiatric defects rather than as actions considered deviant by social and legal definitions. Fourth, psychological theories of deviance cannot explain why deviant behavior is engaged in by individuals not classifiable as pathological personalities. Finally, psychological theories, with their emphasis on pathology—deviants are "psychopaths" or "antisocial" personalities—suggest eugenic solutions to the crime problem that are unacceptable to some segments of society. For example, because more deviance occurs among certain racial and ethnic groups, birth control might be seen as a solution to the crime problem that is the most consistent with psychological theories.

This brings us to sociological explanations of deviance. The specific theories of deviance will be discussed within the frameworks of functionalism, symbolic interactionism, and conflict theory.

Functionalism and Deviance [R1]

Functionalism sheds light on deviance, both in a general sense and via the strain theory of Robert Merton. We will examine both of these contributions as well as that of control theory.

Costs and Benefits of Deviance

Functionalism attempts to explain both the negative and the positive effects of social forces on society. It is easy to think of deviance as having negative social

CHECK YOURSELF 7.2 [R2]

Biological and Psychological Explanations of Deviance
1. Recent research has established a definite causal relationship between certain human biological characteristics and deviant behavior. T or F?
2. According to James Q. Wilson and Richard Herrnstein,
   ___ a. studies of adopted children cannot help in understanding possible biological antecedents of criminal behavior.
   ___ b. intelligence is not correlated with criminality.
   ___ c. emotionally supportive families cannot help prevent criminal behavior.
   ___ d. constitutional factors predispose individuals to criminality.
3. Which of the following is not one of the psychological approaches to deviance?
   ___ a. extroversion
   ___ b. race
   ___ c. unconscious conflicts
   ___ d. IQ
4. Psychological theories of deviance still have not developed the breadth to be able to explain occupational crime. T or F?

Answers: 1. F; 2. d; 3. b; 4.T

consequences. It is harder to imagine benefits of deviance, but functionalism tells us that there are some.

Q What are the negative effects of deviance on society? Widespread violation of norms threatens the foundation of social life. What would happen if bus drivers decided to create their own routes each morning, if local television stations aired what they preferred rather than what had been scheduled, if parents took care of their children's needs only when it was convenient? The result of such nonconformity is social disorder from which follows unpredictability, tension, and conflict.

Deviance erodes trust. If bus drivers do not follow the planned route, if television stations constantly violate their schedules, if parents support their children only sporadically, trust is undermined. A society characterized by widespread suspicion and distrust cannot function smoothly. Take, for instance, the effects of rape. As pointed out in "Using the Sociological Imagination," rape overwhelmingly occurs between people who know one another. Almost one-fourth of college women report being victims of rape. Consequently, increasing female distrust often creates a barrier to normal dating relationships.

Unpunished deviance may encourage others to be nonconformists. If bus drivers regularly pass people waiting for the bus, those people might bombard the buses with rocks. If television stations offer random programming, customers may damage their facilities in protest. If parents neglect their children, more teenagers may turn to delinquency. Deviance stimulates more deviance.

Deviant behavior is also expensive. For one thing, it diverts resources, both human and monetary. Police may have to spend their time dealing with wayward bus drivers, irate passengers, and mobs of annoyed television viewers rather than performing more serious duties. And if delinquency skyrockets, the criminal justice system will be even more jammed than it already is.

Q How does deviance benefit society? Despite its negative effects, deviance can sometimes benefit society. Emile Durkheim observed that deviance clarifies norms. By exercising social control, society defines, adjusts, and reaffirms norms; it defends its values. When parents are taken to court or lose their children because of neglect, for example, society's expectations are demonstrated to other parents and children.

Deviance can be a temporary safety valve. Teenagers listen to music, watch television programs, and wear clothes that adults may view as deviating from expected behavior. Involvement in this relatively minor deviant behavior may relieve some of the pressure teenagers feel from the social demands of the adult world (parents, teachers, clergy).

Deviance increases unity within a society or group. When deviance reminds people of something they

value, it strengthens their commitment to that value. The exposure of government spies selling secrets to an enemy intensifies feelings of patriotism. Learning of parents who abuse their children may encourage other parents to rededicate themselves to proper child care.

Deviance promotes needed social change. Suffragettes who took to the streets in the early 1900s scandalized the nation but helped bring women the right to vote. Prison riots in the past have led to the reform of inhumane conditions. As deplorable as it sounds, the discovery of sexual molestation of young children has led to an improvement of day-care facilities. Looting and other deviant behavior in inner cities has promoted some government efforts to revitalize urban American.

Strain Theory

According to Durkheim (1964; originally published in 1893), **anomie** is a social condition in which norms are weak, conflicting, or absent. In the absence of shared norms, individuals are uncertain as to how they should think and act, and societies become disorganized. Robert Merton (1968) has adapted this concept of anomie to deviant behavior. He calls it strain theory.

According to Merton's **strain theory**, deviance is most likely to occur when there is a discrepancy between a culturally prescribed goal (e.g., economic success) and a legitimate means of obtaining it (education). The resulting strain leads some people to engage in deviant behavior. Merton asserts that culture determines the things people should want (goals) and the legitimate ways (means) of obtaining these things. In American society, an important goal is success and the acquisition of the material possessions that usually accompanies it. Although everyone is taught to value material success, contends Merton, some are denied access to the legitimate means for achieving it (Passas and Agnew 1997).

How do people respond to strain? Merton suggests five general modes of adaptation. By way of illustration, Merton uses the American goal of success (see Table 7.1). One possible response is *conformity*—pursuing culturally approved goals through legitimate means. Here, people accept the goal and the means to achieve it. The very wealthy come to mind. But this category also includes poor people who continue to work hard in conventional jobs in the hope of improving life for themselves and their children. By definition, conformity is not deviant behavior. All of the other four responses are considered deviant, however.

In *innovation*, the individual accepts the goal of success but adopts illegitimate means for achieving it. Teenagers may steal an expensive automobile. Others may use prostitution, robbery, drug dealing, or other lucrative criminal behavior to be successful. Innovation is the most widespread and obvious type of deviant response.

TABLE 7.1

Conforming and Deviant Responses in Merton's Strain Theory

Describe the deviant behavior of some people you know using two of Merton's deviant responses.

Success as a Culturally Approved Goal	Hard Work as the Socially Accepted Way to Succeed	Conformity Response	Deviant Responses	Examples
Accepts goal of success	• Accepts hard work as the apppropriate way to succeed	**Conformity** —works hard to succeed		Business executive
Accepts goal of success	• Rejects hard work as the appropriate way to succeed		**Innovation**—finds illegal ways to succeed	Criminal
Rejects goal of success	• Accepts hard work as the appropriate way to succeed		**Ritualism**—acts as if he wants to succeed but does not exert much effort	Unmotivated teacher
Rejects goal of success	• Rejects hard work as the appropriate way to succeed		**Retreatism**—drops out of the race for success	Skid-row alcoholic
Rejects goal of success	• Rejects hard work as the appropriate way to succeed		**Rebellion**—substitutes new way to achieve new goal	Militia group member

Source: Adapted from Robert K. Merton, *Social Theory and Social Structure*, rev. ed. (New York: Free Press, 1968).

In *ritualism*, the individual rejects the goal (success) but maintains the legitimate means. People go through the motions without really believing in the process. One example is the bureaucrat who continues to go about the daily routines of work while abandoning any idea of moving up the ladder. A college student may come to believe that college is without meaning, that the whole experience is a disappointment, that his or her goal of extreme economic success will not be realized. Yet, because of family expectations or lack of alternatives, he or she may continue to go through the motions needed to graduate.

Retreatism is a deviant response in which both the legitimate means and the approved goals are rejected. Skid-row alcoholics, drug addicts, and bag ladies have dropped out. Retreatists fail to be successful by either legitimate or illegitimate means; they do not even seek success.

In *rebellion*, people reject both success and the approved means for achieving it. At the same time, they substitute a new set of goals and means. Some militia group members in the United States illustrate this response. They may live in near isolation while pursuing their goal of changing society. They may use such means as creating their own currency, deliberately violating gun laws, and threatening (or engaging in) violent behavior against law enforcement officers.

Q **How has strain theory been applied?** Strain theory has been used most extensively in the study of juvenile delinquency. Albert Cohen (1977) uses the theory to explain the prevalence of gang delinquency among lower-class youth. According to Cohen, lower-class youth are poorly equipped to succeed in the middle-class world of school, which rewards verbal skills, academic success, neatness, and the ability to delay gratification. To protect their self-esteem, the youth reject these rules of success and self-worth and create their own status standards—standards they are able to achieve. Being tough, destructive, and daring is a vital part of this status system.

According to Richard Cloward and Lloyd Ohlin (1998), deviance does not always result from the strain created by a discrepancy between cultural goals and socially approved means for reaching these goals. Cloward and Ohlin refine strain theory, emphasizing that deviant behavior is not an automatic response; like any other type of behavior, deviance must be learned. And learning must take place through observation of others. Thus, deviance is more likely to occur as observation of others increases.

The Cloward and Ohlin concept helps explain why deviance occurs more in some parts of a society than in others. In middle- and upper-class homes, young people are encouraged to value education—the most important socially approved means for success—and are exposed constantly to people who are, through legitimate means, successful. Poor young people, on the other hand, can more easily model their behavior after pimps, drug dealers, and other types of criminals who have illegitimately acquired material symbols of success—money, clothes, cars, and women. And when juvenile delinquents are sent to reform schools or prisons, they increase their opportunity to learn criminal behavior because they associate with well-practiced veterans. Cloward and Ohlin's use of strain theory overlaps with the symbolic interactionist approach to deviance, discussed in the next section.

Q **How can strain theory be evaluated?** Merton's strain theory has had great staying power, in part because of its applicability to juvenile delinquency and crime. Another advantage is its emphasis on social structure rather than on individuals.

Strain theory has some shortcomings. Because it is in the functionalist tradition, it assumes a consensus in values; it assumes that everyone values success and defines success in economic terms. Also, strain theory does not seem to explain an individual's preference for one mode of adaptation over another. Why, for instance, do some people choose to conform rather than to rebel? Finally, although strain theory helps explain crime and delinquency, it offers no help in explaining other types of deviance, such as mental illness or drug abuse.

Control Theory

Travis Hirschi's (1972) control theory is also based on Durkheim's concept of deviance. According to **control theory**, conformity to social norms depends on a strong bond between individuals and society. If that bond is weak or is broken for some reason—if anomie is present—deviance occurs. In control theory, then, social bonds *control* the behavior of people; it is the social bond that prevents deviance from occurring. Individuals conform because they fear that deviance will harm the relationships they have with others. They don't want to "lose face" with family members, friends, or classmates.

Q **What are the basic elements of social bonds?** According to Hirschi, the social bond has four intertwined dimensions:

1. *Attachment.* The likelihood of conformity varies with the strength of the ties one has with parents, friends, and institutions such as schools and churches. The stronger the attachment, the more likelihood of conformity.
2. *Commitment.* The greater one's commitment to legitimate social goals such as educational attainment and occupational success, the more likely one is to conform. The commitment of adults exceeds that of teenagers; and the commitment of individuals who believe their hard work will be rewarded is greater than the commitment of those who think they cannot compete within the system.
3. *Involvement.* Participation in legitimate social activities increases the probability of conformity, both because it positively focuses time and energy and because it encourages contact with others whose good opinion one values.

4. *Belief.* Subscription to norms and values of society promotes conformity. Respect for the rules of social life strengthens one against the temptations of deviance.

In short, when social bonds are weak, the chances for deviance increase. Individuals who lack attachment, commitment, involvement, and belief have little incentive to follow the rules of society.

Q **How has control theory been received by other social scientists?** Generally speaking, empirical support for Hirschi's control theory has been relatively strong. Several studies demonstrate the theory's power to explain both nondelinquent and deviant behavior (Bernard 1987; Rosenbaum 1987; Sampson and Laub 1990).

Scientific support weakened, though, when Hirschi attempted to broaden his control theory of delinquency into a more general theory encompassing all types of crime (Gottfredson and Hirschi 1990; Hirschi and Gottfredson 1990). Critics are skeptical that a specific theory of conformity and delinquency can explain crime in all its varieties, ranging from insider trading to murder. The existence of weak social bonds may satisfactorily account for pimps, drug dealers, and carjackers. But it is much more difficult for control theory to explain socially well-integrated individuals who embezzle corporate funds, use public monies for private purposes, or dump toxic waste into rivers (J. Hagan 1994; McCaghy et al. 2007). In fairness, expansion of control theory needs further research.

Symbolic Interactionism and Deviance [R1]

According to theories based on symbolic interaction, deviance is learned through socialization. Concepts such as the looking-glass self, significant others, primary group, reference group, and the generalized other, discussed in Chapter 4, underlie both cultural transmission theory and labeling theory.

Cultural Transmission Theory

Q **What is cultural transmission theory?** Cultural transmission theory emerged from the "Chicago School" during the 1920s and 1930s. According to **cultural transmission theory**, deviance is part of a subculture; it is transmitted through socialization. Clifford Shaw and Henry McKay (1929) observed that delinquency rates stay high in certain neighborhoods, even though the ethnic composition changes over the years. According to Shaw and McKay, delinquency in these neighborhoods persists because it is transmitted through play groups and gangs. As new ethnic groups

Functionalism and Deviance

1. Which of the following is *not* one of the benefits of deviance for society?
   ____ a. It decreases suspicion and mistrust.
   ____ b. It promotes social change.
   ____ c. It increases social unity among members of a society.
   ____ d. It provides a safety valve.
   ____ e. It promotes clarification of norms.

2. According to _____ theory, deviance is most likely to occur when there is a discrepancy between culturally prescribed goals and the socially approved means of obtaining them.

3. A college professor who simply goes through the motions of teaching classes without any thought of success is an example of which of the following responses in strain theory?
   ____ a. rebellion
   ____ b. conformity
   ____ c. ritualism
   ____ d. innovation
   ____ e. retreatism

4. The higher commitment to societal values and norms among adults than teenagers is consistent with the principles of _____ theory.

Answers: 1. a; 2. strain; 3. c; 4. control

enter the neighborhoods, they learn delinquent behavior from the neighborhood residents (Warr 2002).

Edwin Sutherland and Donald Cressey (1992) helped to extend cultural transmission theory to deviance that occurs from generation to generation and from one ethnic group to another. According to **differential association theory**, deviant behavior—like religious choice, political affiliation, or sport preference—is learned, principally, in primary groups. The more individuals are exposed to people who break the law, the more likely they are to become criminals.

At least three other factors impinge on the likelihood of deviance through differential association. First, an individual's vulnerability is affected by the ratio of exposure to deviants and nondeviants. Second, a person is more likely to become a deviant if his or her significant others are deviants. Finally, the earlier a person is exposed to deviants, the more likely that person will become a deviant.

Q How do sociologists evaluate cultural transmission theory? Cultural transmission theory shows that conformity in one setting may be deviant in another. Beyond this, cultural transmission theory explains why individuals placed in prison may become even more committed to deviance; in prison one is exposed almost exclusively to criminals. **Recidivism**—a return to crime after prison—makes sense in the light of cultural transmission theory because ex-convicts normally return to the significant others, primary groups, and reference groups through which they originally learned to be deviants.

Cultural transmission theory leaves unanswered questions. It cannot account for the reason some individuals become deviant without exposure to great numbers of people who advocate breaking the law. Middle-class delinquents are an illustration. Conversely, cultural transmission theory cannot explain why most people reared in crime-ridden environments do not become deviants. Cultural transmission theory is limited in scope because it deals only with crime. Finally, although cultural transmission theory explains how deviance is learned, it fails to explain why some behaviors are considered deviant whereas others are not. An explanation of this relativity of deviance is a major strength of labeling theory.

Labeling Theory

Q Is deviance defined by the act or the label? Although strain theory and cultural transmission theory help us understand why deviance occurs, neither explains the relativity of deviance. **Labeling theory** attempts to fill this gap. In this theory, no act is inherently deviant; deviance is a matter of social definition. According to labeling theory, deviance exists when some members of a group or society label others as deviant. Howard Becker, a pioneer of labeling theory, states the heart of this perspective:

Social groups create deviance by making the rules whose infraction constitutes deviance, and by applying these rules to particular people and labeling them as outsiders. From this point of view, deviance is not a quality of the act the person commits, but rather a consequence of the application by others of rules and sanctions to an "offender." The deviant is one to whom that label has successfully been applied; deviant behavior is behavior that people so label. (Becker 1991:9)

Labeling theory explains, for instance, why a middle-class youth who steals a car may go unpunished for "borrowing" the vehicle, whereas a lower-class youth goes to court for stealing. Too often, lower-class youth are "expected" to be criminals while middle-class youth are not.

Q **Does deviant behavior necessarily carry a label?** Edwin Lemert's (2000) distinction between primary and secondary deviance helps clarify the labeling process. In cases of **primary deviance**, a person engages only in isolated acts of deviance. For example, when college students are asked to respond to a checklist of unlawful activities, most admit to having violated one or more norms, such as cheating, plagiarism, rape, assault, harassment (Hickson and Roebuck 2009). Yet, the vast majority of college students have never been arrested, convicted, or labeled as criminals. Certainly, those who break the law for the first time do not consider themselves criminals. If their deviance stops at this point, they have engaged in primary deviance; deviance is not a part of their lifestyle or self-concept. Juveniles, likewise, may commit a few delinquent acts without becoming committed to a delinquent career or regarding themselves as delinquents.

Some young people decorated this Duke of Wellington statue in Glasgow, Scotland, with a traffic cone. Were they engaged in primary or secondary deviance?

Bullying we think of as primary deviance, a hurtful practice abandoned as one matures. One study, however, found that 60 percent of boys who were bullies as middle schoolers had criminal records before reaching age twenty-five. Additional evidence indicates that bullies have psychological problems and that these problems can extend into adulthood, into secondary deviance ("Battling Bullies" 2010).

Secondary deviance refers to deviance as a lifestyle and a personal identity. Secondary deviants identify themselves as deviants and organize their behavior largely in relation to deviant roles. Other people label them as deviant as well and respond to them accordingly. When this occurs, these individuals usually begin to spend most of their time committing acts of deviance; deviance becomes a way of life, a career (Kelly 1996). Secondary deviance is reflected in the words of Carolyn Hamilton-Ballard, known as Bubbles to her fellow gang members in Los Angeles:

Because of my size, I was automatically labeled a bully-type person.... I mean, people saw that Bloods jacket and since everybody thought I was crazy, I started acting crazy. At first it was an act, but then it became me. After being the target for drive-bys and going through different things, that became my life-style. I started retaliating back and I got more involved. (Johnson and Johnson 1994:209)

Q **What are the consequences of labeling?** Erving Goffman illuminates negative effects of labeling when he wrote about **stigma**—an undesirable characteristic or label used by others to deny the deviant full social acceptance (Falk 2001). Stigmatic labels—such as child pornographer, jailbird, crazy, fat, homeless, and cripple can spoil an individual's entire social identity (Heatherton et al. 2000; Hudak and Kihn 2001; Link and Phelan 2001).

One label can discredit an individual's sense of self worth. The words of a forty-three-year-old bricklayer, who was unemployed during the Depression, illustrate this point:

How hard and humiliating it is to bear the name of an unemployed man. When I go out, I cast down my eyes because I feel myself wholly inferior. When I go along the street, it seems to me that I can't be compared with an average citizen, that everybody is pointing at me with his finger. I instinctively avoid meeting anyone. Former acquaintances and friends of better times are no longer so cordial. They greet me indifferently when we meet. They no longer offer me a cigarette and their eyes seem to say, "You are not worth it, you don't work." (Goffman 1963:17)

Obviously, it is the labeling of an attribute rather than the attribute itself that causes psychological pain and suffering. What matters, for example, is the manner in which an attribute is acquired. Someone with a severe speech impediment caused by a war injury in Iraq is not likely to be labeled by those who know the origin of the impediment.

The application of stigmas varies by time and place. Today's active membership in a political party in the United States is considered a sign of good citizenship. To the generation of George Washington and Thomas Jefferson, being an advocate of a political party was a major stigma that made one unacceptable for national office. Even campaigning for office was a sign of unworthiness (Ellis 2007).

Q Does labeling cause deviance? According to labeling theory, labeling is all that is required for an act to be deviant. Deviance, however, cannot be defined solely by the reactions of others. If an act is not deviant unless it is labeled, there can be no such thing as undetected deviance.

Deviance cannot be defined without some reference to norms, but this does not mean that labeling processes are unimportant. Future behavior may be affected by the way others respond to an individual's deviance. In this sense, labeling produces deviants. To assign a person the label of delinquent, drug addict, or prostitute is a form of social penalty that may lead to rejection and exclusion from conventional groups and consequently may evoke further deviant acts. Labeling leads to deviance when it produces secondary deviance.

Recall the study of the Roughnecks and the Saints, two teenage high school gangs. According to Chambliss (1973), labeling the Roughnecks as deviants promoted additional deviance. Labeling the Saints as upstanding young men promoted conformity to most conventional norms (see "Consider This Research").

It is especially interesting to examine mental illness from the labeling perspective, because mental disorders, being a part of the medical field, are assumed to have an objective basis like cancer or arteriosclerosis. Labeling theory offers a unique way of viewing mental illness.

Mental Illness and Labeling Theory

Q How does labeling theory approach mental illness? By virtue of its foundation in symbolic interactionism, labeling theory views mental illness as the result of social interaction in which others respond to us and we imagine what those responses mean. Mental illness is considered a matter of social definition (Collier 1993).

According to psychiatrist Thomas Szasz (1986), mental illness, as defined by the medical community, is a myth. Szasz sees the behaviors associated with mental disorder as adaptations to interaction-based stresses threatening to overwhelm an individual. In response to "problems of living," people (primarily unconsciously) impersonate a sick person to obtain help from others.

Thomas Scheff (1974, 1999) formulated a theory of mental illness (based on the labeling perspective) in which most psychiatric symptoms of mental illness are seen as violations of social norms. Because of temporary pressures, contends Scheff, anyone might exhibit behaviors that violate norms—withdrawing socially, becoming overly suspicious, muttering to oneself. Others usually consider this primary deviance as transitory and ignore it. If others exaggerate and distort this rule breaking, it can lead to a label—mentally ill. If the process of labeling goes far enough, mental illness may become a career path; it may reach the stage of secondary deviance in which it becomes part of a person's self-concept. Thus, a social process may label a person mentally ill when, in fact, the original deviance may have been only temporary acts to handle temporary pressures.

Scheff's critics present data showing that the prime factor determining the negative reaction of others to mental patients is the patients' behavior, not the label such people have acquired (D. Phillips 1963, 1964; Link and Cullen 1983). More recent research concludes that labels do matter and that labeling theory cannot be dismissed as a framework for understanding responses to the mentally ill (Link 1987; Link et al. 1987).

Q How do sociologists assess the value of labeling theory? Labeling theory has contributed several insights. First, it established that deviance is a matter of social definition and that deviance is relative. Second, labeling theory highlights, through concepts such as secondary deviance and stigma, the acquisition of a deviant self-concept that is likely to lead to a career of deviance. Third, labeling theory applies to a greater variety of deviance than the other theories. It can be applied to mental illness and prostitution as easily as to drug dealing and homosexuality.

Labeling theory also has its limitations. It does not explain habitual deviants who have never been detected and labeled, nor does it deal with isolated acts of deviance (primary deviance). It is also possible that labeling may halt rather than create deviance, as in the case of a man who frequents pornographic movie houses until he is suddenly discovered and labeled by his friends. Also, with its accent on relativity, labeling theory tends to overlook the fact that some acts, such as murder and incest, are banned in virtually all societies. Finally, labeling theory tends to generate sympathy for deviants, who are depicted as innocent victims of labeling.

Labeling theory implies that those who react against deviants are the culprits. Lawmakers do not cause people to commit criminal acts. It seems inappropriate to say that a police officer who arrests a person is somehow at fault. If the criminal law were abolished, acts that result in injuries would not disappear. In other words, a "mugging by any other name hurts just as much" (Nettler 1984).

CHECK YOURSELF **7.4** R2

Symbolic Interactionism and Deviance

1. Which of the following did Edwin Sutherland mean by differential association?
   ____ a. Crime is more likely to occur among individuals who have been exposed more to unfavorable attitudes toward the law than to favorable ones.
   ____ b. People become criminals through association with criminals.
   ____ c. Crime is not transmitted culturally.
   ____ d. Crime comes from differential conflict.
2. _____ theory is the only sociological theory that takes into account the relativity of deviance.
3. _____ refers to deviance as a lifestyle and personal identity.
4. _____ is an undesirable characteristic used by others to deny the deviant full social acceptance.
5. According to labeling theory, mental illness is a matter of _____.

Answers: 1. a; 2. Labeling; 3. Secondary deviance; 4. Stigma; 5. social definition

Conflict Theory and Deviance R1

Deviance in Capitalist Society

Of the several conflict perspectives of deviance, Marxist researchers have forged an influential line of theory and research (Quinney 1980; Chambliss and Seidman 1982; Swaaningen 1997; Arrigo 1999). Focusing on class conflict, Marxist criminologists see deviance as a product of the exploitative nature of the ruling class. Deviance is behavior that the rich and powerful see as threatening to their interests. Consequently, the rich and powerful determine which acts are deviant and to what extent deviants are punished. (See Table 7.2 for examples of deviant behavior according to funtionalism, conflict theory, and symbolic interactionism.)

According to the Marxian interpretation, the rich and powerful use the law to maintain their position. They can do this, argue the Marxists, because a society's beliefs, values, and norms (including, of course, laws) exist to protect the interests of the ruling class.

Q By what means do capitalism and deviance become linked? Steven Spitzer (1980) theorized some basic ways in which the culture of a capitalist society supports its economic system. First, critics of capitalism are considered deviants because their beliefs challenge the economic, political, and social basis of capitalism. Second, because capitalism requires a willing workforce, those who will not work are deviants. Third, those who threaten private property, especially that belonging to the rich, are prime targets for punishment. Fourth, because society needs respect for authority, it treats people who show a lack of respect for authority—agitators on the job, people who stage nonviolent demonstrations

TABLE 7.2

FOCUS ON THEORETICAL PERSPECTIVES: Illustrating Deviance

This table provides illustrations of deviance using concepts associated with a particular theoretical perspective. Construct some examples of your own.

Theoretical Perspective	Sociological Concept	Examples of Deviance
Functionalism	Anomie	• Delinquent gangs sell drugs because they do not agree with the norms and values against drug use advocated in the larger society.
Conflict theory	White-collar crime	• A convicted Wall Street stock manipulator (a more powerful member of society) may spend less time in prison than a factory worker (a less powerful member of society) found guilty of the same crime.
Symbolic interactionism	Labeling	• Some high school students reject dating because they have been consistently treated and described as "not cool."

against established practices—as deviants. Fifth, certain activities and characteristics are encouraged or discouraged, depending on their congruence with the requirements of the economic system. Athletics are approved because they foster competition, achievement, teamwork, and winning. Nonathletic males are wimps (Eder 1995; Adler and Adler 1998).

The Marxian perspective is not the only way to understand deviance from the conflict viewpoint. The relationship between minorities and the judicial system is another approach; white-collar crime is yet another (J. W. Coleman 1987, 1989; G. S. Green 1997; F. E. Hagan 2010).

Race, Ethnicity, and Crime

Q **What is the relationship among race, ethnicity, and crime?** Advocates of conflict theory point to the differential treatment minorities receive in the American criminal justice system. They cite statistics showing that, at all points in the criminal justice process, African Americans and Latinos are dealt with more harshly than whites— from arrest through indictment, conviction, sentencing, and parole (Walker, Spohn, and Delone 2007; Reiman and Leighton 2010; Schaefer 2010). Even when the criminal offense is the same, African Americans and Latinos are more likely than whites to be convicted, and they serve more time in prison than whites.

From a variety of studies reviewed by the Death Penalty Information Center, it is clear that race influences both the conviction rate and the execution rate for murder. Research consistently shows that those who murder white victims have a significantly higher probability of receiving a death sentence than those who kill black victims. Almost 80 percent of completed capital murder cases involve white victims, even though only half of all murder victims are white. Thus, even though nearly one-half of all homicide victims in the United States are African American, more than 80 percent of prisoners on death row are there for murdering whites.

Q **Why do minorities have a higher probability of being arrested, convicted, and severely punished?** Conflict theory suggests several reasons for differences in the way minorities and whites are treated in the criminal justice system. For one thing, conflict theorists point to the fact that minorities generally do not have the economic resources to buy good legal services. Thus, the outcomes of their trials are not likely to be as favorable to them.

Sociologists who follow the conflict perspective believe that people who commit crimes against whites tend to be punished more severely by the courts than people who commit crimes against minorities because society sees minority interests as less important than the interests of whites. **Victim discounting** reduces the seriousness of crimes directed against members of lower

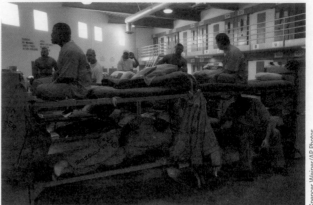

Even when they have committed the same crimes, African Americans and Latinos are more severely punished than whites.

Spencer Weiner/AP Photos

social classes (Gibbons 1985). According to the logic behind victim discounting, if the victim is less valuable, the crime is less serious, and the penalty is less severe.

Michelle Alexander (2010) believes that advocates of the conflict perspective are accurate. In her book, *The New Jim Crow,* Alexander contends that a black social caste in America is not gone, it has merely mutated into a new form. Jim Crow and legal racial segregation, she writes, have been replaced by mass imprisonment as a way to control and dominate blacks. As we shall see later in this chapter, young black men do comprise the majority of American prison inmates. According to Alexander, this "warehousing" of inner-city black youths is a new version of Jim Crow, which shuts many black men out of full participation in American society because the stigma of a prison record makes it almost impossible to enter the mainstream. Alexander traces this situation to the War on Drugs which, she contends, was spawned by a racially coded backlash to the civil rights movement, masked under the banner of public indifference to racial issues than to racial bias. James Unnever and Francis Cullen (2010), however, offer evidence that racial resentment does help to sustain the "get tough on crime" movement.

Occupational and Corporate Crime

Q **What is the distinction between occupational crime and corporate crime?** According to Edwin Sutherland (1940, 1983), the originator of the term, **white-collar crime** is any crime committed by respectable high-status people in the course of their occupations. Or, as one researcher put it, lower-status people commit crimes of the streets; higher-status people engage in "crimes of the suites" (Nader and Green 1972; D. R. Simon 2007). Officially, the term *white-collar crime* is reserved for economic crimes such as price fixing, insider trading, illegal rebates, embezzlement, bribery of a corporate customer, manufacture of hazardous products, toxic pollution, and tax evasion (Geis, Meier, and

Bernie Madoff is currently America's most recognized white-collar criminal. In 2009, he received a 150-year prison sentence for bilking investors of some $65 billion.

Salinger 1995; J. W. Coleman 1997; Calavita, Pontell, and Tillman 1999; Weisburd and Waring 2001).

Since Sutherland, sociologists have refined the idea of white-collar crime, recognizing the difference between crimes committed by individuals (*occupational crime*) and crimes committed by organizations (*corporate crime*). **Occupational crime** refers to illegal acts by people either in their employment or in their personal financial pursuits. In 2009, Bernie Madoff, founder of Bernard L. Madoff Investment Securities, single-handedly, and for his own benefit, bilked his clients of some $65 billion. The only consolation for those who lost their life's saving was the 150-year prison sentence Madoff received, the most time the judge could give (Healy 2009). A subspecies of occupational crime is **corporate crime,** crime committed on behalf of organizations. Corporate crime involves illegal collusion between employees and employers in pursuit of corporate benefit (Munice, Talbot, and Walters 2010). U.S. citizens were dismayed in 2002 to discover that many large corporations, including Enron and WorldCom, had illegally underreported their earnings in order to inflate their stock value. Moreover, they were shocked to learn, these corporations were aided in this deception by some accounting firms—such as Arthur Andersen—that were supposed to audit them. And all the while, brokers with national investment houses such as Merrill Lynch were encouraging investors to purchase stock they actually believed to be worthless in order to protect their firms' lucrative investment banking contracts with some of these same large corporations. Due to the subsequent collapse of stock values, thousands of workers lost their jobs (and their retirement nest eggs), and individual stockholders and pension funds lost billions.

There are more recent examples of large-scale corporate crime. Matt Taibbi reports on the role investment banking giant Goldman Sachs played in the global housing bubble disaster of the first decade of this century. By 2006, at the pinnacle of the housing boom, Goldman was issuing some $4.5 billion worth of investment securities based on the massive bundling of mortgages. Many of these investment vehicles contained toxic mortgages issued fraudulently. We know that Goldman was aware that it was selling some worthless investments because it was betting against them in the stock market as it sold them to many institutional investors like pension funds and insurance companies (Taibbi 2010). Lehman Brothers, the fourth largest Wall Street bank prior to its collapse in 2008, also issued massive amounts of these same kinds of high-risk or worthless mortgage-backed securities. According to Lawrence McDonald, a vice president at the company at the time, Lehman continued to sell these junk securities even after learning that they were based on mortgages sure to be defaulted (McDonald 2009). Ameriquest Mortgage was also a big player in the housing bubble. Michael Hudson reports that Ameriquest deliberately copied the techniques in the white-collar crime movie *Boiler Room* to train its employees to sell overpriced subprime loans to unsuspecting people wishing either to buy new homes or to refinance the homes they already owned (Hudson 2010).

Q **How does the conflict perspective view occupational and corporate crime?** Advocates of conflict theory point out that occupational and corporate crime is extremely harmful to society. Its perpetrators, however, are treated more leniently than other criminals because of their class position (Henry and Lanier 2001).

The costs of occupational and corporate crime are higher than is generally thought. According to the U.S. Department of Justice, occupational and corporate crime costs in excess of $200 billion annually—an amount eighteen times greater than the costs of street crime. Illegal working environments (e.g., factories that expose workers to toxic chemicals) account for about one-third of all work-related deaths in the United States. Five times more Americans are killed each year from illegal job conditions than are murdered on the streets. None of these figures, of course, reflect the costs to society of a demoralized citizenry bombarded by news of criminal acts by corporate, political, and religious leaders (D. R. Simon 2007).

Despite this social harm, much more tolerance is shown to occupational and corporate criminals than to felons in the lower classes. Penalties are both tougher and more frequent for crimes committed by lower-class people than for those committed by higher-status people. Drug law violators (more likely to be from the lower class), for example, receive more harsh treatment than embezzlers. Although fewer than 400 embezzlers are in prison, thousands of drug law violators are incarcerated. In federal court, where most occupational and corporate cases are tried, probation is granted to

CHECK YOURSELF 7.5 R2

Conflict Theory and Deviance

1. Marxist criminologists see deviance as a product of the exploitative nature of the _____.

2. Which of the following is *not* one of the basic ways the culture of a capitalist society supports the society's economic system?

    ____ a. People whose beliefs clash with capitalism are labeled deviants.

    ____ b. Capitalism requires a willing workforce.

    ____ c. Innovation is rewarded.

    ____ d. People who fail to show respect for authority are likely to be considered deviant.

3. The process of reducing the seriousness of crimes based on the lower social value placed on the victims is called _____.

4. _____ is any crime committed by people in their employment or in their personal financial pursuits.

Answers: 1. ruling class; 2. c; 3. victim discounting; 4. Occupational crime

40 percent of antitrust violators, 61 percent of fraud defendants, and 70 percent of embezzlers. In general, these criminals are less likely to be imprisoned; and if they are, they receive shorter sentences. Consider this. None of the executives of Wall Street bank and financial corporations went to jail, despite their criminal role in the loss of trillions of dollars worldwide (Taibbi 2011). Moreover, when sentenced, occupational and corporate criminals are more likely to be placed in a facility with extra amenities (e.g., tennis courts or private rooms), which critics have dubbed "Club Fed" (Gest 1985; U.S. Department of Justice 1987; Reiman and Leighton 2010).

What are the strengths and weaknesses of the conflict approach to deviance? Of course, not all definitions of deviance can be attributed to the exploitation of the weak by the powerful. Laws against murder and rape are meant to protect both the rich and the poor. Moreover, some laws—consumer and environmental laws—exist despite the opposition of big business. Even proponents of the conflict perspective would not conclude that deviance exists only because of cultural and social arrangements supportive of the ruling class. Nevertheless, the conflict approach, like labeling theory, underscores the relativity of deviance. Perhaps the greatest strength of conflict theory is its ability to link deviance to social inequality and power differentials.

Crime in the United States R1

Measurement of Crime

Crime is the most consequential type of deviance in modern society. Most Americans think of **crime**—acts in violation of the law—as including a narrow range of

behavior. On the contrary, in the United States, more than 2,800 acts are considered federal crimes, and many more acts violate state and local statutes. (See

The job of the forensic scientist is to examine evidence—fingerprints, DNA, handwriting, firearms for indications that a crime has occurred. Here Eric Szmanda, one of the stars of the television series CSI, is pretending to be a forensic scientist.

Cyber Criminals Want Your Identity

Cyber theft is one of the crimes reported by the Bureau of Justice Statistics. The FBI defines *cyber theft* as crimes in which a computer is used to steal money or other things of value. Violations include embezzlement, fraud, theft of intellectual property, and theft of financial or personal data (U.S. Bureau of Justice 2010). One of our most valued possessions is our identity. The frequency of identity theft began skyrocketing around the turn of the present century (O'Brien 2000; Grabosky and Smith 2001; O'Harrow 2001). The results to victims can be devastating. Veronica, a California college student, cannot get a student loan because someone in Michigan is using her identity to open credit card accounts and obtain telephone service. In another case, Meredith rented a room in her house to another woman. After discovering Meredith's Social Security number, this boarder used it to fill out several credit card applications in Meredith's name and to run up more than $70,000 in charges. In yet another example, Graciela has been a victim of identity theft for more than ten years. A thief gained access to her Social Security number, birth certificate, and driver's license. With this information, the imposter has obtained credit cards, purchased furniture, bought cars, and obtained welfare. (All of these examples and more are available through the Privacy Rights Clearinghouse at www.privacyrights.org, 2008.)

Beth Givens of the Privacy Rights Clearinghouse (a nonprofit group for consumers' privacy rights) explains that identity theft can occur in many ways. A thief can steal a wallet or purse, get copies of credit card slips from trash, or steal someone's mail. There are also high-tech methods of identity theft. The most common method is hacking into the computers of credit-rating companies. These companies maintain credit reports that provide valuable information about a consumer—Social Security number, birth date, credit card numbers, address. Although credit-rating companies try to prevent the cybercrime of identity theft, the very nature of their service makes this information accessible through computer terminals. This access is an open invitation to criminals (Muncie, Talbot, and Walters 2010).

The victims of identity theft obviously suffer great damage. Unless the thief is caught in the act, there seems to be little the police can do to stop this kind of crime. At the same time, many victims report that their victimization is compounded by abusive collection agencies. Victims also have to spend time and money cleaning up the mess imposters have created for them—sometimes up to ten years or more. Victims are often scarred emotionally, feeling violated, hopeless, and angry.

The main goal of imposters in identity theft is to purchase items at no cost. In these cases, the victims still maintain their identities. But what if identity theft also involved actually losing one's identity?

What would happen if a person's identity were actually "stolen"? A movie— *The Net*—showed what it might be like to have your identity taken away. In this movie, a woman's entire identity is obliterated by thieves. By stealing the documents that would prove her identity and destroying all of her existing computer records, the criminals hijack her identity. Using her photograph and Social Security number, the villains in the movie create a whole new identity for her, including a new name, bad credit report, and criminal record. As the woman in the movie laments, "They knew everything about me. It was all on the Internet!"

Think About It

Which theoretical perspective would be most useful in analyzing identity theft? Explain your choice, and apply that perspective to identity theft.

"See Sociology in Your Life" for a growing type of nonviolent crime.)

In order to prevent and control crime, society must be aware of just how much crime and what types of felonies are being committed. A major source of America's crime statistics is the FBI's *Uniform Crime Report* (UCR). These official statistics are submitted voluntarily by law enforcement agencies across the country.

Q What is the trend in United States? Crime increased sharply from the 1960s to the early 1990s. For example, the FBI index of violent crime increased from a big-city offense rate per 100,000 of 860 in 1969 to over 1,100 in 2001. The U.S. violent crime rate is considerably higher than in most other industrialized countries. (For a picture of violent crime variations by state, see "Sociology Eyes America 7.1.")

Both violent and property crime, however, declined considerably since the 1990s. Figure 7.3 shows that crime continued to decline during 2009 and 2010 (*Crime in the United States* 2010). The number of reported violent crimes decreased by 6.2 percent, while the number of reported property crimes decreased by 2.8 percent. Reported instances of violent crime were down substantially in the Midwest (4.6 percent), the South (6.6 percent), and the West (5.6 percent), and the Northeast (3.5 percent).

SOCIOLOGY EYES AMERICA **7.1**

Violent Crime

Violent Crime Rate by State

- Low
- Medium
- High

Source: Federal Bureau of Investigation, 2009.

Although experiencing a recent decline, the U.S. has one of the highest violent crime rates of the major industrialized countries. In fact, the U.S. has the highest murder, rape, and robbery rates, and keeps pace in burglaries and auto thefts. This map indicates the number of violent crimes by state per 100,000 residents.

Interpret the Map

1. Create a graph showing how the violent crime rate in your state compares with the rates in other states.
2. Pose a question that relates to the relative ranking of your state with other states.
3. What sociological conclusion can you draw from this map?

Q How reliable is *Uniform Crime Report*? Although the FBI statistics provide considerable information about crime, they have serious limitations. Some critics portray the FBI statistics as overrepresenting the lower classes and minorities but undercounting the middle and upper classes. Amateur thefts and minor assaults are not as likely to be reported to the police as murders and auto thefts. Prostitutes and intoxicated persons are subject to arrest in public places, but they are relatively safe in private settings, where the police cannot enter without a warrant.

About half of violent crimes and almost 40 percent of property crimes are not reported to the police (Truman

FIGURE 7.3

U.S. Crime Rates

Inasmuch as this figure overlays the time period of our worst economic recession since the 1930s, are you surprised that crime continues to decline? Any idea why?

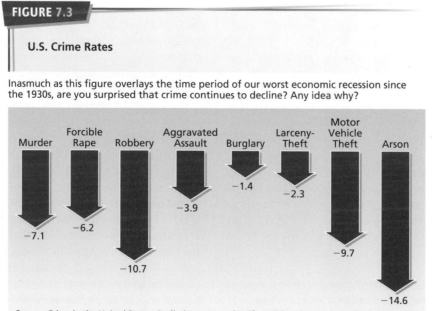

Murder −7.1, Forcible Rape −6.2, Robbery −10.7, Aggravated Assault −3.9, Burglary −1.4, Larceny-Theft −2.3, Motor Vehicle Theft −9.7, Arson −14.6

Source: *Crime in the United States: Preliminary Annual Uniform Crime Report* (Washington D.C.: Federal Bureau of Investigation, December, 2010).

and Rand, 2010). In addition, crime reporting varies from jurisdiction to jurisdiction and from crime to crime. For instance, official crime statistics seldom include government officials, corporate executives, and other white-collar offenders. Finally, in such areas as unfair advertising and job discrimination, special administrative boards enforce the laws rather than the criminal justice system (Ermann and Lundman 1996: J.W. Coleman 1997).

In response to these criticisms, the National Crime Victimization Survey (NCVS) was launched in the early 1970s. The U.S. Census Bureau conducts this survey semi-annually for the Bureau of Justice Statistics, using state-of-the-art survey research techniques. At points, the NCVS and the *Uniform Crime Report* contradict each other. For example, the NCVS indicates that the FBI statistics significantly underestimate the total amount of crime victimization in the United States.

However, both the *UCR* and the NCVS agree that crime is declining in the United States (Truman and Rand 2010). According to the NCVS, both violent and property crime decreased from 2008 to 2009. Violent crime dropped by 11.2 percent and property crime went down by 5.5 percent. In fact, violent crime rates and property crime rates have declined significantly after 2000 (see Figures 7.4 and 7.5). Violent and property crime are now at their lowest level since the survey began in 1973.

Q **Do we need two different reports on crime?** Both the *Uniform Crime Report* and the NCVS have their strengths. Because most people know relatively little about the technical definitions of crime, a major strength of the *Uniform Crime Report* is its use of experienced police

FIGURE 7.5

U.S. Property Crime Rates, 2000–2009

Property crimes overall went down by 29% from 2000 to 2009.

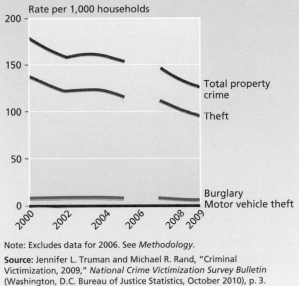

Note: Excludes data for 2006. See *Methodology*.

Source: Jennifer L. Truman and Michael R. Rand, "Criminal Victimization, 2009," *National Crime Victimization Survey Bulletin* (Washington, D.C. Bureau of Justice Statistics, October 2010), p. 3.

officers who decide if an act has violated a statute. The NCVS has two attractive advantages. First, it helps to compensate for the massive underreporting of crime. Second, the surveys are scientifically sound. At the very least, the NCVS is an increasingly important supplement to the FBI's official statistics. Together, these two sources provide a relatively complete account of the extent and nature of crime in the United States.

Juvenile Crime

Juvenile crime refers to violations of the law committed by young people less than eighteen years old. Juvenile offenders are the third largest age category of criminals in the United States, accounting for 12 percent of violent crime arrests and 26 percent of property crime arrests in 2008 (Puzzanchera 2009). From 2006 to 2008 the juvenile arrest rate for violent crime fell by 5 percent and the juvenile arrest rate for property crime increased by 9 percent. A look at the juvenile arrest rate since 1980 provides a more nuanced picture.

Q **What is the trend in juvenile crime?** The total juvenile arrest rate fell dramatically between 1997 and 2008. The pattern is a bit more complicated when we examine violent crime and property crime separately. As shown in Figure 7.6, the juvenile violent crime arrest rate declined to a historic low in 2004, a reduction of 49 percent from its 1994 pinnacle. This ten-year decline

FIGURE 7.4

U.S. Violent Crime Rates, 2000–2009

Overall, violent crime rates declined by 39 percent from 2000 to 2009.

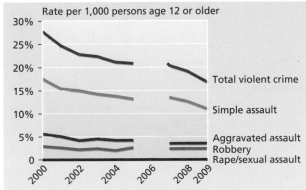

Note: Excludes data for 2006. *See Methodology*.

Source: Jennifer L. Truman and Michael R. Rand, "Criminal Victimization, 2009," *National Crime Victimization Survey Bulletin* (Washington, D.C.: Bureau of Justice Statistics, October 2010), p. 2.

FIGURE 7.6

U.S. Juvenile Violent Crime Arrest Rates

In 1994, the juvenile violent crime arrest rate reached its highest level since 1980. Following 1994, the rate declined to below its 1980 level. Can you explain this downturn?

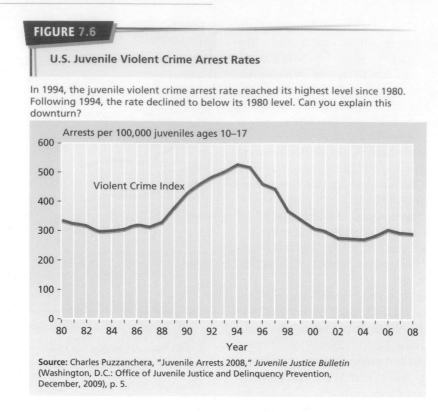

Source: Charles Puzzanchera, "Juvenile Arrests 2008," *Juvenile Justice Bulletin* (Washington, D.C.: Office of Juvenile Justice and Delinquency Prevention, December, 2009), p. 5.

was followed by a 12 percent uptick over the next two years, and a subsequent 5 percent downturn from 2006 to 2008. In spite of the recent increase, the 2008 juvenile property crime arrest rate was 49 percent below its 1991 peak (see Figure 7.7). Juvenile violent and property crime arrests, in short, have declined today to rates below the years prior to the crack epidemic that began in the mid-1980s. This overall diminution is the most dramatic for property crime arrests (Puzzanchera 2009).

Several factors are said to account for this decline in juvenile crime. First, there is a decline in the demand

FIGURE 7.7

U.S. Juvenile Property Crime Arrest Rate

Despite the recent upturn, the 2008 juvenile property crime arrest rate is 49 percent below its 1991 high point. This trend, combined with the downward slope of the juvenile violent crime arrest rate shown in Figure 7.6, attests to a reduction in juvenile criminal behavior following the 1990s.

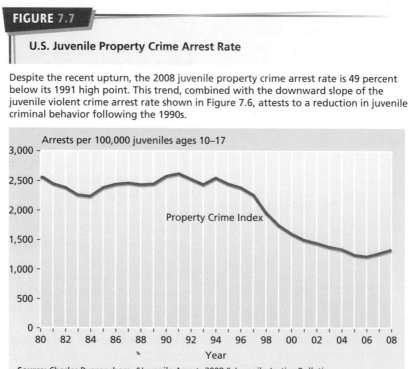

Source: Charles Puzzanchera, "Juvenile Arrests 2008," *Juvenile Justice Bulletin* (Washington, D.C.: Office of Juvenile Justice and Delinquency Prevention, December, 2009), p. 5.

Crime in the United States

1. According to the FBI's *Uniform Crime Report*, crime in the United States has increased since 1989. T or F?
2. According to the National Crime Victimization Survey, does the *Uniform Crime Report* underestimate or overestimate the amount of crime in America? _____

Answers: 1. F; 2. underestimate

for crack cocaine. Second, remaining crack gangs that provided guns to juveniles reached truces. Third, police clamped down on illegal guns, and repeat violent juvenile offenders were given stiffer sentences.

Q **How are juvenile arrest rates related to race?** Blacks are overrepresented in juvenile arrests (Puzzanchera 2009). While African Americans constituted 16 percent of the U.S. juvenile population ages 10 to 17 in 2008, they were involved in 52 percent of all juvenile violent crime arrests and 33 percent of all juvenile property crime arrests. In 2008, the violent crime arrest rate for black juveniles was about five times the rate for white juveniles (which included Latinos), six times the rate for Native American juveniles, and thirteen times the rate among Asian American juveniles. For property crime arrests, black juveniles had a rate twice that of white and Native American juveniles, and almost six times that of Asian American juveniles.

Turning to the trend, the violent crime arrest rate for African American juveniles was between six and seven times that of whites in the 1980s. This ratio went down to 4 to 1 from 1999 to 2004, and increased to 5 to 1 after 2004. The change following 2004 is the product of an increase in black juvenile violent crime arrests (24 percent) and a reduction in white violent crime arrests (3 percent). Among whites, the juvenile violent crime arrest rate in 2008 was far below its 1993 zenith (down 69 percent), its lowest level since 1980. The black rate in 2008 was 76 percent under its 1993 high point, despite a 40 percent increase after 2004. Over the period from 1994 to 2008, the property crime arrest rate fell sharply for all juveniles (down 42 percent).

Q **What is the relationship between juvenile crime and gender?** Females are arrested at a significantly lower rate than males, accounting for 30 percent of all juvenile arrests in 2008. From 1999 to 2008, overall arrests of juvenile females declined less than arrests of male juveniles. This discrepancy was due to the sizeable decrease in male juvenile arrests for property crime over this period. The male juvenile arrest rate for property crimes went down by 28 percent; for females the rate increased by 1 percent. For violent crime arrests, the gender difference was relatively small. The female juvenile rate declined 10 percent compared to an 8 percent decrease among male juveniles (Puzzanchera 2009).

Global Crime R1

Crime rates vary within any society. Sociological factors such as gender, age, race, ethnicity, social class, geographical region, and neighborhood each contribute to these variations. Crime rates also vary from society to society. One way to examine cross-cultural differences in crime is to compare crime rates in the United States with those of other countries.

New York City firefighters work near Ground Zero after Osama bin Laden sent jet airplanes through the Twin Towers on September 11, 2001. How do terrorists differ from other types of criminals?

FORGET Patrick/SAGAPHOTO.COM / Alamy

Global Crime Comparisons

Despite a decline in crime, the United States continues to have more violent crime than other industrialized countries and maintains its high rank in overall crime. Of the major industrialized countries, the United States has the highest murder, rape, and robbery rates and keeps pace, as well, in burglaries and auto thefts. Despite the rise in crime rates in other countries, crime remains a significantly greater problem in the United States than in any other country. Nevertheless, many European countries are gaining on the United States. Denmark and Finland, for example, with a long-standing record of low crime, are now experiencing high rates of street crime. Even Japan, hardly given a thought on the crime front, is experiencing an increase in crime (Harrendorf, Heisanen, and Malby 2010).

Q **Can cross-cultural crime data be trusted?** You read earlier about the difficulties with gathering accurate U.S. crime data. So, it is not unreasonable to question the accuracy of data coming from many different cultures. There are problems associated with data recording, data collection, and varying definitions of crime from one country to another. Despite some notable dissenters (Balrig 1988; Gerber 1991), experts generally agree, though, that the differences in crime rates across societies are too great and too consistent to be denied credibility.

Q **How do the levels of crime across the globe compare with crime in the United States?** The latest and most creditable information on international crime comes from the United Nations Survey of Crime. The following discussion is based on the United Nation's most recent survey, covering the years 1996–2006 (Harrendorf, Heiskanen, and Malby 2010).

Overall, rape and robbery increased somewhat, assault rose markedly, and burglary decreased. Homicide rates declined or held flat. We will consider each of these crimes in more detail.

For most countries, including the United States, *homicide* rates decreased or remained stable between 2003 and 2008. The lowest global homicide rates are found in Western, Southern, and Northern Europe, Oceania, and Eastern Asia. The highest murder rates appear in Southern Africa, Central America, and the Caribbean.

Assault, physical action against another person, ranges from simple attacks such as pushing and slapping to aggravated assault such as wounding and maiming. Total assault rose between 1996 and 2006. North America (United States and Canada) shows a rate of aggravated assault second only to West, Central, and Southern Africa.

Rape, sexual intercourse without legitimate consent, is relatively infrequent in number because most go unreported to the police. Therefore, the data on rape should be viewed as an underestimation. The general trend in rape is increasing. North America, followed by Southern Africa and Oceania, has the highest recorded rape rates. Asia has the lowest.

Robbery, crime against property involving violence or the threat of violence, ranges from mugging to theft with violence. Like assault, the trend of robbery is upward. Robbery is clearly most prevalent in Southern Africa, Latin America and the Caribbean, and North America, in that order. Asia shows the lowest robbery rate, with an extremely wide gulf between it and the top three. The middle is taken by Europe, North Africa, and Oceania.

The United Nations defines *burglary* as breaking into property using force with the intent to steal goods. Overall, the trend of burglary is downward. By far the highest burglary rate is found in Oceania (especially in Australia and New Zealand). North America, Southern Africa, and West and Central Europe follow in that order. The other regions of the world have startling low burglary rates.

CHECK YOURSELF **7.7** **R2**

Global Crime

1. Of all industrialized countries _____ has the most violent crimes.
2. In which of the following categories of crime is the United States *not* the leader in the world?
   ____ a. homicide
   ____ b. rape
   ____ c. robbery
   ____ d. burglary
   ____ e. none of the above
3. According to the overall trend in crime, the world is becoming a safer place. T or F?

Answers: 1. United States; 2. a; 3. T

The overall trend in crime suggests that the world is becoming slightly safer, although that conclusion is a hard sell to the American public. Terrorism is the exception.

Global Terrorism [R1]

Before September 11, 2001, introduced Americans to Al Qaeda, terrorism was something "they" did "over there." The concepts of *bioterrorism* and *cyberterrorism* surfaced only in movies and on television, if at all. At the time of the Oklahoma City bombing in 1995, the general public was not aware enough of terrorism to see the murderous act of Timothy McVeigh and Terry Nichols as a terrorist attack. Americans now acknowledge terrorism for the global crime it has come to be.

The Nature of Global Terrorism

Terrorism was defined in Chapter 3 as the illegal use of violence to intimidate a government, or a group, or an individual in pursuit of a political, religious, economic, or social goal. So, by definition, terrorism is a crime. But that is only the beginning of a sociological examination of terrorism.

Q What are the types of terrorism? Terrorism comes in two varieties (Mooney, Knox, and Schacht 2011). **Transnational terrorism** involves terrorists in one country committing terrorist acts against targets in another country. On 9/11, Americans had their introduction to transnational terrorism. Other countries the world over already knew about this type of terrorism. **Domestic terrorism** occurs against targets in the same country as the perpetrators. Two examples previously mentioned are the Oklahoma City bombing of a federal building, killing 168 and injuring more than 200, and antiabortion attacks.

Q How prevalent is terrorism? The latest, more comprehensive documentation of global terrorism appears in the U.S. Justice Department's 2008 report on terrorism. Almost 12,000 terrorist attacks against noncombatants occurred around the world in 2008, involving the killing, wounding, or kidnapping of over 54,000 people. Of the 11,700 reported attacks, nearly 40 percent occurred in the Near East. About 35 percent of the attacks occurred in South Asia, particularly in Afghanistan and Pakistan ("2008 Report on Terrorism," 2009).

Q What is the difference between terrorists and other criminals? The major commonality between terrorists and ordinary criminals is the illegality of their activity. They otherwise share few, if any, characteristics (White 2009). Terrorists belong to dedicated organizations, share deeply held belief systems, and adhere to an ideology. Ordinary criminals, in contrast, usually work alone or in very small groups, are not committed to a religious or political ideology, and share only the belief that the possessions of others should be theirs. Ordinary criminals are undisciplined, untrained, and opportunistic. Terrorists are well trained, disciplined in their action, and committed to meticulous advanced planning.

Q Is modern terrorism religiously motivated? As Figure 7.8 shows, religion in 2008 did play a major role in terrorist murders. But, deadly terrorist attacks can be secularly and politically motivated, and can be waged by Christians as well as followers of Islam. While it has not always been the case, it is true that a sizeable proportion of current terrorist acts is religiously motivated.

Crime is significantly greater in the United States than in any other industrialized country. But, as global crime rates increase, so too the prison populations, even in traditionally low-crime countries. We can expect the above prison in France to reflect this trend.

Anthony Correia/Shutterstock.com

FIGURE 7.8

Deaths by Terrorist Category, 2008

Does this information change your perception of terrorism? Explain.

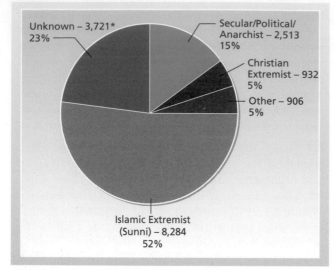

Unknown – 3,721*
23%

Secular/Political/
Anarchist – 2,513
15%

Christian
Extremist – 932
5%

Other – 906
5%

Islamic Extremist
(Sunni) – 8,284
52%

*15,765 Total Death

Source: "2008 Report on Terrorism," *Juvenile Justice Bulletin* (Washington, D.C.: The National Counterterrorism Center, 2009), p. 22. Available at http://www.nctc.gov/.

Q **What social conditions breed terrorism?** Terrorism is most likely to emerge under certain social conditions. For example, terrorism occurs more frequently in politically weak states or in nations that have undergone long years of political violence. Countries with a foreign occupier are also fertile ground for terrorist activity. Other social conditions engendering terrorism are widespread racial or ethnic discrimination and

the presence of extreme secular or religious ideologies (Mooney, Knox, and Schacht 2011). Social conditions such as these are generally necessary but not sufficient causes of terrorism. Terrorism is unlikely to develop in the absence of one or more of them, and may not occur even when one or more does exist.

Crime Control in the United States **R1**

The **criminal justice system** comprises the institutions and processes responsible for enforcing criminal law. It includes police, courts, and a correctional system (Tonry 2000; Inciardi 2009; Siegal 2010, 2011). A criminal justice system may draw on four approaches to crime control—deterrence, retribution, incarceration, and rehabilitation—which may be used in varying combinations. This section explores the use of these four approaches in the United States.

Deterrence

In 1994, Michael Fay, an American teenager convicted of car vandalism, was lashed four times with a four-foot rattan cane in a Singapore prison (M. Elliott 1994). The experience of being "caned" is said to be sufficiently bad that future crime is effectively discouraged. Singapore is by no means alone in the use of corporal punishment. Practices such as caning are designed to protect society through deterrence. The **deterrence** approach emphasizes intimidation, using the threat of punishment to discourage criminal actions. There is considerable debate on the effectiveness of deterrence (DiIulio and Piehl 1991).

CHECK YOURSELF **7.8** **R2**

Global Terrorism
1. The Oklahoma City bombing of a federal building is an example of _____ terrorism.
2. Surprisingly, terrorists and ordinary criminals share a lot of characteristics. T or F?
3. Practically all global terrorism is committed by the followers of Islam. T or F?
4. Under which of these social conditions is terrorism most likely to occur?
    ____ a. countries that are politically weak
    ____ b. countries with a long history of political violence
    ____ c. nations with a foreign occupier
    ____ d. all of the above
    ____ e. none of the above

Answers: 1. domestic; 2. F; 3. F; 4. d

Q Does punishment deter crime? Until the mid-1960s, social scientists generally rejected the idea that punishment deters crime. This rejection was based partly on earlier studies, which indicated that the death penalty did not deter murder any more effectively than life imprisonment. More recent research has led to a reevaluation of the relationship between punishment and crime. Although the evidence to support this point is inconclusive, social scientists may have discounted the deterrence doctrine prematurely (Greenberg and Kessler 1982; Logan 1982; Hook 1989; Yunker 2001; Liptak 2008a).

Investigation of the complicated relationship between punishment and crime is only in its infancy, but some research indicates that the threat of punishment does deter crime if potential lawbreakers know two things: that they are likely to get caught and that the punishment will be severe. In the United States, however, punishment for crime is usually not certain, swift, or severe. Consequently, punishment does not have the deterrent effect that it could have.

Capital punishment is a special case. Murder is usually committed not after a rational consideration of the act or its consequences but during an outburst of emotion. Under such irrational circumstances, one would not expect the fear of capital punishment to be a deterrent, and research shows that it is not. If the death penalty were a deterrent to murder, then a decline in its use should be followed by an increase in the murder rate. But research in many countries, including the United States, indicates that the murder rate remains constant or even drops following a decline in the use of the death penalty. Other research indicates that the use of capital punishment as a sanction is neither swift nor certain (Acker, Bohm, and Lanier 1998; Sarat 1998; Schonebaum 1998; M. E. Williams 2004).

Q How do Americans feel about capital punishment? Actually, American attitudes toward capital punishment have shifted dramatically over the years. In colonial America, murderers, robbers, arsonists, counterfeiters, and many other types of criminals were regularly hung in the public square before large crowds. By the 1780s, the death penalty was beginning to be a sign of social backwardness by many. By the Civil War, three northern states had abolished it and the other northern states reserved it for murderers. Later in the nineteenth century, the death penalty lost even more public favor. In the late 1960s, the death penalty was abolished, only to gain acceptance less than a decade later.

According to a 2008 Gallup poll, about 64 percent of the American population currently supports the death penalty for murder. However, support for the death penalty decreases to 47 percent when life imprisonment without parole is an alternative (Saad 2008). Attitude toward the death penalty in the United States varies according to race and ethnicity. Seventy-three percent of whites favor the death penalty, compared with 55 percent of African Americans (Lynch, Patterson, and Childs 2008; Russell-Brown 2008). This variation in attitude toward the death penalty is not surprising, considering that African Americans are disproportionately sentenced to death row. Although African Americans constitute about 13 percent of the U.S. population, they make up over 40 percent of death row inmates (U.S. Department of Justice 2006; "Facts About the Death Penalty" 2010).

Capital punishment is one of the most controversial issues in American society today.

Only about one-third of Americans are convinced that the death penalty is a deterrent to murder; the same is true for only 5 percent of America's top academic criminologists ("Facts About the Death Penalty" 2010). Of those Americans who favor the death penalty, more than three-fourths say that they would continue to favor it even if confronted with conclusive evidence that the death penalty is not a deterrent to murder. Rather than a need for deterrence, feelings of revenge and a desire for retribution, then, appear to contribute more to the support of capital punishment (Zimring 2004; Gallup 2008).

Increasing American uneasiness about the death penalty is reflected in politics. Partly in response to the release of death row inmates based on DNA evidence, Congress passed the Innocence Protection Act in 2004 (Moore 2007; K. Johnson 2008; Lynch, et al. 2008; McKinley 2010). Between 1976 and 2010, the frequency of executions in the United States spiked. Following 2000, however, the number of inmates sentenced to death and execution dropped. Fifteen states no longer have the death penalty and in 2010, twenty-three of the thirty-five states with the death penalty executed no one.

Q Why is the United States the only Western nation to preserve the death penalty? In his book, *The Peculiar Institution,* David Garland argues that the death penalty is a uniquely American institution and is retained because it is embedded in American history and culture (Garland 2010). The singular tenacity of the death penalty in America, Garland writes, is entrenched in our country's commitment to federalism and local democracy and in our legacy of racism and violence. Elites of other nations have sufficient power to impose bans on capital punishment, even against public wishes. American elites are incapable and unwilling to override the local majority opposition to a ban. The Supreme Court refuses to declare the death penalty to be cruel and unusual punishment out of deference to public opinion and local political leaders.

Retribution

Q What is the philosophy behind the retributive approach to criminal punishment? The public may demand retribution—that criminals pay compensation equal to their offenses against society. When an eye is taken, an eye must be returned. Although the law allows designated officials to exact retribution, it does not tolerate acts of personal vengeance. The legal system removes responsibility for the punishment of a criminal from the hands of individuals and places it in the hands of officials. A convicted criminal repays the state rather than the harmed individual(s). Retribution, in the name of justice, is a social rather than a personal matter. If an individual whose husband is a

victim of homicide exacts the price of wrongdoing by shooting her husband's killer, she is also responsible to society.

The retributive philosophy is concerned with past rather than future crime. Like deterrence, the incarceration and rehabilitation approaches to punishment, to which we now turn, focus on preventing further crime by existing offenders.

Incarceration

Q What is the justification for incarceration? Criminals who are not on the street cannot commit crimes. The **incarceration** approach removes criminals from society. In repressive societies, such as Nationalist China and the former Soviet Union, people may spend their entire lives in prison camps for crimes ranging from political opposition to murder. In recent decades, the United States is seeing an increasing emphasis on incarceration (Grapes 2000; Mauer 2006). Compared with a historical average of the 1925–1970 period, the current rate of imprisonment in the United States increased five times. For the first time, more than one in every 100 adult Americans is in jail or prison (Warren 2008). The incarceration rate is even more startling for minorities. Among white men ages 18 to 64, one in eighty-seven is behind bars. The ratio is much lower for Latino men (one in thirty-six) and black men (one in twelve) of the same age. Of men ages 20–34, the ratio for black men is one in nine and is one in twenty-seven for Latino men. One in twenty-eight American children has a parent in jail. The same is true for one in nine black children ("Collateral Costs" 2010).

Moreover, the current incarceration rate in the United States is six to eight times the rates of Western European countries. With less than 5 percent of the world's population, the United States has almost a quarter of its prisoners (Garland 2001; Western and Pettit 2002; Aizenman 2007; Liptak 2008b).

Rehabilitation

Q How is rehabilitation viewed in the United States? **Rehabilitation** is an approach to crime control that attempts to resocialize criminals. Traditionally, rehabilitative programs are introduced within the prisons, with programs aimed at giving prisoners both social and work skills that will help them adjust to society after release.

Q Do prisons rehabilitate criminals? Unfortunately, because 30 and 60 percent of those released from penal institutions will be back in prison two to five years later, it is difficult to believe that rehabilitation programs in the United States are working (Elikann 1996; Zamble

Juvenile boot camps are an alternative to confinement in juvenile corrections facilities. These boot camps focus on discipline and physical conditioning, and typically are restricted to nonviolent or first-time offenders.

Steve Starr/CORBIS

and Quinsey 1997). This high rate of recidivism—past offenders returning to prison—can be attributed partly to characteristics of the offenders and the problems they face while in the criminal justice system (such as the stigma of being an ex-convict). The tendency toward recidivism may also be due to the inadequacies of prisons. Prisons are schools for crime: Ex-convicts often leave prison more committed as criminals and with a higher likelihood of continued criminal involvement (Abramsky 2001).

Social scientists also recognize that it is difficult to change attitudes and behavior within the prison subculture. Although prison guards and officials hold the power, the informal rules of the prison subculture have greater effect on prisoners' behavior. Conformity with the "inmate code" stresses loyalty among inmates as well as opposition to correctional authorities. This conformity is enforced verbally and physically. Consequently, involvement within prison criminal networks often increases in prisons, promoting a continued life of crime (J. Hagan 1993; Sherman 1993a).

Q **If prisons do not rehabilitate, what are some alternatives?** Some states are experimenting with several alternatives. One is the combination of prison and probation. A mixed, or split, sentence, known as *shock probation*, is designed to shock offenders into recognizing the realities of prison life. Prisoners must serve part of their sentence in an institution. The remainder of the sentence is then suspended, and the prisoner is placed on probation.

Another approach relies on community-based programs designed to reintroduce criminals into society. By getting convicts out of prison for at least part of the day, community-based programs help break the inmate code. At the same time, prisoners have a chance to become part of society, participating in the community but under professional guidance and supervision.

A third strategy, *diversion*, is aimed at preventing, or greatly minimizing, the offender's penetration into the criminal justice system. Diversion involves referring lower-risk offenders to community-based treatment programs rather than to penal institutions or probationary programs. Because offenders are handled outside the formal system of criminal law, the lawbreakers are not as likely to acquire stigmatizing labels and other liabilities (N. Morris and Tonry 1990; Lanier and Henry 2004; Warren 2010).

Another strategy removes obstacles to employment after prison release. While the public expects ex-offenders to take jobs like everyone else, those released from prison face barriers created by the negative effects of incarceration on their economic prospects. Some programs have been successful in lowering these barriers. Providing education and job training to prisoners, both before and after their release, has helped former prisoners find jobs and avoid reincarceration. Subsidizing transitional work programs has also been effective, providing money above the minimum wage exconvicts usually earn initially. Another successful program involves supporting employment with housing and substance abuse treatment ("Collateral Costs" 2010).

CHECK YOURSELF 7.9 [R2]

Crime Control in the United States

1. Match the approaches to punishment on the left side with the examples on the right.

   ____ a. rehabilitation   (1) imprisonment without parole
   ____ b. deterrence   (2) the practice of caning
   ____ c. retribution   (3) employment and educational programs in prison
   ____ d. incarceration   (4) death penalty for murder

2. Prisons currently do an adequate job rehabilitating inmates. T or F?
3. It appears that social scientists have prematurely discounted the deterrence doctrine. T or F?
4. Research supports capital punishment as a deterrent to murder. T or F?
5. The United States has invested heavily in precrime programs. T or F?

Answers: 1. a. (3), b. (2), c. (4), d. (1); 2. F; 3. T; 4. F; 5. F

Because of its emphasis in recent years on deterrence and incarceration, the United States has been slow to embrace these kinds of alternatives. As we shall see later in this chapter, this stance may be changing.

Q What about preventing crime in the first place? The above approaches target current criminals. A different sentiment for crime prevention concentrates on steering potential offenders away from criminal activity in the first place, by providing treatment for addicts; mentoring and counseling poor children; creating living-wage jobs in poor neighborhoods; improving public education for poor children; and funding after-school and late-night recreation programs. Americans, given their long-standing punitive philosophy of corrections, do not heavily invest in "precrime" programs, as with rehabilitation.

Global Crime Control [R1]

Differences in Crime Control

All countries use deterrence and incarceration. They vary significantly, however, in their emphasis on imprisonment and capital punishment (Christie 2000).

Q What are some of these differences? Even Western European countries, which share many cultural traditions, have varying imprisonment rates. England and Wales are near the top in inhabitants per 100,000 in prison among Western European countries. Spain is near the middle, and France and Germany are near the bottom. The United States, however, clearly separates itself from the rest of the world in crime control.

Q What is unique about the U.S. approach to crime control? As stated earlier, the imprisonment rate in the United States is six to eight times that of any Western European country. Actually, the United States is at the very top worldwide in the number of prison inmates. No other industrialized country is even in the world's top ten. The United States has more inmates than the top thirty-five largest European countries combined. Furthermore, the United States is the only democracy to continue serious use of the death penalty. The European Union formally stated its opposition to the death penalty in 2007. By 2006, ninety countries had eliminated the death penalty (see "Think Globally 7.1"). In 2007, the United Nations General Assembly called for a moratorium on executions, with the intent of ultimately abolishing the death penalty.

Q What measures are some other countries taking to control crime? Many other nations have had good results with innovative programs aimed at crime prevention and rehabilitation ("The United States Versus the World" 2005). Programs to preempt initial entrance into the world of crime concentrate on such things as encouraging the social development of children and families and helping at-risk children finish school. To reduce crime and recidivism, New Zealand created Project Turnaround in which offenders, victims, and community representatives try to create an action plan for repairing the damage to victims and communities. Less than 10 percent of offenders have been taken back to court for failure to complete the plan.

Other countries have adopted programs to improve prisoner treatment. Sweden emphasizes rehabilitation, treatment, and job training. Among the Japanese, criminals are resocialized to come to terms with their moral shortcomings and to take responsibility for moral improvement (Feeley and Simon 1992). In Cuba, accent is

THINK GLOBALLY 7.1

Death Penalty Policy

Countries vary in their approach to the control of crime. The most extreme form of social control, the death penalty, is utilized in many countries, while some countries have abolished capital punishment completely. This map shows variations in national policy regarding the death penalty.

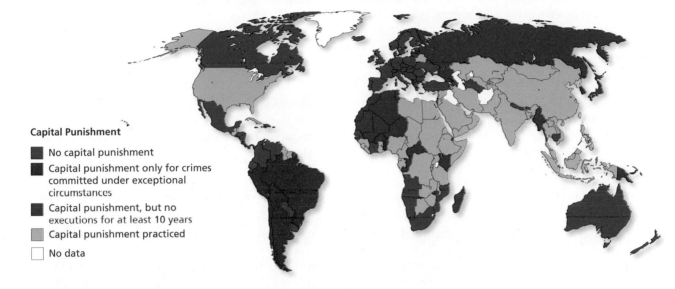

Capital Punishment

- No capital punishment
- Capital punishment only for crimes committed under exceptional circumstances
- Capital punishment, but no executions for at least 10 years
- Capital punishment practiced
- No data

Source: John L. Allen and Christopher J. Sutton. *Student Atlas of World Politics* 9th ed. New York: McGraw-Hill, 2011, p. 79.

Interpret the Map

1. Do you notice any pattern in the use of the death penalty? Describe it.

2. What additional information would you need to determine if capital punishment is an effective deterrent to crime? Explain.

placed on rehabilitating and returning prisoners to normal life rather than on punishing or isolating them:

Prisoners are allowed to wear street clothes, earn a comparable income (to that of a free person who holds the same occupation), and are incarcerated in their home province no matter what their security level is. Additionally, prisoners become eligible for a conditional release program halfway through their sentence (for sentences of under five years), through which they work on farms or in factories with co-workers who are not informed of their prisoner status. Through this program, offenders are also able to visit their families at home (unsupervised) twice a month for three days at a time. Of those prisoners, who participate in alternative programs such as the conditional release program, the recidivism rate is about 15%. ("The United States Versus the World" 2005:2)

Q How does the American public respond to crime control? As mentioned earlier, the United States has not yet made a strong commitment to crime prevention

and rehabilitation. There are, though, signs of a decline in America's traditional, punitive approach to crime control ("Changing Public Attitudes Toward the Criminal Justice System" 2002; Weil 2002; Kiefer 2004). Although a majority of Americans (65 percent) think that the criminal justice system is "not tough enough" on crime, this is less than the 83 percent in the early 1990s. Moreover, fewer Americans now believe that strengthening law enforcement is the best way to lower the crime rate. Sixty-nine percent of Americans prefer attacking the social and economic conditions that promote crime through better education and job training to preventing crime by improving law enforcement with more prisons, police, and judges. Two-thirds of all Americans now prefer to reduce crime through programs like job training, family counseling, and more neighborhood youth activity centers rather than through stricter and longer sentences, capital punishment for more crimes, and fewer paroles.

CHECK YOURSELF **7.10** R2

Global Crime Control

1. The United States is the only industrialized country to practice capital punishment. T or F?
2. The imprisonment rate in the United States is six to eight times that of any Western European country. T or F?
3. Cuba has shown the merits of imprisonment over rehabilitation. T or F?
4. The American public remains firm in its preference for deterrence and incarceration over crime prevention and rehabilitation in the fight against crime. T or F?

Answers: 1. T; 2. T; 3. F; 4. F

Q Why the change in attitudes? Since 1980, most states, it is true, have opted for longer prison sentences and more prisons to hold the burgeoning prison population (Steinhauer 2009). Americans, nonetheless, are beginning to doubt the effectiveness of the get-tough approach to crime control, and they recognize the drag their current approach is having on state budgets. Economics, more than humanitarianism, may be driving these changing attitudes toward incarceration and deterrence. Because state governments can no longer afford to devote annually some $50 billion-plus to prison costs, they are looking for alternatives to deterrence and incarceration (Warren 2008). Alternatives include improved sentencing methods, early and more frequent parole, streamlined probation, and new treatment programs (especially for drug offenders), all of which emphasize rehabilitation and prevention (Richburg 2009). And it may be significant that for the first time since 1980, incarceration in the United States has recently grown at a slower pace.

On to Chapter 8

We examined the nature of social structure and introduced three major types (societies, organizations, groups). We, then, turned to deviance within and between social structures. In Chapters 8 through 10, we will continue to explore social processes within and between social structures. Specifically, Chapter 8 begins the exploration of social inequality, a social process that exists in all social structures, from international social structures to two-person groups.

S INTEGRATED GOALS AND SUMMARY

1. **Define deviance, and explain its relative nature.**
   - Although social life requires conformity and order, it also involves deviance, behavior that violates norms. Deviance is difficult to define because it is a relative matter. What is considered deviant depends on the characteristics of the individuals, the social context, and the historical era.
2. **Define social control, and identify the major types of social control.**
   - All societies need some means of social control to promote conformity to their norms. Internal social control, promoted through the socialization process, enables individuals to control their own behavior. External social control is applied by other people.
3. **Describe the biological and psychological explanations of deviance.**
   - According to biological explanations of deviance, there is a link between physical characteristics and deviant behavior. Early on, Cesare Lombroso believed that

criminals were throwbacks to an earlier stage of human evolutionary development. William Sheldon attributed crime to body shape. Despite later research efforts, there is still no convincing proof that physical characteristics are related to deviance.
   - Psychological theories of deviance attribute deviant behavior to pathological personality traits. Sociologists remain skeptical of comprehensive psychological explanations for deviance.
4. **Discuss the positive and negative consequences of deviance.**
   - According to functionalists, deviance has both negative and positive consequences for society. On the negative side, deviance encourages social disorder, erodes trust, encourages further nonconformity in others, and diverts resources from other social needs. On the positive side, deviance helps clarify norms, offers a safety valve, increases social unity, and brings about needed social change.

5. **Differentiate the major functional theories of deviance.**
   - According to strain theory, deviance occurs because of a discrepancy between cultural goals and socially acceptable means of achieving those goals. Control theory attempts to explain conformity rather than deviance. Conformity, which of course excludes deviance, is based on the existence of a strong bond between individuals and society.

6. **Compare and contrast cultural transmission theory and labeling theory.**
   - The symbolic interactionist perspective yields two theories of deviance. Cultural transmission theory contends that deviance is learned, just like any other aspect of culture. According to labeling theory, an act is deviant only if other people respond to it as if it were deviant. Isolated norm violation may have no serious consequences for individuals. If individuals are labeled as habitual deviants, however, they may organize their lives and personal identities around deviance. Mental illness illustrates this theory.

7. **Discuss the conflict theory view of deviance.**
   - The conflict perspective, when applied to the study of deviant behavior, emphasizes social inequality and power differentials. The most powerful members of a society are said to determine group norms and, consequently, the definition of deviant. Conflict theorists relate deviance to capitalism, pointing to the relationship among race, ethnicity, and crime.

8. **Compare crime in the United States and the world.**
   - The official crime statistics—the *Uniform Crime Reports* published annually by the FBI—are useful in providing an estimate of crime, but they underestimate national crime in America. The National Crime Victimization Survey was launched to overcome this limitation. There is some inconsistency in the findings of these two sources.

   - The United States has the greatest crime problem in the world. The gap between the United States and other countries remains substantial, despite the rising crime rates in Europe during the 1990s.

9. **Discuss the nature of global terrorism.**
   - Terrorism is a type of crime most Americans, indeed, came to know on 9/11. Since that date, sociologists, as you might imagine, have invested much more research energy into the nature of global terrorism.

10. **Compare and contrast crime control domestically and globally.**
    - The four approaches to crime control are deterrence, retribution, incarceration, and rehabilitation. The United States is torn between the less punitive approach of rehabilitation and the harsher approaches of deterrence, retribution, and incarceration.
    - Increasingly, sociologists recognize that prisons are not successful at rehabilitating criminals. In the past, reform programs took place within prisons. In recent years, there has been an interest in rehabilitating criminals outside the prison system. During the 1970s, Americans began to take a harsher view of criminals. Even social scientists are beginning to believe that punishment can deter crime under certain circumstances, although there is no convincing evidence that capital punishment affects the homicide rate.
    - Since 1980, the United States has increasingly moved toward incarceration as a solution to crime control. The imprisonment rate in the United States is currently six to eight times that of any Western European country and nearly double that of the former Soviet Union. The United States lags behind many countries in adopting innovative rehabilitation and prevention programs designed to reduce crime.

CONCEPT REVIEW

Match the following concepts with the definitions listed below them.

_____ a. labeling theory
_____ b. differential association theory
_____ c. retribution

_____ d. control theory
_____ e. social control
_____ f. anomie
_____ g. occupational crime

_____ h. cultural transmission theory
_____ i. deviance
_____ j. recidivism

1. behavior that violates norms
2. a social condition in which norms are weak, conflicting, or absent
3. the conception that conformity is based on the existence of a strong bond between individuals and society
4. the theory that deviance is part of a subculture transmitted through socialization
5. the public demand of compensation from criminals equal to their offense against society
6. the theory that crime and delinquency are more likely to occur among individuals who have been exposed to more

unfavorable attitudes toward the law than to favorable ones
7. the theory that deviance exists when some members of a group or society label others as deviants
8. means for promoting conformity to a group's or society's rules
9. a crime committed by people in their employment or in their personal financial pursuits
10. a return to crime after imprisonment

CHECK YOURSELF REVIEW

1. Recent research has established a definite causal relationship between certain human biological characteristics and deviant behavior. T or F?

2. It appears that social scientists have prematurely discounted the deterrence doctrine. T or F?

3. The imprisonment rate in the United States is six to eight times that of any Western European country. T or F?

4. A major problem that sociologists have in defining deviance is its _____.

5. According to labeling theory, mental illness is a matter of _____.

6. The process of reducing the seriousness of crimes based on the lower social value placed on the victims is called _____.

7. Which of the following is *not* one of the benefits of deviance for society?
   ____ a. It decreases suspicion and mistrust among members of a society.
   ____ b. It promotes social change.
   ____ c. It increases social unity.
   ____ d. It provides a safety valve.
   ____ e. It promotes clarification of norms.

8. Which of the following did Edwin Sutherland mean by differential association?
   ____ a. Crime is more likely to occur among individuals who have been exposed more to unfavorable attitudes toward the law than to favorable ones.

   ____ b. People become criminals through association with criminals.
   ____ c. Crime is not transmitted culturally.
   ____ d. Crime comes from differential conflict.

9. In which of the following categories of crime is the United States *not* the leader in the world?
   ____ a. homicide
   ____ b. rape
   ____ c. robbery
   ____ d. burglary
   ____ e. none of the above

10. Match the approaches to punishment with the examples below.
   ____ a. rehabilitation
   ____ b. deterrence
   ____ c. retribution
   ____ d. incarceration
   (1) imprisonment without parole
   (2) the practice of caning
   (3) employment and educational programs in prison
   (4) death penalty for murder

11. Under which of these conditions is terrorism most likely to occur?
   ____ a. countries that are politically weak
   ____ b. states with a long history of political violence
   ____ c. nations with a foreign political occupier
   ____ d. all of the above
   ____ e. none of the above

GRAPHIC REVIEW

A decade ago "terrorism" was vaguely a part of the American vocabulary. That, of course, changed with 9/11. Figure 7.8 displays deaths by terrorists in 2008.

1. Are you surprised at the number of deaths from terrorism? Explain. Does the frequency of death at the hands of terrorists change your perspective of the number of deaths on 9/11? Elaborate.

   _____

   _____

   _____

2. How would you describe the distribution of deaths by terrorist category? Is this distribution surprising to you in any way? Why or why not?

   _____

   _____

   _____

CRITICAL-THINKING QUESTIONS

1. Identify a time in your life when you were considered a deviant by others. Discuss the attempts at social control you experienced. Be specific as to the types of social control and their concrete application to you.

_____

_____

2. Name some type of deviant behavior you would like yourself and/or others to engage in because you think society would benefit from it. State the sociological case for the social benefit of this type of deviance.

_____

_____

3. Describe someone you know who falls into one of the four deviant responses identified by strain theory. Use specific characteristics of this person to show that he or she fits the response you selected and not the other three responses.

_____

_____

4. Everyone has observed someone who has been labeled deviant by some members of society. Discuss the consequences of this labeling for the person identified as a deviant.

_____

_____

5. The text outlined several distinct approaches to crime control. Choose one approach and explain why you believe it has been successful or unsuccessful in relation to functionalism, conflict theory, or symbolic interactionism.

_____

_____

ANSWER KEY

Concept Review

a. 7
b. 6
c. 5
d. 3
e. 8
f. 2
g. 9
h. 4
i. 1
j. 10

Check Yourself Review

1. F
2. T
3. T
4. relativity
5. social definition
6. victim discounting
7. a
8. a
9. a
10. a. 3
    b. 2
    c. 4
    d. 1
11. d

8 Social Stratification

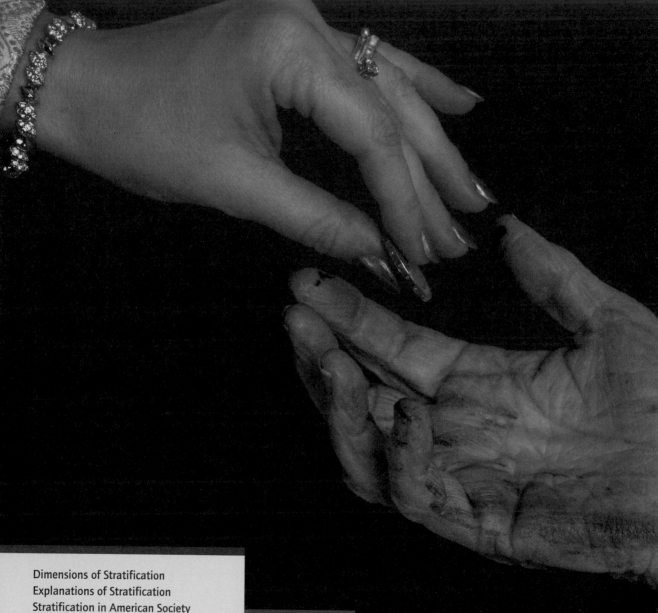

Ankya/Used under license from Shutterstock.com.

S GOALS

- Explain the relationship between social stratification and social class.
- Compare and contrast the three dimensions of stratification.
- State the major differences among the functionalist, conflict, and symbolic interactionist approaches to social stratification.
- Identify the distinguishing characteristics of the major social classes in America.
- Discuss the extent of poverty and the perceptions of poverty in the United States.
- Evaluate U.S. commitment to poverty programs.
- Outline some of the consequences of social stratification.
- Describe upward and downward social mobility in the United States.
- Discuss the major features of global stratification.

USING THE SOCIOLOGICAL IMAGINATION

Is federal spending on social welfare programs excessive? A significant proportion of the U.S. population is unhappy with the amount of tax dollars being spent on the poor. Americans, however, seriously overestimate the proportion of the federal budget that is spent on welfare. Less money in real terms was spent on welfare recipients in 2002 than in 1997. Besides, these welfare expenditures account for less than 1 percent of total federal expenditures, a reduction of three-fourths since 1970, and less than one-fifth of 1 percent of the total gross national product (GNP) of the United States.

Negative attitudes toward welfare recipients are part of American culture, and these attitudes stigmatize the poor. Although all societies have social inequality, not all societies develop negative (and false) stereotypes of those at the bottom. We will return to this topic later in this chapter, but for now we turn to the dimensions on which social classes are created.

Image courtesy of the Everett Collection, inc

In George Orwell's *Animal Farm*, the animals overthrow their human master to form their own soon-to-be stratified society.

Dimensions of Stratification R1

Because of the human tendency to rank one another, inequality emerges. Soon some people are at the top of the hierarchy and others are at the bottom. This tendency is a recurring theme in literature. Dr. Seuss writes of the Sneetches, birds whose rank depends on whether or not they have a large star on their stomach. Star-bellied Sneetches have high status; plain-bellied Sneetches have low status. In the classic novel *Animal Farm*, George Orwell created a barnyard society where the pigs ultimately take over the previously classless animal society by altering one of their cardinal rules from "All animals are equal" to "All animals are equal—but some animals are more equal than others."

Inequality among nonhuman animals is widespread. The higher primates know, from experience, who in the group is currently dominant, relative to whom. Baboons, rhesus monkeys, and chimpanzees are adept at tracking the complicated changes in status of other group members. Apes are even more sophisticated at discerning changing patterns of inequality (Hrdy 2009). Building on that inherited capacity, humans can take social ranking to heights undreamed of by Sneetches or apes. Sociologists call this social ranking *social stratification*.

Q What is the difference between social stratification and social class? **Social stratification** is the creation of layers (strata) of a population who possess unequal shares of scarce desirables, the most important of which are income, wealth, power, and prestige (R. Levine 2006). Each of the layers is a **social class**—a segment of the population whose members hold a relatively similar share of scarce desirables and who share values, norms, and an identifiable lifestyle. The number of social classes within a stratification structure varies. A stratification structure might include upper upper, middle upper, lower upper, upper middle, middle middle, lower middle, upper lower, middle lower, and lower lower classes. Or, like old coal-mining towns in America or like underdeveloped countries, there might be only an upper class and a lower class. (See "Consider This Research" for a stratification structure closer to your own experience.)

Karl Marx and Max Weber made the most significant early contributions to the study of social stratification. Marx demonstrated the importance of the economic foundations of social classes, while Weber accented the prestige and power aspects of stratification. Together, the work of these two great minds reveals to us that stratification is multidimensional (Gerth and Mills 1958; McCall 2001).

The Economic Dimension

Although both Marx and Weber were concerned with inequality, their emphases were different. For Marx, the economic factor was an independent variable

Donna Eder—Who's Popular, Who's Not?

Can you remember what it was like to be in middle school? Donna Eder (1995) formed a research team to answer this question. Focusing on the rituals and daily speech routines of twelve- to fourteen-year-olds, Eder paints a portrait of teenage school culture.

At Woodview Middle School, Eder and her research team observed lunchtime interaction and attended extracurricular activities—talent shows, athletic practices, athletic contests, cheerleading tryouts, cheerleading practice, and choir and band practices and performances. After several months of observation, the research team conducted informal interviews with individuals and groups. To capture interaction for closer study, the researchers obtained student and parental permission for audio and video recordings. Our discussion is confined to Eder's findings about social stratification in middle school.

In the sixth grade, there were no elite groups. Woodview seventh and eighth graders, however, did not see each other as equals. This central fact was evident to the researchers after only a few days of observation. Popular seventh graders were divided along gender lines, with popular boys in one group and popular girls in another. By the eighth grade, the two groups intermingled. In both grades, popularity was based not on who was best liked, but on who was most visible in the school. Being visible meant that many others knew who you were and wanted to talk with you.

Status differences could arise during the seventh and eighth grades because cheerleading and team sports existed as a vehicle to high visibility. Realizing the source of their prestige, male athletes took every opportunity to display symbols of their team affiliation. Team uniforms, jerseys, and athletic shoes were among the most important items of dress. Bandages, casts, and crutches were worn with pride.

Girls could not use sports to gain visibility because female athletics were not valued by faculty, administrators, or students. But because boys' athletic events were the most important and best-attended school activities, girls used cheerleading to make

themselves widely known. Besides appearing at basketball and football games, cheerleaders appeared in front of the entire student body at pep rallies and other school events.

Boys made fun of this high-status female activity by mockingly imitating cheers. One male coach joined the mockery by telling football players to either practice harder or he would get them cheerleading skirts. He then pretended to cheer in a falsetto voice.

Girls, on the other hand, regarded cheerleaders highly. Popular girls in the seventh and eighth grades either were cheerleaders or were friends of cheerleaders. Flaunting their status (just as the male athletes did), cheerleaders put on their uniforms as far ahead of games as possible and wore their cheerleading skirts for extracurricular school activities. Some girls even had T-shirts emblazoned with "cheerleader" on the back.

Evaluate the Research

1. Was the stratification structure at your school similar to Woodview's? Explain why or why not, giving examples to support your conclusion.
2. Is there a stratification structure among students at your college or university? Compare and contrast it to your middle school stratification structure.

explaining the existence of social classes. Weber, on the other hand, viewed the economic dimension as a dependent variable. That is, Weber was more concerned with the economic consequences of stratification.

Marx identified several social classes in nineteenth-century industrial society—laborers, servants, factory workers, craftspeople, proprietors of small businesses, moneyed capitalists—but predicted that capitalist societies would ultimately be reduced to two social classes. Those who owned capital (the means of production)—the **bourgeoisie**—would be the rulers. Those who worked for wages—the **proletariat**—would be the ruled. The propertied capitalist class could exploit the

labor of those without property. Even though the workers performed all the labor, they would be kept at a subsistence wage level, and the capitalists would enjoy the economic surplus created by that labor. In short, Marx predicted that because the capitalists owned the means of production (factories, land), they would both rule and exploit the working class. The working class would have nothing to sell but its labor.

Marx's analysis went deeper: Marx contended that all aspects of capitalist society—work, religion, government, law, morality—were economically conditioned. Consequently, the capitalists controlled all social institutions, which they used to their advantage. They could structure the legal system, educational system, and government to suit their own interests. For Marx, all of capitalist society was a superstructure resting on an economic foundation; the economy determined the nature of the society.

Whereas Marx foresaw only two social classes, Weber envisioned several social classes. Marx focused on the relationship to the means of production as the cause of social stratification; Weber examined the consequences of people's relationships to the economic institution. These consequences Weber termed **life chances**—the likelihood of securing the "good things in life," such as housing, education, good health, and food. The probability of possessing these desirables was directly related to economic resources, such as real estate, wages, inheritance, and investment profits.

By almost any measure—food, clothing, housing, or health—the standard of living has steadily improved in Europe and America. Still, there is considerable economic inequality, even within Western countries; and the United States is no exception. To understand the extent of economic inequality, it is necessary to distinguish income from wealth. **Income** is the amount of money received (within a given time period) by an individual or a group. **Wealth** refers to all the economic resources possessed by an individual or a group.

Q **What is the extent of economic inequality in America?** America was not supposed to have much economic inequality. As Richard Morin puts it:

> It was the great story of the American Century: the fusing after World War II, of the broadest and most prosperous middle class the world had ever seen. In its ticky-tack ramblers and backyard barbecues and unbridled sense of confidence lay a historic reversal—the steady closing of physical and economic gaps between America's rich and poor. (Morin 1994:14)

Income inequality has not turned out that way. It has been increasing for the past few decades. Between 1980 and 1990, the share of America's wealth held by the top 1 percent of the population almost doubled, increasing from 22 percent to 39 percent. Since then the top 1 percent has accumulated more than 70 percent of all earnings growth. In fact, the United States is now the most economically polarized of the major Western countries and continues to become even more unequal (K. Phillips 2002; Palast 2004; Sherman 2007). In 2009, more than 43.6 million Americans were living in poverty (U.S. Bureau of the Census 2010). At the other extreme, there are nearly 7 million millionaires and some 800 billionaires. And from 1990 to 2005, CEO pay increased almost 300 percent (adjusted for inflation), while production workers gained only 4.3 percent (Sawhill and Morton 2007; Alperovitz and Daly

2008; Domhoff 2010). To put it another way, in 1982 the average CEO of an S&P 500 company was paid 42 times as much as the average worker. In 2009, the ratio was 261 to 1, down from 500 to 1 in 2000. Economist Paul Samuelson describes income inequality in America this way:

> If we made an income pyramid out of building blocks, with each layer portraying $500 of income, the peak would be far higher than Mt. Everest, but most people would be within a few feet of the ground. (Samuelson and Nordhaus 2010:24)

Government figures on the distribution of income support Samuelson and Nordhaus's statement. Annual income is currently more concentrated at the top than it has been in ninety-five years (Aron-Dine 2007; Juliano 2007; Sherman 2007; Domhoff 2010). The share of after-tax income now going to the top 1 percent of American households is the highest ever recorded. Similarly, the shares of after-tax income going to the middle and bottom fifths of households are the smallest on record. Between 1979 and 2005, the richest 1 percent of households showed a gain of 228 percent in after-tax income ($745,000). On the other hand, the poorest fifth gained 6 percent ($900) and the middle fifth gained 21 percent ($8,700; see Figure 8.1). Consequently, in 2005 the richest 1 percent of households received seventy times as much in average after-tax income than the poorest one-fifth of households and twenty times as much as the middle one-fifth of households. Since 1979, the top 1 percent has doubled its share of America's income, while the share for the bottom 90 percent has shrunk. The share of aggregate income received by each fifth of the U.S. population in 2009 is illustrated in Figure 8.2. While the bottom fifth of the American population received 3.4 percent, the top fifth received 50.3 percent. The top 5 percent received 21.7 percent of the aggregate income (DeNavas-Walt, Proctor, and Smith 2010). And the pace of this widening gap between the haves and the have-nots is accelerating (Allen 2007; Johnston 2007b; Domhoff 2010).

Although these income distribution figures reveal persistent economic inequality, they do not show the full nature of the concentration of wealth (what one owns) in America. Because the federal government regularly publishes data on national income, income comparisons are not difficult to calculate. Accurate data on wealth holdings are much harder to obtain. Still, some research provides a picture of the concentration of wealth in the United States. The top 1 percent of American households hold almost 34 percent of the nation's wealth; the next 10 percent has almost 38 percent of the wealth; the bottom 50 percent of households owns 2.5 percent of the nation's wealth (see Figure 8.3). Since

FIGURE 8.1

Change in Average Real After-Tax Income 1979-2005

To what percentages do the labels "lowest fifth," "middle fifth," and "top fifth" refer?

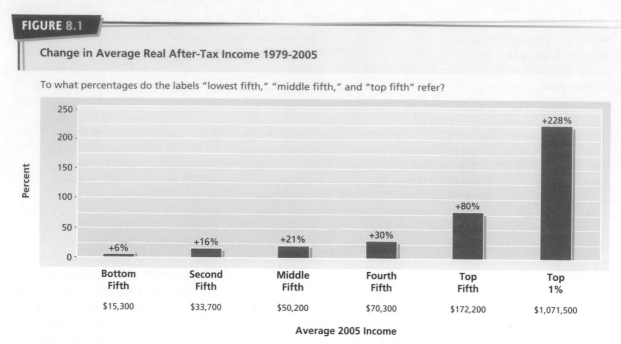

Average 2005 Income

Bottom Fifth	Second Fifth	Middle Fifth	Fourth Fifth	Top Fifth	Top 1%
+6%	+16%	+21%	+30%	+80%	+228%
$15,300	$33,700	$50,200	$70,300	$172,200	$1,071,500

Source: Arloc Sherman, "Income Inequality Hits Record Levels, New CBO Data Show." Center on Budget and Policy Priorities, 2007.
http://www.cbpp.org/12-14-07inc.htm

FIGURE 8.2

Shares of Aggregate Income by Percentile

Is this distribution of income what you expected? What surprised you? Explain.

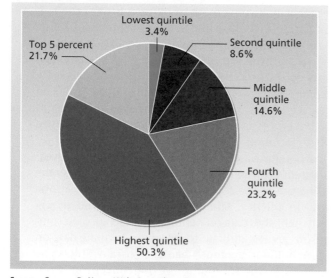

Source: Carmen DeNavas-Walt, Bernadette D.Proctor, and Jessica C. Smith, U.S. Census Bureau. "Income, Poverty and Health Insurance Coverage in the United States: 2009," *Current Population Reports* Washington, D.C.: U.S. Government Printing Office, 2010).

FIGURE 8.3

Distribution of Wealth in the United States

Describe this distribution of wealth in the United States to someone who is not in this class. What do you think their reaction will be? What was your reaction?

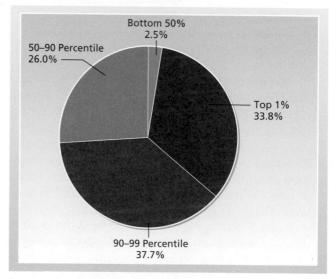

Source: Institute for Policy Studies

the early 2000s, movement toward the concentration of wealth has become even more dramatic (Collins and Yeskel 2005; D. A. Gilbert 2010).

Q What are the consequences of growing income inequality? Inferior health care, loss of leisure time, restricted diets, low-quality housing, and poor police protection are just a few of the disadvantages brought about by the growing disparity between rich and poor in the United States. But, this is the widest rich–poor gap since the Depression in 1929, and it has other less visible negative consequences. The growing economic disparity between the rich and the poor is lowering relative educational levels because college attendance goes up with income level. This, in turn, decreases the proportion of the workforce with college backgrounds, thereby retarding the growth of the skilled workforce. The quality of the workforce is further damaged because the increase of low-income students leads to poorer overall academic performance at all grade levels. The rate of job growth is affected by the income gap, and the rich are even more empowered to influence government for their own interests (Bernstein 1994; Zepezauer and Naiman 1998; Palast 2004; Mishel 2006).

The Power Dimension

You will recall that **power** is the ability to control the behavior of others, even against their will. Individuals or groups who possess power are able to use it to enhance their own interests, often—but not necessarily—at the expense of society.

Q Why is power a separate dimension of stratification? According to Marx, those people in a society who own and control capital have the power. Sociologists agree that economic success heightens the chances of increased power. The wealthy, for example, have the power to influence tax laws in their favor. However, many sociologists, beginning with Weber, argue that economic success and power do not necessarily overlap. This argument is based on several points. First, the fact that money can be used to exert power does not mean that it will be used in this way. Money is a resource that can be used to enhance power, but a decision must be made to use it for that purpose. For example, there are other families as wealthy as the Kennedys who have not used their economic resources to gain political power.

Second, money and ownership of the means of production are not the only resources for power. Expert knowledge can be used to expand power, too. For example, many lawyers convert their expertise into substantial amounts of political power. Eloquence as a speaker is another possible resource. And fame was a factor in 1952, when Albert Einstein was offered the presidency of Israel. He refused by saying, "I know a little about nature, and hardly anything about men."

Power is also attached to the social positions we hold. In organizations, elected officers have more power than rank-and-file members do. People in top executive positions in the mass media are powerful, even if they themselves do not have great wealth.

Finally, we can overcome a scarcity of resources if we have large numbers of people on our side or if we are skillful at organizing our resources. Hitler, for example, was able to transform limited resources into a mass political movement. He gained absolute power by promising to deliver Germany from the economic destitution it suffered following World War I.

The Prestige Dimension

A third dimension of social stratification is **prestige**—recognition, respect, and admiration attached to social positions. Prestige is defined by one's culture and society (J. M. Berger et al. 1998; Webster and Hysom 1998). In the first place, favorable social evaluation is based on the norms and values within a group. Honor, admiration, respect, and deference are extended to dons within the Mafia, but despite America's fascination with the underworld, Mafia chiefs do not have high prestige outside their own circles. Second, prestige is voluntarily given, not claimed. Scientists cannot proclaim themselves Nobel Prize winners; journalists cannot award themselves Pulitzer Prizes; corporate executives cannot grant themselves honorary doctorates. Recognition must come from others. Third, those accorded similar levels of prestige share identifiable lifestyles. The offspring of upper-class families are more likely to attend private universities and Episcopalian churches; children from lower-class homes are less likely to attend college at all and tend to belong to fundamentalist religious groups. In fact, some sociologists view social classes as subcultures.

Q How is conspicuous consumption related to the prestige dimension? People with sufficient economic resources may use their wealth to enhance their prestige; they may consume goods and services to display their wealth to others (Frank 2000). Thorstein Veblen (1995; originally published in 1899) called this phenomenon **conspicuous consumption**. Examples of conspicuous consumption are as numerous as they are astonishing (Frank 2008). Millionaire Malcolm Forbes's son paid $156,450 for an almost 200-year-old bottle of wine believed to have belonged to Thomas Jefferson (McGinn and Peterson 2002). Of course, conspicuous consumption is not limited to the United States. In India, the rich are expected to live extravagantly. In 2010, the richest man in India built himself a $1 billion, twenty-seven-story home, containing three helipads, nine

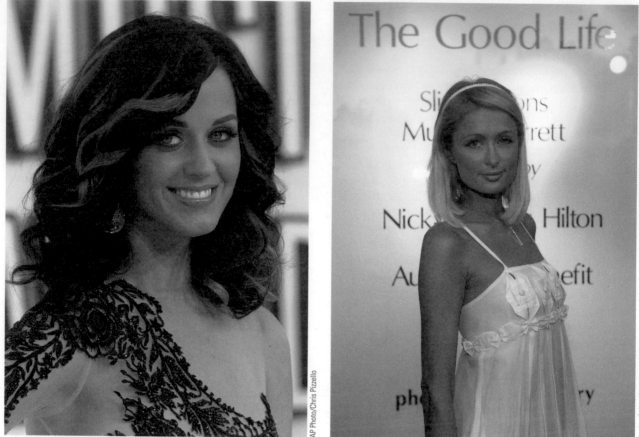

AP Photo/Chris Pizzello

Charley Gallay/Getty Images

Popular celebrities such as Katy Perry and Paris Hilton have considerable wealth. Their prestige rating is stronger in some circles than in others.

elevators, and a movie theater. Companies are constantly creating products that promote conspicuous consumption. Chanel, for example, has introduced a line of diamond-studded handbags priced at $260,150.

Q How is prestige distributed? Prestige distribution coincides with a society's value system. People in statuses that are considered the most important—that are valued the most highly—have the most prestige. Because Americans value the acquisition of wealth and power, they tend to assign higher prestige to persons in positions of wealth and power. The most stable source of prestige in modern society is associated with occupations (Nakao, Hodge, and Treas 1990; Nakao and Treas 1990).

The prestige rankings of selected occupations in the United States are presented in Table 8.1. Obviously, white-collar occupations (doctors, ministers, schoolteachers) tend to have higher prestige than blue-collar occupations (carpenters, plumbers, mechanics). As expected, physicians, lawyers, and dentists have high occupational prestige, whereas janitors, cab drivers, and garbage collectors have low prestige. You may find it somewhat surprising, however, that college professors

have more prestige than bankers—a demonstration that even though wealth and power usually determine prestige, there are exceptions.

Q What is the basis for occupational prestige? According to Robert Hodge, Paul Siegel, and Peter Rossi (1964), all societies rely on comparable factors when determining occupational prestige. In fact, Robert Hodge, Donald Treiman, and Peter Rossi (1966) have shown that the ranking of occupations based on prestige is similar in advanced as well as underdeveloped societies. Occupational prestige scores vary according to the following factors: compensation; education, skills, and ability required; power associated with the occupation; the importance of the occupation to the society; and the nature of the work (mental, or white-collar, work versus manual, or blue-collar, work). More recently, occupational prestige has been shown to be affected by gender.

Q Why do different cultures evaluate occupations similarly? Donald Treiman (1977) attempted to answer this question through an examination of nearly 100 studies of occupational prestige in sixty countries. From

TABLE 8.1

Prestige Rankings of Selected Occupations in the United States

Occupation	Prestige Score
Surgeon	87
Lawyer	75
College professor	74
Engineer	71
School principal	69
Pharmacist	68
Registered nurse	66
Accountant	65
Professional athlete	65
Public grade school teacher	64
Banker	63
Druggist	63
Veterinarian	62
Police officer	61
Actor	60
Journalist	60
TV anchorman	60
Businessperson	60
Nursery school teacher	55
Social worker	52
Funeral director	49
Jazz musician	48
Mail carrier	47
Insurance agent	46
Secretary	46
Bank teller	43
Automobile dealer	43
Evangelist	41
Sales clerk	36
Bus driver	32
Waitress	29
Garbage collector	28
Janitor	22
Prostitute	14
Panhandler	11

Why do you think the highest-listed prestige score is 87? What occupations might rate a higher score?

Source: General Social Survey, National Opinion Research Center, 1996.

societies develop similar occupational positions because of the functions that each must perform. This is clearly a functionalist explanation.

Not only do societies around the world develop similar occupational positions, but these positions tend to be arranged in occupational prestige hierarchies that are substantially similar throughout the world:

> In all societies, ranging from highly industrialized nations like the United States to peasant villages in up-country Thailand, the basic pattern of occupational evaluations is the same—professional and higher managerial positions are most highly regarded, lower white-collar and skilled blue-collar jobs fall in the middle of the hierarchy, and unskilled service and laboring jobs are the least respected. (Treiman 1977:103)

This is the case, according to Treiman, because certain occupations in all societies have greater control over scarce resources than do other occupations. Differential access to these resources—skill, authority, property—creates differential power. The power created by control over scarce resources is used to acquire special privilege. Power and privilege, in turn, are used to garner prestige. In this way, a single worldwide occupational prestige hierarchy is created. This is a conflict explanation.

Q Are the economic, power, and prestige dimensions related? Generally, there is a close relationship among these three dimensions of stratification. Those who are high on one dimension tend to be high on the other two. Power, particularly political power, is a decided economic advantage to its holders. For example, the wealthy pay for political favors either directly (as with money) or indirectly (as through inside information on lucrative business deals). Of the 535 members of the U.S. Congress, 261 are millionaires, representing nearly half of the total body (Levinthal 2010). Ten members of President George W. Bush's first cabinet were millionaires (Edsall 2002b; Keller 2002). Although Obama's cabinet has fewer high-net-worth individuals than Bush's, practically all of his senior advisors in the White House are millionaires. And former President George H. W. Bush and his son George W. Bush are by no means the only Americans who have used their wealth as springboards to the presidency of the United States.

Prestige and wealth are also closely intertwined. High prestige is heavily dependent on economic resources. The lifestyle usually associated with high prestige cannot be maintained without the economic clout to purchase such necessities as a nice home in the proper neighborhood or to send one's children to the best schools. But those with high prestige normally

these studies, which included countries of Western and Eastern Europe, North America, Africa, and South America, Treiman concluded that all societies must accomplish certain objectives. For example, domestic peace must be maintained, and a variety of goods—including food, housing, clothing, and transportation—must be produced and distributed. Culturally dissimilar

have no cause for concern, for with prestige come special economic rewards and unique business opportunities for generating wealth. Most of the wealth amassed by Tiger Woods, who is in billionaire range, did not come directly from prize money in professional golf tournaments. Because of his prestige, many people will buy any product he even implicitly endorses. So despite the blow to his prestige following his well-publicized serial marital infidelities, Tiger retains a multimillion-dollar payout from seven corporations including Nike, EA sports, and Golf Digest.

Prestige and power often mix quite well. Prestige is attached to social positions requiring important decision making. And prestige may be converted into power. Ronald Reagan and Arnold Schwarzenegger are both actors who became governors of California. Reagan, of course, went on to become president.

Explanations of Stratification R1

Obviously, social class exerts a powerful influence on social life. The social class into which people are born and to which they rise or fall affects their existence as much as any other social factor. For this reason, if for no other, it is of benefit to understand why the process of stratification is a mainspring of society.

In most societies, inequality—in income, wealth, power, and prestige—seems to be a basic fact of life (Chris Tilly 1999). Even societies deliberately organized to eliminate inequality are not classless. Despite the former Soviet Union's attempt to create an unstratified society, great differences in rank and rewards developed. Leading members of the Communist Party, the dominant elite, were able to obtain privileges for themselves and their families. For example, Politburo members and national secretaries

of the Communist Party drove black Zil limousines, hand-tooled cars worth more than $100,000 each, while the majority of Russian people had no chance of ever owning any kind of car. The Chinese Communist Party has also apparently become an entrenched, self-interested ruling class (Wortzel 1987). Why is stratification a universal feature of social life? There are several explanations.

The Functionalist Theory of Stratification

According to the functionalist theory of stratification, inequality renders a service. The most qualified people fill the most important positions and perform their tasks competently; they are then rewarded for their efforts. The functionalist theory recognizes that inequality exists not only because certain jobs are more important than others but also because these jobs often involve special talent and training.

To encourage people to make the sacrifices (years of education and so forth) necessary to fill these jobs, society attaches special monetary rewards and prestige to these positions. For example, doctors make more money and have more prestige than bus drivers because a high level of skill is required in the medical profession and our society's need for highly qualified doctors is great. Once qualified people assume positions, however, they must be motivated to do their jobs competently. It is not happenstance, then, that greater rewards go to those who do the superior work. Thus, the more competent doctors, secretaries, and salespersons usually receive more of the "just desserts" than those who perform their tasks less well.

The functionalist theory has dominated sociological thinking for a long time, but it has been a very difficult theory to test. Although some studies support at least some aspects of the functionalist theory (Grandjean 1975; Cullen and Novick 1979), several weaknesses should be noted.

According to conflict theory, inequality is a result of the elite exploiting the less powerful. Financier J. P. Morgan represents the power of nineteenth-century industrialists.

Q. What are the weaknesses of the functionalist theory?
Although the functionalist theory is elegant, concise, and consistent with traditional American beliefs about inequality, it has several failings (Tumin 1953). First, there are many people who have power, prestige, and wealth whose contributions to society do not seem very important. Many top athletes, film stars, and rock singers make much more money than the president of the United States. Why should scientists make almost no money for groundbreaking books reporting their research, whereas screenwriters regularly receive $500,000 plus per script? Twenty–five hedge fund managers made billions before the economic crisis began in 2007. Do hedge fund managers contribute enough to society to merit that payout? Are CEOs 300 times more valuable to society than average workers?

Second, the functionalist theory ignores the barriers to competition faced by some members of society—the poor, women, the aged, African Americans, and various other ethnic groups. A wealth of talent exists among people in these categories, but not much of it is ever tapped, because such people do not experience equal opportunity to compete. They have not had the educational opportunity because they are poor, the wrong color, or the wrong sex. And even if they are technically qualified, they may lose higher-level positions to less qualified individuals who happen to possess particular social characteristics.

Third, the functionalist theory overlooks the inheritance of social class level. In some societies, one's social class is determined at birth. Even in modern societies, in which the rate of mobility is supposed to be high, children tend to remain in or near the social class of their parents. This means that talented daughters and sons from lower-class homes cannot compete on an equal basis with the offspring of middle- and upper-class people. Consequently, many talented individuals—who might have preferred being surgeons, lawyers, or executives—are truck drivers, plumbers, and short-order cooks.

Finally, the functionalist theory of stratification has an ethnocentric bias. That is, it assumes that all people in all societies will be motivated to compete for a greater portion of the scarce desirables. In fact, in some societies, greater emphasis is placed on a more or less equitable distribution of wealth, power, and prestige than on individual competition for larger shares.

The Conflict Theory of Stratification

Melvin Tumin (1953) concluded that stratification exists not because it is necessary for the benefit of society but because it helps people holding the most power and economic resources to maintain the status quo. From his perspective, the functionalist theory is used as a justification for keeping some people at the top of the class structure and some at the bottom. This viewpoint is consistent with the conflict theory of stratification.

Q. How does conflict theory account for inequality?
According to the conflict theory of stratification, inequality exists because some people are willing to exploit others. The elite hold a monopoly over the desirables, and they use their monopoly to dominate others. Stratification, from this perspective, is based on force rather than on consent. Those with wealth, power, and prestige are able to maintain, perhaps even increase, their share of desirables in a society (Perrucci and Wysong 2007).

This conflict theory of stratification is based on Marxian ideas regarding class conflict. For Marx, all of history has been a class struggle between the powerful and the powerless, the exploiters and the exploited. Capitalist society is the final stage of the class struggle. Although (according to conflict theorists) the capitalists are outnumbered, they are able to control the workers by creating a belief system that legitimates the status quo. Those who own the means of production are able to disseminate their ideas, beliefs, and values through the schools, the media, the churches, and the government. In this way, the dominant ideas of the elite become the dominant ideas of the ruled. Marx used the term **false consciousness** to refer to working-class acceptance of the dominant ideology (even though the ideology worked against working-class interests).

Because Marx believed that class conflict occurs in every historical epoch, he predicted that the working class would eventually shed its false consciousness—and its chains—for a revolution based on a true class consciousness. That is, it would realize its exploitation and reject the dominant belief system. After overthrowing the capitalists, the working class would create a socialist society in which the means of production and all property would be owned equally by the people. This would be a transitional stage between capitalist society and the classless society of communism. Ultimately, socialism would be replaced by communism, which would put an end to human misery and exploitation.

Marx's work was somewhat neglected by American sociologists for a time, although it has indirectly influenced the field through the negative reactions of many sociologists. Why has Marx been neglected? For one thing, many of his ideas—exploitation, revolution, classless society, communism—do not fit well with the American emphasis on capitalism, achievement, and upward mobility. In addition, many of Marx's predictions appear to have been wrong. Socialist revolutions have occurred in noncapitalist societies; communism did not produce classless societies; the middle class rather than the working class has expanded in capitalist societies.

Marxists do not consider that any of the preceding factors disprove Marx's theory. First, the so-called socialist and communist revolutions in precapitalist societies were essentially the result of a misinterpretation of Marx, who insisted that capitalism was an essential precondition that must occur before a communist society is possible. Second, Marx's theory defines the middle class as part of the working class. This is because the middle class also does not own the means of production, and its gradual expansion fulfills Marx's prediction of the increasing "proletarianization" of labor (i.e., more and more people, including small-business owners, doctors, and other professionals, lose ownership of their labor power and come to work for someone else). Finally, according to Marxists, it is premature to assert that Marx was wrong simply because capitalism has not yet disappeared. Marx gave no timetable for the socialist revolution, and Marxist theorists see evidence of increasing contradictions within capitalism (Therborn 1982, 1984; E. O. Wright 1985, 2000).

Some sociologists have begun to look past the apparent miscalculations in Marx's theories to appreciate some of the assumptions on which they are based.

They have substantial appreciation for his insight into the ways the elite use society's institutions, including the state, to achieve their own ends.

German sociologist Ralf Dahrendorf (1959) has advocated shifting from the Marxist emphasis on class conflict to conflict between groups, such as unions and corporations. Dahrendorf attributes stratification more to the possession of power than to ownership of property. The wealthy use America's legal system, for example, for their own benefit; education helps the elite perpetuate their power; the political system is skewed toward the interests of the powerful. For the followers of the conflict perspective, then, the struggle for scarce resources creates classes (Domhoff 1996; Giddens 1987, 2002).

The Symbolic Interactionist Theory of Stratification

Why was the inequality between former Soviet political leaders and average Russian people tolerated by the masses? Why does the poorest one-fifth of Americans not revolt against the richest one-fifth of the population? Social stratification systems can persist over the long haul only if people believe in their legitimacy.

Q **How is the legitimacy of a stratification structure incorporated into the minds of individuals?** Social stratification persists only as long as its legitimacy is accepted. Symbolic interactionism helps us understand the legitimation process; it must occur through socialization. Symbols, in the form of language, explain to the young the existence of stratification structure and the reasons for people being located in particular strata. According to this perspective, American children are taught that one's place in the stratification structure is the product of talent and effort. Those "on top" have worked hard and have used their abilities, and those "at the bottom" have lacked the talent and motivation to succeed; therefore, it is not fair to challenge the system. In this way, people come to believe in the fairness of the existing system.

The legitimacy of a stratification structure penetrates even deeper. Legitimacy views are incorporated into an individual's self-concept.

Q **How do ideas about inequality become part of the self-concept?** Certain self-images are implied in the legitimization of stratification. Those at the bottom of the stratification structure suffer from lower self-esteem. How could it be otherwise when messages from all sides tell them of their inferiority? After all, as the symbolic interactionists document, self-esteem is based on our perceptions of others' opinions. The looking-glass process is at work (see Table 8.2; see "Sociology in Your Life").

TABLE 8.2

FOCUS ON THEORETICAL PERSPECTIVES: Social Stratification

This table summarizes issues of social stratification that might be of interest to each of the major perspectives and predictions that they would make. Why would the symbolic interactionists be more likely than the functionalists to look at issues of self-esteem?

Theoretical Perspective	Research Topic	Expected Result
Functionalism	• Relationship between job performance and pay	• Pay levels increase with job performance.
Conflict theory	• Relationship between social class level and the likelihood of punishment for a crime	• The chances for prosecution decrease as social class level increases.
Symbolic interactionism	• Link between social class level and self-esteem	• Self-esteem is higher among the upper class than the lower class.

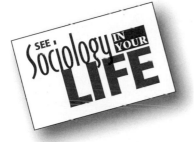

Cyber Bullying and Stratification

As noted, social stratification exists whenever scarce desirables are unequally distributed. In school, among peers, prestige is a most cherished and scarce valuable. Because prestige is such a scarce commodity in school, the charmed circle is small. Those excluded from valued cliques experience varying degrees of social anxiety and loss of self-esteem. And it is the most socially isolated young people who are at the greatest risk of being bullied.

Bullying involves intentional aggression promoted by differences in power or strength (Wang, Nansel, and Iannoti 2001). We are less interested here in bullying based on coercion (through physical strength) than bullying based on status differences. While bullying is age-old, *cyber bullying* has emerged only in the last decade and obviously entails the use of technology. Cyber bullying may be direct (sending messages to someone else personally) or by proxy

(enlisting the help of others, with or without their knowledge) (Aftab 2006).

Cyber bullying is perpetrated through a wide range of technological devices, including e-mails, instant messaging, and cell phone cameras. While traditional bullying is upclose and personal, cyber bullying is often anonymous and occurs among people who have never met. A physical bully can be avoided; a cyber bully is almost impossible to avoid.

Victims of cyber bullying suffer from social anxiety and low self-esteem, both associated with low social status in the youth culture (Kowalski, Limber, and Agaston 2008; Wang, Nansel, and Iannoti, 2010). Megan Meier is a case in point. After a period of name-calling and exclusion from valued school cliques, Megan craved emotional connection. Her mother thought that a MySpace page would be good for her sensitive, socially isolated daughter. But Megan's neediness only made her a highly vulnerable target for abuse. This thirteen-year-old girl became the victim of a group attack on MySpace, labeling her a liar, a whore, and worse. Megan fought back for a while, but the avalanche of hate messages, and the variety of the sources sending them, led her to hang herself with a belt.

Megan's case has an added twist, illustrating that cyber bullying is not limited to the young. She was the victim of

a hoax. Another neighborhood mother, after creating a shadow MySpace profile of a boy named "Josh Evans," had her daughter join her in convincing Megan that Josh liked her. A few weeks later, Josh sent Megan MySpace messages telling her that he hated her. Other girls, most not aware that Josh was fictitious, piled on with vicious insults. Megan's subsequent depression led to her suicide (Maag 2007).

There is a significant gender difference between cyber bullying and traditional bullying (Kowalski, 2008). Females are more likely than males to be cyber bullies and to be targets of cyber bullies. Since cyber bullying is an indirect form of aggression, this is consistent with research indicating that females bully more through social exclusion and rumor spreading while males are more likely to bully physically.

Think About It

1. Which theory of stratification do you think best encompasses cyber bullying? Defend your choice.
2. Describe the research methods you think most appropriate for studying cyber bullying.
3. Do you have any personal knowledge of cyber bullying? Does the case you have in mind conform to the description of cyber bullying given here? Elaborate.

Explanations of Stratification

1. Match the theories of stratification with the examples.
   ____ a. functionalist theory
   ____ b. conflict theory
   ____ c. symbolic interactionism
   (1) Corporate executives make more money because they determine who gets what in their organizations.
   (2) Engineers make more money than butlers because of the education they possess.
   (3) Ghetto children tend to have low self-esteem.
2. Which of the following is *not* a criticism of the functionalist theory of stratification?
   a. There are people at the top whose jobs do not seem very important.
   b. It has a bias toward cultural relativism.
   c. It overlooks the barriers to competition.
   d. It glosses over the inheritance of social class level.
3. The conflict theory of stratification is based on Marx's ideas on class _____.
4. According to the symbolic interactionists, the deepest penetration of the beliefs supporting the stratification structure comes as a result of
   a. the "I"
   b. evolution
   c. conflict
   d. the self-concept

Answers: 1. a. (2), b. (1), c. (3); 2. b; 3. conflict, 4. d

Moreover, a person's sense of self-worth affects the amount of rewards he or she feels entitled to receive. Thus, people at the bottom of the heap tend not to challenge the stratification structure because of the conviction that they are undeserving. Those at the top blame the victims; the victims blame themselves.

The reverse is true for the higher classes. Those profiting most from the stratification structure tend to have higher self-esteem. This, in turn, fuels their conviction that the present arrangement is just. In short, people's self-concepts help preserve the status quo.

Stratification in American Society R1

Class Consciousness

Americans have always had a sense of inequality, but they have never had a sophisticated understanding of **class consciousness**—a sense of identification with the goals and interests of the members of one's own social class (Centers 1949; Hodge and Treiman 1968; Jackman and Jackman 1983). In part because the American public has historically shown relatively little interest in class differences, American scholars began to investigate inequality rather late. It was

not until the 1920s that sociologists began to systematically identify social classes in American communities. Since that time, however, the material available on this subject has been voluminous. Early efforts to study stratification were through intensive case studies of specific communities (W. L. Warner and Lunt 1941; Hollingshead 1949; Hollingshead and Redlich 1958; W. L. Warner 1960). Only relatively recently have attempts been made to describe the stratification structure of America as a whole (Rossides 1997; Chris Tilly 1999; Perrucci and Wysong 2007; D. A. Gilbert 2010).

Identification of Social Classes

Any attempt to describe the social class structure of American society is hazardous. Social classes are fluid, replete with exceptions, and abstract. Nevertheless, sociologists have identified the major features of the American class structure. According to Daniel Rossides (1997), the upper class comprises about 1 percent of the population, the upper middle class about 14 percent, the middle middle class about 30 percent, the working class about 30 percent, and the lower class about 25 percent. Despite the hazards involved, a brief description of each of these social classes follows. (Figure 8.4 presents a similar picture of the American class structure.)

FIGURE 8.4

American Class Structure

What does the shape of the American class structure indicate about stratification in the United States?

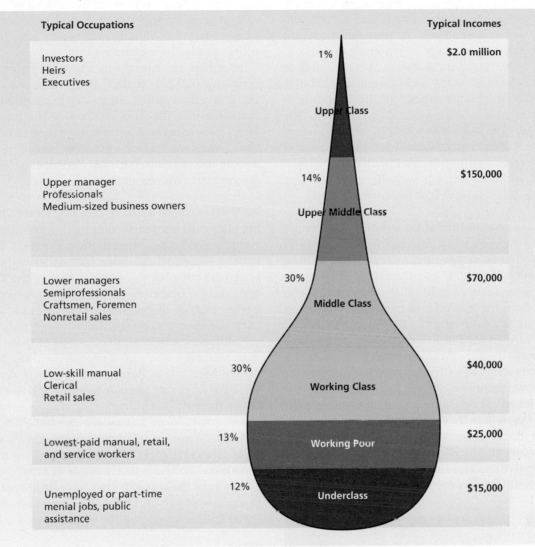

Typical Occupations		Typical Incomes
Investors Heirs Executives	1% **Upper Class**	$2.0 million
Upper manager Professionals Medium-sized business owners	14% **Upper Middle Class**	$150,000
Lower managers Semiprofessionals Craftsmen, Foremen Nonretail sales	30% **Middle Class**	$70,000
Low-skill manual Clerical Retail sales	30% **Working Class**	$40,000
Lowest-paid manual, retail, and service workers	13% **Working Poor**	$25,000
Unemployed or part-time menial jobs, public assistance	12% **Underclass**	$15,000

Source: Adapted from Dennis Gilbert, *The American Class Structure*, 8th ed. (Thousand Oaks, CA: Pine Forge Press, 2010), p. 14.

Q **Are members of the upper class all alike?** Despite America's emphasis on the openness and fluidity of its class structure, its upper class contains only a fraction of its population (1 to 3 percent). Moreover, there is even stratification within the upper class. At the pinnacle rests the upper upper class, the 1 percent of the American population that we recognize as the aristocracy. Its members represent the "old" money amassed for generations by families whose names appear in the Social Register—Ford, Rockefeller, Vanderbilt, du Pont. Gaining entrance into this most elite of clubs is a long-run proposition because the basis of

membership is blood rather than sweat and tears. Money must age over generations to have any chance of entering the orbit of the blue bloods. Obviously, members of the upper upper class pay enormous attention to lineage, which they protect in several ways: sending their children to the best private secondary schools and universities, maintaining rather exclusive interaction with one another, and promoting a high rate of intramarriage.

The lower upper class, the "new rich," are in the upper class more often because of achievement rather than birth; membership is based more on earned income than inherited wealth (Frank 2008). The lower upper class is composed of people with much more varied socioeconomic backgrounds. Many members of the lower upper class inherited some wealth, although usually not fortunes. Others may have amassed fortunes by being shrewd investors on the stock market, creating a chain of hardware stores, becoming a Metropolitan Opera star, or earning millions from athletic talent. Although they may actually be better off financially, people who have entered the lower upper class in their own lifetimes are generally barred from the exclusive social circles in which members of the upper upper class travel.

The upper class as a whole wields tremendous power over domestic and international decisions and over events affecting vast numbers of people (Dye 2001). If the United States has a power elite, this is it (see Chapter 13, "Political and Economic Institutions").

Q What is the composition of the middle class? The upper middle class (10 to 15 percent of the population) is composed of those who are successful in business, the professions, politics, and the military. Basically, this class is made up of individuals and families who benefited from the tremendous corporate and professional expansion following World War II. Members of this class earn enough to live pretty well and to save some money. They are typically college educated and have high educational and occupational aspirations for their children. Although they do not exercise national or international power, their influence is felt in their communities, where they tend to be active in voluntary and political organizations.

The middle middle class is large (30 to 35 percent of the population) and heterogeneous. Its members include small-business owners; small farmers; small,

This family fulfills the American image of comfortable middle-class living.

independent professionals (small-town doctors and lawyers); semiprofessionals (clergy, teachers, nurses, firefighters, social workers, and police officers); middle-level managers; and sales and clerical workers. Their income level, which is at about the national average, does not permit them to live as well as the upper middle class. Typically, these people have only a high school education, although many may have had some college or may have completed college.

Members of the middle class are interested in civic affairs. Their participation in political activities is less than in the classes above them but higher than in either the working class or the lower class. The 1980s witnessed a dramatic decrease of middle class Americans. In fact, since 1980, the proportion of middle-income Americans has declined by 20 percent (Morin 1991; Wallich and Corcoran 1992).

Q What is unique about the working class? The working class (often referred to as the lower middle class) comprises about one-third of the population. Its members typically include either blue-collar workers who work with their hands—roofers, delivery truck drivers, and machine operators—or lower-level salespeople and clerical workers (Rubin 1994). The economic resources of its members are, on the whole, fewer than those of the aforementioned, although some of these workers (e.g., plumbers) may earn more than some middle-class people. Members of the working class experience considerable economic pressure because their incomes are below the national average, their employment is less stable, and they are generally without the hospital insurance and retirement benefits enjoyed by those in the middle class. The specter of unemployment or illness is both real and haunting. Outside of union activities, members of the working class have little opportunity to exercise power, and their participation in organizational life, including politics, is scant (Zweig 2000).

Q What groups of people fall into the lower class, and what is their most common shared characteristic? Lumped into the lower class (20 to 25 percent of the population) are the working poor, the frequently unemployed, the underpaid, and the permanently unemployed. The most common shared characteristic of the lower class is lack of value in the labor market. There are many routes into the lower class—birth, physical or mental disability, old age, loss of a marriage partner, lack of education or training, occupational failure, alcoholism. There are, however, very few paths out (W. J. Wilson et al. 1988; M. B. Katz 1993; D. A. Gilbert 2010).

The **working poor** (about 13 percent of the population) consist of people employed in low-skill jobs with the lowest pay. Its members are typically the lowest-level clerical workers, manual workers (laborers), and service workers (fast-food servers). The backbone

CHECK YOURSELF **8.3** R2

Stratification in American Society

1. _____ refers to a sense of identification with the goals and interests of the members of one's social class.
2. The upper upper class in the United States contains about _____ percent of the total population.
3. A major difference between the upper upper class and the lower upper class is that the latter has relied on _____ rather than birth.
4. The _____ is composed of people with an intergenerational history of unemployment.

Answers: 1. Class consciousness; 2. 1; 3. achievement; 4. underclass

of the country, the working poor, helps the economy function. They serve food, clean offices and homes, care for children and the elderly, turn out products on assembly lines, and help harvest crops. There are more than 10 million low-income working families in the United States, accounting for almost one-third of all working families. In other words, one in three working families in the United States works hard just to survive (Roberts, Povich, and Mather 2010).

The **underclass** (about 12 percent of the population) is composed of people who are usually unemployed and who come from families with a history of unemployment. They either work in part-time menial jobs (unloading trucks, picking up litter) or are on public assistance. In addition to a lack of education and skills, many of the members of the underclass have other problems. Physical or mental disabilities are common, and many are single mothers with little or no income. We explore the underclass in the following section on poverty in the United States as well as in Chapter 9 on racial and ethnic minorities.

Poverty in America R1

Widespread poverty existed throughout the United States when Michael Harrington helped to make it a political issue in his book *The Other America* (1962). Fifty years later, scholars continue to underscore the presence of poverty in affluent America (Newman 1999, 2007; Gilbert 2010). We turn now to the measurement of poverty.

Measuring Poverty

On an absolute scale, poverty embodies a lack of housing, food, medical care, and other necessities for maintaining life. **Absolute poverty** is the absence of enough money to secure life's necessities. On a relative scale, though, it is possible to have those things required to remain alive—and even to live in reasonably good physical health—and still be poor. **Relative poverty** is measured by comparing the economic condition of those at the bottom of a society with that of other strata. Because poverty is determined by the standards that exist within a society, a measure of poverty is not the same in India as in the United States.

Q How can relative poverty be measured? According to advocates of the relative measurement of poverty, the poverty threshold should be raised as the standard of living in a country rises. An increasing amount of spendable income does not make people feel less poor if the income levels of those around them are increasing at the same or a faster rate. A common measure of relative poverty is an income comparison between the lowest fifth of the population and the other four-fifths. Such a measure means, of course, that a segment of the population will always be poor unless the total income distribution approaches equality.

Q How can absolute poverty be measured? An absolute measurement of poverty begins with a "poverty line," an annual income level below which people are considered poor. In the United States in 2009, that figure was set at $21,954 for a family of four. The poor, as measured by this federal government standard, comprises more than 14.3 percent of the American population (see Figure 8.5). The following description of America's poor is based on this absolute measure of poverty (See "Sociology Eyes America" 8.1).

Identifying the Poor

The economic downturn that began in 2007 swelled the ranks of poor Americans. Between 2007 and 2009, the poverty rate and the number in poverty increased almost 2 percent and over 6 million. The number of Americans in poverty is the highest ever since the federal government began publishing poverty estimates over fifty years ago (DeNavos-Walt, Proctor, and Smith 2010). The most disadvantaged groups living in the United States today are the people who live in female-headed households, children under eighteen years of age, elderly people, minorities, and people with disabilities.

FIGURE 8.5

Number of Poor and Poverty Rate: 1959–2009

This graph shows two types of information: (1) the number of poor in the total population and (2) the poverty rate as a percentage of the total population. Why is it often helpful to have related information plotted on the same graph?

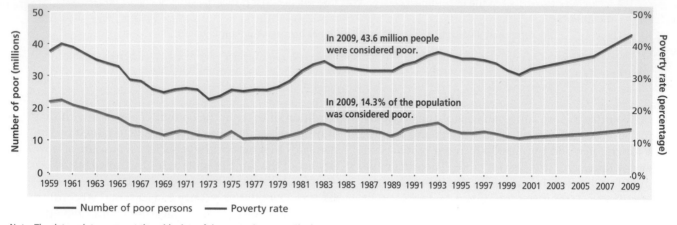

In 2009, 43.6 million people were considered poor.

In 2009, 14.3% of the population was considered poor.

—— Number of poor persons   —— Poverty rate

Note: The data points represent the midpoints of the respective years. The latest recessionary period began in July 1990.
Sources: Carmen DeNavas-Walt, Bernadette D. Proctor, and Jessica C. Smith, U.S. Census Bureau. "Income, Poverty and Health Insurance Coverage in the United States: 2009," *Current Population Reports* (Washington, D.C.: U.S. Government Printing Office, 2010).

Q How are race and ethnicity related to poverty? Nearly 43 percent of the poor in America today are non-Latino white (see Figure 8.5). The poverty rate for African Americans and Latinos is much higher than that for whites, however. The poverty rate for whites is 12.3 percent; for African Americans and Latinos the rate is more than 25 percent. African Americans and Latinos together account for just over one-fourth of the total population, but they make up over half of the poor population (see Figure 8.6).

SOCIOLOGY EYES AMERICA 8.1

Percentage of Population in Poverty

Percentage of Population in Poverty

- ■ 17.0% or above
- ■ 14.0%–16.9%
- ■ 11.0%–13.9%
- ■ 8.0%–10.9%
- □ 7.9% or below

Although the U.S. economy is prosperous, some people are concerned that many have not benefited from this prosperity. In fact, many people still live in poverty. This map shows the average percentage of the poor by state for 2006 to 2008.

Interpret the Map

1. Can you make any generalization about poverty from this map?
2. If you were the governor of your state, what would your platform on poverty be? Be specific.

Source: U.S. Bureau of the Census, *2006–2008 American Community Survey Three-Year Estimates*, 2009.

FIGURE 8.6

The Distribution of Poverty in the United States

What are the most important conclusions you would reach from this figure?

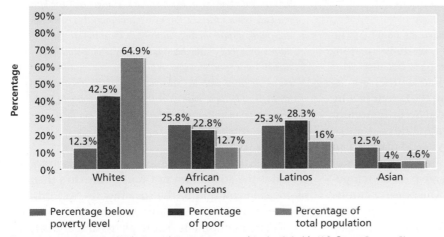

- ■ Percentage below poverty level
- ■ Percentage of poor
- ■ Percentage of total population

Sources: Carmen DeNavas-Walt, Bernadette D. Proctor, and Jessica C. Smith, U.S. Census Bureau. "Income, Poverty and Health Insurance Coverage in the United States: 2009," *Current Population Reports* (Washington, D.C.: U.S. Government Printing Office, 2010).

Q How are gender, age, and health related to poverty? Female-headed households make up another large segment of the poor population. We can look at this issue in two different ways. We can look at all poor households as a group and determine what proportion of them is headed by females with no husband present. When we do this, we find that about one-half of poor households are female-headed. In contrast, when we look at nonpoor households, we find that only about 19 percent are headed by females. Another approach would be to look at all female-headed households as a group and determine what proportion of them is poor. We find that the poverty rate for these households is about 30 percent, compared with just over 11 percent for all families.

By either measure, then, households headed by females are poorer than those headed by males. A related factor is the poverty rate for children under eighteen years of age. The current rate for this is 17.4 percent—the highest rate for any age group in the United States. The high poverty rates for women and children reflect a trend in U.S. society. Between 1960 and today, women and children make up a larger proportion of the poor. Sociologists refer to this trend as the **feminization of poverty** (Edin and Lein 1997; Edin and Kefalas 2006; Sidel 1998, 2006).

There are several reasons women have a higher risk of being poor. As we discuss in more detail in Chapter 10 ("Inequalities of Gender"), women who work full time all year earn only 77 cents for every dollar earned by men. Also, women with children find it more difficult to find and keep regular, long-term employment.

A lack of good child-care facilities adds to the likelihood that women will be incapable of further employment.

A smaller percentage of Americans 65 years and older are poorer than other age groups (DeNavas-Walt, Proctor, and Smith 2010). About 20 percent of children under eighteen are in poverty, and 13 percent of adults eighteen to sixty-four years of age are below the poverty line. The economic situation of the elderly is covered in greater detail in Chapter 15 ("Health Care and Aging").

Poverty is greatest among American children under six years of age.

Ewing Galloway/Jupiter Images

People with disabilities comprise another large segment of the poor. This group is three times as likely to live in poverty as people who are able-bodied. Also, people who have severe disabilities are more likely to live in poverty than are those who have less severe disabilities (Freedman, Martin, and Schoeni 2004).

Q Is this an accurate picture of America's poor? At the very least, this absolute measure of poverty is a reasonable approximation—reasonable, in part, because prior to 1963 the federal government had neither a definition nor a measure of poverty at all. Developed by Mollie Orshansky (1965) of the Social Security Administration, the federal government's absolute measure of poverty was based on an "economy" food plan: a plan designed by the U.S. Department of Agriculture as nutritionally adequate for use in emergencies or, temporarily, when family funds are low. The poverty cutoffs (based on factors such as family size, gender of the head of the household, and place of residence) were based essentially on the amount of income left after allowing for an adequate diet at minimum cost.

Critics point to some shortcomings of this approach. This definition reflects inflation, but it ignores social and economic changes such as the feminization of poverty and the higher costs of child care, transportation, and health care. The federal poverty level also considers the cost of living to be uniform across all states (except Hawaii and Alaska): A family living in Manhattan in New York is assumed to spend the same amount on food, shelter, and clothing as a family in Manhattan, Kansas (Bhargava and Kuriansky 2002). According to Mark Rank (2003), the number of people ever in poverty is a better indicator of the extent of poverty than the number of people in poverty in any particular year. By age seventy-five, he contends, 59 percent of Americans will have spent at least a year below the poverty line during adulthood, and 68 percent will have experienced near poverty.

Such problems with the government's current measure of poverty have led to bipartisan pressure in Washington to create a new measure. The National Academy of Science's formula, which doubles the extent of poverty in America, has sufficient credibility that the U.S. Census Bureau is working with the Academy and leading scholars to devise a new measure to supplement the present one. To be unveiled soon, this new measure is expected to provide a more accurate picture of the poor (Swarns 2008; Yen 2009; Nelson and Haskins 2010).

Perceptions of the Poor

Q How do Americans view the poor? The traditional American view of the poor has roots extending to ancient Greece. In the seventh or eighth century B.C.E.,

the Greek poet Hesiod expressed for his contemporaries his view about work and the poor:

Work! Work, and then Hunger will not be your companion, while fair-wreathed and sublime Demeter will favor you and fill your barn with her blessings. Hunger and the idling man are bosom friends. Both gods and mortals resent the lazy man, a man no more ambitious than the stingless drones that feed on the bees' labor in wasteful sloth. Let there be order and measure in your own work until your barns are filled with the season's harvest. Riches and flocks of sheep go to those who work. If you work, you will be dearer to immortals and mortals; they both loathe the indolent. (Hesiod 1983:74–75)

There is another example of this approach to poverty: it is the adaptation of Charles Darwin's theory of biological evolution to the social world. According to Darwin, only the fittest plants and animals survive in a particular environment. Those plants and animals that survive carry physical characteristics that give them a competitive edge for survival. The process of natural selection ensures that the fittest survive. When applied to human society, this view is called *social Darwinism*. It contends that the fittest individuals survive as a result of social selection and that the inferior are eliminated by the same process (Strickland and Shetty 1998).

Although social scientists have long rejected social Darwinism, this philosophy has contributed to that part of America's basic value system that is variously labeled the work ethic, the achievement and success ideology, and the ideology of individualism (Gilens 1999). Individualism in America involves several central beliefs:

1. Each individual should work hard and strive to succeed in competition with others.
2. Those who work hard should be rewarded with success (seen as wealth, property, prestige, and power).
3. Because of widespread and equal opportunity, those who work hard will, in fact, be rewarded with success.
4. Economic failure is an individual's own fault and reveals lack of effort and other character defects. (Feagin 1975:91–92)

According to the ideology of individualism, those at the bottom are where they belong because they lack the ability, energy, and motivation to survive in a competitive social world. From this vantage point, it is the poor who are to blame for their condition; those who fail deserve to do so (Ryan 1976; O'Toole 1998; N. P. Barry 1999; Zinn 2003). In its most extreme form, the ideology of individualism contends that legislation to protect the poor is harmful because protective legislation interferes with the process of natural selection, thus slowing social evolution (Lux 1990).

To test whether the ideology of individualism continues to affect the American public's view of the poor, James Kluegel and Eliot Smith (2009) conducted a nationwide survey. Respondents were asked to judge the reasons usually cited to explain poverty in America. They found that individualistic explanations were the most popular. Lack of thrift, lack of effort, lack of ability, and loose morals and drunkenness—all individualistic causes—were considered the most important reasons for poverty. Much less emphasis was placed on structural explanations that locate the causes of poverty in social and economic factors, factors beyond the control of the poor (see Table 8.3). Although, recently, structural explanations for poverty have grown in importance, the individualistic interpretation remains dominant, particularly among affluent, higher-status, white, older Americans, those furthest from the situation being studied (W. J. Wilson 1997; Goode and Maskovsky 2001; "National Survey on Poverty in America" 2001; Draut 2002; Eitzen and Smith 2008).

Q **Does race influence attitudes toward the poor?** In a complicated way, it does. Americans do not reject welfare in principle; the poor who are not lazy and who try to find jobs deserve help, most say. It is the "undeserving" poor—those perceived as shiftless—who are the target of public scorn (R. C. Lieberman 1998; M. K. Brown 1999; Neubeck and Cazenave 2001). This is where race is thought to enter the mix. Due, in part, to the media's long-standing negative portrayal of the African American poor, welfare has become enshrouded in racial stereotypes. While Americans do not dislike welfare because African Americans benefit from it, many do believe that welfare benefits undeserving African Americans who prefer a government handout to work (Gilens 1999; Blank and Haskins 2001).

Americans, of course, do not condemn just the African American poor. While race complicates the issue, many Americans are opposed to welfare for *all* "undeserving" poor, regardless of their race and ethnicity.

Q **How accurate is the negative image of the poor?** Not very. About 22 million of the poor in America are over eighteen years of age. Of these, about half worked either full time or part time in 2009. In other words, 45 percent of poor Americans are working. Fifty-five percent are ill, disabled, retired, at home or

---

TABLE 8.3

Perceived Reasons for Poverty in the United States

Reasons for Poverty	Percentage Replying		
	Very Important	Somewhat Important	Not Important
Individualistic Explanations			
• Lack of thrift and proper money management by poor people	64%	30%	6%
• Lack of effort by the poor themselves	53	39	8
• Lack of ability and talent among poor people	53	35	11
• Loose morals and drunkenness	44	30	27
Structural Explanations			
• Low wages in some businesses and industries	40	47	14
• Failure of society to provide good schools for many Americans	46	29	26
• Prejudice and discrimination against blacks	31	44	25
• Failure of private industry to provide enough jobs	35	39	28
• Being taken advantage of by rich people	20	35	45

How would you have answered this survey? Explain your answers.

Source: Adapted with permission from James R. Kluegel and Eliot R. Smith, *Beliefs About Inequality: Americans' Views of What Ought to Be* (p. 79). Copyright © 1990 by James R. Kluegel and Eliot R. Smith.

not working for family reasons, or looking for work. About 11 percent are in school, or not working for some unspecified reason. At any particular point in time, about one-third of welfare mothers are working. Nearly all of the poor in America are either under-age children, working people, or persons not working for legitimate reasons. This evidence contradicts the prevailing assumption that the poor are able-bodied individuals simply waiting for others to take care of them.

Research challenges the view that the poor, whatever their race or ethnicity, are lazy, opposed to work, and prefer to live off others. In a recent study of the working poor in the inner city (Harlem), Katherine Newman (1999) documents the many African Americans and Latinos who are trying to form families, work steadily, and support themselves. If, Newman argues, Americans realized that most minorities are members of the hard-working poor, Americans would be less ready to label them as undeserving. From his research on the working poor, David Shipler (2005) writes sympathetically of these "invisible" Americans who perform the most menial jobs. Americans who encounter the working poor every day fail to see them for what they are. Their jobs—serving Big Macs, helping customers find merchandize at Wal-Mart, cleaning buildings, and assembling products—trap them for life in poorly paid work. Yet, they keep working, battling personal shortcomings and societal barriers that prevent them from being upwardly mobile.

For years, welfare mothers, the most maligned of the poor, have told researchers that they prefer employment to staying at home. Most welfare mothers say they are not presently working because of their children, housework, bad health, or lack of skills (Poddel 1968; Warren and Berkowitz 1969). A national survey indicates a strong work ethic among the poor. A representative sample of poor Americans was asked, "Which do you think is more important in life: working hard and doing what is expected of you or doing the things that give you personal satisfaction and pleasure?" Over three-fourths subscribed to the idea of hard work, which was a bit higher than for the nonpoor in the sample. In addition, the poor favored the idea of workfare—requirement by the government that physically able poor people work before they can receive poverty benefits—to a somewhat greater degree than the nonpoor. The poor, it turns out, believe in the same work-related values and attitudes as other Americans (I. A. Lewis and Schneider 1985). David Shipler found the same attitudes among middle school children in poverty-ridden neighborhoods. Practically all of these children wanted to go to college and aspired to higher level occupations (lawyer, doctor, optometrist, nurse, mechanic, police officer) than their unemployed or

unskilled parents. Other studies report no difference in desire to work between the poor and the nonpoor. Whether male or female, black or white, young or old, poor people appear to share the middle-class identification of self-esteem with work and self-support. The aspirations of the poor match those of the nonpoor; both groups desire an adequate education and a home in a good neighborhood (W.J. Wilson 1997; Lichter and Crowley 2002).

In summary, many Americans tend to blame the poor for their poverty, despite evidence that the poor are not the lazy, shiftless, willingly dependent people they are popularly thought to be. Both the attitudes and the behavior of the poor contradict the negative label often applied to them (Blee and Billings 1999; O'Connor 2002).

Responses to the Problem of Poverty

Before the mid-1960s, fighting poverty was not a major goal of the federal government (O'Connor 2002). Some programs, such as Social Security and Aid to Families with Dependent Children (AFDC), had been enacted during the Great Depression. These measures did not usually reach the lowest levels of needy citizens, however. Finally in 1964, President Lyndon Johnson marshaled the forces of the federal government to begin a War on Poverty.

Q **What were the goals of the War on Poverty?** The philosophy behind the War on Poverty was to help poor people help themselves (Jacoby 1997; Barry 1999; Patterson 2000). President Johnson's predecessor, John F. Kennedy, believed that if the chains of poverty were to be broken, it had to be through self-improvement, not temporary relief. Accordingly, almost 60 percent of the first poverty budget was earmarked for youth opportunity programs and the work experience program (work and job training designed primarily for welfare recipients and unemployed fathers).

Hopes for positive results from the War on Poverty were high. However, not all of the programs were as successful as predicted. Indeed, some have come under severe criticism. These criticisms center around supposed widespread abuses and the fear that the system encourages people to become dependent upon the government longer than is necessary. "Fixing" the way social welfare should be provided and payments should be distributed has been the focus of many hot political debates.

Welfare Reform

Prior to 1996, the main source of welfare assistance for the needy was AFDC (Dervarics 1998). The most recent legislation on welfare reform, enacted in 1996, replaced

AFDC with a program known as Temporary Assistance for Needy Families (TANF).

Q What is the nature of welfare reform? Enacted to encourage welfare recipients (mostly single mothers) to remain in the job market and to improve the chances of their children moving up the economic ladder, welfare reform dramatically changed the way public assistance is distributed. Gone is the assurance of remaining on welfare long term. In place of this guarantee there now are work requirements and limits on the amount of time those able to work can receive welfare assistance. For example, in order to receive benefits for their children, unwed teenage mothers must remain in school. Furthermore, the government terminates cash aid to able-bodied adults if they fail to get a job after two years.

Q Is welfare reform working? According to the Administration of Children and Families, the government agency that administers TANF, welfare rolls have decreased substantially since the new welfare-to-work program went into effect. In 1996, for example, more than 12 million people were receiving welfare. In 2007, the total number of TANF recipients was slightly less than 4 million (*Statistical Abstract of the United States 2010*). This number represents almost 1.6 million families. Only a small percentage of recipients have been removed from the rolls because of the new time limits on benefits.

There is a darker side, however. Most of the people forced from the welfare rolls could find only low-wage jobs in industries such as food service, home health care, and retail sales. And the recession that began in 2007 is causing many of these jobs to disappear. At the same time, wages grew more slowly or actually fell. As a result, many of those who left the welfare rolls continue to live in or near poverty. Research suggests that while welfare reform reduces the welfare rolls and increases lower-income mothers' employment, it does not reduce poverty and hampers the long-term economic well-being of former recipients (McNamara 2004; Haskins and Ellwood 2010). Household income is increased only when these mothers are allowed to remain on welfare while working.

From the very few studies of the effects of welfare reform on children, the results appear mixed. Young children experience small benefits from their mothers being employed as measured by test scores, health, and behavior. However, adolescents, with reduced parental monitoring, tend to show lower school performance and increased problem behavior. Since parental income heavily influences a child's future income, the economic future of these children does *not* appear promising.

CHECK YOURSELF **8.4** **R2**

Poverty In America

1. _____ poverty is defined as the absence of enough money to secure life's necessities.
2. _____ poverty is measured by comparing the economic condition of those at the bottom of a society with that of other segments of the population.
3. Which of the following is *not* one of the major categories of the poor in the United States?
   a. children under eighteen
   b. able-bodied men who refuse to work
   c. the elderly
   d. the disabled
   e. people who live alone or with nonrelatives
4. According to the ideology of _____, those at the bottom of the stratification structure are there because of their own inadequacies.
5. The philosophy behind the Economic Opportunity Act of 1964 was
   a. to provide temporary relief for the poor.
   b. to make the poor dependent on the federal government.
   c. to make it easy for the poor to receive help.
   d. to help poor people help themselves.
6. The problem with the poor is that they have lower economic and educational aspirations than the nonpoor. T or F?

Answers: 1. Absolute; 2. Relative; 3. b; 4. individualism; 5. d; 6. F

Consequences of Stratification ℞

The unequal distribution of income, wealth, power, and prestige has additional consequences for people (Tilly 1999; *Class Matters* 2005; Andersen and Collins 2010). Two broad categories of class-related social consequences are *life chances* and *lifestyle*.

Life Chances

Life chances refers to the likelihood of possessing the good things in life: health, happiness, education, wealth, legal protection, and even life itself. The probability of acquiring and maintaining the material and nonmaterial rewards of life is significantly affected by social class level. Power, prestige, and economic rewards increase with social class level. The same is true for education, the single most important gateway to these rewards. Life chances, then, are in good part the product of inequality in the distribution of education, power, prestige, and economic rewards (Putnam 1996; Pennar 1997; Lewis and Burd-Sharps 2010).

Q How does social class affect life chances? The probability of possessing life itself—the most fundamental, precious life chance—decreases as social class level declines. Whether measured by the death rate or by life expectancy, the likelihood of a longer life is enhanced as people move up a stratification structure. This

disparity is generated by differences in such things as neighborhood safety, possession of health insurance, quality of medical care, value placed on medical attention, and concern with proper nutrition (Pear 2008; Lewis and Sharps 2010).

In light of differences in life expectancy, it is not surprising that physical health is affected by social class level. Those lower in a stratification structure are more likely to be sick or disabled and more apt to receive inferior medical treatment once they are ill. The social effects of inequality start early and stay late (Gravlee 2009). Compared to Americans in higher social classes, adults at age fifty who were raised in poverty have a 40 percent greater chance of heart disease. They are also 46 percent more likely to be asthmatic, 75 percent more likely to suffer from hypertension, 83 percent more likely to be diabetic, and 225 percent more likely to have had a heart attack or stroke. Moreover, poor health diminishes the likelihood of adults improving their economic status (Lewis and Burd-Sharps 2010). It is no different for mental health. Persons at lower class levels have a greater probability of becoming depressed or mentally disturbed and are less likely to receive therapeutic help, adequate or otherwise (Miech and Hauser 1998; Weitz 2010; "Depression in Rheumatoid Arthritis Patients Linked to Social Status" 2011).

Innumerable other life chance inequalities exist. For example, the poor often pay more for the same goods and services (Squires 2004). They are more likely to get caught for committing a crime, and when they are apprehended, they stand a greater chance of being convicted and serving prison time (Reiman

These community college students are attempting to improve their life chances and lifestyle.

Sondra Davies/The Image Works

and Leighton 2010). They often receive class-related inferior public service, as in the neglected poor in New Orleans (mostly African Americans) during the evacuation process prior to Hurricane Katrina and in subsequent efforts to deal with the devastating consequences.

In addition, from an intensive study of twelve families (six white, five black, one interracial), Annette Lareau (2003) concludes that class differences in child-drearing create differential advantages to children. Middle-class children participate in a variety of organizational activities, from ballet to soccer. In the process, they learn to express and assert themselves with unfamiliar people. Children from working-class and poor families interact mostly with relatives. Their lack of exposure to organizations and strangers hinders their ability to get ahead in the impersonal, bureaucratic adult world.

Lifestyle

Q **How does social class affect lifestyle?** The rich and the poor are separated by more than money. **Lifestyle** refers to social class differences in patterns of living in areas like education, marital and family relations, child rearing, political attitudes and behavior, and religious affiliation.

People in higher social classes tend to marry later, experience lower divorce rates, and have better marital adjustment. While working-class and middle-class parents are more alike in child-rearing practices than in the past, some differences remain. Compared with the middle class, lower-class parents tend to be less attentive to their children's social and emotional needs; in disciplining, they are more inclined to use physical punishment rather than reasoning. Middle-class parents are more interested in helping their children develop such traits as concern for others, self-control, and curiosity. Finally, working-class parents emphasize conformity, orderliness, and neatness, whereas middle-class parents stress self-direction, freedom, initiative, and creativity.

The incidence of voting and political involvement increases with social class level. The middle and upper classes are more likely to be Republicans, whereas the working and lower classes tend to register as Democrats. Those in the lower class tend to be more liberal than middle- and upper-class Americans are on economic issues, but more conservative on social issues. Thus, lower-class people are more in favor of labor unions, government control of business, and social welfare programs but tend to exhibit less tolerance and sympathy than do higher social classes for social issues involving civil rights and international affairs.

The rate of church membership and attendance is lowest at the extremes of the stratification structure. Episcopalian, Congregational, and Presbyterian churches are significantly less populated by members of the lower class. Lower-class Americans lean more toward Baptist and fundamentalist churches. Methodist and Lutheran denominations fall in between (see Chapter 14, "Religion, Science and Sociology").

Social Mobility **R1**

Social mobility refers to the movement of individuals or groups within a stratification structure. In the United States, the term *mobility* implies an elevation in social class level. Beyond this, it is possible either to move down in social class or to move with little or no change in social class.

Types of Social Mobility

Social mobility can be horizontal or vertical. Both types of mobility can be measured either within the career of an individual—**intragenerational mobility**—or from one generation to the next—**intergenerational mobility.**

CHECK YOURSELF **8.5** **R2**

Consequences of Stratification

Identify the following as examples of life chances (LC) or lifestyle (LS).

_____ a. divorce rate

_____ b. quality of neighborhood street repair

_____ c. life expectancy

_____ d. child-rearing practices

_____ e. voting behavior

_____ f. church attendance

Answers: a. (LS), b. (LC), c. (LC), d. (LS), e. (LS), f. (LS)

Q **How does horizontal mobility differ from vertical mobility?** A change from one occupation to another at the same general status level is called **horizontal mobility**. Examples of intragenerational horizontal mobility are familiar: An army captain becomes a public school teacher, a minister becomes a psychologist, a restaurant server becomes a taxi driver. The daughter of an attorney who becomes an engineer illustrates intergenerational horizontal mobility. Because horizontal mobility involves no real change in occupational status or social class, sociologists are not generally as interested in investigating it.

Vertical mobility, however, is investigated extensively. In **vertical mobility,** occupational status or social class moves upward or downward. Vertical mobility can also be intragenerational or intergenerational. The simplest way to measure intragenerational mobility is to compare an individual's present occupation with his or her first one. Someone who began as a dockworker and later became an insurance salesperson has experienced upward intragenerational mobility. Intergenerational mobility involves the comparison of a parent's (or grandparent's) occupation with the child's occupation. If a plumber's daughter becomes a physician, upward intergenerational mobility occurs. If a lawyer's son becomes a carpenter, downward intergenerational mobility is occurring.

Caste and Open Class Stratification Systems

The extent of vertical mobility varies from society to society. Some societies have considerable mobility; others have little or none. This is the major difference between caste systems and open class systems.

Q **How much mobility can we expect in a caste system?** In a **caste system,** there is no social mobility because social status is inherited and cannot be changed. In a caste system, statuses (including occupations) are ascribed or assigned at birth; individuals cannot change their statuses through any efforts of their own. By reason of religious, biological, magical, or legal justification, those in one caste are allowed to marry only within their own caste and must limit relationships of all types with those below and above them in the stratification structure. Apartheid, as practiced in South Africa before the election of Nelson Mandela, was a caste system based on race.

The caste system in India is based on occupation and religion and is as complex as it is rigid. Hindus believe that there are four primary caste categories, ranked according to their degree of religious purity. The Brahmin, the top caste, is composed of priests and scholars. Next come the Kshatriyas—noble and warrior caste. Merchants form the third caste, called the Vaishyas. Finally, there is the Shudra caste, containing farmers, menial workers, and craftspeople. Actually, there is a fifth category called the "untouchables"—Indians thought to be so impure that any physical contact contaminates the religious purity of higher caste members.

Q **How is the caste system kept intact?** Traditional rules in India prevented movement into a higher caste. Not only were members of different castes not permitted merely to eat together, but higher-caste people would hardly accept anything to eat or drink from lower-caste persons. Untouchables, who had to live apart from everyone else, couldn't even drink water from the wells used by higher castes. Although the long-standing legal prohibition against dating or marrying someone in a higher caste no longer exists, such crossings are still infrequent. Another sign of the breaking up of the caste system is the rise of a woman named Mayawati, who went from the former "untouchable" community to candidate for prime minister of India (Chu 2008). The caste system has not completely disappeared due to power of those in the higher castes, who use their political power, wealth, and prestige to retard change.

Q **How does an open class system differ from a caste system?** In an open class system, an individual's social status is based on merit and individual effort. Individuals move up and down the stratification structure as their abilities, education, resources, and commitment permit. Although inequality exists in an open class system, it is supposed to be based on monetary worth and personal accomplishment.

Just as some exceptions of social mobility occur in a caste system, exceptions develop within an open class stratification structure as well. Prominent illustrations in American society today—which is relatively, but not purely, an open class system—are African Americans, Native Americans, and Latinos (see Chapter 9, "Inequalities of Race and Ethnicity").

Mobility in American Society

Americans often tend toward optimism. This tendency is captured in the American notion of social mobility.

Q **How do Americans view their chances for upward mobility?** The classic Horatio Alger stories—in which a down-on-his-luck boy makes good through honesty, pluck, and diligence—embody the long-standing belief that America is the land of opportunity. The only thing standing between any American citizen and success, it is argued, is talent, a strong work ethic, and perseverance (Kluegel and Smith 2007). Despite the historic recession of the first decade of this century, Americans continue to believe that upward mobility is within

Using Microsoft founder Bill Gates as an example promotes the myth of unlimited upward social mobility in American society.

their control. Just as most Americans believe that poverty is an individual choice, they believe that ambition and hard work determine mobility, not outside social forces. Supporting this conclusion, a major survey reports that nearly 80 percent believe it is possible to get ahead. Even lower-income, less educated, and unemployed Americans agree ("Economic Mobility Project" 2009). Almost three-fourths of Americans believe that individual characteristics, like hard work and ambition, supercede external factors, like current economic conditions or family background. Let's see how this picture squares with reality.

Q How much upward mobility actually exists in America?
The careers of people like Oprah Winfrey, Tiger Woods, Bill Gates, Shawn (P. Diddy) Combs, and Mark Zuckerman appear to support this idea of unlimited mobility in American society. In reality, though, these individuals are exceptions to the rule. Upward mobility has never been as great as the rags-to-riches myth would have us believe (Schwarz 1997). This does not mean that upward mobility does not occur in American society. It does mean, however, that great leaps in social class level are rare. Earlier studies, comparing fathers' and sons' occupational level, consistently showed that upward mobility, when it occurred, was usually

slight (Sorokin 1927; Jackson and Crockett 1964; Blau and Duncan 1967; Featherman 1971; F. J. Davis 1982; D. A. Gilbert 2010). For example, the son of a janitor becomes a bus driver, or the daughter of a retail sales worker becomes a commercial artist.

More recent research measuring social mobility using income levels (rather than occupations) shows the same pattern of intergeneration inheritance and it holds true for both daughters and sons (Isaacs 2007a). Children from homes on the bottom of the income structure are likely (42 percent) to remain at that level as adults. Those born to parents on the top income rung are also quite likely to stay there (39 percent). This is consistent with other research showing that one of the most dependable predictors of an American child's economic future is the characteristics of his or her parents, a factor children cannot control (Sawhill and Morton 2007).

Looking at social mobility among American men, Dennis Gilbert (2010) found a high degree of occupational inheritance from father to sons. That is, sons most typically are in jobs at or near the same occupational level as their fathers. Fifty-eight percent of the sons of upper manual workers are in either upper manual or lower manual jobs. The same is true for lower manual workers, with the largest percentage of lower manual workers in the same kinds of lower manual jobs as their fathers. Among women, Gilbert concluded that, like men's, their occupational attainment is strongly influenced by class origins. For example, over half of the daughters of upper white-collar fathers are in upper white-collar (managerial and professional) jobs, including doctors, lawyers, teachers, and nurses. Daughters of lower manual workers are more likely to be in clerical, sales, technical, and service jobs.

Q Why is upward intergenerational mobility so limited?
Mobility is heavily influenced by the extent of "intergeneration assistance" (Holland 2007; Haskins 2010). Children from more affluent families enjoy more aid in the form of college tuition payments, down payments for homes, capital to generate a career, or inheritance of an existing business. Because these offspring emerge from college with little or no debt, they often hit the ground running. Beyond financial assistance, the social class level of one's parents affects things like attitudes toward education, contacts for networking, knowledge of economic opportunities, and optimism about careers. Consequently, children from poorer families are less likely to move up and children from wealthier families are less likely to move down.

Q Why, then, is there any social mobility at all? According to Peter Blau and Otis Dudley Duncan (1967), there are three basic determinants of upward mobility. First, as less qualified workers take lower-level jobs, the more qualified people fill higher-level positions. Second, because the higher social classes have fewer children, members of the lower social classes are needed to fill higher-level positions. Third, as an economy advances, technology creates higher-level jobs faster than lower-level jobs. Shrinking job opportunities at the lower end preclude the children of lower-level manual and farm workers from following in their parents' occupational footsteps. They have to prepare themselves to move up somewhat. This type of social mobility, which occurs because of changes in the distribution of occupational opportunities, is called **structural mobility** (Hope 1982; DiPrete 1996; Sobel, Becker, and Minick 1998; Isaacs 2007a).

One example of structural mobility in the United States is the change in labor markets due to the new technology and the globalization of business. Emboldened by computer-driven production, improved means of communication, and better transportation, many U.S. companies are moving their manufacturing operations overseas as they seek to lower costs and increase profits. And they are doing so often. As a result, many blue-collar jobs are being transferred to lower-paid international workers, forcing Americans upward, even if only slightly.

Of course, on the downside, with fewer higher-paying manufacturing jobs, and without the education needed to perform the new, more technologically sophisticated and financially rewarding jobs, many U.S. workers are being forced to take lower-paying jobs (structural downward mobility). Compared to their parents, more U.S. workers are now experiencing downward mobility (Newman 1999; Bernhardt et al. 2001; Frank 2007; Isaacs 2007a,b).

Q **Still, don't Americans experience more upward mobility than people in other rich countries?** In fact, the reverse seems to be true. Using parents' and children's incomes as an indicator of mobility, data show that many high-income countries, including Denmark, Norway, Finland, Canada, Sweden, Germany, and France, permit greater mobility than the United States (see Figure 8.7). Canadians, for example, have 2.5 times more mobility than Americans ("Chasing the Same Dream, Climbing Different Ladders" 2010). This means that family economic background affects mobility more in the United States than in other high-income countries. Specifically, the income of American men is nearer the income of their fathers than is typical for men in other countries (Issacs 2010).

Q **Why is upward mobility more difficult for Americans today?** Gilbert (2010) compared the occupational mobility of younger workers in the 1970s with workers around 2000. Over this period of time, upward mobility declined and downward mobility increased. He attributes

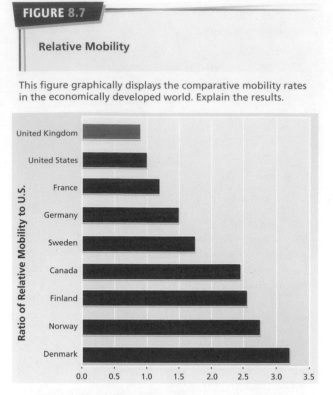

FIGURE 8.7

Relative Mobility

This figure graphically displays the comparative mobility rates in the economically developed world. Explain the results.

Source: Isabel Sawhill and Joe E. Morton. "Economic Mobility: Is the American Dream Alive and Well?" Washington, D.C.: the Pew Charitable Trusts, 2007, p.5.

this change to a reduction in upward structural mobility as the earlier expansion of higher-level jobs and shrinkage of some lower-level jobs waned.

Holland (2007) identifies three other factors making it harder today for working Americans. He discusses educational differences, the accelerating loss of high-paying manufacturing jobs, and the weaker social safety net in the United States.

The United States now has a relatively inferior K–12 educational system as measured by international assessments, increased need for remedial work in college, and employers' complaints about workers' basic skills. A weak educational system disadvantages students from poorer homes. Because, for example, the U.S. education system is largely funded by state and local property taxes, quality of education is determined by the wealth of the community in which children live.

On the college scene, no one has to tell students that tuition costs are going through the roof. With average tuition costs for a year of college exceeding $10,000, a public university education is tougher to finance than it was a generation ago. This is due, in large part, to the fact that the United States is the only advanced country without direct federal government involvement in its educational system. This makes higher-quality education even more dependent on family resources.

The loss of higher-paying manufacturing jobs also disadvantages the lower classes for upward mobility.

CHECK YOURSELF **8.6** **R2**

Social Mobility

1. _____ refers to the movement of individuals or groups within a stratification structure.
2. Match the major types of social mobility with the illustrations.

    ____ a. intergenerational mobility   (1) A restaurant waiter becomes a taxi driver.

    ____ b. vertical mobility   (2) An auto worker becomes a manager.

    ____ c. horizontal mobility   (3) The daughter of a hairdresser becomes a college professor.

3. In a _____ system, social status is inherited at birth from one's parents and cannot be changed.
4. In an _____ system, rank based on the stratification structure is achieved.
5. Upward mobility in America usually involves only a small improvement in status. T or F?
6. The son of a steelworker finds that the steel industry has shrunk so much that a job in the mill is not available. Instead of following in his father's footsteps, he attends a community college and becomes a computer operator. This is an example of

    a. horizontal mobility.

    b. intragenerational mobility.

    c. caste mobility.

    d. structural mobility.

Answers: 1. Social mobility; 2. a. (3), b. (2), c. (1); 3. caste; 4. open class; 5. T; 6. d

At one time, these higher-paying manufacturing jobs were a stepping-stone into the middle class because working parents could afford to support a son or daughter in college. The college-educated sons and daughters of high school-educated parents could more easily become teachers, doctors, and lawyers.

Finally, there is an inverse relationship between the quality of a country's safety net and the extent to which children of working families can experience upward mobility. In the event of job loss and/or serious illness, American parents with a weak or nonexistent safety net (e.g., unemployment and health care benefits) find it even more challenging to educate their children. Children in advanced countries with a stronger safety net, then, enjoy an advantage over U.S. children.

Global Inequality **R1**

Predictably, levels of income inequality vary around the world, from low-income inequality in Sweden and Ukraine to moderate income inequality in the United States to high-income inequality in Bolivia (see Figure 8.8). The United States has greater income inequality than most developed countries.

Despite strong economic growth that created millions of new jobs over the past twenty years, global income inequality increased markedly in most areas of the world (*World of Work Report 2008*). The *Human Development Report 2010* corroborates this trend. It's not that there isn't some progress. Economic growth in Sub-Saharan Africa led to a recent drop in income

inequality. In some Latin American countries, like Brazil, Ecuador, and Paraguay, progressive economic and government policies promote lower income inequality. But for every country in which income inequality decreases, it increases in more than two others. Especially hard hit are former Soviet Union countries, where employment guarantees and lengthy state unemployment payments shriveled. For most nations in East Asia and the Pacific, income inequality worsened compared to a few decades ago. This is partially due to rapidly industrializing urban areas leaving behind the rural areas, with slow agricultural growth. In countries like China and Viet Nam the switch from central economic planning to more market-based principles contributes to higher income inequality.

Identification of Economies

Thus far, the focus has been on inequality within societies. But scarce desirables—income, wealth, prestige, and power—are also differentially distributed across nations. The gross domestic product (GDP) of a country—the total value of the goods and services it produces in one year—is a reasonably good indicator for classifying countries into economic categories. GDP is useful both because it is a single, measurable economic indicator and because a nation's economic rank is highly correlated with the extent of its prestige and power.

Q **Where are the high-income economies, and how wealthy are they?** The richest countries, nearly all capitalistic, include countries such as England, Germany,

FIGURE 8.8

Levels of Income Inequality Vary Around the World

The numbers in this figure represent points on the Gini index. Income inequality increases as the numbers increase. A score of zero represents perfect income equality (everyone has the same income), while a score of 100 corresponds to perfect income inequality (all the income is held by only one person). The median score across the world's countries is 39. Are you surprised by any of the countries' scores? Explain.

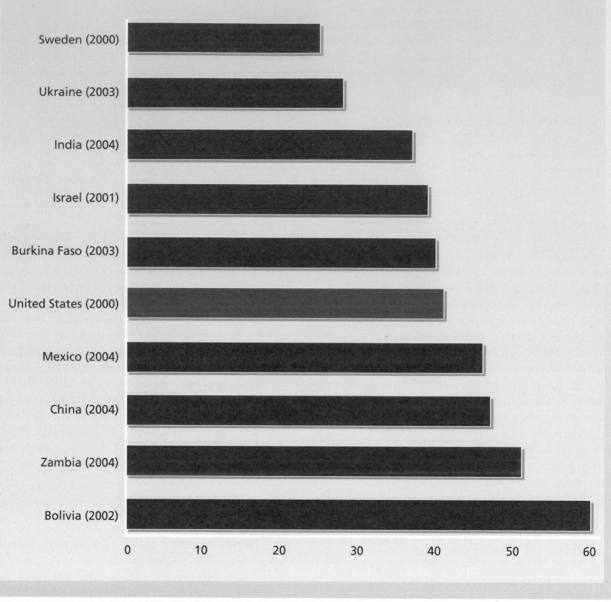

Source: World Bank, World Development Indicators, online database (http://publications.worldbank.org/WDI/, accessed May 25, 2007). It also appears on the 2007 World Population Data Sheet. (Washington, DC: Population Reference Bureau), 2007.

France, Norway, Finland, Denmark, Sweden, and Switzerland in Western Europe; the United States and Canada in North America; Australia and New Zealand in Oceania; and Japan in Asia (see "Think Globally 8.1"). A few oil-rich nations, such as Kuwait and the United Arab Emirates, also have high-income economies. High-income economies, spanning approximately one-quarter of the Earth's land surface, have only 15 percent of the world's population (approximately 800 million people). Yet, these countries are in

THINK GLOBALLY 8.1

The Relative Wealth of Nations

The map below displays the World Bank's classification of countries in terms of per capita purchasing power. The United States is one of the few nations with a "high income" economy—one that has a per-capita purchasing power of more than $25,000.

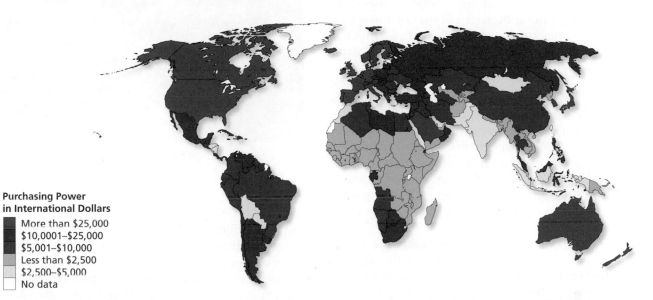

Purchasing Power in International Dollars

- More than $25,000
- $10,0001–$25,000
- $5,001–$10,000
- Less than $2,500
- $2,500–$5,000
- No data

Source: John L. Allen and Christopher J. Sutton, *Student Atlas of World Politics,* 9th ed. (p. 106). Copyright © 2011 by The McGraw-Hill Companies. Reproduced by permission of McGraw-Hill Contemporary Learning Series.

Interpret the Map

1. Is per-capita purchasing power a better measure of economic inequality than per capita income? Explain.

2. How would you describe the pattern of inequality evident in this map?

3. Discuss the distribution of wealth in terms of dependency theory.

control of most of the wealth. Due to this concentration of wealth, the standard of living of nearly all the people living in these countries, even most of the poor people, is higher than that for the average person in low-income economies.

Q What comprises middle-income economies? Middle-income economies include, but are not limited to, nations historically founded on or influenced by socialist or communist economies. This encompasses members of the former Soviet Union, many of them renamed and now part of the new Commonwealth of Independent States that was created in 1991. Other countries that fell into the Soviet orbit but are not part of the Commonwealth of Independent States include Poland, Bulgaria, the Czech Republic, the Slovak Republic, Hungary, Romania, Estonia, Latvia, Lithuania, and Cuba.

From the end of World War II until 1989, all these countries, under the political, economic, and military control of the former Soviet Union, constituted the Eastern bloc in the Cold War against the West. These countries are no more densely populated than high-income economies—they occupy 15 percent of the Earth's land with only 10 percent of the world's population (about 500 million people). Although more prosperous than low-income countries, citizens of middle-income economies do not enjoy the standard of living characteristic of high-income economies. The extent of industrialization in these countries is variable. Most inhabitants of these countries live in urban areas; in comparison to countries with high-income economies, though, a greater percentage of their people live in rural areas and participate in agricultural economic activities.

In 1989, Eastern European countries (freed of Soviet domination, its socialist economy, and government-controlled bureaucracy) turned to capitalism and its market mechanism. A major source of current political and economic turmoil in the former Soviet Union revolves around the struggle between the socialist and capitalist roads to economic development (see Chapter 13, "Political and Economic Institutions").

The middle-income category contains other countries that have never been part of the old Soviet bloc. These countries are spread from Mexico, Latin America, and South America to parts of Africa to Thailand, Malaysia, and New Guinea in the Far East.

Q What is distinctive about low-income economies? The economic base of low-income economies is primarily agricultural. These countries span the globe from south of the United States border to Africa to China to Indonesia. Population density within these countries as a whole is very high. In fact, just over two-thirds of the world's population (more than 5 billion people) live on 60 percent of the Earth's land (Livernash and Rodenburg 1998).

No single economic system is typical of these economies. Capitalism, socialism, and various combinations of each are practiced. If these countries share no economic ideology, they do share one important economic characteristic: They are unimaginably poor. Problems of the poor in high-income countries, which have already been explored in this chapter, are real and significant. But most people in low-income economies live annually on less than 10 percent of the official poverty line in the United States. The plight of the poor in low-income countries is particularly bleak because they are trapped in a double bind. Their populations are exploding (due to declining infant mortality rates while they maintain their traditionally high birth rate).

Global Poverty

Poverty persists despite a $400-trillion-plus global economy. A variety of sources document the extent and distribution of global poverty.

Q What is the state of global poverty at the beginning of the twenty-first century? Despite progress, one-quarter of the Earth's population remains in extreme poverty. More than one-half of the world's population (over 3 billion) lives below the internationally established poverty line of less than $2.50 a day. Poverty by this standard is most extensive in Southern Asia, sub-Saharan Africa, and Eastern and South-Eastern Asia (*World Population Data Sheet* 2007; Shah 2010).

In the more economically developed world, the greatest increase in poverty in the last 15 years is

This slum housing in Indonesia illustrates the subsistence level of living in low-income economies.

found in eastern European countries and among member nations of the former Soviet Union. Whereas poverty in these areas was formerly not widespread, about a third of these people (120 million) now have incomes below $4 daily. Even in industrial nations, more than 100 million people subsist below the established poverty line.

Q What are the consequences of global poverty? The consequences of poverty are fairly well known. It is the scope of these consequences that is surprising (Shah 2010). Over 1 billion people in developing countries have inadequate access to water, and 2.6 billion are without basic sanitation. Nearly half of all people in developing countries are victims of disease caused by water and sanitation deficiencies. Among children, there are 1.4 million deaths annually due to unsafe drinking water and insufficient sanitation. Another 2.2 million children die every year for lack of immunization. And almost one-fourth of the world's children under age five are underweight. According to the Global Hunger Index published by the International Food Policy Research Institute, over 1 billion people are undernourished (Stephenson 2010; 2010 *Global Hunger Index* 2010). The worldwide economic crisis and the rise in grain prices in 2008 resulted in the most extreme food crisis in a generation (Bia 2008; Rizzo 2009).

Q Is there any progress in combating global poverty? Poverty has declined in many areas of the world. In fact, in all regions of the world poverty has decreased more in the last fifty years than in the preceding five centuries. In less than twenty years, China and fourteen other countries, whose populations exceed 1.6 billion, have halved the proportion of their people in poverty. An additional ten nations, who number almost 1 billion, have reduced their poverty rate by one-fourth. Still poverty is pervasive throughout the world, and, in fact, has increased lately due to the global economic crisis (De La Dehsea 2007; *The Millennium Development Goal Report* 2010).

Q What causes global poverty? There are a variety of explanations for global poverty. Two of these explanations are associated with modernism and postmodernism (Sernau 2011).

Modernists rely on functionalism's view of inequality. They blame economic inequality in general, and poverty in particular, on traditionalism. Low-income societies are poor, and remain poor, because they cling to traditional ideas, attitudes, technologies, and institutions. But it's only a matter of time, they claim, before modernization comes to these countries, bringing more efficient ways of creating a prosperous economy.

In common with conflict theory, postmodernists attribute persistent poverty in low-income countries to continued exploitation, domination, and manipulation by high-income countries. This view is known as **dependency theory**. Poorer countries cannot establish economic independence because of their dependence on richer countries for large amounts of capital and for foreign markets for their natural resources. Latin America, for example, continues to be poor because it sells raw materials on foreign markets at low prices and imports finished products at inflated prices. This disadvantageous relationship, which serves the needs of the richer nations, is said to be a more sophisticated form of neocolonialism. This neocolonialism is supported by the debt dependency created by powerful institutions like the World Bank and International Monetary Fund, the need for foreign aid, and the deals made between huge, foreign multinational corporations and corrupt government leaders of poorer countries. Moreover, the economies of poorer nations are now so intertwined with the neocolonial powers that they cannot function outside of the global capitalist system.

Obviously, the cause of global poverty is in dispute. It matters tremendously which explanation will eventually be more accurate.

On to Chapter 9

This chapter is a general introduction to the process of creating and maintaining inequality domestically and globally. Chapter 9 continues to examine inequality, this time concentrating on racial and ethnic minorities in the United States.

CHECK YOURSELF 8.7 R2

Global Inequality

1. Classify the following examples as high-income (HI), middle-income (MI), or low-income (LI) economies.
   ____ a. Commonwealth of Independent States
   ____ b. agricultural economic base
   ____ c. movement toward capitalism
   ____ d. 800 million people
   ____ e. double population bind
   ____ f. one-fourth of the Earth's land surface
2. Do you think that classifying all the nations of the world into three broad categories leads to some distortion of reality? Explain.
3. What proportion of the Earth's population is considered poor today?
   a. one-tenth
   b. one-fifth
   c. one-fourth
   d. one-third
4. _____ is the view that low-income countries remain poor because high-income countries continue to exploit, dominate, and manipulate them.
5. Over the past fifty years, global poverty has actually decreased. T or F?

Answers: 1. a. (MI), b. (LI), c. (MI), d. (HI), e. (LI), f. (HI); 3. c; 4. Dependency theory 5. T.

1. **Explain the relationship between social stratification and social class.**
   - There is a universal tendency for humans to create inequality. When individuals are ranked by wealth, prestige, and power, social stratification exists. Any stratification structure is composed of either social classes or segments of a population whose members hold a similar share of community resources. What's more, these class members share attitudes, values, norms, and an identifiable lifestyle.

2. **Compare and contrast the three dimensions of stratification.**
   - A stratification structure is based on economic, power, and prestige dimensions. Income inequality has always existed in American society, but it has increased dramatically since 1980. Prestige, especially in developed societies, is based primarily on occupation. Occupations with the greatest prestige generally pay the most; require the greatest amount of training, skill, and ability; provide the most power; and are considered the most important.
   - Those individuals who are ranked high on one dimension of stratification are usually high on the other dimensions. Wealth, power, and prestige tend to go together.

3. **State the major differences among the functionalist, conflict, and symbolic interactionist approaches to social stratification.**
   - Functionalists contend that stratification is necessary. It motivates people to prepare themselves for difficult and important jobs, and it motivates them to perform well once they are in those jobs. According to the conflict theory of stratification, inequality exists because some people have more power than others and are willing to use it to promote their self-interest.
   - The functionalist and conflict theories shed light on reasons for stratification. Symbolic interactionism aids in understanding the manner in which stratification structures are perpetuated. This perspective emphasizes the legitimization of a stratification structure through symbols. These symbols, of course, are learned through socialization.

4. **Identify the distinguishing characteristics of the major social classes in America.**
   - Although most sociologists believe that class lines in America are difficult to draw, they agree with the following social class distinctions: upper class, middle class, working class, and lower class. Sociologists agree that the poor exist as an underclass.

5. **Discuss the extent of poverty and perceptions of poverty in the United States.**
   - Poverty can be measured in two ways—absolute or relative. Absolute poverty is determined by annual income. Anything below a determined (absolute) amount is categorized as poverty. Relative poverty is a comparative measure; it contrasts income groups at the bottom of the stratification structure with those above them. Because of the continuing influence of social Darwinism, Americans tend to blame the poor for their own situation, despite evidence to the contrary.

6. **Evaluate the U.S. commitment to poverty programs.**
   - The federal government became serious about combating poverty during the mid-1960s. There have been objections, from some quarters, ever since. The debate on the role of government continues.
   - Americans do not wish to abolish all welfare benefits, but they do want a system that forces the able-bodied off the rolls. In 1996, the U.S. Congress passed a sweeping welfare reform act that dramatically changed the relationship between the poor and their government.

7. **Outline some of the consequences of social stratification.**
   - Social classes can be thought of as subcultures. For this reason, distinctive patterns of thinking, feeling, and behaving are associated with the various social classes. Both life chances and lifestyle characteristics are affected by one's social class level.

8. **Describe upward and downward social mobility in the United States.**
   - Social mobility, the movement of individuals or groups within the stratification structure, is usually measured by changes in occupational status. Sometimes movement within a stratification structure is horizontal. Sociologists, however, are much more interested in upward or downward (vertical) mobility, whether within an individual's lifetime or from one generation to the next.
   - Caste societies, such as India's, permit little vertical mobility; open class societies, such as those in industrialized countries, allow considerable upward mobility. Even in open class societies, however, an upward move tends to be a small one.

9. **Discuss the major features of global stratification.**
   - Nations are also stratified. Richer nations, primarily in the West, are classified as high-income economies. Other less developed industrialized nations, including member nations of the former Soviet Union, can be classified as middle-income economies. The rest of the world, poor and resting primarily on an agricultural base, is classified as low-income. In these societies, poverty is widespread. The cause of global poverty is in dispute.

CONCEPT REVIEW

Match the following concepts with the definitions listed below them.

____ a. life chances　　　　____ e. relative poverty　　　____ i. conspicuous consumption
____ b. horizontal mobility　____ f. power　　　　　　　　____ j. structural mobility
____ c. caste system　　　　 ____ g. social mobility　　　　____ k. dependency theory
____ d. intergenerational mobility　____ h. wealth

1. all the economic resources possessed by an individual or a group
2. the consumption of goods and services to display one's wealth to others
3. social mobility that takes place from one generation to the next
4. the ability to control the behavior of others, even against their will
5. movement of individuals or groups within a stratification structure
6. the type of stratification structure in which there is no social mobility because social status is inherited and cannot subsequently be changed

7. the likelihood of securing the "good things in life," such as housing, education, good health, and food
8. the view that low-income nations remain poor because high-income nations continue to exploit, dominate, and manipulate them
9. the measurement of poverty by a comparison of the economic condition of those at the bottom of a society with that of other segments of the population
10. a change from one occupation to another at the same general status level
11. mobility that occurs because of changes in the distribution of occupational opportunities

CHECK YOURSELF REVIEW

1. The top 1 percent of American households hold nearly 40 percent of the total wealth. T or F?
2. In America, working-class individuals who fail to experience upward mobility claim that it is the system rather than themselves. T or F?
3. The most stable source of prestige in modern societies is associated with _____.
4. The conflict theory of stratification is based on Marx's ideas about class _____.
5. A major difference between the upper upper class and the lower upper class is that the latter has relied on _____ rather than birth.
6. _____ is the view that low income countries remain poor because high-income countries continue to exploit, dominate, and manipulate them.
7. Which of the following is *not* a criticism of the functionalist theory of stratification?
   a. There are people at the top whose jobs do not seem very important.
   b. It has a bias toward cultural relativism.
   c. It overlooks the barriers to competition.
   d. It glosses over the inheritance of social class level.
8. The son of a steelworker finds that the steel industry has shrunk so much that a job in the mill is not available. Instead of following in his father's footsteps, he attends a community college and becomes a computer operator. This is an example of
   a. horizontal mobility.
   b. intragenerational mobility.

c. caste mobility.
d. structural mobility.

9. Match the concepts with the examples.
   ____ a. life chances
   ____ b. power
   ____ c. prestige
   ____ d. conspicuous consumption
   (1) the respect accorded doctors
   (2) a politician conforming to the interests of a lobby
   (3) living in a neighborhood with good police protection
   (4) a lavish wedding
10. Match the theories of stratification with the examples.
   ____ a. functionalist theory
   ____ b. conflict theory
   ____ c. symbolic interactionism
   (1) Corporate executives make more money because they determine who gets what in their organizations.
   (2) Engineers make more money than butlers because of the education they possess.
   (3) Ghetto children tend to have low self-esteem.
11. Match the major types of social mobility with the illustrations.
   ____ a. intergenerational mobility
   ____ b. vertical mobility
   ____ c. horizontal mobility
   (1) A restaurant waiter becomes a taxi driver.
   (2) An auto worker becomes a manager.
   (3) The daughter of a hairdresser becomes a college professor.

GRAPHIC REVIEW

Figure 8.4 graphically portrays the American class structure.

1. Write a paragraph using the information in Figure 8.4 to describe the American class structure.

_____

_____

_____

2. Discuss the most surprising findings in Figure 8.4.

_____

_____

_____

CRITICAL-THINKING QUESTIONS

1. Stratification can occur in any social setting. Think about a group with which you are familiar that is stratified. Discuss the "unequal shares of scarce desirables" used to rank members.

_____

_____

2. Consider the existence of a class at the bottom of the American social stratification structure. Compare the explanations for the enduring presence of this class that would be given by functionalism and conflict theory.

_____

_____

3. More and more of the poor in the United States are women and children. Relate the feminization of poverty

to the prevailing view of the poor held by most Americans. Is there an inconsistency? Why or why not?

_____

_____

4. You are a member of a particular social class. Discuss your life chances and lifestyle in sociological terms.

_____

_____

5. Analyze the social mobility that has occurred in your family across as many generations as you can. Use specific sociological concepts in your analysis.

_____

_____

ANSWER KEY

Concept Review

a. 7
b. 10
c. 6
d. 3
e. 9
f. 4
g. 5
h. 1
i. 2
j. 11
k. 8

Check Yourself Review

1. T
2. F
3. occupations
4. conflict
5. achievement
6. dependency theory
7. b
8. d
9. a. 3
   b. 2
   c. 1
   d. 4
10. a. 2
    b. 1
    c. 3
11. a. 3
    b. 2
    c. 1

Inequalities of Race and Ethnicity

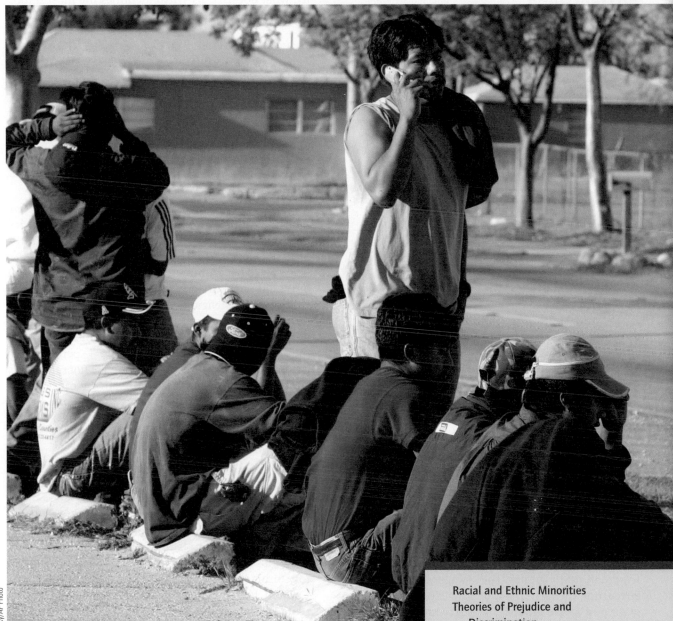

Lynne Sladky/AP Photo

S GOALS

- Distinguish among the concepts of minority, race, and ethnicity.
- Describe patterns of racial and ethnic relations.
- Differentiate prejudice from discrimination.
- Illustrate the different views of prejudice and discrimination taken by

    functionalists, conflict theorists, and symbolic interactionists.
- Describe, relative to the white majority, the condition of minorities in the United States.
- Describe the increasing global and domestic ethnic diversity.

USING THE SOCIOLOGICAL IMAGINATION

Have African Americans reached income parity with white Americans? Many people believe that as a result of the 1960s civil rights legislation, African American and white family incomes are now approaching comparable levels. In reality, evidence reveals a very different picture. The average income of African American households is considerably less than that of white households. Moreover, at each level of education (the gateway to jobs), African American males gain less income than do white males. On average, for example, white high school graduates can expect to earn annually nearly as much as African American college graduates.

Like all minorities, African Americans suffer the consequences of prejudice and discrimination. Latinos, Native Americans, Jewish Americans, white ethnics, and other minorities have felt the same sting of prejudice and unequal treatment. More recently, attention has been called to other categories of people who are subject to the fallout from prejudice and discrimination, particularly women and the elderly. Inequalities of gender and age are covered in subsequent chapters.

Racial and Ethnic Minorities ▣

All Americans are either immigrants or the descendants of immigrants. Even Native Americans are thought to have migrated to this continent many centuries ago. In part because of this large, diverse migration to the United States, prejudice and discrimination developed toward minority groups. The emergence of minorities is a recurring theme in the American experience, as immigrant and native groups alike encounter barriers to full integration into American society. Due to the nature of prejudice and discrimination, the conflict perspective informs much of the research on minorities.

The Definition of Minority

Customarily, a *minority* refers to a relatively small number of people. A sociological definition of a minority, however, can apply to a people numerically larger than others in a society. Before the end of apartheid, for example, blacks in South Africa were a minority—even though they outnumbered whites. Women in the United States are referred to as a minority, and they outnumber men. Obviously, for sociologists, something more than size distinguishes a minority (M. E. Williams 1997).

If small numbers do not necessarily make a minority, what does? Louis Wirth identifies the most important characteristics of a **minority:**

> We may define a minority as a group of people who, because of their physical or cultural characteristics, are singled out from the others in the society in which they live for differential and unequal treatment, and who therefore regard themselves as objects of collective discrimination. The existence of a minority in a society implies the existence of a corresponding dominant group with higher social status and greater privileges. Minority carries with it the exclusion from full participation in the life of the society. (Wirth 1945:347)

This definition expresses several key ideas. First, a minority has distinctive physical or cultural characteristics. Such characteristics can be used as a reminder that the minority person is different. This is more evident for physical characteristics such as skin color, facial features, or disabilities. Minority cultural characteristics might include accent, religion, language, or parentage. Culturally, a minority member can pass as a member of the majority by a change in name, the loss of an accent, or the adoption of the majority's culture. Experience suggests, however, that where differences are not sufficiently visible to allow easy identification, other means of identification may be imposed. During the Nazi regime, for example, Jewish Germans were forced to wear yellow stars to separate them from non-Jewish Germans.

Second, a society's stratification structure reflects minority status. Almost any society has desired goods, services, and privileges. Largely because the majority is the dominating group, it holds an unequal share of the desired goods, services, and privileges. Further, minority members have less access to the desirable resources. Minorities, for example, often have difficulty getting good jobs because of inferior schooling or discriminatory hiring.

Third, because of the distinctive cultural or physical traits of a minority, a majority can judge the minority to be inferior to their own and can be used to justify unequal treatment. In other words, the alleged inferiority of a minority can become part of the majority's ideology—a set of ideas used to justify and defend the interests and actions of those in power (Eagleton 1994). A majority practices job discrimination more easily if, for example, its ideology depicts a minority as shiftless or lazy.

Fourth, because members of a minority regard themselves as objects of discrimination, they have a sense of common identity. Within the minority there is a "consciousness of kind." It is from this sense of common identity that a *we* and *they* vocabulary is accepted

How many races are represented in this photo? On what basis did you make that determination?

within the minority. This vocabulary reflects a strong sense of solidarity and loyalty.

Finally, membership in a minority is an ascribed status. People do not make an effort to join a minority; they become members by birth. One does nothing to achieve this status, and there is little one can do to avoid it or shed it. Although some members of ethnic minorities may, through great effort and a name change, leave this ascribed status behind, it is nearly impossible for members of racial minorities to do so.

Throughout history, various peoples have experienced treatment as a minority. For this reason, it is important to understand the nature of race and ethnicity (Smaje 2000; Parrillo 2005a).

The Significance of Race

Q **What is race?** A **race** is a category of people who allegedly share certain biologically inherited physical characteristics that are considered socially important within a society. Biologists have used such physical characteristics as skin color, hair color and texture, facial features, head form, eye color, and height to create broad racial classifications. The most commonly used system of racial classification has three major racial categories—Negroid, Mongoloid, and Caucasoid—along with some unclassified racial categories (Walton and Caliendo 2011).

Q **Are racial classifications valid?** Sociologists now consider racial classifications, first developed by nineteenth-century biologists, arbitrary and misleading.

Ashley Montagu (2000) refers to *race* as "man's most dangerous myth." Although certain physical features have been associated with particular races, scientists have known for a long time that there is no such thing as a "pure" race. This long-standing belief has been reinforced recently through DNA studies. Geneticist Kenneth Kidd of Yale University concludes from the DNA samples he investigated that there is

> *a virtual continuum of genetic variation around the world. There's no place where you can draw a line and say there's a major difference on one side of the line from what's on the other side. If one is talking about a distinct, discrete, identifiable population...there's no such thing as race in [modern] Homo sapiens.* (Quoted in Marshall 1998:654)

Consequently and frequently, features—or markers—typical of one race show up in other races. For example, some people born into African American families are assumed to be white because of their facial features and light skin color (Appiah and Gutmann 1998).

Even defenders of racial classification acknowledge that their number of identifiable categories exceeds thirty. If racial classification categories are this numerous, scientists conclude, they lose any meaningful capacity to differentiate physical characteristics (Dobzhansky 1970; Hirschfeld 1998; S. Olson 2002, 2003; Wells and Read 2003).

If arbitrary racial classifications are the rule, then it is possible for social definitions to develop from rather superficial physical differences. For example, in the United States prior to the Civil War, a person born of African American and white parents was traditionally "black." If "white" blood were merely a matter of biology, there would have been no legal penalty attached to biracial offspring who claimed to be Caucasian. However, attempting to "pass for white" carried heavy legal sanctions. Some southern and border states defined a person as legally African if one of the great-grandparents was African (one-eighth) or if one of the great-great-grandparents was African (one-sixteenth). In practice, though, it took far less than one-sixteenth of the blood to be "black": anyone with any known African ancestry was usually considered black. This was known as the "one-drop" rule (Spickard 1992; Korgen 1998). Absent the socially imposed restrictions attached to "black" blood, these individuals could have classified themselves as "white" if they had preferred. Fortunately, the legal system in the United States now recognizes the arbitrariness of these racial labels, and parents are able to decide for themselves into which census category to classify their children. For the first time, the 2000 Census allowed residents to select more than one racial category.

Q **What is the origin of racism?** Race, as we have seen, is a matter of physical features, of identifiable biological *differences* in appearance among people. When *evaluations* are made about physical differences, racism enters the picture. **Racism** connects biological differences with judgments of innate superiority or inferiority (van den Berghe 1978; Weivorka 1995; Hurley 1998).

For most of human history, there was no connection between skin color and slavery. Slaves could be any color. The idea of racial evaluations did not emerge in the West prior to the 1600s (Aronson 2007). In that regard, historian Nell Irvin Painter offers a history of the development of racism among European and American thinkers. Painter points out that racism first developed as part of an effort to identify some light-skinned people as superior to other light-skinned people. The application of racism to whites is clear in the harsh treatment of early light-skinned American immigrants like the Irish. It takes little mental effort to imagine where dark-skinned people would fit into this ranking of groups of people based on lightness of skin color.

Q **What is the relationship between alleged racial physical characteristics and mental capacity?** Racist thinkers, from Count de Gobineau in the mid-nineteenth century to Adolf Hitler in the twentieth century, have attempted to link physical differences among people to innate mental and physical superiority or inferiority. Scientific evidence, however, debunks racism. According to past research, physical characteristics are superior only in the sense that they provide advantages for living in particular environments. For example, a narrow opening between eyelids protects against bright light or extreme cold such as found in Siberia or Alaska. A darker skin is better able to withstand a hot sun. But these physical differences are controlled by a very few genes. In fact, geneticists claim that there is more genetic difference between a tall person and a short person than between two people of different races who are the same height. Only about six genes in the human cell control skin color, while a person's height is affected by dozens of genes. Thus, a six-foot white male is genetically closer to a black male of similar height than to a five-foot white male. Research has found no biologically inherited differences in intelligence among the various races. Most social scientists endorse the following statement from a UNESCO Statement on Race, prepared by a distinguished group of social scientists:

> *According to present knowledge, there is no proof that the groups of mankind differ in their innate mental characteristics, whether in respect of intelligence or temperament. The scientific evidence indicates that the range of mental capacities in all ethnic* [or racial] *groups is much the same.* (Klineberg 1950:466)

A subsequent review of research supports UNESCO's earlier conclusion ("Statement on Race and Intelligence"

1969). Both of these reports attribute any differences in measured IQ among racial groups to differences in social environment, training, and education.

While social scientists generally pronounce as dead the idea of innate racial differences, recent DNA research is resuscitating race as a biological reality (Harmon 2007; Kashef 2007; Saletan 2007). When scientists first decoded the human genome in 2000, they offered it as evidence of the essential similarity among all humans. A comparison of any two people revealed a 99 percent DNA overlap. Lately, DNA research has begun exploring the possible importance of the remaining 1 percent difference. Noting some continental variations in DNA, these studies are again raising the question of biologically based racial differences. Relevance of these small DNA differences to the concept of race remains highly doubtful.

Q **What do social scientists mean by *social* races?** The consequences of racial discrimination based on alleged differences are real. Those people professing innate racial differences can make judgments regarding superiority/inferiority and then attempt to justify prejudice and discrimination. For this reason, many social scientists are interested in "social" races (J. E. Farley 1995; Banton 1998; Feagin and McKinney 2005). African Americans, Native Americans, Latinos, and Asian Americans are examples of socially defined races that, in America, often continue to face barriers. It seems reasonable to conclude that race remains an influential part of the American experience (Omi and Winant 1994; Feagin 2001; Loury 2003).

The Significance of Ethnicity

A society can consider people a racial category at one time and not at another time. Anglo-Saxon Americans, for example, once considered Irish and Italians as racial groups. Later, as it became clear that they had no distinctive physical characteristics, the Irish and Italians became ethnic minorities.

Q **What is an ethnic minority?** The term *ethnicity* comes from the Greek word *ethnos*, originally meaning "people" or "nation" (Ibrahim 2011). Thus, the original Greek word referred to cultural and national identity. Today we identify socially an **ethnic minority** by its unique characteristics related to culture or nationality. Just as physical characteristics define racial minorities, cultural differences define ethnic minorities.

Because of their differences from the host culture, ethnic minorities are subcultures. They have a way of life based on their own language, religion, values, beliefs, norms, and customs. Like any subculture, they are part of the larger culture—their members work in the majority (or host) economy, send their children through the dominant educational system, and are subject to the laws of the land—but they are also separate from the larger culture. This separation persists either because an ethnic minority wishes to maintain its cultural and national origins or because the majority erects barriers that prevent the ethnic group from blending in with the larger culture. Michael Novak (1996), himself a Slovak, contends that members of white ethnic minorities from Southern and Eastern Europe—Poles, Slavs, Italians, Greeks—have not been able to blend completely into American society because they are more culturally different from white Anglo-Saxon Protestants (WASPs) than are immigrants from Western and Northern Europe. Western Europeans, for example, have an alphabet similar to English and practice religions similar to Americans.

Q How are ethnic minorities received? Negative attitudes toward ethnic minorities exist in part because of ethnocentrism (the judgment of others based on one's own cultural standards). Many of the majority—out of loyalty to and preference for their own values, beliefs, and norms—may respond to other cultural ethnic views as inferior. Because members of ethnic minorities do not meet the majority's definition of appropriate ways of behaving, the majority may assume that something is wrong with the ethnic members. Ethnocentric judgments, of course, are often expressed via prejudice and discrimination. Jews, for example, have had to contend with prejudice and discrimination based on their religious beliefs. The heated immigration debate is fueled by negative stereotypes of Latino immigrants such as the false claim that they rely heavily on welfare.

A society's attitudes toward ethnic (and racial) minorities vary from minority to minority and from time to time. Figure 9.1 illustrates the changing opinions of Americans toward immigrants. Whether you are white or a member of an ethnic or racial minority, you may want to compare your attitudes with those depicted in Figure 9.1.

Recently, in some quarters, Latino immigrants and Muslims have become a target of intense negative social reactions. Latinos are said, by a vocal segment of Americans, to be threatening jobs, overwhelming social services, and making streets unsafe. Because of often intense prejudice, more than one-half of Latino adults worry about deportation for themselves or someone close to them (Martin and Midgley 2006; Carroll 2007; Reich 2008). Substantial pockets of Americans hold negative feelings or prejudices for Muslims and support extra security measures regarding Muslims and potential terrorism (Saad 2008). A majority of Muslim Americans think it is more difficult to be a Muslim in the United States since the September 11, 2001, terrorist attacks ("Muslim Americans: Middle Class and Mostly Mainstream," 2007).

Patterns of Racial and Ethnic Relations

When people of various racial and ethnic backgrounds interact, a wide range of outcomes are possible (Wallace 1997). It is helpful, however, to divide these many outcomes into two major types: patterns of assimilation (minority groups are accepted) and patterns of conflict (minority groups are rejected).

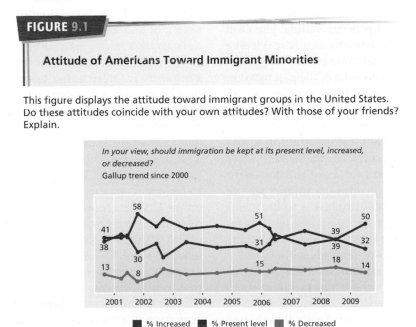

FIGURE 9.1

Attitude of Americans Toward Immigrant Minorities

This figure displays the attitude toward immigrant groups in the United States. Do these attitudes coincide with your own attitudes? With those of your friends? Explain.

In your view, should immigration be kept at its present level, increased, or decreased?
Gallup trend since 2000

■ % Increased   ■ % Present level   ■ % Decreased

Source: Lymari Morales, *Americans Return to Tougher Immigration Stance*. Gallup, Inc. (August 5, 2009, Available at http://www.gallup.com/poll/122057/Americans-Return-Tougher-Immigration-Stance.aspx). Copyright © 2009 the Gallup Organization. Reprinted by permission.

Assimilation involves "those processes whereby groups with distinctive identities become culturally and socially fused together" (Vander Zanden 1990:274). It is the integration of a racial or ethnic minority into a society where minority members are given full participation in all aspects of the society. The classic studies of assimilation are those of Milton Gordon, who defined three basic assimilation patterns in American society: Anglo-conformity, melting pot, and cultural pluralism (M. M. Gordon 1964, 1978).

Q What is the most common pattern of assimilation? *Anglo* is a prefix indicating an American of English descent. So *Anglo-conformity* maintains traditional American institutions. Basic to this pattern of assimilation is the acceptance of immigrants as long as they conform to the "accepted standards" of the host society. Anglo-conformity has been the most prevalent pattern of assimilation in America. It is the least egalitarian assimilation pattern because the immigrant minority must conform and, by implication, either give up or suppress its own values.

Q Is America more like a melting pot or a tossed salad? A second pattern of assimilation is the *melting pot*, in which all ethnic and racial minorities blend together. Although the ethnic and racial pot did simmer, especially in American cities, there is a question as to how much melting of differences and resulting fusion have really taken place. Instead of a melting pot, many sociologists are now using the idea of a "tossed salad," where traditions and cultures exist side by side.

The third assimilation pattern is *cultural pluralism*. Unlike the ideal of a unified culture underlying the Anglo-conformity and melting-pot patterns, cultural pluralism recognizes the immigrants' desire to maintain at least a remnant of their "old" ways. Ethnic enclaves, or settlements, characterized American cities of the past two centuries, and many survive today. Such enclaves allowed immigrants to maintain many of their traditional ways while accommodating American values and norms.

Accommodation, an extreme form of cultural pluralism, occurs when a minority, despite its familiarity with the beliefs, norms, and values of the dominant culture, maintains its own culturally unique way of life. An accommodated minority learns to deal with the dominant culture when necessary, but remains independent in language and culture. Cubans in Miami are an example of a distinct community within a larger community (K. L. Wilson and Martin 1982). Cultural pluralism emphasizes the ethnic and racial diversity that still characterizes American society and is a more democratic and egalitarian pattern of assimilation than either Anglo-conformity or the melting pot. Yet, we know that there is more to American race and ethnic relations than assimilation and equalitarian outcomes.

Conflict is the inevitable consequence of continuing inequities.

Q What are the patterns of conflict? Conflict patterns are associated with the dominance of a majority over racial and ethnic minorities. Three basic patterns of conflict are subjugation, population transfer, and genocide (Mason 1970).

Subjugation is the most common pattern of conflict and most clearly reflects the characteristics of a minority relationship: The majority enjoys greater access to the culture and lifestyle of the larger society. Inequities appear in such areas as power, economics, and education as well as in other important indicators of the quality of life, such as health and longevity. In subjugation, the majority and the minorities may live in the same general area and may participate together in at least some aspects of social life, but members of the minority remain clearly subordinate. Subjugation may be based on the law—**de jure subjugation**—as in the segregation of African Americans following Reconstruction in the United States or as in the former apartheid system of law in South Africa. It may also be based in actual everyday practice—**de facto subjugation**—regardless of what the law is. In this case, subjugation is visible primarily in indicators like political underrepresentation and low occupational achievement. The continuing practice of housing discrimination in the United States is an illustration of subjugation. This practice has existed over many decades, even in the face of direct efforts, including open housing laws, designed to overturn it. African Americans, Latinos, and other minorities still experience considerable discrimination when they attempt to rent or purchase a home.

Population transfer is another way in which a society dominates a minority. In this pattern of conflict, a minority is forced either to move to a remote location or to leave entirely the territory controlled by the majority. Population transfer was the most common policy used against Native Americans, especially during the late 1800s. The Cherokees, for example, were once a single nation in the southeastern United States until 20,000 Cherokees were forcibly removed to Oklahoma reservations, where they became dependent on the U.S. government. Four thousand of these Cherokees died because of harsh conditions along the Trail of Tears. Although Cherokee reservations can be found today in North Carolina and Oklahoma, many Native Americans have migrated to cities to find work, a move that in itself threatens the survival of some tribes. In another example, some believe that the 1999 Serbian aggression in Kosovo was actually closer to an attempt at population transfer than it was to genocide, because the Serbian intent was not to annihilate the Albanians but to move them (Wiesel 1999).

CHECK YOURSELF 9.1 R2

Racial and Ethnic Minorities

1. Which of the following is *not* always a characteristic of a minority?
   a. distinctive physical or cultural characteristics
   b. smaller in number than the majority
   c. dominated by the majority
   d. denied equal treatment
   e. a sense of collective identity
2. _____ is an ideology that links a people's physical characteristics with their alleged intellectual superiority or inferiority.
3. A(n) _____ is a people within a larger culture that is treated as a minority because of its distinctive cultural characteristics.
4. _____ refers to those processes whereby groups with distinctive identities become culturally and socially fused.
5. The pattern of conflict in which one people is forced to move to a remote location is called _____.

Answers: 1. b; 2. Racism; 3. ethnic group; 4. Assimilation; 5. population transfer

Genocide, the most tragic expression of dominance, refers to politically motivated mass murder of most or all of a targeted population (Fein 1993; Chirot and Seligman 2001; Muck 2011). One of the least-known examples occurred between 1492 and 1650 when Christopher Columbus totally eliminated 250,000 Arawak Indians of the Bahamas (Zinn 2005). One of the best-known examples is the Holocaust, Adolph Hitler's attempt to destroy all European Jews during the 1930s and 1940s. (See Figure 9.2.) The Nazis succeeded in killing some 6 million Jews before World War II ended in 1945. A more recent instance of genocide is the killing of more than 400,000 blacks by Arab militias in the Darfur region of Sudan, Africa (Caplan 2006).

At any given time, the patterns of race and ethnic relations are many, diverse, and often coexisting. Also, in the history of relations between two peoples, we can find wide variation through time in the ways the people interact. Many factors can influence the pattern of racial and ethnic relations adopted: the nature of the first contact, the reasons for contact and interaction, visibility of minority groups, views held by respective members, and general social conditions.

FIGURE 9.2

Impact of the Holocaust

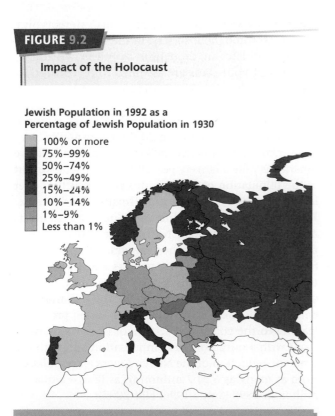

Jewish Population in 1992 as a Percentage of Jewish Population in 1930

- 100% or more
- 75%–99%
- 50%–74%
- 25%–49%
- 15%–24%
- 10%–14%
- 1%–9%
- Less than 1%

One of the worst examples of genocide was the Nazis' attempt, in the 1930s and 1940s, to exterminate the European Jewish population. This map shows the decline in Jewish population in European countries as a result of the Holocaust.

Theories of Prejudice and Discrimination R1

A variety of theories offer explanation for prejudice and discrimination. But first let's look at the nature of prejudice and discrimination.

The Nature of Prejudice and Discrimination

Q How is a sociological definition of prejudice different from the popular view of the term? Students can be prejudiced against professors, professors against university administrators, Catholics against Protestants, and employees against employers. In sociology, however, the concept of **prejudice** has a more precise meaning. *Prejudice* refers to widely held preconceptions of a group (minority or majority) and its individual

Mike Derer/AP Photos

Prejudice can lead to discrimination such as the act committed by the person(s) outside this Jewish cemetery.

members. Because such attitudes are based on strong emotions and rooted in unchallenged ideas, they are difficult to change, even in the face of overwhelming invalidating evidence. New information that contradicts one's prejudices tends to be denied because of selective perception. It is easier to explain an individual who doesn't fit the stereotype as an exception rather than reexamine a whole set of established beliefs. Consequently, prejudiced attitudes generally are not altered either by new personal experiences or by favorable accounts from others. An Anglo student may prefer to believe that an Asian classmate who does poorly in math is the "exception to the rule," that Asians have a "gift" for mathematics.

Prejudice involves an either/or type of logic: A minority (or majority) is either good or bad, and it is assumed that every member possesses the characteristics attributed to the group. Prejudice, then, involves overgeneralization based on biased or insufficient information. Such overgeneralizations are usually defended by one of two responses: citing limited personal experiences with minority members or reciting stories told by others about their experiences.

Q How is discrimination different from prejudice? Whereas prejudice refers to biased attitudes, **discrimination** refers to unequal treatment. Discrimination can take various forms: avoiding social contact with members of minority groups, denying them positions that carry

authority, or blocking their access to exclusive neighborhoods. It can also involve such extremes as physically attacking or killing targeted people (Allport 1979).

Q What is the relationship between prejudice and discrimination? Prejudice is usually considered the cause of discrimination. Although it usually does, prejudice need not lead to discrimination. The Roman High Empire (98 to 180 A.D.) considered conquered people to be barbarians and themselves as "Heaven's representatives among mankind." Yet Romans of this period were very tolerant of the same people, making them Roman citizens and permitting them extraordinary upward mobility (Chua 2007). Discrimination may also cause prejudice. For example, unskilled workers may believe that their jobs are in jeopardy because of the massive immigration of a new ethnic group. This fear of economic threat may lead to unequal treatment of the ethnic members. To justify this discrimination, threatened workers may attempt to show why a minority deserves unequal treatment. This occurs in part through the application of stereotypes. This is exactly what happened to Chinese Americans during the nineteenth and early twentieth centuries (Lyman 1974).

Q What is a stereotype? Like prejudice, stereotyping can appear throughout society. In the United States, for example, athletes are thought to be "all brawn and no brain," and politicians are assumed to be corrupt. As used in sociology, a **stereotype** is a set of ideas based on distortion, exaggeration, and oversimplification and applied to all members of a social category (Stangor 2000; Loury 2003: Pickering 2001). For example, very early relationships between the colonists and Native Americans were relatively peaceful and cooperative, but as the population of the colonies grew, conflicts over land and resources became more frequent and intense. To justify expansion into Indian territory, the colonists nurtured a stereotype of Native Americans as lying, thieving, murdering, heathen savages. This picture was frequently not held by the trappers and traders who moved individually among the Indians and, because of friendly contact, tended to judge the Indian differently. But the prejudice of the farmer–settler prevailed, leading to the continued seizure of Native American lands with a minimum of compensation and with the dramatic reduction of the Native American population from as many as 5 to 7 million to as few as a quarter million in 1890 (Snipp 1996; Ellis 2007).

Discrimination based on stereotypes continues today. Remember the field experiment designed to measure racial discrimination in the labor market described in Chapter 2 in "Consider This Research"? Marianne Bertrand and Sendhil Mullainathan (2002) sent résumés in response to help-wanted ads appearing in Boston and Chicago newspapers. To manipulate the

Spinning a Web of Hate

White supremacists, neo-Nazis, and other hate groups have discovered the Internet as an effective means of spreading hatred of Jews, African Americans, homosexuals, and fundamentalist Christians (Sandberg 1999). The Web boosts the recruiting efforts of these groups from leaflets and small meetings to a mass audience—more than 100 million worldwide. Reaching this audience is inexpensive and allows hate groups to present their message unedited and uncensored.

If you had browsed the World Wide Web in 1995, you would have found only one hate site, Stormfront. According to the Anti-Defamation League, there are now 2,000 Websites advocating racism, anti-Semitism, and violence. Aryan Nation identifies Jews as the natural enemy of whites; White Pride Network offers a racist joke center; Posse Comitatus defends alleged abortion clinic

bomber Eric Robert Rudolph; World Church of the Creator is violently anti-Christian.

Because they use high technology to deliver their message to a mass audience, organized racists are no longer easily identifiable. While members of hate groups used to be recognized by their white hoods or neo-Nazi swastikas, they can now just as easily be wearing business suits instead of brown shirts. The Southern Poverty Law Center is especially concerned about the repackaging of hate-based ideologies to make them appear more respectable to mainstream America. To reach the young, hate groups' Websites offer such child-friendly attractions as crossword puzzles, jokes, cartoons, coloring books, contests, games, and interactive comic strips.

One of the most prominent racist groups is the Council of Conservative Citizens (CCC). This organization, founded in 1985, now has more than 15,000 members in at least twenty-two states. Its members include scores of state legislators in Mississippi, and it has sought the political support of several state governors and U.S. senators and representatives. The CCC is an outgrowth of the White Citizens Councils from the 1950s and 1960s, whose primary purpose was to block the civil rights movement and school desegregation. While the CCC disavows

racism, billing itself as "a conservative organization that tries to defend the Constitution," its Website regularly publishes racist material. One of its featured columnists, H. Millard, made this prediction about the outcome of the interracial melting pot: "What will emerge will be just a slimy brown mass of glop. The genocide being carried out against white people hasn't come with marching armies....Genocide via the bedroom chamber is just as long-lasting as genocide via the gas chamber."

Not all hate group activity comes from white supremacists who target African Americans. The Southern Poverty Law Center also tracks the activities of black separatists and documents several recent hate crimes committed by blacks against whites. In addition, the continued immigration of Asians and Central and South Americans is drawing the angry attention of hate groups of all types. More information on hate group activities can be found at the Southern Poverty Law Center Website: www.spl-center.org.

Think About It

When the economy is not performing well, membership in hate groups rises; membership declines when the economy is doing well. Relate this fluctuating membership pattern to scapegoating you may have observed or heard about.

---

perception of race, each résumé was randomly assigned either a very white-sounding name or a very African American–sounding name. Résumés with white names drew about 50 percent more callbacks than those with African American names. In addition, the researchers introduced variations in the quality of credentials. Among whites, the higher-quality résumés elicited 30 percent more callbacks than the lower-quality ones. Among African Americans, in contrast, the higher-quality résumés did not elicit significantly more callbacks. In short, whites benefited from improving their credentials; African Americans did not.

Q What is a hate crime? In 1999, James Byrd Jr., an African American from Texas, was chained to a pickup truck and

then dragged to death. That same year saw Matthew Shepard, a gay college student at the University of Wyoming, tied to a fence and beaten to death. There were two more dramatic cases in 2010. Rutgers University student, Tyler Clementi, committed suicide after his roommate secretly filmed him having gay sex and streamed it to the Internet. Nine members of a Bronx street gang beat and tortured three men because they thought them gay. (See "Sociology Eyes America 9.1".)

All of these incidents are **hate crimes,** criminal acts motivated by prejudice. Hate or "bias" crimes involve discrimination related to race, religion, sexual orientation, national origin, or ancestry (U.S. Department of Justice 2009). Victims include, but are not limited to, African Americans, Native Americans, Latinos, Asian

SOCIOLOGY EYES AMERICA 9.1

Active U.S. Hate Groups

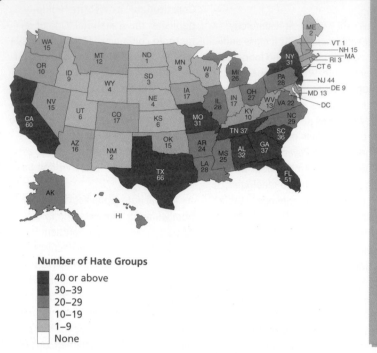

Number of Hate Groups

- 40 or above
- 30–39
- 20–29
- 10–19
- 1–9
- None

Source: From Southern Poverty Law Center, 2010. Reprinted by permission.

Hate groups are formed to direct prejudice and discrimation toward one or more categories of people such as blacks, Jews, Muslims, immigrants, or gays. The Southern Poverty Law Center documents 932 active hate groups in the U.S. in 2009. These hate groups (not just individuals) variously are involved with criminal acts, demonstrations, marches, speeches, meetings, and publications.

Interpret the Map

1. Describe any regional pattern(s) you see in the distribution of hate groups across the U.S.
2. How would you explain any pattern you see?
3. Does the number of hate groups active in the U.S. surprise you? Why or why not?

Neil Redmond/AP Photo

These arson investigators are searching through the ashes of an African American church in North Carolina. What would make this case of arson a hate crime?

Americans, Jews, Muslims, gay men and women, and people with disabilities (Ehrlich 2009).

The term *hate crime* is relatively new; the behavior is not. Even though the federal government has kept statistics since 1900, the official tally of hate crimes appears to be a serious underestimation. National surveys report that nearly 200,000 people say they have been the targets of a hate crime, while only half informed the police (Schaefer 2011). In 2009 alone, there were approximately 7,000 hate crimes in the United States (U.S. Department of Justice 2009).

The Southern Poverty Law Center, which traces violent hate groups in the United States, found a huge spike in the growth of domestic hate groups. Between 2000 and 2008, the number of identifiable hate groups grew from 602 to 926, a 35 percent increase ("Confronting the New Faces of Hate" 2009). All but five states (Arkansas, Georgia, Indiana, South Carolina, and Wyoming) have enacted hate crime laws, though they vary widely in nature.

Obviously, no single factor can account for prejudice and discrimination. The causes are varied. Psychology, functionalism, conflict theory, and symbolic interactionism each contribute to the understanding of prejudice and discrimination.

The Psychological Perspective

Psychological explanations of prejudice and discrimination focus on the prejudiced person's personality, how it developed, and how it functions in the present. Accordingly, questions like these are asked about prejudiced persons: What was their relationship with their parents or with their significant others? What are their values, attitudes, and beliefs? How high is their self-esteem? Two prominent psychological explanations of prejudice and discrimination are the frustration-aggression explanation and the authoritarian personality.

Q How can frustration lead to prejudice and discrimination? According to the *frustration-aggression* explanation, prejudice and discrimination are the products of deep-seated hostility and aggression that stem from frustration. Aggression is most likely when built-up hostility cannot be directed at the actual source of frustration. Pent-up hostility and frustration may subsequently be redirected toward some substitute object that is less threatening than the one causing the frustration. These substitute objects, known as **scapegoats**, serve as convenient and less feared targets on which to place the blame for one's own troubles, frustrations, failures, or sense of guilt.

John Dollard (Dollard et al. 1939), originator of the frustration-aggression explanation, contended that the frustrations experienced by the Germans after World War I helped account for their acceptance of anti-Semitism.

The loss of the war, the disappearance of international prestige, the forced acceptance of the Treaty of Versailles, and a ruined economy all contributed to tremendous frustration among the German people. Because direct aggression against the Allies was not an alternative, the Germans channeled their aggression toward other targets, one of which was the Jews. The best scapegoats are those who have already been singled out by the majority for unequal treatment and who therefore have the least chance to defend themselves.

Q What personality type may tend toward prejudiced attitudes? Another psychological explanation contends that there is a personality type—the **authoritarian personality**—that tends to be more prejudiced than other types. The authoritarian personality is characterized by excessive conformity; submissiveness to authority figures; inflexibility; repression of impulses, desires, and ideas; fearfulness; and arrogance toward persons or groups thought to be inferior. T. W. Adorno and his colleagues, the creators of this theory, summarized it this way:

> The most crucial result of the [study of the authoritarian personality] is the demonstration of the close correspondence in the type of approach and outlook a subject is likely to have in a great variety of areas, ranging from the most intimate features of family and sex adjustment through relationships to other people in general, to religion, and to social and political philosophy. Thus a basically hierarchical, authoritarian, exploitative parent–child relationship is apt to carry over into a power-oriented, exploitatively dependent attitude toward one's sex partner and one's God and may well culminate in a political philosophy and social outlook which has no room for anything but a desperate clinging to what appears to be strong and a disdainful rejection of whatever is relegated to the bottom. (Adorno et al. 1950:971)

The Functionalist Perspective

Functionalists have focused on the dysfunctions of prejudice and discrimination, and as the last half of this chapter will demonstrate, the negative consequences of prejudice and discrimination are wide and deep. The social, political, educational, and economic costs of the exploitation and oppression of minorities are extremely high. Furthermore, the safety and stability of the larger society are at risk because violence periodically erupts between the groups. (See Table 9.1 for a comparison of the three sociological perspectives.)

Q Do functionalists see any positive contributions of prejudice and discrimination? Because functionalists look for positive contributions that each aspect of a

TABLE 9.1

FOCUS ON THEORETICAL PERSPECTIVES: Prejudice and Discrimination

This table illustrates how a particular theoretical perspective views a central sociological concept. Switch the concepts around and illustrate how each theoretical perspective would view a different concept. For example, discuss some functions and dysfunctions of differential power or the self-fulfilling prophecy.

Theoretical Perspective	Concept	Example
Functionalism	Ethnocentrism	• White colonists used negative stereotypes as a justification for taking Native American land.
Conflict theory	Differential power	• African Americans accuse Latinos of using their political clout to win advantages for themselves.
Symbolic interactionism	Self-fulfilling prophecy	• Members of a minority fail because of low expectations they have for their own success.

culture makes to that society's stability and continuity, they have identified some potential benefits. As noted in Chapter 7, Emile Durkheim identified the ways in which deviance contributes to the cohesiveness of society. The functionalist theory of stratification, as shown in Chapter 8, contends that social inequality helps society to channel the most qualified people into the most important positions and to ensure that people in these positions are motivated to perform their tasks competently. Another potential benefit is the social solidarity of the majority. This happens because the attempted exclusion of outside groups rests in part on ethnocentrism—the tendency to judge others based on one's own cultural standards. Once a majority is convinced of its superiority, it can unite around its own way of life. This strengthens the boundaries of the majority.

Q **But what is the downside of ethnocentrism?** As you know, what is functional for one part of society may be dysfunctional for other parts. The price of national unity via ethnocentrism is extremely high for its targets. Passage of the U.S. Constitution in 1789 permitted the retention of slavery. This consigned black slaves to nearly another 100 years of bondage. Documentation of the persistent damage of this extreme oppression to African Americans is covered in this chapter. This early sense of national unity has also been expensive to the entire society. Consequences of the Civil War, which saw our country violently divided in the nineteenth century, still reverberate through regional factions.

The Conflict Perspective

According to conflict theory, a majority uses prejudice and discrimination as weapons of power in the domination of a minority. This theory, then, traces the existence of prejudice and discrimination to majority interests rather than to personality needs. Domination by the majority is often motivated by its desire to gain or increase its control over scarce goods and services. When those with power in a society are able to persuade the majority that a minority *should* be subjugated, the minority have been effectively eliminated or neutralized as competitors (W. J. Wilson 1973).

David Frazier/PhotoEdit

Functionalists see conflict between racial and ethnic groups as dysfunctional. Why?

Q According to the conflict perspective, how do minority groups view one another, and what effect does this have for the majority? Members of a majority tend to think of minorities as people unlike them but similar to one another. Despite being a common target of the majority's prejudice and discrimination, minorities tend to view one another as competitors, rather than as allies, in their struggle for scarce resources (Olzak and Nagel 1986). Conflict among minorities, particularly African Americans and Latinos, is increasing in the United States as whites leave cities and African Americans assume political power. On the one hand, many urban blacks believe that Latinos are benefiting from the civil rights movement waged by African Americans. On the other hand, many Latinos believe that African Americans are using their political clout to push an agenda that favors blacks. A Latino member of Chicago's board of education has charged the five African American members on the board with imposing "apartheid" on Latino children. The board members had voted to send more African American children to integrated schools while disregarding the overcrowding suffered by Latino students. It remains to be seen if urban African Americans and urban Latinos will become allies for their mutual welfare or if they will engage in fierce conflict over the scarce resources available to them.

From a Marxian viewpoint, the ruling class (capitalists) benefits from a continuation of conflict among minority groups. If various minorities fight with one another and attribute their job losses to one another, then the ruling elite can, with little or no resistance, downsize, move jobs offshore, and replace workers with technology. In other words, so long as the conflict is not too extreme, capitalists are the beneficiary of a divided working class.

Prejudice and discrimination cannot be accounted for solely by functionalist and conflict explanations. These theories do not explore the factors involved in learning prejudice and discrimination.

The Symbolic Interactionist Perspective

According to the symbolic interactionist perspective, we acquire prejudice and discrimination, as we do other aspects of culture, through socialization. Members of a society learn prejudice in much the same way that they learn patriotism (Van Ausdale and Feagin 2001). Gordon Allport (1979) described two stages in the learning of prejudice. In the first stage—*the pregeneralized learning period*—children are exposed to prejudice, but they have not yet learned to categorize people. The idea that Asian Americans form a distinct category is beyond their understanding. Later, when children enter the second stage of learning prejudice—*total rejection*—they are able to use physical clues to sort people into groups. At this point, if children hear their parents systematically denigrate a minority, they will reject all members of the group on all counts and in all situations. By this stage, the child has learned the name of the minority he or she is supposed to dislike and can identify individuals who belong to it. A nine-year-old Kosovar Albanian child who wants to "kill Serbs" when he grows up is in the stage of total rejection (Nordland 1999).

Language itself can provide a context supportive of prejudice and discrimination (James M. Jones 1972). For example, in Anglo culture, although it is good to be "in the black" financially, many references using the term *black* are negative. Such terms as *blackball*, *blacklist*, and *black mark* illustrate the negative connotations associated with the term *black*. During the 1960s, militant African American groups coined the slogan "Black is beautiful" to combat this negative connotation. By comparison, it is difficult to think of similar instances in which *white* is used negatively. Such cultural referents, learned as a part of everyday culture, create a context in which some people may erroneously assume that the well-dressed African American male standing outside a fine restaurant is the doorman rather than a customer. Such responses support the continuation of prejudice and discrimination.

CHECK YOURSELF **9.2** **R2**

Theories of Prejudice and Discrimination

1. _____ refers to the unequal treatment of individuals based on their membership in a minority.
2. A _____ is a set of ideas based on distortion, exaggeration, and oversimplification that is applied to all members of a social category.
3. The _____ is characterized by excessive conformity; submissiveness to authority figures; inflexibility; repression of impulses, desires, and ideas; fearfulness; and arrogance toward those thought to be inferior.
4. According to Gordon Allport, children learning prejudice move from a pregeneralized learning period to a stage of total _____.
5. A _____ occurs when an expectation leads to behavior that causes the expectation to become a reality.

Answers: 1. Discrimination; 2. stereotype; 3. authoritarian personality; 4. rejection; 5. self-fulfilling prophecy

Symbolic interactionists also underscore the labeling process. In 1996, Texaco Inc. agreed to pay more than $115 million as reparation for the economic effects of racism within the company. This settlement was fueled in part by a tape recording made by a high corporate official. On this tape, one executive appeared to impose racial labels (Solomon 1996).

What's more, symbolic interactionism underlies the concept of the **self-fulfilling prophecy**—when an expectation leads to behavior that then causes the expectation to become a reality (Merton 1968). For example, if two nations are convinced they are going to war, they may engage in hostile interaction that actually leads to war. Similarly, if members of a minority are constantly treated as if they are less intelligent than the majority, the minority members may eventually accept this limitation. This, in turn, may lead them to place less emphasis on education. Then, indeed, the minority members appear to themselves and others as less intelligent. Or members of a minority may be socialized to believe that they are not capable of holding important positions in a society and may begin to accept this definition. Given this negative image, and the lack of opportunity to develop their abilities, members of minorities may become locked in lower-level jobs.

Institutionalized Discrimination R1

Although it is popular to think of the United States as a society in which everyone has an equal opportunity to achieve his or her chosen goals, such freedom has always been limited. This is the "American dilemma" of which Gunnar Myrdal wrote with regard to African Americans (Myrdal 1944; Obie 1996). At various times in American history, such practices as slavery and the internment of Japanese Americans during World War II reflected the open and legal practice of discrimination against members of various minorities (Muller 2007). Virtually all minorities have encountered such practices to a greater or lesser degree (Feagin and Feagin 1986; Luhman 2002; Schaefer 2007).

In the 1960s, many Americans felt that the passage of the civil rights laws would eradicate racism. Although these statutes did stop many discriminatory practices, many people in this country still suffer from **institutionalized discrimination**. This type of discrimination is the result of unfair practices that are part of the structure of society and have grown out of traditionally accepted behaviors. The legacy of 300 years of discrimination is not easily erased from American life, even though it continues to be publicly exposed. For example, blacks in New Orleans (mostly poor) were

provided less protection and suffered disproportionately more deaths in the wake of Hurricane Katrina.

Q How does direct institutionalized discrimination differ from indirect institutionalized discrimination? To help clarify discriminatory practices, Joe and Clairece Feagin (1986) distinguish between direct and indirect institutionalized discrimination. **Direct institutionalized discrimination** refers to organizational or community actions intended to deprive a racial or ethnic minority of its rights. **Indirect institutionalized discrimination** refers to unintentional behavior that negatively affects a minority. Examples of direct institutionalized discrimination are laws that segregated African Americans or that denied Mexican American children the right to speak their native language in public schools. High school exit exams provide an example of indirect institutionalized discrimination. When required for graduation, these exit exams are disadvantageous to minority students, who are more likely to drop out because they are less likely than white and Asian American students to pass on their first attempt. Seniority systems (promotion and pay increase with years of service) discriminate against the promotion of newly hired people—many of whom are minority workers. Because of past institutionalized discrimination, members of minorities are just now beginning to enter jobs with seniority systems. Because they have to wait their turn for advancement and because they have fewer years of service than members of the majority, who have been in the system for years, members of minorities often find that their chances for quick promotion are slight, even though the seniority systems may not have been intentionally designed to obstruct minority progress.

Another example of institutionalized discrimination can be found in public education. Schools with large numbers of minority students are more common in large urban areas than in the wealthier suburbs. This is partly because of "white flight" to the suburbs and housing discrimination against minorities. As a result, minority children are more concentrated in school districts with a tax base too low to provide resources equal to those in the suburbs. This lack of funding has many repercussions: Teachers in minority schools receive fewer opportunities for training; textbooks, when students have them, are outdated; there is little, if any, money for new technology; and buildings are badly in need of repair. Moreover, parental and community support is generally not as strong in these school districts as in the suburbs.

Institutionalized discrimination in the United States is reflected in the experiences of minorities—African Americans, Latinos, Native Americans, Asian Americans, white ethnics, and Jewish Americans. For each minority, the social and economic costs of discrimination are enormous (Andrews 1996; Aguirre and Turner 1997; Spencer 1997; Pollard 1999; Smelser, Wilson, and Mitchell 2001).

Institutionalized discrimination has contributed to the deterioration of many inner-city public schools, such as the Thomas Alva Edison High School in Philadelphia.

African Americans

African Americans make up one of the two largest minority groups in the United States, numbering just over 36 million, or 12.1 percent of the total population (see Figure 9.3). They are also one of the oldest minorities, first brought to America as indentured servants in 1619 and subsequently as slaves. Because of slavery, African Americans represent a special case of institutionalized discrimination. To capture this uniqueness, Robert

Blauner (1969, 1972) describes the situation of blacks in America as "internal colonialism."

Q **What is internal colonialism?** Colonialism, of course, was originally applied to the domination and oppression of one nation by another (outside) nation, such as the Europeans in Africa and India (Muck 2011). The concept of **internal colonialism**, or domestic colonialism, refers to the domination and oppression of one group by another group within the same society

FIGURE 9.3

U.S. Population by Racial and Ethnic Group, 2008

United States Total Population 304,060,000

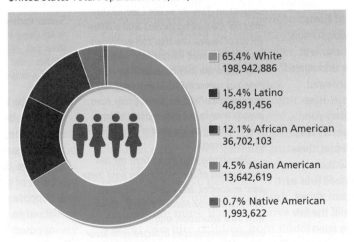

- 65.4% White
  198,942,886
- 15.4% Latino
  46,891,456
- 12.1% African American
  36,702,103
- 4.5% Asian American
  13,642,619
- 0.7% Native American
  1,993,622

Source: U.S. Bureau of the Census, *Statistical Abstract of the United States: 2010*, 129th ed. (Washington, D.C.: U.S. Bureau of the Census, 2009), Table 10, p. 14.

FIGURE 9.4

Majority and Minority Median Household Incomes

Explain why sociologists consider Asian Americans a minority group despite their relatively high annual income.

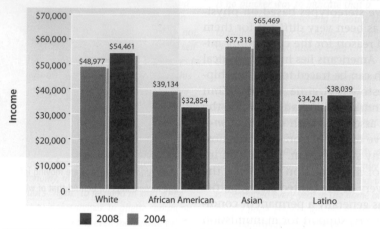

Source: U.S. Census Bureau, *Statistical Abstract of the United States: 2010* (129th ed.), Washington, DC, 2009.

TABLE 9.2

Socioeconomic Characteristics of Minorities

This figure presents some important social and economic characteristics of the majority and larger minorities in the U.S. Can you make sociological generalizations about income level and education based on these data?

	White, Not Latino	African American	Latino	Asian American
Percent of Families in Poverty	9.4%	25.8%	25%	12.5%
Median Income	$54,461	$32,854	$38,039	$65,469
Percent with High School Diploma	87.1%	83.0%	62.3%	88.7%
Percent with College Degree	29.8%	19.6%	13.3%	52.6%

Source: *U.S. Census Bureau, Statistical Absract of the United States: 2010* (129th ed.), Washington, DC, 2009.

distribution, while the same is true for only 16 percent of white children. Finally, black children from poor families are more likely to remain poor in adulthood than poor white children (54 percent versus 31 percent).

Not surprisingly, there is also a vast gulf in wealth (home and car equity, net business assets, net liquid assets). The average African American family holds less than one-quarter of the wealth of the average white family.

Q How do African Americans fare in the job market? According to recent "social audit" studies, African Americans experience employment discrimination despite stronger legal prohibitions. Audit studies involve sending white and minority researchers with comparable résumés to the same firms, applying for the same jobs. Research consistently shows that employers are more likely to interview or hire white applicants. This discrimination now takes more sophisticated and covert forms. For example, discriminatory employers interview or offer jobs to all white applicants before tapping their list of black applicants. Discriminatory firms also offer white applicants higher salaries and higher-status positions (Herring 2002). Such employment practices perpetuate the long-standing minority overrepresentation in low-prestige, low-paying jobs. About one-third of African American men are employed in the highest occupational categories: professional, managerial, technical, and administrative, whereas about one-half of white men have jobs in these categories. Similarly, about 60 percent of African American women are employed in these occupational categories, compared to three-fourths of white women. African Americans are almost twice as likely as whites to work in low-level service jobs.

New long-term economic trends threaten to make matters worse. These trends include a shift from higher-paying manufacturing jobs to lower-paying service jobs, technological replacement of workers, and transfer of high-wage jobs to low-wage countries. Reduced job opportunities for African Americans and other minorities, especially in segregated neighborhoods, are an important negative consequence.

Patterns of unemployment also affect the economic status of African Americans. The jobless rate among African Americans is almost double that of whites (Ehrenreich and Muhammad 2009; *State of Black America* 2009). And these rates do not take account of all unemployed persons. Traditional unemployment rates are based on the number of unemployed people who are looking for jobs. They do not include so-called **hidden unemployment**—discouraged workers who have stopped looking or part-time workers who would prefer full-time jobs. When hidden unemployment is considered, the jobless rate for African Americans approaches one in four workers, the rate during the Great Depression of the 1930s.

It is among African Americans ages sixteen to nineteen that the greatest unemployment problem exists. According to official statistics, about one out of every two African American teenagers is unsuccessfully looking for full-time work (U.S. Department of Labor 2001a). With hidden unemployment taken into account, an even greater percentage of all African American teenagers are unemployed. Consequently, thousands of African American youths are becoming adults without the job experience vital to securing good employment.

Q Are there gender differences in education among African Americans? Knowledge of the nationwide gap between men and women would lead you to answer *yes*. And you would be right. The long-standing advantage of black males over black females, however, appears to be eroding somewhat. At every educational level, black men still earn more than black women do. But African American women with college degrees earn substantially more than the median for all African American men. That is not true for white men and women. And African American college-educated women earn as much as white women with college degrees. Given that a college education opens more doors for African American women, the additional good news for them is their increasing educational level. While more than a third of African American women enter college, only a fourth of black men do. Contrast this to 1970, when African American men and women had a roughly equal level of college enrollment (U.S. Bureau of the Census 2001; Cose 2003).

Q What are the educational opportunities for African Americans? Education is the traditional American path to economic gain and occupational prestige. The educational story for African Americans is mixed. As of 2008, 87 percent of whites had finished high school compared with 83 percent of African Americans. Similarly, whereas almost 30 percent of whites had completed college, only about 20 percent of African Americans had done so. (See Table 9.2.) Moreover, higher educational attainment doesn't pay off for African Americans as it does for whites. Although income tends to rise with educational level for both African Americans and whites, it increases much less for African American men (and for women of both races) than for white men. At each level of schooling, African American men tend to gain less than their white peers do.

Q What is the African American presence in politics? African Americans have enjoyed some political success since 1970. This progress is due in part to legal changes that occurred in the 1950s and 1960s, including the increase in African American voter registration. Also, African Americans constitute a growing political majority in many large cities. Consequently, more than 5,400 African Americans are serving as city and county officials, up from 715 in 1970. There are more than 9,000 African American elected officials in the United States, a sixfold increase since 1970.

Some see the slow emergence of a "biracial politics"—election of African Americans in predominantly white areas—as a hopeful sign (Kilson 2002). According to Richard Zweigenhaft and William Domhoff, some African Americans, though still vastly underrepresented, have entered the "power elite" of America:

Although the power elite is still composed primarily of Christian white men, there are now...blacks...on the boards of the country's largest corporations; presidential cabinets are far more diverse than was the case forty years ago; and the highest ranks of the military are no longer filled solely by white men. (Zweigenhaft and Domhoff 2006:176)

Greg Wahl-Stephens/AP Photo

Barack Obama made helping working families a top priority prior to his run for the presidency of the United States.

There are several prominent examples of blacks recently entering the political elite. In 1991 Clarence Thomas became the second African American in history to serve on the Supreme Court. Colin Powell and Condoleezza Rice both served as Secretary of State in George W. Bush's administration. Many took Barack Obama's election as president in 2008 as a sign of at least some decline in the significance of race in American society. Of course, even Obama's election does not signal a post-racist America (Feagin 2006; Bonilla-Silva 2007). There is more on the significance of race in America later in this chapter.

It is in the statehouses (only two African American governors have been elected) and at the national level (there is only one black Senator) that African Americans have experienced the least political gain. Less than 1 percent of national political offices are held by African Americans. This is true even though there have been more African Americans in the U.S. House of Representatives in the last four Congresses (forty-one in 2010) than at any other time in American history. This is more than double the number of African American House members in 1981. Still, blacks comprise 12.1 percent of the U.S. population and only 10 percent of the House. In 2008, there was only one African American in the U.S. Senate. Although African Americans are an emerging political force, they must accomplish much before they can claim proportionate political representation.

In fact, a 1995 U.S. Supreme Court decision appears to represent a roadblock to political power for African Americans. The Court ruled that race could no longer be the "predominant factor" in determining congressional districts (Fineman 1995). The Court created, at the same time, a legal test that makes it difficult, if not impossible, to keep in place government programs that give an advantage to minorities and women. In fact, "antipreference" forces are making significant progress toward repealing affirmative action laws. The Universities of California and Texas have abandoned all racially based admissions preferences, and the state of California has repealed its affirmative action laws.

Voting patterns reflect another dimension of political inequality among African Americans. Because politicians respond most favorably and consistently to the desires of those who vote, it is in the interest of African Americans to make their presence known on election day. Yet, the African American voting registration rate is typically several percentage points lower than the white registration rate (61 and 71 percent, respectively; Breed 2008). Adding significance is the fact that African Americans are swamped, numerically, by whites.

African Americans vote at a lower rate than whites for at least two reasons. First, African Americans are disproportionately represented in the working class, among the working poor, and in the underclass—the socioeconomic categories least likely to vote. Second, because African Americans have much less confidence in the political system than whites, they are more likely to believe that their votes will count less. This distrust of politics is nurtured by voting experiences like the 2000 presidential election. Intense nationwide scrutiny was given to the undercounting of low-income minority voters in Florida (Parker and Eisler 2001). Unfortunately, Florida is not the exception. Undercounting of low-income and minority voters is a nationwide pattern. Voters in low-income, high-minority congressional districts had greater than triple the likelihood of having their votes discarded than were voters in affluent, low-minority districts (Dooley 2001). In 2008, the U.S. Supreme Court heard a case on a 2005 Indiana law requiring voters to show photo identification before being permitted to vote, a law that critics claim will discourage minority voters (Urbina 2008). Given this situation, it is easy to understand why many African Americans believe that they live in a "still-white" society (Roediger 2003).

Q **What is meant by "two black Americas"?** During the 1960s and 1970s, some occupational progress was made. The number of African Americans in professional and technical occupations—doctors, engineers, lawyers, teachers, writers—increased by 128 percent. The number of African American managers or officials is more than twice as high as it was in 1960. Due to the recent upward mobility of educated African Americans, some scholars predict the emergence of two black Americas—a black **underclass** composed of the permanently poor trapped in inner-city ghettos and a growing black middle class (W. J. Wilson 1984; Landry 1988; Kilson 1998; Pattillo-McCoy 2000). In Richard Freeman's (1977) terms, a black elite is said to be emerging in America. David Swinton offers this view of the mixed state of African Americans:

> The empirical evidence does show that some individual blacks have made impressive economic gains. In fact, there has been an increase in the proportion of blacks who can be classified as upper middle class. This limited upward mobility for the few cannot offset the stagnation and decline experienced by the larger numbers of black Americans whose economic status has deteriorated. The central tendency for the group as a whole is revealed by the trends in the averages. And these trends tell a consistent story of stagnation or decline. (Swinton 1989:130)

U.S. Census data confirm the existence of two black Americas—the rich and the poor. The number of African American households earning a minimum of $50,000 annually has more than tripled since 1970. About 30 percent of African American households earn between $25,000 and $50,000 each year. As shown earlier, the percentage of poor African Americans, however, continues to dwarf that of whites.

The concept of two black Americas may not adequately capture black diversity today. According to Eugene Robinson, the division within the African American population has increased dramatically as a result of decades of desegregation, affirmative action, and immigration. Instead of one, or even two black Americas, Robinson sees four: a middle-class majority; a large contingent of hopelessly poor; a wealthy, powerful, and influential elite; and two new immigrant groups (Robinson 2010).

Q Is the significance of race declining for African Americans? The argument for the declining significance of race is applied to both successful African Americans and the black underclass. Let's examine each in turn.

Although African Americans remain behind whites on all dimensions of stratification, gains made since the 1960s have led some to conclude that race is declining in significance in America (Cose 1995; Thernstrom and Thernstrom 1999). According to some analysts, race is now less important than resources in determining the life chances of young, well-educated African Americans. Well-educated African Americans, it is argued, can now compete on equal ground with whites. African Americans with finances and education are said to be no longer shut out because of their color (W. J. Wilson 1990, 1993a, 1997, 2002).

William Julius Wilson concurs that race is now less important than economic class for successful African Americans. Wilson goes further by saying that race is declining in significance even for the African American urban poor who are part of the underclass—those in poverty who are either continuously unemployed or underemployed due to the absence of job opportunities and/or required job skills. In some of his early work on this topic, Wilson stated it this way:

> The recent mobility patterns of blacks lend strong support to the view that economic class is clearly more important than race in predetermining job placement and occupational mobility. In the economic realm, then, the black experience has moved historically from economic racial oppression experienced by virtually all blacks to economic subordination for the black underclass. (W. J. Wilson 1980:152)

In his book *The Truly Disadvantaged*, Wilson (1990) elaborates on the thesis of the declining significance of race in the United States. It is true, Wilson acknowledges, that many African Americans (and other minority group members) are in the underclass as a result of historical patterns of discrimination. This, however, is in the past. Moreover, the argument continues, African Americans remaining in the underclass are there not because of prejudice and discrimination, but because of features of the American economy. Inner-city African Americans are adversely affected by the deindustrialization of the American economy. In the past, African Americans were drawn to Detroit, Chicago, and other large cities by the availability of high wages and stable employment in factories. These manufacturing jobs, which traditionally required little education, have gone to low-income countries where labor is cheap and labor unions are nonexistent. Consequently, today's inner-city poor are denied the type of jobs used for upward mobility. A second contributing economic factor is the internal movement of business and industry from central cities to the suburbs. A third economic factor contributing to the perpetuation of the underclass is the movement of upwardly mobile African Americans to the suburbs. Lacking the positive role models available in the past, the inner-city poor now see drug dealing, prostitution, and other illegal economic activities as the primary avenues to success (Vobejda 1991; O. Clayton 1996; Massey and Denton 1996; Small and Newman 2001).

If economic factors are perpetuating the underclass, Wilson argues, solutions are to be found in the economic sphere. Wilson calls for a federal economic policy designed to create a higher employment rate and better jobs for all Americans. Wilson looks to such things as higher-paying jobs, improved education, job training, relocation support to encourage members of the underclass to secure and keep decent jobs, publicly supported day care for the low-income employed, a markedly higher minimum wage, and medical insurance for the employed in low-paying jobs (W. J. Wilson 1993b, 1997).

Use of the term *underclass* has been questioned (M. B. Katz 1993). Wilson, himself, suggests substituting the term *ghetto poor* because the concept of underclass seems to be a code word for inner-city African Americans and is often used by journalists to highlight unflattering behavior in the ghetto (W. J. Wilson 1991). Herbert Gans (1990) sees the term *underclass* as a pejorative, value-laden term now being used to describe the "undeserving" poor. Joining a growing number of social scientists, Gans believes that the term *underclass* is hopelessly mired in ideological connotations of undeservingness and blameworthiness. These social scientists, including Wilson, do not wish to obscure the harsh reality faced by the urban poor by continuing to use the term *underclass* if such use contributes to victim blaming. It remains to be seen whether the term *underclass* will lose its currency in sociological terminology. At any rate, some term, perhaps Wilson's *ghetto poor*, will be utilized to capture the problems associated with the inner-city poor.

There is some evidence that young African American college graduates are reaching an economic par with their white peers and that many African Americans in general have made significant gains in the past twenty-five years (R. Farley 1984; Payne 1998). It is not certain, however, that this situation is a permanent one. The strides since the 1960s may simply be the result of tremendous changes in the past two decades that will not be maintained in the future.

Many critics disagree with the idea that race is a declining force for African Americans, whether or not progress has been made (Thomas and Hughes 1986; Carnoy 1994; Hacker 1995; Cancio, Evans, and Maume 1996; Hughes and Thomas 1998; Pulera 2002). Doris Wilkinson (1995) believes that discrimination still determines the life chances of African Americans. The current racial dominance, she argues, is simply more sophisticated and subtle. Others point to inferior education in America's inner cities, a situation tied in part to racial discrimination. Still other critics point to housing discrimination and segregation as an enduring barrier to large-scale African American migration to the suburbs, where many jobs are located (Massey and Denton 1987; Massey 1990; Massey and Eggers 1990; Pattillo-McCoy 2000). According to the 2000 Census, U.S. inner cities are more segregated today than they were before segregation was outlawed in the 1960s (Ware and Allen 2002). Others point to the high rate of incarceration among black males, who are eight times more likely to enter prison than white males (Western and Pettit 2002). Finally, some argue that the concept of a black underclass applies to rural areas. According

to this viewpoint, the black underclass is more densely concentrated in rural parts of the South than in the inner cities of the North (O'Hare 1992a, 1992b; O'Hare and Curry-White 1992).

Latinos

Sociologists have not applied the term *internal colonialism* to Latinos in the United States. But according to Cobas, Duany, and Feagin (2009), Latinos have been "racialized." That is, the fact that Latinos comprise an ethnic group rather than a race has not stopped the white majority from labeling them a racial group. Latinos, because of this racialization, have become part of the racial hierarchy that places whites at the top and blacks at the bottom. As a consequence, Latino Americans experience some of the prejudice and discrimination so familiar to blacks. Racialization continues even though Latinos do not fit the scientific definition of a race and are too diverse to be placed in any single category.

Q **How diverse is the Latino population?** Latinos in the United States number almost 47 million (15.4 percent of the population). They are composed of many diverse ethnic minorities, including Mexican Americans, Puerto Ricans, Cubans, and increasing numbers of people from Central and South American countries (see Figure 9.5). High birth rates and immigration rates combine to make Latinos one of the most rapidly

FIGURE 9.5

Composition of the Latino Population in the United States, 2006

The Latino population will clearly become the largest minority in the United States during this century. This figure displays the diversity within that population itself. Do you see any reason why the composition of the Latino population will change over the next fifty years?

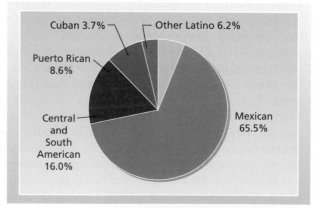

Source: U.S. Census Bureau, *Statistical Abstract of the United States: 2010* (129th ed.), Washington, DC, 2009. Calculated from Table 39, p. 43.

growing minorities in the United States. In fact, early in this century, Latinos will become America's largest ethnic minority. By 2050, the Latino population is projected to reach nearly 100 million, constituting 24 percent of the U.S. population. According to immigration figures, Latinos comprised nearly half of the more than 1 million people naturalized in 2008 (Gamboa 2009).

Just less than two-thirds of Latinos today are of Mexican descent; Puerto Ricans make up a little less than one-tenth the total Latino population. Most Puerto Ricans are concentrated in or near New York City, although greater geographical dispersion is occurring. Cubans make up the third most populous category of Latinos, with about 1 million people, most of whom are located in the Miami area (Suarez-Oroozco and Paez 2008).

Each group of Latinos came to the United States under different circumstances and retains a sense of its own identity and separateness. In addition, there are significant internal differences within individual Latino minorities (Delgado and Stefancic 1998; Suarez-Orozco and Paez 2002; Hernández-León 2008; Telles 2010). For example, the first large group of Cuban immigrants to enter the United States included successful middle- and upper-class people who fled from Cuba when Fidel Castro instituted a communist government there in the late 1950s. These Cuban Americans were substantially more educated than later Cuban immigrants were (Darder and Torres 1997; Stavans 2001).

Q What is the socioeconomic status of Latinos?
Latinos fall behind white Americans in formal education. In 2008, 62 percent of Latinos age twenty-five or over had completed high school, 87 percent of non-Latino whites had done so (see Table 9.2). Mexican Americans have the lowest levels of educational attainment, Cubans the highest. This is due to the migration pattern and the history of these peoples. Mexican immigrants came to the United States with little education; they were unable to speak English and were willing to accept the lowest-level jobs. Cubans, on the other hand, tended to be middle- and upper-middle-class immigrants who had been educated and economically successful in an economy similar to that of the United States (Valdivieso and Davis 1988; Delgado and Stefancic 1998; Lewis and Burd-Sharps 2010).

As shown in Figure 9.4, the average income for Latinos ($38,039) is higher than that of African Americans, but significantly lower than that of non-Latino whites ($54,461). Cubans are the most affluent Latinos, but even their median income is only about 75 percent that of whites. The poorest among the large Latino groups are the Puerto Ricans, whose income is about 51 percent that of whites. Approximately 25 percent of Latino families were living below the poverty level in 2009, compared with 9.4 percent of non-Latino whites (see Table 9.2). Puerto Rican families have the highest poverty rate, Cubans the lowest.

As one might expect from these income figures, Latinos tend to be concentrated in lower-paying and lower-status jobs as semiskilled workers and unskilled laborers (Lippard and Gallaher 2010). Farmwork is still common, especially among Mexican Americans. A study of hundreds of poor Latino immigrants in the South, many of whom are undocumented, describes

The meager wages earned by migrant farm laborers keep many children out of school where they could receive an education.

Sisse Brimberg/National Geographic Image Collection

an environment, which many liken to the Jim Crow era. According to the report, these Latino laborers "are routinely cheated out of their earnings and denied basic health and safety protections. They are regularly subjected to racial profiling and harassment by law enforcement. They are victimized by criminals who know they are reluctant to report attacks" ("Under Seige" 2009: 4). This treatment is justified by false propaganda spread by politicians and the media. Cuban men belong to the only Latino minority that approaches the occupational profile of Anglos (Moore and Pachon 1985; Trueba 1999).

Q How well are Latinos politically represented in the United States? Politically, Latinos are becoming a more nationally visible force shaping American politics (Rodriguez 1999; de La Isla 2003). There are now twenty-five Latinos in the U.S. House of Representatives—a tripling from 1981. Of these members of Congress, the majority are Mexican Americans. In 2002, Cuban American Robert Menendez, then a U.S. Representative, became the third highest-ranking Democrat, the highest post ever held in Congress by a Latino. At present, Robert Menendez and Mel Martinez are the only two U.S. Senators. Susana Martinez, the nation's first Latina governor, succeeded Latino Bill Richardson, governor of New Mexico in 2010. Brian Sandoval became Nevada's first Latino governor in 2010, and Marco Rubio won the U.S. Senate race in Florida (Lopez 2010). On the state and local levels, there were almost 6,000 elected Latino public officials. Latinos, of course, still have a long way to go to achieve political parity. In 2010, Latinos represented only 5 percent of the U.S. House of Representatives (twenty-five members, as just noted) and had only two U.S. Senators and one governor, despite constituting 15 percent of the population. Issues of education and immigration, as well as income and the quality of life, promise to keep Latinos politically active (Vazque and Torres 2002).

Native Americans

Q What is the composition of the Native American population? If a single word can be used to describe Native Americans, it is *diversity*: they are divided into 500 (or so) tribes and bands. This diversity is generally unrecognized because of stereotypes perpetuated by old Hollywood films and cheap paperback adventures of the frontier West of the United States. Most Americans don't know that the Navajo and Sioux are entirely different nations with different cultures, social structures, and problems. Tribal groups are as different from one another as they are from the dominant culture, or as different as Anglo Americans are from Italians or Brazilians. Today, Native Americans number around 4.5 million, three-fourths of whom do not live on reservations (Lobo and Peters 2001; U.S. Census Bureau 2007).

Q What has been the U.S. policy toward Native Americans? Ambivalence in government policy toward Native Americans was present from the founding. George Washington attempted to establish government policies promoting a just accommodation with the Native Americans. Only a few years later, Thomas Jefferson encouraged state governors and military commanders to sign supply contracts designed to impoverish the eastern tribes, thereby accelerating their elimination or removal to the western land newly acquired by the Louisiana Purchase (Ellis 2007). Over the years, the federal government has vacillated between a policy of paternalism (i.e., domination and care) and a policy of neglect. In the past, impoverishment, oppression, and deceit have typically, although not always, characterized relations between the government of the United States and various tribal governments (Marger 2008). Jonathan Turner sums up both past and present government policy toward Native Americans:

> The legacy of economic exploitation, especially the great "land grabs" by whites in this century, has forced Indians into urban areas because they can no longer support themselves on their depleted reservations. Yet the legacy of isolation on the reservation prevents many Indians from making the cultural and psychological transition to urban, industrial life. And the burden of change has been placed on the individual Indian, for white institutions—from factories to labor unions and welfare agencies—display little flexibility in adjusting to Indian patterns. The contemporary Indian is therefore faced with impoverishment no matter what course of action he chooses: to stay on the reservations results in poverty, but to leave the reservation and encounter the hostile white economic system in urban areas also results in poverty. (Turner 1976:185)

Both the paternalistic and neglectful approaches have left Native Americans outside the mainstream of social and economic opportunity (K. M. Dudley 1997; T. R. Johnson 2000).

Q What is the current situation of Native Americans? This neglectful approach is evident in the fact that the U.S. Census Bureau does not regularly report data for Native Americans. Other than a special study performed in the early 1990s, little data are available to describe their current status. Thus, although many of the descriptions that follow are dated, they are the most current available.

Abject poverty remains a major fact of life among Native Americans, especially for many who remain on reservations. Approximately 25 percent of the Native

American population live below the poverty line. The median income is less than $35,000 per year, and about 15 percent have an income greater than $50,000 per year, as compared with some 30 percent of the white population.

A gap in education also exists. Of Native Americans twenty-five years of age or older, 76 percent were high school graduates, compared with 87 percent of the non-Latino white U.S. population. Only 14 percent had completed four years or more of college, compared to almost 30 percent of the white population.

Native Americans have made only scant penetration into the upper levels of the occupational structure. Although some gains were made during the 1960s and 1970s, only 20 percent of all employed Native American men and women currently hold professional, managerial, or administrative positions. One-third are in blue-collar jobs (craftsworkers, supervisors, operatives, and nonfarm laborers). Currently, there is no Native American member of the U.S. Senate and only two in the House of Representatives.

Q Are conditions better or worse on the reservations? For the approximately one-fourth of Native Americans living on reservations, the situation is considerably worse than for those living off the reservations. One-half of those on reservations live below the poverty line (compared with 24 percent for the total Native American population). The rate of college education for Native Americans living on reservations is only about half that of those living off reservations.

A relatively recent development on reservations is the introduction of casino-type gaming establishments. Given the traditionally poor social and economic conditions on reservations, it is not surprising that many Native Americans embrace the gaming industry as a source of income. Because only a few of the tribes received the bulk of this money, its long-term effects remain to be seen.

Q Is there any momentum for change? Recently, the relationship between the U.S. government and various tribal governments has been changing. According to Vine Deloria and Clifford Lytle, government policy now grants tribes special political status. As a result, many tribes have proclaimed their nationhood, demanding some form of representation in the United Nations (Deloria and Lytle 1984; Wilkins 2001).

Deloria and Lytle cite several other possible directions for change. There is, first of all, the need for reform in tribal governments themselves to allow continuity with the past as well as movement into the future. There is also a need to establish a place for Native American cultures in the modern world. Another need is the creation of relationships with federal, state, and local governments based on mutual respect and parity.

Change will not come easily, given the tradition of inequality and discrimination that has characterized Native American life.

Asian Americans

Q Is the Asian American population increasing, decreasing, or stabilizing? Less than 15 million Asians live in the United States, comprising 4.5 percent of the total population. Asian Americans, a more recent fast-growing minority in the United States, increased in population by 49 percent between 1990 and 2000. In 1984 alone, more Asian immigrants entered the United States than during the entire thirty years between 1930 and 1960. In 1996, approximately 220,000 Asians were permitted to immigrate to the United States. The Asian American population is predicted to double by 2050.

Like Latinos, Asians come from many different national and ethnic backgrounds. The largest groups are from China, the Philippines, Japan, India, Korea, and Vietnam. If a success story can be told for any minority groups in America, those groups are the Chinese and Japanese Americans, particularly the latter (S. M. Lee 1998). Even for Chinese and Japanese Americans, however, the road has not been smooth (Kitano and Daniels 2005; Espiritu 1996; Gatewood and Zhou 2000; Wu and Song 2000; Kibria 2003).

Q How have Chinese Americans fared over the years? Heavy Chinese immigration to California in 1848 caused a furor. Americans feared that the presence of another race would encourage the institution of slavery, cause internal discord, and introduce incurable diseases. Although Chinese labor was accepted, even exploited, in the mining and railroad industries in the West, there was fear that the Chinese immigrants would migrate across the country. Added to this fear was the belief that the Chinese would deprive white men of work in the declining mining and railroad industries. These fears, combined with long-standing prejudice—that existed even prior to their immigration—resulted in an anti-Chinese movement that lasted into the first part of the twentieth century. During this period of more than fifty years, there was much violence against the Chinese, including riots, lynchings, and massacres. In the late 1880s, when a group of Chinese in Tonapah, Nevada, asked for time to collect their belongings before being expelled from the town, they were robbed and beaten; one of them died as a result (Lyman 1974).

Finally, the "Chinese question" became a political matter of high priority. Many state laws were created to restrict Chinese from holding jobs that could deprive whites of employment. The Chinese Exclusion Act passed by the U.S. Congress in 1882 prohibited, for a ten-year period, the entry of any skilled or unskilled

Chinese laborers or miners. Strict federal legislation against Chinese immigration continued to be passed until after 1940. During this period, Chinese Americans were driven into large urban ghettos known as Chinatowns, where they are still concentrated today.

Although Chinese Americans in many ways remain isolated from American life, their situation began to improve after 1940 (Loo 1998). American-born Chinese college graduates began to enter professional occupations, and Chinese American scholars and scientists began to make publicly recognized contributions to science and the arts. Their dedication to hard work and education and their contributions to American society have been widely recognized.

Q What has been the history of Japanese Americans? The earliest relations between Americans and Japanese were positive (unlike the Chinese experience). Early diplomatic relations were warm and cordial. Beginning in 1885, large numbers of Japanese men immigrated to the West Coast of the United States, but the timing for this massive immigration was wrong. The entry of the Japanese came on the heels of America's attempt to exclude Chinese immigrants. Although the Japanese suffered prejudice and discrimination during these early years, they moved from being laborers in certain industries (railroad, canning, logging, mining, meat packing) to being successful farmers (Kitano 2005).

When the Japanese began to compete with white farmers, however, anti-Japanese legislation was passed. The California Alien Land Bill of 1913, for example, permitted Japanese to lease farmland for a maximum of three years; it did not allow land they owned to be inherited by their families. In 1924, the U.S. Congress halted all Japanese immigration, and the 126,000 Japanese already in the United States became targets for prejudice, discrimination, stereotyping, and scapegoating. In 1942, Japan's attack on Pearl Harbor brought the United States into World War II. Wartime hysteria generated fear of a possible Japanese invasion. This situation led President Roosevelt to issue Executive Order 9066, which sent more than 110,000 of the 126,000 Japanese in America—two-thirds of whom were American citizens—into internment camps (euphemistically referred to as "relocation centers") away from the West Coast (Nagata 1993; Robinson 2001). It was argued that Japanese Americans posed a security threat during World War II. Even though the same argument could have been made about German and Italian immigrants—their countries were also at war with the United States—they were not relocated (U.S. Commission on Wartime Relocation and Internment of Civilians 1983). Eventually, in 1987, the Supreme Court ruled that the internment of Japanese Americans was "based upon racism rather than military necessity."

Despite their internment, Japanese Americans have not had to overcome the centuries of prejudice and discrimination endured by African Americans and Native Americans. Nevertheless, they have overcome great hardship and have become one of the most successful racial minorities in the United States. Through an emphasis on education and hard work, Japanese Americans have experienced some economic and occupational success (Montero 1981; Zweigenhaft and Domhoff 2006).

Q Why have Asian Americans been relatively successful? Asian Americans have been particularly successful at using the educational system for upward mobility (S. M. Lee 1998; Marger 2008). This fact is reflected in the academic achievement of school-age Asian Americans, whose average Scholastic Aptitude Test (SAT) scores are forty-five points higher than that of the general high school population. Furthermore, over 50 percent of Asian Americans have completed four years of college, compared with 30 percent of whites (see Table 9.2).

Some claim that Asian Americans are academically successful because they are innately more intelligent than other Americans. Most scholars believe that Asian academic excellence is due to culture, socialization, and influence of the family (Gibson and Ogbu 1991; Caplan, Choy, and Whitmore 1992). Most Asians see education as the key to success. Moreover, in the Confucian ethic (which is so much a part of the Chinese, Japanese, Vietnamese, and Korean cultures), academic excellence is the only way of repaying the debt owed to parents. According to school principal Norman Silber, "Our Asian kids have terrific motivation. They feel it is a disgrace to themselves and their families if they don't succeed" (McGrath 1983:52). In addition, Asian immigrants are accustomed to a tougher academic regimen. For example, the average number of school days in America is 180, but it is 225 days in Japan. Whatever the reasons, many Asian Americans are successful in part because of their willingness to work hard inside and outside of school (Barrett 1990).

The struggle, of course, is not over. Although Asian Americans have been more successful than other American racial minorities, they still feel the effects of prejudice and discrimination. In fact, the relative success of Asian Americans has hurt them in some ways. The stereotype of success has led the public to conclude erroneously that Asian Americans are all well educated, are over represented in higher-level occupations, and are making as much money as white Americans—maybe even more. The facts speak otherwise. Actually, vast socioeconomic differences exist among groups within Asian American communities. Popular emphasis on success has led to a disregard of those Asian Americans who have not done very well (Buckley 1991; Chou and Feagin 2008). Moreover, the accent on success camouflages the fact that even "successful" Asian Americans are worse off than are similarly educated and employed white Americans (Kim and Sakamoto 2010). Due to the stereotype of success, many experts believe that Asian Americans have been neglected and ignored by government agencies, educational institutions, private corporations, and other sectors of society (U.S. Commission on Civil Rights 1980; Qin 2008).

In 1996, Gary Locke became the first Asian American governor on the U.S. mainland (Puente 1996). In 2010, five Asian Americans held seats in the House of Representatives and two in the Senate.

White Ethnics

Q Who are white ethnics? White ethnics, sometimes referred to as *Euro-Americans*, first came to the United States as part of the second great wave of immigration that occurred during the nineteenth and early twentieth centuries (Marger 2012). White ethnics are largely the descendants of immigrants from eastern and southern European nations, particularly Italy and Poland, but they also include Greek, Irish, and Slavic peoples (Rubin 1994). Their descendants account for about 20 percent of the current U.S. population. Most white ethnics live in small communities surrounding large cities in the eastern half of the United States (Palen 2008).

Largely Catholic and Jewish, white ethnics stood out in traditionally Protestant America. The combination of being religiously different and poor led to considerable prejudice and discrimination against them. The Irish, for example, were stereotyped as dumb, illiterate, hard-drinking, and hot headed, a picture already painted of them by the English. Italian Americans were closely identified with criminal activity, the assumption being that all Italians are part of organized crime. These stereotypical depictions of Irish and Italian Americans, mythical though they are, endure today. Fortunately for white ethnics, the prejudice and discrimination directed at them was not as extreme as among African Americans, Latinos, Native Americans, and Asian Americans (Marger 2012). Still, during the 1960s, white ethnics gained the undeserved reputation of being conservative, racist, pro-war, and "hardhats."

Q Is this an authentic description? This portrait of white ethnics is not an accurate one. In fact, the evidence is just the contrary. Surveys conducted during the 1960s showed white ethnics to be more against the Vietnam War than white Anglo-Saxon Protestants were. Catholic blue-collar workers were found to be more liberal than either Protestant blue-collar workers or the country as a whole: They were more likely to favor a guaranteed annual wage, more likely to vote for an African American

presidential candidate, and more concerned about the environment. Finally, white ethnics, when compared with WASPs, were more likely to be sympathetic to government help for the poor and were more in favor of integration (Greeley 1974).

According to David Featherman (1971), white ethnics have not been long-term victims of occupational and income discrimination, although it existed from the start for certain minorities such as Italian Americans and Irish Americans. In fact, Andrew Greeley (1976) contended that white ethnics have ultimately been so successful that it is inaccurate to label them working class, as some have done. White ethnic success has not generally been recognized, according to Greeley, because America's elite is not willing to abandon the myth of the blue-collar ethnic.

Despite their relative success, many white ethnics have in recent years become notably conscious of their cultural and national origins (R. T. Schaeffer 2007) and have formed a white ethnic "roots" movement. The black power movement of the 1960s, when many African Americans expressed a desire to preserve their cultural and racial identities, influenced the new trend toward white ethnic identity. Many white ethnics believe that "white ethnicity is beautiful" and that the price of abandoning one's cultural and national roots is simply too high.

Lillian Rubin (1994) links the continuing accent on white ethnicity to the economic decline of white ethnics over the past twenty-five years and the rising demands of minorities. White ethnics, she contends, are attempting to establish a public identity that enables them to take a seat at the multicultural table.

On the other hand, some sociologists contend that white ethnicity is fading. According to Richard Alba (1985, 1990), the remaining relatively small number of white ethnics may not survive long. Ethnic identity, he argues, cannot be maintained in the face of disappearing ethnic families, neighborhoods, and communities. Mary Waters (1990) agrees with Alba's description and sees this as the "twilight" of white ethnics. In researching white ethnics, she found ethnicity not very important to those she studied. Although her respondents feel that being Italian, Polish, or Irish might make one distinctive in some way, ethnicity had little effect on where they live, whom they marry, or what they do for a living. Schaefer (2011) describes the remaining white ethnicity as "symbolic ethnicity." Symbolic ethnicity expresses itself in a preference for ethnic food, celebrations of long-standing ceremonial holidays, and so forth.

Jewish Americans

The United States and Israel are virtually tied for the largest Jewish population at 5.3 million each. Between them, they hold more than 80 percent of the world's Jews (*American Jewish Year Book* 2006). The majority of Jewish Americans are concentrated in several northeastern states, including New York, New Jersey, Massachusetts, and Connecticut, although a sizable number live in California, Florida, and Pennsylvania. The most recent immigrants—primarily well educated and highly skilled—come from Israel and the former Soviet Union. It is estimated that about 10 percent of all Jewish Americans have been in the United States less than ten years.

When Jews landed in New Amsterdam in 1654, all of the colonies discouraged them from immigrating. The colonies, in fact, legally prohibited them from holding political office or voting. Still, by the 1840s, Jews began to arrive in large numbers. Anti-Semitism reached its peak in the 1920s and 1930s, particularly among America's upper and upper middle classes. New York was often called "Jew York," and Jewish Americans were subjected to occupational and social segregation (F. J. Davis 1978; Parrillo 2005b).

Q **How do Jewish Americans demonstrate success, and how do they respond socially?** Throughout the first half of the twentieth century, Jewish Americans were excluded from top positions in most major industries, denied membership in social and recreational organizations, and subjected to quotas in colleges and universities. Although originally limited in their opportunities for movement into the top circles of the most economically powerful American corporate entities, Jewish Americans became one of the most successful ethnic groups ever to migrate to the United States. This is partly because Jewish men, particularly later immigrants, entered the country as skilled workers in a proportion far above the norm for immigrant groups. In addition to bringing skills necessary to fit into industrial society, they valued hard work, sacrifice, perseverance, family responsibility, and education. Although working at skilled blue-collar jobs, Jewish parents urged their children to pursue higher education, to become teachers, lawyers, and doctors. Consequently, Jewish Americans represent an above-average proportion of college graduates; they comprise 2 percent of the population, but account for 5 percent of college graduates. In 2010, there were fourteen Jews in the U.S. Senate, thirty Jews in the U.S. House of Representatives, and three Jews on the U.S. Supreme Court.

Because of the exclusion they experienced, Jewish Americans in the past have tended to remain socially isolated from the rest of American society. This is undergoing some change. Whereas 10 percent of Jewish Americans who married did so outside the faith in 1965, 52 percent now do so. And in 2000 Joe Lieberman became the first Jewish American to run, as a major political party candidate, for the vice presidency of the United States. Although the social isolation of Jewish Americans has diminished, some separation will probably continue for two basic reasons. First, anti-Semitic sentiment appears to be increasing again. And second, many Jewish Americans do not want to abandon their cultural roots.

Middle Easterners

Prior to September 11, Americans seldom seemed concerned about Middle Eastern immigrants. After the attacks on the World Trade Center and the Pentagon, however, interest in these immigrants (old and new) became intense.

Q **Who are Middle Easterners?** Understandable emotions following September 11 led to confusion about Middle Easterners. For starters, Arabs and Muslims are thought by most Americans to be synonymous, an assumption that is false. Arabs are people from the Middle East (Pakistan, Bangladesh, Afghanistan, Turkey, the Levant, the Arabian peninsula) and Arab North Africa. Muslims are followers of Islam. Arabs encompass diverse, ethnic groups. Muslims are religious followers of Mohammed. Not all Arabs are Muslims and not all Muslims are Arabs, particularly in the United States. Although the Mideast is nearly all Muslim (98 percent), only about 75 percent of the Middle Eastern immigrants in the United States are Muslims, up from 15 percent in 1970.

Q **How many Middle Easterners are in the United States?** One of the most rapidly growing immigrant groups in America, Middle Easterners have increased their population from 200,000 in 1970 to over 1.5 million today. This does not include some 1 million U.S.-born children (under age eighteen) who have at least one parent born in the Middle East. Nor does it include illegal Middle Easterners residing in the United States, a number that increases the total population by about 10 percent. Over 80 percent of Middle Eastern Americans are citizens; over 60 percent were born in the United States.

Q **What is the socioeconomic status of Middle Easterners in the United States?** Education level is important because it is the best single predictor of the degree of success in the labor market. Immigrants from the Middle East are actually the second most highly educated immigrant group, following the Asians. About half of them are college graduates and over 20 percent hold graduate or professional degrees.

Considering their education level, the economic success of Middle Eastern immigrants should not be surprising. Given the same amount of education, Middle Eastern men earn on a par with immigrants in general.

And their rate of self-employment exceeds that of the native born and other immigrant groups.

Not everything is positive for Middle Easterners in the United States. Middle Eastern immigrants lag behind natives in home ownership. Somewhat surprisingly, Middle Eastern immigrants have a higher poverty rate and use welfare more often than natives. Thus, while most Middle Eastern immigrants experience economic success in this country, a significant portion is not as fortunate. In addition, due to September 11, Middle Eastern immigrants are now victims of stereotyping.

Q **Where is the evidence for the stereotyping of Middle Easterners?** Since most Americans assume a correspondence between being Arab and being Muslim, the increase in stereotyping of *all* Middle Easterners can be inferred from research on American attitudes toward Muslims. Research does, in fact, reveal prejudice among Americans with respect to Muslims (Marvasti et al. 2004; Saad 2006; "Boorstein 2010; "In U.S., Religious Prejudice Stronger Against Muslims" 2010). Fifty-three percent of Americans view Islam unfavorably, and more than four in ten Americans (43 percent) say they are at least "a little" prejudiced against Muslims, more than twice the percentage that admit to prejudice against Jews (15 percent), Christians (18 percent), or Buddhists (14 percent). Since Americans do not like to admit to prejudice against other groups, these figures surely underestimate the extent and degree of negative attitudes toward Muslims. As Figure 9.6 indicates, U.S. tolerance for Muslims and immigrants in America has declined.

Bias against Middle Easterners in general is also reflected in racial profiling. The U.S. Justice Department defines **racial profiling** as police action based on personal characteristics (race, religion, ethnicity, national origin) rather than on personal behavior (Schaefer 2011). The assumption of guilt based on appearance is obvious as well as dangerous, and some attitudes toward the potential treatment of Muslims are not encouraging. Four in ten Americans advocate more stringent security measures for Muslims than for other U.S. citizens. To help prevent terrorism, 43 percent of Americans favor requiring Muslims (including those who are U.S. citizens) to present a special ID card on demand, and to undergo special, more intensive, security procedures before boarding airplanes in the United States (Saad 2006).

Specific cases also reveal deep suspicion of Muslims among at least a portion of Americans. Consider the heat generated by the proposal to build a mosque a few blocks from Ground Zero, the site of the 9/11 terrorist attacks in New York City. Or think about the feelings of suspicion among Oklahomans who, in 2010, approved a referendum barring Shari law, a strict code of living in Islam, in the state (Dionne and Glaston 2010).

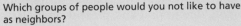

FIGURE 9.6

Limits of Social Tolerance

This figure displays changes in levels of tolerance (as measured by finding a group acceptable as a neighbor) for Muslims, immigrants, and gays. Describe the patterns of change between 1990 and 2006.

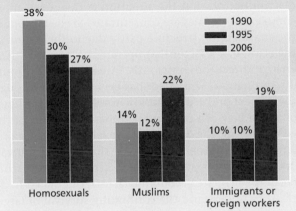

Source: Gallup Organization, nationally representative telephone survey of adults in the United States, adapted from Sarah Lageson and Shannon Golden, "The Limits of Tolerance" *Contexts 9(2)* (Spring 2010): p. 10.

These actions alarm many America Muslims and non-Muslims alike, as does the stabbing of a Manhattan cab driver by Michael Enright, a man who was carrying a diary full of anti-Muslim rantings.

Gays and Lesbians

Gays and lesbians are one of America's minorities, subject to the same vicious prejudice and discrimination. Until 2010, the military barred them from serving if they were open about their sexual orientation: they remain targets of sodomy laws; and in most states, they cannot marry a same-sex partner. They are a unique minority because of their invisibility. The idea that gays and lesbians are identifiable by their behavior or mode of dress is a myth. Since the majority of gays and lesbians can hide their minority status, many do so, avoiding the prejudice and discrimination awaiting them if they "come out." Their invisibility has precluded the systematic application of institutionalized discrimination visited on more visible minorities such as blacks, Latinos, Asians, and Native Americans. The repeal of the "Don't Ask, Don't Tell" law in 2010 gives gays and lesbians some additional legal legitimization. They hope this hastens the disappearance of other forms of institutionalized discrimination against them at a more rapid pace than occurred for African Americans, who, for example, gained full civil rights only in the 1960s after hundreds of years of slavery and the Jim Crow laws that followed.

Beyond Direct Institutionalized Discrimination

The socioeconomic gap between many minorities in the United States and the general white population is largely due to past and present prejudice and discrimination. But the situation is now even more complex. Minorities are concentrated at the bottom of the stratification structure partly due to the nature of the economy, a factor that operates beyond the influence of direct, or consciously intended, institutional discrimination. This factor has been explored through the context of the **dual labor market**—the existence of a split between core and peripheral segments of the economy and the division of the labor force into preferred and marginalized workers (Hodson and Sullivan 2008). This perspective, which attributes persisting racial inequality to economic factors, originated in an effort to understand the continuing survival of large-scale racial (and gender) inequalities in the face of programs designed to overcome such disparities (Hodson and Kaufman 1982).

Q **What is the dual labor market theory?** Traditionally, it has been assumed that only one labor market existed in which all workers competed for jobs. It was also assumed that occupational advancement was based on hard work, education, and training. These

assumptions have been successfully challenged by advocates of conflict theory. The existence of a dual labor market means that the rewards for hard work, education, and training vary in different segments of the labor market. Workers involved in the core sector of the labor market—durable manufacturing and petroleum industries, for example—enjoy high wages, good opportunities for advancement, and job security. Those involved in the peripheral sector, including such industries as textile manufacturing and retail trades, are employed in low-paying jobs with little hope for advancement. African Americans and other minority peoples tend to be trapped in these secondary labor markets and lack the resources to alter their situation. Thus, it is concluded, historical practices of racial and ethnic discrimination now interact with contemporary economic processes to lock a significant and growing number of minority peoples out of the core economy, thereby reducing the likelihood of any improvement in their life chances and lifestyles (Bonacich 1976; Szymanski 1976; Cummings 1980; Lord and Falk 1982).

Q **How does indirect institutionalized discrimination operate in the dual labor market?** Minority groups, who are overrepresented in the peripheral sector of the American economy and consequently tend to hold low-skill, low-paying jobs, are subjected to indirect institutionalized discrimination. A long-standing division of labor automatically reduces minority access to jobs in the core sector despite their education and training. In addition, minority members are disproportionately

CHECK YOURSELF **9.3** R2

Institutionalized Discrimination

1. _____ discrimination refers to unintentional organizational or community actions that negatively affect a racial or ethnic minority.
2. The attitudes and practices associated with _____ in the American slave system help account for the long-term prejudice and discrimination experienced by African Americans.
3. The evidence clearly shows that race is declining in importance in America. T or F?
4. Which of the following Latino ethnic minorities is in the best socioeconomic condition?
   a. Puerto Ricans
   b. Cubans
   c. Mexican Americans
5. The federal government's policy toward Native Americans has vacillated between _____ and almost total neglect.
6. Contrary to popular opinion, white ethnics in the United States are politically more liberal than Protestant blue-collar workers. T or F?
7. Anti-Semitism in America during the 1920s and 1930s was most prevalent among the _____ and upper middle classes.
8. Police actions based on personal characteristics rather than on personal behavior are called _____.
9. Within the dual labor market, minorities tend to be disproportionately trapped in the _____ sector.

Answers: 1. Indirect institutionalized; 2. manumission; 3. F; 4. b; 5. paternalism; 6. T; 7. upper; 8. racial profiling; 9. secondary or peripheral

shut out of the more desirable jobs and out of the education and training needed to move into core sector jobs on the grounds that they actually prefer, and are better suited to, the marginal jobs they hold (Hodson and Sullivan 2008).

Global and U.S. Ethnic Diversity ▨

Global Ethnic Diversity

Establishing the number of different societies, cultures, and ethnic groups is difficult because there is such a wide variety (see "Think Globally 9.1"). Moreover, differences among them are not always clear because contact over the years leaves them intermingled. This process continues through ongoing immigration.

Normally, immigration is from developing countries to more developed countries, with people seeking better jobs, wages, and living conditions. But immigration also occurs for religious, ethnic, or political reasons. There are now over 15 million people who are refugees in countries other than their own due to conflict or persecution ("The Millennium Development Goals Report 2010"). As a result, more people are becoming **transnationals**, immigrants who maintain ties in more than one country. Dominican Republic immigrants to the United States, for example, consider themselves Americans without severing relationships in their home country (Schaefer 2011).

Q Is there an obvious trend in global immigration? As globalization inexorably leads to increased cross-national immigration, it is having a dual effect. Some people in poorer countries are attracted ("pulled") to more prosperous countries. At the same time, people are being "pushed" from countries undergoing economic, political, and social damage due to exploitation by richer countries. Consequently foreign-born populations are rising in both industrialized and developing countries. Many countries in Western Europe have seen an increasing influx of migrants from both former colonies in Asia and African (to the Netherlands) and Eastern Europe (to Ireland). Several developing countries such as Costa Rica are a magnet for both refugees fleeing political upheaval in neighboring countries and those looking for work. Botswana is drawing political refugees and economic migrants from southern African neighbors (*World Population Data Sheet* 2007).

As a product of all this population movement, it is estimated that there are now almost 200 million immigrants worldwide, double the number in 1960. Between 1990 and 2005, there were 36 million immigrants, an average of 2.4 million migrants annually. Almost all of these immigrants (33 million) moved to industrialized countries (Shah 2008).

Q What are the consequences of increased immigration? The effects of this immigration are felt most in the United States and Western Europe because they attract the most immigrants. On the plus side, immigration helps employers because immigrants will often do work avoided by the native population, and they will work longer for less pay. If accepted by their new country, immigrants can promote increased tolerance and understanding of diversity. Educated immigrants provide a talent pool benefiting their new country. On the negative side, employers exploit immigrants because they work more cheaply at unpleasant jobs. At the same time, the poorer countries from which many immigrants come experience a talent pool drain, further hindering their own progress.

There are also negative consequences for the host country. For one thing, immigration may bring increased criminal activity. For another, immigrant minorities can create conflict within a society. For example, the presence of significant minorities contributed to the disintegration of the Soviet Union. Moreover, the new states formed by the breakup contain minority populations that jeopardize their economic growth and political stability (Allen and Sutton 2011). This ethnic conflict sometimes leads to the resurgence of tribalism when minorities resort to violence to assert their independence from the larger society. A good example is the division of Yugoslavia into ethnically "purified" areas. Tribalism is also credited with sparking genocidal conflicts in African countries such as Somalia, Congo, and Rwanda (Pieterse 2007).

Reactions to ethnic minorities may also lead to civil rights issues. Slaughtered Rwandans were clearly deprived of their civil rights. Critics contend that America's "war on terror" has resulted in numerous civil rights violations. In their view, the use of "extraordinary measures" to obtain information from enemy combatants is actually torture in violation of the Geneva Conventions. They offer detention of prisoners without due legal process as another violation of civil rights. The debate about civil rights in the context of ethnic diversity promises to not end soon (Kymlicka 2007; Shah 2010).

Immigration can become a political issue in times of economic stress, as it is in the United States today. This hostility is directed at "illegal aliens" (itself a pejorative term) who are accused of taking jobs from citizens and of receiving educational and health-care benefits they don't deserve. Of course, this scapegoating of unauthorized immigrants by native citizens may also be directed at foreign-born American citizens, an important point covered in the next section.

Ethnic diversity may lead to conflict, as in the case of Hutu rebels beating and raping Congolese women.

Marc Hofer/AFP/Getty Images

Diversity in the United States

When people of the world speak of ethnic diversity, they could be thinking about the United States. America's reputation as the most ethnically diverse country is well deserved. In fact, except for Native Americans and some Mexican Americans, all Americans can trace their ancestry to immigrants. From the 1600s on, immigrants have continuously flowed into the Unites States (Marger 2012). Although the period between the 1600s and 1820 saw fairly low levels of immigration large, successive waves of immigrants followed thereafter. The first great wave of immigrants came between 1820 and 1880. The largest contingents were from Germany and Ireland, though many came from other Western European countries, China, Canada, and Mexico. The second wave, between the early 1880s and 1914, was heavily Catholic and Jewish. They were poorer people than those in the first wave, and they were largely European. The third wave, beginning in 1960, primarily involved immigrants from Asia, Latin America, and the Caribbean. Of course, many came from the Middle East.

Q How many foreign-born people are now in the United States? The foreign-born population of the United States has steadily risen over the past forty years. Between 1970 and 2009, the number of resident foreign-born increased from 9.6 million (4.7 percent of the total population) to 38.5 million (12.5 percent). Even more remarkable is the change in countries of origin. In 1960, three-fourths of the foreign-born were from European countries. Today, over half (53 percent) are from Latin America (see Figure 9.7). Another 28 percent originate from Asia, while Europeans represent only 13

percent. Mexico is the largest single source of foreign-born today (30 percent).

The United States is currently moving from a predominately white population of Western origin to a society comprised of large white and non-white racial and ethnic minorities from non-European countries. Whereas the total population of the United

FIGURE 9.7

Percentage of Total Populations by Nativity and Foreign-Born Populations by Region of Birth: 2009

This figure shows the percentage of Americans who are native born and foreign born. It also displays the areas from which the foreign born come to the United States. What surprises you about these figures? Explain.

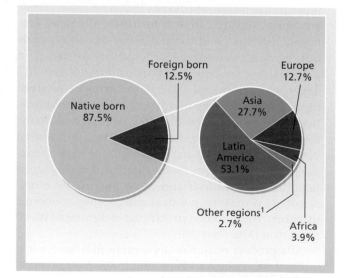

Native born 87.5%

Foreign born 12.5%

Europe 12.7%

Asia 27.7%

Latin America 53.1%

Other regions[1] 2.7%

Africa 3.9%

[1]Other regions include Oceania and Northern America.
Source: U.S. Census Bureau, *American Community Survey*, 2009.

States is projected to increase by 23 percent by 2025, the minority population is expected to expand by 64 percent. This new form of diversity is one of the most important developments in the United States.

Q What is the minorities' share of the U.S. population? In 2008, the combined number of African Americans, Latinos, Asian Americans, and Native Americans exceeded 100 million, up from just fewer than 10 million in 1900 and 21 million in 1960. If these minority groups resided in a separate country, they would be the twelfth most populous nation in the world. Great Britain, France, Italy, and Spain would all be smaller. There are now more minority members than there were people in the United States in 1910 (Martin and Midgley 2006; U.S. Census Bureau, 2009).

In addition to immigration, the large number of births among Asian, Black, and Latino women is fueling this trend. Minority births now constitute 18 percent of all births in the United States, and are expected to surpass non-Latino white births by 2012 (Roberts 2010). For most of the twentieth century, America's minority population constituted a relatively constant percentage of the total population—the share of the population represented by minorities increased from 13.1 to only 14.9 percent between 1900 and 1960. Since then, however, the minority proportion of the population has increased to about 30 percent and is now expected to constitute a near majority of all Americans by 2050, possibly by 2040 if the rate of immigration increases and the birth rates of minorities remain high.

Q What growth can Americans anticipate for minority groups in the future? While the predominant minority in the United States for most of the twentieth century was African American, Latinos have now surpassed them. Further change in the relative growth rate of minorities is expected by 2050. Although the African American population is expected to expand by about 60 percent, Latinos are projected to increase by almost 200 percent, and Asian Americans will mushroom by over 240 percent. (Figure 9.8 shows changes in the relative percentages minorities will represent by 2050.)

These changes in the relative size, proportion, and diversity of the minority population promise to alter the nature of American society. Social, political, and economic reconsideration of racial and ethnic minorities is predictable. In the meantime, a different kind of reconsideration is already occurring involving legal and unauthorized immigrants.

Q What sort of reconsideration is occurring? Pressure for reconsideration is coming especially from the growth in legal foreign-born workers and unauthorized immigrants. It is coming in the form of defensiveness and

FIGURE 9.8

The U.S. Population by Race and Ethnicity, 2008 and 2050

The racial and ethnic composition is expected to look very different by 2050. Discuss some social consequences of this changing composition.

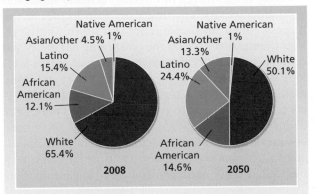

Note: Percentages do not total 100% due to rounding. The White, African American, and Asian/other categories exclude Latinos, who may be of any race.
Source: U.S. Bureau of the Census 2004; Philip Martin and Elizabeth Midgley, "Immigration: Shaping and Reshaping America," *Population Bulletin* 61 (December 2006): 16–17, U.S. Census Bureau, *Statistical Abstract of the United States: 2010* (129th ed.) Washington, DC, 2009, Table 10, p. 14.

anger (Morin 2009). An extreme example is the resurgence of militia groups whose history is rooted in race hate. Not only has a black man been elected leader of the free world, but militia groups are also disturbed about the growing number of legal and unauthorized immigrants as well as the increasing proportion of non-whites in the population.

Q What are the reactions to legal immigrants? The negative reaction to the increasing number of legal immigrants entering the U.S. labor force is not limited to extremist groups. It appears across a wide spectrum of American society. Americans at the lower end of the occupational structure consider unskilled immigrants to be competitors in the job market, competitors who undercut them by working for lower wages and longer hours. This defensiveness is reinforced when they see evidence of foreign-born workers recovering from the recession faster than they are (Kochlar 2010). In contrast, Americans at the upper end of the occupations structure welcome immigrants who help them by working more cheaply in factories, fields, and restaurants. However, these same people are threatened by educated immigrants who come to the labor market with credentials and abilities to perform professional and managerial jobs (Marger 2012). For example, they point to the growing proportion of health-care workers (doctors and nurses) who are immigrants.

Q Is the fear of economic competition from legal immigrants justified? While economists emphasize the general economic benefits of immigration, threatened Americans understandably view the matter from a more personal point of view. Still, this fear of immigrant competition appears to be overblown. According to recent research, the arrival of immigrants actually stimulates economic activity, creating a net gain in jobs in the process. American corporations can see this in the effects immigrants have on the off shoring of jobs. When companies relocate offshore, they remove higher-level jobs such as managers and technical workers, along with low-wage jobs. A bigger pool of immigrant workers reduces the need to hire cheaper labor out of the country in the first place. Consequently, offshoring declines in an economic sector as the relevant immigrant labor pool expands. Because more jobs remain in the United States, immigrants are in competition more with offshore workers than with American workers (Cowen 2010). In addition to providing employers a new labor pool that reduces offshoring, immigrants contribute as new consumers of products and additional contributors of taxes to governments.

Q What about the antipathy toward unauthorized immigrants? Today, there are just over 11 million unauthorized immigrants in the United States, 8 million of whom are in the nation's workforce (Passel and Cohn 2011). Unauthorized immigrants have recently become even more of a political hot button than legal immigrants. Americans of all class levels are concerned that unauthorized immigrants (more than half of which are Mexican) are costing them money by using taxpayer-supported services such as hospitals, schools, and public assistance programs. Most of the heat has come from border states like Arizona, California, and Texas, states that have

---

THINK GLOBALLY 9.1

Ethnic Diversity

The degree of worldwide ethnic diversity is displayed in this map. The color code indicates the proportion of a national population represented by members of an ethnic, racial, or national minority.

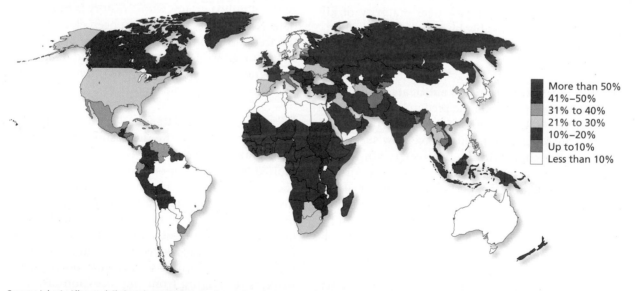

Legend:
- More than 50%
- 41%–50%
- 31% to 40%
- 21% to 30%
- 10%–20%
- Up to 10%
- Less than 10%

Source: John L. Allen and Christopher J. Sutton, *Student Atlas of World Politics, 9th ed.* (p. 42). Copyright © 2011 by The McGraw-Hill Companies. Reproduced by permission of McGraw-Hill Contemporary Learning Series.

Interpret the Map

1. Were you surprised by the comparative degree of ethnic diversity between any particular countries? Describe some differences between your expectations regarding national ethnic diversity and the actual degree of diversity.

2. Write a paragraph detailing your conclusions regarding the extent of ethnic diversity across the globe.

3. Do you believe that the extent of ethnic diversity will increase or decrease during the twenty-first century? Explain your position.

CHECK YOURSELF 9.4 R2

Global and U.S. Ethnic Diversity

1. Immigrants who maintain ties in more than one country are called _____.
2. The number of immigrants worldwide _____ between 1990 and 2005.
3. Which of the following is *not* discussed as a consequence of global immigration?
   a. fear of economic competition
   b. anchor babies
   c. increased conflict
   d. civil rights issues
   e. tribalism
4. Rank order (1–4) the following minority groups to indicate their relative proportion of the total American minority population projected for 2050.
   a. _____ Asian Americans
   b. _____ Native Americans
   c. _____ Latinos
   d. _____ African Americans
5. About _____ percent of all Americans are expected to be members of minority groups by 2050.
6. Economists are beginning to agree with those who believe illegal immigrants to be a serious economic threat. T or F?

Answers: 1. transnationals; 2. doubled; 3. b; 4. a. (3), b (4), c (1), d (2); 5. 50; 6. F

large numbers of Mexican immigrants. California, for example, passed a referendum denying unauthorized immigrants access to public services. Anger only increased when a federal court ruled the new law unconstitutional (Marger 2012). In 2010, Arizona enacted the most restrictive immigration law in America, making failure to carry immigration documents a crime and giving police the right to detain anyone suspected of being undocumented (Archibald 2010; Kornblut and Hsu 2010).

Q Is there an economic basis for the hostility toward unauthorized immigrants? Many Americans believe that unauthorized immigrants do not pay taxes and place additional strain on already overburdened public services.

It appears that unauthorized immigrants do pay an average of $80 less annually than native-born Americans. This is offset, however, by the fact that they use fewer public services, which more than compensates for the lost tax revenue (Lewis and Burd-Sharps 2010).

On to Chapter 10

Over the last two chapters we have covered various aspects of inequality, including inequality among racial and ethnic minorities in this chapter. The part of the text focusing on inequality will end after Chapter 10 on gender inequality.

S INTEGRATED GOALS AND SUMMARY

1. **Distinguish among the concepts of minority, race, and ethnicity.**
   - A minority consists of more than small numbers. A minority possesses some distinctive physical or cultural characteristics, is dominated by the majority, and is denied equal treatment. Minorities also have a sense of collective identity, tend to marry within their own kind, and inherit their minority status at birth.
   - A race is a category of people who share certain biologically inherited physical features. Racists use these physical characteristics as an index of a race's superiority or inferiority. Despite the lack of scientific support for this viewpoint, prejudice and discrimination are often justified by alleged differences in intelligence and ability.
   - Ethnic minorities have distinct subcultures. Unique cultural characteristics of ethnic minorities are used by the majority as a justification for prejudice and discrimination.
2. **Describe patterns of racial and ethnic relations.**
   - Patterns of racial and ethnic relations assume two general forms: assimilation and conflict. Patterns of assimilation include Anglo-conformity, melting pot, and cultural pluralism. Genocide, population transfer, and subjugation are the major patterns of conflict.
3. **Differentiate prejudice from discrimination.**
   - Prejudice—negative attitudes toward some minority—is difficult to change because prejudiced individuals reject information that contradicts their existing

attitudes. Whereas *prejudice* refers to attitudes, *discrimination* refers to behavior. When members of a minority are denied equal treatment, they are being discriminated against. Although prejudice usually leads to discrimination, there are exceptions. In fact, in some instances, discrimination against a minority may lead to the creation of prejudiced attitudes, usually embodied in racial or ethnic stereotypes.

4. **Illustrate the different views of prejudice and discrimination taken by functionalists, conflict theorists, and symbolic interactionists.**
   • Many attempts have been made to explain the existence of prejudice and discrimination. Some psychologists attribute prejudice and discrimination to deep-seated frustration. Hostility and frustration are said to be released on scapegoats who had nothing to do with causing their development in the first place. Other psychologists point to the existence of a personality type—the authoritarian personality—that tends to be very prejudiced against those thought to be inferior. Although functionalism emphasizes the negative consequences of prejudice and discrimination, it also points to some benefits. According to conflict theory, prejudice and discrimination are used by the majority as weapons of power to dominate subordinate minorities. Symbolic interactionism concentrates on the learning of prejudice and discrimination through socialization.

5. **Describe, relative to the white majority, the condition of minorities in the United States.**
   • Virtually all minorities have felt the consequences of institutionalized discrimination. Institutionalized discrimination may be direct, as in segregation laws; or it may be indirect, as in the form of seniority systems that prevent upward mobility of newly hired minorities.

   • Institutionalized discrimination has been harmful to America's minorities. As a result, African Americans, Native Americans, Latinos, some Asian Americans and Middle Easterners, and white ethnics lag behind the white majority occupationally, economically, and educationally. Successful cases do exist, but the gains of minorities remain fragile.
   • Some scholars contend that the disadvantages that minorities are currently experiencing are due to economic as well as social factors. Because of the dual labor market, minorities are trapped in the peripheral labor market, which offers low-paying, dead-end jobs.

6. **Describe the increasing global and domestic ethnic diversity.**
   • Racial and ethnic diversity is increasing across the globe. As a result, the number of immigrants has doubled over the last 20 years. By the middle of the twenty-first century, one-half of the entire American population will be minority group members. There are differential growth rates among minorities. African Americans, traditionally the predominant minority in the United States, have been surpassed by Latinos.

7. **Discuss the consequences of global and domestic ethnic diversity.**
   • The consequences of global immigration are many and varied. Immigrants can contribute economically and promote understanding of diversity. Negative effects appear in the draining of talent in the abandoned countries, increasing conflict, and emerging civil rights issues. Issues of growing diversity in the United States revolve around a perceived economic threat from legal and illegal immigrants. The negative reaction on the part of many native-born Americans to immigrants, both legal and unauthorized, appears to be exaggerated, while the benefits of immigration are overlooked.

CONCEPT REVIEW

Match the following concepts with the definitions listed below them.

____ a. ethnic minority ____ e. minority ____ i. self-fulfilling prophecy
____ b. underclass ____ f. de facto subjugation ____ j. discrimination
____ c. transnationals ____ g. assimilation ____ k. ideology
____ d. race ____ h. racial profiling

1. the integration of a racial or ethnic minority into a society
2. subjugation based on common, everyday social practices
3. unequal treatment of individuals based on their minority membership
4. a people who are socially identified and set apart by others and themselves on the basis of their unique cultural or nationality characteristics
5. a set of ideas used to justify and defend the interests and actions of those in power in a society
6. police action based on personal characteristics rather than on personal behavior
7. a people who possess some distinctive physical or cultural characteristics, are dominated by the majority, and are denied equal treatment

8. a distinct category of people who are alleged to share certain biologically inherited physical characteristics
9. when an expectation leads to behavior that causes the expectation to become a reality

10. those in poverty who are continuously unemployed or underemployed because of the absence of job opportunities and/or required job skills.
11. immigrants who maintain ties in more than one country.

CHECK YOURSELF REVIEW

1. The evidence clearly shows that race is declining in importance in America. T or F?
2. Contrary to popular opinion, white ethnics in the United States are politically more liberal than Protestant blue-collar workers. T or F?
3. According to Gordon Allport, children learning prejudice move from a pregeneralized learning period to a stage of total _____.
4. The attitudes and practices associated with _____ in the American slave system help account for the long-term prejudice and discrimination experienced by African Americans.
5. Almost _____ percent of all Americans will be members of minority groups in 2050.

6. Which of the following is *not* always a characteristic of a minority?
   a. distinctive physical or cultural characteristics
   b. smaller in number than the majority
   c. dominated by the majority
   d. denied equal treatment
   e. a sense of collective identity
7. Rank order (1–4) the following minority groups to indicate their relative proportion of the total American minority population projected for 2050.
   ____ a. Asian Americans
   ____ b. Native Americans
   ____ c. Latinos
   ____ d. African Americans

GRAPHIC REVIEW

Some attitudes of Americans toward immigrant minorities are summarized in Figure 9.1.

1. If you had to write a one-sentence summary of Figure 9.1 for the CNN evening news, what would you say?

2. What do the data in Figure 9.1 suggest regarding the future of ethnic relations in the United States?

CRITICAL-THINKING QUESTIONS

1. Evaluate the definition of minority used by sociologists.

2. Do you think that both the pattern of assimilation and the pattern of conflict accurately describe the state of racial relations between blacks and whites in America today? State your position using terms and evidence from the text.

3. Compare and contrast the functionalist and conflict perspectives on prejudice and discrimination. Is one a better

explanation than the other? Are they complementary? Defend your conclusion.

4. Taking into account the past and present situations of African Americans in the United States, construct a line of argument for or against affirmative action. Be specific.

ANSWER KEY

Concept Review

a. 4
b. 10
c. 11
d. 8
e. 7
f. 2
g. 1
h. 6
i. 9
j. 3
k. 5

Check Yourself Review

1. F
2. T
3. rejection
4. manumission
5. 50
6. b
7. a. 3
   b. 4
   c. 1
   d. 2

Inequalities of Gender 10

Laurence Mouton/Getty Images

S OUTLINE

S GOALS

- Distinguish among the concepts of sex, gender, and gender identity.
- Demonstrate the relative contributions of biology and culture to gender formation.
- Outline the perspectives of gender expressed by functionalists, conflict theorists, and symbolic interactionists.
- State the relationship between sex stereotypical and gender values.

- Describe the position of women in the United States with respect to work, law, and politics.
- Report the state of global gender inequality.
- Discuss factors promoting resistance to change in traditional gender roles as well as factors promoting change in gender roles in the United States.
- Describe the future of gender roles.

275

How well does the United States compare with other industrialized countries on gender income equality? Even if Americans recognize that women are not paid on a par with men, most believe that at the very least the United States is making more progress than other countries. On the contrary, among modern countries, America is surprisingly near the bottom in male–female income parity. Only Luxembourg and Japan have wider gender gaps than the United States. Whereas French women in manufacturing jobs, for example, earn 93 percent of the wages paid men, women in the United States earn only 80 percent of the wages paid men—for the same work.

Throughout history, men have predominantly performed the social, political, and economic functions outside the home, while women have assumed responsibility for child-care and household tasks. Although this division of labor does not necessarily imply any status difference between the sexes, in practice it certainly has this effect. The female domestic tasks are undervalued in industrial societies, where women—thought to be dependent, passive, and deferring—have usually been considered subordinate to independent, aggressive, and strong men. Historically, the division of labor based on sex has almost always led to gender inequality. And this chapter will demonstrate other disadvantages attached to the female gender role as well. But first let's delve into the cultural and social underpinnings of gender roles.

Antecedents of Gender R1

In the past, people believed that anatomy was destiny. Behavioral differences between men and women were popularly attributed to **sex**—the biological distinction between male and female. Males were assumed to be naturally more aggressive than women and to be built for providing and protecting. Thought of as being naturally more passive, females were believed to be designed for domestic work (Valian 1999). This way of thinking is called **biological determinism**—the attribution of behavioral differences to inherited physical characteristics. If this popular conception were true, all men and all women in all societies would behave uniformly in their unique biologically determined ways because of inborn biological forces beyond their control.

As will be shown, biological determinism lacks scientific validation. Although biology may create some behavioral tendencies in the sexes, such tendencies are so weak that they are easily overridden by cultural and social influences (Ridley 1996; Sapolsky 1997; Bearman and Bruchner 2002; Powell and Graves 2002). Therefore, **gender**—the expectations and behaviors associated with a sex category within a society—is acquired through socialization (Jackson and Scott 2001).

From the moment of birth, males and females are treated differently. Parents stress the characteristics and behavior that fit the society's image of the ideal male or female, including modes of dress, ways of walking and talking, play activities, and life aspirations. In response, girls and boys gradually conform to these definitions and learn to behave as expected. From this process comes **gender identity**—an awareness of being masculine or feminine, based on culture. Margaret Andersen succinctly captures the difference between sex and gender:

> Sociologists use the term gender to refer specifically to the social and cultural patterns that we associate with women and men in society. Sex refers to the biological identity and is meant to signify the fact that one is either male or female. . . . Gender is a social, not a biological, concept. Simply put, being "female" and "male" are biological facts; being a woman or a man is a social and cultural process— one that is constructed through the whole array of social, political, economic, and cultural experiences in a given society. (Andersen 2010:30)

Controversy over explanations for gender differences persists; the nature (biology) versus nurture (socialization) distinction remains at the heart of the debate (J. Q. Wilson 1993; Canary et al. 1998). All the same, a notable difference exists today: Research is beginning to replace bias and opinion. Explanations for masculinity and femininity are now based on research rather than on tradition and common knowledge. This research investigates the biological and cultural antecedents of gender (Moir 1991; Hrdy 1999; Andersen 2010).

Biological Evidence

Q **In what ways are men and women biologically different?** The obvious biological differences between the sexes include distinctive muscle and bone structure and fatty tissue composition. The differences in reproductive organs, however, are much more important because they result in certain facts of life: Only men can impregnate; only women (including transsexual men who were formally female) are able to produce an ovum, carry and nurture the developing fetus, and give birth; and only women can secrete milk for nursing infants. In addition, the genetic composition of the body cells of men and women is different. All human beings have twenty-three pairs of chromosomes (the components of cells that determine heredity), but one of those pairs is sex distinctive. Males have an X and a Y chromosome in the pair that determines sex, and females have two X chromosomes. At about the eighth week of prenatal development, the information coded into the chromosomes determines whether the embryo—which is still sexually neutral—will begin to develop testicles or ovaries. These reproductive glands discharge the hormones that are characteristic of either females or males: estrogen and progesterone in females, testosterone and androgens in males. These hormone combinations influence development in both males and females throughout life (Geary 1998).

Some subsequent research indicates that the brains of men and women are somewhat different in structure (Gur et al. 1995; Fisher 1999; Pinker 2009; Brizendine 2007, 2010). For example, men show more activity in a region of the brain thought to be more tied to adaptive, evolutionary responses such as fighting. Women have more activity in a newer region of the brain; this region is more highly developed and thought to be linked to emotional expression. The female brain is less specialized than the male brain. Women tend to use both sides of the brain simultaneously when performing a task. For example, whereas men tend to process verbal tasks on the left side of the brain, women are more likely to use both sides. Women tend to use both ears when listening, and men tend to use the right ear. And while males are more muscular and stronger as a group than females, females have greater physical endurance and generally outlive males.

Q **Do biological differences necessarily lead to differences in social behavior?** Biological determinists point to research indicating that men and women in dozens of different cultures (at varying stages of economic development) are associated with some distinctly different ways of behaving. For example, men and women differ in what they look for in romantic and sexual partners. Men value physical appearance more than women do. Women place more emphasis on social class and income. Men tend to prefer slightly younger mates, while women favor slightly older ones. In addition, males in general tend more toward physical aggressiveness in conflict situations (Buss 1994a, 1994b, 1995; Maccoby 1997; Wodak 1997; Buss, Malamuth, and Winstead 1998).

On the other hand, researchers investigating behavioral differences between the sexes have been unable to consistently establish biological differences as an independent variable (Fausto-Sterling 1987; Stockard and Johnson 1992; Kimmel 2000; Andersen 2010; Fine 2010). One researcher's findings tend to contradict another's. Furthermore, many studies seek to find differences between males and females but ignore the similarities. To compound the problem, researchers often fail to document the variation in characteristics that exists *within* sex categories. Some men, for example, tend to be submissive, weak, and noncompetitive, and some women are aggressive, strong, and competitive. Either may be assertive, strong, and sensitive.

Cultural Evidence

Q **Is there cross-cultural evidence that gender-related behavior is not solely the product of biology?** In her classic study of three primitive New Guinean peoples, Margaret Mead (1950) demonstrated the influence of culture and socialization on gender role behavior. Among the Arapesh, Mead found that both males and females were conditioned to be cooperative, unaggressive, and empathetic. Both men and women in this tribe behaved in a way that is consistent with the more traditional concept of the female gender role. Among the Mundugumor, both men and women were trained to be "masculine"—they were aggressive, ruthless, and unresponsive to the needs of others. In the Tchambuli tribe, the gender roles were the opposite of those found in Western society. Women were dominant, impersonal, and aggressive, and men were dependent and submissive. On the basis of this evidence, Mead concluded that human nature is sufficiently malleable to rule out biological determination of gender roles. Cross-cultural research since Mead's landmark work substantiates her findings that gender roles are not fixed at birth (Janssen-Jurreit 1982; Montagu 2000).

For example, look at the gender behavior of the five-nation League of the Iroquois, which was in territory now part of Pennsylvania and upper New York. In a matrilineal society (family line traced through females) the Iroquois women enjoyed power and respect. Senior women chose the male members of the ruling council, and if the men failed to follow the women's wishes, the males were removed from office. Male dominancy and female subordination were absent in a culture where women took charge of village affairs, including military activities (Zinn 2005).

Studies have also been conducted on infants whose parents intentionally treated their children as if they belonged to the opposite gender. Apparently, individuals can fairly easily be socialized into the gender of the opposite sex. What's more, after a few years, these children resist switching back. These studies indicate that biological tendencies can be greatly influenced by culture and society (Schwartz 1987; L. Shapiro 1990; Ridley 1996; Sapolsky 1997).

Q **What are the most common male and female roles?** Societies such as the Arapesh, Mundugumor, and Tchambuli are exceptions to the rule. The general pattern in cross-cultural studies of gender roles in preliterate societies is one of male dominance and female nurturance (Zelditch 1955; Barry, Bacon, and Child 1957; Collins 1971; Reiss 1976; G. R. Lee 1977; Sinclair 1979). Although both men and women perform economic tasks that provide for family welfare, women's tasks usually involve domestic chores, child rearing, and emotional harmony. Men, on the other hand, are more likely to provide financially for the family and to represent the family in activities outside the home (Tilly and Scott 1978). This is probably because, beginning with early hunting societies, men have had the advantage of greater size and physical strength, and women have had the capability of childbearing and breast-feeding. Larger physical size has led to social, economic, and political advantages for men. Rarely, if ever, have these advantages been shared equally with women.

Q Do gender definitions change? Cultural definitions of gender roles can and do change. In his book *American Manhood*, E. Anthony Rotundo (1993) identifies three distinct culturally created conceptions of manhood. These definitions and redefinitions of gender roles developed in the North American middle class prior to the twentieth century. The first phase, *communal manhood*, was prominent in the socially integrated society of colonial New England. During this period, the definition of manhood was embedded in one's obligations to community. A man's social class at birth gave him his place in the community. He fulfilled himself through public usefulness more than through economic success. As head of the household, a man expressed his value to his community and bestowed a social identity on his wife and children. Before 1800, men were considered superior to women, and in particular, more virtuous. Thought to possess greater powers of reason, men, the culture taught, were better able than women to control passions such as ambition and envy.

The second phase, *self-made manhood*, became the dominant male gender definition in the first decades of the nineteenth century. A social identity based on personal achievement replaced the significance of social status at birth. A man's work role became his source of male identity. "Male" passions were allowed more fullness of expression. Because a man was supposed to prove his superiority, his drive for dominance was virtuous. As males turned from the tradition of public usefulness to the pursuit of self-interest, a redefinition of females emerged. Women assumed a stronger moral sense than men and were responsible for protecting the common good in an age of rampant male individualism. Despite her moral superiority, a woman still depended on her husband's place in society for her own social identity, and she, of course, could not participate in the pursuit of individualism. Her primary purposes were to control men's passions, to make others happy, and to take care of her husband and children.

Although gender stereotypes keep some people from pursuing certain activities, there are actually very few behaviors that cannot be performed by either sex.

Late in the nineteenth century there came another shift. The third phase, *passionate manhood*, emphasized not just achievement, but ambition, combativeness, and aggression. Male toughness was admired, tenderness scorned. The gender definition of men and women changed over these periods, but there was a constant: the exclusion of women from economic, political, and social power. In these arenas, women were consistently relegated to a subservient position.

Antecedents of Gender

1. _____ is the biological distinction between male and female.
2. _____ refers to the expectations and behaviors associated with a sex category within a society.
3. Gender is acquired through the process of _____.
4. _____ is an awareness of being masculine or feminine.
5. Societies that do not follow traditional gender definitions are exceptions to the rule. T or F?

Answers: 1. Sex; 2. Gender; 3. socialization; 4. Gender identity; 5. T

Q **Where does the nature/nurture debate stand?** The nature/nurture controversy has unfortunately been posed as an either/or situation by both the mass media and some researchers. In general, researchers investigating behavioral differences between the sexes have not been able to prove that any particular behavior has a biological cause (Fausto-Sterling 1987; Stockard and Johnson 1992; Andersen 2010). In this light, it is reasonable to credit *both* biology and culture for gender differences. Biological characteristics exist, but they can be modified through social influences (Parker and Easton 1998). In other words, men and women can learn to be submissive or aggressive by mirroring the behaviors of influential role models, such as parents or siblings. Also, this is a good time to remind ourselves that human behavior is the result of multiple causes.

Theoretical Perspectives on Gender R1

The functionalist perspective focuses on the origins of gender differences, whereas conflict theory concentrates on the reasons gender differences continue to exist. Symbolic interactionism attempts to explain the role of socialization in gender-based behavior.

Functionalism and Gender

If some pattern of behavior is not beneficial to society, functionalists argue, it will ultimately cease to be important. According to functionalism, the division of responsibilities between males and females survived because it was beneficial for human living. Early humans found sex-based division of labor efficient. In part because of their size and muscular strength, men performed hunting and defense tasks. In addition, men were responsible for these tasks because men were more expendable than women. Because these duties were more dangerous and because one male was enough to ensure sufficient procreation to sustain the survival of a group (the same is not true of a single woman with several men), it hurt the group's chances of survival less to lose a man. Women performed domestic and child-care tasks. This sexual division of labor endured, assert the functionalists, because it promoted the survival of the species. (See Table 10.1 for "Focus on Theoretical Perspectives.")

Gerald Maxwell (1975), like most sociologists, concedes that the traditional division of labor may have been appropriate at one time. Today, however, argues Maxwell, rapid social change has undermined the value of functionalist theory in understanding gender. Maxwell believes that it is to the advantage of modern

TABLE 10.1

FOCUS ON THEORETICAL PERSPECTIVES: Gender Inequality

Each of the major theoretical perspectives can focus on gender inequality in its own unique way. Explain why the examples given fit each theoretical perspective. How would each of the other theories approach the same social arrangement differently?

Theoretical Perspective	Social Arrangement	Example
Functionalism	• Gender-based division of labor	• Women are expected to perform household tasks for the benefit of society.
Conflict theory	• Patriarchy (male domination)	• Women are denied high-status occupations for the benefit of men.
Symbolic interactionism	• Favoring males over females in the classroom	• Few females believe they can become scientists.

Photodisc/Alamy Limited

This family is structured along traditional gender roles. How would the functionalist interpret this arrangement?

society to treat people based on their ability rather than on an outdated conception of instrumental and expressive roles. According to Maxwell and other critics, then, the contribution of the functionalist view of gender is restricted to an explanation of the development of gender.

In response to Maxwell's criticism, functionalists recognize that the traditional division of labor has dysfunctions, especially for modern society. Consequently, they point to harmful gender definitions resulting from this division of labor. A later discussion on gender inequality will examine these dysfunctions.

Conflict Theory and Gender

Conflict advocates are concerned not only with the origins of the traditional conception of gender but also with gender's persistence (Andersen and Collins 2007). The focus here is on the latter. According to conflict theory, men and women have differential access to the necessary resources for outside-the-home success. It is to the advantage of men (higher-status members of the society) and the disadvantage of women (lower-status members of the society) that women not gain access to political, economic, and social resources. By keeping the traditional division of labor intact, men can maintain the status quo and preserve the privileges they enjoy.

Perhaps the most recent example of maintaining the gender status quo was found in Afghanistan, when the then ruling Taliban militia practiced "gender apartheid." This gender war trapped women in a way of life unknown elsewhere in the modern world (O'Dwyer 1999; Rashid 2001). The Taliban prohibited girls from attending school, banned women from all work outside the home, punished women who left home without a male relative, enforced the wearing of black sacks over the body with only a wire mesh for vision, required windows of houses to be painted black, forced women to wear silent shoes, and required women to remain mute in public.

Conflict theorists see traditional gender roles as outdated. Although these conventional gender roles may have been appropriate in hunting and gathering, horticultural, and agricultural societies, they are inappropriate for the industrial and postindustrial era. Male physical strength may have been important when hunting was the major means of subsistence, but work in modern society does not position men with that advantage. In addition, demographic changes make women more available for outside work. Women are marrying later, are having fewer children, are younger when their last child leaves home, are remaining single in greater numbers, and are increasingly choosing to be single parents. According to conflict theorists, women who prefer careers in fields formerly reserved for men have every right to make that choice, whether or not it is "functional" for society. For example, any potential harm to the family must now be weighed against the damage done to women who are not permitted to develop their occupational potential. According to conflict advocates, research suggests that there are benefits to the family associated with working wives and mothers (Hoffman and Nye 1975; Moen 1978; Kate 1998; Zuo and Tang 2000; Hochschild 2001). Also, they say, the barriers blocking women from entry into higher-level jobs waste talents and skills that modern societies need.

Marxist and socialist feminists see the position of women in capitalist society as the result of two interrelated influences: patriarchal (male-dominated) institutions and the historical development of industrial capitalism. Historically, women held subordinate roles because their unpaid labor in the home produced the future labor force. Home work provides for the care and feeding of workers, the creation of new workers and consumers (through childbearing and child rearing), and the creation of people who can devote their time to the consumption activities necessary to keep factories running and workers working. In addition, women provide a reserve of cheap labor for times of crisis (e.g., war) and for expansion of the labor force when there is a need for more workers. Thus, the subordination of women is seen as a key component in the maintenance of the political and economic institutions in capitalist society (Sokoloff 1980; Chafetz 1984, 1990; Jaggar and Rothenberg 1993; Nierenberg 2002).

Q How is sexual harassment related to conflict theory?
The conflict perspective is built into the concept of **sexual harassment**—the use of one's superior power in making unwelcome sexual advances. Sexual harassment may be experienced as raw superior physical power. Sexual harassment in the military is frequent (Thomas and Vistica 1997; Aulette, Wittner, and Blakely 2009; Burn 2010). According to a 1995 U.S. Army survey, 4 percent of all female soldiers reported that they had been the victim of an actual or attempted rape or sexual assault within the previous year. That is almost ten times greater than the rate of rape and sexual assault in the general population. In fact, evidence of the prevalence of sexual harassment in the military surfaced again in early 2003 at the Air Force Academy, when the country learned of more than fifty reported cases of male cadet rape or sexual assault of female cadets. As the number of cases increased, the Air Force Secretary James G. Roche admitted that the actual number of rapes is probably three times the reported number ("Air Force Reports 54 Rapes, Assault" 2003; Lorch 2003). Many observers consider this assessment as far too conservative.

In addition to physical superiority, sexual harassment can be a matter of social and economic power. A prominent case illustrates the difficulties involved in legally establishing sexual harassment. In 1991 Anita Hill, a law professor, brought the issue of sexual harassment to public attention when she testified in televised Senate Judiciary Committee confirmation hearings of now Supreme Court Justice Clarence Thomas. Professor Hill accused Justice Thomas of sexually harassing her during the time she worked on his staff. The Senate committee, then totally composed of men, initially discounted the sexual harassment charge and subsequently confirmed Justice Thomas.

Symbolic Interactionism and Gender

Symbolic interactionists focus on **gender socialization**—the social process in which boys learn to act the way society assumes boys will behave and girls learn to act in ways society expects of them. This process occurs in large part through interaction with parents, teachers, and peers as well as through the mass media. This socialization process is very powerful, with gender being incorporated into the self-concept through role taking and the looking-glass self.

Q How do parents contribute to gender socialization?
Parents are vital in gender socialization because they transfer values and attitudes regarding the ways boys and girls should behave. The learning of gender behavior begins at birth and is well established by the time the child is two and a half years old (Mussen 1969; Frieze et al. 1978; Davies 1990). Actually, parents begin laying the groundwork for gender socialization before the child is born. Parents often painstakingly select a name to represent the gender-related characteristics they expect their child to possess. Immediately after the baby's birth, friends and relatives give gifts "appropriate" to the child's sex—blue or pink blankets, the baseball playsuits or frilly dresses, balls and trucks or dolls. Numerous studies report that gender definitions lead to differential treatment of boys and girls. Studies of infant care have found that girls are cuddled more, talked to more, and handled more gently. Parents expect boys to be more assertive, and they discourage boys from clinging.

Parental differential treatment of the young does not stop at infancy. For example, the bedrooms of preschoolers reflect masculine and feminine themes. Girls' rooms contain dolls and household items, whereas the rooms of boys are more likely to contain guns, footballs, and trucks. Gender is even taught and reinforced in the assignment of family chores. In an investigation of almost 700 children between the ages of two and seventeen, Lynn White and David Brinkerhoff (1981) found that boys were often given "masculine" jobs, such as cutting grass and shoveling snow, whereas girls were more often assigned "feminine" chores, such as washing dishes and cleaning up the house.

As parents respond to their children's behavior, they usually intentionally as well as unconsciously continue to transfer their gender-related values. Parents often even evaluate children according to their level of conformity to gender definition.

Q In what ways do schools reinforce gender socialization?
Although the most critical period of gender socialization occurs within the family during early childhood, gender socialization occurs through interaction in schools as well (K. A. Martin 1998). Teachers may not recognize that they encourage different behaviors from boys and girls, but observation of preschool teachers reveals a clear sex-based difference in many teacher–student relationships. This pattern continues into the elementary school years. Myra and David Sadker, in an extensive study of fourth-, sixth-, and eighth-grade students, found boys to be more assertive in class: Boys were eight times more likely than girls to call out answers, whereas girls sat patiently with their hands raised. They linked this classroom behavior to the differential treatment given to boys and girls by teachers. Teachers, report these researchers, are more likely to

accept the answers given by boys who call out answers. Girls who call out in class are given such messages as, "In this class we don't shout out answers, we raise our hands." According to Sadker and Sadker, the message is subtle and powerful: "Boys should be academically assertive and grab teacher attention; girls should act like ladies and keep quiet" (Sadker and Sadker 1985:56).

In their later book *Failing at Fairness*, the Sadkers (1995) examine sexism from elementary school through college. The conclusion is consistent with their earlier findings: Through differential treatment, America's schools often shortchange females; gender bias results in an inferior education for girls. Academically, girls typically outperform boys in the early years of school. Through the transmission of gender role values, well-intentioned teachers often dampen female competitiveness. Girls, the study concludes, are systematically taught passivity, a dislike of math and science, and a deference to the alleged superior abilities of boys. Females carry this impairment into adult life—into the working world, where its disadvantageous effects take full toll.

Q How do peers contribute to gender socialization?
Even children in day-care centers and nursery schools are aware of and encourage gender definitions. When three-year-olds behave according to their gender definition, their peers encourage, praise, and imitate them. Children who imitate the opposite sex meet considerable opposition within the group. This opposition includes criticism as well as efforts to modify the behavior (Lamb, Easterbrooks, and Holden 1980).

Interaction among adolescent peers also affects gender conceptions because adolescence is the time when an individual is establishing an identity, and identity is closely linked with definitions of masculinity and femininity (Erikson 1973, 1982; Adler and Adler 1998). Because adolescents want approval from their peers, acceptance or rejection by one's friends can significantly influence a teenager's self-concept. Teens who most closely mirror traditional gender definitions—such as football players and cheerleaders—generally receive the greatest respect, whereas "feminine" boys and "masculine" girls often maintain a low status. This peer group pressure encourages teenage conformity to society's idealized role models. To do otherwise is to risk rejection and a significant loss of self-esteem.

Q What is the role of media in gender socialization?
All members of society are subject to the continental bombardment of images from the Internet, television, books, magazines, radio, movies, and advertising. Many studies document the distorted view of women's roles prevalent in the media and the ways in which this distorted view affects people. In general, the media present the most stereotypical version of gender definitions, thus reflecting and reinforcing the limits on the options

Most Americans accept this conception of beauty. Because slimness is fundamental to this conception, women tend to compare themselves to fashion models.

Jeff Olson/HO, Sports Illustrated/AP Photo

available to both sexes (Craig 1992; Kilbourne 2001; Shields and Heinecken 2001; Dines and Humez 2002; Gauntlett 2002). For an extreme example, in the video game *Grand Theft Auto: Vice City* players can have sex with a female prostitute and earn additional points by beating and murdering her. Harlequin romance books are another example of the staying power of gender role stereotypes in books. In excess of 160 million of these books are published in more than twenty languages. In fact, Harlequin romance book sales account for almost one-third of trade paperbacks sold in the United States and Canada annually. In Harlequin books, women are consistently depicted as more sexually passive; men are the sexual aggressors (Grescoe 1997).

Television continues to reflect traditional gender roles. Despite a reduction in gender bias, most of those women on television who are portrayed as working outside the home are in female-dominated jobs. Male characters are either heroes or villains, whereas females tend to be adulterers or victims. In general, television consistently depicts men as aggressive, independent, and in charge of events. Women are portrayed as dependant and passive. There are signs of change in television programming. Female stars of shows such as *Sex and the City, Alias, Desperate Housewives,* and *CSI* certainly do not play traditional female roles.

CHECK YOURSELF 10.2 R2

Theoretical Perspectives on Gender

1. According to the _____ perspective, the division of labor based on sex has survived because it is beneficial and efficient for human living.

2. According to the _____ perspective, traditional gender definitions exist because they provide greater rewards and privileges to men than to women.

3. _____ is the theoretical perspective that attempts to explain how gender is acquired.

4. Which of the following is *not* a true statement?
   a. Boys are less assertive in class than girls.
   b. Mass media tend to present the most stereotypical version of gender definitions.
   c. Parents' perceptions of the physical characteristics of their children are heavily influenced by their children's gender.
   d. Nursery school children who fail to conform to their "appropriate" gender are met with resistance from their peers.

Answers: 1. functionalist; 2. conflict; 3. Symbolic interactionism; 4. a

Nowhere in the mass media are gender role stereotypes more prevalent than in advertising. Gender is used to promote everything from automobiles to food (Sharp and Wade 2010). Despite an increasing number of gender role reversal ads, men usually appear in advertising as symbols of dominance and aggression and women are portrayed as submissive (Thomas and Treiber 2000). This depiction actually starts targeting audiences quite early in life. Advertising designed for children uses the same stereotypes without sexual overtones–girls are more often cast as frivolous and helpless, and boys are more likely to play dominant and aggressive roles (Browne 1998).

Sex Stereotypes and Gender Roles R1

Sex Stereotypes

In Chapter 9, **stereotype** was defined as a set of ideas based on distortion, exaggeration, and oversimplification that is applied to all members of a social category. A **sex stereotype** is used to portray one sex as innately superior to the other. Men in American society are expected to be virile, brave, sexually aggressive, unemotional, logical, rational, mechanical, practical,

These active girls do not fit the stereotypical image of male football player/female cheerleader.

Jim West/Image Works

Gender-Based Hierarchy

In the not-too-distant past, most doctors were men, who worked closely on a daily basis with female nurses and receptionists who were clearly subordinate to them. This pattern has not disappeared despite the influx of women into the ranks of physicians. In many occupational settings today, most of the executives, supervisors, or higher-level professionals are men, assisted by female secretaries, clerks, aides, or lower-level managers. . . .

When women enter a workplace, they frequently find a male hierarchy already established. Whether a woman's entry creates tensions for herself or others in the workplace presumably depends on the level of the job she takes and the source of any authority inherent in the job. She may come in at a subordinate level as a clerk or receptionist. But if she comes in at the same level as male coworkers, she will be faced with the unaccustomed process of jockeying for position among them, and competing with them for the attention and approval of the people higher up in the hierarchy. If she comes in as a manager or supervisor who has male subordinates, she must learn how to deal with people who may want her job, or who may find it difficult to adjust to being supervised by a woman. Some men believe so strongly in male superiority that they resist women's advancement up the workplace hierarchy. Such men sometimes say quite explicitly that it would be "an insult to their intelligence" to be supervised by a woman.

. . . And there are fairly widespread male beliefs concerning the "natural" (male-dominant) relation between the sexes. In adulthood there is a strong stereotype associating power with masculinity . . . just as there was in childhood, so that women in supervisory positions generate ambivalent reactions in men: are they to treat this woman as a powerful person or a feminine person? If she is seen as feminine, then a man with traditional attitudes might feel it is appropriate to be protective and chivalrous, or at least courteous, while at the same time failing to take her seriously where work-related matters are concerned; clearly, he would expect to be the person who "takes charge" when they interact. Can he forget that a female supervisor is female and adapt himself to a situation where she is the one who takes charge? It is much easier for men—perhaps for many women too—to slip into a traditional male boss/female secretary or male doctor/female nurse kind of work relationship in which the "appropriate" power relationships between the sexes are maintained in the workplace hierarchy. Such traditional attitudes may be weakening, but they are still prevalent enough to impede the promotion of women in many situations.

Think About It

Talk to several men and women with work experience. Ask them a few open-ended questions that you make up to test Maccoby's contention. In your verbal or written report, be specific about similarities or differences in male and female answers.

Source: Excerpted from Eleanor Maccoby, *The Two Sexes: Growing Up Apart, Coming Together.* Cambridge, MA: Howard University Press, 1997, pp. 247–248.

---

dominating, independent, aggressive, confident, and competitive. Women are expected to be the opposite: weak, fearful, sexually passive, emotional, insecure, sentimental, "arty," dependent, submissive, modest, shy, and noncompetitive (Williams and Best 1990). In American society, these stereotypes reflect a belief in the innate superiority of men and the inferiority of women. (See "See Sociology in Your Life.")

Gender Roles

Gender roles involve culturally based expectations associated with each sex. In a sense gender roles represent an ideal, because in reality people do not always behave as expected. Although mothers are expected to be patient and loving with their children, many are not. Consequently, individuals can decide to emphasize different aspects of their gender according to their preferences, abilities, and social circumstances. Thus, as noted earlier, there is a wide range of actual feminine and masculine behavior (Rahman and Jackson 2010; Zinn Hondagneu-Stelo, and Messner 2011). Not all men try to be strong, fearless, and aggressive; not all women attempt to be sweet, submissive, and deferring. For example, in 2009 a California high school student was elected prom queen and a George Mason University student reigned as homecoming queen. Both are male.

Albeit the individual variations in gender role performances, gender roles are sufficiently influential to create conformity most of the time. Males usually value their masculinity and females normally honor the ideals of femininity. Nevertheless, conformity to gender roles is conditioned by a number of sociological variables. Men and women enact and experience gender roles in the context of their social class, racial or ethnic heritage, age, nationality, physical ability, and sexual preferences (Zinn, Hondagneu-Sotelo, and Messner 2010). The impact of these factors on the performance of gender roles sometimes creates confusion about the nature of gender roles. As in all sociological questions, we will concentrate on recurrent patterns of social relationships. We will focus on gender roles within social structures.

Role Conflict and Role Strain

Q **What female role conflicts and strains are created by gender roles?** Women suffer from conflicts and strains built right into the female role. And, a changing society is creating even greater conflicts. Because married women are increasingly working outside the home (see Figure 10.1), they must balance the requirements of work with the demands of housework and child care (Burros 1993; Hochschild 2003; Burn 2011). Married women must juggle, first, the expectation that they will move from one place to another as they or their husbands climb occupationally and, second,

their concern for the effects of rootlessness on their children.

While most married women now share responsibility for the breadwinner role, men, by and large, are slow to share domestic responsibilities. Furthermore, no other institution in society—whether public or private—has stepped in to help working women. As a result, women shoulder the responsibilities of work and family largely on their own (Reskin and Padavic 2002; Auletta, Wittner, and Blakely 2009). According to past research, housewives report higher rates of illness than women in the labor force (Nathanson 1980). This apparent positive health effect of women working outside the home, however, may now be offset by the increasing stress that accompanies the combined demands of work and family (Rosenfield 1989). In addition, greater stress and depression occur among women whose husbands do not support their working than among women with supportive husbands (Ulbrich 1988). Poorer health is also more likely among minority working women with husbands opposed to their employment.

Q **What male role conflicts and strains are created by gender roles and sex stereotypes?** Like women, men experience conflicts and strains within the traditional masculine role. Many working-class men, whose wives must work just to help support their families, are

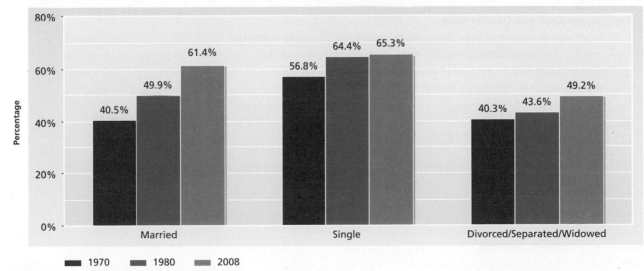

FIGURE 10.1

Marital Status of Women in the U.S. Civilian Labor Force

These data show the relationship between marital status and employment. Write a paragraph describing the important trends you can see.

Source: U.S. Bureau of the Census, *Statistical Abstract of the United States, 2008* (Washington, DC: U.S. Government Printing Office, 2009), table 584.

bothered by a feeling of having failed at their task of provider:

> A guy should be able to support his wife and kids. But that's not the way it is these days, is it? I don't know anybody who can support a family anymore, do you? . . . Well, I guess those rich guys can, but not some ordinary Joe like me. (Rubin 1994:78)

Men are expected to be occupationally and economically successful while simultaneously devoting time to their wives and children. Men are encouraged to admire other women sexually, but they are expected to remain faithful to their wives. The "macho man" ideal conflicts with women's preferences for warm, gentle, romantic lovers. Men also have to handle the inconsistency of being cool and unemotional at work but loving at home (Doyle 1995).

Role conflict and role strain for men are intensifying in today's environment of changing gender roles. Although many women want to be liberated from male domination, they sometimes still expect men to be protective of them. This is partly because appropriate gender role behavior is currently conditioned by the situation. For example, some women want to be treated as equal to men while at work but treated in more traditional ways off the job. Other women resent any attempt by men to treat them differently from the way they would treat other men. Consequently, men are often confused about what women expect. Moreover, although many men wish to shed the John Wayne image, they are less certain than women about the role model that should replace it (Wetcher, Barker, and McCaughtry 1991; Faludi 2000).

Q **Why do strains associated with changing gender roles tend to be greater within working-class families?** In *Worlds of Pain*, Lillian Rubin (1992) reports that working-class Americans advocate more traditional gender roles; yet, for economic reasons, the women are more likely to work outside the home. She also reports that working-class husbands with wives in the labor force do not participate very much in domestic tasks. Other research bolsters this assertion: Less educated, lower-income men are less likely to share household labor when their wives work outside the home (Miller and Garrison 1982; Sweet, Bumpass, and Call 1988). In addition, Rubin concludes, working-class husbands of working women see their wives' employment as a challenge to their self-esteem and masculinity. The contradiction between traditional gender role attitudes and the sharing of the provider, household, and child-care roles among working-class couples, Rubin asserts, leads to personal strain. Rubin wrote that, among other things, this contradiction led working-class men to demand more submission and obedience from their wives and children in order to bolster their own egos and sense of masculinity.

In *Families on the Faultline*, Rubin (1994) reports that although more contemporary working-class men now believe in a woman's right to full independence, most still want women with sufficient dependency and need to make them feel manly. Nearly all the working-class men Rubin studied did some work inside the family—washing dishes, vacuuming, grocery shopping—but only 16 percent shared family work equally with their wives. Almost all of these men, however, either worked different shifts than their wives or were unemployed. The high price paid

---

CHECK YOURSELF **10.3** **R2**

Sex Stereotypes and Gender Roles

1. A sex stereotype is used to portray men as innately _____ to women.
2. _____ roles involved culturally based expectations with each sex.
3. The idea that victory is the most positive reinforcement for all men is an example of
   a. sex
   b. sex stereotype
   c. gender role
   d. a value uniquely held by men
   e. role strain
4. The retention of traditional sex stereotypes causes the most role strain for _____.
   a. working-class men
   b. upper-class men
   c. middle-class women
   d. occupational mobility men
   e. working-class women

Answers: 1. superior; 2. Gender; 3. b; 4. e

for the retention of traditional sex stereotypes and gender roles remains much higher for working-class women.

Gender Inequality in the United States ⬛

Women as a Minority Group

Most scientists consider biological determinism a moral threat because historically it has been used to rationalize the treatment of some categories of people as inferior. This view, in short, has led to racism and sexism. Minorities suffer the effects of racism; women are hurt by **sexism**: a set of beliefs, norms, and values used to justify sexual inequality. Sexist ideology—the belief that men are naturally superior to women—has been used and is still being used to justify men's leadership and power positions in the economic, social, and political spheres of society. It explains women's dependence on men as well (Clayton 1996; Swann, Langlois, and Gilbert 1998; Benokraitis 2004).

Although there is no factual basis to support the maintenance of sexism, its influence remains. Women are easily identified, biologically and culturally, and are subject to many forms of discrimination (Mrkic, Johnson, and Rose 2010).

It is still unusual to see a woman, such as Indra Nooyi, serve as chairman and CEO of a corporation like PepsiCo.

Q **But isn't sex discrimination disappearing?** The answer is *yes* and *no*. Some segments of American society have more positive attitudes about women. And a few women now hold positions traditionally reserved for men. For example, there are now fifteen female CEOs of Fortune 500 companies, and only about 16 percent of corporate officers of these companies are female. Women now head almost one-fourth of colleges, including a number of top universities, (Princeton, Brown, Harvard, Duke, Chicago, Virginia, and Michigan). The proportion of women in the U.S. military has reached 20 percent. They are increasingly performing jobs traditionally assigned to men only (Aulette, Wittner, and Blakely 2009; Bumiller 2010). For example, there are almost 150 female Army combat pilots, some of whom fought in the Iraq and Afghanistan wars. Still, a careful examination reveals many remaining gaps in rights, privileges, and rewards for women in the United States. Although these gaps have closed somewhat in recent years, American women continue to experience occupational, economic, legal, and political inequality (Bianchi and Spain 1996; Riley 1997; Lorber 2005).

Occupational and Economic Inequality

By far the most important U.S. labor market development over the past fifty years is the dramatic increase of women in the workforce (Burn 2011). In 1960, the percentage of women who worked outside the home was below 40 percent; by 2008, that figure reached 60 percent (see Figure 10.2). Furthermore, women now represent almost 47 percent of the entire U.S. labor force (men and women), up from 32 percent in 1960 (see Figure 10.3). The increase in labor force participation among married women is particularly steep. For example, the labor force participation rate of married women between the ages of twenty-five and forty-four skyrocketed from 43 percent in 1960 to 72 percent today (U.S. Census Bureau 2009).

Q **Has increased labor force participation eliminated occupational inequality?** Despite their increased participation in the labor force, women are still concentrated in different occupations than men. This is known as **occupational sex segregation** (Perlmann and Margo 2001; Tomaskovic-Devey and Skaggs 2002; Burn 2011). Women are underrepresented in high-status occupations and overrepresented in low-status occupations. To begin with, females fill only about 14 percent of architecture and engineering positions and about one-third of attorney jobs. By contrast, women occupy nearly all of the pink-collar jobs—secretaries, clerks—whose purpose is to support those higher up the occupational ladder. Moreover, when women are in high-status occupational groups, they are concentrated in lower-prestige, lower-paid jobs. Even within

Harriet Bradley—Men's Work, Women's Work

In a 1989 study, Harriet Bradley focused on occupational sex segregation and job sex-typing in Britain after the Industrial Revolution, around 1750. She presented case studies of various industries and occupations—food and raw material production, agriculture, fishing, mining, manufacturing, pottery, hosiery, shoemaking, shopwork, medicine, and teaching. In these studies, Bradley documented the development of the division of labor along gender lines. Her database consisted of a combination of secondary sources in the form of previously published research, along with new material she collected from primary sources. This study is an excellent example of the integration of sociology and history.

According to Bradley, pervasive sex-typing of jobs—the allocation of certain work-related activities to men and others to women—results in men and women rarely being allocated the same types of jobs. Even when men and women are working side by side, Bradley points out, they are doing different things. This allocation of certain work to men and certain work to women, she argues, is based

on a simple principle: Men occupy jobs that place them in control, and women do work that requires obedience. In the fields, men cut and women gather; in the factory, men stamp out parts and women sew them together; in the office, men handle accounts and women do the typing and filing.

The social definition of what is "women's work" and what is "men's work" may vary from time to time and place to place. Jobs thought of as the province of women may have historically been assigned to men, or vice versa. Prior to the industrialization of the cotton industry, for example, men were weavers, while women did the spinning. These roles were flip-flopped when power-driven machinery replaced hand labor. What does not vary, Bradley asserts, is the assignment of jobs based on the principle of men as superordinate and women as subordinate. Weavers had higher status prior to industrialization and lower status afterward.

Although occupational sex segregation and job sex-typing existed in preindustrial society, Bradley contends that capitalism dramatically increased both. From the case studies, she concludes that the tremendous expansion of capitalist production in the 1880s and 1890s created the foundation for the current patterns of gender job segregation and job sex-typing.

During the capitalist expansion, according to Bradley, hiring women in jobs labeled as "women's work"

served the interests of capitalists as well as male workers. Capitalists could increase their profits by hiring women for lower wages because of the low value placed on female labor. In addition, capitalists used women to challenge the control male workers held as a result of their expertise in preindustrial craft production techniques. As men fought back by demanding that certain jobs remain "men's work," occupational sex segregation deepened; and women were forced into low-paying "female" jobs. Males and females, Bradley concludes, continued to be steered into socially appropriate lines of work. This played into their desire to assert unique sexual identities. Gender-based ideologies emphasize sex differences. She quotes from C. Cockburn:

> What a man "is," what a woman "is," what is right and proper, what is possible and impossible, what should be hoped and what should be feared. The hegemonic ideology of masculinism involves a definition of men and women as different, contrasted, complementary and unequal. It is powerful and it deforms both men and women. (C. Cockburn 1986:85)

Evaluate the Research

1. Which theoretical framework do you think Bradley used? Explain your choice.
2. Do you think that the current changes in gender relations in the United States will alter the state of occupational sex segregation described by Bradley? Support your conclusion.

female-dominated occupations, men fill a disproportionate share of higher positions (See "Consider This Research"). Occupational sex segregation, then, produces a **dual labor market**—a split of the economy into a core segment of preferred workers and a peripheral segment of the marginalized workers.

Q Have women and men reached financial equality? Earnings inequality has followed a pattern since the

1960s. After increasing in the late 1960s, earnings inequality stabilized for most of the 1970s, increased slightly during the 1980s, and has increased somewhat since (Grubb and Wilson 1992; Wasserman 2007; see Figure 10.4). Thus, there remains a wide discrepancy between the earnings of American women and men (U.S. Department of Labor 2010). By 2009, women who worked full time earned only 80 cents for every dollar earned by men. To put it another way, women

FIGURE 10.2

U.S. Labor Force Participation Rates by Sex: 1890–2008

This figure tracks changes in the percentage of women and men in the U.S. labor force since 1890. The participation gap between the sexes has changed radically. Describe this shift using specific percentages.

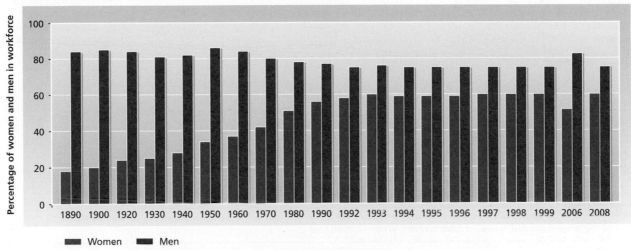

Sources: U.S. Department of Labor; Bureau of Labor Statistics, *Employment in Perspective: Women in the Labor Force*, No. 865 (Washington, DC: U.S. Government Printing Office, 1993), p. 1; U.S. Department of Labor, Bureau of Labor Statistics, *Employment and Earnings*, (Washington, DC: U.S. Government Printing Office, 1997), p. 6; and U.S. Bureau of the Census, *Statistical Abstract of the United States, 2001* (Washington, DC: U.S. Government Printing Office, 2001), p. 367, U.S. Bureau of the Census, *Statistical Abstract of the United States, 2010* (Washington, DC: U.S. Government Printing Office 2009, table 579).

FIGURE 10.3

Composition of the U.S. Labor Force, by Sex: 1870–2050

As this figure demonstrates, the male-female composition of the U.S. labor force has steadily moved toward parity. The female percentage of the labor force has moved from less than 15 percent in 1870 to about 46 percent today. What do you think is the most important social consequence of this change?

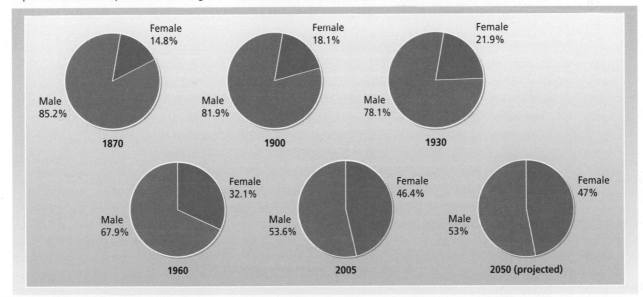

Source: U.S. Department of Labor, Bureau of Labor Statistics, 2006.

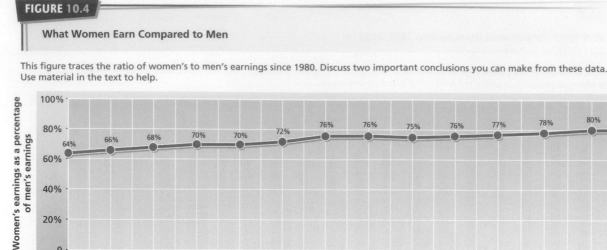

FIGURE 10.4

What Women Earn Compared to Men

This figure traces the ratio of women's to men's earnings since 1980. Discuss two important conclusions you can make from these data. Use material in the text to help.

Source: U.S. Department of Labor, Bureau of Labor Statistics, "Highlights of Women's Earnings in 2009," June 2010, p. 2.

INTERNET LINK For additional information on employment and earnings of women and men in the United States, you can visit the Website of the Department of Labor, Bureau of Labor Statistics, at http://stats.bls.gov/

now work about seven days to earn as much as men earn in five days. On the one hand, there is some good news: This salary gap has decreased since 1980, when women were earning 64 percent as much as men.

In virtually every occupational category, men outstrip the earning power of women. The earning gap persists, regardless of educational attainment. Women in the same professional occupations as men earn less than their male counterparts (see Figure 10.5). This is true even for women who have pursued careers on a full-time basis for all of their adult lives. Furthermore, males in female-dominated occupations typically earn more than women (Aulette, Wittner, and Blakely 2009; Burn 2011).

FIGURE 10.5

Female-to-Male Earnings: 2009

On average, women in the United States earn about 80 cents for every dollar a man earns. In what way do the data in this figure support the contention that gender inequality is real?

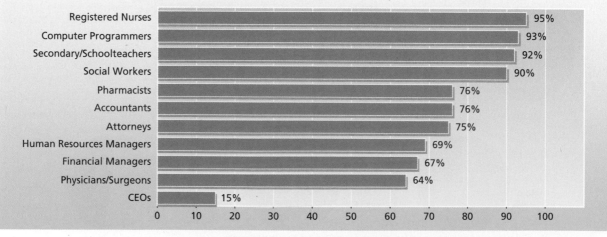

Women's Earnings as a Percentage of Men's Earnings

Source: U.S. Department of Labor, Bureau of Labor Statistics, 2010.

Q How do race and ethnicity affect women's earnings, compared with men's? As noted, women as a whole in the United States earn about 80 percent of what men earn. Throwing race and ethnicity into the mix provides additional information. Unaltered, of course, is the fact that women of all races and ethnic groups earn less than men (Kaufman 2010). Yet, African American and Latino women have a significantly lower wage gap with their male counterparts than white and Asian women experience. Asian women have a little less of a pay gap than white women. Among white women, the pay gap actually increases (see Figure 10.6). Not shown in Figure 10.6 is the fact that white and Asian women earn considerably more than their African American and Latino counterparts. Consequently, the gender pay gap is even more important to black and Latino women.

Q Is there hope of closing the salary gap? Although the salary gap will likely remain indefinitely, there are a few signs of hope. Probably the most encouraging word is that two-thirds of the women currently entering the labor force are taking jobs historically dominated by men. For instance, as more women became computer programmers over the past few years, their earnings rose from 70 percent to almost 85 percent of what their male counterparts earned.

More generally, as the percentage of females in professional, managerial, and technical occupations has increased, the female-to-male income ratio has improved in a number of these occupations. Also, increasing numbers of women are leaving the wage system behind as they become entrepreneurs. Excluding large corporations, women now own about one-fourth of all businesses. However, females are still more likely than males to hold jobs that pay relatively low wages; and as you have seen, the differential in female-to-male earnings persists within occupational categories.

Q Why does the salary gap persist? Research on wage differences has shown that even taking into account all possible factors that might reasonably account for wage differences between women and men—such as age, experience, amount of absenteeism, and educational background—a large difference remains. With the elimination of all other explanations, the conclusion reached from these studies is that sex discrimination is the major source of economic differences.

One of the most serious indicators of economic inequality is the disproportionate number of women living in poverty. More than half of poor families have a female head of household. Individuals living in female-headed households are about three times as likely to live below the poverty level; female-headed households among minority groups are about four times as likely to live in poverty. This, of course, reflects the feminization of poverty discussed in Chapter 8. This trend is fueled by increases in teenage pregnancy, singlehood, and divorce.

Q What about the comparative economic success of men and women? Men and women in the United States tend to have levels of income similar to their own parents with one exception. Daughters of low-income parents experience less income mobility than sons of low-income parents.

FIGURE 10.6

Women's Wages Compared with Men's Wages, by Race and Ethnicity

This figure compares what women of various races and ethnicities earn compared to men. Which group of women has the highest female-to-male earnings ratio?

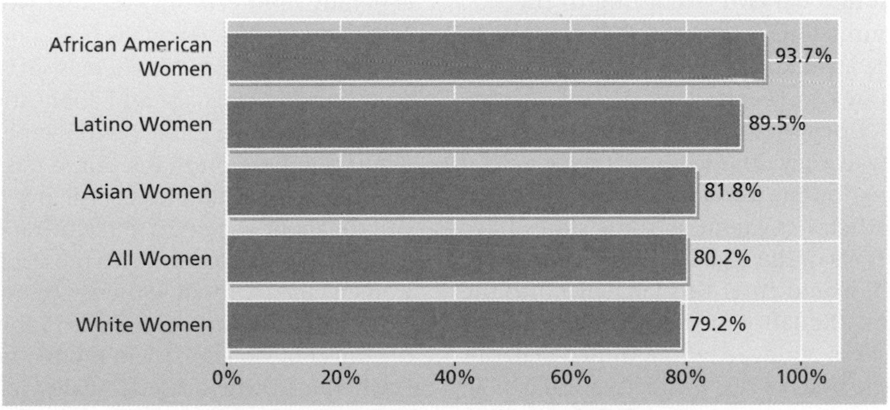

African American Women	93.7%
Latino Women	89.5%
Asian Women	81.8%
All Women	80.2%
White Women	79.2%

Source: Adapted from U.S. Department of Labor, Bureau of Labor Statistics, "Highlights of Women's Earnings in 2009," June 2010, p. 2.

The income of American working women is three-quarters that of men. The gap in earnings between men and women is not obliterated even when education and occupation are comparable. This female professor in all probability is paid less than her male counterparts.

Patrick Clark/Getty Images

It must be noted that women in their thirties today make considerably more in inflation-adjusted dollars than women of the same age in their mothers' generation. Despite making more than their female contemporaries, men in their thirties today make less than men in their fathers' generation. Also men's employment rates, hours worked, and wages have been flat or declining between 1974 and 2004, while women have seen a substantial increase in all three components (Isaccs 2007b).

Legal and Political Inequality

Sexism is similarly built into America's legal and political institutions. National, state, and local legal codes reflect sexual bias; and important differences exist between women and men in positions of political power.

Q **Is sexism built into the law?** According to the U.S. Civil Rights Commission, more than 800 sections of the U.S. legal code are sexually biased. Legal inequities and complexities are compounded by overlapping state and local jurisdictions. Because state and local statutes apply as long as they do not conflict with federal law, the legal situation for women varies greatly from one place to another. For example, some states have enacted state versions of the Equal Rights Amendment, which, if enacted, would enter this language into the U.S. Constitution: "Equality of rights under the law shall not be denied or abridged by the United States or by any state on the basis of sex" (Andersen 2010:352). Other states, however, have retained archaic nineteenth-century laws based on the idea that women are

the property of either a husband or a father. Georgia, for example, has an 1863 law that "defines a woman's legal existence as 'merged in the husband.'"

Due to the passage of Title VII of the Civil Rights Act of 1964, many laws placing women in a dependant position have been preempted; but despite the prohibition by such laws, some practices still linger. Moreover, the Family and Medical Leave Act of 1993, which requires that employees be given up to twelve weeks without pay for childbirth, adoption, serious illness, and so forth, inadvertently affects women negatively. Because women are more likely than men to take parental leave, this legislation gives employers another reason to hire men rather than women.

There are gender differences in criminal law as well. Certain crimes are typically associated with one gender or the other. For example, laws against prostitution are generally enforced only against women, while male customers go free. Rape has been one of the most controversial legal areas. Nowhere is sexism more explicitly built into the language and application of the law. For example, no other crime besides rape requires independent corroboration that a crime has been committed. There are two assumptions of many rape laws: Women will lie about the occurrence of rape, and unless evidence of rape is produced, no prosecution can occur. For women raped without witnesses (presumably the majority of cases), or for women who submit to rape due to the threat of violence, there is often no legal protection. Furthermore, when cases actually do come to trial, the victim is often treated more harshly than the defendant. Many observers have described rape trials as trials of the victims, with evidence of the victims' past sexual activity used to undermine their testimony and to acquit the accused. Even convicted rapists have been allowed to go free on the grounds of provocation. A notorious case involved a Wisconsin judge who refused to send a convicted rapist to prison on the grounds that the way women dress today causes men to lose control. One possible explanation for political bias is the underrepresentation of women in positions of political power.

Q Does the legal system ever work in favor of women? Yes, sometimes women benefit from the criminal justice system. For example, sexual relations with a minor female, even though she consents, may result in prosecution of the man for statutory rape. More broadly, some sociologists point to the **chivalry hypothesis.** That is, females are treated more leniently than males because the men who control the criminal justice system have a protective (paternalistic) attitude toward women (Siegel 2010).

Larry Siegel reports other instances of female favoritism. Evidence indicates that women are treated more generously as they move up the criminal justice hierarchy. Judges, for example, are more likely to be favorably biased toward women than police officers. This bias favors African American and Latino women, as well as white women. Because judges view females as more trustworthy, women spend less time in pretrial detention and have lower monetary bail requirements.

Q How does sexism relate to political power? In cities of 100,000 or more people, only 13 percent had female mayors in 2010. In the same year, about one-fourth of state legislators were women (see Figure 10.7 and "Sociology Eyes America" 10.1). The proportion of statewide elective executive offices occupied by women across the country stood at about 23 percent ("Women in Elective Office 2010" 2010).

A record number of women serve in the U.S. Congress. Still, while women comprise more than one-half of the U.S. population, in 2010 they occupy only about 17 percent of the seats in the U. S. House of Representatives (ninety members). And although the number of female U.S. Senators has increased from two to seventeen over the last fifteen years, women still represent just 17 percent of the Senate. Women in Congress seldom rise to positions of power.

Over the past two decades, a few women have reached the national political stature previously held exclusively by men. In 1988, Geraldine Ferraro became the first female vice presidential candidate in the history of the United States; Madeleine Albright was named the first female Secretary of State in 1996; Elizabeth Dole ran for her party's presidential nomination in 2000. In 2002, Democrat Nancy Pelosi became the first female House minority whip and was subsequently elected House minority leader. George W. Bush appointed Condoleezza Rice as the second female Secretary of State in 2005. In 2006, Nancy Pelosi became Speaker of the House,

FIGURE 10.7

Percentage of Women in Elective Offices

This graph shows the degree of female success in the elective politics from 1979 to today. Explain why the figures are still so low.

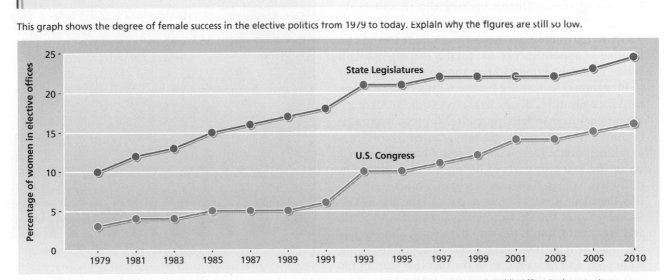

Source: "Women in Elective Office 2010," Center for American Women and Politics, National Information Bank on Women in Public Office, Eagleton Institute of Politics, Rutgers University.

SOCIOLOGY EYES AMERICA 10.1

Women Holding State Public Offices, 2008

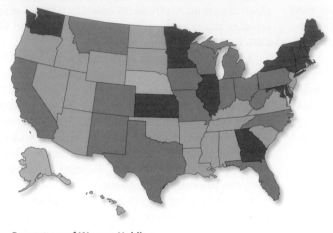

Percentage of Women Holding State Public Offices

- 31 or above
- 23–30
- 15–22
- 14 or less

Source: U.S. Bureau of the Census, *Statistical Abstract of the United States 2010*, Table 402, p. 252.

Hillary Clinton's bid for the presidency as a U.S. Senator is one reflection of the relatively recent accessibility of political office to women. The map at left shows the number of women holding state public offices.

Interpret the Map

1. Identify any patterns you see in the distribution of female office holders across the United States.
2. Are you surprised or disappointed at the place of women in state politics? Explain your answer.

the highest-ranking position a female has ever held in Congress. At the same time, as the newly named Chair of the House Republican Conference, Deborah Pryce became the highest-ranking Republican woman ever to serve in Congress. In 2008, having served as senator from New York since 2000, Hillary Clinton became the first woman to enter the presidential primaries as a leading candidate. Also in 2008, Sarah Palin became the first woman to run for vice president of the United States on the Republican ticket. Then in 2009, Hillary Clinton became the third female Secretary of State.

Although there have been recent increases in the number of appointments, the total is extremely small. When President Jimmy Carter appointed four women to his cabinet, he quadrupled the number ever to have held such positions at one time. President Bill Clinton, almost twenty years later, appointed thirteen women to cabinet posts. George W. Bush appointed five women to cabinet-level positions, and Barack Obama appointed six in the first two years of his presidency. Still, only thirty-five women have ever served as cabinet-level officers. President Ronald Reagan appointed the first female Supreme Court Justice, Sandra Day O'Connor, in 1981; and President Clinton elevated Ruth Bader Ginsburg to the high court in 1993. Barack Obama appointed Sonia Sotomayer and Elena Kagan in the first two years of his first term, raising the current number of female justices to three (because a male replaced O'Connor upon her

CHRIS KEANE/Reuters/Landau

American women are still not well represented in political office. Hillary Clinton, who unsuccessfully ran for the presidential nomination in the Democratic party, was right to say that the number of votes she received in the primaries represents 18 million cracks in the glass ceiling.

retirement in 2009). Only a small percentage of federal judges are women. Even though women comprise more than 40 percent of the federal workforce, they have only recently begun to gain access to the higher pay grades. About 40 percent of women are employed in midlevel grades. Women hold less than one-third of the supervisor and manager positions and account for only one-fifth of senior executives.

On the positive side, about 90 percent of women and men say they would vote for a woman as their political party's nominee (Newport and Carroll 2007). When Gallup first asked this question in 1937, only 33 percent of Americans said they would vote for a female presidential candidate. On the downside, about half of the American public believes that a man would be a better president than would a woman.

Richard Zweigenhaft and William Domhoff (2006) do point out that women are now part of the power elite. The power elite is no longer the exclusively male enclave it used to be. Still, women are seriously underrepresented. And most of those women who do make it come predominantly from upper-class backgrounds.

Global Gender Inequality **R1**

Worldwide Attitudes Toward Gender Inequality

As Americans become increasingly aware of gender inequality, they embrace gender equality as a value. As we have just seen, however, belief in gender equality has not led to actual gender equality. Not surprisingly, the same disjunction between belief and results is repeated all over the world. A poll by the Pew Research Center helps explain the persistence of gender inequality in the face of professed public opposition to it (Kohut 2010).

Q Why the discrepancy between the belief about gender equality and the existence of gender inequality? The Pew Research Center draws the following picture from its twenty-two–nation survey of gender equality. Worldwide, solid majorities endorse gender equality and support women working outside the home. Majorities also agree that the most satisfying marriages are those in which both spouses assume financial and household responsibilities. And majorities in most countries agree that higher education is no more important for males than for females. Still, as in the United States, Kohut found that peoples across the globe acknowledge the continued existence of gender inequality in their countries. According to these respondents, men continue to get more opportunities than equally qualified women for higher-paying jobs and men have a better life in general than women.

The Extent of Global Gender Inequality

An examination of global gender inequality requires moving beyond comparisons between the United States and the rest of the world. Consideration must be given to where the world as a whole stands in terms of progress toward gender equality. Then we will return to a United States–world comparison.

Q Has there been progress toward gender equality in the world? The short answer is *yes*. The longer answer is *it's complicated*. The findings of three major international reports converge in support of two conclusions: More progress toward gender equality has occurred in developed countries than in developing countries, and gender parity remains a future goal around the world, despite some progress over the last two decades (*Human Development Report* 2010; Mrkic, Johnson, and Rose 2010; *The Millennium Development Goals Report* 2010). We will look at educational, economic, and political inequality.

CHECK YOURSELF 10.4 **R2**

Gender Inequality

1. _____ is a set of beliefs, norms, and values used to justify sexual inequality.
2. On the average, women earn about _____ of what men earn.
   a. 80 percent
   b. one-half
   c. two-thirds
   d. 95 percent
3. The idea that females are treated more leniently than males in the criminal justice system is called the _____ hypothesis.
4. The exclusion of women from political power applies mainly to elective offices. T or F?

Answers: 1. Sexism; 2. a; 3. chivalry; 4. F

Q What about educational gender equality? Over the last twenty years, in all regions of the world, enrollments in primary and secondary schools have risen more rapidly for girls than for boys. While the educational level for girls and boys in primary and secondary schools is close to parity in developed countries, equality remains out of reach for many developing regions. For primary education, the greatest educational inequality is in Oceania, Sub-Saharan Africa, and Western Asia. The gender gap in secondary education is the greatest in Sub-Saharan Africa, Western Asia, and Southern Asia.

Among developed countries, near-parity has been reached in higher education. But in most developing nations, many more males than females are enrolled in colleges and universities. In Sub-Saharan Africa, for example, only 67 females for every 100 males are enrolled in institutions of higher education. Gender inequality is also evident in the difference in areas of study pursued in college by males and females. Women are more concentrated in the humanities and social sciences and are still discouraged from studying science, technology, and engineering. Also, men are more likely to graduate than women.

Differences in wealth and place of residence make the situation even more complicated. Girls of primary-school age from the wealthiest families are three times more likely to remain in school than girls from poorer families. Females of secondary-school age from richer families are twice as likely to be in school as girls from poorer families. Girls living in rural areas are significantly less likely to remain in school than their urban peers.

Q Are the world's women achieving economic progress? Worldwide, there are some signs of improvement. Women now comprise 41 percent of those employed outside of agriculture, a reflection of the general movement of labor from the land to industry. In developing regions, of course, the female share of the nonagricultural labor force is often down in the 20 to 30 percent range. Moreover, women who are in industry disproportionately hold the most vulnerable jobs. These are low paying, highly insecure jobs, providing no economic or social protection during periods of unemployment.

Women in nonagricultural employment also experience occupational sex segregation, as men maintain a near monopoly on higher-level positions. Across the globe, women represent only one out of every four senior officials or managers. In some developing regions (Western Asia, Southern Asia, and Northern Africa), women hold only one in ten higher-level positions.

FIGURE 10.8

Women's Monthly Wages Compared with Men's Wages in Nonagricultural Employment, 2006-2008

This figure reveals where the United States stands worldwide in wage parity. Explain this fact based on information in this chapter.

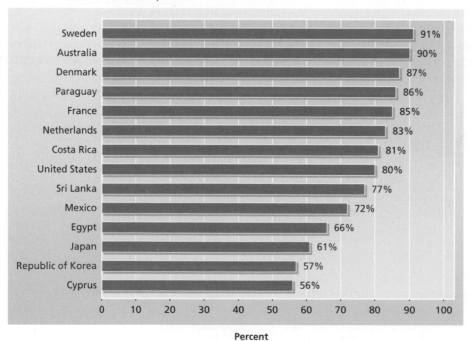

Percent

Source: Srdjan Mrkic, Tina Johnson, and Michael Rose, *The World's Women 2010: Trends and Statistics,* Department of Economic and Social Affairs, New York: United Nations, 2010, p. 97.

The gender wage gap, despite some bridging, continues to be significant (Burn 2011; see Figure 10.8). In a majority of countries, women earn between 70 and 90 percent of men's wages. There, however, is a wide disparity within the total range. Australia and Sweden are outliers at 90 and 91 percent, respectively. Cyprus and the Republic of Korea represent the lower end of the spectrum (56 and 57 percent, respectively).

Q Where do the world's women stand politically? Forty years ago about thirty countries denied their citizens the right to vote and to run for public office. This withholding of civil rights, aimed primarily at women, has almost completely disappeared. The right to vote is now granted to practically all people in the world, with notable exceptions such as Saudi Arabia, which continues to refuse full civil rights to its female citizens.

Although women constitute half of the world's electorate and possess voting rights almost everywhere, they are still grossly underrepresented politically (see Figure 10.9). Female representation in national parliaments slowly increased, from 11 percent in 1995 to 19 percent in 2010. In twenty-six countries, women comprise 30 percent of lower houses of parliament and 40 percent or above in seven nations. On the other hand, in fifty-eight countries women make up 10 percent or less of parliamentary chambers and there are no women in the governing body of nine nations.

Though the number of women in parliamentary leadership posts has increased somewhat (from twenty-four women in 1995 to thirty-five in 2010), their presence at the top remains uncommon. As of 2009, women headed a scant 21 of 176 lower or single chambers of parliaments, and only 10 of 73 upper chambers had female leaders. The executive branch magnifies the failure of women to achieve leadership positions.

FIGURE 10.9

Proportion of Seats Held by Women in Single or Lower Houses of National Parliaments, 2000 and 2010 (Percentage)

If you took this figure home to your parents, how would you describe the results to them? What would be your assessment of progression in the legislative representation of women throughout the world?

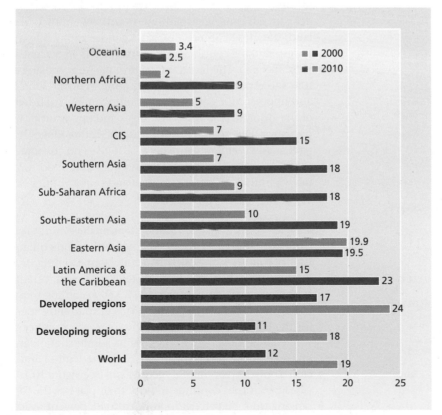

Source: *The Millenium Developmental Goals Report 2010*, New York: The United Nations, 2010, p. 25.

In 2010, a mere 9 of 151 elected heads of state were female, and only 11 of 192 heads of government were women. There has been only slight improvement in the representation of women in cabinet posts. On average across the globe, women hold only 17 percent of cabinet positions, up from 8 percent a decade ago.

Women are also underrepresented in the judicial branch of government, except for Eastern Europe. In Western Europe and Western Asia, women hold less than 50 percent of judgeships, and the percentage for most of these countries is in the 20 to 40 range.

In Eastern European countries, in contrast, the average percentage of female judges is 64.

To this point, we have refrained from systematic comparisons between the United States and the rest of the world. This is appropriate for three reasons. First, constant comparisons would detract from the global picture. Second, it would be impossible to compare the United States to other countries on the many separate dimensions, measured in so many different ways across countries. Third, comparisons would make this section unnecessarily long for you. There is, however, a shortcut that permits a generalized comparison between the United States and the world. This shortcut comes in the form of the Global Gender Gap Index, a composite measure of global gender inequality created by the World Economic Forum.

A United States–World Comparison

Q **What is the Global Gender Gap Index?** First published in 2005, the Global Gender Gap Index ranks 134 major and emerging economies in terms of the extent to which they close the gap between women and men (Hausmann, Tyson, and Zahidi 2010). Covering almost all of the world's population, the Index is a composite measure of four central dimensions of gender equality: employment and economic opportunity, educational achievement, political power, and health. The higher a country scores on this Index, the greater its progress toward closing its gender gap. For example, the highest-ranking country (Iceland) has closed 85 percent of its gender gap, while the lowest-ranking country (Yemen) has closed 46 percent of its gender gap. The Index is a relative measure, looking at how successful a country is in allocating its own resources and opportunities among men and women, regardless of the absolute amount of resources and opportunities it possesses. The relativity built into the Index makes it a particularly useful measure because it gives no advantage to richer nations with greater resources and opportunities. Countries with few resources and opportunities can compete with wealthier countries.

Q **Where does the United States stand on the world stage?** Until 2010, the United States did not rank among the top twenty countries in closing its gender gap. Coming in at number 19 in 2010, the United States improved its ranking by twelve places compared to 2009. According to the latest Global Gender Gap report, this upward movement for the United States is due to the increased number of women in leading roles in the Obama administration and improvements in the wage gap. Still, the United States closed only 74 percent of its gender gap (see Figure 10.10). Nordic countries continue to hold their place at the top, ranging from 80 percent in Sweden to 85 percent in Iceland. "Think Globally" 10.1 provides a panoramic view of progress toward gender equality around the world.

FIGURE 10.10

Top 20 Countries on the Global Gender Gap Index

Where would you have expected the United States to rank among these countries? Why do you think the United States did not rank as high as the Nordic countries? Do you expect this to happen soon?

	Country	Score
1.	Iceland	0.8496
2.	Norway	0.8404
3.	Finland	0.8260
4.	Sweden	0.8024
5.	New Zealand	0.7808
6.	Ireland	0.7773
7.	Denmark	0.7719
8.	Lesotho	0.7678
9.	Philippines	0.7654
10.	Switzerland	0.7562
11.	Spain	0.7554
12.	South Africa	0.7535
13.	Germany	0.7530
14.	Belgium	0.7509
15.	United Kingdom	0.7460
16.	Sri Lanka	0.7458
17.	Netherlands	0.7444
18.	Latvia	0.7429
19.	United States	0.7411
20.	Canada	0.7372

Source: *The Global Gender Gap Report 2010*, New York: World Economic Forum, 2010.

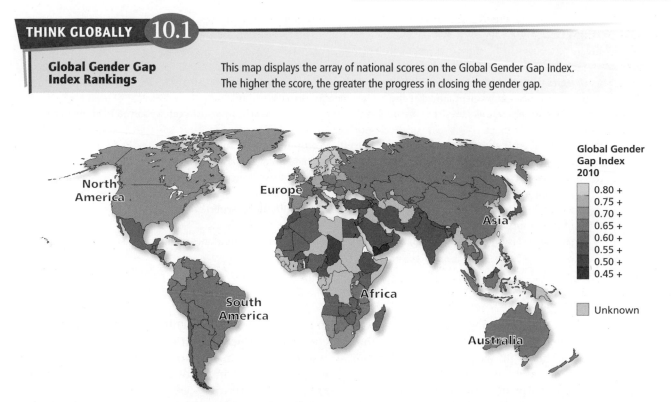

THINK GLOBALLY 10.1

Global Gender Gap Index Rankings

This map displays the array of national scores on the Global Gender Gap Index. The higher the score, the greater the progress in closing the gender gap.

Global Gender Gap Index 2010

0.80 +
0.75 +
0.70 +
0.65 +
0.60 +
0.55 +
0.50 +
0.45 +

Unknown

Source: Ricardo Hausmann, Laura D. Tyson, and Saadia Zahidi, *The Global Gender Gap Report 2010*. (Geneva, Switzerland: World Economic Forum, 2010).

Interpret the Map

1. Rank the areas of the world in terms of their general progress toward closing the gender gap.

2. Assess the likelihood of further change in these areas over the next twenty years.

Changing Gender Roles in the United States R1

Gender Roles and Social Change

Q Why is there resistance to change in gender roles?
First, although men may not be aware that their suppression of women is to their own advantage, like all dominant groups, they can see little reason to change the way things have always been. Second, even if men were willing to relinquish their dominant position, it would be costly to them to do so. Third, some women resist giving up some advantages they see for themselves in the traditional gender role arrangement. Some fear losing the option to be full-time mothers or homemakers and, in addition, do not want to relinquish their husbands' legal obligation to provide for them and their children. Others do not wish to lose conventional male courtesies and protection. Finally, an ideology still exists that supports members of both sexes who wish to maintain their traditional gender roles.

Q What trends are promoting change in gender roles?
There are a number of agents promoting change. Demographic trends—longer life expectancy, smaller families, higher education, increased numbers of jobs requiring skilled labor—have a profound impact on everyone's lives. For women, these trends led to their increased participation in activities outside the home—in school, work, politics, and voluntary organizations. In 2009, 72 percent of all married women held jobs outside the home. Another source of change in gender roles is the "women's movement." Although the goals and objectives of the women's movement appear radical to some, its central ideas are not new (Walters 2005; Lorber 2009).

The Feminist Movement

The **women's movement** is a social movement aimed at the achievement of sexual equality—socially,

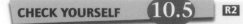

CHECK YOURSELF **10.5** R2

Changing Gender Roles

1. The women's movement can be traced as far back as the _____ century.
2. _____ is a social movement aimed at the achievement of sexual equality.
3. A central assumption of the feminist movement is that the problems created by sexism can be solved by individuals. T or F?
4. Match the gender role alternatives for the future with the descriptions beside them.

____ a. emergent pluralism	(1) Male and female gender roles are basically identical.
____ b. conservative pluralism	(2) Traditional gender roles exist along with alternatives.
____ c. melting pot	(3) Traditional gender roles continue.
____ d. assimilation to the male model of success	(4) Women are socialized into the masculine role.
____ e. female exclusion	(5) Men's and women's roles are different but equally valued.

Answers: 1. eighteenth; 2. Feminism; 3. F; 4. a. (2), b. (5), c. (1), d. (4), e. (3)

legally, politically, and economically. It is best viewed as the reemergence of a long historical struggle that began as far back as 1792 with the publication in England of *A Vindication of the Rights of Women*, by Mary Wollstonecraft. The movement picked up tempo in the United States in 1848, when a group of women abolitionists drew up the *Declaration of Sentiments*, which demanded equal rights for women. By the end of the nineteenth century, it had become a mass movement (Kraditor 1971; S. M. Evans 1989; West and Blumberg 1990; Tobias 1997; Andersen 2010).

The women's movement almost perished in 1920 when, with the passage of the Nineteenth Amendment, women gained the right to vote. However, many of the problems that had prompted it in the first place—the economic dependence of women and the restriction of their full participation in work and politics—remained. These remaining problems, coupled with other developments, such as effective birth control technology and the growth of certain sectors of the labor market (clerical, sales, technical), kept the women's movement alive (V. Taylor 1989).

During the 1960s, the women's movement again gained national attention through its efforts for gender role and societal changes. Beginning with a few isolated voices, such as the publication of Betty Friedan's (1963) enormously influential book *The Feminine Mystique*, the women's movement gained momentum. By the 1970s, it was a mass movement with widespread support (S. M. Evans 1980; Freeman 2008; Collins 2009).

Q **What is the distinction between the women's movement and feminism?** Two points of clarification. First, it is necessary to distinguish between the women's movement and feminism. In Chapter 1, **feminist theory** is defined as a branch of conflict theory that links the lives of women (and men) to the structure of gender relationships. While feminist theory is a scientific matter pursued in the context of theory and research, the women's movement lies in the nonscientific sphere. It involves groups and organizations engaged in activities designed to promote gender equality (Burn 2011).

The popular conception of feminism, and therefore the women's movement as well, may conjure up images of bra burning, political correctness, and angry women—images associated with the rejection of femininity and the desire to emasculate men. Feminist theory and the women's movement are none of those things, but popular conception of feminism denigrates both.

Second, it is helpful to think of the women's movement as one broad, ongoing movement that takes different forms in different eras and in different countries. The movement waxes and wanes across the globe. When it suddenly gains public attention, it may appear to be a new movement, but it actually is another iteration of an enduring struggle with long historical roots.

Gender Roles in the Future

Q **What will gender roles be like in the future?** Women are living longer, bearing fewer children, becoming better educated, and entering the labor force in greater numbers than at any other time in history (Reskin and Padavic 2002). If these trends continue—and there is every reason to believe that they will—certain gender role changes should occur. For example, we can expect more and more women to plan for and pursue careers. No longer will female gender roles define work and career as unfeminine pursuits, nor will certain occupations be off-limits to women. The increasing enrollment of women in medical, law, and business schools indicates that this development is already under way. It is difficult to predict how gender roles will

CHECK YOURSELF **10.6** **R2**

Global Gender Inequality

1. Worldwide, solid majorities endorse gender equality. T or F?
2. Virtually no progress has been made toward gender equality around the world. T or F?
3. Politically, the major problem for women around the globe is the lack of voting rights. T or F?
4. Despite its wealth and educational levels, the United States has been less successful in closing its gender gap than Nordic countries such as Iceland and Finland. T or F?

Answers: 1. T; 2. F; 3. F; 4. T

change in the future because unforeseen events could result in the reversal of present trends. However, the changes that have already occurred suggest a future in which more alternatives will be available to both men and women.

On to Chapter 11

This is the last of three chapters on social inequality in social structures. The next few chapters examine social institutions as a specific type of social structure.

S **INTEGRATED GOALS AND SUMMARY**

1. **Distinguish among the concepts of sex, gender, and gender identity.**
   - All societies have definitions of gender—expectations and behaviors associated with a sex category. Through socialization, members of a society acquire an awareness of themselves as masculine or feminine.
2. **Demonstrate the relative contributions of biology and culture to gender formation.**
   - Aside from obvious biological differences, such as genital characteristics and muscular structure, there are no established, genetically based behavior differences between the sexes. Behavioral differences between men and women are culturally and socially created.
   - Anthropological research reveals cultural diversity in gender characteristics. All in all, though, the traditional gender roles remain the predominant pattern.
3. **Outline the perspectives of gender expressed by functionalists, conflict theorists, and symbolic interactionists.**
   - Functionalists and conflict theorists have different explanations for traditional gender definitions. According to functionalists, a division of labor based on sex was a convenient and obvious solution for preindustrial societies. Conflict theorists, who are more concerned with the continued existence of traditional roles than with their origins, contend that men want to maintain the status quo; they want to protect their dominance of women and society. According to conflict advocates, traditional gender definitions are not appropriate in the modern world.
   - According to symbolic interactionism, gender definitions are imparted through the socialization process.

They are learned and reinforced through interaction with parents, teachers, peers, and the media. This interaction is especially important because gender becomes intertwined with the self-concepts of those affected by it. Gender socialization, which begins before birth and continues throughout life, occurs through elements of the mass media such as books, television, and advertising.

4. **State the relationship between sex stereotypes and gender roles.**
   - Gender roles permit some deviation from the ideal, but sex stereotypes are labels applied to all members of each sex. Sex stereotypes are employed to encourage all men to be masculine and all women to be feminine and allow for no variation from the generalized picture.
   - Sex stereotypes and gender roles are damaging to both men and women. Among other things, they intensify role conflict and strain for men and women.

5. **Describe the position of women in the United States with respect to work, law, and politics.**
   - Although both men and women are damaged by sexism, it is women who feel its full effect. Women, like other minorities, are subject to prejudice and discrimination occupationally, economically, athletically, politically, legally, and socially.

6. **Report the state of global gender inequality.**
   - There seems to be a contradiction between the level of global support for gender equality and the degree of gender inequality that actually exists. Despite some reduction in gender inequality globally, gender inequality continues to be a future goal rather than a past achievement.

7. **Discuss factors promoting resistance to change in traditional gender roles as well as factors promoting change in gender roles in the United States.**
   • Barriers to change in gender roles come from both men and women. Like any dominant group, men are, in principle, reluctant to relinquish their power. Men also realize that gender equality would be costly to them. Many women also resist change, preferring to retain the perceived advantages traditional gender roles provide them. All of this is buttressed by an ideology justifying the status quo. At the same time, demographic trends and the feminist movement are undermining traditional gender roles.

8. **Describe the future of gender roles in the United States.**
   • Given the factors promoting and hindering gender role changes, it is risky to make predictions about the future of gender roles. Most likely, the exclusion of women from traditionally male domains will continue to diminish, and both sexes will increasingly be able to choose from a variety of gender role alternatives.

CONCEPT REVIEW

Match the following concepts with the definitions listed below them.

____ a. sex
____ b. gender
____ c. patriarchy
____ d. feminism
____ e. sex stereotype
____ f. occupational sex segregation
____ g. sexual harassment
____ h. dual labor market
____ i. chivalry hypothesis

1. a split between core and peripheral segments of the economy and the division of the labor force into preferred and marginalized workers
2. the type of society that is controlled by men who use their power, prestige, and economic advantage to dominate women
3. a social movement aimed at the achievement of sexual equality—socially, legally, politically, and economically
4. the expectations and behaviors associated with a sex category within a society
5. the concentration of women in different occupations than men
6. used to portray one sex as innately superior to the other
7. the biological distinction between male and female
8. the use of one's superior power in making unwanted sexual advances
9. the idea that females are treated more leniently than males in the criminal justice system

CHECK YOURSELF REVIEW

1. Societies that do not follow traditional gender roles are exceptions to the rule. T or F?
2. Sex stereotypes and gender roles are essentially the same thing. T or F?
3. Despite its wealth and high educational levels, the United States has been less successful in closing its gender gap than Nordic countries such as Iceland and Finland. T or F?
4. Gender is acquired through the process of _____.
5. According to the _____ perspective, the division of labor based on sex has survived because it is beneficial and efficient for human living.
6. According to the _____ perspective, traditional gender definitions exist because they provide greater rewards and privileges to men than to women.
7. _____ is the theoretical perspective that attempts to explain how gender is acquired.
8. The _____ hypothesis is the idea that females are treated more leniently than males in the criminal justice system.

9. Which of the following is *not* a true statement?
   a. Boys are less assertive in class than girls.
   b. Mass media tend to present the most stereotypical version of gender definitions.
   c. Parents' perceptions of the physical characteristics of their children are influenced very little by their children's gender.
   d. Nursery school children who fail to conform to their "appropriate" gender are met with resistance from their peers.
10. The idea that victory is the most positive reinforcement for all men is an example of
   a. sex
   b. a sex stereotype
   c. a gender role
   d. a value uniquely held by men
   e. role restrain

GRAPHIC REVIEW

Figure 10.4 displays American women's median annual earnings as a percentage of men's from 1955 to 2009.

1. How would you explain this trend to your sixteen-year-old daughter (if you had one)?

_____

_____

_____

2. Assuming that the upward trend since 1980 continues, which of the five gender role patterns outlined in the text would be most descriptive? Why?

_____

_____

_____

CRITICAL-THINKING QUESTIONS

1. Suppose that one of your high school teachers invites you back to speak to her class on the nature versus nurture gender debate. Write a brief essay you could use to summarize the scientific knowledge and to initiate class discussion.

_____

_____

2. Describe the major influences on the development of your gender identity. Use the categories of influence mentioned in this chapter in laying out the specifics of your experiences.

_____

_____

3. Some sociologists draw a parallel between racism and sexism. Discuss the consequences of sex stereotypes to substantiate or refute this assertion.

_____

_____

4. Draw on the information in this chapter to discuss the need for affirmative action programs. Substantiate a case either for or against continuation of these programs.

_____

_____

5. Use information throughout this chapter to predict the future of gender roles. Choose one of the five alternatives for the future of gender roles as the framework for your analysis.

_____

_____

ANSWER KEY

Concept Review

a. 7
b. 4
c. 2
d. 3
e. 6
f. 5
g. 8
h. 1
i. 9

Check Yourself Review

1. T
2. F
3. T
4. socialization
5. functionalist
6. conflict
7. Symbolic interactionism
8. chivalry
9. a
10. b
11. a. 2
    b. 5
    c. 1
    d. 4
    e. 3

11 Family

S GOALS

- Describe the types of family structure, dimensions of family structure, societal norms for mate selection, and types of marital arrangements.
- Compare and contrast views of the family proposed by functionalists, conflict theorists, and symbolic interactionists.
- Describe the modern American family.

- Outline the extent and cause of divorce in America.
- Give an overview of family violence in the United States.
- Describe contemporary alternatives to the traditional nuclear family structure.
- Discuss the future of the American family.

Jim Craigmyle/Getty Images

U.S. divorce rates are soaring! Family life is on the ropes. Yes? No? Films, television, music, and print media suggest that America's family life is in jeopardy. Actually, data on divorce provide grounds for some optimism. Although a dramatic rise in the divorce rate did begin in the early 1960s, the divorce rate began a decline in 1985.

The facts regarding divorce are not as clear-cut as commonly believed, and the family is not as simple an institution as it appears. It is a complex social unit with many dimensions. In addition, there is great diversity in the family structure—across various societies and even within one society (United Nations 1996; Sussman, Steinmetz, and Peterson 1999).

Marriage and Family Defined **R1**

In the simplest terms, a **marriage** is a legal union based on mutual rights and obligations, and a **family** is a group of people related by marriage, blood, or adoption. These brief definitions mask some modern complexities (Eshleman and Bulcroft 2005; Knox and Schacht 2010). By tradition, a marriage in the United States involves a legal relationship between a man and a woman. The recent push for legal recognition of same-sex couples attempts to challenge this tradition. So far, only six states recognize as legitimate a marriage between two men or two women. Other states have tried and failed to legalize gay marriage. A few states recognize "civil unions," some of which grant legal rights associated with heterosexual married couples. The traditional definition of family also fails to include cohabiting couples, which, along with same-sex domestic partners, we cover later in this chapter (Powell, et al. 2010).

There are several types of families and types of marriages. Some of these appear in all cultures, others appear only in certain cultures at certain times.

Q **What types of families are common to all cultures?** The **family of marriage** is established upon marriage. The marriage ceremony signifies that it is legal (officially sanctioned) for a couple to have offspring and to give the children a family name. The family of marriage becomes the family of orientation for the children created from that marriage. The

family of orientation is the family a person is born into, or the family of birth. It provides children with a name, an identity, and a heritage. In other words, it gives the child an ascribed status in the community. The family of birth "orients" children to their neighborhood, community, and society. The forms you fill out to register for college typically ask: What is your father's name? What is your mother's name? Where do you live? Where do your parents work? The answers to these questions indicate who you are and to whom you belong. The family of orientation locates you in the world.

All known societies have families and marriage; the permutations, however, are staggering. Exposure to these variations requires something of an anthropological excursion.

Cross-Cultural Analysis of Family and Marriage **R1**

The structure of family and marriage involves many variations within many cultures. This cross-cultural analysis examines the predominant family and marriage forms in modern society as well as an appreciation for alternative lifestyles.

Variations in Types of Family Structure

The **nuclear family**, the smallest group of individuals that can legitimately be called a family, is generally composed of a mother, a father, and any children. Because the nuclear family is usually based on marriage, it is sometimes called the *conjugal family*. However, the two are not always synonymous. A single parent and child can compose a nuclear family, as well as a brother and sister. The **extended family** consists of two or more adult generations of the same family whose members share economic resources and live in a common household. Extended families may contain grandparents, children, grandchildren, aunts, uncles, and so forth. Because it is based on blood ties, the extended family is often identified as the *consanguine family*.

In general, extended families are most characteristic of preindustrial societies and rural parts of industrial societies. This is not to say, however, that nuclear families were not common in preliterate societies or in preindustrial Europe (Nydeggar 1985). Moreover, it would be inaccurate to conclude that the nuclear family—most characteristic of modern society—exists in isolation from a larger kinship network. Both of these issues—the association of the nuclear family with industrialization and the question of the isolation of the modern nuclear family—require elaboration.

Monkey Business Images/Used under license from Shutterstock

Monkey Business Images/Used under license from Shutterstock

In terms of structure, how would sociologists distinguish these two families?

Q How are industrialization and the nuclear family related? As Figure 11.1 indicates, there is a curvilinear relationship between types of family structure and industrialization. Before humans began to domesticate animals and cultivate crops, most economies were based on hunting and gathering. Small bands of nuclear families followed herds of animals and changing seasons, moving around constantly, never staying long in any one place. When humans learned to domesticate animals to help with tilling the soil and cultivating crops (about 9,000 years ago), they no longer needed to be mobile to maintain a food supply. Families began to farm, settle down, and establish roots. Large families were then needed to plow, harvest, and fulfill the many other tasks needed to live.

FIGURE 11.1

Economy and Family Structure

The nature of family structure varies with the type of economy. Agricultural society promotes the extended family because of the need for labor from a large number of people. The nuclear family is more compatible with hunting and gathering societies and modern societies.

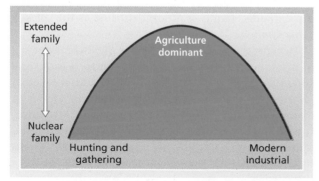

Source: Richard R. Clayton, *The Family, Marriage, and Social Change,* 2nd ed (Lexington, MA: D.C. Heath, 1979), p. 95. Reprinted by permission of the publisher.

Thus, the emergence of family farms and permanent residences encouraged the development of the extended family. When agriculture became the dominant economic base, the extended family became the major type of family. In general, when societies move from agricultural economies to industrialized ones, the extended family is replaced by the nuclear family because large families are no longer needed to supply the necessities of life (W. J. Goode 1970).

Q What accounts for the relationship between industrialization and nuclear family structure? One factor is increasing geographical mobility. People in rural areas must leave their relatives to secure industrial employment in cities. Furthermore, for occupational reasons, those already living in urban areas come to accept frequent changes in residence. Either way, geographical mobility makes it difficult to maintain close ties with large numbers of relatives; usually, only the most immediate kin can be taken along. Also, before industrialization, family members were expected to care for the sick and the elderly. (Actually, they scarcely had a choice, because there were few outside resources.) With the growth of special-purpose organizations and government programs, however, the sick can go to hospitals—for which insurance companies often pay—and the elderly can live in assisted living homes—paid for in part by their Social Security payments. In short, because outsiders provide many of the services formerly performed by the family, relatives do not depend on one another as much as they once did. Thus, certain conditions associated with industrialization are more compatible with the nuclear family than with the extended family.

Q How isolated is the modern nuclear family? Although families in industrialized societies tend to have a nuclear structure and maintain separate residences, there is evidence that they are no longer as isolated from their relatives. Recent changes in the American nuclear family are now occurring in other industrialized societies as well. For one thing, modern transportation and communication make it easier for relatives to maintain family ties even though separated geographically. For another, because of metropolitan growth, children no longer need to leave their parents and other relatives to go to college or to pursue their occupations.

Early on, Marvin Sussman (1953) observed considerable cooperative effort and mutual aid between adults in urban nuclear families and their parents. According to Sussman, families of orientation and procreation are linked together through a kin network. He found, for example, parents offering a variety of services to their married children, including financial aid, home repair and maintenance, baby-sitting, and various kinds of help during illnesses. Subsequent researchers have also found this network of kin relationships (Litwak 1960; Adams 1968, 1970; Troll 1971). A study of Muncie, Indiana, by Theodore Caplow and his colleagues (1982) showed that a high proportion of the close kin of the residents surveyed lived within fifty miles of the city. Most of the residents with parents still living saw their parents at least once a month, and nearly half saw them either weekly or more often. Apparently, the overwhelming majority of Americans maintain frequent contact with a substantial number of relatives. At the very least, the modern family has either a modified nuclear or extended family structure that falls somewhere between the isolated nuclear family and the classic extended family (De Luca 2001).

Whatever the basic family type—nuclear or extended—several dimensions of family structure must be recognized. These patterns take into consideration three circumstances: descent and inheritance, authority within the family, and place of residence.

Dimensions of Family Structure

Q Who owns what? Different arrangements exist for determining descent (who becomes head of the family) and inheritance (who owns family property). If the arrangement is **patrilineal,** descent and inheritance are passed from the father to his male descendants. Iran, Iraq, and Tikopia in the Western Pacific are examples of patrilineal societies. Should descent and inheritance be transmitted from the mother to her female descendants, the arrangement is a **matrilineal** one. Some Native American tribes, such as the five belonging to the League of the Iroquois in Pennsylvania and upper New York, were matrilineal (Zinn, Fitzen, and Wells 2010). In other societies, descent and inheritance are bilateral, passed equally through both parents. Thus, both the father's and mother's relatives are part of the

kinship structure, as is the case for most American families today.

Q Who has authority? With **patriarchal control,** the oldest man living in a household has authority over the rest of the family members—as in Jordan, Iraq, and China (Khouri 2005). In the purest form of patriarchy, the father is the absolute ruler. Usually, patriarchal families are extended families structured along bloodlines. So rare is **matriarchal control,** in which the oldest woman living in a household holds the authority, that controversy exists over whether any society has ever had a genuinely matriarchal family structure. With **democratic control,** authority is split evenly between husband and wife. Many families in the Scandinavian countries and in the United States follow the democratic model.

Q Who lives where? In a nuclear family, a married couple establishes a new residence of its own. Such a residential arrangement is a **neolocal residence.** Extended families, of course, have different residence norms. A **patrilocal residence,** as in premodern China, calls for living with or near the husband's parents. Residing with or near the wife's parents is expected under a **matrilocal residence,** such as the Nayar caste of Kerala in southern India.

Mate Selection

In the United States, most people assume they will have the freedom to choose their mate. It is true that American parents generally no longer arrange marriages for their children. American women no longer fill hope chests with quilts, china, silverware, and other household goods in anticipation of marriage. An American man does not negotiate, with a future father-in-law, a price for the woman he wishes to marry. Therefore, we assume that freedom of choice prevails in the selection of a marriage partner. Actually, this is a false assumption. All societies, including the United States, have norms regarding who may marry whom.

Q What does society tell us about whom to marry? **Exogamy** refers to mate selection norms requiring individuals to marry someone outside their kind. Exogamous norms are usually referred to as incest taboos. In the classic Chinese culture, for example, two people with identical family names could not marry unless their family lines were known to have diverged at least five generations previously (Queen, Habenstein, and Quadagno 1985). In the United States, you are not legally permitted to marry a son or daughter, a brother or sister, a mother or father, a niece or nephew, or an aunt or uncle. Twenty-nine states prohibit marriage to a first cousin, and it is illegal to marry a former mother-in-law or father-in-law. Incest is almost universally prohibited.

In fact, incest seldom existed as an established pattern of mate selection. Royalty in ancient Europe, Hawaii, Egypt, and Peru were prominent exceptions. Even in these instances, most members of the royal families chose partners to whom they were not blood related.

Endogamy involves mate selection norms that require (or at least encourage) individuals to marry within their own kind. An endogamous norm requires that marriage partners be of the same race, ethnicity, religion, and/or social class.

Q What is the difference between endogamy and homogamy? While endogamy refers to cultural pressure to marry someone similar, **homogamy** refers to the tendency to marry someone similar to oneself based on personal preference. Such choices are made because of the greater likelihood of being attracted to and becoming intimate with someone like ourselves. Some factors leading to homogamous choice are age, educational background, degree of physical attractiveness,

shared interests, and extent of religious commitment. Of course, endogamy and homogamy can converge when norms encouraging mate selection with one's race, religion, or social class are so completely internalized that they determine personal preference. But people do tend to marry someone based on one or more shared characteristics. Most marriages in the United States occur between individuals who are about the same age. Most people who have never before married become married to someone who also has always been single. Divorced people tend to marry those who have been previously married. Finally, people tend to choose marriage partners from their own communities or neighborhoods.

Although still the exception in the United States, **heterogamy** is rising. In heterogamous marriages, partners are dissimilar with respect to some important social characteristics. Presently, in America, more marriages are crossing traditional barriers of race and ethnicity.

This trend is due to several factors. America has become more racially and ethnically integrated. This change is especially evident among newlyweds. According to a Pew Research Center analysis of Census Bureau data, nearly 15 percent of all new marriages in the United States in 2008 were between mates of different races or ethnicities (Passel, Wang, and Taylor 2010). Although they represent a relatively small percentage of all marriages in the United States, mixed marriages have increased dramatically since 1980. (Figure 11.2 shows the racial and ethnic breakdown of new marriages.) Racial and ethnic lines are crossed with greater frequency also because more Americans from racial and ethnic groups are attending college together. In addition, younger Americans are very supportive of interracial marriages ("Almost All Millennials Accept Interracial Dating and Marriage" 2010). Finally, the traditional cultural taboos against mixed marriages are weakening.

As you can see, who may marry whom in a society is not completely a matter of choice. Norms of mate selection limit the field of eligible marital partners (Kephart and Jedlicka 1997; Kennedy 2003; Romano 2006).

Types of Marriages

Whatever form an American wedding ceremony takes, be it in a synagogue or on a mountain top, it is an important ritual announcing to the world that a man and woman are husband and wife, that they form a new family, and that any children born to the couple can legitimately inherit the family name and property. But this traditional marital arrangement in the United States is merely one of several possibilities.

Nruboc/Dreamstime LLC

Are these two just-married individuals in a homogenous or heterogamous relationship? Explain.

FIGURE 11.2

Intermarriage Types, Newly Married Couples in 2008

Although only 8 percent of marriages in the U.S. are mixed, the percentage of newly married couples is nearly two times higher.

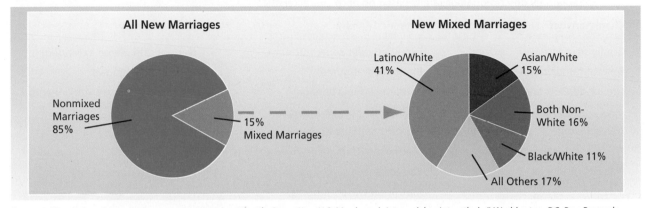

Source: Jeffrey S. Passel, Wendy Wang, and Paul Taylor, "One-in-Seven New U.S. Marriages is Interracial or Interethnic," Washington, DC: Pew Research Center, 2010, pp.1, 2. http://pewsocialtrends.org/pubs/755/trend-attitudes-interracial-interethnic-marriage.

Q What are the possible types of marriage? **Monogamy**—the marriage of one man to only one woman at a time—is the most widely practiced form of marriage in the world today. **Polygamy,** on the other hand, which is the marriage of a male or female to multiple partners of the other sex, takes two forms: polygyny and polyandry. **Polygyny** is the marriage of one man to two or more women at the same time. The most obvious example of polygyny can be found in the Old Testament of the Bible, in which King Solomon is reported to have had 700 wives and 300 concubines. George Murdock (1957) found the practice of polygyny in 75 percent of the 575 preliterate societies he studied. However, polygyny is not legal in any Western society (Paddock 1999), and as stated in its 1948 statement on human rights, the United Nations explicitly frowns on this type of marriage. **Polyandry**—the marriage of one woman to two or more men at the same time—is an even rarer form of marriage, found exclusively in the South Asian countries of Tibet, Nepal, and India (Stockard 2002). It was common in only two societies: in Tibet and among the Todas of India (Queen, Habenstein, and Quadagno 1985). Where polyandry existed, it usually consisted of several brothers sharing a wife (fraternal polyandry). Instances of a father sharing a wife with his sons are very rare. A group marriage consists of two or more men married to two or more women which is also rare. In fact, researchers have not identified even one society in which group marriage was the norm. There have, however, been communes that practiced group marriage (Berger, Hackett, and Millar 1972; Kanter 1972; Ferrar 1977).

This analysis of the family and marriage is complicated because of the large number of concepts. Table 11.1 summarizes these concepts within the context of the traditional (extended) and modern (nuclear) family structures.

Theoretical Perspectives and the Family [R1]

The family is as central to society as it is complex. It is not surprising that each of the major theoretical perspectives sheds light on this institution.

Functionalism

You were born into a family with whom you have lived for almost twenty years. You are likely to marry, and despite the high rate of divorce, the overwhelming majority of your adult life will be spent within a family.

The family performs many essential functions. First, it provides the initial learning experiences that make people human. Second, it generally provides a supportive and loving atmosphere that fulfills basic human social and emotional needs. Third, it is the only legitimate source of reproduction for a society. Fourth, it regulates sexual activity. Fifth, it places people in a social class at birth. Finally, the family serves an important economic function. Because of these vital functions, the family is often referred to as the basic institution of society. Each function deserves elaboration.

Q How does the family contribute to the socialization process? A major function of the family begins with the birth of a baby. In addition to caring for an infant's physical needs, parents begin the vital process of

TABLE 11.1

Major Characteristics of Extended and Nuclear Families

Examine the major characteristics of extended and nuclear family structures. Do you live in a nuclear or extended family? Explain by describing your family based on each characteristic.

Characteristics	Extended Family	Nuclear Family
Family structure	Extended (also some nuclear)	Nuclear (also some extended)
Basis of family bond	Blood (consanguine)	Marriage (conjugal)
Line of descent and inheritance	Patrilineal (male lineage)	Bilateral (dual parental lineage)
	Matrilineal (female lineage)	
Locus of control	Patriarchal (male dominance)	Democratic (sexes share power)
	Matriarchal (female dominance)	
Place of residence	Patrilocal (husband's parents)	Neolocal (independent)
	Matrilocal (wife's parents)	
Marriage structure	Monogamy (one spouse)	Monogamy (one spouse)
	Polygyny (several wives)	
	Polyandry (several husbands)	
	Group (several husbands and wives)	

teaching the child necessities for participating in society. During the first year, the infant mimics words and, later, sentences. During the second and third years, parents begin to teach the child customary ways of behaving. By providing role models, training, and education, the process of family socialization continues as the child enters new stages of development.

Q What is the socioemotional function of the family?
Another major function of the family is "socioemotional

maintenance" (Nimkoff 1965). This begins in the first year with intimate holding, touching, stroking, and talking to the baby. Generally, the family provides the one supportive environment in society in which an individual is unconditionally accepted and loved. Family members accept one another as they are; every member is special and unique. Without this care and affection provided by parents (or other adults), children will not develop normally. They may have low self-esteem, fear rejection, feel insecure, and eventually find it

CHECK YOURSELF **11.1** **R2**

Marriage and Family Defined

1. A _____ is a group of people related by marriage, blood, or adoption.
2. A family of _____ is the family into which a person is born.
3. A family of _____ is the family established upon marriage.
4. The _____ family consists of two or more generations of the same family sharing a common household and economic resources.
5. There is a _____ relationship between types of family structure and industrialization.
6. Industrialization promotes the shift from the extended family to the _____ family.
7. In a _____ family, the oldest man living in the household controls the rest of the family members.
8. Indicate which type of mate selection norm is reflected in each of the following situations.
   ____ a. Jews are supposed to marry Jews.   (1) exogamy
   ____ b. A father is not permitted to marry his daughter.   (2) endogamy
   ____ c. Members of the same social class marry.   (3) homogamy
9. _____ is the marriage of a woman to two or more men at the same time.

difficult to adjust to marriage or to express affection to their own children. In fact, some young children who do not receive love and attention become retarded or die (see Chapter 4). Even individuals who are well integrated into society require support when adjusting to changing norms and when developing and continuing healthy relationships. Here again, the family can provide socioemotional maintenance. (See Table 11.2 for American children's view of how well their parents fulfilled the socioemotional functions.)

TABLE 11.2

American Youths Grade Their Parents

In a national survey, Americans in the seventh through the twelfth grades were asked to "grade" their mothers and fathers. The results are shown below. The left-hand column lists various aspects of child rearing, and the remaining columns indicate the percentage of students who assigned each grade. For example, on the dimension "Raising me with good values," 69 percent gave their fathers an A, 17 percent a B, and so forth.

Grading Dad — Assigned Grade

Aspect of Child Rearing	A	B	C	D	F
Raising me with good values	69%	17%	8%	4%	2%
Appreciating me for who I am	58%	21%	11%	8%	2%
Encouraging me to enjoy learning	58%	24%	12%	4%	2%
Making me feel important and loved	57%	22%	13%	6%	2%
Being able to go to important events	55%	22%	13%	5%	5%
Being there for me when I am sick	52%	20%	16%	8%	4%
Establishing traditions with me	41%	26%	15%	11%	7%
Being involved in school life	38%	24%	19%	12%	7%
Being someone to go to when upset	38%	22%	15%	12%	13%
Controlling his temper	31%	27%	20%	10%	12%
Knowing what goes on with me	31%	30%	17%	12%	10%

Grading Mom

Aspect of Child Rearing	A	B	C	D	F
Being there for me when I am sick	81%	11%	5%	2%	1%
Raising me with good values	74%	15%	6%	3%	2%
Making me feel important and loved	64%	20%	10%	5%	1%
Being able to go to important events	64%	20%	10%	3%	3%
Appreciating me for who I am	63%	18%	8%	6%	5%
Encouraging me to enjoy learning	59%	23%	12%	3%	3%
Being involved in school life	46%	25%	13%	10%	6%
Being someone to go to when upset	46%	22%	13%	8%	9%
Spending time talking with me	43%	33%	14%	6%	4%
Establishing traditions with me	38%	29%	17%	10%	6%
Knowing what goes on with me	35%	31%	15%	10%	9%
Controlling her temper	29%	28%	19%	12%	11%

1. Based on these data, what conclusions would you draw about the closeness of families in America?
2. Select the three aspects of child rearing you think are the most important, and compare the grade you would give your parent or parents on these aspects with the grades in this national sample.

Source: Ellen Galinsky, *Ask the Children* (New York: Harper Collins, 2000).

Q What is the reproductive function of the family? Society cannot survive without new members. The family's reproductive function provides an orderly mechanism for producing generation after generation. So important is this function that for many cultures and religions, it is the primary purpose for sexual relations. In many societies in developing nations, the failure of a wife to bear children can lead to divorce. Residents of places like the Punjab region of northern India, for example, view children as an economic necessity. The significance of having children is also seen in the hundreds of rituals, customs, and traditions associated with pregnancy and childbirth in virtually all cultures around the world. It is customary in the United States, for instance, to honor the mother-to-be with a baby shower. After birth, babies are displayed in hospital nurseries so that friends and relatives can marvel at them. Among the Sirono Indians of eastern Bolivia, there are three days of rituals celebrating the birth of a child. These rituals are designed to protect the life of the infant and to ensure the child's good health (Holmberg 1969).

Q In what ways does the family regulate sexual activity? In no known society are people given total sexual freedom. Even in sexually permissive societies, like that of the Hopi Indians, there are rules for mating and marrying (Queen, Habenstein, and Quadagno 1985).

Norms regarding sexual activities vary from place to place, but whatever the norms, it is almost always the family who enforces them. To illustrate, the Trobriand Islands society off the coast of Papua, New Guinea, encourages all children to engage in premarital sex (Malinowski 1929). Thus, much of childhood is spent going from partner to partner, as a bee goes from flower to flower. By contrast, other societies, like those in Iran or Afghanistan, go to great lengths to prevent any contact between unrelated single males and females. In Muslim countries, for instance, the bride's family must guarantee that she is a virgin; the honor of the family rests on that guarantee (E. L. Peters 1965). In the United States, the norm traditionally falls between these two extremes.

Sexual norms also change within a society. For instance, in colonial America, sex outside of marriage was considered a sin, but after Alfred Kinsey's studies of sexual behavior hit the American public like a bombshell (Kinsey, Pomeroy, and Martin 1948; Kinsey and Gebhard 1953), a sexual revolution occurred.

Q How does the family transmit social status? Transmission of social class occurs primarily through the family, partly because it is the family that provides economic resources that open and close occupational doors. If people move up or down the stratification structure, it is usually only a very slight move. The sons and daughters of high-income professionals,

More than 25 percent of working wives earn more than their husbands. How do you think the fact that the wives out earn their husbands changes the balance of power and responsibility in these marriages?

Stephen Wilkes/Getty Images

for example, are more likely to attend college and graduate school than are the children of blue-collar workers. Consequently, the children of professionals are more likely as adults to enter professional occupations. The family also transmits values that later affect social status. The children of professionals, to cite only one illustration, tend to feel a greater need to pursue a college degree than do their counterparts from blue-collar families. In these and many other ways, the family affects the placement of children in the stratification structure.

Q What is the economic function of the family? At one time, families were self-sufficient economic units whose members all contributed to the production of needed goods—growing food, making cloth, and taking care of livestock. Malls, corporations, and supermarkets were not part of the scene. In contrast, the modern American family is a unit of consumption rather than production. Adult members, increasingly including working mothers, work outside the home and pool their resources. But the end result is the same: The family provides the economic necessities of life.

Conflict Theory

Functionalism emphasizes the ways in which the family attempts to contribute to the order and stability of society. The conflict perspective draws attention to social concerns such as sexual inequality. (See Table 11.3 for a comparison of the theoretical perspectives with respect to the family.)

Q How was the conflict perspective first applied to the family? One can trace the conflict perspective of family gender inequality to Friedrich Engels, a collaborator of Karl Marx. Engels saw women's oppression as the result, first, of women's loss of a productive role, and second, of men's interest—with the development of private property and surplus wealth—in utilizing monogamy to confirm paternity (Engels 2001; originally published in 1884). To Engels, then, males historically used the family to preserve their domination of females.

Q How do the ideas of early feminist writers fit with Engels's approach? Some feminists share with conflict theorists the belief that families reflect social inequality and experience conflict over resources (Benokraitis 2007). Because these feminists focus on patriarchy (control by men over women), they point out that the domination by men over women predates private ownership of property and capitalism (P. Mann 1994). Conflict in the family, according to these feminists, is primarily the result of women's attempt to gain more power within the family structure.

Q Do conflict theorists currently endorse this viewpoint? This theme, prevalent among contemporary conflict theorists, bears on at least three issues: the domination of women by men, family rules of power and inheritance, and the male-dominated economic division of labor. Because most family structures throughout history have been patriarchal, women have traditionally been the property of men—first of fathers, then

of husbands. Only since 1920 have American women had an opportunity to vote in federal elections (after a tremendous struggle), and only since 1974 have women gained the right to make contracts and obtain credit independently of husbands or fathers. Even so, the treatment of women as the property of men often continues, and because most arrangements have been patrilineal, male control of family members and male ownership of property typically have been through male bloodlines (Collins 1971). This has created built-in gender inequality in most family systems because male dominance is considered "natural" and "legitimate."

The predominant patrilineal and patriarchal family patterns are also related to the traditional economic division of labor, which again perpetuates gender inequality. In the traditional division of labor, males work outside the home, while women remain at home to prepare meals, keep house, and care for the children. Women are unpaid laborers who make it possible for men to earn wages. This economic power enables males to maintain dominance over the economically dependent wife and mother.

Industrialization has altered these traditional patterns, but the persistent social, economic, occupational, political, and legal inequality of women continues, as we saw in Chapter 10.

Symbolic Interactionism

Q What is the relevance of symbolic interactionism to the study of the family? According to this popular perspective of marriage and the family, a key to understanding behavior within the family lies both in the interactions among family members and in the meanings that members assign to these interactions. Within the family, you can observe all the major concepts of symbolic interactionism—socialization, looking-glass self, role taking, primary group, reference group, significant others, symbolic interpretation of events, and symbolic communication (Waller and Hill 1951; Leslie and Korman 1989).

TABLE 11.3

FOCUS ON THEORETICAL PERSPECTIVES: Perspectives on the Family

Both functionalism and conflict theory are more concerned with the ways social norms affect the nature of the family. Symbolic interactionism tends to examine the relationship of the self to the family. If functionalism and conflict theory were used to focus on the self, what examples would you give?

Theory	Topic	Example
Functionalism	Sex norms	Children are taught that sexual activity should be reserved for married couples.
Conflict theory	Male dominance	Husbands use their economic power to control the ways money is spent.
Symbolic interactionism	Developing self-esteem	A child abused by her parents learns to dislike herself.

CHECK YOURSELF **11.2** R2

Theoretical Perspectives and the Family

1. Which of the following functions of the family is not shared with any other institution?
   a. socialization
   b. reproduction
   c. socioemotional maintenance
   d. sexual regulation

2. Match the following examples with the major theoretical perspectives:
   ____ a. a father "giving away" the bride
   ____ b. sexual regulation
   ____ c. development of self-concept
   ____ d. a newly married couple adjusting to each other
   ____ e. child abuse
   ____ f. social class passed from one generation to another

   (1) functionalism
   (2) conflict theory
   (3) symbolic interactionism

Answers: 1. b; 2. a. (2), b. (1), c. (3), d. (3), e. (2), f. (1)

Socialization begins within the family. As family members share meanings and feelings, children develop self-concepts and learn to put themselves mentally in the place of others. Interaction with adults permits children to acquire the personality and social characteristics associated with human beings. With the repertoire of personality and social capabilities learned within the family, children can develop further as they interact with people outside the home.

According to symbolic interactionists, relationships within the family are constantly being redefined. A newly married couple will spend many months (perhaps years) testing their new relationship. As time passes, the initial relationship changes, along with some aspects of the partners' personalities—including self-concepts. These changes occur as the partners grapple with such problem issues as distribution of responsibilities, personality clashes, and in-law distractions. With the arrival of children comes a new set of adjustments. Parental views may differ on number of children desired, child-rearing practices, and education for the children. The family becomes even more complex as the new member(s) add(s) to the interaction patterns.

Family and Marriage in the United States R1

The Nature of the American Family

The **marriage rate**—the number of marriages per year for every 1,000 members of a population—has fluctuated in the United States since 1940. As shown in Figure 11.3, the marriage rate peaked at over 16 per

1,000 immediately following World War II. Since then, the marriage rate, with some ups and downs, has fallen by more than half. Marriage among Americans is at an all-time low of 52 percent for adults eighteen and over.

Some claim that there is no "typical American family." After all, the United States is a large, diverse society in which various groups—reflecting vastly different cultural heritages—have blended together. The early white settlers came primarily from Holland and England. Not

FIGURE 11.3

Divorce and Marriage Rates: 1940–2009

Can you apply what you learned in history to interpret this chart? (a) What happened in the mid-1940s that caused the dramatic rise in the marriage rate during this period? (b) Why do you think the marriage rate dropped so low in the 1950s? (c) What are some possible reasons the divorce rate peaked in the 1980s?

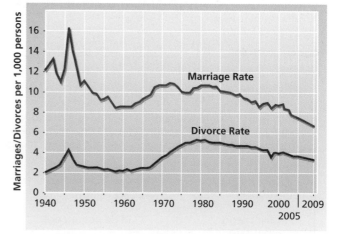

Sources: National Vital Statistics Reports; *Statistical Abstract of the United States,* and *The World Almanac and Book of Facts 2011,* New York: World Almanac Books, 2011, p.172.

long after they arrived, many Africans were brought in as slaves. Subsequently came waves of immigrants from northern Europe, Ireland, Italy, the Slavic and Baltic countries, China, Japan, Southeast Asia, and, more recently, countries in Latin America.

Still, there are more similarities than differences among American families. As the various ethnic groups assimilate into American life, most families tend to follow the American pattern: containing only the parents and children in the same household (nuclear), tracing lineage and passing inheritance equally through both parents (bilateral), dividing family decision making equally (democratic), establishing a separate residence (neolocal), and following the norm of one woman married to one man at any particular time (monogamous).

A large family was once the norm in American society. In 1971, almost three-fourths of American adults thought that three or more children would be the most desirable number (Roper Organization 1985). In 2007, the average number of children born to American women was 2.0, enough to replace the country's population for the first time in thirty-five years (*World Population Data Sheet* 2010).

Q Why have large families declined in popularity? Many factors contribute to the smaller American family. Both men and women are marrying later and staying in school longer. Increasing numbers of women are in the labor force, for financial rewards as well as personal fulfillment. Legalized contraception and abortion also reduce family size. Two additional factors promoting a lower fertility rate are the high cost of children and the removal of the stigma on childless marriages. (More is said about childless marriages later in this chapter.)

Americans are increasingly choosing alternatives to the family pattern of mother (as homemaker), father (as breadwinner), and children: Slightly less than one-fourth of American households consist of a married couple with children under age eighteen. These new family and marriage arrangements include single-parent families, childless marriages, dual-employed marriages, single life, cohabitation, and gay and lesbian couples, all to be discussed later in this chapter.

Romantic Love as the Basis for Marriage

Overwhelmingly, American men and women rated "being in love" as the most important reason to marry (93 percent; "The Decline of Marriage and Rise of New Families" 2010; Hull, Meier, and Ortyle 2010). But this view of love and marriage has not always been the case. Among the British feudal aristocracy, romantic love was a game of pursuit played outside of marriage. Marriage was not thought to be compatible with deeply romantic feelings. In ancient Japan,

love was considered a barrier to the arrangement of marriages by parents. Among Hindus in India today, parents or other relatives are expected to find suitable mates for the young. Criteria for mate selection include caste, wealth, family reputation, and appearance. Love is not absent in Hindu marriages, but love follows marriage rather than the other way around (F. D. Cox 2006; see "See Sociology in Your Life").

Are modern marriages based on romantic love alone? In modern societies, romantic love is almost always a priority for marriage, but it is seldom the only one. People marry for many reasons, and love may or may not be one of them. People may marry to obtain regular sex partners, to legitimate living together, to enter a rich and powerful family, or to advance a career. One of the strongest motivations for marriage is conformity. Throughout our formative years, we are told what to do: "Feed yourself," "Join the Girl Scouts," "Learn to drive," "Go to college," "Get a job." Many parents also expect their children to marry after a certain age and worry about them—perhaps even pressure them—if they remain single very long. Peers are another source of pressure. Because about 90 percent of all adults in the United States do marry, conformity must certainly be a motivating factor (Saad 2006a). Although the age of first marriage is increasing, most Americans are married by their mid-twenties.

Although Americans typically believe that a marriage that is not based on romantic love cannot last, it may be more accurate to say that a marriage based only on romantic love is almost sure to fail. According to research, love may be a good start, but it is only the beginning. For a marriage to last, a couple must build a relationship that goes beyond romantic love (J. F. Crosby 1985; Knox and Schacht 2010).

Divorce

Q What is the current divorce rate? The **divorce rate** is the number of divorces annually for every 1,000 members of the population. Except for a peak and decline after World War II, the divorce rate in the United States increased slowly between 1860 and the early 1960s. A dramatic increase in the divorce rate occurred over the next twenty years. It more than doubled from 2.2 in 1960 to 5.3 in 1981. Since then, as indicated in Using the Sociological Imagination at the beginning of this chapter, the rate has leveled off, declining slightly since 1985 (Cherlin 2010). The divorce rate, which peaked at 5.3 in 1981, stood at just less than 4 in 2009 (see Figure 11.3).

In 1940, the marriage rate was 12.1 per 1,000 people, whereas the divorce rate was only 2 per 1,000 persons. Now the rate of divorce is half the rate of marriage. Based on these data, it is correct to say only that the divorce rate in the United States is now half its marriage rate. It is wrong to conclude that half of all marriages

Looking for Mr. or Ms. Right

This activity will give you some ideas for evaluating whether a current boyfriend or girlfriend is a good candidate for a successful long-term relationship.

From the list on the right (and on a separate sheet of paper), list the ten most important qualities to you. (Number 1 as the most important, number 2 the next more important, and so forth.) Then fold your paper in half. In the right-hand column, either have your partner fill out the questionnaire or rank the characteristics yourself according to how you think your partner would.

Which of the items listed on the right do you think are the most important in predicting marital success? According to research, the last seven items (17–23) are the most important. High compatibility between you and your partner on these seven characteristics would probably increase your chances of marital success. A low degree of matching does not, of course,

ensure an unhappy marriage or a divorce, but it does suggest areas that may cause problems in the future.

Adapted from the Department of Human Development and Family Studies, Colorado State University.

Think About It

Do you think that the qualities listed in the questionnaire are relevant to your choosing a wife or a husband? Why or why not? Are there characteristics more important to you and your friends? Explain.

I am looking for a partner who…

Partner Self

1. _____ _____ is honest and truthful.
2. _____ _____ is fun to be with.
3. _____ _____ is of the same educational background.
4. _____ _____ will take care of me.
5. _____ _____ wants to have children.
6. _____ _____ communicates well with me.
7. _____ _____ will share household jobs and tasks.
8. _____ _____ is a good friend with whom I can talk.
9. _____ _____ is of the same religious background.
10. _____ _____ makes decisions.
11. _____ _____ earns good money.
12. _____ _____ is physically attractive.
13. _____ _____ is in love with me and I with him or her.
14. _____ _____ encourages me to be my own person.
15. _____ _____ has interests like mine in making money and having fun.
16. _____ _____ makes me feel important.
17. _____ _____ is faithful.
18. _____ _____ shares mutual interests in home, children, romantic love, and religion.
19. _____ _____ has had a happy childhood with happily married parents.
20. _____ _____ is emotionally mature.
21. _____ _____ is prepared to support a family.
22. _____ _____ is interested in waiting to marry until age twenty-two or older.
23. _____ _____ wants a six-month to two-year engagement period.

end in divorce, because the divorce and marriage rates are snapshots of a single year and do not take into account the total number of divorces and intact marriages from all years past.

This is why sociologists also employ the **divorce ratio**—the number of divorced persons in the population divided by the number of persons who are married and living with their spouses. In the United States in 2006, there were 23 million divorced persons and 128 million persons married and living with their spouses. Dividing the number of divorced persons by

the number of married persons yields a divorce ratio of 180. This divorce ratio is five times the 1960 ratio of 35. Women generally have a higher divorce ratio than men (204 versus 153 in 2006), reflecting the greater tendency of men to get remarried after divorce and to do so more quickly than women (U.S. Bureau of the Census 2007).

These figures provide some basis for optimism for the future of the American family, just as do the divorce rates of recent years. Between 1960 and 1970, the divorce ratio in the United States increased by an annual average of 1.2 (from 35 in 1960 to 47 in 1970). During the 1970s, the average annual increase rose sharply to 5.2 (from 47 in 1970 to 100 in 1980). Since 1980, the average annual increase has actually declined. In other words, although the divorce ratio is rising each year, its rate of increase has declined since 1980 (Cherlin 2002). Still, the U.S. divorce rate is high among industrialized countries (F. D. Cox 2005; U.S. Census Bureau, 2009).

Q Why the high U.S. divorce rate? There are no easy answers to this question; like family and marriage, divorce is a complex matter. Those who study marriage and divorce have sought answers at both individual and societal levels.

At the individual level, the following factors seem to be associated with divorce (Knox and Schacht 2008). First, the earlier one marries, the greater the likelihood of divorce. Second, the longer a couple remains married, the lower the probability that their marriage will end in divorce. The average length of first marriages ending in divorce in the United States is about six years. However, the largest number of first marriages ending in divorce occurs between the second and third anniversaries. This suggests that poor decisions in mate selection may be as important as marital conflict. Third, as might be expected, divorce is related to the nature and quality of the marital relationship: The more respect and flexibility between partners, the lower the chance of divorce.

At the societal level, several factors seem to affect the divorce rate. First, divorce rates increase during economic prosperity and decrease during economic recession or depression. This is probably because economic prosperity permits people to concentrate on issues beyond survival and to consider options other than marriage for their personal happiness. Second, the rise in the divorce rate in the United States in the 1960s reflects the passage of the baby boom generation into the marriageable ages. Not only are there greater numbers of them, but baby boomers as a group are much more forgiving of divorce and remarriage than earlier generations. Third, because women are more economically independent and because they have a wider range of child care options, they are less hesitant to dissolve a bad marriage. Finally, American values and attitudes about marriage and divorce have changed. The stigma once associated with divorce is much weaker today (R. Farley 1998).

Q What about future divorce rates? The recent decline in the U.S. divorce rate and divorce ratio may continue for several reasons. First, we know that the later people marry, the less likely they are to divorce. (This happens in part because more mature individuals have more realistic expectations about their relationships and because they have fewer economic and career problems

that create emotional strain.) The average age at first marriage is, in fact, increasing in the United States (see Figure 11.4). In 1970, the average age at first marriage was 23.2 for men and 20.8 for women. The average age has increased to 28 for men and 26 for women (Cherlins 2010). This trend is likely to continue well into the twenty-first century. Second, the average age of the population of the United States is increasing as baby boomers grow older. It was this exceptionally large generation that set records for divorce in the late 1960s and 1970s. Baby boomers now range in age from late thirties to mid-fifties, removing them from the age bracket that produces the highest divorce rates. Third, American couples are having fewer children and the children are spaced farther apart. This reduces pressure.

The recent decline in the U.S. divorce rate is encouraging. At the very least, it is the first break in a long-term increase. Still, many experts are cautious about predicting the future, pointing to the fact that the extent of the divorce rate is cyclical and that the recent decline may be only temporary.

Q Is a high divorce rate unique to the United States? The media often leave the impression that the United States is experiencing a high divorce rate due to social factors peculiar to this country. In fact, since 1960 the divorce rate has risen more than fivefold in Canada and the United Kingdom, almost tripled in France, and doubled in Germany and Sweden. The divorce rate has also gone up in Japan but to a lesser degree. On the other

FIGURE 11.4

Median Age at First Marriage

This figure displays changes in the median age at first marriage in the United States since 1900. The marrying age for both men and women has been on the increase since the 1970s. Discuss the implications of this trend for the future divorce rate.

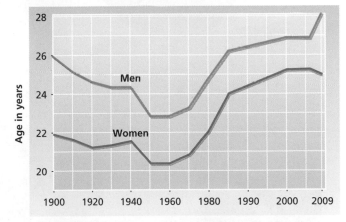

Source: U.S. Bureau of the Census, *Current Population Reports*, Series P20-537, "America's Families and Living Arrangements: 2000," and earlier reports; at www.census.gov/prod/2001pubs/p20-537.pdf. *The World Almanac and Book of Facts 2011* (New York: World Almanac Books, 2011, p.172).

hand, countries in Asia, Central America, and South America have significantly lower divorce rates.

To understand this worldwide variation in divorce rates, it is necessary to identify the major socioeconomic factors influencing these rates. Increasing prosperity, to cite one important factor, is associated with higher divorce rates. Consider China, whose divorce rate has risen with its recent economic development. China's divorce rate is now twice as high as it was in 1990. Because of social and economic development, more women are initiating divorce as their economic opportunities and rights increase.

The correlation between economic development and divorce rate is far from perfect. For example, the divorce rate is higher in Belarus despite its lower economic development, while the divorce rate is lower in a highly prosperous country such as Japan. This is because the divorce rate is affected by additional social factors.

Religion is a second factor affecting divorce rates, particularly in less developed countries. The predominance of Roman Catholicism in Central and South America, for example, diminishes the frequency of divorce. Religion also affects divorce, independently of level of socioeconomic development, as seen in Roman Catholic–dominated Italy and Ireland.

A third factor retarding the divorce rate is a patriarchal power structure. The more patriarchal a society, the lower its divorce rate. In many Middle Eastern countries, for example, a husband can dissolve his marriage by saying "I divorce thee" three times in the presence of witnesses. A woman wishing a divorce, however, must convince a court of her husband's economic neglect and his morally corrupting influence on the family. And only recently have Egyptian women

even been allowed to file for divorce in the absence of extraordinary maltreatment. Unless they give considerable wealth to a willing husband, Taiwanese women are reluctant to seek divorce because their children will automatically be in the sole custody of their husbands (Chang 1998).

Family Violence

Americans, like the rest of the world, have traditionally denied the existence of widespread family violence (*The World's Women* 2010). Its occurrence was mistakenly associated most often with lower-class families, with maybe a few exceptional cases in the middle and upper classes.

There is a good reason for this erroneous picture. Early research used law enforcement and public medical records. Because law enforcement officials and public hospitals were more likely to be aware of lower-class family violence, the statistics were skewed toward these families. Middle- and upper-class families disproportionately conceal their domestic violence (S. Weitzman 2000).

However, the past few decades brought heightened public attention to domestic violence (Ingrassia and Beck 1994; Smolowe 1994; Jasinski 2000; Anderson 2010). The media make every effort to give Americans the details of dramatic legal cases. Erik and Lyle Menendez admitted planning and carrying out the murder of parents they accused of abusing them. Evidence indicates that O.J. Simpson abused his wife before she was murdered. Claiming past abuse, humiliation, and forced sex, Lorena Bobbitt severed her husband's penis while he slept. Actor Mel Gibson was captured on tape threatening to kill his wife, who, he said, needs a "bat on the side of the head."

In patriarchal societies, the divorce rate is lower. Why?

Arabian Eye/Getty Images

Q **How widespread is family violence?** Although the family does, as the functionalists contend, usually provide a safe and warm emotional haven, it can also be a hostile environment (Johnson 2009). Assault and murder are more likely to be the acts of someone living in the home. More than one-fifth of all reported cases of aggravated assault involve domestic violence. The situation is actually much worse because most episodes of domestic violence go unreported. Perhaps as little as 10 percent of information about such cases reaches the authorities (Gelles 1997; Gelles et al. 2004; The World's Women 2010). Domestic violence is not reserved for any particular members of the family. It involves children, spouses, siblings, and older people ("Violence Against Women" 2002; Barnett, Perrin, and Miller-Perrin 2004).

Parental abuse of children may begin in the womb. A large percentage of assaults on wives by their husbands occur during pregnancy; birth defects and miscarriages are common results. In fact, such abuse may lead to more birth defects than all other childhood diseases combined. Nor do all children grow up in a loving home, nurtured by caring parents (Miller-Perrin and Perrin 2006). About one-quarter of adults in the United States report being physically abused as children. In most cases, physical violence involves a slap, a shove, or a severe spanking. However, kicking, biting, punching, beating, and threatening with a weapon are examples of abusive violence by many parents. Furthermore, according to estimates, one of every four girls and one in ten boys are victims of sexual aggression either within the home or outside. Child sexual abuse goes beyond physical contact. Some children are forced into pornography or are made to view pornography in the presence of the abuser. What's worse, the abuser is usually someone the child trusts—a parent, friend of the family, child caregiver, brother, or sister. About 750,000 children in the United States were victims of child abuse in 2007. About 44 percent of the victims were five years of age or younger (U.S. Census Bureau, 2009).

Q **What does research reveal about husband abuse?** Each year, almost 5 million women are victims of intimate partner-related physical assaults and rapes. And about 1,500 women die from intimate partner violence annually (Centers for Disease Control and Prevention 2009). Male domestic abuse is frequently overlooked. Although intimate relationship are generally male dominated, there is considerable abuse perpetrated by women (Steinmetz, 1988; Wiehe 1990; Straus and Steinmetz 2006). The Centers for Disease Control and Prevention reports that men are the target of almost 3 million intimate partner-related physical attacks annually, 300 of which result in death. Much of the violence on the part of women, it should be noted, involves self-protection or retaliation. Whoever initiates the violence, women are more likely to suffer greater injury because the average man is ordinarily bigger, stronger, and more physically aggressive (Gelles 1997). The extent of domestic abuse is surely underestimated, in part because three-fourths of spousal violence occur during separation or after divorce and most research is conducted among married couples. Other factors depressing reports of domestic violence include reconciliation, fear of partner retaliation, and the shame of publicly admitting the abuse. (See Figure 11.5 for data on levels of domestic violence against women in selected countries.)

Q **Is abuse always physical?** Domestic violence, of course, is not limited to physical abuse. Verbal abuse and psychological abuse are a part of many families (M. D. Schwartz 1997; Jacobson and Gottman 1998; Knox and Schacht 2008). This is seen in parent–child relationships as well as spousal relationships. Furthermore, psychologists report that the feelings of self-hate and worthlessness that are often the effects of such abuse can be as damaging as physical wounds. In addition, neglect, a condition of being ignored rather than abused, occurs at four times the rate of physical abuse, involving more than half a million children in 2007 (U.S. Census Bureau 2009).

Q **What other forms of family violence are of concern?** Probably the most frequent and most tolerated violence in the family occurs among children (see "Consider This Research"). Much violence occurs among children who are too young to channel their frustrations in nonphysical channels. Abuse among siblings may be based on rivalry, jealousy, disagreements over personal possessions, or incest. Although violence among siblings declines somewhat with age, it does not disappear. Sibling violence appears to be prevalent and on the rise.

Little is known about the abuse of elderly people because less research is available in this area. Abuse of older people usually takes the form of physical violence, psychological mistreatment, economic manipulation, or neglect. Normally, the abuser is a family member (Pillemer and Finkelhor 1988). Over 3 million elderly people are victims of crime annually (Gelles 1997; U.S. Census Bureau, 2009). There is fear of an increase in abuse of older people as the population bulge, represented by the baby boomers, enters old age. For one thing, there will be fewer working adults to support a growing, aging segment of the population. The most likely to be abused are white Protestant women over seventy-five years of age who are mentally, physically, or financially disadvantaged (Garbarino 1989). Older women represent a higher proportion of the abused, in part because they live longer than men. There are simply more elderly women with greater dependency

FIGURE 11.5

Proportion of Women Experiencing Partner Physical Violence

The level and recency of intimate partner physical violence against women clearly varies from country to country. How would you explain the variations?

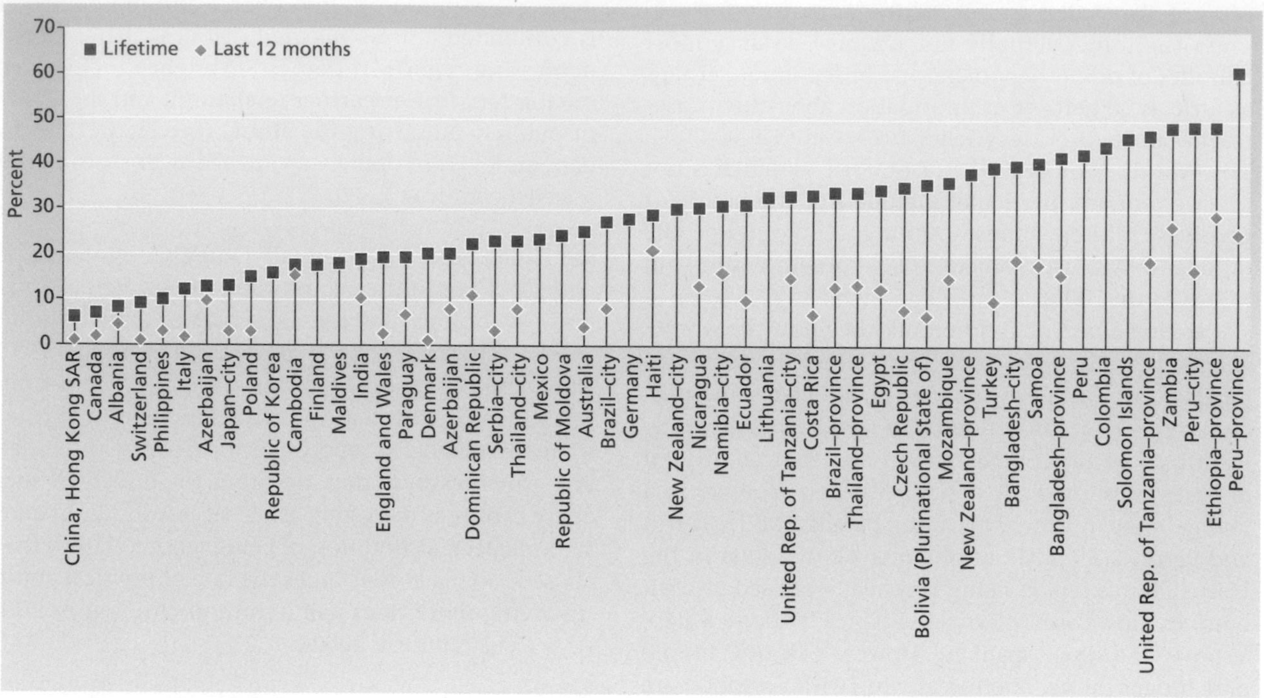

Source: *The World's Women 2010: Trends and Statistics*, New York: United Nations, 2010, p. 132.

needs. Abuse of the elderly is partly due to the psychological, physical, and economic strain of caring for elderly persons. These strains of caretaking may lead to hostility and depression, followed by violence. Elder abuse may involve a dependent adult child who has moved back into his or her parents' home as a result of divorce or financial problems (Gelles 1997), or it may occur in nursing homes.

The high incidence of divorce, violence, and abuse motivates sociologists to examine the strength and durability of the American family. One area of research focuses on *family resiliency*.

Family Resiliency

Q What is family resiliency? Synonyms for the word *resilient* include *flexible, supple,* and *buoyant*. Thus, resiliency implies an ability to cope successfully with shock. **Family resiliency** refers to the family's capacity to emerge from crises as stronger and more resourceful. A resilient family is able to flourish despite distress.

Q What factors promote family resiliency? Sociologists have identified four sets of factors promoting resiliency.

First, family resiliency is enhanced by *individual* characteristics such as self-esteem, autonomy, sense of humor, and problem-solving skills. Second, resiliency is engendered by *family* characteristics such as emotional support, commitment, warmth, affection, and cohesion. Third, resiliency is nurtured by *community* characteristics such as ample opportunities for participation in community life, emphasis on helping others, avenues for communication with friends and adults, and availability of youth activities. Fourth, resiliency is increased via family-friendly *public policy*. Because it is the most abstract factor, public policy requires some elaboration.

Q What role does public policy play in promoting family resiliency? Public policy is a broad course of governmental action expressed in specific laws, programs, and initiatives; it is created and changed in democratic societies through the interplay of government, lobbyists, and interest groups (Parenti 2007; Bardes, Shelly, and Schmidt 2010; Patterson 2011). The making of public policy involves trade-offs, compromises, winners, and losers. The 1993 Family and Medical Leave Act granted American workers the right to twelve weeks of

Murray A. Straus, David B. Sugarman, and Jean Giles-Sims — Spanking and Antisocial Behavior

Many children in the United States experience spanking and other legal forms of physical punishment from their parents. In the 1980s, more than 90 percent of parents used corporal punishment on young children, and more than half persisted in its use during the early teen years. Although high, this extent of corporal punishment was less than in the 1950s (99 percent) and in the mid-1970s (97 percent). Despite a further decline since 1985, nearly all American children still experience some form of corporal punishment.

The use of corporal punishment to correct or control the behavior of children is a part of American culture. "Spare the rod and spoil the child" is a warning deep in our national consciousness. Murray Straus,

David Sugarman, and Jean Giles-Sims (1997), however, present evidence contradicting the supposed salutary effects of corporal punishment on children's behavior.

These researchers interviewed more than 800 mothers of children, aged six to nine years, in a national longitudinal (involving before and after measurement) study. This research compared parents' use of corporal punishment with antisocial behavior in children. The study defined corporal punishment as "the use of physical force with the intention of causing a child to experience pain, but not injury, for the purpose of correction or control of the child's behavior" (Straus et al. 1997:761). Slapping a child's hand or buttocks and squeezing a child's arm are examples. A measure of antisocial behavior was based on the mothers' reports of their children's behavior: "cheats or tells lies," "bullies or is cruel or mean to others," "does not feel sorry after misbehaving," "breaks things deliberately," "is disobedient at school," and "has trouble getting along with teachers."

Because this was a longitudinal study, data on the frequency of parents' use of corporal punishment were collected *prior* to reports on subsequent antisocial behavior. Contrary to common expectation, Straus and colleagues found that the higher

the use of corporal punishment, the higher the level of antisocial behavior two years later.

Straus and his colleagues suggest that the reduction or elimination of corporal punishment could have significant benefits for lowering antisocial behavior in children. In addition, given the research indicating a relationship between childhood antisocial behavior and violence on the one hand and other crime in adulthood on the other, society at large could benefit from abandoning the use of corporal punishment in child rearing.

Evaluate the Research

1. Explain why a longitudinal study inspires greater confidence that a relationship is causal.
2. Suppose that you are on a panel reporting on child rearing to the president of the United States. Describe the study you would conduct on a possible relationship between childhood corporal punishment and adult crime.
3. How do you anticipate corporally punished children will discipline their own children later in life?
4. Describe what you think would be more effective means of discipline.
5. How were you disciplined? How will you discipline your children? Why?

unpaid leave for family emergencies without the threat of job loss. But the United States remains the only major industrialized country without paid maternity leave. Germany, for example, provides new parents with fourteen weeks of fully paid leave. In the United States, this lack of a universal public policy places the American family at a disadvantage in coping with the unique pressures of modern life.

For example, the lack of a national health insurance program has resulted in some 40 million uninsured Americans with millions more underinsured.

This adds to the stress of low-income, poor, and unemployed families already disproportionately characterized by high rates of divorce, violence, and abuse. The United States also reduces family resiliency through the absence of paid parental leaves surrounding childbirth. Longer paid family leaves promote such vital conditions as improved maternal health, lower infant mortality, enhanced infant and child development, and greater likelihood of women resuming employment after childbirth. These conditions, in turn, encourage family resiliency.

CHECK YOURSELF 11.3 R2

Family and Marriage in the United States

1. Which half of each of the following pairs best describes the typical American family?
   a. nuclear/extended
   b. patrilineal/bilateral
   c. authoritarian/democratic
   d. neolocal/matrilocal
   e. polygynous/monogamous
2. The idea of love as a crucial factor in the mate selection process did not become common practice until which century?
   a. seventeenth
   b. eighteenth
   c. nineteenth
   d. twentieth
3. The _____ is the number of divorces in a particular year per 1,000 members of the total population.
4. Which of the following is *not* stated in the text as one of the factors associated with divorce?
   a. decline of religious influence
   b. age at first marriage
   c. length of marriage
   d. economic conditions
5. Contrary to what one would expect from the traditional male dominance in American family life, women are spousal abusers almost as frequently as men are. T or F?
6. _____ refers to the family's capacity to emerge from crises as stronger and more resourceful.

Answers: 1. a. nuclear, b. bilateral, c. democratic, d. neolocal, e. monogamous; 2. d; 3. divorce rate; 4. a; 5. T; 6. Family resiliency

New Family Forms R1

Since 1960, American marital and familial arrangements have been undergoing dramatic change, with a decline in marriage and the emergence of new family forms. In 1960, over 70 percent of all adults were married; today, about 56 percent of adults are married at any given time. Generational differences are even more startling. While 68 percent of adult Americans in their twenties were married in 1960, today that is true of only 25 percent of males and 34 percent of females (U.S. Census Bureau 2009). Social approval of most of these new family forms is a continuing long-term trend, despite the unease many Americans feel (particularly older ones) (Thornton and Young-DeMarco 2001; "Decline in Marriage and Rise of New Family Forms" 2010; Skolnick and Skolnick 2010).

Blended Families

The relatively high divorce rate in the United States has led to the creation of the **blended family**—a family formed when at least one of the partners in the marriage has been married before and has one or more children from a previous marriage. A blended family, otherwise known as a stepfamily, a remarried family, or a reconstituted family, is the most rapidly growing type of family in the United States. Four-in-ten American adults are part of a blended family (Parker 2011). This type of family can become extremely complicated (Ganong and Coleman 1994; Herbert 1999). Consider the number and complexity of relationships in the following blended family:

Former husband (with two children in the custody of their natural mother) marries new wife with two children in her custody. They have two children. Former wife also remarries man with two children, one in his custody and one in the custody of his former wife, who has also remarried and had a child with her second husband who also has custody of one child from his previous marriage. The former husband's parents are also divorced and both have remarried. Thus, when he remarries, his children have two complete sets of grandparents on his side, plus one set on the mother's side, plus perhaps two sets on the stepfather's side. (F. D. Cox 2006:530)

Part of this complexity arises because more marriages are ending through divorce rather than death (Sweeney 2010). For children, a parent is being added, not replaced. Along with the third parent come his or her relatives. Blended families, then, create a new type of extended family, a family that is not based strictly on blood relationships. As the preceding excerpt shows, it is possible for a child in a blended family to have eight grandparents, if each of the child's biological parents remarries. Although not all blended families are this complicated, they are sufficiently complicated to suggest that stepfamilies often fail to "blend" harmoniously enough to make the term blended family somewhat of a misnomer (Sweeney, Wong, and Videon 2009; Sweeney 2010).

Q **What are the reasons for greater instability in blended families?** Although many blended families are harmonious, especially if they make adjustments during the first few years, children from previous marriages are one factor in the higher divorce rate among second marriages (Baca Zinn and Eitzen 2006). Sociologists point to three major problems facing blended families: financial difficulties, stepchildren's antagonism, and unclear roles (Lamanna, Riedmann, and Riedmann 2005).

- *Financial difficulties.* Incomes are lower in stepfamilies. This is compounded by the financial demands from both the former and present families. Remarried husbands are often legally obligated to support children from their previous marriage. Second wives may resent the income denied their own children to support children from that previous marriage.
- *Stepchildren's antagonism.* Hoping for a reunion of their original parents, stepchildren may attempt to undermine the new marriage. Even five years after divorce, about a third of stepchildren continue to strongly disapprove of their original parents' divorce. This is especially true for teenagers, who can be very critical of their stepparent's values and personality.
- *Unclear roles.* The roles of stepparents are often vague and ambiguous. Stepchildren often don't consider their parent's new spouse as a "real" father or mother. It is also uncertain to stepparents or stepchildren how much power the new spouse really has. As a result, questions of control and discipline can become very contentious, especially when teenagers are involved.

Single-Parent Families

Q **How widespread are single-parent families?** **Single-parent families** (families headed by an unmarried adult) are on the rise in the United States (*2010 Kids Count Data Book* 2010). Approximately 23 million children now live in single-parent families, almost 2 million more than in 2000. The percentage of children in single-parent families has increased slightly since

A debate exists over the appropriateness of celebrities, like Sharon Stone, choosing to be single mothers.

2000, going from 31 percent to 32 percent. The percentage of children in single-parent families ranges from 18 percent in Utah to 45 percent in Mississippi (see "Sociology Eyes America" 11.1). About 95 percent of children living with one parent are in female-headed households.

The situation is more stark when we examine racial and ethnic differences in single-parent families. In 2008, almost two-thirds of African American children lived in single-parent families, as did 50 percent of Native American children, and 38 percent of Latino children (see Figure 11.6). African American, Native American, and Latino children are more likely than white children to live with single parents because of high divorce and out-of-wedlock birth rates, combined with lower rates of marriage and remarriage. While the proportion of single-parent families has increased for all races since 1970, the gap between them has remained relatively constant (Dunifon 2009).

Q **To what degree is social class an ingredient in single-parent households headed by women?** Although, in cases of separation and divorce, courts today are more sensitive to fathers' claims, women in all social classes are still more likely to win custody of their children. Frequently, though, there are factors unique to poor single-parent women. The poor single-parent

SOCIOLOGY EYES AMERICA 11.1

Percent of Children in Single-Parent Families: 2008

This map shows, by state, the percentage of children living in single-parent families.

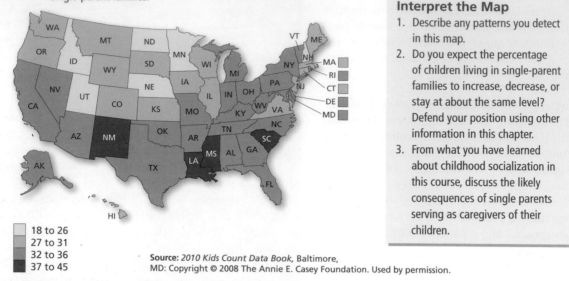

18 to 26
27 to 31
32 to 36
37 to 45

Source: *2010 Kids Count Data Book,* Baltimore, MD: Copyright © 2008 The Annie E. Casey Foundation. Used by permission.

Interpret the Map

1. Describe any patterns you detect in this map.
2. Do you expect the percentage of children living in single-parent families to increase, decrease, or stay at about the same level? Defend your position using other information in this chapter.
3. From what you have learned about childhood socialization in this course, discuss the likely consequences of single parents serving as caregivers of their children.

households are generally created by unwed mothers or by women abandoned by their husbands and/or the fathers of their children. And poor women are able to marry (or remarry) at a very low rate.

Although significantly fewer, there is an increasing number of well-educated, professional women who head single-parent households. With the stigma of unwed motherhood declining, more affluent unmarried women are choosing to have children and to care for them alone. In addition, these women have the economic resources to support an independent family. Finally, well-educated women are adopting higher standards for selecting husbands (Seligmann 1999; Hertz 2006).

Q Economically, how do children fare in single-parent families? Typically, children in single-parent families are without the same economic resources available in two-parent families. In 2008, about one-third of single-parent families with related children lived in poverty, compared to 7 percent of married-couple families with children.

Although single mothers comprise only about one-fifth of all family households, they account for about half of households with minor children living below the poverty line. Because only about 16 percent of the single-parent families headed by men are below the poverty line, experts are now writing about the feminization of poverty (see Chapters 8 and 10). Earning a living is a problem for these single-parent mothers, not only due to the difficulty of arranging for child care (which all working mothers must face) but also because most of these women do not have the educational credentials for the job market. Many were housewives or part-time workers before a divorce; others are young, uneducated women who never married. Thus, if they do not get an education or marry a solidly employed male, these mothers are unlikely to work their way out of poverty. Their

FIGURE 11.6

Percent of Children in Single-Parent Families by Race and Hispanic Origin: 2008

This figure compares the percentage of White, African American, Native American, Latino, and Asian children living in single-parent households. What generalizations can you make from these data?

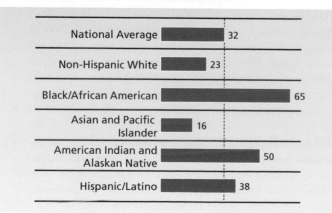

National Average	32
Non-Hispanic White	23
Black/African American	65
Asian and Pacific Islander	16
American Indian and Alaskan Native	50
Hispanic/Latino	38

Source: *2010 Kids Count Data Book,* Baltimore, MD: Copyright © 2008 The Annie E. Casey Foundation. Used by permission.

children, of course, suffer the consequences along with them.

Q What are the effects of single-parent families on the well-being of children? Most research indicates that growing up with a single parent negatively affects a child's well-being. Children in single-parent homes exhibit more behavioral problems, have higher teenage pregnancy rates, and perform lower academically than children living with their biological parents (McLanahan 2003; Dunifon 2009). Sheppard Kellam, Margaret Ensminger, and R. Jay Turner (1977) found that children from one-parent families consistently score lower on tests of psychological well-being and are less able to adapt in social settings, such as school, than their counterparts from two-parent or two-adult families. They conclude that the problem lies not so much in the absence of the father, but in the aloneness of the mother, because children living in two-adult families fared almost as well as children from two-parent families.

Adolescents who live with one parent or with a stepparent have much higher rates of deviant behavior than adolescents living with both natural parents (Dornbush et al. 1985; Popenoe 1999; Sweeney, Wang, and Videon 2009). David Popenoe's study (1999) of a national sample of twelve- to seventeen-year-olds indicates that arrests, school discipline, truancy, runaways, and smoking occur more often in single-parent and stepparent families, regardless of income, race, or ethnic background. Adults who grew up in single-parent homes are also more likely to be divorced, have an illegitimate child, be receiving psychological counseling, be school truants, and use alcohol and drugs (Bianchi 1990; P. Taylor 1991; McLanahan and Sandefur 1996).

A lifelong effect of growing up in a single-parent home is also reflected in the relative economic success of children. Daniel Mueller and Philip Cooper (1986), in a study of nineteen- to thirty-four-year-olds, found that compared to individuals from two-parent families, children raised by single parents (especially single mothers) tend to have lower educational, occupational, and economic success. And children from homes with continuously married parents achieve greater social mobility than children from either single-parent or divorced homes (DeLeire and Lopoo 2010).

Q How much variation do we find among single-parent families? Researchers recognize the diversity among single-parent homes (Dunifon 2009). First, the composition of a single-parent family varies. Many unmarried parents do not actually live alone. They may be cohabiting or living with other family members such as grandparents. Second, children come to be in single-parent homes in a variety of ways. Some are born to unwed mothers; others are born to two married adults who subsequently divorce. Third, children

have different experiences in single-parent families. Some live with a single parent until they leave home. Other children may live through one or more periods when another adult is present and then leaves, either through marriage or cohabitation. Finally, children across subgroups have different experiences. For example, one study found that white children in single-parent families have a lower sense of well-being than black children in single-parent families (Dunifon and Kowaleski-Jones 2002).

Q How do the variations in single-parent homes differentially affect the well-being of children? The variations in single-parent families are reflected in factors thought to most heavily influence social and behavioral outcomes for children. Prominent among these are income inequality, lack of quality child care, and family instability (Dunifon 2009).

Income inequality accounts for a large part of the adverse effects of single parenting on the well-being of children (Sigle-Rushton and McLanahan 2002). Children reared in single-parent families headed by a mother have a five times higher probability of living in poverty than those in homes with married parents. Not only do poor single parents have only one income, they are also less educated, limiting them to lower paying jobs forever. Their children, consequently, grow up in inferior neighborhoods, attending inferior schools.

Because single parents face severe time and energy constraints, they have less time and energy to supervise their children or to spend time with them (Kissman and Allen 1993). Studies show that single parents are with their children less, monitor children less closely, provide less emotional support, and exert less control over them (Astone and McLanahan 1991; Thomson, Hanson, and McLanahan 1994; Sandberg and Hofferth 2001). Evidence indicates that the resulting low-quality child care during the early years has important, enduring negative effects on a child's academic performance and general behavior (Vandell, et al. 2010). This study followed a sample of children through their first fifteen years, suggesting that these tendencies are sufficiently established to last a lifetime.

Low-quality child care is not confined to single-parent families. Children living with stepparents suffer more ill effects than children residing with their married parents (Sweeney, Wang, and Videon 2009). And having a cohabiting adult in the home (even if it is the parent) does not necessarily improve the well-being of children (Brown 2004).

Instability is another factor affecting the well-being of children in single-parent families. In some cases, single-parent families are created by divorce, a situation known to be detrimental to many children, particularly in the short run (Kilmann, Carranza, and

Vendemia 2006; Lambert 2007). In other instances, family instability comes from a series of disruptions as parents remarry (and maybe divorce again) or from the presence of one or more cohabiting partners over time. In other single-parent families, lack of economic resources may result in frequent residential moves.

Childless Marriages

In the past, there was a stigma attached to marriages without children. Due in part to the assumption that all women have a maternal instinct, married women without children were seen as failing to fulfill their biological destiny. In addition, as we learned in Chapter 5, children of that time were needed for farm labor. As the traditional negative societal response to childless marriages diminishes, more American couples are choosing not to have children.

Q **To what extent are married couples in the United States choosing to be childless?** In 2008, one in five American women ages 40–44 was childless, up 80 percent since 1970, when only one in ten had never borne a child. Even though childlessness is rapidly increasing among black, Latino, and Asian women, white women still exhibit a higher rate of childlessness. More highly educated women are the most likely to remain childless (Livingston and Cohn 2010). According to experts, the proportion of married couples choosing childlessness is likely to increase (Kornblum 2008; Benokraitis 2010).

Q **Why are some married women choosing not to have children?** The reasons are diverse. An important factor, of course, is the disappearing social stigma attached to childless marriages. Also, some women are so involved in their careers that they see children either as an impediment or as too important to shortchange if brought into the world. Sometimes women want their independence in order to pursue personal goals. According to others, today's world is a questionable place into which to bring a child. Some women simply do not enjoy the presence of children. For some couples, having children has been delayed so long that it becomes difficult to make the necessary adjustments for raising a family. Finally, some childless marriages are not a result of choice but are due to physical or mental limitations.

Q **Aren't childless couples missing an important part of life?** Because of the strains placed on a marriage, the presence of children tends to reduce marital happiness and satisfaction. Marital satisfaction is higher at the start of marriage, lowest during children's teenage years, and higher again when the children leave home. It is true, however, that among childless couples who want children, marital happiness is generally lower than for married couples with children (Singh and Williams

1981). This is not the case among women who prefer not to have children. Most voluntarily childless couples appear to be happier, less stressed, and more satisfied with their marriages and lives than couples with children (Defago 2009; Scott 2009).

Dual-Employed Marriages

In a **dual-employed marriage,** both husband and wife are in the labor market. This is quite different from the marriage in which the wife works at a job merely to supplement the family income, a pattern long observed in the lower and working classes (Bielby and Bielby 1989; Jacobs and Gerson 2004). Although a relatively new trend, the dual-employed marriage is now the norm, as suggested in Chapter 10 (Hertz and Marshall 2001; Moen 2003).

Q **Do dual-employed marriages create special stress?** Women in dual-employed marriages are apparently expected to handle the bulk of household tasks and child-care responsibilities in addition to the pursuit of full-time jobs (Goldscheider and Waite 1991; Thompson and Walker 1991; Spain and Bianchi 1996; Gerson 2010). Combining employment with child-care and domestic tasks, married working women work

Dual-employed couples face special strains. It hurts these parents to leave their baby with a nanny. The baby doesn't look too happy either.

about fifteen hours more a week than men do. This additional month of twenty-four-hour days a year Arlie Hochschild calls the "second shift (Hochschild 1997; Hochschild and Machung 2003)." Although men spend an average of sixteen hours per week (up from twelve hours in 1965) in household and child-care duties, women nevertheless, bear the larger burden (Williams, Swisher, and Stalcup 1997; Parker 2009).

In addition to this greater workload, women in dual-employed marriages often must cope with role conflict. They are torn between the time requirements of their jobs and their desire to spend more time with their children and husbands (Rubenstein 1991).

Despite their general unwillingness to assume household responsibilities equal to their wives, men in dual-employed marriages also may feel the negative effects of conflicting roles and excessive demands on their time (Moen 1992). In addition, having an employed wife, particularly if she earns more, may not fit with a man's image of himself as provider. This problem promises to be more acute as a larger proportion of American women becomes more highly educated and more highly paid than their husbands (Menaghan and Parcel 1991; G. Spitze 1991; Fry and Cohn 2010).

The challenge in the future will be to find ways of reducing the strains placed on members of dual-employed families. Some pressure on working women could be relieved if men became more participative in domestic duties. Many experts believe that the combined pressures of job and family will lead to accommodative changes in the workplace. Alterations in company policies and practices will likely involve more flexible working schedules, family leaves for both males and females, work-at-home situations, and on-site child-care centers (L.A. Gilbert 1993; Gerson 2011).

Q Are there no benefits to dual employment? Thus far, emphasis has been on the stress experienced by dual-employed couples. There is a positive side. Most recent research reveals beneficial effects for the psychological well-being of women (Moen 1992; Crosby 1993; F. D. Cox 2006). Working outside the home can provide a wider set of social relationships and greater feelings of control, independence, and heightened self-esteem. Employment also appears to provide a socioemotional cushion for women when their children leave home. Compared with women who do not work outside the home, employed women tend to have more alternative channels for self-expression (Adelmann et al. 1989; Wolfe 1997).

As economic pressures ease, more discretionary money is available for purchases that improve the quality of life of all family members. In addition, sons and daughters of working mothers can benefit in noneconomic ways. Daughters of working mothers may see themselves as working adults, as capable of being economically independent, and as benefiting from

further education. Sons may choose wives with similar attitudes toward education and employment.

For men, benefits of a dual-employed marriage may include freedom from sole economic responsibility, increased opportunity for job changes, and opportunity for continuing an education. Men with employed wives can often share the triumphs and defeats of the day with someone who is in a similar situation. If their wives are happier working outside the home, husbands also enjoy a better marital relationship. Those husbands who take advantage of the opportunity can form a closer relationship with their children by being more active parents (Booth and Crouter 1998).

Q Is there a role for government in reducing the negative effects of dual employment? Whatever happens between partners, there seems to be a role here for government (Gilbert 2010). As Table 11.4 shows, when compared with the United States, other industrialized countries are more diligent in requiring employers to participate in relief for the dual employed. In fact, at least 178 other countries guarantee paid leave for new mothers, and over 50 underwrite paid leave for new fathers ("Failing Its Families"2011). The United Kingdom has one of the most advanced parental leave policies. Following the birth of an employee's child, UK employers are required to provide twenty-five weeks of work furlough at 100 percent of pay for the mother and up to one year at a further-reduced compensation rate.

In 1993, under the Clinton administration, the Family and Medical Leave Act was passed. Prior to this, there was no federal law requiring employers

TABLE 11.4

Government Mandated Maternity Leave Policies, United States vs. Selected Countries

This table compares the paternal and maternity leave policies of selected countries. Does the rank of the United States among these industrialized countries surprise you? Why?

Country	Leave Duration (Weeks)	Percentage of Pay/Weeks
United Kingdom	26	100%
Italy	25	100%
Netherlands	16	100%
Sweden	14	100%
Iceland	12	100%
Norway	9	100%
United States	12	0

Source: "Family Leave in the U.S., Canada, and Global," Catalyst, Accessed 11/3/10. http://www.catalyst.org/file/455/qt_family_leave.pdf.

to offer family leave for childbirth or medical emergency. This act requires that employers with fifty or more employees provide up to twelve weeks of unpaid leave for either the father or mother of a newborn child, the adoption of a child, the placement of a foster child, or for some other family member's medical emergency. A serious health condition is broadly defined to include illness, injury, and mental problems. The employer must permit the employee to return to the same or an equivalent job and must continue group health insurance for the employee during the leave period (Snarr 1993; Stranger et al. 1993).

There are several shortcomings to this step, which is relatively modest in comparison to government policies in other industrialized societies. First, because most American workers are employed in organizations with fewer than fifty employees, this benefit is unavailable to them. Second, less than 40 percent of dual-employed couples can afford to take an unpaid six-week leave. Third, employees must have been employed by their company for at least twelve months to be eligible (Shaller and Qualiana 1993; Wisensale 2001; Reskin and Padavic 2002).

Q **What are the consequences of the lack of paid parental leave?** A recent study by Human Rights Watch examines the consequences of a lack of legally backed paid parental leave, or sick days; the scant support for pumping breast milk on the job; and the meager protection against work-related discrimination surrounding caregiving duties ("Failing Its Families" 2011). Such weak work-family support can contribute to postponed immunization and doctor visits for infants, postpartum depression, early termination of breastfeeding, increased debt, and job loss. Businesses also suffer lower productivity, higher turnover, and reduced employee morale.

Q **Do mothers really prefer to enter the work force?** Over the past ten years, full-time work outside the home has become less popular among mothers ("Fewer Mothers Prefer Full-Time Work" 2007). There are now almost 6 million stay-at-home moms in the United States, accounting for one in four married women with children under age fifteen. In 1997, 32 percent of working mothers with children under age seventeen said that full-time work is ideal for them. Ten years later only 21 percent stated the same preference. Sixty percent of today's working mothers prefer part-time work, up from 48 percent in 1997. Reversing a twenty-five year trend, there is a recent decline in employment among women with infants under one year of age, from 60 percent in 1998 to 55 percent in 2006. It would be premature to predict a continuing decrease in working mothers with infants. Moreover, there has been no decrease in employment among mothers of older children (Bachu and O'Connell 2001; Knox and Schacht 2010). It is interesting to know which mothers are staying at home with their children. Stay-at-home mothers are more likely to be younger, less educated, and less affluent. They also tend to be Latino or foreign-born (George 2009). This evidence contradicts the popular idea that more highly educated women are "opting out" of the work force to be at home with their children (Stone 2008).

Single Life

To what extent are Americans remaining single? The increased age at first marriage for both sexes and the high divorce rate have combined to create an increase in the percentage of single adults. In 1990, about 18 million women and 22 million men over the age of eighteen had never been married. By 2006, these numbers had increased to 25 million for women and almost 30 million for men. More than 30 million Americans over the age of fifteen now live alone, an increase of almost 50 percent since 1980. Although many of these people will eventually marry, an increasing percentage will remain single all their lives.

Q **Why are more Americans choosing to live alone?** Remaining single was always an alternative, but it carried a stigma. Colonial society taxed bachelors more heavily than married men and viewed spinsters as millstones around the necks of their families. They expected adults to marry and to begin having children as soon as morally and physically possible. Failure to do so was a form of inadequacy and deviance.

The stigma attached to remaining single has faded since colonial times, especially in the past two decades, and more Americans are either choosing this alternative or at least marrying later than previous generations. In addition to the lifting of the stigma, there are other factors contributing to the popularity of singlehood. More single Americans are choosing to remain childless, to obtain sexual gratification outside of marriage, to pursue careers, to rear children from a former marriage, to adopt children, to have strictly homosexual relationships, or to rear out-of-wedlock children (DePaulo 2007).

Q **Will the current trend continue?** It is too early to predict confidently whether the increase in singlehood among the young will eventually lead to a decline in marriage at all ages. It is safe to say that singlehood is an increasingly popular alternative to traditional marriage. This is not necessarily a rejection of marriage, but it does imply a desire to expand the period of "freedom" after leaving home and an unwillingness to rush into the responsibilities of early marriage and parenthood.

Cohabitation

Q **What is cohabitation, and how widespread is it?**
Cohabitation—living with someone in a marriagelike arrangement without the legal obligations and responsibilities of formal marriage—has emerged as an alternative to traditional monogamy. While cohabitation is more common among people with less education, it is increasing at higher educational levels (Cherlin 2010). It is not known if cohabitation has increased because more Americans are delaying marriage or because cohabitation is being substituted for marriage.

At any rate, cohabitation is on the rise. In 2009, cohabitation increased by 13 percent, twice the average annual increase of the preceding few years. Cohabitation has almost doubled since 1990. In a Pew Research Survey, 44 percent of all adults and over half of all adults between thirty and forty-nine years of age say they have cohabited. Among those who have cohabited, about two-thirds believe that living together is a step toward marriage ("The Decline of Marriage and the Rise of New Families" 2010).

It is impossible to predict whether cohabitation will become a commonly accepted practice experienced by

While marriage is still a thriving institution, more American couples, like these young people, are choosing to delay or to reject marriage through cohabitation.

virtually everyone. Certainly, as the average age at first marriage goes up, increased toleration for this lifestyle is a possible outcome; given the high divorce rate, it may be that cohabitation will become a more popular practice in the selection of a second marital partner as well.

Q **Is cohabitation a workable alternative to marriage?**
Research reports on cohabitation are not encouraging. Only about 25 percent of cohabiting couples stay together more than four years, reflecting a lower level of certainty about commitment than is found in marriage. This lack of commitment is probably an important reason for the lower satisfaction among cohabiting couples than among married couples (Nock 1995). Another factor is the higher rate of abuse among cohabiting women than among married, divorced, or separated women. There is no evidence that the marriages of those cohabiting before marriage are any stronger than those who did not and there is some evidence that those cohabiting before are more likely to divorce after marriage (F. D. Cox 2005; Poponoe 2007).

Same-Sex Domestic Partners

Q **How prevalent is homosexual cohabitation?** Because of the stigma surrounding homosexuality, it is impossible to know what proportion of the American population is gay. This makes it difficult to obtain an accurate count of the frequency of same-sex cohabitation. And the Census Bureau will not help, claiming that the federal Defense of Marriage Act prohibits the agency from recognizing same-sex marriage even in those states where it is legal ("Census Will Not Record Same-Sex Marriages" 2010). We do know that the incidence of same-sex partners living together is increasing, although their number remains small compared with heterosexual marriages. Comparing the same-sex cohabitation rate among gays, lesbians, and heterosexuals provides additional information. According to surveys in California, 37 to 46 percent of gay men are cohabitating with a partner of the same sex. Lesbians are cohabiting at a rate more comparable to heterosexuals, over 60 percent (Carpenter and Gates 2008). The relatively high rates of cohabitation among both gays and lesbians is hardly surprising since cohabitation is the sole form of domestic partnership available to them except where same-sex marriage is legal. And, as we shall see, at the present time, this alternative is available in only six states and the District of Columbia (Cherlin 2010).

Q **How do Americans feel about same-sex marriage?** More Americans oppose same-sex marriage than approve it (48 percent versus 42 percent). Opposition, however, declined after 2003, when 64 percent disapproved of gay and lesbian marriage ("Majority Continues to Support Civil Unions" 2009; "Gay Marriage Gains More Acceptance" 2010).

Q Are younger Americans really more supportive of same-sex marriage? Yes, there are significant generational differences in attitudes toward same-sex marriage. A majority of Americans born after 1980, Millenials, endorse gay and lesbian marriage (53 percent). More Gen Xers, born between 1965 and 1980, now favor same-sex marriage (48 percent) than oppose it (43 percent). The age gap is evident among baby boomers (born between 1946 and 1964) who oppose same-sex marriage by a 38 percent to 52 percent margin. The Silent Generation (born between 1928 and 1945) feels even more strongly, opposing same-sex marriage by a 59 percent to 29 percent difference ("Gay Marriage Gains More Acceptance" 2010).

Several recent legal, social, and political occurrences also reflect some change in the social landscape for same-sex partners. In 1996, the U.S. Supreme Court ruled that gays have equal rights under the Constitution (E. Thomas 2003), and the Supreme Court struck down the nation's antisodomy laws in 2003. In 2003, only Massachusetts had legalized gay marriage. Vermont, New Hampshire, Connecticut, Iowa, New York, and the District of Columbia have since joined Massachusetts. Civil unions are an alternative to gay marriage but still fall short of legalized same-sex marriage. **Civil unions,** arrangements many gay marriage supporters see as "separate but equal," are legal agreements between same-sex couples providing them many of the rights enjoyed by married couples. Thirteen states have legalized civil unions. In 2011, Obama announced that the Defense of Marriage Act, a federal law limiting marriage to between a man and a woman, would no longer be defended in court by the Department of Justice. As he must, Obama stated that his administration would continue to enforce the law until the Congress or the Supreme Court says otherwise.

Homosexual families—same-sex partners living together with children—are also increasing in number, although their number is small compared with heterosexual marriages (Gates and Romero 2009; Powell et al. 2010). Homosexual families are created in several ways. A divorced person may take his or her children into a new homosexual relationship. In fact, about 15 percent of lesbian mothers are currently given custody of their children, and homosexual fathers are beginning to seek custody as well. Homosexual couples are also adopting children, a movement encouraged by a 1979 New York case in which the court gave permanent custody of a thirteen-year-old boy to an openly homosexual minister who had been caring for the boy (Maddox 1982). Even before this case, welfare agencies in large cities were placing orphaned children with homosexual

couples. Although it is as yet uncommon, lesbian couples can purchase frozen semen from sperm banks and have their families by artificial insemination, and homosexual male couples can hire surrogate mothers who are inseminated with the couple's mixed semen.

Debate may become even more complicated if recent laboratory research on animals proves applicable to humans. In 2003, scientists reported turning ordinary mouse embryo cells into egg cells in laboratory dishes. In 2007, researchers unveiled a technique for turning ordinary skin cells of mice into stem cells (Stolberg 2007; Weiss 2007). If the same can be done with human cells, then gay male couples could technically produce children. This would make it possible for male gay partners whose ordinary cells are transformed into eggs to become biological mothers even though gestation would take place in females. There are even more extreme complications. If it ever becomes possible to make sperm from stem cells, then a lesbian couple could reproduce a child in complete independence from males (R. Weiss 2003). Researchers can now create a synthetic (made from chemicals in a bottle) genome capable of self-replication. Production of a synthetic cell is the first step toward creating artificial life ("Artificial Life [Synthetic DNA] Created by Scientist" 2010).

Other countries are beginning to legalize same-sex marriages In 2000, the Netherlands became the first country to legalize same-sex marriage, with the same rights enjoyed by heterosexual married couples. Belgium followed the Netherlands in 2003. Canada and Spain did the same in 2005, and six countries have since followed suit. Uruguay became the first Latin American country to legalize gay civil unions in 2007, joining a group of nineteen other nations (see "Think Globally 11.1").

Adult Children Returning Home

Young American adults (eighteen- to thirty-four-year-olds) have a much higher probability of living in their parents' home than they did thirty years ago. For example, the percentage of adults aged eighteen to twenty-four living at home increased from 49 percent in 1960 to 17 percent in 2000 (Bianchi and Casper 2000). In 2009, the total percentage of boomerang children stood at 14 percent. The percentage of adults returning home increases with age, ranging from 7 percent among eighteen-to-twenty-nine-year-olds to 30 percent among offspring sixty-five years and older (Wang and Morin 2009). These offspring carry the label *boomerang kids* because they are returning to their parents after having lived away from home (Quinn 1993; Goldscheider and Goldscheider 1994; Mitchell 2007).

Q Why are more adult children returning home? Several factors combine to produce this higher proportion of

THINK GLOBALLY 11.1

Gay Marriage

This map shows those countries around the world with laws permitting either gay marriage, civil unions, or domestic partnerships.

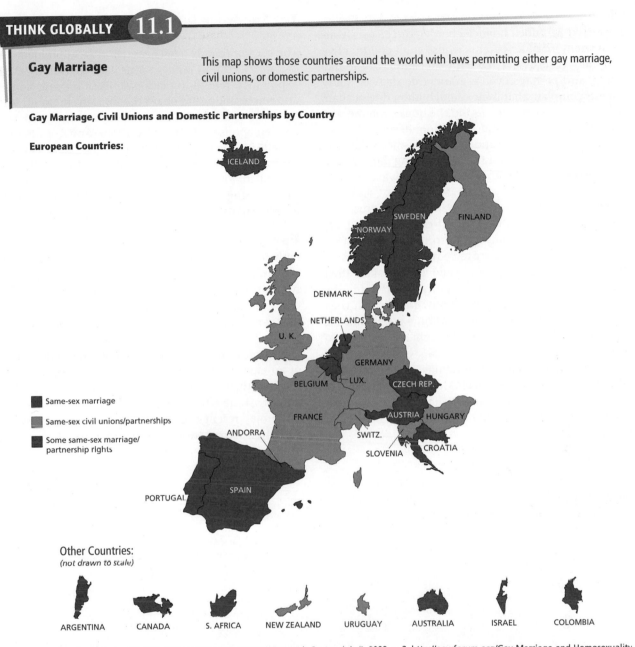

Gay Marriage, Civil Unions and Domestic Partnerships by Country

European Countries:

Legend:
- ■ Same-sex marriage
- ■ Same-sex civil unions/partnerships
- ■ Some same-sex marriage/partnership rights

Other Countries:
(not drawn to scale)

ARGENTINA CANADA S. AFRICA NEW ZEALAND URUGUAY AUSTRALIA ISRAEL COLOMBIA

Source: "Gay Marriages Around the World", Washington, DC: Pew Research Center. July 9, 2009, p .2. http://pewforum.org/Gay-Marriage-and-Homosexuality Gay-Marriage-Around-the-World.com

Interpret the Map

1. What conclusions do you reach from studying this map?

2. Is there more or less openness to same-sex legal arrangements than you had expected from your exposure to American media? Explain.

3. Discuss what you think a world map displaying same-sex laws will look like in 2050?

young adults living with their parents (Ward, Logan, and Spitze 1992; F. D. Cox 2005). Because young adults are marrying later, more stay at home longer. In addition, more of them are continuing their education and find living at home the best solution to the challenges of self-support and school expenses. Many young adults return home (or remain home) even after completing their education because the high cost of living outstrips their earning capacity. The high divorce rate also increases the proportion of young adults living at home because parents tend to accept their children in the home more readily after a failed marriage. Of course, the flow of boomerang increases during periods of high unemployment.

Q What are some possible consequences of this boomerang effect? An added financial burden can create significant strain for older parents whose adult children live at home—costs associated with education, day-to-day living, and perhaps even a grandchild or two. Many parents complain that their adult children do not share in expenses, fail to help around the house, rob them of their privacy, and prevent them from developing relationships with spouses and friends. It is not surprising that higher marital dissatisfaction among middle-aged parents is associated with adult children living at home (Glick and Lin 1986).

Adult children who find themselves in this situation could suffer as well. Adult children who have returned home normally do so from necessity rather than choice. They are likely to be having difficulties associated with balancing school and work, making their way economically, forming a family, or surviving the aftermath of a divorce. They know the burden they represent. In addition, returning home usually means forfeiting some freedom and being subject to unwanted parental control.

Despite these strains, most families appear to adjust well with the return of older children (Mitchell and Gee 1996). This is especially true when the returning older child contributes financially and helps with household duties.

The Sandwich Generation

The current middle-aged generation faces problems associated with new family forms. Due to prolonged life expectancy, refusal to place parents in nursing homes, and fewer siblings to share the burden, more middle-aged adults are finding mothers or fathers (their own or their spouse's) living with them. **Sandwich generation** is the term applied to adults caught between caring for their parents and caring for the family they formed after leaving home (Zal 2001; Abramson 2004). Sandwiching, of course, can occur whether or not the elderly parent(s) lives with the younger couple.

Q What are the repercussions? On the positive side, elderly parents unable to take care of themselves usually receive better care from those who love them and feel responsible for their well-being. Older children may enjoy taking care of those who reared them. The caregiving is usually not one-way. Aging parents can offer emotional support and financial resources.

There are also negative repercussions. Taking care of an elderly parent is often not easy. A parent with severe arthritis or Alzheimer's disease demands close and constant attention. Younger adults in this situation may resent the social and emotional intrusion and then experience guilt feelings because of this

CHECK YOURSELF 11.4 R2

New Family Forms

1. A family composed of at least one remarried man or woman with at least one child from a previous marriage is a _____ family.
2. Although the proportion of single-parent families has increased for both blacks and whites since 1970, the gap between them has
   a. decreased somewhat.
   b. increased significantly.
   c. remained the same.
   d. decreased significantly.
3. Voluntarily child-free couples are generally
   a. less educated than couples with children.
   b. less emotional than couples with children.
   c. less satisfied with their marriages and lives than couples with children.
   d. more satisfied with their marriages and lives than couples with children.
4. In a _____ marriage, both husband and wife are in the labor market.
5. In 1997, approximately _____ percent of women and _____ percent of men in America between the ages of twenty-five and twenty-nine had never married.
6. _____ involves living with someone of the opposite sex in a marriage like arrangement without the legal obligations and responsibilities of formal marriage.
7. The percentage of adults aged eighteen to twenty-four who live with their parents now stands at more than _____ percent.

Answers: 1. blended; 2. c; 3. d; 4. dual-employed; 5. 35, 51; 6. Cohabitation; 7. 53

resentment. They may even suffer a loss of self-esteem because they perceive themselves to be selfish. The older parents, too, may feel guilt and anger about the burden they are placing on those they love, in part because they do not have long-term healthcare to cover expenses. They also experience stress and depression from the problems they see their adult children, their spouses, and their grandchildren undergoing (Pillemer and Suiter 1991).

One additional negative consequence deserves special mention. The burden of elder-care falls much more heavily on women; it is typically daughters who care for an aging parent. According to one study, about two-thirds of unpaid caregivers are female (Johnson and Weiner 2006). The average woman in the United States is now likely to devote more years caring for her aging parents than she did caring for her own children.

Looking Forward ⓡ1

Q Is the nuclear family deteriorating? If the frequency of marriage and remarriage is any indication, the nuclear family is not disappearing (see "Sociology Eyes America" 11.1). Fifty-six percent of men and women are married at any given time; only 23 percent have never married (U.S. Census Bureau 2009). It is estimated that two-thirds of all divorced persons remarry. In fact, almost half of all weddings each year are remarriages. Sixty percent of second marriages end in divorce, but three-fourths of people twice divorced marry a third or even a fourth time. This is known as *serial monogamy*, an alternative that is on the rise.

Despite all the current experimentation with alternatives, the nuclear family remains the most popular choice among Americans. In 2007, 51 percent of all households were composed of married couples. Moreover, 69 percent of children under eighteen live with two parents (Kreider and Elliott 2009). Furthermore, three-fourths of American adults cite family as the most important part of their lives; they claim they are very satisfied with their family life ("The Decline of Marriage and Rise of New Families" 2010). We are not, then, abandoning the nuclear family. Contrary to a long-standing fear, most Americans are not avoiding marriage permanently; they are simply postponing it or sampling it often (Popenoe 2007).

Q What about the modifications of family? This is not to say that change in the American family is not occurring. The proportion of all households with the traditional husband as wage earner, wife as homemaker, and two children is expected to continue to account for less than one-fourth of all American households. Social scientists expect continued increases for other family forms such as the dual-employed family and the single-parent family (Nock 2009; see Figure 11.7). As sociologist Judith Stacey notes, there is no longer "a single culturally dominant family pattern to which the majority of Americans conform or aspire" (1990:17).

But, change is not equivalent to obliteration. Contrary to Arlie Hochschild's (1997) highly influential thesis, a shift toward women's view of work as more satisfying than family life does not appear to be the case. In the first longitudinal study on this question, K. Jill Kiecolt (2003) reports an increase

Belief that the family will continue is found even in the most futuristic views.

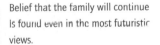

FIGURE 11.7

Families in the Labor Force

The nature of families in the United States has changed since 1975. What do you believe will be the most significant trend by 2025? Explain.

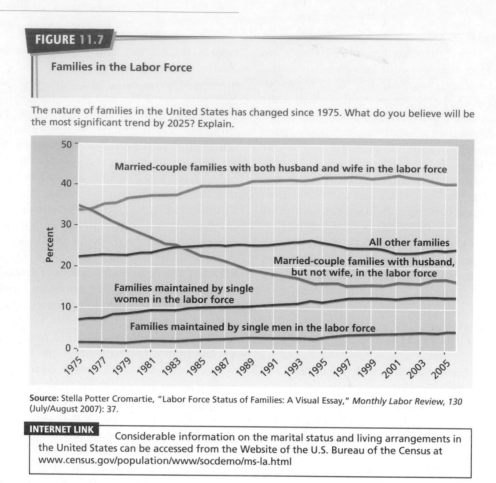

Source: Stella Potter Cromartie, "Labor Force Status of Families: A Visual Essay," *Monthly Labor Review, 130* (July/August 2007): 37.

INTERNET LINK Considerable information on the marital status and living arrangements in the United States can be accessed from the Website of the U.S. Bureau of the Census at www.census.gov/population/www/socdemo/ms-la.html

in satisfaction with home over work among women since 1973. And a relatively stable proportion of younger Americans continue to value marriage and family life, complete with children (Thornton and Young-DeMarco 2001; "The Decline of Marriage and the Rise of New Families 2010).

Although variations will become more prevalent and socially acceptable, the family system is not about to disappear from American society. In the United States, as well as in other modern societies, the nuclear family will remain the bedrock of the family system, despite the growing diversity in family form (Knox and Schacht 2010; Powell, et al. 2010).

Q What about immigrant and minority families? We cannot think about the future of the American family without anticipating the influence of our growing minority and immigrant population (Ingoldsby and Smith 2006; Trask and Hamon 2007; Burton, et al. 2010). While the American family described in this chapter most often reflects the long-standing white majority model, the American family is evolving, as we saw in our analysis of new family forms and in the many variations among minority subgroups. In the future, the unique features of various minority and immigrant families will probably be even more prominent. It cannot be otherwise if, as predicted, the current non-Latino white majority comprises only half of the U.S. population by 2050. The magnitude of the impact of minority and immigrant families hinges on the path these families take in the future. If minority and immigrant families assume increasingly new shapes, the effects will be significant. If minority and immigrant families become more "Americanized," the blend will be less dramatic (Lichter and Brown 2009). The future is ours to conjecture, but not yet to see.

On to Chapter 12

Family is the most basic social institution. Another important institution is education, the social structure one formally enters in kindergarten. Chapter 12 examines education primarily through the lens of the three major theoretical perspectives.

S INTEGRATED GOALS AND SUMMARY

1. **Describe the types of family structure, dimensions of family structure, societal norms for mate selection, and types of marital arrangements.**
   - A family is a group of people related by marriage, blood, or adoption. Each of us may belong to two families—the family into which we were born and the family we create upon marrying.
   - The extended family and the nuclear family are two basic types of family structure. A curvilinear relationship exists between family structure and industrialization. In hunting and gathering societies, the nuclear family was the most prevalent type. With the rise of agriculture as the means of subsistence, the extended family came to prevail. The nuclear family regained popularity in modern industrial society.
   - Whether the family is nuclear or extended, there are several important dimensions of family structure. These dimensions pertain to descent and inheritance, family authority, and residence pattern.
   - Mate selection is never completely a matter of individual choice. Exogamous, endogamous, and homogamous mate selection norms exist in all societies.
   - There are four basic types of marriages: One man and one woman may marry, one man and several women may marry, one woman and several men may marry, or two or more men may marry two or more women.

2. **Compare and contrast views of the family proposed by functionalists, conflict theorists, and symbolic interactionists.**
   - In all societies, the family has been the most important institution. It is the institution that produces new generations, socializes the young, provides care and affection, regulates sexual behavior, transmits social status, and provides economic support.
   - Although functionalism emphasizes the benefits of the family for society, the conflict perspective depicts the traditional family structure as the instrument of male domination over women. Evidence of this domination, they assert, is reflected in the traditional ownership of women by men, family rules of power and inheritance, and the male-dominated economic division of labor.
   - Symbolic interactionism is used frequently in the study of the family. It is within the family that socialization of children begins and children develop a self-concept. Most of the interactions within families can be analyzed within this theoretical perspective.

3. **Describe the modern American family.**
   - The marriage rate in the United States is one-half that of 1940. At the same time, the reduction in family size is dramatic. Modern marriages are primarily based on love. This is a relatively new development in the formation of marriages.

4. **Outline the extent and causes of divorce in America.**
   - The divorce rate in the United States rose dramatically in recent times. Factors promoting divorce include the quality of the marital relationship, the increasing economic independence of women, and the social acceptability of divorce. The dissolution of marriage, however, is not expected to continue to escalate. In fact, the divorce rate has declined slightly.

5. **Give an overview of family violence in the United States.**
   - Although the American family provides social and emotional support for its members, violence in this intimate setting is not uncommon. Spouses use violence against each other, parents abuse children, siblings are physically violent with one another, and the elderly experience abuse.
   - Problems such as the high divorce rate and frequent family violence and abuse have raised the question of the strength and durability of the American family. Some researchers approach this area of research via the concept of family resiliency—the family's capacity to emerge from crises as stronger and more resourceful.

6. **Describe contemporary alternatives to the traditional nuclear family structure.**
   - There is considerable experimentation with new patterns of marriage and family: blended families, single-parent families, child-free marriages, people remaining single, cohabitation, gay and lesbian couples, adult children returning home, and the sandwich generation. In addition, the American family encounters the rise of the dual-employed marital arrangement.

7. **Discuss the future of the American family in the United States.**
   - Despite the adoption of alternatives within the family institution, these practices will not replace the nuclear family in any broad scale. Given the frequency of the marriage and remarriage, the nuclear family is enduring reasonably well. The American family is definitely changing; it is not, however, on the way to extinction.

CONCEPT REVIEW

Match the following concepts with the definitions listed below them.

____ a. matrilineal descent   ____ f. blended family   ____ k. divorce ratio
____ b. exogamy   ____ g. marriage   ____ l. monogamy
____ c. nuclear family   ____ h. democratic control   ____ m. family resiliency
____ d. family   ____ i. patrilineal descent
____ e. polyandry   ____ j. family of marriage

1. composed of a remarried man or woman and at least one child from a previous marriage
2. the form of control in which authority is split evenly between husband and wife
3. the number of divorced persons per 1,000 persons who are married and living with their spouses
4. mate selection norms requiring individuals to marry someone outside their kind
5. a group of people related by marriage, blood, or adoption
6. the family group established upon marriage
7. a heterosexual union in which public approval is given to sexual activity, having children, and assuming mutual rights and obligations
8. the familial arrangement in which descent and inheritance are passed from the mother to her female descendants
9. the form of marriage in which one man is married to only one woman at a time
10. the smallest group of individuals (mother, father, and children) that can be called a family
11. the familial arrangement in which descent and inheritance are passed from the father to his male descendants
12. the form of marriage in which one woman is married to two or more men at the same time
13. the family's capacity to survive crises

CHECK YOURSELF REVIEW

1. Contrary to what one would expect from the traditional male dominance in American family life, women are spousal abusers almost as frequently as men are. T or F?
2. Although the nuclear family is not disappearing, Americans are spending less and less of their lives married. T or F?
3. Industrialization promotes the shift from the extended family to the _____ family.
4. In a _____ family, the oldest man living in the household controls the rest of the family members.
5. In 1997, approximately _____ percent of women and _____ percent of men in America between the ages of twenty-five and twenty-nine had never married.
6. Which of the following functions of the family is not shared with any other institution?
   a. socialization
   b. reproduction
   c. socioemotional maintenance
   d. sexual regulation
7. Which of the following is not stated in the text as one of the factors associated with divorce?
   a. decline of religious influence
   b. age at first marriage
   c. length of marriage
   d. economic conditions

8. Although the proportion of single-parent families has increased for both blacks and whites since 1970, the gap between them has
   a. decreased somewhat.
   b. increased significantly.
   c. remained the same.
   d. decreased significantly.
9. Indicate which type of mate selection norm is reflected in each of the following situations.
   ____ a. Jews are supposed to marry Jews.
   ____ b. A father is not permitted to marry his daughter.
   ____ c. Members of the same social class marry.
   (1) exogamy
   (2) endogamy
   (3) homogamy
10. Match the following examples with the major theoretical perspectives.
   ____ a. a father "giving away" the bride
   ____ b. sexual regulation
   ____ c. development of self-concept
   ____ d. a newly married couple adjusting to each other
   ____ e. child abuse
   ____ f. social class passed from one generation to another
   (1) functionalism
   (2) conflict theory
   (3) symbolic interactionism

GRAPHIC REVIEW

U.S. trends in age at first marriage for males and females are graphically depicted in Figure 11.4.

1. If this upward trend in age at first marriage for both sexes continues, what do you predict will happen to the divorce rate?

2. Explain the reasons for the relationship between age at first marriage and the divorce rate you assumed in answering the first question.

CRITICAL-THINKING QUESTIONS

1. The text outlines six functions of the family. Describe how you have experienced these functions within your family of orientation. Be specific.

2. What do you think the divorce rate trend line in the United States will be in the twenty-first century? Develop your answer within the context of information in this chapter.

3. Given all the current marital and familial lifestyle variations in the United States today, many observers argue that the nuclear family will become a choice of the minority of Americans. Do you agree or disagree? Use data and social trends to support your position.

ANSWER KEY

Concept Review

a. 8
b. 4
c. 10
d. 5
e. 12
f. 1
g. 7
h. 2
i. 11
j. 6
k. 3
l. 9
m. 13

Check Yourself Review

1. T
2. T
3. nuclear
4. patriarchal
5. 35, 51
6. b
7. a
8. c
9. a. 2
   b. 1
   c. 3
10. a. 2
    b. 1
    c. 3
    d. 3
    e. 2
    f. 1

12 Education

Digital Vision/Jupiter Images

S GOALS

- Describe the relationship between industrialization and education.
- Discuss schools as bureaucracies and the attempts to debureaucratize education in the United States.
- Compare the competitors of traditional public schools.
- Outline the basic functions (manifest and latent) of the institution of education.
- Evaluate the meritocratic model of public education.
- Discuss educational inequality.
- Describe the ways in which schools socialize students.
- Identify and describe the dominant issues in higher education today.

Is federally funded Head Start another example of government waste? Americans tend to believe that the federal "bureaucracy," including its efforts in Head Start, is doomed to failure. This is government "interference" in our lives. Research, to the contrary, has consistently shown the Head Start program to produce positive benefits for underprivileged children: improvements in intelligence tests, general ability tests, and learning readiness.

Education serves many functions in modern society, including the promotion of a common identity among all members of society. Due to educational inequality among minority groups, the achievement of this integrative function has been retarded in the United States. Although Head Start has helped in this regard, barriers in the educational system remain. Before turning to the issue of educational inequality, however, some other topics require coverage, beginning with the development and structure of the American educational institution.

The Development and Structure of Education 🔲

Before industrialization, the family, the rural community, and the church were the major socializing groups in a child's life. The family taught children the values, norms, and farming skills needed to survive in an agricultural society; as societies industrialized, however, this knowledge increasingly lost its relevance. And as knowledge increased in volume and complexity, family members gradually lost the ability to adequately educate their children. As a consequence, the educational institution developed.

Q What was the objective of early schools? The founding fathers considered education an investment in democracy because it would create a literate, active, and informed public. Schools, they believed, would create some minimal "democracy of knowledge," thus preventing the privileged few from having a monopoly on knowledge. Between 1850 and 1910, the teaching of democratic values and marketable skills became especially popular in urban areas inundated by the many ethnic groups who immigrated to the United States. During this period, most proponents of public education believed the objective of the early school to be

not so much . . . *intellectual culture, as the regulation of the feelings and dispositions, the extirpation of vicious propensities, the preoccupation of the wilderness of the young heart with seeds and germs of moral beauty, and the formation of a lovely and virtuous character by the habitual practice of cleanliness, delicacy, refinement, good temper, gentleness, kindness, justice, and truth.* (M. B. Katz 1975:31)

Thus, public schooling in nineteenth-century America was not designed primarily to teach sophisticated intellectual skills; it was a mechanism of social control. Otherwise, children would grow up "vicious," or the "wilderness of the young heart" would lack "seeds of moral beauty."

Q How did education develop after the turn of the twentieth century? As farming gave way to manual factory labor in the latter part of the nineteenth century, relatively simple manual skills began to be less and less important. By the beginning of the twentieth century, new middle-management and clerical jobs were highly desired by Americans seeking to better their own lives and, more important, their children's future. Business leaders and parents began to demand more advanced training in schools. School administrators responded by developing secondary schools that emphasized advanced learning. The success of this push for education is reflected in the increasing percentage of Americans (including major racial and ethnic groups) graduating from high school (See Figure 12.1).

Bureaucracy in Education

Early school administrators based their organizational structure on the factory model. Schools would educate children in much the same way as factories mass-produced cars:

Schooling came to be seen as work or the preparation for work; schools were pictured as factories, educators as industrial managers, and students as the raw materials to be inducted into the production process. The ideology of school management was recast in the mold of the business corporation, and the character of education was shaped after the image of industrial production. (Cohen and Lazerson 1972:47)

Although this philosophy softened considerably, the concept of bureaucratized public education remains prevalent, with its specialization, rules and procedures, and impersonality.

Q In what ways are schools bureaucratic? The bureaucratic model divides the process of education into specializations: administrators who run schools; teachers who either concentrate on one or two topics or teach a specific grade level; specialists who

FIGURE 12.1

High School Graduates, 1970 and 2007

Displayed in this figure are the percentages, by racial and ethnic category, of persons twenty-five years old and above who have completed high school. Note that the proportion of high school graduates in each group has increased sharply between 1970 and 2007. As a result, each of these groups is placing more pressure on public schools to accommodate the needs of their members.

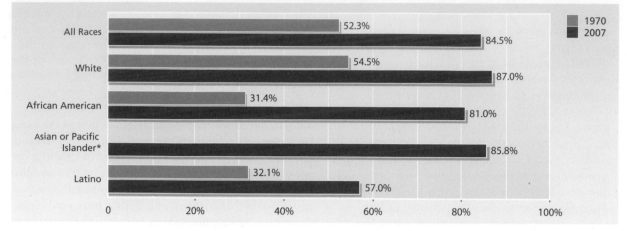

*Note: No data available for Asian or Pacific Islander for 1970.
Source: U.S. Census Bureau, *Statistical Abstract of the United States*, 2004–2005, U.S. Census Bureau, *Statistical Abstract of the United States: 2010*, 29th ed. (Washington, D.C.: U.S. Government Printing Office, 2009), Table 36, p. 40.

purchase materials; specialists who test and counsel students; and specialists who manage libraries. There are even specialists who drive buses, serve lunches, and type memos.

According to the bureaucratic model, education for large numbers of students is more efficient when students are homogeneous in development and ability. In this way, a teacher can focus attention on one set of learning materials for large numbers of students. Age-graded classrooms, in which all students receive the same instruction, reflect the impersonal, bureaucratic nature of schools.

It is also thought more efficient (the ultimate goal of a bureaucracy) to have all teachers of a given subject teaching the same, or at least similar, material. Materials can be approved and purchased in bulk, and testing can be standardized. In addition, if parents need to know what subjects are being taught at any given time, school administrators can readily advise them. This practice also allows students to transfer from one school to another without losing continuity of curriculum. Rules and procedures exist to ensure that this happens.

Schools are also part of a much larger bureaucratic system. This system begins with the federal government and progresses layer by layer through state and local governments.

Critics of the bureaucratic model claim that children are not inorganic materials to be processed on an assembly line. Children are human beings who come into school with previous knowledge and who interact socially and emotionally with other students. How can we know what takes place inside a child's head? According to critics of formal schooling, the school's bureaucratic nature is unable to respond to the expressive, creative, and emotional needs of individual children.

Reforms in the Classroom

Q **Are there alternatives to the bureaucratic model?** American educational reform occurs in cycles. The U.S. progressive education movement of the 1920s and 1930s was a reaction to the Victorian authoritarianism of early-nineteenth-century schools. Educational philosopher John Dewey (1859–1952) led the progressive education movement, with a child-centered focus and an emphasis on work-related knowledge (Dewey 2001). This movement virtually disappeared in the 1950s but resurged in the 1960s and 1970s in the humanistic education movement. The humanistic movement advocated such steps as the elimination of restrictive rules and codes and the involvement of students in the educational process. The aim was to create a more democratic, student-focused learning environment (Ballantine and Spade 2007). This movement spawned a number of educational philosophies aimed at classroom reform. Three formulations of the humanistic educational impulse are the open classroom, cooperative learning, and the integrative curriculum.

Q **What is the open classroom?** The **open classroom** is a nonbureaucratic approach to education based on democratic relationships, flexibility, and non-competitiveness:

> In the 1960s, advocates of the open classroom proposed alternatives to the bureaucratically organized school. They agreed on an underlying philosophy: Children are naturally curious and motivated to learn by their own interests and desires. The most important condition for nurturing this natural interest is freedom, supported by adults who enrich the environment and offer help. In contrast, coercion and regimentation only inhibit emotional and intellectual development. (Graubard 1972:352)

The open classroom philosophy advocates elimination of the following customs: the sharp authoritarian line between teachers and students, the predetermined curriculum for all children of a given age, the constant comparison of students' performance, the use of competition as a motivator, and the grouping of children according to performance and ability. In short, schools adhering to the open classroom approach wish to avoid the bureaucratic features of traditional public schools (Silberman 1973; Kozol 1985; Kohl 1988; Holt 1995).

The open classroom approach did not definitively fulfill expectations. Money, student–teacher ratio, and teacher endorsement all affected the outcome. So the debate continues (Hallinan 1995). Some argue that schools must operate bureaucratically because limited money requires the less expensive mass instruction. Others claim that concern for children should supersede administrative needs and that individualized programs developing the child's whole personality should hold priority. According to another viewpoint, the bureaucratic nature of schools prepares children for the bureaucratic society to which they must ultimately adapt.

Although further experimentation continues and appears warranted, it remains to be seen whether Americans are in the mood for it. In fact, the "back-to-basics" movement, which emerged in the mid-1980s and 1990s, conflicts explicitly with the open classroom philosophy. The back-to-basics movement represents an attempt to reinstate a traditional curriculum ("reading, writing, and arithmetic") based on more bureaucratic methods.

Q **What led to the back-to-basics movement?** In 1983, America received an "educational wakeup call" when the National Commission on Excellence in Education issued a report dramatically entitled *A Nation at Risk* (1984). Catching the attention of politicians and the general public, the report warned of a "rising tide of mediocrity" in America's schools (see "See Sociology in Your Life").

Because of deficiencies in its educational system, the report claimed, America is at risk of being overtaken by some of its economic world competitors (D. P. Gardner 1983). As evidence, the report pointed to several indicators:

- Twenty-three million American adults, 40 percent of minority young people, and 13 percent of all seventeen-year-olds are functionally illiterate.
- Scholastic Aptitude Test (SAT) scores dropped dramatically between the early 1960s and 1980.
- Only one-third of all seventeen-year-olds can solve a mathematics problem requiring several steps.
- American children are being outperformed by children of other nations on achievement tests.

Unlike the recommendations of the progressive and humanistic reform movements, most of the solutions offered by the commission tended toward the bureaucratic. The report urged a return to fundamental skills such as reading and mathematics. High school graduation requirements should include four years of English, three years of mathematics, three years of science, three years of social studies, and a half-year of computer science. School days, the school year, or both should be longer. Students should take standardized achievement tests as they move from one level of schooling to another. Teachers should assign significantly more homework. Discipline should be tighter through the development and enforcement of codes for student conduct.

The commission's report stirred intellectual debate (Adelson 1984; Bunzel 1985; Gross and Gross 1985) and aroused the public. Americans generally favor the commission's recommendations, especially its call for more homework and greater discipline (Barrett 1990).

In a series of books, English professor E. D. Hirsch contends that American schoolchildren are not being taught the knowledge they need in today's world (Hirsch 1987, 1999, 2004). Hirsch labeled American schoolchildren "culturally illiterate." Surprising numbers of schoolchildren don't know when the American Revolution occurred, who George Washington Carver was, or where Washington, D.C., is located. Although concerned for all Americans, Hirsch is particularly concerned that the failure of schools, and the accompanying cultural illiteracy, is dooming children from poor and illiterate homes to perpetual poverty. Keeping poor and illiterate children in the same condition as their parents is, for Hirsch, an unacceptable failure of American schools (see "Think Globally" 12.1).

Q **How did our government respond?** Late in 1987, U.S. Secretary of Education William Bennett, under President Ronald Reagan, proposed a back-to-basics curriculum for American high schools. Emphasis was on a

Are Americans Losing Their Minds?

That America is dumbing down is not a new charge. In 1837, Ralph Waldo Emerson observed that "The mind of this country, taught to aim at low objects, eats upon itself." So begins Susan Jacoby's current examination of anti-intellectualism and anti-rationalism in America (Jacoby 2008a, 2008b).

Jacoby identifies Richard Hofstadter's (1966) *Anti-Intellectualism in American Life* as the classic book in this area. Hofstadter saw anti-intellectualism as cyclical, waxing and waning as broad social forces change. Jacoby believes that the prevalence and depth of "dumbness" in our culture would shock even Hofstadter if he were still alive.

Jacoby offers some facts to bolster her claim of a current wave of anti-intellectualism. For example:

Reading has declined not only among the poorly educated, according to a report last year by the National Endowment for the Arts. In 1982, 82 percent of college graduates read novels or poems for pleasure; two decades later, only 67 percent did. And more than 40 percent of Americans under 44 did not read a single book—fiction or nonfiction—over the course of a year. The proportion of 17-year-olds who read nothing (unless required to do so for school) more than doubled between 1984 and 2004. (Jacoby 2008a)

Of the several broad social forces promoting anti-intellectualism today, Jacoby sees the triumph of video culture over print culture as paramount. With rising use of personal computers, instant messages, video games, YouTube, Facebook, and MySpace, we have seen a decline in book, newspaper, and magazine reading. This trend, Jacoby contends, is most obvious among the young.

Some supporters of the new technology see the ability of children to spend long periods of time in front of video games and computers as a sign of an ability to focus (S. Johnson 2006). Jacoby attempts to debunk this contention through research on children. She cites a study of babies between eight and sixteen months who watch videos such as *Baby Einstein*. This University of Washington research team reported that children this age recognize an average of six to eight fewer words for every hour spent watching videos each day. A study of toddlers ages one to three at Children's Hospital in Seattle found a positive correlation between the amount of television watched and attention problems at age seven. For each hour of television watched daily, the chances of developing attention-deficit hyperactivity disorder rose by almost 10 percent. This disorder is associated with difficulties in concentrating, organizing, and controlling impulsive behavior (Brody 2004).

It is not just that 20 percent of Americans believe the sun revolves around the Earth, or that almost half of Americans between ages eighteen and twenty-four do not care to know the locations of countries where significant news is being made. Really worrying Jacoby is what she sees as "the alarming number of Americans who have smugly concluded that they do not need to know such things in the first place" (Jacoby 2008a:37). It is arrogance about the lack of knowledge that she considers anti-intellectual or anti-rationalist.

Think About It

1. As a member of the first generation to experience video culture as Jacoby describes it, do you agree or disagree with her thesis? Defend your answer.
2. As a future (or present) parent, do you think it is necessary to protect your children from video culture? Why or why not?

---

minimum core curriculum that all students must take (Bennett 1988). In 1991, the first President Bush's secretary of education, Lamar Alexander, formulated a national educational reform plan with six goals (*America 2000* 1991):

1. Every child must begin school ready to learn.
2. The national high school graduation rate must be 90 percent.
3. Competence in core subjects must be shown after grades 4, 8, and 12.
4. American students should be the best educated in the world in math and science.
5. All adults must be literate and possess the skills necessary for citizenship and competition in a global economy.
6. Schools should be free of drugs and violence.

Implementation of the plan included a longer school year, national standards, state exams, and merit pay for teachers.

The latest manifestation of the back-to-basics philosophy is the "high-stakes" testing movement. As part of this movement, President George W. Bush signed in January 2002 a bill he considered the cornerstone of his administration's domestic policy. Known as *No Child*

THINK GLOBALLY 12.1

Literacy Rates

One of the functions of education is to promote literacy—the key to continued learning, problem solving, and information analysis. This map shows rates of illiteracy among persons fifteen years of age and older in various countries of the world. Because of cultural norms and discrimination, more men than women are able to read and write.

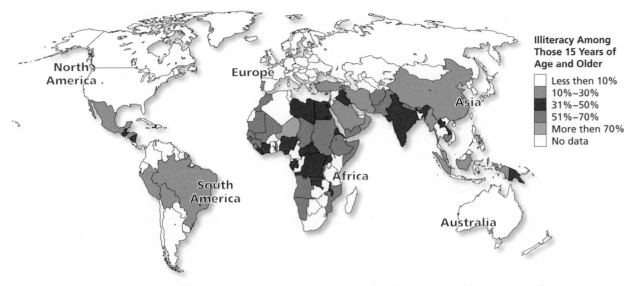

Illiteracy Among Those 15 Years of Age and Older

- Less then 10%
- 10%–30%
- 31%–50%
- 51%–70%
- More then 70%
- No data

Source: John L. Allen and Christopher J. Sutton, *Student Atlas of World Politics, 9th ed.* (p. 88). Copyright © 2011 by The McGraw-Hill Companies. Reproduced by permission of McGraw-Hill Contemporary Learning Series.

Interpret the Map

1. Do you see a pattern in the rates of Illiteracy? Explain.

2. How does the United States measure up?

Left Behind, this federal law requires that each student racial and demographic subgroup improve each year (grades 3–8) on mandatory standardized tests. Schools failing to accomplish this improvement for two years running must help students transfer to better schools and use public money for tutoring students. A school that continues to fall short of the federal standard must either replace its principal and teachers or reopen as a charter school (Fletcher 2003; *From the Capital to the Classroom* 2003).

Q **Do we see confirmation for the bureaucratically oriented solutions?** To date, there is no evidence that the back-to-basics movement, on its own, can live up to its advanced billing (Kantrowitz 1993a; Hancock and Wingert 1995; Wingert 1996). In fact, the implementation of some of the solutions actually inflicts greater harm. The dropout rate increases as school hours increase, achievement testing expands, and homework assignments grow. The pressure only exacerbates the low self-esteem of many low-performing students. Stricter grading and increases in academic requirements discourage low-income and minority students even more. So, despite the efforts of the back-to-basics

movement and the No Child Left Behind push, it appears that the nation's educational system remains at risk (Wagner 2003; Dillon 2008; Anderson and Turque 2010; Ravitch 2010).

Public opinion reflects perceived shortcomings of the most recent back-to-basics reform. Americans showed very mixed feelings in 2008 as Congress prepared to debate renewal of the No Child Left Behind Act. Fifty-eight percent of Americans polled believed that the law either made schools worse or had no impact; 34 percent said that the law improved schools. Of Americans with children in public school, only 30 percent claimed that No Child Left Behind upgraded their children's schools ("No Child Left Behind Gets Mixed Grades" 2008).

Q **How does cooperative learning contribute to a less bureaucratic classroom?** Evidence indicates that a less bureaucratic approach to education should not be dismissed (R. A. Horwitz 1979; Hurn 1993). In fact, the open classroom philosophy that became prominent in the 1960s and 1970s is currently being implemented again (emerging alongside the back-to-basics movement). The philosophy this time is in the form of cooperative learning. **Cooperative learning** takes place in a nonbureaucratic classroom structure in which students study in groups, with teachers acting as guides rather than as the controlling agents:

> *Cooperative learning approaches are based in part on the assumption that students learn best when actively working with others in small heterogeneous groups. . . . It occurs when teachers have students work together in small groups on a task toward a group goal—a single product (a set of answers, a project, a report, a piece or collection of creative writing, etc.) or achieving as high a group average as possible on a test—then reward the entire group on the basis of the quality or quantity of its product according to a set standard of success.* (Oakes 1985:208, 210)

According to the cooperative learning method, students learn more if they are actively involved with others in the classroom (Sizer 1996). The traditional teacher-centered approach rewards students for being passive recipients of information and requires them to compete with others for grades and teacher recognition. Cooperative learning, with its accent on teamwork rather than individual performance, is designed to concentrate on results rather than on performance comparisons among students. Cooperation replaces competition. Students typically work in small groups on a specific task. Credit for the task is given only if all group members do their part.

Research has documented some benefits of the cooperative learning approach. Uncooperativeness and stress among students is less; academic performance is higher; students have more positive attitudes toward school; racial and ethnic antagonism decreases;

and self-esteem increases (Oakes 1985; Aronson and Gonzalez 1988; Children's Defense Fund 1991).

Although Japanese schools have been using group learning in the early grades for years, resistance remains strong among many American teachers (Kantrowitz 1993b). They fear loss of control with younger children and disciplinary problems among older students, especially teenagers. Many American teachers and principals believe that mapping a student's progress is more difficult in a cooperative learning setting. This approach also requires more preparatory work for teachers, who must plan lessons allowing for less frequent teacher intrusion. Grading is also more complex when blending an individual and group evaluation.

Q **What is the integrative curriculum?** The **integrative curriculum,** another extension of the open classroom, is an approach to education based on student–teacher collaboration. Where the traditional classroom predetermines the curriculum for students, students and teachers together create the curriculum for the integrative approach. Because students are asked to participate in curriculum design and content, the integrative curriculum is democratic in nature. Giving students such power obviously deviates from the traditional subject-centered curriculum (Barr 1995). Rather, subject matter is selected and organized around certain real-world themes or concepts, as exemplified in a Washington State sixth-grade unit of study on water quality:

> *The unit became a part of an actual water quality project that originated in the Great Lakes region of the United States but now spans the globe. Lessons were organized*

Working cooperatively in groups was one of the most democratic school reforms of the twentieth century.

PhotoLink/Getty Images

CHECK YOURSELF **12.1** **R2**

The Development and Structure of Education

1. The _____ institution developed to fulfill society's need to transmit knowledge to the young.
2. Contemporary public education is important primarily because of
   a. the quality of teachers in modern schools.
   b. efficient operation of school bureaucracies.
   c. historical changes in the economic and social structures of industrial societies.
   d. lack of qualified individual tutors.
3. Early public schooling in America was viewed as a mechanism of _____.
4. Schools in America today are based on the _____ model of organization.
5. _____ attempt to avoid most of the bureaucratic features of traditional public schools.
6. _____ is a nonbureaucratic classroom structure in which students study in groups with teachers acting as guides rather than as the controlling agents determining all activities.

Answers: 1. educational; 2. c; 3. social control; 4. bureaucratic; 5. Open classrooms; 6. Cooperative learning

around the actual work of determining water quality in Puget Sound. These lessons culminated in students' reporting to community groups about the quality of the water. In this way learning was relevant to a real-world problem that the students contributed to solving. (Simmons and El-Hindi 1998:33)

Instruction in this unit was organized around hands-on experience and a "multiple intelligence" approach, recognizing that students in a classroom are not identical. Students bring to any unit of study a variety of learning styles, interests, and abilities, and different units of study will engage students in varying ways.

Competitors of Traditional Public Schools **R1**

While the debate over the most effective classroom methods continues, educators, parents, and politicians are looking for answers beyond the classroom, to the way schools are organized, funded, and administered (Boyles 2004; Pedroni 2007). The latest back-to-basics reform is based on **school choice**—alternatives predicated on the free enterprise model, thereby creating competition for the public school system. According to school choice advocates, parents and students should be able to select the school that best fits their needs and provides the greatest educational benefits (Corwin and Schneider 2005; Ravitch 2010). There are several approaches to education that are consistent with the school choice philosophy: voucher systems, charter schools, magnet schools, for-profit schools, and home schooling.

Q **What is a voucher system?** Proponents of **vouchers** contend that the government should make available to families with school-age children a sum of money that they can use in private or parochial schools. Families who chose a public school would pay nothing, just as in the current system. Parents who chose a religious or other private school would have the tuition paid up to the amount of the government voucher and would have to make up the difference (if any) between the amount of the voucher and the tuition amount. A voucher plan in Cleveland, for example, provided publicly funded scholarships of just over $2,000 annually to almost 4,000 city children. Most parents chose to spend the money at private schools rather than to keep their children in public schools. In Wisconsin, adoption of a voucher plan ($5,300 per voucher for students whose parents earn less than $30,000 for a family of four) increased from fewer than 10 schools to 103 (M. A. Fletcher 2001).

Proponents point to the freedom vouchers give parents, the increased quality that would presumably come from schools competing for students, and the ability to place students in educational environments best suited to their particular needs. Critics fear that free choice of school would make urban schools even more of a dumping ground for the poor and minorities, because poor and minority parents in the inner cities cannot make up the difference between the amount of the voucher and the cost of sending their children to higher-quality schools. Critics contend that the use of vouchers will erode national commitment to public education, leaving the public school system in even worse shape (Kozol 1992; Kahlenberg 2003; Weil 2003; Pedroni 2007).

Claiming that vouchers violate separation of church and state, courts traditionally ruled voucher systems unconstitutional. However, a 1998 U.S. Supreme Court ruling validated a Wisconsin law allowing state money for low-income students to attend either private or parochial schools (Perry and McGraw 1999). And in a 2001 decision, the Supreme Court declared the Cleveland vouchers to be neutral with respect to religion because parents still retained choice of where and how to school their children (Morse 2002).

Evidence on the effectiveness of the voucher system is inconsistent. Although some voucher programs have improved student test scores (compared with public schools), other programs produced no improvement (Toch and Cohen 1998; Moe 2001; Witte 2000; *School Vouchers* 2001; Blum and Mathews 2003; Ravitch 2010). Rand Corporation researchers conclude that many of the key questions about vouchers still await answers. With regard to academic achievement, these researchers found that privately funded small-scale experimental voucher programs aimed at low-income students may have a modest academic benefit for African American students after one to two years in these programs. While even this effect must be tentatively reported, no conclusion at all can be drawn regarding children of other racial or ethnic groups (Gill et al. 2001).

The harshest critics draw several negative conclusions: Public schools lose money to private voucher schools, making public education less able to be successful; voucher programs do not necessarily lead to higher academic performance; and voucher schools are not accountable to taxpayers (Miner 2000). American public opinion appears to be swinging toward the critics. With increased approval of public schools, support of vouchers declined from 44 percent in 1997 to 22 percent in 2004 (Ray 2004). More generally, the momentum of the school choice movement is declining.

Charter Schools

Q What are charter schools? **Charter schools** are publicly funded schools operated like private schools by public schoolteachers and administrators. Freed of answering to local school boards, charter schools have the latitude to use nontraditional teaching methods and to shape their own curricula (Murphy 2002; Zimmer, Buddin, and Chau 2003). For example, the Mosaica Academy in Bensalem, Pennsylvania, is not organized along public school lines. The school day is nearly two hours longer and the school year is twenty days longer. This school created its own curriculum with the goal of immersing students in a study of civilizations that developed over a period of 4,000 years (Symonds 2000). The number of charter schools reached about 5,000 by 2011, with more than 1 million students (U.S. Census Bureau 2009). Washington, D.C., for example, has sixty charter schools on ninety-two campuses with 26,000 students (Keating and Labbe-DeBose 2008).

After some fifteen years of charter school operations, the results have been disappointing (Gabriel 2010). According to one study, charter schools spend more on administration and less on instruction than public schools do; student performance is generally no better, and often worse; and charter schools are more homogeneous with respect to race and class than their public counterparts (Wingert 2002; Dillon 2007). UCLA researchers in the Civil Rights Project review a number of studies, concluding that, if anything, charter schools across the nation produce fewer academic benefits than public schools (Frankenberg, Siegel-Hawley, and Wang 2010). Moreover, charter schools increase school segregation. Partly due to their predominantly urban location, charter schools have a larger proportion of black students than traditional public schools ("Choice Without Equity" 2010). Nationally, 70 percent of black charter school students are in heavily segregated minority charter schools. Half of Latino charter school students are also enrolled in homogeneous minority schools. In the West and in part of the South, charter schools serve as havens for white students fleeing public schools.

Q What is unique about magnet schools? **Magnet schools** are public schools that attempt to achieve excellence by specializing in a particular area. One school may emphasize the arts; another may stress science. If their public school district includes magnet schools, families can decide which particular school best suits their children's needs. Normally, public school children are required to attend the school nearest their home. However, magnet schools provide the opportunity to attend a school outside the zoned boundaries. Unlike charter schools and for-profit schools, magnet schools operate under the same administrative structure as public schools (Chen 2007).

Advocates of magnet schools point to their promotion of diversity. Because parents choose their own magnet school, this approach is advertised as a way of avoiding forced busing while encouraging voluntary desegregation. They also praise the introduction of school choice and the positive effects magnet schools have on curriculum and teaching in the regular public schools. Critics counter with evidence that magnet schools have not fulfilled their promises with respect to diversity (Frankenberg, Siegel-Hawley, and Wang 2010). Critics, as we shall see, also question the existence of a truly free market in education and doubt the claimed effects magnet schools are supposed to have on public schools. They also worry that magnet schools will harm public schools by draining off the best and the brightest students and by absorbing scarce school funds.

This urban magnet school emphasizing the arts is one alternative to the public school system.

Amy Conn-Gutierrez/AP Photo

For-Profit Schools

Q **What is the nature of for-profit schools?** Some reformers believe government to be incapable of improving the educational system, because government is wasteful and ineffective. Instead, they say, why not look to market forces to solve the problems facing schools today? **For-profit schools,** supported by government funds but run by private, profit-seeking companies, are proposed as a superior alternative to the traditional public schools. By borrowing from modern business practices, the argument goes, these schools will be efficient, productive, and cost-effective. Marketplace forces, they allege, will ensure that the "best" schools survive.

The most comprehensive for-profit organization is Edison, which launched itself with a $40 million, three-year campaign in 1992. Edison schools claim to feature challenging curricula, along with a schedule that has children in school almost a third longer than in the average public school. Beginning in the third grade, students are equipped with a computer and modem that they can take home to access the Edison's intranet system (Symonds 2000). Edison's annual revenue is in the neighborhood of $2 billion. Despite recent expansion, for-profit schools still handle a relatively small portion of America's school students.

Supporters of for-profit schools point to several advantages. Their competitive model, they argue, forces regular public schools to improve their performance. Otherwise, public schools will lose students to the for-profits. Competition motivates for-profit schools to constantly improve or they will have fewer students (and profits). Since for-profit schools have the burden of attracting students, supporters claim they must be responsive to parent preferences.

Critics of for-profit school are not silent. Where is the evidence to support these claims, they ask? In one of the few studies of for-profit schools, researchers found no increase in student achievement for the first ten years of Edison schools operation (Miron and Applegate 2000). For-profit schools are also seen as a drain on scarce public funds. Many detractors are offended by the very idea of mixing profit with children's education; they see profit and education as antithetical, to the detriment of children. For example, they charge, extracurricular activities such as sports and social clubs are often squeezed out to reduce expenses. Finally, critics are concerned about the lack of oversight of for-profit schools, thereby denying voters the power to influence school officials and educational policy (Saltman 2001, 2007).

Homeschooling

Homeschooling, another alternative to either private or public schools, has a long history in the United States. Of course, prior to laws mandating school attendance, children were educated at home or in informal community schools. Recently, some critics of the public schools have advocated a return to homeschooling. Most prominent among the early critics of public schools is John Holt, an educator who wrote two early influential books excoriating public schools (Holt 1995a, 1995b; originally published in 1964 and 1967). In these books, Holt did not propose homeschooling as an alternative to public schools. At the time, his aim was to improve public schools that he believed were failing children by placing excessive pressure on them; he wished to make schools child friendly. Later, Holt went further, asking what could be friendlier than being taught at home by parents (Holt 2003).

Many parents agree. From 1999 to 2007, the percentage of homeschooled children increased by 74 percent, now involving some 1.5 million students. The most salient reason parents give for homeschooling is the desire to provide religious or moral instruction.

What do critics fear about homeschooling?

viki2win/Shutterstock.com

A second tier of motivations involve parental concern about things such as safety, drugs, and peer pressure in the school environment and dissatisfaction with academic instruction. Other reasons include family time, finances, travel, and distance. A smaller percentage of parents simply opt for a nontraditional approach to education, or they have a child with health problems or special needs. White students comprise most of homeschooled children (77 percent). Homeschooled children are overwhelmingly in two-parent families (89 percent; "Fast Facts" 2009).

Detractors of homeschooling lack confidence in the credentials homeschooling parents bring to the table. How can parents possibly bolster their children's education with the dynamic topics of science, biology, and computer technology? What about extracurricular activities? And where are homeschooled children going to get the social experience needed to function in the modern world? Skeptics also fear that removing children from public schools will affect school budgets that usually are based on the number of students in the classroom. Though homeschooling has not made a significant impact on school budgets thus far, its growth represents a threat, particularly when combined with other competitors such as charter schools, magnet schools, and for-profit schools.

Q **Where does this leave school choice?** Vociferous critics Ronald Corwin and E. Joseph Schneider call school choice a hoax. There simply is no free market, they contend. Given education laws compelling school enrollment, the public school system will always have students, no matter how they perform. Public schools don't have to compete to survive. Moreover, Gorwan and Schneider assert, the government, not

CHECK YOURSELF **12.2** **R2**

Competitors of Traditional Public Schools

1. School choice is undergirded by the _____ model.
2. A school that concentrates on science in its curriculum is known as a
   a. magnet school
   b. interactive school
   c. segregated school
   d. for-profit school
   e. charter school
3. Charter schools, contrary to expectations, have increased school integration. T or F?
4. One of the advantages of for-profit schools is that they operate without government funds. T or F?
5. The most salient reason parents give for homeschooling is the desire to provide religious or moral instruction. T or F?

Answers: 1. free enterprise; 2. e; 3. F; 4. F; 5. T

the market, regulates the competition. Politicians can determine winners and losers because they control the money needed by all of the schools (Corwin and Schneider 2005).

Diane Ravitch, too, believes that the free choice movement (as well as No Child Left Behind) is a failure, though she doesn't see it a hoax. She was after all, as assistant secretary of education under George W. Bush, one of the moving forces behind the most recent back-to-basics reform. There is something soothing, she writes, about the idea that the invisible hand of the market will automatically improve schools in the long run. The public and politicians can stop worrying about school improvement because infallible market forces will do the job for them. However, Ravitch asserts, schools are not business organizations. Consequently, the application of business principles is no substitute for the hard work of grappling with the unique problems of schools. Knowledge of management, marketing, finance, and accounting does not compensate for a lack of expertise in education.

The Functionalist Perspective **R1**

Functions of Education

According to the functionalists, social institutions develop because they meet one or more of society's basic needs. The educational institution performs several vital functions in modern society: cultural transmission; social integration; selection and screening of talent; promotion of personal growth and development; and the dissemination, preservation, and creation of knowledge. (See Table 12.1 for a comparison of the three major theoretical perspectives on education.)

Q How does the educational institution transmit culture? Cultural transmission must occur if a society is to endure. Indeed, the educational institution perpetuates a society's cultural heritage from one generation to the next. When we see evidence of the teaching of Marxist-Leninist doctrine in communist societies, we call it indoctrination. We are less aware of the process of indoctrination when, through the study of Washington, Jefferson, and Lincoln, we Americans learn about the merits of democracy. Thus, although schools teach basic academic skills such as reading, writing, and mathematics, they also transmit culture by instilling in students the basic values, norms, beliefs, and attitudes of the society. The value of competition, for example, is taught through an emphasis on grades, sports, and school spirit. (More is said about this function later.)

Q How does education contribute to social integration? Although television is now a strong competitor, the educational system remains the major agent of social integration. Formal education transforms a diverse population into a community with a common identity. Learning an official language, sharing in national history and patriotic themes, and being exposed to similar informational sequences facilitate a shared identity. The result is a society with relatively homogeneous values, norms, beliefs, and attitudes. Even newly arrived immigrant children without the ability to speak and write English attend local schools and soon learn to participate in the American way of life.

The current debate on bilingual education touches on this function. People who emphasize the need for

TABLE 12.1

Investigating Education

This table illustrates differences in the ways the major theoretical perspectives investigate education as a social institution. It is, of course, possible for a theoretical perspective to study education using one of the concepts associated in this table with another perspective. Explain, for example, how conflict theory would interpret the hidden curriculum and tracking.

Theoretical Perspective	Concept	Example
Functionalism	Tracking	• Schools shape the occupational future of children by placing them in educational programs based on test scores and early school performance.
Conflict theory	Meritocracy	• Students attending better schools have an occupational advantage over students from poorer schools.
Symbolic interactionism	Hidden curriculum	• Schools teach children the values of conformity and achievement.

Do you consider the student opportunity to flirt with the opposite sex a positive or negative function of schools?

Huy Lam/Getty Images

students pursue careers consistent with their abilities. (The concept of tracking plays an important role in the conflict perspective of education, discussed shortly.)

Q How do schools promote personal growth and development? Schools expose students to a wide variety of perspectives and experiences that encourage them to develop creativity, verbal skills, artistic expression, intellectual accomplishment, and cultural tolerance. In this way, education provides an environment in which individuals can improve the quality of their lives. In addition, schools promote personal growth and development by preparing students for their occupational pursuits.

Q How does education encourage the dissemination, preservation, and creation of knowledge? Educational organizations disseminate knowledge not only via the classroom but through contributions such as written or audiovisual materials that can reach hundreds of thousands of people. Preservation of knowledge is perpetuated by the transmission of knowledge from generation to generation. The task of preserving knowledge is also achieved by such activities as deciphering ancient manuscripts; protecting artifacts; and recording knowledge in written, video, or audio form. *Innovation*—the creation or discovery of new knowledge through research or creative thinking—can take place at any level within the educational system, but it traditionally receives more emphasis at the university level.

Latent Functions of Education

The functions of schools discussed to this point are recognized and intended—**manifest functions.** The educational institution has other functions as well that are unrecognized and unintended—**latent functions.**

Q What are the latent functions of education? We do not usually count among the functions of schools the provision of day-care facilities for dual-employed couples and single parents. Nor do we think that our tax money goes to schools so that people can find marriage partners. Also, schools are not consciously designed to prevent delinquency by holding juveniles indoors during the daytime. Nor are schools intended as training grounds for athletes. Finally, schools are not generally recognized for inoculating the discipline needed to follow orders in a bureaucratized society (DeYoung 1989; also see "Consider This Research" in Chapter 4).

Though we consider each of the above latent functions a positive contribution to society, some consequences, of course, are negative, or dysfunctional. Determining what is dysfunctional depends on the reference point. Most see tracking, for example, as a

recognizing and honoring cultural diversity *(multiculturalists)* usually support instruction in the student's own language, at least for some period of time. Opponents of bilingual education argue that it hinders the development of a common American cultural identity and that it is not a proven success for helping students succeed academically. A conservative political backlash to the bilingual approach has led twenty-three states to adopt English as their official language.

Q How do schools select and screen students? Scores on intelligence and achievement tests are used for grouping students. The stated purpose of testing (administered for more than fifty years now) is to identify an individual's talents and aptitudes. Test scores are also used for **tracking**—placing students in curricula consistent with the school's expectations for the students' eventual occupations (Oakes 1985; Oakes and Lipton 1996; Taylor, Peplau, and Sears 1997). Counselors use test scores and early performance records to predict careers for which individuals may be best suited. Counselors usually feel a moral obligation to ensure that

CHECK YOURSELF 12.3 R2

The Functionalist Perspective

1. Placing students in curricula consistent with the school's expectations for students' eventual occupations is called _____.
2. Schools serve as day-care facilities for dual-employed couples and single parents. This is an example of a
   a. progressive function
   b. manifest function
   c. parental function
   d. latent function
   e. none of the above

Answers: 1. tracking; 2. d

manifest, positive function of schools. On the other hand, according to the conflict perspective, tracking serves a latent dysfunction: it is a mechanism for perpetuating the social class structure. Moreover, evidence suggests that tracking is harmful to those placed on "slower" tracks (Hurn 1993; Oakes and Lipton 1996). The conflict perspective of education is presented in the following discussions on meritocracy, educational inequality, and cognitive testing. These topics are central to the relationship between education and social inequality, a topic of research in the sociology of education since World War II (Hallinan 1988).

The Conflict Perspective R1

Meritocracy

In a **meritocracy,** social status is based on ability and achievement rather than social class or parental status (M. Young 1967; Bell 1976). According to the meritocratic model, all individuals have an equal chance to succeed and to develop their abilities for the benefit of themselves and their society. A meritocratic society is free of barriers that might prevent individuals from developing their talents. Meritocracy, then, by definition, involves competition. For this reason, sports are seen as the ultimate meritocracy. Although some sports have glaring shortcomings in this regard, they do fit very closely the definition of **competition** as "a social process that occurs when rewards are given to people on the basis of how their performances compare with the performances of others doing the same task or participating in the same event" (Coakley 2006:78).

Q Is America a meritocracy? Many Americans believe that the United States is a meritocratic society. However, a number of recurring problems suggest that the model does not always work the way we think it does (Lieberman 1993; Lemann 2000).

Although America purports to be a meritocratic society, researchers recognize barriers to true merit-based achievement. For example, critics argue that public education primarily serves the economic elite. Because schools are not equal for children of all social classes, students do not all have an equal starting point (Bowles and Gintis 1976; Giroux 1983; Gittell 1998; See "Sociology Eyes America 12.1 and 12.2).

Randall Collins (2007) contends that America is not a meritocratic society but is composed of various status groups competing with one another for wealth, power, and prestige. **Status groups** are made up of individuals who share a sense of status equality based on their participation in a common culture, with similar manners, hobbies, opinions, and values. In their struggle for advantage in society, individuals frequently turn to others like themselves as a resource in their struggle with other status groups. In America, for example, white Anglo-Saxon Protestant males dominate most of the positions of wealth, power, and prestige. Collins argues that this elite has structured public schools to reinforce the shared culture of their group. Entry into higher-status positions requires acceptance of their values. People from higher-status homes who have been educated in "better" schools, for example, have an easier time getting into the higher-level jobs. Those who are from lower social classes; who are of a different color or sex; or who do not possess the appropriate values, manners, language, and dress find it more difficult to enter better colleges and universities and to obtain higher-level jobs.

In an earlier book, Collins (1979) takes the conflict interpretation even further with the concept of **credentialism**—the idea that credentials (educational degrees) are unnecessarily required for many jobs. Why, he asks, must American physicians be trained almost into middle age when communist countries produce qualified doctors in a relatively short time? The required credentials, according to Collins, empower those who can afford them to maintain a strong hold

SOCIOLOGY EYES AMERICA 12.1

School Expenditures

School Expenditures Per Person

- $1,200 or less
- $1,201 to $1,300
- $1,301 to $1,400
- $1,401 to $1,500
- Over $1,500

Source: U.S. Census Bureau, *Statistical Abstract of the United States: 2010*, 129th ed. (Washington, D.C.: U.S. Bureau of the Census, 2009), Table 253, p. 165.

Everyone has heard "You get what you pay for." Because of this idea, many people use the amount of money spent on public schools as a measure of the quality of education. The accompanying map shows that some states spend more than twice as much per student as other states.

Interpret the Map

1. How does your state compare with other states in school expenditures?
2. Do you see a regional pattern in public school funding? Explain.
3. What other factors might you want to know to determine if the amount of money spent affected the quality of education delivered?

SOCIOLOGY EYES AMERICA 12.2

Median Household Income

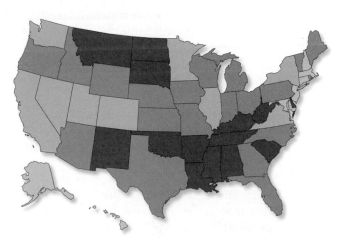

- $37,404–$45,542
- $46,107–$53,096
- $55,327–$61,154
- $63,989–$70,005

Source: U.S. Census Bureau, *American Community Survey, 2008*.

This map displays the median household income by state. You would expect to see a positive relationship between state median household income and state school expenditures.

Interpret the Map

1. Looking at Sociology Eyes America 12.1 and 12.2, how would you describe the correlation between state median household income and state school expenditures? Explain your answer.
2. How does your state compare with other states with respect to median household income and school expenditures?
3. What is the relationship between income and school expenditures in your community? Be as specific as you can in your answer.

on the elite occupations. Otherwise, why would people spend so much time in school learning things that are useless to them on the job (Labaree 1997)?

Racial and ethnic minorities face related barriers to achievement. An important example is the lower performance on college entrance examinations.

Q How do minorities perform on college entrance exams, and why? African Americans, Latinos, and Native Americans have lower average scores on the Scholastic Assessment Test (SAT) than whites (see Table 12.2). Sociologists attribute this fact, in part, to the differences in school quality noted earlier. And both school quality and SAT performance are related to social class levels of parents. Children from upper-class and upper-middle-class families attend more affluent schools. These children also have higher SAT scores. Social class clearly affects SAT performance.

Q How does SAT performance influence occupational and economic achievement? The original purpose of the SAT, created in 1926, was to enable talented youth, regardless of social class background, to attend premier colleges and universities (Lemann 2000). Ironically, as we have just seen, social class is a major factor in SAT performance. Consequently, social class nevertheless influences (through SAT performance) who will attend the elite institutions, which are the gateway to America's higher social classes.

Q But don't the rewards accompanying high SAT performance indicate that America is a meritocracy? On the surface, it does seem so. After all, it is those who perform better academically who enjoy higher levels of success.

But there are two problems. First, the advantage some people have because of their parents' social class can create an uneven playing field; talent in the lower social classes often goes unrecognized and undeveloped. Second, conflict theorists question the assumption that SAT performance measures academic ability and the likelihood of success in both college and life. For example, African American students who attend the most prestigious schools—including students with SAT scores below 1000—complete college at a higher rate than black students attending less rigorous institutions. They are also more likely to go on to graduate or professional schools (Bowen and Bok 2000).

At the least, these findings raise doubts. Recognizing this, an official at the Educational Testing Service (ETS)—developer and marketer of the SAT—announced in 1999 that ETS was creating a "Strivers" score. The idea was to adjust a student's SAT score to factor in social class as well as racial and ethnic characteristics thought to place him or her at a competitive disadvantage. Any student whose original score exceeded by 200 points the score predicted for his or her social class or racial or ethnic category would be considered a striver. The striver's score would be made available for colleges and universities to use, if they desired, in their

TABLE 12.2

SAT Scores by Race and Ethnicity

An examination of this table reveals the gap in average SAT scores for whites and Asian Americans versus African Americans, Latinos, and Native Americans. Interpret these data as a conflict theorist would in the context of the United States as a meritocracy.

Racial/Ethnic Category	SAT Critical Reading Mean Scores	SAT Math Mean Scores	Totals
Native American	485	492	977
Asian	519	591	1110
African American	429	428	851
Latino Background			
Mexican American	454	462	916
Puerto Rican	454	452	906
Other Latino	454	462	916
White (excluding Latino origin)	528	536	1,064

Source: The College Board, 2010.

Social class is a strong predictor of success on the SATs. How is race related to social class?

Mary Ann Chastain/AP Photo

admissions decisions (Glazer 1999; Wildavsky 1999). A firestorm of criticism influenced a quick withdrawal of the proposal. But, concern did not die. By 2005 the SAT was transformed from an IQ-like test to a measure of academic preparedness (J. E. Barnes 2002).

Of course, the basic problem is not an SAT score deficiency (Darragh Johnson 2002). The larger issue is educational inequality.

Educational Inequality

Q How has the definition of educational inequality changed? From the beginning, American public education stressed equality (Demaine 2001). That originally meant, for all children, a free public education, exposure to identical curricula regardless of social and economic background, attendance within a given locality, and equal financing for their schools by local tax dollars (Coleman 1969; E. W. Gordon 1972; Brint and Brint 1998).

Despite this ideal, argue conflict theorists, not all children received a formal education—specifically Native Americans and African Americans. During the 1850s, many believed that slaves could not and should not be educated. It was not until slavery was abolished and former slaves began to assume industrial jobs that African Americans were among those Americans thought to be educable. Even then, African Americans did not receive equal educational treatment. In the *Plessy v. Ferguson* decision of 1896, the Supreme Court made "separate but equal" part of America's legal framework. This doctrine held that African Americans and whites would have substantially equal facilities, even when these facilities were separate.

It was not until 1954 that the judicial system seriously challenged the separate-but-equal doctrine. In the

Brown v. Board of Education of Topeka decision of 1954, Chief Justice Earl Warren wrote, as part of the Court's opinion:

> *Does segregation of children in public schools solely on the basis of race, even though the physical facilities and other "tangible" factors may be equal, deprive the children of the minority group of equal educational opportunities? We believe that it does.*

Warren went on to say that the separate-but-equal doctrine had no place in America's public educational structure and that separate educational facilities are inherently unequal. Still, it took the civil rights movement of the 1950s and 1960s to make the long-existing educational inequality for African Americans and other minorities a socially recognized problem for America. Thus the Civil Rights Act of 1964 prohibits discrimination on the grounds of race, color, religion, or national origin in any educational program or activity receiving financial support from the federal government.

Q What is meant today by educational equality? The most recent notion of **educational equality** addresses "effects" of schooling. Educational equality exists when schooling produces the same results (achievement and attitudes) for lower-class and minority children as it does for other children. Results, not resources, are the test of educational equality (Coleman et al. 1966; Hallinan 2006).

The emphasis on the effects of schooling does not mean that resources are unimportant in school success. In most states and communities, schools in the poorest neighborhoods are funded least. This means that less money can be spent per pupil in poorer neighborhood schools. Less money per pupil translates into fewer support staff, larger class sizes, less qualified teachers, and absence of preschool programs, all factors known to negatively affect student achievement (Lewis and Burd-Sharps 2010).

There are, however, factors beyond the obvious one of underfunding. Two of these factors are teacher evaluation and tracking and reliance on tests of cognitive ability.

Q How do teacher evaluation and tracking affect educational equality? According to Ray Rist (1977), even the best-intentioned teachers often evaluate students' potential based on their social class, their racial characteristics, and their ethnic heritage rather than on their objective abilities. There is evidence to support this allegation. For example, in his classic study of "Elmstown's" youth, August Hollingshead (1949) found that when middle- and upper-class children had difficulty in class, their parents were usually called in to discuss learning problems. Similar learning difficulties, however, were interpreted as behavioral problems when they occurred among lower-class children. Aaron Cicourel and John Kitsuse (1963) later found the same phenomenon in their study of high school counseling procedures. When test scores were consistent with the counselor's expectations, there was no problem. The counselor, however, was much more willing to find excuses for poor performance among high-status students than among low-status ones. Rist (1977) reported a similar pattern among classroom teachers. When asked questions in class, the students perceived as more capable by teachers were given more time to answer than "less able" students were given. Also, lower-status students were more likely to be considered by teachers as less capable.

Most high schools have a series of curricula (tracks): college preparatory, commercial, vocational, and general for those who are undecided about their occupational futures (Kilgore 1991; Gamoran 1992). Researchers report that social class and race heavily influence the placement of students in these curricula—regardless of their intelligence or past academic achievement (Oakes and Lipton 1996; Taylor, Peplau, and Sears 1997).

Regardless of earlier school performance or intelligence, the overall academic performance of those bound for college increases, whereas the performance of those on a noncollege track decreases. Through tracking, then, schools may deny educational equality to many students, especially minority children, who often come from disadvantaged families (Oakes 1985; Gibson and Ogbu 1991). In part because tracking has been linked to educational inequality, American high schools are retreating from the practice. Some research, however, casts doubt on the idea that detracking promotes greater educational equality (Lucas 1999). Rather

than assigned courses based on students' course-specific abilities, mathematical achievement is now a gateway to the college-prep courses.

Tests of Reliance on Cognitive Ability

The technical term for intelligence, today, is **cognitive ability**—the capacity for thinking abstractly. Dating back to the turn of the twentieth century, there has been an attempt to measure cognitive ability. Because cognitive ability testing is an important element in sorting and tracking students, it contributes to educational inequality. Whenever cognitive ability tests are discussed, the question of inherited intelligence always arises.

Q Is intelligence inherited? In the past, most people assumed that individual and group differences in measured intellectual ability were due to genetic differences. This assumption, of course, underlies social Darwinism.

A few researchers still take this viewpoint. More than forty years ago Arthur Jensen (1969), an educational psychologist, suggested that the lower average intelligence score among African American children may be due to heredity. A more recent book by Richard Herrnstein and Charles Murray (1996), entitled *The Bell Curve*, is also in the tradition of linking intelligence to heredity. According to these authors, humans inherit 60 to 70 percent of their intelligence level. Herrnstein and Murray further contend that the fact of inherited intelligence makes largely futile the efforts to help the disadvantaged through programs such as Head Start and affirmative action.

Social scientists have generally criticized these advocates of genetic differences in intelligence for failing to consider adequately the effects of the social, psychological, and economic climate experienced by children of various racial and ethnic minorities. Even those social scientists who grant genetics an important role in intelligence criticize both the interpretations of the evidence and the public policy solutions contained in *The Bell Curve*. They point to the body of research that runs counter to Herrnstein and Murray's thesis. More specifically, they see intelligence not as an issue of nature versus nurture, but as a matter of genetics and environment (Morganthau 1994; L. Wright 1995; Fischer et al. 1996). We know, for example, that city dwellers usually score higher on intelligence tests than do people in rural areas, that African Americans with higher socioeconomic status score higher than lower-status African Americans, and that middle-class African American children score about as high as middle-class white children. We also have discovered that as people get older, they usually score higher on intelligence tests. These findings, and others like them, have led researchers to conclude that environmental factors affect test performance at least as much as genetic factors (Samuda 1975; Schiff and Lewontin 1987; Jencks and Phillips 1998; Arrow, Durlauf, and Bowles 2000). One of these environmental factors is a *cultural bias* in the measurement of cognitive ability.

Q How can intelligence tests be culturally biased? Robert Williams (1974) is one of many early social scientists who argued that intelligence tests have a **cultural bias**—an unfair measure of cognitive abilities for people in certain social categories. Specifically, intelligence tests are culturally biased because they are designed for middle-class children and because the results measure learning and environment as much as intellectual ability. Consider this intelligence test item cited by Daniel Levine and Rayna Levine (1996:67):

A symphony is to a composer as a book is to what?
☐ *paper* ☐ *sculptor* ☐ *author* ☐ *musician* ☐ *man*

According to critics, higher-income children find this question easier to answer correctly than lower-income children because higher social class members are more mindful of classical music. (Critics made the same charge of a recent SAT question that used a Bentley automobile as its illustration.) Several studies indicate that because most intelligence tests assume fluency in English, minorities cannot respond as well. Some researchers suggest that many urban African American students are superior to their white classmates on several dimensions of verbal capacity, but because intelligence tests do not measure these areas, this ability remains unrecognized (S. J. Gould 1981; Goleman 1988; Hurn 1993).

The testing situation itself can affect performance. Low-income and minority students, for example, score higher on intelligence tests when tested by adult members of their own race or income group. Apparently, they feel threatened when tested in a strange environment by someone dissimilar to them. Middle-class children are frequently eager to take the tests because they have learned the importance of tests and academic competitiveness. Because low-income children do not recognize the importance of tests and are not academically competitive, they ignore some of the questions or look for something more interesting to do. In addition, nutrition seems to play a role in test performance. Low-income children with poor diets may do less than their best when they are hungry or when they lack particular types of food over long periods of time.

Promoting Equality in Education

Although it is difficult to overcome the barriers of economics and social class, policy makers and educators are exploring avenues for educational equality. Four of the avenues—school desegregation, compensatory education, community control, and private schooling—are discussed here.

Q Does school desegregation improve academic achievement of minority children? An early study by James Coleman (1966) reported that African American children in classrooms that are more than one-half white scored higher on achievement tests. Many additional studies verify that minority children perform better academically when placed in desegregated, middle-class schools (Frankenberg, Siegel-Hawley, and Wong 2010). It does not seem coincidental that the period of higher school desegregation

Some evidence suggests that ethnic and racial integration in schools improves attendance and academic achievement. Despite these potential advantages, over two-thirds of African American and Latino students are in segregated classrooms.

Monkey Business Images/Index Open

witnessed major academic progress for African American students and that the resegregation of the 1990s is associated with a growing gap in racial academic achievement (Kaufman 2000, 2001).

Several studies show that racially balanced classrooms can have either positive or negative effects on the academic achievement of minority children. Mere physical desegregation without adequate support may have detrimental effects on children. However, desegregated classrooms with an atmosphere of respect and acceptance promote improved academic performance (U.S. Commission on Civil Rights 1967; I. Katz 1968; Longshore 1982a, 1982b; Patchen 1982; Orfield et al. 1992). For example, a study of seniors at a racially and ethnically diverse high school in Cambridge, Massachusetts, revealed a positive effect of diversity on higher-education aspirations ("The Impact of Racial and Ethnic Diversity on Educational Outcomes" 2002).

Q Does school desegregation have positive effects beyond school? Some postschooling benefits of desegregation include higher occupational positions and higher incomes for minority students who attended desegregated public schools than for minority students who attended segregated schools. These differences cannot be attributed solely to differences in educational attainment. Rather, increased social contact with middle-class students also contributes to college attendance and better employment opportunities, because middle-class students provide norms of behavior, dress, and language often required by employers in the middle-class hiring world (Crain 1970; Crain and Weisman 1972; W. D. Hawley 1985). Today, more than ever, the social and economic benefits of school equality are an important consideration. Good jobs require postsecondary education. Those well-paying factory jobs that require minimal education are a shrinking part of the economy (Orfield 2001).

Evidence suggests that school desegregation may also lead to better racial and ethnic relations because students are exposed to people of different backgrounds (W. D. Hawley 1985; Hawley and Smylie 1988; Kurlaender and Yun 2000; Eaton 2001). Support for this finding also appeared in the aforementioned study of seniors in a racially and ethnically diverse high school. These students felt well prepared for life as adults in a diverse community, indicated increased understanding of different points of view, and expressed enhanced appreciation of the background of other groups ("The Impact of Racial and Ethnic Diversity on Educational Outcomes" 2002).

On such evidence rests the promise of the application of **multiculturalism to schools**: an approach to education in which the curriculum accents the viewpoints, experiences, and contributions of minorities—including women as well as ethnic and racial minorities

(Katsiaficas and Kiros 1998; Watson 2000). Multiculturalism attempts to dispel stereotypes and to make the traditions of minorities valuable assets for the broader culture. According to an earlier study, school attendance and academic performance have increased in some schools with multicultural curricula (Marriott 1991).

Q But, are America's public school desegregated? As noted earlier, public schools in the United States are drifting back toward segregation. In a reversal of the trend toward integration from the mid-1960s until the late 1980s, minority youngsters are once again becoming more racially and ethnically segregated. This intensification of school resegregation throughout the 1990s is hardly surprising given the three major U.S. Supreme Court decisions permitting a shift back toward segregated neighborhood schools. And, as you may recall, charter schools failed to desegregate schools, and magnet schools do not entirely fulfill their promise for integration either ("Choice Without Equity" 2010; Frankenberg, Siegel-Hawley, and Wang 2010). In *The Shame of the Nation*, Jonathan Kozol (2005) laments the steady decline of inner-city schools into resegregation. As a result, he writes, more minority children are in segregated schools than at any time since 1968. Around three-fourths of African American students are now in classrooms with predominately minority enrollments (Orfield and Eaton 1997; Orfield 2001; Frankenberg and Lee 2002; Orfield and Lee 2006; Frankenberg and Orfield 2007).

Q Does compensatory education increase school achievement for disadvantaged children? It appears so (Entwisle and Alexander 1989, 1993; Ramey and Campbell 1991; Zigler and Styfco 1993; Campbell and Ramey 1994). The best-known attempt at remedial education is the Head Start program, a federally supported program for preschoolers from disadvantaged homes. Head Start originated as part of the Office of Economic Opportunity in 1965. It was, in part, a means of preparing disadvantaged preschoolers for entering the public school system. Its goal is to provide disadvantaged children an equal opportunity to develop their potential (Waldman 1990–1991). Initial studies on the progress of Head Start report positive long-term results. Low-income youngsters between the ages of nine and nineteen who had been in preschool compensatory programs performed better in school, had higher achievement test scores, and were more motivated academically than low-income youth who had not been in compensatory education programs (Bruner 1982; Etzioni 1982).

Follow-up research also supports the benefits of Head Start (Schweinhart 1992; Zigler and Muenchow 1992; K. Mills 1998). For example, in one study children entering a Head Start program scored lower on intelligence than a group of their peers, but follow-up research revealed benefits for those Head Start students: better school attendance, completion of high school at a higher rate, and entrance into the workforce in greater proportion (Passell 1994).

As noted in Using the Sociological Imagination at the beginning of this chapter, children's scores on IQ tests, general ability tests, and learning readiness assessments significantly improve after exposure to Head Start programs. Studies report that the scores of Head Start participants eventually reach the national average on tests of general ability and learning readiness. Attitudinal, motivational, and social progress have been observed as well.

Q What is the relationship between community control and educational equality? The authority to finance and administer elementary and high schools lies within the states rather than with the federal government. The states in turn delegate most of this authority to local school systems. Ultimately, then, the power rests with school administrators who carry out policies established by the local school boards.

The local school board is thought to represent the interests of the community residents while, it is assumed, administrators represent the professional needs of teachers and the educational needs of students. Many challenge these assumptions, arguing that the current school governance arrangement is so centralized and bureaucratic that accountability to parents and neighborhood is rare. Furthermore, political decentralization in urban areas, which would place direct control of each school in the hands of neighborhood residents, is desirable because the current remote, bureaucratic structure fails to meet the needs of children—needs that vary from one neighborhood to another. Minorities claim this to be a particular disadvantage because, they charge, schools are oriented toward white students' needs and are not responsive to the problems of minority students.

Whereas many school administrators have agreed to share major educational decisions with parents, it remains to be seen whether they are willing to share their power as well. There is also the question of whether neighborhood schools can raise enough money to ensure quality education. Finally, there is the possibility that community control will increase school segregation.

Q Do private schools offer a better teaching environment for the disadvantaged? Amid the controversy surrounding educational opportunity in public schools has come some interesting research by James Coleman and his colleagues (Coleman, Hoffer, and Kilgore 1981; Coleman, Kilgore, and Hoffer 1982; Coleman et al. 1982a, 1982b). Coleman and his colleagues attempted to investigate whether actual achievement among students attending private schools was better than that among public school students. Much to the dismay of many public school educators, the private schools studied produced higher student achievement levels in mathematics and vocabulary, even when controlled for background characteristics of students. Of particular interest to the researchers was the observation that minority children in these private schools, particularly Catholic schools, performed better than their counterparts in public schools. The authors argued that higher academic standards, stricter discipline, more homework, and the accompanying student perceptions of academic emphasis accounted for the differences in

CHECK YOURSELF 12.4 R2

The Conflict Perspective

1. _____ refers to a social system in which social status is a function of ability and achievement rather than background or parental status.
2. The idea that some educational requirements are necessary for many jobs today is called
   a. status grouping.
   b. credentialism.
   c. meritocracy.
   d. conflict.
3. A significantly larger proportion of higher social class children attend college than lower-class children. This is largely due to differences in ability among social classes. T or F?
4. Educational equality exists when schooling produces the same _____ for lower-class children and minorities as it does for other children.
5. _____ is an approach to education in which the curriculum accents the viewpoints, experiences, and contributions of women and diverse ethnic and racial minorities.

Answers: 1. Meritocracy; 2. b; 3. F; 4. results; 5. Multiculturalism

achievement levels. Coleman and his associates used these finding to argue for changes in public school policies that could enhance achievement levels for all students and to suggest that the growing private school movement might have beneficial consequences for many of America's children.

The results of the Coleman study drew criticism. For example, Arthur Goldberger and Glen Cain (1981, 1982) accuse the researchers of being biased toward private schools. Others contend that Coleman overstated his conclusions. These criticisms should not overshadow the results of the Coleman study. Diane Ravitch places the debate into proper focus:

> *What it [the Coleman study] does show is that good schools have an orderly climate, disciplinary policies that students and administrators believe to be fair and effective, high enrollment in academic courses, regular assignment of homework, and lower incidence of student absenteeism, class-cutting, and other misbehavior. These conditions are found more often in private than in public schools (though they are not present in all private schools, and they are not absent in all public schools).* (Ravitch 1982:10)

Symbolic Interactionism R1

Schools are in the business of transmitting culture, and it is in this socialization that symbolic interactionists are interested. Socialization takes place primarily through three sources: the hidden curriculum, textbooks, and teachers.

The Hidden Curriculum

Q How does the hidden curriculum contribute to socialization? Modern society places considerable emphasis on the verbal, mathematical, and writing skills an adult needs to obtain a job, read a newspaper, balance a checkbook, and compute income taxes. However, schools teach much more than these basic academic skills. They also, through a **hidden curriculum,** transmit to children a variety of nonacademic values, norms, beliefs, and attitudes (Sadker and Sadker 1995; Ballantine and Spade 2007). The hidden curriculum teaches children skills such as discipline, order, cooperativeness, and conformity. These skills are thought to be necessary for success in modern bureaucratic society, whether one becomes a doctor, a college president, a computer programmer, or an assembly-line worker. Over the years, schools, for example, socialize children for the transition from their closely knit, cooperative families to the loosely knit, competitive, adult occupational world. The school provides systematic practice for children to operate independently in the pursuit of personal and academic achievement. Individual testing

and grading emphasize the values of conformity and achievement. Because teachers evaluate young people as students—not as relatives, friends, or equals—students participate in a model for future secondary relationships (e.g., employer–employee, salesperson–customer, or lawyer–client).

Textbooks and Teachers

Q How do textbooks socialize children? A by-product of the hidden curriculum is the development of patriotism and a sense of civic duty. Partly for this reason, courses such as history and government generally slant in favor of a particular view of history. Accounts of the American Revolution, for example, are not the same in British and American textbooks. Few societies are willing to admit imperfections, and school materials often reinforce this reluctance. Most U.S. history textbooks, for example, do not accurately portray the government's treatment of Native American peoples. And the resistance to critical accounts of history is especially apparent when a teacher attempts to introduce a controversial book, such as Alice Walker's *The Color Purple*.

Textbooks implicitly convey values and beliefs. Sociologists interested in gender stereotypes point out that older primary textbooks tended to present men in challenging and aggressive activities while portraying women as homemakers, mothers, nurses, and secretaries. Women were not only seen in traditional roles, they also appeared far less frequently than men. Underprivileged children who compared their homes with middle-class homes felt out of place. Parents of low-income or inner-city children complained that such pictures of middle-class life harmed their children (Trimble 1988; Gibson and Ogbu 1991). Today, active parent groups, minority special interest groups, and state boards of education are working with textbook authors and publishers to ensure that a more balanced picture of society is presented to students.

Q How do teachers socialize children? Teachers, usually a child's first authority figures outside the family, intentionally socialize students by having them perform academic tasks in predetermined ways. But teachers unintentionally affect children as well, as can be seen in a study by Robert Rosenthal and Lenore Jacobson (1989). In their book *Pygmalion in the Classroom*, Rosenthal and Jacobson demonstrate the **self-fulfilling prophecy**—when an expectation leads to behavior that causes the expectation to become a reality (Merton 1968). (Self-fulfilling prophecy was discussed in Chapter 9.) In the study, elementary schoolteachers were given a list of children in their classrooms who, according to the researchers, were soon to blossom intellectually. Actually, these children were picked at random from the school roster and were no different from the student body in general. At the end of the year, the authors found that this randomly selected group of children had scored significantly higher on the same intelligence test they had taken at the beginning of the year. Their classmates as a group did not. According to Rosenthal and Jacobson, the teachers expected these "late bloomers" to spurt academically. Consequently, the teachers treated these students as if they were special. This behavior by the teachers encouraged the students to become higher academic achievers (see "Consider This Research"). Subsequent research generally supports dramatic effects of teacher (and parent) expectations (Leacock 1969; Gamoran 1986). To quote the Children's Defense Fund: "Educational research shows that children adjust their performance and self-image to meet adult expectations, and children who are placed in lower ability classes soon come to believe that they cannot excel in school" (Children's Defense Fund 1991:80).

In the 1990s, another teacher influence gained national prominence. A report by the American Association of University Women, entitled "How Schools Shortchange Girls," reviewed hundreds of research studies, concluding that schools at every level discriminate against girls (AAUW 1992). Shortly thereafter several other researchers documented a gender bias in schools that is detrimental to girls (Raffali 1994; Orenstein 1995; Sadker and Sadker 1995).

Q How do teachers foster sexism? Myra Sadker and David Sadker (1995) contended that well-meaning teachers unconsciously transmit sexist assumptions, basing these assumptions on stereotypes for appropriate gender behavior. America's teachers, therefore, are often unfair to girls, crippling them through differential classroom treatment. Girls, for example, learn to talk softly, avoid certain subjects (especially math and science), defer to the alleged intellectual superiority of boys, and emphasize appearance over intelligence. Boys are more talkative in class, raise their hands more often, move around more, argue with teachers more, and get more of the teachers' attention than do girls. All of this tends to make young women mature as second-class citizens, these researchers conclude, depriving the world of important contributions women can make.

While the gender bias in schools has not been obliterated, there has been some success in reducing its effects on girls (*Gender Gaps* 1999). Sadker, Sadker, and Zittleman (2009) report that over 40 percent of high school athletes are females. Girls currently enroll in science-oriented courses (biology, chemistry, and pre-calculus) as frequently as boys, and all colleges and universities are now open to females.

In fact, the gender equity debate created the counterargument that males are the disadvantaged gender (Sommers 2001). A report entitled "Where the Girls Are" examines this argument, concluding that the increasing success of girls does not come at the expense of boys (Corbett, Hill, and Rose 2008). If this were the case, these researchers write, we would see males' test scores decline as females' scores increase.

What evidence has been presented about the advantage of single-gender schools?

Catherine Ledner/Getty Images

CHECK YOURSELF **12.5** R2

Symbolic Interactionism

1. According to symbolic interactionists, schools are very much in the business of transmitting _____.
2. The _____ teaches children such things as discipline, order, cooperativeness, and conformity—skills thought to be necessary for success in a modern bureaucratic society.
3. _____ are the first authority figures children encounter on a daily basis outside the family.
4. The _____ occurs when an expectation leads to behavior that causes the expectation to become a reality.
5. Match the following research topics with the three theoretical perspectives.

    ____ a. functionalism
    ____ b. conflict theory
    ____ c. symbolic interactionism

    (1) requirement of unnecessary credentials by schools
    (2) benefit of schools for society
    (3) effects of teacher reactions on the self-esteem of students

Answers: 1. culture; 2. hidden curriculum; 3. Teachers; 4. self-fulfilling prophecy; 5. a. (2), b. (1), c. (3)

This has not happened. Scores on standardized tests in elementary school, secondary school, and college have increased or remained constant for both genders. And, while females graduate from college at a slightly higher rate than males, both genders are graduating from high school and college at the highest rates ever.

There have been recent important refinements in the research on gender bias. One is the recognition of "intra-gender" differences, that all girls (and boys) are not alike. Some girls may shy away from science courses, while others excel in them. These individual differences are important considerations for schools authorities. School officials and teachers should avoid assuming that all girls are deficient at science or that all girls can be good at science (*Gender Gaps* 1999). A second refinement is recognition of the differential treatment of both genders within racial and ethnic groups. For instance, white boys receive the most teacher attention. They are followed in descending order by minority boys, white girls, and minority girls (Aulette, Wittner, and Blakely 2009).

Higher Education Today R1

College Attendance

Following World War II, as a result of the G.I. Bill and the influx of veterans, enrollment in institutions of higher education began to grow; it has not stopped. Today, about 18 million students are enrolled in American colleges and universities. Since 1980, the percentage of high school graduates attending college increased from 49 percent to 67 percent (U.S. Census Bureau 2009). This expansion occurred despite predictions of a downturn in college enrollment, a prediction based on a decline in the number of eighteen- to twenty-four-year-olds, the traditional college-age category.

Q **Why didn't college enrollment drop as anticipated?** Several trends account for the continued increase. First, despite a decline in the number of eighteen-to-twenty-four-year-olds, a substantially larger proportion of this age category is attending college. Second, the number of students over age twenty-four attending college, particularly women, continues to grow. Third, the number of students remaining in college after their first year has increased.

At least four factors account for these trends. First, fearful of declining enrollments, colleges and universities have mounted strong student recruitment campaigns. This has stimulated student demand and enlarged university applicant pools. Second, low-paying service jobs increasingly replace high-paying manufacturing jobs, resulting in fewer attractive noneducational options for those with only high school diplomas. With the loss of high-wage unionized jobs in blue-collar industries such as automobiles and steel, the incentive to attend college increases. Third, the increase in the number of community and branch colleges offers an opportunity for many who could not otherwise have enrolled to continue their education (Arenson 2008). Finally, the recession that began in 2008, with its persistently high unemployment, is fueling the increase as well.

Q **What can we expect in the future?** A new baby boom is about to hit colleges and universities. The leading edge of the children and grandchildren of baby boomers—the so-called "baby boomlet"—is beginning to work its way into colleges. The year 2009 had the largest high school graduating class in the history of the United States—over 3 million students. The college enrollment of 12 million in 1985 reached 19 million in 2010, a 27 percent increase (see Figure 12.2).

FIGURE 12.2

College Enrollment in the United States: 1965–2014

This figure traces the increase in college enrollment in the United States since 1965. Explain why college enrollment continues to increase.

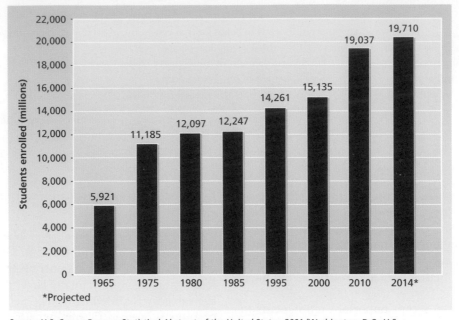

Source: U.S. Census Bureau, *Statistical Abstract of the United States: 2001* (Washington, D.C.: U.S. Government Printing Office, 2001), Table 205; U.S. Bureau of the Census, *Statistical Abstract of the United States: 2008* (Washington, D.C.: Government Printing Office, 2007), Table 207; U.S. Bureau of the Census, *Statistical Abstract of the United States: 2010*, 129th ed. (Washington, D.C.: U.S. Government Printing Office, 2010), Table 216.

State Budgets and the Cost of College

At the same time that college enrollments are accelerating, state revenue shortfalls across the nation are spawning deep cuts in higher education budgets. Thus, the train wreck between student demand and limited college financial resources continues. Colleges, therefore, must scramble to revamp their enrollment policies, to expand services, to create adequate housing and class space, and to generate new sources of funding. The Association of Governing Boards of Universities and Colleges describes the situation as "the new depression in higher education." Even the budgets of the most prestigious public universities are being cut, causing them to become semipublic institutions at best. The University of California system, consistently one of the world's finest, is seeing the proportion of its state-funded financial base shrink from a high of 70 percent thirty years ago to less than 25 percent today. The University of Michigan receives less than 20 percent of its funding from the state; the University of Colorado receives only 10 percent of its budget from the state.

Q How are public colleges and universities responding to budget cuts? State colleges and universities have responded to reduced state funding by increasing both private funding and tuition charges. As a result, the cost of a college education is skyrocketing. The low-cost, high-quality system of higher education that was provided the veterans after World War II, as well as their "baby boomer" children who were born between 1946 and 1964, is being denied the postboomer generation. In response to recent public outcry, tuition increases have leveled off, going from an increase of 9 percent in 2003 to an increase of 6 percent in 2007 (College Board 2007).

Q What are the consequences of reduced public funding? For one thing, parents and students are experiencing sticker shock. Between 1981 and 2008, tuition quadrupled at both private and public colleges and universities, whereas family income rose only 18 percent (U.S. Census Bureau 2009). In 2010, tuition and fees at public four-year colleges cost an average of $7,605 for in-state students and $11,990 for out-of-state students. At four-year private colleges, annual tuition and fees average almost $28,000. These expenses do not include "indirect costs" such as books, supplies, transportation, personal expenses (cell phone and pizza), and room and board. Exclusive of room and board, which varies widely for on-campus and off-campus residents, indirect costs are estimated at over $4,000 annually ("What It Costs to Go to College" 2010).

Another important consequence of reduced public funding is the diminution of democratization of higher education. Prior to World War II, only a small elite attended colleges. Through extensive federal and state investment after 1945, the United States became the first country to support mass higher education. As government financial backing declines, the costs of higher education are increasingly shifting to students and their parents. While most students feel the pinch, the most damaged are from low-income, immigrant, and minority families. In 2007, non-Latino whites earned almost three-fourths of the college degrees in the United States. The remainder of the degrees went to blacks (9.6 percent), Latinos (7.5 percent), Asians (6.9 percent), and Native Americans (0.6 percent). Reduced access jeopardizes the promise of higher education as a means to upward social mobility (Symonds 2003; U.S. Census Bureau 2009).

In addition, reduced public support has encouraged a new relationship between leading research universities and business. In the past, large corporations—like RCA, Xerox, and AT&T—housed internal research facilities, essentially research university-like labs within private companies. However, universities are now opening their own research facilities to corporations, thus spearheading the replacement of the corporate labs. Business views this relationship as more cost efficient and productive. Universities use the collaboration to bring in significant amounts of money. Stanford, for example, received $100 million from Exxon Mobil over a ten-year period (Zachary 2007). Many professors, at these universities, do not welcome this move. They worry about contamination of the research process by the profit motive. They fear that their disinterested pursuit of knowledge will be corrupted by corporate desire for self-interested answers.

Increased student debt is another unwelcome consequence of reduced public funding (Kamenetz 2006). College seniors graduating in 2009 had an average of $24,000 in student loan debt, an increase of 6 percent over 2008 (Mooney 2008; Steinberg 2010). Increased college costs and debt burden community college students even further. Most community college students are beyond the typical college age and are supporting themselves. Independent of their families and denied financial aid because they have incomes, many community college students find this additional obstacle the last straw; they drop out. Others reduce the number of hours they take each term and/or work more hours. These alternatives further retard their often already slow progress caused by work and/or family responsibilities.

Economic Benefits of College

The public furor over mounting college costs and student debt has sparked a debate over whether college costs are worth it. Let's consider the question.

Q Is college worth the investment? You hear it said that education is the ticket to better jobs and higher incomes. And it turns out that a college degree is that. The average college graduate can expect to earn about two-thirds more than the average high school graduate over the same period ("Life Time Earnings" 2010). And, as first noted in Chapter 2, college education results in higher annual income, regardless of race or gender. Among African American and white males with a college degree, annual average income is more than triple that of high school dropouts. White male high school graduates earn annually about 52 percent of that earned by white college graduates. African American males with high school diplomas earn about 56 percent of that earned by African American male college graduates. White female high school graduates earn only about 58 percent of that earned by white college graduates. African American females with high school diplomas earn only 60 percent of the earnings of African American female college graduates (see Figure 12.3). Although African Americans and women benefit from a college education, they clearly suffer in comparison to white males with identical educational credentials. (See Chapters 9 and 10 for more detailed analysis of the socioeconomic situation of African Americans and women in the United States.)

Q How strong is the relationship between occupational status and education? If anything, the benefits of college are even more apparent occupationally. For African Americans, whites, males, and females, occupational status (measured by blue-collar versus white-collar status) increases dramatically with higher education. The percentage for all race and gender combinations employed in white-collar occupations rises dramatically with educational level, whereas the percentages in blue-collar jobs decline sharply. Although African Americans and females are more concentrated in lower-level jobs within the higher-status occupations, the significant relationship between occupational status and higher education cannot be dismissed (D. A. Gilbert 2010).

FIGURE 12.3

Median Annual Income by Gender, Race, and Education

Clearly, this figure documents the income advantage that white males in the United States have over white females and African Americans of both sexes. Explain how this situation can be used to challenge the existence of a true meritocracy.

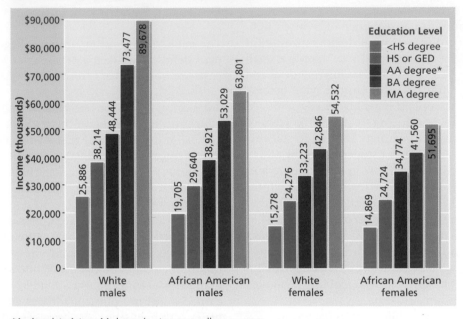

*An Associate Arts or AA degree is a two-year college program.
Source: U.S. Census Bureau, *Statistical Abstract of the United States: 2010*, 129th ed. (Washington, D.C.: U.S. Government Printing Office, 2009), Table 227, p. 149.

INTERNET LINK To learn more about income in the United States, visit the U.S. Bureau of the Census Website at www.census.gov. On its home page, select "Subjects A to Z," then select "I" ("Income"), and then your choice of topics.

Community Colleges

Q Are enrollments in community colleges static or fluid? As noted earlier, college enrollment is at an all-time high. The enrollment surge in America's 12,000 community colleges contributes heavily to this continued growth of college enrollment. Between 2007 and 2008 enrollment in four-year colleges remained stable, while enrollment in two-year colleges increased by 9 percent (Fry 2009). In 2011, two-year schools accounted for over 43 percent of the total number of students in public institutions of higher education (U.S. Census Bureau 2009).

Q What contributions are community colleges making to higher education? While four-year institutions concentrate on state or national matters, community colleges attend to local students and local issues. For students who cannot relocate for financial, family, or work reasons, community colleges provide a chance at higher education otherwise unavailable. Plus, their open enrollment policy offers a second chance to those who are not yet academically qualified for a four-year school or who earned a GED after dropping out of high school. Community colleges,

whose students average twenty-nine years of age, also serve an older population unable or reluctant to attend a four-year college. Flexibility is another positive feature of community colleges, allowing students to schedule classes around work and/or family responsibilities. This is important because over 80 percent of community college students work at least part time. Nearly two-thirds of community college students are part time. The relatively low cost of community colleges compared to four-year schools is another feature that opens economic opportunity to students who otherwise would not attend college, such as low-income students and students who must work to pay for their education. Community colleges provide the first step up the occupational ladder to low-income and minority students. Over a lifetime, a graduate with an associate's degree will earn an average of $250,000 more than a high school graduate. About half of all African American, Latino, Asian, and Native American undergraduates are enrolled in community colleges. Almost one-third of community college students are minorities. Because four-year colleges frequently respond favorably to community college transfers, students may eventually attend colleges that were not available to them out of high school.

Community college enrollment is at an all-time peak. Enrollment at two-year schools now accounts for more than 43 percent of all public college enrollments.

Andrew Payne/Alamy

Q So, how are community colleges responding to their new role? One response of community college leaders is the appeal for more money. They have a good case. Community colleges have traditionally operated on budgets one-fifth the size of four-year college budgets. Trying to operate on smaller budgets is being further complicated by the combination of budget cuts and rising enrollments (Whoriskey 2010). Community colleges, created with the idea that all interested students be able to enroll, are so overcrowded that students are being turned away or placed on long waiting lists. Citing the crucial role community colleges must play in educating the future workforce, Obama is exhorting community colleges to graduate an additional 5 million students by 2020. To help them reach this goal, Obama has advanced a two-pronged initiative. In 2009, he announced his American Graduation Initiative, which will pump $12 billion into community colleges, thereby opening the door to more students unable to afford four-year universities and to older workers in need of new skills (Shear and deVise 2009). This initiative was followed in 2010 by a "Skills for America" program seeking to create at least one partnership between community colleges and a large U.S. corporation in each state.

Over the past forty years, several additional trends have altered dramatically the environment of higher education. Prominent among these are the introduction of curriculum change, the adoption of distance learning, and the appearance of for-profit colleges and universities.

Curriculum Change

Q How has the college curriculum changed? A market mentality toward higher education emerged in the mid-1960s, as reflected in student demand for courses and programs more directly related to their specific

employment goals. In an effort to attract "customers," colleges and universities began to package their curricula more appealingly. This change is evident in the increased demand for vocational programs in community colleges, the shift of students from liberal arts into business and economics, and grade inflation.

Stanley Aronowitz and Henry Giroux (1994) are concerned about the influence of these labor market considerations. They point to the rise of business school enrollments and the concomitant decline in liberal arts majors. They see social science and humanity departments becoming service departments for nonmajors. They witness the diminution of graduate programs and faculty in liberal arts. As a result, they contend, a generation of liberal arts scholars has been lost. Moreover, colleges and universities have lost some of their ability to shape the intellectual development of students (see "Consider This Research").

A similar, but much broader, indictment is delivered by Martha Nussbaum in her book, *Not for Profit* (Nussbaum 2010). American higher education, she asserts, is taking a wrong turn, fueled by market-driven, career-oriented motives. Colleges and universities are now seen primarily as producers of workers sufficiently skilled to enhance economic growth. A near-term concentration on developing profitable skills is replacing an emphasis on thinking critically, imaginatively, and creatively. The college curricular is now deemphasizing the humanities and the arts, viewing them as unaffordable and unproductive frills, in favor of engineering, science, and economics. This trend not only deprives students of an important part their intellectual and social development but also undermines their ability to participate in the democratic process. Originally, education in America was viewed as a major vehicle for creating a citizenry capable of participating intelligently in the public square.

George Ritzer—The McDonaldization of Higher Education

Max Weber, you remember, was concerned that rationalization would go too far. He feared that rationalization would spread to all aspects of society, resulting in an "iron cage of rationality." This dehumanizing cage of rationality, Weber asserted, would eventually deprive everyone of freedom, autonomy, and individuality.

George Ritzer uses the metaphor of the "McDonaldization of society" to illustrate Weber's image of the iron cage. McDonaldization, Ritzer states, is the process of increasing efficiency, calculability, predictability, and control by replacing human technology with nonhuman technology. *Efficiency* refers to the relationship between effort and result. An organization is most efficient when the maximum results are achieved with minimum effort. For example, fast-food restaurants are efficient in part because they transfer work usually done by employees to customers. *Calculability* involves estimation based on probabilities. High calculability exists when the output, cost, and effort associated with products can be predicted. A McDonald's manager trains employees to make each Big Mac within a rigid time limit. *Predictability* pertains to consistency of results. Predictability exists when products turn out as planned. Big Macs are the same everywhere. *Control* is increased by replacing human activity with technology. McDonald's drink machines stop after a cup has been filled to its prescribed limit. McDonald's restaurants, Ritzer argues, ideally reflect the dehumanizing effects of extreme rationality.

> *The fast-food restaurant is often a dehumanizing setting in which to eat or work. People lining up for a burger, or waiting in the drive-through line, often feel as if they are dining on an assembly line, and those who prepare the burgers often appear to be working on a burger assembly line. Assembly lines are hardly human settings in which to eat, and they have shown to be inhuman settings in which to work.* (Ritzer 2004:12)

Ritzer (1998) uses a wide variety of materials to document the McDonaldization of many important aspects of American society. His sources of information include newspapers, books, magazines, and industry publications. As a college student, you will find Ritzer's conclusions on the "McUniversity" of immediate interest. Higher education, Ritzer concludes, is well on the way to becoming another consumer item. Increasingly, students and parents view a college degree as a necessary credential to compete successfully in the job market.

This consumer orientation, Ritzer asserts, can be observed on most college campuses in the United States. For example, students want education to be conveniently located and available as long as possible each day. They seek inexpensive parking, efficient service, and short waiting lines. Students want a high-quality service at the lowest cost. A "best buy" label in national academic rankings catches the attention of parents and students.

Public colleges and universities, Ritzer contends, are responding to this consumer orientation. They are doing so in part because government funding for higher education is becoming scarcer. To meet reduced funding, colleges and universities are cutting costs and paying more attention to "customers." For example, Ritzer points to student unions, many of which are being transformed into mini malls with fast-food restaurants, video games, and ATMs.

Ritzer predicts that a far-reaching customer-oriented tactic will be to McDonaldize through new technology. The McUniversity will still have a central campus, but it will also have convenient satellite locations in community colleges, high schools, businesses, and malls:

> *Students will "drop by," for a course or two. Parking lots will be adjacent to McUniversity's satellites (as they are to fast-food restaurants) to make access easy.* (Ritzer 1998:156)

McDonaldization, Ritzer contends, will dehumanize the process of education. Most instructors at satellites will be part-timers hired to teach one or more courses. They will come and go quickly, depriving students of the opportunity to form relationships with permanent, tenured faculty. To make the courses alike from satellite to satellite, course content, requirements, and materials will be highly standardized, losing the flavor individual professors bring to their classes. Students will not be able to choose a particular instructor for a course because there will be only one per satellite. In fact, there may be no teacher physically present at all. More courses will be delivered by professors televised from distant places.

It is not, Ritzer states, that colleges and universities will become a shopping mall or a chain of fast-food restaurants. Institutions of higher education will retain many traditional aspects. But there will undoubtedly be a significant degree of McDonaldization.

Evaluate the Research

1. Ritzer's study is based on one of the three theoretical perspectives. Explain which one you think it is and why.
2. Could you use another perspective instead? Why or why not?
3. Analyze the functions and dysfunctions of the McDonaldization of higher education.

Moreover, Nussbaum's concern is not limited to the United States. The world, she believes, is contributing to the evasion of the bedrock of democratic citizenship, caught in the fervor of globalization and national economic development. To curb this erosion of democracy, Nussbaum concludes, America (and the world) must reconnect education to the humanities and the arts. Then we can develop citizens able to think critically, rise above local loyalties, and imagine sympathetically the situation of other people and other nations. Well-developed global citizens, she believes, will be empowered to advocate for democracy and the development of all people, and to work with people unlike themselves to solve global problems shared by all.

Another concern about change in higher education is the alleged influence of "political correctness" on the university curriculum. An explosion was ignited in 1987 when Allan Bloom, a University of Chicago professor, published *The Closing of the American Mind*. According to these critics of higher education, academia is now under the control of administrators and faculty who were part of the radical left in the 1960s. Universities, they believe, are using a radical egalitarian philosophy to elevate works of popular culture to the level of Platonic studies and are eliminating some classic works by white male authors in favor of less important women and minority authors. A basic fear of these academic critics is that the gender, racial, and ethnic background of authors is inappropriately supplementing merit as a basis for designing programs, courses, and reading lists. This is a debate that promises to continue for some time.

Distance Learning

Q **What is the nature of distance learning in higher education?** Distance learning first reached college and university campuses in the form of closed-circuit television. Professors were filmed giving their normal lectures in front of a television camera and assorted technicians. Once captured on film, these lectures were delivered to small groups of students at designated locations off-campus. An instructor might or might not be present to take student questions by phone. The Internet, of course, revolutionized distance learning. The cumbersome logistics of closed-circuit technology was replaced by computer technology. Now students don't have to leave home to take courses, and they can communicate with their instructors by e-mail at will.

Q **What are the advantages of distance learning to colleges and universities?** Online instructional technology allows faculty to deliver pretty much the same content that they present in class. Thus, colleges can maintain the integrity of traditional instruction at relatively low

Colleges and universities are changing from being a completely geographically bound institution to a more virtual one.

operating costs. Moreover, they can offer these Web-based courses anywhere, anytime, and they can use the courses repeatedly. Adjunct instructors or graduate assistants can perform grading and other administrative tasks associated with Web-based courses, thus either reducing the need for expensive new faculty and/or increasing the number of students and courses with fixed labor costs (Fisher 2006).

Q **How is distance learning changing higher education?** The technology-driven information age is transforming colleges and universities from geographically bound campuses to virtual ones. Although the traditional residence-based system will continue, higher education will increasingly involve geographically dispersed faculty and students (Kamenetz 2010). Distance learning will be necessary in part because it saves money and expands the outreach of colleges and universities, and because it provides flexibility and convenience to students. Web-based instruction is also compatible with the change in higher education from a set number of semesters and courses to a lifelong process of learning for many students. For example, anyone, of any age, can view one of Yale University's most popular philosophy professors sitting on his or her desk, talking about the meaning of life. MIT is offering 1,800 classes online, practically the entire curriculum open to all at no charge. Of the 35 million people who have tried MIT's online courses, almost half are people just curious to learn (Kinzie 2007). This trend, reinforced by a rapidly changing global economy, will surely accelerate (Brody 1997; Ritzer 1998).

For-Profit Colleges and Universities

The availability of Web-based technology has two broader effects. It enables colleges and universities to enter the for-profit arena, which some have done. More importantly, Web-based technology permits the for-profit arena to come to the university in the form of a competitor (Kinser 2006; Tierney and Hentschke 2007).

Q How prevalent are for-profit colleges and universities? The idea of purely profit-driven institutions seems antithetical to the traditional view of higher education. We have always viewed colleges and universities as selfless organizations dedicated to a unique form of service, if anything, "ivory towers" too far removed from the "real world." Yet, in recent years strictly for-profit colleges and universities have arrived on the scene. Their arrival is based both on the availability of technology capable of generating a profit and on the connection Americans have made among postsecondary education, income, employment, and quality of life (Hentschke, Lechuga, and Tierney 2010).

For-profit colleges and universities have about 3 million students annually. Compared to the total college student population of some 18 million, this is not particularly large. Currently, they award a relatively small proportion of all degrees in higher education, only 15 percent of associate degrees and 4 percent of bachelor's degree. However, for-profit colleges and universities are growing rapidly. They went from less than 1 percent of all college students in 1970 to about 10 percent today. And while the number of public institutions remains fairly constant, the number of for-profits increases rapidly, currently accounting for 39 percent of all institutions of higher education (Hentschke, Lechuga, and Tierney 2010). In fact, for-profit colleges and universities have become sufficiently visible to gain public attention, most of it unfavorable.

Q What are the complaints against for-profit colleges and universities? Complaints come from inside and outside the university. Most educators believe that for-profit colleges and universities undermine the intellectual integrity of higher education. They charge that underqualified instructors are teaching underdeveloped courses. Educators also lament the loss of personal interaction between teachers and students and between students and other students. Moreover, there is the problem of accreditation and transfer of credits. Most non-profits are nationally accredited, whereas traditional colleges and universities are regionally accredited. National accreditation usually covers only vocational, career, or technical programs.

Regional accreditation requires rigorous examination of academically oriented programs. Consequently, many regionally accredited institutions refuse credits from nationally accredited schools. Some students, then, are caught in the middle with college credits they can't transfer to a traditional college or university.

Besides, the expense of for-profit colleges and universities is in the spotlight. Partly because for-profit colleges spend about 30 percent of their revenue on advertising and marketing, their degrees are more expensive than nonprofit schools (Lewin 2010). This, combined with their built-in profit margin, leaves their graduates more in debt than graduates from nonprofit institutions. Over half of 2007–2008 for-profit bachelor's degree recipients left school $30,500 or more in debt, compared to 24 percent of private not-for-profit college students and 12 percent of public four-year college students (Baum and Steele 2010).

Because for-profit graduates have high debt-to-income ratios, they have low loan repayment rates. Although for-profits have only about 10 percent of all college students, they have almost half of student loan defaults. And students aren't the only ones to suffer. Taxpayers also pay a price, because most of the revenue for for-profit colleges comes from federal student aid. Kaplan Higher Education, for example, receives over 90 percent of its revenue from Pell grants, Stafford loans, and military and veteran benefits. Overall, for-profit colleges are given one-fourth of the student federal aid each year. Uncollectable student loan defaults, therefore, come at the expense of the taxpayers (Lewin 2010; Vasquez 2010).

Both the public and the government are calling attention to charges of fraudulent business practices by for-profit colleges. The Florida attorney general, for example, is scrutinizing eight for-profit colleges regarding allegations of deception in financial aid, recruitment, enrollment, accreditation, placement, and graduation rates (Lewin 2010). At the federal level, the Government Accountability Office (GPO) conducted on investigation regarding deceptive recruiting practices, including misrepresentation of costs and future earnings. The GPO, using hidden cameras, documented either deception or fraud at all fifteen for-profit colleges sampled. Unethical or illegal practices included failing to disclose actual tuition costs, withholding actual graduation rates, misrepresenting accreditation status, exaggerating probable future earnings, and falsifying student loan applications. Congress is considering federal legislation to counteract unethical practices and to punish criminal violations.

CHECK YOURSELF **12.6** R2

Higher Education Today

1. As expected, college enrollment in the United States declined in the 1980s because of a decrease in the number of eighteen- to twenty-four-year-olds. T or F?
2. Which of the following has suffered the most under continuing state budget cuts?
   a. community colleges
   b. four-year colleges
   c. private colleges
   d. for-profit colleges
   e. female colleges
3. Although a college education pays off financially for white males, it does not benefit African American men and women. T or F?
4. Community colleges account for _____ percent of all college students in the United States.
   a. 51 to 54
   b. 13
   c. 26
   d. 43
   e. 34
5. According to Martha Nussbaum, U.S. colleges and universities should put more or less emphasis on business education?
6. Contrary to predictions, for-profit colleges and universities are more expensive than public institutions. T or F?

Answers: 1. F; 2. a; 3. F; 4. d; 5. less; 6. T

On to Chapter 13

The socialization process begun in the family continues through the educational institution. Parents begin the process and, at an early age, entrust their children to schools to continue their preparation for life as adults. Upon leaving school as young adults, these children enter the political and economic institutions in a serious way. That is the subject of Chapter 13.

5 **INTEGRATED GOALS AND SUMMARY**

1. **Describe the relationship between industrialization and education.**
   - With industrialization and urbanization, the ability of the family to prepare its young for the future declined. As a result, formal schooling became necessary. The early emphasis in American schools was on "civilizing" the young; but after the turn of the twentieth century, the emphasis shifted to education for jobs.
2. **Discuss schools as bureaucracies and the attempts to debureaucratize education in the United States.**
   - Early schools were modeled after businesses and have increasingly become more bureaucratic. Advocates of open classrooms and cooperative learning contend that bureaucratically run schools fail to take into account the emotional and creative needs of individual children. The evidence suggests that some aspects of these alternatives provide benefits that should not be overlooked. The back-to-basics movement, however, seems to clash with the open classroom philosophy.

3. **Compare the competitors of traditional public schools.**
   - Beyond improvements to the public school classroom, some educators, parents, and politicians promote competitors to traditional public schools. These advocates of "school choice" support voucher systems, charter schools, magnet schools, and homeschooling.
4. **Outline the basic functions (manifest and latent) of the institution of education.**
   - Functionalists see the emergence of the educational institution as a response to society's needs. The manifest functions of education include the transmission of culture; social integration; selection and screening of talent; promotion of personal growth and development;

R3 REVIEW GUIDE

and the dissemination, preservation, and creation of knowledge. Schools also serve latent functions.

5. **Evaluate the meritocratic model of public education.**
   - America is supposed to be a meritocracy in which social status is achieved rather than determined by family background. Advocates of the conflict perspective point to flaws in the meritocratic model, contending that the elite use the educational institution to preserve their privileged position.

6. **Discuss educational inequality.**
   - Many of the flaws in the meritocratic model appear within the context of educational inequality, which exists when schooling produces different results for lower-class and minority children than it does for other children. Schools themselves promote educational inequality by reacting to students' social class backgrounds and racial or ethnic characteristics rather than to their abilities and potential. Schools use intelligence testing—which ignores the environmental deficiencies of lower-class students—to channel students into noncollege tracks.
   - Although there is disagreement, some evidence suggests that school desegregation reduces educational inequality. Three other approaches to promoting educational equality are compensatory education, increased community control of schools, and private schooling.

7. **Describe the ways in which schools socialize students.**
   - Symbolic interactionists emphasize the nonacademic socialization that occurs within schools. Through the hidden curriculum, children are taught a variety of values, norms, beliefs, and attitudes thought to be desirable by a society. This nonacademic socialization is accomplished in large part through textbooks and teachers. The self-fulfilling prophecy and gender bias are two ways that teachers exert influence over students.

8. **Identify and describe the dominant issues in higher education.**
   - Contrary to expectation, college enrollment increased and evidently will continue to increase in the future. Budget cuts in higher education have occurred along with rising enrollment. Colleges and universities are responding by increasing private funding and raising tuition. This places an extra financial burden on parents and students, resulting in increased student (or parent) debt. A college education still pays off handsomely in the United States. Both income and occupational level increase with higher education.
   - Large increases in community college enrollment are fueling the overall growth in higher education. Added enrollment heightens the need for additional funding of community colleges, which already had significantly lower government support prior to the enrollment spike. Other important changes in higher education include the introduction of curriculum change, the adoption of distance learning, and the expanding role of for-profit colleges and universities.

CONCEPT REVIEW

Match the following concepts with the definitions listed below them.

____ a. multiculturalism   ____ d. cooperative learning   ____ g. manifest function
____ b. hidden curriculum   ____ e. self-fulfilling prophecy   ____ h. school choice
____ c. vouchers   ____ f. dysfunction

1. a negative consequence of some element of a society
2. the nonacademic agenda in schools that teaches children skills thought to be necessary for success in modern bureaucratic society
3. an intended and recognized consequence of some element of a society
4. an approach to education in which the curriculum accents the viewpoints, experiences, and contributions of women and diverse ethnic and racial minorities

5. the idea that the best way to improve schools is by using the free enterprise model
6. when an expectation leads to behavior that causes the expectation to become a reality
7. a nonbureaucratic classroom structure in which students study in groups with teachers acting as guides rather than as the controlling agents determining all activities
8. tax allowances granted to cover part of the costs for an academic year at the school selected

CHECK YOURSELF REVIEW

1. Charter schools, contrary to expectations, have increased school integration. T or F?
2. Public commitment to higher education is as strong for the postboomer generation as it was for their parents. T or F?

3. Early public schooling in America was viewed as a mechanism of _____.
4. Educational equality exists when schooling produces the same _____ for lower-class children and minorities as it does for other children.

5. According to symbolic interactionists, schools are very much in the business of transmitting

_____.

6. School choice is undergirded by the _____ model.

7. Contemporary public education is important primarily because of
   a. the quality of teachers in modern schools.
   b. efficient operation of school bureaucracies.
   c. historical changes in the economic and social structures of industrial societies.
   d. lack of qualified individual tutors.

8. The idea that some educational requirements are unnecessary for many jobs today is called
   a. status grouping.   c. meritocracy.
   b. credentialism.   d. conflict.

9. Match the following research topics with the three theoretical perspectives:
   ____ a. functionalism
   ____ b. conflict theory
   ____ c. symbolic interactionism
   (1) requirement of unnecessary credentials by schools
   (2) benefit of schools for society
   (3) effects of teachers' reactions on the self-esteem of students

GRAPHIC REVIEW

The trend in educational level among whites and major minority groups since 1970 is displayed in Figure 12.1. Answer these questions, referring to the data in this figure.

1. Relate the educational levels in the various categories to the process of industrialization.

_____

_____

_____

2. Would functionalists and conflict theorists interpret the gap between the educational level of whites and the educational attainment of African Americans and Latinos differently, or in the same way? Explain.

_____

_____

_____

CRITICAL-THINKING QUESTIONS

1. The open classroom philosophy represents an alternative to the bureaucratic model of education. Use the symbolic interactionist perspective to convince a local school board of the desirability of adopting the open classroom approach.

_____

_____

2. Assume for the moment that schools cannot provide educational equality. Analyze the consequences of the persistence of educational inequality within the context of the functions of education discussed in the text.

_____

_____

3. With the hidden curriculum in mind, think back to your early school years. Provide specific examples from your own experience to support the existence of the hidden curriculum.

_____

_____

4. Identify what you believe are the two biggest issues facing higher education in the twenty-first century. Develop recommendations for solving these problems.

_____

_____

ANSWER KEY

Concept Review

a. 4
b. 2
c. 8
d. 7
e. 6
f. 1
g. 3
h. 5

Check Yourself Review

1. F
2. F
3. social control
4. results
5. culture
6. free enterprise
7. student consumerism
8. c
9. b
10. a. 2
    b. 1
    c. 3

13 Political and Economic Institutions

Alex Wong/Getty Images

S GOALS

- Distinguish among power, coercion, and authority, and identify three basic forms of authority.
- Discuss the nation-state, comparing and contrasting the functionalist and conflict approaches to this form of political authority.
- Identify the major differences among democracy, totalitarianism, and authoritarianism.
- Delineate the major types of terrorism.
- Differentiate the views of functionalism and conflict theory on the distribution of power in America.

- Describe the major characteristics of capitalism, socialism, and mixed economic systems.
- Discuss the effects of the modern corporation on American society.
- Describe the changing workforce composition in highly developed economies.
- Portray the changing occupational structure in modern economies.
- Discuss corporate downsizing and its consequences.

Do Japanese or Americans work more hours per week? Less than a decade ago, Americans looked at workers in Japan with awe. Stories of men and women slaving away for ten or more hours per day, six days per week, made the rounds of corporate America and surprised many American workers. The reality today is different. The average American works longer than workers in any other industrialized country, including Japan. Between 1977 and 2000, the average workweek among salaried American workers lengthened from forty-three to forty-eight hours. In that same period, the number of workers putting in more than fifty hours per week went from 24 percent to 37 percent. In fact, Americans work an equivalent of eight weeks longer every year than Western Europeans. In this chapter on political and economic institutions, we examine where, why, and how Americans vote and work.

Power and Authority ▣

All societies must deal with the challenges of economics and politics. Economic issues exist because of the need for goods and services. The institution that carries out the production and distribution of goods and services is the **economy**. Because economic decisions affect organizations and the general public, severe conflicts often arise. Every society must develop some means of handling these conflicts. This responsibility lies in the **political institution**—the institution that obtains and exercises power.

The 1997 strike by the Teamsters Union against United Parcel Service (UPS) illustrates the interaction between the economy and the political institution. This labor confrontation was based on a strong objection to the UPS corporate policy of downsizing—changing permanent jobs into temporary ones. UPS, by asking President Clinton to intervene early in the dispute, demonstrated the intimate interdependence between business and government in modern society. The interplay of these two institutions will become apparent in this chapter.

Defining Power and Authority

Max Weber (1946), a founder of political sociology, defined **power** as the ability to control the behavior of others, even against their will. One form of power can exist in a leader's personal appeal or magnetism. For example, in his classic study of power and decision making, Floyd Hunter (1953) wrote about James Treat, a man whose extensive power was not evident from his simple, nonthreatening appearance. Treat's power was based not on his visible personal characteristics but on his ability to influence the actions of others—including Georgia's governor. His power existed in his relationships with others.

Weber recognized another form of power, power through force, or **coercion**. A blackmailer might extort money from a politician. A government might confiscate, without compensation, the property of one of its citizens. In neither case do the victims recognize this use of power as valid. Moreover, because victims of coercive power see it as illegitimate, they normally are resentful and wish to fight back. Weber recognized that a political system based on coercive power is inherently unstable.

Because force produces compliance only in the short run and only when those in power can exercise surveillance, Weber believed that a political institution must rest on a more stable form of power. This more stable form of power is **authority**—power accepted as legitimate by those subjected to it. For example, students take exams and accept the evaluations they receive because they believe that their teachers have the right to determine grades. Citizens pay taxes because they believe that their government has the right to collect the money. Because authority is based on others' acceptance, it is the most stable form of power. Its existence reduces the likelihood that coercion will be needed to maintain order.

Forms of Authority

Weber identified three forms of authority—*charismatic*, *traditional*, and *rational-legal*. Those invested with these forms of authority can expect compliance from others, who recognize authority figures as holders of legitimate power.

Q **What is charismatic authority? Charismatic authority** arises from a leader's personal characteristics. Charismatic leaders can lead because of their magnetic personalities or the feelings of trust they inspire. Martin Luther King, Jr., Nelson Mandela, and César Chávez are examples of charismatic leaders. The power of a charismatic figure may be unlimited while it lasts; but for modern nation-states, charismatic authority alone is too unstable to provide a permanent basis of power. It is linked to an individual and is therefore difficult to transfer to another. When charismatic leaders die, they relinquish their authority, leaving no traditional norms for the continuation of power. Adolf Hitler, himself a charismatic leader, made a futile attempt at the end of World War II to name his successor. But as historian John Toland has noted:

Hitler's death brought an abrupt, absolute end to National Socialism. Without its only true leader, it burst like a bubble. . . . What had appeared to be the most powerful and fearsome political force of the twentieth century vanished overnight. No other leader's death since Napoleon had so completely obliterated a regime. (Toland 1976:892)

So, even governments controlled by charismatic leaders must eventually come to rely on other types of authority. The two alternatives identified by Weber are traditional authority and rational-legal authority.

Q **What is traditional authority?** In the past, most states relied on **traditional authority**, authority in which the legitimacy of a leader is rooted in custom.

Early kings, for example, often claimed rule by divine right. Orderly perpetuation was a key benefit. This peaceful transfer of power was possible because only a few individuals were eligible to become the next ruler. Until recently, custom was sufficiently strong to legitimate one's inherited right to rule. Because, for example, the kings in eighteenth-century Europe could depend on the custom of loyalty from their subjects, their traditional authority provided a stable political foundation—more stability than charismatic authority could have provided.

Q **How does rational-legal authority limit the power of government officials?** Most modern governments base their power on a system of **rational-legal authority**. In this case, the power of government officials comes from offices they hold—with specific rules and procedures that define and limit their rights and

Employee Rights

The Supreme Court of the United States has historically granted employers a great deal of power over their employees. In 1878, a New York company posted a list of rules that told employees, among other things, "On the Sabbath, everyone is expected to be in the Lord's House" and "All employees are expected to be in bed by 10:00 p.m." At the turn of the nineteenth century, Henry Ford's automobile workers were carefully watched by management for signs of bad character. Many Ford Motor Company employees lost their jobs for smoking, drinking, or criticizing the firm.

Even today, some employee rights are curtailed at work. The Constitution, for example, protects free speech for all citizens. Employees, however,

can be prevented from printing and distributing a critical newsletter to customers of their companies. Of recent concern is the right of employers to track workers' movements on the Internet and to read personal e-mails.

Today, a growing employee rights movement is pushing for greater political and legal protection on the job. Here is a partial list of the rights that many workers feel should be theirs today.

- The right to a job.
- The right to protection from arbitrary or sudden termination.
- The right to privacy of possessions and person in the workplace, including freedom from arbitrary searches, use of polygraphs, surreptitious surveillance, and intrusive psychological or medical testing.
- The right to a clean, healthy, and safe environment on the job, including freedom from undue stress, sexual harassment, cigarette smoke, and exposure to toxic substances.
- The right to be informed of records and information kept and to have access to personnel files.

- The right to freedom of action, association, and lifestyle when off duty.
- The right to freedom of conscience and to inform government or media about illegal or socially harmful corporate actions.
- The right to due process for grievances against the employer.

Many of these rights already exist; others need to be discussed with employers. There is one thing most employees and employers agree on, however. If employees take a balanced approach to pursuing their rights on the job, both individuals and organizations will benefit.

Think About It

1. Some observers believe that violations of employee rights contradict the rational-legal basis of organizational authority. Do you agree?
2. Discuss the previous list of rights with some workers. Ask them if they know whether or not these rights exist in their workplaces. Are there any rights not on the list that they believe should be added?

responsibilities. Therefore, with power invested in positions rather than in individuals, officials lose their authority when they leave their formal positions. This approach presupposes that citizens will follow the directives of the political leaders, and that leaders will stay within the boundaries of their legal authority. (The same is true for managers in business. See "See Sociology in Your Life.") If not, and if abuse is excessive, even leaders of countries (e.g., Egypt's Mubarak) can lose their authority.

Q **How are these forms of authority ideal-typical?** In the real world, people may hold more than one form of authority. Weber knew this, but he intentionally distinguished these three forms of authority through use of the ideal-type method defined in Chapter 6. As you may recall, this method involves isolating the most basic characteristics of some social entity. The purpose here is to crystallize the meaning of some social entity by removing that entity from the context in which it is embedded with other entities. Stripped of the surrounding complexity, the essential characteristics of a social entity are identifiable.

Although the power of any American president is fundamentally one of rational-legal authority, authority forms are somewhat mixed. The concept of the "imperial presidency," for example, suggests that some element of traditional authority may be a part of the office. Particular presidents (Theodore Roosevelt, John Kennedy, Ronald Reagan) add charismatic authority, whereas other presidents (Gerald Ford, Jimmy Carter) may not.

No matter the form, because authority depends on acceptance, it is the most stable expression of power. This is particularly true of modern nation-states.

The Nation-State ⓡ

Distinguishing Between Government and Nation-State

By combining several independent political units, a nation-state consolidates power over a large geographical area. The United States, for instance, became a nation through the Constitutional Convention of 1787, whereby particular powers of individual states transferred to the federal government.

Historically, the nation-state is a recent development. For 99 percent of human history, people lived in small hunting and gathering bands, with little need for large legal systems of control. Even the Roman Empire, with a few exceptions, consisted of self-governing cities (A. H. M. Jones 1966; Service 1975; Bottomore 1993; P. James 1996). Nation-states began to emerge in Europe during the fifteenth century, but as recently as 100 years ago, there were still politically unclaimed territories in the world. Many people lived without formal political rule. No more. Presently, the Earth is divided into more than 100 nation-states, and nearly everyone is a member of one of them. One is born, lives, and dies only by the official recognition of a nation-state (Alford and Friedland 1985; Skocpol 1985; Skocpol and Amenta 1986; P. James 1996).

Q **What is a nation-state?** Although the nature of nation-states may vary, the **nation-state** is always the political authority over a specified territory (Charles Tilly 1990). One key characteristic of a nation-state is the absolute sovereignty it has over its citizens. Citizens can appeal no higher than the laws of the state,

---

CHECK YOURSELF **13.1** ⓡ

Power and Authority

1. The institution within which power is obtained and exercised is the _____ institution.
2. _____ is the ability to control the behavior of others, even against their will.
3. Power that is considered legitimate by those subjected to it is called _____.
4. On which of the following types of authority are kingships based?
   a. charismatic
   b. traditional
   c. rational-legal
5. Which of the following types of authority places the strongest limits on government officials' freedom of action?
   a. charismatic
   b. traditional
   c. rational-legal

Answers: 1. political; 2. Power; 3. authority; 4. b; 5. c

The behavior of these Chinese citizens at the opening of the 2008 Olympics is a display of nationalism.

Nick Laham/Getty Images

and the state has supreme authority over its citizens. Only state representatives have a legal right to act on behalf of the state. Only they, for example, can impose taxes, imprison criminals, or declare war. A second key characteristic of a nation-state is its devotion to **nationalism**—a people's commitment to a common destiny based on a recognition of a common past and a vision of a shared future (Stoessinger 1981).

It is important to distinguish between a state, which has ultimate authority over a territory, and a **government**—the political structure that rules a nation. All societies have government; arrangements for settling disputes are always necessary. A state exists as an entity, however, only if governmental functions are separated from other institutions, such as the family and religion. As societies modernize, states become increasingly common, with officials overseeing governmental functions.

The emergence of the state parallels advances in agriculture and industry. In hunting and gathering societies, most decisions are made through consensus. Agricultural and industrial developments, on the other hand, lead to surpluses that certain segments of society can convert into wealth and power. When conflict arises over control of surpluses, a clearly defined state develops to maintain order (Nolan and Lenski 2010). Both functionalists and conflict theorists offer explanations for the emergence of nation-states.

A Functionalist View of the Nation-State

According to functionalism, nation-states form because society needs them. Unless a strong state exists, argued English philosopher Thomas Hobbes (1958; originally

published in 1651), people will act only according to their own selfish interests. Without a state to control these selfish impulses, there will be a "war of every one against every one" and life will be "solitary, poor, nasty, brutish, and short." To escape such chaos, people agree to create nation-states on the basis of a "social contract" of cooperation (Lilla 2007).

Emile Durkheim developed a similar argument (1964; originally published in 1893). He feared the rapid and extensive social change experienced within modern societies. Without sufficient controls, admonished Durkheim, modern societies will experience disruptive internal conflicts. Although attempting to act in their self-interest, people will actually create a situation in which disruption prevents the achievement of personal goals. For Durkheim, the role of the state is to provide centralized regulation of economic life. Like Hobbes, Durkheim believed that the absence of a state invites chaos.

Talcott Parsons (1959) agrees with Hobbes; humans must have external constraints. Through social constraints, a government can perform necessary functions. Government officials can mobilize resources to plan, coordinate, and achieve commonly shared goals. They can formulate policy decisions reflecting society's highest values. State representatives can oversee relationships with other nation-states—whether political, economic, or military.

A Conflict Perspective of the Nation-State

According to the conflict perspective, nation-states exist primarily to serve the interests of a society's elite. One of Hobbes's earliest critics was the French philosopher

Jean-Jacques Rousseau. In the original state of nature, Rousseau argued, people were noble savages living in harmony with their environment. They were probably socially indifferent rather than at war with one another. There was no reason to start fighting until the creation of private property led to the rise of social inequality. At this point, Rousseau agreed, a social contract may indeed restore order by creating a state. This social contract, however, carries advantages primarily for the privileged. He described the contract in this fashion:

> *You need me, for I am rich and you are poor. Let us therefore make a contract with one another. I will do you the honor to permit you to serve me under the condition that you give me what little you have left for the trouble I shall take in commanding you.* (quoted in Cassirer 1951:260)

Rousseau argued for a new social contract in which obedience to the privileged class is replaced by obedience to the "common will," a will aimed at the welfare of all, rich and poor alike.

Karl Marx offers the most influential expression of the conflict perspective. The nature of a society, Marx contended, is determined by the relations between those who own property and those who do not. Industrial societies, in Marx's view, are dominated by the relatively small number of people who own factories, machines, and other productive resources. As noted in Chapter 1, those who own productive property are the ruling class, and those who do not own property are the workers. The **bourgeoisie** (the few in the ruling class) and the **proletariat** (the mass of workers) form the major social classes in capitalist societies.

According to Marx, political life is a reflection of relations between these two social classes. Because the ruling class controls the resources, the government serves its needs: "The executive of the modern State is but a committee for managing the affairs of the whole bourgeoisie. . . ." (Tucker 1972:337; originally published by Marx in 1867). The state, through the power of force, provides a means for controlling workers. In most cases, however, the use of force is unnecessary, because the state draws on common values and experiences to promote an ideology that encourages general acceptance of the system. Marx used the term **false consciousness** to describe acceptance of a system that works against one's own interests.

According to Marx, then, those in charge of the state in capitalist societies—the government, military, police, bureaucracy—make decisions to benefit the ruling class. It is only through the revolution of the proletariat that the state will serve the interests of everyone. A short-term "dictatorship of the proletariat" had to exist during the transition from the capitalist state to communism, the final stage of historical development. Because Marx spent his time analyzing the problems of capitalist society, he did not refine a conception of the communist society. It does seem, however, that the state under communism had to be nonauthoritarian and nonbureaucratic and to exist for purely administrative reasons. Ownership of the means of production, including land, had to be in public hands, not in the hands of a few. To ensure that state functionaries did not form a new elite class, their pay had to be kept commensurate with those outside government.

Marx failed to foresee the difficulties in reducing the power of state bureaucracy and in persuading government officials to relinquish their positions and power. Modern conflict theorists broaden Marx's concept of class conflict to encompass social conflict of all types, whether between classes or between political interest groups.

CHECK YOURSELF 13.2 R2

The Nation-State

1. A _____ is the political entity that holds authority over a specified territory.
2. A _____ is the political structure that rules a nation.
3. According to Thomas Hobbes and Emile Durkheim, nation-states exist
   a. to serve the interests of powerful, privileged social classes.
   b. because of custom.
   c. to control the selfish impulses that would otherwise make social order impossible.
4. According to Jean-Jacques Rousseau, it is primarily the privileged classes who benefit from the existence of the state. T or F?
5. According to Karl Marx, those in charge of the state in capitalist societies make decisions that serve the interests of the owners of the means of production. He used the term _____ to describe acceptance of a system that works against one's own interests.

Answers: 1. nation-state; 2. government; 3. c; 4. T; 5. false consciousness

Global Political Systems ㋛

Nation-states embrace two polar types of political systems—*democracy* and *totalitarianism*. Because few societies are pure enough to maintain all characteristics of each polar type, the real world contains variations between the two (Orum 1983).

Democracy

One conception, inspired by the ancient Greeks, assumes a form of self-government that involves the political participation of *all* citizens. This classical conception of democracy applies both to Athens in the fifth century B.C. and to old New England town meetings. A second, more familiar conception, based on realities of modern times, conceives **democracy** as a system of elected officials responsible for fulfilling majority wishes. The United States is the oldest representative democracy (republic) in the world (Ellis 2002).

Q **What are the assumptions of a representative democracy?** Representative democracy is based on two assumptions. The first assumption recognizes that not everyone in modern society can actively participate in all political decisions. A representative government does not expect its people to be involved deeply in politics; citizens merely need to vote. Given the minute division of labor in contemporary society, it would be hopelessly inefficient for all qualified citizens to be preoccupied with political activities. Who would manage companies, teach school, design buildings, prepare taxes, rear children? The classical practice of democracy in ancient Greece could exist only because the masses (women and slaves), excluded from the political process, were available to perform nonpolitical functions. In the second assumption of representative democracy, citizens will not elect (or reelect) politicians who fail to satisfy the wishes of the majority.

In the two-party system of the United States, we have a "winner take all" form of representative democracy. Here, the party with the most votes wins the election. In many European countries, where third-party systems are common, parties participate in government to the extent that they win representation in general elections. For example, one party might win 40 percent of the vote and control 40 percent of the legislature. Three other parties might take 20 percent each and still control a combined 60 percent of the legislature. This proportional representation system seems to be more democratic; it tends to encourage compromises and cooperation. Governments formed under this system can be fragile, however, and shifting political alliances may force new elections, even after relatively short periods of time.

Q **Is democracy escalating throughout the world?** Data from the United Nations Development Programme show a worldwide trend toward democratization (*Human Development Report 2010*). Forty years ago, approximately thirty countries did not give voting rights or the right to run for political office to all of their citizens. The percentage of countries with democratic governments went from under one-third in the early 1970s to over half today. As Figure 13.1 indicates, the share of countries with democratic governments increases with the level of development. Most highly developed countries are democracies and have been democracies for a long time. The lowest percentage of democracies appears among the least developed countries. However, the sharpest increase in democratization is occurring among the least developed countries, rising from zero in 1971 to 30 percent in 2008. The protests across North Africa and the Middle East (including Egypt, Tunisia, Libya, Jordan, Yemen, and Bahrain) in 2011 illustrate this push for democracy.

While documenting an important trend toward democratization around the world, the report recognizes that the simple dichotomy between "democratic" and "nondemocratic" obscures the complexity introduced when considering the *degree* of democratization. Only about half of the new democracies are fully democratic: Some will not continue their transition to democracy, others will be back into authoritarianism or war. For the most part, "free" political systems are associated with advanced economic development and are found primarily in a few nations: Japan; Western Europe; and some former European colonies, notably Canada, Australia, some Latin American countries, several African nations, and the United States (Karatnycky 1995; Vanhanen 1997; *Human Development Report* 2002).

Totalitarianism

Q **What is the nature of totalitarianism?** **Totalitarianism**, which lies at the other end of the political spectrum from democracy, is the type of political system in which a ruler with absolute power attempts to control all aspects of social life (see Figure 13.2). Totalitarian states are replete with "not-free" characteristics: a detailed ideology designed to encompass all phases of individuals' lives, a single political party typically controlled by one person, a well-coordinated system of terror, total control of all means of communication, a monopoly over military resources, and a planned economy directed by a state bureaucracy (Friedrich and Brzezinski 1965). Classic illustrations of totalitarian states are Nazi Germany and the former Soviet Union. A brief description of Nazi Germany in relation to its totalitarian characteristics is enlightening.

FIGURE 13.1

More Countries Adopting Democracy

Why do you think there is a relationship between the level of development of societies and the adoption of democratic governments?

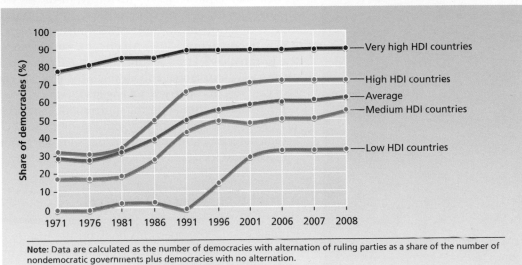

Note: Data are calculated as the number of democracies with alternation of ruling parties as a share of the number of nondemocratic governments plus democracies with no alternation.

Source: *Human Development Report 2010,* United Nations Development Programme, New York: United Nations 2010, P. 68.

Q How extreme was Hitler's Nazi government? Hitler's National Socialist (Nazi) government, which came to power in Germany in the early 1930s, offers a good example of the way a totalitarian system works. Hitler, in his autobiography, *Mein Kampf,* laid the ideological foundation for the National Socialist Party. At the center of this ideology is the myth of Aryan racial superiority and its role in saving the world, in part by destroying Jews. Despite presenting a facade of democracy, Hitler and the National Socialist Party held the power. In fact, Hitler helped solidify his own power by setting up identical offices in the state bureaucracy and the party. The ensuing competition allowed Hitler to divide and conquer any opposition. Hitler bolstered his absolute control by the Gestapo (secret police) and SS troops, whose terrorist practices squelched all dissenters and eliminated state enemies. With few exceptions, the party either seized or eliminated all news media. Hitler dominated the armed forces, often devising his own military plans over the opposition of his generals. Nazi Germany's four-year economic plans included strategies for budgets, production, organization of factories, and forced labor.

Authoritarianism

Because authoritarianism is a residual (leftover) category between democracy and totalitarianism, it is more difficult to define than either polar type. As a type of political system, it is, of course, closer to totalitarianism than to democracy. **Authoritarianism** refers to a political system controlled by nonelected rulers who generally permit some degree of individual freedom (Linz 1964). Countless regimes have leaned toward totalitarianism but have fallen short of all its defining characteristics. These authoritarian governments include monarchies (King Fahd of Saudi Arabia), military seizures of power (Pakistan's General Musharraf Parvez), and dictatorships (Saddam Hussein of Iraq).

FIGURE 13.2

The Political Continuum

Political institutions offer varying degrees of freedom for their members.

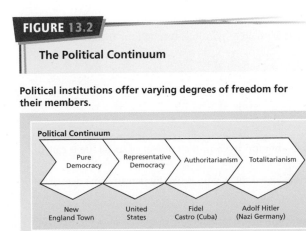

AP Photos

At the opposite end of the political spectrum from democracy is totalitarianism, the type of political system in which an absolute ruler controls all aspects of society. This photo chillingly illustrates a totalitarian state.

Political Terrorism R1

Terrorism, first defined in Chapter 3, entails the illegal use of violence or threats of violence against a government, a group, or an individual in pursuit of a political, religious, economic, or social goal. Terrorism is clearly multidimensional and is therefore pertinent to more than one chapter in this textbook (White 2009). Terrorism, for example, is discussed in Chapter 3 within the context of violent subcultures, and it appears again in that chapter on religion. Obviously, in the present chapter the focus is on the political and economic aspects of terrorism. To most Americans, terrorism is a new phenomenon. Sure, Americans were aware of the terrorist attacks occurring "over there," but such attacks were impersonal and abstract, the way war can be if you or your country is not engaged. Terrorism suddenly became personal on the morning of September 11, 2001, when New York City and Washington, D.C., became targets of airplanes used as missiles. But terrorism, like most social phenomena, is not new.

A Brief Biography of Terrorism

Randall Law (2009) opens his book on the history of terrorism, by observing that terrorism is as old as human civilization and as new as today's online news. While the weapons, methods, and objectives of terrorists change over time and place, the bedrock characteristics present at the dawn of terrorism remain. Even before the creation of the word *terrorism* during the French Revolution, violent acts or threats of violent acts intimidated others as a means to satisfy the goals of the perpetrators. Murderous gangs coerced enemies in ancient Rome, the Sicarii of Judea used terrorism to provoke war with their Roman rulers, twelfth-century hit men murdered their Muslim competitors, and scholars in the Middle Ages used the Bible to support the assassination of hated political leaders. In subsequent eras, terrorism continued to appear in many diverse new forms.

CHECK YOURSELF **13.3** R2

Global Political Systems

1. _____ is the type of political system in which elected officials are held responsible, through the mechanism of voting, for fulfilling the wishes of the majority of the electorate.

2. The United States is characterized as a
   a. classical democracy.
   b. lineage democracy.
   c. representative democracy.
   d. democracy of hegemony.

3. The type of political system in which a ruler with absolute power attempts to control all phases of social life is called _____.

4. _____ refers to the type of political system controlled by nonelected rulers who generally permit some degree of individual freedom.

Answers: 1. Democracy; 2. c; 3. totalitarianism; 4. Authoritarianism

The Klu Klux Klan mounted a counter-revolution against former slaves and their supporters during Reconstruction following the Civil War. Common methods of terror included lynching, whipping, beating, and burning. The Nazi genocide and the organized violent oppression of the Soviet Union demonstrated other ways to terrorize opponents. The most recent manifestation of terrorism is that of Jihadist Muslim religious fanatics, who have internationalized terrorism. (Chapter 14 on religion will cover more of this topic.)

Types of Political Terrorism

Our understanding of sociological phenomenon always improves when a multidimensional analysis replaces a unitary view. By differentiating among several types of political terrorism, we can avoid the error of assuming all terrorists are the same. Rosemary O'Kane (2007) identifies the major types of political terrorism. Four of these are revolutionary terrorism, totalitarian terrorism, state terrorism, and international terrorism.

Revolutionary terrorism involves acts of violence aimed at replacing an existing government. Much

Saddam Hussein, former leader of Iraq, practiced state terrorism. His government targeted Kurds, killing 200,000 in one instance and uprooting 1.5 million in another.

Peter Jordan/Alamy

of the violence in revolutionary terrorism actually occurs after the government has been toppled, because of the perceived need to quell a counter revolution. The Jacobin reign of terror in eighteenth-century France, the classic case, succeeded in murdering the king and queen, while killing tens of thousands of civilians in the process. In modern times, a reign of terror followed the Iranian Revolution in 1979. After months of strikes, riots, and demonstrations, the Shah surrendered power to Ayatollah Khomeni, the religious and political leader who led the revolution. Although the level of terrorism gradually diminished, it was 1984 before it ended.

Totalitarian terrorism, perpetrated by an established and legitimate government, intimidates and controls its own population through violence and fear. Prime examples are Nazi Germany between World War I and World War II and the Soviet Union under Stalin in the 1930s. The targets of totalitarian governments extend beyond dissenters to include any group(s) the regime wishes to terrorize. For example, the Jews under Hitler and the Kulaks (prosperous farmers) under Stalin were not political dissidents. They were just Jews and Kulaks, groups that Hitler and Stalin, respectively, wished to eliminate. The instruments of totalitarian terrorism include labor camps, prisons, death camps, forced marches, and purges.

State terrorism manipulates through normal government agencies rather than by special coercive forces, is short term, and targets only specific groups (Green 2010). In the mid-1990s, a Hutu group with close ties to the president of Rwanda, as well as the country's army, police, and mass media, murdered half a million innocent Tutsi men, women, and children in what can only be described as genocide. Between 1987 and 1989, the Iraqi government, under Saddam Hussein, killed almost 200,000 Kurds and deported hundreds of thousands more from northern Iraq. Many Kurds left the country, fleeing death threats, burned out villages, bombs, and chemical weapons. After the failed invasion of Kuwait in 1991, the same thing happened again, sending 1.5 million Kurdish refugees to Iran and Turkey.

In her description of these types of terrorism, O'Kane notes that given the interconnectedness brought on by globalization, even domestic terrorism has an international aspect. Minimally, terrorist groups may receive supplies, weapons, information, or money from sources outside their country. Consequently, she limits *international terrorism* to instances involving a foreign country, through either an actual terrorist act abroad, collaboration with terrorist agents in another country, or negotiation of terrorist demands with a foreign government (see "Think Globally" 13.1). A prime example of international terrorism is the current struggle between the East and the West, one result of which America experienced on September 11, 2001.

To provide historical perspective, Loretta Napoleoni (2005) compares the Christian crusades with the contemporary crusade conducted by Islamic extremists.

THINK GLOBALLY 13.1

International Terrorist Incidents

The world outside the United States was familiar with terrorists attacks before 9/11/01 and is still the major theatre for terrorists attacks today. The following map illustrates the pattern of geographic distribution of terrorist attacks between 2001 and 2006.

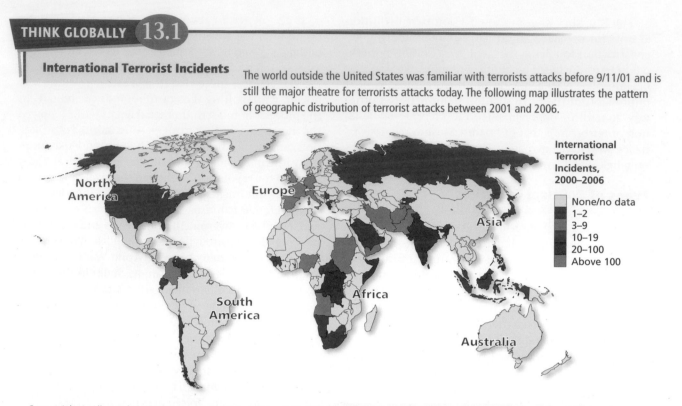

International Terrorist Incidents, 2000–2006

- None/no data
- 1–2
- 3–9
- 10–19
- 20–100
- Above 100

North America
Europe
Asia
Africa
South America
Australia

Source: John L. Allen and Christopher J. Sutton, *Student Atlas of World Politics, 9th ed.*(pp. 68-69). Copyright © 2011 by The McGraw-Hill Companies. Reproduced by permission of McGraw-Hill Contemporary Learning Series.

Interpret the Map

1. Write a brief paragraph describing the pattern of terrorist attacks you see in the map.

2. Write a second paragraph describing how the pattern will change over the next twenty years.

3. Explain any surprises you see in the geographic distribution of terrorist attacks.

In 1095, Pope Urban II launched the Christian Crusades when he urged the people of Western Christendom to take up arms to rescue Eastern Christendom from what he described as marauding Turks, said to be invading Christian territory, mistreating its inhabitants, and defiling its religious shrines. The people should cease killing one another, and under God's banner and leadership, fight a righteous war described as God's work. As added motivation, Pope Urban II promised God's holy warriors an escape from this mean earthy existence to a heavenly paradise complete with absolution of all sins. Sound familiar? The pope's words are eerily similar to those of Osama bin Laden almost a thousand years later. In 1996, bin Laden railed against the Zionist crusaders and their allies, whom he claimed had been persecuting followers of Islam for far too long. The infidels, he wrote, have slaughtered Muslims around the world while Israel continues to occupy Jerusalem, oppress the Palestinians, and violate the two Holy Places in Saudi Arabia, Mecca and Medina. Muslims, he exhorted, must stop fighting one another, unite, and focus their energies on enemies aligned with the West.

Like Pope Urban II, bin Laden offers eternal rewards for death in the struggle. The martyrs, upon entering Paradise, will find their sins forgiven and marital bliss with seventy-two beautiful virgins.

Napaleoni describes the economic dimension of bin Laden's crusade against the West and its Muslim aiders and abettors. According to Napaleoni, Jerusalem and Israel, though very important, are sideshows compared to the economic motive underlying the *Jihad*. (In English, *jihad* translates as "struggle." We will make an important distinction between religious and political jihad in Chapter 14.) The conflict between East and West is at base, she writes, a struggle between the capitalist giants of the West and the masses of the East. Some Muslim leaders, argues bin Laden, adopted secularism, modernized their countries on the Western capitalist model, and supported the West. These Muslim elites, educated in the West, opened the door to the West, leading to the exploitation of Eastern resources and markets. According to bin Laden, these Muslim elites are rewarded with wealthy oligarchies, while the East is pillaged economically and left dependent on the West.

CHECK YOURSELF **13.4** R2

Political Terrorism

1. _____ is the illegal use of violence or threats of violence against a government, a group or an individual in pursuit of a political, religious, economic, or social goal.
2. If Al Qaeda can be destroyed, the world can once again be free of terrorism. T or F?
3. The terrorism of Iran's Ayatollah Khomeini illustrates _____ terrorism.
   a. international
   b. preemptive
   c. revolutionary
   d. totalitarian
   e. state
4. The international terror campaign being waged by Al Qaeda has an underlying economic motive. T or F?

Answers: 1. Terrorism; 2. F; 3. c; 4. T

Political Power in American Society R1

Political elitism is inevitable, even in democratic societies, because the public, which cannot govern directly, must delegate political decisions and governing responsibilities to representatives. This act of delegation then creates an elite group (Dye 2001). Still, citizens in democratic societies are supposed to influence the actions of their representatives, through voting (usually via political parties) and through interest groups. So, following a discussion of the vote, we will consider interest groups within the context of the pluralist model.

The Vote

Like all contemporary democracies, the United States emphasizes political participation through voting. Voting, supposedly, is an important source of power for citizens, and it does, in fact, enable people to remove incompetent, corrupt, or insensitive officials from office and to influence issues at the local, state, and national levels. Unfortunately, American political parties are more concerned with winning elections than with maintaining a clear-cut ideological position, contributing to a politics of "blandness."

Q How much actual power do Americans exercise through the ballot box? In current U.S. practice, voting has severe limitations as a means of exercising power. In the first place, the range of candidates from which to choose is restricted, because of the power of political parties—organizations designed to gain control of the government through the election of candidates to public office (Bardes, Shelley, and Schmidt 2010). Because the United States has only two major political parties,

and because only candidates endorsed by those parties have any chance of winning a major political office, the political views of candidates for any particular office often resemble one another more than they differ. Consequently, many groups are not effectively represented (S. Hill 2003). Second, the high cost of political campaigns reinforces the limited choice of political candidates. Only wealthy people or people who are able to attract large contributions from others can mount effective campaigns. For example, Barrack Obama and John McCain jointly raised $1.3 billion for their presidential election campaigns in 2008 (U.S. Census Bureau 2009). Not only are such people often not representative of the public, but they must face powerful contributors who expect favors once their candidates are in office (VandeHei and Hamburger 2002; Dye 2009).

A third limitation lies in the exercise of power by those at the top of the American political structure. According to Howard Zinn (2003), the ballot box is a poor tool for coping with such matters as racial discrimination, economic justice, and the formation of foreign policy. Singling out foreign policy as the most clear-cut example, he documents the powerlessness of voters with respect to waging war. The Constitution gives Congress the power to declare war, but Zinn cites examples throughout U.S. history of presidents waging war on the advice of a few *appointed* officials, even after campaigning as peacemakers (Dreyfuss and Vest 2004). And once war is declared, presidents are rarely seriously challenged by elected representatives or the people.

Q How fully do Americans take advantage of the voting privilege? American interest in voting is relatively low, partly because of the public's relatively low confidence in political leaders (Jones 2006, 2007a). In the 2008 presidential election, 64 percent of eligible U.S. voters exercised their right up from 50 percent in 1996

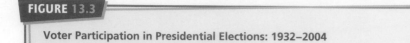

FIGURE 13.3

Voter Participation in Presidential Elections: 1932–2004

Is there any correlation between the confidence level and the voter participation rate? Explain.

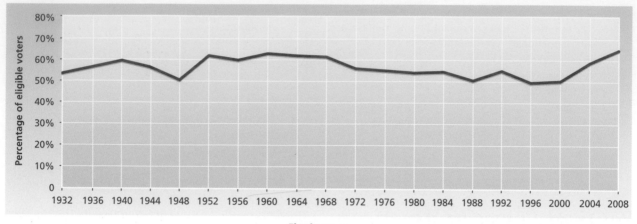

Election year

Source: U.S. Bureau of the Census, *Statistical Abstract of the United States, 2004-2005* and *Current Population Survey* (November 2004). U.S. Census Bureau, *Statistical Abstract of the United States:* 2010, Table 408.

(File and Crissey 2010; see Figure 13.3 and "Sociology Eyes America" 13.1). U.S. voter participation is even lower in off-year (nonpresidential) elections. Only 36 percent of eligible voters went to the polls in the 2006 off-year elections (U.S. Census Bureau 2009). In fact, the United States has one of the lowest voter turnout rates in the industrialized world (Center for Voting and Democracy 2002; T. E. Patterson 2009).

In general, the lower social classes and the working class in the United States tend to vote in smaller proportions than the middle and upper classes. Members of minorities, people with less education, and people with less income are less likely to vote in both congressional and presidential elections (Walsh 2000).

Q **On what do Americans base their vote?** Most attitudes and beliefs that are expressed as political opinions are gained through a learning process called *political socialization*. This can be formal, as in government class, or informal, as through the family, the media, economic

SOCIOLOGY EYES AMERICA 13.1

Distribution of Electoral College Votes

■ Obama victory   ■ Mccain victory

Source: Federal Election Commission, www.fec.gov, November 2008.

As the American population learned during the 2000 presidential election, it is the electoral college rather than the popular vote that determines the winner. This map shows the states won by Obama and McCain in 2008. The winner of the popular vote in a state garners all of its electoral votes.

Interpret the Map
1. What does the distribution of electoral votes across the country (without respect to the candidates) say about political power in the United States? Explain.
2. Look now at the states McCain and Obama won. What does the pattern of states won by each candidate indicate about differences in the characteristics of Republican and Democrat supporters? Explain.

status, and education. Studies have shown that most political socialization is informal:

- *The family.* Children learn political attitudes the same way they learn values and norms, by listening to everyday conversations and by watching the actions of other family members. In one study, more high school students could identify their parents' political party affiliation than any other of their parents' attitudes or beliefs.
- *Education.* Level of education influences political knowledge and participation. For example, more highly educated men and women tend to show more knowledge about politics and policy. They also tend to vote and participate more often in politics.
- *Mass media.* Television is the leading source of political and public affairs information for most of us. Television and other mass media determine which issues, events, and personalities are in the public eye. By publicizing some issues and ignoring others and by giving some stories high priority and others low priority, the media decide the relative importance of issues. While it is clear that the media play an important role in shaping public opinion, the extent of that role is unclear. Studies indicate that the mass media have the greatest effect on those people who have not yet formed an opinion about the issue being discussed.
- *Economic status and occupation.* Economic status clearly influences political views. Disadvantaged people are more likely to favor government assistance programs than wealthier people, for example. Similarly, where you work affects how you vote. Corporate managers are more likely than hourly factory workers to favor tax shelters and aid to businesses.
- *Age and gender.* On most issues, young adults are a bit more liberal than older Americans. Young adults,

for example, tend to be more progressive than older persons on racial and gender equality. Women tend to be more liberal on abortion rights, women's rights, health care, and government-supported child care.

Pluralism: The Functionalist Approach

In a democratic society, two major models of political power are evident—*pluralism* and *elitism.* According to **pluralism**, decision making is the result of competition, bargaining, and compromise among diverse special interest groups. In this view, no one group holds the majority of power; rather, power is widely distributed throughout a society or community. The second major model of political power, elitism, is in direct contrast to pluralism. According to **elitism**, a community or society is controlled from the top by a few individuals or organizations. Whereas the elitist model is based on the conflict perspective, the pluralist model is consistent with the functionalist perspective (see Table 13.1).

Q **How do pluralists view the distribution of power?** According to David Riesman (2001), major political decisions in the United States are made via competition among special interest groups, each of which has its own stake in the issue. In addition to attaining their own ends, interest groups try to protect themselves from opposing interest groups (Ethridge and Handelman 2008).

Q **What is an interest group?** An **interest group** is a group organized to influence political decision making. Group members share one or more goals—either of their own members (as in the case of the National Rifle Association) or of a larger segment of society (as in the case of ecology-oriented groups such as the Sierra Club).

TABLE 13.1

FOCUS ON THEORETICAL PERSPECTIVES: Characteristics of Two Models of Political Power

This table illustrates the way the functionalist and conflict perspectives view political power. Several key features of the political system are compared. Which theory do you think best describes power in the United States? Explain.

Characteristics	FUNCTIONALIST PERSPECTIVE Pluralist Model	CONFLICT PERSPECTIVE Power Elite Model
Who exercises power?	Bargaining and compromising interest groups	National political, economic, and military leaders
What is the source of power?	Resources of interest groups	Leadership positions in major institutions
Where is power located?	Spread widely among interest groups	Concentrated in hands of elites
How much influence do nonelites have?	Considerable influence on public policy	Very little influence on public policy
What is the basis for public policy decisions?	Goals and values are shared by the general public	Preferences of the elites

In the movie *An Inconvenient Truth* Al Gore makes the case for global warming. Does he represent an interest group?

Interest groups are not new to American politics. In the nineteenth century, they were active in extending women's rights and promoting the abolition of slavery. Furthermore, a history of twentieth-century America would have to include a wide range of interest groups, such as the Women's Christian Temperance Union and the early labor union movement. The 1960s—with controversies surrounding civil rights, the Vietnam War, the environment, the women's movement, and corporate power—strengthened many interest groups and led to the creation of new ones (Clemens 1997).

New interest groups continue to form. The environmental lobby is one example. There were relatively few environmental interest groups prior to the passage of major environment legislation (such as the Clean Water Act) in the 1960s. The success of the then existing environmental groups that lobbied for this legislation spawned additional groups, now numbering three times the total number of groups before the legislation. This added clout produced additional environmental legislation (e.g., the 1990 Clean Air Act Amendments), which subsequently led to the creation of still other interest groups (Bardes, Shelley, and Schmidt 2010). The popularity of Al Gore's global warming film, *An Inconvenient Truth*, and his subsequent receipt of the Nobel Prize, has provided even greater impetus to the environment lobby.

In all of this, responsibility falls on government leaders for balancing the public welfare with the desires of special interest groups. (Table 13.2 contains a sample of interest groups and their primary issues.)

Q **How prevalent are interest groups?** Alexis de Tocqueville depicted Americans as a nation of joiners:

> As soon as several Americans have conceived a sentiment or an idea that they want to produce before the world, they seek each other out, and when found, they unite. Thenceforth they are no longer isolated individuals, but a power conspicuous from the distance whose actions serve as an example; when it speaks, men listen. (Tocqueville 1955:488; originally published in 1835)

The presence of more than 100,000 associations in the United States today, however, might have surprised even Tocqueville. About two-thirds of all Americans belong to some voluntary formal association. Most of these, of course, are not interest groups attempting to affect government policy. The Washington, D.C., telephone directory contains listings for some 3,000 organizations whose names begin with "National Association of." These organizations, along with many other interest groups, energetically push the economic interests of their members. In Washington, the number of lobbyists attempting to influence Congress is estimated at about 27,000 and rising (E. Brown 2006).

From a study of New Haven, Connecticut, Robert Dahl (2005) made an interesting observation: Power in New Haven was not concentrated in the hands of one elite group. The groups, for example, trying to influence political decisions on public education were not the same groups competing, bargaining, and compromising on the issue of highway construction. Power was sufficiently dispersed that few segments of the community were without power. This system of checks and balances worked on the local level just the way James Madison, in *The Federalist Papers*, predicted it would in a large republic (Ellis 2002).

Pluralists point to the beneficiaries of the 2010 tax-cut bill. Tax breaks came not only to the wealthy, but to all income groups as well as groups with more modest resources, such as churches and people with mental disabilities. We can further examine the pluralist model by focusing on political action committees.

Political Action Committees

American political parties were influential in the past because they controlled the nominations for major offices, because they oversaw campaign financing, and because many citizens tended to vote the straight party ticket. These bases of political party power appear, however, to be eroding. Fewer than one-fourth of Americans indicate that party affiliation makes a great deal of difference in their decision to vote for a candidate for Congress, whereas more than one-third say that party affiliation would have little or no influence on their vote. More than one-third of Americans consider themselves "independents." With the decline of citizen participation in political parties, political interest groups are currently most often represented by political action committees that in turn lobby the political parties (Greider 1993; Birnbaum 2000; M. Green 2002).

Q **What are political action committees and what do they do?** **Political action committees (PACs)** are organizations established by interest groups to raise and

TABLE 13.2

Types of Interest Groups

The U.S. government is influenced by a wide variety of interest groups. This table illustrates the most important types of interest groups. Do you believe that the influence of all these interest groups promotes or hinders democracy? Explain your answer using conflict theory or functionalism.

Example	Membership	Objectives
ECONOMIC GROUPS		
Business Groups		
U.S. Chamber of Commerce	3 million	Lobby for policies favorable for all businesses
Agricultural Groups		
American Farm Bureau Federation	4 million	Lobby for agribusiness and owners of large farms
Professional Groups		
American Medical Association (AMA)	300,000	Oppose government involvement in medical practices
Labor Groups		
AFL-CIO	19 million	Lobby to protect member unions from business influence in government
CITIZEN'S GROUPS		
Public Interest Groups		
Common Cause	265,000	Advocate political reform such as more restrictive campaign financial laws
Single-Issue Groups		
Greenpeace USA	2,100,000	Pursue environmental protection
Ideological Groups		
National Organization for Women (NOW)	250,000	Protect rights of women

Sources: Adapted from Thomas E. Patterson, *The American Democracy*, 10th ed., Boston: McGraw-Hill, 2011.

distribute funds for the purpose of electing or defeating candidates. PACs can channel up to $5,000 per election (primary, general, special) into any candidate's election campaign and up to $15,000 annually to a national political party. Moreover, there is no legal restriction on the number of PACs that may support a candidate (Federal Election Committee 2010).

Since the authorization of PACs in the mid-1970s, their number has mushroomed. Whereas only about 600 political action committees existed in 1974, there are now about 4,500 (see Figure 13.4). Moreover, contributions from PACs are beginning to dwarf the role of political parties in financing political campaigns. PACs contribute more than ten times as much support to congressional candidates as do political parties. Dollar amounts of PAC contributions to federal

candidates (so-called hard money, limited by legal restrictions) increased from just under $12 million in 1974 to over $400 million in 2007–2008 (U.S. Census Bureau, 2009).

A relatively recent type of advocacy group called 527s (because they are tax-exempt organizations under section 527 of the Internal Revenue Code) raise money for such political activities as voter mobilization efforts and issue advocacy. Although 527s may be PACs, many raise only unlimited soft money, which cannot be used to expressly favor the election or defeat of a federal candidate.

During the 2004 election cycle, 527s raised and spent more than a half-billion dollars, double the amount spent during the 2002 cycle. The 2004 election marked the first time they made a considerable impact on the

FIGURE 13.4

Growth in the Number of PACs: 1974–2009

This figure graphically depicts the sharp increase in the number of PACs in the United States. Evaluate the presence of PACs within the context of pluralism and elitism.

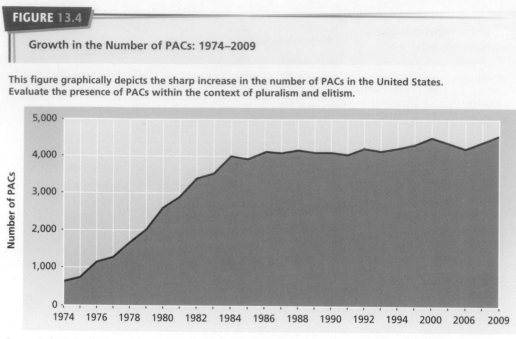

Source: Federal Election Commission, 2007; U.S. Census Bureau, *Statistical Abstract of the United States: 2010* (Washington, DC: U.S. Government Printing Office, 2009), Table 410.

results of a national election. For example, the 527 popularly known as the Swift Boat Veterans played a major role in the 2004 presidential election through its persistent questioning of John Kerry's military honors.

In addition to spending money on candidates, PACs (and interest groups in general) lobby for political decisions. Lobbyists attempt to gain the ear of politicians through a smorgasbord of gifts (Williamson 2007a). The extent to which these activities occur is reflected in the cases of Randy "Duke" Cunningham and Jack Abramoff. In 2005, Cunningham, an eight-term U.S. representative, was sentenced to eight years in prison after pleading guilty to charges of conspiracy to commit bribery, fraud, and tax evasion (Hettena 2007). In 2006, Abramoff pled guilty to illegally soliciting Republican lawmakers' votes with a wide variety of gifts, including expense-free trips to foreign golf resorts, jobs for their spouses, and skybox sports seats and was sentenced to ten years in prison (Kaiser 2010). More recently, health insurers spent almost $40 million lobbying Congress in 2009 to influence the new health care plan. Members of Congress were outnumbered eight to one by health care lobbyists. This spending pales beside $123 million the U.S. Chamber of Commerce spent on lobbying in 2009, $86 million of which was given secretly to the Chamber by the health insurance lobby to kill the bill. The Chamber disbursed almost $10 million into House races and additional millions on Senate contests during the last few months of the 2010 midterm elections, much of which surely came from American (and some say foreign) corporations (Fang 2010; Jilani 2010; Lipton, McIntire, and van Natta 2010).

Q Do PACs contribute to pluralism? The original intent of PACs was to provide a mechanism for small contributors to become involved in politics, allow candidates without personal wealth to run for office, and encourage independence from the viewpoints of political parties. Critics are concerned, however, that PACs may be undermining pluralism, because most PACs are connected with business-related interests (Watzman, Youngclaus, and Shecter 1997; Bardes, Shelley, and Schmidt 2007; Hartung 2011).

House and Senate candidates are vulnerable to the influence of PAC money, in part because of the high cost of running for office. Between 1974 and 2006, the average cost of winning a Senate seat went from $743,000 to about $8 million. The cost of winning a House seat rose comparably, from $56,500 in 1974 to $1.3 million in 2006 (Kaiser 2010). Two books, one by Charles Lewis (1998) and one by Robert Kaiser (2010), make a strong case for the potential influence of PAC money on members of Congress. Their books, entitled *The Buying of Congress* and *So Damn Much Money,* are replete with examples of PAC contributions to House and Senate members prior to particular votes. As one illustration, consider the possible political influence by business-related PACs associated with the Tax Reform Act of 1986. As the congressional tax-writing panels were considering tax reform, PACs contributed $6.7 million—$119,643 per member—to fifty-six members of the House Ways and Means and Senate Finance Committees. This was two and a half times more money than the members of those same committees received from PACs two years earlier.

There are more recent examples. In 2007, the sugar industry successfully campaigned to preserve its $1 billion, ten-year government subsidy. During the housing boom, the subprime mortgage industry successfully avoided the enactment of laws regulating what proved to be ruinous lending practices to home buyers (Morgan 2007; Simpson 2007). The relationship between PAC money and votes doesn't have to have one-to-one correspondence (as in paying a congressman for a vote), though sometimes this is the case. Rather, money is thrown into the mix as a politician considers a vote within the context of what he or she thinks is best for the country, best for his or her constituents, and best for his or her reelection. It will vary as to degree, but money almost always has influence.

Campaign finances likewise influence who runs for office and who wins elections (M. Green 2002; K. Phillips 2002; Palast 2004). For instance, according to the Federal Election Commission (FEC), the candidates who raised the most money won about 90 percent of the primary races in the 2010 congressional primary elections. In fact, victorious candidates raised four times as much as their opponents. And, as in past elections, relatively few large donors, many of whom were out-of-state residents, contributed most of this money. In the 2010 midterm elections, slightly more than 95 percent of U.S. House races and 75 percent of Senate races were won by the candidate who spent the most money. At that same time, 237 members of Congress were millionaires. That means that 44 percent of the national legislative branch of government are millionaires, compared to 1 percent of the American Public ("Report: 237 Millionaires in Congress" 2009).

Q **Does this mean the degree of financial support determines election outcomes?** Generally, candidates with the deepest pockets win elections. Money alone, however, does not assure political victory (Farnam 2010). Among the seventeen congressional campaigns in 2010 costing more than $60 per vote, ten were by Democrats, of which only three sit in the new congress. And in the majority of races won by Republicans, the candidates had less money than their Democratic opponents. More dramatically, Sharron Angle lost her Senate race with Harry Reid, even though she spent almost $30 more per vote received than Reid. And Linda McMahon lost her Senate race despite spending $47 million of her own money. Meg Whitman's personal outlay of $140 million of her own money did not win her the California governor's chair.

No, money alone doesn't always win the political day, but as one Washington political adviser put it, you can't win without it. Even the less well-funded winners noted earlier had huge amounts of campaign funds themselves. For example, while Sharron Angle spent $32 million in her race, her victorious opponent, Harry Reid, spent $25 million.

Moreover, the Supreme Court in 2010 issued its opinion on the *Citizens United* case, in which, by a 5–4 vote, it struck down the provision in the McCain-Feingold Act prohibiting corporations and unions from spending their money to elect or defeat a candidate even in ways that are independent of a candidate's campaign: Such "independent expenditures," the Court ruled, constitute free speech and are protected by the First Amendment of the Constitution. Thus was born what are called "super" PACs. These PACs can engage in unlimited spending so long as they conduct their activities independently of candidates and their campaign funds, and report their donors to the FEC. Critics depict this as a landmark decision eviscerating campaign finance laws and permitting corporations and unions to spend unlimited amounts of money in independent support of candidates. In fact, the 2010 midterm elections brought massive corporate and union spending, estimated at five times the amount PACS spent in 2006 (Barnes and Eggen 2010; Farnam and Eggen 2010). And because they channeled this money primarily through nonprofit groups, donors avoided public disclosure (Stone 2010).

Another possible threat to pluralism is the increasing number of groups refusing to reveal the identity of their donors. Part of the reasoning in the *Citizens United* case relied on existing law that required disclosure of donors. Public disclosure, the Supreme Court argued, provides the openness needed by the public to evaluate the sources of information. A growing number of groups, however, are stretching the law by claiming that disclosure applies only to monies devoted to campaign ads. For example, as much as $110 million of so-called dark money (undisclosed) was given by political groups during the 2010 elections (Narayanswamy 2010). As long as the FEC continues not to challenge this interpretation, the number of secret donors will increase ("Fading Disclosure" 2010).

Q **Does this mean that the pluralist model is invalid?** Despite the mixed results of PACs, pluralism remains a part of the American political landscape. Individuals in American society are represented to the extent that they belong to groups—whether political parties or interest groups—that are capable of influencing political decision making. Therefore, interest groups are one of the most important avenues for political representation. Groups representing civil rights, the environment, and consumer concerns have won concessions that otherwise would not have been the case. They have accomplished this through lobbying, making contributions to political campaigns, gathering information, generating publicity to express their viewpoint, and filing lawsuits. The National Rifle Association, for example, launches major letter-writing campaigns whenever gun control legislation is introduced. Many environmental organizations have taken legal action against companies that violate pollution laws and have forced some government regulatory agencies to investigate illegal environmental practices.

Q Doesn't the public have any influence over its government? Political pressure is routinely channeled through voting, despite the limitations of the ballot box. Two recent cases demonstrate that an aroused public can project a political voice above the din of special interest groups. Popular will inspired the passage of the Brady handgun bill in 1993 and the ban on the sale of assault weapons in 1994, despite strong opposition by the National Rifle Association (Lacayo 1993; J. Alter 1994). The tobacco lobby, similarly, is on the wrong side of public opinion. This, of course, does not mean that the gun and tobacco lobbies are dead. According to functionalism and the pluralist model, interest groups will continue their influence. They are part of the fabric of the American political system. At the same time, claim the functionalists, don't assume that the public is missing from all political decisions, because the public can express its will through a strong collective voice. There is, however, a competing viewpoint (J. Q. Wilson 1995).

Elitism: The Conflict Approach

According to elitism, power is concentrated in the hands of a relatively few individuals and organizations. Fear of elitism is as old as the American

From your knowledge of John Adams and the other founders, do you think they were acting as functionalists or conflict theorists?

National Portrait Gallery, Smithsonian Institution/Art Resource, Inc.

Revolution. The intellectual leaders of the Revolutionary generation, being familiar with old Europe, held concentrated power as the paramount threat to the new republic. John Adams, the second president of the United States, expressed this concern: "When economic power became concentrated in a few hands, then political power flowed to those possessors and away from the citizens, ultimately resulting in an oligarchy or tyranny." Abraham Lincoln shared this concern. The Civil War had enthroned corporations, he said, ensuring an era of corruption at the top. The concern about elitism imprints the conflict perspective (Conason 2008).

Q What is the power elite? The pluralist model has been dominant in American social science since the mid-twentieth century. But C. Wright Mills (1956) and others (F. Hunter 1953, 1980) developed an influential alternative view. According to Mills, the United States no longer has separate economic, political, and military leaders; rather, the prominent people in each sphere overlap to form a unified elite. Whereas most pluralists saw two levels of power—special interest groups and the public—Mills outlined three levels. Overshadowing special interest groups and the public is the **power elite**—a unified coalition of top military, corporate, and government leaders (the executive branch in particular). Mills placed U.S. Senators and representatives at the middle levels of power rather than at the higher levels. It is at the higher levels where decisions are made regarding national policy, war, and domestic affairs (Hartung 2011).

According to Mills, members of the power elite share common interests and similar social and economic backgrounds. Members of the elite tend to be educated in select boarding schools, military academies, and Ivy League schools; belong to the Episcopalian and Presbyterian churches; and come from upper-class families. Members of the power elite have known one another for a long time, have mutual acquaintances of long standing, share many values and attitudes, and intermarry. All this makes it easier for them to coordinate their actions and obtain what they want.

Although advocates of elitism do not always use Marxian analysis, Marx's perspective often influences their explanations. Like Marx, elitist theorists tend to see political leaders as captives of business and corporate interests (Wolfe 1999). Pluralists, who are more likely influenced by classical theorists of democracy than by Marx, view political leaders as referees among competing interest groups.

In a democratic society, in which power is supposed to rest with the people, the powerful prefer that their activities not be advertised. The elite, according to conflict theory, exercises its power behind the scenes through informal channels. Although the invisibility of power is an obstacle for social scientists, it does not stop them from investigating it (Zweigenhaft and Domhoff 2006; Parenti 2010).

Q Is there a national power elite in America? G. William Domhoff (1990, 2009) has spent much of his career investigating a ruling class, as described by Mills. Using such measures as membership in private schools, prestigious urban clubs, and the Social Register, Domhoff concluded that the very top of the upper class actually consists of less than 1 percent of the population (perhaps as little as 0.5 percent). Thomas Dye corroborates this conclusion. He reviewed studies of eminent leaders in political, military, and corporate positions. These institutional leaders are not typical Americans: "They are recruited from the well-educated, prestigiously employed, older, affluent, urban, white, Anglo-Saxon, upper- and upper-middle-class male populations of the nation" (Dye 2001:189). For example, about half of the elite group graduates from only twelve prestigious private universities, only 5 percent are female, and only one-fourth graduates from public universities.

The extensive socioeconomic homogeneity among military, political, and corporate institutional leaders does not *prove* the existence of the power elite. To make a convincing case for the existence of a power elite, it is necessary to document the presence of an elite group that is unified and that cooperates for the promotion of its shared interests.

Although it is impossible to definitively identify a national power elite, conflict supporters offer evidence for its existence. Thomas Dye (2001) identified 7,314 first-rate national positions in fourteen different institutions: education, industrial corporations, banking, investments, insurance, mass media, law, government, utilities, foundations, the military, civic/cultural organizations, transportation, and communications. The "elite" are those individuals who occupy the top-drawer positions in these institutional sectors. They control one-half of America's industrial and financial assets, almost one-half of the assets of private foundations, and more than two-thirds of the assets of private universities. In addition, they control the mass media, the most prestigious civic and cultural organizations, and all three branches of the federal government.

At the time of Dye's study, 5,778 individuals occupied these 7,314 top positions. The existence of fewer occupants than positions means that some individuals held more than one top position. Approximately 15 percent of the elite held more than one top position at a time. What's more, almost one-third of all top positions were interrelated because some individuals held three or more positions. Some even held six or more top positions at the same time. The members of this inner group of multiple position holders are situated to allow communication with one another and to coordinate the activities of a wide variety of powerful institutions. Still, it must be remembered that 85 percent of the top position holders were not interrelated. While this leaves considerable room for disunity and conflict among the top institutional leaders at any given time, this latitude was offset by the fact that some of these individuals held top leadership positions in a number of institutional areas over their careers. A study by Kevin Hallock found 9,804 director seats in 602 large American corporations occupied by 7,519 persons (Hallock 1997). In addition, we know that prominent people move from business to government, from government to universities, from universities to foundations, and so on (Useem 1984; B. Mintz and Schwartz 1985; Zweigenhaft and Domhoff 2006).

Whether or not a power elite exists, the wealthy are a powerful force in American politics. The top 1 percent of American earners forms something of a "superrich" elite. The net worth of the top 1 percent is over 200 times that of the average American household (Frank 2007, 2010; Isidore 2010). The scale of the economic divide between the superrich and the rest of Americans becomes even more obvious when the income of the top 1 percent is compared to the 19 percent of Americans just below them, who are very well off themselves. From 1979 to 2006, the average household after-tax income increased 256 percent among the top 1 percent, compared to 55 percent among the next 29 percent (Hacker and Pierson 2010).

Q Why is the gap between the superrich and the rest of Americans so large? According to Jacob Hacker and Paul Pierson (2010), this "winner-take-all" economy is not just the product of superior education, hard work, and luck. Nor, they assert, is the income disparity the result of foreign trade, financial globalization, or technology, the most commonly cited explanatory factors. Rather, they attribute the winner-take-all economy to America's winner-take-all political system. The ascendancy of the wealthiest elite began, they write, in the late 1970s, with big business and its allies beginning a forty-year campaign to reduce government regulation and to eliminate the progressive tax structure, both of which had worked to maintain a more equitable distribution of income prior to the late 1970s (Johnston 2005, 2007a; Stiglitz 2010). The success of this campaign continues. With the extension of the Bush tax cuts in 2010, the annual tax break for the average American household ($55,000) is $2,700 compared to $70,000 for the top 1 percent. Only two groups will face tax increases: individuals making less than $20,000 and families with income below $40,000. Moreover, the 15 percent tax rate on capital gains and dividends, due to increase, was extended, along with a new estate tax exemption of $5 million per person and $10 million per couple ("Bush Era Tax Cuts" 2010).

CHECK YOURSELF 13.5 R2

Political Power in American Society

1. The model of political power known as _____ depicts political decision making as the outcome of competition, bargaining, and compromise among diverse special interest groups.
2. The model of political power known as _____ contends that political control is held by a unified and enduring few.
3. The majority of political action committees (PACs) are now associated with
   a. labor unions.
   b. citizen groups.
   c. political parties.
   d. corporations and other businesses.
4. Interest groups are an important means by which the nonelite can influence political decision making. T or F?
5. The operation of PACs in America today invalidates the pluralist model. T or F?
6. According to C. Wright Mills, which of the following is *not* part of the power elite?
   a. military organizations
   b. U.S. Senators and representatives
   c. large corporations
   d. executive branch of the government

Answers: 1. pluralism; 2. elitism; 3. d; 4. T; 5. F; 6. b

Global Economic Systems R1

Our earlier discussion of interest groups established the fact that many groups are tied to corporate and other business interests. Discussions of elitist and pluralist models revealed that business interests play an important role in the distribution of power. These two points illustrate the close link between the polity and the economy. Societies differ, however, regarding the kinds of political and economic systems they develop. Variations in economies play particularly important roles in relationships among nations because fundamental differences in worldviews are likely to underlie differing solutions to problems associated with the production and distribution of goods and services.

Q What is the basic distinction between capitalism and socialism? Capitalism, as an economic system, is founded on two assumptions: the sanctity of private property and the right of individuals to profit from their labor. Successful individuals, according to capitalists, deserve to own and control land, factories, raw materials, and the tools of production. In addition, economic success is most likely promoted by free competition with no government interference. Other economic systems assume that property belongs to the society. These economies are carefully planned by a centralized government. This latter type of economy, in which production is owned by the people and the economy is controlled by the government, is called **socialism** (Samundson and Nordhaus 2010).

When we speak of the political/economic systems of capitalism and socialism, we are referring to ideals rather than actual operating systems. As we saw in Chapter 6, much can be learned by considering ideal types that involve an isolation of the most basic characteristics of some social entity. No society is likely to embody all principles described in the ideal type, but a contrast of ideal types can help us understand how societies become very different by placing different degrees of emphasis on particular sets of ideals.

Capitalism

Capitalist societies are founded on the belief that private individuals and organizations have the right to pursue their own private gain and that society will benefit from their activities. Although the pursuit of profit is the motivation of capitalism, the individuals and organizations that are pursuing profit run the risk of losing money:

> In a typical year [in the United States] *about four out of ten corporations report net losses. Of ten business firms started in an average year, five close down within two years, and eight within ten years—lack of success being the main reason.* (Ebenstein, Ebenstein, and Fogelman 2000:132)

This combination of profit seeking and risk taking is possible only under certain economic ownership arrangements.

Q Who owns the property in a capitalist system? Under capitalism, most property belongs to private individuals and organizations rather than to the state or the community. The bedrock of private ownership is a conviction that people have an inalienable right to hold and to control their own property. While advocates of capitalism recognize that private ownership leads to concentrations of power, they believe that distributing power among a large number of owners trumps concentrating power in the state. Moreover, because of private ownership, the pursuit of profit is possible. And, defenders of capitalism argue, private ownership benefits society.

Q How is capitalism thought to benefit society? According to Adam Smith, eighteenth-century Scottish social philosopher discussed in Chapter 1, a combination of both private ownership of property and the pursuit of profit brings advantages to society. Competition from other capitalists, Smith stated, will motivate individual capitalists to provide the goods and services desired by the public at prices the public is willing and able to pay. Capitalists who produce inferior goods or who charge too much will soon be out of business because the public will turn to their competitors. The public, Smith reasoned, will benefit through the "invisible hand" of market forces. Not only will the public receive high-quality goods and services at reasonable prices, but capitalists will always be searching for new products and new technologies to reduce their costs. As a result, capitalist societies will use resources efficiently. Efforts by government to control the economy will distort the economy's ability to regulate itself for the benefit of everyone.

Q Do contemporary capitalist economies work this perfectly? We cannot say how perfectly or imperfectly a purely capitalist economy operates, because none exists. At the same time, the United States is generally considered the purest existing capitalist system. Most Americans view their own affluence as evidence that capitalism works. The rest of the world is not so sure. According to a worldwide survey, only 11 percent of respondents think free market capitalism works well, while 23 percent believe it is fatally flawed ("Global Poll: Wide Dissatisfaction with Capitalism 20 Years After Fall of Berlin Wall" 2009). Only half of the people surveyed say additional regulation and reform can solve capitalism's problems. Only in the United States and Pakistan did as much as a fifth of the people agree that capitalism functions well as is (see Figure 13.5).

FIGURE 13.5

Global attitudes Toward Free Market Capitalism

Describe the global attitudes toward free market capitalism you see in this figure as you would to your parents. Imagine their response and your reply.

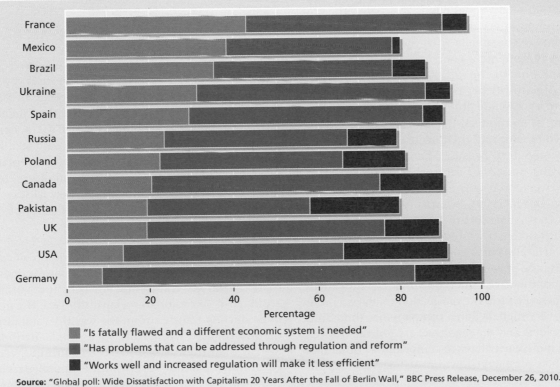

■ "Is fatally flawed and a different economic system is needed"
■ "Has problems that can be addressed through regulation and reform"
■ "Works well and increased regulation will make it less efficient"

Source: "Global poll: Wide Dissatisfaction with Capitalism 20 Years After the Fall of Berlin Wall," BBC Press Release, December 26, 2010. http://news.bbc.co.uk/2/hi/8347409.stm

Intellectually, economist Joseph Stiglitz feels the pain of the doubters. However, he tends to agree with that half of the people in the survey above that more regulation and reform can solve the problems (Stiglitz 2010). Stiglitz's offers his basic premise that markets are necessary for prosperous economies, but that markets malfunction if left too "free." The great recession beginning in 2008, he believes, is the result of a dominant ideology based on the alleged infallibility of free markets, the assumption that unfettered markets alone lead to greater economic growth and wealth. This erroneous assumption, Stiglitz writes, permeated the globe so that when markets faltered, the whole world felt the repercussions. He favors an economy grounded on a balance, a balance among the role of government, the role of markets, and the role of forces outside of both markets and the government. This theme will re-emerge later in an exploration of the global cultures of capitalism.

Q What are some deficiencies of the capitalist model? In practice, there are important deviations from the ideal capitalist model, one of which involves the tendency to form a **monopoly**, a single company controlling a particular market, or an **oligopoly**, a combination of companies controlling a market. This muzzling of competition is reflected in several ways. When capitalist organizations experience success, they tend to grow until they become giants within their particular industries. When this happens, new organizations and entrepreneurs find it difficult to enter the industry. There is little hope of competing on an equal basis. Worse yet, the creation of monopolies and oligopolies permits price fixing, leaving consumers with the choice of either buying or not buying a good or service (Ebenstein, Ebenstein, and Fogelman 2000). In the 1990s, for example, Microsoft began to insist that computer manufacturers include only its Internet browser, Explorer, on its computers. If they refused, Microsoft threatened to withhold their license to sell Windows on their computers. Because Microsoft had so much power, other makers of Internet browsers, such as Netscape, were essentially excluded from the market (Chandbasekaran 1999). Eventually, the federal government took Microsoft to court, where it was decided that Microsoft was engaging in monopolistic practices (*The Economist* 2002).

Also, the rise of widespread stock ownership can affect the profit motive. When one or a few individuals own or operate a firm, the motivation to make a profit is usually very high. When a company has thousands of shareholders and the managers are not the owners, the profit motive may have to compete with other motives, such as company growth or self-aggrandizement by the managers.

Q How does the government contribute to the U.S. economy? People often misinterpret Adam Smith as saying that government should take a hands-off approach where the economy is concerned. Although Smith did strongly oppose overregulation by government, he reserved a place for it. In fact, the U.S. government has always had a hand in the workings of the economy.

The Constitution expressly provided a role for the national government in the promotion of a sound economy. Government functions included the regulation of commerce, development of a strong currency, creation of uniform standards for commerce, and the provision of a stable system of credit. In 1789, Congress supported our shipping industry through a tariff on goods imported by foreign ships, and since this initial move into the economy, the federal government has continued to augment business, labor, and agriculture. More recently, for example, in 2009, the federal government took several steps to prop up banks and auto companies. In addition to the $700 billion bailout labeled TARP, the government committed over $12 trillion ("Adding Up the Government's Total Bailout Tab" 2010). U.S. labor receives government support through minimum wages, maximum working hours, health and safety conditions, and unemployment relief. The agricultural industry feels the influence of government through price controls, price supports, and grain embargoes against other countries. Small farmers and agri-businesses receive financial assistance that runs into the billions of dollars each year (Katznelson, Kesselman, and Draper 2005; T. E. Patterson 2011). See Table 13.3 for additional examples of government economic and regulatory assistance.

Socialism

The quest for private property and the pursuit of profit, according to many critics of capitalism, leads to serious inequities because workers are paid less than the value of their products. In keeping with Karl Marx, contradictions within the capitalist system would lead to its overthrow by the proletariat, who would replace it first with socialism and later with communism. Marx, however, was not the first to propose a socialist system. Plato's *Republic* and some portions of the Bible also contain elements of socialist thought.

Q What are the distinguishing characteristics of socialist economies? Despite differences, socialist economies share several key features (Samuelson and Nordhaus 2010). First, according to socialist thinkers, the means of production transfers from the wealthy capitalists to the government. This means, for example, nationalizing key industries such as banks and airlines. Second, government planning in socialist economies replaces the disorder and unpredictability of the market.

TABLE 13.3	

Examples of Government Economic and Regulatory Assistance

The government is extensively involved in the U.S. economy. What would Adam Smith say about this?

Public Utilities are often owned and operated by state or local governments.

The agricultural industry feels the influence of government through price controls and embargoes on exports to other countries.

Antitrust legislation exists to control the growth of corporations.

The federal government is heavily involved in the defense industry.

Business could not survive without publicly financed roadways, airports, and waterways.

Publicly funded public schools, colleges, and universities supply business with a skilled workforce and provide basic research for product development.

The U.S. military protects American international business interests.

Government supports business through tax breaks.

Legislation requires labor and business to obey labor laws.

Government, not the invisible hand of the market, decides which industries to develop. Third, the state ensures all members of society a share of the nation's wealth. High taxation reduces the accumulation of wealth at the upper income levels. These taxes, in turn, provide the citizens health care, retirement benefits, and a myriad of social services.

Q Who owns property in a socialist system? According to socialist thinkers, the means of production must not lie in the hands of wealthy capitalists. The state, as the people's representative, should own and control property. The state is expected to ensure all members of society a share in the monetary benefits.

Q How is socialism thought to benefit society? Capitalist thinkers, of course, see a role for the state in a capitalist economy—military protection, a system of criminal justice, and a limited number of public works and institutions (e.g., highways and public schools). Socialist thinkers envision a far more ambitious role for the state. They see state control of the economy as a means for the people to maintain control over the production and distribution of goods.

Socialist theory also points to important benefits for workers. Whereas workers under capitalism receive wages below the value that their labor produces and experience little control over their work, workers under socialism should profit because both the state and the workplace exist for their benefit (J. E. Elliott 1985).

Q Do contemporary socialist economies work this perfectly? Cases of pure socialism have been as rare as cases of pure capitalism. In the socialist economy of the former Soviet Union, for example, some agricultural and professional work was performed privately by individuals who worked for a profit, and significant portions of housing were privately owned as well. Managers received salaries that were considerably higher than those received by workers, and managers were eligible for bonuses such as automobiles and housing.

Private enterprise existed in Poland under Russian communist rule. Service businesses, such as restaurants and hotels, had a significant degree of private ownership. In fact, multinational chains typically built and managed hotels. Because Poles could travel abroad, they formed business relationships, learned about capitalist methods, imported goods to fill demand, and brought back hard currency. They then used the hard currency earned abroad to create private businesses (Schnitzer 2000).

Some socialist societies even introduced economic incentives for higher productivity—a step that would seem to encourage the workers' desire for profit. Socialist systems have not eliminated income inequalities, nor have they developed overall economic plans that guarantee sustained economic growth.

Mixed Economic Systems

Because capitalist and socialist economic systems are based on different assumptions, their relationships are often strained. The historic tension between the United States and Russia illustrates the point. This conflict is often predicated on seeing the other as a pure case. In reality, however, every nation violates some of the assumptions of its economic system, and most nations fall between the extremes of capitalism and socialism. Countries in Western Europe, for example, have developed capitalist economic systems in which both public and private ownership play important roles. In these nations, highly strategic industries (banks, transportation, communications, and some others) are owned and operated by the state, while other industries are privately owned but are more closely regulated than in the United States (Esping-Andersen 1996; C. D. Harris 1997; Ollman 1998; Amsden 2003).

Q Is there movement toward mixed systems in socialist societies? As the former Soviet Union lost control over its republics and Eastern Europe, many of the formally socialist countries began to move toward a market system (Elster, Offe, and Preuss 1998; Stark and Bruszt 1998). In Hungary, state-owned enterprises can become privately owned companies. More than 1 million Hungarians now have the right to buy land, businesses, buildings, or other property taken over by the Russians in 1949. Nearly all of the state-owned small businesses are now in the hands of private owners. Agricultural co-operatives are also private initiatives (Schnitzer 2000). In 1991, Cuba's Communist Party adopted some degree of capitalism by permitting handymen, plumbers, carpenters, and other tradespeople to work for profit.

Economic change thrives beyond the Soviet-bloc countries. In 2002, the Communist nation of North Korea announced the creation of a free capitalist zone near its Chinese border. Freed of central government control for fifty years, this zone will solicit private capital from its neighbors and the West (French 2002). After the death of Mao Zedong, the longtime communist leader of the People's Republic of China, the Chinese began market-related economic reforms (Hung 2009). The changes initiated in 1979—restoration of financial incentives, free market prices, education, and economic

relations with the West—accelerated in the early 1980s. Private enterprise was legitimated in the Chinese Constitution in 1999. Market forces increasingly replace central economic planning as farmers are permitted to work the land freely (rather than pay the government a predetermined amount of produce), markets and local entrepreneurship develop, foreign businesses open facilities on the mainland, and capitalists join the Community Party (Nee and Stark 1989; Ollman 1998; Muldavin 1999; Pomfret 2001).

High inflation and public demand for greater political freedoms (to match the newly granted economic liberation in the late 1980s) led to political turmoil. Communist hardliner Li Peng gained control after a popular revolt in Tiananmen Square in June 1989 was suppressed. Mainland China, nevertheless, did not revert to central economic planning. It continues its rapid move toward what its now-deceased leader, Deng Xiaoping, called the creation of a "socialist market economy" (Nelan 1993a, 1993b; Schell 1997). When ownership of the port city of Hong Kong reverted to China in 1997, the Chinese government pledged not to interfere with the city's capitalistic economy and so far has lived up to that promise (Kraar 1997). Most recently, China's Community Party began a path to "state capitalism." In this system, the government promotes the success of selected companies via supports such as tax breaks, contracts, and land deals. The payback from these companies comes in the form of party and government loyalty, taxes, and kickbacks (Pomfret 2002). In 2002, China's party revised its constitution to permit membership of private entrepreneurs, formerly considered capitalist "exploiters" (Liu 2002).

According to some scholars, the demise of communism ensures the triumph of capitalism. The twenty-first century, it is argued, will see a global economy dominated by capitalism (Thurow 2003a; Fukuyama 2006; Reich 1993, 2001, 2007). Whether or not socialism passes from the economic and political scene, capitalism is clearly spreading.

The Global Cultures of Capitalism

Q What are the cultures of capitalism? We can collapse the several variants of capitalism into two basic types (Hampden-Turner and Trompenaars 1995). **Individualistic capitalism** promotes the principles of self-interest, the free market, profit maximization, and the highest return possible on stockholder investment. This variant of capitalism dominated the world in the nineteenth century (the United Kingdom) and twentieth century (the United States). **Communitarian capitalism,** which emphasizes the interests of employees, customers, and society, exists in Europe and Japan. These two types of capitalism deserve the label "cultures of capitalism" because, as we will see, each rests on a distinctive value base.

As the Yangshuo KFC restaurant reflects, elements of capitalism are being introduced into China.

Lee Snider/The Image Works

Q What is culturally distinctive about individualistic capitalism? Individualistic capitalism is based on the ideas of John Locke and Adam Smith. Locke, a seventeenth-century philosopher who strongly influenced the leaders of the American war for independence and the nature of the U.S. Constitution, placed individual rights, including the right to own property, at the heart of his *Second Treatise of Government* (1980; originally published in 1690). Government is needed to protect the property of individuals from others, Locke argued, but it must have very limited powers. Although Smith has been widely misinterpreted (Shepard, Shepard, and Wokutch 1991; Werhane 1991; Muller 1993), some of his ideas were used to shape individualistic capitalism and continue to be used to maintain it. The concept of the "invisible hand," mentioned only once in his *Wealth of Nations* (2000; originally published in 1776), has been particularly influential in individualistic capitalism. According to the popular interpretation, if individuals are free to pursue their own self-interest, their separate activities will, through the free market mechanism, automatically benefit everyone else by increasing the supply of consumable goods and services.

These cultural underpinnings are easy to observe in individualistic capitalism (Thurow 2003a). Both individuals and firms have their own economic strategies for success. The individual wants to prosper, and firms wish to satisfy their stockholders. Firms seek to maximize profits because shareholders invest to maximize profits. Customers and employees are the firm's means to reach the goal of higher shareholder return. Because higher wages cut into profits, firms try to keep them as low as possible and lay off employees whenever necessary. Short-term thinking in the name of profit maximization is the norm. Employees can leave one job for another if they can get higher wages. Employees and employers have no mutual obligations outside the legal employment contract.

Within individualistic capitalism, government is not to interfere with the workings of the free market. Government is to make minimal rules and act as an umpire to settle disputes (M. Friedman 2002). There is no place for government in investment funding or economic planning. As long as government protects private property rights, the pursuit of profit maximization will ensure the greatest prosperity.

Q What is the value base of communitarian capitalism? Communitarianism, not to be confused with communism, is a form of "soft capitalism" also rooted in the ideas of a philosopher. Jean-Jacques Rousseau, writing in the eighteenth century, was, like Locke, a social contract theorist. Both believed that individuals forfeit some of their freedom to obtain protection from a central government. Locke saw the social contract as an individualistic device, but Rousseau thought it a communitarian one. Locke's notion of individualism appeared in the seventeenth century and influenced the

American Revolution. Rousseau's idea of the "General Will" emerged in the eighteenth century and helped to fuel the French Revolution. The General Will always puts the community first: "The French state thus became an instrument of intervention in the interest of the General Will, to plan and guide the nation's institutions" (Lodge 1975:13).

Japan shares a communitarian viewpoint with France and many other Western European countries. They each emphasize cooperation, interpersonal harmony, and the subordination of the individual to the community. Roots of Japanese communitarianism, however, lie in its own philosophical and religious ideas and in its unique demographic and geographical situation.

In communitarian capitalism, individuals and firms have strategies, as well (Thurow 2003a). But given the cultural foundations just outlined, those strategies are very different from strategies in individualistic capitalism. Individuals in communitarian capitalism attempt to select the best firm and then work hard to be part of the company team; personal success or failure is identified with the fate of the company. Job switching is not widespread. In fact, in many Japanese firms, the person who voluntarily leaves a company is a "traitor" ("Graduates Take Rites of Passage into Japanese Corporate Life" 1991). At the same time, both Japanese and German workers are less often laid off.

Communitarian firms place the interests of shareholders behind those of their employees and customers. Because employees are of first importance, high wages are a top priority. Maintenance of high wages and job security supersedes profits. The emphasis is on long-range planning over profit maximization, and shareholders, in fact, earn relatively low returns.

In both Europe and Japan, the government assumes a significant role in economic funding, planning, and growth. There is cooperation between business and government as well as between business and labor. Labor officials sit on the boards of directors of German firms, and German banks are major stockholders in German companies. Job training is the responsibility of both business and government. In short, there is no line of demarcation between private and public interests.

The contrast between the two cultures is conceptually clear, although in actual practice, it is more complicated. Individualistic capitalists in Britain, Holland, and the United States believe that by concentrating on individual self-interest, they will automatically better serve customers and society. Communitarian or so-called soft capitalists, on the other hand, presume that by concentrating on benefiting customers and society, they will automatically serve their own interests (Kuttner 2007; Phillips 2008).

Q Which culture of capitalism is superior? Some scholars believe that in the long run, communitarian capitalism outperforms individualistic capitalism (Lodge

CHECK YOURSELF   13.6   R2

Global Economic Systems

1. Which of the following is *not* characteristic of capitalist thought?
   a. Private individuals have a right to pursue private gain.
   b. Society will benefit from attempts to make a profit.
   c. The state must make an active attempt to control the economy.
   d. Individuals pursuing a profit must be willing to risk losing money.

2. Under _____, most property belongs to private individuals and organizations rather than to the state or the community as a whole.

3. As capitalist systems mature,
   a. the economy is increasingly dominated by small businesses.
   b. the willingness to take risks increases.
   c. consumer goods become very scarce.
   d. many industries are dominated by a few large firms.

4. According to economic theorists, which system should have the greatest degree of control by the state?
   a. capitalism
   b. socialism
   c. democratic socialism
   d. welfare capitalism

5. Proponents of socialism contend that it will
   a. prevent workers from exerting significant control over social policy.
   b. lead to increased profits for owners.
   c. allow workers to exert significant control over work organizations.
   d. result in very inactive governments.

6. Currently, there seems to be a movement toward mixed economic systems in socialist societies. T or F?

7. Several characteristics of capitalist economic systems are listed here. Indicate in the space beside each characteristic whether it best describes individualistic capitalism (IC) or communitarian capitalism (CC).
   ____ a. government and business cooperation
   ____ b. high job mobility
   ____ c. profit maximization
   ____ d. more value placed on the interests of employees and consumers
   ____ e. self-interest paramount
   ____ f. long-range economic planning

Answers: 1. c; 2. capitalism; 3. d; 4. b; 5. c; 6. T; 7. a. (CC), b. (IC), c. (IC), d. (CC), e. (IC), f. (CC)

and Vogel 1987; Albert 1993; Thurow 2003a). In fact, according to George Lodge, the American economy has already moved, albeit kicking and screaming, toward communitarian capitalism (Lodge 1986). However, only future unfolding events will answer our question.

The Corporation R1

Within capitalist and mixed economic systems, corporations are extremely important actors. In their provocative book, *America Inc.*, Morton Mintz and Jerry Cohen contend that large corporations now own and operate the United States. Government power is a derivative of corporate power:

The danger that this superconcentration poses to our economic, political and social structure cannot be over-estimated.

Concentration of this magnitude is likely to eliminate existing and future competition. It increases the possibility for reciprocity and other forms of unfair buyer-seller leverage. It creates nation-wide marketing, managerial and financing structures whose enormous physical and psychological resources pose substantial barriers to smaller firms wishing to participate in a competitive market. . . . [This] superconcentration creates a "community of interest" which discourages competition among large firms and establishes a tone in the marketplace for more and more mergers. This leaves us with the unacceptable probability that the nation's manufacturing and financial assets will continue to be concentrated in the hands of fewer and fewer people. (Mintz and Cohen 1972:39)

The political and economic effects of modern corporations are seen at the local, national, and international levels, a point discussed later. For now, let's examine the nature of modern corporations.

The Nature of Modern Corporations

The economy of the United States has experienced substantial and continual growth. The gross domestic product (GDP)—the domestic output of goods and services—has steadily increased since 1933. Along with this increase in the GDP was an increasing domination of the economy by large business corporations. While the emergence of giant business organizations contributed to economic growth, it also created problems. These problems will be better understood if we first examine the nature and extent of modern corporations.

Q What is a corporation? A **corporation** is an organization owned by shareholders who have limited liability and limited control over organizational affairs. A key feature is the separation of ownership from control (Berle and Means 1968; originally published in 1932). Although shareholders receive reports of gains and losses from the corporation's transactions, they are not legally liable for them. And although shareholders are formally entitled to elect a board of directors, in reality they routinely approve the candidates recommended by the existing board. The actual control of a corporation rests with the board of directors and the corporate managers. Some critics contend, however, that this widely assumed separation between ownership and management is a myth.

Q How important are corporations today? At the beginning of the twentieth century, America had only a few industries, such as railroads, shipping, steel, oil, and mining, organized as corporations (Roy 1999; Perrow 2005). Today, U.S. corporations dominate the economy, providing everything from diapers to retirement communities.

Total corporate assets are concentrated in the hands of a relatively few giant corporations. The top 100 corporations, which account for less than 0.1 percent of all corporations in the United States, control more than 9 percent of total corporate assets; the top 200 corporations control nearly 11 percent. This has changed little since 1960. There is also a very high concentration of assets *within* the top corporations. The top 100 corporations have three-fourths of the assets held by the top 500 corporations, and the top 200 corporations possess almost 90 percent of the assets held by the top 500 corporations. Although only 0.2 percent of American corporations have assets of $250 million or more, these corporations control about 80 percent of the corporate assets in the United States. In sharp contrast, the 98.5 percent of corporations with assets of less than $10 million control only about 7 percent of the nation's corporate assets.

The Effects of Modern Corporations

Corporations represent massive concentrations of economic resources. Because of their economic muscle, corporations such as Wal-Mart Stores, Exxon-Mobil, and Bank of America make their voices heard by government decision makers. Many government policies, such as those regarding consumer safety, tax laws, and relationships with other nations, reflect corporate influence.

Q How do corporations affect political decision making? The tremendous political influence of corporate officials exists for several reasons. First, corporate leaders develop influential political and social ties. For example, Robert McNamara was president of the Ford Motor Company before becoming secretary of defense in the Kennedy administration; Michael Blumenthal was chairman of Bendix Corporation before becoming Jimmy Carter's secretary of the treasury; and Donald Regan was chairman of the board and chief executive officer (CEO) of Merrill Lynch before entering Ronald Reagan's cabinet as secretary of the treasury. In addition to being a CEO himself, George W. Bush picked a former CEO as his running mate and appointed three former CEOs to his cabinet and one as his White House Chief of Staff (M. Moore 2001; Page 2002). The movement between government and corporate positions occurs on lower levels as well. For example, after authoring the 2003 Medicare drug program sought by the drug companies, U.S. Representative Billy Tauson left Congress to become the chief lobbyist for the pharmaceutical industry.

Second, corporate officials—because of their personal wealth and organizational connections—are able to reward or punish elected government officials through investment decisions. It is unlikely, for example, that Detroit's $500 million Renaissance Center would have been constructed without the personal and financial support of Henry Ford II. On a more ominous note, financially troubled International Harvester extracted considerable concessions from both Springfield, Ohio, and Fort Wayne, Indiana, by announcing that it would close its plant in one of the two cities. The decision to allow the Springfield plant to remain open was reached only after the city found $30 million in local and state funds to buy the plant and lease it back to the company.

Third, in addition to affecting political processes through investment decisions, wealthy members of society, including corporate officials, affect a political candidate's chance of being elected in the first place. State and national politicians hesitate to jeopardize their chances for election (or reelection) by offending corporate officials or wealthy potential contributors, who are frequently the same people (Keen 2002).

Fourth, the political clout of large corporations is multiplied because of **interlocking directorates**—members of corporations sitting on one another's boards of directors. Although interlocking directorates are illegal if the corporations are competitors, this does not prevent noncompeting corporations with common interests from forming interlocking directorates. For example, members of the General Motors board of directors are also on the boards of many other corporations, including Eastman Kodak, Bristol-Myers Squibb, and Merck and Company. Moreover, these interlocks are only the beginning. The corporations having interlocking directors with General Motors have interlocks with hundreds of other corporations. In addition, there are indirect interlocks that permit two board members of competing firms to be members of a third corporation. It is not difficult to imagine the political power emanating from this spider's web of interlocks among America's most powerful corporations (Mintz and Schwartz 1981a, 1981b, 1985; Useem 1984; Dye 2001).

Fifth, the political power of corporations is enhanced through conglomerates. A **conglomerate** is a network of unrelated businesses operating under a single corporate umbrella. The parent corporation does not actually produce a product or provide a service; it simply has controlling interest in a set of diverse enterprises. RJR Nabisco, Inc., for example, owns companies in such different areas as tobacco, pet foods, candy, cigarettes, food products, bubble gum, research, and technology. A list of the company's North American subsidiaries covers almost an entire page in *Who Owns Whom* (*Lexis-Nexis Corporate Affiliations* 2010).

The informal contacts and global power, then, give corporations important advantages in the political decision-making process. And although corporate officials may disagree with one another and may not share all of the same goals, they have the ability, when they see their interests threatened, to effectively use their organizational resources. This influence is reflected in what critics call **corporate welfare**—economic benefits government regularly gives to corporations. Corporate welfare comes in many forms, including tax breaks, subsidies, and lax regulation and law enforcement for white-collar crimes. Mark Zepezauer and Arthur Naiman (1996) estimate that the government dispenses over half a trillion dollars annually to big business and wealthy individuals.

In the *Shock Doctrine,* Naomi Klein identifies privatization of public resources as a source of government-sponsored corporate power. She documents the government's use of disasters over the last thirty years to elevate the free market ideology to a level last seen in the nineteenth century. For example, she argues, George Bush used the nationwide fear following 9/11 to outsource to corporation's some central functions of government—"from providing health/care to soldiers, to interrogating prisoners, to gathering and 'data mining' information on all of us" (Klein 2007:15).

Consequently, the newly created "homeland security industry," economically unimportant before 2001, is now a $200 billion sector of the economy, largely in the hands of private contractors. Klein calls this ruling partnership between very large corporations and wealthy politicians a *corporatist* elite.

Globalization and Multinational Corporations

Globalization, as defined in Chapter 1, is the process by which crumbling geographical barriers permit members of different societies to become aware of increasingly similar economic, political, and social arrangements. To say globalization is to say interconnectedness. Nowhere are the effects of globalization more visible than in the penetration of *multinational corporations* into all economies of the world.

Increasingly influencing the globe, **multinational corporations** are firms in highly industrialized societies with operating facilities throughout the world. Multinationals are concentrated in a few industries, each controlled by a small number of giant companies. The oil and automobile industries alone account for about half of all multinational activity. Although multinational corporations existed for centuries, they became more powerful after World War II. Improvements in communication and transportation technology allowed them to exert extensive control over their worldwide operations (Chandler and Mazlish 2005).

Q How powerful are multinational corporations? While the financial and political power of multinationals is undeniable, it is difficult to measure (Roach 2005). Of the world's hundred largest political and economic entities, over fifty are multinational corporations rather than nation-states. If the 300 largest multinational corporations were to band together, their combined economic resources would be exceeded only by the combined wealth of the United States and Japan. Figure 13.6 compares the annual revenue of the top ten U.S. multinational corporations with the GDP of selected nations.

The political power of multinational corporations is even more problematic to document than their economic power. Evidence of political power is always more elusive than evidence of economic power. This is partly because the exercise of political power is often covert. Also, measures of economic power are much more collectable and accurate because of their quantitative nature. Political power is not as subject to metrics, but is identified through specific examples and inferred from the outcomes of political battles. For instance, the political power of multinationals can be surmised from the governmental approval of international trade agreements that permit corporations to challenge the

FIGURE 13.6

Total Revenue of Multinational Corporations versus National Gross Domestic Products

This figure compares the revenue of the top 10 American corporations to the gross domestic product (value of all goods produced and consumed domestically) of some countries. Were you surprised by any of the information?

Wal-Mart Stores $408.2 Billions (Revenue)	vs.	Austria $413.5 Billions (GDP)
Exxon-Mobil $284.7 Billions (Revenue)	vs.	Columbia $243.7 Billions (GDP)
Chevron $163.5 Billions (Revenue)	vs.	Chile $169.6 Billions (GDP)
Bank of America $150.5 Billions (Revenue)	vs.	Egypt $165.0 Billions (GDP)
ConocoPhillips $139.5 Billions (Revenue)	vs.	Hungary $154.7 Billions (GDP)
AT&T $123.0 Billions (Revenue)	vs.	Kazakhston $132.5 Billion (GDP)
Ford Motor $118.3 Billions (Revenue)	vs.	Peru $128.9 Billions (GDP)
JPMorgan Chase $115.6 Billions (Revenue)	vs.	New Zealand $126.4 Billions (GDP)
Hewlett-Packard $114.6 Billions (Revenue)	vs.	Puerto Rico $97.5 Billions (GDP)
Berkshire Hathaway $112.5 Billions (Revenue)	vs.	Viet Nam $90.6 Billion (GDP)

Source: United Nations Department of Economic and Social Affairs, *The World Statistics Pocketbook, 2009* (New York: United Nations, 2010); *The World Almanac and Book of Facts 2011* (New York: World Almanac Books, 2011), p. 62.

regulations of even democratic nations. Political power is particularly displayed in the United States, where multinationals have been successful in obtaining favorable tax rates, giant subsidies, and freedom from responsibility for some of the costs it imposes on society. Uncompensated environmental damage, whose costs are borne by taxpayers, is a prime illustration of the freedom from responsibility for negative social effects (Roach 2005). Our exploration into multinational corporate power continues into the next section, which discusses the effects of multinational corporations.

Q What are some effects of multinational corporations? Defenders of multinationals argue that the corporations provide developing countries access to technology, capital, foreign markets, and products that would otherwise be unavailable. Critics claim that multinationals actually harm economies of host nations—exploiting their natural resources, disrupting local economies, introducing inappropriate technologies and products, and increasing income inequality. Multinationals, these critics note, often rely on inexpensive labor or abundant raw materials in the developing nations while returning their profits to corporate headquarters and shareholders in rich nations. Multinationals'

domination of their industries makes it difficult for the economically developing nations to establish new companies that can effectively compete with the multinationals. As a result, multinationals retard rather than promote the economic development of some regions of the world. The relative lack of economic development in host countries is visible in two areas: job creation and economic prosperity.

One argument advanced for the benefits of multinational corporations is their provision of jobs in developing countries. Critics point out that these jobs are largely unskilled and low-paying. Moreover, multinationals don't create the number of jobs expected, considering the magnitude of their revenues, profits, and assets. In 2002, the *Fortune* Global 500 corporations accounted for only 1.6 percent of the global workforce. And, while the profits of the world's fifty largest corporations rose by 167 percent between 1983 and 2001, their employment increased by only 21 percent (Roach 2005).

Another primary justification for globalization (and accompanying multinational corporations) is its contribution to the economic prosperity of developing countries. Why do developing countries so often end up with greater debt and increased economic instability? Economist Joseph Stiglitz traces this failure to the connection between the United States and the International Monetary Fund, the World Bank, and the World Trade Organization (Stiglitz 2003, 2007). The United States, for example, has virtual veto power over International Monetary Fund policy because economic size determines the number of votes in the organization. In addition, the president of the United States appoints the head of the World Bank. Consequently, these organizations respond to the wishes of wealthy countries. This concentration of power works to aid richer nations more than the poorer nations they are pledged to help.

Corporations dominate the American economic system and influence the economies of nations worldwide. Even farming, historically a family business, is not immune to the corporate form of organization.

CHECK YOURSELF **13.7** R2

The Corporation

1. A(n) _____ is an organization owned by shareholders who have limited liability and limited control over organizational affairs.
2. Which of the following is *not* one of the reasons behind corporate political influence?
   a. Corporate managers and directors have informal and organizational ties that lead them to be consulted about matters of political policy.
   b. Many corporate officials have reward and coercive power over elected government officials.
   c. Many elected officials are also top corporate officials.
   d. Interlocking directorates exist.
   e. Conglomerates are present.
3. Indirect interlocks permit two board members of different corporations to sit on each other's boards of directors. T or F?
4. Firms with operating facilities in several different countries are called _____.
5. Multinational corporations are concentrated in a few industries, each dominated by a small number of giant companies. T or F?
6. Multinational corporations
   a. are easily manipulated by the governments of low-economy nations.
   b. sometimes create problems involving unsafe working conditions and inappropriate products.
   c. are known to have overthrown large numbers of low-economy governments.
   d. carefully avoid environmental damage in their areas of operation.

Answers: 1. corporation; 2. c; 3. F; 4. multinational corporations; 5. T; 6. b

Q **How would critic Joseph Stiglitz curtail the negative effects of multinational corporations?** The power and reach of large multinational corporations is enough to leave reformers in despair. Certainly, the moral appeal to corporations that good ethics in good business does not work. Serious critics of multinational abuses look to government regulations as a solution. Joseph Stiglitz (2007) outlines some regulatory actions government could take: limit corporate power, improve corporate governance, and create international laws.

With their monopolistic power and size, multinationals most likely will increase abuses. Microsoft operating systems, for example, has about 90 percent of the world PC market. U.S. and European courts have, in fact, ruled that Microsoft abused its monopoly power. We need global competition laws and a global authority to enforce them, Stiglitz writes. Criminal and civil law applied to anti-competitive behavior could lower prices and stimulate innovation.

Another approach involves regulating corporate governance, forcing multinationals to operate internally in ways consistent with the public interest. Making corporate officials legally responsible for corporate abuses is one example. Another is to simplify the process of obtaining compensation for corporate damage such as endangering employee health and safety and harming the environment. Other laws could permit parties from one country to sue abusive corporations in their home

nation, and allow enforcement of judgments from foreign courts in corporate home countries.

Finally, the creation of international law and international courts could curb multinational abuse. This would provide the opportunity for complainants from several countries to file class action suits against multinationals. Requiring advanced industrial nations to give legal assistance to developing countries in international courts would buttress any new international legal framework.

Work in the Contemporary American Economy R1

The U.S. economy is dynamic, reflected, for instance, in the radical alterations of workforce composition. Significant change is likewise taking place in hiring and firing practices as management relies increasingly on downsizing and contingent employment. Social scientists expect these changes to accelerate, with some serious consequences (Rifkin 1995; Milkman 1997; Mazaar 1999; Hodson and Sullivan 2011).

Changes in the Workforce Composition

To understand work in modern society, it is necessary to be familiar with the three basic economic sectors: primary, secondary, and tertiary.

Q **How do the economic sectors differ?** The **primary sector** of an economy depends on the natural environment to produce economic goods. The jobs in this sector vary widely—farmer, miner, fishery worker, timber worker, cattle rancher. The **secondary sector** manufactures products from raw materials. Occupations in this sector include blue-collar workers of all types, from those who produce computers to those who construct *Grand Theft Auto* video games as well as associated white-collar employees in management and office positions. Employees in the **tertiary sector** provide services. If you went to class, filled your car with gas, stopped by the bank, and visited your doctor today, you spent most of your time and money in the tertiary (service) sector. Other service industries include insurance, real estate, retail sales, and entertainment. Employees in the tertiary sector are primarily white-collar workers.

Q **Historically, how have the three sectors evolved?** Obviously, the primary sector dominated the preindustrial economy. At that stage of economic development, most citizens were involved in the battle for economic survival. This sector made goods by hand. Very few people could be spared for religious, medical, or educational purposes.

This balance began to change with the mechanization of farming in the agricultural economy. Mechanical innovations (cotton gin, plow, tractor), along with the application of science (seed production, fertilization, and crop rotation) reduced the proportion of the labor force needed in the primary sector. During the 1800s, the average farmer could feed five workers or so. Today, the figure is eighty. Not surprisingly, the proportion of workers in the farming sector declined from almost 40 percent in 1900 to about 2 percent today.

Along with the mechanization of farming came other technological advancements (power looms, motors of all types, electrical power), followed by the shift of agricultural workers from farms to factories, all ushering in the secondary sector. The percentage of the U.S. labor force engaged in blue-collar jobs reached almost 40 percent in 1900.

Just as in agriculture, technological developments in the secondary sector permitted greater production with fewer workers. After World War II, the fastest-growing occupations were the white-collar jobs—managers, professionals, sales workers, clerical workers. In 1956, white-collar workers for the first time accounted for a larger proportion of the U.S. labor force than did blue-collar workers. In manufacturing industries, white-collar workers tripled the number of blue-collar workers.

Technological progress did not stop with the secondary sector. As relative growth of workers in goods-producing jobs was decreasing, the demand for labor in the tertiary section was increasing. Fueled by computer

FIGURE 13.7

Distribution of Workers by Occupational Category

This table shows the percentage of American workers who are employed in each occupational category. It also shows how each occupational category is broken down by gender.

Occupational category	Percent of total	Percent male	Percent female
Management, professional, and related occupations	36.2	49.8	50.8
Service occupations	16.8	43	57
Sales and office occupations	24.5	36.8	63.2
Natural resources, construction, and maintenance occupations	10.2	95.8	4.2
Production, transportation, and material moving occupations	12.2	77.6	22.4

Source: U.S. Census Bureau, *Statistical Abstract of the United States: 2010*, (129 Edition), Washington, DC, 2009, Table 603.

technology, the U.S. economy moved from a manufacturing base to a "knowledge" base (see Chapter 5). Demand for people who could manage information and deliver services became the new workforce hallmark. This development, along with the growth of white-collar employment in the secondary sector, increased the proportion of white-collar workers in the United States from just below one-third in 1930 to about three-fourths today (see Figure 13.7 for the proportion of American workers in major occupational categories). The ever-increasing number of women employed outside the home has influenced the American workplace as well.

Occupational Structure

We read in Chapter 9 about America's dual labor market. The emphasis there was on institutionalized discrimination suffered by minorities. Actually, the implications of the dual labor market are much broader.

Q **What is the nature of the two-tiered occupational structure?** One tier—the **core tier**—contains dominant positions in large firms. Computer technology, pharmaceutical, and aerospace firms are prime examples. Between 30 and 40 percent of U.S. workers are in the core. The **peripheral tier** is composed of jobs in smaller firms that either are competing for business excluded from core firms or are engaged in less profitable industries such as agriculture, textiles, and small-scale

The American economy is shifting from assembly-line production with blue-collar workers to a service economy with white-collar employees.

retail trade. Most U.S. workers—60 to 70 percent—are employed in the peripheral tier.

Historically, jobs in the core pay more, offer better benefits, and provide longer-term employment. This is not surprising, since the firms involved are large and highly profitable. Peripheral jobs are characterized by low pay, little or no benefits, and short-term employment (Weakliem 1990; Hudson 2000). These features follow from the weaker competitive position and the smaller size of the employing firms.

Q How are the core and peripheral tiers changing? During the last twenty five years, the core industries scaled back, laying off experienced workers. As early as 1983, for example, a steel mill in Hibbing, Minnesota, that once employed 4,400 people had a payroll of only 650 ("Left Out" 1983). Since 1983, the Weirton Steel Company cut its production capacity by 30 percent and laid off more than half of its workforce. In fact, since 1979, the United States has eliminated more than 43 million jobs. More than 570,000 job cuts were announced in the United States in 1998, more than half of which occurred in manufacturing plants (McNamee and Muller 1998; Riederer 1999). American corporations created more than 21,000 mass layoffs in 2001, affecting nearly 2.5 million workers (Marchese 2002). Of course, as these top-tier jobs disappear, peripheral jobs become a larger share of the total jobs (see "Consider This Research" for an example of the consequences of restructuring for workers).

Newer industries, such as those based on microchip technology, are beginning to replace manufacturing jobs in some areas. These industries, however, provide few jobs suited to the skills and backgrounds of laid-off manufacturing workers. Moreover, most jobs in high-tech industries pay minimal wages and offer few chances for promotion. A very small proportion of high-tech employees hold responsible positions with high pay.

Q What does this mean for U.S. workers? The U.S. economy is losing higher-paying jobs and gaining lower-paying jobs. This helps explain why, since the 1970s, most workers are losing economic ground. Whereas one American worker could support a family thirty years ago, the dual-employed married couple is the norm today. This process, known as "downwaging," is expected to continue, propelled, in part, by the movement offshore of higher wage blue-collar jobs and higher income white-collar jobs as a result of globalization policies such as NAFTA (North American Free Trade Agreement; Thurow 2003a). Many researchers believe that these trends of job loss and downwaging will threaten the American Dream (Newman 1993; Barlett and Steele 1996; Frank 2007).

Q How useful is the dual labor market perspective? Criticisms of the dual labor market perspective include the need to clarify some of its assumptions and recognition of the fact that it does not always accurately predict labor market experiences. Studies within each sector reveal considerable variation in individual experiences. Despite a need for refinement, however, dual labor market theory alerts us to shifts in industries and firms that will be offering jobs in the future (Hodson and Kaufman 1982; M. R. Kelley 1990; Sakamoto and Chen 1991; Hudson 2000).

Downsizing and Contingent Employment

Clearly, the American labor landscape is changing, due in part to corporate management decisions. Two interrelated steps by management—downsizing and contingent employment—deserve special attention (Mazaar 1999).

Q Why do corporations downsize? Downsizing refers to the reduction in a corporation's workforce designed to cut costs, increase profits, and enhance stock values. To justify downsizing, business leaders point to several factors: rising health-care costs, the need to become leaner and less hierarchically structured in an increasingly competitive global environment, and the necessity to eliminate levels of middle management that can be replaced by computers and information technology (Gleckman et al. 1993; Huber and Korn 1997).

Q To what extent is downsizing occurring? Downsizing became popular during the 1990s (Boroughs 1996; Sloan 1996; Belton 1999; Burke and Cooper 2000; Cohen and Thomas 2001). Since 1985, more than 8 million employees were downsized, half of whom held white-collar jobs. In 2001, corporate layoffs increased nearly 40 percent over the previous year (Marchese 2002). For a multitude of reasons, the momentum for downsizing and layoffs continues. In 2005 General Motors announced plans to close twelve factories and eliminate 30,000 factory jobs. Ford Motor Company followed with the intention of eliminating 25,000 jobs and closing fourteen manufacturing plants in North America. In fact, between 2000 and 2006, the auto industry cut 200,000 jobs.

Q How do employers approach downsizing? Part of the motivation for downsizing is top management's belief that their companies employ a surplus of people and that fewer employees can do the work without reducing efficiency and effectiveness. On the other hand, the desire to shrink the size of the workforce is not the only incentive. Part of the impetus for downsizing is less expensive alternatives to permanent, full-time employees.

Profitable companies are increasingly using the services of **contingent employees**—individuals hired on a part-time, short-term, or contract basis. These contingent employees replace full-time employees ("The New World of Work" 1994; T. S. Moore 1996; Cappelli et al. 1997; Sullivan 2004). The contingent label is appropriate because their employment is contingent on daily, weekly, or seasonal company need. References to them as "marginal" and "disposable" workers attest to their lack of traditional job and economic security (Kirkpatrick 1988; Castro 1993).

Contingent employees now make up more than one-third of the U.S. labor force (more than 40 million people), increasing more than 250 percent since 1982. These temporary employees earn about 60 percent of average full-time workers and do not receive health insurance or retirement benefits. The contingent labor force traditionally includes groups from the bottom of the occupational structure—minorities, women, youth, the elderly. They are often recent immigrants who will work for less pay and lower benefits. Though most contingent workers are in low-level, low-paying clerical, retail, and service jobs, downsizing is increasingly affecting higher-level white-collar people—engineers, accountants, nurses, managers, and physicians (Heckscher 1995; Rifkin 1995; Altman 2002).

In addition to domestic employment, contingent employment takes the form of job *offshoring*, or moving operations outside the United States. Initially, offshoring involved only factory workers. But white-collar jobs are no longer immune. Increasingly information technology, legal, accounting, customer service, and insurance jobs are leaving the United States for places like India and Mexico. According to a recent survey by the Pew Research Center, 77 percent of Americans believe that outsourcing jobs to other countries is hurting American workers. There are no signs that this concern is deterring corporate offshoring. In 2010, U.S. firms created 1.4 million jobs overseas, compared to fewer than 1 million domestically ("U.S. Companies Hiring at Rapid Pace . . . Overseas" 2010).

Q What are the effects of these actions by employers? These actions by management, heightened considerably by the deepest recession since the Great Depression, may portend a fundamental change in the relationship between American workers and their employers. Critics fear a fundamental fracture in the social contract (job security and good pensions in exchange for high productivity) between businesses and employees (Greenhouse 2009). Similarly, Robert Reich, former Secretary of Labor under President Clinton, expresses concern for greater polarization between those who control capital and those who do not (Reich 2010).

According to a survey of the U.S. workforce, there is a growing split in employees' attitudes toward their work and their employers (2010 *Global Workforce Study* 2010). Although employees express high job satisfaction, confidence in management is extremely low (Saad 2010). Workers seem to be losing faith in management's commitment to them. Robert Reich (2010) writes of a growing perception in the general public that the economic system is rigged in favor of the rich and powerful. The growing compensation gap between top corporate executives and employees heightens this sense of injustice (Kuttner 2007). And Wall Street further fueled the cynicism when it announced in 2010 that its annual bonuses, the first since their rescue by the government, would run into

Kathryn Marie Dudley— The End of the Line

Because she grew up near Chrysler's auto plant in Kenosha, Wisconsin, researcher Kathryn Marie Dudley had an interest in studying the cultural fallout from the plant's closing in 1988. She offers Kenosha as a representative example of the cultural consequences of the current restructuring of the U.S. economy. As Dudley indicates, the plant relocations, downsizings, and job eliminations undertaken by large corporations over the past few decades are seen as part of the shift from industrial to postindustrial society:

What was once a fundamental segment of the American economic structure—heavy industry and durable goods manufacturing—has now become a marginal part of the national portfolio. As this sector of the economy gives way to the new "knowledge industries," workers in this sector are being superseded as well. In America's new image of itself as a postindustrial society, individuals still employed in basic manufacturing industries look like global benchwarmers in the competitive markets of the modern world. (Dudley 1997:161)

Dudley's research is a case study of a large plant in a one-industry community experiencing the ongoing shrinking of core jobs in postindustrial society.

During the year following the shutdown, Dudley conducted in-depth interviews with autoworkers and with a wide variety of professionals in the Kenosha area. Interview questions were open-ended to give informants freedom to roam where their thoughts and feelings took them. Dudley's only restriction was that the interviews be geared to the cultural meaning of repercussions suffered by the community because of its declining employment base.

For Dudley, the demolition of the auto plant was a metaphor for the dismantled lifestyle of U.S. blue-collar workers in core manufacturing industries. These increasingly displaced blue-collar workers, contends Dudley, find themselves caught between two interpretations of success. On the one hand, middle-class professionals justify their place in society by reference to their educational credentials and "thinking" jobs. Blue-collar workers, on the other hand, legitimize their place in society by the high market value placed on their hard labor. One ex-autoworker, whom Dudley calls Al Tirpak, captures the idea beautifully:

We're worth fifteen dollars an hour because we're producing a product that can be sold on the market that'll produce that fifteen dollars an hour. . . . I don't know if you want to [base a person's value] strictly on education. You can send someone to school for twelve years and they can still be doing something that's socially undesirable and not very worthwhile for society. I don't know if
they should get paid just because they had an education. In my mind, yuppie means young unproductive parasite. We're gonna have an awful lot of yuppies here in Kenosha that say they are doing something worthwhile when, really, they aren't. (Dudley 1997:169)

Due to the massive loss of high-paying factory jobs, Dudley contends that the blue-collar vision of success is coming to "the end of the line." They have lost their cultural niche in a postindustrial world where work is based on education and the application of knowledge.

Dudley documents the blue-collar workers' view of this new reality. From her extensive interviews, she constructs a portrait of their struggle to preserve their cultural traditions in a social world that is removing the type of employment on which these traditions were built. The penalty for not creating new cultural supports for a sense of social worth, Dudley concludes, will be life in a state of confusion with a sense of failure.

Evaluate the Research

1. What does Dudley mean when she says that the blue-collar workers caught in the wave of corporation restructuring are experiencing the shift from industrial to postindustrial society?
2. Do you think that Dudley's research methods are strong enough to support her conclusion?
3. Do you believe that Dudley can be objective in this study of her hometown? Explain.

the billions (Fletcher 2010; Tse 2010). Trust and loyalty are difficult to maintain when employees do not believe that their companies' policies treat them fairly.

We do not know the full consequences for companies or employees. One conclusion, however, seems clear: If we are to realize future economic benefits, management will have to take into account the problems of downsizing survivors and initiate appropriate remedial responses. The needs are basic: maintaining honest and constant communication between top management and survivors of layoffs, setting goals with survivors, further empowering survivors on the job, exercising accessible and sensitive leadership, and creating a positive organizational culture for survivors.

On to Chapter 14

As adults, we must participate in the political and economic institutions. Not so with the next major

institution, religion. While our parents may not give us, as youngsters, a choice about religious faith and worship attendance, we, as adults, are free to choose. And, despite secularization, most Americans do participate in the religious institution, sharing certain basic tenets of some religious faith. Even Americans who reject religious faith must deal with religion because it is embedded in our culture.

CHECK YOURSELF 13.8 R2

Work in the Contemporary Economy

1. Which of the following is *not* one of the major labor-force trends discussed in the text?
   a. decrease in primary sector employment
   b. decline in agricultural employment
   c. increased employment of service workers
   d. increase in blue-collar jobs
   e. increase in white-collar proportion of the labor force
2. Most of the jobs that were added to the American economy over the past thirty years were in which of the following sectors?
   a. service and white-collar
   b. manufacturing
   c. mining
   d. skilled blue-collar
3. The _____ industrial sector contains large, profitable firms with dominant positions within major industries.
4. The _____ industrial sector contains small, less profitable firms operating in more competitive industries.
5. _____ is the decision on the part of top management to reduce its workforce to cut costs, increase profits, and enhance stock values.

Answers: 1. d; 2. a; 3. core; 4. peripheral; 5. Downsizing

INTEGRATED GOALS AND SUMMARY

1. **Distinguish among power, coercion, and authority, and identify three basic forms of authority.**
   - The economic and political institutions are closely related. The economy is the institution designed for the production and distribution of goods and services, and it is the political institution that obtains and exercises power.
   - Power is the ability to impose one's will on others whether or not they wish to comply. Authority is power accepted as legitimate by those subjected to it. Max Weber identified three types of authority: charismatic authority, which is unstable; traditional authority, which is too outdated to serve as the primary basis of power for modern nation-states; and rational-legal authority, which is the authority of most nation-states today. The power of most modern government officials, then, is limited by legal rules and regulations.

2. **Discuss the nation-state, comparing and contrasting the functionalist and conflict approaches to this form of political authority.**
   - A nation-state is the political entity that holds authority over a specified territory; a government is the political structure that rules a nation. The nation-state is relatively new in human history, emerging with the rise of agriculture and industrial production. According to functionalism, the nation-state developed to maintain social order. From the conflict perspective, nation-states exist primarily to promote the interests of the societal elite.

3. **Identify the major differences among democracy, totalitarianism, and authoritarianism.**
   - Democracy and totalitarianism are the two polar types of political systems. In modern societies, democracies

are representative with minimal citizen involvement in political affairs. Totalitarian political systems have absolute rulers who control all aspects of social life. Between these two polar types lies authoritarianism. This third type of political system involves nonelected rulers who possess absolute control but frequently permit some individual freedom.

- Voting seems to have limitations as an effective means for the nonelite to influence political decision making. This is partly because America does not have a high voter participation rate and partly because the most disadvantaged tend to be nonvoters.

4. **Delineate the major types of Terrorism**
   - Four types of terrorism are distinguishable. Revolutionary terrorism involves acts of violence aimed at replacing an existing government. Totalitarian terrorism is intimidation, through violence and fear, of a population by its own established and legitimate government. State terrorism controls through normal government agencies rather than by special coercive forces. International terrorism involves either collaboration with a nondomestic terrorist group, a terrorist act committed outside the country, or negotiation over demands with a foreign country.

5. **Differentiate the views of functionalism and conflict theory on the distribution of power in America.**
   - The two major models of power distribution are pluralism and elitism. Pluralists, whose view is associated with functionalism, depict power in the United States as widely distributed among diverse special interest groups. Interest groups appear to be on the rise as the public becomes more politically sophisticated and as the influence of political parties declines. The growing importance of political action committees (PACs) reflects the same social conditions. Some powerful interest groups, notably those PACs associated with business interests, thwart public opinion by using their power for the attainment of narrow, selfish goals. Still, interest groups provide one of the few mechanisms for the representation of nonelite segments of a society. Some of these interest groups have successfully challenged the political and economic establishment.
   - Advocates of the conflict perspective contend that American society is controlled by a unified and enduring elite. This is a "power elite" comprised of a unified coalition of top military, corporate, and government leaders. Although some evidence documents the existence of a national power elite, no research definitively confirms its presence.

6. **Describe the major characteristics of capitalism, socialism, and mixed economic systems.**
   - Economies differ in their organization and underlying assumptions. Capitalist economies are committed to private property and the pursuit of profit without government interference. In socialist economies, the

people own the means of production, and government has an active role in planning and controlling the economy. There is movement toward capitalism in socialist countries. Capitalist and socialist ideologies appear to be becoming less of a barrier in the relationships among nations.

- Individualistic capitalism and communitarian capitalism are the two basic variants of capitalism. Self-interest, the free market, profit maximization, and highest return possible on stockholder investment are foundational principles of individualistic capitalism. In communitarian capitalism, the emphasis is on the interests of employees, customers, and society.

7. **Discuss the effects of the modern corporation on American society.**
   - The rise of the corporate economy intensifies the link between political and economic institutions. Some critics contend that vast corporations now control the political institution in the United States. Furthermore, a relatively small segment of the population owns the assets of these corporations.
   - Corporations are rapidly increasing in size, number, and power. Their influence is felt domestically and internationally. Corporations affect domestic political decision making and also influence the political and economic institutions of countries around the world.

8. **Describe the changing workforce composition in highly developed economies.**
   - Modern economies are composed of three basic sectors: primary, secondary, and tertiary. In preindustrial societies, the primary sector, in which the natural environment is used to produce economic goods (mining, fishing), predominates. The secondary sector, in which manufactured goods are made from raw materials, grows in importance with the mechanization of farming in the agricultural economy. The tertiary sector, the service sector, expands when manufacturing requires fewer workers.

9. **Portray the changing occupational structure in modern economies.**
   - Core manufacturing industries have reduced the number of their employees over the last twenty-five years. The laid-off manufacturing workers do not have the skills needed by expanding high-tech industries. Also, most jobs in high-tech industries pay minimal wages and provide few opportunities for advancement. Consequently, workers lose economic ground.

10. **Discuss corporate downsizing and its consequences.**
    - More American corporations are downsizing and replacing full-time employees with contingent, or temporary, workers. Granted, we do not yet know the full implications of these changes for workers and for the future of American society, but evidence is beginning to establish some negative consequences.

CONCEPT REVIEW

Match the following concepts with the definitions listed below them.

____ a. individualistic capitalism	____ g. monopoly	____ m. power elite
____ b. political action committees	____ h. downsizing	____ n. rational-legal authority
____ c. oligopoly	____ i. communitarian capitalism	____ o. bourgeoisie
____ d. government	____ j. authoritarianism	____ p. elitism
____ e. nation-state	____ k. terrorism	____ q. interest group
____ f. democracy	____ l. traditional authority	____ r. corporation

1. the type of political system controlled by nonelected rulers who generally permit some degree of individual freedom
2. members of a society who own productive property
3. the type of political system in which elected officials are held responsible for fulfilling the goals of the majority of the electorate
4. the theory of power distribution that sees society in the control of a few individuals and organizations
5. a group organized to achieve some specific, shared goals by influencing political decision making
6. a situation in which a single company controls a market
7. the political entity that holds authority over a specified territory
8. organizations established by interest groups for the purpose of raising and distributing funds to selected political candidates
9. a unified coalition of top military, corporate, and government leaders

10. authority based on rules and procedures associated with political offices
11. the political structure that rules a nation
12. legitimate power rooted in custom
13. the type of capitalism that emphasizes the interests of employees, customers, and society
14. the decision of top management to reduce its workforce to cut costs, increase profits, and enhance stock values
15. the type of capitalism founded on the principles of self-interest, the free market, profit maximization, and the highest return possible on stockholder investment
16. The use of violence or threats of violence against a government, a group, or an individual in pursuit of a political, religious, economic, or social goal
17. a situation in which a combination of companies controls a market
18. an organization owned by shareholders who have limited liability and limited control over organizational affairs

CHECK YOURSELF REVIEW

1. According to Jean-Jacques Rousseau, it is primarily the privileged classes who benefit from the existence of the state. T or F?
2. The operation of PACs in America today invalidates the pluralist model. T or F?
3. According to Karl Marx, those in charge of the state in capitalist societies make decisions that serve the interests of the owners of the means of production. He used the term _____ to describe acceptance of a system that works against one's own interests.
4. _____ refers to the type of political system controlled by nonelected rulers who generally permit some degree of individual freedom.
5. Firms with operating facilities in several different countries are called _____.
6. The _____ industrial sector contains large, profitable firms with dominant positions within major industries.
7. Most political action committees (PACs) are now associated with
   a. labor unions.
   b. citizen groups.
   c. political parties.
   d. corporations and other businesses.
8. Which of the following is *not* one of the reasons behind corporate political influence?
   a. Corporate managers and directors have informal and organizational ties that lead them to be consulted about matters of political policy.
   b. Many corporate officials have reward and coercive power over elected government officials.
   c. Many elected officials are also top corporate officials.
   d. Interlocking directorates exist.
   e. Conglomerates are present.
9. Which of the following is *not* one of the major labor force trends discussed in the text?
   a. decrease in primary sector employment
   b. decline in agricultural employment
   c. increased employment of service workers
   d. increase in blue-collar jobs
   e. increase in white-collar proportion of the labor force
10. Several characteristics of capitalist economic systems are listed here. Indicate in the space beside each

characteristic whether it best describes individualistic capitalism (IC) or communitarian capitalism (CC).

_____ a. government and business cooperation

_____ b. high job mobility

_____ c. profit maximization

_____ d. more value placed on the interests of employees and consumers

_____ e. self-interest paramount

_____ f. long-range economic planning

GRAPHIC REVIEW

Figure 13.7 displays the percentage of American male and female workers in major occupational categories.

1. Ask your parents to comment on the information in this figure. Do you agree or disagree with them? Explain.

_____

_____

_____

2. Describe Figure 13.7 in terms of gender equity.

_____

_____

_____

3. Discuss the most important implications regarding employment in the United States that can be suggested from these data.

_____

_____

_____

CRITICAL-THINKING QUESTIONS

1. Like all organizations, universities are based on some form of authority. Discuss each of the three types of authority, and show which type is most basic to the university structure. Be careful to show why each type of authority is applicable or inapplicable to the university's organizational structure.

_____

_____

2. Functionalism and conflict theory each have a unique perspective on the nature and purpose of the nation-state. Do you think that one of these perspectives more accurately describes American society than the other? Why or why not?

_____

_____

3. Define the concept of the power elite. Is American society best characterized as a pluralist society or a society controlled by a power elite? Defend your position.

_____

_____

4. Distinguish between the two global cultures of capitalism. Do you envision a convergence of these two approaches to capitalism within the rapidly developing global marketplace? Support your viewpoint.

_____

_____

5. American corporations have in recent years turned to the practices of downsizing and contingent employment. State the reasons for this managerial strategy, and discuss whether or not it will promote the organizational goals it is designed to reach.

_____

_____

ANSWER KEY

Concept Review

a. 15
b. 8
c. 17
d. 11
e. 7
f. 3
g. 6
h. 14
i. 13
j. 1
k. 16
l. 12
m. 9
n. 10
o. 2
p. 4
q. 5
r. 18

Check Yourself Review

1. T
2. F
3. false consciousness
4. Authoritarianism
5. multinational corporations
6. core
7. d
8. c
9. d
10. a. CC
    b. IC
    c. IC
    d. CC
    e. IC
    f. CC

14 Religion

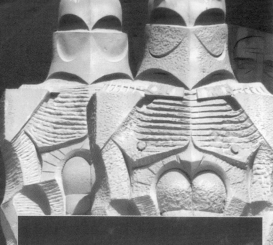

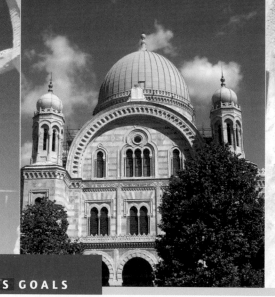

Rolmat/Dreamstime; LLC/ARTEKI/Used under license from Shutterstock;Mikhail Nekrasov/Used under license from Shutterstock

GOALS

- Explain the sociological meaning of religion.
- Demonstrate the different views of religion taken by functionalists and conflict theorists.
- Distinguish among the basic types of religious organization.
- Discuss the meaning and nature of religiosity.
- Define secularization, and describe its relationship to religiosity in the United States.
- Differentiate between civil and invisible religion in America.
- Describe the current resurgence of religious fundamentalism in Christianity and Islam.
- Identify a wide variety of religious movements in America.
- Discuss social class and politics as correlates of religion.
- Compare and contrast five world religions.

Religion and Sociology

USING THE SOCIOLOGICAL IMAGINATION

Is secularization destroying religion in the United States? Many self-proclaimed prognosticators fear the decline of religion in the United States. On the contrary, evidence reveals that America, compared with other industrialized nations, remains a fairly religious nation.

Religion in America, then, remains a viable topic to explore. Before doing so, we will view religion within the context of sociology, define religion as an institution, examine religion from the functionalist and conflict perspectives, explore religious organization, and identify the ways people express their religious beliefs.

Religion, Science, and Sociology [R1]

Religion and Science

Q Can religion and science coexist? Because religion involves matters beyond human observation and because science is all about observation, these two institutions can potentially conflict. It is not that scientists cannot be religious. Rather, scientists separate their professional work (based on reason and observation) from their religious life (based on faith and the unobservable).

Science and religion do conflict, however, when people try to mix the two. Some American religious fundamentalists do just that when they argue that *creationism* (explanation of the natural world through the Bible) is as scientifically based as evolutionary biology. The evolution versus creation debate has intensified in several states (Nelson 2002).

Q Will science replace religion? Science need not, and doubtless will not, eradicate religion. Because all societies have some form of religion, we can assume that humans seek answers to some fundamental questions about existence: Is there a higher purpose to life? Why does life unfold for us in particular ways? Is there an afterlife? Answers to such questions are simply beyond science. We can therefore expect religion to endure as long as human life exists. Furthermore, it is likely that science and religion will continue on their historical path of separation and coexistence.

Religion and Sociology

The study of religion attracted the attention of sociologists in the nineteenth century. These early sociologists were interested in the place religion holds in social life. Auguste Comte, the man who coined the term *sociology*, saw sociology as a new religion (a religion of science) and sociologists as high priests. Other pioneering sociologists, such as Emile Durkheim, Max Weber, and Karl Marx, viewed the practice of religion as a key to some of the mysteries of social life. Religion, they believed, could help explain the presence of social order and the cultural variation of societies. Despite this early scholarly interest, the sociological study of religion disappeared during the first half of the twentieth century. Only after World War II did social scientists again become interested in the scientific study of religion (Sharot 2001; Clarke 2009).

Sociologists of religion neither explain nor endorse particular religions but rather are interested in all sociological aspects of religion. This interest must begin with a sociological definition of religion.

Q What is the sociological meaning of religion? Religion is a unified system of beliefs and practices relating to sacred things. This definition comes from Emile Durkheim, who based his studies on the Australian aborigines in the late nineteenth century. According to Durkheim, every society distinguishes between the **sacred**—entities that are set apart and given a special meaning that transcends immediate human existence—and the **profane**—nonsacred aspects of life. (Profane in this context does not mean unholy or defiled but simply commonplace and not involving the supernatural.)

Sacred things take on a public character that makes them important in themselves; the profane do not. Temple Mount in Jerusalem is a particularly illuminating example because its sacred meaning is not the same for the three religions that revere it. Jews hold sacred the Temple Mount "Wailing Wall" because it is the remnant of the First and Second Temples destroyed by the Romans in 70 A.D. Christians consider it holy because it was a site of Jesus' preaching. For Muslims, it is sacred as a place from which Mohammed ascended to heaven. Because Hindus do not share any of these religious beliefs, Temple Mount is part of their nonsacred, or profane, world.

Interestingly, some nonreligious aspects of culture can assume something of a sacred character. Babe Ruth's bat illustrates the difference between the sacred and the profane:

When Babe Ruth was a living idol to baseball fans, the bat he used to slug his home runs was definitely a profane object. It was Ruth's personal instrument and had little

Buddhas, like this one at a Mongolian monastery, are sacred objects in the Far East and Southeast Asia, and wherever Buddhists live. What makes an object sacred?

Christineg/Dreamstime LLC

social value in itself. Today, however, one of Ruth's bats is enshrined in the Baseball Hall of Fame. It is no longer used by anyone. It stands, rather, as an object which in itself represents the values, sentiments, power, and beliefs of all members of the baseball community. What was formerly a profane object is now in the process of gaining some of the qualities of a sacred object. (Cuzzort and King 1976:27)

Babe Ruth's bat illustrates two points about the sociological study of religion. First, a profane object can become sacred, and vice versa. Second, sociologists can deal with religion without becoming involved in theological issues. By focusing on the cultural and social aspects of religion, sociologists avoid questions about the ultimate validity of any particular religion. This point needs elaboration.

Q How do sociologists avoid theological issues? Religion involves a *transcendent reality*—a set of meanings attached to a world beyond human observation (Lilla 2007). Because sociologists must deal with this dimension of unobservability, their task is particularly difficult. For example, in this realm, sociologists face unique problems: Can an empirical science actually study the unobservable? Can scientific objectivity be maintained while investigating something as value laden as religion? Can sociologists retain religious faith after scientifically probing religion? Each of these questions deserves a brief answer.

Obviously, sociologists cannot study the unobservable. As part of an empirical science, sociologists who investigate religion must formulate theories and hypotheses and apply scientific methods to aspects of religion. Consequently, sociologists avoid the strictly spiritual side of religion and focus on social aspects of religion that we can measure and observe.

Objectivity, as we saw in Chapter 2, is a goal for which scientists strive. Because there are so many emotional overtones in the study of religion, researchers must be especially vigilant of their own biases. Thus, sociologists investigating religion do not attempt to determine the truth or falseness of any religion. Because scientists avoid definitions of good or bad, truth or falsity, theological issues lie beyond the sociology of religion. Sociologists can point out that conceptions of God, religious beliefs, and religious practices vary from culture to culture without attempting to make value judgments of any of the beliefs and practices involved. Because the validity of any religion is founded in faith, sociologists restrict themselves to the social manifestations of religion.

For this reason, it is possible for sociologists to retain a personal religious faith while investigating the social dimensions of religion. In fact, sociologists, like other people, vary in their religious orientations. They have varying degrees of religious commitment, exhibit myriad religious behaviors, and belong to quite different religious organizations.

Theoretical Perspectives **R1**

The functionalist and conflict perspectives have different views of the sociological dimensions of religion. We begin with functionalism, which examines the role of religion in relation to the functions it serves for society.

Functionalism and Religion

We know from archaeological discoveries and anthropological observations that religion has existed in some form in virtually all societies (Nielsen et al. 1993). The earliest evidence of religion dates as far back as 50,000 B.C., when humans had already begun to bury their dead—a practice that suggests belief in some existence after death. In early Rome, there were specific gods for objects and events—a god of trees, a god of money, a goddess of fever. According to the ancient Hebrew religious texts (both the Book of Genesis and the Book of Leviticus), pigs were unclean animals whose pollution would spread to all who touched or tasted them. To the tribes of New Guinea and the Pacific Melanesian Islands, on the other hand, pigs are holy creatures worthy of ancestral sacrifice (M. Harris 1974).

Emile Durkheim, the first sociologist to examine religion scientifically, wondered why it is that all societies have some form of religion. In one of his books, *The Elementary Forms of Religious Life* (1995; originally published in 1915), Durkheim offered a sociological explanation for the ubiquity of religion, an explanation rooted in the function religion performs for society. The essential function of religion, he believed, was to provide through sacred symbols a mirror for members of society to see themselves. Through religious rituals, people worship their society and thereby remind themselves of their shared past and future existence. Following Durkheim's lead, sociologists identify the following social functions of religion: (1) to legitimate social arrangements, (2) to encourage a sense of social unity, (3) to provide a sense of meaning, and (4) to promote a sense of belonging.

Q **How does religion legitimate social arrangements?** *Legitimation* justifies and explains the status quo. It explains why a society is—and should be—the way it is. Legitimations tell us why some people have power and others do not, and why some are rich and others poor. Many such legitimations are based on religion. According to Durkheim, legitimation is the central function of religion. For him, ideas of the sacred within a society represent the society itself. When people think of their souls, Durkheim believed, they are really thinking of the social element within themselves—an element that is superior to them and will live on after them.

If, as Durkheim believed, religion is a representation of society, its power to provide legitimation for society is considerable. Through its system of beliefs, a religion explains the nature of social life, the existence of evil, and the imperfect nature of the world. Religion has been used to justify slavery in America (many ministers in the nineteenth-century South preached that African Americans were descendants of Ham, a son of Noah whose ancestors were condemned to slavery) and male superiority (Eve was created from one of Adam's ribs, and it was her encouragement that led Adam to eat the forbidden apple). One of the most important and widely agreed-on social functions of religion, then, is the legitimation or justification of social arrangements.

Q **How does religion promote social unity?** Religion, according to Durkheim, is a glue that holds society together. Without religion, society would be chaotic. As Cuzzort and King have stated, Durkheim "provided the greatest justification for religious doctrine ever granted by a social scientist when he claimed that all societies must have religious commitments. Without religious dedication there is no social order" (Cuzzort and King 1976:43). In some cases, however—Northern Ireland being one example—religion provokes societies to fragment, even to the point of civil war. Thus, whereas it is accurate to say that religion is usually a source of social unity, it can also divide a society (Lilla 2008; Putnam and Campbell 2010).

Q **How does religion provide a sense of meaning?** Religion not only legitimates existing social arrangements and encourages social unity but also provides individuals meaning beyond day-to-day life. People mark important events in life—birth, sexual maturity, marriage, death—with religious ceremonies and explain such events in religious terms. Religion gives believers cosmic significance and gives eternal significance to a short and uncertain earthly existence.

Q **How does religion promote a sense of belonging?** Religious organizations provide opportunities for people to share significant commonalties—ideas, a way of life, an ethnic background. Religion supplies a kind of group identity. People usually join religious organizations freely and feel a degree of influence within these organizations. For many people in modern society, membership in a religious organization provides a sense of community. This counteracts depersonalization, powerlessness, and rootlessness.

Of course, religious organizations are not unique in providing a sense of belonging. Fraternal groups, clubs, and other voluntary associations do the same thing. Because of religion's other functions, however, the sense of belonging to a religious organization can be particularly appealing.

Conflict Theory and Religion

As noted, Durkheim believed that religion supports societies by providing legitimation for social arrangements. Durkheim's ideas are still debated, however, and other sociological theorists have identified quite different relationships between religion and society.

Georg Friedrich Hegel, an eighteenth-century German philosopher, believed that ideas and beliefs, including religious ones, determine the nature of social life. Ideas and beliefs, Hegel thought, cause social life to be structured in certain ways. Hegel's position was very popular within the religious and intellectual establishment of his day, but it was not without critics. By the early nineteenth century, a group of critics known as the young Hegelians had begun to develop a radical makeover of Hegel's position. They claimed to set Hegel "on his head." Social structure determines

ideas and beliefs, not the other way around. More specifically, the economic structure of a society determines the nature of the society's religion. Karl Marx, deciding the group had gone too far the other way, developed a view encompassing both ideas and structure.

Q **How did Marx view religion?** Marx believed that once people create a unified system of sacred beliefs and practices, they act as if it were something beyond their control. They become "alienated" from the religious system they set up. Although humans have the power to change (or, better yet, in Marx's mind, to abandon) the religion they have created, they don't do so because they see it as a binding force to which they must conform.

The ruling class, Marx wrote, uses religion to justify its economic, political, and social advantage over the oppressed. The elite attribute poverty, degradation, and misery to God's will. So to eliminate inequalities and injustices is to tamper with God's plan. Change is sacrilegious to the elite. Many illustrations of ties between the elite and religion exist; in fact, a close relationship between the dominant classes and the church is the rule in human history. The Catholicism of medieval Europe, for example, was so closely identified with the upper classes that the lower and lower middle classes welcomed the Protestant Reformation. In his classic study *Millhands and Preachers*, Liston Pope (1942) documented a case of religious control by the managers of a mill in a North Carolina community (Gastonia):

> *The churches were inextricably bound to mill management by their finances if not by their ideology. Organized religion was a key instrument in creating a manipulable labor force and in resisting the union's effort to break with the exploitative status quo. Ministers not only justified management practices; they were mute in reaction to the violent recriminations exerted by the community against the union organizers.* (Pope 1942:xx)

In a restudy of Gastonia, churches were still providing latent support for long-standing economic relations in the community.

In addition, Marx contended, the oppressed employ religion to explain and justify their deplorable existence and to provide hope for a better life after death. In this way, they can find self-fulfillment in their oppression. Marx thought of religion as a narcotic for the oppressed:

> *Religious suffering is at the same time an expression of real suffering and a protest against real suffering. Religion is the sign of the oppressed creature, the sentiment of a heartless world, and the soul of soulless condition. It is the opium of the people.* (quoted in Bottomore 1963:43–44; originally published by Karl Marx in 1844)

We know from artifacts that religion is an important part of almost all societies. Consider this painting of the Pope being carried on his papal throne around 1600.

Hutton Archive/Getty Images

If people abandoned the religion of their oppressors, Marx alleged, they would turn from the comforts offered by an afterlife and instead concentrate on the present. This would lead them to reject their oppressed economic condition and decide to do something about it. Nonetheless, Marx recognized that it would be difficult for the oppressed to view their religion as a manipulation of the elite. A contemporary scholar of ideology highlights the latter point:

> The most efficient oppressor is the one who persuades his underlings to love, desire and identify with his power, and any practice of political emancipation thus involves that most difficult of all forms of liberation, freeing ourselves from ourselves. (Eagleton 1994:xiii–xiv)

Capitalism and the Protestant Ethic

How did Weber view the place of religion in social life? Whereas Marx contended that religion retards social change because the elite wish to maintain the status quo, Max Weber (1958; originally published in 1904) supposed that religion sometimes encourages social change. Weber looked for a case that would demonstrate his point and found it in the relationship between the ideas of early Protestantism and the rise of capitalism.

Weber began with the fact that capitalism was widespread only in northwestern Europe and America. Why had this happened? Why had capitalism not emerged as the basic economic system in other parts of the world? Through an extensive study of various religions of the world, Weber (1951, 1952, 1958, 1964) found a possible answer in the basic compatibility between what he termed the spirit of capitalism and the Protestant ethic.

Q **What is the relationship between the spirit of capitalism and the Protestant ethic?** Capitalism, Weber noted, involved a radical redefinition of work. With capitalism, work became a moral obligation rather than a mere necessity. Capitalism also required the reinvestment of profits, if businesses were to grow. Because capitalism involved the reinvestment of capital, investment for the future was more important than immediate consumption. All of this Weber called the **spirit of capitalism.**

Although most major religions did not define hard work as an obligation or demand the reinvestment of capital for further profits (rather than for immediate enjoyment), some Protestant sects did. Here, then, embodied in Protestantism, was a cluster of values, norms, beliefs, and attitudes that favored the emergence of modern capitalism. Weber referred to this cluster of values and attitudes stressing hard work, thrift, and discipline as the **Protestant ethic.**

Q **What is the nature of the Protestant ethic?** Weber found the roots of the Protestant ethic in the seventeenth-century Puritan theology of Calvinism.

The theology of sixteenth-century theologian John Calvin formed the basis for the Protestant ethic.

Of particular importance was the Calvinist belief that every person's eternal fate was unalterably predetermined by God, at birth—predestination. Society, the Calvinists believed, was divided into the few who were elected to salvation and the many who were predestined to spend eternity in hell. Individuals could do nothing to alter their fate.

Calvinism taught its followers to look for signs of God's blessing because, according to Calvin, God identifies his elect by rewarding them in this world. This was translated into the belief that the more successful people were in this life, the more sure they were of being a member of God's select few. In addition, consumption beyond necessity was considered sinful; those who engaged in self-pleasure were agents of the devil. Finally, Calvinists believed that there was an underlying purpose of life: glorification of God on earth through one's occupational calling. Because everyone's material rewards were actually God's and the purpose of life was to glorify God, profits should be multiplied (through reinvestment) rather than used in the pursuit of personal pleasures.

Other Protestant religious beliefs may have contributed to the development of capitalism. For example, Protestants endorsed the idea that salvation came from unselfish good works here on earth. Therefore, the Protestants' beliefs encouraged them to do more and more work while receiving less and less of the material rewards.

Q Does the Protestant ethic still exist? The debate over Weber's Protestant ethic continues (MacKinnon 1988a, 1988b; Zaret 1992; Lehrmann and Roth 1993; R. F. Hamilton 1996; J. Cohen 2002). However, any link between Protestantism and economic behavior that may have existed 200 years ago appears to be rather weak today. Surveys show that Protestants do not value success and hard work any more than Catholics do. Moreover, Jews have higher incomes and are more successful occupationally than Protestants. If the Protestant ethic still exists, it does not appear to be the exclusive property of Protestants. As a matter of fact, it may not be the property of any religious group.

Q Did Protestantism precipitate the development of capitalism? Weber did not contend that capitalism developed *because* of Protestantism. (Capitalism had actually flourished among Catholics in some parts of the world before the Protestant Reformation.) He did, however, suggest that early Protestantism seems to have provided a social environment *conducive* to the emergence of this economic system. Weber's emphasis on the influence of ideas on social structure remains important as a counterpoint to Marx's accent on the effect of social structure (economy) on ideas. He recognized that capitalism could exist apart from Protestant dogma. Weber himself pointed out that capitalism helped destroy many of the foundations of Protestantism. He was well aware that from the seventeenth century on, religion gradually lost its hold over capitalist society. Jere Cohen (2002) concludes that Weber's exaggeration of the effects of Protestantism on the development of modern capitalism should not cause us to overlook the real economic impact of Protestantism.

Gender and Religion

Conflict theorists view religion as a primary source of division and strife within societies and between societies. They point out that most wars are grounded in religious conflict. The Arab–Israeli–United States conflict is only one of the most current illustrations. War, however, is only one manifestation of religious-based conflict. Less visible forms of conflict are generated by the efforts of religious elites to maintain control over an entire society or subgroups within a society. An important instance is male domination of women that exists in most of the world's major religions (McGuire 2001).

For starters, feminists see the assumed maleness of the Supreme Being, in all major religions, as blatant sexism. Female inferiority and subordination, they argue, is prominent in all sacred texts of the major religions. Orthodox Jewish males thank God daily that they were not born female. In the Muslim Koran, the superiority of men over women comes from God-given gender differences. The account of creation in the Christian

Bible blames Eve for the eating of forbidden fruit and announces an eternal punishment for women: "In sorrow thou shalt bring forth children; and thy desire shall be to thy husband, and he shall rule over you" (Genesis 3:16).

Despite the plethora of positive statements about women attributed to Jesus in the New Testament, the negative view in Genesis has historically dominated the Christian view of gender. And even after the many significant contributions women made to American religious denominations over the centuries, gender inequalities in modern religious practices and organization continue to reflect the maintenance of male patriarchy (Benowitz and Vowels 1998).

Since the early 1980s, feminists have worked against male patriarchy in Christian religious organizations. Their results are meager. This is partly because many major religious organizations, including Roman Catholics, Eastern Orthodox churches, conservative and Orthodox Jews, and Missouri Synod Lutherans, continue to bar female ordination. And women are at an extreme disadvantage even within religious organizations that accept their ordination. Although the increasing number of female seminarians and ordained ministers is one important consequence of feminist efforts to eradicate sexism in churches, their number remains small. Even after ordination, women face a glass ceiling, salaries below those of male ministers, and assignment to small congregations. These conditions frustrate female ministers as well as discourage women from preparing for ordination.

An Evaluation

Interpretations of the relationship between religion and social change, as the preceding paragraphs show, are varied. Marx, writing from the conflict perspective, believed that religion retards social change in part because of its ties to an economic elite. Unlike Marx, Weber argued that religion could encourage social change by supporting new social arrangements.

Although the two views appear contradictory, each may be viable under particular conditions. Meredith McGuire (2008) suggested that the relationship between religion and social change depends on several situations: quality of religious beliefs and practices existing in a society, dominant ways of thinking in a culture, social location of religion within a larger society, and internal structure of religious organizations and movements. For example, McGuire argues that religion is likely to promote change if it provides a critical standard against which the established social system can be measured. When religion provides such a standard, it allows the social critic to say, "This is what we say is the right way to act, but look how far our group's actions are from these standards!" For

example, during the American civil rights movement religious leaders pointed to American values of equality and opportunity and their incompatibility with racial discrimination.

The degree of a society's network for change is another factor. In many Latin American countries, for example, the Roman Catholic Church plays an important role in social change and protest because it is the sole dissenting grassroots organization with an established network and sympathetic leanings. When other channels for action exist—such as interest groups—religion may play a minor role in social change.

The relationship of religion to social change, then, is quite variable. Although the interpretations developed by Marx and Weber call attention to specific aspects of that relationship, no single interpretation appears applicable to all situations.

Symbolic Interactionism and Religion

Sociologist Peter Berger (1990) captured the relationship between religion and **symbolic interactionism** in his book *The Sacred Canopy*. In this book, Berger explores the idea that humans create from their religious traditions a canopy, or cover, of symbolic meanings to lay over the secular world. These meanings are used to illuminate the difference between the sacred and the profane and to guide everyday social interaction. A canopy of religious beliefs, rituals, and ideas provides stability and security in a changing and uncertain existence.

Symbolic interactionism, for example, helps us understand the expression "There are no atheists in foxholes." Insecurity and uncertainty, of course, are at a peak in the life-and-death situation of war, and the desire to regain security and certainty is a natural human response. Religious meanings, especially those related to a possible afterlife, can offer some relief. Like the Japanese kamikaze pilots in World War II, Middle Eastern terrorists can infuse into suicidal behavior the meaning of a reward beyond life. Less dramatically, people enduring troubled marriages can be strengthened by their commitment to uphold their holy vows of matrimony spoken in a place of worship.

So far, we portray the interplay between religion and society as one-way. Religion does bestow meanings on social life, but the reverse is also true; social change within a society also influences religious beliefs, rituals, and ideas. As scientific knowledge began to increase with the Enlightenment, religious beliefs in the West also began to change. Gradually, the belief that devils inhabited witches weakened. An understanding of the universe slowly emptied the prisons of scientists who disputed the theological truism of an earth-centered solar system. In our own time, most Protestants now commit the former heresy

TABLE 14.1

FOCUS ON THEORETICAL PERSPECTIVES: Religion

This table shows that in examining religion, the three major perspectives focus on different aspects. Discuss the conclusion on any one of the theories in light of your experience with the institution of religion.

Theoretical Perspective	Concept	Example
Functionalism	• Religion makes specific contributions to society.	• Legitimates social arrangements • Promotes social unity • Provides a sense of understanding • Encourages a sense of belonging
Conflict theory	• Elites use religion to manipulate the masses.	• Religion is used by the most powerful to justify their economic, political, and social advantage.
Symbolic interactionism	• People create symbolic meanings from their religious beliefs, rituals, and ideas.	• People use their socially created symbolic meanings to guide everyday social interaction.

of practicing birth control, without negative church sanction. Given the widespread practice of birth control among the Catholic laity, one can almost imagine the distant acceptance of birth control methods by the Church itself. And tide of gender equality seems certain to erode the rejection of female ministers within Protestant faiths (Eck 2002).

Each of the three major theoretical perspectives aids the scientific study of religion. Table 14.1 shows the unique light each perspective sheds.

Religion: Structure and Practice [R1]

Religious Organization

Major religious faiths in the world include Christianity, Judaism, Islam, Hinduism, and Buddhism. Because most people practice religion through some organizational

CHECK YOURSELF **14.2** [R2]

Theoretical Perspectives

1. According to Karl Marx, religion is a force working for
   a. the good of all people.
   b. the good of the proletariat.
   c. maintenance of the status quo.
   d. the creation of conflict between the classes.
2. According to Marx, religion is created by the _____ to justify its economic, political, and social advantages over the oppressed.
3. The _____ is the belief that work is an obligation and that capital should be reinvested for further profits rather than used for immediate enjoyment.
4. According to Max Weber,
   a. early Protestantism provided a social environment conducive to capitalism.
   b. capitalism developed because of Protestantism.
   c. capitalism strengthened Protestantism.
   d. religion will always be linked with economy.
5. Religion
   a. has been found to promote social change under almost all conditions.
   b. is unrelated to social change.
   c. promotes social change only under certain conditions.
   d. always supports the interests of underprivileged groups in society.

Answers: 1. c; 2. elite; 3. Protestant ethic; 4. a; 5. c

The Amish are a religious sect. How does a sect differ from a church, denomination, or cult?

Andre Jenny / Alamy

structure, religious organization is an important component of the sociological study of religion. Early scholars identified four basic types of religious organization: ecclesia, denomination, sect, and cult (Troeltsch 1931; Niebuhr 1968; originally published in 1929). A religious faith may be practiced through any one of these types of religious organizations.

Q **How do sociologists distinguish among the basic types of religious organization?** The rarest type of religious organization today is the **ecclesia,** a state religion either headed by religious leaders or heavily influenced by a religious elite. Under this type of religious organization there is no separation between church and state. Since there is no separation between church and state, there is no separation between citizenship and church membership. Everyone born into the country is automatically a member of the church. Outsiders wishing to live in the country must either convert or face considerable discrimination or expulsion.

Examples of ecclesia from the past include England (Anglican), France (Roman Catholic), and Sweden (Lutheran). There is a struggle to establish Islamic ecclesia in the Middle East today. Political and religious leaders are virtually the same in Saudi Arabia and Iran. In Afghanistan, Islam is the official religion to which virtually all Afghans belong. The state religion of Pakistan is Islam and is practiced by all except a small percentage of Christians, Hindus, and various other religions. None of these countries have pure ecclesia. Saudi Arabia, for example, does not require citizens or visitors to be Muslim and the Afghan government allows the practice of other religions so long as they conform to the Islam-centered law. Still, the ecclesia in the Middle East

comes close to the ideal, as in Saudi Arabia where converting from Islam to another religion carries the death penalty for citizens, and where religious freedom is severely restricted.

A **denomination** is one of several religious organizations that most members of a society accept as legitimate. Because denominations are not tied to the state, membership in them is voluntary, and competition among them for members is socially acceptable. Being one religious organization among many, a denomination generally accepts the values and norms of the secular society and the state, although it may at times be in opposition to them. Most American "churches"—Methodist, Episcopalian, Presbyterian, Baptist, Roman Catholic, Reformed Jewish—are actually denominations (Mead, Hill, and Atwood 2010).

A **sect** is a religious organization formed when members of an existing religious organization break away in an attempt to reform the "parent" group. Generally, sect members believe that some valuable beliefs or traditions were lost by the parent organization, and they form their own group to save these features. Thus, they see themselves not as establishing a new religious faith but as redeeming an existing one. The withdrawal of a sect from the parent group is usually psychological, but some sects go further and form communal groups apart from the larger society. The Pilgrims, who landed in Jamestown in 1609, wished to reform the Church of England from which they had separated. Another example is the Amish, a sect formed in 1693 when a Swiss bishop named Jacob Amman broke from the Mennonite Church in Europe (Kraybill and Olshan 1994). Less extreme sects in the United States today include the Seventh-Day Adventists, the Quakers, and the Assemblies of God.

A **cult**, by contrast, is a religious organization whose characteristics are not drawn from existing religious traditions within a society (Karson 2000; Kaplan and Loow 2002). Whether imported from outside the society or created within the society, cults bring something new to the larger religious environment. We may think of cults as engaging in extreme behavior (see "Sociology in Your Life"). The world was shocked in 1997, for example, when reports came of the ritualistic suicides of thirty-nine members of the Heaven's Gate cult in California (E. Thomas 1997). Dwarfing this incident was the mass killing of approximately 1,000 members of the Ugandan cult called the Movement for the Restoration of the Ten Commandments of God ("Cult Killings Exceed Jonestown Toll" 2000). Cults do not usually appear in such an extreme and bizarre form, however. More conventional examples of cults are the Unification Church, the Divine Light Mission, and the Church of Scientology (C. S. Clark 1993).

Although the term *cult* covers a wide range of groups and organizations, the religious cults in the United States today share several characteristics. At their center are an authoritarian structure, rejection of the secular world's laws and ways, strict discipline of adherents, rigidity in thinking, conviction of sole possession of truth and wisdom, belief in the group's moral superiority, and discouragement of individualism (Appel 1983; J. J. Collins 1991; Lewis 2004). More is said about cults later.

Religiosity

For many years, Charles Glock and Rodney Stark (1965, 1968) explored religious experiences in relation to **religiosity**—the ways in which people express their religious interests and convictions. These authors' work focuses on the types of religious attitudes and behavior people display in their everyday lives.

Q How do people display religiosity? Glock and Stark distinguish five dimensions of religiosity: belief, ritual, intellectual, experience, and consequences. *Belief* refers to what a person considers to be true. People may, for example, believe that Christ died on the cross for everyone, or that there is no God but Allah. A *ritual* is a religious practice that members of a religion perform. A ritual may be private (personal prayer) or public (attending mass). The *intellectual* dimension of religiosity may involve knowledge of the Bible or an interest in such religious aspects of human existence as evil, suffering, and death. A society expects religious persons to be informed about their faith. *Experience* encompasses certain feelings attached to religious expression. This dimension is the hardest to measure, but James Davidson (1975) contended that researchers can ascertain experience by asking people whether or not they think specific religious experiences are desirable and whether or not they have had any specific religious experiences themselves. *Consequences* are the

---

CHECK YOURSELF 14.3 **R2**

Religion: Structure and Practice

1. Match the following descriptions with the types of religious organizations.
   - ____ a. church
   - ____ b. sect
   - ____ c. denomination
   - ____ d. cult
   - ____ e. ecclesia

   (1) a religious organization whose characteristics are not drawn from existing religious traditions within a society

   (2) an exclusive and cohesive religious organization based on the desire to reform the beliefs and practices of another religious organization

   (3) a life-encompassing religious organization to which all members of a society belong

   (4) one of several religious organizations within a society that are considered legitimate

2. _____ refers to the ways people express their religious interests and convictions.

3. Match the dimensions of religiosity with the examples beside them.
   - ____ a. Belief
   - ____ b. ritual
   - ____ c. intellectual
   - ____ d. experience
   - ____ e. consequences

   (1) prayer in church
   (2) knowing the content of the Koran
   (3) having seen an angel
   (4) conviction that the Bible is divinely inspired
   (5) marching in support of prayer in schools

Answers: 1. a. (3), b. (2), c. (4), d. (1); 2. Religiosity; 3. a. (4), b. (1), c. (2), d. (3), e. (5)

Understanding the Danger of Cults

In late November 1978, news began to arrive in the United States that a semireligious, socialistic colony in Guyana, South America, headed by the Reverend Jim Jones—founder of the California-based People's Temple—had been the scene of a shocking suicide-murder rite in which some 900 people died from cyanide poisoning. Many Americans wondered how people could have become involved in something like that.

Some dismissed the participants as ignorant or mentally unbalanced. But as more news came out, it became known that many of the members were fairly well-educated young people and that Jones was trusted and respected by some members of the California political establishment. We also learned that such events, although rare, have occurred before.

Why are people willing to join extremist religious groups? Sociology can help us understand the motivations.

- Most converts to extremist religious groups seek friendship, companionship, acceptance, warmth, and recognition. These groups can provide a supportive community that helps overcome past loneliness and isolation. They can provide emotional ties that converts have not found at home,

school, church, or work. Many groups even adopt kinship terms to give recruits new identities to separate them from their former lives.
- Most extremist religious groups emphasize immediate experience and emotional gratification. Converts "feel" religion rather than merely think about it. Whether by meditation, speaking in tongues, or singing hymns, followers have frequent and intense emotional experiences they have not found elsewhere.
- Extremist religious groups emphasize security through strict authority. Under a firm authority structure and a clear, simple set of beliefs and rules, converts have something in which they can believe. Converts think they can exchange uncertainty, doubt, and confusion for trust and assurance through absolute obedience.
- Extremist religious groups claim to offer authenticity and naturalness in an "artificial" world. By emphasizing such things as natural foods, communal living apart from civilization, and a uniform dress code, these groups attempt to show they are not part of the flawed outside world.

Religious movements may not actually be able to meet their followers' needs any better than the outside world. Many of these religious groups lead to disillusionment, frustration, and bitterness when members realize that they cannot completely escape the outside world, which is full of uncertainty, confusion, fuzzy choices, and shades of gray. Moreover, many of these religious groups have joined the consumer society they profess to deplore, attractively packaging

and selling themselves to the public. Not only may the new religious groups not solve the problems people in modern society must face, many are as inauthentic as they accuse society of being.

Some key questions exist to evaluate the authenticity of any religious group's claims. For purposes of self-protection, these questions should be answered carefully before committing to an extremist religious group.

- Does it require that you cut yourself off from family and friends?
- Does it consider drugs to be a major vehicle for true religious experiences?
- Is corporal punishment or intensive, hours-long psychological conditioning a part of its program?
- Does it claim to have special knowledge that can be revealed only to insiders?

If the answer to any one of these questions is *yes*, you stand a chance of getting "hooked." If the answers to several of these questions are positive, the chances of getting hooked increase dramatically.

Think About It
1. Do you agree or disagree with the reasons given for why people join extremist religious groups? Discuss each reason and explain why you agree or disagree.
2. Can you think of other reasons people may be attracted to such groups? Show that any reason you identify that does not fit into one of the four reasons stated.
3. If you had a friend considering membership in an extremist religious group, how would you use the information in this See Sociology In Your Life section to discourage him or her?

decisions and commitments people make as a result of religious beliefs, rituals, knowledge, or experiences. Consequences may be social (opposing or supporting capital punishment or abortion) or personal (restricting one's sex life to marriage or telling the truth regardless of the cost).

Why use a dimensional approach to religiosity? Although the dimensions of religiosity may be related to one another (Clayton and Gladden 1974), they may also operate independently at times. People who attend a place of worship (ritual dimension), for example, may know little about religious doctrines (intellectual dimension). And some people who worship regularly may believe that people who do not frequent religious services will spend eternity in hell (belief dimension).

Religion in the United States ®

The nature rites of South Sea Islanders and the well-ordered church of the Middle Ages were relatively simple and stable forms of religion. By comparison, advanced industrial society presents a challenge to the sociological study of religion.

The Development of Religion in America

Although the search for religious freedom was only one of the reasons the Puritans came to America, there was a genuine religious element in the American colonization and revolution (Brauer 1976; Marty 1985). Robert Bellah described the American religious connection this way:

> In the beginning, and to some extent ever since, Americans have interpreted their history as having religious meaning. They saw themselves as being a "people" in the classical and biblical sense of the word. They hoped they were a people of God. (Bellah et al. 1991:2)

Religion in the colonies was varied, but beginning in the second half of the eighteenth century, the leaders of the Enlightenment—Bentham, Voltaire, Diderot, Hume, and many others—in Europe and the British Isles increasingly influenced the approach to religion. The same ideas that inspired the questioning of arbitrary colonial government and the writing of the Declaration of Independence also led to a critical examination of religion and its relationship to the state. Although the framers of the U.S. Constitution seldom raised arguments against religious faith, they were sharply critical of any entanglement between religion and the state. Indeed, the ideas of separation of church and state and freedom

of religious expression are cornerstones of American life. Despite this tradition, there have been incidents of religious persecution, including some directed at immigrant groups.

Secularization: Real or Apparent?

Religion has been an important influence during most of human history, including the history of the United States. However, the industrialization (and accompanying secularization) of many nations diluted the influence of religion (Wade 2009). As Figure 14.1 shows, religiosity tends to decline as wealth (per capita GDP) increases, except for the United States. More will be said about this fact, but first secularization needs to be defined.

Q **What is secularization?** **Secularization** is a profane process through which the sacred loses influence over society (see "Consider This Research"). Through this process, other social institutions possess less religious content and are free from religious control (B. Wilson 1982; Swatos and Olson 2000; Lilla 2008). Religion itself becomes a specialized, isolated institution. This is in sharp contrast to preindustrial society, where religion and social life were inseparable. Religious leaders and peers forced Hester Prynne, for example, the central character of Nathaniel Hawthorne's novel *The Scarlet Letter*, to live forever with shame and ostracism for her act of adultery. Religion and social life were so intertwined in seventeenth-century Puritan America that the discovery of Hester's adultery led to her loss of a normal social existence.

Q **Is America becoming more secular?** Evidence is mixed concerning the relative importance of religion in the United States today (Miller 2007; See Sociology Eyes America 14.1). There are some indications of a diminution of the importance of religion in the United States. The percentage of Americans claiming that religion is very important in their lives declined from 75 percent in 1952 to 56 percent in 2010, increased a bit since hitting a low of 52 percent in 1978, and is now declining a bit (see Figure 14.2). The Princeton Religion Index, comprised of six to eight leading indicators, also shows a decline since the 1940s. Fourteen percent of the public in 1957 indicated that religion was losing influence on American life; in 2007, 61 percent of the public saw a lessening of religion's influence on American life (Lyons 2005; Newport 2007).

Finally, while only 15 percent of Americans claim no preference for a religious faith, it is double the percentage who claim not to have been affiliated with a particular faith as children. The religiously unaffiliated are now the country's third largest "religious group." And there appears to be evidence of a further generational

FIGURE 14.1

Wealth and Religiosity

This figure shows at least two things. First, the religiosity of countries decreases as wealth increases. Second, the relatively high degree of religiosity in the United States makes it an outlier among Western nations. Why do you think this is so? Do you think the situation will remain the same or change? Why?

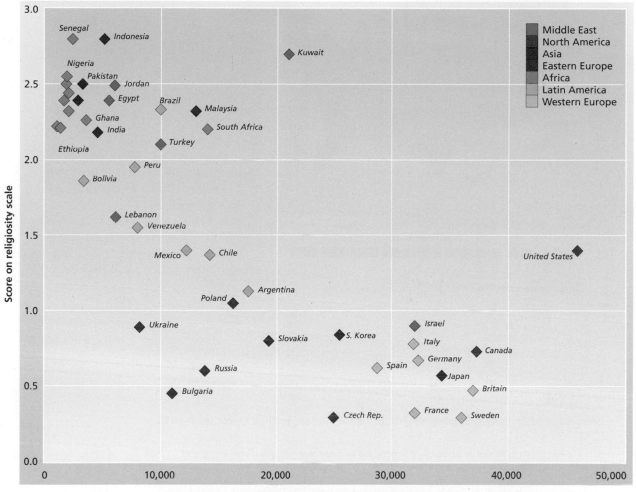

Per capita GDP (in U.S. dollars, adjusted for price differences between countries)

Source: "Among Wealthy Nations... the U.S. Stands Alone in its Embrace of Religion." Washington, DC: The Pew Center Research Center for the People and the Press, Pew Global Attitudes Project, 2002. This graphic is also adapted from Alan Wolfe, "And the Winner Is..." *The Atlantic* (March 2008):59.

shift today. Young adults between eighteen and twenty-nine are much more likely than those seventy or over to indicate a lack of affiliation with any particular religion (29 percent versus 7 percent; "U.S. Religious Landscape Survey" 2008; Kosmen and Keysar 2009; Putnam and Campbell 2010; "Religion Among the Millennials" 2010).

Q Why is the number of the religiously unaffiliated increasing? Secularization, you say? True, but some researchers think we can be more specific. Based on a national survey of college freshmen, Putnam and Campbell (2010) document the decline of religious

affiliation among America's youth. Their evidence attributes this trend to the politicalization of religion in the United States that began in the 1980s. Because young Americans are more politically moderate than the conservative (and Republican) evangelicals, they are less likely to associate themselves with religion in general.

Q So religion is becoming less important in American society? Not exactly. Researchers characterize America as being unusually religious among industrialized nations. Putnam and Campbell themselves report data showing that Americans are somewhat more religious

SOCIOLOGY EYES AMERICA 14.1

Importance of Religion in One's Life

Percentage of each state's population that says religion in their life is:
Very important

Source: Pew Forum on Religion and Public Life, 2010.

Among industrialized nations, America is unusually religious. Even in the U.S., however, the evidence on the importance of religion to people is mixed. The map below displays the percentage of each state's population agreeing that religion is very important in their life.

Question Wording: How important is religion in your life – very important, somewhat important, not too important, or not at all important?

Interpret the Map

1. From the data in this map, how would you characterize the importance of religion in the lives of Americans?
2. How important is religion to peoples' lives in your state? Is religion more or less important to you than the people in your state? Why?
3. Describe any regional pattern you see in this map. If you see no pattern, summarize what you do see.

FIGURE 14.2

Percentage of Americans Saying Religion Is Very Important in Their Lives: 1952–2010

This figure tracks changes in the percentage of Americans who say that religion is very important in their lives. Why do you think the percentage was so high in the early 1950s? What prediction do you make for the next ten years?

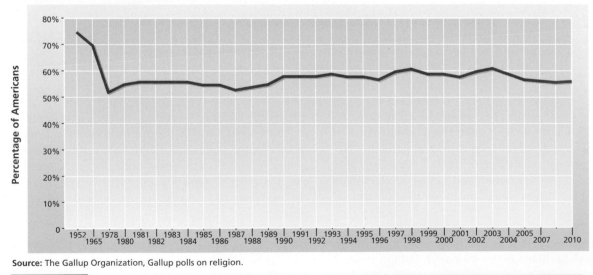

Source: The Gallup Organization, Gallup polls on religion.

INTERNET LINK The Gallup Organization compiles a tremendous amount of data on the American public's views. You can go to its website at www.gallup.com/.

Fenggang Yang and Helen Rose Ebaugh— The Secularization of Religion?

Yang and Ebaugh (2001) challenge the long-standing view that religious pluralism accompanying modernization secularizes religions. They present evidence for a new view: Instead of promoting the decline of religions, religious pluralism leads to their revitalization. Organizational and theological transformations provoked by exposure to a wide variety of religions are said to energize religions.

Their research is based on the study of immigrants who came to the United States after 1965. These "new immigrants" arrive in much larger numbers from Asia and Latin America than from Europe, the predominant home of "old immigrants." Whereas earlier European immigrants left mainly Judeo-Christian countries, many of the new immigrants from Asia are Muslim, Hindu, Buddhist, or adherents to other religions (Eck 2002). Even immigrants from South and Central America grew up with forms of Catholicism and Protestantism distinct from U.S. versions.

Data came from thirteen immigrant churches, ranging from Buddhist temples to Protestant churches. In 1997–1998, intensive interviews were conducted with clerical and lay leaders, new immigrants, and more established residents.

According to Yang and Ebaugh, these churches have prospered by adopting new organizational and theological forms. New immigrant religions are becoming congregational, theologically pure, and open to outsiders.

Adopting Congregation Forms
New immigrants often abandon the religious institutional forms brought from their home countries in favor of U.S. Protestant-style congregations, which are communities that gather voluntarily. Rather than remaining for life in their religions of birth, new immigrants feel freer to join or leave a religious group. Also, these new immigrants had been taught reliance on periodic visits to formal religious leaders at their often-isolated temples and monasteries. These immigrants now emphasize lay leadership within their local congregations, and they are providing social services and recreational centers.

Returning to Theological Roots
New immigrants come from societies dominated by one or two religions. In such societies, religion is intertwined with the culture. Consequently, being a Muslim in one country may be different in certain ways from practicing Islam in another. For example, in the United States, Pakistani Muslim men, accustomed to praying with their caps on, find themselves worshipping with Arab Muslims, who pray bareheaded. Which custom does one's pluralistic congregation adopt? Rather than attempting to make a host of such decisions, American Muslim congregations return to the original teachings of Prophet Muhammad, which they share worldwide. Various culturally based adaptations of Islam are dropped as congregations seek commonalities. Reference to original theological foundations provides culturally diverse Muslim congregations with a unified rationale for determining what aspects of their faith to keep and to discard.

Openness to Outsiders
Diverse congregations forge a distilled theological base. By reducing religious idiosyncrasies, new immigrant congregations can incorporate members from their own faith as well as from other religious traditions. Not only can Pakistani and Arab Muslims worship together, they can also attract native-born American converts. This is appealing because it speeds up the process of Americanization.

Evaluate the Research
1. Why would these organizational and theological processes of change work to prevent a weakening of the new immigrants' religions?
2. Explain the interrelationships among these three processes of change.
3. Discuss the link between these processes of change and secularization.

than the Iranians (see Figure 14.3). There are more than 300 recognized denominations and sects and thousands of independent congregations in the United States (Linder 2010; see Figure 14.4). As noted earlier, only 15 percent of the American population is without affiliation with some religious faith, and about three-fourths identify themselves with the Christian religion. About six out of ten Americans belong to some religious organization, and about half of these claim to be active in their congregations. Only about 20 percent of adult Americans say they never attend religious services, which means that eight out of ten Americans attend worship services at least "seldom." Almost 40 percent say they attend church once a week. Ninety-two percent of Americans

FIGURE 14.3

Global Comparison of Church Attendance

As this figure indicates, the United States has a higher rate of weekly attendance at religious services than other advanced industrial countries. In fact, weekly church attendance in the U.S. is a bit higher than it is among Iranians. What do you make of the large disparity in church attendance between the U.S. and the rest of the highly industrialized world?

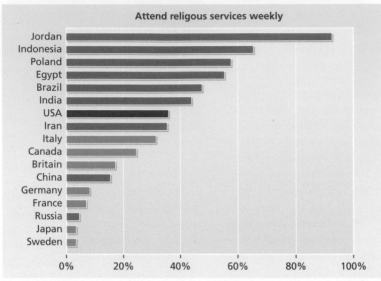

Attend religous services weekly

Source: "American Grace: How Religion Divides and Unites Us," The Pew Forum on Religion and Public Life, December 16, 2010, p. 3, http://pewforum.org/American-Grace-How-Religion-Divides-and-Unites-Us.aspx

FIGURE 14.4

Membership in Selected Religious Organizations in the United States

On the basis of these data, how would you describe the religious composition of the U.S.?

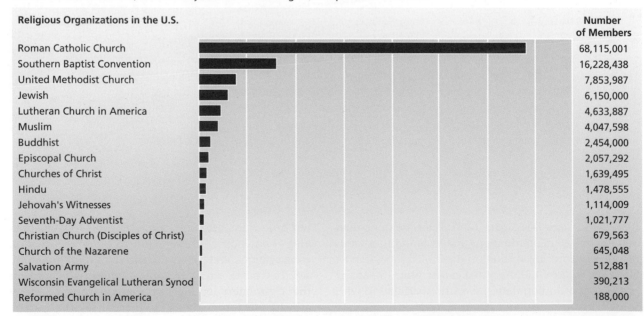

Religious Organizations in the U.S.	Number of Members
Roman Catholic Church	68,115,001
Southern Baptist Convention	16,228,438
United Methodist Church	7,853,987
Jewish	6,150,000
Lutheran Church in America	4,633,887
Muslim	4,047,598
Buddhist	2,454,000
Episcopal Church	2,057,292
Churches of Christ	1,639,495
Hindu	1,478,555
Jehovah's Witnesses	1,114,009
Seventh-Day Adventist	1,021,777
Christian Church (Disciples of Christ)	679,563
Church of the Nazarene	645,048
Salvation Army	512,881
Wisconsin Evangelical Lutheran Synod	390,213
Reformed Church in America	188,000

Source: Eileen W. Lindner (ed.), *Year Book of American and Canadian Churches 2010,* Nashville, TN: Abingdon Press, 2010.

believe in the existence of God or a universal spirit. Moreover, 71 percent say they are absolutely certain of God's existence. A majority of Americans believe that God directly affects their daily lives. Eighty percent say they use God in making decisions; 70 percent attribute good and bad occurrences to God's plan; 60 percent give God credit for the course their lives are taking (Ortyl and Minyard 2010).

Even Americans unaffiliated with a particular religion have religious beliefs and practices. Among the unaffiliated, 41 percent say that religion is at least somewhat important in their lives, 70 percent believe in God, 41 percent believe in Heaven, 35 percent pray at least once a week, and one-fourth attend religious services at least a few times annually ("U.S. Religious Landscape Survey" 2008).

Q Why is there a continuing interest in religion? Theodore Caplow and his colleagues (Caplow, Bahr, and Chadwick 1983) suggest that religion is sought as a buffer against the insatiable demands of the state. According to Gallup, Americans are searching for spiritual moorings for three basic reasons: the threat of nuclear war, loneliness, and disenchantment with what is perceived as a society without rules. Several sociologists contend that religion remains important in helping many Americans deal with problems of grief, misery, fear of the unknown, hopelessness, hunger, death, and the search for meaning beyond life in this world (Wind and Lewis 1994; Greeley 1996; Stark and Finke 2000).

Q Does this mean that secularization is not an important force in American society today? No, it does not. As Robert Wuthnow (1985) emphasizes, when Weber, Durkheim, and Marx wrote about secularization, they were not thinking of short-term, individual religious attitudes and behavior such as belief in God or synagogue attendance. They were observing major historical trends in European history since the Middle Ages, such as the separation of church and state. From this long-term, large-scale perspective, secularization accompanied modernization throughout the industrial world, including the United States (Bruce 2002; Chaves 2002).

In addition to reducing the social influence of religion, secularization promotes the mixing of the sacred and the profane (Fenn 1978). American places of worship are becoming more secular, and the American clergy are increasingly involved in community affairs. Religious leaders were heavily involved in the civil rights movement and the Vietnam War protests of the 1960s (Hadden and Rymph 1973) and are still concerned with such political issues as world peace and poverty. Although the clergy's participation in public affairs has receded in favor of parishioners' spiritual needs, the clergy remain involved in solving such social

problems as drug abuse, juvenile delinquency, hunger, malnutrition, homelessness, and school violence. Secular society is entering religion in other ways as well. Worship services, for example, use "worldly" musical instruments such as saxophones and electric guitars, as well as jazz and rock liturgies. The televangelists of the "electronic church" use many marketing and show-business techniques to attract viewers and bring in vast amounts of money (Hadden and Swann 1981; Hoover 1988).

According to C. Kirk Hadaway, Penny Long Marler, and Mark Chaves (1993), characterizations of religious commitment in America typically rely on poll data. Self-reports of church attendance, they contend, inflate estimates of church attendance. Comparing church attendance rates based on actual counts of those who attend church with self-reported rates of church attendance, these researchers conclude that religious service attendance rates for Protestants and Catholics in the United States are actually about one-half the generally cited rates.

Robert Wuthnow (1976, 1978, 1990) argues that secularization, like increased religious fervor, is a process that fluctuates in strength. He claims that the religious revival of the 1950s waned because of opposition to it within the countercultural generation of the 1960s. Wuthnow thinks that a return to religious commitment may occur as successive age groups, unaffected by the counterculture, mature.

Civil and Invisible Religion

There is yet other evidence of the enduring religious influence on American society. Look at the existence of civil religion and invisible religion.

Q What is civil religion? Every American president's inaugural address (except Washington's second one) has made reference to God. Similar religious references exist throughout American life: Thanksgiving Day is a day of public thanksgiving and prayer; our currency proclaims "In God We Trust"; the Pledge of Allegiance to our flag contains the phrase "under God"; many formal public occasions open with prayer. Even voluntary organizations such as the Rotary Club and the Boy Scouts carry out this religious theme.

None of these public religious allusions, however, involve any specific religion. References are not made to Jesus Christ, Moses, or the Virgin Mary but are made to the general concept of God, a concept compatible with nearly all religions. **Civil religion,** then, is a public religion that expresses a strong tie between a deity and a culture; it is broad enough to encompass almost the entire nation. Robert Bellah (1967, 1992; Bellah and Hammond 1980; Lilla 2008), the sociologist

Megachurches are among the fastest-growing faith groups in the United States.

Jessica Kourtoonis/AP Photos

most closely identified with the concept of civil religion, summarizes it this way:

> *The separation of church and state [in America] has not denied the political realm a religious dimension. Although matters of personal religious beliefs, worship, and association are considered to be strictly private affairs, there are, at the same time, certain common elements of religious orientation that the great majority of Americans share. These have played a crucial role in the development of American institutions and still provide a religious dimension for the whole fabric of American life, including the political sphere. This public religious dimension is expressed in a set of beliefs, symbols, and rituals that I am calling the American civil religion.* (Bellah and Hammond 1980:171)

The concept of civil religion continues to generate debate (Gehrig 1981; Demerath and Williams 1985; Audi and Wolterstorff 1996; Horsley 2003), but many studies support Bellah's claim for the existence of a civil religion in the United States (Wimberley et al. 1976; Christenson and Wimberley 1978; Wimberley and Christenson 1980; Kearl and Rinaldi 1983; Warner 1994; Heclo and McClay 2002). Martin Marty (1985) points out that civil religion is alive and well today, thanks in part to its adoption by the conservative evangelical churches, which in the 1980s linked God and nationalism. The public outcry over a federal court's ruling that bans the phrase "under God" from the Pledge of Allegiance provides strong evidence of civil religion in the United States.

Q **What is invisible religion?** Those focusing only on traditional religious beliefs and practices underestimate the religiosity of Americans (Luckmann 1967; Yinger

1969, 1970). Many Americans who do not belong to churches or sects nevertheless practice a type of religion. These individuals, according to Luckmann, practice an **invisible religion**—a private religion that is substituted for formal religious organizations, practices, and beliefs.

In a study of 208 households in Baton Rouge, Louisiana, Richard Machalek and Michael Martin (1976) found support for the existence of an invisible religion, even in a region of the United States that is deeply religious in the conventional sense. The authors asked participants in their survey to list the most important concerns of life, beyond immediate daily problems, and to indicate the means they used to cope with them. They found that 18 percent of the respondents cited such traditional religious concerns as life after death, salvation, and the existence of heaven. More significantly, 8 percent listed a variety of less religiously conventional concerns, such as consideration and love for others, the need for less selfishness in the world, national corruption, lack of political leadership, poverty, the need for social equality, and the meaning of life. One-third of the sample relied on conventional religious practices—prayer, Bible study, formalized church activities, and informal religious study groups—to help them handle their daily concerns. For two-thirds of the sample, coping strategies were not related to institutionalized religion. They relied on such humanistic strategies as reflection and meditation, participation in civic organizations, and informal discussion groups composed of family and friends.

Even people who ordinarily remain outside formal religion tend to observe religious ceremony during such rites of passage as birth, marriage, and death. For example, Gorer (1965) found that although 25 percent of his sample did not believe in life after death, 98 percent arranged religious rites when they buried their relatives.

Whether or not the United States is as religious as in the past, it is clear that religious effects abound throughout the American way of life. Americans join congregations, enter synagogues, and attend services in comparatively large numbers, and civil religion and private religion influence their lives daily. Moreover, there has recently been a revival of religious fundamentalism.

The Resurgence of Fundamentalism

Since the late 1960s, most mainline American Protestant denominations—Methodists, Lutherans, Presbyterians, Episcopalians—either declined in membership or fought to hold their own. In contrast, contemporary fundamentalist denominations—the conservatives of Protestantism—are growing. Fundamentalists (also referred to as *born-again* or *evangelical Christians*) exist in all Protestant organizations, but they are predominantly in such religious bodies as the Assemblies of God, the Seventh-Day Adventists, the Southern Baptists, and the Jehovah's Witnesses (Finke and Stark 1992; Aldridge 2000; Antoun 2001). About half of Protestants identify themselves as born-again or evangelical Christians (Gallup 2002; Green 2008).

It is, of course, inaccurate to limit fundamentalism to Protestants alone. Fundamentalism is in all religions, including the Catholics, Muslims, Hindus, and Mormons (Aulette, Wittner, and Blakely 2009). In this section, however, we will concentrate on Protestant and Islamic fundamentalism.

What is the nature of fundamentalism? Fundamentalism rejects secularization and adheres closely to traditional beliefs, rituals, and doctrines (Bruce 2007; Berger and Zijderveld 2009). It is not surprising that most religious fundamentalists are politically conservative, given that the roots of contemporary religious fundamentalism are in the latter part of the nineteenth century. Two issues disturbed the early fundamentalists. First, fundamentalists were concerned about the spread of secularism. Science was challenging the Bible as a source of truth; Marxism was portraying religion as an opiate for the masses; Darwinism was challenging the biblical interpretation of creation; and religion was losing its traditional influence on social institutions. Second, fundamentalists rejected the movement away from the traditional message of Christianity toward an accent on social service (Johnstone 2006).

The theological agenda of today's fundamentalists is very close to that of their nineteenth-century forebears. Today's Protestant fundamentalists believe in the literal truth of the Scriptures, being "born again" through acceptance of Jesus Christ as the Son of

Reverend John Hagee epitomizes fundamentalism with his strong resistance of secularization and rigid adherence to traditional beliefs, rituals, and doctrines.

God, the responsibility of all believers to give witness for God, the presence of Satan as an active force for evil, and the destruction of the world prior to the Messiah's return to establish his kingdom on earth (H. Cox 1996; Hunt, Hamilton, and Walter 1998; C. Smith and Emerson 1998).

Q **How do fundamentalists differ among themselves?** Variations exist, of course, among fundamentalists. The term *evangelical*, for example, is often used as a synonym for fundamentalism. However, when compared with evangelicals, most fundamentalists are more theologically rigid and less accommodating in their opposition to the rest of the world. Most evangelicals are on the political right or in the center, but some are on the ideological left. Evangelicals share much of the traditional theology of fundamentalism, but often reject its political and social conservatism (Quebedeaux 1978; J. D. Hunter 1987; Roof 2001). Other religious organizations that share in much of the fundamentalist theology have some unique beliefs and practices of their own (C. Smith 2000). Neo-Pentecostalism—or the charismatic movement, as it is sometimes called—has occurred for the most part within traditional religious organizations, particularly the Roman Catholic and Episcopal churches. Those involved in this movement often speak of being "born again" or of receiving "the baptism of the Holy Spirit." But central to most neo-Pentecostal groups is the experience of "speaking in tongues" *(glossolalia)*, which believers claim is a direct gift of the Holy Spirit (H. Cox 1992).

Q Why has fundamentalism reappeared? There are several reasons for the revival of fundamentalism. First, many Americans feel their world is out of control. The social order of the 1950s has been shattered by a string of traumatic events beginning with the civil rights movement and progressing through campus violence, political assassinations, the Vietnam War, Watergate, and destruction of the World Trade Center towers. Fundamental religion, with its absolute answers and promise of eternal life, provides a strong anchor in a confusing, bewildering world. Second, by placing emphasis on warmth, love, and caring, fundamentalist churches provide solace to people who are witnessing and experiencing the weakening of family and community ties. Mainline churches are more formal and impersonal. Third, fundamentalist churches offer what they consider a more purely sacred environment, in contrast to mainline denominations that fundamentalists see as accommodating to secular society.

Islamic Fundamentalism

Fundamentalists, you recall, reject the secular world and support a return to traditional beliefs, rituals, and doctrines. Originally, "fundamentalists" referred to Christians who not only believed everything in the Bible to be literally true but also rejected any scientific evidence conflicting with their scripture. Denial of the theory of evolution and the Big Bang explanation of creation are examples. In this context, fundamentalism can carry negative connotations, and unfortunately, these negative connotations often accompany a description of Islamic fundamentalism. Adding to this derogatory baggage is the erroneous association made between Islam fundamentalism and terrorism. This is ironic given that Islam literally means a religion of peace through submission to God (Esposito 2010).

Aware of this problem, scholars have attempted to distinguish among Islamic fundamentalism, Islam, and radical Islam (Davidson 2003; Haugen 2007; Esposito 2011). Just as we don't equate Christianity with fundamentalism (not all Christians are fundamentalists), scholars differentiate between Islamic fundamentalism and Islam. Like nonfundamentalist Christians, Muslims follow the tenets of their faith without rejecting all aspects of the modern world. Muslims, for example, generally support women being educated, active in social and political life, and employed. Islamic fundamentalism, on the other hand, vigorously dismisses all things Western as corrupt. They see home as the only proper place for women and think the sexes should not interact in public. In other words, Islamic fundamentalism is a subset of Islam. Radical Islam, which advocates the use of terror against the Western world, is a subset of fundamentalism (Roy 1998). Failure to make those distinctions leads to *Islamophobia*.

Q How is Islamophobia similar to anti-Semitism and racism? *Islamophobia* is fear of all Muslims based on false, negative stereotypes. The seeds of Islamophobia germinate in the erroneous assumption that all Muslims are fundamentalists and all fundamentalists are terrorists. These seeds then grow into the equivalent of anti-Semitism and racism with Muslims being judged by their "different" physical appearance as well as their religious and cultural beliefs (Esposito 2010, 2011). A constant media barrage of reports on Middle Eastern hijackers and suicide bombers only serves to further ignite the phobia (Davidson 2003).

Islamophobia denies Muslims in the United States the basic civil rights and religious freedom guaranteed all Americans. On the rise since September 11, Islamophobia reveals itself via discrimination, racism, hate speeches, physical assaults, and anti-Muslim campaigns. The debate in New York City over the proposed Islamic center near the World Trade Center site is an expression of Islamophobia, as is the desecration of existing mosques and Islamic centers. In schools, work places, and real estate offices, Muslims face discrimination, hostility, and denial of goods and services.

Q How does *Jihad* play into Islamopobia? Much of Islamophobia in the United States is due to confusion regarding the Muslim concept *Jihad*. *Jihad* is best translated as simply "struggle." The vagueness of the term *struggle* to the untutored ear makes it easy for most Americans to view *jihad* as a violent, "holy war" against the West (Esposito 2002; Schindler 2007). However, to the overwhelming majority of Muslims *jihad* refers to the daily struggle in attempting to follow the moral teachings of their faith. It is helpful to understand a further distinction between political and religious *jihad*. Political *jihad* is practiced by militant Islamic groups, and involves battling not only Jews and Christians but also Muslims who are straying from the right path. This is an external struggle. Religious *jihad* is an internal struggle between base human tendencies and adherence to Islamic high moral principles. Most Muslims pursuing a religious *jihad* find acts of violence in the name of Islam just as abhorrent as most non-Muslims do (Wike and Smith 2009; Esposito 2002, 2010).

Q What fuels Islamic fundamentalism? According to Lawrence Davidson (2003), Islamic fundamentalists believe that Westerners and Islamic modernists have failed to solve the problems confronting the Muslim world. Fundamentalists, he writes, see an erosion of their religion, culture, and political system by imperialism and secularization, absent any compensating improvement in their economic condition. So it isn't just religion that fuels anti-Western Islamic fundamentalism, but cultural and economic factors as well.

Davidson delineates four assumptions shared by Islamic fundamentalists. First, they blame the centuries of political, economic, and ethical decay on a lack of proper respect for and practice of traditional Islamic principles. Second, this deterioration has enabled the West to pollute the Muslim world with immoral and secular ways of thinking and behaving. Third, to rid itself of this decay and pollution, the Muslim world must return to basic Islamic teachings. This must involve the adoption of *Shariah* or Muslim law, while eliminating the corrupting aspects of Western influence. Fourth, re-Islamizing Muslim society requires the strong politicization of Islam. Islamic fundamentalist leaders must replace Muslim government leaders failing to conform to traditional Islamic principles. Only then will religious, cultural, political, and economic justice prevail.

Religious Movements in the United States

Other religious movements have emerged alongside the resurgence of fundamentalism (Bainbridge 1997; Bromley 1998; Lewis 2004). Speaking broadly, these religious movements embrace such varied organizations as the Jesus People (on the fringe of the Christian establishment), the Guru Maharaj Ji, the Hare Krishnas, the Messianic Jews, and politically oriented movements such as the Christian Coalition.

Religious cults are an interesting part of these religious movements. Four examples, varying in their closeness to Christianity, are the Raelians, the Unification Church, Scientology, and neo-paganism.

Q Who are the Raelians? In January 2003, a religious cult known as the Raelians proclaimed to the world their successful attempt to clone the first human being (named "Eve"). The group's promise to verify this claim with DNA evidence from the baby and the egg donor, however, was never kept. Claiming 55,000 adherents in more than eighty countries, Claude Vorilhon (a.k.a. Raël) the founder of this cult, was a French-born Canadian auto racer whose messianic vision was sparked when he was aboard an alien spaceship for a trip to a distant planet whose inhabitants created life on earth through cloning themselves in a laboratory 25,000 years ago. Raël's mission is to replace the "myth of God" with a scientific vision of creation. As part of this mission, the Raelians see human cloning as a path to achieving external life. The Raelians are preparing a nucleus of attractive females ("Order of the Angels") to welcome the return of their alien creators sometime prior to 2035 (Adler 2003).

Q What is the Unification Church? One of the most controversial religious movements is the Reverend Sun Myung Moon's Unification Church, a religion whose adherents are generally (and negatively) referred to as Moonies. Moon is a Korean industrialist turned prophet–minister–messiah–newspaper publisher who proclaims a religion that is a combination of Protestantism and anticommunism (Barker 1984).

Several interesting sociological observations can be made about the Unification Church. First—as in some of the other new mystical movements, such as the Hare Krishnas—the Unification Church expects total conformity of its members. Second, despite parental fears, its morality is generally conservative, sometimes rigidly so. More often than not, it endorses such basic American values as a powerful God, a strong sense of family, and a belief in individualism. Third, the more the Unification Church grows, the more it resembles a denomination. For example, it now has its own seminary with faculty members who belong to respected national professional societies.

Although the Unification Church is small, it has attracted considerable attention. It forced society to deal with the legal rights of converts whose family members believe their kin were brainwashed (Richardson 1982; W. Shepherd 1982; Bromley and Shupe 1984). The Unification Church has been in the public spotlight because of its economic activities. The Reverend Moon's movement now controls more than $10 billion in business assets around the world. These assets include an automobile plant in Asia, the University of Bridgeport (Connecticut), the *Washington Times* newspaper, pharmaceutical companies, banks, publishing ventures, and other enterprises.

Q What is Scientology? Scientology, a spiritual therapy inspired by the late science fiction writer L. Ron Hubbard, has gained notoriety because of the behavior of one of its famous adherents, movie star Tom Cruise. Hubbard claimed to have discovered the therapy and technique of Dianetics, a new approach to mental health that was received with faddish seriousness in the 1950s. Later, Hubbard developed an elaborate system of Scientology that included far more metaphysical speculation, particularly the doctrine of reincarnation. Hubbard and his followers claim the ability to perform mental and physical healing. Its practitioners charge for their services; they have very little formal religious ritual; and, like the Unification Church and some other religious movements, they demand absolute conformity to stated doctrines. In recent years, however, the requirement that followers sever all non-Scientological connections is more relaxed (Hubbard 1998).

Q Are Neo-Pagans nonbelievers? Neo-Paganism, the new religious movement least related to Christianity, originated in mid-twentieth-century England. Of course, its lineage extends much further back in history when early Jews, Christians, and Muslims used the term *pagan* to identify nonbelievers or "heathens." Neo-Pagans do, in fact, worship pre-Christian gods and goddesses. They characterize themselves as nature-worshippers and see the anthropomorphic Divine as Gods and Goddesses. Neo-Paganism is composed of many different traditions and is without the usual centralized control usually characteristic of religious organizations. Most Neo-Pagan groups, however, do share some key components like magic, shamanism, and environmental consciousness.

Q Are these religious movements unique? These religious movements resemble older religions in many ways. The New Testament, for example, demands that Christians place the gospel ahead of family and friends. And throughout the history of Western Christendom, movements have periodically arisen that demand absolute conformity, self-denial, and separation from family and friends who are not converted (Beckford 1985). Similarly, the political activities of religious fundamentalists have many parallels in American history, and political involvement by fundamentalist religious groups also occurs in other nations (Marty 1980; Yinger and Cutler 1982).

Nor are exotic cults new to our nation. Consider David Koresh who was a charismatic cult leader. In 1993, under FBI assault, he and many of his Branch Davidians (some sixty people, including seventeen children) went up in flames in their Waco, Texas, compound. Koresh saw himself as Jesus Christ in sinful form, and his devoted followers probably believed they were on their way to join Jesus in heaven after the Apocalypse (Edmonds and Potok 1993; Gibbs 1993a).

Why are people willing to go to extremes? Sociology cannot answer this question, but it can help us understand why people may be disposed to join religious cults.

Q Why do cults emerge? Earlier we discussed reasons for movements closely related to fundamentalism. However, such movements are not the likes of David Koresh's Branch Davidians. In this section we look exclusively at some explanations for the current rise of cults and why people join them.

Thomas Robbins, Dick Anthony, and James Richardson (1978) contend that cults are the product of a value crisis or normative breakdown in modern industrial society. In this view, some people attempt to escape moral ambiguity—a sense of personal helplessness, doubt, and uncertainty—by grasping onto a new "truth."

No one has brought Scientology to public attention more than actor Tom Cruise, a vocal advocate for the movement.

Applied Scholastics via Getty Images

According to Charles Glock and Robert Bellah (1976), interest in cults is a reaction to the excessive emphasis on self-interest in American Protestantism. The exaggeration of the parts of the Bible emphasizing self-interest has resulted in a failure to provide either social benefits or a sense of personal worth in complex urban society. The religious yearning seen in cults is geared toward socialism and mysticism, which are incompatible with American denominations that emerged from an agricultural or frontier environment.

Harvey Cox (1977) identifies four seductive features of religious cults. First, most of the cult converts are looking for friendship, companionship, acceptance, warmth, and recognition. The cult provides a supportive community that helps overcome past loneliness and isolation. The Eastern religious cults provide emotional ties that converts cannot find at home, school, church, or work. Many of them even use kinship terms to give recruits new identities—sister, brother, Hare Krishna. Often a convert is renamed. Entertainer Steve Allen's son Brian joined the Church of Jesus Christ at Armageddon in Seattle and was "reborn" under the name Logic Israel.

Second, most of the Eastern religious cults emphasize immediate experience and emotional gratification rather than deliberation and rational argument. Converts report "experiencing" religion rather than merely thinking about it. Whether by meditation, speaking in tongues, or singing hymns, adherents have the frequent and intense emotional experiences they could not find elsewhere.

Third, Eastern religious cults emphasize authority. By having a firm authority structure and a clear, simple set of beliefs and rules, they offer converts something in which to believe. Converts profess to exchange uncertainty, doubt, and confusion for trust and assurance.

Finally, these cults purport to offer authenticity and naturalness in an otherwise artificial world. By emphasizing natural foods, communal living apart from "civilization," a uniform dress code, and sometimes nudity, these groups attempt to show that they are not part of the "plastic society."

Social Correlates of Religion

Social class and politics are two important social correlates of religious preference. Before discussing them, however, it will be helpful to glance at a picture of religious affiliation in the United States.

Q **What are the religious preferences of Americans?** About 85 percent of Americans profess some religious affiliation (see Table 14.2). Although there are more than 300 denominations and sects in the United States, Americans are largely Protestant (about 50 percent)

TABLE 14.2

Self-Identification by Religious Tradition

Religious Tradition	Percent of U.S. Population
Catholic	25.1
Baptist	15.8
Mainline Christian	12.9
Other Protestant	20.8
Mormon	1.4
Jewish	1.2
Buddhist	0.05
Muslim	0.6
New Religious Movements	1.2
No Religion	15.0
Agnostic	0.9
Atheist	0.7

Source: Barry A. Kosmin and Ariela Keysar, "American Religious Identification Survey," Hartford CT: Trinity College, 2009, p. 5.

and are concentrated in a few major denominations—Baptist (16 percent), Methodist (5 percent), Lutheran (4 percent), Presbyterian (2 percent), and Episcopalian (1 percent). Fourteen percent prefer other Protestant denominations. Catholics constitute a relatively large proportion of the American population (25 percent) and Jews a small proportion (1 percent; Kosmin and Keysar 2009).

Q **What is the relationship between social class and religious characteristics?** There are marked differences in social class (as measured by education and income) among the adherents of various religions in the United States. Generally speaking, Presbyterians, Episcopalians, and Jews are on the top of the stratification structure. Below them are Lutherans, Catholics, and Methodists. When measured by education and income, Baptists, on the average, come out the lowest. Because these are average figures, there are, of course, many individual exceptions to these rankings.

The social class differences are due partly to self-selection: People tend to prefer churches with members who have socioeconomic characteristics similar to their own. The socioeconomic differences occur partly because religious organizations place varying emphasis on worldly success versus otherworldly rewards (Niebuhr 1968). Finally, a historical dimension exists. With the exception of the Jewish groups, the higher-status denominations have experienced this social benefit for a long time. Thus, members of these denominations have had tremendous socioeconomic advantages. Lutherans and Roman Catholics, in

Some evidence suggests that many baby boomers, who left their churches in large numbers earlier, are returning to their religious roots. This trend, however, has not produced the shock wave baby boomers typically cause when they touch an institution.

Michael Blann/Getty Images

contrast, tend to be later immigrants who have not had as many opportunities to achieve higher status (Johnstone 2009).

Differences in religiosity exist between the upper and lower classes. Reflecting Marx's view of religion as an opiate of the masses, many early sociologists saw religion primarily as a source of solace for the deprived poor. Research in the 1940s challenged this entrenched view, showing higher denominational affiliation among the wealthy. Further research in the 1950s and 1960s revealed religion as important at both extremes of the stratification structure. It is just that the upper and lower classes express their religious beliefs in different ways. The upper classes display their religiosity through church membership, church attendance, and observance of ritual, whereas lower-class people more often pray privately and have emotional religious experiences (Stark and Bainbridge 1985).

Q **What is the relationship between religion and politics?** Because American religious groups vary widely in socioeconomic characteristics, we must be careful when interpreting empirical correlations between religion and politics (Audi and Wolterstorff 1996). Some of

the apparent influence of religion on political attitudes and behavior is due to social class.

Followers of the Jewish faith are particularly aligned with the Democratic Party; they are followed in strength of support by the religiously unaffiliated, Catholics and Protestants. This is predictable because Protestants generally are more politically conservative than the unaffiliated, Catholics, or Jews, and the Democratic Party is not associated with political conservatism. Of the major Protestant denominations, the greatest support for the Republican Party is among Episcopalians and Presbyterians, which is hardly surprising, because the upper classes are more likely to be identified with the Republican Party ("U.S. Religious Landscape Survey" 2008).

The religion-related voting pattern in 2010 was similar to recent elections (Smith 2010). Protestants, particularly white Protestants, voted overwhelmingly Republican (69 to 29 percent). Religiously unaffiliated voters supported Democrats by a similarly wide margin (66 to 32 percent). Catholic voters, who generally prefer Democrats to Republicans, voted somewhat more heavily for Republicans (44 to 54 percent). Republican support from white Catholics was a bit stronger (39 to 59 percent). White evangelicals or born-again Christians (including some Catholics and members of some non-Protestant religions) cast the vast majority of their votes for Republicans (78 to 20 percent).

World Religions **R1**

This section is about religions of the world. But it is not about all religions of the world. There are too many, some 4,000 (Matthews 2010). By convention, though, there are three major Western religions: Judaism, Christianity, and Islam. The two major Eastern religions are Hinduism and Buddhism. The contrast between Eastern and Western religions primarily revolves around the practice of polytheism or monotheism rather than by physical location. (See "Think Globally 14.1" for the geographic distribution of the world's religions.) Our characterizations of each religion's fundamentals will begin with Eastern religions. Each description of a religion will include its origins, key figures, beliefs, and practices (see Table 14.3).

Eastern Religions: Hinduism and Buddhism

Q **What are the fundamentals of Hinduism?** Hinduism, the oldest of the religions covered here, originated over 2,000 years ago in India. In fact, the word *Hindu* literally refers to any person living in India. Hinduism is unique among the five religions in not having a specific founder associated with it. Rather, Hinduism comes from an ancient oral tradition not committed to writing until the Middle Ages (Pollock 2008). Hinduism is a

CHECK YOURSELF 14.4 R2

Religion in the United States

1. _____ is based on the rejection of the effects of modern society on traditional religious beliefs, rituals, and doctrines.

2. Which of the following is *not* one of the reasons presented for the resurgence of fundamentalism in the United States?
   a. fear that the world is out of control
   b. provision of solace by fundamentalist organizations
   c. the electronic church
   d. the rise of invisible religion

3. The origins of religious movements in the United States appear to lie in
   a. social conditions in modern industrial society.
   b. desecularization.
   c. the rising influence of the Middle East.
   d. the decline of civil religion.

4. Which of these groupings of religious organizations is at the top of America's stratification structure?
   a. Jewish, Presbyterian, Episcopalian
   b. Lutheran, Jewish, Catholic
   c. Catholic, Episcopalian, Methodist
   d. Methodist, Baptist, Presbyterian

5. Contrary to popular opinion, Islamic fundamentalism is fueled by a combination of religious, cultural, and economic factors. T or F?

6. According to Glock and Bellah, interest in cults is a reaction to the excessive emphasis on _____ in American Protestantism.

7. Which of the following religions is most closely identified with the Democratic party?
   a. Christianity
   b. Catholicism
   c. Muslims
   d. Judaism

Answers: 1. Fundamentalism; 2. d; 3. a; 4. a; 5. T; 6. self-interest; 7. d

very open faith, recognizing the divine in all existence and accepting other religious traditions. Because Hindus believe other faiths to be inadequate rather than wrong, they may adopt another religion while remaining a Hindu. The new faith does not replace Hinduism; it merely folds into it. The nature of its gods also reveals the openness of Hinduism. Rather than believing in a single god, polytheistic Hindus are free to choose which of the myriad of divine beings they prefer to worship; and they may choose different deities at different times in their lives. Most prominent among the Hindu deities are Vishnu, Brahma, and Shiva (Pollock 2008).

In Hinduism, events happening to you today are due to decisions you made in the past. *Karma* is the term by which we know this belief. Likewise, what you do today determines your fate tomorrow. Moreover, the nature of one's *karma* (good or bad) from a former life is reflected in a new life after rebirth (reincarnation). Belief in *karma* and reincarnation is related to the quest for freedom from the transmigration of the soul, the ultimate spiritual goal of Hinduism. Though there are Hindu temples and priests called Brahmins, there is no strict organizational structure in Hinduism. Hinduism is absolutely integral to everyday living; so much so that virtually any time a believer chooses is a time for worship. There are no special days of religious celebration, and worshipers, for the most part, conduct their spiritual practices at home, usually equipped with likenesses of particular gods and goddesses (Pollack 2008).

There are about 780 million Hindus today. Nearly all Hindus live in South Asia, particularly India, whose population is 80 percent Hindu. (See Figure 14.5 for the portion of world population accounted for by the five major religions.)

Q **What is the nature of Buddhism?** Buddhism originated in sixth-century B.C.E. India as an alternative interpretation of Hinduism. Its founder, Siddhartha Gautama, lived between 560 and 480 B.C.E. According to legend, his father, a king, learned at Gautama's

THINK GLOBALLY 14.1

Religions of the World   For historical reasons, all of the major religions originated in the Middle East and Asia. This uneven distribution of religions has continued from that point.

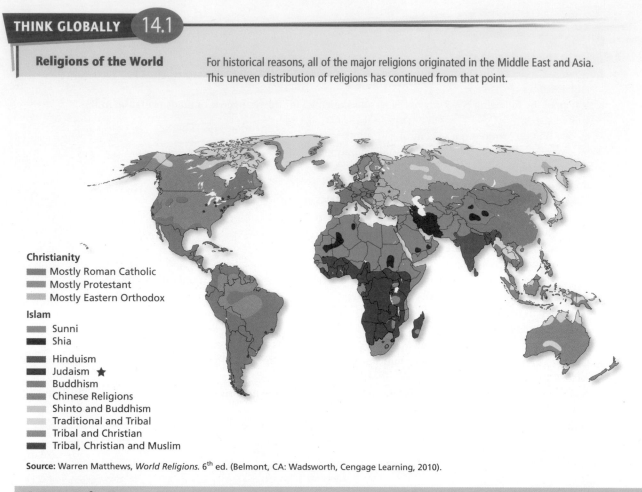

Christianity
- ▬ Mostly Roman Catholic
- ▬ Mostly Protestant
- ▬ Mostly Eastern Orthodox

Islam
- ▬ Sunni
- ▬ Shia

- ▬ Hinduism
- ▬ Judaism ★
- ▬ Buddhism
- ▬ Chinese Religions
- ▬ Shinto and Buddhism
- ▬ Traditional and Tribal
- ▬ Tribal and Christian
- ▬ Tribal, Christian and Muslim

Source: Warren Matthews, *World Religions.* 6th ed. (Belmont, CA: Wadsworth, Cengage Learning, 2010).

Interpret the Map
1. Write a paragraph describing any distribution patterns you see in this map.

2. Of these patterns, which two or three surprise you the most?

---

birth that his son would become a powerful king provided he never witnessed human misfortune or the inner peace of monks. Therefore the king surrounded Siddhartha with only beauty and light. However, the gods led the child in another direction—to view the contrast between his life and the human misery in the world and the tranquility of monks. Because of these experiences, in his early teens, Gautama decided to meditate until he reached enlightenment. Consequently, Gautama became known as the Buddha (*Enlightened One*). His first sermon after enlightenment introduced the idea of balanced living, a rejection of both extreme self-denial and extreme self-indulgence. With his friends who accepted these teachings, Gautama created a Buddhist monastic order (*sangha;* Hopfe and Woodward 2009).

As an unorthodox Hindu, the Buddha taught that all people, regardless of sex and caste, could reach enlightenment. Buddha followers were to avoid lying, stealing, and killing, as well as the worldly pleasures of improper sex and intoxicating substances. These prohibitions formed the five basic rules of ethical living. The Buddha subscribed to many Hindu beliefs regarding its many gods, but he considered the gods to be mortals. Therefore, enlightenment is a state individually attained rather than one received as a gift from the deities. Typical of Indian religious followers, the Buddha taught that each person is bound to a never ending cycle of birth, death, and rebirth. Enlightenment, achieved through intense meditation and good deeds, brings release from this cycle (*nirvana*). The goal is to free oneself from desire, thirst, and craving (*tanha*). Then once free of human temptations, an enlightened individual escapes the cycle of birth, death, and rebirth, a cycle accompanied by suffering. Upon attaining *nirvana*, one becomes a saint (*arhat*). There is no evidence

TABLE 14.3

Major World Religions

This table summarizes characteristics and beliefs of the major world religions being widely practiced today.

Religion	Origination	Key Figure	Beliefs	Main Geographic Areas	Number of Followers
Hinduism	Before 2000 B.C.E.	Unknown	• Worship many deities. Life is determined by the law of karma (the spiritual force generated by one's own actions, which determines one's next reincarnation).	India	785 million
Judaism	About 2000 B.C.E.	Abraham	• The one true God has established a covenant with the people of Israel, who are called to lives of justice, mercy, and obedience to God.	Israel, eastern Europe, USA	17 million
Buddhism	About 500 B.C.E.	Siddhartha Gautama	• The existence of God is not assumed. Through adherence to the Eightfold Path (correct thought and behavior), one can escape from desire and suffering and achieve nirvana (a state of bliss reached through extreme denial of the self).	Far East, Southeast Asia	360 million
Christianity	About 1 C.E.	Jesus	• Jesus is the Son of the one true God. Through God's grace and profession of faith, people have eternal life with God.	Europe, North America, South America	2 billion
Islam	About C.E. 600	Muhammad	• Muhammad received the Koran (holy scriptures) from the one true God. Believers go to an eternal Garden of Eden.	Africa, Middle East, Southeast Asia	1.2 billion

FIGURE 14.5

Division of World Population by Religions*

This graph compares the number of all religious believers belonging to a particular religion to the total estimated world population.

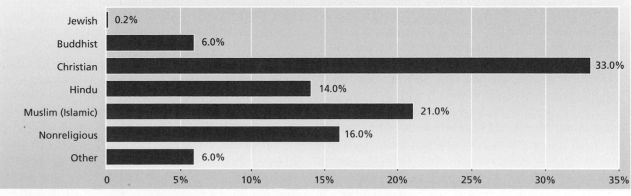

Percent of world population

*Figures shown are estimates and do not total to 100 due to rounding errors.

to suggest that the Buddha meant to establish a new religion. Only later did the Buddha's teachings coalesce into an organizational form recognizable as a distinct religion with laws and scriptures (*dharma;* Hopfe and Woodward 2009).

Because most Buddhist rituals involve an attempt to achieve merit either for oneself or for someone else, they embrace service to and respect for others. And like Hinduism, Buddhist rituals are grounded in the idea of *karma.* Formal worship takes many forms because its nature reflects local culture. Worship can occur in the home, but reverence practiced in a temple facilitates the goals of Buddhist teachings (Kurtz 2007).

Buddhists, numbering approximately 360 million, are concentrated in the Far East and Southeast Asia. This covers an area from Sri Lanka to Japan (O'Brien and Palmer 2007).

Western Religions: Judaism, Christianity, and Islam

Q What is distinctive about Judaism? The seeds of Judaism grew from a relationship of Abraham and his wife, Sarah, with a clan God. Abraham and Sarah were enmeshed in an eighteenth-century B.C.E. migration from present-day Iraq to today's Israel. Subsequently, because of a famine in thirteenth century B.C.E., the descendents of Abraham and Sarah migrated to Egypt, where they were enslaved. Moses, a Jew living in Pharaoh's palace at the time, received a directive from his ancestors' God to free the enslaved descendents of Abraham and Sarah. After the liberation, while wandering in the desert, Moses and his people created a covenant with the clan God of his ancestors. According to this covenant, Jews are to obey God's law and receive God's blessings in return. Upon giving the Ten Commandments to Moses, the clan God became the single God (monotheism) of the Israelites, and Judaism became an established religion (Kutz 2007; Matthews 2010).

Judaism is a religion of God's law as expressed in the Scripture (*Torah*). Central to the law are the Ten Commandments issued from God through Moses to the people. These commandments emphasize just treatment of others and obedience to God. We think of a *synagogue* as a physical structure, but it is more accurately a gathering of ten adult Jewish males with a copy of the Torah. Such an assembly may take place in a designated building or in a home or even in a park. A synagogue usually involves a rabbi, who is a teacher more than a priest or minister. A rabbi is a scholar who has studied the Torah and functions as an interpreter and teacher of God's word to a community of Jews. Thus, the Jewish faith is based on the written word rather than on an oral tradition, which was more common at the time of origin (Hopfe and Woodward 2009).

As reflected in the Ten Commandments, Israel's God required the practice of high moral principles in everyday life. These principles, to be applied especially to the most disadvantaged, are consistent with Judaism's history of slavery and impoverishment in Egypt. Because ritual supersedes doctrine in the Jewish faith, its adherents are free to subscribe to a wide variety of beliefs. Certain practices, such as dietary restrictions, observance of Sabbath, and religious holidays are, however, binding in traditional Judaism. Holiday rituals center on the preparation of selected foods according to *Kosher* laws forbidding the eating of certain animals, prohibiting the mixing of meat and dairy, and requiring the application of strict rules regarding the preparation and consumption of food. Prominent among Jewish religious holidays are Passover, celebrating the Israelites' liberation from Egypt, and the ten days from Rosh Hashanah (New Year) to Yom Kippur (Day of Atonement). The latter is a period of repentance. All holidays reflect Judaism's agricultural heritage, its history of oppression by the Egyptians, and its liberation by God. The rituals surrounding these holidays reinforce the Jews' obligation to help the oppressed, just as God, through Moses, helped them (Kurtz 2007).

It is out of the Jewish religious tradition that Christianity and Islam emerged. Not only did Christianity adopt Jewish scripture, it is founded on the Jewish belief in the coming of a messiah, who will establish peace and justice on earth. For Christians only, Jesus is that messiah.

There are about 17 million followers of Judaism, 5 million of whom reside in Israel. The remainder is found mainly in Eastern Europe and the United States. In fact, 80 percent of the world's Jews are in the United States and Israel (O'Brien and Palmer 2007).

Q In what ways does Christianity differ from Judaism? First, let's recognize the similarities between Christianity and Judaism, which are few in number, but important (Lee 2002). Both religions are monotheistic, worship the same God, and trace their ancestry to Abraham, a Jewish patriarch. Both faiths share the Old Testament scripture. Even the most important distinctions defining Christianity and Judaism are drawn from similar assumptions, differently interpreted.

The fundamental division between early Christians (who were themselves Jews) and Jews is traced to the founder of Christianity (Bowker 2006). While the Jews expected the appearance of a messiah (savior), they did not believe him to be Jesus, the messiah recognized by Christians. Christians embraced Jesus of Nazareth (4 B.C.E. –30 C.E.), born of the Virgin Mary, as the Son of God, sent by the Father in the body of a man, to save the faithful. All who accepted Jesus as the Son of God would have eternal life in the Kingdom of God. Jesus was an itinerant preacher, who traversed the Mediterranean, performing miracles; teaching love, forgiveness, and the need to accept God; and foretelling His death as the will of God. The Romans crucified Him on a cross in about 30 C.E., but Christians believe Jesus rose from the dead to return to His Father in Heaven. On judgment day, Jesus is expected to reappear on earth to claim all those who believe in His divinity. Believers are to have an everlasting and blissful life in heaven, while nonbelievers will spend eternity in hell (Matthews 2010).

Like the Jews, Christians also had a covenant (a binding alliance) with God. But theirs is a "new" covenant. The "old" covenant between the Jews and God was an agreement to obey God's commandments in exchange for the protection of God as His chosen people. The new covenant promises eternal life to all those who accept Jesus as the Son of God and as their savior. The difference between the two covenants is the fundamental difference between Judaism and Christianity. To be one of God's chosen people, early Jews had only to be born into a Jewish community. The Christian covenant had no ethnic or tribal qualifications. Early Christians only had to accept Jesus as the Lord, and then be baptized. Not only could anyone who believed in Jesus be a Christian, it was the duty of Christians to actively seek new members. Christians yet fulfill their faith with missionary zeal (Kurtz 2007).

This open membership policy promotes the idea that belief is more important than ritual. While followers formally worship in churches on Sunday morning, personal prayer to God is appropriate any time, anywhere. In fact, church membership and attendance is not required to enter the kingdom of heaven. The major worship rituals are Communion and Baptism, both of which reflect the new covenant. Communion entails small portions of wine and bread, consumed as emblematic of the blood and body of Jesus, who died for man's sins. Baptism, by sprinkling or immersion, symbolizes the anointment of water that Jesus received from John the Baptist.

The open arms policy of Christianity has made it the world's largest and most diverse religion. With over 2 billion adherents, Christianity, extending over the globe, claims one-third of the world's population, and is still growing. South Korea, Russia, and Sub-Saharan Africa are especially good recruiting grounds today. The diversity of Christianity is reflected in its almost 35,000 denominations located in 238 countries. In fact, a prime characteristic of Christianity is the continuous formation of new religious groups who split from a parent group (O'Brien and Palmer 2007).

Q **What are the fundamentals of Islam?** Islam shares its Abrahamic origin with Jews and Christians. Like Judaism and Christianity, Islam is monotheistic, also believing in the one true all-knowing, all-powerful, but forgiving and merciful God who created the universe and all that it contains. Founded by the Prophet Muhammad (570–632 C.E.) who received his first revelation from God in 610 C.E., Islam also claims a new covenant with God, different still from the Jewish and Christian covenants. This third covenant supersedes the covenants of the Jews and Christians, whom Islams believe have corrupted their original revelations from God. Merciful God has sent the final revelation to Muhammad with the command to summon all people to "submit" (*Islam* literally means submission or surrender) to God and become members of the Islamic community under Islamic rule (Esposito, Fasching, and Lewis 2009).

The final word of God is contained in the Koran, scripture revealed to Muhammad over his lifetime. Despite the diversity of Islam and the continual debate over the intent of the Koran, all Muslims subscribe to the Five Pillars of Islam (Smith 1991; Esposito, Fasching, and Lewis 2009). The first pillar of Islam is a declaration of faith: "There is no god but God, and Muhammad is His Prophet." The first part of this declaration recognizes the existence of only one true God (monotheism). The second part accepts the authenticity of Muhammad as God's Prophet and, implicitly, the validity of the Koran. Upon making this statement of faith, one becomes a Muslim. The second pillar of Islam is a commitment to pray five times each day—at dawn, noon, midafternoon, sunset, and evening. Muslims may conduct prayer anywhere, but they must face Mecca, where the Prophet was born and where he received God's word. The basic purpose of prayer is to reaffirm one's submission to God's will, to remind each follower that God is at the center of all things, not human beings. Therefore, prayer is an act of worship to honor God, not to ask God for special favors. The third pillar of Islam is charity. While accepting the fact of economic inequality, Muslims have a duty to help those on the low end of the economic scale. Haves are obligated to make life better for the have-nots. The Quran stipulates that all Muslims must pay an annual tax equivalent to 2.5 percent of all their wealth, not just of their income. Poor people are not obligated to pay any tax. Since God has given wealth, adherents must share it with the less well-off members of the Muslim community. The fourth pillar of Islam is to keep the fast of Ramadan, which occurs during the ninth month of Islam's lunar calendar, marking the month when Muhammad received his first revelation from God and when (ten years later) made his historic migration from Mecca to Medina (the two holy sites of Islam in Saudi Arabia). On each day of Ramadan, all healthy Muslims are to refuse food, drink, tobacco, and sex from dawn to dusk. At dusk the fast is broken with a light meal. Ramadan serves several purposes.

CHECK YOURSELF **14.5** R2

World Religions

1. In terms of deities, Hinduism is
   a. monotheistic
   b. nontheistic
   c. polytheistic
   d. controlled by government
   e. practiced only by monks
2. Which of the following is *not* a central concept in Buddhism?
   a. *nirvana*
   b. repentance
   c. enlightenment
   d. *sangha*
   e. *karma*
3. Ritual supersedes doctrine in Judaism. T or F?
4. Christianity and Judaism share an ethnic qualification test for membership. T or F?
5. Which of these is *not* a pillar of Islam?
   a. prayer
   b. pilgrimage
   c. declaration of faith
   d. reincarnation
   e. charity

Answers: 1. c; 2. d 3. T; 4. F; 5. d

It teaches self-discipline needed in daily life to resist temptations. Fasting reminds Muslims of their own weakness and God's strength. Denying bodily and psychological needs also breeds compassion for the less fortunate who know deprivation year around. Islam's fifth pillar is a pilgrimage to Mecca in Saudi Arabia at least once in a lifetime by all Muslims physically and economically able. A pilgrimage to the House of Allah in Mecca, where God made His final revelations, is intended to increase one's devotion to God's will. It also reminds pilgrims of the magnitude of equality in God's sight: at Mecca, two unadorned sheet-like garments are to replace daily clothing, which can reflect status differences.

Jihad, sometimes referred to as the sixth pillar of Islam, refers to the struggle for goodness and personal accomplishments of commendable works, as God commands. This is its nonviolent essence. Jihad has another historically based interpretation, which may involve armed conflict in pursuing the goals of Islam. These two messages of Jihad are said to be recognized by Muhammad who, returning from battle, spoke these words: "We return from the lesser Jihad to the greater Jihad." By greater Jihad, Muhammad meant the more difficult and more significant struggle against one's own weaknesses of selfishness, greed, and evil (Esposito, Fasching, and Lewis 2009).

The Five Pillars specify deeds required of a Muslim. There are also things a Muslim should not do. Among these is lying, gambling, drinking spirits, eating pork, stealing, and being sexually promiscuous (Smith 1991).

Today, there are about 1.6 billion Muslims, representing 24 percent of the world's population. Over the next two decades, the Muslim population is expected to increase at twice the rate of the non-Muslim population, reaching 2.2 billion by 2030. Islam is the state religion of twenty-five nations. While present in other areas of the world, Muslims are concentrated in the Middle East, the rest of Asia and Africa (82 percent; "The Future of the Global Muslim Population" 2011).

On to Chapter 15

The next major social institution is health care. Due to rising health-care costs, the growth of huge medical organizations, and the aging of the world's population, health care has become a major social institution around the world.

S INTEGRATED GOALS AND SUMMARY

1. **Explain the sociological meaning of religion.**
   - Religion is a unified system of beliefs and practices about sacred things. From his studies of Australian aborigines, Emile Durkheim concluded that every religion distinguishes between the sacred and the profane.
   - Because religion involves a set of meanings attached to a world beyond human observation, sociologists who study it scientifically face some unique problems. They do not evaluate the validity of various religions, leaving theological issues to theologians and philosophers.

2. **Demonstrate the different views of religion taken by functionalists and conflict theorists.**
   - Religion is found in nearly all societies. Its importance is due in part to the functions it serves. Religion legitimates the structure of society, promotes social unity, and provides a sense of meaning and belonging.
   - Writing from the conflict perspective, Karl Marx contended that religion is used by the elite to justify and maintain their power, and it is used by the oppressed to soothe their misery and maintain hope for improvement. Religion, in his view, is the opiate of the masses.
   - According to the conflict interpretation, religion retards social change because those in power wish to maintain the status quo. Max Weber, on the other hand, believed that religion could promote social change. He attempted to support this idea by connecting the Protestant ethic with the rise of capitalism. The Protestant ethic emphasizes hard work and reinvestment for profit, characteristics that were highly compatible with the needs of emerging capitalism.
   - Most of the world's major religions suppress women. Starting in the early 1980s, feminists have challenged the male patriarchy characteristic of Christian religious organizations.

3. **Distinguish among the basic types of religious organization.**
   - Two of the most important components of religion are religious organization and religiosity. The major forms of religious organization are ecclesia, denominations, sects, and cults.

4. **Discuss the meaning and nature of religiosity.**
   - Sociologists analyze the ways people express their religious interests and convictions (religiosity) by looking at five dimensions: belief, ritual, intellectual, experience, and consequences.

5. **Define secularization, and describe its relationship to religiosity in the United States.**
   - Through secularization, the sacred and the profane are increasingly intermixed in modern society. The existence of secularization does not mean, however, that a society is not religious.

6. **Differentiate between civil and invisible religion in America.**
   - Although many observers have noted a decline in the role of religion in the United States, others contend that religion may be stronger than supposed. For one thing, Americans practice both a civil (public) religion and an invisible (private) religion.

7. **Describe the current resurgence of religious fundamentalism in Christianity and Islam.**
   - Moreover, there has been a revival of religious fundamentalism in the United States. This fundamentalism, which is occurring largely outside the mainline religious organizations, shares a theological conservatism with nineteenth-century American fundamentalism. In addition, contemporary fundamentalism has its own conservative social and political agenda.
   - Islam, Islamic fundamentalism, and radical Islam are not synonymous terms. Islamic fundamentalism is a subset of Islam and radical Islam is a subset of Islamic fundamentalism. Failure to make these distinctions has led to Islamophobia in the non-Muslim world. A complex of religious, cultural, and economic dimensions fuel Islamic fundamentalism.

8. **Identify a wide variety of religious movements in America.**
   - The rise of other religious movements since the 1960s may also be an indication of a religious revival. The Raelians, the Unification Church, Scientology, and other religious movements may be a response to contemporary feelings of confusion, doubt, helplessness, and uncertainty.

9. **Discuss social class and politics as social correlates of religion.**
   - Two important social correlates of religion are social class and politics. Sociologists rank the major religious faiths by educational level, income, and occupational prestige. Also, the upper and lower classes express their religiosity in quite different ways.

10. **Compare and contrast five major world religions.**
    - This chapter introduces five major world religions. Two religions, Hinduism and Buddhism, are polytheistic (belief in many gods). Judaism, Christianity, and Islam follow a monotheist faith (belief in one God). We usually distinguish between Eastern and Western religions by their practice of polytheism or monotheism rather than by geographic location.

CONCEPT REVIEW

Match the following concepts with the definitions listed below them.

____ a. secularization   ____ d. ecclesia   ____ g. denomination
____ b. invisible religion   ____ e. profane
____ c. sacred   ____ f. civil religion

1. a state religion either headed by religious leaders or heavily influenced by a religious elite
2. a public religion that expresses a strong tie between a deity and a society's way of life
3. the process whereby religion loses its influence over society as a whole
4. one of several religious organizations that members of a society accept as legitimate
5. a private religion that is substituted for formal religious organizations, practices, and beliefs in a secular society
6. nonsacred aspects of our lives
7. things that are set apart and given a special meaning that transcends immediate human existence

CHECK YOURSELF REVIEW

1. Sociologists who study religion are normally forced to abandon their religious beliefs and convictions. T or F?
2. Contrary to popular opinion, Islamic fundamentalism is fueled by a combination of religious, cultural, and economic factors. T or F?
3. Christianity and Judaism share an ethnic qualification test for membership. T or F?
4. According to Marx, religion is created by the _____ to justify its economic, political, and social advantages over the oppressed.
5. _____ is based on the rejection of the effects of modern society on traditional religious beliefs, rituals, and doctrines.
6. According to Glock and Bellah, interest in cults is a reaction to the excessive emphasis on _____ in American Protestonism.
7. According to Karl Marx, religion is a force working for
   a. the good of all people.
   b. the good of the proletariat.
   c. maintenance of the status quo.
   d. the creation of conflict between the classes.
8. According to Max Weber,
   a. early Protestantism provided a social environment conducive to capitalism.
   b. capitalism developed because of Protestantism.
   c. capitalism strengthened Protestantism.
   d. religion will always be linked with economy.
9. Which of the following is *not* one of the reasons presented for the resurgence of fundamentalism in the United States?
   a. fear that the world is out of control
   b. provision of solace by fundamentalist organizations
   c. the electronic church
   d. the rise of invisible religion
10. The origins of religious movements appear to lie in
   a. social conditions in modern industrial society.
   b. desecularization.
   c. the rising influence of the Middle East.
   d. the decline of civil religion.
11. Which of these groupings of religious organizations is at the top of America's stratification structure?
   a. Jewish, Presbyterian, Episcopalian
   b. Lutheran, Jewish, Catholic
   c. Catholic, Episcopalian, Methodist
   d. Methodist, Baptist, Presbyterian
12. Match the dimensions of religiosity with the examples beside them.
   ____ a. Belief   (1) prayer in church
   ____ b. ritual   (2) knowing the content of the Koran
   ____ c. intellectual   (3) having seen an angel
   ____ d. experience   (4) conviction that the Bible is divinely inspired
   ____ e. consequences   (5) marching in support of prayer in school

GRAPHIC REVIEW

Figure 14.2 displays the percentage of Americans saying religion is very important in their lives since 1952.

1. Describe the trend you see in Figure 14.2. Include any significant shifts in the importance of religion that you identify.

_____
_____
_____

2. Explain the reasons for the most significant changes you see in the importance of religion to Americans.

_____
_____
_____

CRITICAL-THINKING QUESTIONS

1. Does the distinction between the sacred and the profane still have validity in America today? Explain why or why not, using examples.

_____
_____

2. Consider the four functions of religion identified by sociologists. Which of these functions are being performed by religion in the contemporary United States? Illustrate each.

_____
_____

3. Describe Weber's Protestant ethic. Explain why Marx could not have endorsed the relationship between the Protestant ethic and the spirit of capitalism proposed by Weber.

_____
_____

4. What do you think is the relationship, at the present time, between secularization and religiosity in the United States? Develop your answer with material from the text.

_____
_____

5. Evaluate the place of civil religion and invisible religion in America today.

_____
_____

6. Identify what you think are the three most important effects of fundamentalism on religion in contemporary America. Support your case with specifics.

_____
_____

ANSWER KEY

Concept Review

a. 3
b. 5
c. 7
d. 1
e. 6
f. 2
g. 4

Check Yourself Review

1. F
2. T
3. F
4. elite
5. Fundamentalism
6. self-interest
7. c
8. a
9. d
10. a
11. a
12. a. 4
    b. 1
    c. 2
    d. 3
    e. 5

15 Health Care and Aging

GOALS

- Define the concept of a health care system, and identify its major components.
- Apply functionalism, conflict theory, and symbolic interactionism to the health care system in the United States.
- Compare health care performance within developing countries and between developed and developing countries.

- Discuss current health care reform in the United States.
- Describe the aging of the world's population.
- Discuss the graying of America.
- Distinguish between age stratification and ageism.
- Summarize the relationship between health care and aging in the United States.

Is Canada our only model for a national health care system? Canada is not the only industrialized country with a health care system organized and operated by the federal government. In fact, the United States is the only highly developed nation that does *not* provide a federally centralized, free (or inexpensive) health insurance program, a service for all citizens on an equal access basis.

To this point, we have explored the most thoroughly developed institutions in modern society—family, education, polity, economy, and religion. Neither modern society nor sociology is static, however. As society changes, sociology expands to encompass the study of new social phenomena. Several additional institutions, such as health care and sports, are beginning to assume increasing relevance in contemporary society. In this chapter we explore one of these emerging institutions—the health care system. Sport is covered Chapter 16.

Health Care as a Social Institution R1

Health Care and Society

Health is an issue in every society. Whether they rely on shamans, barber-surgeons, magic, rituals, herbs, or hospitals, people develop cultural patterns to cope with sickness and death. In the 1830s, Alexis de Tocqueville noted the concern Americans tend to express for their well-being. But the current mania over physical health among Americans might overwhelm even de Tocqueville. Burgeoning industries supply the needs of joggers, weight lifters, health food devotees, tennis players, and aerobic dancers.

This American propensity for personal health is embedded in culture. Americans tend to respond aggressively to their health care needs. Lynn Payer (1996) contends that U.S. medical practice, as compared with other industrialized countries, reflects this aggressiveness. Compared with their European colleagues, for example, American physicians practice extremely aggressive medicine, and their patients expect it. Thus, American physicians are much more likely than their European counterparts are to perform surgery, run tests, and prolong life, even for individuals facing imminent death.

The Nature of the Health Care System

The **health care system** embraces the professional services, organizations, training academies, and technological resources committed to the treatment, management, and prevention of disease. The American health care system constitutes a very large sector of the total national economy. Its growing claim on national resources reveals it to be an institution of increasing import. As shown in Figure 15.1, Americans will spend over $4 trillion on health care in 2018, up from approximately $200 billion in 1960. When viewed as a proportion of the gross domestic product (GDP)—the monetary value of all the goods and services produced by the economy during a given year—these numbers reveal even more clearly the size of the health care system (see "See Sociology in Your Life"). Health care expenditures now account for about 16 percent of the GDP; the comparable figure in 1960 was about 5.4 percent.

Americans have always been health conscious, a point made by Alexis de Tocqueville in the 1830s. Yoga has recently become a popular form of exercise in the United States.

iophoto/Used under license from Shutterstock

FIGURE 15.1

U.S. Health Care Costs

This figure compares U.S. health care costs in 1960 to the present time. The direction is dramatically upward. Given these soaring costs, why do you think it took so long for Congress to pass broad health care reform?

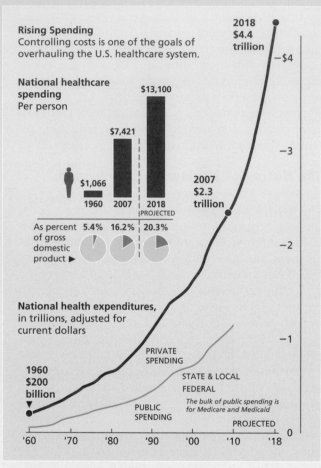

Rising Spending
Controlling costs is one of the goals of overhauling the U.S. healthcare system.

National healthcare spending
Per person

$13,100

$7,421

$1,066

1960   2007   2018
(PROJECTED)

As percent of gross domestic product ▶   5.4%   16.2%   20.3%

2018
$4.4 trillion

2007
$2.3 trillion

National health expenditures, in trillions, adjusted for current dollars

1960
$200 billion

PRIVATE SPENDING

STATE & LOCAL
FEDERAL

PUBLIC SPENDING

The bulk of public spending is for Medicare and Medicaid

PROJECTED

'60   '70   '80   '90   '00   '10   '18

Source: U.S. Department of Health and Human Services

Q **What are the components of the health care system?**
By way of introduction, let us briefly discuss four major components of the health care system: physicians, nurses, hospitals, and patients (L. D. Weiss 1997; Weitz 2010). We will cover each of these components later in greater depth.

Although physicians constitute only about 10 percent of health care workers in the United States, they establish the working framework for everyone else. In most states, only physicians have the authority to diagnose illness, prescribe medicine, and certify such events as birth and death. Though many professionals and nonprofessionals alike may attend hospitalized patients, only physicians make decisions about diagnosis and treatment. High levels of social prestige and monetary rewards, of course, match American physicians' responsibilities.

Nursing became a recognized profession only in the late nineteenth century, and its identity continues to undergo change. When Florence Nightingale left (at her insistence) with nurses and supplies to help British army doctors in Turkey in 1854, she encountered substantial resistance. One colonel wrote: "The ladies seem to be on a new scheme, bless their hearts.... I do not wish to see, neither do I approve of, ladies doing the drudgery of nursing" (quoted in Mumford 1983:289). After finally winning acceptance, Nightingale influenced the establishment of nursing schools in England and elsewhere. Although this represented a major advance in medical care, Nightingale's vision of the nurse's role was narrower than most nurses would now accept:

> She insisted that nurses should be "clean, chaste, quiet, and religious." She saw the nurse as providing wifely support, keeping the hospital going so the physician could do his important work. (Mumford 1983:290)

Possibly as a result of this initial orientation, nursing experiences frequent controversy regarding education, professional roles, and compensation.

Training programs for nurses shifted from three-year diploma programs in hospitals to associate, baccalaureate, and master's degrees in colleges and universities. Despite a need for increasingly sophisticated knowledge, college and university nursing programs were slow to develop because hospital administrators enjoyed the plentiful supply of cheap labor generated within their own hospital training programs. The shift of nurses' training to colleges and universities is now well established, but the fact that it took an interminable half a century symbolizes the professional and economic problems of nurses (Lynaugh and Brush 1996).

Hospitals provide specialized medical services to a variety of inpatients and outpatients. Hospitals range from small facilities specializing in short-term, uncomplicated care to large medical centers providing long-term care with complex technology. Typically, medical centers, as well as some large hospitals, combine research and training with patient care.

People usually enter the health care system only because others defined them as ill or injured. The definition of illness or injury hinges upon some complex social process. Symptoms that may be proof of illness in some circumstances are not in others. The elderly, for example, are labeled "ill" far more easily than young adults because of the common assumption that illness is a normal aspect of old age. Whether or not a patient's designation as sick is biologically justifiable, this social definition places the patient in a complex set of rights and responsibilities that Talcott Parsons calls the *sick role*. This leads directly to the theoretical perspectives, because the analysis of patients in relation to the sick role is part of the functionalist approach to the health care system.

Virtual Health Care?

No industry is structured like health care. The patient, in most cases, is not the person who directly pays most of the bill. The primary payer is almost always a third party, such as an insurance company or a government agency. Knowledge that the patient is not paying most of the bill has been a disincentive to cost cutting. Therefore, doctors have provided as much care as possible at the highest cost. Given this setup, medical providers have had little reason to invest in information technology such as Internet services. It was not until the advent of managed care in the mid-1990s that concern over rising health insurance premiums became an issue in the health care industry (Francis 1999).

At the start of the twenty-first century, the Internet promises to make a significant impact on health care costs. First, the Internet is selling medical "stuff" such as prescription drugs, medical supplies, and durable medical equipment. Insurance claims are also being filed, investigated, and paid online (Francis 1999; McTighe 1999). These mundane business tasks, however, do not directly affect the delivery of medical care.

Advances in the actual care of patients through the Internet have been longer in coming. Because the health care industry is fragmented (thousands of individual physicians treat patients and gather information without a central means of communication), patients and doctors have not been able to access information easily. The Internet, with its standardized language and communication formats, is overcoming this obstacle and providing vast stores of easily accessed information. This central store of data makes analysis of medical research much easier and allows patients to obtain much more information about illnesses, diseases, and doctors. These improvements in health care are expected to produce better quality care and more informed patients (Nobel and Cherry 1999). Another potential benefit is the ability of patients to communicate with one another in chat rooms and to form support groups (McTighe 1999).

One example of improvement in quality and efficiency is the treatment of chronic illnesses such as diabetes, asthma, and heart disease, which are becoming more prevalent due to increased longevity of the American population. This field of medicine, known as disease management, seeks to keep patients away from expensive health care as much as possible while delivering high-quality service. The Internet permits this because patients can take medical readings from equipment provided by physicians and transmit them to health care providers. The data, transmitted over the Internet, are then analyzed by

computer, and patients requiring special attention are made known to the physician (Nobel and Cherry 1999).

Although e-mail communication between doctors and patients is the exception, the American Medical Association states that more than one-quarter of physicians now use e-mail with some of their patients. Obvious advantages are less phone tag for doctors and fewer office visits and more rapid Check Yourself for patients.

There are concerns about the use of the Internet in health care. The most notable of these worries is the possible breach of patients' privacy and information security. As you can imagine, the information about patients' health is very sensitive and must be well protected (McTighe 1999). Another concern is the relative lack of software programs to gather, compile, sort, analyze, and access medical data. This latter problem is expected to be solved in the near future, as software developers turn their attention to the health care field (Francis 1999). Physicians also worry about reimbursement and increased liability. With respect to increased liability, many doctors fear harming patients through a misdiagnosis by e-mail and subsequent patient malpractice lawsuits (Kritz 2003).

Think About It

If the predicted changes in the health care industry are realized, what effects will they have on the social status of your physician? Use one or more of the three sociological perspectives in your analysis.

CHECK YOURSELF   15.1   **R2**

Health Care as a Social Institution

1. The _____ embraces the professional services, organizations, training academies, and technological resources that are committed to the treatment, management, and prevention of disease.
2. Health care expenditures now account for about _____ percent of the American GDP.
   a. 5
   b. 10
   c. 16
   d. 21

Answers: 1. health care system; 2. c

Theoretical Perspectives and the Health Care System 🔲

Functionalism

Talcott Parsons (1951, 1964a, 1964b, 1975) proposed a view of sickness that was distinctively sociological, rather than merely medical. For the first time, sickness became relevant to sociological theory and research. Parsons assumed, first, that health problems are a threat to society. If people are sick and cannot fulfill their roles, society will not function smoothly. Either functions will not be performed at all, or they will be performed in an inferior manner by others who substitute for the sick. According to Parsons, society responds in two ways. As a deterrent to fake illness, society defines sham sickness as a form of deviant behavior. But society also institutionalizes legitimate patterns of behavior for a sick role (Weiss and Lonnquist 1996).

Q What is the sick role? The **sick role** is a confluence of appropriate behavior patterns for people who are ill. It serves to remove the sick from active involvement in daily routines, give these individuals special protection and privileges, and set the stage for their return to normal social roles. Parsons identifies four major aspects of the sick role:

1. *They may withdraw temporarily from other roles or at least reduce their involvement in them.* As long as others agree with the sick prescription, the ailing person can miss work or school or not perform usual household duties.
2. *Society assumes that the sick cannot simply will the sickness away.* Consequently, ill citizens avoid negative sanctions because others agree that the malady is not the patient's fault. Illness is defined as a physical rather than a moral matter.
3. *The culture expects the sick to define their condition as undesirable.* They are expected to neither resign themselves to illness nor take unfair advantage of an ailment's benefits (relief from normal activities, displays of sympathy, service from others). Thus, because the sick are to prefer good health again, individuals who feign an illness have no valid claim to the sick role.
4. *The sick must seek and follow the advice of competent health care providers.* Although not blamed for the onset of their illness, the sick are responsible for their own improvement. If the sick fail to cooperate in efforts to cure themselves, society will tag them as deviants.

If any of these elements are missing, the patient may lose the privileges of the sick role. For example, the quality of care given to those who are "uncooperative" may decrease. Some illnesses, including those linked to obesity and anorexia, may negate the usual privileges if people judge the disorders to be self-imposed. The existence of the sick role and the relationships surrounding it demonstrate the social nature of illness.

Q What are the criticisms of the concept of the sick role? Several criticisms are leveled. One criticism depicts the sick role as too narrow in scope: It speaks only to Western society; it does not capture all aspects of illness; and it does not seem to apply to such conditions as pregnancy. According to another objection, the sick role applies primarily to acute illnesses, such as viral infections, which are curable. In the case of an incurable disease, such as inoperable cancer, the patient cannot leave the sick role. Also, charge some critics, the sick role does not apply to stigmatized illnesses such as AIDS and mental illness. Some also contend that the sick role is related to the professional health care system and ignores other means of coping with sickness, such as self-treatment or the use of religious faith. Although analyzing sickness sociologically requires more than the concept of the sick role, Parsons's effort was pioneering and remains quite useful (Twaddle 1981; Twaddle and Hessler 1987; Aronowitz 1998).

Q Why has the American medical profession risen to its present heights? A second relevant issue to the functionalist perspective is the medical profession's rise to preeminence in American society. In his Pulitzer Prize–winning book, *The Social Transformation of American Medicine*, Paul Starr (1983) offers a functionalist explanation for the advancement of American physicians. Using a pluralist orientation, Starr contends that physicians gained the recognition of medicine as a profession through the efforts of the American Medical Association (AMA), especially after its reorganization around the turn of the twentieth century. As an interest group, the AMA was able to wield power vis-à-vis other competing interest groups such as patent medicine producers. The patent medicine companies were direct competitors with the doctors because early physicians, in addition to treating patients, often prepared their own drugs, and the patent medicine producers offered therapy and advice in addition to selling medicine.

According to Starr, the AMA persuaded Americans that they "needed" physicians to handle their health problems. The combination of a convincing lobby and a responsive American public elevated physicians in the eyes of the American public.

Conflict Theory

The conflict perspective challenges many health care practices. Among the concerns are an alternative explanation of the medical profession's prestige,

Andy Guest/Alamy Limited

While functionalists attribute the handsome income of physicians to their talent and training, advocates of conflict theory credit the medical establishment with limiting the number of available physicians. In either case, the American Medical Association building stands as a symbol of power.

the medical institution. Thus it was not merely persuasion that promoted the interests of the physicians but, more importantly, the coercive and repressive power physicians possess because of the capitalist power structure. Navarro would point, for example, to physician attempts at monopolization through repression of alternative (competing) approaches to health care—spiritual healing, acupuncture, osteopathy (based on the idea that disease results from loss of structural integrity), and homeopathy (treatment of disease by administering minute doses of a remedy that would in healthy persons produce symptoms of the disease being treated). In fact, a U.S. Supreme Court decision ruled the AMA guilty of unfair restraint of trade in its efforts to keep osteopaths from practicing. It is these continuous conflicts and struggles, claims Navarro, that determine alterations in American society and in medicine.

Q Why do physicians receive a hefty reward? Conflict theorists reject the functionalist explanation for the high financial and prestige rewards of physicians. According to functionalist theory, the high rewards accorded any occupation, including that of physicians, are necessary for attracting talented people into demanding professions that require extensive training. But, according to the conflict perspective, occupational groups use various mechanisms (licensing, credential requirements) to limit competition. Thus, physicians' rewards are high in part because the medical establishment keeps medical school enrollments artificially low, thereby limiting price competition among physicians (Weeden 2002).

Whatever the reason, not all physicians have enjoyed the privileges accorded those in the United States today. In eighteenth-century England and early-twentieth-century France, physicians were poorly paid and were socially marginal. In the former Soviet Union, physicians received only about 75 percent as much income as the average industrial worker. Contemporary Great Britain has a few specialists who command very high incomes, but most general practitioners are only moderately well paid. Although physicians in most contemporary societies have higher status than was the case in ancient Rome (where physicians were primarily slaves, freedmen, and foreigners and medicine ranked very low as an occupation), the situation in the United States is unusual (P. E. Starr 1983).

Q Can physicians maintain their rewards? Whether physicians in the United States will maintain their privileged and powerful position is an unknown. For one thing, the number of physicians for every 10,000 people in the United States has risen sharply since 1950 (Brownlee 2007). Also, because of declines in population growth, increasing costs of malpractice

an explanation of the high income and status of physicians, the professional and economic problems of nurses, and the inequality of health care and the power of the pharmaceutical industry (Waitzkin 2000; Scambler 2002).

Q How do conflict theorists explain the prestige of the medical profession? According to Vicente Navarro (1976, 1986), the evolution of American medicine reflects the values and beliefs of American society. Navarro credits Starr with recognizing the role of the AMA in persuading American people of the need for physicians and the resulting preeminence of medicine. Nevertheless, Navarro offers a very different interpretation.

Navarro begins with American power differentials based on class, race, and gender. The success of the medical profession, Navarro claims, is due to the power it possesses because of its alliances with the dominant capitalist class, the white race, and the male gender.

The same political and economic forces that determine the nature of capitalism determine the nature of insurance, and the movement from general practice to specialized medicine, physicians are becoming less likely to work as independent professionals. Increasing numbers of physicians are taking salaried positions with organizations, or they are going into group practice and managed care organizations where expenses are shared. As these changes occur, individual physicians are beginning to lose control over their work:

> Perhaps the most subtle loss of autonomy for the profession will take place because of the increasing corporate influence over the rules and standards of medical work. Corporate management is already thinking about the different techniques for modifying the behavior of physicians, getting them to accept management's outlook and integrate it into their everyday work. (Starr 1983:447–448)

Medicine retains enough mystery that physicians are unlikely to lose all of their social status. As long as physicians use professional jargon, write illegible prescriptions, maintain control over patients' records, and force patients to wait in a waiting room "because the doctor's time is so valuable" (Mumford 1983:334), many members of society will hold them in awe. It appears, however, that their ability to dictate the nature of the medical system is eroding.

One reflection of a growing sense of powerlessness is the 2003 strike of more than two dozen surgeons in West Virginia. They were protesting the rise in malpractice insurance premiums. Pennsylvania averted a similar walkout only because the state's governor proposed a $220 million fund to partially offset insurance premiums. In early 2003, protests, work slowdowns, and work stoppages occurred in New Jersey, Florida, and Mississippi. Other doctors are protesting rising malpractice costs by refusing to perform high-risk procedures, taking early retirement, or moving from states with the highest malpractice insurance premiums (L. Parker 2003; R. Stein 2003).

Q What are some of the professional and economic problems nurses face? Role expectations and authority relationships are problematic for nurses (Shalala and Burns 2010). Although nurses tend to patients far more frequently than do physicians, the nurses lack the authority to make any but the most routine decisions. In many situations, when nurses convey recommendations to physicians, they must appear to be passive. Leonard Stein illustrates this problem of domination in a hypothetical telephone conversation between a nurse and a physician:

> This is Dr. Jones.
>
> (An open and direct communication.)
>
> Dr. Jones, this is Miss Smith of 2W—Mrs. Brown, who learned today of her father's death, is unable to fall asleep.

> (This message has two levels. Openly, it describes a set of circumstances, a woman who is unable to sleep and who that morning received word of her father's death. Less openly, but just as directly, it is a diagnostic and recommendation statement; i.e., Mrs. Brown is unable to sleep because of her grief, and she should be given a sedative. Dr. Jones, accepting the diagnostic statement and replying to the recommendation statement, answers.)
>
> What sleeping medication has been helpful to Mrs. Brown in the past?
>
> (Dr. Jones, not knowing the patient, is asking for a recommendation from the nurse, who does know the patient, about what sleeping medication should be prescribed. Note, however, his question does not appear to be asking her for a recommendation. Miss Smith replies.)
>
> Phenobarbital mg 100 was quite effective night before last.
>
> (A disguised recommendation statement. Dr. Jones replies with a note of authority in his voice.)
>
> Phenobarbital mg 100 before bedtime as needed for sleep, got it?
>
> (Miss Smith ends the conversation with the note of a grateful supplicant.)
>
> Yes I have and thank you very much doctor.
> (L. Stein 1967:700)

Despite the difficult tasks and inconvenient hours associated with nurses' work, nurses' pay ranks below that of most professionals. As noted in Chapter 10, women receive substantially lower pay for their work than men do. This is certainly the case for nurses compared with physicians. The low pay received by nurses may relate to the fact that more than 90 percent of registered nurses are female. In contrast, less than 30 percent of physicians are female.

Hospitals resisted past efforts by nurses to improve their salaries, but the nature of contemporary medical work could change that. Medical work is increasingly defined as more than prescribing medicine and performing surgery. As demonstrated by Anselm Strauss and his colleagues (1985), successful treatment requires attention to safety, comfort, emotion, and the coordination of a variety of activities. Nurses, they note, play critical roles in these tasks. Nursing itself is becoming increasingly specialized, and the need for coordination with other professionals is accelerating (Kovner 1990; Bodenheimer and Grumbach 2008).

Q How do conflict advocates view inequality in health care in the United States? The concern of conflict advocates for health care inequality begins with **epidemiology**—the study of the distribution of diseases within a population. Social epidemiologists study the relationship of illness to the social and physical environment

(Rockett 1994, 1999). Conflict theorists are interested in the reasons minorities and the poor have shorter life expectancies and higher incidence of certain diseases than the general American population. (They are aware that certain illnesses are associated with some minorities more than others. For example, African Americans are more prone to heart disease, Irish Americans to alcoholism.) Conflict proponents trace the proclivity for ill health among minorities and the poor to the nature of capitalist society. Specifically, they point to the role of the health care establishment in maintaining unequal access to medical care (Navarro 1976, 1986; McKinlay 1985; Waitzkin 1986; Weitz 2010). In addition, underprivileged people more often live in areas with heavy industrial pollution.

Q **How does the medical establishment promote unequal access to health care?** The market philosophy promotes unequal access to medical care, making medical care a market commodity. Those without the money to purchase health care are likely to be ill more often, have more serious diseases, and die younger. Unable to purchase good health care, they suffer the consequences. Health care reform is discussed later in this chapter.

Q **Why is affordable health care not provided to the poor in the United States?** According to conflict theorists, medical care is a capitalistic industry, an industry that brings to its participants—hospitals, nursing homes, nurses, physicians, pharmaceutical companies, medical schools, medical suppliers, and pharmacies—almost $2 trillion dollars annually. According to conflict theorists, these combined vested interests ensure the perpetuation of health care inequality.

Q **How powerful is the pharmaceutical industry?** The pharmaceutical industry ("Big Pharma") is powerful enough to be a primary source of rising health care costs. Rose Weitz (2010) provides an excellent portrait of the power of the pharmaceutical industry. Huge profits reflect the power of the pharmaceutical industry: It stands as the most profitable industry in the United States. This has been true since the industry's rise began in the early 1980s with the efforts of its lobby in Congress. Its lobby, the largest in Washington, has produced significant benefits for the industry. For one thing, legislation permits federally funded researchers (many of whom are university professors) to patent new drugs and subsequently license the patents to pharmaceutical firms. This arrangement farms out research and, of course, provides significant savings for drug companies. Other laws, nearly doubling the length of drug patents, extend the period during which a company can hold a monopoly. Moreover, "new" drugs that hardly differ from an original product can lengthen the life of a patent. Drugs created this way account for three-fourths of all new drugs (Angell 2004). This monopoly, of course, means the drug companies are free to set their own price without fear of being underpriced. In addition, new laws permit pharmaceutical companies to advertise directly to consumers. This marketing tool sends millions of Americans to their doctors with a request for a particular drug, and the overwhelming percentage of doctors consent (Appleby 2008). The pharmaceutical lobby continues to be successful. For example, pharmaceutical industry personnel, for the most part, wrote the Bush Medicare drug benefit program enacted in 2008, under which the federal government subsidizes the costs of prescription drugs for Medicare recipients. Its existence increased profits in part because the law prohibits Medicare from negotiating with drug companies to reduce prices.

Symbolic Interactionism

As we have seen repeatedly, symbolic interactionism is grounded in the concepts of socialization and symbols. This section examines the socialization of physicians,

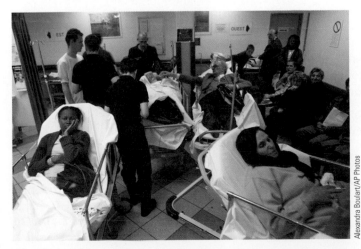

The market philosophy of the American health care system promotes unequal access to medical care. The poor more often turn to emergency rooms as a source of medical services.

Alexandra Boulart/AP Photos

the personal attributes and socialization of nurses, and the influence of labeling.

The socialization process of most physicians begins early. Those who decide to become doctors tend to do so early in life, many by the time they are sixteen years old. This is not accidental. Early decision occurs in part because many of those who enter medical school have been influenced by relatives who are themselves physicians. This, of course, also helps explain why physicians tend to come from the higher social classes. This presocialization, however important in the decision to become a physician, does not prepare medical students for the socialization they experience in medical school.

Q **What are the most common socialization experiences of medical students?** That medical students acquire technical knowledge and skills and learn to diagnose and treat illness goes without saying. In addition, medical school socializes students to accept the beliefs, norms, values, and attitudes associated with the medical profession. They learn, for example, to be dispassionate and unemotional about illness, suffering, and death; to never criticize another physician publicly; and to avoid revealing a lack of knowledge. They also learn gradually to view themselves as doctors and to display a confident, professional appearance (Colombotos and Kirchner 1986; Twaddle and Hessler 1987; Kronenfeld 1998). Medical school also transforms students from eager neophytes who wish to absorb all medical knowledge to more experienced individuals who realize that their human limitations require a selective learning strategy. They must determine what is considered safe not to learn by assessing what they think the faculty wants them to learn, a social process involving meanings, symbols, and subjective interpretations (see "Consider This Research").

Q **How are nurses socialized?** Although nurses are both male and female and come from all social classes, they tend to be white, middle-class females. Compared with the general female college student population, nursing students are more altruistic, benevolent, and generous and are less interested in power, control, and self-advancement. They prefer to make their own decisions, and they want to be treated empathetically. The four years of undergraduate nursing education supports these characteristics:

> *During their four years of nursing education, students are socialized to a nurse role that values individualized, direct patient care, rational knowledge, and innovation, and they are taught to think of themselves as autonomous, professional persons.* (Twaddle and Hessler 1987:215)

Nursing students place high value on making their own medical decisions and on their being treated with empathy. These expectations usually are not met in the inflexible organizational setting in which they work.

Upon graduation, however, nurses face a rigid, bureaucratized work environment. Their work lives are in a setting that contradicts the values they brought to their education and that their school socialization reinforced. This creates the potential for many conflicts and difficulties because nurses are constantly attempting to interpret their occupational world with symbols and meanings that do not fit their work situation (S. Gordon 2006).

Q **How is the labeling perspective applied to illness?** As discussed in Chapter 7, the labels and stigmas applied to people affect the way others behave toward them, which in turn affects the behavior of the labeled people. "Sickness" and "illness" are social labels that can stigmatize people.

Because culture varies, definitions and labels associated with health and illness are also diverse. Mark Zborowski (1952, 1969) found Jews and Italians more likely to talk openly about their pain, whereas "old Americans" and the Irish, with objectively the same levels of pain, tended not to complain. Similarly, Irving Zola (1966) reported that although the Irish did not see any relationship between their illnesses and their social relationships, the Italians presented relationship problems as a significant part of their illnesses.

Given this background, the existence of labels and stigma associated with certain illnesses is not surprising. There is no more timely illustration than the traditional view of AIDS in the United States. Because initially AIDS became apparent among homosexual men, who are already stigmatized in American society, nonhomosexual people who acquire AIDS from such sources as blood transfusions or heterosexual partners also carry the label and stigma (Dennis Altman 1986). The stigma often attaches a taint of

Howard S. Becker— Socialization of Students in White

Using participant observation, sociologist Howard Becker (1961) examined the socialization of medical students. Using a symbolic interactionist approach, his picture of student culture in medical school is not glamorous. Medical students grapple with a sense of eroding idealism, diminished concern for patient well-being, and bewilderment over the shortcomings of medicine.

Bright college graduates who enter medical school face a rude awakening. The gratifying thoughts of helping others through the practice of a high-status, honored profession are, in the first year in medical school, supplanted by the recognition of unforeseen barriers. Before becoming a physician, it is first necessary to learn to be a medical student. The medical student preoccupation blots out any images of how to perform as a doctor in the future.

Much of Becker's book concentrates on the ways students recognize and solve problems posed by their teachers. Medical students turn their eyes from the glorious distant mountain to the swamp that threatens to overwhelm them. Becker, in short, focuses on the social interaction between medical students and their instructors as they undergo a prolonged rite of passage from student to doctor.

Becker began his research without firm, testable hypotheses and without preset data-gathering research instruments. Because he wished to "discover" how the medical school as an organization influenced the basic perspectives of physicians in the making—something Becker did not know beforehand—he could not design formal research instruments in advance. This is not to say, however, that he lacked any research design. He states that his commitment to symbolic interactionism led him to use participant observation as the major research technique. Although he and his colleagues did not pose as medical students, they did "participate" in the life of medical students. The researchers attended classes and laboratories with students, listened to student conversations outside of class, accompanied students on rounds with attending physicians, ate with students, and took night calls with students.

In the end, Becker challenged the view (on the part of both the public and the medical school faculty) that medical students shed their idealism for cynicism as they progress through their training. Often-cited evidence for this alleged shift from idealism to cynicism is the detached way medical students come to view their patients. Death and disease become depersonalized for medical students. Because medical students view death and disease unemotionally, as a medical responsibility rather than a tragedy, they are viewed by laypeople as cruel and heartless.

Becker does not deny that medical students appear to become cynical and detached in medical matters. He attributes this appearance not to the loss of an idealistic long-range perspective but to the need to survive the overwhelming demands of the training experience. A cadaver, for example, is not viewed as somebody's daughter or mother but as a necessary means for gathering information for a forthcoming examination. Successful medical students ask not what they can do for a cadaver but what a cadaver can do for them. It is, in short, the manifestations of the urgent and immediate need to survive medical training that give the appearance of cynicism to outsiders.

As graduation approaches, another change occurs. As medical students lose concern for the immediate situational demands of school, they begin to display the concern for service to others they had felt upon entering medical school. This new idealism, however, is more informed than the original.

The erroneous conclusions regarding cynicism are made more understandable within the framework of symbolic interactionism. The cynicism fails to acknowledge that individuals can hold conflicting values and rely on the relevant one in a particular situation. As the situation varies, so does an individual's definition of the situation. Thus, as the students' circumstances revert near graduation, the dormant values of idealism replace the expressions of cynicism. Corresponding alterations in behavior follow.

Evaluate the Research

1. Do you think the method of investigation is appropriate? Why or why not? What other methods could have been used?
2. Does the symbolic interactionist interpretation of medical school socialization ring true? Explain.
3. If you think they would be appropriate, explain how functionalism and conflict theory could be brought to bear on the study of the socialization of medical students. If you don't think one or both of these two theoretical perspectives are applicable, explain why.

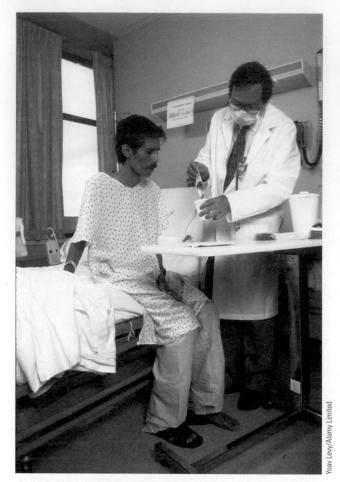

The high costs associated with AIDs make its victims particularly vulnerable in the American health care system.

Yoav Levy/Alamy Limited

deviance and immorality to AIDS patients. Reflecting this stigma, for example, are some Americans who believe that AIDS is a punishment for the decline in moral standards.

The foregoing depiction of health care, via the major theoretical perspectives, was from the macro level. By shifting our concentration to a single health problem, we can gain a deeper understanding of these theoretical perspectives. Let's take a look at disability.

Sociological Views of Disability

Q What is disability? Intuitively, defining disability seems a simple, straight forward matter (Freedman, Martin, and Schoeni 2004). We all think we know a person with a disability when we see one—a soldier with two legs missing, a child who stutters so badly that he or she can't answer questions in class, a young man with migraine headaches so frequent and severe that he can only work at jobs with very flexible schedules. That is obvious, we assume. But thanks to sociology, our various perspectives enable us to look below the surface.

An examination of disability from each of the major theoretical perspectives illustrates the way perspective frames definition. So rather than define disability, let's see what the theoretical perspectives have to tell us.

Q How do functionalists view disability? According to functionalism, disability is a medical problem. For functionalists, people with disabilities are deviants, unable to perform according to society's expectations. All responsibility for the disability lies with the individual. This perspective leads to a definition of disability much like the one used by the World Health Organization: a physical or psychological impairment making someone unable to engage fully in an activity under normal role expectations (Barbotte et al. 2001; Weitz 2010).

Q What is the conflict conception of disability? The conflict perspective gives us two related slants on disability. First, placing all responsibility for disability on the individual amounts to society "blaming the victim." If a society assumes that people are the cause of their own disabilities, then that society can claim no responsibility for accommodating those people. Second, according to conflict theorists, those with disabilities constitute a minority group, whose lives are controlled by those with power in business, government, and the health care industry, most of whom defend the status quo. The conflict perspective, then, would define disability as a physical or psychological condition preventing the performance of an activity and for which society bears little or no responsibility.

Q What is the take of symbolic interactionism on disability? Because disabled persons often cannot play normal parts on society's stage, they are labeled as different. Labeling someone as different in this context also means labeling that person as inadequate. "Cripple" is a label as effective as "queer" or "crazy" for setting others apart from the majority group. Stigmatizing people in this way may lead to the adoption of a personal identity based on feelings of inferiority and the properties of the stigma. By this reasoning, symbolic interactionists would define disability as a physical or psychological condition to which we in society identify, label, stigmatize, and isolate into a category of people.

The three theoretical perspectives provide very different insights into our health care system, as we expect. In fact, in the absence of a single unifying theory, sociology is fortunate to have three powerful theoretical perspectives. Together, these theoretical approaches underscore the social nature of sickness and health care (see Table 15.1).

TABLE 15.1

FOCUS ON THEORETICAL PERSPECTIVES: Health Care in the United States

Each theoretical perspective opens unique avenues for research on health care. Can you think of other research questions for each theory?

Theoretical Perspective	Research Topic	Hypothesis
Functionalism	Sick role	• Society requires (needs) a timely exit from the state of illness.
Conflict theory	Power of physicians	• Physicians repress competing approaches to health care.
Symbolic interactionism	Stigmatization of illness	• AIDS victims are labeled as immoral and deviant.

CHECK YOURSELF **15.2** **R2**

Theoretical Perspectives on the Health Care System

1. The _____ serves to remove people from active involvement in everyday routines, give them special protection and privileges, and set the stage for their return to normal social roles.
2. If a sick person in American society does not attempt to recover, he or she will be labeled a _____.
3. According to the _____ perspective, physicians rose to dominance in the American health care system by taking such actions as attempting to create a monopoly on medical services.
4. AIDS appears most frequently among homosexuals and intravenous drug users. This is an example of _____.
5. According to _____ theory, affordable health care is not provided to the poor in the United States because of the desire for profit.
6. Nurses are caught in a conflict between their values and their work environment. Which of the following perspectives best helps us understand this situation?
   a. functionalism
   b. conflict theory
   c. symbolic interactionism
   d. exchange theory
7. America's negative reaction to AIDS victims illustrates the effects of _____.
8 The _____ perspective views disability as a problem of blaming the victim.

Answers: 1. sick role; 2. deviant; 3. conflict; 4. epidemiology; 5. conflict; 6. c; 7. labeling; 8. conflict

Global Health Care R1

Health Care in the Developed World

No way can we reach an accurate perspective of American health care without examining its global context. The U.S. health care system is unique in the world, but probably not entirely as you imagine (Reid 2009).

Q **How does the U.S. approach to national health insurance fare with the rest of the world?** Of the highly developed countries of the world, the United States is the only one without national health insurance for all its

citizens. Moreover, except for the Veterans Administration hospital system, the military, and the Indian Health Service, the United States is without any direct mechanism for the delivery of health care services (Waitzkin 2001; Kovner and Knickman 2008; Bodenheimer and Grumback 2009). As mentioned in Using the Sociological Imagination at the beginning of this chapter, most modern societies provide free or relatively inexpensive health care through their governments. The United Kingdom, although it has a system of private medical care, promotes equality of medical care through its National Health Service, which provides the vast majority of its services without charge. Canada also has a public health care delivery system committed to providing equal access. As in the United Kingdom, the government finances health care in Canada.

The United States has the dubious distinction of having the most expensive health care and one of the worst performing health care systems in the developing world. So opens a comprehensive report comparing health care in the United States with six other developed countries: Australia, Canada, Germany, the Netherlands, New Zealand, and the United Kingdom (Davis, Schoen, and Stremikis 2010). But let's start with an international comparison of health care spending.

Q By how much does the United States outspend its peers?
A lot. Look at the data in Figure 15.2. Citizens of the United States spend over $7,000 per person for health care annually (*Health at a Glance 2009*). Inhabitants of the next closest comparison country, Canada, spend a little more than half that much ($3,895). Following Canada in descending order are the Netherlands ($3,837), Germany ($3,588), Australia ($3,137), United Kingdom ($2,992), and New Zealand ($2,510).

As noted earlier, U.S. health care expenditures as a share of GDP are the highest in the world (16 percent; see Figure 15.3). Switzerland, the next highest comparison country, spends 10.8 percent of its GDP on health care. In descending order come Canada (10.1 percent), the Netherlands (9.8 percent), New Zealand

(9.2 percent), Australia (8.7 percent), and the United Kingdom (8.4 percent).

Let's turn now to the bang each of these seven countries gets for its money. As shown in Figure 15.4, the United States ranks last overall on five dimensions of health performance. Despite its high price tag, the United States finishes last on access to medical care, organizational efficiency, equity of treatment, and health results, next to last on quality care. The Netherlands achieves the highest performance overall, followed closely by the United Kingdom and Australia. Germany and New Zealand are middle-level performers, and Canada finishes just ahead of the United States. Let's look more closely at the five measures of performance.

Q How does the United States fare on quality of care?
The United States shows its "best" performance on preventive and patient-centered care. Its low scores on chronic care management and coordinated care drag it down to next-to-last on quality overall. Other nations have made more progress than the United States in incorporating information technology and managing chronic health problems. Until the United States makes better use of information technology, its physicians will have difficulty in identifying and monitoring patients suffering from chronic illnesses.

FIGURE 15.2

Per Capita Health Expenditures

This figure compares a number of developed countries in terms of their annual per capital public and private health care expenditures. What are biggest surprises for you?

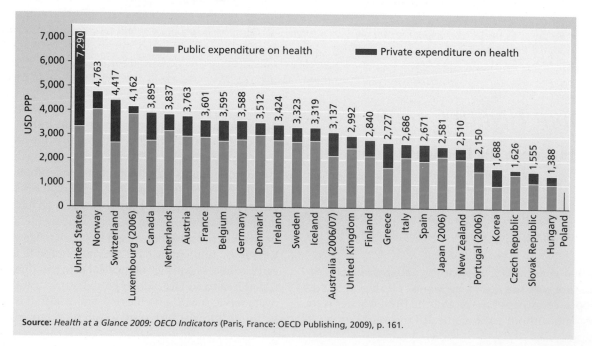

Source: *Health at a Glance 2009: OECD Indicators* (Paris, France: OECD Publishing, 2009), p. 161.

FIGURE 15.3

Health Care Expenditures as a Share of GDP

This figure shows the percentage of GDP each country spends on health care annually. Public and private expenditures are presented separately. What conclusions do you draw from the array of numbers?

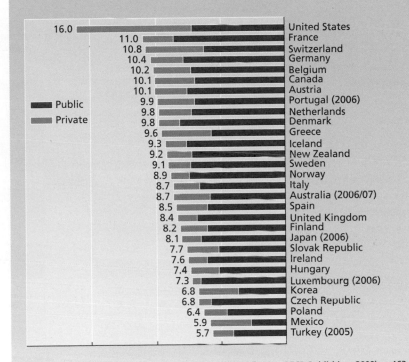

Source: *Health at a Glance 2009: OECD Indicators* (Paris, France: OECD Publishing, 2009), p. 163.

Q **How good is access to patient care in the U.S. health care system?** Because the United States lacks universal health care coverage, inhabitants go without medical attention more often than people in the other six nations. Lack of insurance and cost are the biggest barriers to health care access for Americans. For Americans with insurance and/or money, access to general health care and specialized services is no problem. In countries such as the United Kingdom and Canada, those seeking medical services are not inhibited by cost, but they do have to wait for specialized treatment. Patients in the Netherlands and Germany have the best of both worlds, with little out-of-pocket costs and rapid access to specialized care.

Q **Where does the United States rank on efficiency of health care?** The United States ranks at the bottom of the seven countries on efficiency of delivery, while the United Kingdom and Australia rank first and second, respectively. The United States performs poorly in terms of national health care expenditures, administrative costs, information technology, readmittance to hospital, and duplicative medical testing.

Q **Is equality a problem in the U.S. health care system?** In fact, the United States ranks last on almost all indicators of equal access to treatment. The expense of health care in the United States makes it extremely difficult for low-income Americans to see a physician or dentist, obtain a recommended test, receive treatment or follow-up care, and fill prescriptions. Almost half of lower-income adults in the United States go without needed care, due to costs. The Netherlands, United Kingdom, and Germany finished one, two, and three, in the order listed.

Q **But, don't Americans have longer, healthier, and productive lives?** Actually, the United States ranks dead (excuse the pun) last on each of the measures of health outcomes. Along with the United Kingdom, the United States has significantly higher death rates from treatable medical problems than Canada and Australia. Overall, Australians enjoy the longest, healthiest, and most productive lives.

The authors of this report conclude that all countries have room for improvement in delivering health care

FIGURE 15.4

National Rankings on Key Health Indicators

Below is a comparison between the United States and six other developed countries on five major indicators of health care performance. Write a short paragraph summarizing what you think are the two most important points.

Country Rankings		AUS	CAN	GER	NETH	NZ	UK	US
	1.00–2.33							
	2.34–4.66							
	4.67–7.00							
OVERALL RANKING (2010)		3	6	4	1	5	2	7
Quality Care		4	7	5	2	1	3	6
Effective Care		2	7	6	3	5	1	4
Safe Care		6	5	3	1	4	2	7
Coordinated Care		4	5	7	2	1	3	6
Patient-Centered Care		2	5	3	6	1	7	4
Access		6.5	5	3	1	4	2	6.5
Cost-Related Problem		6	3.5	3.5	2	5	1	7
Timeliness of Care		6	7	2	1	3	4	5
Efficiency		2	6	5	3	4	1	7
Equity		4	5	3	1	6	2	7
Long, Healthy, Productive Lives		1	2	3	4	5	6	7
Health Expenditures/Capita, 2007		$3,357	$3,895	$3,588	$3,837	$2,454	$2,992	$7,290

Source: Karen Davis, Cathy Schoen, and Kristof Stremikis, "Mirror, Mirror on the Wall: How the Performance of the U.S. Health Care System Compares Internationally," Common Wealth Fund Pub. No. 1400 (Washington, DC: The Commonwealth Fund, 2010), p.v.

services. But, they emphasize that the United States is spending significantly more on health care per person and as a percent of GDP than the other six countries, while performing below them. Therefore, the U.S. health care system has considerable room for improvement in obtaining a return on the nation's heavy investment in health care services. The authors express some optimism for improvement in the United States in light of the national health legislation signed by Obama in 2010 (Davis, Schoen, and Stremikis 2010). We will return to this point later.

So far, the focus has been on health care among wealthier countries, and the comparisons among countries have been relative to one another. All of these countries have health care systems far superior to poorer countries. A fuller picture of global health care demands an examination of the medical situation in developing countries.

Health Care in the Developing World

Developed countries have made significant advances in health care services over the last forty years. Nevertheless,

among developing countries where some advancement is occurring, progress is much more modest and uneven (Cockerham and Cockerham 2010). The poor always suffer more, and the poorest of the poor suffer most.

Q To what extent has health care progressed in developing countries? Assessing medical care in developing countries requires two comparisons: one between developed and developing countries, another within developing and developed countries. Figure 15.5 helps in this regard. This figure's depiction of progress on three key health indicators (infant mortality, female adult mortality, and male adult mortality) makes both comparisons. For simplicity's sake, we can consider infant mortality alone because the same trend holds for the adult mortality of both sexes. Since the 1970s, progress occurred in both rich and poor countries, but developed countries started out far ahead. During the 1970s, developed countries annually experienced 17 deaths per 1,000 live births compared to 89 instances of infant mortality each year in

FIGURE 15.5

Progress on Key Health Indicators

In this figure, developed and developing countries are compared in terms of infant and adult mortality. State two conclusions one can make from the data.

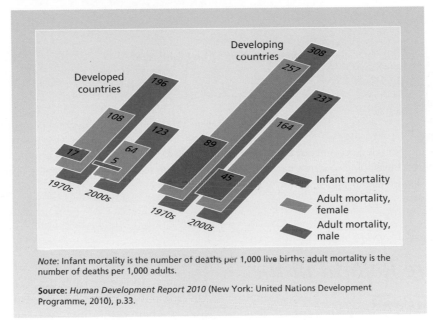

Note: Infant mortality is the number of deaths per 1,000 live births; adult mortality is the number of deaths per 1,000 adults.

Source: *Human Development Report 2010* (New York: United Nations Development Programme, 2010), p.33.

developing countries. By the 2000s, the infant mortality rate within richer countries was down to 5 (a 70 percent reduction), while it stood at 45 within developing countries (a 49 percent decrease).

We can draw three conclusions. First, in absolute terms, developing countries made more progress in reducing infant mortality than developed countries. Infant mortality went down 44 deaths per 1,000 births in developing countries, compared to a decline of 12 deaths per live births in developed countries. Second, the percentage decline was faster in developing countries than in poorer ones (71 percent versus 49 percent). Third, poorer countries remain much worse off than richer countries because of their high infant mortality starting point.

The good news is that both rich and poor countries have had a significant increase in life expectancy. A baby's expectation of living longer in almost any country is historically high. The bad news is that poorer countries are still far behind, and progress is beginning to slow down. According to an international report, health advancement began to slow down after 1990. This, the report states, is due to increasing mortality rates (infant and adult) in nineteen developing countries, particularly in Africa and parts of the former Soviet Union (*Human Development*

Report 2010). While this is true in both rich and poor countries, again the poorest of the poor suffer a more dismal effect.

Q **How does income affect health care and health outcomes?** Another international study reported on the health condition of the poorest women and children around the world (Gwatkin, et al. 2003). The rankings used in the study are relative. That is, a quantitative measure of wealth within each country determines which are the "poorest" and/or "richest" groups. Consequently, the poorest in one country may be, in absolute terms, much worse off than the poorest in another nation because almost everyone in his or her country is poor by international standards ("The Wealth Gap in Health" 2004). The poorest women and their children around the world are less knowledgeable about health issues, make less use of health care services, and have higher health risks. Poorer women are twice as likely to be malnourished and five times less likely to be with a qualified medical person at childbirth. The children of the poorest mothers are three times more likely to have low height for their age and twice as likely to die at birth than children of richer mothers.

CHECK YOURSELF   15.3   R2

Global Health Care

1. Which of the following countries receives the least return on its investment in health care?
   a. Canada
   b. United States
   c. The Netherlands
   d. New Zealand
   e. Australia

2. What percentage of its GDP does the United States spend on health care?
   a. 5 percent
   b. 13 percent
   c. 16 percent
   d. 22 percent
   e. 25 percent

3. Out of seven most developed countries, the United States finished _____ in terms of health care performance.

4. In absolute terms, developing countries have made more progress in reducing infant mortality over the last forty years than developed countries. T or F?

Answers: 1. b; 2. c; 3. last; 4. T

Health Care Reform in the United States R1

The Need for Health Care Reform

Americans have conflicting ideas about the health care system (Haugen 2008). Almost 60 percent of Americans say they are satisfied with their health care and health care coverage. This is at odds with their attitudes regarding the need for health care reform. Americans consistently identify health care as a top domestic issue for government. Three-fourths of the public believes that the present health care system is either "in a state of crisis" or "has major problems." A large majority of Americans believe that the U.S. health care system requires reform. Just over one-fourth favor a total revamping of the system; 51 percent believe that fundamental change is needed; only 22 percent see the need for little or no change. Moreover, almost three-fourths of Americans approve of a government-backed health care program for children, and almost 60 percent prefer a universal health care system (Vtz, Hollingshaus, and Dien 2010).

Q Why is there a need for health care reform? One motivation for health care reform, as we have seen, is economic. America annually devotes a larger share of its GDP (16 percent) to health care than any other nation. This amounts to more than $7,000 annually for every man, woman, and child. And as you saw at the beginning of this chapter, the costs of health care are skyrocketing. The escalating costs of medical

care also negatively affect the overall health of the economy. According to critics, economic resources of government—desperately needed in other areas of public life—are being siphoned off by a health care system critics believe is out of control (Marmor and Barr 1992; Andersen, Rice, and Kominski 2007).

A second reason for reform is the substantial proportion of Americans who, except on an emergency basis, do not have access to medical care (see Figure 15.6). A large segment of the over 46 million uninsured

FIGURE 15.6

Percentage of Persons Not Covered by Health Insurance in the United States by Age: 2009

This figure displays the percentage of various age categories in the United States without health insurance. If you were running for the presidency of the United States, what would you say about this situation?

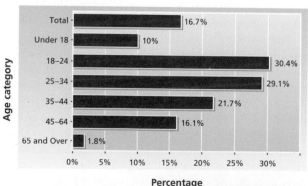

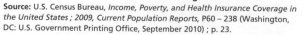

Source: U.S. Census Bureau, *Income, Poverty, and Health Insurance Coverage in the United States ; 2009, Current Population Reports,* P60 – 238 (Washington, DC: U.S. Government Printing Office, September 2010) ; p. 23.

Americans are the most disadvantaged, those on the bottom of the stratification structure (Dressler, Oths, and Gravlee 2005; Barr 2008). Even with Medicaid, over one-fourth of America's poor are without medical coverage. Poor children are particularly vulnerable. This vulnerability extends beyond the poor. In 2009, one-fifth of those earning between $25,000 and $50,000 were uninsured as were 16 percent of those earning between $50,000 and $75,000 (DeNavas-Walt, Proctor, and Smith 2010). Increasingly, either employers are requiring employees to pay both high premiums and deductibles for the coverage of their children and spouses, or they are providing health plans that simply do not cover dependents. Nearly one-half of uninsured children live with parents who are insured. Ten percent of children in the United States under eighteen years of age were without health insurance in 2009.

Quality of life is a third reason for health reform. One obvious aspect of a lowered quality of life is the lack of health care or inferior health care. One-third of Americans indicate they or a family member has

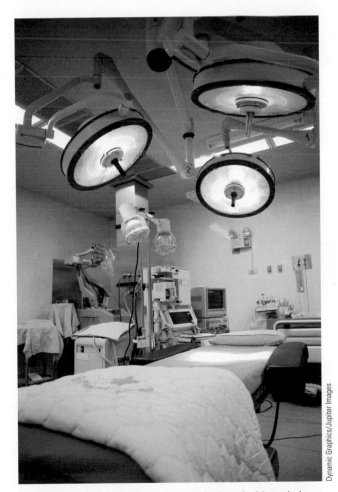

Much of the skyrocketing cost of medical care in the United States is due to the changing nature of hospitals. This operating room displays the sophisticated technology that most hospital administrators and physicians appear to desire.

Dynamic Graphics/Jupiter Images

postponed medical treatment because of cost (Rheault 2007). Perhaps less obvious is the fear and desperation that the uninsured feel. They know that an illness or accident experienced by themselves or a member of their family could either go untreated or absorb whatever economic resources they have. Moreover, even the insured live with the prospect of losing coverage should they lose their jobs. As you saw in Chapter 13, more Americans, both blue- and white-collar, are experiencing job loss or, even if employed, lower compensation. In addition, companies are requiring employees to pay for more of their health care coverage.

A fourth reason for health care reform is the aging of the American population. As the baby boomers age, strains in the present health care system are expected to increase dramatically. The remainder of this section dwells on options for health care reform.

Health Care Reform Options

Americans support a variety of health care reforms, ranging from a national health care system to government deregulation promoting competition among private health care providers. Strength of support varies with different proposals. Seventy-seven percent of Americans support government deregulation to create competition. A narrow majority (54 percent) favor establishing a national health care system (Saad 2007b).

Q **What are the health care reform options?** There are a few basic options to delivering health care services (Reid 2009; Samuelson and Nordhaus 2010). *Modified competitiveness* bases its approach on market principles such as consumer cost sharing. This attempt, however, depends on universal health coverage as a precondition to health care reform.

A second option, *managed competition*, relates to the first option but is a combination of free market forces and government regulation. Health care could embody several large plans modeled after health maintenance organizations (HMOs). To increase their competitive edge, employers could form large purchasing networks, with health care providers bidding on their business. President Bush's Medicare drug prescription plan enacted by Congress in 2003 reflects this approach through its reliance on competition among numerous health care insurance providers. The idea is to create competition and to reward those health care providers that exhibit superior performance in cost, quality, and patient satisfaction.

A third option is the *single payer approach*, like the Canadian model. The government finances medical services. Canadians choose their doctors and hospitals and bill the government according to a standardized fee structure. A public opinion comparison of the U.S. and Canadian health care systems favors the Canadian system. The Canadian approach engenders higher levels of consumer satisfaction with patient services and possesses much more favorable regard than the U.S. system (H. Taylor 1994, Budrys 2001).

A fourth option—based primarily on the German model—uses a *play or pay mechanism*. Here, employers either offer employees health coverage (play) or pay into a public fund for covering the uninsured. This access to universal medical care in Germany, considered among the best in the world, is a guarantee for life (R. Atkinson 1994; Budrys 2001).

The Health Reform Road Taken

Health care reform has eluded every American president who has attempted it since 1965 when Lyndon Johnson made Medicare legal. George W. Bush, who introduced a Medicare prescription drug plan in 2003, achieved partial success. Consequently, health insurance in the United States has been a privilege largely enjoyed, with the exception of the elderly, by those who have full-time jobs with well-established firms. Over the years, contend conflict theory proponents, those with the power—including business interests and the medical establishment—have successfully frustrated all efforts to reform the health care system. By invoking threats of socialized medicine and profit reduction, powerful forces have prevented equality of access to medical care for all Americans (Weissert and Weissert 2006).

No wonder, then, that excitement among health care advocates reached a fever pitch in 2010 when Congress debated a new health care reform bill introduced to fulfill one of Obama's campaign promises.

Advocates pushed for guaranteed universal coverage for all Americans, a requirement for each of the four health care reform alternatives just outlined. Though Obama and Congress managed to pass a major reform package, they failed to get guaranteed coverage for all Americans. Consequently, the road taken to reform fell short of advocates' aspirations. Still, supporters of reform saw some important improvements in the health care system.

Q **What is new in America's health care reform law?**
While the new law fails to introduce government-sponsored universal coverage, it does require most citizens and legal residents to purchase health insurance. This so-called individual mandate imposes a tax penalty for those who fail to purchase coverage. The bill also penalizes employers with more than fifty employees who do not offer some form of health coverage. Employers with more than 200 employees must automatically enroll their workers into employer-offered health insurance plans. The reform legislation extends coverage to some 32 million uninsured people through Medicaid, particularly providing health coverage for all uninsured children. Also included are subsidies for purchasing health insurance provided by the government to lower income families. The legislation establishes health-insurance exchanges designed to promote more competitive insurance coverage rates. There are additional specific aspects of the new law that improve the health care system. Insurance companies can no longer deny coverage to those with preexisting conditions. Children can remain on their parents' health policies until age twenty-six. And there can now be no lifetime cap on the amount of coverage

CHECK YOURSELF **15.4** **R2**

Health Care Reform in the United States

1. Approximately _____ million Americans are without health insurance.
2. Which of the following highly industrialized countries does not have national health care coverage?
   a. Germany
   b. France
   c. United States
   d. Canada
3. The major reason the United States does not have a national health care program is because its citizens want different results from health care programs than citizens of other developed societies. T or F?
4. Of those Americans without health care protection, the poor and children comprise the majority. T or F?
5. The approach to health care delivery under which medical services are financed governmentally is called
   a. managed competition.
   b. single payer.
   c. all payer.
   d. play or pay.
6. The 2010 health reform law fails to provide universal health insurance coverage. T or F?

Answers: 1. 46; 2. c; 3. F; 4. T; 5. b; 6. T

the insured with preexisting conditions can receive, including children ("A Giant Step Toward Universal Healthcare" 2010; *Landmark 2010*; "Summary of New Health Reform Law" 2010).

The extent to which this new law overcomes some of the shortcomings identified earlier remains to be seen. For one thing, the reform is phased in over several years. For another, opponents in Congress are vowing to repeal the entire legislation. Also, advocates fear that reform doesn't go nearly far enough because the health insurers successfully shaped the bill for their own benefit (Terhune and Epstein 2009). Americans, by a margin of 2 to1, believe the law should have been stronger ("Repeal? Most Americans Think Health Reform Did Not Go Far Enough, Poll Finds" 2010).

The Graying of America 🔲

In the second half of this chapter we will look at aging and its ramifications. But because America is not alone in its growing proportion of older persons, we will again first look at the United States within a global context.

A Global Context

Economic development carries with it a train of factors, not the least of which is improved medical care and knowledge of birth-control methods (see Chapter 17). These factors increase life expectancy while reducing the birth rate. For example, the proportion of the world's population sixty-five and older is increasing at a rate of about 6 percent annually, whereas the world's population as a whole has a growth rate under 2 percent. Consequently, the world in the twenty-first century will be an older world ("Why Population Aging Matters: A Global Perspective" 2007; Bremner et al. 2010). In fact, the count of the world's older population has been rising for centuries, but the difference is the increase in the rate of increase. The global population of the elderly (sixty-five years or over) will triple from some 516 million today to 1.53 billion in 2050. This means that the elderly, who account for less than 8 percent of the population, will comprise 16 percent of the world's population by 2050. And those eighty-five and over will be the fastest growing age group, two-thirds of which will be women. China expects its percentage increase in population aged sixty-five and over, for example, to increase by more than 238 percent by 2025. If this occurs, the proportion of China's elderly population will increase to nearly 20 percent by the end of the first quarter of this century. Today, the situation is even more extreme in Japan where people age sixty-five and over comprise 23 percent of the population, a proportion projected to increase to 40 percent by 2050. By that same time, more than one-half of the world's elderly will inhabit East and South Asia. In Africa, where the most dramatic increases in the growth of the aged population are expected, the population aged sixty-five and over will have gone from 23 million persons in 1980 to more than 100 million in 2025 (Curran and Renzetti 2000).

Aging in the United States

An **age cohort** consists of persons born during the same time period in a particular population. The baby boomers, for example, constitute an age cohort born

Population graying is a worldwide phenomenon. In China, the population sixty-five and over is projected to increase by over 238 percent by 2025.

Becky Reed/Alamy Limited

FIGURE 15.7

Percentage of the U.S. Population 65 and Over

This graph charts the increase in elderly Americans from 1900 to 2040. Why has this trend occurred?

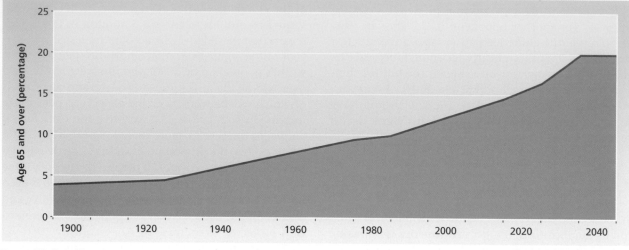

Source: U.S. Census Bureau.

between roughly 1946 and 1964. The important thing about an age cohort is that its members pass through life together. Consequently, an age cohort not only exerts a certain influence on the rest of society but also experiences in common some effects of the particular nature of its society (Frey 2007).

The age cohort of persons sixty-five years and over—37 million strong—comprises 12 percent of the total U.S. population (Kinsella and Phillips 2005). Because the first baby boomers turned sixty-five in 2011, there will be about 82 million elderly Americans representing 20 percent of the nation's population by 2040 (see Figure 15.7). The median age of the population will be forty-three years by 2080; it was about sixteen in 1800 and thirty-six in 2000. Due to the baby-boom generation, there will be an increasing proportion of elderly in the advanced age cohort. The number of Americans sixty-five to eighty-four will increase from about 30 million in 1990 to more than 50 million in the middle of the twenty-first century. Moreover, the number of Americans over age eighty-five will increase from about 4 million in 2000 to about 8 million in 2010 to more than 17 million by 2050 (see "Sociology Eyes America 15.1").

Population pyramids are graphic representations illustrating the age and sex distribution of a population. Their use enhances understanding of an aging society. The pyramid on the left in Figure 15.8 shows the number of American males and females by age group in 1945. This is the classic pyramid shape, representing a population that has many younger people at the bottom, fewer adults in the middle, and a still smaller number of older people at the top. The pyramid on the right in Figure 15.8 portrays the projected age structure of the United States in 2050. Obviously, this is more of a rectangle or square than a geometric pyramid, with a similar number of people in all age groups from infancy to old age. This **age structure**—the distribution of people of different ages within a society—results from the combination of the low fertility rate (after the baby-boom years of 1946 to 1964) and increased longevity due to the low mortality rate.

Q **What accounts for the rapid growth in the number of older Americans?** The maximum size of the elderly population at any given time is due primarily to the number of births sixty-five or more years ago (Himes 2001). Between 2010 and 2030, those born in the post–World War II baby boom will dramatically increase the pool of the elderly. After this "senior boom," the rate of growth will fall significantly as those born in the so-called baby bust of the mid-1960s and 1970s reach retirement age. Around 2045, another dramatic increase in the elderly will occur as the children of the baby boomers reach age sixty-five. This uneven growth rate will see the number of elderly increase from 26 million in 1980 to more than 53.7 million in 2020 and then to almost 82 million in 2050.

The second most significant factor in the growth of the elderly population is the decline in the death rate. Thanks to medical advancements such as improved sanitation, antibiotics, and vaccines, the death rate among infants and children dropped precipitously between 1900 and 1954. Although only 40 percent

SOCIOLOGY EYES AMERICA 15.1

Projected Growth of Senior Population (2000–2030)

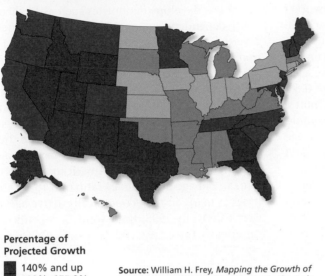

Percentage of Projected Growth

- 140% and up
- 100%–139.9%
- 70%–99.9%
- under 70%

Source: William H. Frey, *Mapping the Growth of Older America: Seniors and Boomers in the Early 21st Century* (p. 12). Copyright © 2007 The Brookings Institute. Reprinted by permission.

The "graying of America" refers to the growing senior population. Improved medical care, better nutrition, and healthier lifestyles have all contributed to longer life expectancies in the United States. This map shows the projected growth of the population that is aged sixty-five years old and over in each state.

Interpret the Map

1. Describe the distribution pattern of senior people across the United States. Create a chart representing the distribution pattern.
2. Where is your state in this distribution?
3. Research the voting rate for seniors in your state. Is it higher or lower than the national average?

of those Americans born at the turn of the century had a life expectancy of sixty-five, today more than 80 percent are expected to reach this age. The life expectancy figures are, of course, even better than this. The average male life span, now seventy-six years, is expected to increase to seventy-seven by 2020. Among females, the life span is projected to increase from the current eighty-one years to eighty-two years in 2020 (U.S. Census Bureau 2009).

Immigration has had its effect through the massive pre–World War I immigration into the United States. Most of those immigrants were young adults with a very high fertility rate. Their children, born in the United States, are now among the elderly.

FIGURE 15.8

Age and Sex Structure of the United States: 1945 and 2050

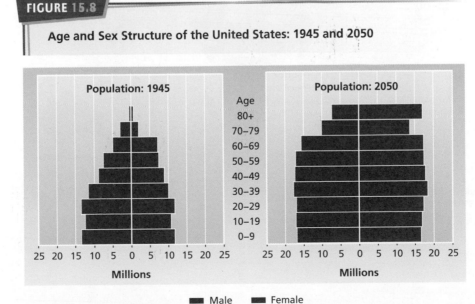

Source: U.S. Census Bureau.

Q **Why is this trend important to you?** A look at the "dependency ratio" will tell us. The **dependency ratio** is the proportion of persons in the dependent ages (under fifteen and over sixty-four) in relation to those in the economically active ages (fifteen to sixty-four). A higher dependency ratio indicates that each worker has to support more dependent people; a lower ratio indicates that each worker has fewer people to support. Suppose a population was composed of 45 juveniles, 15 seniors, and 100 people of economically active ages. This would yield a dependency ratio of 60/100 or 0.60, denoting that each worker supports just over half a dependent person; to put it another way, there would be just over one dependent for every two working-age people. There are two subtypes of dependency: *youth dependency* and *old-age dependency*. The fictitious population just described would have a youth dependency ratio of 0.45 (45/100) and an old-age dependency ratio of 0.15 (15/100). That is, for every youthful dependent, there would be two-and-a-fraction workers; for every

elderly person, there would be over six and a half workers. Less developed nations have much higher youth dependency than more developed nations. More developed nations have significantly higher old-age dependency (see "Think Globally" 15.1).

For less developed countries such as Mexico, a high youth dependency means that national income must be diverted from savings (and the capital needed for economic development) to take care of its large population of children (food, housing, education). In more developed countries such as the United States, rising old-age dependency creates other challenges. There are fewer working-age people in the labor force to support the growing number of seniors. For example, in the United States in 1985, there were about 19 persons age sixty-five and over for every 100 Americans fifteen to sixty-four, an old-age dependency ratio of 0.19, or about five times as many in the economically active ages as there were elderly. By 1995, there were 25 dependent elderly Americans for every 100 economically active ones

THINK GLOBALLY 15.1

Old-Age Dependency

This map displays the old-age dependency ratio for countries around the world. A ratio of 15, for example, signifies that there are 15 economically active persons to support each dependent elderly person.

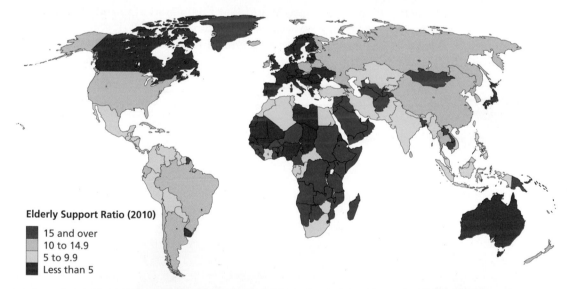

Elderly Support Ratio (2010)

- 15 and over
- 10 to 14.9
- 5 to 9.9
- Less than 5

Source: U.N. Population Division, *World Population Prospects: The 2008 Revision*, 2009. Cited in *2010 World Population Data Sheet* (Washington, DC: Population Reference Bureau, 2010).

Interpret the Map

1. Describe the relationship between level of economic development and old-age dependency demonstrated in this map. Use specific areas of the world to illustrate the relationship.

2. Explain why there is a relationship between level of economic development and old-age dependency.

3. Looking at the old-age dependency ratio in the United States, what are the implications for your future?

The Graying of America

1. The aging of the population is confined to only the most highly industrialized societies. T or F?
2. By 2050, the size of the elderly population in the United States will constitute _____ percent of the population.
   a. 13
   b. 17
   c. 20
   d. 33
3. By 2050, the population pyramid of the United States is expected to resemble a
   a. triangle.
   b. a classic pyramid.
   c. a rectangle.
   d. an inverted pyramid.
4. By 2030, the old-age dependency ratio in the United States is expected to
   a. more than double its 1985 level.
   b. just about triple its 1985 level.
   c. remain relatively stable.
   d. be about half its 1985 level.

Answers: 1. F; 2. c; 3. c; 4. a

(ratio of 0.25), or just about four times as many Americans fifteen to sixty-four years of age as there were Americans sixty-five and older. In 2030, there will be 50 dependent elderly individuals for every 100 Americans of working age (ratio of 0.50). In other words, every two working-age Americans will have to support one elderly person. This shift will dramatically increase the burden on the economically active to pay for Social Security and Medicare (Kent and Mather 2002; Bremner et al. 2010). This economic burden will be even heavier because of escalating health care costs and the need for increasing health care services, prescription drugs, and institutional arrangements for the long-term care of an aging population.

Q Is there no good news for America's younger generation in all this? There is some comfort. The United States remains the world's fastest growing industrialized nation, up almost 10 percent since 2000. Because the United States has a fertility rate near replacement level (an average of 2.1 children per woman), its population will increase, at least through the following generation. Thus, relative to most of the world's countries, the United States will have an enviable balance between its younger and older people. In addition, the negative effects of the coming tide of some 80 million retiring baby boomers may be cushioned by their view of retirement (Jacobe 2004; Carroll 2005; Saad 2006, 2007a), which is different than previous and current generations. Surveys indicate that although a majority of baby boomers intend to retire at around age sixty-four, they plan to reject either full-time leisure

or full-time work. In a Gallup Poll, for example, only 35 percent of baby boomers express the hope to never work for pay again, and only 12 percent wish to work full time. Fifty-one percent want to alternate periods of work and leisure by working part time (Saad 2006). In fact, a government report estimates that 93 percent of the increase in the U.S. labor force from 2006 to 2016 will be among workers ages fifty-five and over ("Recession Turns a Graying Office Grayer" 2009).

This view of retirement reflects several factors. First, baby boomers are healthier, more highly educated, and living into their eighties. Second, the majority of baby boomers express enjoyment provided by employment. Third, a significant proportion of baby boomers are worried about not having enough money in retirement because of soaring health care costs and diminishing pensions (Chaddock 2004).

Age Stratification R1

Thus far in our exploration of social inequality, we have examined race, ethnicity, and gender as major factors in the differential distribution of the scarce desirables (power, wealth, privileges) in a society. Because chronological age is another basis for social ranking, sociologists are interested in **age stratification**—the age-based unequal distribution of scarce desirables in a society. Although age can operate to the advantage or disadvantage of any age group in a society, sociologists focus especially on the inequality among older Americans because as the median age of the U.S. population grows older, this form of stratification affects more and more people (Henretta 2001; Spencer 2003; Baars et al. 2006).

Q **What is the economic condition of the elderly?** Because the economic situation among America's elderly has improved since 1960, the public thinks of the elderly as not only well-off, but as taking economic resources from the young (Duff 1995). It is true that the poverty rate for Americans over sixty-five years of age has declined since 1960 from 35 percent to 9 percent (see Figure 15.9). The conclusion that the elderly are therefore well-off economically, however, fails to capture the complexity of their economic condition (Carr 2010). Among the factors masking the true economic situation of the elderly are distorted measures of poverty and factors of race, ethnicity, and gender.

Q **What is being left out of the rosy economic picture?** The measurement of poverty among older people distorts the reality: The poverty line is drawn at a higher dollar amount for the elderly than for younger Americans. Although the elderly spend proportionately more on health care and housing than younger people do, the federal government assumes a lower cost of living for the elderly. If our government applied the same standard for both younger and older age categories, the poverty rate for the elderly would increase from 10 to 15 percent. Gross poverty rates also fail to take into account the just over 7 percent of the elderly who

are officially considered "near poor." Counting these at-risk elderly people, about one in six of those over age sixty-five is poor. Nor do official statistics include the "hidden poor" among the elderly population, who live either in institutions or with relatives because they cannot afford to live independently. Inclusion of these people would substantially raise the poverty rate for America's elderly.

Diversity is another factor complicating an evaluation of the economic situation of the elderly (Lee and Haaga 2002). There is a wide financial gap among the elderly. Some older people have moderate to high incomes based on dividends from assets, cash savings, and private retirement programs. Most elderly Americans, however, do not have sources of income beyond Social Security benefits. The existence of a small percentage of high-income older people gives the false impression that most elderly people are economically well-off (Himes 2001).

Q **How do race and ethnicity compound age inequality?** The elderly who are members of racial or ethnic minority groups are generally in worse condition than older white Americans. Whereas the median income of whites over age sixty-five was $19,372 in 2008, the median income for elderly African Americans was $14,357; for elderly Latinos, it was about $11,957 (see Table 15.2). This means that older blacks have incomes that are 74 percent of whites, and older Latinos have incomes that are 62 percent that of whites. The poverty

---

FIGURE 15.9

Poverty Rates Among Americans 65 and Over, 1960–2009

This figure documents the changing poverty rate among Americans 65 and over since 1960. Explain why it would be misleading to cite the current poverty rate as evidence that older people are economically well-off.

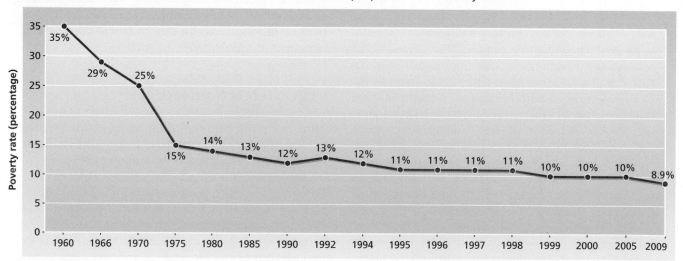

Source: U.S. Census Bureau, *Income, Poverty, and Health Insurance Coverage in the United States: 2009, Current Population Reports* P60 – 238 (Washington, DC: U.S. Government Printing Office, 2001); U.S. Census Bureau, *Statistical Abstract of the United States: 2008* (Washington, DC: U.S. Government Printing Office, September 2010), p. 17.

TABLE 15.2

Selected Socioeconomic Characteristics of Elderly Americans

From this table, some comparative statements can be made about the economic situation of elderly Americans. What are two important statements that can be supported by these data?

	Whites	African Americans	Latinos	Women	Men
Medium Income	$19,372	$14,357	$11,957	$14,429	$25,344
Percent in Poverty	8.9%	19.9%	19.3%	12%	6.7%

Source: Patrick Purcell, "Income and Poverty Among Older Americans in 2008," CRS Report for Congress, Congressional Research Office, October 2, 2009.

rate among the African American elderly is over twice that of whites (19.9 percent versus 8.9 percent). For older Latinos, the poverty rate is also over two times that of white Americans (19.3 percent versus 8.9 percent). Unquestionably, this disparity is intimately linked to the lifetime of prejudice and discrimination experienced by these racial and ethnic groups. The problem just becomes magnified in old age (Calisanti and Slevin 2001; L. Olson 2001; Purcell 2009).

Q How does gender heighten age inequality? Because women the world over live longer than males, there is a global trend toward the *feminization of poverty* among the elderly. Because the highest poverty rates exist among single women, the longer life expectancy of women means that, if poor, they will live longer than men will in that condition. Elderly women constitute one of the poorest segments of American society. Women over age sixty-five are almost twice as likely to live in poverty as are their male counterparts (12 percent versus 6.7 percent). Elderly women most likely to be poor are single women who have never married or who are divorced, separated, or widowed. The median income of elderly women is $14,429 and $25,344 for males. Thus, the average income of elderly women is only about 57 percent of elderly males, lower than the amount that American women under sixty-five earn relative to working males (Purcell 2009). This is not surprising, because the roots of poverty among older American women lie in the work-related experiences women have had throughout their lives (Sidel 1998). The consequences of gender inequality are compounded by the inequalities of age.

Q Are America's elderly a minority group? Jack Levin and William Levin (1980) contend that the field of **social gerontology**—the scientific study of the social dimensions of aging—has in the past blamed the elderly for their situation in much the same way that

Americans in general have blamed the poor for their plight. Because early researchers tended to study older people in institutions, their studies focused on people with diminished mental and physical capacities. This perspective coincides with the American public's negative view of the elderly. Many scholars, however, join Levin and Levin in their quest to avoid blaming the elderly for their situation and view them instead as a minority (M. L. Barron 1953; Comfort 1976; Palmore 1978; Hillier and Barrow 2011).

Richard Posner (1996) suggests that it is not necessary to consider the elderly (or women) as a minority to recognize them as victims of prejudice and discrimination. The existence of ageism alone substantiates the persistence of age-based inequality in America (Rubin 2007).

Age stratification, like most aspects of a society, must exist within a social and cultural context: It must make sense to those involved, and it must be socially justified. The justification for negative age stratification among the elderly in a society comes in the form of **ageism**—a set of beliefs, attitudes, norms, and values used to justify age-based prejudice and discrimination (Roscigno 2010). **Stereotypes** are ideas based on distortion, exaggeration, and oversimplification and applied to all members of a social category. As with racism and sexism, ageism develops from such stereotypes.

Q What are the stereotypes of the elderly? Years ago gerontologist Robert Butler summarized negative stereotypes of the elderly, many of which exist today:

An older person thinks and moves slowly. He does not think as he used to or as creatively. He is bound to himself and can no longer change or grow. He can learn neither well nor swiftly and, even if he could, he would not wish to. Tied to his personal traditions and growing conservatism, he dislikes innovations and is not disposed to new ideas. Not only can he not move forward, he often moves backward. He enters a second childhood, caught up in increasing egocentricity and demanding more from his environment than he is willing to give to it. Sometimes he becomes an intensification of himself, a caricature of a life-long personality. He becomes irritable and cantankerous, yet shallow and enfeebled. He lives in his past; he is behind times. He is aimless and wandering of mind, reminiscing and garrulous. Indeed, he is a study in decline, the picture of mental and physical failure. He has lost and cannot replace friends, spouse, job, status, power, influence, income. He is often stricken by diseases which, in turn, restrict his movement, his enjoyment of food, the pleasures of well-being. He has lost his desire and capacity for sex. His body shrinks, and so too does the flow of blood to his brain. His mind does not utilize oxygen and sugar at the same rate as formerly. Feeble, uninteresting, he awaits his death, a burden to society, to his family, and to himself. (Butler 1975:6–7)

Q Are these stereotypes accurate? By definition stereotypes are usually inaccurate because they do not apply to all members of a group. Stereotypes of older

This healthy couple represents the legions of Americans who contradict the negative stereotypes of the aging.

Monkey Business Images/Used under license from Shutterstock

people are no exception, as much research demonstrates. Most elderly people are not senile. Old age is not a sexless period for the majority of those over sixty-five. There are few age differences in response to job-related challenges; most elderly people are able to learn new things and can enthusiastically adapt to change (Palmore 1980, 1981; Hendricks and Hendricks 1987; Atchley 2004).

Q What do seniors themselves say about the accuracy of these stereotypes? A survey asked a sample of persons sixty-five years and older about their experience with such matters as illness, memory loss, inability to drive, loss of sexual activity, loneliness and depression, and difficulty paying bills ("Growing Old in America: Expectations vs. Reality" 2009). On every issue, seniors report experiencing them at lower levels (frequently far lower) than younger people in the sample expected to experience them as they age. This survey also found that the older people feel younger than their age, while younger people feel older than their age. Among eighteen- to twenty-nine-year-olds, about half report feeling their age and one-fourth report feeling older than their age. Surprisingly, 60 percent of seniors say they feel younger than their age, and 32 percent say they feel precisely their age. Only 3 percent of seniors report feeling older than their age. And the gap between real and "felt age" increases with age. Almost half of respondents fifty and older report feeling at least ten years younger than their age. Among respondents between sixty-five and seventy-four, one-third says they feel ten to nineteen years younger than their age. And one in six claims to feel at least twenty years younger than their chronological age.

In summary, there is enough evidence to challenge the popular stereotypes about older people. It is, of course, true that some older people fit one or more of these stereotypes (as do some younger people) and that more individuals are likely to fit one or more of them as they reach age eighty. This, however, does not justify applying these stereotypes to all seniors, at any age or for mindlessly applying them to individuals in their fifties and sixties.

Q Why are age-related stereotypes important in the context of health care? It is not a stereotype to say that health care costs of the elderly in America will place a strain on the economy. But the elderly are unfairly harmed when age-related stereotypes are used to deny them proper health care.

Robert Butler (1989) points out that stereotypes lead the younger generation to view the elderly as different from them. As we have seen in the study of racism and sexism, judgments of difference within

CHAPTER 15: HEALTH CARE AND AGING **473**

CHECK YOURSELF **15.6** **R2**

Age Stratification

1. _____ is age-based in equal distribution of scarce desirables in a society.
2. Of the following, which is an *accurate* statement?
   a. Since 1960, the economic situation for the elderly in the United States has deteriorated.
   b. The poverty rate for Americans over sixty-five is lower than the official count indicates.
   c. The elderly who are members of racial or ethnic minorities are in much worse condition than other older people are.
   d. Only about one-fourth of American families in poverty have female heads of household.
3. _____ is a set of beliefs, attitudes, norms, and values used to justify age-based prejudice and discrimination.
4. Age-related _____ are used to justify prejudice and discrimination against the elderly in the context of health care.

Answers: 1. Age stratification; 2. c; 3. Ageism; 4. stereotypes

a category of people usually become powerful reasons to treat them as less deserving of humane treatment. The younger generation is concerned that the impending avalanche of elderly will create a disproportionate economic burden on them. This concern may promote support for reductions in government spending on Medicare and other social support programs for the elderly.

On to Chapter 16

Presented in Chapter 16, sport is the last social institution covered. While clearly not as central an institution as family, education, economy, polity, religion, and health care, sport has significant effects in the United States and abroad.

S INTEGRATED GOALS AND SUMMARY

1. **Define the concept of a health care system, and identify its major components.**
   - All societies must develop ways of coping with the issues of health care and dying. Modern societies have evolved large and complex health care systems. In the United States, for example, health care expenditures alone account for 14 percent of the gross domestic product.
   - The major components of the health care system are physicians, nurses, patients, and hospitals. Physicians control the health care system in the United States and receive rewards of power, prestige, and money. Partly because nursing began as a low-status, female-dominated occupation, it suffers from low power and pay.
2. **Apply functionalism, conflict theory, and symbolic interactionism to the health care system in the United States.**
   - Functionalists conceptualize a sick role, which carries with it prescriptions for the treatment and behavior of patients. Patients are expected to reduce activities in other roles, seek the advice of physicians, and attempt to recover. Failure to cooperate in recovery efforts may result in loss of accommodating privileges.

- Functionalists and conflict theorists offer opposing views of the U.S. medical profession. The medical profession, functionalists contend, has become preeminent because Americans perceive it as essential. Conflict theorists attribute the dominance of the medical profession, the prestige of physicians, the professional and economic problems of nurses, and the inequality of health care to the power of the medical establishment.
- Symbolic interactionism highlights the socialization of physicians and nurses. This perspective, of course, deals with the labeling process in illness. It explains, for example, the attachment of a stigma to certain illnesses.
- The theoretical perspectives provide insight into health care at the macro level. At the macro level, the perspectives help us understand the social nature of a specific health problem such as disability.
3. **Compare health care performance within developed countries and between developed and developing countries.**
   - The United States does not get an appropriate return on its investment in health care. Spending considerably

R3 REVIEW GUIDE

more than other developed countries on health care, but performing below them at the same time, is not an enviable combination. And the United States is the only developed country without national health insurance.

- Developing countries have made notable progress in health care over the last forty years. Their sharp decline in infant and adult mortality reflect this achievement. Because they started with such high levels of mortality, they are still far behind the developed world. And progress has slowed in recent years.

4. Discuss health care reform in the United States.

- The public and politicians agree that the United States, the only major industrial power in the world without national health insurance for everyone, must undergo major health care reform. There are several distinct options for such reform, but the surrounding political, social, and economic conflicts cloud the path.

5. Describe the aging of the world's population.

- The aging of the population is occurring in all highly industrialized societies. It is, therefore, not surprising that the graying of America is one of the most significant changes in the American population. Whereas persons over sixty-five years of age comprise 13 percent of the population today, they will constitute 20 percent in 2040.

6. Discuss the graying of America.

- One of the important consequences of the graying of America is the rising dependency ratio. Thus, as the population ages, there will be proportionately fewer employed people to support the growing retired population.

7. Distinguish between age stratification and ageism.

- Age stratification is the distribution of scarce desirables based on chronological age. A culture justifies its inequality reflected in age stratification through ageism—a set of beliefs, attitudes, norms, and values that permit age-based prejudice and discrimination.

8. Summarize the relationship between health care and aging in the United States.

- Although the economic situation of America's elderly has improved over the last several decades, their poverty rate still stands at about 10 percent. Moreover, the gross poverty rate masks the true economic situation of most elderly Americans. The elderly who are members of racial or ethnic minorities or who are female are in the worst economic condition.
- Age-related stereotypes have important implications for the health care of the elderly. A society can use them to justify lower health care benefits for seniors.

CONCEPT REVIEW

Match the following concepts with the definitions listed below them.

____ a. sick role
____ b. ageism
____ c. age cohort
____ d. stereotypes

____ e. population pyramids
____ f. health care system
____ g. age stratification
____ h. social gerontology

____ i. dependency ratio
____ j. epidemiology
____ k. age structure

1. the professional services, organizations, training academies, and technological resources committed to the treatment, management, and prevention of disease
2. a set of beliefs, attitudes, norms, and values used to justify age-based prejudice and discrimination
3. the unequal distribution of scarce desirables in a society based on age
4. persons born during the same time period in a particular population
5. a social definition serving to remove people from active involvement in everyday routines, give them special protection and privileges, and set the stage for their return to their normal social roles

6. the distribution of people of different ages within a society
7. the proportion of persons in the dependent ages relative to those in the economically active ages
8. graphic representations illustrating the age and sex distribution of a population
9. the scientific study of the social dimensions of aging
10. ideas based on distortion, exaggeration, and oversimplification that are applied to all members of a social category
11. the study of disease distribution patterns within a population

CHECK YOURSELF REVIEW

1. The major reason the United States does not have a national health care system is because its citizens want different results from health care programs than citizens of other developed societies. T or F?

2. The aging of the population is largely confined to the most highly industrialized societies. T or F?
3. In absolute terms, developing countries have made more progress in reducing infant mortality than developed countries. T or F?

4. The _____ embraces the professional services, organizations, training academies, and technological resources that are committed to the treatment, management, and prevention of disease.

5. If a sick person in American society does not attempt to recover, he or she will be labeled a _____.

6. According to _____ theory, affordable health care is not provided to the poor in the United States because of the desire for profit.

7. _____ refers to a set of beliefs, attitudes, norms, and values used to justify age-based prejudice and discrimination.

8. The _____ perspective views disability as a problem of blaming the victim.

9. Health care expenditures now account for about _____ percent of the American GDP.
   - a. 5
   - b. 10
   - c. 16
   - d. 21

10. Nurses are caught in a conflict between their values and their work environment. Which of the following perspectives best helps us understand this situation?
    - a. functionalism
    - b. conflict theory
    - c. symbolic interactionism
    - d. exchange theory

11. Of the following, which is an *accurate* statement?
    - a. Since 1960, the economic situation for the elderly in the United States has deteriorated.
    - b. The poverty rate for Americans over sixty-five is lower than the official count indicates.
    - c. The elderly who are members of racial or ethnic minorities are in much worse condition than other older people are.
    - d. Only about one-fourth of American families in poverty have female heads of household.

12. By 2050, the population pyramid of the United States is expected to resemble
    - a. a triangle.
    - b. a classic pyramid.
    - c. a rectangle.
    - d. an inverted pyramid.

GRAPHIC REVIEW

Figure 15.8 depicts the age and sex structure of the United States as of 1945 and its projected age and sex structure in 2050. Answer the following questions to check your understanding of this information as it relates to the material in this chapter.

1. What was the largest age cohort in 1945?

_____

_____

2. What factors contribute to the change in the shapes of the population pyramids in 1945 and 2050?

_____

_____

3. Why is the seventy to seventy-nine age cohort markedly smaller than nearly all of the other age cohorts in the 2050 population pyramid? Check your answer against what you know about the baby boomers, Generation X, and Generation Y.

_____

_____

CRITICAL-THINKING QUESTIONS

1. Evaluate the idea that under certain circumstances sickness is seen as a form of deviant behavior. Draw on the concept of the sick role in forming your answer.

_____

_____

2. The medical profession in the United States enjoys a lofty position in the stratification structure. Compare the functionalist and conflict explanations of this fact.

_____

_____

3. Do you think the health care system in the United States will be reformed in the next ten to fifteen years? Why or why not? If it is reformed, describe the basic direction you think it will take.

_____

_____

4. Discuss factors that led to the graying of America.

_____

5. Based on information in this chapter, would you expect that the dependency ratio has increased, decreased, or

remained stable over the past fifty years? What other factors influence the dependency ratio? How will America's dependency ratio affect you as you enter the labor force?

_____

_____

6. Examine the stereotypes commonly associated with the elderly. Based on your personal experience with older people, do you think those stereotypes are accurate? Why or why not?

_____

_____

ANSWER KEY

Concept Review

a. 5
b. 2
c. 4
d. 10
e. 8
f. 1
g. 3
h. 9
i. 7
j. 11
k. 6

Check Yourself Review

1. F
2. F
3. T
4. Health care system
5. deviant
6. conflict
7. ageism
8. conflict
9. c
10. c
11. c
12. c

Diademimages/Dreamstime LLC

Sport as a Reflection of Society
Theoretical Perspectives and Sport
Mobility, Inequality, and Sport
Globalization and Sport

S GOALS

- Justify sport as an American institution.
- Compare and contrast sport in America from a functionalist, conflict, and symbolic interactionist perspective.
- Understand the relationship between American sport and social mobility.
- Cite evidence of sexism and racism in American sport.
- Discuss social issues associated with the globalization of sport.

Is sport the way to upward social mobility for minorities? It may appear so on the surface.

Collegiate football and basketball have made it possible for many African Americans to go to college who would not have done so otherwise. There are many wealthy Latino baseball players. But there is evidence that sport actually impedes upward mobility for minorities. The chances of becoming a collegiate or professional player are very small. Minority youth, attracted by the lure of fame and wealth, often fail to obtain the education they need to advance in life.

The issue of social mobility and sport will be covered later in this chapter, along with sport and racism and sport and sexism. The topic of sport as a social institution, however, is our starting point.

Sport as a Reflection of Society R1

For most of us, sport brings to mind certain leisure activities, exercise, and spectator events. Actually it is more complex. Sociologists define **sport** as a set of competitive activities, within a set of established rules, and in which physical performance determines winners and losers. While sport is an important aspect of recreation, many forms of recreation are not sport. Sport sociologist Jay J. Coakley (2009) sees a spontaneous race between two skiers as more of a contest than a sport. Although a contest between skiers involves physical activity and competition, it does not involve definite rules or standardized conditions.

Sport as a Social Institution

Although the five most commonly recognized social institutions—family, education, government, economy, and religion—take different forms in different societies, they appear in every society because they fulfill needs common to all societies.

And, because societies may have additional needs, there may be additional social institutions. In American society, sport is one of these additional institutions. It not only teaches some basic values of a culture, it also promotes attachment to and identification with society. As a prominent sport in ancient Rome, chariot racing illustrates the extent athletes would risk their lives in part to reflect their self-identification as Romans.

The individual, even when free, did not belong to himself; he was strictly subordinated to the city. His life, his death, were only episodes in the history of the group. To confront death was not an act of exceptional heroism; it was the normal way of proving oneself a Roman. (Auguet 1972:198)

Q How does sport create and reinforce American Culture?

American sport embodies American values—striving for excellence, winning, individual and team competition, and materialism. Parents want their children to participate in sport because participation teaches them the basic values of American society and builds character. (Eitzen 2009a:3)

Although sociologists agree that sport mirrors society, and that the relationship is complex, they disagree over the social implications of sport. Sport sociologist Stanley Eitzen has written a book on the paradoxes, or contradictions, of sport in America (see Table 16.1).

Q Can you name another value in sport that exemplifies that same value in our larger society? Sport plays a central role in American society in part because it reflects the culture's emphasis on achievement (Mandelbaum 2004a).

People who visit the United States from other countries are often amazed at the extent to which competition [in sport] is used to distribute rewards and evaluate the work of human beings. (Coakley 2009:82)

Chariot Race (gouache on paper), Jackson, Peter (1922–2003)/Private Collection. © Look and Learn/ The Bridgeman Art Library Internat onal

The chariot races of the Roman Empire involved considerable skill and courage. Charioteers delivered the violence required to please the crowd.

TABLE 16.1

Sport Paradoxes

Stanley Eitzen, a highly respected sport sociologist, argues that sport is inherently contradictory. Here are a few of the paradoxes Eitzen identifies. Do you agree with Eitzen that these paradoxes exist?

Social Integration
Sport can unite different social classes and racial/ethnic groups
but
sport can heighten barriers that separate groups

Fair Play
Sport promotes fair play by teaching the importance of following the rules
but
sport's emphasis on winning tempts people to cheat

Physical Fitness
Sport promotes muscle strength, weight control, endurance, and coordination
but
sport can lead to the use of steroids and other drugs, excessive weight loss or gain, and injuries.

Academics
Sport contributes to higher education through scholarships and fund raising
but
sport takes money away from academics and emphasizes athletic performance over learning and graduation.

Social Mobility
Sport allows athletes who might otherwise not attend college to obtain an education
but
only a few can achieve the promise of fame and wealth in the professional ranks.

Source: D. Stanley Eitzen, Fair and Foul, 4th ed. (Lanham, MD: Rowman & Littlefield Publishers, Inc. 2009).

The prevailing American view of sport is the one reportedly expressed by the late Vince Lombardi, coach of the Green Bay Packers of the National Football League during the 1960s: "Winning isn't everything. It's the only thing." For the most part, sport continues to be dominated by achievement-oriented values.

Q **Where, in sport, can we find a reflection of our society's discrimination?** It is not surprising that males dominate the sports world just as they do many other aspects of American society. Females are second to men overall in power, income, and job opportunities in sports just as they are in business, education, medicine, and law (Eitzen 2009a).

Some progress toward equality is being made, however. The women's basketball teams at both the University of Tennessee and the University of Connecticut have, at different times, held the best single-season record in men's or women's basketball history. Women are making inroads in professional golf and tennis, and the women's professional basketball league (WNBA) has many fans. Mia Hamm and her teammates gave women athletics a healthy boost in 1999 when they won soccer's World Cup. Equality of opportunity for women in sports, though, remains a distant goal.

Q **Is the institution of sport, then, a unified reflection of its host culture?** The short answer is *no*. There are groups, **sport subcultures**, within the larger context of sport that have their own distinct roles, values, and norms. These subcultures are organized around a sport activity, and beliefs vary widely. Sociologist Michael Smith (1979) wanted to know if violence among hockey players is due to involvement in a "subculture of violence." In this kind of subculture, violence is the expected response to a perceived challenge or insult—a jostle, a glance, or an offensive remark. Following this norm is essential in acquiring and maintaining honor, especially when challenges are associated with masculinity.

Smith found that hockey players favor violence more than nonplayers. Because of the expectations of coaches and teammates, many hockey players act violently during games. In fact, players criticize teammates who aren't violent. As one National Hockey League player put it:

I don't think that there's anything wrong with guys getting excited in a game and squaring off and throwing a few punches. That's just part of the game. It always has been. And you know if you tried to eliminate it, you wouldn't have hockey any more. You look at hockey from the time it was begun, guys gets excited and just fight, and it's always been like that. (Eitzen 2009a:165)

What values are at the center of the unique jockey subculture?

Kent Pearson (1981) researched subcultures involving water-related sports in Australia and New Zealand. He found major cultural differences between surfboard riders and surf lifesavers. Surfboard riders avoid formal organizations, work with loose and flexible definitions of the territory in which their sport will occur, place a heavy emphasis on physical prowess and individualism, and generally oppose the larger society. In contrast, surf lifesaving clubs are highly organized entities that stage competitions involving swimming, boating, and lifesaving. The territory for such competitions is precisely defined, and formal rules are employed.

Even in nonteam sports, subcultures emerge Thoroughbred jockeys have developed a subculture with a strong emphasis on displaying dignity, poise, and integrity. The ideal within the subculture of jockeys is a fiery animal with a cool rider.

> The cool jockey can wait patiently with a horse in a pocket and get through on the inside, risking the possibility that there will be no opening. Coolness is waiting far back in the pack, risking the possibility that his horse will not "get up" in time. Coolness is sparing the whip on a front-running horse when another animal has pressed into the lead, risking the possibility that once his horse is passed he will not get started again. All these activities are taken by observers as instances of a jockey's character. In short, moral character is coolness in risky situations. (Scott 1981:146–147)

Jockeys take such chances partly because their subculture requires it. Jockeys who fail to display gallantry, integrity, and coolness—qualities expected of them by horse owners, trainers, and other jockeys—do not receive their choice of horses and therefore win few races. Failing to take risks leads to lost opportunities.

Theoretical Perspectives and Sport

Functionalists tend to concentrate on the benefits of sport. Conflict theorists see a downside. Symbolic interactionists focus on personal meanings derived from sport, on the self-concepts and relationships developed through sport activities.

Functionalism

Q How do functionalists view the role of sport in society? Functionalists think sport contributes to society through the following functions (Eitzen and Sage 2009):

- *Sport teaches basic beliefs, norms, and values.* Sport readies us for adult roles. Games, for instance, prepare participating athletes for work in organizations.

CHECK YOURSELF 16.1

Sport as a Reflection of Society
1. _____ is a set of competitive activities in which winners and losers are determined by physical performance within a set of established rules.
2. A group within the larger context of sport that has some of its own distinct roles, values, and norms is a _____.
3. Which of the following is *not* an example of sport?
   a. a baseball game between two major league teams
   b. a baseball game between two minor league teams
   c. a spontaneous race between two cyclists
   d. a swim meet involving amateur athletes

Answers: 1. Sport; 2. Subculture; 3. c.

Young people who are exposed to competitive sport become more motivated to achieve than those who are not. And the earlier the exposure occurs, the higher the orientation toward achievement. This is important because achievement–motivation is essential to productivity in the modern economy.

- *Sport promotes a sense of social identification.* A team binds people to their community and nation. Clevelanders are united in their love of the Browns, Indians, and Cavaliers. The citizens of Green Bay, Wisconsin, seem to live or die on the fortunes of their beloved Packers.

- *Sport offers a safe release of aggressive feelings generated by the frustrations, anxieties, and strains of modern life.* It is socially acceptable to yell and scream for an athletic team. Similar behavior directed at a teacher, a principal, a parent, or an employer can have negative consequences.

- *Sport encourages the development of character.* Coaches, school officials, and parents often draw a parallel between sport and "life." "When the going gets tough, the tough get going" is a sentiment expressed in most locker rooms. The hard work, discipline, and self-sacrifice demanded by team sports become part of an athlete's value system.

Q What are the social dysfunctions of sport? Functionalists identify some drawbacks to sport. Because sport reflects society, it draws on achievement-oriented values that can be intensified to an extreme degree (Kohn 1992). When achievement and winning come to be seen as the primary goals of sport, any method of winning—including violence and cheating—may be encouraged.

We need not look far to see examples of violence in sport. Coaches and fans expect athletes to place their

Functionalists have identified some drawbacks to sport. Competition can lead to cheating, as when the New England Patriots under head coach Bill Belichick illegally taped opposing team signals during games.

physical well-being on the line. Players in many sports are expected to resort to violence. High school football may defend aggressive behavior as preparation for "real-life" competition. Pressures intensify at the professional level, where many sports develop the informal role of *enforcer*—a team member whose major responsibility is to intimidate, provoke, and even injure opponents (Coakley 2009). Boston Bruins hockey player Marty McSorley used his hockey stick to deliver a vicious blindside slash to the head of opposing player Donald Brashear in February 2000. The attack was the culmination of a game marked by injuries and was the result of the long-standing rivalry between two "top enforcers."

Cheating may not be as easy as violent behavior to identify, but it is often present nonetheless. In 2008, Marion Jones received a six-month prison sentence for lying to federal agents investigating illegal steroid use (O'Connor 2008). Bill Belichick, the coach of the New England Patriots, received a $500,000 fine by the National Football League for videotaping opponents' defensive signals. And cheating can extend beyond players, as when a Utah state committee used illegal inducements to attract the 2002 Winter Olympics.

Conflict Theory

Some sociologists raise disturbing questions that we can better understand through the conflict perspective. Conflict theorists are interested in who has the power

Sport promotes a sense of social identification. These Oakland Raiders fans are carrying social identification to the extreme.

TABLE 16.2

Social Effects of Sport

This table illustrates how each theoretical perspective might study an issue involving sport. For each assumption, provide a specific example from your own experience or from a tem you folllow.

Theoretical Perspective	Concept	Power Elite Model
Functionalism	Social integration	Athletic teams promote togetherness and belonging in a community.
Conflict Theory	Social conflict	Deep social conflict exists within a community and persists despite widespread attachment to athletic teams.
Symbolic Interactionism	Social concept	Participation in a team sport may promote or harm self-esteem depending upon factors such as emphasis on winning and fair play.

and how elites use power to satisfy their own interests. To conflict theorists, sport is a social institution in which the most powerful oppress, manipulate, coerce, and exploit others. Conflict theorists highlight the ways in which sport mirrors the unequal distribution of power and money in society. They also emphasize the role of sport in maintaining inequality (Cozzillio 2005).

While functionalists see sport as contributing to the unification of society, conflict theorists do not (see Table 16.2). While people from all major segments of a community or society may join in cheering for the same team, their union is only temporary.

When the game is over, the enthusiasm dies, the solidarity runs short, and disharmony in other relations reasserts itself. Much as one hour a week cannot answer to the religious impulse, one game a week cannot answer to the solidarity needs of a racist, sexist, or elitist society. (Young 1986)

Basic social class divisions, in other words, will continue to exist and to affect social relationships in a community even if the local team has won the World Series or the Super Bowl.

Conflict theorists likewise question the molding of character. Among college athletes, studies show that the degree of sportsmanship apparently declines as athletes become more involved in the sports system. As sociologist Stanley Eitzen (2009a) notes, nonscholarship athletes display greater sportsmanship than those with athletic scholarships, and those who have not earned letters exhibit more sportsmanship than letter winners.

Conflict theorists can point to any number of past and present scandals where athletes, in high school, college, and professional ranks, are taking drugs, cheating in school, or accepting illegitimate cash "gifts." One university after another is being investigated and penalized by the National Collegiate Athletic Association (NCAA). Coaches as well as players are involved in misconduct.

Athletes may use performance-enhancing drugs such as steroids and amphetamines to achieve a "competitive edge." . . . Big-time college coaches in their zeal to win have been found guilty of exploiting athletes, falsifying transcripts, providing illegal payments, hiring surrogate test takers, paying athletes for nonexistent summer jobs, and illegally using government Pell grants and work study monies for athletes. So much, I would argue, for the myth that "sport builds character." (Eitzen 2009a:189)

Symbolic Interactionism

Symbolic interactionism further contributes to our understanding of sport as a social institution. This theoretical perspective concentrates on personal meanings, social relationships, and self-identity processes. The meanings and interpretations of the symbols associated with sport are important because they affect the self-concepts, as well as the relationships, of those involved (see "Sociology Eyes America 16.1").

The social context of Little League baseball illustrates this perspective. For three years, Gary Alan Fine (1987) studied American adolescent suburban males

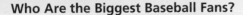

SOCIOLOGY EYES AMERICA 16.1

Who Are the Biggest Baseball Fans?

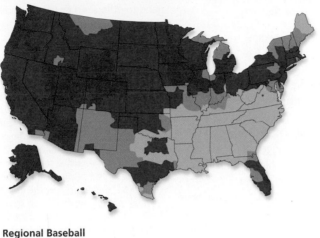

**Regional Baseball
Viewership on Television**

- High
- Above average
- Below average
- Low

Adapted from *Latitudes and Attitudes: An Atlas of American Tastes, Trends, Politics, and Passions.* Boston: Little, Brown.

Baseball fans used to be young working-class white males. Today's fans are older and more affluent but still predominantly white and male. The relative lack of African American fans might be traced to baseball's traditional racist policies on the field and in the front office.

Interpret the Map

1. Do you see any regional patterns in the rates of baseball viewership? Describe.
2. How do you explain these patterns?
3. As a baseball fan, are you similar to or different from the general pattern in your state? Why?

who played Little League baseball. He discovered and documented a variety of ways in which the boys assigned meanings to their team activities. In addition, he described how these meanings and interpretations influenced the boys' social interactions and affected their self-definitions.

Q What were these meanings? Much of the activity of coaches and parents centered on teaching the rules of the game and teaching values, such as team play, hard work, fair play, competition, and winning. But these ten-to twelve-year-old boys formed their own interpretation of these messages. The boys misinterpreted the

Do you think participation in a team sport at an early age promotes or harms self-esteem?

Vicky Kasala/Alamy Limited

Tough Guys, Wimps, and Weenies

Donna Eder researched the nature of middle-school sports using the case study method. Following the framework of symbolic interactionism, Eder assumes that the social world of teenagers is constructed through interaction with others. Thus, everyday exchanges—insults, greetings, gossip—give teenagers a sense of their self and the social world.

Middle-school coaches accented the value of toughness. In the world of athletics, having a "mean" attitude is masculine and being nice is effeminate. Wrestlers, for example, were told to make opponents "suffer." Football coaches did not tolerate fighting off the field, but as a means to handle conflict among athletes, these same coaches encouraged physical force on the field.

I said that I had heard that Coach Paulson wasn't pleased with the way the team played. Walter and Carl both agreed. Walter [the team manager] said that the team didn't hit like they should have and that made the coach

mad. Carl said, "Yeah, but I really socked that guy. Man, I threw him down on the concrete. Did you hear Coach James yelling, "Way to go, Orville"? (Eder 1995:62)

Evidence of weakness was greeted by derogatory names like "wuss," "wimp," and "girl." Ritual insults promoted stereotypically masculine behavior, particularly among higher-status boys. Stories of physical force in sports were repeated with pride. Even soccer players bragged about kicking opponents in the shins or throwing a ball into an opponent's face.

The most forcefully combative boys were the most respected. Although the coaches tried to curb physical violence outside of games and matches, many players considered fighting an appropriate way to handle all peer conflicts.

[The] importance of being tough extended to behavior off the playing field as well as on it. Boys were continually challenged to develop more aspects of toughness, including the ability to deny pain and suppress feelings as well as respond combatively to verbal and physical attacks. Boys who rejected these messages were sometimes subject to ridicule by girls as well as boys, showing the difficulty boys faced when trying to escape the pressures of being masculine within this school setting. (Eder 1995:72)

Insult exchanges could be won by getting another boy to become angry.

By losing his cool, the other boy lost his image of toughness. Some boys would insult another boy just to look good to others. An example is provided by one of the researcher's notes on Hank, the highest-status boy in the seventh grade, who had a reputation for verbal assault:

Hank does seem to enjoy conflict or competition on a one-on-one basis. A couple of times today he left the table just to go down and abuse some kid at the end of the table, calling him a pud, a squirrel, or a wimp. Then he would come back and tell the group how the guy had done nothing when he had said this. Hank would get a big smile on his face and was really pleased. (Eder 1995:73–74)

Insults and counter-insults delivered several messages. First, boys learned not to care about the feelings of others. Second, insulting, or even humiliating, their peers was a socially approved means of achieving or displaying higher status. Third, boys who humiliated low-status peers were rewarded with social recognition. This was true even if the target of ridicule had a disability or was overweight.

Evaluate the Research
1. Do you think this study describes sports at your school? Explain.
2. Do female athletes treat one another differently from the way boys treat one another? Explain.

---

adult values of hard work, competition, and so forth as the "masculine" values of dominance, "toughness," and risky behavior (see "Consider This Research").

Q How were social interaction and self-concepts affected? In the first place, the boys' behavior convinced coaches and parents that the youngsters understood and accepted their values. For example, the aggressive behavior that the boys considered as evidence of their masculinity was, to the coaches and parents, evidence of "hustle," a dedication to competition, and the desire to win. The praise the coaches and parents showered

on the boys encouraged them to continue their aggressiveness. "Weaker" peers, younger children, and girls in general frequently experienced the disdain of these Little Leaguers, and this disrespect often led to low self-esteem for children who suffered the brunt of the Little Leaguers' scorn.

Q What are some limitations of each perspective? Although the functionalist perspective makes important points regarding the positive and negative roles of sport in society, critics contend that many sports are so closely tied to elite interests that they

CHECK YOURSELF 16.2 R2

Theoretical Perspectives and Sport

1. Which of the following is *not* one of the functions of sport discussed in the text?
   a. Sport solidifies social class identification.
   b. Sport teaches basic beliefs, norms, and values.
   c. Sport provides a sense of identification.
   d. Sport offers a safe release of aggressive feelings.
   e. Sport encourages the development of character.
2. Several social aspects of sport are listed below. Indicate which would most interest functionalists (F), conflict theorists (C), and symbolic interactionists (SI).
   ____ a. intensification of achievement-oriented values
   ____ b. maintaining social inequality
   ____ c. character building
   ____ d. self-identification
   ____ e. sport scandals

Answers: 1. a; 2. a. (F), b. (C), c. (F), d. (SI), e. (C)

contribute more to private profit than to the general well-being of society. To investigate this point, the conflict perspective concentrates on some major flaws of sport, such as racism and sexism (discussed in the next section). On the other hand, critics claim conflict theorists tend to overlook the positive contributions of sport, place too much emphasis on the extent to which the elite manipulate and control sport, and underestimate the character-building benefit. Indeed, symbolic interactionism contributes greatly to understanding the socialization process in sport, but, because it concentrates on social interaction, it fails to include the broader social and cultural context. For example, symbolic interactionism does not address the functions of sport in society or explore sport within the context of power and social inequity.

Mobility, Inequality, and Sport R1

Sport contributes to upward mobility among collegiate athletes, but the opportunities are too few. In addition, minorities face discrimination (see "See Sociology in Your Life") and women suffer from gender-based stereotypes.

Social Mobility in Sport

The autobiographies of star athletes often point to sport as their way out of poverty. One educator once predicted that "football would enable a whole generation of young men in the coal fields of Pennsylvania to turn their backs on the mines that employed their fathers". Many athletes do use sport as a means out of their equivalent "coal fields," and many minority

members work their way out of poverty through sport. It is also true that the average salaries of professional athletes are extremely high. Even so, let's examine this alleged relationship between sport and social mobility.

Jonathan Kim/Alamy Limited

The phenomenal success of basketball star Michael Jordan is frequently used as proof that sport is a path to upward social mobility for minorities. How typical is Jordan's experience?

How to Avoid Bigotry in Sports

Sports sociologist Jay Coakley supports the concerns of many Native Americans on the issue of team names. He wrote the following article about this issue.

Most of us are not very concerned about the use of Native American names by many athletic teams. But to Native Americans, war whoops and tomahawk chopping portray negative stereotypes.

Using stereotypes to characterize Native Americans in the United States is so common that most people don't even realize they are doing it. . . .When these stereotypes are used as a basis for team names, mascots, and logos, sports become a way of perpetuating

an ideology that exploits, trivializes, and demeans the history and cultural heritage of Native Americans.

If teachers, administrators, and students in U.S. schools had a deep knowledge of the rich and diverse cultures of Native Americans and realized the discrimination native peoples currently face, they would not use names such as Indians, Redskins, Chiefs, Braves, Savages, Tribe, and Redmen for their teams; they would not allow Anglo students to entertain fans by dressing up as caricatures of Native Americans; and they would not allow fans to mimic Native American chants or act out demeaning stereotypes of war-whooping, tomahawk-chopping Native Americans.

Schools should not use any Native American name or symbol in connection with sport teams unless they do the following:

1. Sponsor a special curriculum to inform students of the history, cultural heritage, and current living conditions of the native group after which their sport teams are named. Unless

70 percent of the students can pass annual tests on this information, schools should drop the names they say they used to "honor" native people.
2. Publish two press releases per year in which information about the heritage and current circumstances of the native peoples honored by their team names is described and analyzed; publish similar materials annually in school newspapers and yearbooks.
3. Once per year, during homecoming or a major sport event, sponsor a special ceremony designed by and for native peoples in the local area, with the purpose of informing students and parents about the people they say they honor with their team names.

Think About It

Is there a sport symbol in your community or state that might be offensive to Native Americans? Has the existence of this offensive symbol hurt your community or state economically? Explain.

Source: Jay J. Coakley, *Sport in Society*, 6th ed. (Boston: McGraw-Hill, 2006, pp. 272–273).

Q Is there social mobility among athletes? Participation in sport does improve the chances of college athletes moving up the stratification structure. Whatever sport they play, college athletes tend to be better educated, earn more money, and have higher occupational prestige than their fathers. This is the very definition of upward social mobility. And, in these terms, college athletes as a whole are more successful than college students who do not participate in sports (Leonard 1998). Although this finding is meaningful, it does not settle the debate regarding the degree to which sport promotes upward mobility for minorities.

Q Does sport promote upward mobility for minorities? Some people argue that sport is a social class escalator for minorities. They point to Tiger Woods, Kobe Bryant, and Venus and Serena Williams, among others. A different viewpoint argues that the emphasis on sport is harmful because it diverts attention from learning the academic and business-related skills necessary for

success in mainstream American society. Because of the lure of high salaries and prestige, many aspiring minority athletes fail to develop alternative career plans. Minority members who spend their youth sharpening their athletic skills at the expense of their general education will very likely be casualties of an unrealizable dream of wealth and glory (Lapchick and Matthews 2004; Lapchick and General 2007).

Some convincing evidence supports those who see sport as a barrier to upward mobility for minorities. Table 16.3 shows that there are more than 1 million high school players. Fewer than 60,000 of these players become college football players. And only 1,600 of these college players become professional players. Thus, the probability that a high school football player will make it to the pros is less than two-tenths of 1 percent. Similarly a high school baseball player has a 0.2 percent chance of becoming a major leaguer. The odds are even worse for a high school basketball player, who has a 0.1 percent probability of making it

TABLE 16.3

Athletes' Chances of Advancing to the Pros

This table shows the slim chance that high school athletes have to play a professional sport. Does this surprise you?

	Number of Players in High School	Percentage Advancing from High School to College	Number of Players in College	Percentage Advancing from College to Professional Level	Number of Players at Professional Level	Percentage Advancing from High School to Professional Level
MALES						
Football	1,002,734	6%	57,593	3%	1,643	0.16%
Basketball	541,130	3%	15,874	2%	348	0.06%
Baseball	451,701	6%	25,938	3%	750	0.17%
Ice hockey	27,245	13%	3,647	18%	648	2.38%
Total	2,022,811	5%	103,052	3%	3,389	0.17%
FEMALES						
Basketball	451,600	3%	14,445	1%	132	0.03%
Golf	49,690	6%	3,108	2%	52	0.10%
Tennis	159,740	5%	8,314	2%	150	0.09%
Total	661,030	4%	25,867	1%	334	0.05%
Grand Total	**2,683,841**	**5%**	**128,919**	**3%**	**3,723**	**0.14%**

Source: National Federation of State High School Associations, 1999–2000.

to the National Basketball Association. Moreover, those who become professional athletes have short careers: one to seven years for baseball players, four to six years for basketball players, and four-and-one-half years for football players.

Of course, this does not mean minority athletes should not enjoy the benefits of a collegiate sport. To be sure, some athletes, who may otherwise not have the chance, receive college degrees. It does argue, however, that no high school athlete—minority or white—should rely solely on sport as a ticket up the stratification structure.

Racial and Ethnic Inequality in Sport

Stacking—assigning players to less central positions on the basis of race or ethnicity—is an obvious indication of systemic discrimination. "Central" positions are those that involve leadership and decision-making responsibilities and thus offer a greater likelihood of influencing the outcome of a game. Historically, minorities have positions requiring relatively little interaction and coordination with other players. In football, for example, African American quarterbacks traditionally

are rare, while the proportions of African Americans in many defensive and other less central positions are high (see Figure 16.1).

Such discrimination has important economic consequences: the less central positions occupied by most African Americans have high injury rates that cut careers short, which in turn reduce both salaries and pension benefits.

Q Is there salary fairness in professional sports? Discrimination in salary at the professional level exists. African Americans in the major professional sports are, on the average, paid as much as or more than their white counterparts. It is only when level of performance is controlled that discrimination appears—African Americans have lower average salaries than whites for the same level of performance. In other words, African Americans must perform better than whites to avoid pay discrimination (Eitzen and Sage 2009).

Q Where else do we find discrimination? Minority former athletes profit much less than their white colleagues from personal appearances and commercial endorsements. They also lose out in sports-related

FIGURE 16.1

National Football League Positions, by Race

Do you think that these data support the presence of stacking in the NFL?

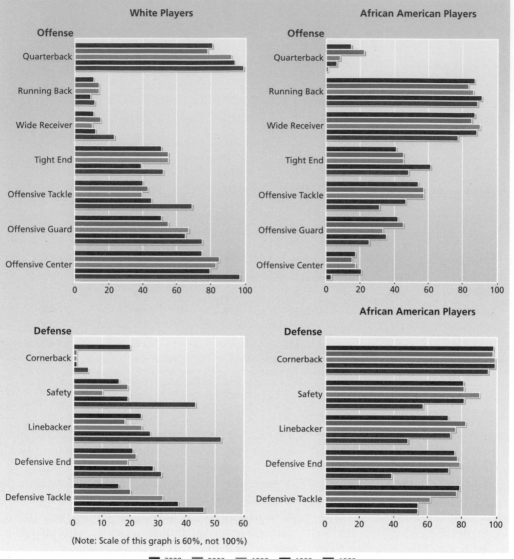

Source: The Institure for Diversity and Ethics in Sport, 2004 and Richard Lapchick, "The 2010 Racial and Gender Report Card : National Football League," The Institute for Diversity and Ethics in Sport, University of Central Flordia, September 29, 2010.

careers when their playing days are over. In professional sports overall, minorities are grossly underrepresented in the power structure—head coaches, general managers, owners, executives, commissioners. In 1989, Bill White became the first African American to head a major professional sports league. In 2010, 82 percent of players in the National Basketball Association (NBA) were people of color, while only 21 percent held team senior administrative positions. In the NBA League Office, only 36 percent of management was African American, Latino, Asian, Native American, or "other."

Michael Jordan is the only minority member to hold majority ownership in a professional basketball team. There was only one Asian and eight African Americans head coaches (Lapchick 2010a).

At the start of the 2010 season, African Americans accounted for 67 percent of National Football League (NFL) players. In the League Office, only one-fourth of management was African American, Latino, Asian, Native American, or "other." There were just six African Americans head coaches. Only 17 percent of team senior administrative personnel were minorities.

Minorities are well represented as players in major U.S. sports. However, after their playing days are over, minorities are underrepresented in administrative positions within their sport.

Mayskyphoto/Used under license from Shutterstock

No person of color has ever held majority ownership of an NFL franchise. Less than 20 percent of the radio and television announcers were Latino or African American (Lapchick, 2010b).

The situation in Major League Baseball (MLB) is somewhat better because minorities comprise a smaller percentage of the players. Forty percent of MLB's players were people of color at the beginning of the 2010 season. At the director and managerial level in MLB's Central Office people of color represented 20 percent of the employees. There were two Latino and three African American general managers (17 percent of the total number of general managers). Only 16 percent of senior team administrators were people of color. One person of color owned a franchise. There were nine team minority managers: three African American, five Latino, and one Asian American (30 percent of all MLB managers; Lapchick 2010c).

Q **What about racial and ethnic inequality in college sports?** Much of what has been said about professional sports applies to collegiate sports, only more so. According to Richard Lapchick (2009), positions of power at the collegiate level are overwhelming held by white men. In Divisions I, II, III of the NCAA, over 90 percent of all university presidents, athletic directors, head coaches, faculty athletic representatives, and sports information directors are white men. Excluding historically black colleges and universities, white men hold 100 percent of the conference commissioner positions in Division I. Only two Asian males and one Native American male were in leadership positions.

Gender Inequality in Sport

Racial and ethnic minorities are not the only victims of prejudice and discrimination in sport. Women experience sexism in athletics. The cultural roots of sexism date back at least as far as the ancient Greeks. Greek gods were depicted as athletic, strong, powerful, competitive, rational, physical, and intellectual. Most Greek goddesses were passive, beautiful, physically weak, supportive, unathletic, and sexually attractive. (The few active strong goddesses were usually not attractive to nor attracted by men. To Greek males, women who were physically or intellectually superior to them were unfeminine.) Twenty-five hundred years later we feel the influence of these gender definitions in sport just as we do in other aspects of social life.

Q **What are some of the consequences of sexism?** Stereotypes traditionally discouraged females from playing sports. For centuries, to be an athlete, the culture warned, was to be unfeminine. This stigma discouraged many females from participating in athletics and tyrannized many of those who did. Another barrier was the old, discredited argument that sports harm a woman's health, particularly her ability to have children.

In addition, sexism has explicitly denied females equal access to organized sports, and, at the local level, resistance to female participation in sports continues to exist (McDonagh and Pappano 2008). It was not until the mid-1970s that, under legal threat, the national Little League organization ended its males-only policy. And, only in 1972 did the Educational Amendment Act

Although sexism in sports has been decreasing, women athletes continue to suffer from inequalities.

Amy Sancetta/AP Photos

(Title IX) require public high schools and colleges to offer females equal access to sports. Originally, Title IX was interpreted as providing equal opportunity in "all" sport programs of institutions receiving federal funds. But, ambiguities in Title IX led to many legal suits and unresolved issues. Currently, the courts favor matching the ratio of males and females in a school's athletic programs to their proportionate numbers in the student body of that school (Hannon 2003; Orecklin 2003; Messner 2007).

Q Why do we have a decline in the percentage of women in collegiate leadership positions? It is true that in the early 1970s, women did lead most women's intercollegiate teams. But at this point, men coach 60 percent of the NCAA women's teams (see Figure 16.2), and administer about 80 percent of women's programs. Females hold only 41 percent of all administrative jobs in women's programs (Acosta and Carpenter 2004).

Ironically, Title IX may be one reason for this decline. As the money and prestige associated with

FIGURE 16.2

Percentage of College Women's Athletic Teams Coached by Women (Division 1)

What is most interesting to you about these data?

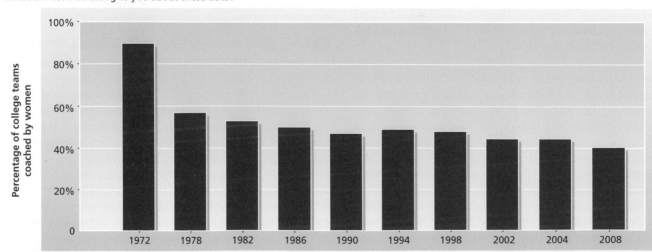

Source: R. Vivian Acosta and Linda Jean Carpenter, "Women in Intercollecgiate Sport." Brooklyn College, 2004; Richard Lapchick, "The 2009 Racial and Gender Report Card : College Sport," The Institute for Diversity and Ethics in Sport, University of Central Flordia, March 11, 2010.

CHECK YOURSELF 16.3 R2

Mobility, Inequality, and Sport

1. One positive thing about sports is that they eliminate discrimination. T or F?
2. Sport can impede the social mobility of minorities. T or F?
3. _____ involves the assignment of players to less central positions on the basis of race or ethnicity.
4. Minority former athletes benefit less than their white colleagues from personal appearances and commercial endorsements. T or F?
5. Females are denied equal access to organized sports because of _____.

Answers: 1. F; 2. T; 3. Stacking; 4. T; 5. sexism

women's programs increase, men find these coaching jobs much more attractive. And conflict theorists believe that men, who are overwhelmingly in charge of athletic programs and who have the power to make hiring decisions, are more likely to choose men as coaches (Fazioli 2004).

Q How are women represented at the national level? Currently, professional sports for women include a Women's National Basketball Association (WNBA), a volleyball league, a golf tour, and a tennis circuit. As we have seen, few athletes make it to the professional ranks. But, even those women who become professionals earn significantly less than their male counterparts. Golf, for example, is one of the few professional sports offering significant opportunities for women. Still, the leading money winner on the men's tour earns far more than twice as much as the leading money winner on the women's tour. This disparity is reflected in the 2010 prize money earned by the top men's Professional Golfers' Association (PGA) player and the top Ladies Professional Golf Association (LPGA) player—$5 million versus $2 million.

There are some positive, if small, signs of change. Tennis sensation Venus Williams has product endorsement contracts with American Express, McDonald's, and Wilson Racquet Sports. In 2003, Serena Williams signed a five-year contract with Nike worth close to $40 million. And shortly after sixteen-year old golfer Michelle Wie turned professional in 2005, she signed endorsement deals worth $10 million a year.

Globalization and Sport R1

Globalization, you know by now, embodies many societies of the world and their awareness of mutual economic, political, and social commonalities. Commonalities are most prominent in popular culture—music, dance, dress, movies, television shows, and entertainment in general. And sport is one of the primary forms of entertainment shared across national borders, in part because sport is

seen as less threatening socially and politically than music, dance, or dress.

The globalization of sport began in the 1870s as Britain spread cricket and soccer into its imperial holdings and along its trading routes in Europe and South America (Giulianotti and Robertson 2007). The transnationalizing of sport accelerated in the twentieth century and continues today (Smart 2007). Most emblematic of the globalization of sport is the Olympic Games run by the International Olympic Committee (See "Think Globally" 16.1). Additional examples include the popularity of baseball in Japan, the recent encroachment of the "other" game of football (soccer is the original) into British culture, and the establishment of an NFL-type league abroad. Sport appeals to something universal in human beings, a fact recognized by a secretary of the United Nations who pronounced soccer as more universal than the UN. The FIFA World Cup, he asserted, brings together the family of nations in celebration of our common humanity (Annan 2006).

An aspect of culture so shared worldwide as sport is bound to create significant social issues. Prominent among these issues, as articulated by conflict theorists, are the economic and cultural influences of multinational sport corporations and the growth of a worldwide consumer culture.

Influence of Transnational Corporations

Sport is now part of global capitalism. The global sport market generates some $300 billion in sales annually. The most rapidly expanding markets are in South Asia, Central Asia, the Middle East, and Central and Eastern Europe. Growth in the global sports market follows, as it must, the money. Expansion of sales is occurring in those countries experiencing the largest increases in economic development. More discretionary income permits people to purchase sports equipment, clothing, and shoes. As in the United States, brand name sports goods are worn as status symbols ("Global Sports Equipment, Apparel, and Footwear Market Nearly $280B" 2011).

THINK GLOBALLY 16.1

Olympic Success

Sport also plays an important role in today's global society. For some time, the winning of Olympic medals has been a source of regional and global prestige. This map shows the number of medals earned by each country in the 2008 Summer Olympic Games.

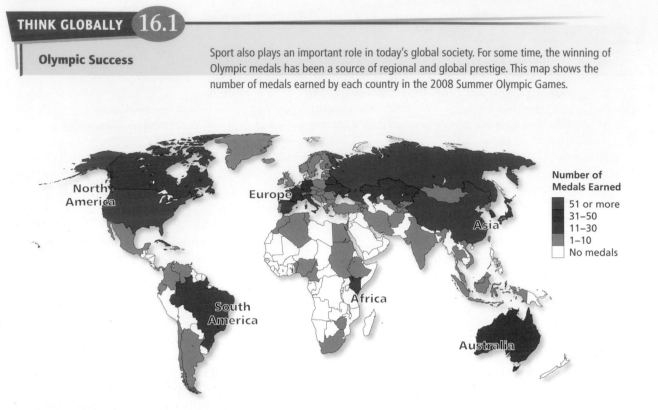

Number of Medals Earned

- 51 or more
- 31–50
- 11–30
- 1–10
- No medals

Source: *The World Almanac and Book of Facts, 2010,* p. 858.

Interpret the Map

1. Why do you think there is such wide variation in the number of Olympic medals earned?

2. Do the Olympics illustrate connection between sport and politics? Explain.

Q **What is the economic impact of multinational corporations on host countries?** Nike illustrates the influence of large sport corporations in the countries where they locate (Eitzen 2009b). Founded primarily as a shoe company in 1964, Nike had sales of $19 billion in 2010, from the work of some 450,000 employees in Southeast Asia and 120,000 workers in China. Nike runs over 900 independent international factories and has 3,000 stores in China alone. D. Stanley Eitzen (2009b) describes Nike as a classic case of capitalism at work in the global market

Capitalism in sport is nowadays global. This young boy selling souvenir pens in Albania sports the Nike brand.

Maciej Dakowicz / Alamy

place. Its 35,000 American employees accomplish Nike's product research, design, development, and marketing. The actual production of sports goods occurs elsewhere. Low-wage countries without labor laws and environmental protection regulations are where the labor-intensive, assembly-line work takes place. Companies like Nike move their production sites to locations where wages are the lowest and governments are the friendliest to their profit-maximizing interests. In the latter part of the 1980s, for example, Nike left South Korea and Taiwan, where wages were rising, into countries like Indonesia and Thailand. Later, operations were moved to China and Southeast Asia for the same reason.

As a result of this business strategy, conflict theorists argue, corporations are making higher profits while undercutting local labor markets and exploiting workers. Three-fourths of Nike's factory workers are young women, who routinely work ten to thirteen hours daily, six days a week, for as little as $1.60 to $2.20 a day. And they do so under appalling physical conditions and abusive management. Alongside them often are children also working in a sweatshop environment, despite efforts by human rights groups to introduce protective child labor laws. The shoes sold in the United States for $100 and more, thus, are made by children and young women who continue to live in poverty and work under conditions long ago outlawed in developed countries. And if too many demands are made to ameliorate this situation—like demanding cost-of-living increases and better working conditions—multinational sport corporations either threaten to leave the country or actually do move their operations to countries where people are just as poor but less demanding (Coakley 2009).

In fairness, Eitzen notes that Nike simply represents the norm among transnational sport corporations. He highlights Nike only because its profits are sufficiently large that it could operate more humanely. And global sport corporations defend themselves by pointing to their creation of jobs where few employment opportunities exist and to their role in introducing and promoting capitalism within host countries.

Q **How do transnational sport corporations affect the local cultures of host countries?** In order to create markets for their products, multinational sport corporations alter local cultures in two ways. The rather subtle first path is designed to avoid rejection and promote acceptance for their products. Toward accomplishing this goal, a corporation often hires researchers to investigate the popular activities and preferred clothing of a society's young people. Based on this research, a corporation produces goods—sports shoes, clothing, etc.—that mirror the local customs and tastes. The corporation then re-creates these preferences and, thereupon, launches a media campaign illustrating (or proclaiming) the compatibility between the company's "new" products and

the original preferences of the local culture. Through this advertising process, multinationals bombard potential consumers with messages and images that ultimately modify, some say undermine, a culture's initial patterns of thinking, feeling, and behaving.

George Ritzer (2004) refers to the above process as *glocalization*. This concept, a synthesis of the words *global* and *local*, captures the interplay between global influence and local influence, and assumes that different cultures will incorporate global influences in ways unique to their local cultures. Ritzer adds another concept, *grobalization*, which is the second path multinationals can take to alter local culture. Grobalization highlights the imperative for *growth* inherent in the ideology of multinational corporations. While glocalization entails the modification of global values as they are incorporated into local cultures, grobalization captures the attempt to make local cultures a part of global culture. Inherent in grobalization is the effort by multinationals to create a universal consumer culture common to all societies.

Creation of a Consumer Culture

Howard Nixon (2008) does an excellent job of elaborating on globalization and the diffusion of a consumer culture around the world. Nixon's starting point is what he calls the *Golden Triangle*, a power elite in global sports formed by sport organizations (such as the International Olympic Committee), corporate media (such as television networks), and corporate sponsors (such as Nike). Actually, as Nixon recognizes, there are multiple golden triangles formed around specific global sport venues such as the Olympics and the FIFA World Cup. At any rate, the driving imperative of the elite is to grow markets for their products, particularly where none exists (Giulianotti and Robertson 2007).

Q **By what means do golden triangles expand their markets?** Golden triangles attempt to create as many potential consumers as possible by generating a universal sports culture (grobalization). Television, especially, provides an avenue for transnational corporate interests to grobalize. You can see its importance in the increasing prices television networks can charge corporate sponsors. For example, the U.S. broadcast rights fee for the Summer Olympics rose from $400,000 for the 1960 Games in Rome to $894 million for the 2008 Olympics in Beijing (Coakley 2009). The global influence of television on sport is also obvious in the enormous worldwide audience attracted by the Olympic Games (over 3 billion in 2008), the FIFA World Cup (over 2 billion in 2010), and the Superbowl (over 100 million in 2010).

Multinationals further expand their sports markets via sports celebrities, whom they use to endorse products internationally. For example, they use NBA star Yao Ming successfully to promote an interest in basketball in China.

CHECK YOURSELF 16.4 R2

Globalization and Sport

1. The global sport market generates about _____ in sales annually.
2. According to conflict theorists, global sport corporations move foreign production facilities from country to country in order to.
   a. take advantage of low wages.
   b. create jobs where few exist.
   c. employ American workers abroad.
   d. serve as an ambassador for Western culture.
   e. promote capitalism throughout the world.
3. The concept _____ captures the interplay between the influence of global corporations and local cultures.
4. Around which of the following does a "golden triangle" *not* evolve
   a. sport organizations
   b. media organizations
   c. political leaders
   d. corporate sponsors

Answers: 1. $300 billion; 2. a; 3. glocalization; 4. c

With this increased interest, the huge Chinese market for all sorts of sports equipment and apparel is now open.

In addition, Eitzen (2009b) credits the outreach efforts of U.S. professional baseball, football, and basketball organizations with spreading their sports around the globe. The U.S. baseball All-Star team has conducted a tour of Japan for years. Since 2000, Major League Baseball International has sent high school and college baseball coaches to twenty-nine countries to teach young people the game. Interested audiences in a variety of countries can view certain games on television by request. An audience in more than 200 nations can watch the World Series and the All-Star Game. The NFL plays a minimum of one exhibition game annually in another country. Over 200 countries receive the telecast of the Superbowl. The NFL International established a developmental league for players in Europe in 1995. It is composed of six teams from the Netherlands, Spain, and Germany. Soccer is the largest sport in the world, but basketball is the fastest growing. This is not accidental. The NBA encourages foreign athletes to play on U.S. teams, and, in turn, markets these players in their native countries. Preseason games are held each year in Europe, Latin America, and Asia. Over 200 nations can watch NBA games in forty languages. According to the NBA Commissioner, the league is expecting to soon receive half of its revenue from international markets.

On to Chapter 17

We are leaving the section of the text dealing with social institutions. While we have documented change in social institutions, the accent has been on social structures in their present form. The final two chapters shift the focus specifically to change in social structures. Chapter 17 concentrates on population and urbanization, two important influences contributing to social change.

S INTEGRATED GOALS AND SUMMARY

1. **Justify sport as an American institution.**
   - As a social institution, sport fulfills some important societal needs. One of these is helping individuals identify with others members of society.
   - Sport subcultures have developed around both team and individual sports. For this reason, sport is a reflection of society.
2. **Compare and contrast sport in America from a functionalist, conflict, and symbolic interactionist perspective.**
   - Functionalists see sport positively, as a means for socializing young people, promoting social integration, providing a release for tensions, and developing sound character. Conflict theorists believe that organized sports can be harmful to character development. Symbolic interactionists focus on the self-concepts and relationships developed through sport activities.
3. **Understand the relationship between American sport and social mobility.**
   - There are two dimensions to the relationship between social mobility and collegiate athletics: mobility for all college athletes and mobility for minority athletes.

Overall, college athletes benefit from participation in sport. They tend to be better educated, earn more money, and have higher occupational prestige than their fathers. Reliance on sport for upward mobility, however, is detrimental to minority athletes.

4. Cite evidence of sexism and racism in American sport.
- Minorities continue to face discrimination in sport. Discrimination against minority athletes exists in assigned playing positions, salary levels, commercial endorsements, and post-career leadership opportunities.
- Females in sport suffer from gender-based stereotypes. Discrimination begins early, with a relative lack of opportunity in youth leagues. It continues in secondary, collegiate, and professional sport. Although intercollegiate female athletes do not receive treatment equal to

males, this situation is slowly improving. Fewer women are able to become professional athletes and are paid less than males when they do.

5. Discuss social issues associated with the globalization of sport.
- Transnational sport corporations affect cultures of host countries, economically as well as socially. Economically, conflict theorists cite transnational sport corporations for undercutting local labor markets and exploiting local workers. Corporations want credit for creating jobs and fostering economic development in poor countries. Socially, global sport corporations alter the societies they enter either by tailoring their products to fit a local culture or by attempting to impose global culture on a local population.

CONCEPT REVIEW

Match the following concepts with the definitions listed below them.

____ a. stacking   ____ b. sport subculture   ____ c. sport

1. A set of competitive activities in which winners and losers are determined by physical performance within a set of established rules.
2. The assignment of players to less central positions on the basis of race or ethnicity.
3. A group within the larger context of sport that has some of its own distinct rules, values, and norms.

CHECK YOURSELF REVIEW

1. Which of the following is *not* one of the functions of sport discussed in the text?
   a. Sport solidifies social class identification.
   b. Sport teaches basic beliefs, norms, and values.
   c. Sport provides a sense of identification.
   d. Sport offers a safe release of aggressive feelings.
   e. Sport encourages the development of character.
2. One positive thing about sports is that they eliminate discrimination. T or F?
3. Sport can impede the social mobility of minorities. T or F?
4. Minority former athletes benefit less than their white colleagues from personal appearances and commercial endorsements. T or F?
5. _____ involves the assignment of players to less central positions on the basis of race or ethnicity.
6. _____ is a set of competitive activities in which winners and losers are determined by physical performance within a set of established rules.

7. A group within the larger context of sport that has some of its distinct roles, values, and norms is a _____.
8. Females are denied equal access to organized sports because of _____.
9. Several social aspects of sport are listed below. Indicate which would most interest functionalists (F), conflict theorists (C), and symbolic interactionists (SI).
   ____ a. intensification of achievement-oriented values
   ____ b. maintaining social inequity
   ____ c. character building
   ____ d. self-identification
   ____ e. sport scandals
10. Which of the following does a "golden triangle" *not* involve?
   ____ a. sport organizations
   ____ b. media organizations
   ____ c. political leaders
   ____ d. corporate sponsors

GRAPHIC REVIEW

Table 16.3 shows an athlete's chances of making it to next level in their respective sports.

1. Describe any patterns you see in the data in this table.

_____

_____

2. Discuss the implications of these data for the chances of upward social mobility for male and female athletes.

_____

_____

CRITICAL-THINKING QUESTIONS

1. Athletes with superior skills are often given extraordinary help in meeting school requirements. Many students feel this is unfair. Others point out that athletics bring in lots of money for colleges. They also say that athletes have skills as rare as high intelligence and so deserve their sports scholarships. What do you think?

_____

_____

2. Some schools have made efforts to change their school nicknames and mascots so as not to offend various groups that might have been negatively portrayed by these mascots and nicknames. Do you think that schools and teams have an obligation to take such actions? Or should teams be allowed to retain their traditional nicknames and mascots?

_____

_____

3. In the National Basketball Association draft, the best players go to the teams that competed the previous season with the worst records. Why do you think the NBA uses this approach instead of allowing the best players to go to the teams with the most prestige, status, and monetary resources? Should the NBA use a different method?

_____

_____

ANSWER KEY

Concept Review

a. 2
b. 3
c. 1

Check Yourself Review

1. a
2. F
3. T
4. T
5. stacking
6. sport
7. subculture
8. sexism
9. a. F
   b. C
   c. F
   d. SI
   e. C
10. c

Population and Urbanization 17

S GOALS

- Distinguish among the concepts of demography, formal demography, and social demography.
- Distinguish the three population processes.
- Discuss the major dimensions of the world population growth problem.
- Predict future world and U.S. population trends.
- Differentiate among the basic measures of urbanization.

- Trace the historical development of preindustrial and modern cities.
- Describe some of the consequences of suburbanization.
- Discuss world urbanization.
- Compare and contrast four theories of city growth.
- Compare and contrast traditional and contemporary views on the quality of urban life.

USING THE SOCIOLOGICAL IMAGINATION

Do you perceive urbanites as being part of the "lonely crowd," living amid a sea of strangers? If so, you can find support in the pioneering studies of urbanism. Subsequent research, however, presents another depiction: Urban residents engage in personal relationships and these social ties contribute to a positive emotional state of mind. There are those without such social relationships, but they tend to be recently relocated residents who have not yet had time to form close human connections.

The quality of urban life is an important consideration. There are, of course, many other issues associated with population growth and urbanization. As a prelude to these issues, the chapter begins with the concept of demography.

The Dynamics of Demography ◾

The Nature of Demography

Q Why is demography essential in the discussion of population change? Demography, the scientific study of population, encompasses all measures of population: size, distribution, composition, age structure, and change. Although basically a social science, demography draws from many disciplines, including biology, geography, mathematics, economics, sociology, and political science.

Demographic research includes two subareas. **Formal demography** deals with gathering, collating, analyzing, and presenting population data. For example, formal demography looks at the data demonstrating changes in the entire American population. Another example of formal demography is the documentation of the dramatic increase in the Latino population of California and Texas. **Social demography,** on the other hand, is the study of population patterns within a social context. For example, social demography examines the relationship between population growth and congressional districting. Historically, social demographers have found that the projected growth of minorities in the United States benefited Democrats more than Republicans (Tilove 1999). Regardless of political affiliation, the growth of minorities affects the drawing of congressional districts and is one reason census-taking can be a controversial topic. For a second

example, to help plan for hospitals and long-term nursing facilities, a social demographer might study trends in the population shifts of aging baby boomers.

Q Why study population trends? There is a demographer in all of us, observing and recording important events related to population change—births, deaths, the relocation of friends and family. The professional demographer considers these events in two ways: first, by gathering, organizing, and analyzing the patterns of population size, structure, composition, and distribution; and second, by attempting to identify and understand relationships between demographic and social processes. In other words, the demographer studies the link between the quantity of people and the quality of their lives.

Knowledge of population trends has never been more important. The study of population provides information about population growth, the characteristics of population, the location of population, and the probable long- and short-run effects of demographic trends. Demography plays a major role in policy formation, planning, and decision making in both public and private sectors of modern economies. Population information is crucial, for example, to plan for the health, education, transportation, and recreation needs of virtually every community in the United States. Demographers assist government policy makers and decision makers in meeting the needs of various socioeconomic groups, including the young, the poor, the unemployed, and the elderly. Demography generates information for identifying variable demands for products and services (see "See Sociology in Your Life").

Three population processes—fertility, mortality, and migration—are responsible for population growth and decline. Any alterations in population characteristics originate from these three processes, which sociologists use to chart population shifts, past and future (Namboodiri 1996; McFalls 2007). Figure 17.1 looks at the key demographic statistics by world regions.

Fertility

Q How is fertility related to population growth? Fertility measures the number of children born to a woman or to a population of women. Whereas *fertility* refers to the "actual" number of children women produce, **fecundity** is the maximum rate at which women can potentially produce children. The estimate for the upper limit of a society's average fecundity is fifteen births per woman. The record fertility rate for a group probably is held by the Hutterites, who migrated from Switzerland to North and South Dakota and Canada in the late nineteenth century. Hutterite women in the 1930s produced an average of more than twelve

FIGURE 17.1

World Birth Rates, Death Rates, and Infant Mortality Rates

Would you always expect to see a correlation between crude birth rates and total fertility rates for a country? Between crude death rates and infant mortality rates?

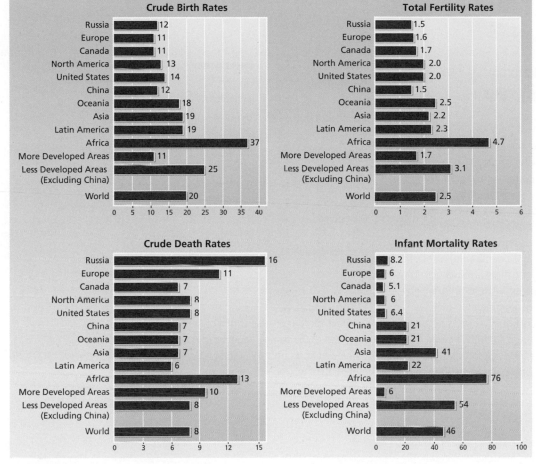

Source: Washington, DC: Population Reference Bureau, 2010.

children each (Westoff and Westoff 1971). The Hutterites give us a good estimate of fecundity, because they are the best example of *natural fertility*—the number of children born to women in the absence of conscious birth control. No other known society has exhibited the fertility level of the Hutterites (Weeks 2012).

Q How is fertility measured? The **crude birth rate** is the annual number of live births per 1,000 members of a population. Birth rate varies considerably from one country to another. The birth rate for the United States is 14 per 1,000. Uganda, in East Africa, experiences a very high birth rate of 47 per 1,000; and Germany, a very low rate of 8 per 1,000 (2010 *World Population Data Sheet* 2010).

To calculate birth rate, one simply needs to know the number of births in a year and the size of the population. One then divides the annual number of live births by the total population and multiplies that number by 1,000. As a formula, it would appear as

$$\text{Crude birth rate} = \frac{(\text{live births} \times 1{,}000)}{(\text{Total population})}$$

This formula is "crude," however, because, being based on the entire population, it fails to identify those women in the population most likely to give birth; and it ignores the age structure of the population—two factors that affect the number of live births in any given year. Consequently, in addition to the crude birth rate, demographers use the **fertility rate**—the annual number of live births per 1,000 women ages fifteen to forty-four. **Age-specific fertility** is the number of live births per 1,000 women in a specific age group,

in many other product and service categories.

Studies of the U.S. population have identified seven distinct groups described in the accompanying table. Which cohort are you? Your parents?

Demography for Businesses

Businesses have discovered that they can grow bigger by targeting smaller groups of consumers. These groups, called *generations*, or *cohorts*, are defined by important life experiences. Events occurring when people first become economic adults (usually between ages seventeen and twenty-one) affect their lifelong attitudes and values. These attitudes and values are unlikely to change as a person ages. So the kind of music that is popular during these formative years often remains the preferred type of music for life. Similarly, early lifetime experiences influence preferences

Cohort	Description	Born Between Years	Popular Music Styles
The Depression cohort	The G.I. generation	1912–1921	Big Band
The World War II cohort	The Depression generation	1922–1927	Swing
The postwar cohort	The silent generation	1928–1945	Frank Sinatra/ Rat Pack
The boomers I cohort	The Woodstock generation	1946–1954	Rock and roll
The boomers II cohort	The zoomer generation	1955–1976	Grunge, rap, Country western
The boomlet cohort	The echo-boom generation	1977–	Retro-swing, Latin

Think About It

Conduct short interviews with members of at least two of the demographic business cohorts profiled here. Identify a number of differences in preferences for products among the members of different cohorts.

Source: Erin N. Berkowitz, Robert A. Kerin, Steven W. Hartley, and William Rudelius, *Marketing*, 5th ed. (Chicago: Irwin, 1997).

---

such as twenty to twenty-four or thirty-five to thirty-nine. The rate easiest to comprehend is the **total fertility rate**—the average number of children born to a woman during her lifetime. Currently, total fertility rates in the world range from 4.7 in Africa to 1.6 in Europe. In the United States, the total fertility rate stands at 2.0 (see "Sociology Eyes America 17.1").

Mortality

Q **What are the dimensions of mortality?** **Mortality** refers to deaths within a population. The important dimensions of mortality are life span and life expectancy. **Life span**—the most advanced age to which humans can survive—can be inferred only from the person with the greatest authenticated age, a Japanese man who lived nearly 121 years (Russell 1987). Although this reveals that people are biologically capable of

living to be 120 years old, few even approach this age. **Life expectancy** is the average number of years that persons in a given population born at a particular time can expect to live. World life expectancy is sixty-nine years (2010 *World Population Data Sheet* 2010).

Morbidity refers to rates of disease and illness in a population. For example, in early twentieth-century America, influenza, pneumonia, and tuberculosis accounted for nearly 25 percent of all deaths; but their share of all deaths has declined to less than 3 percent. As more people survive to older ages, chronic degenerative diseases such as heart disease, stroke, and cancer have come to represent an increasing share of deaths (nearly seven out of ten). These diseases represent the consequences of an industrialized lifestyle, including stress, alcohol consumption, cigarette use, and pollution.

SOCIOLOGY EYES AMERICA 17.1

Teen Birth Rate

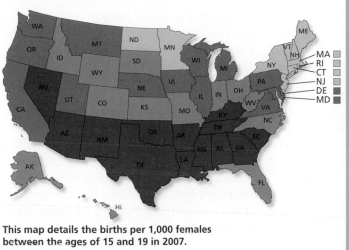

MA
RI
CT
NJ
DE
MD

This map details the births per 1,000 females between the ages of 15 and 19 in 2007.

- 20 to 30
- 31 to 40
- 41 to 51
- 52 to 72

Source: *2010 Kids Count Data Book*, p. 27. Copyright © 2010 The Annie E. Casey Foundation. Used by permission.

Interpret the Map

1. Describe any patterns you see in this map and describe how you would account for each.
2. Of the several birth rate measures demographers use, which one is portrayed in this map? Explain your choice by comparing the measure used in this case with the other possible measures.
3. What do these data tell you about the likely population growth in different geographic regions? Are these data sufficient to predict population growth? If not, what other information would be necessary?

Q How is mortality measured? The **crude death rate** is the annual number of deaths per 1,000 members of a population. Similar to the crude birth rate, the death rate is figured by dividing the annual number of deaths by the total population and multiplying by 1,000. Like the crude birth rate, the crude death rate varies widely throughout the world. The worldwide average death rate is 9 per 1,000 persons. Looking at specific regions of the world, the death rate varies from a low of 5 per 1,000 in Central America to a high of 16 per 1,000 in Middle Africa. The death rate in the United States is about 8 per 1,000 (2010 *World Population Data Sheet* 2010).

Demographers are also interested in the variations in birth rates and death rates for specific groups. They have devised **age-specific death rates** to measure the number of deaths per 1,000 persons in a specific age

How might fertility drugs affect the crude birthrate?

Robert Llewellyn/PhotoLibrary

group, such as fifteen to nineteen or sixty to sixty-four. This measure allows one to compare the risk of death to members of different groups. Although death eventually comes to everyone, the rate at which it occurs depends on many factors, including age, sex, race, occupation, social class, standard of living, and health care.

The **infant mortality rate**—the number of deaths among infants under one year of age per 1,000 live births—is a good indicator of the health status of any group, because infants are extremely susceptible to variations in food consumption, availability of medical care, and public sanitation. Infants in less developed countries are greater than seven times more likely to die before their first birthday than infants in more developed nations; this fact illustrates the wide variation in living standards among these nations.

Migration

Q **In what two ways can we describe migration?** **Migration** refers to the movement of people from one geographical area to another for the purpose of establishing a new residence. We can describe migration in relation to a move either within a country or from one country to another. A current example of international migration is the resettlement of Asian refugees from Vietnam and Cambodia to the United States and other countries around the world. Many of the refugees who settle in the United States in one particular city or region later move to another region, thus becoming internal migrants, as when people move from New York State to Arizona (Weeks 2012).

Q **How is migration measured?** The **gross migration rate** is the number of persons per 1,000 members of a population who, in a given year, enter (immigrants) or leave (emigrants) a geographical area. Net migration is the combined effect of immigration and emigration on the size of a population. Thus, the **net migration rate** is the annual increase or decrease per 1,000 members of a population resulting from movement into and out of the population. The United States, for example, has a net migration rate of about 3 per 1,000 population. That is, 3 more persons per 1,000 population enter the country than leave the country (2010 *World Population Data Sheet* 2010).

When the U.S. Census Bureau reports migration rates, it refers only to the number of legal immigrants. Many people violate immigration quotas in the United States. In the 1970s, illegal entry into the United States—primarily from Latin American and Caribbean countries—became a major concern. It continues to be controversial. There are no precise statistics on either the illegal immigration rate or the total number of illegal immigrants living in the United States, but researchers estimate that one-half of the foreigners in the United States entered illegally (Martin and Midgley 2006).

As of 2010, almost 43 million immigrants were living in the United States, triple the number (13.5 million) reached in 1910 during the last massive influx of immigrants. Thus, immigration has become the determinate factor in U.S. population growth, accounting for about 30 percent of the U.S. population increase between 1980 and 2000. In 2010, the foreign-born comprised

Not all migration is voluntary. Those leaving New Orleans because of Hurricane Katrina were being "pushed."

REUTERS/Jason Reed/Landov

The Dynamics of Demography

Match the following terms and definitions.

_____ a. fertility
_____ b. crude death rate
_____ c. crude birth rate
_____ d. demography
_____ e. fecundity
_____ f. age-specific fertility
_____ g. age-specific death rate
_____ h. infant mortality rate
_____ i. migration
_____ j. gross migration rate
_____ k. net migration rate
_____ l. morbidity

(1) the number of deaths per 1,000 members of a population per year
(2) the movement of people from one geographical area to another for the purpose of establishing a new residence
(3) the increase or decrease per 1,000 members of a population per year as a result of people leaving and entering the population
(4) the number of live births per 1,000 women aged fifteen to forty-four years
(5) the number of deaths per 1,000 persons in a specific age group
(6) the study of the growth, distribution, composition, and change of a population
(7) the number of live births per 1,000 women in a specific age group
(8) the number of persons per 1,000 members of a population who enter or leave the population each year
(9) the number of deaths to infants under one year of age per 1,000 live births
(10) rates of disease and illness in a population
(11) the maximum rate at which women can physically produce children
(12) the number of live births per 1,000 members of a population per year

Answers: a. 4; b. 1; c. 12; d. 6; e. 11; f. 7; g. 5; h. 9; i. 2; j. 8; k. 3; l. 10

just over 12 percent of the total population—the largest proportion in seventy years. Given current trends, the end of this decade will see the immigrant portion of the total population exceed the previous high of 15 percent, documented in 1890 (Camarota 2002; Martin and Midgley 2006).

Q Why do people migrate? The most general explanation for migration is the so-called push–pull theory. That is, people move either because they are attracted elsewhere or because they feel impelled to leave their present location. Often "push and pull" factors exist simultaneously. The people who settled the United States were fleeing economic, religious, and social circumstances and were attracted by the promise of a better future. People, of course, may not migrate despite significant pushing and pulling factors. Certain barriers, such as the cost of moving or bad health, may outweigh the push–pull factors.

In cases of voluntary movement, economic reasons are the most compelling. Voluntary migration is also associated with stages in the life cycle. The greatest movement is found among young people leaving home to attend college, take a job, marry, or join the military. Retired people may move from a metropolitan area to a rural community or from a colder climate to a warmer one.

Unfortunately, not all migrants make their decisions freely. People may be forced to leave an area or prevented from leaving a locale, both of which occurred among Jews in Hitler's Germany and in Bosnia and Yugoslavia. An environmental crisis or an inhospitable climate producing famine or drought may give people no choice but to abandon their place of residence.

Population Growth R1

World Population Growth

On October 12, 1999, the United Nations officially declared that the world's population had reached 6 billion. How big is 6 billion? If you counted 100 numbers every minute for eight hours a day, five days a week, it would take you 500 years to reach 6 billion!

According to Population Connection, the world's population is growing at a rate of 83 million people per year. If asked about the cause of rapid world population growth, what would you say? Like most people, you would probably refer to the high birth rate in poorer countries. You could point out that 135 million new infants are born each year, enough people to more than duplicate Japan's population. You could note that every time you watch a thirty-minute television program, 4,860 infants are born. This explanation, however, is only half the story. It leaves out the death-rate side of the equation. Developing countries have passed through the stage when both birth rates and death rates were high. Now these countries are growing rapidly because their birth rates remain high while their death rates have dropped sharply, thanks to modern medicine, improved sanitation, and better hygiene. The growth and the distribution of the world's population—almost 7 billion—vary greatly among the nations of the world. Not only that, but population has grown at markedly different rates throughout history (Livi-Bacci 1997; Haupt and Kane 2004; McFalls, 2007; see Figure 17.2).

Q How fast is the world's population growing? When describing population growth, it is impossible to avoid a certain amount of conjecture, because there has never been a complete worldwide numeration of the population. Although most countries now take a census, there are still national populations that do not. Furthermore, the quality of census data varies a great deal from country to country. Nevertheless, it is possible to indicate world population growth patterns by using historical information and recently collected data (Gelbard, Haub, and Kent 1999).

Rapid world population growth—now standing at 1.2 percent, or about 83 million people per year—is a relatively recent phenomenon: Your grandparents "born before 1950 have seen more population growth during . . . [their] lifetimes than occurred during the preceding four million years, since our early ancestors first stood upright" (L. R. Brown 1996:3). It is estimated that only about 250 million people were on the Earth in A.D. 1. It was not until 1650 that the world's population doubled, to half a billion (see Figure 17.2). Subsequent doublings have taken less and less time. The second doubling occurred in 1850, bringing the world population to just over 1 billion. By 1930, only eighty years later, another doubling had taken place. Only forty-five years later, in 1976, a fourth doubling raised the world's population to 4 billion. At the current growth rate, the world's population will double again in approximately fifty-one years and will reach almost

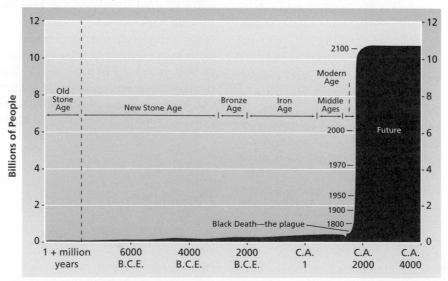

FIGURE 17.2

World Population Growth Through History

This figure shows estimated world population growth from the Old Stone Age to 2100. Population growth since 1800 has been phenomenal. The first doubling of the world's population occured between 8000 B.C.E. and 1650 C.A. The fourth doubling had occurred by 1976, and world population is on schedule to double for the fifth time in 2025.

Sources: Population Reference Bureau and United Nations, *World Population Projections to 2100* (1998). Adapted from Joseph A. Falls Jr., *Population*, 5th ed. (Washington, DC: Population Reference Bureau, 2007), p. 25.

11 billion persons by the year 2100 (McFalls 2007; 2010 *World Population Data Sheet* 2010). Obviously, the time between each doubling of the population is getting shorter and shorter.

Q Why is the world growing so rapidly? The population is increasing dramatically, in part because of the mathematical principle by which population increases. We are accustomed to thinking in terms of linear growth—arithmetical increases of a constant amount within a given time period (as in the progression 1, 2, 3, 4, 5 . . .). If you save $100 a year for ten years, you will end up with $1,000, accumulated in ten equal amounts. Population, however, does not grow linearly. It increases geometrically (as in 2, 4, 8, 16, 32 . . .), following the principle of **exponential growth**—the absolute growth that occurs within a given time period becomes part of the base for the growth rate in the next time period. This means that if the growth rate of a population remains the same for two successive years, the absolute growth will be larger in the second year.

Suppose that a city of 100,000 has an annual growth rate of 5 percent for two years. At the end of the first year, its population will increase by 5,000 (100,000 × 0.05). During the second year, the population will increase by an additional 5,250 (105,000 × 0.05). Consider a concrete case. The world population grew at about 2 percent per year between 1960 and 1970, which produced an increase of 650 million people. At the same rate, by 1980, the world population would increase by 800 million. This was nearly the case. In 1970, the world population was 3,261 million; in 1980, it stood at 4,414 million, an actual increase of 1,153 million.

A classic story offers an example of exponential growth. The story tells of a clever courtier who presented a beautiful chess set to his king and in return asked only that the king give one grain of rice for the first square on the chess board, two grains, or double the amount, for the second square, four (doubling again) for the third, and so forth. The king, being mathematically naive, agreed and ordered the rice brought forth. The eighth square required 128 grains, and the twelfth took more than a pound of rice. Long before reaching the sixty-fourth square, the king's coffers were depleted. Even today, the world's richest king could not produce enough rice to fill the final square. It would require more than 200 billion tons, or the equivalent of the world's current total production of rice for the next 653 years.

A term often used in analyzing population growth is **doubling time**—the number of years needed to double the original population size (given its current rate of growth). If a population is growing at 1 percent per year, it takes only seventy years to double. The number of people added each year becomes part of the total population, which then increases by another 1 percent in the following year.

Whereas the current world population growth rate of 1.2 percent may not seem high, it represents an increase of nearly 220,000 people every day. At this rate, the world's population grows every seven days as much as the size of the entire population of Utah (2010 *World Population Data Sheet* 2010). To put it another way, the human population is growing at the rate of 152 per minute, nearly 220,000 per day, about 83 million per year. The pace of growth is so rapid that additions to the world's population could equal the population of the United States in just over three years. At this rate, more people will be born in the year 2050 than were born in the 1,500 years after the birth of Christ.

On the encouraging side, the rate of world population growth has been declining since the 1970s. Data from fifty-six countries with an estimated population of 10 million or more indicate that the average annual rate of natural increase dropped from 2.1 percent in 1970 to 1.7 percent in the 1980s, to 1.2 percent in 2007, where it stands in 2010 (2007 *World Population Data Sheet* 2007; 2010 *World Population Data Sheet* 2010).

Figure 17.3 shows the population in various regions of the world, along with the projected populations for 2050. Compare the projected population increase in the less developed regions (44 percent) with more developed nations (7 percent). Doubling time for less developed regions is 46 years, while the doubling time for more developed nations is 680 years. To put it another way, nearly 99 percent of the world's population growth will take place in less developed countries, while deaths exceed births annually in Europe (2010 *World Population Data Sheet* 2010).

Q What difference does one child make? Population projections for the United States can illustrate the importance of limiting family size, even by one child (see Figure 17.4). Even though the United States is not going to a three-child average in the future, the hypothetical American case can help us understand the importance of population control. Figure 17.4 contrasts the projected population of the United States in the year 2070 for an average family size of two children and an average family size of three children. When we assume small decreases in the crude death rate and a stable net migration, an average two-child family size would result in a population of 300 million in 2015. Taking the hypothetical average family size of three children, the U.S. population would grow to 400 million by 2013. As time passed, the difference of only one extra child per family would assume added significance. By 2070, the two-child family would produce a population of 350 million, but the three-child family would push the population to close to 1 billion! To say it another way, with an average family of two children, the U.S. population would not quite double itself between 1970 and 2070. But should the three-child family be the average,

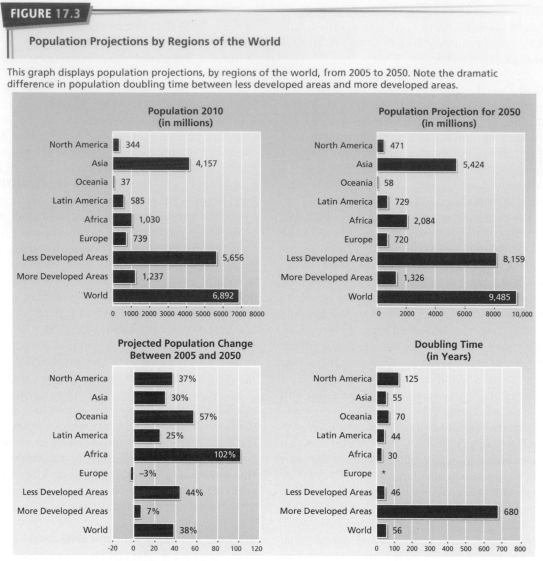

FIGURE 17.3

Population Projections by Regions of the World

This graph displays population projections, by regions of the world, from 2005 to 2050. Note the dramatic difference in population doubling time between less developed areas and more developed areas.

Population 2010 (in millions)

North America	344
Asia	4,157
Oceania	37
Latin America	585
Africa	1,030
Europe	739
Less Developed Areas	5,656
More Developed Areas	1,237
World	6,892

Population Projection for 2050 (in millions)

North America	471
Asia	5,424
Oceania	58
Latin America	729
Africa	2,084
Europe	720
Less Developed Areas	8,159
More Developed Areas	1,326
World	9,485

Projected Population Change Between 2005 and 2050

North America	37%
Asia	30%
Oceania	57%
Latin America	25%
Africa	102%
Europe	−3%
Less Developed Areas	44%
More Developed Areas	7%
World	38%

Doubling Time (in Years)

North America	125
Asia	55
Oceania	70
Latin America	44
Africa	30
Europe	*
Less Developed Areas	46
More Developed Areas	680
World	56

Source: Adapted from *2010 World Population Data Sheet*, 2010.
* Doubling not projected to occur.

the population would double itself twice during this same period.

Thus when we recognize the effect of one child added to a family, the importance of limiting population in developing regions becomes clear. Moreover, the addition of one child per family has a greater effect as the population base gets larger; not only is one extra person added, but theoretically that one person will be involved with the reproduction of yet another three; and on it goes. The largest populations are found in developing countries, which also have the largest average number of children per family.

The Malthusian Perspective

Although concern about population growth is strong, it is not new. In 1798, Thomas Robert Malthus, an English minister and economist, published *An Essay on the Principle of Population*, one of the most important works ever written on population growth and its repercussions. Thanks to the pessimism of Malthus's thesis, economics earned the label "dismal science."

In his essay, Malthus proposed a set of relationships between population growth and economic development:

1. Population, if left unchecked, will tend to exceed the available food supply. This is because population increases exponentially; the food supply does not.

2. Checks on population can be positive—those factors that increase mortality, such as famines, disease, wars—or preventive—those factors that decrease fertility, such as later marriages or abstaining from sexual relations in marriages. (At the time, there was no reliable birth control. For this conservative minister, sexual abstinence was the only

FIGURE 17.4

Projected Population of the United States, Comparing a Two-Child Average per Family (Replacement Level) to a Three-Child Average

This figure illustrates the importance of reaching the population replacement level (two children per family). Are you surprised with the difference in U.S. population growth caused by an average three children per family versus two children? Relate this difference to the principle of exponential growth.

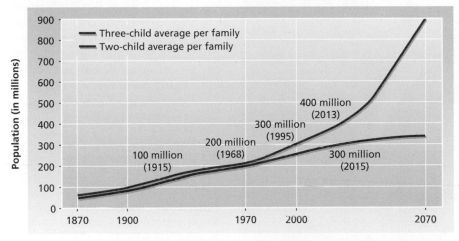

Source: *World Population Data Sheet*, Washington, DC: Population Reference Bureau, 2000.

morally acceptable—and practical—way to reduce the number of births.)

3. For the poor, any improvement in income is lost to additional births; this leads to reduced food consumption and lower standards of living and eventually to the operation of positive checks.

4. The wealthy and better educated already exercise preventive checks.

This last point leads to some of Malthus's suggestions for solving the "population problem." Because the wealthy and better educated had achieved controlled fertility, the method of extending this to the poor would be through universal education, which would offer all members of the population the chance for improving their situation: "The desire of bettering our condition, and the fear of making it worse, has been constantly in action and has been constantly directing people into the right road" (Malthus 1798:477). Raising people's aspirations for a higher standard of living, Malthus suggested, would enhance the beneficial effects of universal education on population control. A society could accomplish this by raising wages above the minimum required for subsistence, thus providing the poor an opportunity to choose between more children at a minimal standard of living or smaller families with a higher quality of life.

Q **Has the Malthus perspective had any effect?** Malthus's writings have profoundly influenced the study of population change. Events during the late nineteenth and

early twentieth centuries brought his predictions into question. The last half of the twentieth century, however, has again raised the specter of a Malthusian crisis: population growth outstripping both food resources and the ability of different societies to provide even minimal quantities of basic necessities (housing, health care, education, employment). Some social scientists—the neo-Malthusians—modified Malthus's propositions in an attempt to explain the current world situation and to predict possible futures. First, neo-Malthusians note that the development of reliable contraceptives has not distorted marital relations as Malthus feared that it might. Second, historical developments since Malthus's time indicate that values promoting, and norms supporting, smaller families are positively related to certain kinds of social and economic changes. In other words, values on family size and norms for fertility regulation adapt to socioeconomic conditions, enabling society to avoid Malthusian checks through self-regulation. Third, neo-Malthusians argue that many nations have a rate of population growth that overloads this self-regulating process because population growth is excessive to the extent that resources are diverted from socioeconomic change to population maintenance (Humphrey and Buttel 1986).

A debate is taking place between those who believe that the world's population is exploding beyond control and those who are convinced that the population explosion will be defused. Those predicting a slackening of the current high population growth rate often

English minister and economist Thomas Malthus wrote about the inability of the food supply to keep up with population growth.

base their optimism on the increasing worldwide acceptance of birth control. You can better appreciate this debate within the context of the *demographic transition*.

The Demographic Transition

Q How does the demographic transition develop? To the extent that developed nations have defied Malthus's theory, they have done so through the **demographic transition**—the process by which a population, as a result of economic development, gradually moves from high birth rates and death rates to low birth rates and death rates (see Figure 17.5). The number of stages in the demographic transition ranges from three to five, depending on the distinctions within each process. The description that follows is a four-stage model with examples:

Stage 1.   Both the birth rate and the death rate are high, and population growth is modest. This is characteristic of preindustrial societies.

Stage 2.   The birth rate remains high, but the death rate begins to drop sharply because of modernization—sanitation, increased food production, medical advances. The rate of population growth is very high. Most Sub-Saharan African countries are presently at this stage.

Stage 3.   The birth rate declines sharply; but because the death rate continues to drop, population growth is still rapid.

Stage 4.   Both the birth rate and the death rate are low, and the population grows slowly if at all. North America, Europe, and Japan are at this stage today. Europe, in fact, is in what is being called the "second demographic transition."

Q What is the second demographic transition? According to Figure 17.3, the expected population decrease for Europe between 2005 and 2050 is 13 percent. This reflects the "second demographic transition," which Europe alone is experiencing. Europe's first demographic transition began with a gradual death-rate decline in the early nineteenth century, followed by a birth-rate decline beginning around 1880. The transition to both low birth rate and low death rate was completed by the 1930s. Europe's second demographic transition began in the mid-1960s.

The primary demographic characteristic of the second demographic transition is the decline in fertility from slightly above **replacement level**—the birth rate at which a couple replaces itself in the population—to a fertility level of 1.7. Should Europe maintain this lower fertility rate, and if immigration does not interfere, Europe's population will decline, something that is already the case in Italy, Sweden, Germany, Hungary, and Russia. The original formulation of the demographic transition, as noted earlier, ended with stable or nongrowing population.

Q Does the demographic transition occur in developing societies? Traditionally, demographers assumed that developing societies would proceed through the same stages as the developed world. This assumption is being criticized for its ethnocentric bias. Why? Because developing societies did not begin the transition at the same point as Western societies. For example, less developed countries started the transition with birth rates and death rates higher than existed in the now-developed societies when they began the transition. And mortality declined in the West because of domestic industrialization rather than from the importation of sophisticated techniques of disease control.

FIGURE 17.5

Stages of the Demographic Transition

This figure illustrates the demographic transition. Stage 1 begins with smaller population growth due to a balance between birth rates and death rates (both at high levels). In Stage 2, population grows dramatically because the death rate decreases so much faster than the birth rate. Population growth begins to slow in Stage 3, when the birth rate belatedly drops sharply. Stage 4 is again a condition of smaller population growth because birth rates and death rates come into balance (both at low levels). Given this description, what would you call the gap between the two graphs representing birth and death rates?

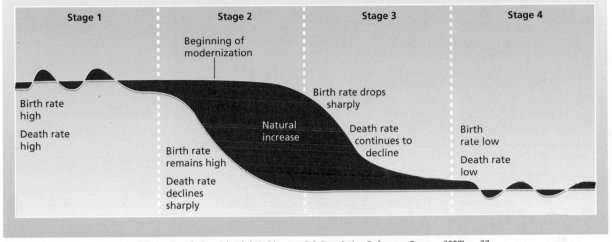

Source: Adapted from Joseph A. Falls Jr., *Population*, 5th ed. (Washington, DC: Population Reference Bureau, 2007), p. 27.
Note: Natural increase or decrease is produced from the difference between the number of births and deaths.

Population Control

Because death rates in both developing and developed nations have already dropped dramatically, efforts to curb world population growth must concentrate on lowering birth rates. Thus, **population control** is the conscious attempt to regulate population size through national birth control programs.

Q **What is the history of birth rates?** Historically, many societies were more concerned with increasing their population size than with overpopulation. High birth rates were needed to offset the high death rates from disease and poor hygiene. For some societies, larger populations enhanced security because of the ability to maintain larger armies. Agricultural societies needed large numbers of people to work the land. Aging parents wanted to be more secure in old age. High birth rates were also prevalent in countries with religious prohibitions against birth control.

Since the mid-twentieth century, however, more governments have come to view high birth rates as a threat to their national well-being. By 1990, most countries had in place formal programs to reduce birth rates—either voluntary or compulsory.

Q **What is voluntary population control, and how successful has it been?** Voluntary population control is generally known as **family planning**—making it

technically possible for women to choose the number of children they will have. Beyond making contraceptive devices available, family planning programs provide birth prevention information and other services. Although women in the poorest countries still have the highest fertility, their overall fertility decreased by 50 percent after 1969 (Kluger and Dorfman 2002).

Even when effective, family planning programs merely enable families to achieve their *desired* family size. Unfortunately for effective population control, in many nations the desired family size is quite high. The World Fertility Survey reported that the average preferred family size of women in African nations is 7.1; in Middle Eastern nations, 5.1; in Latin American nations, 4.3; and in Asian Pacific nations, 4.0. In European countries, the average preferred family size ranges from 2.1 to 2.8.

Family planning has worked in Taiwan, where by the turn of the twenty-first century, the birth rate declined below replacement level. Taiwan launched its family planning efforts under very favorable conditions. When the Japanese withdrew from Taiwan after World War II, they left behind a labor force trained for industrial work. Consequently, the Taiwanese used this advantage to build an expanding economy. With economic development came a decline in both death rates and birth rates. In short, they went through the demographic transition fairly rapidly.

India was a different story. Family planning there got off to a very slow start, and the country has been unable

Family planning in Africa has failed to control population growth. Consequently, this scene of mothers and malnourished children waiting for medical treatment is all too familiar.

AFP/Getty Images

to reduce the rate of population growth through voluntary means. Family planning efforts failed because government officials and family planners underestimated the barriers to birth control—they did not take the broader social context into account. For one thing, India did not have Taiwan's advantage of relatively rapid economic development. In addition, the Indian officials and planners made insufficient efforts to overcome cultural and religious opposition to birth control. Nor did they address the lack of channels to effectively distribute birth control information and technology. Finally, the implementation of the national birth control policy was left in the hands of individual state governments.

Efforts at population control began to succeed in India only after the government turned to a sterilization program in 1976. Although the government did not use the force of law, a system of disincentives had the effect of compulsion. Those who could not produce official proof of a sterilization were denied such things as business permits, gun licenses, and ration cards for the purchase of basic goods (Weeks 2012). Still, India currently has a total fertility rate of 2.6 children per woman (the United States has a total fertility rate of about 2.0 children per woman). India is expected to have the largest population in the world by about 2050.

Q **Have any countries successfully enforced compulsory population control methods?** Both China and Singapore have required population control policies that seem to achieve their goals. In an attempt to reach zero population growth, the Chinese government first tried to discourage a third child in a family. The second step was to push for the one-child family. China successfully reduced its total fertility rate from 7.5 in 1963 to 1.5

today through coercion and a system of rewards and punishments. In cities, couples with only one child can obtain a one-child certificate. This certificate ensures them a monthly allowance for the costs of children up to age fourteen. One-child families receive a larger retirement pension and enjoy preference in housing, school admission for their children, and employment. Families with more than one child are subject to an escalating tax on each child, and they get no financial aid from the government for the medical and education costs of their extra children.

Singapore, an island city-state on the Malaysian peninsula, began formally discouraging large families in 1969, installing some economic penalties to encourage replacement-level fertility. The government included the following measures: denial of a paid eight-week maternity leave, loss of an income tax allowance, diminished access to public housing, increased maternity costs for each additional child, and lower likelihood of children entering the better schools.

These policies worked so well that the total fertility rate in Singapore dropped from 4.5 children per woman to 1.4 between 1966 and 1985. Worried over the reduction in population size, the government in 1987 switched to the guideline of three or more children for people able to afford them (Yap 1995). Despite this effort, Singapore's total birth rate is now 1.2, still below replacement level.

Future World Population Growth

World population growth has reached a watershed. After more than 200 years of acceleration, the annual population growth rate is declining. From 1950 to 1975, world population rose 64 percent; since 1975 it has increased 48 percent (Kluger and Dorfman 2002). The current growth rate of 1.2 percent compares favorably with the peak of 2.04 percent in the late 1960s. Moreover, the rate is projected to drop to zero by the end of the twenty-first century (United Nations Population Division 2000). The birth rate is already low in developed countries and, as noted earlier, is now declining in many developing countries. Similarly, the population growth rate is declining somewhat in both developed and developing areas of the world.

Demographers are unsure of future world population growth in part because they do not know for sure how many children today's youth will have. Nor do they know what will happen to change life expectancy, particularly in developing countries.

Some analysts are now foreseeing a potential shift from concern about a "population explosion" to worry about a "population implosion" or decline due to lower fertility rates (Eberstadt 2001; Pearce 2010). Other demographers, however, point out that there are two very different worlds of population growth. In developed countries, fertility rates are at or below two children per couple (Europe; the United States; Canada; Japan; and some rapidly developing countries such as China, South Korea, and Thailand). In developing societies, women average four children each (most of Africa, Asia, and Latin America). If the accelerating population growth that the world has known since the 1950s is to stop, there must be a dramatic decrease in fertility in developing countries (Gelbard and Haub 1998; Ashford 2001).

Q **What is the future of world population growth?** The United Nations offers three possible world population growth scenarios (see Figure 17.6). These three futures vary, depending on their assumptions regarding the average number of children women will bear. For the medium scenario to come true, women will have to average two children. If so, world population will rise to more than 9 billion by 2100. The medium scenario depicts **zero population growth**—when deaths are balanced by births so that the population does not grow. To make the high scenario a reality, women worldwide will have to average about 2.5 children. If this happens, world population will rise to 14 billion in 2100 and continue to grow indefinitely, exceeding 27 billion 100 years later. In the low scenario, fertility will have fallen to 1.6 children per woman or less. World population, under this condition, will peak at 8 billion in 2050 and drop to 6 billion by 2100.

But as we have seen, despite the reduction in the annual growth rate and birth rate, the world's population will continue to increase. Throughout the first half of the twenty-first century, demographers expect the annual growth rate to decline until world population stabilizes at about 12 billion people. At this point, the world will have reached zero population growth, when deaths are balanced by births so that the population does not increase.

Contrary to popular opinion, limiting the average family size to two children does not immediately produce zero population growth. This is because there is a time lag of sixty to seventy years, due to the high proportion of young women of childbearing age. Even if each of these women had only two children, global population would grow because there are so many young women. Only when this disproportionate number of young mothers disappears, will the world reach zero population growth.

The time lag is what demographers call **population momentum**—a population continues to grow, regardless of a recent drop in the birth rate, because of the existing population base created by past growth. The increase in the world's population, like a huge boulder careening down a mountain, cannot suddenly cease. But the sooner we halt the momentum of current population growth, the better. The sooner the world fertility rate reaches the replacement level, the sooner zero population growth will be reached. The ultimate size of the world's population, when it does stop growing, depends greatly on the timing of the replacement level. To state it another way, each decade it takes to reach replacement level, fertility will increase the world's population by 15 percent.

Population Growth in the United States

The population of the United States has increased dramatically since the first census in 1790, growing steadily from less than 4 million in 1790 to 309 million in 2010 (Pollard and Mather 2010). At the same time, the population growth rate has, with some deviations, tended to decline since 1790. Between 1990 and 2000, however, the American population surged by nearly 33 million, after growing more slowly between 1970 and 1990. The population of the United States, according to demographers, will continue growing despite the average American family reproducing at the replacement level of 2.0 children per family. In fact, contrary to other industrialized nations, the United States is undergoing a *baby boomlet*. The 4.3 million births in 2007 was the largest number of children born in the United States in almost fifty years. In part, this trend is due to the baby-boom bulge in the age structure that produced the large number of women whose children and grandchildren are now part of the population (the "baby boomlet"). In addition to fertility, American population growth will experience the effect of its mortality and migration rates. If the current predictions of fertility, mortality, and immigration rates are accurate, the total U.S. population will reach 423 million by 2050. This would represent an almost 50 percent increase,

FIGURE 17.6

The World's Population Explosion

As this figure illustrates, the future growth of world population is uncertain. Which of these scenarios do you think is most likely to occur? Defend your answer with information from this chapter or from additional research.

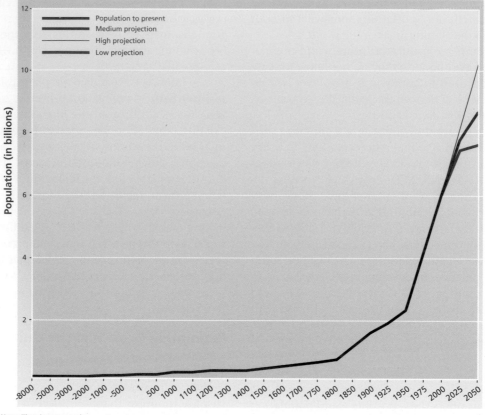

Note: Time is not to scale.

Source: Adapted from John R. Weeks, *Population*, 11th ed. (Belmont, CA: Wadsworth, 2012), p. 35. Original projections are from the United Nations Population Division, 2009.

considerably higher population growth than we expect in other more developed countries. In fact, as projected in Figure 17.7, U.S. population growth will increase between now and 2050, while population growth in other more developed countries will decline. Thus, the United States will remain the largest of the more developed countries.

Q Why will the U.S. population grow faster than other more developed countries? Generally, fertility is the primary factor in population change. The United States is no exception. Its population experienced **natural increase** (excess of births over deaths) each decade of the twentieth century. This trend continued between 2000 and 2001, when 4 million births were offset by only 2.4 million deaths. This natural increase of 1.6 million accounted for just over 60 percent of the total population growth that year (2.7 million).

Demographers often use the total fertility rate (the average number of children born to a woman during her lifetime) to predict population change. The total fertility rate ebbed and flowed during the twentieth century. In the first few decades of that century, native-born white women had an average of 3.5 children over their lifetimes. In part because of a lower total fertility rate, natural increase hit a low during the Great Depression of the 1930s. This declining natural increase reversed after World War II when the baby boom occurred. Another total fertility rate low occurred in the early 1970s (1.7 children per woman), followed by an upswing beginning in the late 1970s. This small natural increase in the late 1970s and 1980s did not approach that of the baby boom of the 1950s, during which women were once again averaging 3.5 children.

A positive net migration rate has always, except during the Great Depression in the 1930s, played a larger

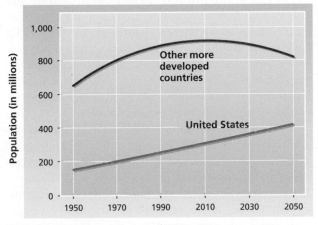

FIGURE 17.7

Population Growth in the United States and Other More Developed Countries: 1950–2050

This figure compares the curves of population growth in the United States with the rest of the more developed world. Describe any differences you see between 1950 and 1990. Describe the current differences in population growth between the two areas. Explain.

Note: "Other more developed countries" includes all European countries, Australia, Canada, Japan, and New Zealand.
Source: U.S. Census Bureau, International Data Base, October, 10, 2002, release; www.census.gov/ipc/www/idbayg.html (accessed October, 12, 2002).

role in the population growth in the United States than in most other nations. Among more developed countries, the United States has the largest foreign population, by a considerable margin (Camarota 2001; "The Longest Journey" 2002). The traditional importance of immigration to U.S. population growth has intensified over the last few decades because fertility among U.S.-born women has remained at or below replacement level. During the 1980s, immigration was responsible for about one-third of U.S. population growth. The contribution of immigration to population growth increased in the 1990s, accounting for 40 percent of growth between 2000 and 2001. Because of high immigrant fertility, the contribution of immigration to population growth is even greater than suggested by the number of foreign-born people entering the United States. Approximately one-fifth of births in 2000 were among immigrant women. Should current immigration and fertility trends continue for 100 years, four in ten Americans will be post-1980 immigrants or their descendants.

During the 1950s, almost half of all immigrants came from Northern and Western Europe, whereas only two in ten came from less developed nations. Since 1960, the sources of immigration have shifted

CHECK YOURSELF 17.2 R2

Population Growth

1. According to the principle of _____, the absolute growth that occurs within a given time period becomes part of the base on which the growth rate is applied for the next time period.
2. Thomas Malthus saw famines as a _____ check on population growth.
3. The process by which a population gradually moves from high birth and death rates to low birth and death rates as a result of economic development is called the _____.
4. Europe's second demographic transition involves what kind of population growth?
   a. stable
   b. increasing
   c. declining
5. Which of the following figures is the world's population most likely to reach before it stops growing?
   a. 4 billion
   b. 8 billion
   c. 12 billion
   d. 25 billion
6. _____ exists when deaths are balanced by births so that the population does not increase.
7. Between now and 2050, the U.S. population is expected to
   a. remain stable.
   b. increase by almost 50 percent.
   c. decrease by 33 percent.
   d. dip in 2036 and start growing again.
8. A population with an excess of births over deaths will experience _____.

Answers: 1. exponential growth; 2. positive; 3. demographic transition; 4. c; 5. c; 6. Zero population growth; 7. b; 8. natural increase

from Europe to Latin America, the Caribbean, and Asia. Less than one-fifth of the legal immigrants now come from Europe and Canada, whereas about three-fourths arrive from Latin American, the Caribbean, and Asia. Mexico, India, and China are the top three countries from which immigrants came between 2000 and 2008 (Kleniewski and Thomas 2011).

Although mortality rates can influence population growth rates, they have little effect among more developed countries, where mortality is already low (Kent and Mather 2002). At 8 deaths per 1,000 persons, the death rate in the United States is relatively low, but because of its aging population, the number of deaths has been increasing slightly since the early 1980s. Life expectancy, of course, has increased as the death rate has declined. On the average, an American born now can expect to live seventy-eight years, up from seventy-one years at the beginning of the 1970s. Life expectancy remains lower for males (seventy-five years) than for females (eighty years).

Actually, mortality rates could affect future U.S. population growth because they are higher at most ages than in other more developed countries, outside Eastern Europe. U.S. mortality rates could decline further if we lowered the preventable deaths due to such factors as poor medical care and poverty among younger Americans, particularly among African Americans. Death rates could also be lower at later ages with improved medical care and the adoption of healthier diets and lifestyles (Kent and Mather 2002).

Urbanization ⬛

For centuries, people have lived in large population settlements. The nature of those settlements has undergone important changes, and as the settlements mutated, the language to discuss them also shifted. As an aid to understanding the volatile conditions in urban areas, we first examine the terminology used to describe such areas.

Basic Concepts

Q What defines a community? Long before the rise of cities, people depended on communities for their common needs. In fact, a **community** is a concentration of people who can satisfy their major social and economic needs within the area where they live. It is easy to identify the network of social relationships and organizations that fulfill basic social and economic needs in a small community of several hundred people, but the situation is far more complex when several million people live within a given geographical area. Some sociologists even doubt that we can describe such large concentrations of people as communities. Consequently, social scientists

now concentrate on cities and metropolitan areas rather than on communities.

Q When does a village become a city? The census bureaus of most nations define cities as population aggregates exceeding a certain size. In Denmark and Sweden, an area with 200 inhabitants officially qualifies as a city. Japan uses a much higher cutoff point—30,000 inhabitants. The minimal cutoff point used by the U.S. Census Bureau to define a city is a population of 2,500. These relatively low definition points reflect a time when urbanization had just begun and population concentrations were small. Because 2,500 people are clearly low for modern times, the Census Bureau has come up with additional urban designations. Of course, using mere numbers of inhabitants to define a city overlooks other important aspects of cities. In addition to containing a reasonably large number of people, cities represent permanence, density, heterogeneity, and occupational specialization of inhabitants. In brief, a city is a dense and permanent concentration of people who live in a limited geographical area and who earn their living primarily through nonagricultural activities.

The Census Bureau has several terms to distinguish urban areas of varying size (Palen 2008; Kleniewski and Thomas 2011). An **urban area** is a census block with a population density of no less than 1,000 persons per square mile. **Urban clusters** are areas over 10,000 but under 50,000. An **urbanized area** is composed of a central city, or cities, of 50,000 or more and the surrounding densely inhabited territory. The 2000 Census identified 1,371 "urbanized areas" and "urban clusters." A **micropolitan statistical area (MicroSA)** has at least one urban concentration of no less than 10,000 but less than 50,000 population, plus adjoining territory that is highly integrated with the core. In 2005 10 percent of the population resided in 577 MicroSAs. A **metropolitan statistical area (MetroSA or MSA)** is a grouping that contains at least one city of 50,000 inhabitants or more or an urbanized area of at least 50,000 inhabitants and the surrounding integrated population.

The establishment of criteria for designating MicroSAs and MetroSAs allows the Census Bureau to identify large areas whose populations have interdependent relationships with a central city. This is important because the influence of any city extends far beyond its official boundaries. As of 2005, 83 percent of America's people lived in 361 MetroSAs. Even a MetroSA is too limited to identify some urban areas because many do not exist in isolation. For example, one must consider Newark, New Jersey, which qualifies as a MetroSA, in relation to surrounding MSAs, including New York City. Because of such situations, the Census Bureau identifies a **combined statistical area (CSA)**—two or more adjacent MSAs or a MetroSA and one or more MicroSAs. As of 2005, there were 124 CSAs.

The Urban Transition

Urbanization is the process by which an increasingly larger portion of the world's population lives in urban areas (see "Think Globally" 17.1). Urbanization has been such a prevalent trend that it is now taken for granted in many parts of the world. As you have just seen, this process has resulted in cities so large and interdependent that it is now necessary to think of strips of interlocking cities. At the beginning of the twenty-first century, almost as many people live in urban areas as in rural areas (Pacione 2005; Scripps-Howard 2002). This is a fairly recent development in human history.

Q **What was the population of the early cities?** The size of the first cities—founded only 5,000 years ago—was quite small by contemporary standards. Ur, located at the point where the Tigris and Euphrates Rivers meet (in modern-day Iraq), was one of the world's first major cities; but at its peak, it held only about 24,000 people. Later, during the time of the Roman Empire, it is unlikely that many cities had populations larger than 33,000. The population of Rome itself was probably under 350,000 (A. H. Hawley 1971).

In addition to their small size, the cities of ancient and medieval periods contained only a small portion of the world's population. As recently as 1800, less than 3 percent of the world's population lived in cities of 20,000 or more (K. Davis 1955). By contrast, 50 percent of the world's population now lives in urban areas (see Figure 17.8). In North America, 79 percent of the population lives in cities (2010 *World Population Data Sheet* 2010). Only about 5 percent of the American population lived in urban areas in 1790 (U.S. Census Bureau 1993).

THINK GLOBALLY 17.1

Urban Population as a Proportion of Total Population

As discussed in the text, the Industrial Revolution encouraged the rapid growth of cities. The map below shows that many countries now have urban populations that comprise 60 percent or more of their total populations.

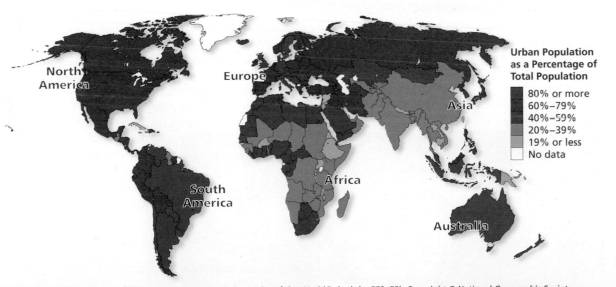

Urban Population as a Percentage of Total Population

- 80% or more
- 60%–79%
- 40%–59%
- 20%–39%
- 19% or less
- No data

Source: From John L. Allen and Christopher J. Sutton, *Student Atlas of the World* 3rd ed. (p. 552–53). Copyright © National Geographic Society. Reprinted by permission.

Interpret the Map

1. The map shows that countries such as the United Kingdom, Germany, and Sweden have urban populations that make up over 80 percent of their total populations. This can be explained by the effects of the Industrial Revolution, since these countries' economies are highly developed. However, other countries, such as Venezuela, Argentina, and Libya, which are not highly developed, also have urban populations that comprise over 80 percent of their totals. Can you think of reasons why this is so? Explain.

2. What effects will increased urbanization have on countries and the world?

Q What accounts for this increase in urbanization? To find the answer to this question, we must take a closer look at urbanization before and after the Industrial Revolution. Although rapid urbanization is a fairly recent occurrence, its groundwork has been developing for several centuries.

Preindustrial Cities

Because people in cities hold primarily nonagricultural jobs, they require an agricultural surplus. Before 3500 B.C.E., few areas of the world were capable of producing a dependable supply of extra food for nonagriculturally productive people. For this reason, cities were initially slow to develop (Robert Adams 1965).

Q What enabled the first cities to develop? According to anthropological research, the first urban settlements were established around 3500 B.C.E in Mesopotamia (in southwestern Asia between the Tigris and Euphrates rivers). The Mesopotamian region is among the world's most fertile areas, and at that time, its people were relatively advanced in the development of plant cultivation. So this area provided the necessary surplus of food for people in cities.

The existence of a surplus food supply clarifies the location of cities, but it does not explain people's attraction to them. Cities tended to attract four basic types of people: the elite, functionaries, craftspeople, and the poor and destitute. For the elite, who comprised but a small segment of the population, the city provided a setting for consolidating political, military, or religious power. The jewelry and other luxury items found in the tombs of the elite acknowledge the benefits these people gained from their consolidation of power and

control. The functionaries were the political or religious officials who carried out the plans of the elite and whose lives were undoubtedly easier than those of the peasant-farmers in the countryside. Craftspeople, still lower on the stratification structure, came to the city to work and sell their products to the elite and functionaries. The poor and destitute, who responded to the lure of the city for economic relief, were seldom able to improve their condition (Gist and Fava 1974).

Q Do preindustrial types of cities still exist? Many parts of Africa, Asia, and Latin America are not industrialized and therefore still have some preindustrial types of cities. This is particularly true of capital cities, which attract migrants from rural areas because of the symbolic importance of these cities and the promise of a better life. Unfortunately, those who migrate to many of these cities are disappointed, because the expected employment opportunities do not exist. Also, many cities in developing nations often lack the housing, sanitation, transportation, and communication facilities needed to accommodate their residents. As a result, many city dwellers in developing nations live in makeshift housing with few or none of the facilities that most people in modern societies consider necessities. Although cities in developing nations are unable to fulfill the social and economic needs of their residents, many people feel driven to them because their life chances in the over-populated rural areas and small towns are even worse.

Rise of the Modern City

As merchants gained power and wealth during the late medieval period, they often established small industries that would give them a stable supply of goods. As these

Kolkata (Calcutta), India, remains essentially a preindustrial city.

industries gradually increased in size, the stage was prepared for rapid city growth.

Q How did the Industrial Revolution encourage the growth of cities? The Industrial Revolution, beginning in the eighteenth century, created major changes in transportation, agriculture, commerce, and industry. Technological developments during this period allowed for better food production and more efficient transportation systems with less human labor. As food production and transportation became more dependable, it became possible for more people with nonagricultural jobs to live in cities. The major reason for the growth of cities following the Industrial Revolution, however, was the increased use of factories.

The goal of factories was not to encourage the growth of cities, but they almost immediately had that effect; one factory tends to attract others to the same location. While taking advantage of natural features such as water power and river transport, factories located together can share raw materials and transportation costs. And at a time when transportation and communication were slow and undependable, it was desirable for producers of machinery and equipment to be near the factories they were supplying. The concentration of industry led to dense population settlements of factory workers, which in turn attracted retailers, innkeepers, entertainers, and a wide range of people offering services to city dwellers. Of course, the greater availability of urban services often enticed still more factories, keeping the cycle fluid. Although subsequent technological and social developments affected the growth of cities in different ways, the overall trend toward urbanization was set. The industrial world was becoming urbanized.

Q How does modern suburbanization differ from life on the outskirts of cities during preindustrial times? The direction of life in preindustrial times was directed toward the city's center. The walls, moats, and other protective devices found in these cities symbolized their role in defending the cities' inhabitants. It was safer to live in cities than outside them. Residential patterns also reflect the importance of the center of the city in preindustrial times. Members of the upper class lived near the center of preindustrial cities, which gave them access to the most important government and religious buildings and, as a rule, the main market. The poor and those with low-status craft occupations, such as tanning and butchering, populated the outskirts (including what we would now consider the suburban areas). These people lived on the outskirts partly because more privileged residents wanted to have minimal contact with them. More important, though, the outskirts were the least desirable areas due to their lack of accessibility to the central city (Sjoberg 1966).

Modern cities, like preindustrial cities, located their major economic and government activities in their central core. Cities in industrialized nations, however, are connected by sophisticated communication and transportation networks, which have had the opposite effect of the walls and other protective devices of preindustrial cities. Thus, industrial cities tend to have an outward orientation. Most of their development occurs away from the central city in the surrounding suburban areas. In industrialized nations, population movement from rural to urban areas accompanies suburbanization. In fact, many central cities are now losing population to the areas surrounding them (Brockerhoff 2000).

Suburbanization

Suburbanization—which occurs when central cities lose population to the area surrounding them—is a hallmark of contemporary American urban growth (Baldassare 1992; Gober 1993). By 1980, seventeen of the twenty-six central cities with a population of half a million or more in 1970 registered losses in population. Still, the population outside central cities is expanding several times as fast as the central cities themselves. According to the U.S. Census Bureau, the population of the central cities of the 255 MSAs increased by only 3.9 percent between 1990 and 1998, whereas the population of MSA areas outside the central cities (almost entirely suburbs) increased by 12.5 percent during the same period (U.S. Bureau of the Census 2000). During 1991–1992, the percentage of Americans moving from central cities to suburbs was twice the rate of movement from suburbs to central cities (U.S. Census Bureau 1993). This is a continuation of a trend that more than doubled the proportion of the population living in suburbs since 1950. Thus, the United States is now predominantly suburban.

Q What makes suburbanization possible? Suburbanization has become an important trend partly as a concomitant of technological developments. Improvements in communication—such as telephones, radios, television, and (later) computers, fax machines, and the Internet—allow people to live away from the central city without losing touch with its activities. Developments in transportation (especially highways, automobiles, trucks, and metro systems) make it possible both for people to commute to work and for many businesses to leave the central city for suburban locations (Baxandall and Ewen 2000).

Technology is not the only cause of suburbanization, however. Both cultural and economic pressures have encouraged the development of suburbs. Partly because of America's frontier heritage, American culture has always had a bias against urban living. Some Americans prefer urban life, but most report that they would rather live in a rural setting. Even those who, on balance, choose to live in the city believe they are giving up some advantages. Suburbs, with their low-density housing, allow many people to escape the problems of urban living without completely leaving the urban areas. Suburbs are attractive because of decreased crowding and traffic congestion, lower taxes, better schools, less crime, and reduced pollution.

Also, the scarcity and high cost of land in the central city encourage suburbanization. Developers of new housing, retail, and industrial projects often find suburban locations to be far less expensive than those near the central city.

Finally, government policy has often increased the impact of economic forces. Federal Housing Administration regulations, for example, favor the financing of new houses (which can be built most cheaply in suburban locations) rather than the refurbishing of older houses in central cities (Steinnes 1982).

As people move to suburban areas, increasing numbers of businesses and jobs follow. In fact, suburbanization is leading to the development of edge cities, and "boomburgs" that are changing the face of urban America.

Q **What are edge cities and boomburgs?** Originally, most suburbs were merely places where people lived. Suburbanites commuted daily from their "bedroom" communities to their jobs in the central city. Over the last decade, the nature of suburbanization has changed to include the movement of jobs and businesses to the suburbs as well. This change in suburbanization has created the **edge city**—a suburban unit specializing in a particular economic activity (Garreau 1991; Bingham and Bowen 1997). Employment in one edge city may focus on computer technology, another on financial services or health care. An edge city, of course, will have many other types of economic activities—industrial tracts, office parks, distribution and warehousing clusters, and home offices of national corporations. These are actually little cities in themselves with a full range of services, including schools, retail sales, restaurants, malls, medical facilities, hotels, motels, recreational complexes, and entertainment centers.

Edge cities do not have legal and physical boundaries separating them from the larger urban area in which they are located. This does not prevent names from being attached to several of them: Tyson's Corner is located in northern Virginia near Washington, D.C.; Las Colinas is close to the Dallas–Fort Worth airport; and King of Prussia is northwest of Philadelphia. Some edge cities bear the name of highways, such as Route 128 outside of Boston.

Boomburgs are places of more than 100,000 residents that are not the largest cities in their metropolitan areas but they experience double-digit population

growth in recent decades (Lang and Simmons 2001). According to the U.S. Census Bureau, the United States has fifty-three boomburgs, forty-one of which exceed 100,000 people. Accounting for 51 percent of the 1990s growth are cities between 100,000 and 400,000 residents, boomburgs now contain one-fourth of all Americans living in cities of this size.

Despite developing into large cities, most boomburgs retain their suburban character. They are not without traditional urban problems, however, such as sprawl, overused government services, and traffic congestion.

Consequences of Suburbanization

When suburbanization first became noticeable in the 1930s, only the upper and middle classes could bear the cost. It was not until the 1950s that the working class joined them. But until the 1970s, the suburbs remained largely white, despite federal legislation prohibiting housing discrimination (Feagin and McKinney 2005).

Central-city minorities are beginning to move to the suburbs in greater numbers (Frey 1984, 1985; Massey and Denton 1987; R. Farley 1998; R. Farley and Haaga 2005). Although America's suburban counties remain predominantly white, minorities, over the past ten years, have poured into the suburbs. A greater number of Latinos and Asian Americans, in fact, now reside in suburban counties than live in central cities. The percentage of African Americans living in suburbs increased substantially since 1980, standing now at 40 percent (Kleniewski and Thomas 2011).

Despite this decline in the degree of residential segregation, African Americans remain the most isolated ethnic or racial minority in the United States (O'Hare et al. 1990; Farley and Frey 1994; South and Crowder 1997; Palen 2008). The situation is better for Latinos and Asians, as already noted. Not only are Latinos and Asians more suburbanized—and thus less concentrated in the central cities—than African Americans, they are also less segregated in suburban areas (R. Farley 1997; Palen 2008). Even this progress has a downside. As the more successful minority members move to the suburbs, the "underclass" accounts for a larger proportion of the remaining central-city population (Frey and Farley 1996; Massey and Denton 1996; Orfield 2001; see Chapter 9).

Q **What is the central-city dilemma?** Suburbanization created a major problem in the United States. The problem is not merely that minorities remain trapped in inner cities. Businesses have now followed the more affluent people to the suburbs, where they can find lower tax rates, less expensive land, less congestion, and their customers who have already left the city. Accompanying the exodus of the middle class, the manufacturers, and the retailers is the shrinking

Minorities are increasingly choosing to live in suburban communities. Despite this increase in residential integration, African Americans remain the most isolated minority in the United States.

Bill Bachmann/PhotoEdit

of the central-city tax base (Mouw 2000). As a result, the central city has become increasingly populated by the poor, the unskilled, and the uneducated. The result is a **central-city dilemma**—the concentration of a large population in need of public services (schools, transportation, health care) but without the money to provide for them (Wolfe 1999).

Q What are the consequences of the central-city dilemma? Poor inner-city African American children are handicapped by inferior educational facilities and teachers, and the dropout rate among them is considerably higher

than among whites (Kozol 1992, 2006). During prosperous times, their unemployment rate is at least twice as high as it is for urban whites, and it skyrockets when the economy falters. Those who are employed generally must take dead-end, low-paying jobs because the more desirable jobs go to the better educated. A catalog of social ills flows from this socioeconomic condition in the inner city (see "Consider This Research"). African Americans in large-city slums exist in a world of poverty, congestion, prostitution, drug addiction, broken homes, and brutality. Crime rates, for example, appear to increase in central cities that undergo suburbanization, both

Dennis MacDonald/PhotoEdit

The movement of whites back to the central city has led to gentrification.

John Hagedorn— Gang Violence

Gangs were a constant feature of the American urban landscape during most of the twentieth century. John Hagedorn (1998), however, contends that the extent and nature of gang violence has substantially changed with the emergence of postindustrial society in the 1960s. Hagedorn's conclusions are based on a combination of three methods: a review of the research of others, secondary analysis of precollected data (data collected by other researchers), and original data he gathered.

Gangs (mostly male) in the industrial period were tied to specific neighborhoods and new immigrant groups. These gangs emerged among unsupervised teens whose fathers worked in factories. Gang violence primarily centered on "turf" battles among neighborhood peer groups. Pride in violence came from defending the gang's space. Violence provided excitement and a sense of place in a group. Nevertheless, these working- and lower-class boys would eventually move on to hold decent jobs, have families, and live in better neighborhoods.

Gangs today still tend to form around racial and ethnic groups and neighborhoods. Currently, gangs tend to be African American, Latino, or Asian, just as earlier gangs were mostly European immigrants, such as those from Ireland, Italy, or Eastern Europe. Gangs form in the same poor urban areas, and members continue to come from dysfunctional families who do not supervise them. Juvenile gangs continue to engage in small-time crime, substance abuse, and periodic violence.

According to Hagedorn, however, the extent and nature of violence in postindustrial gangs underwent a major change. First, gang violence significantly increased. Second, gang-related homicides rose dramatically.

The question is, why? In answering this question, Hagedorn pinpoints important changes in postindustrial gangs, particularly gang functions. Gang violence, he notes, skyrocketed at the same time that American corporations were moving well-paying jobs from the central city. As legitimate work disappeared in inner cities, gangs turned from their earlier territorial emphasis to participation in the illegitimate drug market. The common outlook of gang members today is expressed by this gang member:

I got out of high school and I didn't have a diploma, wasn't no jobs, wasn't no source of income, no nothing. That's basically the easy way for a . . . young man to be—selling some dope—you can get yourself some money real quick, you really don't have nothing to worry about, nothing but the feds. You know everybody in your neighborhood. Yeah, that's pretty safe just as long as you don't start smoking it yourself. (Hagedorn 1998:390)

Significantly, this gang member was not a teenager. More urban gang members today remain members into adulthood. Rather than getting a job, marrying, and settling down, more inner-city young adults hang out on the street, making a living on the drug trade.

Although drug selling was a small part of the gang scene before the 1980s, it was not a business. By contrast, Hagedorn found more young African American males in drug trafficking than any other area of employment.

There is still movement out of urban gangs, however. A minority of gang members remain committed to the drug economy, but most seek "legit" jobs as they approach their thirties.

Evaluate the Research

1. Relate Hagedorn's findings to Merton's strain theory in Chapter 7.
2. What do you think is the most important step in solving this problem? Justify your answer.

---

because suburbanization creates stratification along city-suburban lines and because it contributes to an absolute decline in the socioeconomic status, the economic and tax base, and the physical structure of the central city (Farley and Hansel 1981; Ganz 1985; Yinger 1995).

Q Can the central-city dilemma be solved? Some countertrends exist. There are city governments now requiring certain public employees to live in the city.

Some parts of inner cities are being restored through **gentrification**—the development of low-income areas by middle-class home buyers, landlords, and professional developers ("Race, Place, and Segregation" 2002). Finally, there is a fairly significant movement of whites back to the central city. This movement is particularly evident among baby boomers who are remaining single or establishing childless or two-income families. Because these people are not as heavily involved in child-rearing, they prefer central-city living more than the previous generation (Palen 2008). The importance of these countertrends for easing the central-city dilemma remains to be seen. They certainly have not been sufficiently important to stop the emergence of edge cities.

World Urbanization

Urbanization is a worldwide movement. From 1800 to the mid-1980s, the number of urban dwellers increased almost a hundredfold, whereas the population increased only about fivefold. Fifty percent of the world's population now lives in urban areas, and this is expected to reach 60 percent in 2025 (see Figure 17.8). In more developed countries, 75 percent of the population lives in urban areas compared with 44 percent in less developed countries (2010 *World Population Data Sheet* 2010).

The pattern of urbanization is different in more developed countries than it is in less developed countries. One distinction is the rapidity of the urban growth rate. In less developed countries, most of the urban growth before the turn of the twentieth century occurred through colonial expansion. Western countries, which were involved in colonial expansion after the late fifteenth century, held half the world under colonial rule by the latter part of the nineteenth century. Only since World War II have many of these colonial countries become independent nations (Bardo and Hartman 1982). Since gaining independence, these former colonies have experienced rapid urbanization. In fact, urbanization in these areas is now proceeding faster than it did in the West, even during that area's biggest urban expansion period from 1850 to 1950 (Gelbard, Haub, and Kent 1999).

Q **What are some additional distinctions of urbanization in less developed and more developed countries?** In the first place, industrial developments in less developed countries have not kept pace with urbanization. In the cities of less developed countries, the supply of labor from the countryside exceeds the demand for labor. A high rate of unemployment is the obvious result. The term **overurbanization** describes a situation in which a city is unable to supply adequate jobs and housing for its inhabitants. In the Western experience, on the other hand, industrial development kept pace with urbanization, and cities of North America and Europe had jobs for most migrants from rural areas.

FIGURE 17.8

Urbanization Has Grown Dramatically Since the 1970s

As recently as 1975, one in three persons worldwide lived in urban areas, with most of those 1.5 billion urbanites living in areas of fewer than 1 million persons. (Many urban dwellers, in fact, live in communities of fewer than 5,000 residents.) Over the past 30 years, the urban population has increased so that more than half of the world population will be living in cities by 2008. Parallel to this overall urban growth (and the continued rise of smaller cities) is the emergence of "mega-cities—urban areas of at least 10 million persons. Between 1975 and 2010, the number of such large cities has mushroomed from three (two of which were in industrialized countries) to 20 (15 of which are in developing countries). Did you think that the world was more or less urban than shown below?

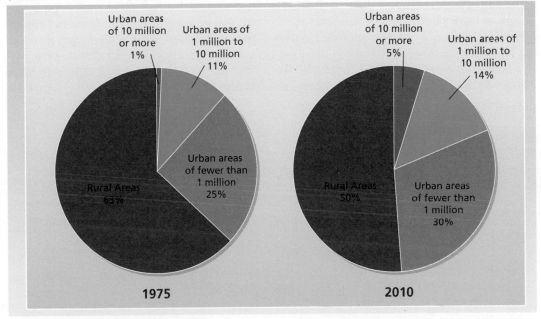

Source: Adapted from *World Population Data Sheet, 2010.*

FIGURE 17.9

World's Largest Urban Areas: 1950, 2009

This figure compares the world's largest urban areas in 1950 and 2010. What is the most surprising aspect of these data to you?

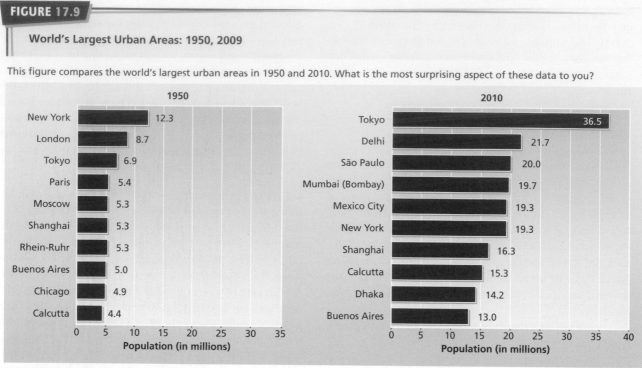

Source: *The World Almanac and Book of Facts, 2011.*

Another difference between urbanization in more developed and less developed countries is the number and size of cities. When grouped by size, cities in developed countries form a pyramid: a few large cities at the top, many medium-sized cities in the middle, and a large base of small cities (Light 1983). In the less developed world, many countries have only one big city, a tremendously large city that dwarfs a large number of villages. Calcutta, India, and Mexico City are examples. In 1950, of the world's ten largest cities, only two—Shanghai and Kolkata—were in less developed areas. By 2000, seven of the top ten largest urban areas were in less developed countries. In 2005, there were twenty "megacities" with populations of 10 million or more, and that number is expected to increase to 22 million by 2015. Of these, fifteen were in developing countries, including the most impoverished societies in the world. Similarly, nine of the world's largest urban areas are in less developed countries (Weeks 2012; see Figure 17.9).

Q Why do people in developing countries move to large cities where they will find inadequate jobs and housing? Urban sociologists point to the operation of push–pull factors in the rural-to-urban migration in less developed countries. Peasants are pushed out of their villages because the existing agricultural economy cannot support the expanding rural populations. Peasants are also pulled into cities by perceived opportunities for better education, employment, social welfare support, and availability of good medical care, even though they are likely to be disappointed (Firebaugh 1979; Sassen 2006).

CHECK YOURSELF 17.3 R2

Urbanization

1. A _____ is a concentration of people whose major social and economic needs are satisfied within the area in which they live.
2. _____ is the process by which an increasingly large proportion of the world's population lives in urban areas.
3. Thanks to worldwide urbanization, preindustrial cities no longer exist. T or F?
4. The _____ exists because diminishing public revenues are not sufficient to cope with the influx of the poor, unskilled, and uneducated.
5. _____ occurs when a city is unable to supply adequate jobs and housing for its inhabitants.

Answers: 1. community; 2. Urbanization; 3. F; 4. central-city dilemma; 5. Overurbanization

Theories of City Growth R1

Every city is unique, but we can interpret the patterns of all cities through **urban ecology**—the study of the relationships between humans and their urban environments.

In the 1920s and 1930s, sociologists at the University of Chicago studied the effects of the city environment on urban residents. It turns out that the effects varied in different parts of the city. For example, Harvey Zorbaugh (1929) found significant differences between Chicago's wealthy Gold Coast and its slum areas. The realization that such differences existed led to additional questions: Why do differences exist among areas of a city? How do different areas affect one another? What are the processes through which areas are changed? To answer these and other questions, the University of Chicago sociologists developed theories of urban ecology, including theories of city growth (Micklin and Poston 1998; Flanagan 2001; Kleniewski and Thomas 2011).

There are four major theories of city growth. **Concentric zone theory** describes urban growth in relation to circular areas that grow from the central city outward. **Sector theory** emphasizes the importance of transportation routes in the process of urban growth. **Multiple-nuclei theory** focuses on specific geographical or historical influences. These three theories, developed more in the early part of the twentieth century, are joined by a more contemporary model, the **peripheral theory,** which accents the growth of suburbs around the central city. These four theories lead to quite different images of urban space (see Figure 17.10). Indeed, all four tell us more when considered together than they tell us separately. To understand why this is so, we must first examine each theory.

Concentric Zone Theory

Q **How does Chicago represent the concentric zone theory of growth?** Ernest Burgess (1925), like other early sociologists at the University of Chicago, was interested in the causes and consequences of Chicago's growth. His work led to the concentric zone theory, which describes city growth in relation to distinctive zones that develop from the central city outward, in a circular pattern. As illustrated in Figure 17.10, the innermost circle is the *central business district*, the heart of the city, containing major government and private office buildings, banks, retail and wholesale stores, and entertainment and cultural facilities.

FIGURE 17.10

Theories of City Growth

This figure displays in graphic form the four major theories of city growth. Discuss one important advancement these theories make to understanding urban growth.

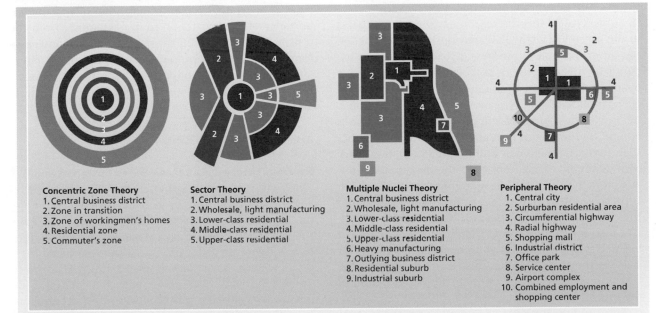

Concentric Zone Theory
1. Central business district
2. Zone in transition
3. Zone of workingmen's homes
4. Residential zone
5. Commuter's zone

Sector Theory
1. Central business district
2. Wholesale, light manufacturing
3. Lower-class residential
4. Middle-class residential
5. Upper-class residential

Multiple Nuclei Theory
1. Central business district
2. Wholesale, light manufacturing
3. Lower-class residential
4. Middle-class residential
5. Upper-class residential
6. Heavy manufacturing
7. Outlying business district
8. Residential suburb
9. Industrial suburb

Peripheral Theory
1. Central city
2. Surburban residential area
3. Circumferential highway
4. Radial highway
5. Shopping mall
6. Industrial district
7. Office park
8. Service center
9. Airport complex
10. Combined employment and shopping center

Source: Chauncy D. Harris and Edward L. Ullman, "The Nature of Cities," *The Annals* (1945):13. Copyright © 1945 by The American Academy of Political and Social Science; and Chauncy D. Harris, "'The Nature of Cities' and Urban Geography in the Last Half Century," *Urban Geography* 18(1997):17. Used by permission of V.H. Winston & Son, Inc.

Sam Diephuis/zefa/CORBIS

Explain which theory of urban growth best accounts for this suburban office building.

The central business district exerts an especially strong influence on other parts of a city. This influence is especially clear in the zone immediately surrounding it. Burgess called this the *zone in transition* because it is in the process of change. As new businesses and activities enter the central business district, the district expands by invading the next zone. This area may have been a residential area inhabited by middle- or upper-class families, who left because of the invasion of business activities. Most of the property in this zone is bought by those with little interest in the area. Rather than investing money in building maintenance, landowners simply extract rent from the property or sell it at a profit after the area becomes more commercialized. Until the zone in transition is completely absorbed into the central business district (which may never occur), it is used for slum housing, warehouses, and marginal businesses that are unable to compete economically for space in the central business district itself. In short, the invasion of business activities creates deterioration in the transition zone.

Surrounding the zone in transition are three zones devoted primarily to housing. The *zone of workingmen's homes* contains modest but stable neighborhoods populated largely by blue-collar workers. In the northern United States, the zone of workingmen's homes is often inhabited by second-generation immigrants who have enough financial success to leave the deteriorating zone in transition. Next comes a *residential zone* containing mostly middle-class and upper-middle-class neighborhoods. Single-family dwellings dominate this zone, which is inhabited by managers, professionals, white-collar workers, and some well-paid factory workers. On the outskirts of the city, often outside the official city limits, is the *commuter's zone*, which contains upper-class and upper-middle-class suburbs.

Sector Theory

Q How is transportation related to the sector theory of city growth? Based on a study he performed for the Federal Housing Administration, Homer Hoyt (1939) developed sector theory. Hoyt's study indicated that patterns of land use do not necessarily change according to distance from the central business district. Instead, land is more strongly affected by major transportation routes. As Figure 17.10 shows, sectors tend to be pie-shaped wedges radiating from the central business district to the city's outskirts. Each sector is organized around a major transportation route. Once a given type of activity is organized around a transportation route, its nature tends to be set. Thus, some sectors will be predominantly industrial, others will contain stores and professional offices, others will be "neon strips" with motels and fast-food restaurants, and still others will be residential sectors, each with its own social class and ethnic composition.

As in concentric zone theory, sector theory depicts cities as generally circular in shape. But due to the importance of transportation routes extending from the central business district, the boundaries of many cities form a star-like pattern, rather than a uniformly circular shape. The exact shape of a city, however, is not a major issue in sector theory. Emphasis here is on land patterns around transportation routes.

Multiple-Nuclei Theory

Q What theory does Beacon Hill in Boston exemplify? Many cities have areas that cannot be explained by either concentric zone or sector theory. For example, the Beacon Hill area of Boston defies concentric zone theory; it remains an expensive, prestigious neighborhood despite its location near the central business district. Because of such cases, Chauncy Harris and Edward Ullman (1945) have suggested that cities do not always follow a pattern contingent on a central district. (Figure 17.10 shows one example of a multiple-nuclei city pattern.) A city may have several separate centers, some devoted to manufacturing, some to retail trade, some to residential use, and so on. These specialized centers can develop because of the availability of automobiles and highways. They reflect such factors as geography, history, and tradition. Because the factors affecting land use are unique to each city, multiple-nuclei theorists do not predict any particular pattern of land use that would apply to all cities.

Peripheral Theory

Q Why have urban geographers developed a peripheral theory? The preceding three theories of urban growth were developed more than fifty years ago. Despite their age, the insights of each theory demonstrate how cities have expanded from the center outward. This is especially the case for older cities such as Chicago and San Francisco. Many cities today, however, no longer have a central-city core to which other parts of the metropolitan area are oriented.

More flexible means of transportation, such as cars and trucks, replace dependence on shipping, railroads, and heavy manufacturing. Highways now encircle large urban areas. New technologies (fax machines, cell phones, computers, the Internet) are also loosening the ties of most parts of the city to the central core. As a result, many cities are now oriented *away* from the older urban core.

As mentioned earlier, many Americans have moved from the city to the suburbs. They have done so in part because many businesses—offices, factories, schools, retail stores, restaurants, health centers—are in the suburbs. To encompass changes in urban areas

today, urban geographer Chauncy Harris (1997) has formulated the peripheral theory. The dominant feature of this model, obviously, is the growth of suburbs (and edge cities) around and away from the central cities (see Figure 17.10). Peripheral theory brings urban growth research up to date.

Q Of what value are these diverse theories of city growth? Although each of these theories calls attention to the dynamics of city growth, no single theory describes the growth pattern of all cities. In recognition of this, some researchers explain patterns of land use by combining the insights of these theories. Several researchers, for example, report that people distribute themselves in cities in a way that combines both concentric zone theory and sector theory (Berry 1965; Timms 1971; Berry and Kasarda 1977).

Regardless of the ultimate fate of the concentric zone, sector, multiple-nuclei, and peripheral theories, they definitely perform a service. By calling attention to the factors influencing land use in urban areas, these theories remind us that cities do not grow in a random manner.

The Quality of Urban Life **R1**

As just noted, sociologists from the University of Chicago contributed to our understanding of urban land use. Their interests were not, however, confined simply to the ecological characteristics of cities. These sociologists were also concerned with the effects of

---

CHECK YOURSELF **17.4** **R2**

Theories of City Growth

1. Match the following zones of the concentric zone theory with the appropriate descriptions.

    ____ a. central business district

    ____ b. commuter's zone

    ____ c. residential zone

    ____ d. zone in transition

    ____ e. zone of workingmen's homes

    (1) zone that is the next zone out from the zone in transition

    (2) site of major stores and offices

    (3) zone with physical deterioration stemming from few repairs

    (4) zone the wealthiest people live in

    (5) zone that is largely middle class in composition

2. The theory that emphasizes the importance of transportation routes is called _____ theory.

3. The _____ theory contends that the growth of cities does not necessarily follow any specific pattern.

4. _____ theory of city growth brings urban growth research up to date.

5. One of the ultimate contributions of the four major theories of city growth is their demonstration that cities do not grow in a random fashion. T or F?

Answers: 1. a. (2), b. (4), c. (5), d. (3), e. (1); 2. sector; 3. multiple-nuclei; 4. Peripheral; 5. T

cities on people. Their basic conclusion: People in cities live a unique way of life. The researchers designated this distinctive way of life—**urbanism.**

Cities have always produced a wide variety of lifestyles. During medieval times, cities were places to escape the domination of powerful landowners, and it was said that "city air makes one free." Many of today's citizens consider cities sources of intellectual and cultural diversity, sophistication, and freedom. Louis Wirth (1938), a University of Chicago sociologist and the first to develop the idea of urbanism as a way of life, agreed in part with the intellectual tradition that associated the city with freedom and tolerance. He believed that because urban residents confront a variety of lifestyles, they are more tolerant of diversity and less ethnocentric than residents of small towns or rural areas (T. C. Wilson 1985, 1991). However, Wirth also drew on an intellectual tradition that saw impersonality and social disorganization in urban areas, a tradition represented in the work of German sociologist Ferdinand Tönnies. Later sociologists, as noted in "Using the Sociological Imagination" at the beginning of this chapter, have a more positive view of the quality of urban social life. (See Table 17.1 for an illustration of how the three major theoretical perspectives might view urban society.)

The Traditional Perspective on Urbanism: Loss of Community

Q What was Tönnies's viewpoint? Although he did not use the term *urbanism*, Tönnies was the first sociologist to contrast the culture in rural and urban settings. As noted in Chapter 5, Tönnies distinguished between *gemeinschaft* (community) and *gesellschaft* (society). In the **gemeinschaft**—the type of society existing before the Industrial Revolution—social relationships were intimate because people knew one another. Daily life revolved around family and was based on tradition. There was a sense of a shared way of life and an interest in the common good of the community. Urbanization changes all that, according to Tönnies. In the **gesellschaft**, social relationships are impersonal because most people with whom one interacts are strangers. Although the immediate family is still important, the wider kinship network disappears. With the fading of tradition goes the sharing of common values. Interest shifts from the community's welfare to self-interest.

Q How did Wirth conceptualize urbanism? In Wirth's view, the urban conditions that promote sophistication, freedom, and diversity also involve a high cost. Urbanism, Wirth said, brings a depersonalization of human relationships. Rather than involving their total personalities in interaction, urban residents interact on the basis of rigidly defined roles. For example, a customer in a rural store may combine shopping with a lengthy conversation, but interactions in most urban stores are confined to the exchange of money and products. This emphasis on rigid role prescriptions, Wirth concluded, makes it difficult for urban residents to maintain a sense of their own individuality; it makes them indifferent and blasé. Heavy reliance on roles occurs partly because of sheer number: It is impossible to know everyone. Urbanites may actually know more people than do rural residents, but they know fewer people well enough to interact with them on a personal basis.

According to Wirth, urban residents behave as they do because of three demographic characteristics of cities: large size, high density (a large number of residents per square mile), and great diversity within the population. Wirth contended that as cities become larger,

---

TABLE 17.1

FOCUS ON THEORETICAL PERSPECTIVES: Urban Society

This table illustrates how functionalism, conflict theory, and symbolic interactionisms might approach the study of urban society. State a research topic for the study of population for which any one of the theories would be appropriate.

Theoretical Perspective	Concept	Sample Research Topic
Functionalism	Urbanization	• Study of the relationship between population density and the suicide rate
Conflict theory	Overurbanization	• Investigation of the relationship between the distribution of scarce resources and social class
Symbolic interactionism	Urbanism	• Research on the effect of the degree of urbanization and the extent to which social interaction is based on shared meanings

more densely settled, and more socially diverse, residents become more sophisticated and more reliant on impersonal relationships.

The Contemporary Perspective on Urbanism: Community Sustained

The most frequent criticism of Wirth's theory of urbanism points to its overgeneralization. Some critics charge that Wirth's view of urbanism mistakenly assumes that all urban residents share a common lifestyle (I. M. Young 1990; Macionis and Parillo 2006). A leading spokesperson for this opposing line of thought is Herbert Gans (1962b, 1968).

Q **Do all urban residents share the same way of life?** Gans described five basic population groups found within inner-city areas, the first three of which live in the inner city by choice and are protected from the extreme negative consequences depicted by Wirth:

- *Cosmopolites*. People in this category are well educated and have high incomes. The inner-city attracts them to the area's cultural advantages, such as art museums, theaters, and symphony orchestras.
- *The unmarried and childless*. People in this category also live in the inner city by choice. They may not feel a strong commitment to the inner city, but living there allows them to meet other people, and the area is convenient to jobs and entertainment facilities.
- *Ethnic villagers*. People in this category live in inner-city neighborhoods with strong ethnic identities. Residents of such neighborhoods are suspicious of

the city as a whole and participate little in its affairs. The neighborhood itself, however, is an important source of intimate, enduring relationships.

- *The trapped*. Some people—such as the elderly living on pensions or public assistance—cannot afford to leave the inner city. They may identify with their own neighborhood, but this does not prevent them from becoming annoyed over changes in the central-city area that they consider undesirable.
- *The deprived*. Poor minorities, the psychologically and physically challenged, some divorced mothers, and other deprived people see the city as a source of increased opportunities for employment or welfare assistance. The poverty, however, prevents such individuals from choosing where they will live in the city. These people are therefore vulnerable to the most extreme effects of population size, density, and diversity.

According to Gans, then, no blanket statement (such as that formulated by Wirth) applies to every urban resident. Although the trapped and the deprived are unable to escape many of the adverse effects described by Wirth, members of the other three categories choose to live in the inner city. They would not make this choice had they not seen many advantages.

Q **Are city dwellers isolated, with no personal relationships?** According to Wirth's theory, urban residents have relatively few opportunities for participation in informal relationships. Subsequent research shows, however, that urban residents do participate in informal relationships, and such relationships play an important role in maintaining a positive emotional state (Kadushin 1983; Creekmore 1985; C. S. Fischer

---

CHECK YOURSELF **17.5** **R2**

The Quality of Urban Life

1. The distinctive way of life allegedly developed in urban areas is referred to as _____.
2. According to Ferdinand Tönnies, urbanism corresponds to _____ (gemeinschaft/gesellschaft).
3. Louis Wirth relied on three characteristics to explain the development of urbanism as a way of life. What were they?
   a. age of city, population density, political structure
   b. population size, economic base, political structure
   c. population size, population density, population diversity
   d. economic base, political structure, population structure
4. According to Herbert Gans, which of the following groups have relatively little choice within the inner city?
   a. cosmopolites, the unmarried and childless
   b. ethnic villagers, the deprived
   c. the unmarried and childless, ethnic villagers
   d. the trapped, the deprived
5. Research shows that urban residents are largely isolated from family and friends. T or F?

Answers: 1. urbanism; 2. gesellschaft; 3. c; 4. d; 5. F

1982, 1984, 1995). In an intentional test of Wirth's theory, John Kasarda and Morris Janowitz (1974) found that population size and density do not necessarily produce a lack of involvement in local friendship, kinship, or other social relationships. Those who are not highly involved in such relationships in a large city tend to be those who have not lived there long enough to become a part of it. John Esposito and John Fiorillo (1974) found essentially the same thing in a study of working-class neighborhoods in New York City.

Other evidence indicates that families continue to provide urban residents with emotional support and mutual aid (see Chapter 12). Studies based on observations of actual behavior in areas as diverse as lower-class slums and middle-class suburbs are showing the importance of personal relationships among family members and friends. For example, Gans (1962a) observed the West End of Boston, where many aspects of Italian rural life continue to be honored. Personal relationships exist there, some argue, because one ethnic group dominates the area. However, neighborhoods in general appear to be important sources of interaction and support. Take, for example, research of a Chicago slum (Addams) by Gerald Suttles (1968): Even a low-income area populated by four different ethnic groups developed a social order of informal and personal relationships.

On to Chapter 18

Population and urbanization both reflect social change and lead to further modifications. The first half of Chapter 18 focuses more explicitly on the nature and sources of social change. The last half introduces collective behavior, the least structured form of social behavior.

S | INTEGRATED GOALS AND SUMMARY

1. **Distinguish among the concepts of demography, formal demography, and social demography.**
   - Demography is the scientific study of population. Formal demography gathers, collates, analyzes, and presents population data. Social demography examines population data within a social context.

2. **Distinguish the three population processes.**
   - Demographers use three population processes to account for population change: fertility, mortality, and migration. Fertility is measured in three ways: the crude birth rate (the annual number of live births per 1,000 members of a population); the fertility rate (annual number of live births per 1,000 women between the ages fifteen and twenty-four; and the age-specific fertility (number of live births per 1,000 women in a specific age group). Mortality is measured by the crude death rate, age-specific death rate, and the infant mortality rate. Migration has two measures: the gross migration rate (the number of persons per 1,000 members of a population that enter or leave) and the net migration rate (the annual increase or decrease per 1,000 members of a population produced by people entering and leaving).

3. **Discuss the major dimensions of the world population growth problem.**
   - Because population grows exponentially, it increases more each year in absolute numbers, even if the rate of growth remains stable. Most developed nations have undergone what is known as the demographic transition. This is the process accompanying economic development in which a population gradually moves from high birth and death rates to low birth and death rates. Europe seems to be experiencing a second demographic transition, which involves an eventual decline in population size.
   - In more developed societies, economic growth has led to a lower fertility rate for a number of reasons. But this type of economic development, along with continued inequalities, has not led to a reduction in fertility in less developed countries. These latter countries may or may not pass through the demographic transition.

4. **Predict future world and U.S. population trends.**
   - Although the world's population growth rate is declining after 200 years of acceleration, the world's population will continue to grow. It is projected that world population growth will cease at just greater than 12 billion by the end of the twenty-first century.
   - America grows more rapidly than other developed countries due to a combination of its total fertility rate, low mortality rates, and high net migration rate.

5. **Differentiate among the basic measures of urbanization.**
   - As urban areas increased in size, sociologists gradually shifted their attention from communities to larger units, such as metropolitan statistical areas (MetroSAs or MSAs) and combined statistical areas (CSAs). However, the basic unit of study is the city, which is characterized by a large number of inhabitants, permanence, density, and occupational specialization of inhabitants.

6. **Trace the historical development of preindustrial and modern cities.**
   - Although the process of urbanization is now commonplace throughout the world, the first cities developed only 5,000 to 6,000 years ago. The first preindustrial

cities developed in fertile areas where plant cultivation was sufficiently advanced to support a nonagricultural population. A surplus food supply permitted relatively large numbers of people to live in cities and perform nonagricultural work. Preindustrial types of cities still exist in underdeveloped parts of the world.

- The Industrial Revolution, with its technological innovations and alterations in social structure, caused a major increase in the rate of urbanization. The development of factories was an especially important influence on the location of cities. Although cities and metropolitan areas are important in industrialized societies, they feel strongly the effects of suburbanization and a recent tendency for medium-sized metropolitan and nonmetropolitan areas to grow more rapidly than large metropolitan areas.

7. **Describe some of the consequences of suburbanization.**
- Suburbanization has created severe problems for central cities and their residents. The problems are particularly serious for minorities, the poor, and the elderly in the inner city.

8. **Discuss world urbanization.**
- Less developed countries are having a different experience with urbanization than did the West. In less developed countries, the urban growth rate has been faster, industrialization has been slower, and a base of small- and middle-sized cities has not developed. Still, peasants in less developed countries migrate to cities both because they are forced off the land and because cities appear to provide unique opportunities.

9. **Compare and contrast four theories of city growth.**
- Urban ecologists study the adjustment processes of human populations to their environments. They developed four major models of spatial development in cities: concentric zone theory, sector theory, multiple-nuclei theory, and peripheral theory. Each of these theories receives some empirical support, but it appears that combining insights from all of them is the most useful.

10. **Compare and contrast traditional and contemporary views on the quality of urban life.**
- According to the traditional view of urbanism, cities provide a free and sophisticated environment but are characterized by impersonality and social disorganization. According to more recent empirical research, this description is not applicable to all urban residents; many people in urban areas are involved in personal and social relationships.

CONCEPT REVIEW

Match the following concepts with the definitions listed below them.

___ a.	gemeinschaft	___ h.	age-specific fertility	___ o.	morbidity
___ b.	multiple-nuclei theory	___ i.	social demography	___ p.	demography
___ c.	crude death rate	___ j.	doubling time	___ q.	net migration rate
___ d.	urban ecology	___ k.	urbanization	___ r.	metropolitan statistical area
___ e.	fecundity	___ l.	community		(MetroSA or MSA)
___ f.	replacement level	___ m.	gross migration rate	___ s.	fertility rate
___ g.	sector theory	___ n.	combined statistical area (CSA)	___ t.	life span

1. the birth-rate level at which married couples replace themselves in the population
2. rates of disease and illness in a population
3. the maximum rate at which women can physically produce children
4. a description of the process of urban growth emphasizing the importance of transportation routes
5. the branch of demography that studies population in relation to its social setting
6. a grouping that contains at least one city of 50,000 inhabitants or more or an "urbanized area" of at least 50,000 inhabitants and the surrounding integrated population
7. Tönnies's term for the type of society based on tradition, kinship, and intimate social relationships
8. a concentration of people who can fulfill their major social and economic needs within the area where they live
9. the annual number of live births per 1,000 women ages fifteen to forty-four
10. the annual number of deaths per 1,000 members of a population

11. the annual increase or decrease per 1,000 members of a population resulting from people leaving and entering the population
12. the scientific study of population
13. a description of the process of urban growth that emphasizes specific and historical influences on areas within cities
14. the most advanced age to which humans can survive
15. the number of live births per 1,000 women in a specific age group
16. the study of the relationships between humans and their environments within cities
17. an urban area composed of two or more sets of neighboring primary metropolitan statistical areas (MetroSAs) or one or more MicroSAs
18. the number of years needed to double the size of a population
19. the process by which an increasingly larger proportion of the world's population lives in urban areas
20. the annual number of persons per 1,000 members of a population who enter or leave a geographical area

CHECK YOURSELF REVIEW

1. Thanks to worldwide urbanization, preindustrial cities no longer exist. T or F?

2. One of the ultimate contributions of the four major theories of city growth is their demonstration that cities do not grow in a random fashion. T or F?

3. Thomas Malthus sees famine as a _____ check on population growth.

4. _____ is the process by which an increasingly large proportion of the world's population lives in urban areas.

5. A population with an excess of births over deaths will experience _____.

6. _____ occurs when a city is unable to supply adequate jobs and housing for its inhabitants.

7. The distinctive way of life allegedly developed in urban areas is referred to as _____.

8. Which of the following figures is the world's population most likely to reach before it stops growing?
   a. 4 billion
   b. 8 billion
   c. 12 billion
   d. 25 billion

9. Europe's second demographic transition involves what kind of population growth?
   a. stable
   b. increasing
   c. declining

10. Which of the following characteristics is not included in the definition of a city?
    a. permanence
    b. dense settlement
    c. advanced culture
    d. occupational specialization in nonagricultural activities

11. According to Herbert Gans, which of the following groups have relatively little choice within the inner city?
    a. cosmopolites, the unmarried and childless
    b. ethnic villagers, the deprived
    c. ethnic villagers, the unmarried and childless
    d. the trapped, the deprived

12. Match the following zones of the concentric zone theory with the adjacent descriptions.
    ___ a. central business district
    ___ b. commuter's zone
    ___ c. residential zone
    ___ d. zone in transition
    ___ e. zone of workingmen's homes
    (1) zone that is the next zone out from the zone in transition
    (2) site of major stores and offices
    (3) zone with physical deterioration stemming from few repairs
    (4) zone the wealthiest people live in
    (5) zone that is largely middle class in composition

GRAPHIC REVIEW

Population projections by world regions appear in Figure 17.3. Answer these questions to test your grasp of world population growth between 2005 and 2050.

1. Compare the projected population growth by world region between 2005 and 2050. Explain any surprises. If you were not surprised, explain why projections went just as you expected.

   _____
   _____
   _____

2. Compare the population doubling time in less and more economically developed areas. Explain the difference.

   _____
   _____
   _____

CRITICAL-THINKING QUESTIONS

1. Suppose that the average number of children per family in the United States increased from 1.8 to 3. Discuss the short- and long-term effects this would have on population growth.

   _____
   _____

2. Should the slow-growing nations, such as the United States, have immigration policies that help relieve the population pressures on countries with high-growing populations? Defend your position using sociological concepts.

   _____
   _____

3. Explain and evaluate the usefulness of the following theories of city growth: concentric zone theory, sector theory, multiple-nuclei theory, and peripheral theory.

4. According to Louis Wirth, what are the major characteristics of urbanism as a way of life? Evaluate the accuracy of Wirth's explanation in view of more recent research findings.

ANSWER KEY

Concept Review

a. 7
b. 13
c. 10
d. 16
e. 3
f. 1
g. 4
h. 15
i. 5
j. 18
k. 19
l. 8
m. 20
n. 17
o. 2
p. 12
q. 11
r. 6
s. 9
t. 14

Check Yourself Review

1. F
2. T
3. positive
4. Urbanization
5. natural increase
6. Overurbanization
7. urbanism
8. c
9. c
10. c
11. d
12. a. 2
    b. 4
    c. 5
    d. 3
    e. 1

18 Social Change and Collective Behavior

Dominic Favre/AP Photos

GOALS

- Illustrate three social processes contributing to social change.
- Discuss, as sources of social change, the role of technology, population, the natural environment, conflict, and ideas.
- Explain the why and how of social change within the context of the functionalist and conflict perspectives.
- Discuss the unique nature of collective behavior in sociology.

- Describe social activities engaged in by dispersed collectivities.
- Describe the nature of a crowd, and identify the basic types of crowds.
- Contrast contagion theory, emergent norm theory, and convergence theory.
- Define the concept of social movement, and identify the primary types of social movements.

Do successful revolutions bring radical social change? It seems so, almost by definition. There are dramatic examples of truly revolutionary changes in a society: France in the eighteenth century, China in the twentieth century, and Russia in the early twentieth century. Generally, however, victory celebrations are not followed by a new social order. Change after the American Revolution was not radical; it was gradual and long term. It is also a fact that the revolution was merely *one* of the precipitative factors creating change.

Revolution is only one factor contributing to the alteration of social structure. After defining social change, we turn immediately to several of its sources.

Social Change 🔲

Social Change a Constant

Imagine for a moment the history of the Earth as a 365-day period, with midnight January 1 marking the starting point and December 31 being today. Within this time span, each "day" represents 12 million years. The first form of life, a simple bacterium, appeared in February. More complex life, such as fish, appeared about November 20. On December 10, the dinosaurs appeared; by Christmas they were extinct. The first recognizable human beings did not appear until the afternoon of December 31. *Homo sapiens* emerged shortly before midnight that last day of the year. All of

recorded history occurred in the last sixty seconds of the year (Ornstein and Ehrlich 2000).

All societies change. In Egypt, where Islamic law permits a man to divorce his wife by declaring to her "You are divorced," one man, inspired by new technology, did the deed by text messaging his wife, "I divorce you" (Knickmeyer 2008). The speed of change may vary from the glacial to the mercurial. Nonetheless, social change is a constant. Sociologists define **social change** as societal alterations with long-term and relatively important consequences (Abu-Lughod 2000).

Q **Why is it difficult to predict social change?** Predicting precise change is a challenge, partly because a society absorbs change in ways consistent with its own culture. For instance, two societies, both adopting a form of democracy, may develop their government in very different ways. Both Britain and the United States are democracies. But their histories prior to becoming democracies (Britain had a royal tradition) led to divergent forms of government. In addition, people in a society can modify their behavior and consciously decide for themselves the ways in which change will occur. They can, for example, deliberately avoid a predicted state of affairs (Caplow 1991). These facts should not, however, discourage an attempt to understand alterations in society. But in doing so, one must base predictions on sound assumptions, just as Frenchman Alexis de Tocqueville did during the early 1800s in his remarkably penetrating study of American society (see Table 18.1).

Q **Why do some societies change faster than others?** This is a complex question with no easy answer. Technology, discussed shortly, is a prime force in social change. Technologically complex societies change much faster than technologically simple societies (Nolan and Lenski 2010). This is because technology increases human

TABLE 18.1

Key Assumptions in Predicting Social Change in America

The most accurate prognosticator of trends in American society has been the Frenchman Alexis de Tocqueville. Tocqueville's *Democracy in America*, which was published in the 1830s, displayed an amazing grasp of American society. Tocqueville's success has been attributed to several key assumptions he made.

- *Major social institutions would continue to exist.* Unlike many of his contemporaries—and many of ours— Tocqueville did not expect the family, religion, or the state to be greatly changed.
- *Human nature would remain the same.* Tocqueville did not expect men and women to become much better or worse or different from what history had shown them to be.
- *Equality and the trend toward centralized government would continue.*
- *The availability of material resources (such as land, minerals, and rich soils) limits social change.*
- *Change is affected by the past, but history does not strictly dictate the future.*
- *There are no social forces aside from human actions.* Historical events are not foreordained by factors beyond human control.

Source: Adapted from Theodore Caplow, *American Social Trends* (New York: Harcourt Brace Jovanovich, 1991), p. 216.

control over the physical world. And as control over the environment increases, nontechnological changes occur in other parts of society—family, economy, education, medicine. For example, new technologies associated with the computer and information processing are radically changing health care. There are patients today who are diagnosed by physicians they will never meet in person.

Technology is, however, not the only reason some societies change faster than others. Sociologists have identified three important social processes and several more specific factors that influence the pace of social change.

Processes for Change

Three interrelated social processes lead to social change. Although related, the processes of discovery, invention, and diffusion are distinct.

Q **How does each of these three social processes promote social change?** In the **discovery** process, something is either learned or reinterpreted. Early ocean navigators, with skill and courage, demonstrated by experience the rounded shape of the Earth. With this new interpretation, then, many worldwide changes followed, including new patterns of migration, intercontinental commerce, and colonization. Likewise, prehistoric peoples used fire for warmth and cooking, and later (in about 7000 B.C.) the first agriculturists used fire to clear fields and to create ash for fertilizer. Fire, of course, was central to the ensuing transition to agricultural society.

Invention is the creation of a new element by combining two or more already existing elements, with a spawning of new rules for its use. Examples of inventions come easily to mind. It was not so much the materials Orville and Wilbur Wright used to make an airplane (most of the parts were available), but the way they manipulated and combined the elements, that led to their successful flight at Kitty Hawk.

The pace of social change through invention is closely tied to the complexity of the cultural and social base. As the base becomes more complex and varied, the number of elements, as well as the possible combination of elements, increases dramatically. Consequently, the more complex and varied a society, the more rapidly it will change. This helps explain why even though several million years passed between the evolution of the human species and the invention of the airplane, we reached the moon in less than seventy years after the Wright brothers' first flight. Social change, of course, occurs faster when an invention can integrate with many other aspects of a society. NASA (National Aeronautics and Space Administration) was able to reach the moon relatively quickly because the United States was already advanced in physics, aerodynamics, and the manufacturing of specialized materials.

When one group borrows something from another group—norms, values, roles, styles of architecture—change occurs through the process of **diffusion.** Whereas the extent and rate of invention depend on the complexity of a society, the extent and rate of diffusion depend on the degree of social contact. Borrowing from others may involve entire societies, as in the American importation of cotton growing that was first developed in India. Or diffusion may take place among groups within the same society, as in the social and

By which social process did this advertisement for a Mariah Carey concert reach Beirut, Lebanon?

Norbert Schiller/epa/CORBIS

Social Change

1. _____ refers to alterations in social structures that have long-term and relatively important consequences.
2. The more complex a society, the more rapidly it will change through invention. T or F?
3. The process of _____ usually involves modification and selectivity.

Answers: 1. Social change; 2. T; 3. diffusion

cultural spin-offs of the jazz subculture, which was created by African American musicians.

As noted earlier, a borrowed element must harmonize with the group culture. Despite the upsurge of unisex fashions in America today, wearing a Scottish kilt on the job could get a construction worker laughed off the top of a skyscraper. Wearing kilts still clashes with the American definition of manhood. If skirts are ever to become as acceptable for American men as pants are for women, society will have to either alter their form or modify the cultural concept of masculinity.

Integrating a borrowed element may involve merely a selection of certain aspects. The Japanese, for example, accept capitalism but resist the American form of democratic government, the American style of conducting business, and the American family structure. Diffusion, then, almost always involves selectivity and modification.

In modern society, most aspects of culture are borrowed rather than created. The processes of discovery and invention are important, but usually far more elements enter a society through cultural diffusion.

Sources of Social Change ⬛R1

Discovery, invention, and diffusion are social processes through which social change occurs. A multitude of factors affect society through these processes. Most important among the factors encouraging social change are technology, population, the natural environment, revolution and war, and ideas.

Technology

Time magazine selected Albert Einstein as the man of the century, a choice reflecting the significance of science and technology in the twentieth century (Golden 1999). **Technology** is knowledge and hardware combined to achieve practical goals. Historically, we view technology as a precursor to social change (Teich 1993; MacKenzie and Wajcman 1999; Volti 2003). For instance, Karl Marx placed the importance of technology in sharp perspective: "The windmill gives you society with the feudal lord; the steammill, society with the industrial capitalist" (Marx 1920:119). Although the relationship between technology and social change is

not this simple and direct—and Marx knew it—their interconnectedness is firmly established.

Q To what extent can technological advances create social change? Although originally thought to be a mere means of transportation, the automobile had countless effects on society. It changed dating and courtship patterns, contributed to a new sexual morality, created new industries, promoted industrial expansion, produced suburbanization, and contributed immeasurably to environmental pollution. The creation of the silicon chip introduced technological change at an unprecedented rate (see Figure 18.1). The societal transformations wrought by the microprocessor are many and far-reaching. Changes in the workplace are as consequential as those of the Industrial Revolution (Fukuyama 1999). The microprocessor radically changes surgical techniques, from microsurgeries to radio wave therapy

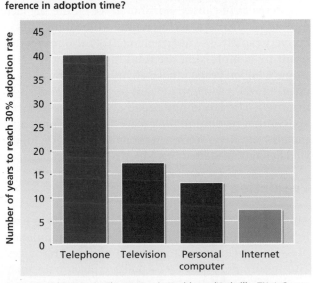

FIGURE 18.1

Becoming Wired: Time It Took for 30 Percent of Americans to Acquire Selected Technologies

It took forty years for 30 percent of American homes to have telephones. How much time elapsed before 30 percent of Americans were online? How would you account for the difference in adoption time?

Source: David R. Francis, *The Internet in Healthcare* (Nashville, TN: J. C. Bradford, August 1999), p. 11.

(Cowley and Underwood 1998). And we can only begin to imagine the artificial intelligence implications of IBM's super computer, "Watson," that soundly trashed the best "Jeopardy" players humans have to offer (Borenstein and Robertson 2011).

The sequencing of the human genome promises even more dramatic social change. Now that scientists have cloned sheep, cows, pigs, domestic cats, a human embryo from adult cells, and artifical DNA, who can know where this capability will lead ("Hello, Dolly" 1997; R. Weiss 2000; J. Fischer 2001; Kluger 2002; Fukuyama 2003; "To Clone a Human" 2008)? The national debate on stem-cell research policy may seem mild given where "synthetic biology" may take us. Think of this 2010 revelation from a human genetic engineering lab: We have created a living cell controlled only by man-made genetic instructions. Say again! Synthia, the first artificial microorganization, has computer-designed DNA created from a few, inexpensive basic chemicals. When placed in a host cell, it reproduces itself independently of human biology (Brown 2010; "'Synthia': And Then There Was Life" 2010). This ability to design and create new forms of life will most assuredly affect our future. But, how?

Q Why should we be skeptical of technological determinism? Technological determinism assumes that technology is the primary determinate of a society. This is a seductive theory, but, actually, the relationship between technology and social change is more complicated (Lauer 1991). First, social change can occur without technological developments. Second, the introduction of technology does not necessarily lead to social change. Third, the particular effects of technology will vary from society to society because any given society filters the adoption and use of technology through its own culture.

Although it seems inadvisable to view technology as a necessary and sufficient cause of social change, it is essential not to underestimate its contribution as part of a network of causes. Nor should we ignore the fact, as noted earlier, that technological innovation can occur very rapidly. David Freeman (1974) also makes this point by compressing the total lifetime of the Earth (some 5 billion years) into an eighty-day period and calculating when some significant technological changes occurred: The Stone Age began six minutes ago, the agricultural revolution took place fifteen seconds ago, metals were first used ten seconds ago, and the Industrial Revolution started three-tenths of a second ago.

Population

Alterations in population size and composition have interesting effects. By way of illustration, population pressures in China led to a conservation of resources. This in turn produced a state policy replacing the more expensive, traditional burial rites with cremation ceremonies. Yet another consequence of population stress is found in the conflict and strain within Chinese families. Moreover, China instigated a national population control program to create the one-child family. This is already affecting Chinese social structure, as in the dishonesty engendered by some anxious local officials who underreport birth statistics to meet the government quotas. Less developed countries offer another illustration; they are undergoing many dramatic changes because their declining mortality is not being matched by lowered fertility.

America's baby boom following the return of American soldiers at the end of World War II is illustrative as well. The increased birth rate of Americans born between 1946 and 1964 required expanded medical personnel and facilities for child health care and then, in the 1950s and 1960s, created the need for more teachers and schools. On the other hand, the generation following the baby boomers, now in their thirties and in the labor market, is experiencing increased competition for jobs and fewer opportunities to move up the career ladder. As the baby boomers retire, problems of health care and Social Security loom large. Longer working hours, retraining programs, and reeducation for senior people will probably become prevailing patterns. As our population continues to age, more attention is being paid to our senior citizens. Already, there are more extended-care homes for the aged, an increase in geriatric emphasis, and more television advertising and programming targeting the aging population.

The Natural Environment

Interaction with the natural environment, from the earliest times, has transformed American life. The vast territory west of the thirteen colonies permitted expansion, ultimately to the Pacific Ocean. This western movement helped shape our cultural identity and wrought untold changes, most tragically the destruction of many Native American cultures. Climate change, caused in part by human behavior, promises truly catastrophic consequences. Two authoritative reports describe some implications of unchecked climate change, including rising conflict between rich and poor nations, tensions due to massive migrations, a proliferation of diseases, and realignment in global power driven by accessibility of natural resources (Campbell et al. 2007; United Nations Climate Change Conference 2007).

Q How can change in natural resources ripple through a society? Christopher Steiner (2009), in his book *$20 Per Gallon*, offers an ideal example. He discusses oil as the most important natural resource in the modern and modernizing world. In addition to fuel, oil provides ingredients for countless consumer products from food, to carpets, to clothing, to everything plastic. Consequently, a shortage of oil ripples through economies worldwide. This is why reaching "peak oil" (the point at which more oil is consumed than is found) is a global turning point. In *$20 Per Gallon,* Steiner (2009) attempts to document the social changes tied to our reaching peak oil and the resulting inevitable rising cost of petroleum. He predicts life at $6 a gallon: Hybrids replace SUVs, mass transit begins to supplant automobiles, and more walking and biking make people thinner. At $8 a gallon, flying is a luxury, families live closer together, students attend colleges nearer home, and trips to ski resorts, Las Vegas, and Disney World diminish drastically. $12 per gallon gasoline shifts populations from the suburbs to cities, makes apartments and condos competitive with McMansions, causes subways to burgeon, and allows local residential stores to successfully challenge malls. $20 per gallon will make the planet greener as we take a sharp turn from oil to hydro, solar, wind, geothermal, and nuclear power.

Revolution and War

From the Greek historian Polybius to Karl Marx, many early thinkers viewed conflict as the central form of human interaction. Marx and more contemporary conflict theorists, who see social conflict as the prime impetus for social change, are covered in the next major section. For now, let's focus on revolution and war as sources of social change that involve conflict (see Think Globally 18.1).

Q What is a revolution? A **revolution** occurs when a new political elite topples an entrenched governing regime, with the goal of changing its society's social structures. Leaders of a revolution aspire to make subsequent significant transformations. Marx, for example, expected workers' revolutions to eliminate class-based inequality and therefore to profoundly affect the social and economic structures of the societies in which they occurred.

Q Are revolutions normally followed by radical changes? As suggested in "Using the Sociological Imagination" at the beginning of this chapter, revolutions are normally not followed by radical social change. In Crane Brinton's (1990) view, the changes introduced by revolutionary leaders are followed eventually by restoration of a social order similar to that existing in prerevolutionary days. In other words, even successful revolutions fail to tear down the old order and bring in an entirely new one. Radical changes are rarely permanent; after victory celebrations are over, a society operates with a great deal of continuity with the past—a compromise between the new and the old.

Q What sorts of changes do follow revolutions? There is a middle ground between Marx's position that revolutions produce major changes and Brinton's position that revolutions have little lasting effect. Tilly (1978, 1997) argues that revolutions *do* have lasting effects if there is a genuine transfer of power. Most revolutions,

Tilly writes, *do not* have lasting effects because revolutionaries seize control of a government too weak to effect change. Eighteenth-century French revolutionaries, in contrast, took control of a powerful, centralized state, allowing them to seize and redistribute the property of aristocrats and churches. Despite a backlash, the French Revolution had lasting effects.

In the 1940s, a cornerstone of the communist revolution in China was sexual equality; liberation from sexism was a revolutionary plank. The situation for Chinese women has improved, but complete sexual equality is still a far-distant dream ("Closing the Gap" 1995). Revolutions, then, can be a powerful mechanism for social change, whether or not they create the total change promised by those who lead them and expected by those who participate in them.

Q What is the relationship between war and social change? War—armed conflict that occurs within a society or among nations—and change are closely intertwined (Nisbet 1989). Change is created through diffusion as war breaks down insulating barriers among societies. The crossbreeding and intermingling of people and cultures during and following a war leave participating societies different than they were before the conflict. Wars also promote invention and discovery. During World War I (1914–1918), the U.S. government, due to the pressure of war, promoted and financed the development of such technologies as the airplane, automobile,

Wars often bring social change because culturally dissimilar societies, such as the United States and Iraq, come into increased contact.

nylon, radio, and computer—each of which contributed to the social and cultural revolution that followed the war. It is too early to know the changes the wars in Iraq and Afghanistan will bring.

Ideas

Indeed, ideas can lead to social change. Max Weber, for example, believed that the ideas inherent in Calvinism produced behavior conducive to the development of industrial capitalism. Ideas about the family affect a society's birthrate (see Sociology Eyes America 18.1).

Alfred North Whitehead wrote, "A general idea is always a danger to the existing order" (Whitehead 1933:22). We have seen the validity of this observation in the earlier discussion on revolution. In the next section, we will see that two major theories of social movements also emphasize the crucial influence of ideas.

Q **What are some examples of ideas retarding social change?** During the Middle Ages, Christian religious ideas forestalled change (Gay 1977). In fact, the Catholic Church based its strength on total resistance to change (Manchester 1993). Economic development slowed in part because the Church considered usury (charging interest on loans) a sin. Another example is the defense of slavery in the United States on the basis of fallacious ideas that depicted African Americans

as inferior. Similar unreasoned ideas have been used to deny women equal opportunity in many societies, including the United States.

Q **How are these sources of change interrelated?** Several, or all, of these factors can be operating in combination. Consider abortion. Abortions are possible because of medical inventions that have been widely diffused. Underlying the ability to perform abortions is medical technology. This technology affects the population by lowering the birth rate, which in turn affects family size and a number of other social conditions (child-free marriages, dual-employed couples, sexual freedom). A lowered birth rate also reduces demand on limited natural resources. Conflict between pro-life and pro-choice forces in the United States has existed ever since the Supreme Court legalized abortion in 1973 in the *Roe v. Wade* decision. This conflict, of course, arises from disparate ideas regarding the moment at which a fetus constitutes a human being.

Theoretical Perspectives **R1**

It is through theory that we go beyond description of social change toward explanation. Before our theoretical discussion of functionalism, conflict theory, and symbolic interactionism, let's look, briefly, at some

---

SOCIOLOGY EYES AMERICA **18.1**

Children in Single-Parent Families

The increasing prevalence of children in single-parent families is due to several changes in family forms in the United States. More single-parent families are inevitable in a culture where divorce, single life, and unstable cohabitation arrangements are becoming more common. Nationally, the percent of children in single-parent families stood at 32 percent in 2008. Almost 2 million more children lived in single-parent homes in 2008 than in 2000. This map shows the percentage of children in single-parent families, by state.

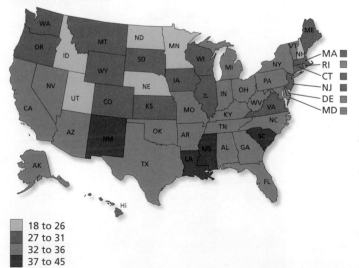

18 to 26
27 to 31
32 to 36
37 to 45

Interpret the Map

1. Contrast and compare the functionalists and conflict perspectives explaining the existence of so many American children in single-parent families.

2. Regarding the percentage of children living in single-parent families, how does your state compare with other states and with the national average?

Source: *2010 Kids Count Data Book*, p. 37. Copyright © 2010 The Annie E. Casey Foundation. Used by permission.

THINK GLOBALLY 18.1

Political Violence

This map identifies the worldwide distribution of political violence since 2000. Also indicated are the length and magnitude of conflict in an area.

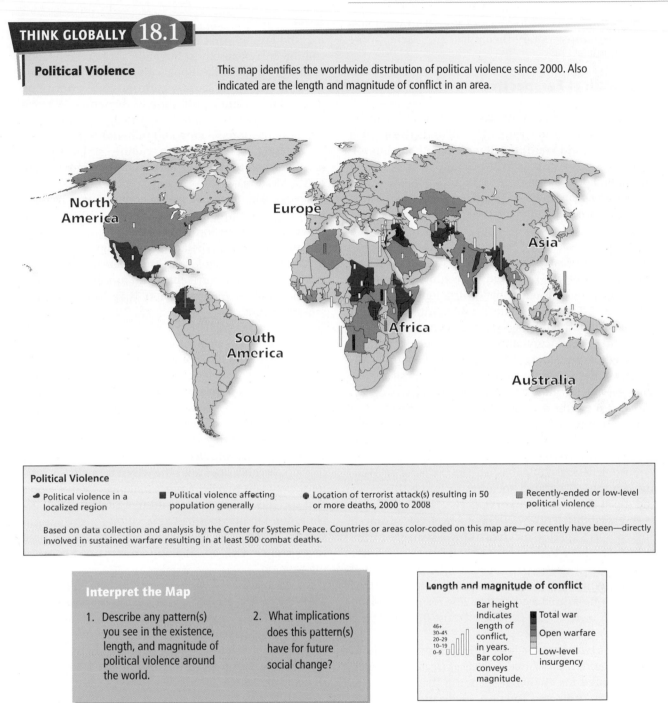

Political Violence

- ➡ Political violence in a localized region
- ◼ Political violence affecting population generally
- ● Location of terrorist attack(s) resulting in 50 or more deaths, 2000 to 2008
- ◼ Recently-ended or low-level political violence

Based on data collection and analysis by the Center for Systemic Peace. Countries or areas color-coded on this map are—or recently have been—directly involved in sustained warfare resulting in at least 500 combat deaths.

Interpret the Map

1. Describe any pattern(s) you see in the existence, length, and magnitude of political violence around the world.

2. What implications does this pattern(s) have for future social change?

Length and magnitude of conflict

Bar height indicates length of conflict, in years. Bar color conveys magnitude.

46+
30–45
20–29
10–19
0–9

- ◼ Total war
- ◼ Open warfare
- ◻ Low-level insurgency

Source: From John L. Allen and Christopher J. Sutton, *Student Atlas of the World,* 3rd ed. (Washington, D.C.: National Geographic Society, 2009), pp. 52–53. Copyright © 2009 National Geographic Society. Reprinted by permission.

CHECK YOURSELF 18.2 R2

Sources of Social Change

1. The theory of social change that assumes technology to be the primary cause of the nature of social structure is called _____.
2. The baby boom in the United States is a good example of the effects of _____ on an entire society.
3. _____ is a type of social movement that involves the toppling of a political regime through violent means.
4. Contrary to conventional wisdom, war retards social change. T or F?
5. Was it Karl Marx or Max Weber who emphasized the role of ideas in creating social change? _____

Answers: 1. technological determinism; 2. population; 3. Revolution; 4. F; 5. Weber

early theories specific to social change. This will make the three contemporary theoretical approaches more meaningful.

The Cyclical Perspective

Scholars were baffled. Why would the most developed nations in the world spend $337 billion between 1914 and 1918 (World War I) to kill more than 8 million soldiers? This was very poor evidence indeed for a belief in the natural progression of civilization. Scholars began to ask whether change was necessarily progress. Was Western civilization on the road to improvement or deterioration?

Q How did advocates of the cyclical perspective describe the effects of social change? The dramatic upheaval during the early part of the twentieth century led scholars to consider the possibility that civilizations rise and fall rather than develop in a straight line. British historian Edward Gibbon published six large volumes, between 1776 and 1788, documenting the rise and fall of Rome. Although many scholars disagreed with Gibbon's conclusions, they did not miss the point that social change may very well follow a pattern of growth and decay. Three of the most prominent advocates of the cyclical perspective were historians Oswald Spengler (1880–1936), Arnold Toynbee (1889–1975), and sociologist Pitirum Sorokin (1889–1968).

Spengler (1926–28) published *The Decline of the West*, in which he compared societies to living things, as did social Darwinist Herbert Spencer (1820–1903), but with a vital difference. Whereas Spencer saw advanced societies as superior survivors of the struggle of the fittest, Spengler believed that civilizations are born, ripen, decay, and perish. Specifically, he predicted that a civilization from Asia would replace Western civilization—which had traded zest for materialism. Spengler's work is now considered more literature than scientific explanation.

Almost twenty years later, British historian Arnold Toynbee (1946) published *A Study of History*, in which he presented his challenge-response theory of social change. According to Toynbee, civilizations rise only when a proper challenge in the environment is presented to a people who can respond successfully to it. If there is no challenge from the environment or if the society fails to meet a challenge, that society will either fail to rise in the first place or will decline.

Like Spengler and Toynbee, Sorokin did not see in history any linear pattern of change. To him, sociocultural history moves through three types of culture. *Ideational* cultures believe that truth and value come from God. Emphasis is on the spiritual and the next world. In *sensate* cultures, truth comes through empirical observation by the senses. It is experience in the current

world—gained through touching, smelling, hearing, seeing, and tasting—that reveals truth and reality. Sensate cultures are not absolutist but allow for reinterpretation of reality. People in ideational cultures focus on spiritual needs; members of sensate cultures place priority on physical needs and gratification of the senses. Whereas ideational cultures tend to be spiritual, sensate cultures are more pleasure-seeking and materialistic. Sorokin's third cultural type, the *idealistic* culture, is a blend of the ideational and the sensate, with somewhat more accent on the ideational.

For Sorokin, then, history is a continuous movement from the predominance of one type of culture to another. According to Sorokin, sensate culture dominated in Christ's time. Christian medieval Europe typified the shift from the sensate to the ideational. Idealistic culture emerged in thirteenth- and fourteenth-century Europe. Modern Western society is again grounded in sensate culture.

Q Regarding the cyclical approach to social change, what kinds of questions are left unanswered? Because history tells us that societies do, in fact, rise and fall, cyclical perspectives are especially appealing. The proof is there. Cyclical perspectives have a major problem, however. They are not so much explanations for change as descriptions of change. Spengler does not indicate why societies mature and decay; he just tries to show that they do. Toynbee does not state why a formerly successful society fails to meet a new challenge; he just writes that societies failing to respond to a challenge will decline. Sorokin provides no explanation for the cyclical pattern he describes; he just attempts to substantiate its existence with an amazing amount of historical information.

Q Is the cyclical perspective even worth considering? Yes it is. First, it represents an early, historically important attempt to understand social change. Second, it helped legitimate the scientific study of social change. Third, it offers a backdrop for distinguishing between description and explanation.

The Evolutionary Perspective

Q What was the nature of early evolutionary theory? "Every day in every way, things get better and better." In simple terms, this idea of progress, of societies constantly moving toward improvement, was at the heart of the evolutionary perspective that dominated nineteenth-century social thought. In its nineteenth-century form, the evolutionary perspective held that societies must pass through a set series of stages, each of which results in a more complex and advanced stage of development.

The evolutionary perspective became popular during the nineteenth century in part because of the times. During the middle and late nineteenth century, Western Europeans prided themselves on their superiority over other peoples. Progress and territorial expansion were watchwords. During colonial expansion, contact with preliterate people only offered ethnocentric Europeans further proof that their societies were the most highly civilized ever to exist. "Primitives" simply represented early stages of social evolution.

Another important influence of the evolutionary perspective was the work of Charles Darwin (1809–1882), which provided an intellectual framework for interpreting the place of primitive and advanced societies in the world. Darwin's idea that all living things tend to improve and become more complex as they develop seemed to fit the fact that some societies were more advanced than others.

English sociologist Herbert Spencer transformed Darwin's biological ideas into Social Darwinism. Spencer drew a parallel between living organisms and societies and coined the expression "survival of the fittest" to explain why some peoples had become "civilized" whereas others remained "savages" and "barbarians." Social Darwinism was so widely accepted in the Western world that governments in Western Europe and America believed that they had the right to dominate, protect, and tutor less developed societies. Such was thought to be the destiny and burden of nature's hardiest people.

Social Darwinism and classical evolutionary perspectives survived into the first part of the twentieth century, but social scientists no longer believe that societies necessarily improve as they change or that developing societies are destined to follow the Western model. Nevertheless, more recent perspectives on social change have overcome some of the faults of the classical evolutionary perspective (Sanderson 1990; Chirot 1994).

Q **So how does modern evolutionary theory contribute to our view of social change?** The contemporary evolutionary perspective looks at the social and cultural diversity around the world and rejects the unilinear, or single-direction, assumption of earlier perspectives. Because we know that societies can develop in many ways—some even toward greater deterioration and unhappiness—evolution must be multilinear, or multidirectional. Deliberately missing from the current evolutionary perspective, then, are the ideas of definite and orderly stages of development and of change inevitably producing progress and greater happiness. There are many paths and directions to evolutionary change (Steward 1979).

The most recent sociocultural evolutionary theory comes from Patrick Nolan and Gerhard Lenski (2010), whose initial assumption is that social scientists must consider both change and stability if human societies are to be understood. Despite the dramatic changes that have taken place in the world over the past 10,000 years, they argue, most individual societies have successfully resisted change. This, of course, is a paradox; how can rapid social change occur when individual societies successfully resist change? To resolve this apparent paradox, Nolan and Lenski offer a proposition: A total system can change despite resistance to change in most of its parts, providing the parts that fail to change do not survive. This, they assert, is precisely the case in the "world system of societies." Of those societies that did not change or changed only a little, almost none are around today. Conversely, nearly all surviving societies are those that did alter their social structures. Thus, say Nolan and Lenski, in the world system of societies, a process of natural selection operates to favor innovative societies over those that resist change.

Modern sociocultural evolutionary theory, then, helps us understand how societal changes are made. It shows that as subsistence technologies improve, societies have the means for gradually progressing from a hunting and gathering to a postindustrial form. As we shall see, modern evolutionary theory is related to both functionalist and conflict theories.

The Functionalist Perspective

Because functionalism emphasizes social stability and continuity, it may seem contradictory to refer to a functionalist theory of social change. However, two functionalist theories of social change—proposed by William Ogburn and Talcott Parsons—are especially interesting. Both of these theories are based on the concept of *equilibrium* discussed in Chapter 1.

Q **What is the connection between functionalism and the concept of equilibrium?** The word *equilibrium* implies balance and consistency. Concerned with equilibrium, the tightrope walker on a narrow rope inches his way across a deep chasm, continually shifting his body and using his long balancing pole to counterbalance the effects of the wind as well as the effects of his own motions. When applied to social life, equilibrium connotes attempts to reestablish stability after some disturbance. According to functionalists, societies act as inherently stable wholes that react to changes by making adjustments and eventually assimilating change into a new state of equilibrium. A society in change, then, moves from stability to

Social equilibrium was seriously shaken in New Orleans after Hurricane Katrina.

temporary instability and back to stability. Sociologists refer to this as a "dynamic," or "moving," equilibrium. For example, in 1972, a broken dam led to the destruction of the community of Buffalo Creek, West Virginia. Along with the physical destruction of the community was death and the rending of the old fabric of life. Despite the ensuing chaos, residents of the community pulled their lives together again. Although things were not the same as before, a new equilibrium was built out of the physical, social, and human wreckage (K. T. Erikson 1976). The 1960s were a time when the norms of sexual behavior changed radically. But, after skyrocketing during the sixties, teenage pregnancy is now declining. Although Americans do not follow the norms of the 1950s, a retreat from extremes is occurring as new norms of sexual behavior are being established.

Functionalism is based on the concept of equilibrium. Kingsley Davis writes:

It is only in terms of equilibrium that most sociological concepts make sense. Either tacitly or explicitly, anyone who thinks about society tends to use the notion. The functional-structural approach to sociological analysis is basically an equilibrium theory. (Davis 1949:634)

Although not all sociologists would agree that most sociological concepts make sense only in relation to equilibrium, most would concur that functionalism involves the concept of equilibrium (see Table 18.2).

Before turning to two specific functionalist theories of social change, we should consider the similarity and difference between the evolutionary and functionalist approaches, because both of the functionalist theories of change we will examine draw on evolutionary theory. Both the evolutionary and functionalist perspectives view society as composed of many highly differentiated parts, all contributing to the maintenance of a smooth-running, stable society. However, whereas the traditional evolutionary

TABLE 18.2

FOCUS ON THEORETICAL PERSPECTIVES: Social Change

This table gives examples of how the functionalist, conflict, and symbolic interactionist perspectives view social change. Describe how a functionalist would look at an interest group and how a conflict theorist would view equilibrium.

Theoretical Perspective	Concept	Example
Functionalism	Equilibrium	• The nature of the presidency has continuity, despite scandals in the Nixon and Clinton administrations.
Conflict theory	Interest group	• Civil rights laws were enacted in the 1960s as a result of the struggle over racial equality.
Symbolic interactionism	Urbanism	• A smaller proportion of social interaction in a large city is based on shared meanings.

perspective emphasizes a constant forward direction spurred by change, the functionalist perspective places emphasis on society's ability to recover its balance if equilibrium is upset by change. Functionalists view the various parts of society as highly integrated so that if a change occurs in one part, other parts are affected. The chain reaction is supposed to eventually restore balance because change is absorbed and distributed among a society's elements until equilibrium is reestablished. The emphasis in the functionalist approach is always on a return to stability and order after some restructuring takes place.

Q **What is Ogburn's theory of social change?** If a new equilibrium is achieved, the parts of society, asserted William Ogburn (1964; originally published in 1922), do not all reach the new balance at the same time. Some parts lag in time behind others. Ogburn applied the term **cultural lag** to any situation in which disequilibrium is caused by one segment of a society failing to change at the same rate as an interrelated segment. More specifically, Ogburn believed that changes in the nonmaterial dimensions of culture (norms, values, beliefs) lag behind alterations in the material culture (technology, inventions). Significant social change occurs when the nonmaterial culture is forced to change because of a prior change in the material culture. Ogburn's best-known example is the lag between the technological ability to cut down entire forests and the subsequent emergence of the conservationist movement. Cultural lag still exists. More recently, we can point to the sexual norms, values, and beliefs now in the process of attempting to catch up with the widespread distribution of birth control technology that occurred years ago. The Roman Catholic Church, officially, continues to oppose birth control, while many members of the church are waging personal struggles over contraception. The continuing conflict (sometimes violent) between pro-choice and pro-life advocates over the issue of abortion is a prime illustration of cultural lag.

Q **How does Parsons approach social change?** The concept of equilibrium is at the heart of Talcott Parsons's theory of social change. In his early work, Parsons (1937, 1951) did not emphasize social change. He depicted societies as systems attempting to resist change in order to maintain their current state of equilibrium. It was only later that Parsons (1966, 1971, 1977) began to depict change as a contribution to a new equilibrium with novel characteristics.

Consistent with his roots in evolutionary theory, Parsons was interested in the processes by which societies become more complex. In the first process, *differentiation*, aspects of a society are broken into separate parts. In simple societies, the family was responsible for nearly all functions—economic, educational, medical, emotional, and recreational. As societies became more complex, these functions began to differentiate from the family. Factories supplied jobs, schools provided education, doctors and hospitals cared for medical needs, community offered emotional support, and nonfamilial sources supplied a variety of amusement.

Differentiation brought on the need for the second process—*integration*. All the newly evolving social units formed workable links for a new equilibrium different from the previous one. Ways developed for schools and families to mesh, for parents to accept their children's leaving for work in the factories, and for parents to cope with their offspring's independent lives outside their local communities. The process of integration not only leads to a new state of equilibrium but also, in conjunction with the process of differentiation, helps to produce a much more complex type of society.

Q **What are the contributions and criticisms of the functionalist perspective on social change?** A major contribution of the functionalist perspective is its attempt to explain both stability and change. Ogburn tries to show that a society's ways of thinking, feeling, and behaving are constantly attempting to catch up with prior technological change. Technology, for him, is an independent variable leading to further social change. Parsons identifies differentiation and integration as processes integral to the maintenance of a moving equilibrium. In addition, he emphasizes that change does not imply total change; continuity as well as change exists.

The concept of equilibrium, argue some critics, assumes internal societal resistance to change. Also, the equilibrium model of functionalism depicts change as external to societies: Societies are changing not because of their own internal dynamics, but as a result of outside forces. By failing to explore internal sources of change, it is argued, functionalists ignore many forces for change that influence a society. Finally, some fault functionalists for focusing on gradual change and failing to consider radical change (R. Collins 1975; Giddens 1979, 1987; Giddens 2007). The conflict perspective addresses these criticisms.

The Conflict Perspective

Whereas the functionalist perspective assumes society to be inherently stable, conflict theorists depict society as unstable. Whereas functionalism views society as an integrated whole whose various parts work

Katherine S. Newman— The Withering of the American Dream?

After the economic recovery from the Great Depression, each subsequent generation of Americans expected a standard of living higher than that of their parents. A boost to this expectation was given by the unprecedented economic expansion following World War II. Upwardly spiraling affluence was assumed to be America's destiny.

Instead, according to Katherine Newman (1993), social and economic change is placing the American dream in jeopardy. The downscaling of jobs and pay that occurred during the 1980s and 1990s has replaced earlier optimism with anger, doubt, and fear. The traditional middle-class way of life is threatened by declining work compensation and a staggering national debt.

Newman analyzes this new reality among middle-class Americans as she tries to understand the effects on family life, political attitudes, and personal identities as well as the "rage, disappointment, and . . . sense of drift in communities across the land" (Newman 1993:x).

Bypassing the "bloodless" statistics, Newman talked with the Americans whose lives lie behind the graphs and dire popular media accounts. She spent two years conducting personal interviews with 150 Americans living in "Pleasanton," a representative suburban community. The population of Pleasanton corresponds to the hallmark of suburbia: a mix of skilled blue-collar workers and white-collar professionals from a variety of ethnic and religious origins. Her respondents were schoolteachers, guidance counselors, and sixty families whose children were then grown.

The promise of America had taken an unexpected wrong turn, and the residents of Pleasanton were trying to make sense of it. Newman attempted to understand the residents' view of this downward mobility. She looked for hidden meanings of culture as much as the more apparent behavior and norms. The stresses associated with changing economic conditions, she believed, would bring cultural expectations, disappointments, and conflicts close enough to the surface for a trained social scientist to see. In fact, she saw intergenerational conflict, marital discord, and racial and ethnic division. The following statement reveals a baby boomer's shattered confidence in the American dream:

> I'll never have what my parents had. I can't even dream of that. I'm living a lifestyle that's way lower than it was when I was growing up and it's depressing. You know it's a rude awakening when you're out in the world on your own. . . . I took what was given to me and tried to use it the best way I could. Even if you are a hard worker and you never skipped a beat, you followed all the rules, did everything they told you you were supposed to do, it's still horrendous. They lied to me. You don't get where you were supposed to wind up. At the end of the road it isn't there. I worked all those years and then I didn't get to candy land. The prize wasn't there, damn it. (Newman 1993:3)

After a detailed and often personal exploration of what Newman calls the "withering American Dream," she turns to the larger social and political implications for society. She explores the transition from a society of upward mobility based on effort and merit to a society in which social classes of birth increasingly dictate future social and economic positions.

According to Newman, the soul of America is at stake. She raises these questions: Will Americans turn to exclusive self-interest, or will they care for others as well as themselves? Will suburbanites turn a blind eye to the rapidly deteriorating inner cities? Will the generational, racial, and ethnic groups turn inward, or will they attempt to bridge the divides that threaten to separate them further?

A partial answer to these questions is reflected in public opinion about federal, state, and local tax revenues. If the residents of Pleasanton are any guide, Americans do not wish to invest in the common good. Public schools, colleges, universities, and inner cities, for example, are receiving a rapidly declining share of public economic support. In conclusion, Newman states:

> This does not augur well for the soul of the country in the twenty-first century. Every great nation draws its strength from a social contract, an unspoken agreement to provide for one another, to reach across the narrow self-interests of generations, ethnic groups, races, classes, and genders toward some vision of the common good. Taxes and budgets—the mundane preoccupations of city hall—express this commitment, or lack of it, in the bluntest fashion. Through these mechanistic devices, we are forced to confront some of the most searching philosophical questions that face any country: What do we owe one another as members of a society? Can we sustain a collective sense of purpose in the face of the declining fortunes that are tearing us apart, leaving those who are able to scramble for advantage and those who are not to suffer out of sight? (Newman 1993:221)

Evaluate the Research

1. Think about your experiences at home and in other social institutions (schools, churches). State the conception of the American dream these experiences provided. Critically analyze the ways in which society shaped your conception.
2. Newman's research was done in the early 1990s. Do you believe that she is right about the fate of the American dream? Explain.
3. If the American dream is withering, many social changes are in store. Describe the major changes you foresee.
4. Suppose Katherine Newman had decided to place her study in the context of sociological theory. Write a conclusion to her book from the theoretical perspective—functionalism, conflict theory, or symbolic interactionism—that you think is most appropriate.

harmoniously to achieve balance, the conflict perspective emphasizes the separate parts of society and the conflict that occurs among them. According to the conflict perspective, social change is the result of struggles between groups for scarce resources. Social change is created as these conflicts are resolved.

Q **What are the origins of the conflict perspective?** Many of the basic assumptions of the conflict perspective emerge from the writings of Karl Marx, who wrote that "without conflict, no progress: this is the law which civilization has followed to the present day" (Marx; in Feuer 1959:7). Ralf Dahrendorf, a modern advocate of the conflict perspective, summarizes Marx's view of society in this succinct passage:

> *For Marx, society is not primarily a smoothly functioning order of the form of a social organism, a social system, or a static social fabric. Its dominant characteristic is, rather, the continuous change of not only its elements, but its very structural form. This change in turn bears witness to the presence of conflicts as an essential feature of every society. Conflicts are not random; they are a systematic product of the structure of society itself. According to this image, there is no order except in the regularity of change.* (Dahrendorf 1959:28)

More specifically, according to Marx, the struggle for scarce economic resources, particularly property, is the primary stimulus for change. By way of review, Marx claims that change in capitalist society is authored by class struggle, and as a capitalist society develops, it begins to divide into two classes: those who possess property and own the means for production (the bourgeoisie) and the exploited workers who sell their labor merely to survive (the proletariat). These two classes polarize as the rich get richer and the poor get poorer. At some point, a revolution permits the oppressed proletariat to seize power. With the proletarian revolution comes the development of a classless society. The absence of classes eliminates the source of conflict.

Q **What are the contributions and criticisms of Marx's approach to social change?** Defenders of Marx contend that contrary to the charge, Marx avoided economic determinism. Although Marx contended that the economic base of any society is the ultimate determinant of the society's nature and course, he also allowed for noneconomic influences on this economic base. They also credit Marx with effectively showing that how people think, feel, and behave reflects the basic underlying economic foundation of their society (see "Consider This Research"). In addition, Marx refined the view that social conflict is built into all stratification structures and that the distribution of power is rooted in the economic system (Lauer 1991).

According to critics, Marx placed too much emphasis on economic factors as the determinants of social change while downplaying relevant social and cultural forces. Others criticized Marx for failing to see that conflict can integrate societies as well as tear them apart and for not recognizing the prevalence of cooperation over conflict within societies. They also challenged Marx's views on revolution. Contrary to Marx's prediction, the critics assert, most revolutions of this century have come from the middle class rather than the working class. Also, the critics continue, communist revolutions did not occur in highly industrialized Western societies such as the United States, Great Britain, or Germany but in the agrarian societies of China, Russia, and Cuba. Finally, non-Marxists note the lack of a polarization of capitalist societies into ruling classes and working classes. They point to the emergence of a large middle class—composed of neither workers nor owners—in modern capitalist societies (Vago 2003).

Q **Were there changes in the reemergence of the conflict perspective?** Although the conflict perspective had little influence in sociology during the first half of the twentieth century, it has reemerged. This revitalization was the work of sociologists, like Ralf Dahrendorf, who follow some of Marx's ideas while rejecting others (Dahrendorf 1958a, 1958b, 1959). Although Dahrendorf attributes change to the struggle over resources, the resources at stake are more than economic. Dahrendorf credits the quest for power—conflict over who controls whom—as the cause of social change. Whereas Marx envisioned two opposing social classes, Dahrendorf sees conflict among groups at all levels of society. Rather than change emerging from a single grand conflict, it comes from a multitude of competing interest groups. By rejecting Marx's contention that it is class conflict alone that creates history, Dahrendorf recognizes conflict among all types of interest groups—political, economic, religious, racial, ethnic, gender based. Thus, society changes as power relationships among interest groups change.

Historical events seem to support Dahrendorf's interpretation. Class conflict has not occurred in any capitalist society; social classes are not polarized into major warring factions. Rather, capitalist societies incorporate countless competing groups. In America, for example, racial groups struggle over the issue of equal economic opportunity; and environmentalists and industrialists debate the proper balance between environmental protection and economic development.

Some sociologists conclude that no single perspective on social change is clearly superior in all respects. They assert that social and cultural change is too complex for any single theory, given our present state of knowledge. They believe that because each perspective has its strengths and weaknesses, the best way to explain social change is through a combination of theories called functionalist conflict theory (R. Collins 1994).

Reconciling the Functionalist and Conflict Perspectives

Q **What attempts have sociologists made to accommodate the differences in these two perspectives?** There has been no fully successful synthesis of the functionalist and conflict perspectives but some attempts are interesting. Although he does not reconcile all the differences between these two perspectives, Pierre van den Berghe (1978) points to some commonalities. First, both perspectives observe society as systems with interrelated parts. Second, both perspectives are capable of viewing conflict as a contributor to social integration and integration as a producer of conflict. Third, both theoretical perspectives assume an evolutionary view of social change. Finally, van den Berghe sees both perspectives as equilibrium models.

Like Marx, Lewis Coser (1998) sees the pressure for social change coming from conflict: Competing groups and classes rise and fall in the struggle for power and for protection of their interests. Unlike Marx, however, Coser does not believe that cataclysmic social change necessarily follows social conflict or that change produced by conflict must necessarily come about abruptly. In fact, Coser distinguishes between change *within* a system and change *of* a system. A society flexible enough to adjust to a new environment will experience change while maintaining its basic structure. Examples of change within a society would be the civil rights and women's movements in the United States. If a society is not flexible enough, a change of the system may occur as a result of conflict. The Chinese Communist Revolution illustrates change of a society.

According to Coser, the behavior of a society's elite strongly influences the outcome of conflict, affecting whether conflict will produce a readjustment within the society or a breakdown and formation of a new society. If the dominant groups are flexible enough to allow free expression of complaints and make appropriate adjustments, change within the society is more likely to occur. Should those with the power choose to protect their interests by resisting change and stifling grievances, they run the risk of intensifying conflict and producing a change of the society.

Radical change of a society may occur suddenly, but it does not necessarily have to, according to Coser. Although basic institutions, values, and social relationships did change immediately following the Chinese Communist Revolution, change following the American War of Independence was gradual. The United States is a fundamentally different society than it was before 1776, but this restructuring cannot be linked to any specific event. In other words, for Coser, the fundamental restructuring of a society can take place as a result of gradual, cumulative changes within the society.

Nolan and Lenski (2005) also attempt to combine the functionalist and conflict perspectives. In the first place, they give equal weight to stability and change. Second, they explicitly incorporate conflict into their theory. For example, Nolan and Lenski contend that when societies have come into conflict with one another for territorial and other vital resources, those that have been technologically more advanced have usually been dominant. They make ample provision for conflict between societies, pointing out the need for societies to defend themselves and their territories from invasion by outsiders. Nor do they ignore conflict within societies, highlighting, for example, the struggle in industrializing agrarian societies between the elite in control of their society's resources and the masses who supply the labor for subsistence-level returns.

Q **So regarding social change and the attempts at reconciliation of theories, do we abandon the functionalist and conflict perspectives?** Although these attempts at reconciliation may be interesting, they do not eliminate the need for separate functionalist and conflict perspectives. Continued work by functionalists will tell us more about the processes involved in the maintenance of a dynamic equilibrium—how societies maintain stability and order while undergoing change. Conflict theorists continue to provide insights into how change occurs as a result of the struggles between those with differential power and opposing interests.

Collective Behavior and Dispersed Collectives R1

Another area of sociological study—collective behavior—often focuses on short-term behavior. Some forms of collective behavior are thought to be inconsequential; other forms have far-reaching consequences.

Hong Kong from the air looks like a modern Western city. Would social life on the ground look similar or different from that of a modern Western city?

We will examine both (see Table 18.3 for a sketch of the various forms of collective behavior).

Collective behavior is the relatively spontaneous and unstructured social behavior of people who are responding to similar stimuli. It is *collective* because it usually occurs among a large number of people. The phrase "responding to similar stimuli" emphasizes collective behavior as a reaction by people to some person or event outside themselves, such as the attacks on the World Trade Center and Pentagon on September 11, 2001. Collective behavior involves social interaction in which loosely connected participants influence one another's behavior.

The study of collective behavior poses some problems. In the first place, sociologists are accustomed to studying structured behavior. Second, how will researchers investigate a social phenomenon that occurs spontaneously? Despite these obstacles, sociologists are conducting fascinating research and formulating serviceable theories of collective behavior. It turns out that there is more structure and rationality to collective behavior than appears on the surface.

Initiating our discussion are the more disorganized, unplanned, and short-term forms of collective behavior—rumors, mass hysteria, panics, fads, and

CHECK YOURSELF 18.3 R2

Theoretical Perspectives

1. According to the cyclical perspective on social change, societies rise and fall rather than move continuously toward improvement. T or F?
2. Cyclical theories explain the reason social change occurs. T or F?
3. Classical evolutionary theory assumed that change leads to improvement. T or F?
4. According to modern evolutionary theory, social change is _____. (unilinear/multilinear)
5. According to the _____ perspective, society is inherently stable, and any change that occurs is eventually assimilated so that a new state of equilibrium is achieved.
6. _____ refers to any situation in which disequilibrium is caused by one aspect of a society failing to change at the same rate as an interrelated aspect.
7. According to the _____ perspective, social and cultural change occurs as a result of the struggles among groups representing different segments of a society.

Answers: 1. T; 2. F; 3. T; 4. multilinear; 5. functionalist; 6. Cultural lag; 7. conflict

TABLE 18.3

Major Forms of Collective Behavior

You can test your understanding of these forms of collective behavior by suggesting an additional example for each one.

Forms of Collective Behavior	Definition	Example
Rumor	• A widely circulating piece of information that is not verified as being true or false	• Continuously repeated prediction that airplanes would crash on a massive scale on January 1, 2000
Urban legend	• A moralistic tale that the teller swears happened to someone he or she knows or to an acquaintance of a friend or family member	• Fierce alligators in New York City's sewer system
Fad	• An unusual behavior pattern that spreads rapidly and disappears quickly	• Swing dancing
Fashion	• A widely accepted behavior pattern that changes periodically	• Wearing Nike shoes
Crowd	• A temporary collection of people who share an immediate interest	• New Year's celebrants at Times Square in New York City
Mob	• An emotional crowd ready to use violence for a specific purpose	• Lynch mob
Riot	• An episode of largely random destruction and violence carried out by a crowd	• Destructive behavior following the acquittal of police officers who were filmed using extreme force against Rodney King
Social movement	• Movement whose goal is to promote or prevent social change	• Civil rights movement

fashions. Crowds are covered next. A discussion of social movements, the most highly structured, enduring, and rational form of collective behavior, closes the chapter.

In the more structured forms of collective behavior, such as crowds and social movements, people are in physical contact. Other forms of collective behavior occur among dispersed members of a mass society. These

Collective behavior is popularly thought of as unstructured and irrational. What does this photo of volunteers unloading supplies after the World Trade Center disaster say about this conception?

Bill Kostroun/AP Photos

dispersed collectivities engage in the less structured forms of collective behavior—rumors, mass hysteria, panics, fads, and fashions. Behavior among members of dispersed collectivities is not highly individualized. Members of dispersed collectivities are not physically connected, but they do uniformly respond to some common object of attention; they are aware of being a member of a collectivity:

> When people are scattered about, they can communicate with one another in small clusters of people; all of the members of a public need not hear or see what every other member is saying or doing. And they can communicate in a variety of ways—by telephone, letter, Fax machine, computer linkup, as well as through second-, or third-, or fourth-hand talk in a gossip or rumor network. (Goode 1992:255)

Rumors

In the *Aeneid*, Virgil wrote these lines:

> Rumor! What evil can surpass her speed? In movement she grows mighty, and achieves strength and dominion as she swifter flies.

Rumor, as Virgil's words underscore, has a negative connotation. Rumors may be benign, as in the case of continual Elvis Presley sightings, or they can do considerable damage. They are often communicated as the truth when in fact they may be false. At best, rumors are usually inaccurate and misleading. In any event, the likelihood of an individual spreading a rumor depends in part on the degree of anxiety a person feels, the extent of uncertainty about events that the person is experiencing, the credibility of the person passing the rumor, and the relevance of the rumor to that particular person (Rosnow 1988, 1991).

Q **Why is rumor considered an unstable form of collective behavior?** A **rumor** is a widely circulating story of questionable truth. Rumors usually focus on people or events that are of great interest to others. Segments of the mass media exploit the public's fascination with rumors: entertainment magazines devoted exclusively to rock idols and movie stars; tabloid newspapers loaded with titillating guesswork, half-truths, and innuendos; even mainstream news publications catering to accounts of the rich, famous, and offbeat. As these examples suggest, rumors and gossip are closely related.

Following Hurricane Katrina, the national media reported rumors of a cholera outbreak, a dead baby in a trashcan, rampant rape, children with slit throats, and scores of bodies stacked inside a freezer in the New Orleans Superdome. During the 2008 presidential campaign, Barack Obama fought the rumor that he was a part of a Muslim conspiracy against America, and that, if elected president, he would replace the Bible with the Quran at his inauguration. Obama, in fact, is not a Muslim (Bacon 2007). The rumor that President Obama is not an American citizen remains current among so-called "birthers," who claim he was born in Kenya. Similarly, also lingering is the rumor that his health-care reform law legalizes "death panels." None of these rumors proved true, but they were spread and believed, in part because they touched on people's insecurities, uncertainties, and anxieties (Rosnow 1991; Fine and Turner 2004). Debunking rumors is becoming even more difficult because many believe that if it's on the Internet, it must be true.

Q **How is an urban legend dissimilar from a rumor?** Akin to rumors are what Jan Harold Brunvand calls **urban legends** (Brunvand 2001, 2002). Although urban legends may incorporate current rumors, they tend to have a longer life and wider acceptance. They are moralistic tales passed along by people who swear the stories happened to someone they know, or to an acquaintance of a friend or family member (Heath, Bell, and Sternberg 2001). The tales often focus on current places, concerns, and fears such as AIDS and inner-city gangs. A typical story tells about a man who wakes up in a hotel room missing a kidney. Another describes alligators roaming the sewer systems of big cities. As cautionary tales, urban legends warn us against engaging in risky behaviors by pointing out what has supposedly happened to others who did what we might be tempted to try. Like rumors, urban legends permit us to play out some of our hidden fears and guilt feelings by being shocked and horrified at others' misfortune.

Mass Hysteria and Panics

Q **What breeds mass hysteria?** **Mass hysteria** is a collective anxiety created by the acceptance of one or more false beliefs. Orson Welles's famous "Men from Mars" radio broadcast in 1938, though based entirely on H. G. Wells's novel *The War of the Worlds*, caused nationwide hysteria. About 1 million listeners became frightened or disturbed and thousands of Americans hit the road to avoid the invading Martians. Telephone lines were jammed as people shared rumors, anxieties, fears, and escape plans (Houseman 1948; Cantril 1982; J. Barron 1988). A more recent example occurred in Georgia, one of the Soviet Union's former member states, where citizens panicked following a television report that their president had been assassinated and that Russian tanks were entering the country. Missing the disclaimer accompanying the telecast, people filled the streets, overloaded the phone system, and at the point of exhaustion, entered hospitals with anxiety and heart attacks ("The World at a Glance . . . 'Russian Invasion' Hoax" 2010).

Q What is the difference between mass hysteria and a panic? A **panic** occurs when people react to a real threat in fearful, anxious, and often self-damaging ways. Panics usually occur in response to such unexpected events as fires, invasions, and ship sinkings. For example, 117 people died in two nightclubs in Chicago and Rhode Island in 2003, when panic reactions to a fire caused a jamming of escape routes (D. Johnson 2003a).

Interestingly enough, people often do not continue to panic after the initial chaos triggered by natural disasters such as earthquakes and floods. Although panic may occur at the outset, major natural catastrophes usually involve highly structured behavior (K. T. Erikson 1976, 1995; Dynes and Tierney 1994; Quarantelli 2001). An example of both initial panic and subsequent structured behavior occurred during the terrorist attacks of September 11, 2001. Some occupants of the buildings panicked, jumping from windows, whereas firefighters exhibited highly structured behaviors during their rescue efforts (see "See Sociology in Your Life"). Agreeing that rational behavior usually accompanies a catastrophe, Lee Clark writes:

> When the World Trade Center started to burn, the standards of civility that people carried with them everyday did not suddenly dissipate. The rules of behavior in extreme situations are not much different from rules of ordinary life. . . . When danger arises, the rule—as in normal situations—is for people to help those next to them before they help themselves. (Clark 2002:24)

Panics and episodes of mass hysteria are based on repulsion. Other forms of collective behavior, such as fads, crazes, and fashions, are rooted in attraction.

Fads, Crazes, and Fashions

Q Do fads have staying power? No. **Fads** are unusual behavior patterns that spread rapidly, appeal to a particular segment of society, and then disappear after a short time. The widespread zeal of a fad rests largely on its novelty. The "streaking" fad (running naked across college grounds or through occupied classrooms) delighted students in the early 1970s (Aguirre, Quarantelli, and Mendoza 1988). More recent fads include skinny jeans and Silly Bandz. Fads are not limited to hobbies, clothing, and entertainment; they also

emerge regarding serious matters. Ron Insana (2002) documented past investment fads, including the bull market of the 1990s.

Q What is the distinction between a fad and a craze? A **craze** is a type of fad that can have serious consequences for its adopters. The fads previously mentioned are primarily recreational and harmless in nature. But consider the potential downside to fads such as losing weight through extreme diets, getting "high" from cold medication, and using the date rape drug "roofies."

Q Do fashions reflect a society's culture? Yes. **Fashions** are behavior patterns that evolve over time and receive wide approval, but change periodically (Crane 2001). As societies modernize, fashion becomes more salient and may change more rapidly. Seasonally, contemporary American society introduces "in" fashions for the clothing industry. Women get "on top" of the defined dress or pant length, and men question if pant cuffs are fashionable or passé. High school students wishing to be fashionable wear clothes with the hottest labels.

Although the most widely recognized examples of fashion are related to appearance (clothing, jewelry, hairstyles), fashions also come and go in such diverse arenas as automobile design, home decorating, architecture, and politics. Slang, another example, goes in and out of favor (J. Lofland 1993). What self-respecting teenager today would be caught calling something "neat"? *Cool, groovy, tubular, tough, fine, rad, bad, phat,* and *sick* were all slang terms of approval among young people at some point in time.

Q Why is fashion particularly prevalent in modern society? In the first place, modern societies are based on growing economies fueled by mass consumption. For employment and profit in a society, styles in clothing, automobiles, eyewear, and sporting equipment must change. Second, without traditions to supply the brakes, people in modern societies are eager to respond to the tempting new fashions that entrepreneurs and corporations are constantly creating. Finally, the relative affluence in modern societies provides enough disposable income for people to indulge in fashion novelty and change.

Crowds ⓡ₁

Distinguishing Characteristics of Crowds

The most dramatic form of collective behavior is the crowd, because it involves intense emotions. Look at the content of local and national television news. If this is any indication, people are alternately fascinated

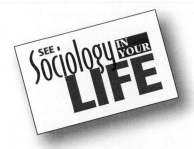

Terrorist Attacks and Disaster Myths

You fail a test, lose a boyfriend or girlfriend, have a minor auto accident, or suffer defeat by an archrival's basketball team. You might well describe each of these occasions as a "disaster." For sociologists, however, the term *disaster* is limited to events with the following characteristics.

- Extensive damage to property
- Great loss of human life
- Massive disruption to everyday living
- Unpredictability and suddenness of a short term event

Researchers typically divide disasters into "natural disasters" such as floods, earthquakes, and hurricanes and "technological accidents" such as airline crashes, nuclear plant meltdowns, and ship sinkings. But how can we classify the September 11, 2001, attacks on the World Trade Center in New York City and the Pentagon in Washington, D.C.? They were neither natural nor an accident. But, they had all the characteristics of a disaster. In fact, terrorism is introducing a new type of disaster, one that involves technology and is intentionally caused by humans.

The World Trade Center and Pentagon attacks obviously met the criteria of a disaster. Less obviously, they also exposed as false many popular beliefs about human behavior

in disasters. Let's consider four such myths within the context of this national tragedy.

1. **Victims of disasters panic.** Contrary to this myth, disaster victims do not generally panic. While some individuals in disasters may panic and while mass panics may follow disasters, the prevailing response is one of general composure and problem-solving behavior. Some inside the World Trade Center did respond with incapacitating emotion. One secretary in shock, for example, had to be carried out by a fellow worker. Some people jumped from the towers. But the disaster failed to set off a widespread panic. Many who heeded the first building-wide instructions died after calmly remaining in their offices. And many of the survivors remained as interested observers, forcing police to broadcast an urgent plea for them to hurry away for their own safety.

2. **Disaster victims respond as isolated individuals.** Typically, we picture disaster victims as individuals trying to save only themselves. Actually, according to research, people immediately engage in group efforts to help others. People in the World Trade Center with cell phones offered them to other victims desperate to call family or friends. Scores of New York police and more than 300 firefighters died while working together to rescue trapped victims.

3. **Disaster victims leave the scene as soon as possible.** Contrary to this myth, the majority of victims remain near the disaster site. Rather than fleeing, most victims remained to help others, to witness the fire and rescue efforts, or to think about returning to their

offices. Large numbers of volunteers and off-site emergency personnel actually rushed to the scene. Bellevue Hospital at one point had five doctors for each emergency ward patient. Four firefighters who were playing golf on Staten Island saw the first plane hit the north tower. Three of those four lost their lives in rescue efforts, and they were just a few of the hundreds of firefighters who died after entering the disaster site. To help rescuers searching for survivors under the rubble, ironworkers, many of whom had built the World Trade Center, labored together in twelve-hour volunteer shifts clearing away twisted steel.

4. **Crime is prevalent during disasters.** Rather than increasing, crime actually decreases after a disaster. While some isolated instances of criminal behavior occur, the crime rate in a disaster falls. After the World Trade Center disaster, some looting in surrounding buildings was reported, and a Picasso drawing valued at $320,000 was stolen from a Madison Avenue art gallery. More importantly, the overall crime rate in New York City declined 34 percent in the week following the disaster. According to the NYPD, arrests were down 64 percent compared to the same seven days the previous years.

Think About It

1. Think of some event you formerly considered a disaster. Explain why it was not a disaster from a sociological viewpoint.

2. Do you think that the behavior following the terrorist attack on the World Trade Center is best explained by functionalism, conflict theory, or symbolic interactionism? Explain your choice.

In modern societies, fashion becomes more important and changes more rapidly. Penelope Cruz arrives at the Oscars dressed in the latest creation of fashion designer Armani Privé.

Q **How dissimilar is a crowd from an aggregate of people?** A **crowd** is a temporary collection of people who share an immediate common interest. The temporary residents of a large campground, each occupied with his or her own activities, constitute an *aggregate*. But if some event, such as the landing of a hot-air balloon or the appearance of a bear, serves as a common stimulus to draw the campers together, the aggregate becomes a crowd. What will happen next is highly unpredictable. The specific subject of mutual interest—the common stimulus—is not important. What is significant is the collection of individuals into a situation that has the potential to stimulate an emotional reaction.

A crowd situation involves ambiguity and uncertainty; participants have no predefined ideas about the way they should behave toward one another or toward some target on which their attention is converging. Members of a crowd, however, are certain about one thing: They share the urgent feeling that something either is about to happen or should be made to happen (McPhail 1991; Marx and McAdam 1994).

Q **How do crowds differ from one another?** Although it is accurate to make generalizations about crowds, not all crowds are alike. Herbert Blumer (1969a) distinguishes four basic types of crowds. A *casual crowd* is the least organized, least emotional, and most temporary type of crowd. Although members of a casual crowd share some point of interest, it is minor and fades quickly. Members of a casual crowd may gather with others to observe the aftermath of an accident, to watch someone threatening to jump from a building, or to listen to a street-rap group.

A *conventional crowd* has a specific purpose and follows accepted guidelines for appropriate behavior. People watching a film, flying on a chartered flight to a university ballgame, or observing a tennis match are in conventional crowds. As in casual crowds, there is little interaction among members of conventional crowds.

and horrified by passions that are unleashed in crowds. We are engrossed by reports of crowds, mobs, and rioters, whether they are celebrating a joyous event or lamenting a sad one.

CHECK YOURSELF 18.4 **R2**

Collective Behavior and Dispersed Collectives

1. A _____ is a widely circulating story whose truth is questionable.
2. _____ exists when collective anxiety is created by acceptance of one or more false beliefs.
3. A _____ occurs when people react to a genuine threat in fearful, anxious, and often self-damaging ways.
4. Unusual patterns of behavior that spread rapidly, are embraced zealously, and disappear after a short time are called _____.
5. _____ are patterns of behavior that are widely approved but expected to change periodically.

Answers: 1. rumor; 2. Mass hysteria; 3. panic; 4. fads; 5. Fashions

The fact that the activity of the conventional crowd follows some established procedures distinguishes this type of crowd from a casual crowd.

Expressive crowds have no significant or long-term purpose beyond unleashing emotion. Their members are collectively caught up in a dominating, all-encompassing mood of the moment. Free expression of emotion—yelling, crying, laughing, jumping—is the defining characteristic of this type of crowd. Hysterical fans at a rock concert and the people gathered at Times Square on New Year's Eve are examples of expressive crowds. Following the assassination of presidential candidate Benazir Bhutto, hundreds of thousands of Pakistani mourners thronged the mausoleum of their countries' most famous political dynasty in an outpouring of emotion.

Finally, a crowd that takes some action toward a target is an *acting crowd*. This type of crowd concentrates intensely on some objective and engages in aggressive (sometimes violent) behavior to achieve it. The some 5 million demonstrators who congregated across the United States and the world in protest to the 2003 impending war on Iraq were acting crowds (Campo-Flores 2003; Tyler 2003). Sometimes acting crowds become *mobs* or *riots*. Think of mobs and riots as acting crowds gone wild.

Q What is unique about mobs? A **mob** is an emotionally stimulated, disorderly crowd that is ready to use destructiveness and violence to achieve a specific purpose. Through group understanding, a mob knows what it wants to do and considers all other things as distractions. In fact, individuals who are tempted to deviate from the mob's purpose are pressured to conform. If a mob is storming a seat of government, for example, it is inappropriate for participants to waste their time raping or stealing, although that may come later. Strong leadership maintains concentration on the main event.

Mobs have a long and violent history. The French Revolution is a classic example of mob action. With the cry "To the Bastille! To the Bastille!" a Parisian mob stormed this symbol of oppression on July 14, 1789. The overthrow of royalty and the desire for political freedom were the larger objectives of the French Revolution, but this mob's more specific and limited goal was to destroy the symbol of tyranny, oppression, and fear (Tilly 1992). Ultimately, yet another mob escorted King Louis XVI and Queen Marie Antoinette to Paris for execution.

The formation of mobs is not limited to revolutions. For instance, beginning in the late nineteenth century, some mobs in the American South acted as judges, juries, and executioners in the lynching of African Americans (as well as some whites). During a protest of the Kenyan presidential election in 2008, a mob burned a church containing hundreds of citizens seeking refuge. That same year, a group of protestors in Tibet went into a rampage, killing 19 people and injuring more than 600 (Drew 2008).

Q How do riots differ from mobs? Some acting crowds, although engaging in deliberate destructiveness and violence, do not display a mob's sense of common purpose. These episodes of crowd destructiveness and violence are **riots.** Riots involve a much wider range of activities than mob action. Whereas a mob surges to burn a particular building, to lynch an individual, or to throw bombs at a government official's car, riots may include actions of several different crowds, with rioters often directing their violence and destructiveness at targets simply because they are convenient. People who participate in riots typically lack power and engage in destructive behavior as a way to express their frustrations. A riot, usually triggered by a single event, is best understood within the context of long-standing tensions. The 1967 summer ghetto riots tore through many large American cities, occurring against a background of massive unemployment, uncaring slum landlords, poverty, discrimination, and charges of police brutality. The rioters in the twenty-odd cities involved did not, however, lash out at the underlying cause of the riots—the enduring gap between black and white America (*Report of the National Advisory Commission on Civil Disorders* 1968). Although the rioters were protesting against discrimination and deprivation, and although white-owned businesses were damaged more frequently than those owned by African Americans, the fact remains that African Americans did more damage to themselves (the overwhelming majority of the dead were African American) and their neighborhoods than they did to the establishment. As further evidence of random behavior in riots, many participants saw the riots as a way to loot stores or to have some destructive, violent fun.

Q Are these distinctions this clear cut? As you can tell, it can be difficult to distinguish among peaceful acting crowds, mobs, and riots. Throw revolutions into the mix and it really gets complicated. Truth is, these forms of collective behavior often bleed (another unintended pun) into each other. A peaceful acting crowd may ultimately involve mobs and riots and may even become transformed into a revolution. It is only after the event that the situation makes complete sense.

The massive protests that occurred in Egypt in 2011 is an excellent example. Protestors in the streets of Cairo began as a peaceful acting crowd with the goal of unseating their dictatorial president, Hosni Mubarak. A mob scene developed when thousands of pro-Mubarak forces, sometimes on horseback or camelback, attacked the peaceful demonstrators with clubs, swords, straight razors, and machetes. The prodemocracy protestors attempted to defend themselves, resulting in street battles with rocks, sticks, and firebombs. Several deaths and hundreds of injuries occurred on the first day of fighting (Englund, Witte, and Wilgoren 2011). After two days of fighting, the peaceful protest resumed, culminating in Mubarak's resignation under threat of his own military, which took power. While the news media immediately portrayed this as a revolution, it is too early to reach that conclusion. If Mubarak's regime is simply replaced by people sympathetic to totalitarianism, a revolution will not have occurred. Should a new governing elite be successful in creating widespread change, a revolution will have taken place. Whatever happens, the role of social media, such as Facebook and twitter, in facilitating the protest is worth exploring in itself. As usual, opinions vary.

Social Media and Crowds

Over the next decade, Howard Rheingold predicts, mobile communications (including cell phones) and pervasive computer technologies will "change the way people meet, mate, work, fight, buy, sell, govern, and create" (Rheingold 2003:xiii). These new technologies, for example, permit people to join together in collective action not possible before. In 2003, 400,000 antiwar activists protested without hitting the streets. They jammed White House and congressional switchboards with phone calls, faxes, and e-mails. This is said to be the first national virtual demonstration (Taylor 2003). Rheingold calls collectivities organized through these new technologies *smart mobs*.

Q Can social media actually create an acting crowd? Important questions attract conflicting opinions. The effect of social media on crowd behavior is no exception. The extremes run from those envisioning social media as an all-powerful galvanizing force. "Get on the Internet and make a revolution," they declare. Skeptics counter that Facebook and twitter may draw a crowd, but often not a very committed one.

The truth, as it almost always turns out to be, is more complicated. Most everyone agrees that the Internet can draw a crowd fast. But, as Andrew Woods (2011) argues, at least two additional conditions are required to create a successful acting crowd via social media. People are much more likely to act on a belief if they know that their peers feel the same way. Who was going to show up in Tahrir Square to protest Egypt's Mubarak by themselves or with a few close friends? Thousands of Egyptian citizens staged mass protests only after they learned, partly through social media, that their antigovernment sentiments were widely shared. Then, the speed of social media became a truly valuable asset. The Mubarak government understood this, at times cutting access to the Internet.

Under the right circumstances, then, social media can contribute greatly to the formation of an acting crowd. Creation of a *successful* acting crowd usually requires another condition—the existence of an organizational structure complete with leaders directing the action. The power of social media then becomes an important tool for sustaining an acting crowd.

Rheingold envisions both positive and negative social consequences of the new technologies. Negative repercussions include the potential loss of privacy in a

These Egyptian pro-democracy protestors marched in 2011 demanding political change and the ouster of President Mubarak. Mubarak is no longer in power, but the jury remains out on the degree of ensuing political change.

Barry Iverson/Alamy

surveillance state, the increased capacity for terrorists to operate undercover, and the creation of new opportunities for criminal behavior. On the positive side, social media-driven "smart mobs" can overthrow dictators and organize mass protests. At this early point, the uprising in Egypt is being hailed as the first social media revolution.

Theories of Crowd Behavior

The three most important theories of crowd behavior are contagion theory, emergent norm theory, and convergence theory.

Q **What is the focus for contagion theory?** **Contagion theory** emphasizes the irrationality of crowds that is created by participants stimulating one another to higher and higher levels of emotional intensity. As emotional intensity in the crowd increases, people temporarily lose their individuality to the "will" of the crowd. This makes it possible for a charismatic or manipulative leader to direct behavior, at least initially.

This theory has its roots in the classic work of Gustave Le Bon (1960; originally published in 1895), a French aristocrat who disdained crowds composed of the masses. People in crowds, Le Bon thought, were reduced to a nearly subhuman level:

> *By the mere fact that he forms part of an organized crowd,*
> *a man descends several rungs in the ladder of civilization.*
> *Isolated, he may be a cultivated individual; in a crowd,*
> *he is a barbarian—that is, a creature acting by instinct.*
> *He possesses the spontaneity, the violence, the ferocity, and*
> *also the enthusiasm and heroism of primitive beings.*
> (Le Bon 1960:32)

Herbert Blumer (1969a) offers another version of contagion theory, but he avoids Le Bon's elitist bias. Blumer's theory is more refined but still implies that crowds are irrational and out of control. For Blumer, the basic process in crowds is a "circular reaction"—people mutually stimulating one another. There are three stages to this process. In *milling*, the first stage, people move around in an aimless and random fashion, much like excited herds of cattle or sheep. Through milling, people become increasingly aware of and sensitive to one another.

The second stage, *collective excitement*, is a more intense form of milling. At this stage, crowd members become impulsive and highly responsive to the actions and suggestions of others. Individuals begin to lose their personal identities and take on the identity of the crowd.

The last stage, *social contagion*, is an extension of the other stages. Excitement begins to spread. Behavior in this stage lacks caution and judgment and is a nonrational transmission of mood, impulse, or behavior. For example, fans at soccer games in Europe have launched attacks on referees to such proportion that games have been interrupted and people killed or injured. Taking a less extreme case, people who observe an auction can find themselves buying white elephants because they have become immersed in the contagious excitement of bidding.

Blumer's theory is more refined than Le Bon's, but it still implies that people in crowds are irrational and out of control. Sociologists today, though, realize that much of crowd behavior, even within an acting crowd such as a mob, is actually very rational (McPhail 1991). Take, for example, a concert by The Who in 1979, at which eleven young people died and several others were injured. According to the news reports, this tragedy was caused by people "stampeding" over one another to secure better seating. This sounds like social contagion. Norris Johnson (1987), however, concludes otherwise after researching police records and newspaper articles. Rather than the unregulated competitive behavior popularly associated with everyone in a panic, Johnson documents the presence of considerable socially structured behavior in the form of participants cooperating to help one another avoid harm. *Emergent norm theory* and *convergence theory* further illustrate the structure and rationality of crowd behavior.

Q **Where is the emphasis for emergent norm theory?** **Emergent norm theory** stresses the similarity between daily social behavior and crowd behavior. In both situations, norms guide behavior (R. H. Turner 1964; Turner and Killian 1987). So, even within crowds, rules develop. These rules, of course, are *emergent* norms, because the crowd participants are not aware of the rules until they find themselves in a particular situation. These norms develop on the spot as crowd participants pick up cues for expected behavior. Emergent norm theory contends, in short, that crowd behavior is no different from noncrowd behavior, except that crowds do not have ready-made norms.

Also, whereas contagion theory proposes a collective mind that motivates crowd members to action, emergent norm theory views people in a crowd as present for a variety of reasons; they do not all behave in the same way (McPhail and Wohlstein 1983; Zucher and Snow 1990). Conformity may be active (some people in a riot may take home as many watches and rings as they can carry) or passive (others may simply not interfere with the looters, although they take nothing for themselves). In Nazi Germany, for instance, some people destroyed the stores of Jewish merchants while others watched silently, either in support or afraid to disagree for fear that others would ridicule or hurt them.

Q **What is convergence theory?** Both the contagion and emergent norm theories of crowd behavior assume that individuals are merely responding to those around them. It may be a more emotional response

Many Americans have visited the memorial site in Oklahoma City. It commemorates the 1995 terrorist bombing that destroyed a U. S. government complex, killing 168 people. How does this behavior relate to convergence theory for crowd behavior?

Jeff Mitchell/Landov Media

(as in contagion theory) or a more rational response (as in emergent norm theory). In other words, the independent variable in crowd behavior is the crowd itself. In contrast, in **convergence theory,** crowds are formed by people who deliberately congregate with others whom they know to be like-minded. According to convergence theory, the independent variable in crowd behavior is the desire of people with a common interest to come together.

Many Americans have visited the memorial site at Oklahoma City. It commemorates the 1995 terrorist bombing that destroyed a U.S. government complex, killing 168 people. How does this behavior relate to convergence theory for crowd behavior?

There have been many instances of crowds gathering in front of clinics to discourage abortions. This behavior, say convergence theorists, does not simply occur because people happened to be at the same place and are influenced by others. Such a crowd is motivated to form because of shared values, beliefs, and attitudes (Berk 1974).

Contemporary sociologists view crowd behavior as a more structured and rational phenomenon than is apparent on the surface. Sociologists also agree that a social movement—discussed in the next section—is an even more highly structured, rational, and enduring form of collective behavior (Goode 1992; Marx and McAdam 1994).

CHECK YOURSELF 18.5 R2

Crowds

1. A _____ is a temporary group of people who are reacting to the same event or individual.
2. An _____ crowd has no purpose or direction beyond the unleashing of emotions.
3. *Mob* and *riot* are simply two terms for the same type of crowd. T or F?
4. Much crowd behavior is structured and rational. T or F?
5. Some individuals at a lynching do not participate or give verbal support, but do not attempt to stop it. Which of the following theories of crowd behavior best explains this response?
   a. contagion theory
   b. crowd decision theory
   c. emergent norm theory
   d. casual crowd theory

Answers: 1. crowd; 2. expressive; 3. F; 4. T; 5. c

Social Movements R1

The Nature of Social Movements

The next time you observe a **social movement,** you will be aware of its four defining elements: a large number of people, a common goal to promote or prevent social change, some degree of leadership and organization, and activity sustained over a relatively long period of time. It is the form of collective behavior that has the most structure, lasts the longest, and is the most likely to create social change (Lofland 1996). Most social movements mount to stimulate change. This was as much the case for Nazism and the American Revolution as it is for the U.S. militia movement (Cozic 1997; Snow, Soule, and Kriesi 2007; McAdam and Snow 2009). The pro-life, environmental, and Tea Party movements are more contemporary examples.

Despite commonalities, various social movements have unique characteristics. It is difficult to compare the civil rights movement with the environmental movement or the environmental movement with the Tea Party movement. This predicament led sociologists to study differences among social movements (Crossley 2002; Goodwin and Jasper 2008).

Q What are the primary types of social movements? David Aberle (1991) has identified four basic types of social movements. A **revolutionary movement** attempts to change a society totally. An example is the revolutionary movement led by Mao Zedong in China; it entrenched a communist form of government. A **reformative movement** aims to effect only partial change in a society; it can either advocate change or resist change. Many reformative movements seek to promote change. The women's liberation movement illustrates this type of social movement (Baxandall and Gordon 2000, 2001). Other reformative social movements oppose change. Conservative political and fundamentalist religious organizations have mounted a concerted effort to oppose abortion (Chesler 2001). A **redemptive movement** focuses on changing individuals. The religious cult of David Koresh (the Branch Davidians) was a redemptive movement. Finally, an **alternative movement** seeks only limited changes in individuals. Population Connection (formerly known as Zero Population Growth) illustrates such a movement. It attempts to persuade people to limit the size of their families, but it does not advocate sweeping lifestyle changes, nor does it advocate legal penalties for large families.

Social movements are the most highly structured form of collective behavior. Three illuminating theories of social movements are relative deprivation theory, value-added theory, and resource mobilization theory.

Relative Deprivation Theory

It is the frustrated and discontent who want change and who are the most willing to fight for it. Discontent with present conditions, in short, is necessary for collective action. People must see existing conditions as undesirable, unfair, and unjust (Rose 1982). Thus, American colonists protested taxation without representation; Fidel Castro pointed to the vast gap between rich and poor Cubans; and Iranian revolutionaries in 1979 felt strongly that the Shah had gone too far with the processes of modernization, Westernization, and secularization. Discontent is more likely to lead to a social movement if it is linked with relative deprivation and unfulfilled rising expectations.

Q When does one feel relative deprivation? Relative deprivation occurs when people compare themselves with others and believe that they should have as much as those others have. Women's liberationists compare the situation of women to men, and gays in the United States underscore the penalties they suffer when they reveal their sexual preference. Government statistics indicate that African Americans receive less income than whites of comparable educational background. African Americans who are aware of this fact are likely to experience relative deprivation. Because a comparison is made between one's own situation and the situation of others, deprivation of this type is purely relative. There is no absolute standard for comparison—only the conviction among certain people that they, wrongfully, have less than some specific others have.

Q Why do some social movements follow progress in a society? Unfulfilled rising expectations occur when newly raised hopes for a better life either are not satisfied at all or are not satisfied as rapidly as people had expected. For example, newly industrializing countries are likely to experience some revolutionary discontent when people who have been poor all their lives are suddenly promised a better life. They revolt not just because of their poverty but because their expectations about their material well-being have changed more rapidly than their actual material condition. The phenomenon of unfulfilled rising expectations helps explain why many revolutionary situations arise only after people have experienced some economic and social improvement. Alexis de Tocqueville (1955; originally published in 1835) observed improvement in the French peasant's economic situation:

It is a singular fact that this steadily increasing prosperity, far from tranquilizing the population, everywhere promoted a spirit of unrest. The general public became more and more hostile to every ancient institution, more and more discontented; indeed, it was increasingly obvious that the nation was heading for a revolution.

> *Moreover, those parts of France in which the improvement in the standard of living was most pronounced were the chief centers of the revolutionary movement. Such records of the Ile-de-France region as have survived prove clearly that it was in the districts in the vicinity of Paris that the old order was soonest and most drastically superseded. In these parts the freedom and wealth of the peasant had long been better assured than in any other pays d'élection.* (Tocqueville 1955:175)

James Davies (1979) links unfulfilled rising expectations to revolutionary social movements. According to Davies's J-curve theory, a revolutionary movement is most probable when a decline in the fortunes of the masses follows a period of rising expectations accompanied by actual economic improvement (see Figure 18.2). According to this model, once expectations begin to rise, they continue to do so. As long as expected need satisfaction and actual need satisfaction are reasonably close, people will tolerate the gap between what they want and what they are getting. It is when actual need satisfaction falls off sharply (note the upside-down J formed by the curve in Figure 18.2) that the gap between what people want and what they have becomes intolerable. At this point, a revolutionary social movement is most likely to occur.

Q **What is the major shortcoming of relative deprivation theory?** This theory cannot explain why some social discontent can exist without a subsequent social movement. Although African Americans had long been discontented and suffered from relative deprivation, they did not mount a social movement until the 1950s. We must conclude, then, that although discontent and deprivation are necessary conditions of social movements, they are not sufficient ones. Discontent and deprivation must precede a movement, but they cannot alone produce one. The other two theories of social movements point to other factors.

Value-Added Theory

One of the strengths of Neil Smelser's (1971) **value-added theory** is its applicability to many forms of collective behavior. Although the theory applies to such types of collective behavior as panics and riots, we describe it here only within the context of social movements.

Q **What is value-added theory?** Smelser's contribution is based on an economic theory. In the economic value-added process, each step in the creation of a product contributes (adds value) to the final entity. Smelser gives an example involving automobile production:

> *An example of [the value-added process] is the conversion of iron ore into finished automobiles by a number of stages of processing. Relevant stages would be mining, smelting, tempering, shaping, and combining the steel with other parts,*

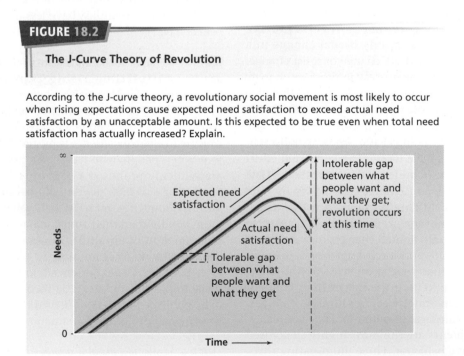

FIGURE 18.2

The J-Curve Theory of Revolution

According to the J-curve theory, a revolutionary social movement is most likely to occur when rising expectations cause expected need satisfaction to exceed actual need satisfaction by an unacceptable amount. Is this expected to be true even when total need satisfaction has actually increased? Explain.

Source: James Chowning Davies, "The J-Curve of Rising and Declining Satisfactions as a Cause of Revolution and Rebellion," in Hugh Davis Graham and Ted Robert Gurr (eds.), *Violence in America*, rev. ed. (Beverly Hills, CA: Sage, 1979), p. 416. Reprinted by permission of J. C. Davies and the publisher, Sage Publications, Inc. (Beverly Hills/London).

painting, delivering to retailer, and selling. Each stage "adds its value" to the final cost of the finished product. . . . Every stage in the value-added process, therefore, is a necessary condition for the appropriate and effective condition of value in the next stage. The sufficient condition for final production, moreover, is the combination of every necessary condition, according to a definite pattern. (Smelser 1971:13–14)

According to Smelser's theory, six conditions are necessary and sufficient for the development of a social movement. That is, Smelser specifies conditions that must exist if a social movement is to occur and that will lead to a social movement if they are present.

Q **What are Smelser's necessary conditions for the development of a social movement and how do these conditions apply to the Tea Party movement?** The Tea Party is not truly a political party. Unlike political parties, the Tea Party is without consensus on leaders, rules, or organizational structure. It is a political movement ignited more by what it opposes than by what it supports. In a phrase, Tea Party members want to "take back our country" (LePore 2010; The Rise of the Tea Party" 2010).

Structural conduciveness, the first of Smelser's conditions, refers to an environment that is social movement friendly. For the Tea Party movement, with its loosely affiliated often conflicting factions, technology provided Smelser's condition of conduciveness. Conservative talk radio, television, and the blogosphere delivered the initial message. You Tube and the Internet further communicated their viewpoint. Once aware of their common cause, Tea Party members used the political process to stage public protests. As, for example, they did in the summer of 2009 at local political forums on Obama's health-care bill, held by both Republicans and Democrats.

A second condition promoting the emergence of a social movement is the presence of *structural strains*—conflicts, ambiguities, and discrepancies within a society. Without some form of strain, there is no impetus for change. The major structural strains that produced the Tea Party movement centered on ideological differences about the role of government in daily life. Since the 1930s the federal government has increasingly become more active. We see this in such areas as the regulation of financial institutions, the auto industry, and the food industry. Social Security, Medicare, and health care for the general public are further examples of the expanding role of government. This expansion is precisely the target of the Tea Party movement, reflecting its desire to decrease the size of government.

The combination of structural conduciveness and structural strains increases the probability that a social movement will occur. When a third condition—*generalized beliefs*—is also present, a social movement is even more likely. Generalized beliefs include a general recognition not only that there is a problem, but that something should be done about it. The Tea Party movement, based on the assumption that government should be doing less, articulates a number of generalized convictions, which are more important to some of its factions than to other factions. All Tea Party members cite the federal government's "fiscal irresponsibility." Hence, the movement calls for lower taxes, balanced budgets, and a termination of government spending on projects like corporate bailouts, stimulus spending, and health care. Of interest to one specific faction of the Tea Party is the "meddling" of courts in social issues such as abortion and gay marriage. Another faction focuses on illegal immigration, while yet another faction is opposed to gun control. Whatever the faction, it is clear members want government "moved off of our backs" and "into our hands" (Lepore 2010; "The Rise of the Tea Party" 2010; Wolraich 2010).

Even when structural conduciveness, structural strains, and generalized beliefs exist, a social movement might not occur. One or more *precipitating factors* must occur to galvanize people into action. The precipitating factor for the Tea Party movement came in 2009 when a blogger, Keli Cavender, proposed a protest of the federal government's $781 billion economic stimulus package. A local protest drew about 100 people. That small gathering went viral on the conservative blogosphere, leading to similar protests in other cities. CNBC's Rick Santelli's followed shortly with a diatribe opposing the use of tax-payer money to bail out banks and rescue individuals unable to pay their mortgages. He ended with a call for the formation of a new Boston Tea Party ("The Rise of the Tea Party" 2010).

Once these first four conditions exist, the only remaining step to the emergence of a social movement is the *mobilization of participants for action*. Usually, it is at this point that leaders become very important. In the case of the Tea Party, which lacked agreed-upon leaders, it was the media that mobilized the movement. After Santelli's diatribe, some protestors began to call themselves Tea Partiers. Soon the word *tea* came to stand for Taxed Enough Already. At that point, Fox News began to strongly support the movement. On April 15, a date deliberately selected because it is tax filing deadline, Tea Party protesters across the country, took aim at Obama's health-care bill ("The Rise of the Tea Party" 2010).

The sixth determinant of a social movement is ineffective *social control*—efforts on the part of society (media, police, courts, community leaders, political officials) to prevent, minimize, or interrupt the momentum for a social movement. If society applies appropriate techniques of social control, it may prevent a social movement, even though the first five determinants are present. Sometimes, officials apply social controls after a panic, riot, or mob action has already started. At that point, control efforts may block the social movement, minimize its effects, or make matters worse. Given the nature of the Tea Party, attempting to apply social control was inappropriate and would have failed if tried. Political speech is free speech in the United States.

The anger, which fuels most populist movements, eventually dissipates. This may or may not happen to the Tea Party movement. Having elected five members to the U.S. Senate and forty members to the U.S. House of Representatives in 2010, the Tea Party now has a legitimate and continuous voice in national political debate. Given the dismal survival record of third political parties in the United States, the future of the Tea Party depends on whether it converts the Republican political establishment or whether the Republican mainstream co-opts and thereby weakens the movement.

Q **What are the strengths and weaknesses of value-added theory?** According to value-added theory, more than discontent and deprivation are necessary for a social movement to emerge. Beyond structural strains there must be structural conduciveness, generalized beliefs, precipitating factors, and the mobilization of participants for action. Critics reject the traditional view of social movements as irrational, spontaneous, and initially unstructured (Oberschall 1973; Tilly 1978; Opp 1989; Gamson 1990; Opp and

Roehl 1990). According to other critics, the value-added approach works best for crowd behavior, but even in that type of collective behavior, all six factors are not always present (Goode 1992). In addition, say critics, value-added theory fails to consider the importance of resources—funds, people, abilities—for the emergence and success of social movements (Olzak and West 1991).

Resource Mobilization Theory

Q **According to resource mobilization theory, what is a key to galvanizing people for collective action?** **Resource mobilization** is the process through which members of a social movement secure and use the resources needed to advance their cause. Resources encompass human skills such as leadership, organizational ability, and labor power as well as material goods such as money, property, and equipment (Cress and Snow 1996; McCarthy and Wolfson 1996; Freeman and Johnson 1999). The civil rights movement of the 1960s succeeded because of the commitment of African Americans and because people of other races, and college students in particular, contributed money, energy, and skills necessary to stage repeated protests. In contrast, the gay movement in the United States experienced difficulty partially because of a relative shortage of money, foot soldiers, and affluent supporters.

John Lofland (1979) writes of the 1970s "white-hot" mobilization efforts of the Unification Church ("Moonies"). Upon taking up residence in the United States

A human need to belong is a prime motivator for joining social movements such as represented by Reverend Sun Myung Moon's Unification Church. What other motivations might cause people to join a social movement?

Ahn Young-Joon/AP Photos

in 1971, the Reverend Sun Myung Moon was shocked by the scant resource mobilization work that had been done. He set out to change the situation, establishing a set of long- and short-term goals for the movement, including new-member and fund-raising quotas. He staged elaborate publicity campaigns and events, including speaking tours and rallies, established an organizational structure, and created a national training center. He sent trainees across the country in evangelistic teams, dividing the United States into ten regions, each headed by a regional director. Each regional director supervised several state directors who were in charge of local center directors. These efforts required about $15 million to be generated each year, some of it coming from Korean and Japanese branches of the movement. (Allegations were made that some of the money came from the South Koreans and American CIA.) Many local groups made money from their own businesses, such as housecleaning services, gas stations, and restaurants. Between 1971 and 1974, membership increased from 500 to 2,000. (For more detail on the current resources of the Unification Church, see Chapter 14.)

The case of the Unification Church makes a point central to resource mobilization theory: The collective action is organizationally based and led by rational people who calculate the likelihood of achieving their ends (A. D. Morris 1981, 1984). Resource mobilization advocates contend that although other theories of social movements depict organization as something that emerges as the movement develops, resource mobilization theory sees preexisting organizational structure (and associated resources) as central to launching a social movement.

Several scholars emphasize the role of "outsiders" in the creation of modern social movements (McCarthy and Zald 1977; Zald and McCarthy 1987; Burstein 1991). Outsiders may be volunteers who care about the plight of a category of people, or they may be professionals knowledgeable about the organization and management of social movements. For example, white students and adults from the North brought commitment and organizational skills to the civil rights movement in the 1960s.

Q **What do critics think of resource mobilization theory?** Although critics praise resource mobilization theory for shedding light on the importance of resources in mounting and sustaining social movements, they fault it for deemphasizing the necessary social discontent and strain needed for a social movement to emerge. Resources are of little use if people are not sufficiently dissatisfied with current conditions (Jenkins 1983; Klandermans 1984). Although recognizing the importance of organization and planning, some social movement theorists foresee a danger in dismissing the important role of spontaneity in the emergence and development of social movements. Social movement theorists, critics write, must not lose sight of the emotional factors that lead people to join a movement whose likelihood of success is small, and they must also consider the ways in which the unpredictable, spontaneous actions of the people involved affect the organization leaders (Killian 1984; Opp 1988; Rule 1989; A. Scott 1995).

The Future Direction of Social Movement Theory

The three theories of social movements just discussed are more complementary than they are mutually exclusive. Relative deprivation theory emphasizes discontent from a social-psychological, or micro, viewpoint. Value-added theory implies discontent (within the concept of structural strain) but focuses on the operation of several factors at the macro level of analysis. Value-added theory, also at the macro level, implies the need for resources through its mobilization factor, but resource mobilization theory is needed to spell out this contributing factor to the rise of social movements.

Social movement theory in the future will likely encompass both preexisting structure and spontaneity, both rationality and irrationality. It seems inevitable that those on both sides of the debate will consider viewpoints of resource mobilization theory and other social movement theories.

A distinction is being made between "old" and "new" social movements (Eyerman 1992; Haferkamp and Smelser 1992; Buechler 2000). Old social movements, such as the American civil rights movements and the labor movement, are based more on the interests of the poor and the working class. They are centered on the struggle for power and control over economic conditions within the context of industrial capitalism. New social movements, such as the women's movement, the ecology movement, the peace movement, the gay movement, and the animal rights movement, are not as embedded in economics (although women and gays seek economic equality) and in opposition to capitalism (although environmentalists seek to moderate capitalism). Rather than expressing conflicts of industrial society and industrialization, new social movements rest more on conflicts unique to postindustrial society. Cultural conflicts fuel the new social movements aiming at redefinitions of norms and values rather than at questions of economics and who gets what. New social movements are more global in focus, tend to center on quality-of-life issues, and pertain to the interests of the middle and upper-middle class (Melucci 1980; Kriesi 1989; A. Scott 1995).

CHECK YOURSELF 18.6 R2

Social Movements

1. A _____ is the form of collective behavior that has the most structure, lasts the longest, and is the most likely to create social change.

2. Which of the following is an example of a reformative social movement?
   a. the French Revolution
   b. Zero Population Growth
   c. the Jesus People
   d. Women's Christian Temperance Union

3. _____ is felt when people compare themselves with others and believe that they should have as much as those others have.

4. _____ occur when newly raised hopes for a better life either are not satisfied at all or are not satisfied as rapidly as people expect them to be.

5. Once widespread discontent exists within a society, a social movement is bound to occur. T or F?

6. According to the _____ theory, several conditions are necessary and sufficient for the emergence of a social movement.

7. _____ is the process through which members of a social movement secure and use resources needed to press for social change.

Answers: 1. social movement; 2. d; 3. Relative deprivation; 4. Unfulfilled rising expectations; 5. F; 6. value-added; 7. Resource mobilization

---

S INTEGRATED GOALS AND SUMMARY

R3 REVIEW GUIDE

1. **Illustrate three social processes contributing to social change.**
   - *Social change* refers to social structure alterations that have long-term and relatively important consequences. For most of the world, social change is accelerating at a dramatic rate. Although predicting the precise nature of social change within a society is hazardous, several sources of social change are pretty well understood. Discovery, invention, and diffusion are the major social processes through which social change occurs.

2. **Discuss, as sources of social change, the role of technology, population, the natural environment, conflict, and ideas.**
   - Important sources of social change are technology, population, the natural environment, conflict, and ideas. There are many interrelationships among these sources of social change.

3. **Explain the why and how of social change within the context of the functionalist and conflict perspectives.**
   - Sociologists go beyond identifying sources of social change to developing theoretical perspectives of social change. The evolutionary, functionalist, and conflict perspectives view social change in very different ways. The cyclical perspective, short on explanatory power, envisions societies as changing through the process of growth and decay. Contemporary evolutionary theory emphasizes multilinear change (i.e., various societies may evolve in many diverse directions). The functionalist perspective depicts societies as relatively stable. Following a major change, these integrated systems seek a new equilibrium. According to the conflict perspective, societies are unstable systems that are constantly undergoing change. Attempts to combine the insights of the functionalist and conflict perspectives, although interesting, do not eliminate the need to retain separate perspectives.

4. **Discuss the unique nature of collective behavior in sociology.**
   - Most areas of sociological study assume that social life is predictable, orderly, and recurrent. Collective behavior can be an important exception; much of this behavior is spontaneous, short term, and relatively unstructured. Some forms of collective behavior, though, are planned, structured, and enduring.

5. **Describe social activities of dispersed collectivities.**
   - On the more unstructured end of the collective behavior continuum are dispersed collectivities—rumors,

fads, crazes, panics, mass hysteria, and fashions. Even these forms of collective behavior are structured to some degree.

- Rumors have a negative reputation, usually deserved, because they are composed of inaccurate, distorted, or false information. Rumors can be playful and harmless, or they can be damaging and hurtful. Mass hysteria occurs when people accept false beliefs, then become anxious. Panics take place when there is a collective reaction to a real threat. Unusual patterns of behavior that are adopted quickly, accepted enthusiastically, and disappear soon are called fads. Fashions are patterns of behavior with wide approval but with expectations to change periodically. Fads and fashions are more central to modern than premodern societies.

6. **Describe the nature of a crowd, and identify the basic types of crowds.**
   - Crowd behavior is fascinating to most people because it usually involves intense feelings and sometimes outrageous behavior. There are casual, conventional, expressive, and acting crowds.

7. **Contrast contagion theory, emergent norm theory, and convergence theory.**
   - Three quite different theories attempt to explain crowd behavior. Contagion theory stresses the irrationality of crowds and the buildup of intense emotion—a result

of social interaction within a large collection of people. Emergent norm theory depicts crowd behavior as being more rational. According to emergent norm theory, norms guide crowd behavior that arise spontaneously. In convergence theory, people with a common interest form crowds.

8. **Define the concept of social movement, and identify the primary types of social movements.**
   - Social movements are closer to conventional social behavior than is crowd behavior because social movements are more permanent and more organized. Even so, they are not as permanent and structured as most aspects of social life.
   - There are three major explanations of social movements. According to relative deprivation theory, discontent and unfulfilled rising expectations create a breeding ground for social movements. Value-added theory outlines six necessary and sufficient conditions for the development of a social movement: structural conduciveness, structural strains, generalized beliefs, precipitating factors, mobilization of participants for action, and social control. According to the resource mobilization theory, resources are a crucial ingredient in the mounting of a social movement. Resources include human skills and economic assets, both of which often come from outside the movement.

CONCEPT REVIEW

Match the following concepts with the definitions listed below them.

a.	diffusion	____ e.	collective behavior	____ i.	panic
____ b.	technology	____ f.	mass hysteria	____ j.	rumor
____ c.	invention	____ g.	emergent norm theory	____ k.	crowd
____ d.	social change	____ h.	relative deprivation		

1. the social process that occurs when members of one group borrow social and cultural elements from another group
2. the creation of a new element by combining two or more already existing elements and creating new rules for their use as a unique combination
3. alterations in social structures that have long-term and relatively important consequences
4. the part of culture, including ideas and hardware, that is used to reach practical goals
5. a condition that exists when people compare themselves with others and believe that they should have as much as those others have
6. the relatively spontaneous and unstructured social behavior of people who are responding to similar stimuli

7. the form of collective behavior in which general social anxiety is created by acceptance of one or more false beliefs
8. a widely circulating story whose truth is questionable
9. the theory of crowd behavior that stresses the similarity between typical, everyday social behavior and crowd behavior
10. collective behavior that occurs when people react to a genuine threat in fearful, anxious, and often self-damaging ways
11. a temporary collection of people who share a common point of interest

CHECK YOURSELF REVIEW

1. According to the cyclical perspective on social change, societies rise and fall rather than move continuously toward improvement. T or F?
2. Classical evolutionary theory assumed that change leads to improvement. T or F?
3. *Mob* and *riot* are simply two terms for the same type of crowd. T or F?
4. Much crowd behavior is structured and rational. T or F?
5. The theory of social change that assumes technology to be the primary cause of the nature of social structure is called _____.
6. Was it Karl Marx or Max Weber who most emphasized the role of ideas in creating social change? _____.
7. According to the _____ perspective, social and cultural change occurs as a result of the struggles among groups representing different segments of a society.
8. Unusual patterns of behavior that spread rapidly, are embraced zealously, and disappear after a short time are called _____.

9. An _____ crowd has no purpose or direction beyond the unleashing of emotions.
10. A _____ is the form of collective behavior that has the most structure, lasts the longest, and is the most likely to create social change.
11. Which of the following is *not* one of the major consequences of modernization discussed in the text?
   a. the social and cultural convergence of modernizing countries
   b. increased urbanization
   c. greater equality
   d. more political democracy
   e. widespread development of the nuclear family
12. Some individuals at a lynching do not participate or give verbal support, but do not attempt to stop it. Which of the following theories of crowd behavior best explains this response?
   a. contagion theory
   b. crowd decision theory
   c. emergent norm theory
   d. casual crowd theory

GRAPHIC REVIEW

Figure 18.1 shows the varying speeds with which Americans have adopted certain important technologies. Answer these questions to make sure you understand the information presented.

1. How would you explain the difference in adoption speed for the telephone and the Internet?

_____
_____
_____

2. Discuss some social implications of the increasing use of the Internet.

_____
_____
_____

CRITICAL-THINKING QUESTIONS

1. What do you think is the proper perspective on technological determinism? In the process of answering this question, be sure to incorporate the perspective of Karl Marx.

_____
_____

2. Identify a major social change that has occurred in your lifetime. What do you think are the major sources of this change? Be careful to relate each source of change to the nature of the change itself.

_____
_____

3. Is evolutionary theory compatible or incompatible with functionalism and conflict theory? Make clear the nature of all three perspectives on social change.

_____
_____

4. Are you convinced that modernizing societies are becoming socially and culturally similar? Why or why not?

_____
_____

5. Select a rumor, fad, craze, or fashion to demonstrate your understanding of a dispersed collectivity.

   _____

   _____

6. Sociologists take collective behavior to be a legitimate area of study on the grounds that it is more structured than it appears at first glance. Develop three examples of collective behavior of which you have some knowledge to support this claim by sociologists.

   _____

   _____

7. You have participated in a crowd at some time. Think of an instance and identify it as one of the four types of crowds

described in the text. Using your personal experience, provide examples of behavior within the crowd (yours or someone else's) that illustrate why you think it was a particular type of crowd.

   _____

   _____

8. Which theory of social movements do you think best explains the women's movement? Link the theory to the nature of the women's movement.

   _____

   _____

ANSWER KEY

Concept Review

a. 1
b. 4
c. 2
d. 3
e. 6
f. 7
g. 9
h. 5
i. 10
j. 8
k. 11

Check Yourself Review

1. T
2. T
3. F
4. T
5. technological determinism
6. Max Weber
7. conflict
8. fads
9. expressive
10. social movement
11. a
12. c

Glossary

Absolute poverty The absence of enough money to secure life's necessities.

Achieved status A status within a social structure occupied because of an individual's efforts.

Age cohorts Persons born during the same time period in a particular population.

Age stratification The unequal distribution of scarce desirables based on chronological age.

Age structure The distribution of people of different ages within a society.

Ageism A set of beliefs, norms, and values used to justify age-based prejudice and discrimination.

Age-specific death rate The number of deaths per 1,000 persons in a specific age group.

Age-specific fertility The number of live births per 1,000 women in a specific age group.

Agricultural society A society whose subsistence relies primarily on the cultivation of crops with plows drawn by animals.

Alternative movement The type of social movement that seeks only limited changes in individuals.

Anomie A social condition in which norms are weak, conflicting, or absent.

Anticipatory socialization The process of preparing oneself for learning new norms, values, attitudes, and behaviors.

Ascribed status A status within a social structure that is not earned or chosen, but is assigned.

Assimilation The integration of a social or ethnic minority into a society.

Authoritarian personality A personality characterized by excessive conformity; submissiveness to authority figures; inflexibility; repression of impulses, desires, and ideas; fearfulness; and arrogance toward persons or groups thought to be inferior.

Authoritarianism The type of political system controlled by nonelected rulers who generally permit some degree of individual freedom.

Authority Power accepted as legitimate by those subjected to it.

Beliefs Ideas concerning the nature of reality.

Bilateral descent The familial arrangement in which inheritance and descent are passed equally through both parents.

Biological determinism The attribution of behavioral differences to inherited physical characteristics.

Blended family A family formed when at least one of the marriage partners has been married before and has one or more children from a previous marriage.

Boomburgs Places of more than 100,000 residents that are not the largest cities in their metropolitan areas and have experienced double-digit population growth in recent decades.

Bourgeoisie Members of a society who own the means for producing wealth.

Bureaucracies Formal organizations based on rationality and efficiency.

Capitalism An economic system founded on the sanctity of private property and the right of individuals to profit from their labor.

Case study A thorough, recorded investigation of a small group, an incident, or a community.

Caste system The type of stratification structure in which there is no social mobility because social status is inherited and cannot subsequently be changed.

Causation The idea that events occur in a predictable, non-random way and that one event leads to another.

Central-city dilemma The concentration of a large population in need of public services, but without the tax-generated money to provide them.

Charismatic authority Legitimate power based on an individual's personal characteristics.

Charter schools Publicly funded schools that are operated like private schools by public schoolteachers and administrators.

Chivalry hypothesis The idea that females are treated more leniently than males because the men who control the criminal justice system have a protective (paternalistic) attitude toward women.

City A dense and permanent concentration of people living in a limited geographical area who gain their living primarily through nonagricultural activities.

Civil religion A public religion that expresses a strong tie between a deity and a culture.

Civil unions Legal agreements between same-sex couples providing them some of the rights enjoyed by married couples.

Class conflict The conflict between those controlling the means for producing wealth and those laboring for them.

Class consciousness A sense of identification with the goals and interests of the members of one's own social class.

Clinical sociology The use of sociological theories, principles, and research to diagnose and measure social invention.

Closed-ended questions Questions a person must answer by choosing from a limited, predetermined set of responses.

Coercion Social interaction in which individuals or groups are forced to give in to the will of other individuals or groups.

Cognition The process of thinking, knowing, or mentally processing information.

Cognitive ability The capacity for thinking abstractly.

Cohabitation A marriage-like living arrangement without the legal obligations and responsibilities of formal marriage.

Collective behavior The relatively spontaneous and unstructured social behavior of people who are responding to similar stimuli.

Combined statistical area (CSA) Two or more adjacent metropolitan statistical area (MSAs) or a MetroSA and one or more MicroSAs.

Communitarian capitalism The type of capitalism that emphasizes the interests of employees, customers, and society.

Community A concentration of people who can satisfy their major social and economic needs within the area where they live.

Competition A social process that provides rewards to people based on how their performance compares with that of others.

Concentric zone theory A description of the process of urban growth emphasizing circular areas that develop from the central city outward.

Conflict A form of social interaction in which individuals or groups work against one another to obtain a larger share of the valuables.

Conflict theory The theoretical perspective that emphasizes conflict, competition, change, and constraint within a society.

Conformity Behavior matching group expectations.

Conglomerate A network of unrelated businesses operating under a single corporate umbrella.

Conspicuous consumption The consumption of goods and services to display one's wealth to others.

Contagion theory The theory of crowd behavior that emphasizes the irrationality of crowds that is created by participants stimulating one another to higher and higher levels of emotional intensity.

Contingent employees Individuals hired on a part-time, short-term, or contract basis.

Continuity theory Presumes that most aging people maintain consistency with their past lives and use their life experiences to intentionally continue to develop in self-determined channels.

Control group The group in an experiment that is not exposed to the experimental variable.

Control theory The idea that conformity to social norms depends on the presence of a strong bond between individuals and society.

Convergence theory The theory that crowds are formed by people who deliberately congregate with others whom they know to be like-minded.

Cooperation A form of social interaction in which individuals or groups combine their efforts to reach some common goal.

Cooperative learning A nonbureaucratic classroom structure in which students study in groups, with teachers acting as guides rather than as the controlling agents determining all activities.

Core tier The tier of the occupational structure composed of large firms dominating their industries.

Corporate crime Crime committed on behalf of organizations with illegal collusion by corporations.

Corporate welfare Economic benefits government regularly gives to corporations.

Corporation An organization owned by shareholders who have limited liability and limited control over organizational affairs.

Correlation A statistical measure in which a change in one variable is associated with a change in another variable.

Counterculture A subculture that is deliberately and consciously opposed to certain central aspects of the dominant culture.

Craze A type of fad that can have serious consequences for its adopters.

Credentialism The idea that credentials (educational degrees) are unnecessarily required for many jobs.

Crime Acts in violation of the law.

Criminal justice system A system for controlling crime; comprised of police, courts, and corrections.

Crowd A temporary collection of people who share an immediate common interest.

Crude birth rate The annual number of live births per 1,000 members of a population.

Crude death rate The annual number of deaths per 1,000 members of a population.

Cult A religious organization whose characteristics are not drawn from existing religious traditions within a society.

Cultural bias In regard to intelligence tests, the unfair measurement of the cognitive abilities of people in some social categories.

Cultural lag Any situation in which disequilibrium is caused by one segment of a society's failing to change at the same rate as an interrelated segment.

Cultural particulars The widely varying, often distinctive ways societies demonstrate cultural universals.

Cultural relativism The idea that any given aspect of a particular culture should be evaluated in relation to its place within the larger cultural context of which it is a part rather than according to some alleged universal standard that is applied across all cultures.

Cultural transmission theory The theory that deviance is part of a subculture transmitted through socialization.

Cultural universals General cultural traits thought to exist in all known cultures.

Culture A people's way of life—consisting of material objects as well as the patterns of thinking, feeling, and behaving—that is passed from generation to generation among members of a society.

Culture shock Psychological and social stress experienced when confronted with a radically different cultural environment.

Cyber bullying Bullying through electronic media such as e-mail, instant messaging, chat rooms, Websites, and cell phones.

De facto subjugation Subjugation based on common, everyday social practices.

De jure subjugation Subjugation based on the law.

Democracy The type of political system in which elected officials are held responsible for fulfilling the goals of the majority of the electorate.

Democratic control The form of control in which authority is split evenly between husband and wife.

Demographic transition The process by which a population gradually moves from high birth rates and death rates to low birth rates and death rates as a result of economic development.

Demography The scientific study of population.

Denomination One of several religious organizations that members of a society accept as legitimate.

Dependency ratio The proportion of persons in the dependent ages relative to those who are economically active.

Dependency theory The view that low-income countries remain poor because high-income countries continue to exploit, dominate, and manipulate them.

Dependent variable A variable in which a change (or an effect) can be observed.

Desocialization The process of relinquishing old norms, values, attitudes, and behaviors.

Deterrence Intimidation of members of society into compliance with requirements of the legal system.

Deviance Any behavior that departs from societal or group norms.

Deviant A person who violates one or more of society's most highly valued norms.

Differential association theory The theory that deviant behavior is learned—that the more individuals are exposed to people who break the law, the more likely they are to become criminals.

Diffusion The process by which members of one group borrow social and cultural elements from another group, resulting in change.

Direct institutionalized discrimination Organizational or community actions intended to deprive a racial or ethnic minority of its rights.

Discovery The social process of learning something or reinterpreting something.

Discrimination Unequal treatment of individuals based on their minority membership.

Dispersed collectivities Participants in the less-structured forms of collective behavior such as rumors, panics, and fads.

Divergence The persistence of cultural differences in modernizing societies as a result of intervening idiosyncratic social and cultural forces.

Divorce rate The number of divorces in a particular year for every 1,000 members of the total population.

Divorce ratio The number of divorced persons per 1,000 persons in the population divided by the number of persons who are married and living with their spouses.

Domestic terrorism Involves terrorists in a country targeting members of their own country.

Doubling time The number of years needed to double the size of a population.

Downsizing The process by which companies reduce the size of their full-time workforce.

Dramaturgy The symbolic interactionist approach that depicts social life as theater.

Dual labor market The existence of a split between core and peripheral segments of the economy and the division of the labor force into preferred and marginalized workers.

Dual-employed marriage Marriage in which both husband and wife are employed in the labor market.

Dynamic equilibrium The assumption by functionalists that a society both changes and maintains most of its original structure over time.

Dysfunction A negative consequence of some element of a society.

Ecclesia A state religion either headed by religious leaders or heavily influenced by a religious elite.

Economic determinism The idea that the nature of a society is based on the society's economy.

Economy The institution designed for the production and distribution of goods and services.

Edge city A suburban unit specializing in a particular economic activity.

Educational equality When schooling produces the same results (achievement and attitudes) for lower-class and minority children as it does for other children.

Elitism The theory of power distribution that sees society in the control of a relatively few individuals and organizations.

Emergent norm theory The theory of crowd behavior that stresses the similarity between typical, everyday social behavior and crowd behavior.

Endogamy Marriage within one's own group as required by social norms.

Epidemiology The study of the distribution of diseases within a population.

Ethical relativism The idea that morality (right or wrong) depends on the norms of the group or society in which they exist.

Ethnic minority A group of people who are socially identified by their unique characteristics related to culture or nationality.

Ethnocentrism The tendency to judge others in relation to one's own cultural standards.

Ethnography An approach to field work developed by social anthropologists that attempts a detailed and accurate description of a group's way of life.

Ethnomethodology The study of the processes people develop and use in understanding the routine behaviors expected of themselves and others in everyday life.

Exogamy Mate selection norms requiring individuals to marry someone outside their kind.

Experiment A laboratory procedure that attempts to eliminate all possible contaminating influences on the variables being studied.

Experimental group The group in an experiment exposed to the experimental variable.

Exponential growth When the absolute growth of a population that occurs within a given time period becomes part of the base for the growth rate in the next time period.

Extended family A family consisting of two or more adult generations that share a common household and economic resources.

Fads Unusual patterns of behavior that spread rapidly, are embraced zealously, and disappear after a short time.

False consciousness Acceptance of a system that works against one's own interests.

Family A group of people related by marriage, blood, or adoption.

Family of marriage The family group established upon marriage.

Family of orientation The family into which an individual is born.

Family planning The voluntary use of population control methods.

Family resiliency The capacity of the family to emerge from crises as stronger and more resourceful.

Fashions Behavior patterns that evolve over time and are widely approved, but are expected to change periodically.

Fecundity The maximum rate at which women can potentially produce children.

Feminism A social movement aimed at the achievement of sexual equality—socially, legally, politically, and economically.

Feminist social theory Links the lives of women (and men) to the structure of gender relationships within society.

Feminist theory A theoretical perspective that links the lives of women and men to the structure of gender relationships within society.

Feminization of poverty The trend toward more and more of the poor in the United States being women and children.

Fertility A measurement of the number of children born to a woman or to a population of women.

Fertility rate The annual number of live births per 1,000 women ages fifteen to forty-four.

Field research A research approach for studying aspects of social life that cannot be measured quantitatively and that are best understood within a natural setting.

Folk society A society that rests on tradition, cultural and social consensus, family, personal ties, little division of labor, and an emphasis on the sacred.

Folkways Norms without moral overtones.

Formal demography The branch of demography that deals with gathering, collating, analyzing, and presenting population data.

Formal organization A social structure deliberately created for the achievement of one or more goals.

Formal sanctions Rewards and punishments that may be given only by officially designated persons.

For-profit schools Schools run by private, profit-seeking companies on government funds.

Functionalism The theoretical perspective that emphasizes the contribution (functions) made by each part of a society.

Fundamentalism The rejection of secularization and the adherence to traditional religious beliefs, rituals, and doctrines.

Game stage According to Mead, the stage of development during which children learn to consider the roles of several people at the same time.

Gemeinschaft Tönnies's term for the type of society based on tradition, kinship, and intimate social relationships.

Gender The expectations and behaviors associated with a sex category within a society.

Gender identity An awareness of being masculine or feminine, based on culture.

Gender roles Culturally based expectations associated with each sex.

Gender socialization The social process in which boys learn to act the way society assumes boys will act and girls learn to act in ways society expects of them.

Generalized other An integrated conception of the norms, values, and beliefs of one's community or society.

Genocide Politically motivated mass murder of most or all of a targeted population.

Gentrification The development of low-income areas by middle-class home buyers, landlords, and professional developers.

Gesellschaft Tönnies's term for the type of society characterized by weak family ties, competition, and impersonal social relationships.

Gesture Facial expression, body movement, or posture carrying culturally defined and shared symbolic meanings.

Global culture A homogenized culture spread across the globe.

Globalization The process by which increasingly permeable geographic boundaries lead different societies to share in common some economic, political, and social arrangements.

Goal displacement The situation that occurs when organizational rules and regulations become more important than organizational goals.

Government The political structure that rules a nation.

Gross migration rate The annual number of persons per 1,000 members of a population who enter or leave a geographical area.

Group A number of people who are in contact with one another; share some ways of thinking, feeling, and behaving; take one another's behavior into account; and have one or more interests or goals in common.

Groupthink A situation in which pressures toward uniformity discourage members of a group from expressing their reservations about group decisions.

Hate crime A criminal act motivated by prejudice.

Health maintenance organizations (HMOs) Health plans in which members pay set fees on a regular basis and in return receive all necessary health care at little or no additional cost.

Health-care system The combination of professional services, organizations, training academies, and technological resources that are committed to the treatment, management, and prevention of disease.

Heterogamy Marriage among people with differing social characteristics.

Hidden curriculum The educational curriculum that transmits to children a variety of nonacademic values, norms, beliefs, and attitudes.

Hidden unemployment Unemployment that is not measured because of discouraged workers who have stopped looking for work or part-time workers who would prefer full-time jobs.

Homogamy The tendency to marry someone similar to oneself based on personal preference.

Homosexual families Same-sex partners living together with children.

Horizontal mobility A change from one occupation to another at the same general status level.

Horticultural society A society that solves the subsistence problem primarily through the domestication of plants.

Hospices Organizations designed to provide support for the dying and their families.

Hospitals Organizations providing specialized medical services to a variety of patients, including some who continue to live in their homes and others who will spend a prolonged period in the facility.

Humanist sociology The theoretical perspective that places human needs and goals at the center of sociology.

Hunting and gathering society A society that solves the subsistence problem through hunting animals and gathering edible fruits and vegetables.

Hypothesis A tentative, testable statement of a relationship between particular variables.

Hypothesis of linguistic relativity The idea that one's perception of reality is based on language.

"I" The spontaneous and unpredictable part of the self.

Ideal culture Cultural guidelines publicly embraced by members of a society.

Ideal-type method A method that involves isolating the most basic characteristics of some social entity.

Ideology A set of ideas used to justify and defend the interests and actions of those in power in a society.

Imitation stage The developmental stage during which, according to Mead, a child imitates the physical and verbal behavior of a significant other without comprehending the meaning of what is being imitated.

Incarceration The removal of criminals from society.

Income The amount of money received (within a given time period) by an individual or a group.

Independent variable A variable that causes something to happen.

Indirect institutionalized discrimination Unintentional behavior that negatively affects a racial or ethnic minority.

Individualistic capitalism The type of capitalism founded on the principles of self-interest, the free market, profit maximization, and the highest return possible on stockholder investment.

Industrial society A society whose subsistence is based primarily on the application of science and technology to the production of goods and services.

Infant mortality rate The number of deaths among infants under one year of age per 1,000 live births.

Informal organization A group in which personal relationships are guided by rules, rituals, and sentiments not provided for by the formal organization.

Informal sanctions Rewards and punishments that may be applied by most members of a group.

In-group A group toward which one feels intense identification and loyalty.

Instincts Genetically inherited, complex patterns of behavior that always appear among members of a particular species under appropriate environmental conditions.

Institutionalized discrimination Discrimination that results from unfair practices that are part of the structure of society and have grown out of traditionally accepted behaviors.

Integrative curriculum An approach to education based on student–teacher collaboration.

Interest group A group organized to achieve some specific shared goal by influencing political decision making.

Intergenerational mobility Social mobility that occurs from one generation to the next.

Interlocking directorates Members of corporations sitting on one another's boards of directors.

Internal colonialism The domination and oppression of one group by another group within the same society.

Interorganizational relationship A pattern of interaction among authorized representatives of two or more formally independent organizations.

Intervening variable A variable that influences the relationship between an independent variable and a dependent variable.

Interview A set of questions asked by a trained interviewer.

Intragenerational mobility Social mobility that occurs from one generation to the next.

Invention The creation of a new element by combining two or more already existing elements and creating new rules for their use as a unique combination.

Invisible religion A private religion that is substituted for formal religious organizations, practices, and beliefs in a secular society.

Iron law of oligarchy The principle that power tends to become concentrated in the hands of a few members of any organized group.

Juvenile crime Violations of the law committed by those under eighteen years of age.

Labeling theory The theory that deviance exists when some members of a group or society label others as deviants.

Latent function An unintended and unrecognized consequence of some element of a society.

Laws Norms that are formally defined and enforced by officials.

Liberal feminism The feminist social theory that focuses on equal opportunity for women and heightened public awareness of women's rights.

Liberation sociology The theoretical approach to sociology that seeks to replace human oppression with greater democracy and social justice.

Life chances The likelihood of possessing the good things in life like health, happiness, education, wealth, legal protection, and life itself.

Life expectancy The average number of years that persons in a given population born at a particular time can be expected to live.

Life span The most advanced age to which humans can survive.

Lifestyle Social-class related patterns of living in areas like education, marital and family relations, childrearing, political attitudes and behavior, and religious affiliation.

Looking-glass self One's self-concept based on perceptions of others' judgments.

Macrosociology The level of analysis that focuses on relationships among social structures without reference to the interaction of the people involved.

Magnet schools Public schools that attempt to achieve excellence by specializing in a certain area.

Manifest function An intended and recognized consequence of some element of a society.

Marriage A legal union based on mutual rights and obligations.

Marriage rate The number of marriages per year for every 1,000 members of a population.

Mass hysteria The form of collective behavior in which general social anxiety is created by acceptance of one or more false beliefs.

Mass media Those means of communication that reach large heterogeneous audiences without any personal interaction between the senders and the receivers of messages.

Master statuses Statuses that affect most other aspects of a person's life.

Matching Process in which participants in an experiment are matched in pairs according to all factors thought to affect the relationship being investigated.

Material culture The concrete, tangible objects within a culture.

Matriarchal control The form of control in which the oldest female living in a household has the authority.

Matrilineal descent The familial arrangement in which descent and inheritance are passed from the mother to her female descendants.

Matrilocal residence When a married couple is expected to live with the wife's parents.

"Me" The socialized part of the self.

Mechanical solidarity Social unity based on a consensus of values and norms, strong social pressure for conformity, and dependence on tradition and family.

Meritocracy A society in which social status is based on ability and achievement rather than background or parental status.

Metropolitan statistical area (MetroSA, or MSA) A grouping of counties that contains at least one city of 50,000 inhabitants or more or an "urbanized area" of at least 50,000 inhabitants and the surrounding integrated population.

Micropolitan statistical area (MicroSA) At least one urban concentration of no less than 10,000 but less than 50,000 population, plus adjoining territory that is highly integrated with the core.

Microsociology The level of analysis concerned with the study of people as they interact in daily life.

Migration Movement of people from one geographical area to another for the purpose of establishing a new residence.

Minority A people who possess some distinctive physical or cultural characteristics, are dominated by the majority, and are denied equal treatment.

Mob An emotionally stimulated, disorderly crowd that is ready to use destructiveness and violence to achieve a specific purpose.

Modernism The broad social changes beginning in the late nineteenth century and ending around the time of World War II.

Modernization The great number of social changes accompanying economic development.

Modernization theory Proposes that changes associated with modernization are the result of an evolutionary process by which societies become increasingly complex.

Monogamy The form of marriage in which one man is married to only one woman at a time.

Monopoly A single company controlling a particular market.

Morbidity Rates of disease and illness in a population.

Mores Norms that have great moral significance and that should be followed by the members of a society.

Mortality Deaths within a population.

Multiculturalism An approach that accents the viewpoints, experiences, and contributions of women and diverse ethnic and racial minorities (women as well as ethnic and racial minorities).

Multinational corporations Firms in highly industrialized societies with operating facilities throughout the world.

Multiple causation The idea that an event occurs as a result of several factors operating in combination.

Multiple-nuclei theory A description of the process of urban growth that emphasizes specific geographical and historical influences on areas within cities.

Nationalism In a nation-state, a people's commitment to a common destiny based on recognition of a common past and a vision of a shared future.

Nation-state The political entity that holds authority over a specified territory.

Natural increase Population growth due to an excess of births over deaths.

Negative correlation A statistical measure in which the independent and dependent variables change in opposite directions.

Negative deviance Behavior that underconforms to accepted norms.

Neolocal residence When a newly married couple establishes a residence separate from either of their parents.

Net migration rate The annual increase or decrease per 1,000 members of a population resulting from people leaving and entering the population.

Nonmaterial culture The norms, values, and beliefs of a group of people.

Norms Rules defining appropriate and inappropriate behaviors.

Nuclear family The smallest group of individuals (mother, father, and children) that can be called a family.

Objectivity The principle stating that scientists are expected to prevent their personal biases from influencing the interpretation of their results.

Obligations Roles informing individuals of the behavior others expect from them.

Occupational crime Illegal acts by people in either their employment or their personal financial pursuits.

Occupational sex segregation The concentration of men and women in different occupations.

Oligopoly A combination of companies controlling a market.

Open class system The type of stratification structure in which an individual's social status is based on merit and individual effort.

Open classroom A nonbureaucratic approach to education based on democracy, flexibility, and noncompetitiveness.

Open-ended questions Questions a person must answer in his or her own words.

Operational definition A definition of an abstract concept in terms of simpler, observable procedures.

Organic solidarity Social unity based on a complex of highly specialized roles that makes members of a society dependent on one another.

Organic-adaptive systems Organizations based on rapid response to change rather than on the continuing implementation of established administrative principles.

Organizational environment Consists of all the forces outside an organization that exert an actual or potential influence on the organization.

Out-group A group toward which one feels opposition, antagonism, or competition.

Overurbanization A situation in which a city cannot supply adequate jobs and housing for its inhabitants.

Panic Collective behavior that occurs when people react to a genuine threat in fearful, anxious, and often self-damaging ways.

Participant observation The type of field research technique in which a researcher becomes a temporary member of the group being studied.

Pastoral societies Populations that depend primarily on raising and caring for domesticated animals for food.

Patriarchy The pattern in which the oldest man living in a household has authority over the rest of the family members. Also called *patriarchal control*.

Patrilineal descent The familial arrangement in which descent and inheritance are passed from the father to the male descendants.

Patrilocal residence When a married couple is expected to live with the husband's parents.

Peer group A group composed of individuals of roughly the same age and interests.

Peripheral theory Theory of city growth that emphasizes the growth of suburbs and edge cities around and away from central cities.

Peripheral tier The tier of the occupational structure composed of smaller, less profitable firms.

Personality The relatively organized complex of attitudes, beliefs, values, and behaviors associated with an individual.

Perspective One's outlook on something.

Physician-hospital organizations (PHOs) Joint ventures between hospitals and organized groups of physicians to reach predetermined business objectives.

Play stage According to Mead, the stage of development during which children take on the roles of individuals, one at a time.

Pluralism The theory of power distribution that sees decision making as the result of competition, bargaining, and compromise among diverse special interest groups.

Political action committees (PACs) Organizations established by interest groups for the purpose of raising and distributing funds to selected political candidates.

Political institution The institution within which political power is supposed to be lodged and exercised.

Polyandry The form of marriage in which one woman is married to two or more men at the same time.

Polygamy Marriage of a male or female to multiple partners of the other sex.

Polygyny The form of marriage in which one man is married to two or more women at the same time.

Population All those people with the characteristics a researcher wants to study within the context of a particular research question.

Population control The conscious attempt to regulate population size through national birth control programs.

Population momentum When a population continues to grow, regardless of a recent drop in the birth rate to zero, because of the existing population base.

Population pyramids Graphic representations of the age and sex compositions of populations.

Positive correlation A statistical measure in which the independent and dependent variables change in the same direction.

Positive deviance Behavior that overconforms to social expectations.

Positivism The use of observation, experimentation, and other methods of the physical sciences in the study of social life.

Postindustrial society The type of society in which knowledge and service organizations are the major source of power and the prime mover of social life.

Postmodernism The theory that rejects the idea that individuals are autonomous beings, that reason is a reliable way to interpret the world, and that a discoverable reality exists.

Power The ability to control the behavior of others, even against their will.

Power elite A unified coalition of top military, corporate, and government leaders.

Preferred provider organizations (PPOs) Small groups of physicians providing a limited set of medical services to pre-enrolled patients at reduced prices.

Prejudice Widely held preconceptions of a group (minority or majority) and its individual members.

Presentation of self The ways that we, in a variety of social situations, attempt to create a favorable evaluation of ourselves in the minds of others.

Prestige Social recognition, respect, and admiration that a society attaches to a particular status.

Primary deviance Isolated acts of norm violation.

Primary group People who are emotionally close, know one another well, seek one another's company because they enjoy being together, and have a "we" feeling.

Primary sector That part of the economy producing goods from the natural environment.

Profane Nonsacred aspects of our lives.

Proletariat Members of a society who labor for the bourgeoisie at subsistence wages.

Protestant ethic A set of values, norms, beliefs, and attitudes stressing hard work, thrift, and self-discipline.

Public policy A broad course of governmental action expressed in specific laws, programs, and initiatives.

Qualitative variable A variable that consists of variation in kind rather than in number.

Quantitative variable A variable that can be measured and given a numerical value.

Questionnaire A written set of questions participants fill out by themselves.

Race A category of people who are alleged to share certain biologically inherited physical characteristics that are considered socially important within a society.

Racial profiling Police action based on personal characteristics rather than on personal behavior.

Racism Ideas that attempt to connect biological characteristics with innate racial superiority or inferiority.

Radical feminism The feminist social theory that traces oppression of women to the fact that societies are dominated by men.

Random sample A sample selected on the basis of chance so that each member of a population has an equal opportunity of being selected.

Randomization Process by which subjects are assigned to the experimental or control group on a random or chance basis.

Rationalism The solution of problems on the basis of logic, data, and planning rather than tradition and superstition.

Rationalization The tendency to use knowledge and impersonality in social relationships to gain increased control over society.

Rational-legal authority Authority based on rules and procedures associated with political offices.

Real culture Actual (subterranean) patterns of thinking, feeling, and behaving.

Recidivism A return to crime after prison.

Redemptive movement The type of social movement that focuses on changing individuals rather than society.

Reference group A group one uses to evaluate oneself, and from which one acquires attitudes, beliefs, values, and norms.

Reformative movement The type of social movement that aims to bring partial change to a society.

Rehabilitation The resocialization of criminals into conformity with the legal code of society.

Relative deprivation A condition that exists when people compare themselves with others and believe that they should have as much as those others have.

Relative poverty The designation of poverty resulting from a comparison of the economic condition of those at the bottom of a society with that of other segments of the population.

Reliability The ability of a measurement technique to yield consistent results.

Religion A unified system of beliefs and practices relating to sacred things.

Religiosity The ways in which people express their religious interests and convictions.

Replacement level The birth rate at which a married couple replaces itself in the population.

Replication The duplication of the same study to ascertain its accuracy.

Resocialization The process of learning to adopt new norms, values, attitudes, and behaviors.

Resource mobilization The process through which members of a social movement secure and utilize the resources needed to press for social change.

Retribution The public demand that criminals pay compensation equal to their offenses against society.

Revolution Occurs when a new political elite topples an entrenched governing regime, with the goal of changing their society's social structures.

Revolutionary movement The type of social movement that attempts to change society totally.

Rights Roles informing individuals of the behavior that can be expected from others.

Riots Crowds that engage in episodes of destructiveness and violence without a mob's sense of common purpose.

Role conflict Conflict between the performance of a role in one status with the performance of a role in another status.

Role performance The actual conduct involved in putting a role into action.

Role strain Conflicting roles within a single status.

Role taking The process of mentally assuming the viewpoint of another individual and then responding to oneself from that imagined viewpoint.

Roles Culturally defined rights and obligations attached to social statuses indicating the behavior expected of individuals holding them.

Rumor A widely circulating story of questionable truth.

Sacred Entities that are set apart and given a special meaning that transcends immediate human existence.

Sample A limited number of cases drawn from a population.

Sanctions Rewards and punishments used to encourage conformity to norms.

Sandwich generation The term applied to adults caught between caring for their parents and caring for the family they formed after leaving home.

Scapegoat A substitute object that serves as a convenient and less feared target on which to place the blame for one's own troubles, frustrations, failures, or sense of guilt.

School choice The idea that the best way to improve schools is by using the free enterprise model, thereby creating competition for the public school system.

Secondary analysis The use of information already collected by someone else for another purpose.

Secondary deviance Deviance as a lifestyle and personal identity.

Secondary group A group that is impersonal and task oriented and involves only a segment of the lives and personalities of its members.

Secondary relationships Relationships that are impersonal, that involve only limited aspects of others' personality, and that exist to accomplish a specific purpose beyond the relationship itself.

Secondary sector That part of the economy engaged in manufacturing goods from raw materials.

Sect A religious organization formed when members of an existing religious organization break away in an attempt to reform the "parent" group.

Sector theory A description of the process of urban growth emphasizing the importance of transportation routes.

Secularization The process whereby religion loses its influence over society as a whole.

Self-concept An image of oneself as an entity separate from other people.

Self-fulfilling prophecy The situation in which an expectation leads to behavior that causes the expectation to become a reality.

Sex The biological distinction between male and female.

Sex stereotype A stereotype used to portray one sex as innately superior to the other.

Sexism A set of beliefs, norms, and values used to justify sexual inequality.

Sexual harassment The use of one's superior power in making unwelcome sexual advances.

Sick role A confluence of appropriate behavior patterns for people who are ill, serving to remove them from active involvement in everyday routines, give them special protection and privileges, and set the stage for their return to their normal social roles.

Significant others Those persons whose judgments are the most important to an individual's self-concept.

Single-parent family A family headed by an unmarried adult.

Social aggregate A number of people who happen to be physically located together.

Social category A group of persons who share a social characteristic.

Social change Alterations in social structures that have long-term and relatively important consequences.

Social class A segment of a population whose members have a relatively similar share of the desirable things and who share attitudes, values, norms, and an identifiable lifestyle.

Social control Means for promoting conformity to norms.

Social demography The branch of demography that studies population patterns within a social context.

Social dynamics The study of social change.

Social exchange A form of social interaction in which one person voluntarily does something for another, expecting a reward in return.

Social gerontology The scientific study of the social dimensions of aging.

Social interaction The process by which people influence one another's behavior as they relate.

Social mobility The movement of individuals or groups within a stratification structure.

Social movement A large number of people acting together with some degree of leadership and organization over a relatively long period with the goal of promoting or preventing social change.

Social network A web of social relationships that joins a person to other people and groups.

Social statics The study of stability and order in society.

Social stratification The creation of layers (strata) of people possessing unequal shares of scarce desirables.

Social structure Patterned, recurring social relationships.

Socialism An economic system founded on the belief that the means of production should be controlled by the people as a whole and that government should plan and control the economy.

Socialist feminism The feminist social theory that sees capitalism as the source of female oppression.

Socialization The process of learning to participate in group life through the acquisition of culture.

Society People who live within defined territorial borders and participate in a common culture.

Sociobiology The study of the biological basis of human behavior.

Sociological imagination The set of mind that allows individuals to see the relationship between events in their personal lives and events in their society.

Sociology The scientific study of social structure.

Spirit of capitalism The preference to accumulate capital as a moral obligation (not as a necessity) to reinvest rather than to use for consumption.

Sport A set of competitive activities in which winners and losers are determined by physical performance within a set of established rules.

Sport subculture A group within the larger context of sport that has some of its own distinct roles, values, and norms.

Spurious correlation An apparent relationship between two variables that is actually produced by a third variable that affects both of the original two variables.

Stacking The assignment of players to less central positions on the basis of race or ethnicity.

Status The position that a person occupies within a social structure.

Status groups Groups composed of individuals who share a sense of status equality.

Status set All the statuses that an individual occupies at any particular time.

Stereotypes Ideas based on distortion, exaggeration, and oversimplification that are applied to all members of a social category.

Stigma An undesirable characteristic or label used by others to deny the deviant full social acceptance.

Strain theory The theory that deviance is most likely to occur when there is a discrepancy between culturally prescribed goals and legitimate (socially approved) means of obtaining them.

Stratified random sample A sample drawn from a population that has been divided into categories such as sex, race, or age. (The sample is selected at random from each category.)

Structural differentiation The division of one social structure into two or more social structures that operate more successfully separately than the one alone would under the new circumstances.

Structural mobility Mobility that occurs because of changes in the distribution of occupational opportunities.

Subculture A group that is part of the dominant culture but differs from it in some important respects.

Subjective approach A research method in which the aim is to understand some aspect of social reality through the study of the subjective interpretations of the participants themselves.

Suburbanization The process by which central cities lose population to the areas surrounding them.

Survey A research method in which people are asked to answer a series of questions.

Symbol Something that stands for, or represents, something else.

Symbolic interactionism The theoretical perspective that focuses on interaction among people based on mutually understood symbols.

Taboo A norm so important that its violation is considered repugnant.

Technology Knowledge and hardware combined to achieve practical goals.

Terrorism The illegal use of violence or threats of violence to intimidate a government, group, or individual in pursuit of a political, religious, economic, or social goal.

Tertiary sector That part of the economy providing services.

Total fertility rate In a given population, the average number of children born to a woman during her lifetime.

Total institutions Places in which residents are separated from the rest of society and are controlled and manipulated by those in charge.

Totalitarianism The type of political system in which a ruler with absolute power attempts to control all phases of social life.

Tracking A process used in schools to place students in curricula consistent with the school's expectations of the student's eventual occupation.

Traditional authority Legitimate power rooted in custom.

Trained incapacity The situation that occurs when previous training prevents someone from adapting to new situations.

Transnational terrorism Involves terrorists in one country committing terrorist acts against targets in another country.

Transnationals Immigrants who maintain ties in more than one country.

Underclass People typically unemployed who come from families with a history of unemployment for generations.

Unfulfilled rising expectations When newly raised hopes for a better life are either not satisfied at all or not satisfied as rapidly as people had expected.

Urban area A census block with a population density of no less than 1,000 persons per square mile.

Urban cluster An area with a population over 10,000 but under 50,000.

Urban ecology The study of the relationships between humans and their urban environments.

Urban legends Moralistic tales passed along by people who swear the stories happened to someone they know, or to an acquaintance of a friend or family member.

Urban society A society in which social relationships are impersonal and contractual, kinship is deemphasized, cultural and social consensus are not complete, the division of labor is complex, and secular concerns outweigh sacred ones.

Urbanism The idea that urbanization involves a distinctive way of life.

Urbanization The process by which an increasingly large proportion of the world's population lives in urban areas.

Urbanized area A central city, or cities, of 50,000 or more and the surrounding densely inhabited territory.

Validity The ability of a measurement technique to actually measure what it is designed to measure.

Value-added theory A theory outlining six conditions that are necessary and sufficient for the emergence of a social movement.

Value-free research Research in which personal biases are not allowed to affect the research process and its outcomes.

Values Broad cultural principles that most people in a society consider desirable.

Variable Something that occurs in different degrees among individuals, groups, objects, and events.

Verifiability A principle of science by which any given piece of research can be duplicated (replicated) by other scientists.

Verstehen The method of understanding social behavior by putting oneself in the place of others.

Vertical mobility An upward or downward change in status level.

Victim discounting The act of seeing a crime as less serious if the victim is a member of a minority or a lower social class.

Vouchers Government money made available to families with school-age children for use toward public, private, or parochial schools.

War Armed conflict that occurs within a society or among nations.

Wealth All the economic resources possessed by an individual or a group.

White collar crime Any crime committed by respectable and high-status people in the course of their occupations.

Women's movement Comprised of groups and organizations engaged in activities designed to promote gender equality.

Working poor People employed in low-skill jobs with the lowest pay who do not earn enough to rise out of poverty.

World-system theory A theory of modernization that sees the pattern of a nation's development as largely dependent on that nation's location in the world economy.

Zero population growth When deaths are balanced by births so that a population does not increase.

References

Abbott, Andrew. *Department and Discipline: Chicago Sociology at One Hundred.* Chicago, IL: University of Chicago Press, 1999.

Aberle, David. *The Peyote Religion Among the Navaho.* Norman, OK: University of Oklahoma Press, 1991.

Abramsky, Sasha. "Hard-Time Kids." *The American Prospect* (August 27, 2001):16–21.

Abramson, Alexis. *The Caregivers Survival Handbook.* New York: Penguin Books, 2004.

Abu-Lughod, Janet L. *Rabat.* Princeton, NJ: Princeton University Press, 1980.

Abu-Lughod, Janet L. (Ed.). *Sociology for the Twenty-First Century: Continuities and Cutting Edges.* Chicago, IL: University of Chicago Press, 2000.

Acker, James R., Robert M. Bohm, and Charles S. Lanier (eds.). America's Experiment with Capital Punishment. Durham, NC: Carolina Academic Press, l998.

Acosta, R. Vivian, and Linda Jean Carpenter. "Women in Intercollegiate Sport: A Longitudinal Study—Twenty Seven Year Update, 1977–2004." Brooklyn, NY: Department of Physical Education, Brooklyn College, 2004.

Adams, Bert N. *Kinship in an Urban Setting.* Chicago, IL: Markham, 1968.

Adams, Bert N. "Isolation, Function, and Beyond: American Kinship in the 1960s." *Journal of Marriage and the Family* 32 (November 1970):575–597.

Adams, Rebecca G. "The Sociology of Jerry Garcia." *Garcia: Reflections* 1 (1995):16–18.

Adams, Robert. *The Evolution of Urban Society.* Chicago, IL: Aldine, 1965.

Addams, Jane. *Twenty Years at Hull House.* New York: New American Library, 1981.

Adelmann, Pamela K., Toni C. Antonucci, Susan E. Crohan, and Lerita M. Coleman. "Empty Nest, Cohort, and Employment in the Well-Being of Midlife Women." *Sex Roles* 20 (1989):173–189.

Adelson, Joseph. "Why the Schools May Not Improve." *Commentary* 78 (October 1984):40–45.

Adler, Emily Stier, and Roger Clark. *How It's Done: An Invitation to Social Research,* 2nd ed. Belmont, CA: Wadsworth, 2003.

Adler, Jerry. "Spaced Out." *Newsweek* (January 13, 2003):48–51.

Adler, Patricia A., and Peter Adler. *Peer Power.* New Brunswick, NJ: Rutgers University Press, 1998.

Adorno, Theodor W., Else Frenkel-Brunswik, Daniel J. Levinson, and Nevitt R. Sanford. *The Authoritarian Personality.* New York: Harper, 1950.

Aftab, P. (2006). http://www.wiredsafety.net

"A Giant Step Toward Universal Health Care." *The Week* (April 12, 2010):6.

Aguirre, Adalberto, and Jonathan H. Turner. *American Ethnicity,* 2nd ed. New York: McGraw-Hill, 1997.

Aguirre, Benigno, E. L. Quarantelli, and Jorge L. Mendoza. "The Collective Behavior of Fads: The Characteristics, Effects, and Career of Streaking." *American Sociological Review,* 53 (1988):569–584.

Ahlburg, Dennis A., and Carol J. De Vita. "New Realities of the American Family." *Population Bulletin* 47 (August 1992):1–44.

Ahrens, Frank. "FCC Eases Media Ownership Rules." *Washington Post* (June 3, 2003):A1, A6, A7.

"Air Force Reports 54 Rapes, Assault." *Associated Press* (March 6, 2003).

Aizenman, N. C. "Influx of U.S. Inmates Slowing, Census Says." *Washington Post* (September 27, 2007).

Alba, Richard D. "The Twilight of Americans of European Ancestry: The Case of Italians." *Ethnic and Racial Studies* 8 (January 1985):134–158.

Alba, Richard D. *The Transformation of White America.* New Haven, CT: Yale University Press, 1990.

Albert, Michel. *Capitalism vs. Capitalism.* New York: Four Walls Eight Windows, 1993.

Aldrich, Howard. *Organizations Evolving.* Thousand Oaks, CA: Sage, 1999.

Aldridge, Alan. *Religion in the Contemporary World.* Malden, MA: Blackwell, 2000.

Alexander, Jeffrey C., Bernard Giesen, Richard Munch, and Neil J. Smelser. (Eds.). *The Micro-Macro Link.* Berkeley, CA: University of California Press, 1987.

Alexander, Michelle. *The New Jim Crow.* New York: The New Press, 2010.

Alfino, Mark, John S. Caputo, and Robin Wynyard. *Mcdonaldization Revisited.* Westport, CT: Praeger, 1998.

Alford, Robert R., and Roger Friedland. *Power of Theory.* Cambridge, UK: Cambridge University Press, 1985.

Allen, Jodi T. *A Nation of 'Haves' and 'Have-Nots.'* Washington, DC: Pew Research Center (September 13, 2007). http://pewresearch.org.pubs/593/haves-have-nots

Allen, John L., and Christopher J. Sutton. *Student Atlas of World Politics,* 9th ed. New York: McGraw-Hill, 2011.

Allport, Gordon. *The Nature of Prejudice.* Reading, MA: Addison-Wesley, 1979.

"Almost All Millennials Accept Interracial Dating and Marriage." Washington, DC: Pew Research Center (February 1, 2010). http://pewresearch.org/pubs/1480/millennials-accept-interracial-dating-marriage-friends-different-race-generations.

Alperovitz, Gar, and Lew Daly. *Unjust Deserts.* New York: The New Press, 2008.

Alter, Catherine, and Jerald Hage. *Organizations Working Together.* Newbury Park, CA: Sage, 1992.

Alter, Jonathan. "How America's Meanest Lobby Ran Out of Ammo." *Newsweek* (May 16, 1994):24–25.

Alterman, Eric. *What Liberal Media? The Truth About Bias and the News.* New York: Basic Books, 2003.

Altman, Daniel. "We Saved Your Job, but Gave You More Work." *New York Times* (October 29, 2002):G4.

Altman, Dennis. *AIDS in the Mind of America.* Garden City, NY: Anchor Books, 1986.

America 2000: An Educational Strategy. Washington, DC: U.S. Department of Education, 1991.

American Association of School Administrators. *Sex Equality in Educational Materials.* Executive Handbook Series, vol. IV. Washington, DC: American Association of School Administrators.

"American Grace: How Religion Divides and Unites Us." Washington, DC: Pew Forum on Religion & Public Life (December 16, 2010). http://pewforum.org/American-Grace—How-Religion-Divides-and-Unites-Us.aspx.

American Jewish Year Book, 2006. New York: American Jewish Committee, 2006.

American Sociological Association. *The Health of Sociology.* Washington, DC: Research and Development Department, 2007.

American Sociological Association. *Code of Ethics.* Washington, DC: American Jewish Committee, 2011.

Amsden, Alice H. *The Rise of "the Rest": Challenges to the West from Late-Industrializing Economies.* Oxford, UK: Oxford University Press, 2003.

A Nation at Risk. The National Commission on Excellence in Education. Schaumburg, IL: Research USA Incorporated, 1989.

Andersen, Margaret L. *Thinking About Women*, 8th ed. Upper Saddle River, NJ: Prentice-Hall, 2010.

Andersen, Margaret L., and Patricia Hill Collins. *Race, Class, and Gender*, 7th ed. Belmont, CA: Wadsworth Cengage Learning, 2010.

Andersen, Ronald M., Thomas H. Rice, and Gerald F. Kominski. *Changing the U.S. Health Care System: Key Issues in Health Services Policy and Management*, 3rd ed. New York: John Wiley & Sons, 2007.

Anderson, Craig A. "Longitudinal Effects of Violent Video Games on Aggression in Japan and the United States." *Pediatrics* 122 (November 2008):1067–1072.

Anderson, Craig A., and Brad J. Bushman. "The Effects of Media Violence on Society." *Science* 295 (March 29, 2002):2377–2378.

Anderson, Curt. "Anti-Muslim Hate Crimes Soared Last Year, FBI Says." *The Philadelphia Inquirer* (November 26, 2002).

Anderson, Elijah, and Douglas S. Massey. (Eds.). *Problem of the Century: Racial Stratification in the United States.* New York, NY: Russell Sage, 2001.

Anderson, Nick, and Bill Turque. "Reading Scores Stalled Under 'No Child' Law, Report Finds D.C. Fourth-Graders a Bright Spot in Disappointing 2009 Data." *Washington Post* (March 25, 2010).

Anderson, T. B. "Widowhood as a Life Transition: Its Impact on Kinship Ties." *Journal of Marriage and the Family* 46 (February 1984):105–114.

Andrews, Lori B. *Black Power, White Blood.* New York: Pantheon Books, 1996.

Angell, Marcia. *The Truth About the Drug Companies: How They Deceive Us and What to Do About It.* New York: Random House, 2004.

Annan, K. "Football Envy at the UN." *Guardian* (June 12, 2006):30.

Antoun, Richard T. *Understanding Fundamentalism: Christian, Islamic, and Jewish Movements.* Thousand Oaks, CA: AltaMira Press, 2001.

Appel, Willa. *Cults in America.* New York: Holt, Rinehart and Winston, 1983.

Appleby, Joyce. *Inheriting the Revolution: The First Generation of Americans.* Cambridge, MA: Harvard University Press, 2001.

Appiah, Kwame Anthony, and Amy Gutmann. *Color Conscious: The Political Morality of Race.* Princeton, NJ: Princeton University Press, 1998.

Appleby, Julie. "Survey: Many Request Drugs Advertised on TV." *Arizona Republic* (March 4, 2008):A12.

Archibold, Randal C. "Arizona Enacts Stringent Law on Immigration." *New York Times* (April 23, 2010).

Archibold, Randal C. "U.S.'s Toughest Immigration Law Is Signed in Arizona." *New York Times* (April 23, 2010).

Arenson, Karen W. "Applications to Colleges Are Breaking Records." *New York Times* (January 17, 2008).

Armour, Stephanie. "Faced with Less Time off, Workers Take More." *USA Today* (October 29, 2002):1A.

Aron-Dine, Aviva. "New Data Show Income Concentration Jumped Again in 2005." Washington, DC: Center on Budget and Policy Priorities (2007). http://www.cbpp.org/3-29-07inc.htm

Aronowitz, Robert A. *Making Sense of Illness.* New York: Cambridge University Press, 1998.

Aronowitz, Stanley, and Henry A. Giroux. *Education Still Under Siege*, 2nd ed. Toronto, ON: OISE Press, 1994.

Aronson, E., and A. Gonzalez. "Desegregation, Jigsaw, and the Mexican American Experience." In P. A. Katz and D. A. Taylor (Eds.), *Eliminating Racism.* New York: Plenum Press, 1988, pp. 301–314.

Aronson, Marc. *Race: A History Beyond Black and White.* New York: Atheneum Books, 2007.

Arrigo, Bruce A. *Social Justice/Criminal Justice: The Maturation of Critical Theory in Law, Crime, and Deviance.* Belmont, CA: Wadsworth, 1999.

Arrow, Kenneth Joseph., Steven N. Durlauf., and Samuel Bowles. (Eds.). *Meritocracy and Economic Inequality.* Princeton, NJ: Princeton University Press, 2000.

"Artificial Life (Synthetic DNA) Created by Scientist." *The Tech Journal* (December 6, 2010). http://thetechjournal.com/science/artificial-life-synthetic-dna-created-by-scientists.xhtml

Asch, Solomon E. "Opinions and Social Pressure." *Scientific American* 193 (November 1955):31–35.

Ashford, Lori S. "New Population Policies: Advancing Women's Health & Rights." *Population Bulletin* 56 (March 2001):1–44.

Ashour, Ahmen Sakr. "The Contingency Model of Leadership Effectiveness: An Evaluation." *Organizational Behavior and Human Performance* 9 (June 1973):339–355.

Astone, N. M., and Sara McLanahan. "Family Structure, Parental Practices, and High School Completion." *American Sociological Review* 56 (1991):309–320.

Atchley, Robert C. *Continuity and Adaptation in Aging: Creating Positive Experiences.* Baltimore, MD: Johns Hopkins University Press, 2001.

Atchley, Robert C., and Amanda Barush. *Social Forces and Aging*, 10th ed. Belmont, CA: Wadsworth, 2004.

Atchley, Robert C., and S. Miller. "Types of Elderly Couples." In T. H. Brubaker (Ed.), *Family Relationships in Later Life.* Beverly Hills, CA: Sage, 1983, pp. 77–90.

Atkinson, Paul. "Ethnomethodology: A Critical Review." In W. Richard Scott and Judith Blake (Eds.), *Annual Review of Sociology* 14 (1988):441–465.

Atkinson, Rick. "Germany's Health-Care System Such a Success It Needs Reform." *Washington Post* (June 22, 1994):A1.

Audi, Robert, and Nicholas Wolterstorff. *Religion in the Public Square: Debating Church and State.* Lanham, MD: Rowman & Littlefield, 1996.

Auguet, Roland. *Cruelty and Civilization.* London: George Allen and Unwin, Ltd, 1972.

Aulette, Judy Root, Judith Wittner, and Kristin Blakely. *Gendered Worlds.* New York: Oxford University Press, 2009.

Axtell, Roger E. *Gestures: The Do's and Taboos of Body Language Around the World.* Secaucus, NJ: Castle Books, 2009.

Baars, Jan, Chris Phillipson, Alan Walker, and Dale Dannefer. (Eds.). *Aging, Globalization and Inequality.* Amityville, NY: Baywood Publishing, 2006.

Babbie, Earl R. *The Basics of Social Research*, 5th ed. Belmont, CA: Wadsworth, 2010a.

Babbie, Earl R. *The Practice of Social Research*, 12th ed. Belmont, CA: Cengage, 2010b.

Baca Zinn, Maxine, and D. Stanley Eitzen. "Economic Restructuring and Systems Inequality." In Margaret L. Andersen and Patricia Hill (Eds.), *Race, Class, and Gender: An Anthology*, 6th ed. Belmont, CA: Wadsworth, 2006.

Bacon, Perry Jr. "Foes Use Obama's Muslim Ties to Fuel Rumors About Him." *Washington Post* (November 29, 2007).

Baert, Patrick, and Filipe Carreira Da Silva. *Social Theory in the Twentieth Century and Beyond*, 2nd ed. Cambridge, UK: Polity Books, 2010.

Bagdikian, Ben. *The New Media Monopoly*, 10th ed. Boston, MA: Beacon Press, 2004.

Bahrampour, Tara. "Internet Helped Muslim Convert from Northern Virginia Embrace Extremism at Warp Speed." *Washington Post* (November 2, 2010).

Bailey, Garrick, and Jame Peoples. *Essentials of Cultural Anthropology*, 2nd ed. Belmont, CA: Wadsworth Cengage Publishing, 2011.

Bainbridge, William Sims. *The Sociology of Religious Movements.* New York: Routledge, 1997.

Baldassare, Mark. "Suburban Communities." *Annual Review of Sociology* 18 (1992):475–494.

Bales, Robert F. *Interaction Process Analysis.* Reading, MA: Addison-Wesley, 1950.

Ballantine, Jeanne H., and Joan Z. Spade. (Eds.). *Schools and Society: A Sociological Approach to Education,* 3rd ed. Thousand Oaks, CA: Sage, 2007.

Balrig, Flemming. *The Snow-White Image.* Oslo: Norwegian University Press, 1988.

Banner, Stuart. *The Death Penalty: An American History.* Cambridge, MA: Harvard University Press, 2003.

Banton, Michael. *Racial Theories.* New York: Cambridge University Press, 1998.

Barak, Gregg. (Ed.). *Crime and Crime Control: A Global View.* Westport, CT: Greenwood Press, 2000.

Barbalet, Jack. *Weber, Passion and Profits.* Cambridge, UK: Cambridge University Press, 2008.

Barbotte, Eric, et al. "Prevalence of Impairments, Disabilities, Handicaps and Quality of Life in the General Population: A Review of Recent Literature." *Bulletin of the World Health Organization* 79 (2001):1047–1055.

Bardes, Barbara A., Mack C. Shelley, and Steffen W. Schmidt. *American Government and Politics Start over Today: The Essentials,* 2009–2010 ed. Belmont, CA: Wadsworth, 2010.

Bardo, John W., and John J. Hartman. *Urban Sociology.* Itasca, IL: Peacock, 1982.

Barker, Eileen. *The Making of a Moonie.* London: Basil Blackwell, 1984.

Barlett, Donald L., and James B. Steele. *America: Who Stole the Dream?* Kansas City, MO: Andrews and McMeel, 1996.

Barlett, Donald L., and James B. Steele. *The Great American Tax Dodge: How Spiraling Fraud and Avoidance Are Killing Fairness, Destroying the Income Tax, and Costing You.* Boston, MA: Little, Brown and Company, 2002.

Barnes, Julian E. "The SAT Revolution." *U.S. News and World Report* (November 11, 2002).

Barnes, Robert, and Dan Eggen. "Supreme Court Rejects Limits on Corporate Spending on Political Campaigns." *Washington Post* (January 22, 2010):AOl.

Barnett, Ola W., Robin D. Perrin, and Cindy L. Miller-Perrin. *Family Violence Across the Lifespan,* 2nd ed. Thousand Oaks, CA: Sage, 2004.

Barr, C. "Pushing the Envelope: What Curriculum Integration Can Be." In E. Brazee and J. Capelluti (Eds.), *Dissolving Boundaries: Toward an Integrative Curriculum.* Columbus, OH: National Middle School Association, 1995.

Barr, Donald A. *Health Disparities in the United States: Social Class, Race, Ethnicity, and Health.* Baltimore, MD: Johns Hopkins University Press, 2008.

Barrett, Michael J. "The Case for More School Days." *The Atlantic Monthly* (November 1990):78–106.

Barron, James. "Fondly Recalling a Martian Invasion." *New York Times* (September 16, 1988):B1,B3.

Barron, Milton L. "Minority Group Characteristics of the Aged in American Society." *Journal of Gerontology* 8 (October 1953):477–482.

Barry, Herbert III, Margaret K. Bacon, and Irvin L. Child. "A Cross-Cultural Survey of Some Sex Differences in Socialization." *Journal of Abnormal and Social Psychology* 55 (November 1957):327–332.

Barry, Norman P. *Welfare,* 2nd ed. Minneapolis, MN: University of Minnesota Press, 1999.

"Battling Bullies." *The Week* (November 12, 2010).

Baum, Sandy, and Patricia Steele. "Who Borrows Most? Bachelor's Degree Recipients with High Levels of Student Debt." New York: College Board (2010). www.collegeboard.com/trends

Baumohl, Bernard. "When Downsizing Becomes Dumbsizing." *Time* (March 15, 1993):55.

Baumol, William J., and Alan S. Blinder. *Economics Principles and Policy,* 11th ed. Belmont, CA: South-Western, 2010.

Baumol, William J., Alan S. Blinder, and Edward N. Wolff. *Downsizing in America.* New York: Russian Sage Foundation, 2005.

Baxandall, Rosalyn, and Elizabeth Ewen. *Picture Windows: How the Suburbs Happened.* New York: Basic Books, 2000.

Baxandall, Rosalyn, and Linda Gordon. "Second-Wave Soundings." *The Nation* (July 3, 2000):28–32.

Baxandall, Rosalyn, and Linda Gordon. *Dear Sisters.* New York: Basic Books, 2001.

Beals, Ralph L., Harry Hoijer, and Alan R. Beals. *An Introduction to Anthropology,* 5th ed. New York: Macmillan, 1977.

Bearman, Peter S., and Hannah Bruchner. "Opposite Sex Twins and Adolescent Same-Sex Attraction." *American Journal of Sociology* 107 (March 2002):1179–1205.

Becker, Howard S. *Art Worlds.* Berkeley, CA: University of California Press, 1982.

Becker, Howard S. *Outsiders.* New York: Free Press, 1991.

Becker, Howard S., et al. *Boys in White.* Chicago, IL: University of Chicago Press, 1961.

Beckford, James A. *Cult Controversies.* London: Tavistock, 1985.

Begley, Sharon. "Not Just a Pretty Face." *Newsweek* (November 1, 1993):63–67.

Begley, Sharon. "The 3–Million-Year-Old Man." *Newsweek* (April 11, 1994):84.

Begley, Sharon. "The Science Wars." *Newsweek,* (April 21, 1997):54–57.

Bell, Daniel. "Equality and Equity." *The Seminar on Technology and Culture at MIT.* Boston, MA: Massachusetts Institute of Technology, 1976.

Bell, Daniel. *The Coming of Post-Industrial Society.* New York: Basic Books, 1999.

Bellah, Robert N. "Civil Religion in America." *Daedalus* 96 (Winter 1967):1–21.

Bellah, Robert N. *The Broken Covenant,* 2nd ed. Chicago, IL: University of Chicago Press, 1992.

Bellah, Robert N., and Phillip E. Hammond. *Varieties of Civil Religion.* New York: Harper and Row, 1980.

Bellah, Robert N., et al. *The Good Society.* New York: Knopf, 1991.

Belton, Beth. "Despite Humming Economy, Workers Sweat Job Security." *USA Today* (March 2, 1999):A1.

Bendix, Reinhard. *Max Weber.* Garden City, NY: Doubleday, 1962.

Bennett, William J. "American Education: Making It Work." *Chronicle of Higher Education* 34 (May 4, 1988):29–41.

Bennis, Warren G. "Beyond Bureaucracy." *Transaction* 2 (July/August 1965):31–35.

Bennis, Warren G. "Response to Shariff: Beyond Bureaucracy Baiting." *Social Science Quarterly* 60 (June 1979):20–24.

Benokraitis, Nijole V. *Subtle Sexism.* Thousand Oaks, CA: Sage, 2004.

Benokraitis, Nijole V. *Marriages and Families: Changes, Choices and Constraints,* 7th ed. Upper Saddle River, NJ: Prentice Hall, 2010.

Benowitz, June Melby, and Yvonne M. Vowels. *Encyclopedia of American Women and Religion.* Santa Barbara, CA: ABC-CLIO Inc, 1998.

Bensman, Joseph, and Israel Gerver. "Crime and Punishment in the Factory: The Function of Deviancy in Maintaining the Social System." *American Sociological Review* 28 (August 1963):588–598.

Berends, Mark. (Ed.). *Charter School Outcomes*. United Kingdom: Taylor & Francis, Inc, 2007.

Berger, Bennett M., Bruce Hacket, and R. Mervyn Millar. "The Communal Family." *The Family Coordinator* 21 (October 1972):419–427.

Berger, Joseph, M. Hamit Fisek, Cecilia L. Ridgeway, and Robert Z. Norman. "The Legitimization and Delegitimization of Power and Prestige Orders." *American Sociological Review* 63 (June 1998):379–405.

Berger, Peter L. *Invitation to Sociology*. New York: Anchor Books, 1963.

Berger, Peter L. *The Sacred Canopy: Elements of a Sociological Theory of Religion*. New York: Doubleday, 1990.

Berger, Peter L., and Anton Zijderveld. *In Praise of Doubt*. New York: HarperCollins Publishers, 2009.

Berger, Peter L., and Anton Zijderveld. *In Praise of Doubt*. New York: HarperOne, 2009.

Berger, Peter L., and Thomas Luckmann. *The Social Construction of Reality*. Garden City, NY: Anchor Books, 1967.

Berk, Richard A. *Collective Behavior*. Dubuque, IA: William C. Brown, 1974.

Berle, Adolph A. Jr., and Gardiner C. Means. *The Modern Corporation and Private Property*. New York: Harcourt Brace Jovanovich, 1968.

Bernard, Thomas J. "Structure and Control: Reconsidering Hirschi's Concept of Commitment." *Justice Quarterly* 4 (1987):409–424.

Bernhardt, Annette D., et al. *Divergent Paths: Economic Mobility in the New American Labor Market*. New York: Russell Sage Foundation, 2001.

Bernstein, Aaron. "Inequality: How the Gap Between the Rich and Poor Hurts the Economy." *BusinessWeek*, August 15, 1994:78–83.

Berry, Brian J. L. "Internal Structure of the City." *Law and Contemporary Problems* 30 (Winter 1965):111–119.

Berry, Brian J. L., and John D. Kasarda. *Contemporary Urban Ecology*. New York: Macmillan, 1977.

Bertrand, Marianne, and Sendhil Mullainathan. "Are Emily and Brendan More Employable than Lakisha and Jamal? A Field Experiment on Labor Market Discrimination." Chicago, IL: University of Chicago Graduate School of Business, Working Paper (November 18, 2002):3–28.

Best, Joel. *Damned Lies and Statistics*. Berkeley, CA: University of California Press, 2001.

Best, Joel. *More Damned Lies and Statistics*. Berkeley, CA: University of California Press, 2004.

Best, Joel. *Stat-Spotting*. Berkeley, CA: University of California Press, 2008.

Bhalla, Surjit. *Imagine There's No Country: Poverty, Inequality, and Growth in the Era of Globalization*. Washington, DC: Institute for International Economics, 2002.

Bhargava, Deepak, and Joan Kuriansky. "Really Out of Line." *Washington Post* (September 15, 2002):B2.

Bia, Javier. "World's Hunger 'Close to One Billion.'" *Financial Times* (December 9, 2008).

Bianchi, Suzanne M. "America's Children: Mixed Prospects." *Population Bulletin* 45 (June 1990):3–41.

Bianchi, Suzanne M., and Daphne Spain. *Women, Work, and Family in America*. Washington, DC: Population Reference Bureau, 1996.

Bianchi, Suzanne M., and Lynne M. Casper. "American Families." *Population Bulletin* 55 (December 2000):1–44.

Bickman, Leonard, and Debra J. Rog. (Eds.). *Handbook of Applied Social Research Methods*. Thousand Oaks, CA: Sage, 1997.

Bielby, William T., and Denise D. Bielby. "Family Ties: Balancing Commitments to Work and Family in Dual Earner Households." *American Sociological Review* 54 (October 1989):776–789.

Bierstedt, Robert. "Sociology and General Education." In Charles H. Page (Ed.), *Sociology and Contemporary Education*. New York: Random House, 1963, pp. 40–55.

Bigler, Rebecca, and Lynn Liber. "The Role of Attitudes and Interventions in Gender-Schematic Processing." *Child Development* 61 (1990):1440–1452.

Billson, Janet Mancini, and Bettina Huber. *Embarking Upon a Career with an Undergraduate Degree in Sociology*. Washington, DC: American Sociological Association, 1993.

Bingham, Richard D., and William M. Bowen. (Eds.). *Beyond Edge Cities*. New York: Garland Publishing, 1997.

Birnbaum, Jeffrey. *The Money Men: The Real Story of Political Power in the USA*. New York: Crown, 2000.

Birren, James E., et al. *Handbook of the Psychology of Aging*, 6th ed. Amsterdam, Netherlands: Elsevier, 2005.

Black, Clifford. "Clinical Sociology and Criminal Justice Professions." *Free Inquiry in Creative Sociology* 12 (1984):117–120.

Black, Thomas R. *Doing Quantitative Research in the Social Sciences*. Thousand Oaks, CA: Sage, 2001.

Blackwell, John Reid. "Chance of Higher Cigarette Tax Dims." *Richmond Times Dispatch* (January 23, 2003).

"Black/White Relations in the United States." *The Gallup Poll Social Audit*. Princeton, NJ: The Gallup Organization, 1997.

Blaikie, Norman. *Designing Social Research*, 2nd ed. Cambridge, UK: Polity Brooks, 2009.

Blank, Rebecca M., and Ron Haskins. *The New World of Welfare*. Washington, DC: Brookings Institution Press, 2001.

Blank, Rolf K., Roger E. LeVine, and Lauri Steel. "After 15 Years: Magnet Schools in Urban Education." In Bruce Fuller and Richard F. Elmore (Eds.), *Who Wins, Who Loses?* New York: Teachers College Press, 1996, pp. 154–172.

Blau, Peter M. *Exchange and Power in Social Life*. New Brunswick, NJ: Transaction Books, 1986.

Blau, Peter M., and Marshall W. Meyer. *Bureaucracy in Modern Society*, 3rd ed. New York: Random House, 1987.

Blau, Peter M., and Otis Dudley Duncan. *The American Occupational Structure*. New York: Wiley, 1967.

Blau, Peter M., and W. Richard Scott. *Formal Organizations*. London: Routledge and Kegan Paul, 1982.

Blauner, Robert. "Internal Colonialism and Ghetto Revolt." *Social Problems* 16 (Spring 1969):393–408.

Blauner, Robert. *Racial Oppression in America*. New York: Harper and Row, 1972.

Blee, Kathleen M., and Dwight B. Billings. *The Road to Poverty: The Making of Wealth and Hardship in Appalachia*. Cambridge, UK: Cambridge University Press, 1999.

Bloom, Allan. *The Closing of the American Mind*. New York: Simon & Schuster, 1987.

Blum, Deborah. *Love at Goon Park: Harry Harlow and the Science of Affection*. Cambridge, MA: Perseus Publishing, 2002.

Blum, Justin, and Jay Mathews. "Quality Uneven, Despite Popularity." *Washington Post* (June 19, 2003):A1, A12, A13.

Blumer, Herbert. "Collective Behavior." In Alfred M. Lee (Ed.), *Principles of Sociology*, 3rd ed. New York: Barnes and Noble, 1969a, pp. 65–121.

Blumer, Herbert. *Symbolic Interactionism*. Englewood Cliffs, NJ: Prentice Hall, 1969b.

Bodenheimer, Thomas S., and Kevin Grumbach. *Understanding Health Policy*, 5th ed. New York: McGraw-Hill, 2009.

Bonacich, Edna. "Advanced Capitalism and Black/White Race Relations in the United States: A Split Labor Market Interpretation." *American Sociological Review* 41 (February 1976):34–51.

Bonilla-Silva, Eduardo. *Racism Without Racists*. Lanham, MD: Rowman and Littlefield, 2007.

Boorstein, Michelle. "Americans' Bias Against Jews, Muslims Linked, Poll Says." *Washington Post* (January 21, 2010):A03.

Booth, Alan, and Ann C. Crouter. (Eds.). *Men in Families: When Do They Get Involved? What Difference Does It Make?* Mahwah, NJ: Erlbaum, 1998.

Borenstein, Seth, and Jordan Robertson. "BMI's Watson Wins on Jeopardy!—What Can We Do?" *Associated Press* (February 16, 2011).

Boroditsky, Lera. "Does Language Shape Thought? Mandarin and English Speakers' Conceptions of Time." *Cognitive Psychology* 43 (2001):1–22.

Boroughs, Don L. "Winter of Discontent." *U.S. News & World Report* (January 22, 1996):47–54.

Bottomore, Tom B. *Karl Marx*. New York: McGraw-Hill, 1963.

Bottomore, Tom B. *Political Sociology*, 2nd ed. Minneapolis, MN: University of Minnesota Press, 1993.

Bouvier, Leon F., and Carol J. De Vita. "The Baby Boom—Entering Midlife." *Population Bulletin* 46 (November 1991):1–35.

Bowen, William G., and Derek Bok. *The Shape of the River: Long-Term Consequences of Considering Race in College and University Admissions*. Princeton, NJ: Princeton University Press, 2000.

Bowker, John. *World Religions*. New York: DK Publishing, Inc, 2009.

Bowles, Samuel, and Herbert Gintis. *Schooling in Capitalist America*. New York: Basic Books, 1976.

Boyles, Deron R. *Schools or Markets? Commercialism, Privatization, and Schoolbusiness Partnerships*. United Kingdom: Taylor & Francis, Inc, 2004.

Brafman, Ori, and Rod A. Beckstrom. *Starfish and the Spider*. New York: Penguin Group, 2008.

Brajuha, Mario, and Lyle Hallowell. "Legal Intrusion and the Politics of Fieldwork: The Impact of the Brajuha Case." *Urban Life* 14 (January 1986):454–478.

Brauer, Jerald C. (Ed.). *Religion and the American Revolution*. Philadelphia, PA: Fortress Press, 1976.

Breed, Allen G. "Minority Vote Moves Center Stage." *Associated Press* (January 12, 2008).

Bremner, Jason, et al. "World Population Highlights: Key Findings from PRP's 2010 World Population Data Sheet." *Population Bulletin* 65 (July 2010):1–12.

Breneman, David W., Brian Pusser., and Sarah E. Turner. (Eds.). *Earnings from Learning: The Rise of For-Profit Universities*. Albany, NY: State University of New York Press, 2006.

Brint, Steven, and Steve Brint. *Schools and Societies*. Thousand Oaks, CA: Pine Forge Press, 1998.

Brinton, Crane. *The Anatomy of Revolution*. New York: Knopf, 1990.

Brizendine, Louann. *The Female Brain*. New York: Crown Publishing Group, 2007.

Brizendine, Louann. *The Male Brain*. New York: Crown Publishing Group, 2010.

Brockerhoff, Martin P. "An Urbanizing World." *Population Bulletin* 55 (September 2000):1–44.

Brody, Jane E. "Personal Health; TV's Toll on Young Minds and Bodies." *New York Times* (August 3, 2004).

Brody, William. "Building a New Kind of Academy." *Planning for Higher Education* 25 (Summer 1997):72–74.

Bromley, David G. (Ed.). *The Politics of Religious Apostasy: The Role of Apostates in the Transformation of Religious Movements*. Westport, CT: Praeger, 1998.

Bromley, David G., and Anson D. Shupe Jr. *New Christian Politics*. Macon, GA: Mercer University Press, 1984.

Bronfenbrenner, Urie. *Two Worlds of Childhood*. New York: Russell Sage Foundation, 1970.

Brouilette, John R. "The Liberalizing Effect of Taking Introductory Sociology." *Teaching Sociology* 12 (January 1985):131–148.

Brown, David. "Scientists Create Cell Based on Man-Made Genetic." *Washington Post* (May 21, 2010):A3.

Brown, Elizabeth. *"Lobbying FAQ: What Is Permissible? Out of Bounds? Punishable?"* Washington, DC: The Center for Public Integrity (January 18, 2006).

Brown, Lester R. *State of the World 1996*. New York: Norton, 1996.

Brown, Michael K. *Race, Money, and the American Welfare State*. Ithaca, NY: Cornell University Press, 1999.

Brown, S. "Family Structure and Child Well-Being. The Significance of Parental Cohabitation." *Journal of Marriage and Family 66* (2204), 351–367.

Browne, Beverly A. "Gender Stereotypes in Advertising on Children's Television in the 1990s: A Cross-National Analysis." *Journal of Advertising* 27 (Spring 1998):83–96.

Brownlee, Shannon. "Overdose." *The Atlantic* (December 2007):36–38.

Brubaker, T. H. "Family in Later Life: A Burgeoning Research Area." In A. Booth (Ed.), *Contemporary Families*. Minneapolis, MN: National Council on Family Relations, 1991, pp. 226–248.

Bruce, Steve. *God Is Dead: Secularization in the West*. Malden, MA: Blackwell, 2002.

Bruce, Steve. *Fundamentalism*, 2nd ed. New York: Polity Books, 2007.

Bruggeman, Jereen. *Social Networks: An Introduction*. New York: Routledge, 2008.

Bruner, Jerome. "Schooling Children in a Nasty Climate." *Psychology Today* (January 1982):57–63.

Brunner, H. G., M. Nelsen, X. O. Breakefield, H. H. Ropers, and B. A. van Oost. "Abnormal Behavior Associated with a Point Mutation in the Structural Gene for Monoamine Oxidase A." *Science* 262 (October 22, 1993):578–580.

Brunvand, Jan Harold. "Urban Legends: Folklore for Today." *Psychology Today* 14 (June 1980):50ff.

Brunvand, Jan Harold. *Too Good to Be True: The Colossal Book of Urban Legends*. New York: Norton, 2001.

Brunvand, Jan Harold. *Encyclopedia of Urban Legends*. New York: Norton, 2002.

Buckley, Jack, and Mark Schneider. *Charter Schools*. Princeton, NJ: Princeton University Press, 2009.

Buckley, Stephen. "Shrugging Off the Burden of a Brainy Image." *Washington Post* (June 17, 1991):D1, D6.

Budrys, Grace. *Our Unsystematic Health Care System*. Lanham, MD: Rowman & Littlefield, 2001.

Buechler, Steven M. *Social Movements in Advanced Capitalism*. New York: Oxford University Press, 2000.

Bumiller, Elisabeth. "For Female Marines, Tea Comes with Bullets." *New York Times* (October 2, 2010).

Bunzel, John H. (Ed.). *Challenge to American Schools*. New York: Oxford University Press, 1985.

Burawoy, Michael. "For Public Sociology." *American Sociological Review* 70 (February 2005):4–28.

Burawoy, Michael. *The Extended Case Method*. Berkeley, CA: University of California Press, 2009.

Burgess, Ernest W. "The Growth of the City." In Robert E Park, Ernest W. Burgess, and Robert D. McKenzie (Eds.), *The City*. Chicago, IL: University of Chicago Press, 1925, pp. 47–62.

Burgess, J. K. "Widowers." In C. S. Chilman, E. W. Nunnally, and F. M. Cox (Eds.), *Variant Family Forms*. Beverly Hills, CA: Sage, 1988, pp. 150–164.

Burke, Ronald, and Cary Cooper. (Eds.). *The Organization in Crisis: Downsizing, Restructuring and Privatization*. Cambridge, MA: Blackwell, 2000.

Burn, Shawn Meghan. *Women Across Cultures*, 3rd ed. New York: McGraw-Hill, 2011.

Burns, T., and G. M. Stalker. *The Management of Innovation*, 2nd ed. London: Tavistock, 1966.

Burros, Marian. "Even Women at the Top Still Have Floors to Do." *New York Times* (May 31, 1993):A1, A11.

Burstein, Paul. "Legal Mobilization as a Social Movement Tactic: The Struggle for Equal Employment Opportunity." *American Journal of Sociology* 96 (March 1991):1201–1225.

Buss, David M. "The Strategies of Human Mating: People Worldwide Are Attracted to the Same Qualities in the Opposite Sex." *American Scientist* 82 (May 1994a):238–249.

Buss, David M. *The Evolution of Desire: Strategies of Human Mating.* New York: Basic Books, 1994b.

Buss, David M. "Psychological Sex Differences: Origins Through Sexual Selection." *The American Psychologist* 50 (March 1995):164.

Buss, David M., Neil M. Malamuth, and Barbara A. Winstead. "Sex, Power, Conflict: Evolutionary and Feminist Perspectives." *Contemporary Psychology* 43 (April 1998).

Butler, Robert N. *Why Survive?* New York: Harper and Row, 1975.

Butler, Robert N. "Dispelling Ageism: The Cross-Cutting Intervention." *Annals of the American Academy of Political and Social Science* 503 (1989):138–148.

Calasanti, Toni M. "Participation in a Dual Economy and Adjustment to Retirement." *International Journal of Aging and Human Development* 26 (1988):13–27.

Calasanti, Toni M., and Kathleen F. Slevin. *Gender, Social Inequalities, and Aging.* Walnut Creek, CA: AltaMira Press, 2001.

Calavita, Kitty, Henry N. Pontell, and Robert H. Tillman. *Big Money Crime.* Berkeley, CA: University of California Press, 1999.

Callan, Victor J. "The Voluntarily Childless and Their Perceptions of Parenthood and Childlessness." *Journal of Comparative Family Studies* 14 (Spring 1983):87–96.

Camarota, Steven A. "Immigrants in the United States—2000: A Snapshot of America's Foreign-Born Population." *Backgrounder.* Washington, DC: Center for Immigration Studies, 2001.

Camic, Charles. *Reclaiming the Sociological Classics.* Malden, MA: Blackwell, 1998.

Campbell, Kurt M., et al. "The Age of Consequences: The Foreign Policy and National Security Implications of Global Climate Change." New York: Center for Strategic and International Studies, 2007.

Campo-Flores, Adrian. "Giving Protest a Chance." *Newsweek* (February 3, 2003):28.

Canary, Daniel J., et al. "Diversity—Sex and Gender Differences in Personal Relationships." *Contemporary Psychology* 43(1998):764.

Cancio, A. Silvia, T. David Evans, and David J. Maume Jr. "Reconsidering the Declining Significance of Race: Racial Differences in Early Career Wages." *American Sociological Review* 61 (August 1996):541–556.

Cantril, Hadley. *The Invasion from Mars.* Princeton, NJ: Princeton University Press, 1982.

Caplan, Gerald. "No Lessons Learned 12 Years After the Rwandan Genocide." *Pombazuka News* (April 14, 2006). http://pombazuka.org/en/category/features/33432

Caplan, Nathan, Marcella H. Choy, and John K. Whitmore. "Indochinese Refugee Families and Academic Achievement." *Scientific American* 266 (February 1992):36–42.

Caplow, Theodore. *American Social Trends.* New York: Harcourt Brace Jovanovich, 1991.

Caplow, Theodore, Howard M. Bahr, and Bruce A. Chadwick. *All Faithful People.* Minneapolis, MN: University of Minnesota Press, 1983.

Caplow, Theodore, Howard M. Bahr, Bruce A. Chadwick, Rueben Hill, and Margaret Holmes Williamson. *Middletown Families.* Minneapolis, MN: University of Minnesota Press, 1982.

Carey, Benedict. "Study Quantifies Orphanage Link to I.Q." *New York Times* (December 2, 2007).

Carnoy, Martin. *The Politics and Economics of Race in America.* Cambridge, UK: Cambridge University Press, 1994.

Carpenter, C., and G. J. Gates. "Gay and Lesbian Partnership: Evidence from California." *Demography* 45 (2008):573–590.

Carr, Deborah. "Golden Years? Poverty Among Older Americans." *Contexts* 9 (Winter 2010):62–63.

Carroll, Joseph. "Hispanics' Views on Immigration Unchanged from Last Year." *Gallup News Service* (2007).

Carter, Bill, and Jacques Steinberg. "Off the Air: The Light Goes Out for Don Imus." *New York Times* (April 13, 2007).

Carter, Cynthia, and Kay C. Weaver. *Violence and the Media.* Philadelphia, PA: Taylor and Francis, 2003.

Cashion, Barbara G. "Female-Headed Families: Effects on Children and Clinical Implications." *Journal of Marital and Family Therapy* 8 (April 1982):77–85.

Casler, Lawrence. "The Effects of Extra Tactile Stimulation on a Group of Institutionalized Infants." *Genetic Psychology Monographs* 71 (1965):137–175.

Cassirer, Ernst. *The Philosophy of the Enlightenment.* Princeton, NJ: Princeton University Press, 1951.

Castro, Janice. "Disposable Workers." *Time* (March 15, 1993):47.

Cavanaugh, John C., and Fredda Blanchard-Fields. *Adult Development and Aging,* 4th ed. Pacific Grove, CA: Duxbury, 2001.

Cavanaugh, Stephanie. "The Trophy Kitchen." *Washington Post* (June 10, 1999):T14–T15.

Cavender, Gary, and Mark Fishman. (Eds.). *Entertaining Crime.* Hawthorne, NY: Aldine de Gruyter, 1998.

Censky, Annalyn. "GE: 7000 Tax Returns, $0 U.S. Tax Bill." CNNMoney.com. (2010). http://money.cnn.com/fdcp?1271507499871

"Census Will Not Record Same-Sex Marriages." Associated Press (July 18, 2008). http://query.nytimes.com/gst/fullpage.html?res=9D05EFDF1E3BF93BA25754COA96E9C8

Center for Voting and Democracy. "International Voter Turnout, 1991–2000." (2002). Available online at www.fairvote.org/turnout/intturnout.htm

Centers, Richard. *The Psychology of Social Classes.* New Haven, CT: Yale University Press, 1949.

Chaddock, Gail Russell. "Baby Boomers Face Retirement Squeeze." *Christian Science Monitor* (February 27, 2004).

Chafetz, Janet Saltzman. *Sex and Advantage.* Totowa, NJ: Rowman & Allanheld, 1984.

Chafetz, Janet Saltzman. *Gender Equity.* Newbury Park, CA: Sage, 1990.

Chagnon, Napoleon A. *Yanomamö,* 5th ed. Fort Worth, TX: Harcourt Brace College Publishers, 1997.

Chamberlain, Gary. "Metal Wars." *Design News* (October 4, 1999):115.

Chambliss, William J. "The Saints and the Roughnecks." *Society* 11 (November/December 1973):24–31.

Chambliss, William J., and Robert Seidman. *Law, Order, and Power,* 2nd ed. Reading, MA: Vantage, 1982.

Chandbasekaran, Rajiv. "Microsoft Trial Ends After 8 Months." *Washington Post* (June 25, 1999):A1, A20.

Chandler, Alfred D. Jr., and Bruce Mazlish. (Eds.). *Leviathans: Multinational Corporations and the New Global History.* Cambridge, UK: Cambridge University Press, 2005.

Chandra, Anita, et al. "Does Watching Sex on Television Predict Teen Pregnancy? Findings from a National Longitudinal Survey of Youth." *Pediatrics* 122 (November 2008):1047–1054.

Chang, Kenneth. "Panel Says Bell Labs Scientist Faked Discoveries in Physics." *New York Times* (September 26, 2002):A1, A20.

Changing Public Attitudes Toward the Criminal Justice System. Open Society Institute. Criminal Justice Initiative, 2002.

Charon, Joel M. *Symbolic Interactionism*, 10th ed. Boston, MA: Prentice-Hall, 2010.

Chase-Dunn, Christopher. *Global Formation: Structures of the World Economy.* Lanham, MD: Rowman & Littlefield, 1999.

"Chasing the Same Dream, Climbing Different Ladders: Economic Mobility in the United States and Canada." The Pew Charitable Trusts. Economic Mobility Project, 2010.

Chaves, Mark. "Abiding Faith." *Contexts* 1 (Summer 2002):19–26.

Chen, Grace. "What Is a Magnet School?" Public School Review (December 4, 2007). http://www.publicschoolreview.com/articles/2

Cherlin, Andrew J. "A 'Quieting' of Change." *Contexts* 1 (Spring 2002):67–68.

Cherlin, Andrew J. "Demographic Trends in the United States: A Review of Research in the 2000s." *Journal of Marriage and Family* 72 (June 2010):403–439.

Chesler, Ellen. "New Options, New Politics." *The American Prospect* (Fall 2001):12–14.

Children's Defense Fund. *The State of America's Children–1991.* Washington, DC: Children's Defense Fund, 1991.

Chirot, Daniel. *How Societies Change.* Thousand Oaks, CA: Pine Forge Press, 1994.

Chirot, Daniel, and Martin E. P. Seligman. (Eds.). *Ethnopolitical Warfare: Causes, Consequences, and Political Solutions.* Washington, DC: American Psychological Association, 2001.

Choi, N. G. "Correlates of the Economic Status of Widowed and Divorced Elderly Men." *Journal of Family Issues* 12 (March 1992):38–54.

Choldin, Harvey M., and Claudine Hanson. "Subcommunity and Change in a Changing Metropolis." *Sociological Quarterly* 22 (Autumn 1981):549–564.

"Choice Without Equity: Charter School Segregation and Need for Civil Rights Standards." UCLA, The Civil Rights Project, (February 2010). http://civilrightsproject.ucla.edu/research/k-12-education/integration-and-diversity/choice-wit...

Chou, Rosalind, and Joe R. Feagin. *The Myth of the Model Minority.* Boulder, CO: Paradigm Publishers, 2008.

Christenson, James A., and Ronald C. Wimberley. "Who Is Civil Religious?" *Sociological Analysis* 39 (Spring 1978):77–83.

Christie, Nils. *Crime Control as Industry*, 3rd ed. London: Routledge, 2000.

Chu, Henry. "From Lowest Caste to High Office in India." *Los Angeles Times* (March 30, 2008).

Chua, Amy. *Day of Empire.* New York: Doubleday, 2007.

Chua, Amy. *World on Fire: How Exporting Free Market Democracy Breeds Ethnic Hatred and Global Instability.* New York: Knopf Publishing, 2004.

Cicourel, Aaron, and John Kitsuse. *The Educational Decision Makers.* New York: Bobbs-Merrill, 1963.

Citizens for Tax Justice. "Year-by-Year Analysis of the Bush Tax Cuts Shows Growing Tilt to the Very Rich." (2002). Available online at www.ctj.org/html/gwb0602.htm

Citizens for Tax Justice. "The Bush Tax Cuts: The Latest CTJ Data." (March 2007). Available online at www.ctj.org/pdf/gwbdata.pdf

Clark, Charles S. "Cults in America." *CQ Researcher* 3 (May 7, 1993):385–408.

Clark, Lee. "Panic: Myth or Reality." *Contexts* 1 (Fall 2002):21–26.

Clarke, Peter. (Ed.). *The Oxford Handbook of the Sociology of Religion.* New York: Oxford University Press, 2009.

Clark-Flory, Tracy. "The New Pornographers." *Salon* (February 20, 2009). http://www.salon.com/mwt/feature/2009/02/20/sexting_teens/print.html

New York Times Correspondents. *Class Matters.* New York: Times Books, 2005.

Clausen, John A. *The Life Course.* Englewood Cliffs, NJ: Prentice Hall, 1986.

Clayton, Obie Jr. (Ed.). *An American Dilemma Revisited.* New York: Russell Sage Foundation, 1996.

Clayton, Richard R., and James W. Gladden. "The Five Dimensions of Religiosity: Toward Demythologizing a Sacred Artifact." *Journal for the Scientific Study of Religion* 13 (June 1974):135–143.

Clemens, Elisabeth S. *The People's Lobby.* Chicago, IL: University of Chicago Press, 1997.

"Closing the Gap." *The Economist* (September 2, 1995):74.

Cloward, Richard A., and Lloyd E. Ohlin. *Delinquency and Opportunity.* London: Routledge, 1998.

Coakley, Jay J. (Ed.). *Sports in Society*, 10th ed. Boston, MA: Irwin/McGraw-Hill, 2009.

Cobas, Jose A., Jorge Duany, and Joe R. Feagin. (Eds.). *How the United States Racializes Latinos.* Boulder, CO: Paradigm Publishers, 2009.

Cockburn, Alexander. "Beat the Devil." *The Nation* (January 17, 1994):42–43.

Cockburn, C. "The Relations of Technology." In R. Crompton and M. Mann (Eds.), *Gender and Stratification.* Cambridge, UK: Polity, 1986.

Cockerham, Geoffrey, and William G. Cockerham. *Health and Globalization.* Malden, MA: Polity Press, 2010.

Cohen, Adam, and Cathy Booth Thomas. "Inside a Layoff." *Time* (April 16, 2001):38–40.

Cohen, Adam. "A Curse of Cliques." *Time* (May 3, 1999):44.

Cohen, Albert K. *Delinquent Boys.* New York: Free Press, 1977.

Cohen, David, and Marvin Lazerson. "Education and the Corporate Order." *Socialist Revolution* 2 (March/April 1972):47–72.

Cohen, Jere. *Protestantism and Capitalism: The Mechanisms of Influence.* Hawthorne, NY: Aldine de Gruyter, 2002.

Coleman, James S. *Equal Educational Opportunity.* Cambridge, MA: Harvard University Press, 1969.

Coleman, James S., et al. "Achievement and Segregation in Secondary Schools: A Further Look at Public and Private School Differences." *Sociology of Education* 55 (April/July 1982a):162–182.

Coleman, James S., et al. "Cognitive Outcomes in Public and Private Schools." *Sociology of Education* 55 (April/July 1982b):65–76.

Coleman, James S., et al. *Equality of Educational Opportunity.* Washington, DC: U.S. Government Printing Office, 1966.

Coleman, James S., Sally B. Kilgore, and Thomas Hoffer. "Public and Private Schools." *Society* 19 (January/February 1982):4–9.

Coleman, James S., Thomas Hoffer, and Sally B. Kilgore. "Questions and Answers: Our Response." *Harvard Educational Review* 51 (November 1981):526–545.

Coleman, James W. "Toward an Integrated Theory of White-Collar Crime." *American Journal of Sociology* 93 (September 1987):406–439.

Coleman, James W. *The Criminal Elite: The Sociology of White Collar Crime.* New York: St. Martin's Press, 1989.

Coleman, James W. *The Criminal Elite*, 4th ed. New York: St. Martin's Press, 1997.

"Collateral Costs: Incarceration's Effect on Economic Mobility." The Pew Charitable Trusts, Economic Mobility Project, 2010.

College Board. *Trends in College Pricing 2007.* New York: College Entrance Examination Board, 2007.

Collier, Theresa J. "The Stigma of Mental Illness." *Newsweek* (April 26, 1993):16.

Collins, Chuck, and Felice Yeskel. *Economic Apartheid in America: A Primer on Economic Inequality and Insecurity*, 2nd ed. New York: New Press, 2005.

Collins, Gail. *When Everything Changed: The Amazing Journey of American Women from 1960 to the Present*. United Kingdom: Little, Brown & Company, 2010.

Collins, John J. *The Cult Experience*. New York: Charles C. Thomas, 1991.

Collins, Randall. "Functional and Conflict Theories of Educational Stratification." *American Sociological Review* 36 (December 1971):1002–1019.

Collins, Randall. *Conflict Sociology*. New York: Academic Press, 1975.

Collins, Randall. *The Credential Society: An Historical Sociology of Education*. New York: Academic Press, 1979.

Collins, Randall. *Four Sociological Traditions*. New York: Oxford University Press, 1994.

Collins, Randall. "Conflict Theory of Educational Stratification." In Jeanne H. Ballantine and Joan Z. Spade (Eds.), *Schools and Society: A Sociological Approach to Education*. Belmont, CA: Wadsworth/Thomson, 2007.

Colombotos, John, and Corinne Kirchner. *Physicians and Social Change*. New York: Oxford University Press, 1986.

Comfort, Alex. "Age Prejudice in America." *Social Policy* 17 (November/December 1976):3–8.

Conason, Joe. *It Can Happen Here*. New York: St. Martin's Press, 2008.

"Confronting the New Faces of Hate: Hate Crimes in America." Washington, DC: The Leadership Conference, 2009.

Cook, Ken. "Government's Continued Bailout of Corporate Agriculture." Environmental Working Group, (2010). http://www.ewg.org/farm/subsidies

Cooley, Charles Horton. *Human Nature and the Social Order*. New York: Scribner's, 1902.

Cooley, Charles Horton, and Hans-Joachim Schubert. *On Self and Social Organization*. Chicago, IL: University of Chicago Press, 1998.

Coon, Dennis, and John O. Mitterer. *Introduction to Psychology*, 3rd ed. Belmont, CA: Wadsworth, 2008.

Corbett, Christianne, Catherine Hill, and Andresse St. Rose. "Where the Girls Are: The Facts About Gender Equity in Education." Washington, DC: AAUW Educational Foundation, 2008.

Corwin, Ronald G., and E. Joseph Schneider. *The School Choice Hoax*. Lanham, MD: Rowman & Littlefield Education, 2007.

Cose, Ellis. *The Rage of the Privileged Class*. New York: Harper-Collins, 1995.

Cose, Ellis. "The Black Gender Gap." *Newsweek* (March 3, 2003):48–51.

Coser, Lewis A. *The Functions of Social Conflict*. London: Routledge, 1998.

Cowen, Tyler. "How Immigrants Create More Jobs." *New York Times* (October 30, 2010).

Cowley, Geoffrey, and Anne Underwood. "Surgeon, Drop That Scalpel." *Newsweek* (February 1998, Winter 1997–1998, Special Edition):77–78.

Cox, Frank D. *Human Intimacy*, 10th ed. Belmont, CA: Wadsworth, 2006.

Cox, Harvey. *Turning East: The Promise and Peril of the New Orientalism*. New York: Simon & Schuster, 1977.

Cox, Harvey. *Religion in the Secular City*. New York: Simon & Schuster, 1992.

Cox, Harvey. *Fire from Heaven*. London: Cassell, 1996.

Cozic, Charles P. (Ed.). *The Militia Movement*. San Diego, CA: Greenhaven Press, 1997.

Cozzillio, Michael J. *Sports and Inequality*. Durham, NC: Carolina Academic Press, 2005.

Craig, Steve. *Men, Masculinity and the Media*. Thousand Oaks, CA: Sage, 1992.

Crain, Robert L. "School Integration and Occupational Achievement of Negroes." *American Journal of Sociology* 75 (January 1970):593–606.

Crain, Robert L., and Carol S. Weisman. *Discrimination, Personality and Achievements*. New York: Seminar Press, 1972.

Crane, Diana. *Fashion and Its Social Agendas: Class, Gender, and Identity in Clothing*. Chicago, IL: University of Chicago Press, 2001.

Creekmore, C. R. "Cities Won't Drive You Crazy." *Psychology Today* (January 1985):46–53.

Cress, Daniel M., and David A. Snow. "Mobilization at the Margins: Resources, Benefactors, and the Viability of Homeless Social Movement Organizations." *American Sociological Review* 61 (December 1996):1089–1109.

Crewdson, John. "Fraud in Breast Cancer Study." *Chicago Tribune* (March 13, 1994):A1.

Crime in the United States: Preliminary Annual Uniform Crime Report. Washington, DC: Federal Bureau of Investigation, December 2010.

Crosby, F. E. *Juggling*. New York: Free Press, 1993.

Crosby, John F. *Reply to Myth: Perspectives on Intimacy*. New York: Wiley, 1985.

Crossley, Nick. *Making Sense of Social Movements*. Buckingham, UK: Open University Press, 2002.

Crow, Barbara A. (Ed.). *Radical Feminism: A Documentary Reader*. New York: New York University Press, 1998.

Cullen, John B., and Shelley M. Novick. "The Davis-Moore Theory of Stratification: A Further Examination and Extension." *American Journal of Sociology* 84 (May 1979):1424–1437.

"Cult Killings Exceed Jonestown Toll." *Los Angeles Times* (April 1, 2000):A14.

Cummings, Scott. "White Ethnics, Racial Prejudice, and Labor Market Segmentation." *American Journal of Sociology* 95 (January 1980):938–950.

Curran, Daniel J., and Claire M. Renzetti. *Social Problems: Society in Crisis*, 6th ed. Upper Saddle River, NJ: Prentice Hall, 2000.

Curtiss, Susan. *Genie*. New York: Academic Press, 1977.

Cuzzort, R. P., and E. W. King. *Humanity and Modern Social Thought*, 2nd ed. Hinsdale, IL: Dryden Press, 1976.

"Cybercrime." Bureau of Justice Statistics (2005). http://bys.ojp.usdoj.gov/index. cfm?ty=tp&tid

Cyert, Richard M., and James G. March. *A Behavioral Theory of the Firm*. Englewood Cliffs, NJ: Prentice Hall, 1963.

Dahl, Robert. *Who Governs?* 2nd ed. New Haven, CT: Yale University Press, 2005.

Dahrendorf, Ralf. "Out of Utopia: Toward a Reorientation of Sociological Analysis." *American Journal of Sociology* 64 (September 1958a):115–127.

Dahrendorf, Ralf. "Toward a Theory of Social Conflict." *Journal of Conflict Resolution* 2 (June 1958b):170–183.

Dahrendorf, Ralf. *Class and Class Conflict in Industrial Society*. Stanford, CA: Stanford University Press, 1959.

Daly, Martin, and Margo Wilson. "Crime and Conflict: Homicide in Evolutionary Psychological Perspective." *Crime and Justice* 22 (1997):51–100.

Darder, Antonia, and Rodolfo D. Torres. *The Latino Reader*. Malden, MA: Blackwell, 1997.

Davenport, Paul. "Arizona Governor Signs Bill Revising New Immigration Law." *Washington Post* (May 1, 2010).

Davidson, James D. "Glock's Model of Religious Commitment: Assessing Some Different Approaches and Results." *Review of Religious Research* 16 (Winter 1975):83–93.

Davidson, Lawrence. *Islamic Fundamentalism*, revised and updated ed. Westport, CT: Greenwood Publishing Group, Inc, 2003.

Davies, Bronwyn. *Frogs and Snails and Feminist Tales*. New York: Pandora Press, 1990.

Davies, Christie. "Sexual Taboos and Social Boundaries." *American Journal of Sociology* 87 (March 1982):1032–1063.

Davies, James Chowning. "The J-Curve of Rising and Declining Satisfactions as a Cause of Revolution and Rebellion." In Hugh Davis Graham and Ted Robert Gurr (Eds.), *Violence in America*, rev. ed. Beverly Hills, CA: Sage, 1979.

Davis, F. James. *Minority-Dominant Relations*. Arlington Heights, IL: AHM Publishing Corporation, 1978.

Davis, F. James. "Up and Down Opportunity's Ladder." *Public Opinion* 5 (June/July 1982):11ff.

Davis, Karen, Cathy Schoen, and Kristof/Stremikis. *Mirror, Mirror on the Wall: How the Performance of the U.S. Health Care System Compares Internationally*. New York: The Commonwealth Fund, 2010.

Davis, Kingsley. "Final Note on a Case of Extreme Isolation." *American Journal of Sociology* 52 (March 1947):232–247.

Davis, Kingsley. *Human Society*. New York: Macmillan, 1949.

Davis, Kingsley. "The Origin and Growth of Urbanization in the World." *American Journal of Sociology* 60 (March 1955):429–437.

Dawkins, Richard. *The Selfish Gene*, 2nd ed. New York: Oxford University Press, 1990.

"The Decline of Marriage and Rise of New Families." Pew Research Center, Social and Demographic Trends (November 18, 2010). http://pewsocialtrends.org/2010/11//18/the-decline-of-marriage-and-r . . .

De La Dehesa, Guillermo. *What Do We Know About Globalization: Issues of Poverty and Income Distribution*. Malden, MA: Blackwell Publishing, 2007.

de La Isla, Jose. *The Rise of Hispanic Political Power*. Santa Maria, CA: Archer Books, 2003.

De Luca, Rita Caccamo. *Back to Middletown: Three Generations of Sociological Reflections*. Stanford, CA: Stanford University Press, 2001.

de Waal, Frans B. M. "Cultural Primatology Comes of Age." *Nature* 399 (June 1999):635–636.

Death Penalty Information Center. "Race of Defendants Executed Since 1976." (2008). Available online at www.deathpenaltyinfo.org/dpicrace.html

Deegan, Mary J. *Women in Sociology: A Bio-Bibliographical Source Book*. Westport, CT: Greenwood, 1991.

Deegan, Mary J. *Jane Addams and the Men of the Chicago School, 1892–1918*. New Brunswick, NJ: Transaction Publishers, 2000.

Deegan, Mary Jo, and Michael Stein. "American Drama and Ritual: Nebraska Football." *International Review of Sport Sociology* 3 (1978):31–44.

Deer, Brian. "How the Case Against the MMR Vaccine was Fixed." *British Medical Journal* 342 (January 5, 2011). http://bmj.com/content/342/bmj.c5347.full

Defago, Nicki. *Childfree and Loving It*. London: Vision Paperbacks, 2009.

DeFleur, Melvin L., and Sandra Ball-Rokeach. *Theories of Mass Communication*, 4th ed. New York: Longman, 1982.

DeLeire, Thomas, and Leonard M. Lopoo. "Family Structure and the Economic Mobility of Children." Pew Research Center, Economic Mobility Project, May 2010.

Delgado, Richard, and Jean Stefancic. (Eds.). *The Latino Condition: A Critical Reader*. New York: New York University Press, 1998.

Deloria, Vine Jr., and Clifford Lytle. *The Nations Within*. New York: Pantheon Books, 1984.

Demaine, Jack (Ed.). *Sociology of Education Today*. New York: Palgrave, 2001.

Demerath, N. J., III, and Rhys H. Williams. "Civil Religion in an Uncivil Society." *The Annals* 480 (July 1985):154–166.

DeNavas-Walt, Carmen, Bernadette D. Proctor, and Jessica C. Smith. U.S. Census Bureau. Current Population Reports, P60-238. *Income, Poverty, and Health Insurance Coverage in the United States: 2009*. Washington DC: U.S. Government Printing Office.

DePaulo, Bella. *Singled Out*. New York: St. Martin's Press, 2007.

Desmond, Adrian, and James Moore. *Darwins Sacred Cause*. Boston, MA: Houghton Mifflin Harcourt, 2009.

DeSpelder, L. A., and D. L. Strickland. *The Last Dance*. Mountain View, CA: Mayfield Press, 1991.

Deutscher, Guy. *Through the Language Glass: Why the World Looks Different in Other Languages*. New York: Henry Holt and Company, 2010.

Dervarics, Charles. "Is Welfare Reform Reforming Welfare?" *Population Today* 26 (October 1998):1–8.

Dewey, John. *The School and Society: And the Child and the Curriculum*. Mineola, NY: Dover, 2001.

DeWitt, Karen. "Blacks Prone to Job Dismissal in Organizations." *New York Times* (April 20, 1995):A19.

DeYoung, Alan J. *Economics and American Education*. White Plains, NY: Longman, 1989.

Diamond, Jared. *The Third Chimpanzee: The Evolution and Future of the Human Animal*. New York: HarperPerennial, 1993.

Diamond, Jared. *Guns, Germs, and Steel: The Fates of Human Societies*. New York: Norton, 1999.

DiIulio, John J. Jr., and Anne Morrison Piehl. "Does Prison Pay?: The Stormy National Debate Over the Cost-Effectiveness of Imprisonment." *The Brookings Review* (Fall 1991):28–35.

Dillon, Sam. "Ohio Goes after Charter Schools That Are Failing." *New York Times* (November 8, 2007).

Dillon, Sam. "Under 'No Child' Law, Even Solid Schools Falter." *New York Times* (October 13, 2008).

DiMaggio, Paul. (Ed.). *The Twenty-First-Century Firm: Changing Economic Organization in International Perspective*. Princeton, NJ: Princeton University Press, 2001.

Dines, Gail, and Jean M. Humez. (Eds.). *Gender, Race, and Class in Media: A Text-Reader*, 2nd ed. Thousand Oaks, CA: Sage, 2002.

Dionne, E.J., and William A. Galston, "The Old and New Politics of Faith: Religion and the 2010 Election." Brookings Institution (November 17, 2010). http://www.brookings.edu/papers/2010/1117_faith_dionne_galston.a...

DiPrete, Thomas A. *Collectivist vs. Individualist Mobility Regimes?* Stockholm, Sweden: Stockholm University, 1996.

Directory of Corporate Affiliations. New Providence, NJ: Lexis Nexis Group, 2010.

Dobzhansky, Theodosius. *Mankind Evolving*. Toronto: Bantam Books, 1970.

Dollard, John, et al. *Frustration and Aggression*. New Haven, CT: Yale University Press, 1939.

Domhoff, G. William. *The Power Elite and the State*. Hawthorne, NY: Aldine de Gruyter, 1990.

Domhoff, G. William. *State Autonomy or Class Dominance*. New York: Aldine de Gruyter, 1996.

Domhoff, G. William. *Who Rules America*, 6th ed. New York: McGraw-Hill, 2009.

Dooley, Calvin M. *Income and Racial Disparities in the Undercount in the 2000 Presidential Election*. Washington, DC: U.S. House of Representatives Committee on Government Reform, 2001.

Doreian, Patrick, and Frans N. Stokman. *Evolution of Social Networks*. Amsterdam: Gordon and Breach Publishers, 1997.

Dornbush, Sanford M., et al. "Single Parents, Extended Households, and the Control of Adolescents." *Child Development* 56 (1985):326–341.

Douglas, Mary. "Accounting for Taste." *Psychology Today* 13 (July 1979):44ff.

Doyle, James A. *The Male Experience*, 3rd ed. Madison, WI: Brown and Benchmark, 1995.

Draut, Tammy. *New Opportunities? Public Opinion on Poverty, Income Inequality and Public Policy: 1996–2002*. New York: Demos, 2002.

Dressler, William W., Kathryn S. Oths, and Clarence C. Gravlee. "Race and Ethnicity in Public Health Research: Models to Explain Health Disparities." *Annual Review of Anthropology* 34 (2005):231–252.

Drew, Jill. "Eyewitnesses Recount Terrifying Day in Tibet." *Washington Post* (March 27, 2008):A1.

Dreyfuss, Robert, and Jason Vest. "The Lie Factory." *Mother Jones* 29 (January/February 2004):34–41.

Drucker, Peter F. "The Coming of the New Organization." *Harvard Business Review* 66 (January/February 1988):45–53.

Du Bois, William, and R. Wright. *Applying Sociology: Making a Better World*. Boston, MA: Allyn & Bacon, 2000.

Dudley, William. *Media Violence: Opposing Viewpoints*. San Diego, CA: Greenhaven Press, 1999.

Duff, Christina. "Profiling the Aged: Fat Cats or Hungry Victims." *The Wall Street Journal* (September 28, 1995):B1, B16.

Dunifon, Rachel. "Single Parenthood and Child Well-Being: Trends, Theories, and Evidence." In H. Elizabeth Peters and Claire M. Kamp Bush (Eds.), *Marriage and Family*. New York: Columbia University Press, 2009, pp. 93–113.

Dunifon, Rachel, and L. Kewaleski-Jones. "Who's in the House? Race Differences in Cohabitation, Single Parenthood, and Child Development." *Child Development* 73 (2002):1249–1264.

Durkheim, Emile. *Suicide*. Translated by John A. Spaulding and George Simpson. Edited by George Simpson. New York: Free Press, 1964.

Durkheim, Emile. *The Rules of Sociological Method*. Translated by Sarah A. Solovay and John H. Mueller. Edited by George E. G. Catlin. New York: Free Press, 1966.

Durkheim, Emile. *The Elementary Forms of Religious Life*. New York: Free Press, 1995.

Durkheim, Emile. *The Division of Labor in Society*. New York: Free Press, 1997.

Dye, Robert R., and Bartholomew Sparrow. *Politics in America*, 8th ed. Englewood Cliffs, NJ: Prentice-Hall, 2009.

Dye, Thomas R. *Who's Running America?* 7th ed. Englewood Cliffs, NJ: Prentice Hall, 2001.

Dynes, Russell R., and Kathleen J. Tierney. (Eds.). *Disasters, Collective Behavior, and Social Organization*. Newark: University of Delaware Press, 1994.

Eagleton, Terry. *Ideology*. London: Longman, 1994.

Eagley, Alice H., and Wendy Wood. "The Origins of Sex Differences in Human Behavior: Evolved Dispositions versus Social Roles." *American Psychologist* 54 (1999):408–423.

Eaton, Susan E. *The Other Boston Busing Story: What's Won and Lost Across the Boundary Line*. New Haven, CT: Yale University Press, 2001.

Ebenstein, Alan O., William Ebenstein, and Edwin Fogelman. *Today's Isms*, 11th ed. Upper Saddle River, NJ: Prentice Hall, 2000.

Eccles, Jacquelynne, et al. Development During Adolescence: The Impact of Stage-Environment Fit on Young Adolescents' Experiences in Schools and in Families. *American Psychologist* 48 (February 1993):90–101.

Eck, Diana L. *A New Religious America: How a "Christian Country" Has Become the World's Most Religiously Diverse Nation*. New York: HarperCollins Publishers, 2002.

Economist, The. "On the Right Track?" (March 2, 2002):59–60.

Eder, Donna. *School Talk*. New Brunswick, NJ: Rutgers University Press, 1995.

Edin, Kathryn, and Laura Lein. *Making Ends Meet: How Single Mothers Survive Welfare and Low-Wage Work*. New York: Russell Sage Foundation, 1997.

Edin, Kathryn, and Maria Kefalas. *Promises I Can Keep*. Berkeley, CA: University of California Press, 2006.

Edmonds, Patricia, and Mark Potok. "Followers 'See Themselves on Side of Jesus.'" *USA Today* (April 20, 1993):A1, A2.

Edsall, Thomas B. "Bush Has a Cabinet Full of Wealth." *Washington Post* (September 18, 2002b):A27.

Eggen, Dan, and T. W. Farnam. "'Super PACs' Alter Campaign." *Washington Post* (September 28, 2010):1A, 6A.

Ehrenreich, Barbara. "Helping the Rich Stay That Way." *Time* (April 18, 1994):86.

Ehrenreich, Barbara, and Dedrick Muhammad. "The Economic Fallout Has Decimated the Black Middle Class." *Alternet* (August 10, 2009). http://www.alternet.org/story/141825/

Ehrlich, Howard J. *Hate Crimes and Ethnoviolence*. Boulder, CO: Westview Press, 2009.

Eisenstock, Barbara. "Sex-Role Differences in Children's Identification with Counterstereotypic Televised Portrayals." *Sex Roles* 10 (1984):417–430.

Eitzen, D. Stanley. "Ethical Dilemas in American Sport: The Dark Side of Competition." In D. Stanley Eitzen (Ed.), *Sport in Contemporary Society*, 8th ed. Boulder, CO. Paradigm Press, 2009a, pp. 161–170.

Eitzen, D. Stanley. *Fair and Foul: Beyond Myths and Paradoxes of Sport*, 4th ed. Lanham, MD: Rowman & Littlefield Publishers, Inc, 2009b.

Eitzen, D. Stanley, and George H. Sage. *Sociology of North American Sport*, 8th ed. New York: Paradigm Press, 2009.

Eitzen, D. Stanley, and Kelly Eitzen Smith. *Experiencing Poverty*. Belmont, CA: Wadsworth, 2008.

Eitzen, D. Stanley, and Maxine Baca Zinn. *Globalization: The Transformation of Social Worlds*. Belmont, CA: Wadsworth Cengage Learning, 2009.

Eitzen, George, and Zeynep Atalay. *Readings in Globalization: Key Concepts and Major Debates*. Maldern, MA: Wiley-Blackwell, 2010.

Elikann, Peter T. *The Tough-On-Crime Myth: Real Solutions to Cut Crime*. New York: Plenum, 1996.

Elkin, Frederick, and Gerald Handel. *The Child and Society*, 6th ed. New York: McGraw-Hill, 2001.

Elliott, John E. *Comparative Economic Systems*, 2nd ed. Belmont, CA: Wadsworth, 1985.

Elliott, Michael. "Crime and Punishment." *Newsweek* (April 18, 1994):18–22.

Ellis, Joseph J. *Founding Brothers: The Revolutionary Generation*. New York: Knopf, 2002.

Ellis, Joseph J. *American Creation*. New York: Knopf, 2007.

Elster, Jon, Clause Offe, and Ulrich Preuss. *Institutional Design in Post-Communist Societies*. Cambridge, UK: Cambridge University Press, 1998.

Empey, LaMar T. *American Delinquency*, 2nd ed. Homewood, IL: Dorsey, 1982.

Engels, Friedrich. *The Origin of the Family, Private Property, and the State*. New York: International Publishing, 2001.

Englund, Will, Griffe Witte, and Debbi Wilgoren. "During 2nd Day of Bloody Clashes in Egypt, Foreign Journalists Arrested." *Washington Post* (February 3, 2011).

Entwisle, Doris R., and Karl L. Alexander. "Early Schooling as a 'Critical Period' Phenomenon." In K. Namboodiri and R. G. Corwin (Eds.), *Sociology of Education and Socialization*. Greenwich, CT: JAI Press, 1989, pp. 27–55.

Entwisle, Doris R., and Karl L. Alexander. "Entry into School: The Beginning School Transition and Educational Stratification in the United States." *Annual Review of Sociology* 19 (1993):401–423.

Epstein, T. Scarlett. *Economic Development and Social Change in South India*. New York: Humanities Press, 1962.

Erickson, Rosemary J., and Rita J. Simon. *The Use of Social Science Data in Supreme Court Decisions*. Urbana, IL: University of Illinois Press, l998.

Erikson, Erik H. *Childhood and Society*. Harmondsworth, UK: Penguin Books, 1973.

Erikson, Erik H. *The Life Cycle Completed*. New York: Norton, 1982.

Erikson, Kai T. "A Comment on Disguised Observation in Sociology." *Social Problems* 14 (Spring 1967):366–373.

Erikson, Kai T. *Everything in Its Path*. New York: Simon & Schuster, 1976.

Erikson, Kai T. *A New Species of Trouble: Explorations in Disaster, Trauma, and Community*. New York: Norton, 1995.

Erikson, Kai T. *Sociological Visions*. Blue Ridge Summit, PA: Rowman & Littlefield, 1997.

Ermann, M. David, and Richard J. Lundman. *Corporate and Governmental Deviance*, 5th ed. New York: Oxford University Press, 1996.

Eshleman, J. Ross, and Richard A. Bulcroft. *The Family*, 11th ed. Boston, MA: Allyn & Bacon, 2005.

Esping-Andersen, Gosta. *Welfare States in Transition*. Thousand Oaks, CA: Sage, 1996.

Espiritu, Yen Le. *Asian American Men and Women*. Thousand Oaks, CA: Sage, 1996.

Esposito, John L. *Unholy War: Terror in the Name of Islam*. New York: Oxford University Press, 2002.

Esposito, John L. *The Future of Islam*. New York: Oxford University Press, 2010.

Esposito, John L., Darrell J. Fasching, and Todd Lewis. *World Religions Today*, 3rd ed. New York: Oxford University Press, 2009.

Esposito, John, and John Fiorillo. "Who's Left on the Block? New York City's Working Class Neighborhoods." In Hans Spiegel (Ed.), *Citizen Participation in Urban Development*. Fairfax, VA: Learning Resources, 1974, pp. 307–334.

Ethridge, Marcus E., and Howard Handelman. *Politics in a Changing World*, 4th ed. Belmont, CA: Wadsworth, 2008.

Etzioni, Amitai. *A Comparative Analysis of Complex Organizations*, rev. ed. New York: Free Press, 1975.

Etzioni, Amitai. "Education for Mutuality and Civility." *Futurist* 16 (October 1982):4–7.

Etzioni, Amitai. *The Monochrome Society*. Princeton, NJ: Princeton University Press, 2001.

Evans, Jean. *Three Men*. New York: Knopf, 1954.

Evans, Sara M. *Personal Politics*. New York: Vintage, 1980.

Evans, Sara M. *Born for Liberty: A History of Women in America*. New York: Free Press, 1989.

Eyerman, Ron. *Studying Collective Action*. Newbury Park, CA: Sage, 1992.

Eysenck, Hans. *Crime and Personality*, 3rd ed. London: Routledge and Kegan Paul, 1977.

"Facts about the Death Penalty." Washington, DC: Death Penalty Information Center, Updated October 28, 2010.

Fagot, Joël, Edward A. Wasserman, and Michael E. Young. "Discriminating the Relation between Relations: The Role of Entropy in Abstract Conceptualization by Baboons (*Papio papio*) and Humans (*Homo sapiens*)." *Journal of Experimental Psychology: Animal Behavior Processes* 27 (October 2001):316–328.

"Failing Its Families: Lack of Paid Leave and Work-Related Supports in the U.S." New York: Human Rights Watch (February 2011). www.hrw.org

Faioloa, Anthony. The New Economics of Hunger. *Washington Post* (April 27, 2008).

Falk, Gerhard. *Stigma: How We Treat Outsiders*. Amherst, NY: Prometheus Books, 2001.

Faltermayer, Charlotte. "Cyberveillance." *Time* (August 14, 2000):B22–B25.

Faludi, Susan. *Stiffed: The Betrayal of the American Man*. New York: HarperCollins Publishing, 2000.

Fang, Lee. "Exclusive: Chamber Receives at Least $885,000 from Over 80 Foreign Companies in Disclosed Donations Alone." *Think Progress* (October 13, 2010). http://thinkprogress.org/2010/10/13/chamber.foreign-funded-me

Farley, Christopher John. "The Butt Stops Here." *Time* (April 18, 1994):58–64.

Farley, John E., and Mark Hansel. "The Ecological Context of Urban Crime: A Further Exploration." *Urban Affairs Quarterly* 17 (September 1981):37–54.

Farley, Reynolds. *Blacks and Whites*. Cambridge, MA: Harvard University Press, 1984.

Farley, Reynolds, and John Haaga. "Modest Declines in U.S. Residential Segregation Observed." *Population Today* 25 (February 1997):1–2.

Farley, Reynolds, and John Haaga. *The New American Reality: Who We Are, How We Got There, Where We Are Going*. New York: Russell Sage Foundation, 1998.

Farley, Reynolds, and John Haaga. (Eds.). *American People*. New York: Russell Sage Foundation, 2005.

Farley, Reynolds, and William H. Frey. "Changes in the Segregation of Whites from Blacks During the 1980's: Small Steps Toward a More Integrated Society." *American Sociological Review* 59 (February 1994):23–45.

Farnam, T. W. "At $97 per Vote, Top Spenders Lost." *Washington Post* (November 9, 2010):A5.

Farnam, T. W. "72 Super Pacs Spent $83.7 Million on Election, Financial Disclosure Reports Show." *Washington Post* (December 3, 2010).

Farnam, T. W., and Dan Eggen. "Interest-Group Spending for Midterm UP Fivefold from 2006; Many Sources Secret." *Washington Post* (October 4, 2010).

Farrell, Christopher. "Time to Prune the Ivy." *BusinessWeek* (May 24, 1993):112–118.

Fast Facts. National Center for Education Statistics (2010). http://nces.ed.gov/fastfacts/display.asp?id=91

Fasteau, Marc. "The Male Machine: The High Price of Macho." *Psychology Today* 8 (September 1975):60.

Fattah, Hasson M. "Saudis Rethink Taboo on Women Behind the Wheel." *New York Times* (September 28, 2007).

Fausto-Sterling, Anne. *Myths of Gender*. New York: Basic Books, 1987.

Fazioli, Jennifer K. "The Advancement of Female Coaches in Intercollegiate Athletics." Department of Labor Studies and Industrial Relations, Pennsylvania State University, 2004.

Feagin, Joe R. *Subordinating the Poor*. Englewood Cliffs, NJ: Prentice Hall, 1975.

Feagin, Joe R. The Continuing Significance of Race: Antiblack Discrimination in Public Places. *American Sociological Review* 56 (February 1991):101–115.

Feagin, Joe R. *Racist America: Roots, Current Realities and Future Reparations*, 2nd ed. New York/London: Taylor & Francis, Inc, 2001.

Feagin, Joe R. *Systemic Racism*. New York: Routledge, 2006.

Feagin, Joe R., and Clairece Booker Feagin. *Discrimination American Style*. Malabar, FL: Krieger, 1986.

Feagin, Joe R., and Karyn D. McKinney. *The Many Costs of Racism*. Lanham, MD: Rowman & Littlefield, 2005.

Feagin, Joe R., Hernán Vera, and Pinar Batur. *White Racism*, 2nd ed. New York: Routledge, 2001.

Fears, Darryl. "In Jena and Beyond, Nooses Return as a Symbol of Hate." *Washington Post* (October 20, 2007).

Featherman, David L. "The Socio-Economic Achievement of White Religio-Ethnic Sub-Groups." *American Sociological Review* 36 (April 1971):207–222.

Feeley, Malcolm, and Jonathon Simon. "The New Penology: Notes on the Emerging Strategy of Corrections and Implications." *Criminology* 30 (1992):449–474.

Fein, Helen. *Genocide*. Newbury Park, CA: Sage, 1993.

Fenn, Richard. *Toward a Theory of Secularization*. Storrs, CT: Society for the Scientific Study of Religion, 1978.

Fenwick, Charles R. "Crime and Justice in Japan: Implications for the United States." *International Journal of Comparative and Applied Criminal Justice* 6 (1982):62–71.

Ferber, Abby L. *White Man Failing: Race, Gender, and White Supremacy*. Lanham, MD: Rowman & Littlefield, 1998.

Ferrante, Joan. "Careers in Sociology." Wadsworth Sociology Module. Belmont, CA: Wadsworth, 2009.

Ferrar, Jane W. "Marriages in Urban Communal Households: Comparing the Spiritual and the Secular." In Peter J. Stein, Judith Richman, and Natalie Hannon (Eds.), *The Family*. Reading, MA: Addison-Wesley, 1977, pp. 409–419.

Feuer, Lewis S. (Ed.). *Marx and Engels*. New York: Doubleday, 1959.

"Fewer Mothers Prefer Full-time Work." Washington, DC: Pew Research Center, Pew Social and Demographic Trends Project, July 12, 2007.

Fiedler, Fred E. *A Theory of Leadership Effectiveness*. New York: McGraw-Hill, 1967.

File, Thom, and Sarah Crissey. "Voting Registration in the Election of November 2008." Current Population Reports, P20-562, Washington, DC: U.S. Census Bureau, 2010.

"Findings from a National Survey & Focus Groups on Economic Mobility." The Pew Charitable Trusts. Economic Mobility Project. Greenberg Quinlan Rosner Research, 2009.

Fine, Cordelia. *Delusions of Gender*. New York: W.W. Norton, 2010.

Fine, Gary Alan. *With the Boys: Little League Baseball and Preadolescent Culture*. Chicago, IL: University of Chicago Press, 1987.

Fine, Gary Alan. "The Sad Demise, Mysterious Disappearance, and Glorious Triumph of Symbolic Interactionism." *Annual Review of Sociology* 19 (1993):61–87.

Fine, Gary Alan. *The Culture of Restaurant Work*. Berkeley/Los Angeles, CA: University of California Press, 1996.

Fine, Gary Alan, and Patricia Turner. *Whispers on the Color Line: Rumor and Race in America*. Berkeley, CA: University of California Press, 2004.

Fineman, Howard. "Leadership? Don't Ask Us." *Newsweek* (May 11, 1992):42.

Fineman, Howard. "Shifting Racial Lines." *Newsweek* (July 10, 1995):38–39.

Finke, Roger, and Rodney Stark. *The Churching of America*. New Brunswick, NJ: Rutgers University Press, 1992.

Firebaugh, Glenn. "Structural Determinants of Urbanization in Asia and Latin America." *American Sociological Review* 44 (April 1979):199–215.

Fischer, Claude S. *To Dwell among Friends*. Chicago, IL: University of Chicago Press, 1982.

Fischer, Claude S. *The Urban Experience*, 2nd ed. New York: Harcourt Brace Jovanovich, 1984.

Fischer, Claude S. "The Subcultural Theory of Urbanism: A Twentieth-Year Assessment." *American Journal of Sociology* 101 (November 1995):543–577.

Fischer, Claude S., et al. *Inequality by Design: Cracking the Bell Curve Myth*. Princeton, NJ: Princeton University Press, 1996.

Fischer, David Hackett. *Growing Old in America*. New York: Oxford University Press, 1977.

Fischer, Joannie. "Scientists Have Finally Cloned a Human Embryo." *U.S. News & World Report* (December 3, 2001):51–63.

Flanagan, William G. *Contemporary Urban Sociology*, 4th ed. Boston, MA: Allyn & Bacon, 2001.

Fletcher, Max E. "Harriet Martineau and Ayn Rand: Economics in the Guise of Fiction." *American Journal of Economics and Sociology* 33 (October 1974):367–379.

Fletcher, Michael A. "In Wisconsin, Vouching for Vouchers." *Washington Post* (March 20, 2001):A1, A14.

Florida, Richard, and Martin Kenney. "Transplanted Organizations: The Transfer of Japanese Industrial Organization to the U.S." *American Sociological Review* 56 (June 1991):381–398.

Fonda, Daren. "National Prosperous Radio." *Time* (March 24, 2003):49–51.

Francis, David K. *The Internet in Healthcare: The Final Frontier*. Nashville, TN: J. C. Bradford, 1999.

Frank, Robert H. *Luxury Fever: Money and Happiness in an Era of Excess*. Princeton, NJ: Princeton University Press, 2000.

Frank, Robert H. *Falling Behind: How Rising Inequality Harms the Middle Class*. Berkeley, CA: University of California Press, 2007.

Frank, Robert. *Richistan*. New York: Crown Publishing Group, 2008.

Frankenberg, Erica, and Chungmei Lee. *Race in American Public Schools: Rapidly Resegregating School Districts*. Cambridge, MA: The Civil Rights Project, August 2002.

Frankenberg, Erica, and Gary Orfield. *Lessons in Integration*. Charlottesville, VA: University of Virginia Press, 2007.

Frankenberg, Erica, Genevieve Siegel-Hawley, and Jia Wang. *Choice Without Equity: Charter School Segregation and the Need for Civil Rights Standards*. Los Angeles, CA: The Civil Rights Project/Proyecto Derechos Civiles at UCLA (2010). www.civil/rightsproject.ucla.edu

Fredman, Sandra, Sarah Spencer, and Sandra Spencer. (Eds.). *Age as an Equality Issue*. UK: Hart Publishing, 2003.

Freedman, Jane. *Feminism*. Buckingham, UK: Open University Press, 2001.

Freedman, Marc. *Encore*. New York: Perseus Publishing, 2007.

Freedman, Vicki A., Linda G. Martin, and Robert F. Schoeni. "Disability in America." *Population Bulletin* 59 (September 2004):1–32.

Freedman, Vicki A., Linda G. Martin, and Robert F. Schoeni. "Disability in America." *Population Bulletin* 59 (September 2004):3ff.

Freeman, David M. *Technology and Society*. Chicago, IL: Rand McNally, 1974.

Freeman, Jo. *We Will Be Heard: Women's Struggles for Political Power in the United States*. Lanham, MD: Rowman & Littlefield Publishers, 2008.

Freeman, Jo, and Victoria Johnson. (Eds.). *Waves of Protest: Social Movements Since the Sixties*. Lanham, MD: Rowman & Littlefield, 1999.

Freeman, Linton C. "The Sociological Concept of 'Group': An Empirical Test of Two Models." *American Journal of Sociology* 98 (July 1992):152–166.

Freeman, Richard B. *Black Elite*. New York: McGraw-Hill, 1977.

French, Howard W. "North Korea to Let Capitalism Loose in Investment Zone." *New York Times* (September 25, 2002):A1,A3.

Frey, William H. "Lifecourse Migration and Metropolitan Whites and Blacks and the Structure of Demographic Change in Large Central Cities." *American Sociological Review* 49 (December 1984):803–827.

Frey, William H. "Mover Destination Selectivity and the Changing Suburbanization of Metropolitan Blacks and Whites." *Demography* 22 (May 1985):223–243.

Frey, William H. *Mapping the Growth of Older America: Seniors and Boomers in the Early 21st Century.* Washington, DC: The Brookings Institution, 2007.

Frey, William H., and Reynolds Farley. "Latino, Asian, and Black Segregation in U.S. Metropolitan Areas, Are Multiethnic Metros Different?" *Demography* 31 (February 1996):35–50.

Friedan, Betty. *The Feminine Mystique.* New York: Dell, 1963.

Friedman, Milton. *Capitalism and Freedom.* Chicago, IL: University of Chicago Press, 2002.

Friedman, Thomas. *Lexus and the Olive Tree: Understanding Globalization.* New York: Knopf Publishing Group, 2000.

Friedman, Thomas. *The World Is Flat.* New York: Picador, 2007.

Friedrich, Carl J., and Zbigniew K. Brzezinski. *Totalitarian Dictatorship and Autocracy,* 2nd ed. Cambridge, MA: Harvard University Press, 1965.

Frieze, Irene H., Jacquelynne E. Parsons, Paula B. Johnson, Diane N. Rable, and Gail L. Zellman. *Women and Sex Roles.* New York: Norton, 1978.

From the Capital to the Classroom: State and Federal Efforts to Implement the No Child Left Behind Act. Washington, DC: Center on Education Policy, January 2003.

Fruch, Terry, and Paul McGhee. "Traditional Sex Role Development and Amount of Time Watching Television." *Developmental Psychology* 11 (1975):109ff.

Fry, Richard. "College Enrollment Hits All-Time High, Fueled by Community College Surge." Pew Research Center, October 29, 2009.

Fry, Richard, and D'Vera Cohn. "New Economics of Marriage: The Rise of Wives." Pew Research Center (January 19, 2010). http://pewresearch.org/pubs/1466/economics-marriage-rise-of-wives

Fry, Richard, and D'Vera Cohn. "Women, Men and the New Economics of Marriage." Pew Research Center (January 19, 2010). http://pewsocialtrends.org/pubs/750/new-economicsofmarriage

Fukuyama, Francis. "The Great Disruption." *Atlantic Monthly* 283 (May 1999):55–80.

Fukuyama, Francis. *Our Posthuman Future: Consequences of the Biotechnology Revolution.* New York: Picador, 2003.

Fukuyama, Francis. *The End of History and the Last Man.* New York: Free Press, 2006.

"The Future of the Global Muslim Population." Pew Forum on Religion and Public Life (January 27, 2011). http://www.pewforum.org/The-Future-of-the-Global-Muslim-Populatio...

Gabriel, Trip. "Despite Push, Success at Charter Schools Is Mixed." *New York Times* (May 1, 2010).

Galloway, Joseph L. "In the Heart of Darkness." *U.S. News & World Report* (March 3, 1999):18.

Gallup, George H. Jr. *Religion in America 2002.* Princeton, NJ: The Princeton Religion Research Center, 2002.

Gamboa, Suzanne. "Almost 1 of 2 New Americans in 2008 was Latino." Associated Press, 2009. http://license.icopyright.net/user/viewFreeUse.act?fuid=MzEo0Duong%3D%3D

Game, Ann, and Andrew W. Metcalfe. *Passionate Sociology.* Thousand Oaks, CA: Sage, 1996.

Gamoran, Adam. "Instructional and Institutional Effects of Ability Grouping." *Sociology and Education* 59 (1986):185–198.

Gamoran, Adam. "The Variable Effects of High School Tracking." *American Sociological Review* 57 (December 1992):812–828.

Gamson, William. *The Strategy of Social Protest,* 2nd ed. Belmont, CA: Wadsworth, 1990.

Ganong, Lawrence, and Marilyn Coleman. *Remarried Family Relationships.* Thousand Oaks, CA: Sage, 1994.

Gans, Herbert J. "Reconstructing the Underclass: The Term's Danger as a Planning Concept." *Journal of the American Planning Association* 56 (Summer 1990):271–277.

Gans, Herbert J. *The Urban Villagers.* New York: Free Press, 1962a.

Gans, Herbert J. "Urbanism and Suburbanism as Ways of Life." In Arnold M. Rose (Ed.), *Human Behavior and Social Processes.* Boston, MA: Houghton Mifflin, 1962b, pp. 625–648.

Gans, Herbert J. *People and Plans.* New York: Basic Books, 1968.

Ganz, Alexander. "Where Has the Urban Crisis Gone." *Urban Affairs Quarterly* 20 (June 1985):449–468.

Garbarino, J. "The Incidence and Prevalence of Child Maltreatment." In L. Ohlin and M. Tonry (Eds.), *Family Violence.* Chicago, IL: University of Chicago Press, 1989, pp. 219–261.

Gardner, Carol Brooks. "A Family among Strangers: Kinship Claims Among Gay Men in Public Places." In Don A. Chekki, Spencer E. Cahill, and Lyn H. Lofland (Eds.), *Research in Community Sociology,* Supplement 1. Greenwich, CT: JAI Press, 1994, pp. 95–118.

Gardner, David Pierpont. *A Nation at Risk: The Imperative for Educational Reform.* Report of the National Commission on Excellence in Education. Washington, DC: U.S. Government Printing Office, 1983.

Gardner, Lytt. "Deprivation Dwarfism." *Scientific American* 227 (July 1972):76–82.

Garfinkel, Harold. *Studies in Ethnomethodology.* Cambridge, UK: Polity Press, 1984.

Garland, David. (Ed.). *Mass Imprisonment: Social Causes and Consequences.* Thousand Oaks, CA: Sage, 2001.

Garland, David. *Peculiar Institution: America's Death Penalty in an Age of Abolition.* Cambridge, MA: Harvard University Press, 2010.

Garreau, J. *Edge City: Life on the New Frontier.* New York: Doubleday, 1991.

Garst, Jennifer, and Galen V. Bodenhausen. "Advertising's Effects on Men's Gender Role Attitudes." *Sex Roles* 36 (May 1997):551–572.

Gates, Gary J., and Adam P. Romero. "Parenting by Gay Men and Lesbians." In H. Elizabeth Peters and Claire M. Kamp Bush (Eds.), *Marriage and Family.* New York: Columbia University Press, 2009, pp. 227–246.

Gatewood, James V., and Min Zhou. (Eds.). *Contemporary Asian America: A Multidisciplinary Reader.* New York: New York University Press, 2000.

Gauntlett, David. *Media Gender and Identity: An Introduction.* New York: Routledge, 2002.

"Gay Marriage Gains More Acceptance." Pew Research Center (October 6, 2010). http://pewresearch.org/pubs/1755/poll-gay-marriage-gains-acceptance...

Gay, Peter. *The Enlightenment: The Rise of Modern Paganism.* New York: Norton, 1966.

Geary, David C. *Male, Female: The Evolution of Human Sex Differences.* Washington, DC: American Psychological Association, 1998.

Gecas, Viktor, and Michael L. Schwalbe. "Beyond the Looking-Glass Self: Social Structure and Efficacy-Based Self-Esteem." *Social Psychology Quarterly* 46 (1983):77–88.

Gehrig, Gail. "The American Civil Religion Debate: A Source for Theory Construction." *Journal for the Scientific Study of Religion* 20 (March 1981):51–63.

Geis, Gilbert, Robert Meier, and Lawrence Salinger. (Eds.). *White-Collar Crime: Offenses in Business, Politics and the Professions,* 3rd ed. New York: Free Press, 1995.

Gelbard, Alene, and Carl Haub. "Population 'Explosion' Not Over for Half the World." *Population Today* 26 (March 1998):1–2.

Gelbard, Alene, Carl Haub, and Mary M. Kent. "World Population Beyond Six Billion." Washington, DC: Population Reference Bureau, March 1999, pp. 1–44.

Gelles, Richard J. *Intimate Violence in Families*, 3rd ed. Thousand Oaks, CA: Sage, 1997.

Gelles, Richard J., et al. (Eds.). *Current Controversies on Family Violence*, 2nd ed. Thousand Oaks, CA: Sage, 2004.

Gellman, Barton. "The Secret World of Extreme Militias." *Time* (September 30, 2010).

Gender Gaps: Where Schools Still Fail Our Children. American Association of University Women. New York: Marlowe & Company, 1999.

Gerber, Jurg. "Heidi and Imelda: The Changing Image of Crime in Switzerland." *Criminology* 8 (March 1991):121–128.

George, Linda K. "Sociological Perspectives on Life Transitions." *Annual Review of Sociology* 19 (August 1993): 353–373.

Gershon, Ilana. *The Breakup 2.0: Disconnecting Over New Media*. Ithaca, NY: Cornell University Press, 2010.

Gerson, Kathleen. *The Unfinished Revolution: How a New Generation Is Reshaping Family, Work, and Gender in America*. New York: Oxford University Press, 2010.

Gersoni-Stavn, Deane. *Sexism and Youth*. New York: Bowker, 1974.

Gerth, H. H., and C. Wright Mills. (Eds.). *From Max Weber*. New York: Oxford University Press, 1958.

Gest, Ted. "Are White-Collar Crooks Getting Off Too Easy." *U.S. News & World Report* 99 (July 1985):43.

Gibbons, Tom. "Justice Not Equal for Poor Here." *Chicago Sun Times* (February 24, 1985):1,18.

Gibbs, Nancy. "Oh My God, They're Killing Themselves." *Time* (May 3, 1993):27–43.

Gibson, Margaret A., and John V. Ogbu. *Minority Status and Schooling*. New York: Garland Publishing, 1991.

Giddens, Anthony. *Studies in Social and Political Theory*. London: Hutchinson, 1979.

Giddens, Anthony. *Social Theory and Modern Sociology*. Stanford, CA: Stanford University Press, 2000.

Giddens, Anthony. *Runaway World: How Globalisation Is Reshaping Our Lives*. New York: Routledge, 2002.

Giddens, Anthony, et al. *Introduction to Sociology*, 7th ed. New York: Norton, 2009.

Gilbert, Dennis A. *The American Class Structure in an Age of Growing Inequality*, 8th ed. Thousand Oaks, CA: Sage, 2010.

Gilbert, Lucia Albino. *Two Careers/One Family*. Newbury Park, CA: Sage, 1993.

Gilbert, Neil. *How Feminism, the Market, and Policy Shape Family Life*. New Haven, CT: Yale University Press, 2008.

Gilens, Martin. *Why Americans Hate Welfare: Race, Media, and the Politics of Antipoverty Policy*. Chicago, IL: University of Chicago Press, 1999.

Giles, Jeff. "Generation X." *Newsweek* (June 6, 1994):62–72.

Gill, Brian P., et al. *Rhetoric versus Reality: What We Know and What We Need to Know About Vouchers and Charter Schools*. Santa Monica, CA: The Rand Corporation, 2001.

Giroux, Henry A. "Theories of Reproduction and Resistance in the New Sociology of Education: A Critical Analysis." *Harvard Educational Review* 53 (August 1983):257–293.

Gist, Noel P., and Sylvia Fleis Fava. *Urban Society*, 6th ed. New York: Crowell, 1974.

Gittell, Marilyn J. (Ed.) *Strategies for School Equity: Creating Productive Schools in a Just Society*. New Haven, CT: Yale University Press, 1998.

Giulianotti, Richard, and Roland Robertson (eds.). *Globalization and Sport*. Malden, MA: Blackwell, 2007.

Glazer, Nathan. "The End of Meritocracy." *The New Republic* (September 27, 1999):26.

Gleckman, H., J. Carey, R. Mitchell, T. Smart, and C. Pousch. "The Technology Payoff." *BusinessWeek* (June 14, 1993):51ff.

Glick, P., and S. L. Lin. "More Young Adults Are Living with Their Parents: Who Are They?" *Journal of Marriage and the Family* (February 1986):107–112.

Global Hunger Index. *The Challenge of Hunger: Focus on the Crisis of Child*. 2010.

"Global Poll: Wide Dissatisfaction with Capitalism 20 Years After the Fall of Berlin Wall." BBC Press Release (2009). http://www.bbc.co.uk/pressoffice/pressreleases/stories/2009/11_november/09/pollshtml

"Global Sports Equipment, Apparel and Footwear Market Nearly $280B." Port Washington, NY: NPD Group (2011). http://www.marketingcharts.com/direct/global-sports-equipment-apparel-and-footwear-marke...

Glock, Charles Y., and Robert N. Bellah. (Eds.). *The New Religious Consciousness*. Berkeley, CA: University of California Press, 1976.

Glock, Charles Y., and Rodney Stark. *Religion and Society in Tension*. Chicago, IL: Rand McNally, 1965.

Glock, Charles Y., and Rodney Stark. *American Piety*. Berkeley, CA: University of California Press, 1968.

Glueck, Sheldon, and Eleanor Glueck. *Unraveling Juvenile Delinquency*. Cambridge, MA: Harvard University Press, 1950.

Gober, Patricia. "Americans on the Move." *Population Bulletin* 48 (November 1993):1–40.

Goffman, Erving. *Asylums*. Garden City, NY: Anchor Books, 1961a.

Goffman, Erving. *Encounters*. Indianapolis, IN: Bobbs-Merrill, 1961b.

Goffman, Erving. *Stigma*. Englewood Cliffs, NJ: Prentice Hall, 1963.

Goffman, Erving. *The Presentation of Self in Everyday Life*. New York: Overlook Press, 1974.

Goffman, Erving. *Gender Advertisements*. New York: Harper and Row, 1979.

Goffman, Erving. "The Interaction Order." *American Sociological Review* 48 (February 1983):1–17.

Goldberger, Arthur S., and Glen G. Cain. *The Causal Analysis of Cognitive Outcomes in the Coleman Report*. Madison, WI: Institute for Research on Poverty. University of Wisconsin, December 1981.

Golden, Frederic. "Albert Einstein: Person of the Century." *Time* (December 31, 1999):62–65.

Goldfarb, William. "Psychological Privation in Infancy and Subsequent Adjustment." *American Journal of Orthopsychiatry* 15 (April 1945):247–255.

Goldscheider, Frances K., and Calvin Goldscheider. "Leaving and Returning Home in 20th Century America." *Population Bulletin* 48 (March 1994):1–35.

Goldscheider, Frances K., and Linda J. Waite. *New Families, No Families?* Chapel Hill, NC: University of North Carolina Press, 1991.

Goleman, D. "An Emerging Theory on Blacks' IQ Scores." *New York Times Education Supplement* (April 10, 1988):22–24.

Good, Mary-Jo DelVecchio, Paul E. Brodwin, Byron J. Good, and Arthur Kleinman. (Eds.). *Pain as Human Experience: An Anthropological Perspective*. Berkeley, CA: University of California Press, 1994.

Goode, Erich. *Collective Behavior*. Fort Worth, TX: Sanders College Publishing, 1992.

Goode, Judith, and Jeff Maskovskyk. (Eds.). *The New Poverty Studies: The Ethnography of Power, Politics, and Impoverished People in the United States*. New York: New York University Press, 2001.

Goode, William J. *World Revolution and Family Patterns*. New York: Free Press, 1970.

Goodstein, David. "Scientific Misconduct." *Academe* 88 (January/February 2002):28–31.

Goodwin, Jeff, and James Jasper. (Eds.). *Social Movements Reader*. New York: John W. Wiley, 2008.

Gordon, Milton M. *Assimilation in American Life*. New York: Oxford University Press, 1964.

Gordon, Milton M. *Human Nature, Class, and Ethnicity*. New York: Oxford University Press, 1978.

Gordon, Suzanne. *Nursing Against the Odds*. Ithaca, NY: Cornell University Press, 2006.

Gorer, Geofrey. *Grief and Mourning in Contemporary Britain*. London: Cresset Press, 1965.

Gottfredson, Michael R., and Travis Hirschi. *A General Theory of Crime*. Stanford, CA: Stanford University Press, 1990.

Gould, R. "Growth Toward Self Tolerance." *Psychology Today* (February 1975):47–48.

Gould, Stephen Jay. *The Mismeasurement of Man*. New York: Norton, 1981.

Gouldner, Alvin N. "Metaphysical Pathos and the Theory of Bureaucracy." *American Political Science Review* 49 (June 1955):496–507.

Grabosky, Peter N., and Russell G. Smith. *Electronic Theft: Unlawful Acquisition in Cyberspace*. New York: Cambridge University Press, 2001.

"Graduates Take Rites of Passage into Japanese Corporate Life." *Financial Times* (April 8, 1991):4.

Grandjean, B. "An Economic Analysis of the Davis-Moore Theory of Stratification." *Social Forces* 53 (June 1975):543–552.

Granovetter, Mark. "The Strength of Weak Ties." *American Journal of Sociology* 78 (May 1973):1360–1380.

Grapes, Bryan J. *Prisons*. San Diego, CA: Greenhaven Press, 2000.

Graubard, Allen. "The Free School Movement." *Harvard Educational Review* 42 (August 1972):351–373.

Gravlee, Clarence C. "How Race Becomes Biology: Embodiment of Social Inequality." *American Journal of Physical Anthropology* 139 (2009):47–57.

Greeley, Andrew M. "Political Attitudes Among American White Ethnics." In Charles H. Anderson (Ed.), *Sociological Essays and Research*, rev. ed. Homewood, IL: Dorsey, 1974, pp. 202–209.

Greeley, Andrew M. *Ethnicity, Denomination, and Inequality*. Beverly Hills, CA: Sage, 1976.

Greeley, Andrew M. *Religious Change in America*. Cambridge, MA: Harvard University Press, 1996.

Green, Gary S. *Occupational Crime*, 2nd ed. Chicago: Nelson-Hall Publishers, 1997.

Green, John. *U.S. Religious Landscape Survey*. Washington, DC: Pew Forum on Religion and Public Life, 2008.

Green, Mark. *Selling Out*. New York: HarperCollins Publishers, 2002.

Greenberg, Daniel S. *Science, Money, and Politics: Political Triumph and Ethical Erosion*. Chicago, IL: University of Chicago Press, 2003.

Greenberg, David F., and Ronald C. Kessler. "The Effects of Arrests on Crime: A Multivariate Panel Analysis." *Social Forces* 60 (March 1982):771–790.

Greenhouse, Steven. "17,000 G.E. Workers Strike over Higher Health Costs." *New York Times* (January 15, 2003).

Greenhouse, Steven. *The Big Squeeze: Tough Times for the American Worker*. New York: Anchor Books, 2009.

Greider, William. *Who Will Tell the People?* New York: Simon & Schuster, 1993.

Grescoe, P. *The Merchants of Venus: Inside Harlequin and the Empire of Romance*. Custer, WA: Orca Book Publishers, 1997.

Grieco, Elizabeth M., and Edward N. Trevelyan. "Place of Birth of the Foreign-Born Population: 2009." U.S. Census Bureau, October 2010.

Griffin, John Howard. *Black Like Me*. Boston, MA: Houghton Mifflin, 1961.

Grint, Keith. *The Sociology of Work*. Boston, MA: Polity Books, 2005.

Gross, Beatrice, and Ronald Gross. *The Great School Debate*. New York: Simon & Schuster, 1985.

Gross, L., and S. Jeffries-Fox. "What Do You Want to Be When You Grow Up, Little Girl?" In Gary Tuchman, Arlene Kaplan Daniels, and James Benet (Eds.), *Hearth and Home*. New York: Oxford University Press, 1978, pp. 240–265.

"Growing Old in America: Expectations vs. Reality." Pew Research Center Publications (June 29, 2008). http://pewresearch.org/pubs/1269/aging-survey-expectations-versus-reality

Grubb, W. Norton, and Robert H. Wilson. "Trends in Wage and Salary Inequality, 1967–1988." *Monthly Labor Review* 115 (June 1992):23–39.

Guillen, Mauro F. *The Limits of Convergence: Globalization and Organizational Change in Argentina, South Korea, and Spain*. Princeton, NJ: Princeton University Press, 2003.

Guillen, Mauro F. "Is Globalization Civilizing, Destructive or Feeble? A Critique of Five Key Debates in the Social Science Literature." In George Ritzer and Zeynep Atalay (Eds.), *Readings in Globalization: Key Concepts and Major Debates*. Malden, MA: Wiley-Blackwell, 2010, pp. 4–17.

Gur, R. C., et al. "Sex Differences in Regional Cerebral Glucose Metabolism During a Resting State." *Science* 267 (January 27, 1995):528–531.

Gutman, Henry G. *The Black Family in Slavery and Freedom, 1750–1925*. New York: Pantheon, 1983.

Gwatkin, D. R., S. Rutstein, K. Johnson, E. A. Suliman, and A. Wagstaff. *Initial Country-Level Information About Socioeconomic Differences in Health, Nutrition, and Population*, vols. I and II. Washington, DC: The World Bank, November 2003.

Hacker, Andrew. *Two Nations: Black and White, Separate, Hostile, and Unequal*, expanded and updated ed. New York: Ballantine Books, 1995.

Hacker, Jacob S., and Paul Pierson. *Winner-Take-All Politics: How Washington Made the Rich Richer—And Turned Its Back on the Middle Class*. New York: Simon & Schuster, 2010.

Hadaway, C. Kirk, Penny Long Marler, and Mark Chaves. "What the Polls Don't Show: A Closer Look at U.S. Church Attendance." *American Sociological Review* 58 (December 1993):741–752.

Hadden, Jeffrey K., and Raymond R. Rymph. "The Marching Ministers." In Jeffrey K. Hadden (Ed.), *Religion in Radical Transition*, 2nd ed. New Brunswick, NJ: Transaction Books, 1973, pp. 99–109.

Haferkamp, Hans, and Neil J. Smelser. (Eds.). *Social Change and Modernity*. Chapel Hill, NC: University of North Carolina Press, 1992.

Hagan, Frank E. *Introduction to Criminology*, 7th ed. Thousand Oaks, CA: Sage, Nelson-Hall Publishers, 2010.

Hagan, John. "The Social Embeddedness in Crime and Unemployment." *Criminology* 31 (November 1993):464–492.

Hagan, John. *Crime and Disrepute*. Thousand Oaks, CA: Pine Forge Press, 1994.

Hagedorn, John M. "Gang Violence in the Postindustrial Era." In Michael Tonry and Mark H. Moore (Eds.), *Youth Violence*. Chicago, IL: University of Chicago Press, 1998, pp. 365–419.

Hall, Edward T. "How Cultures Collide." *Psychology Today* 10 (July 1976):66ff.

Hall, Edward T. "Learning the Arabs' Silent Language." *Psychology Today* 13 (August 1979):45ff.

Hall, Edward T. *The Silent Language*. New York: Anchor Books, 1990.

Hall, John. "President's Remarks Leave Settlement Up in the Air." *American Business Review* (September 18, 1997):1.

Hall, Richard H. "Intraorganizational Structural Variation: Application of the Bureaucratic Model." *Administrative Science Quarterly* 7 (December 1962):295–308.

Hall, Richard H., and Pamela S. Tolbert. *Organizations*, 10th ed. Upper Saddle River, NJ: Prentice Hall, 2008.

Hallinan, Maureen T. "Equality of Educational Opportunity." In W. Richard Scott and Judith Blake (Eds.), *Annual Review of Sociology* 14 (1988):249–268.

Hallinan, Maureen T. (Ed.). *Restructuring Schools: Promising Practices and Policies*. South Bend, IN: University of Notre Dame, 1995.

Hallinan, Maureen T. (Ed.). *Handbook of the Sociology of Education*. New York: Springer-Verlag, 2006.

Hallock, Kevin F. "Reciprocally Interlocking Boards of Directors and Executive Compensation." *Journal of Financial and Quantitative Analysis* 32 (September 1997):331–344.

Hamilton, Peter, and Kenneth Thompson. (Eds.). *The Uses of Sociology*. Malden, MA: Blackwell Publishers, 2002.

Hamilton, Richard F. *The Social Misconstruction of Reality: Validity and Verification in the Scholarly Community*. New Haven, CT: Yale University Press, 1996.

Hampden-Turner, Charles, and Fons Trompenaars. *The Seven Cultures of Capitalism*. London: Piatkus, 1995.

Hampton, Robert L., et al. (Eds.). *Family Violence*. Newbury Park, CA: Sage, 1993.

Hancock, LynNell, and Pat Wingert. "A Mixed Report Card." *Newsweek* (November 13, 1995):69.

Hannon, Kelly. "Title IX: History of the Civil Rights Legislation." *Lynchburg News & Advance* (August 8, 2003).

Harlow, Harry F. "The Young Monkeys." *Psychology Today* 5 (1967):40–47.

Harlow, Harry F., and Margaret Harlow. "Social Deprivation in Monkeys." *Scientific American* 207 (November 1962):137–146.

Harlow, Harry F., and Robert R. Zimmerman. "Affectional Responses in the Infant Monkey." *Science* 21 (August 1959):421–432.

Harmon, Amy. "In DNA Era, New Worries about Prejudice." *New York Times* (November 11, 2007).

Harrendorf, Stefan, Markku Heiskanen, and Steven Malby. (Eds.). "International Statistics on Crime and Justice." Helsinki: European Institute for Crime Prevention and Control, 2010.

Harris, Chauncy D. "The Nature of Cities and Urban Geography in the Last Half Century." *Urban Geography* 18 (1997):15–35.

Harris, Chauncy D., and Edward L. Ullman. "The Nature of Cities." *Annals of the American Academy of Political and Social Science* 242 (November 1945):7–17.

Harris, Gardiner. "Cigarette Company Paid for Lung Cancer Study." *New York Times* (March 26, 2008).

Harris, Judith Rich. *The Nurture Assumption: Why Children Turn Out the Way They Do*. New York: Free Press, 1998.

Harris, Marvin. *Cows, Pigs, Wars, and Witches*. New York: Random House, 1974.

Harris, Marvin. *Our Kind: Who We Are, Where We Came From, and Where We Are Going*. New York: HarperTrade, 1990.

Hartman, Laura P. "Technology and Ethics: Privacy in the Workplace." Waltham, MA: Center for Business Ethics (February 28, 2000):1–28.

Hartung, William D. *Prophets of War: Lockheed Martin and the Making of the Military-Industrial Complex*. New York: Nation Books, 2011.

Haskins, Ron. *Wealth and Economic Mobility*. The Pew Charitable Trusts, Economic Mobility Project, 2010.

Haskins, Ron, and David Ellwood. *Welfare Reform and Intergenerational Mobility*. The Pew Charitable Trusts, Economic Mobility Project, 2010.

Haugen, David M. *Health Care*. Detroit: Greenhaven Press, 2008a.

Haugen, David M. *Islamic Fundamentalism*. Detroit: Greenhaven Press, 2008b.

Haupt, Arthur, and Thomas T. Kane. *Population Handbook*, 5th ed. Washington, DC: Population Reference Bureau, 2004.

Hauser, Marc D. *Wild Minds: What Animals Really Think*. New York: Henry Holt, 2001.

Hausmann, Ricardo, Laura D. Tyson, and Saadia Zahidi. *The Global Gender Gap Report*. Geneva, Switzerland: World Economic Forum, 2010.

Haviland, William A., et al. *Cultural Anthropology*, 13th ed. Belmont, CA: Wadsworth, 2011.

Hawkins, Asher. "Will the Silver State Go Green?" *Newsweek* (July 29, 2002):12.

Hawley, Amos H. *Urban Society*, 2nd ed. New York: Wiley, 1971.

Hawley, Amos H. "The Logic of Macrosociology." *Annual Review of Sociology* 18 (1992):1–14.

Hawley, W. D. "Achieving Quality Integrated Education—With or Without Federal Help." In F. Schultz (Ed.), *Annual Editions: Education 85/86*. Guilford, CT: Dushkin Publishing, 1985, pp. 142–145.

Hawley, W. D., and M. A. Smylie. "The Contribution of School Desegregation to Academic Achievement and Racial Integration." In P. A. Katz and D. A. Taylor (Eds.), *Eliminating Racism*. New York: Plenum Press, 1988, pp. 281–297.

Hays, Kim. *Practicing Virtues: Moral Traditions at Quaker and Military Boarding Schools*. Berkeley/Los Angeles, CA: University of California Press, 1994.

Health at a Glance: OECD Indicators. Paris, France: OECD Publishing, 2009.

Healy, Jack. "Madoff Is Sentenced to 150 Years for Ponzi Scheme." *New York Times* (June 30, 2009).

Heath, Chip, Chris Bell, and Emily Sternberg. "Emotional Selection in Memes: The Case of Urban Legends." *Journal of Personality and Social Psychology* 81 (December 2001):1028–1041.

Heatherton, Todd F., Michelle R. Hebl, and Jay G. Hull. (Eds.). *The Social Psychology of Stigma*. New York: Guilford Publications, 2000.

Hechter, Michael, and Karl-Dieter Opp. (Eds.). *Social Norms*. New York: Russell Sage Foundation, 2005.

Heckert, Druann Maria. "Positive Deviance." In Patricia A. Adler and Peter Adler (Eds.), *Constructions of Deviance: Social Power, Context, and Interaction*. Belmont, CA: Wadsworth, 2003, pp. 30–42.

Heclo, Hugh, and Wilfred M. McClay. (Eds.). *Religion Returns to the Public Square: Faith and Policy in America*. Washington, DC: Woodrow Wilson Center Press, 2002.

Heilbrunn, Jacob. *They Knew They Were Right*. New York: Doubleday, 2008.

Helle, H. J., and S. N. Eisenstadt. (Eds.). *Macro-Sociological Theory*, vol. 1. Beverly Hills, CA: Sage, 1985a.

Helle, H. J., and S. N. Eisenstadt. (Eds.). *Micro-Sociological Theory*, vol. 2. Beverly Hills, CA: Sage, 1985b.

"Hello, Dolly." *The Economist* 18 (March 1, 1997):17–18.

Hendricks, Jon, and C. Davis Hendricks. *Aging in Mass Society*, 3rd ed. New York: HarperCollege, 1987.

Henig, Jeffrey R. *Rethinking School Choice*. Princeton, NJ: Princeton University Press, 1994.

Henig, Robin Marantz. "What Is It About 20-Some Things?" *New York Times* (August 18, 2010).

Henretta, John C. *Age and Inequality*. New York: Perseus Publishing, 2001.

Henry, Stuart, and Mark Lanier. (Eds.). *What Is Crime? Controversies over the Nature of Crime and What to Do about It.* Lanham, MD: Rowman & Littlefield, 2001.

Henry, William A., III. "News as Entertainment: The Search for Dramatic Unity." In Elie Abel. (Ed.), *What's News.* San Francisco, CA: Institute for Contemporary Studies, 1981, pp. 133–158.

Hentschke, Guilbert C., Vicente M. Lechuga., and William G. Tierney. (Eds.). *For-Profit Colleges and Universities.* Sterling, VA: Stylus, 2010.

Herbert, Wray. "When Strangers Become Family." *U.S. News and World Report* (November 29, 1999):58–67.

Herman, Arthur. *How the Scots Invented the Modern World.* New York: Crown Publishers, 2001.

Hernández-León. *Metropolitan Migrants: The Migration of Urban Mexicans to the United States.* Berkeley, CA: University of California Press, 2008.

Herring, Cedric. "Is Job Discrimination Dead?" *Contexts* (Summer 2002):13–18.

Herrnstein, Richard J., and Charles A. Murray. *The Bell Curve: Intelligence and Class Structure in American Life.* New York: Free Press Paperbacks, 1996.

Herszenhorn, David M. "Congress Sends $801 Billion Tax Cut Bill to Obama." *New York Times* (December 16, 2010).

Herszenhorn, David M., and Carl Hulse. "Estate Tax Cutoff Draws Special Fire in Congress." *New York Times* (December 10, 2010).

Hertz, Rosanna. *Single by Chance, Mothers by Choice.* New York: Oxford University Press, 2006.

Hesiod. *Theogony, Works and Days, Shield.* Translation, Introduction, and Notes by Apostolos N. Athanassakis. Baltimore: Johns Hopkins University Press, 1983.

Hettena, Seth. *Feasting on the Spoils.* New York: St. Martin's Press, 2007.

Hewitt, John P. *Self and Society: A Symbolic Interactionist Social Psychology*, 9th ed. Boston, MA: Allyn & Bacon, 2002.

Hickson, Mark, III, and Julian Roebuck. *Deviance and Crime in Colleges and Universities: What Goes on in the Halls of Ivy.* Springfield, IL: Charles C. Thomas Pub. Ltd, 2009.

Higginbotham, Elizabeth, and Margaret L. Andersen. *Race and Ethnicity in Society*, 2nd ed. Belmont, CA: Wadsworth, 2011.

Hilbert, Richard A. "Ethnomethodology and the Micro-Macro Order." *American Sociological Review* 55 (December 1990):794–808.

Hill, Michael R., and Susan Hoecker-Drysdale. (Eds.). *Harriet Martineau: Theoretical and Methodological Perspectives.* New York: Routledge, 2001.

Hill, Steven. *Fixing Elections: The Failure of America's Winner Take All Politics.* Bristol, PA: Taylor and Francis, 2003.

Hillier, Susan, and Georgia M. Barrow. *Aging, the Individual, and Society*, 9th ed. Belmont, CA: Wadsworth, 2011.

Himes, Christine L. "Elderly Americans." *Population Bulletin* 56 (December 2001):1–40.

Hirsch, E. D. Jr. *Cultural Literacy.* Boston, MA: Houghton Mifflin, 1987.

Hirsch, E. D. *The Schools We Need and Why We Don't Have Them.* New York: Doubleday, 1999.

Hirsch, E. D. *The New First Dictionary of Cultural Literacy*, 3rd ed. Boston, MA: Houghton Mifflin Company, 2004.

Hirschfeld, Lawrence A. *Race in the Making.* Cambridge, MA: MIT Press, 1998.

Hirschi, Travis. *Causes of Delinquency.* Berkeley, CA: University of California Press, 1972.

Hirschi, Travis, and Hanan Selvin. *Principles of Survey Analysis.* New York: Free Press, 1973.

Hirschi, Travis, and Michael R. Gottfredson. "Substantive Positivism and the Idea of Crime." *Rationality and Society* 2 (October 1990):412–428.

Hobbes, Thomas. *Leviathan.* Edited by Herbert W. Schneider. New York: Liberal Arts Press, 1958.

Hochschild, Arlie R. *The Managed Heart: Commercialization of Feeling*, 20th anniversary ed. Berkeley, CA: University of California Press, 2003.

Hochschild, Arlie R., and Anne Machung. *The Second Shift.* New York: Avon, 2001.

Hochschild, Arlie R., and Anne Machung. *The Time Bind: When Work Becomes Home and Home Becomes Work.* New York: Penguin, 2003.

Hodge, Robert W., and Donald J. Treiman. "Class Identification in the U.S." *American Journal of Sociology* 73 (March 1968):535–547.

Hodge, Robert W., Donald J. Treiman, and Peter H. Rossi. "A Comparative Study of Occupational Prestige." In Reinhard Bendix and Seymour Martin Lipset (Eds.), *Class, Status, and Power*, 2nd ed. New York: Free Press, 1966, pp. 309–321.

Hodge, Robert W., Paul M. Siegel, and Peter H. Rossi. "Occupational Prestige in the United States, 1925–1963." *American Journal of Sociology* 70 (November 1964):286–302.

Hodson, Randy, and Teresa A. Sullivan. *The Social Organization of Work*, 5th ed. Belmont, CA: Wadsworth, 2011.

Hodson, Randy, and Robert L. Kaufman. "Economic Dualism: A Critical Review." *American Sociological Review* 47 (December 1982):727–739.

Hoebel, E. Adamson. *The Law of Primitive Man.* New York: Atheneum, 1983.

Hoffer, Richard. "Bannister and Hillary." *Sports Illustrated* (December 27, 1999):96.

Hoffman, Lois W., and Francis I. Nye. *Working Mothers.* San Francisco, CA: Jossey-Bass, 1975.

Hofstadter, Richard. *Anti-Intellectualism in American Life.* New York: Knopf Publishing Group, 1966.

Hofstadter, Richard. *America at 1750.* New York: Vintage, 1973.

Hogan, Dennis P., and Nan Marie Astone. "Transition to Adulthood." In Ralph H. Turner and James F. Short Jr. (Eds.), *Annual Review of Sociology* 12 (1986):109–130.

Hogg, Michael A., and Dominic Abrams. (Eds.). *Intergroup Relations: Essential Readings.* Philadelphia, PA: Psychology Press, 2001.

Holland, Joshua. "The American Dream Is Alive and Well . . . in Finland." *Alternet* (December 11, 2007). http://www.alternet.org/story/70103/

Hollingshead, August B. *Elmtown's Youth.* New York: Wiley, 1949.

Hollingshead, August B., and Frederick C. Redlich. *Social Class and Mental Illness.* New York: Wiley, 1958.

Holmberg, Allan R. *Nomads of the Long Bow.* Garden City, NY: Natural History Press, 1969.

Holt, John. *How Children Fail*, rev. ed. Reading, MA: Perseus Books, 1995a.

Holt, John. *How Children Fail.* Cambridge, MA: Da Capo Press, 1995b.

Holt, John. *How Children Learn.* Cambridge, MA: Da Capo Press, 1995c.

Holt, John, and Patrick Farenga. *Teach Your Own.* Cambridge, MA: Da Capo Press, 2003.

Hook, Donald D. *Death in the Balance.* Lexington, MA: Heath, 1989.

Hoover, Stewart M. *The Social Sources of the Electronic Church.* Newbury Park, CA: Sage, 1988.

Hooyman, Nancy R., and H. Asuman Kiyak. *Social Gerontology*, 8th ed. Boston, MA: Allyn & Bacon, 2007.

Hope, Keith. "Vertical and Nonvertical Class Mobility in Three Countries." *American Sociological Review* 47 (February 1982):99–113.

Hopfe, Lewis M., and Mark R. Woodward. *Religions of the World*, 11th ed. Upper Saddle River, NJ: Pearson Education, Inc, 2009.

Hornblum, Allen M. *Acres of Skin: Human Experiments at Holmesburg Prison*. New York: Routledge, 1998.

Horsley, Richard A. *Jesus and Empire: The Kingdom of God and the New World Disorder*. Minneapolis, MN: Fortress Press, 2003.

Horwitz, Allan V. *The Logic of Social Control*. New York: Plenum, 1990.

Horwitz, Robert A. "Psychological Effects of the Open Classroom." *Review of Educational Research* 49 (Winter 1979):71–86.

Hougland, James G. Jr., and Willis A. Sutton Jr. "Factors Influencing Degree of Involvement in Interorganizational Relationships in a Rural County." *Rural Sociology* 43 (Winter 1978):649–670.

Houseman, John. "The Men from Mars." *Harper's Magazine* 197 (December 1948):74–82.

How Schools Shortchange Girls: A Study of Major Findings on Girls and Education. Washington, DC: American Association of University Women, 1992.

Hoyt, Homer. *The Structure and Growth of Residential Neighborhoods in American Cities*. Washington, DC: Federal Housing Authority, 1939.

Hrdy, Sarah Blaffer. *The Woman That Never Evolved*, rev. ed. Cambridge, MA: Harvard University Press, (1999). Available online at www.tvb.org/tvfacts/tvbacis/basics6.html

Hrdy, Sarah Blaffer. *Mother Nature: Maternal Instincts and How They Shape the Human Species*. New York: Ballantine Books, 2000.

Hrdy, Sarah Blaffer. *Mothers and Others: The Evolutionary Origins of Mutual Understanding*. Cambridge, MA: Harvard University Press, 2009.

Hubbard, L. Ron. *What Is Scientology?* Los Angeles, CA: Bridge, 1998.

Huber, Peter, and Jessica Korn. "The Plug-And-Play Economy." *Forbes* (July 7, 1997):268–272.

Hudak, Glenn M., and Paul Kihn. (Eds.). *Labeling: Pedagogy and Politics*. New York: Routledge, 2001.

Hudson, Ken. *Duality and Dual Labor Markets*. Revision of a paper presented at the 93rd Annual Meetings of the American Sociological Association, 2000.

Hudson, Michael W. *The Monster: How a Gang of Predatory Lenders and Wall Street Bankers Fleeced America—and Spawned a Global Crisis*. New York: Times Books, 2010.

Huffington, Arianna. *Pigs at the Trough: How Corporate Greed and Political Corruption Are Undermining America*. New York: Crown Publishers, 2004.

Hughes, John A., Peter J. Martin, and W. W. Sharrock. *Understanding Classical Sociology*. Thousand Oaks, CA: Sage, 1995.

Hughes, Michael, and Melvin E. Thomas. "The Continuing Significance of Race Revisited: A Study of Race, Class, and Quality of Life in America, 1972 to 1996." *American Sociological Review* 63 (December 1998):785–795.

Hull, Kathleen E., Ann Meier, and Timothy Ortyl. "The Changing Landscape of Love and Marriage." *Contexts* (Spring 2010):32–37.

Human Development Report 2002. New York: Oxford University Press, 2002.

Human Development Report 2010. The Real Wealth of Nations: Pathways to Human Development. New York: United Nations Development Programme, 2010.

Hummel, Ralph P. *The Bureaucratic Experience*, 3rd ed. New York: St. Martin's Press, 1987.

Humphrey, Craig R., and Frederick H. Buttel. *Environment, Energy and Society*. Malabar, FL: Krieger Publishing, 1986.

Humphreys, Laud. *Tearoom Trade*. New York: Aldine, 1979.

Hung, Ho-Fung. (Ed.). *China and the Transformation of Global Capitalism*. Baltimore, MD: Johns Hopkins University, 2009.

Hunt, Morton M. *The New Know-Nothings: The Political Foes of the Scientific Study of Human Nature*. New Brunswick, NJ: Transactions, 1999.

Hunt, Stephen, Malcolm Hamilton, and Tony Walter. (Eds.). *Charismatic Christianity: Sociological Perspectives*. New York: St. Martin's Press, 1998.

Hunter, Floyd. *Community Power Structure*. Chapel Hill, NC: University of North Carolina Press, 1953.

Hunter, Floyd. *Community Power Succession*. Chapel Hill, NC: University of North Carolina Press, 1980.

Hunter, James Davison. *Evangelicism*. Chicago, IL: University of Chicago Press, 1987.

Hurley, Jennifer A. (Ed.). *Racism*. San Diego, CA: Greenhaven Press, 1998.

Hurn, Christopher J. *The Limits and Possibilities of Schooling*, 3rd ed. Boston, MA: Allyn & Bacon, 1993.

Ibrahim, Vivian. "Ethnicity." In Stephen M. Caliendo and Charlton D. McIlwain (Eds.), *Race and Ethnicity*. London: Routledge, 2011, pp. 12–28.

Ikeda, Keiko. *A Room Full of Mirrors*. Stanford, CA: Stanford University Press, 1998.

"The Impact of Racial and Ethnic Diversity on Educational Outcomes." Cambridge, MA: The Civil Rights Project, January 2002.

Inciardi, James A. *Criminal Justice*, 9th ed. New York: McGraw-Hill, 2009.

Infante, Esme M. "Panel: Nicotine Addictive." *USA Today* (August 13, 1994):A1.

Ingoldsby, Bron B., and Suzanna D. Smith. (Eds.). Families in Global and Multicultural Perspective, 2nd ed. Thousand Oaks, CA: Sage Publications, 2006.

Ingrassia, Michele, and Melinda Beck. "Patterns of Abuse." *Newsweek* (July 4, 1994):26–33.

Inkeles, Alex. *One World Emerging? Convergence and Divergence in Industrial Societies*. Boulder, CO: Westview Press, 1998.

Insana, Ron. *Trendwatching: Don't Be Fooled by the Next Investment Fad, Mania, or Bubble*. New York: HarperCollins, 2002.

"In U.S., Religions Prejudice Stronger Against Muslims." *Gallys Center for Muslim Studies* (January 21, 2010).

Isaacs, Julia B. "Economic Mobility of Black and White Families." Economic Mobility Project. Washington, DC: Pew Charitable Trusts, 2007a.

Isaacs, Julia B. "Economic Mobility of Families Across Generations." Economic Mobility Project. Washington, DC: Pew Charitable Trusts, 2007b.

Isaacs, Julia B. "Economic Mobility of Men and Women." Economic Mobility Project. Washington, DC: Pew Charitable Trusts, 2007c.

Isaacs, Julia B. "*International Comparisons of Economic Mobility*." The Pew Charitable Trusts, Economic Mobility Project, 2010.

Isidore, Chris. "The Rich Are Much Richer than You and Me." CNNMoney.com (December 23, 2010). http://money.cnn/2010/12/23

Isikoff, Michael. "Christian Coalition Steps Boldly into Politics." *Washington Post* (September 10, 1992):A1, A14.

ITO, Mizuko, et al. "Living and Learning with New Media: Summary of Findings from the Digital Youth Project." Chicago, IL: MacArthur Foundation, November 2008. www.macfound.org

Jackman, Mary R., and Robert W. Jackman. *Class Awareness in the United States*. Berkeley, CA: University of California Press, 1983.

Jackson, Elton F., and Harry J. Crockett Jr. "Occupational Mobility in the United States: A Point Estimate and Trend Comparison." *American Sociological Review* 29 (February 1964):5–15.

Jackson, Stevi, and Sue Scott. (Eds.). *Gender: A Sociological Reader*. New York: Routledge, 2001.

Jacobe, Dennis. "Work Is Part of Many Investors' Retirement Plans." *Gallup News Service* (November 16, 2004).

Jacobs, Jerry A., and Kathleen Gerson. *The Time Divide: Work, Family, and Gender Inequality*. Cambridge, MA: Harvard University Press, 2004.

Jacobson, Neil S., and John Gottman. *When Men Batter Women*. New York: Simon & Schuster Trade, 1998.

Jacoby, Sanford M. *Modern Manors: Welfare Capitalism Since the New Deal. Princeton*. Princeton, NJ: Princeton University Press, 1997.

Jacoby, Susan. *The Age of American Unreason*. New York: Knopf Publishing Group, 2008a.

Jacoby, Susan. "How Dumb Can We Get?" *The Week* (February 29, 2008b):36–37.

Jaggar, Alison M., and Paula S. Rothenberg. *Feminist Frameworks*, 3rd ed. New York: McGraw-Hill, 1993.

James, Paul. *Nation Formation*. Thousand Oaks, CA: Sage, 1996.

Janis, Irving L. *Groupthink*, 2nd ed. Boston, MA: Houghton Mifflin, 2006.

Janofsky, Michael. "Rustic Life of Amish Is Changing but Slowly." *New York Times* (July 6, 1997):7.

Janowitz, Morris. *Sociology and the Military Establishment*, 3rd ed. Beverly Hills, CA: Sage, 1974.

Janssen-Jurreit, and Marie Louise. *Sexism*. New York: Farrar Strauss Giroux, 1982.

Jasinski, Jana L. (Ed.). *Partner Violence: A Comprehensive Review of Twenty Years of Research*. Thousand Oaks, CA: Sage, 2000.

Jencks, Christopher. *Inequality*. New York: HarperCollins Publishers, 1981.

Jencks, Christopher, and Meredith Phillips. (Eds.). *The Black-White Test Score Gap*. Washington, DC: Brookings Institution, 1998.

Jenkins, J. Craig. "Resource Mobilization Theory and the Study of Social Movements." In Ralph H. Turner and James F. Short Jr. (Eds.), *Annual Review of Sociology* 9 (1983):527–553.

Jensen, Arthur. How Much Can We Boost IQ and Scholastic Achievement? *Harvard Educational Review* 39 (Winter 1969):1–123.

Jilani, Zaid. "Health Insurers Spent $38 Million Lobbying Congress in 2009." *Think Progress* (January 25, 2010). http://thinkprogress.org/2010/01/25/health-insurers-2009/

Johnson, Charles Richard, and Patricia Smith. *Africans in America: America's Journey Through Slavery*. San Diego, CA: Harcourt Brace and Company, 1998.

Johnson, Darragh. "SAT Scores Dip Slightly Overall: Widening Racial Gap Is Greater Concern." *Washington Post* (August 29, 2002):A03.

Johnson, David W., and Frank P. Johnson. *Joining Together*, 5th ed. Boston, MA: Allyn & Bacon, 1994.

Johnson, Dirk. "A Leap of Fate." *Newsweek* (January 20, 2003a):34.

Johnson, Dirk. "The Night the Music Died." *Newsweek* (March 3, 2003b):40–42.

Johnson, George. *The Ten Most Beautiful Experiments*. New York: Alfred A. Knopf, 2008.

Johnson, Kevin. "DNA Tests Fuel Urgency to Free the Innocent." *USA Today* (February 2, 2008).

Johnson, Michael P. "Differentiating Among Types of Domestic Violence: Implications for Healthy Families." In H. Elizabeth Peters and Claire M. Kamp Bush (Eds.), *Marriage and Family*. New York: Columbia University Press, 2009, pp. 281–300.

Johnson, Norris R. "Panic at 'The Who Concert Stompede': An Empirical Assessment." *Social Problems* 34 (October 1987):362–373.

Johnson, R.W. and J. M. Weiner. "A Profile of Frail Older Americans and Their Caregivers." Urban Institute Report, 2006. http://urban.org/url.efm?ID=311284

Johnson, Steven. *Everything Bad Is Good for You*. New York: Riverhead Books, 2006.

Johnson, Troy R. *Contemporary Native American Political Issues*. Thousand Oaks, CA: AltaMira Press, 2000.

Johnston, David Cay. *Perfectly Legal*. New York: Portfolio, 2005.

Johnston, David Cay. *Free Lunch*. New York: Penguin Books, 2007a.

Johnston, David Cay. "Report Says That the Rich Are Getting Richer, Faster, Much." *New York Times* (December 15, 2007b).

Johnston, David Cay. "Tax Rates for Top Earners Fall as Income Sears, IRS Data." *The Tax Daily for Citizen Taxpayer* (September 30, 2010), Tax.com

Johnstone, Ronald L. *Religion in Society*, 8th ed. Upper Saddle River, NJ: Prentice Hall, 2009.

Jones, A. H. M. *The Decline of the Ancient World*. New York: Holt, Rinehart and Winston, 1966.

Jones, Daniel. (Ed.). *Dylan Thomas: The Poems*. London: J. M. Dent and Sons, 1971.

Jones, James H. *Alfred C. Kinsey: A Public/Private Life*. New York: Norton, 1997.

Jones, James M. *Prejudice and Racism*. Reading, MA: Addison-Wesley, 1972.

Jones, James M. *Bad Blood*, expanded ed. New York: Free Press, 1993.

Jones, Jeffrey M. "Trust in Government Declining, Near Lows for the Past Decade." *Gallup News Service* (September 26, 2006).

Jones, Jeffrey M. "Low Trust in Federal Government Rivals Watergate Era Levels." *Gallup News Service* (September 26, 2007).

Jones, Pip, Shawn Le Boeutillier, and Liz Bradbury. *Introducing Social Theory*, 2nd ed. Cambridge, UK: Polity Books, 2011.

Jones, Robert Alun. *The Development of Durkheim's Social Realism*. New York: Cambridge University Press, 2005.

Juliano, Nick. "Income Inequality Worst Since 1920s, According to IRS Data." *The Raw Story* (October 12, 2007). http://rawstory.com/printstory.phpostory=7882

Kadushin, Charles. "Mental Health and the Interpersonal Environment: A Reexamination of Some Effects of Social Structure on Mental Health." *American Sociological Review* 48 (April 1983):188–198.

Kahlenberg, Richard D. (Ed.). *Public School Choice vs. Private School Vouchers*. New York: The Century Foundation, 2003.

Kahne, Joseph, Ellen Middaugh, and Chris Evans. "The Civic Potential of Video Games." Civic Engagement Research Group of Mills College (September 7, 2008). www.civicsurvey.org

Kaiser, Robert G. *So Damn Much Money: The Triumph of Lobbying and the Corrosion of American Government*. New York: Knopf Doubleday Publishing Group, 2010.

Kamenetz, Anya. *Generation Debt*. New York: Penguin Group (USA), 2006.

Kamenetz, Anya. *DIY U. White River Jet*. Hartford, VT: Chelsea Green Publishing, 2010.

Kanter, Rosabeth Moss. *Commitment and Community*. Cambridge, MA: Harvard University Press, 1972.

Kanter, Rosabeth Moss. *Men and Women of the Corporation.* New York: Basic Books, 1993.

Kantrowitz, Barbara. "The Group Classroom." *Newsweek* (May 10, 1993a):73.

Kantrowitz, Barbara. "A Nation Still at Risk." *Newsweek* (April 19, 1993b):46–49.

Kaplan, Fred. *Daydream Believers.* New York: John Wiley & Sons, 2008.

Kaplan, Jeffrey, and Helene Loow. (Eds.). *Cultic Milieu.* Thousand Oaks, CA: AltaMira Press, 2002.

Karatnycky, Adrian. "Democracies on the Rise, Democracies at Risk." *Freedom Review* 26 (January/February 1995):5–10.

Kardulias, P. Nick (Ed.). *World-Systems Theory in Practice: Leadership, Production, and Exchange.* Lanham, MD: Rowman & Littlefield, 1999.

Karson, Jill. (Ed.). *Cults.* San Diego, CA: Greenhaven Press, 2000.

Kasarda, John D., and Morris Janowitz. "Community Attachment in Mass Society." *American Sociological Review* 39 (June 1974):328–339.

Kashef, Ziba. "Is DNA Research Giving New Life to the Idea That Race Exists?" *Alternet* (October 18, 2007). http://alternet.org/story/65484

Kate, Nancy T. "Two Careers, One Marriage." *American Demographics* (April 1998):28.

Katsiaficas, George N., and Teodros Kiros. (Eds.). *The Promise of Multiculturalism: Education and Autonomy in the 21st Century.* New York: Routledge, 1998.

Katz, Irwin. "Desegregation or Integration in Public Schools?: The Policy Implications of Research." *Integrated Education* 5 (December 1967/January 1968):15–28.

Katz, Michael B. *Class, Bureaucracy and Schools.* New York: Praeger, 1975.

Katz, Michael B. (Ed.). *The "Underclass" Debate.* Princeton, NJ: Princeton University Press, 1993.

Katznelson, Ira, Mark Kesselman, and Alan Draper. *The Politics of Power: A Critical Introduction to American Government,* 5th ed. Belmont, CA: Wadsworth, 2005.

Kaufman, Philip. *Dropout Rates in the United States: 1999.* Washington, DC: National Center for Education Statistics, November 2000.

Kaufman, Philip. *The Nation's Report Card: Fourth Grade Reading 2000.* Washington, DC: National Center for Education Statistics, 2001.

Kaufman, Robert L. *Race, Gender, and the Labor Market.* Boulder, CO: Lynne Reinner Publishers, 2010.

Kearl, Michael C., and Anoel Rinaldi. "The Political Uses of the Dead as Symbols in Contemporary Civil Religions." *Social Forces* 61 (March 1983):693–708.

Keating, Dan, and Theola Labbe-DeBose. "Charter Schools Make Gains on Tests." *Washington Post* (December 15, 2008).

Keen, Judy. "In Capital, Business and Politics Firmly Entwined." *USA Today* (July 31, 2002):1A, 2A.

Kellam, Sheppard G., Margaret E. Ensminger, and R. Jay Turner. "Family Structure and the Mental Health of Children." *Archives of General Psychiatry* 34 (September 1977):1012–1022.

Kelley, Harold H., and John W. Thibaut. "Group Problem Solving." In Gardner Lindzey and Elliot Aronson (Eds.), *The Handbook of Social Psychology,* vol. 4. Reading, MA: Addison-Wesley, 1969, pp. 735–785.

Kelley, Maryellen R. "New Process Technology, Job Design, and Work Organization: A Contingency Model." *American Sociological Review* 55 (1990):191–208.

Kelly, Delos H. (Ed.). *Deviant Behavior,* 5th ed. New York: St. Martin's Press, 1996.

Kendall, Diana. *Sociology in Our Times,* 8th ed. Belmont, CA: Wadsworth, 2010.

Kenneally, Christine. "When Language Can Hold the Answer." *New York Times* (April 22, 2008).

Kennedy, Randall. *Interracial Intimacies: Sex, Marriage, Identity, and Adoption.* New York: Knopf, 2003.

Kent, Mary M., and Mark Mather. "What Drives U.S. Population Growth?" *Population Bulletin* 57 (December 2002):3–40.

Kephart, William M., and Davor Jedlicka. *The Family, Society, and the Individual,* 7th ed. New York: HarperCollins, 1997.

Khouri, Norma. *Honor Lost: Love and Death in Jordan.* New York: Simon & Schuster, 2005. Kibria, Nazli. *Becoming Asian American: Second-Generation Chinese and Korean American Identities.* Baltimore, MD: Johns Hopkins University Press, 2003.

Kiefer, Heather Mason. "Public on Justice System: Fair, but Still Too Soft." *Gallup* (February 3, 2004).

Kilbourne, Jean. "Beauty and the Beast of Advertising." In James M. Henslin (Ed.), *Down to Earth Sociology.* New York: Free Press, 2001, pp. 391–394.

Kilgore, Sally B. "The Organizational Context of Tracking in Schools." *American Sociological Review* 56 (April 1991):189–203.

Killian, Lewis M. "Organization, Rationality and Spontaneity in the Civil Rights Movement." *American Sociological Review* 49 (December 1984):770–783.

Kilmann, P. R., L. V. Carranza, and J. M. C. Vendemia. "Recollections of Parent Characteristics and Attachment Patterns for College Women of Intact vs. Non-Intact Families." *Journal of Adolescence* 29 (2006):89–102.

Kilson, Martin L. "The State of African-American Politics." In Lee A. Daniels (Ed.), *The State of Black America 1998.* New York: National Urban League, 1998, pp. 247–270.

Kilson, Martin L. "African Americans and American Politics 2002: The Maturation Phase." In Lee A. Daniels (Ed.), *The State of Black America 2002.* New York: National Urban League, 2002, pp. 147–180.

Kim, Changttwan, and Arthur Sakamoto. "Have Asian American Men Achieved Labor Market Parity with White Men?" *American Sociological Review* 75 (December 2010):934–957.

Kimmel, Michael S. *Gendered Society.* New York: Oxford University Press, 2000.

Kimmel, Michael. *Guyland: The Perilous World Where Boys Become Men.* New York: HarperCollins Publishers, 2008.

Kinsella, Kevin, and David R. Phillips. "Global Aging: The Challenge of Success." *Population Bulletin* 60 (March 2005):1–40.

Kinser, Kevin. *From Main Street to Wall Street: The Transformation of For-Profit Higher Education.* San Francisco, CA: The ASHE Higher Education Report, 2006.

Kinsey, Alfred C., and Paul Gebhard. *Sexual Behavior in the Human Female.* Philadelphia, PA: Saunders, 1953.

Kinsey, Alfred C., Wardell Pomeroy, and Clyde Martin. *Sexual Behavior in the Human Male.* Philadelphia, PA: Saunders, 1948.

Kinzie, Susan. "Internet Access Is Only Prerequisite for More and More College Classes." *Washington Post* (December 31, 2007).

Kirkpatrick, David. "Smart New Ways to Use Temps." *Fortune* (February 15, 1988):110–116.

Kissman, Kris, and Jo Ann Allen. *Single-Parent Families.* Newbury Park, CA: Sage, 1993.

Kitano, Harry H. *The Japanese Americans,* 2nd ed. New York: Chelsea House, 2005.

Kitano, Harry H., and Roger Daniels. *Asian Americans,* 4th ed. Englewood Cliffs, NJ: Prentice Hall, 2005.

Klandermans, Bert. "Mobilization and Participation: Social Psychological Explanations of Resource Mobilization Theory." *American Sociological Review* 49 (1984):583–600.

Klein, Naomi. *The Shock Doctrine: The Rise of Disaster Capitalism.* New York: Henry Holt & Company, 2007.

Kleniewski, Nancy, and Alexander R. Thomas. *Cities, Change, and Conflict,* 4th ed. Belmont, CA: Wadsworth, 2011.

Klineberg, Otto. "Race Differences: The Present Position of the Problem." *International Social Science Bulletin* 2 (Autumn 1950):460–466.

Kluegel, James R., and Eliot R. Smith. *Beliefs About Inequality: Americans' Views of What Ought to Be.* New Brunswick, NJ: Aldine Transaction, 2009.

Kluger, Jeffrey. "Here, Kitty, Kitty!" *Time* (February 25, 2002):58–59.

Kluger, Jeffrey, and Andrea Dorfman. "The Challenges We Face." *Time* (August 26, 2002):A6–A12.

Knickmeyer, Ellen. "A New Text in Islamic Law." *Washington Post* (January 19, 2008).

Knight, Louise W. *Jane Addams.* New York: W. W. Norton & Company, 2010.

Knox, David, and Caroline Schacht. *Choices in Relationships: Introduction to Marriage and the Family,* 10th ed. Belmont, CA: Wadsworth, 2010.

Kochlar, Rakesh. "After the Great Recession: Foreign Born Gain Jobs; Native-Born Lose Jobs." Pew Research Center (October 29, 2010).

Kocieniewski, David. "G.E.'s Strategies Let It Avoid Taxes Altogether." *New York Times* (March 24, 2011).

Kohl, Herbert. *Growing Minds.* New York: Harper Touchbook, 1988.

Kohn, Alfie. *No Contest: The Case Against Competition,* rev. ed. Boston, MA: Houghton Mifflin Company, 1992.

Kohn, Melvin L., and Carmi Schooler. *Work and Personality: An Inquiry into the Impact of Social Stratification.* Norwood, NJ: Ablex, 1983.

Kohut, Andrew. "Gender Equality Universally Embraced, but Inequalities Acknowledged. Global Attitudes Project." Washington, DC: Pew Research Center, 2010.

Kolbe, Richard, and Joseph C. LaVoie. "Sex-Role Stereotyping in Preschool Children's Picture Books." *Social Psychology Quarterly* 44 (December 1981):369–374.

Konner, Melvin. "Darwin's Truth, Jefferson's Vision." *The American Prospect* (July/August 1999): 30–38.

Koon, Jeff, Andy Powell, and Ward Schumaker. *You May Not Tie an Alligator to a Fire Hydrant: 101 Real Dumb Laws.* New York: Free Press, 2002.

Koppel, Ross. "American Public Policy: Formation and Implementation." In Roger A. Straus (Ed.), *Using Sociology,* 3rd ed. Lanham, MD: Rowman & Littlefield, 2002, pp. 265–228.

Korgen, Kathleen Odell. *From Black to Biracial: Transforming Racial Identity Among Americans.* Westport, CT: Praeger, 1998.

Kornblum, J. "More Women 40 to 44 Remaining Childless." *USA Today* (August 19, 2008):12B.

Kornblut, Anne E., and S. H. Spencer. "Arizona Governor Signs Immigration Bill, Reopening National Debate." *Washington Post* (April 24, 2010):401.

Kosmin, Barry A., and Ariela Keysar. "American Religious Identification Survey." Summary Report. Hartford, CT: Trinity College, March 2009.

Kovner, Anthony R., and James R. Knickman. (Eds.). *Health Care Delivery in the United States.* New York: Springer Publishing Company, Inc, 2008.

Kovner, Christine. "Nursing." In Anthony R. Kovner (Ed.), *Health Care Delivery in the United States,* 4th ed. New York: Springer, 1990, pp. 87–105.

Kowalski, Robin M., Susan P. Limber, and Patricia W. Agatston. *Cyber Bullying: Bullying in the Digital Age.* Malden, MA: Blackwell Publishing, 2008.

Kozol, Jonathan. *Death at an Early Age.* New York: Penguin, 1985.

Kozol, Jonathan. *Savage Inequalities: Children in America's Schools.* New York: HarperCollins, 1992.

Kozol, Jonathan. *The Shame of the Nation: The Restoration of Apartheid Schooling in America.* New York: Three Rivers Press, 2005.

Kozol, Jonathan. *The Shame of the Nation.* New York: Crown Publishing Group, 2006.

Kraar, Louis. The Real Threat to China's Hong Kong. *Fortune* 135 (May 26, 1997):84.

Kraditor, Aileen S. *The Ideas of the Woman's Suffrage Movement 1890–1920.* Garden City, NY: Anchor Books, 1971.

Kraybill, Donald B., and Marc A. Olshan. (Eds.). *The Amish Struggle with Modernity.* Hanover, NH: University Press of New England, 1994.

Kreider, Rose M., and Diana B. Elliott. "America's Family and Living Arrangements: 2007." Current Population Reports. P20-561. U.S. Census Bureau, Economics and Statistics Administration, September 2009, pp. 1–21.

Kriesi, Hanspeter. "New Social Movements and the New Class in the Netherlands." *American Journal of Sociology* 94 (March 1989):1078–1116.

Kritz, Francesca Lunzer. "uncertainty@dr-mail.com." *Washington Post* (April 1, 2003):F1, F5.

Kronenfeld, Jennie Jacobs (Ed.). *Research in the Sociology of Health Care: Changing Organizational Forms of Delivering Health Care,* vol. 15. Greenwich, CT: JAI Press, 1998.

Kruschwitz, Robert B., and Robert C. Roberts. *The Virtues.* Belmont, CA: Wadsworth, 1987.

Kübler-Ross, Elisabeth. *On Death and Dying.* New York: Taylor & Francis, Inc, Touchstone, 2008.

Kübler-Ross, Elisabeth. *Death: The Final Stage.* New York: Simon & Schuster, 2009.

Kumar, Krishan. *From Post-Industrial to Post-Modern Society.* New York: Wiley, 2004.

Kurlaender, Michal, and John T. Yun. "Is Diversity a Compelling Educational Interest? Evidence from Metropolitan Louisville." Cambridge, MA: Civil Rights Project, August 2000.

Kurtz, Lester R. *Gods in the Global Village: The World's Religions in Sociological Perspective,* 2nd ed. Thousand Oaks, CA: Pine Forge Press, 2007.

Kuttner, Robert. "Competitiveness Craze." *Washington Post* (August 12, 1993a):A17.

Kuttner, Robert. "The Corporation in America: Is It Socially Redeemable?" *Dissent* (Winter 1993b):35–49.

Kuttner, Robert. *The Squandering of America.* New York: Knopf Publishing Group, 2007.

Kymlicka, Will. *Multicultural Odysseys: Navigating the New International Politics of Diversity.* New York: Oxford University Press, 2007.

Labaree, David F. *How to Succeed in School without Really Learning: The Credentials Race in American Education.* New Haven, CT: Yale University Press, 1997.

Lacayo, Richard. "Wounding the Gun Lobby." *Time* (March 29, 1993):29–30.

Lachman, Margie E., and Jacquelyn Boone James. "Charting the Course of Midlife Development: An Overview." In Margie E. Lachman and Jacquelyn Boone James (Eds.), *Multiple Paths of Midlife Development.* Chicago, IL: University of Chicago Press, 1997, pp. 1–17.

Lachman, Margie E., et al. "Images of Midlife Development Among Young, Middle-Aged, and Older Adults." *Journal of Adult Development* 1 (1994):201–211.

Lamanna, Mary Ann, Agnes Riedmann, and Agnes Czerwinski Riedmann. *Marriages and Families: Making Choices and Facing Change,* 9th ed. Belmont, CA: Wadsworth, 2005.

Lamb, Michael B., M. Ann Easterbrooks, and George W. Holden. "Reinforcement and Punishment Among Preschoolers: Characteristics, Effects, and Correlates." *Child Development* 51 (1980):1230–1236.

Lambert, A. N. "Perceptions of Divorce—Advantages and Disadvantages: A Comparison of Adult Children Experiencing One Parental Divorce Versus Multiple Parental Divorces." *Journal of Divorce & Remarriage* 48 (2007):55–77.

Lampert, Leslie. "Fat Like Me." *Ladies Home Journal* (May 1993):154ff.

Landes, David S., and Charles Tilly. (Eds.). *History as Social Science.* Englewood Cliffs, NJ: Prentice Hall, 1991.

Landmark: The Inside Story of America's New Health-Care Law and What It Means for Us All. New York: Public Affairs, 2010.

Landry, Bart. *The New Black Middle Class.* Berkeley, CA: University of California Press, 1988.

Lane, Charles. "Ruling Is Landmark Victory for Gay Rights." *Washington Post* (June 27, 2003b):A1, A16.

Lang, Robert E., and Patrick E. Simmons. "'Boomburbs': The Emergence of Large, Fast-Growing Suburban Cities in the United States." Fannie Mae Foundation *Census Note* 6 (June 2001).

Lanier, Mark M., and Stuart Henry. *Essential Criminology*, 2nd ed. Boulder, CO: Westview Press, 2004.

Lapchick, Richard. "The 2008 Racial and Gender Report Card." Orlando, FL: The Institute for Diversity and Ethics in Sport, Central Florida University, 2009.

Lapchick, Richard. "The 2010 Racial and Gender Report Card: Major League Baseball." Orlando, FL: The Institute for Diversity and Ethics in Sport, Central Florida University, April 29, 2010a.

Lapchick, Richard. "The 2010 Racial and Gender Report Card: National Basketball Association." Orlando, FL: The Institute for Diversity and Ethics in Sport. University of Central Florida, June 9, 2010b.

Lapchick, Richard. "The 2010 Racial and Gender Report Card: National Football League." Orlando, FL: The Institute for Diversity and Ethics in Sport, University of Central Florida, September 29, 2010c.

Lapchick, Richard, and Bente General. "The Buck Stops Here: Assessing Diversity Among Campus and Conference Leaders for Division 1A Schools in 2007–08." Orlando, FL: University of Central Florida, DeVos Sport Business Management Program, 2007.

Lapchick, Richard E., and Kevin J. Matthews. *2004 Racial and Gender Report Card.* Center for the Study of Sport in Society: Northeastern University, 2004.

Lareau, Annette. *Unequal Childhoods: Class, Race, and Family Life.* Berkeley, CA: University of California Press, 2003.

Lasswell, Harold. "The Structure and Function of Communication in Society." In Lyman Bryson (Ed.), *The Communication of Ideas.* New York: Harper and Row, 1948.

Lauer, Robert H. *Perspectives on Social Change*, 4th ed. Boston, MA: Allyn & Bacon, 1991.

Law, Randall D. *Terrorism: A History.* Malden, MA: Polity Press, 2009.

Lawrence, Paul R., and Jay W. Lorsch. *Organization and Environment.* Boston, MA: Division of Research, Graduate School of Business Administration, Harvard University, 1967.

Lazarsfeld, Paul. *Survey Design and Analysis.* New York: Free Press, 1955.

Le Bon, Gustave. *The Crowd.* New York: Viking, 1960.

Leach, Edmond. *Social Anthropology.* New York: Oxford University Press, 1982.

Leacock, Eleanor Burke. *Teaching and Learning in City Schools.* New York: Basic Books, 1969.

Lee, Alfred McClung. *Toward Humanist Sociology.* New York: Oxford University Press, 1978.

Lee, Alfred McClung. *Sociology for People.* Syracuse, NY: Syracuse University Press, 1990.

Lee, Arthur Paterson. *Three Faiths, One Father: Judaism, Christianity, and the Challenge of Islam.* Toronto, ON: Clements Publishing, 2002.

Lee, Gary R. *Family Structure and Interaction.* Philadelphia, PA: Lippincott, 1977.

Lee, Jennifer, and Frank D. Bean. "Beyond Black and White: Remaking Race in America." *Contexts* (Summer 2003):26–33.

Lee, Ronald, and John Haaga. "Government Spending in an Older America." Washington, DC: Population Reference Bureau, 2002.

Lee, Sharon M. "Asian Americans: Diverse and Growing." *Population Bulletin* 53 (June 1998):1–40.

"Left Out." *Newsweek* (March 21, 1983):26–35.

Lehrmann, Hartmut, and Guenther Roth. *Weber's Protestant Ethic: Origins, Evidence, Context.* New York: Cambridge University Press, 1993.

Leibenstein, Harvey. *Inside the Firm.* Cambridge, MA: Harvard University Press, 1987.

Lemann, Nicholas. *The Big Test: The Secret History of the American Meritocracy.* New York: Farrar, Straus & Giroux, 2000.

Lemert, Charles. *Postmodernism Is Not What You Think: Why Globalization Threatens Modernity.* Boulder, CO: Paradigm Publishers, 2005.

Lemert, Charles, and Ann Branaman. (Eds.). *The Goffman Reader.* Malden, MA: Blackwell, 1997.

Lemert, Charles, et al. *Globalization: A Reader.* New York: Routledge, 2010.

Lemert, Edwin McCarthy, Michael Winter, and Charles C. Lemert. (Eds.). *Crime and Deviance: Essays and Innovations of Edwin M. Lemert.* Lanham, MD: Rowman & Littlefield, 2000.

Leming, Michael R., and George E. Dickinson. *Understanding Dying, Death, and Bereavement*, 5th ed. Fort Worth, TX: Harcourt Brace, 2002.

Lengermann, Patricia Madoo, and Jill Niebrugge. *The Women Founders: Sociology and Social Theory, 1830–1930.* Long Grove, IL: Waveland Press, Inc, 2007.

Lenhart, Amanda. "Teens and Sexting." Pew Research Center, October 2009. http://pewresearch.org/pubs/1440/teens-sexting-text-messages

Lenhart, Amanda, Kristen Purcell, Aaron Smith, and Kathryn Zickuhr. *Social Media and Young Adults.* Pew Research Center's Internet and American Life Project, 2010.

Lenhart, Amanda, et al. "Teens, Video Games, and Civics." Pew Internet & American Life Project (September 16, 2008). www.pewinternet.org

Lenski, Gerhard E. *Power and Privilege.* Chapel Hill, NC: University of North Carolina Press, 1984.

Lenski, Gerhard E. "Rethinking Macrosociological Theory." *American Sociological Review* 53 (April 1988):163–171.

Leonard, Wilbert Marcellus, II. *A Sociological Perspective of Sport*, 5th ed. Boston, MA: Allyn & Bacon, 1998.

LePore, Jill. *The Whites of Their Eyes: The Tea Party's Revolution of the Battle over American History.* Princeton, NJ: Princeton University Press, 2010.

Leslie, Gerald R., and Sheila K. Korman. *The Family in Social Context*, 7th ed. New York: Oxford University Press, 1989.

Levin, Jack, and James Alan Fox. *Elementary Statistics in Social Research*, 9th ed. Boston, MA: Allyn & Bacon, 2002.

Levin, Jack, and William C. Levin. *Ageism.* Belmont, CA: Wadsworth, 1980.

Levin, Susanna. The Spoils of Victory: Who Gets Big Money from Sponsors, and Why? In D. Stanley Eitzen (Ed.), *Sport in Contemporary Society*, 8th ed. New York: St. Martin's Press, 2008, pp. 367–372.

Levine, Daniel U., and Rayna F. Levine. *Society and Education*, 9th ed. Boston, MA: Allyn & Bacon, 1996.

Levine, Robert V. "The Kindness of Strangers." *American Scientist* (May–June 2003).

Levinson, Daniel J. *Seasons of a Man's Life*. New York: Random House, 1978.

Levinson, Daniel J. "A Conception of Adult Development." *American Psychologist* 41 (January 1986):3–13.

Levinthal, Dave. "Congressional Members' Personal Wealth Expands Despite Sour National Economy." Open Secrets Blog (November 17, 2010). http://www.opensecrets.org/news/2010/11/congressional-members-p . . .

Lewin, Tamar. "Scrutiny Takes Toll on For-Profit College Company." *New York Times* (November 9, 2010).

Lewis, Charles. *The Buying of Congress*. New York: Avon Books, 1998.

Lewis, Charles, and Bill Allison. *Cheating of America: How Tax Avoidance and Evasion by the Super Rich Are Costing the Country Billions—And What You Can Do About It*. New York: Morrow, 2002.

Lewis, David Levering. *W. E. B. Du Bois: The Fight for Equality and the American Century, 1919–1963*, vol. 2. New York: Henry Holt, 2000.

Lewis, David Levering, and W. E. B. Du Bois. *W. E. B. Du Bois: Biography of a Race, 1868–1919*. New York: Henry Holt, 1993.

Lewis, I. A., and William Schneider. "Hard Times: The Public on Poverty." *Public Opinion* 8 (June/July 1985):2ff.

Lewis, Jerry R. (Ed.). *The Oxford Handbook of New Religious Movements*. New York: Oxford University Press, 2004.

Lewis, Kristen, and Sarah Burd-Sharps. The Measure of America 2010–2011. New York: New York University Press, 2010.

Lewis, Lionel. "Working at Leisure." *Society* (July/August 1982):27–32.

Lexis-Nexis Corporate Affiliations. New Providence, NJ: Lexis-Nexis Group. 2008.

Liazos, Alexander. "The Poverty of the Sociology of Deviance: Nuts, Sluts, and Perverts." *Social Problems* 20 (Summer 1972):103–120.

Lichter, Daniel L., and Warren A. Brown. "Race, Immigration, and the Future of Marriage." In H. Elizabeth Peters and Claire M. Kamp Bush (Eds.), *Marriage and Family*. New York: Columbia University Press, 2009, pp. 365–382.

Lichter, Daniel T., and Martha L. Crowley. "Poverty in America: Beyond Welfare Reform." *Population Bulletin* 57 (June 2002):1–36.

Lieberman, Myron. *Public Education*. Cambridge, MA: Harvard University Press, 1993.

Lieberman, Robert C. *Shifting the Color Line: Race and the American Welfare State*. Cambridge, MA: Harvard University Press, 1998.

Liebow, Elliot. *Talley's Corner*. Boston, MA: Little, Brown, 2003.

Light, Ivan. *Cities in World Perspective*. New York: Macmillan, 1983.

Likert, Rensis. *New Patterns of Management*. New York: McGraw-Hill, 1961.

Likert, Rensis. *The Human Organization*. New York: McGraw-Hill, 1967.

Lilla, Mark. *The Stillborn God*. New York: Alfred A. Knopf, 2008.

Lin, Nan, Walter M. Ensel, and John C. Vaughn. "Social Resources and Strength of Ties: Structural Factors in Occupational Status Attainment." *American Sociological Review* 46 (August 1981):382–399.

Lincoln, Taylor, and Craig Holman. "Fading Disclosure: Increasing Number of Electioneering Groups Keep Donors' Identities Secret." *Public Citizen* (September 15, 2010). www.citizen.org

Lincoln, Yvonna S., and Norman K. Denzin. *Turning Points in Qualitative Research: Tying Knots in the Handkerchief*, 3rd ed. Thousand Oaks, CA: AltaMira Press, 2005.

Linden, Eugene. "Can Animals Think?" *Time* (March 22, 1993):55–61.

Linden, Eugene. *The Octopus and the Orangutan*. New York: Dutton, 2002a.

Linden, Eugene. "The Wife Beaters of Kibale." *Time* (August 19, 2002b):56–57.

Linder, Eileen W. (Ed.). *Yearbook of American and Canadian Churches*. Nashville, TN: Abingdon Press, 2010.

Link, Bruce G. "Understanding Labeling Effects in the Area of Mental Disorders." *American Sociological Review* 52 (February 1987):96–112.

Link, Bruce G., and Francis Cullen. "Reconsidering the Social Rejection of Ex-Mental Patients: Levels of Attitudinal Response." *American Journal of Community Psychology* 11 (1983):261–273.

Link, Bruce G., and Jo C. Phelan. "Conceptualizing Stigma." *Annual Review of Sociology* 27 (2001):363–385.

Link, Bruce G., Bruce P. Dohrenwand, and Andrew E. Skodal. "Socio-Economic Status and Schizophrenia: Noisome Occupational Characteristics as a Risk Factor." *American Sociological Review* 51 (April 1986):242–258.

Link, Bruce G., Francis T. Cullen, James Frank, and John Wozniak. "The Social Rejection of Former Mental Patients: Understanding Why Labels Matter." *American Journal of Sociology* 92 (May 1987):1461–1500.

Linz, Juan J. "An Authoritarian Regime: Spain." In Erik Allardt and Yrjo Littunen (Eds.), *Cleavages, Ideologies and Party Systems*. Helsinki, Finland: The Academic Bookstore, 1964.

Lippard, Cameron D., and Charles A. Gallagher. (Eds.). *Being Brown in Dixie: Race, Ethnicity, and Latino Immigration in the New South*. Boulder, CO: FirstForumPress, 2010.

Lipset, Seymour Martin. "Harriet Martineau's America." In Seymour Martin Lipset (Ed.), *Harriet Martineau, Society in America*. Garden City, NY: Doubleday, 1962, pp. 5–41.

Lipset, Seymour Martin. *American Exceptionalism: A Double-Edged Sword*. New York: Norton, 1996.

Liptak, Adam. "Challenges Remain for Lethal Injection." *The New York Times* (April 17, 2008a).

Liptak, Adam. "American Exception: Inmate Count in U.S. Dwarfs Other Nations." *New York Times* (April 23, 2008b).

Lipton, Eric, Mike McIntire, and Don van Natta Jr. "Top Corporations Aid U.S. Chamber of Commerce Campaign." *New York Times* (October 21, 2010).

Lithwick, Dahlia. "What to do about Teens and their Naked Photos of Themselves," 2009. http://www.slate.com/id/2211169

Little, Suzanne. "Sex Roles in Faraway Places." *Ms* (February 1975):77ff.

Litwak, Eugene. "Occupational Mobility and Extended Family Cohesion." *American Sociological Review* 25 (February 1960):9–21.

Litwak, Eugene. "Models of Bureaucracy Which Permit Conflict." *American Journal of Sociology* 67 (September 1961):177–184.

Liu, Melinda. "Party Time in Beijing." *Newsweek* (November 25, 2002):36.

Livernash, Robert, and Eric Rodenburg. *Population Change, Resources, and the Environment*. Washington, DC: Population Reference Bureau, 1998.

Livi-Bacci, Massimo. *A Concise History of World Population*, 2nd ed. Malden, MA: Blackwell Publishers, 1997.

Livingston, E. *Making Sense of Ethnomethodology*. London: Routledge and Kegan Paul, 1987.

Livingston, Gretchen, and D'Vera Cohn. "Childlessness Up Among All Women; Down Among Women With Advanced Degrees." Pew Research Center (June 25, 2010). http://pewsocialtrends.org/pubs/758/rising-share-women-have-no-children-childlessness

Lobo, Susan, and Kurt Peters. (Eds.). *American Indians and the Urban Experience*. Thousand Oaks, CA: AltaMira Press, 2001.

Locke, John. *Second Treatise of Government*. Edited by C. B. Macpherson. Indianapolis, IN: Hackett, 1980.

Lodge, George C. *The New American Ideology*. New York: Knopf, 1975.

Lodge, George C. *The American Disease*. Washington Square, NY: New York University Press, 1986.

Lodge, George C., and Ezra F. Vogel. (Eds.). *Ideology and National Competitiveness*. Cambridge, MA: Harvard Business School, 1987.

Lofland, John. "White-Hat Mobilization: Strategies of a Millenarian Movement." In Mayer N. Zald and John D. McCarthy (Eds.), *The Dynamics of Social Movements*. Cambridge, MA: Winthrop, 1979, pp. 157–166.

Lofland, John. *Polite Protesters*. Syracuse, NY: Syracuse University Press, 1993.

Lofland, John. *Social Movement Organizations*. Hawthorne, NY: Aldine de Gruyter, 1996.

Logan, Charles H. "Problems in Ratio Correlation: The Case of Deterrence Research." *Social Forces* 60 (March 1982):791–810.

Lombroso, Cesare. *Crime*. Boston, MA: Little, Brown and Company, 1918.

"The Longest Journey." *The Economist* (November 2, 2002):3–16.

Longshore, Douglas. "Race Composition and White Hostility: A Research Note on the Problem of Control in Desegregated Schools." *Social Forces* 61 (September 1982a):73–78.

Longshore, Douglas. "School Racial Composition and Blacks' Attitudes toward Desegregation: The Problem of Control in Desegregated Schools." *Social Science Quarterly* 63 (December 1982b):674–687.

Loo, Chalsa M. *Chinese American*, rev. ed. CA, Thousand Oaks: Sage, 1998.

Lopez, Mark Hugo. "The Latino Vote in the 2010 Elections." Washington, DC: Pew Hispanic Center, 2010.

Lopez, Mark Hugo, and Paul Taylor. "Illegal Immigration Blacklash Worries, Divides Nation." Pew Research Center (October 28, 2010).

Lopreato, Joseph. "From Social Evolutionism to Biocultural Evolutionism." *Sociological Forum* 5 (1990): 187–212.

Lorber, Judith. *Gender Inequality: Feminist Theories and Politics*, 3rd ed. Los Angeles, CA: Roxbury Publishing, 2005.

Lorch, Donatella. "Ghosts of Tailhook." *Newsweek* (March 17, 2003):43.

Lord, George F., III, and William W. Falk. "Hidden Income and Segmentation: Structural Determinants of Fringe Benefits." *Social Science Quarterly* 63 (June 1982):208–224.

Lott, Bernice. *Women's Lives: Themes and Variations in Gender Learning*, 2nd ed. Pacific Grove, CA: Brooks/Cole, 1994.

Loury, Glenn C. *Anatomy of Racial Inequality*. Cambridge, MA: Harvard University Press, 2003.

Lucas, Samuel Roundfield. *Tracking Inequality: Stratification and Mobility in American High Schools*. New York: Teachers College Press, 1999.

Luckmann, Thomas. *The Invisible Religion*. New York: Macmillan, 1967.

Luhman, Reid. *Race and Ethnicity in the United States: Our Differences and Roots*. Fort Worth, TX: Harcourt College Publishers, 2002.

Lune, Howard. *Understanding Organizations*. Boston, MA: Polity Books, 2010.

Lupyan, Gary. "The Conceptual Grouping Effect: Categories Matter (and Named Categories Matter More)." *Cognition* 108 (2008):566–577.

Lux, Kenneth. *Adam Smith's Mistake*. Boston, MA: Shambhala, 1990.

Lyman, Stanford M. *Chinese Americans*. New York: Random House, 1974.

Lynaugh, Joan E., and Barbara L. Brush. *American Nursing*. Malden, MA: Blackwell, 1996.

Lynch, Michael J., E. Britt Patterson., and Kristina K. Childs. (Eds.). *Racial and Ethnic Bias in the Criminal Justice System*. Monsey, NY: Criminal Justice Press, 2008.

Lynch, Michael, et al. *Truth Machine: The Contentious History of DNA Fingerprinting*. Chicago, IL: University of Chicago Press, 2008.

Lyotard, Jean-Francois. *The Postmodern Condition*. Minneapolis, MN: University of Minnesota Press, 1984.

Maag, Christopher. "When Bullies Turn Faceless." *New York Times* (December 16, 2007).

Maccoby, Eleanor E. *The Two Sexes: Growing Up Apart, Coming Together*. Cambridge, MA: Belknap Press of Harvard University Press, 1997.

Machalek, Richard, and Michael Martin. "Invisible' Religions: Some Preliminary Evidence." *Journal for the Scientific Study of Religion* 15 (December 1976):311–321.

MacIntyre, Alasdair. *A Short History of Ethics*, Touchstone 1st ed. New York: Simon & Schuster, 1998.

Macionis, John J., and Vincent N. Parrillo. *Cities and Urban Life*, 4th ed. Upper Saddle River, NJ: Prentice-Hall, 2006.

MacKay, Natalie J., and Katherine Corell. "The Impact of Women in Advertisements on Attitudes Toward Women." *Sex Roles* 36 (May 1997):573–583.

MacKenzie, Donald A., and Judy Wajcman. (Eds.). *The Social Shaping of Technology*, 2nd ed. Bristol, PA: Taylor and Francis, 1999.

MacKinnon, Malcolm. "Calvinism and the Infallible Assurance of Grace: The Weber Thesis Reconsidered." *British Journal of Sociology* 39 (1988a):143–177.

MacKinnon, Malcolm. "Weber's Exploration of Calvinism: The Undiscovered Provenance of Capitalism." *British Journal of Sociology* 39 (1988b):178–210.

Maddox, Brenda. "Homosexual Parents." *Psychology Today* 16 (February 1982):62, 66–69.

"Majority Continues to Support Civil Unions." Pew Research Center, The Pew Forum on Religion & Public Life (October 9, 2009). http://pewforum.org/Gay-Marriage-and-Homosexuality/Majority-Continues-To-Support- . . .

Malinowski, Bronislaw. *The Sexual Life of Savages*. New York: Liveright, 1929.

Malthus, Thomas. *An Essay on the Principle of Population*. London: Reeves and Turner, 1798.

Manchester, William. *A World Lit Only by Fire*. Boston, MA: Little, Brown and Company, 1993.

Mandelbaum, Michael. *The Ideas That Conquered the World: Peace, Democracy, and Free Markets in the Twenty-First Century*. New York: Public Affairs, 2004a.

Mandelbaum, Michael. *The Meaning of Sports*. New York: Public Affairs, 2004b.

Mann, Patricia. *Micro-Politics: Agency in a Postfeminist Era*. Minneapolis, MN: University of Minnesota Press, 1994.

Manning, Wendy D., Pamela J. Smock, and Cara Bergstrom-Lynch. "Cohabitation and Parenthood: Lessons from Focus Groups." In H. Elizabeth Peters and Claire M. Kamp Bush (Eds.), *Marriage and Family*. New York: Columbia University Press, 2009, pp. 115–142.

Marchese, Aileen A. "What Companies Need to Know about Employment Practices Liability and Layoffs." (2002). Available online at www.plusweb.org/Downloads/Events/NeedtoKnowAboutEPLI&Layoffs-AileenMarchese.doc

Marcum, Catherine Davis. *Adolescent Online Victimization.* El Paso, TX: LFB Scholarly Publishing, 2009.

Marger, Martin N. *Race and Ethnic Relations: American and Global Perspectives*, 8th ed. Belmont, CA: Wadsworth, 2008.

Markle, Gerald E., and Ronald J. Troyer. "Cigarette Smoking as Deviant Behavior." In Ronald A. Farrell and Victoria Lynn Swigert (Eds.), *Social Deviance*, 3rd ed. Belmont, CA: Wadsworth, 1988, pp. 82–91.

Marklein, Mary Beth. "U.S. Community Colleges Face a 'Turning Point.'" *USA Today* (July 23, 2008):1A.

Marmor, Theodore R., and Michael S. Barr. "Health." In Mark Green (Ed.), *Changing America*. New York: Newmarket Press, 1992, pp. 399–414.

Marriott, M. "Afrocentrism: Balancing or Skewing History?" *New York Times* (August 11, 1991):1, 18.

Marsden, Peter V. "Core Discussion Networks of Americans." *American Sociological Review* 52 (February 1987):122–131.

Marshall, Eliot. "DNA Studies Challenge the Meaning of Race." *Science* 282 (October 23, 1998):654–655.

Martin, Joyce A., et al. "Births: Final Data for 2000." *National Vital Statistics Reports 50* (February 12, 2002).

Martin, Karin A. "Becoming a Gendered Body: Practices of Preschools." *American Sociological Review* 63 (August 1998):494–511.

Martin, Philip, and Elizabeth Midgley. "Immigration: Shaping and Reshaping America." 2nd ed. *Population Bulletin* 61 (2006):1–28.

Martin, S., and K. Oppenheim. "Video Coming: General and Pathological Use." *Trends Tudes* 6 (2007):1–7.

Martineau, Harriet. *Society in America*. Paris: Bandry's European Library, 1837.

Martineau, Harriet. *How to Observe Manners and Morals*. London: C. Knight, 1838.

Martinelli, Alberto, and Neil J. Smelser. *Economy and Society: Overview in Economic Sociology*. Newbury Park, CA: Sage, 1990.

Martinez, Valerie J., R. Kenneth Godwin, Frank R. Kemerer, and Laura Perna. "The Consequences of School Choice: Who Leaves and Who Stays in the Inner City." *Social Science Quarterly* 76 (September 1995):485–501.

Martocchio, B. "Grief and Bereavement." *Nursing Clinics of North America* 20 (1985):327–346.

Marty, Martin E. "Fundamentalism Reborn: Faith and Fanaticism." *Saturday Review* (May 1980):37–42.

Marty, Martin E. *Pilgrims in Their Own Land*. New York: Penguin, 1985.

Marvasti, Amir, B., Karyn D. McKinney, and Joe Feagin. *Middle Eastern Lives in America*. Lanham, MD: Rowman & Littlefield, 2004.

Marx, Gary T., and Douglas McAdam. *Collective Behavior and Social Movements*. Englewood Cliffs, NJ: Prentice Hall, 1994.

Marx, Karl. *The Poverty of Philosophy.* Translated by H. Quelch. Chicago IL: Charles H. Kerr, 1920.

Mason, Philip. *Patterns of Dominance*. New York: Oxford University Press, 1970.

Massey, Douglas S. "American Apartheid: Segregation and the Making of the Underclass." *American Journal of Sociology* 96 (September 1990):329–357.

Massey, Douglas S., and Mitchell L. Eggers. "The Ecology of Inequality: Minorities and the Concentration of Poverty, 1970–1980." *American Journal of Sociology* 95 (March 1990):1153–1188.

Massey, Douglas S., and Nancy A. Denton. "Trends in the Residential Segregation of Blacks, Hispanics, and Asians: 1970–1980." *American Sociological Review* 52 (December 1987):802–825.

Massey, Douglas S., and Nancy A. Denton. *American Apartheid.* Cambridge, MA: Harvard University Press, 1996.

Matthews, Warren. *World Religions,* 6th ed. Belmont, CA: Wadsworth, 2010.

Mauer Marc. *Race to Incarcerate*, 2nd ed. New York: New Press, 2006.

Maxwell, Gerald. "Why Ascription: Parts of a More-Or-Less Formal Theory of the Functions and Dysfunctions of Sex Roles." *American Sociological Review* 40 (1975):445–455.

May, Tim. *Social Research: Issues, Methods and Process*. Buckingham, UK: Open University Press, 2001.

Maynard, Douglas W. "On the Functions of Social Conflict Among Children." *American Sociological Review* 50 (April 1985):207–223.

Mazaar, Michael J. *Global Trends 2005: An Owner's Manual for the Next Decade*. New York: St. Martin's Press, 1999.

Mazlish, Bruce. *A New Science*. University Park, PA: Penn State Press, 1993.

McAdam, Doug, and David A. Snow. (Eds.). Readings on Social Movements. New York: Oxford University Press, 2009.

McArdle, Megan. "Body Counting." *The Atlantic* (April 2008):26, 28.

McCaghy, Charles H., Timothy A. Capron, J. D. Jamieson, and Sondra Harley Carey. *Deviant Behavior*, 8th ed. Boston, MA: Allyn & Bacon, 2007.

McCallum, Dennis. *The Death of Truth*. Minneapolis, MN: Bethany House Publishers, 1996.

McCarthy, John D., and Mark Wolfson. "Resource Mobilization by Local Social Movement Organizations: Agency, Strategy, and Organization in the Movement Against Drinking and Driving." *American Sociological Review* 61 (December 1996):1070–1088.

McCarthy, John D., and Mayer N. Zald. "Resource Mobilization and Social Movements: A Partial Theory." *American Journal of Sociology* 82 (May 1977):1212–1241.

McDonagh, Eileen, and Laura Pappano. *Playing with the Boys: Why Separate is Not Equal in Sports*. New York: Oxford University Press, 2008.

McDonald, Lawrence C. *A Colossal Failure of Common Sense: The Inside Story of the Collapse of Lehman Brothers*. New York: Crown Business, 2009.

McDonald, Scott. "Sex Bias in the Representation of Male and Female Characters in Children's Picture Books." *Journal of Genetic Psychology* 150 (December 1989):389–401.

McFalls, Joseph A. Population: A Lively Introduction. Washington, DC: Population Reference Bureau, 2007.

McGinn, Daniel, and Holly Peterson. "Playground of the Rich." *Newsweek* (November 25, 2002):34.

McGrath, Ellie. "Confucian Work Ethic." *Time* (March 28, 1983):52.

McGuire, Meredith B. *Religion. The Social Context.* Long Grove, IL: Waveland Press, Inc, 2008.

McKinlay, John B. (Ed.). *Issues in the Political Economy of Health Care*. New York: Tavistock, 1985.

McKinley, James C. Jr. "Cleared, and Pondering the Value of 27 Years." *New York Times* (August 12, 2010).

McLanahan, Sara, and Gary Fam Sandefur. *Growing Up with a Single Parent*. Cambridge, MA: Harvard University Press, 1996.

McManus. (Ed.). "The Death Penalty and the Race Factor." *Illinois Issues* 11 (March 1985):47.

McNamara, Justine M. "The Welfare Myth" *Journal of Sociology and Social Welfare* (December 1, 2004).

McNamee, Mike, and Joann Muller. "A Tale of Two Job Markets." *BusinessWeek* (December 21, 1998):38.

McNary, Sharon. "Neighbors Didn't Believe Norco Mother's Tale." *The Inland Southern California Press-Enterprise* (September 11, 1999):B1.

McNeil, Donald G. "U.S. Apologizes for Syphilis Tests in Guatemala." *New York Times* (October 1, 2010).

McPhail, Clark. *Myth of the Madding Crowd*. Hawthorne, NY: Aldine de Gruyter, 1991.

McPhail, Clark, and Ronald T. Wohlstein. "Individual and Collective Behaviors within Gatherings, Demonstrations, and Riots." In Ralph H. Turner and James F. Short Jr. (Eds.), *Annual Review of Sociology* 9 (1983):579–600.

McQuail, Denis. *Mass Communication Theory*, 2nd ed. Beverly Hills, CA: Sage, 1987.

McTighe, Kathryn. "Internet-Healthcare: Ultimate Savior of the System?" *Health Management Technology* 20 (December 1999):24–27.

Mead, Frank S., Samuel S. Hill, and Craig D. Atwood. *Handbook of Denominations in the United States*. Nashville, TN: Abingdon Press, 2010.

Mead, George Herbert. *Mind, Self and Society*. Chicago, IL: University of Chicago Press, 1934.

Mead, Margaret. *Sex and Temperament in Three Primitive Societies*. New York: Mentor Books, 1950.

Mednick, Sarnoff A., William J. Gabrielli, and Barry Hutchings. "Genetic Influences in Criminal Convictions: Evidence from an Adoption Cohort." *Science* 224 (1984):891–894.

Melucci, Alberto. "The New Social Movements: A Theoretical Approach." *Social Science Information* 19 (May 1980):199–226.

Mcnaghan, E. G., and T. L. Parcel. "Parental Employment and Family Life: Research in the 1980s." In A. Booth (Ed.), *Contemporary Families*. Minneapolis, MN: National Council on Family Relations, 1991, pp. 361–380.

Mental Health: A Report of the Surgeon General. Washington, DC: Government Printing Office, 1999.

Mercader, Julio, et al. "4,300-Year-Old Chimpanzee Sites and the Origins of Percussive Stone Technology." *Proceedings of the National Academy of Sciences* 104 (February 27, 2007):3043–3048.

Merton, Robert K. *Social Theory and Social Structure*, enlarged ed. New York: Free Press, 1968.

Merton, Robert K. *On Social Structure and Science*. Chicago, IL: University of Chicago Press, 1996.

Messner, Michael A. *Politics of Masculinities: Men in Movements*. Thousand Oaks, CA: Sage, 1997.

Messner, Michael A. *Taking the Field: Women, Men, and Sports*. Minneapolis, MN: University of Minnesota Press, 2002.

Messner, Michael A. *Out of Play: Critical Essays on Gender and Sport*. Albany, NY: State University of New York Press, 2007.

Meuller, Walt. *Understanding Today's Youth Culture*. Wheaton, IL: Tyndale House, 1999.

Michels, Robert. *Political Parties*. New York: Free Press, 1949.

Micklin, Michael, and Dudley L. Poston Jr. (Eds.). *Continuities in Sociological Human Ecology*. New York: Plenum Press, 1998.

Miech, Richard, and Robert M. Hauser. *Social Class Indicators and Health at Midlife*. Madison, WI: Center for Demography and Ecology, University of Wisconsin–Madison, 1998.

Milberg, William, and Robert L. Heilbroner. *Making of Economic Society*, 12th ed. Englewood Cliffs, NJ: Prentice Hall, 2007.

Milgram, Stanley. "Behavioral Study of Obedience." *Journal of Abnormal and Social Psychology* 67 (1963):371–378.

Milgram, Stanley. "Group Pressure and Action Against a Person." *Journal of Abnormal and Social Psychology* 68 (1964):137–143.

Milgram, Stanley. "Some Conditions of Obedience and Disobedience to Authority." *Human Relations* 18 (1965):57–76.

Milgram, Stanley. "The Small World Problem." *Psychology Today* 1 (1967):61–67.

Milgram, Stanley. *Obedience to Authority*. New York: Harper and Row, 1974.

Milkman, Ruth. *Farewell to the Factory*. Berkeley, CA: University of California Press, 1997.

Mill, John Stuart. *On Liberty and Utilitarianism*. New York: Bantam Books, 1993.

The Millennium Development Goals. New York: United Nations, 2010.

The Millennium Development Goals Report 2010. New York: United Nations Department of Economic and Social Affairs, 2010.

Miller, Ellen, and Nick Penniman. "The Road to Nowhere." *The American Prospect* (August 12, 2002): 14.

Miller, Dale T. (Ed.). *Cultural Divides: Understanding and Overcoming Group Conflict*. New York: Russell Sage Foundation, 1999.

Miller, Joanne, and Howard H. Garrison. "Sex Roles: The Division of Labor at Home and in the Workplace." *Annual Review of Sociology* 8 (1982):237–262.

Miller-Perrin, Cindy L., and Robin D. Perrin. (Eds.). *Child Maltreatment*. Thousand Oaks, CA: Sage, 2006.

Mills, C. Wright. *The Power Elite*. New York: Oxford University Press, 1956.

Mills, C. Wright, and Amitai Etzioni. *The Sociological Imagination*, 40th ed. New York: Oxford University Press, 1999.

Mills, Kay. *Something Better for My Children: The History and People of Head Start*. New York: NAL/Dutton, 1998.

Miner, Barbara. "Who's Vouching for Vouchers?" *The Nation* (June 5, 2000):23–24.

Mintz, Beth, and Michael Schwartz. "Interlocking Directorates and Interest Group Formation." *American Sociological Review* 46 (December 1981a):851–869.

Mintz, Beth, and Michael Schwartz. "The Structure of Intercorporate Unity in American Business." *Social Problems* 29 (December 1981b):87–103.

Mintz, Beth, and Michael Schwartz. *The Power Structure of American Business*. Chicago, IL: University of Chicago Press, 1985.

Mintz, Morton, and Jerry Cohen. *America, Inc*. New York: Dial Press, 1972.

Mintzberg, Henry. *The Structuring of Organizations*. Englewood Cliffs, NJ: Prentice Hall, 1979.

Miron, Gary, and Brooks Applegate. "An Evaluation of Student Achievement in Edison Schools Opened in 1995 and 1996." Kalamazoo, MI: Western Michigan University Evaluation Center, 2000.

Mishel, Lawrence. *State of Working America, 2006–2007*. Ithaca, NY: Cornell University Press, 2006.

Mishel, Lawrence, Jared Bernstein, and Sylvia Allegretto. (Eds.). *The State of Working America, 2006–2007*. Ithaca, NY: Cornell University Press, 2006.

Mitchell, B., and E. Gee. "Boomerang Kids and Midlife Parental Marital Satisfaction." *Family Relations* 45 (October 1996):442–448.

Mitchell, Barbara. *The Bomerang Age*. New Brunswick, NJ: Transaction Publishers, 2007.

Mitford, Jessica. *The American Way of Death Revisited*. New York: Alfred A. Knopf, 1998.

Mizruchi, Mark S., and Linda Brewster Stearns. "Getting Deals Done: The Use of Social Networks in Bank Decision-Making." *American Sociological Review* 66 (October 2001):647–671.

Moe, Terry M. *Schools, Vouchers, and the American Public*. Washington, DC: Brookings Institution Press, 2001.

Moen, Phyllis. "The Family Impact of Maternal Employment: Its Effects on Children." In Sameha Peterson, Judy Richardson, and Gretchen Kreuter (Eds.), *The Two-Career Family*. Washington, DC: University Press, 1978, pp. 182–197.

Moen, Phyllis. *Women's Two Roles*. New York: Auburn House, 1992.

Moen, Phyllis. *It's About Time: Couples and Careers*. Ithaca, NY: Cornell University Press, 2003.

Moir, Anne. *Brain Sex: The Real Difference between Men and Women*. New York: Lyle Stuart, 1991.

Moller, David Wendell. *Confronting Death*. New York: Oxford University Press, 1995a.

Moller, David Wendell. *Death and Dying*. New York: Oxford University Press, 1995b.

Montagu, Ashley. "Don't Be Adultish." *Psychology Today* 11 (August 1977):46–50, 55.

Montagu, Ashley. *The Natural Superiority of Women*, 5th ed. Thousand Oaks, CA: AltaMira Press, 1997.

Montagu, Ashley. *Natural Superiority of Women*. Thousand Oaks, CA: AltaMira Press, 2000.

Montero, Darrel. "The Japanese Americans: Changing Patterns of Assimilation over Three Generations." *American Sociological Review* 46 (December 1981):829–839.

Mooney, Linda A., David Knox, and Caroline Schacht. *Understanding Social Problems*, 7th ed. Belmont, CA: Wadsworth Cengage Learning, 2011.

Mooney, Nan. "College Loan Slavery: Student Debt Is Getting Out of Hand." *AlterNet* (November 12, 2008). http://www.alternet.org/module/printversion/106445

Moore, Joan, and Harry Pachon. *Hispanics in the United States*. Englewood Cliffs, NJ: Prentice Hall, 1985.

Moore, Michael. *Stupid White Men*. New York: HarperCollins, 2001.

Moore, Solomon. "Exoneration Using DNA Brings Change in Legal System." *New York Times* (October 1, 2007).

Moore, Thomas S. *The Disposable Work Force*. Hawthorne, NY: Aldine de Gruyter, 1996.

Moorhead, Gregory, Richard Ference, and Chris P. Neck. "Group Decision Fiascoes Continue: Space Shuttle Challenger and a Revised Groupthink Framework." *Human Relations* 44 (1991):539–550.

Mor, V., et al. (Eds.). *The Hospice Experiment*. Baltimore, MD: Johns Hopkins Press, 1988.

Morgan, C. "Adjusting to Widowhood: Do Social Networks Make It Easier?" *Gerontologist* 29 (1989):101–107.

Morgan, Dan. "Sugar Industry Expands Influence." *Washington Post* (November 3, 2007).

Morganthau, Tom. "IQ: Is It Destiny?" *Newsweek* (October 24, 1994):53–55.

Morganthau, Tom, and Seema Nayyar. "Those Scary College Costs." *Newsweek* (April 29, 1996):52–56.

Morin, Rich. "What Divides America?" Pew Research Center (September 24, 2009).

Morin, Richard. "America's Middle-Class Meltdown." *Washington Post* (December 1, 1991):C1–C2.

Morris, Aldon D. "Black Southern Sit-In Movement: An Analysis of Internal Organization." *American Sociological Review* 46 (December 1981):744–767.

Morris, Aldon D. *The Origins of the Civil Rights Movement*. New York: Free Press, 1984.

Morris, Norval, and Michael Tonry. *Between Prison and Probation*. New York: Oxford University Press, 1990.

Morse, Jodie. "A Victory for Vouchers." *Time* (July 8, 2002):32–34.

Mouw, Ted. "Job Relocation and the Racial Gap in Unemployment in Detroit and Chicago, 1980–1990." *American Sociological Review* 65 (October 2000):730–753.

Mrkic, Srdjan, Tina Johnson, and Michael Rose. "The World's Women 2010: Trends and Statistics." New York: United Nations Department of Economic and Social Affairs, 2010.

Muck, William. "Colonialism/Postcolonialism." In Stephen M. Cahendo and Charlton D. McIlwain (Eds.), *Race and Ethnicity*. London: Routledge, 2011, pp. 29–37.

Mueller, D. P., and P. W. Cooper. "Children of Single Parent Families: How They Fare as Young Adults." *Family Relations* 35 (January 1986):169–176.

Muldavin, Joshua. "Commentary: Market Reforms Breed Discontent." *Los Angeles Times* (June 3, 1999):B9.

Muller, Eric. *American Inquisition*. Chapel Hill, NC: University of North Carolina Press, 2007.

Muller, Jerry Z. *Adam Smith in His Time and Ours*. New York: Free Press, 1993.

Mumford, Emily. *Medical Sociology*. New York: McGraw-Hill, 1983.

Muncie, John, Deborah Talbot, and Reece Walters. *Crime: Local and Global*. Culmcott, Devon, UK: Willan Publishing, 2010.

Murdock, George P. *Our Primitive Contemporaries*. New York: Macmillan, 1935.

Murdock, George P. "The Common Denominator of Cultures." In Ralph Linton (Ed.), *The Science of Man in the World Crisis*. New York: Columbia University Press, 1945, pp. 123–142.

Murdock, George P. "World Ethnographic Sample." *American Anthropologist* 59 (August 1957):664–687.

Murphy, Joseph. *Understanding and Assessing the Charter School Movement*. New York: Teachers College Press, 2002.

"Muslim Americans: Middle Class and Mostly Mainstream." Washington, DC: Pew Forum, 2007.

Mussen, Paul H. "Early Sex-Role Development." In David Goslin (Ed.), *Handbook of Socialization Theory and Research*. Chicago, IL: Rand McNally, 1969, pp. 707–732.

Myers, David G. *Social Psychology*, 6th ed. Boston, MA: McGraw-Hill College, 2001.

Myrdal, Gunnar. *An American Dilemma*. New York: Harper and Row, 1944.

Myrdal, Gunnar. *Objectivity in Social Research*. Middletown, CT: Wesleyan University Press, 1983.

Nader, Ralph, and Mark Green. "Crime in the Suites" *The New Republic* (April 29 1972):17–19.

Nagata, Donna K. *Legacy of Injustice*. New York: Plenum, 1993.

Nakao, Keiko, and Judith Treas. "Computing 1989 Occupational Prestige Scores." General Social Survey Methodological Report Number 70, November 1990.

Nakao, Keiko, Robert W. Hodge, and Judith Treas. "On Revising Prestige Scores for All Occupations." General Social Survey Methodological Report Number 69, October 1990.

Namboodiri, Krishman. *A Primer of Population Dynamics*. New York: Plenum, 1996.

Nanda, Serena, and Richard L Warms. *Cultural Anthropology*, 10th ed. Belmont, CA: Wadsworth, 2011.

Nansel, R., et al. "Bullying Behavior Among U.S. Youth: Prevalence and Association with Psychosocial Adjustment." *Journal of American Medical Association* 285 (2001):2094–2100.

Napoleoni, Loretta. *Terror Incorporated: Tracing the Dollars Behind the Terror Networks*. New York: Seven Stories Press, 2005.

Narayanswamy, Anupama. "Dark Money Groups Spend $110 Million in 168 Races." *Washington Post* (October 30, 2010).

Nathanson, C. A. "Social Roles and Health Status among Women and the Significance of Employment." *Social Science and Medicine* 14 (1980):463–471.

"National Survey on Poverty in America." National Public Radio/ Kaiser Family Foundation/Kennedy School of Government, 2001.

Navarro, Vicente. *Medicine under Capitalism*. New York: Prodist, 1976.

Navarro, Vicente. *Crisis, Health, and Medicine*. New York: Tavistock, 1986.

Nee, Victor, and David Stark. (Eds.). *Remaking the Economic Institutions of Socialism*. Stanford, CA: Stanford University Press, 1989.

Nelan, Bruce W. "More Harm Than Good." *Time* (March 15, 1993a):40–45.

Nelan, Bruce W. "The Dark Side of Islam." *Time* (October 4, 1993b):62–64.

Nelson, Bryn. "Creation vs. Evolution." *Newsday* (March 11, 2002):B-6.

Nelson, Doug, and Ron Haskins. "Census to Redefine Poverty." *Politico* (2010). http://dyn.politico.com/printstory.cfm?uuid=4F915148-18FE-70B2

Nettler, Gwynn. *Explaining Crime*, 3rd ed. New York: McGraw-Hill, 1984.

Neubeck, Kenneth J., and Noel A. Cazenave. *Welfare Racism: Playing the Race Card against America's Poor*. London: Routledge, 2001.

Neugarten, B. L. "Adult Personality: Toward a Psychology of the Life Cycle." In B. L. Neugarten (Ed.), *Middle Age and Aging*. Chicago, IL: University of Chicago Press, 1968, pp. 137–147.

Neuman, William Lawrence. *Social Research Methods: Qualitative and Quantitative Approaches*, 5th ed. Boston, MA: Allyn & Bacon, 2005.

"The New Employment Deal: How Far, How Fast and How Enduring." Towers Watson's 2010 Global Workforce Study, 2010. http://www.towerswatson.com/global-workforce-study

Newman, Katherine S. *Declining Fortunes*. New York: Basic Books, 1993.

Newman, Katherine S. *No Shame in My Game: Working Poor in the Inner City*. New York: Alfred A. Knopf, 1999.

Newman, Katherine S., and Victor Tan Chen. *The Missing Class*. Boston, MA: Beckon Press, 2007.

Newport, Frank. "Americans Have Become More Negative on Impacts of Immigrants." *Gallup News Service* (June 4, 2007).

Newport, Frank, and Joseph Carroll. "Analysis: Impact of Personal Characteristics on Candidate Support." *Gallup News Service* (March 13, 2007).

"The New World of Work." *BusinessWeek* (October 17, 1994):76–86.

Niebuhr, H. Richard. *The Social Sources of Denominationalism*. New York: World, 1968.

Nielsen, Niels C. Jr., et al. *Religions of the World*, 3rd ed. New York: St. Martin's Press, 1993.

Nierenberg, Danielle. *Correcting Gender Myopia: Gender Equality, Women's Welfare, and the Environment*. Washington, DC: Worldwatch Institute, 2002.

Nimkoff, Meyer F. (Ed.). *Comparative Family Systems*. Boston, MA: Houghton Mifflin, 1965.

Nisbet, Robert A. *The Sociological Tradition*. New York: Basic Books, 1966.

Nisbet, Robert A. *The Social Bond*. New York: Knopf, 1970.

Nisbet, Robert A. *The Present Age*. New York: Harper and Row, 1989.

Nobel, Jeramy J., and Julie C. Cherry. "It Helps Manage Patients with Chronic Illness" *Health Management Technology* 20 (December 1999):38–40.

'No Child Left Behind' Gets Mixed Grades" Washington, DC: Pew Research Center for the People and the Press, 2008.

Nock, Steven L. "A Comparison of Marriages and Cohabiting Relationships." *Journal of Family Issues* 16 (January 1995):53–76.

Nock, Steven L. "The Growing Importance of Marriage in America." In H. Elizabeth Peters and Claire M. Kamp Bush (Eds.), *Marriage and Family*. New York: Columbia University Press, 2009, pp. 301–324.

Nolan, Patrick, and Gerhard Lenski. *Human Societies*, 11th ed. Boulder, CO: Paradigm Publishers, 2010.

Nordland, Rod. "Learning the Killing Game." *Newsweek* (September 13, 1999):38–39.

Novak, Michael. *The Unmeltable Ethnics*, 2nd ed. New Brunswick, NJ: Transaction, 1996.

Nursing Homes: More Can Be Done to Protect Residents from Abuse. GAO-02-312. Washington, DC: U.S. General Accounting Office, 2002.

Nussbaum, Martha C. *Not for Profit: Why Democracy Needs the Humanities*. Princeton, NJ: Princeton University Press, 2010.

Nydeggar, Corinne N. "Family Ties of the Aged in Cross-Cultural Perspective." In Beth B. Hess and Elizabeth W. Markson (Eds.), *Growing Old in America*. New Brunswick, NJ: Transaction, 1985.

O'Brien, Joanne, and Martin Palmer. *The Atlas of Religion*. CA, Berkeley: University of California Press, 2007.

O'Brien, Joanne, and Martin Palmer. *The State of Religion Atlas*. New York: Touchstone, 1993.

O'Brien, Timothy L. "Officials Worried over a Sharp Rise in Identity Theft." *New York Times* (April 3, 2000):A1, A19.

O'Connell, Martin. "Where's Papa? Fathers' Role in Child Care." *Population Bulletin* 20 (September 1993):1–20.

O'Connell, Tom. "Jane Addams's Democratic Journey." *Contexts* (Fall 2010):22–27.

O'Connor, Alice. *Poverty Knowledge: Social Science, Social Policy, and the Poor in Twentieth-Century U.S. History*. Princeton, NJ: Princeton University Press, 2002.

O'Connor, Timothy. "Disgraced Olympian Jones Given Six Month Sentence." *USA Today* (January 11, 2008).

O'Dwyer, Thomas. "The Taliban's Gender Apartheid." *Jerusalem Post* (October 27, 1999):6.

O'Hare, William P. *Can the Underclass Concept Be Applied to Rural Areas? Population Reference Bureau*. Staff Working Papers, January 1992b.

O'Hare, William P. "America's Minorities—The Demographics of Diversity." *Population Bulletin* 47 (December 1992a):1–47.

O'Hare, William P., and Brenda Curry-White. "*The Rural Underclass: Examination of Multiple-Problem Populations in Urban and Rural Settings.*" *Population Reference Bureau*. Staff Working Papers, January 1992.

O'Hare, William P., et al. *Real Life Poverty in America: Where the American Public Would Set the Poverty Line*. Washington, DC: A Center on Budget and Policy Priorities and Families USA Foundation Report, 1990.

O'Harrow, Robert Jr. "Identity Thieves Thrive in Information Age." *Washington Post* (May 31, 2001):A1, A9.

O'Kane, Rosemary H. T. *Terrorism*. Harlow, England: Pearson Education Limited, 2007.

O'Neill, Hugh M., and D. Jeffrey Lenn. "Voices of Survivors: Words That Downsizing CEOs should Hear." *Academy of Management Executive* 9 (November 1994):23–34.

Opp, Karl-Dieter. "Grievances and Participation in Social Movements." *American Sociological Review* 53 (1988):853–864.

O'Toole, Patricia. *Money and Morals in America*. New York: Clarkson/Potter Publishers, 1998.

Oakes, Jeannie. *Keeping Track*. New Haven, CT: Yale University Press, 1985.

Oakes, Jeannie, and Martin Lipton. "Developing Alternatives to Tracking and Grading." In Laura I. Rendon and Richard O. Hope (Eds.), *Educating a New Majority: Transforming*

America's Educational System for Diversity. San Francisco, CA: Jossey-Bass, 1996, pp. 168–200.

Oates, Stephen B. *Malice Toward None.* New York: Mentor Books, 1977.

Oberschall, Anthony. *Social Conflict and Social Movements.* Englewood Cliffs, NJ: Prentice Hall, 1973.

Obie, Clayton. *An American Dilemma Revisited: Race Relations in a Changing World.* New York: Russell Sage Foundation, 1996.

Ogburn, William F. *On Culture and Social Change.* Chicago, IL: University of Chicago Press, 1964.

Ollman, Bertel. *Market Socialism.* New York: Routledge, 1998.

Olson, Laura Katz. (Ed.). *Age through Ethnic Lenses.* Lanham, MD: Rowman & Littlefield, 2001.

Olson, Steve. *Mapping Human History: Discovering the Past Through Our Genes.* Boston, MA: Houghton Mifflin, 2002.

Olson, Steve. *Mapping Human History: Genes, Race, and Our Common Origins.* Boston, MA: Houghton Mifflin, 2003.

Olzak, Susan, and Elizabeth West. "Ethnic Conflict and the Rise and Fall of Ethnic Newspapers." *American Sociological Review* 56 (August 1991):458–474.

Olzak, Susan, and Joane Nagel. (Eds.). *Competitive Ethnic Relations.* San Diego, CA: Academic Press, 1986.

Omi, Michael, and Howard Winant. *Racial Formation in the United States.* New York: Routledge and Kegan Paul, 1994.

Opp, Karl-Dieter. *The Rationality of Political Protest.* Boulder, CO: Westview, 1989.

Opp, Karl-Dieter, and Wolfgang Roehl. "Repression, Micromobilization, and Political Protest." *Social Forces* 69 (1990):521–547.

Orecklin, Michele. "Now She's Got Game." *Time* (March 3, 2003):57–59.

Orenstein, Peggy. *School Girls.* New York: Knopf Doubleday Publishing Group, 1995.

Orfield, Gary. "*Schools More Separate: Consequences of a Decade of Resegregation.*" Cambridge, MA: The Civil Rights Project, July 2001.

Orfield, Gary, and Chungmei Lee. *Racial Transformation and the Changing Nature of Segregation.* Cambridge, MA: Civil Rights Project, Harvard University, 2006.

Orfield, Gary, and Susan E. Eaton. *Dismantling Desegregation: The Quiet Reversal of Brown v. Board of Education.* New York: New Press, 1997.

Orfield, Gary A., et al. "Status of School Desegregation: The Next Generation." Report to the National School Board Association. Alexandria, VA: National School Board Association, 1992.

Ornstein, Robert, and Paul Ehrlich. *New World New Mind.* Los Altos, CA: Isak, 2000.

Orshansky, Mollie. "Who's Who Among the Poor: A Demographic View of Poverty." *Social Security Bulletin* 28 (July 1965):3–32.

Ortyl, Tum, and Jeremy Minyard. "Religion: Americans Love God." *Contexts* (Summer 2010):6.

Orum, Anthony M. *Introduction to Political Sociology*, 2nd ed. Englewood Cliffs, NJ: Prentice Hall, 1983.

Pacione, Michael. *Urban Geography: A Global Perspective*, 3rd ed. New York: Taylor and Francis, 2009.

Paddock, Richard C. "Republic Stirs Debate by Allowing for Multiple Wives." *Los Angeles Times* (August 15, 1999):A1, A27–A28.

Page, Susan. "Corporate Credentials Weigh Down Bush's Team." *USA Today* (August 6, 2002):1B.

Painter, Nell Irvin. *The History of White People.* New York: W. W. Norton, 2010.

Palast, Greg. *The Best Democracy Money Can Buy.* New York: Penguin, 2004.

Palen, John J. *The Urban World*, 8th ed. Boulder, CO: Paradigm Publishers, McGraw-Hill, 2008.

Palmore, Erdman. "Are the Aged a Minority Group?" *Journal of the American Geriatrics Society* 26 (May 1978):214–217.

Palmore, Erdman. "The Facts on Aging Quiz: A Review of Findings." *Gerontologist* 20 (December 1980):669–672.

Palmore, Erdman. "More on Palmore's Facts on Aging Quiz." *Gerontologist* 21 (April 1981):115–116.

Parenti, Michael. *Democracy for the Few*, 9th ed. Belmont, CA: Cengage Learning, 2010.

Parker, Kim. "The Harried Life of the Working Mother." Pew Research Center (October 1, 2009). http://pewresearch.org/pubs/1360/working-women-conflicted-but-few-favor-return-to-tra . . .

Parker, Kim. "A Portrait of Stepfamilies. Pew Research Center, Social & Demographic Trends." (January 13, 2011). http://pewsocialtrends.org/2011/01/13/a-portrait-of-stepfamilies/

Parker, Laura. "Surgeons' Strike Forces Hospitals to Juggle Service." *USA Today* (January 20, 2003).

Parker, Laura, and Peter Eisler. "Ballots in Black Fla. Precincts Invalidated More." *USA Today* (April 6–8, 2001):1A, 3A.

Parker, Richard, and Delia Easton. "Sexuality, Culture, and Political Economy: Recent Developments in Anthropological and Cross-Cultural Sex Research." *Annual Review of Sex Research* 9 (1998):1–19.

Parkinson, C. Northcote. *Parkinson's Law.* Cutchogue, NY: Buccaneer Books, 1993.

Parrillo, Vincent N. *Diversity in America*, 2nd ed. Thousand Oaks, CA: Sage, 2005a.

Parrillo, Vincent N. *Strangers to These Shores*, 8th ed. Boston, MA: Allyn & Bacon, 2005b.

Parsons, Talcott. *The Structure of Social Action.* New York: McGraw-Hill, 1937.

Parsons, Talcott. *The Social System.* New York: Free Press, 1951.

Parsons, Talcott. *Politics and Social Structure.* New York: Free Press, 1959.

Parsons, Talcott. "Definitions of Health and Illness in the Light of American Values and Social Structure." In Talcott Parsons (Ed.), *Social Structure and Personality.* New York: Free Press, 1964a, pp. 257–291.

Parsons, Talcott. "A Functional Theory of Change." In Amitai Etzioni and Eva Etzioni (Eds.), *Social Change.* New York: Basic Books, 1964b, pp. 83–97.

Parsons, Talcott. *Societies: Evolutionary and Comparative Perspectives.* Englewood Cliffs, NJ: Prentice Hall, 1966.

Parsons, Talcott. *The System of Modern Societies.* Englewood Cliffs, NJ: Prentice Hall, 1971.

Parsons, Talcott. "The Sick Role and the Role of the Physician Reconsidered." *Health and Society* (Summer 1975):257–278.

Parsons, Talcott. *The Evolution of Societies.* Englewood Cliffs, NJ: Prentice Hall, 1977.

Passas, Nilos, and Robert Agnew. (Eds.). *The Future of Anomie Theory.* Boston, MA: Northeastern University Press, 1997.

Passel, Jeffrey. "U.S. Unauthorized Immigration Flows are Down at Mid-Decade." Pew Research Center (September 1, 2010).

Passel, Jeffrey, and D'Vera Cohn. "U.S. Unauthorized Immigration Flows Are Down Sharply Since Mid-Decade." Pew Hispanic Center (September 1, 2010). http://pewhispanic.org/reports/report.php?ReportID=126

Passel, Jeffrey S., and D'Vera Cohn. "Unauthorized Immigrant Population: National and State Trends, 2010." Pew Hispanic Center (February 1, 2011). www.pewhispanic.org

Passel, Jeffrey S., Wendy Wang, and Paul Taylor. "One-in-Seven New U.S. Marriages is Interracial or Interethnic." Pew Research Center, Social and Demographic Trends (June 4, 2010). http://pewsocialtrends.org/pubs/755/trends-attitudes-interracial-interethnic-marriage

Passell, Peter. "Bell Curve's Critics Say Early I.Q. Isn't Destiny." *New York Times* (November 9, 1994):B10.

Patchen, Martin. *Black-White Contact in Schools*. West Lafayette, IN: Purdue University Press, 1982.

Patterson, James T. *America's Struggle Against Poverty in the Twentieth Century*. Cambridge, MA: Harvard University Press, 2000.

Patterson, Orlando. *Rituals of Blood: Consequences of Slavery in Two American Centuries*. Washington, DC: Civitas/Counterpoint, 1998.

Patterson, Thomas E. *Vanishing Voter: Public Involvement in an Age of Uncertainty*. New York: Knopf, 2009.

Patterson, Thomas E. *The American Democracy*, 10th ed. Boston, MA: McGraw-Hill, 2011.

Pattillo-McCoy, Mary. *Black Picket Fences: Privilege and Peril Among the Black Middle Class*. Chicago, IL: University of Chicago Press, 2000.

Payer, Lynn. *Medicine and Culture*. New York: Henry Holt, 1996.

Payne, Richard J. *Getting beyond Race: The Changing American Culture*. Boulder, CO: Westview Press, 1998.

Pear, Robert. "Gap in Life Expectancy Widens for the Nation." *New York Times* (March 23, 2008).

Pearce, Fred. *The Coming Population Crash*. Boston, MA: Beacon Press, 2010.

Pearson, Kent. "Subcultures and Sport." In John W. Loy, Jr., Gerald S. Kenyon, and Barry D. McPherson (Eds.), *Sport, Culture, and Society*, 2nd ed. Philadelphia, PA: Lee and Febiger, 1981, pp. 131–145.

Peck, Dennis L., and J. Selwyn Hollingsworth. (Eds.). *Demographic and Structural Change: The Effects of the 1980s on American Society*. Westport, CT: Greenwood, 1996.

Pedroni, Thomas. *Market Movements*. United Kingdom: Taylor & Francis, Inc, 2007.

Pendleton, Brian F., Margaret M. Poloma, and T. Neal Garland. "Scales for Investigation of the Dual Career Family." *Journal of Marriage and the Family* 42 (May 1980):269–275.

Pennar, Karen. "The Ties That Lead to Prosperity." *Business-Week* (December 15, 1997):153–155.

Pennings, Johannes M. "The Relevance of the Structural-Contingency Model for Organizational Effectiveness." *Administrative Science Quarterly* 20 (September 1975):393–410.

Peoples, James, and Garrick Bailey. *Humanity: An Introduction to Cultural Anthropology*, 8th ed. Belmont, CA: Wadsworth, 2009.

Peplau, L. Roles and Gender. In Harold H. Kelly et al. (Eds.), *Close Relationships*. New York: Freeman, 1983, pp. 220–264.

Perlmann, Joel, and Robert A. Margo. *Women's Work? American Schoolteachers, 1650–1920*. Chicago, IL: University of Chicago Press, 2001.

Perrow, Charles. *Complex Organizations*, 3rd ed. New York: McGraw-Hill, 1986.

Perrow, Charles. *Organizing America: Wealth, Power, and the Origins of Corporate Capitalism*. Princeton, NJ: Princeton University Press, 2005.

Perrucci, Robert, and Earl Wysong. *The New Class Society*, 3rd ed. Lanham, MD: Rowman & Littlefield, 2007.

Perry, Joellen, and Dan McGraw. "In Cleveland, It's a Back-to-School Daze." *U.S. News & World Report* (September 6, 1999):34.

Peter, Laurence J., and Raymond Hull. *The Peter Principle*. New York: William Morrow, 1996.

Peters, E. L. "Aspects of Family Life among the Bedouin of Cyrenaica." In Meyer F. Nimkoff (Ed.), *Comparative Family Systems*. Boston, MA: Houghton Mifflin, 1965, pp. 121–146.

Peters, Tom. "Restoring American Competitiveness: Looking for New Models of Organizations." *Academy of Management Executive* 2 (May 1988):103–109.

Petersen, Trond, Ishak Saporta, and Marc-David L. Seidel. "Offering a Job: Meritocracy and Social Networks." *American Journal of Sociology* 106 (November 2000):763–816.

Pfeffer, Jeffrey. "The Micropolitics of Organizations." In Marshall W. Meyer and Associates (Ed.), *Environments and Organizations*. San Francisco, CA: Jossey-Bass, 1978, pp. 29–50.

Pfeffer, Jeffrey. *Power in Organizations*. Marshfield, MA: Pitman, 1981.

Pfeffer, Jeffrey. *New Directions for Organization Theory*. New York: Oxford University Press, 1997.

Phillips, Bernard. *Understanding Terrorism*. Boulder, CO: Paradigm Publishers, 2008.

Phillips, Derek. "Rejection: A Possible Consequence of Seeking Help for Mental Disorders." *American Sociological Review* 28 (December 1963):963–972.

Phillips, Derek. "Rejection of the Mentally Ill: The Influence of Behavior and Sex." *American Sociological Review* 29 (October 1964):679–687.

Phillips, John L. *The Origins of the Intellect*, 2nd ed. San Francisco CA: Freeman, 1975.

Phillips, Kevin. *Wealth and Democracy: How Great Fortunes and Government Created America's Aristocracy*. New York: Broadway Books, 2002.

Phillips, Kevin. *Bad Money*. New York: Penguin Group, 2008.

Phu, Vu Duy. Vietnam—Anticipating It. *Vietnam Economic News* (December 14, 1998).

Piaget, Jean. *The Psychology of Intelligence*. Totowa, NJ: Littlefield, Adams, 1981.

Piaget, Jean, and Barbel Inhelder. *The Psychology of the Child*. London: Routledge, 1973.

Piaget, Jean, and Jane Valsiner. *The Child's Conception of Physical Causality*. New Brunswick, NJ: Transaction Publishers, 1999.

Pichanik, V. K. *Harriet Martineau*. Ann Arbor, MI: University of Michigan Press, 1980.

Pickering, Michael. *Stereotyping: The Politics of Representation*. New York: Palgrave, 2001.

Pickering, W. S., and Geoffrey Walford. (Eds.). *Durkheim's Suicide*. New York: Routledge, 2000.

Pieterse, Jan Nederveen. *Ethnicities and Global Multiculture*, New York: Rowman & Littlefield Publishers, Inc, 2007.

Pieterse, Jan Nederveen. *Globalization and Culture*, 2nd ed. Boulder, CO: Rowman & Littlefield Publishers, Inc, 2009.

Pillemer, K., and D. Finkelhor. "The Prevalence of Elder Abuse: A Random Sample Survey." *Gerontologist* 28 (February 1988):51–57.

Pillemer, V., and J. Suiter. "Will I Ever Escape My Children's Problems? Effects of Adult Children's Problems on Elderly Parents." *Journal of Marriage and the Family* (August 1991):585–594.

Pines, Maya. "The Civilizing of Genie." *Psychology Today* 15 (September 1981):28ff.

Pinker, Steven. *The Blank Slate*. New York: Penguin Group, 2003.

Pinker, Steven. *The Language Instinct*. New York: HarperCollins Publishers, 2007.

Pinker, Steven. *The Stuff of Thought*. New York: Penquin Press, 2008.

Pinker, Susan. *The Sexual Paradox*. New York: Simon & Schuster, 2009.

Pipher, Mary, and Susan Cohen. *The Middle of Everywhere: Helping Refugees Enter the American Community*. San Diego, CA: Harcourt Trade, 2002.

Plog, Fred, and Daniel G. Bates. *Cultural Anthropology*, 3rd ed. New York: McGraw-Hill, 1990.

Poddel, Lawrence. "Welfare History and Expectancy." *Families on Welfare in New York City*. Preliminary Report No. 5. New York: The Center for Social Research, City University of New York, 1968.

Pollack, Detlef, and Daniel V. A. Olson. (Eds.). The Role of Religion in Modern Societies. New York: Routledge, 2007.

Pollard, Kelvin. "U.S. Diversity Is More than Black and White." Washington, DC: Population Reference Bureau, 1999.

Pollard, Kelvin, and Mark Mather. "2010 Census Counts Nearly 309 Million Americans." Washington, DC: Population Reference Bureau, 2010.

Pollner, Melvin. "Left of Ethnomethodology: The Rise and Decline of Radical Reflexivity." *American Sociological Review* 56 (June 1991):370–380.

Pollock, Robert. *World Religions*. New York: Fall River Press, 2008.

Pomfret, John. "China Allows Its Capitalists to Join Party." *Washington Post* (July 2, 2001):A1, A14.

Pomfret, John. "Chinese Back New Breed of Capitalism." *Washington Post* (September 29, 2002):A1, A25.

Pope, Liston. *Millhands and Preachers*. New Haven, CT: Yale University Press, 1942.

Popenoe, David. *Life Without Father*. Cambridge, MA: Harvard University Press, 1999.

Popenoe, David. "Essay: The Future of Marriage in America." National Marriage Project. Rutgers University, 2007. http://marriage.rutgers.edu/Publications/SOOU/TEXTSOOU2007.htm

Posner, Richard A. *Aging and Old Age*. Chicago, IL: University of Chicago Press, 1996.

Powell, Brian, et al. *Counted Out: Same-Sex Relations and Americans' Definitions of Family*. New York: Russell Sage Foundation, 2010.

Powell, Gary N., and Laura M. Graves. *Women and Men in Management*, 3rd ed. Thousand Oaks, CA: Sage, 2002.

Powers, Jeanne M. *Charter Schools*. New York: Palgrave Macmillan, 2009.

Preidt, Robert. "Depression in Rheumatoid Arthritis Patients Linked to Social Status." Medicine Plus, U.S. National Library Medicine, NIH National Institutes of Health (April 8, 2011). http://www.nih.gov/medicineplus/news/fullstory-108241.html

Puente, Maria. "Election of Governor a Sign of Growing Political Clout." *USA Today* (November 19, 1996):1A.

Pulera, Dominic J. *Visible Differences: How Race Will Matter to Americans in the Twenty-First Century*. New York: Continuum International Publishing Group, 2002.

Purcell, Patrick. "Income and Poverty Among Older Americans in 2008." CRS Report for Congress, Congressional Research Service (October 2, 2009): pp. 1–25. www.crs.gov

Purcell, Piper, and Lara Stewart. "Dick and Jane in 1989." *Sex Roles* 22 (1990):177–185.

Putnam, Robert. "Who Killed America?" *American Prospect* (March 1996):26–28.

Putnam, Robert. *Bowling Alone: The Collapse and Revival of American Community*. New York: Simon & Schuster, 2001.

Putnam, Robert D., and David E. Campbell. *American Grace: How Religion Divides and Unites US*. New York: Simon & Schuster Adult Publishing Group, 2010.

Puzzanchera, Charles. "Juvenile Arrests 2008." Juvenile Justice Bulletin. Washington, DC: Office of Juvenile Justice and Delinquency Prevention, December, 2009.

Qin, Bibin. *Earnings Attainment of Chinese Americans*. New York: LFB Scholarly Publishing LLC, 2008.

Quarantelli, E. L. "Society of Panic." In *International Encyclopedia of the Social and Behavioral Sciences*. Oxford, UK: Pergamon Press, 2001, pp. 11020–11023.

Quarantelli, E. L., and Joseph Cooper. "Self-Conceptions and Others: A Further Test of the Meadian Hypothesis." *Sociological Quarterly* 7 (Summer 1966):281–297.

Quebedeaux, Richard. *The Worldly Evangelicals*. New York: Harper and Row, 1978.

Queen, Stuart A., Robert W. Habenstein, and Jill S. Quadagno. *The Family in Various Cultures*, 5th ed. New York: Harper and Row, 1985.

Quinn, Jane Bryant. "What's for Dinner, Mom?" *Newsweek* (April 5, 1993):68.

Quinney, Richard. *Class, State and Crime*, 2nd ed. New York: Longman, 1980.

"Race, Place, and Segregation." Cambridge, MA: The Civil Rights Project, May 2002.

Radin, Paul. *The World of Primitive Man*. New York: Henry Schuman, 1953.

Radkau, Joachim. *Max Weber*. Cambridge, UK: Polity Press, 2009.

Rae, John. *Life of Adam Smith*. Fairfield, NJ: Augustus M. Kelley, 1965.

Raffali, Mary. "Why So Few Women Physicists?" *New York Times Supplement* (January 1994):26–28.

Rafter, Nicole. *The Criminal Brain*. New York: New York University Press, 2008.

Raghavan, Sudarson, and Dan Eggen. "Shoe-Throwing Mars Bush's Baghdad Trip." *Washington Post* (December 15, 2008).

Rahman, Momin, and Stevi Jackson. *Gender and Sexuality*. Australia: Polity Books, 2010.

Raine, Adrian. (Ed.). *The Psychopathology of Crime*. San Diego, CA: Academic Press, 1993.

Ramey, Craig T., and Frances Campbell. "Poverty, Early Childhood Education, and Academic Competence: The Abecedarian Experiment." In Aletha C. Huston (Ed.), *Children in Poverty*. New York: Cambridge University Press, 1991, pp. 190–221.

Rank, Mark R. "As American as Apple Pie: Poverty and Welfare." *Contexts* (Summer 2003):41–49.

Rashid, Ahmed. *Taliban: Militant Islam, Oil and Fundamentalism in Central Asia*. New Haven, CT: Yale University Press, 2001.

Ravitch, Diane. "What Makes a Good School?" *Society* 19 (January/February 1982):10–11.

Ravitch, Diane. *The Death and Life of the Great American School System*. New York: Basic Books, 2010.

Ray, Julie. "Public Opinion Still 'Soft' on Voucher Issue." Gallup News Service (September 28, 2004).

Ray, Larry J. *Theorizing Classical Sociology*. Levittown, PA: Open University Press, 1999.

"Recession Turns a Graying Office Grayer." Pew Research Center Publications September 3, 2009. http://pewresearch.org/pubs/1330/american-work-force-is-graying

Redfield, Robert. *The Folk Culture of Yucatan*. Chicago, IL: University of Chicago Press, 1941.

Redhead, Steve. *Subcultures to Clubcultures*. Malden, MA: Blackwell, 1997.

Reich, Robert B. *The Future of Success*. New York: Vintage, 2001.

Reich, Robert B. *Super Capitalism*. New York: Knopf Publishing Company, 2007.

Reich, Robert B. "America's Biggest Divide." *American Prospect* (January 4, 2008). http://www.prospect.org//cs/

Reich, Robert B. *Aftershock*: The Next Economy and America's Future. New York: Alfred A. Knopf, 2010.

Reiman, Jeffrey H., and Paul Leighton. *The Rich Get Richer and the Poor Get Prison*, 9th ed. Boston, MA: Allyn & Bacon, 2010.

Reiss, Ira L. *Family Systems in America*, 2nd ed. Hinsdale, IL: Dryden Press, 1976.

Report of the National Advisory Commission on Civil Disorders. Washington, DC: U.S. Government Printing Office, 1968.

"Religion Among the Millennials: Less Religiously Active Than Older Americans, Tradition in Other Ways." Pew Forum (February 17, 2010). http://religions.pew.forum.org/maps

"Religion in the 2010 Elections: A Preliminary Look." The Pew Forum on Religion & Public Life (November 3, 2010). http://pewforum.org/Politics-and-Elections/Religion-in-the-2010-Election-A-Preliminary-Loo . . .

"Repeal? Most Americans Think Health Reform Did Not Go Far Enough, Poll Finds." The Associated Press (September 25, 2010).

"Report: 237 Millionaires in Congress." Politico (November 6, 2009). http://dyn.politico.com/printstory.cfm?uuid=CA707571-18FE-70B2 . . .

"2008 Report on Terrorism." Washington, DC: The National Counterterrorism Center, 2009. http://www.nctc.gov/

Reskin, Barbara, and Irene Padavic. *Women and Men at Work*, revised 2nd ed. Thousand Oaks, CA: Pine Forge Press, 2002.

Reverby, Susan M. *Tuskegee's Truth*. Chapel Hill, NC: University of North Carolina Press, 2000.

Reynolds, Larry T., and Nancy JHerman-Kinney. (Eds.). *Handbook of Symbolic Interactionism*. Thousand Oaks, CA: AltaMira Press, 2003.

Rheault, Magali. "Three in 10 Have Postponed Medical Treatment Due to Cost." *Gallup News Service* (December 14, 2007).

Rheingold, Howard. *Smart Mobs: The Next Social Revolution: Transforming Cultures and Communities in the Age of Instant Access*. Cambridge, MA: Perseus Publishing, 2003.

Rich, Frank. "Who Will Stand Up to the Superrich." *New York Times* (November 13, 2010).

Richardson, James T. "Conversion, Brainwashing, and Deprogramming." *The Center Magazine* 15 (March/April 1982):18–24.

Richburg, Keith B. "States Seek Less Costly Substitutes for Prison." *Washington Post* (July 13, 2009).

Ridley, Matt. *The Origins of Virtue*. New York: Viking, 1996.

Ridley, Matt. *Nature Via Nurture: Genes, Experience, and What Makes Us Human*. New York: HarperCollins Publishers, 2003.

Ried, T. R. *The Healing of America: A Global Quest for Better, Cheaper, and Fairer Health Care*. New York: The Penguin Press, 2009.

Riederer, Richard K. "Battered by the World Financial Crisis." *Metal Producing* 33 (March 1999):42–45.

Riesman, David. *On Higher Education*. San Francisco, CA: Jossey-Bass, 1980.

Riesman, David, Nathan Glazer, and Reuel Denney. *The Lonely Crowd: A Study of the Changing American Character*. New Haven, CT: Yale University Press, 2001.

Rifkin, Jeremy. *The End of Work*. New York: Tarcher/Putnam, 1995.

Riley, Nancy E. *Gender, Power, and Population Change*. Washington, DC: Population Reference Bureau, 1997.

"The Rise of the Tea Party." *The Week* (February 19, 2010):13.

Risman, Barbara J. *Gender Vertigo: American Families in Transition*. New Haven, CT: Yale University Press, 1998.

Risman, Barbara, and Pepper Schwartz. "After the Sexual Revolution: Gender Politics in Teen Dating. *Contexts* (Spring 2002):16–24.

Rist, Ray C. "On Understanding the Process of Schooling: The Contributions of Labeling Theory." In Jerome Kagan and A. H. Halsey, (Eds.), *Power and Ideology in Education*. New York: Oxford University Press, 1977, pp. 292–305.

Ritzer, George. *The McDonaldization Thesis*. Thousand Oaks, CA: Sage, 1998a.

Ritzer, George. *Postmodern Social Theory*. New York: McGraw-Hill, 1998b.

Ritzer, George. *The Globalization of Nothing*. Thousand Oaks, CA: Pine Forge Press, 2004.

Ritzer, George. *The McDonaldization of Society*, 4th ed. Thousand Oaks, CA: Sage, 2004.

Ritzer, George. *Modern Sociology Theory*, 7th ed. Boston, MA: McGraw-Hill, 2008.

Ritzer, George. *McDonaldization: The Reader*, 3rd ed. Thousand Oaks, CA: Sage, 2009.

Ritzer, George. *Contemporary Social Theory*, 3rd ed. Ed. New York: McGraw-Hill, 2010a.

Ritzer, George. *Globalization: A Basic Text*. Malden, MA: Wiley-Blackwell, 2010b.

Ritzer, George. *Sociological Theory*, 8th ed. Boston, MA: McGraw-Hill, 2011a.

Ritzer, George. *The Mcdonaldization of Society*, 6th ed. Thousand Oaks, CA: Sage, 2011b.

Rizzo, Alessandra. "World Hunger Reaches the 1 Billion People Mark." Yahoo News, 2009. http://news.yahoo.com/slap/20090619/ap_on_re_eu/eu_un_world_hu...

Roach, Brian. "A Primer on Multinational Corporations." In Alfred D. Chandler Jr. and Bruce Mazlish (Eds.), *Leviathans: Multinational Corporations and the New Global Economy*. Cambridge, MA: Cambridge University Press, 2005, pp. 19–44.

Robbins, Richard Howard. *Global Problems and the Culture of Capitalism*, 2nd ed. Boston, MA: Allyn & Bacon, 2004.

Robbins, Stephen P. *Organization Theory*, 3rd ed. Englewood Cliffs, NJ: Prentice Hall, 1990.

Robbins, Thomas, Dick Anthony, and James Richardson. "Theory and Research on Today's New Religions." *Sociological Analysis* 39 (Summer 1978):95–122.

Roberts, Brandon, Deborah Povich, and Mark Mather. "Great Recession Hit Hard at America's Working Poor: Nearly 1 in 3 Working Families in United States are Low-Income." Working Poor Families Project, Winter 2010–2011. www.workingpoorfamilies.org/wpfp@starpower.net

Roberts, Sam. "Projections Put Whites in Minority in U.S. by 2050." *New York Times* (December 18, 2009).

Roberts, Sam. "Birth to Minorities Are Approaching Majority in the U.S." *New York Times* (March 11, 2010)

Robinson, Eugene. *Disintegration: The Splintering of Black America*. New York: Doubleday, 2010.

Robinson, Greg. *By Order of the President: FDR and the Internment of Japanese Americans*. Cambridge, MA: Harvard University Press, 2001.

Rochon, Thomas R. *Culture Moves: Ideas, Activism, and Changing Values*. Princeton, NJ: Princeton University Press, 1998.

Rockett, Ian R. H. "Population and Health: An Introduction to Epidemiology." *Population Bulletin* 49 (November 1994):1–47.

Rockett, Ian R. H. *Population and Health*. Washington, DC: Population Reference Bureau, 1999.

Rodriguez, Gregory. "From Minority to Mainstream, Latinos Find Their Voice." *Washington Post* (January 24, 1999):B1, B4.

Roediger, David R. *Colored White: Transcending the Racial Past*. Berkeley, CA: University of California Press, 2003.

Roethlisberger, F. J., and William J. Dickson. *Management and the Worker*. New York: Wiley, 1964.

Romano, Renee Christine. *Race Mixing: Black–White Marriage in Postwar America*. Gainesville, FL: University Press of Florida, 2006.

Roof, Wade Clark. *A Generation of Seekers*. San Francisco, CA: Harper San Francisco, 1994.

Roof, Wade Clark. *Spiritual Marketplace: Baby Boomers and the Remaking of American Religion*. Princeton, NJ: Princeton University Press, 2001.

Roozen, David, Jackson W. Carroll, and Wade Clark Roof. "Fifty Years of Religious Change in the United States." In Wade Clark Roof, Jackson W. Carroll, and David A. Roozen (Eds.), *The Post-War Generation and Establishment Religion*. Boulder, CO: Westview Press, 1998, pp. 59–85.

Roper Organization. *Virginia Slims Poll*. New York: Richard Weiner, 1985.

Rosaldo, Renato. "Of Head Hunters and Soldiers: Separating Cultural and Ethical Relativism." The Markkula Center for Applied Ethics, 2010.

Roscigno, Vincent J. "Ageism in the American Workplace." *Contexts* 9 (Winter 2010):16–21.

Rose, Jerry D. *Outbreaks*. New York: Free Press, 1982.

Rosen, Jeffrey. *The Unwanted Gaze: The Destruction of Privacy in America*. New York: Random House, 2000.

Rosenbaum, Jill. "Social Control, Gender and Delinquency: An Analysis of Drug, Property and Violent Offenders." *Justice Quarterly* 4 (March 1987):117–132.

Rosenfeld, Anne, and Elizabeth Stark. "The Prime of Our Lives." *Psychology Today* (May 1987):62–72.

Rosenfield, Sarah. "The Effects of Women's Employment: Personal Control and Sex Differences in Mental Health." *Journal of Health and Social Behavior* 30 (March 1989):77–91.

Rosenthal, Robert, and Lenore Jacobson. *Pygmalion in the Classroom*. New York: Irvington Publishers, 1989.

Rosenwein, Rifka. "Why Media Mergers Matter." *Brill's Content* (December 1999/January 2000):92–111.

Rosnow, Ralph L. "Inside Rumor: A Personal Journey." *American Psychologist* 46 (May 1991):484–496.

Rosnow, Ralph L. "Rumor as Communication: A Contextualist Approach." *Journal of Communication* 38 (Winter 1988):12–28.

Rossi, Alice S. (Ed.). *The Feminist Papers*. New York: Bantam, 1974.

Rossides, Daniel W. *Social Stratification*. Upper Saddle River, NJ: Prentice Hall, 1997.

Rothschild, Joyce. "Alternatives to Bureaucracy: Democratic Participation in the Economy." *Annual Review of Sociology* 12 (1986):307–328.

Rothschild, Joyce, and J. Allen Whitt. *The Cooperative Workplace*. New York: Cambridge University Press, 1987.

Rothschild-Whitt, Joyce. "The Collectivistic Organization: An Alternative to Rational Bureaucratic Models." *American Sociological Review* 44 (August 1979):509–527.

Rotundo, E. Anthony. *American Manhood*. New York: Basic Books, 1994.

Rowe, David C. "Biometrical Models of Self-Reported Delinquent Behavior: A Twin Study." *Behavior Genetics* 13 (1983):473–489.

Rowe, David C. "Genetic and Environmental Components of Antisocial Behavior: A Study of 265 Twin Pairs." *Criminology* 24 (August 1986):513–532.

Roy, Olivier. *The Failure of Politial Islam*. Cambridge, MA: Harvard University Press, 1998.

Roy, William G. *Socializing Capital: The Rise of the Large Industrial Corporation in America*. Princeton, NJ: Princeton University Press, 1999.

Rubenstein, Carin. "Guilty or Not Guilty." *Working Mother* (May 1991):53–56.

Rubin, Lillian B. *Worlds of Pain*. New York: Basic Books, 1992.

Rubin, Lillian B. *Families on the Faultline*. New York: HarperCollins, 1994.

Rubin, Lillian B. *60 and Up*. Boston, MA: Beacon Press, 2007.

Ruesch, Hans. *Top of the World*. New York: Pocket Books, 1959.

Ruggiero, Vincent Ryan. *A Guide to Sociological Thinking*. Thousand Oaks, CA: Sage, 2001.

Rule, James B. "Rationality and Nonrationality in Militant Collective Action." *Sociological Theory* 7 (1989):145–160.

Russell, Alan. *Guinness Book of World Records*. New York: Sterling, 1987.

Russell-Brown, Katheryn. *The Color of Crime*. New York, NY: New York University Press, 2008.

"'Russian Invasion' Hoax." *The Week* (March 26, 2010):10.

Ryan, William. *Blaming the Victim*, rev. and updated ed. New York: Vintage, 1976.

Saad, Lydia. "Future 'Retirees' Planning to Keep Busy on the Job." *Gallup News Service* (June 27, 2006a).

Saad, Lydia. "Anti-Muslim Sentiments Fairly Commonplace." *Gallys News Service* (August 10, 2006b).

Saad, Lydia. "This Is Not Your Father's Retirement." *Gallup News Service* (May 14, 2007).

Saad, Lydia. "Anti-Muslim Sentiments Fairly Commonplace." *Gallup News Service* (2008).

Saad, Lydia. "Congress Ranks Last in Confidence in Institutions." *Gallup Poll* (July 22, 2010). http://www.gallup.com/poll/141512/Congress-Ranks-Last-Confidence-Institutions.aspx?e

Sadker, David, Myra Sadker, and Karen R. Littleman. *Still Failing at Fairness: How Gender Bias Cheats Girls and Boys in School and What We Can Do About It*. New York: Scribner, 2009.

Sadker, Myra, and David Sadker. "Sexism in the Schoolroom of the 80s." *Psychology Today* 19 (March 1985):54–57.

Sadker, Myra, and David Sadker. *Failing at Fairness*. New York: Simon & Schuster, 1995.

Sahlins, Marshall D. *Tribesmen*. Englewood Cliffs, NJ: Prentice Hall, 1968.

Sakamoto, Arthur, and Meichu D. Chen. "Inequality and Attainment in a Dual Labor Market." *American Sociological Review* 56 (June 1991):295–308.

"Salary Report, The 1997." *Working Woman* (January 1997):31–76.

The State of Black America 2009. Washington, DC: National Urban League, 2009.

"Statement on Race and Intelligence." *Journal of Social Issues* 25 (Summer 1969):1–3.

Saletan, William. "Race, Genes, and Intelligence." *Slate* (November 19, 2007). http://www.slate.com/id/2178122

Salholz, Eloise. "A Conflict of the Have-Nots." *Newsweek* (December 12, 1988):28–29.

Saltman, Kenneth J. *Collateral Damage: Corporatizing Public Schools: A Threat to Democracy*. Lanham, MD: Rowman & Littlefield, 2001.

Saltman, Kenneth J. *Capitalizing on Disaster*. Boulder, CO: Paradigm Publishers, 2007.

Sampson, Robert J., and John H. Laub. "Crime and Deviance Over the Life Course: The Salience of Adult Social Bonds." *American Sociological Review* 55 (October 1990):609–627.

Samuda, Ronald. *The Psychological Testing of American Minorities*. New York: Dodd, Mead, 1975.

Samuelson, Paul A., and William D. Nordhaus. *Economics*, 19th ed. New York: McGraw-Hill, 2010.

Sandberg, John F., and Sandra L. Hofferth. "Changes in Children's Time with Parents: U.S. 1981–1997." Research Report No. 01-746. Ann Arbor, MI: Population Studies Center, 2001.

Sandberg, Jared. "Spinning a Web of Hate." *Newsweek* (July 19, 1999):28–29.

Sanders, Catherine M. *Surviving Grief*. New York: Wiley, 1992.

Sanderson, Stephen K. *Social Evolutionism*. New York: Basil Blackwell, 1990.

Santrock, John W. *Life-Span Development*, 12th ed. Boston, MA: McGraw-Hill, 2008.

Sapir, Edward. "The Status of Linguistics as a Science." *Language* 5 (1929):207–214.

Sapolsky, Robert. "A Gene for Nothing." *Discover* (October 1997):40–46.

Sassen, Saskia. *Cities in a World Economy*, 3rd ed. Thousand Oaks, CA: Sage Publications, 2006.

Sawhill, Isabel, and John E. Morton. "Economic Mobility: Is the American Dream Alive and Well?" Washington, DC: The Pew Charitable Trusts, 2007.

Sawyer, R. Keith. "Emergence in Sociology: Contemporary Philosophy of Mind and Some Implications for Sociological Theory." *American Journal of Sociology* 107 (November 2001):551–585.

Sayles, Leonard R., and George Strauss. *The Local Union*, rev. ed. New York: Harcourt Brace Jovanovich, 1967.

Scambler, Graham. *Health and Social Change: A Critical Theory.* Buckingham, UK: Open University Press, 2002.

Schaefer, Richard T. *Racial and Ethnic Groups*, 12th ed. Upper Saddle River, NJ: Prentice Hall, 2010.

Schaefer, Richard T. *Race and Ethnicity in the United States*, 6th ed. Boston, MA: Prentice Hall, 2011.

Schaefer, Richard T., and William W. Zellner. *Extraordinary Groups*, 9th ed. New York: Worth Publishers, 2011.

Scheff, Thomas. "The Labeling Theory of Mental Illness." *American Sociological Review* 39 (June 1974):444–452.

Scheff, Thomas. *Microsociology*. Chicago, IL: University of Chicago Press, 1990.

Scheff, Thomas. *Being Mentally Ill: A Sociological Theory*, 3rd ed. New York: Aldine de Gruyter, 1999.

Schell, Orville. "Deng's Revolution." *Newsweek* (August 22, 1997):21–27.

Schellenberg, James A. *The Science of Conflict*. New York: Oxford University Press, 1982.

Schiff, Michel, and Richard Lewontin. *Education and Class.* New York: Oxford University Press, 1987.

Schindler, John R. *Unholy Terror*. Norwalk, CT: MBI Publishing Company, 2007.

Schlesinger, Arthur M. Jr. *The Disuniting of America: Reflections on a Multicultural Society*. New York: Norton, 1998.

Schnitzer, Martin C. *Comparative Economic Systems*, 8th ed. Mason, OH: South-Western College Publishing, 2000.

School Vouchers: Publicly Funded Programs in Cleveland and Milwaukee. U.S. General Accounting Office (GAO). Washington, DC: U.S. Government Printing Office, August 2001.

Schorr, Jonathan. "Giving Charter Schools a Chance." *The Nation* (June 5, 2000):19–22.

Schrag, Peter. "The Voucher Seduction." *The American Prospect* 11 (November 23, 1999):46.

Schriesheim, Chester A., and Steven Kerr. "Theories and Measures of Leadership: A Critical Appraisal of Current and Future Directions." In James G. Hunt and Lars L. Larson (Eds.), *Leadership*. Carbondale, IL: Southern Illinois University Press, 1977, pp. 9–45.

Schuman, Howard. "Sense and Nonsense about Surveys." *Contexts* (Summer 2002):40–47.

Schutt, Russell K. *Investigating the Social World*, 5th ed. Thousand Oaks, CA: Sage, 2006.

Schwartz, Barry. *The Battle for Human Nature*. New York: Norton, 1987.

Schwartz, Martin D. *Researching Sexual Violence against Women.* Thousand Oaks, CA: Sage, 1997.

Schwarz, John E. *Illusions of Opportunity: The American Dream in Question*. New York: Norton, 1997.

Schweinhart, Lawrence J. "How Much Do Good Early Childhood Programs Cost?" *Early Childhood Education and the Public Schools* 3 (April 1992):115–127.

Schwirtz, Michael. "The Lede in." *The New York Times* (December 11, 2007). http://thelede.blogs.nytimes.com/200712/11

Scimecca, Joseph A. "Humanist Sociological Theory: The State of the Art." *Humanity and Society* 11 (1987):335–352.

Scott, Alan. *Ideology and the New Social Movements*. London: Routledge, 1995.

Scott, John, and Gordon Marshall. *Oxford Dictionary of Sociology*. New York: Oxford University Press, 2009.

Scott, Laura. *Two Is Enough*. New York: Avalon Publishing Group, 2009.

Scott, Martin B. "The Man on the Horse." In John W. Loy Jr., Gerald S. Kenyon, and Barry D. McPherson, *Sport, Culture, and Society*, 2nd ed. Philadelphia, PA: Lea and Febiger, 1981, pp. 146–156.

Scott, W. Richard. *Organizations*, 3rd ed. Englewood Cliffs, NJ: Prentice Hall, 1992.

Scripps-Howard. "Soon, Most of World Will Live in Cities." *Quad City Times* (May 16, 2002): A12.

Seale, Clive. *Constructing Death: The Sociology of Dying and Bereavement*. Cambridge, MA: Cambridge University Press, 1998.

Seligmann, Jean. "Husbands No, Babies, Yes." *Newsweek* (July 26, 1999):53.

Sernau, Scott. *Social Inequality in a Global Age*, 3rd ed. Thousand Oaks, CA: Pine Forge Press, 2011.

Service, Elman R. *Origins of the State and Civilization*. New York: Norton, 1975.

Service, Elman R. *The Hunters*, 2nd ed. Englewood Cliffs, NJ: Prentice Hall, 1979.

Settle, Jaime E., Christopher T. Dawes, Nicholas A. Christakis, and James H. Fawler. "Friendships Moderate an Association between a Dopamine Gene Variant and Political Ideology." *Journal of Politics* 72 (October 2010):1189–1198.

Shah, Anup. "Immigration." (May 26, 2008). http://www.globalissues.org/article/537/immigration

Shah, Anup. "Human Rights in Various Regions." (October 1, 2010). http://www.globalissues.org/article/138/human-rights-for-all

Shah, Anup. "Poverty Facts and Stats." 2010. http://www.globalissues.org/print/article/26

Shalala, Donna E, and Linda Burns Bolton. *The Future of Nursing: Leading Change, Advancing Health*. Robert Wood/Johnson Foundation. Washington, DC: The National Academies Press, 2010.

Shaller, Elliot H., and Mary K. Qualiana. "The Family and Medical Leave Act—Key Provisions and Potential Problems." *Employee Relations Law Journal* 19 (Summer 1993):5–22.

Shanahan, Michael J., Shawn Bauldry, and Jason Freeman. "Beyond Mendel's Ghost." *Contexts* 9 (Fall 2010):34–39.

Shanas, Ethel. *Old People in Three Industrial Societies*. New York: Arno Press, 1980.

Shapiro, Laura. "Guns and Dolls." *Newsweek* (May 28, 1990):54–65.

Sharot, Stephen. *A Comparative Sociology of World Religions: Virtuosos, Priests, and Popular Religion*. New York: New York University Press, 2001.

Sharp, Gwen, and Lisa Wade. "Consuming Oppression." *Contexts* (Winter 2010):48–49.

Shaw, Clifford, and Henry McKay. *Delinquency Areas*. Chicago, IL: University of Chicago Press, 1929.

Shear, Michael D., and Daniel de Vise. "Obama Announces Community College Plan." *Washington Post* (July 15, 2009).

Sheehan, Molly O. "Poverty Persists." In *Vital Signs 2002: The Trends That Are Shaping Our Future*. New York: Norton, 2002, pp. 148–149.

Sheldon, William H. *Varieties of Delinquent Youth*. New York: Harper, 1949.

Shepard, Jon M., and James G. Hougland, Jr. "Contingency Theory: 'Complex Man' or 'Complex Organization'?" *Academy of Management Review* 3 (July 1978):413–427.

Shepard, Jon M., and Richard E. Wokutch. "The Problem of Business Ethics: Oxymoron or Inadequate Vocabulary." *Journal of Business and Psychology* 6 (1991):9–23.

Shepherd, William. "Legal Protection for Freedom of Religion." *The Center Magazine* (March/April 1982):30–37.

Sherman, Arloc. *Income Inequity Hits Record Levels, New CBO Data Show*. Washington, DC: Center on Budget and Policy Priorities, 2007. http://www.cbpp.org/12-14-07inc.htm

Sherman, Arloc, and Chad Stone. "Income Gaps Between Very Rich and Everyone Else More Than Tripled in Last Three Decades, New Data Show." Washington, DC: Center on Budget and Policy Priorities, June 25, 2010.

Sherman, Lawrence. "Defiance, Deference, and Irrelevance: A Theory of the Criminal Sanction." *Journal of Research in Crime and Delinquency* 30 (November 1993):445–473.

Shields, Vickie Rutledge, and Dawn Heinecken. *Measuring Up: How Advertising Images Shape Gender Identity*. Philadelphia, PA: University of Pennsylvania Press, 2001.

Shils, Edward A., and Morris Janowitz. "Cohesion and Disintegration in the Wehrmacht in World War II." *Public Opinion Quarterly* 12 (Summer 1948):280–315.

Shils, Edward A., and Morris Janowitz. *Young Heroines*. Berkeley, CA: University of California Press, 2006.

Shipler, David K. *The Working Poor*. New York: Vintage Books, 2005.

Sidel, Ruth. *Keeping Women and Children Last*. New York: Penguin, 1998.

Sidel, Ruth. *Unsung Heroines*. Berkeley, CA: University of California Press, 2006.

Siegal, Larry J. *Criminology*, 4th ed. Belmont, CA: Wadsworth, 2011.

Siegal, Larry J., and Joseph J. Senna. *Introduction to Criminal Justice*, 11th ed. Belmont, CA: Wadsworth, 2010.

Sifford, Darrell. *The Only Child*. New York: Putnam, 1989.

Sigle, Rushton, and Sara McLanahan. "The Living Arrangements of New Unmarried Mothers." *Demography* 39 (2002):415–433.

Silberman, Charles E. *Crisis in the Classroom*. London: Wildwood House, 1973.

Simmel, Georg. *Conflict and the Web of Group Affiliation*. Translated by Kurt H. Wolff. New York: Free Press, 1964.

Simmons, Jerry Lairda. *Deviants*. Berkeley, CA: Glendessary Press, 1969.

Simmons, Sally Lynn, and Amelia E. El-Hindi. "Six Transformations for Thinking about Integrative Curriculum." *Middle School Journal* 30 (November 1998):32–36.

Simon, David R. *Elite Deviance*, 9th ed. Boston, MA: Allyn & Bacon, 2007.

Simon, Herbert A. *Administrative Behavior*, 3rd ed. New York: Free Press, 1976.

Simpson, George Eaton. *Emile Durkheim*. New York: Crowell, 1963.

Simpson, Glenn R. "Lender Lobbying Blitz Abetted Mortgage Mess." *The Wall Street Journal* (December 31, 2007).

Sinclair, Karen. "Cross-Cultural Perspectives on American Sex Roles." In Marie Richmond Abbott (Ed.), *The American Woman*. New York: Holt, Rinehart and Winston, 1979, pp. 28–47.

Singh, B. Krishna, and J. Sherwood Williams. "Childlessness and Family Satisfaction." *Research on Aging* 3 (June 1981):218–227.

Singh, Sarban. "Shift in Focus." *Malaysian Business* (September 16, 1998):54.

Sizer, Theodore. *Horace's Hope: What Works for the American High School*. Boston, MA: Houghton Mifflin, 1996.

Sjoberg, Gideon. *The Preindustrial City, Past and Present*. New York: Free Press, 1966.

Skinner, Denise A. "Dual-Career Families: Strains of Sharing." In Hamilton I. McCubbin and Charles R. Figley (Eds.), *Stress and the Family*, vol. 1. New York: Brunner/Mazel, 1983, pp. 90–101.

Skocpol, Theda. "Bringing the State Back In: Strategies of Analysis in Current Research." In Peter B Evans, Dietrich Rueschemeyer, and Theda Skocpol (Eds.), *Bringing the State Back In*. Cambridge, UK: Cambridge University Press, 1985, pp. 3–37.

Skocpol, Theda, and Edwin Amenta. "States and Social Policies." In Ralph H. Turner and James F. Short Jr. (Eds.), *Annual Review of Sociology* 12 (1986):131–157.

Skolnick, Arlene S., and Jerome H. Skolnick (Eds.). *Family in Transition*, 16th ed. Upper Saddle River, NJ: Prentice-Hall 2010.

Smaje, Chris. *Natural Hierarchies: The Historical Sociology of Race and Caste*. Malden, MA: Blackwell, 2000.

Small, Mario, and Katherine Newman. "Urban Poverty After *The Truly Disadvantaged*: The Rediscovery of the Family, the Neighborhood, and Culture." *Annual Review of Sociology* 27 (August 2001):23–45.

Smelser, Neil J. *Theory of Collective Behavior*. New York: Free Press, 1971.

Smelser, Neil J., William Julius Wilson, and Faith Mitchell. (Eds.). *America Becoming: Racial Trends and Their Consequences*, vols. 1 and 2. Washington, DC: National Academy Press, 2001.

Smith, Adam. *An Inquiry into the Nature and Causes of the Wealth of Nations*. Edwin Cannan (Ed.). New York: Modern Library, 1965.

Smith, Adam. *The Theory of Moral Sentiments*. North Shadeland, IN: Liberty Press/Liberty Classics, 1976.

Smith, Adam, and Edwin Cannan. *The Wealth of Nations*. New York: Random House, 2000.

Smith, Christian, and Michael Emerson. *American Evangelicalism: Embattled and Thriving*. Chicago, IL: University of Chicago Press, 1998.

Smith, Christian. *Christian America*. Berkeley, CA: University of California Press, 2000.

Smith, Heather. "The Promotion of Women and Men." Ph.D. Dissertation, University of Delaware, 1999.

Smith, Huston. *The World's Religions*. New York: HarperOne, 1991.

Smith, Lee. "Burned-Out Bosses." *Fortune* (July 25, 1994):44–52.

Smith, Michael D. "Hockey Violence: A Test of the Violent Subculture Hypothesis." *Social Problems* (27):235–247.

Smolowe, Jill. "When Violence Hits Home." *Time* (July 4, 1994):18–25.

Snarr, Brian B. "The Family and Medical Leave Act of 1993." *Compensation and Benefits Review* 25 (May/June 1993):6–9.

Snipp, C. Matthew. "A Demographic Comeback for American Indians?" *Population Today* 24 (November 1996):4–5.

Snow, David A., Sarah A. Soule, and Hanspeter Kriesi. (Eds.). *The Blackwell Companion to Social Movements*. Malden: MA: Blackwell Publishing, 2007.

Sobel, Michael E., Mark P. Becker, and Susan M. Minick. "Origins, Destinations, and Association in Occupational Mobility." *American Journal of Sociology* 104 (November 1998):687–721.

Sokoloff, Natalie J. *Between Money and Love*. New York: Praeger, 1980.

Solomon, Jolie. "Smoke from Washington." *Newsweek* (April 4, 1994):45.

Solomon, Jolie. "Texaco's Troubles." *Newsweek* (November 25, 1996):48–50.

Sommers, Christina Hoff. *The War Against Boys: How Misguided Feminism Is Harming Our Young Men*. New York: Simon & Schuster Adult Publishing Group, 2001.

Sorokin, Pitirim A. *Social Mobility*. New York: Harper, 1927.

Sourcebook of Criminal Justice Statistics Online. "Characteristics of Federal Prisioners." 2003. Available online at http://www.albany.edu/sourcebook/pdf/t654.pdf

South, Scott J., and Kyle D. Crowder. "Escaping Distressed Neighborhoods: Individual, Community, and Metropolitan Influences." *American Journal of Sociology* 102 (January 1997):1040–1084.

Spain, Daphne, and Suzanne M. Bianchi. *Balancing Act: Motherhood, Marriage, and Employment Among American Women*. New York: Russell Sage Foundation, 1996.

Spencer, Jon Michael. *The New Colored People*. New York: New York University Press, 1997.

Spengler, Oswald. *The Decline of the West*. New York: Knopf, 1926–1928.

Spickard, Paul R. "The Illogic of American Racial Categories." In Maria P. P. Root (Ed.), *Racially Mixed People in America*. Thousand Oaks, CA: Sage, 1992.

Spindler, George D., and Louise Spindler. "Anthropologists View American Culture." *Annual Review of Anthropology* 12 (1983):49–78.

Spitz, René A. "Hospitalism." In Anna Freud et al. (Eds.), *The Psychoanalytic Study of the Child*, vol. 2. New York: International Universities Press, 1946a, pp. 52–74.

Spitz, René A. "Hospitalism: A Follow-Up Report." In Anna Freud et al. (Eds.), *The Psychoanalytic Study of the Child*, vol. 2. New York: International Universities Press, 1946b, pp. 113–117.

Spitze, G. "Women's Employment and Family Relations: A Review." In A. Booth (Ed.), *Contemporary Families*. Minneapolis, MN: National Council on Family Relations, 1991, pp. 381–404.

Spitzer, Steven. "Toward a Marxian Theory of Deviance." In Delos H. Kelly (Ed.), *Criminal Behavior*. New York: St. Martin's Press, 1980, pp. 175–191.

Spotts, Peter N. "Science Labs, Too, 'Cooking the Books.'" *Christian Science Monitor* (July 19, 2002):1, 9.

Squires, Gregory D., and Clarence Page. *Why the Poor Pay More*. Santa Barbara, CA: Greenwood, 2004.

St. George, Donna. "Most Stay-At-Home Moms Start That Way, Study Finds." *Washington Post* (October 1, 2009):A1, A16.

St. George, Donna. "More Wives Are the Higher-Income Spouse, Pew Report Says." *Washington Post* (January 19, 2010):A2.

Stacey, Judith. *Brave New Families*. New York: Basic Books, 1990.

Stangor, Charles. *Stereotypes and Prejudice*. Philadelphia, PA: Psychology Press, 2000.

Stark, David, and Laszlo Bruszt. *Postsocialist Pathways*. Cambridge, UK: Cambridge University Press, 1998.

Stark, Rodney, and Roger Finke. *Acts of Faith: Explaining the Human Side of Religion*. Berkeley, CA: University of California Press, 2000.

Stark, Rodney, and William Sims Bainbridge. "Secularization and Cult Formation in the Jazz Age." *Journal for the Scientific Study of Religion* 20 (December 1981):360–373.

Stark, Rodney, Lori Kent, and Daniel P. Doyle. "Religion and the Ecology of a 'lost' Relationship." *Journal of Research in Crime and Delinquency* 19–20 (January 1982):4–24.

Starr, Paul E. *The Social Transformation of American Medicine*. New York: Basic Books, 1983.

The State of Food Insecurity in the World 2002. Rome, Italy: Food and Agriculture Organization of the United Nations, 2002.

The State of Our Nation's Youth. Alexandria, VA: Horatio Alger Association of Distinguished Americans, 2001.

Stavans, Ilan. *The Hispanic Condition*, 2nd ed. New York: HarperCollins, 2001.

Steele, Stephen F., and Jammie Price. *Applied Sociology*. Belmont, CA: Wadsworth, 2008.

Steen, R. Grant. "Retractions in the Scientific Literature: Do Authors Deliberately Commit Research Fraud." *Journal of Medical Ethics* (November 15, 2010). doi:10.1136/jme.2010.038125

Stein, Joel. "The New View of Pot." *Time* (November 4, 2002):56–66.

Stein, Leonard I. "The Doctor-Nurse Game." *Archives of General Psychiatry* 16 (June 1967):699–700.

Stein, Rob. "Increase in Physicians' Insurance Hurts Care: Services Are Being Pared, and Clinics Are Closing." *Washington Post* (January 5, 2003):A1.

Steinberg, Jacques. "Average College Debt Rose 6 Percent to $24,000 in 2009." *The Choice* (October 22, 2010). http://thechoice.blogs.nytimes.com/2010/10/22/debt-3/

Steiner, Christopher. *$20 Per Gallon*. New York: Grand Central Publishing, 2009.

Steinhauer, Jennifer. "To Cut Costs, States Relax Prison Policies." *New York Times* (March 25, 2009).

Steinmetz, Suzanne K. *Duty Bound: Elder Abuse and Family Care*. Newbury Park, CA: Sage, 1988.

Steinnes, Donald N. "Suburbanization and the 'Malling of America': A Time-Series Approach." *Urban Affairs Quarterly* 17 (June 1982):401–418.

Stephens, Martha. *The Treatment: The Story of Those Who Died in the Cincinnati Radiation Tests*. Durham, NC: Duke University Press, 2002.

Stephens, W. Richard Jr., "What Now? The Relevance of Sociology to Your Life and Career." In Roger A. Straus (Ed.), *Using Sociology*, 3rd ed. Lanham, MD: Rowman & Littlefield, 2002, pp. 347–363.

Stephenson, Emily. "29 Countries' Hunger Levels 'Alarming': Report." Washington, DC: Reuters, 2010. http://www.reuters.com/assets/print?aid=USTRE69A3QP2010

Stern, Kenneth S. *A Force Upon the Plane*. New York: Simon & Schuster, 1996.

Steward, Julian H. *Theory of Culture Change*. Urbana, IL: University of Illinois Press, 1979.

Stiglitz, Joseph E. *Globalization and Its Discontents*. New York: W. W. Norton & Company, Inc, 2003.

Stiglitz, Joseph E. *Making Globalization Work*. New York: W. W. Norton & Company, Inc, 2007.

Stiglitz, Joseph H. *Freefall: America, Free Markets, and the Sinking of the World Economy*. New York: W. W. Norton & Company, 2010.

Stockard, Janice. *Marriage in Culture: Practice and Meaning Across Diverse Societies*. Fort Worth, TX: Harcourt College Publishers, 2002.

Stockard, Jean, and Miriam M. Johnson. *Sex and Gender in Society*, 2nd ed. Englewood Cliffs, NJ: Prentice Hall, 1992.

Stoessinger, John. "The Anatomy of the Nation-State and the Nature of Power." In Michael Smith, Richard Little, and Michael Shackleton (Eds.), *Perspectives on World Politics*. London: Croom Helm, 1981, pp. 25–26.

Stogdill, Ralph M. *Handbook of Leadership*. New York: Free Press, 1974.

Stolberg, Sheryl. "New Method Equalizes Stem Cell Debate." *The New York Times* (November 21, 2007).

Stone, Pamela. *Opting Out? Why Women Really Quit Careers and Head Home*. Berkeley, CA: University of California Press, 2008.

Stone, Peter H. "Campaign Cash: The Independent Fundraising Gold Rush Since 'Citizens United' Ruling." *The Center for Public Integrity* (October, 2010). http://publicintegrity.org/articles/entry/24

Stranger, Janice, Nicole C. Batchelder, William Brossman, and Gerald L. Uslarder. "What the Family and Medical Leave Act Means for Employers." *Journal of Compensation and Benefits* 9 (July/August 1993):12–19.

Strasburger, Victor C. *Adolescents and the Media: Medical and Psychological Impact*. Newbury Park, CA: Sage, 1995.

Straus, Murray A., and Suzanne K. Steinmetz. *Behind Closed Doors*. Piscataway, NJ: Tronaglion Publishers, 2006.

Straus, Murray A., David B. Sugarman, and Jean Giles Sims. "Spanking by Parents and Subsequent Antisocial Behavior of the Child." *Archives of Pediatrics and Adolescent Medicine* 151 (August 1997):761–767.

Straus, Roger A. *Using Sociology*, 3rd ed. Lanham, MD: Rowman & Littlefield, 2002.

Strauss, Anselm, and Juliet Corbin. *Basics of Qualitative Research*, 3rd ed. Thousand Oaks, CA: Sage, 2007.

Strauss, Anselm, Shizuko Fagerhaugh, Barbara Suczek, and Carolyn Wiener. *Social Organization of Medical Work*. Chicago, IL: University of Chicago Press, 1985.

Strickland, S. S., and Prakash S. Shetty. *Human Biology and Social Inequality*. New York: Cambridge University Press, 1998.

Suárez, Orozco, and Mariela Páez. *Latinos*. Berkeley, CA: University of California Press, 2008.

Suchman, Edward A. "The 'Hang-Loose' Ethic and the Spirit of Drug Use." *Journal of Health and Social Behavior* 9 (June 1968):146–155.

Sullivan, Teresa A. "Work-Related Social Problems." In George Ritzer (Ed.), *Handbook of Social Problems*. Beverly Hills, CA: Sage, 2004, pp. 193–208.

"Summary of New Health Reform." Focus on Health Reform. Menlo Park, CA: Kaiser Family Foundation (March 26, 2010). www.kff.org

Sumner, William Graham. *Folkways*. Boston, MA: Ginn, 1906.

Sureeney, Megan M., Hongbo Wang, and Tami M. Videon. "Reconsidering the Association Between Stepfather Families and Adolescent Well-Being." In H. Elizabeth Peters and Claire M. Kamp Bush (Eds.), *Marriage and Family*. New York: Columbia University Press, 2009, pp. 177–226.

Sussman, Marvin B. "The Help Pattern in the Middle Class Family." *American Sociological Review* 18 (February 1953):22–28.

Sussman, Marvin, Suzanne K. Steinmetz, and Gary W. Peterson. *Handbook of Marriage and the Family*. New York: Plenum, 1999.

Sutherland, Edwin H. "White Collar Criminality." *American Sociological Review* 5 (February 1940):1–12.

Sutherland, Edwin H. *White-Collar Crime*. New Haven, CT: Yale University Press, 1983.

Sutherland, Edwin H., and Donald R. Cressey. *Principles of Criminology*, 11th ed. Dix Hills, NY: General Hall, 1992.

Suttles, Gerald D. *The Social Order of the Slum*. Chicago, IL: University of Chicago Press, 1968.

Swaaningen, Renévan. *Critical Criminology: Visions from Europe*. London: Sage, 1997.

Swann, William B. Jr., Judith H. Langlois, and Lucia Albino Gilbert. (Eds.). *Sexism and Stereotypes*. Washington, DC: American Psychological Association, 1998.

Swarns, Rachel L. "Bipartisan Calls for New Federal Poverty Measure." *New York Times* (September 2, 2008).

Swatos, William H. Jr., and Daniel V. Olson. (Eds.). *The Secularization Debate*. Lanham, MD: Rowman & Littlefield, 2000.

Sweet, Jones, Larry Bumpass, and Vaughn Call. *National Survey of Families and Households*. Madison, WI: University of Wisconsin, Center for Demography and Ecology, 1988.

Swidler, Ann. "Culture in Action: Symbols and Strategies." *American Sociological Review* 51 (April 1986):273–286.

Swidler, Ann. *Talk of Love: How Culture Matters*. Chicago, IL: The University of Chicago Press, 2003.

Swinton, David H. "Economic Status of Blacks." In *The State of Black America 1989*. New York: National Urban League, 1989, pp. 129–152.

Symonds, William C. "For-Profit-Schools." *BusinessWeek* (February 7, 2000):64ff.

Symonds, William C. "Colleges in Crisis." *BusinessWeek* (April 28, 2003):72–79.

"'Synthia': And Then There was Life." The Week (June 4, 2010):18.

Szasz, Thomas. *The Myth of Mental Illness*, rev. ed. New York: Harper and Row, 1986.

Szymanski, Albert. "Racial Discrimination and White Gain." *American Sociological Review* 41 (June 1976):403–414.

Taibbi, Matt. *Griftopia: Bubble Machines, Vampire Squids, and the Long Con That Is Breaking America*. New York: Spiegel & Grau, 2010.

Taibbi, Matt. "Why Isn't Wall Street in Jail." *Rolling Stone* (March 3, 2011).

Tannenbaum, Frank. *Slave and Citizen*. New York: Knopf, 1947.

Taylor, Chris. "Day of the Smart Mobs." *Time* (March 10, 2003):53.

Taylor, Humphrey. "The Canadian and U.S. Health Care Systems Compared." *The Harris Poll* (April 26, 1994):1–6.

Taylor, Paul. "Therapists Rethink Attitudes on Divorce: New Movement to save Marriages Focuses on Impact on Children." *Washington Post* (January 29, 1991):A1, A6.

Taylor, Shelley E., Letitia Ann Peplau, and David O. Sears. *Social Psychology*, 9th ed. Englewood Cliffs, NJ: Prentice Hall, 1997.

Taylor, Verta. "Social Movement Continuity: The Women's Movement in Abeyance." *American Sociological Review* 54 (October 1989):761–775.

Teich, Albert H. (Ed.). *Technology and the Future*, 6th ed. New York: St. Martin's Press, 1993.

Tellegen, Auke, David T. Lykken, Thomas J. Bouchard, Jr., and M. McGue. "Heritability of Interests: A Twin Study." *Journal of Applied Psychology* 78 (August 1993):649–661.

Telles, Edward E. "Mexican Americans and Immigrant Incorporation." *Contexts* (Winter 2010):29–33.

Tepperman, Lorne. *Deviance, Crime, and Control*. Cary, NC: Oxford University Press, 2009.

Terhune, Chad, and Keith Epstein. "The Health Insurers Have Already Won." *BusinessWeek* (August 6, 2009).

Terry, James L. "Bringing Women In: A Modest Proposal." *Teaching Sociology* 10 (January 1983):251–261.

Therborn, Goran. *The Power of Ideology and the Ideology of Power*. London: New Left Books, 1982.

Therborn, Goran. "The Prospects of Labor and the Transformation of Advanced Capitalism." *New Left Review* 145 (May/June 1984):5–38.

Thernstrom, Stephan, and Abigail Thernstrom. *America in Black and White: One Nation, Indivisible*. New York: Simon & Schuster, 1999.

Thomas, Evan. "The Next Level." *Newsweek* (April 7, 1997):28–36.

Thomas, Evan. "The War over Gay Marriage." *Newsweek* (July 8, 2003):38–45.

Thomas, Evan, and Gregory L. Vistica. "A Question of Consent." *Newsweek* (April 28, 1997):41.

Thomas, Melvin E., and Michael Hughes. "The Continuing Significance of Race: A Study of Race, Class, and Quality of Life in America, 1972–1985." *American Sociological Review* 51 (December 1986):830–841.

Thomas, Melvin E., and Linda A. Trieber. "Race, Gender, and Status: A Content Analysis of Print Advertisements in

Four Popular Magazines." *Sociological Spectrum* 20 (July/September 2000): 357–371.

Thomas, Susan L. *Gender and Poverty*. New York: Garland, 1994.

Thompson, Kenneth. "The Organizational Society." In Graeme Salaman and Kenneth Thompson (Eds.), *Control and Ideology in Organizations*. Cambridge, MA: MIT Press, 1980, pp. 3–23.

Thompson, L., and A. J. Walker. "Gender in Families." In A. Booth (Ed.), *Contemporary Families*. Minneapolis, MN: National Council on Family Relations, 1991, pp. 76–102.

Thomson, Elizabeth, Thomas L. Hanson, and Sara S. McLanahan. "Family Structure and Child Well-Being: Economic Resources vs. Parental Behaviors." *Social Forces* 73 (1994):221–242.

Thurow, Lester C. *Fortune Favors the Bold: What We Must Do to Build a New and Lasting Global Prosperity*. New York: HarperCollins Publishers, 2003a.

Thurow, Lester C. *Head to Head*. New York: HarperCollins Publishers, 2003b.

Tierney, William G., and Guilbert C. Hentschke. *New Players, Different Game: Understanding the Rise of For-Profit Colleges and Universities*. Baltimore: Johns Hopkins University Press, 2007.

Tilly, Charles. *From Mobilization to Revolution*. Reading, MA: Addison-Wesley, 1978.

Tilly, Charles. "Does Modernization Breed Revolution?" In Jack A. Gladstone (Ed.), *Revolutions*. New York: Harcourt Brace Jovanovich, 1986, pp. 47–57.

Tilly, Charles. *Coercion, Capital, and European States, AD 990–1990*. Cambridge, MA: Blackwell, 1990.

Tilly, Charles. *Coercion, Capital, and European States, AD 990–1992*. Cambridge, MA: Blackwell, 1992.

Tilly, Charles. *Social Processes*. Lanham, MD: Rowman & Littlefield, 1997.

Tilly, Charles. *Durable Inequality*. Berkeley, CA: University of California Press, 1999.

Tilly, Chris. "Beyond Patching the Safety Net: A Welfare and Work Survival Strategy." *Dollars and Sense* (January/February 1999):14, 36–38.

Tilly, Louise, and Joan Scott. *Women, Work, and Family*. New York: Holt, Rinehart and Winston, 1978.

Tilove, Jonathan. "The New Map of American Politics." *The American Prospect* (May/June 1999):34.

Timmons, Heather. "Online Scrabble Craze Leaves Sellers at Loss for Words." *The New York Times* (March 2, 2008).

Timms, Duncan. *The Urban Mosaic*. Cambridge, UK: Cambridge University Press, 1971.

To Establish Justice, to Insure Domestic Tranquility: A Thirty Year Update of the National Convention on the Causes and Prevention of Violence. Washington, DC: The Milton S. Eisenhower Foundation, 1999.

Toch, Thomas, and Warren Cohen. "Public Education: A Monopoly No Longer." *U.S. News & World Report* (November 23, 1998):25.

"To Clone a Human." *The Week* (February 15, 2008):13.

Tocqueville, Alexis de. *The Old Regime and the French Revolution*. Translated by Stuart Gilbert. Garden City, NY: Doubleday, 1955.

Toland, John. *Adolph Hitler*. Garden City, NY: Doubleday, 1976.

Tomaskovic-Devey, Don, and Sheryl Skaggs. "Sex Segregation, Labor Process Organization, and Gender Earnings Inequality." *American Journal of Sociology* 108 (July 2002):102–128.

Tönnies, Ferdinand. *Community and Society*. Translated and edited by Charles P. Loomis. East Lansing, MI: Michigan State University Press, 1957.

Tonry, Michael. (Ed.). *The Handbook of Crime and Punishment*. New York: Oxford University Press, 2000.

Tonry, Michael, and Mary Lynch. "Intermediate Sanctions." In Michael Tonry (Ed.), *Crime and Justice: A Review of Research*, vol. 20. Chicago, IL: University of Chicago Press, 1996, pp. 94–144.

Toynbee, Arnold. *A Study of History*. New York: Oxford University Press, 1946.

Trask, Bahira Sherif, and Raeann R. Hamon. (Eds.). *Cultural Diversity and Families*. Thousand Oaks, CA: Sage Publications, 2007.

Treiman, Donald J. *Occupational Prestige in Comparative Perspective*. New York: Academic Press, 1977.

Trimble, J. E. "Stereotypical Images, American Indians, and Prejudice." In P. A. Katz and D. A. Taylor (Eds.), *Eliminating Racism*. New York: Plenum Press, 1988, pp. 181–202.

Troeltsch, Ernst. *The Social Teachings of the Christian Churches*. New York: Macmillan, 1931.

Troll, Lillian E. "The Family of Later Life: A Decade Review." *Journal of Marriage and the Family* 33 (May 1971):263–290.

Trueba, Enrique T. *Latinos Unidos: From Cultural Diversity to the Politics of Solidarity*. Lanham, MA: Rowman & Littlefield, 1999.

Truman, Jennifer L., and Michael R. Rand. "Criminal Victimization, 2009." National Crime Victimization Survey Bulletin. Washington, DC: Bureau of Justice Statistics, October 2010.

Tse, Tomoeh Murakami. "Fresh Round of Wall Street Bonuses Rekindles Scrutiny." *Washington Post* (January 12, 2010):A11.

Tucker, Robert C. (Ed.). *The Marx-Engels Reader*. New York: Norton, 1972.

Tumin, Melvin M. "Some Principles of Stratification: A Critical Analysis." *American Sociological Review* 18 (August 1953):387–394.

Turner, Jonathan H. *American Society*, 2nd ed. New York: Harper and Row, 1976.

Turner, Jonathan H. *Face to Face: Toward a Sociological Theory of Interpersonal Behavior*. Stanford, CA: Stanford University Press, 2002a.

Turner, Jonathan H. (Ed.). *Handbook of Sociological Theory*. New York: Kluwer Academic/Plenum Publishers, 2002b.

Turner, Jonathan H. *The Structure of Sociological Theory*, 5th ed. Belmont, CA: Wadsworth, 2002c.

Turner, Ralph H. "Collective Behavior." In Robert E. L. Faris (Ed.), *Handbook of Modern Sociology*. Chicago, IL: Rand McNally, 1964, pp. 382–425.

Turner, Ralph H., and Lewis M. Killian. *Collective Behavior*, 3rd ed. Englewood Cliffs, NJ: Prentice Hall, 1987.

Twaddle, Andrew C. *Sickness Behavior and the Sick Role*. Cambridge, MA: Schenkman, 1981.

Twaddle, Andrew C., and Richard M. Hessler. *A Sociology of Health*, 2nd ed. New York: Macmillan, 1987.

Tyler, Patrick E. "Threats and Responses." *New York Times* (February 17, 2003):A1.

U.S. Census Bureau. *1990 Census of Population, Social and Economic Characteristics, United States* CP-2-1. Washington, DC: U.S. Government Printing Office, November 1993.

U.S. Census Bureau. "Percentage Change in Metropolitan Population Inside and Outside Central Cities, by Region and Division," 2000. Available online at www.census.gov/population/estimates/metrocity/ma98-c2.gif

U.S. Census Bureau. *Statistical Abstract of the United States: 2008*. Washington, DC: U.S. Government Printing Office, 2007.

U.S. Census Bureau. *Statistical Abstract of the United States: 2010*, 129th Edition. Washington, D.C.: U.S. Government Printing Office, 2009.

U.S. Commission on Civil Rights. *Racial Isolation in the Public Schools*, vol. II. Washington, DC: U.S. Government Printing Office, 1967.

U.S. Commission on Civil Rights. *Success of Asian Americans: Fact or Fiction?* Clearinghouse Publication 64. Washington, DC: U.S. Government Printing Office, 1980.

U.S. Commission on Wartime Relocation and Internment of Civilians. *Personal Justice Denied.* Washington, DC: U.S. Government Printing Office, 1983.

"U.S. Companies Hiring at Rapid Pace . . . Oversees." The Associated Press (December 28, 2010). http://www.rawstory.com/rs/2010/12/us-companies-hiring-oversees/

U.S. Department of Health and Human Services. "U.S. Birth Rate Reaches Record Low." Washington, DC: HHS News (July 25, 2003). http://www.hhs.gov

U.S. Department of Justice. *White Collar Crime.* Washington, DC: U.S. Government Printing Office, 1987.

U.S. Department of Justice. *Criminal Victimization in the United States, 2006*, (2006a). http://ojp.usdoj.gov/bJS/cvict.htm

U.S. Department of Justice. "Federal Bureau of Investigation." *Uniform Crime Reports, 2006*, (2006b). http://www.fbi.ucr/ucr.htm

U.S. Department of Justice. "FBI Releases 2006 Hate Crime Statistics." Federal Bureau of Investigation. Press Release, November 19, 2007.

U.S. Department of Justice. Federal Bureau of Investigation. "Incidents and Offenses—Hate Crime Statistics," 2009. http://www.2.fbi.gov/ucr/hc2009/incidents.html

U.S. Department of Labor. U.S. Bureau of Labor Statistics. "Highlights of Women's Earning in 2009." Report 1025. June, 2010.

"U.S. Religious Landscape Survey." Pew Forum on Religion and Public Life, 2008. http://religions.pewforum.org/

"U.S. Teenage Sexual Activity 2005." Menlo Park, CA: The Henry J. Kaiser Family Foundation. January 2005. www.kff.org

Ulbrich, Patricia M. "The Determinants of Depression in Two-Income Marriages." *Journal of Marriage and the Family* 50 (February 1988):121–131.

"Undernutrition," 2010. http://ifpri.org/publication/2010-global-hunger-index-0

United Nations Climate Change Conference. United Nations, 2007. http://www.csis.org/

"The United States Versus the World." Political Research Associates, 2005. www.publiceye.org

"Under Siege: Life for Low-Income Latinos in the South." Southern Poverty Law Center, April 2009.

"Understanding Intimate Partner Violence." Fact Sheet, Centers for Disease Control, 2009. www.cds.gov/violenceprevention

United Nations Population Division. *World Population Prospects: The 1998 Revision.* New York: United Nations, 2000.

United Nations. *Family.* New York: United Nations Publications, 1996.

United Nations. *State of the World Population 2007.* New York: United Nations, 2007.

Unnever, James D., and Francis T. Cullen. "The Social Sources of Americans' Punitiveness Models." *Criminology* 48 (February 2010):99–129.

Urban Dictionary, 2008. http://www.urbandictionary.com/

Urbina, Law. "Voter ID Laws Are Set to Face a Crucial Test." *New York Times* (January 7, 2008).

Useem, Michael. *The Inner Circle.* New York: Oxford University Press, 1984.

Utz, Rebecca, Michael Hollingshaus, and Peter Dien. "Public Opinion and Health Care." *Contexts* 9 (Spring 2010):66–67.

Vago, Steven. *Social Change,* 5th ed. Upper Saddle River, NJ: Prentice Hall, 2003.

Valdivieso, Rafael, and Cary Davis. "U.S. Hispanics: Challenging Issues for the 1990s." *Population Trends and Public Policy.* Washington, DC: Population Reference Bureau, 1988.

Valian, Virginia. *Why So Slow? The Advancement of Women.* Cambridge, MA: MIT Press, 1999.

Van Ausdale, Debra, and Joe R. Feagin. *The First R: How Children Learn Race and Racism.* Lanham, MD: Rowman & Littlefield, 2001.

van den Berghe, and Pierre L. "Dialectic and Functionalism: Toward a Theoretical Synthesis." *American Sociological Review* 28 (October 1963):695–705.

van den Berghe, and Pierre L. *Race and Racism,* 2nd ed. New York: Wiley, 1978.

van Gennep, A. *The Rites of Passage.* Chicago, IL: University of Chicago Press, 1960.

Van Zelst, Raymond H. "Sociometrically Selected Work Teams Increase Production." *Personnel Psychology* 5 (Autumn 1952):175–185.

VandeHei, Jim, and Tom Hamburger. "Businesses Prepare New Legislative Wish List for Bush." *The Wall Street Journal* (January 8, 2002):A20.

Vandell, D. L., et al. "Do Effects of Early Child Care Extend to Age 15 Years?" *Child Development* 81 (2010):737–756.

Vander Zanden, James W. *American Minority Relations.* New York: McGraw-Hill, 1990.

Vanhanen, Tatu. *Prospects of Democracy.* London: Routledge, 1997.

Vasquez, Michael. "For-Profit Schools Grow—As Do Complaints." *Miami Herald* (September 4, 2010).

Vazque, Francisco H., and Rodolfo D. Torres. *Latino/a Thought: Culture, Politics, and Society.* Lanham, MD: Rowman & Littlefield, 2002.

Veblen, Thorstein. *The Engineers and the Price System.* New York: Viking, 1933.

Veblen, Thorstein. *Theory of the Leisure Class.* New York: Penguin, 1995.

"Violence Against Women: Research into Practice." Washington, DC: National Institute of Justice, 2002.

Vobejda, Barbara. "The Heartland Pulses with New Blood." *Washington Post* (August 11, 1991):A1, A18.

Volti, Rudi. *Society and Technological Change,* 4th ed. New York: Worth Publishers, 2003.

Voss, Kim, and Rachel Sherman. "Breaking the Iron Law of Oligarchy: Union Revitalization in the American Labor Movement." *American Journal of Sociology* 106 (September 2000):303–349.

Wade, Nicholas. *The Faith Instinct: How Religion Evolved & Why It Endures.* New York: The Penguin Press, 2009.

Wade, Nicholas. *The Faith Instinct.* New York: Penguin Group (USA), 2010.

Wagner, Tony. *Making the Grade: Reinventing America's Schools.* Bristol, PA: Taylor and Francis, 2003.

Wagster, Emily. "Many Workers Hurt Abroad by Culture Shock." *USA Today* (December 17, 1993):1B.

Waitzkin, Howard. *The Second Sickness.* Chicago, IL: University of Chicago Press, 1986.

Waitzkin, Howard. *The Second Sickness: Contradictions of Capitalist Health Care.* Lanham, MD: Rowman & Littlefield, 2000.

Waitzkin, Howard. *At the Front Lines of Medicine: How the Health Care System Alienates Doctors and Mistreats Patients â€¦ and What We Can Do about It.* Lanham, MD: Rowman & Littlefield, 2001.

Waldman, Steven. "The Stingy Politics of Head Start." *Newsweek. Special Issue. Education: A Consumer's Handbook* (Fall/Winter 1990–1991):78–79.

Walker, Samuel, Cassia Spohn, and Miriam DeLone. *The Color of Justice: Race, Ethnicity, and Crime in America,* 4th ed. Belmont, CA: Wadsworth, 2007.

Wallace, Walter J. *The Future of Ethnicity, Race and Nationality.* Westport, CT: Praeger, 1997.

Waller, Willard, and Reuben Hill. *The Family*, rev. ed. New York: Dryden Press, 1951.

Wallerstein, Immanuel. *The Capitalist World Economy.* New York: Cambridge University Press, 1979.

Wallerstein, Immanuel. *The Politics of the World Economy.* Cambridge, UK: Cambridge University Press, 1984.

Wallerstein, Immanuel. *The Essential Wallerstein.* New York: New Press, 2000.

Wallerstein, Immanuel. *The End of the World as We Know It: Social Science for the Twenty-First Century.* Minneapolis, MN: University of Minnesota Press, 2001.

Wallerstein, Immanuel. *Decline of American Power: The U.S. In a Chaotic World.* New York: New Press, 2003a.

Wallerstein, Immanuel. *The Modern World-System III.* UK: Emerald Group Publishing, 2003b.

Wallerstein, Immanuel. *World-Systems Analysis.* Durham, NC: Duke University Press, 2004.

Wallich, Paul, and Elizabeth Corcoran. "The Discreet Disappearance of the Bourgeoisie." *Scientific American* 226 (February 1992):111.

Walsh, Anthony, and Kevin M. Beaver. *Biosocial Criminology: New Directions in Theory and Research.* New York: Routledge, 2009.

Walsh, Edward. "In Midwest, Bush Calls Gore Obstacle to Reform." *Washington Post* (October 24, 2000):A12.

Walters, Margaret. *Feminism.* New York: Oxford, University Press, 2005.

Walton, F. Carl, and Stephen Maynard Caliendo. "Origins and the Concept of Race." In Stephen M. Claiendo and Charlton D. McIlwain (Eds.), *Race and Ethnicity.* London: Routledge, 2011, pp. 3–11.

Wang, Jing, Tonja R. Nansel, and Ronald J. Iannotti. "Cyber and Traditional Bullying: Differential Association with Depression." *Journal of Adolescent Health*, 2010. www.jahenline.org

Wang, Wendy, and Rich Morin. "Recession Brings Young Adults Back to the Nest." Pew Research Center (November 25, 2009). http://pewresearch.org/pubs/1423/home-for-the-holidays-boomeranged-parents

Ward, R., J. Logan, and G. Spitze. "The Influence of Parent and Child Needs on Coresidence in Middle and Later Years." *Journal of Marriage and the Family* (February 1992):209–221.

Ware, Leland, and Antoine Allen. "The Geography of Discrimination: Hypersegregation, Isolation and Fragmentation Within the African-American Community." In Lee A. Daniels (Ed.), *The State of Black America 2002.* New York: National Urban League, 2002, pp. 69–92.

Warner, R. Stephen. *Public Religions in the Modern World.* Chicago, IL: University of Chicago Press, 1994.

Warner, W. Lloyd. *Social Class in America.* New York: Harper and Row, 1960.

Warner, W. Lloyd, and Paul S. Lunt. *The Social Life of a Modern Community.* New Haven, CT: Yale University Press, 1941.

Warr, Mark. *Companions in Crime: The Social Aspects of Criminal Conduct.* New York: Cambridge University Press, 2002.

Warren, Jenifer. "One in 100: Behind Bars in America 2008." The Pew Center of the States, 2008a. www.pewtrusts.org

Warren, Jenifer. "One in 100: Behind Bars in America." Washington, DC: Pew Center on the States and the Public Safety Performance Project, 2008b.

Warren, Martin, and Sheldon Berkowitz. "The Employability of AFDC Mothers and Fathers." *Welfare in Review* 7 (July/August 1969):1–7.

Warrick, Joby, and Peter Finn. "Psychologists Helped Guide Interrogations." *Washington Post* (April 18, 2009).

Wasserman, Gary. *The Basics of American Politics*, 14th ed. New York: Longman, 2010.

Waters, Malcolm. *Globalization*, 2nd ed. New York: Routledge, 2001.

Waters, Mary C. *Ethnic Options.* Berkeley, CA: University of California Press, 1990.

Watson, C. W. *Multiculturalism.* Bristol, PA: Taylor and Francis, 2000.

Watterson, T., "Social Security: Many Widows Don't Get Benefits." *Baltimore Sun* (June 13, 1990):C24.

Watzman, Nancy, James Youngclaus, and Jennifer Shecter. *Cashing In.* Washington, DC: Center for Responsive Politics, 1997.

Wax, Emily. "In Times of Terror, Teens Talk the Talk." *Washington Post* (March 19, 2002):A1, A10.

Waxman, Chaim I. *The Stigma of Poverty.* New York: Pergamon, 1983.

Weakliem, David L. "Relative Wages and the Radical Theory of Economic Segmentation." *American Sociological Review* 55 (1990):574–590.

"The Wealth Gap in Health: Data Women and Children in 53 Developing Countries." Washington, DC: Global Health Council, 2004.

Webb, R. K. *Harriet Martineau, a Radical Victorian.* New York: Columbia University Press, 1960.

Weber, Max. *From Max Weber.* Edited by H. H. Gerth and C. Wright Mills. New York: Oxford University Press, 1946.

Weber, Max. *The Religion of China.* New York: Free Press, 1951.

Weber, Max. *Ancient Judaism.* New York: Free Press, 1952.

Weber, Max. *The Religion of India.* New York: Free Press, 1958.

Weber, Max. *The Sociology of Religion.* Boston, MA: Beacon Press, 1964.

Webster, Murray, Jr., and Stuart J. Hysom. "Creating Status Characteristics." *American Sociological Review* 63 (June 1998):351–378.

Weeden, Kim A. "Why Do Some Occupations Pay More than Others? Social Closure and Earnings Inequality in the United States." *American Journal of Sociology* 108 (July 2002):55–101.

Weeks, John R. *Population*, 10th ed. Belmont, CA: Wadsworth, 2008.

Weil, Amy. "Majority of Americans Think U.S. Criminal Justice System is Broken, Ineffective: See Need for Change." Open Society Foundations, 2002. aweil@sorosny.org

Weinberg, Meyer. *Desegregation Research*, 2nd ed. Bloomington, IN: Phi Delta Kappan, 1970.

Weingart, Peter, et al. (Eds.). *Human by Nature: Between Biology and the Social Sciences.* Mahwah, NJ: Erlbaum, 1997.

Weinstein, Jay. "A (Further) Common on the Differences Between Applied and Academic Sociology." *Contemporary Sociology* (March 2000):344–347.

Weisberg, Jacob. *The Bush Tragedy.* New York: Random House, 2008.

Weisburd, David, and Elin Waring. *White Collar Crime and Criminal Careers.* Cambridge, UK: Cambridge University Press, 2001.

Weiss, Gregory L., and Lynne E. Lonnquist. *The Sociology of Health, Healing, and Illness.* New York: Simon & Schuster, 1996.

Weiss, Lawrence D. *Private Medicine and Public Health.* Boulder, CO: Westview Press, 1997.

Weiss, Rick. "Transplant Researchers Clone 5 Pigs." *Washington Post* (March 15, 2000):A1, A16.

Weiss, Rick. "In Laboratory, Ordinary Cells Are Turned into Eggs." *Washington Post* (May 2, 2003):A1, A12.

Weiss, Rick. "Synthetic DNA on the Brink of Yielding New Life Forms." *Washington Post* (December 7, 2007):A1.

Weissert, Carol S., and William G. Weissert. *Governing Health: The Politics of Health Policy*, 3rd ed. Baltimore, MD: The Johns Hopkins Press, 2006.

Weitz, Rose. *The Sociology of Health, Illness, and Health Care: A Critical Approach*, 5th ed. Belmont, CA: Wadsworth, 2010.

Weitzman, Leonore J., and Deborah Eifler. "Sex Role Socialization in Picture Books for Preschool Children." *American Journal of Sociology* 77 (May 1972):1125–1150.

Weitzman, Susan. *"Not to People Like Us": Hidden Abuse in Upscale Marriages*. New York: Basic Books, 2000.

Well, Danny. *School Vouchers and Privatization*. Santa Barbara, CA: ABC-CL10, 2003.

Weller, Jack E. *Yesterday's People: Life in Contemporary Appalachia*. Lexington, KY: University Press of Kentucky, 1980.

Wells, Spencer, and Mark Read. *The Journey of Man: A Genetic Odyssey*. Princeton, NJ: Princeton University Press, 2003.

Werhane, Patricia H. *Adam Smith and His Legacy for Modern Capitalism*. New York: Oxford University Press, 1991.

West, Candace, and Don H. Zimmerman. "Doing Gender." *Gender and Society* 1 (June 1987):125–151.

West, Guida, and Rhoda Lois Blumberg. (Eds.). *Women and Social Protest*. New York: Oxford University Press, 1990.

Western, Bruce, and Becky Pettit. "Beyond Crime and Punishment: Prisons and Inequality." Contexts 1 (Fall 2002): 37–43.

Westoff, Leslie Aldridge, and Charles F. Westoff. *From Now to Zero*. Boston, MA: Little, Brown and Company, 1971.

Wetcher, Kenneth, Art Barker, and Rex McCaughtry. *Save the Males: Why Men Are Mistreated, Misdiagnosed, and Misunderstood*. Summit, NJ: PIA Press, 1991.

"What It Costs to go to College." College Board, 2010. http://www.collegeboard.com/student/pay/add-it-up/4494.html?print=true

White, Jonathan R. *Terrorism and Homeland Security*, 6th ed. Belmont, CA: Wadsworth Cengage Learning, 2009.

White, Leslie A. *The Science of Culture*, 2nd ed. New York: Farrar, Straus & Giroux, 1969.

White, Lynn, and David B. Brinkerhoff. "The Sexual Division of Labor: Evidence from Childhood." *Social Forces* 60 (September 1981):170–181.

White, Ralph K., and Ronald O. Lippitt. *Autocracy and Democracy*. New York: Harper and Row, 1960.

White, Robert, and Robert Althauser. "Internal Labor Markets, Promotions, and Worker Skill: An Indirect Test of Skill ILMS." *Social Science Research* 13 (December 1984):373–392.

Whitehead, Alfred North. *Adventures of Ideas*. New York: Mentor Books, 1933.

"White House Wealth: President Barack Obama's Team Virtually All Chicago Millionaires." *Chicago Tribune* (April 9, 2009).

Whiten, A., et al. "Cultures in Chimpanzees." *Nature* 399 (June 1999):682–685.

Whorf, Benjamin Lee. *Language, Thought and Reality*. Edited by John B. Carroll. Cambridge, MA: MIT Press, 1956.

Whoriskey, Peter. "Community Colleges Are Getting an Education in Tough Economics." *Washington Post* (November 27, 2010):A1, A11.

"Why Population Aging Matters: A Global Perspective." Washington, DC: National Institute on Aging, 2007.

Whyte, William Foote. *Street Corner Society*, 4th ed. Chicago, IL: University of Chicago Press, 1993.

Whyte, William H., Jr. *The Organization Man*. New York: Simon & Schuster, 1972.

Whyte, William H., and Joseph Nocera. *The Organization Man: The Book That Defined a Generation*. Philadelphia, PA: University of Pennsylvania Press, 2002.

Wiehe, Vernon R. *Sibling Abuse*. Lexington, MA: Heath, 1990.

Wiesel, Elie. "The Question of Genocide." *Newsweek* (April 12, 1999):37.

Wieviorka, Michel. *The Arena of Racism*. Newbury Park, CA: Sage, 1995.

Wike, Richard, and Greg Smith. "Little Support for Terrorism Among Muslim Americans." Pew Research Center Publications, December 17, 2006.

Wildavsky, Ben. "Grading on a Curve: A New Controversy Erupts over Race, Class, and SAT Scores." *U.S. News & World Report* (September 13, 1999):53.

Wiley, Norbert. (Ed.). *The Marx-Weber Debate*. Beverly Hills, CA: Sage, 1987.

Wilkins, David E. *American Indian Politics and the American Political System*. Lanham, MD: Rowman & Littlefield, 2001.

Wilkinson, Doris Y. "Gender and Social Inequality: The Prevailing Significance of Race." *Daedalus* 124 (Winter 1995):167–178.

Will, George. "The Nature of Human Nature." *Newsweek* (August 19, 2002):64.

Williams, J. Allen, Joetta A. Vernon, Martha C. Williams, and Karen Malecha. "Sex Role Socialization in Picture Books: An Update." *Social Science Quarterly* 68 (March 1987):148–156.

Williams, John E., and Deborah L. Best. *Measuring Sex Stereotypes*, rev. ed. Newbury Park, CA: Sage, 1990.

Williams, Mary E. *Minorities*. San Diego, CA: Greenhaven Press, 1997.

Williams, Mary E., Karin Swisher, and Brenda Stalcup. (Eds.). *Working Women: Opposing Viewpoints*. San Diego, CA: Greenhaven Press, 1997.

Williams, Robert L. "Scientific Racism and IQ: The Silent Mugging of the Black Community." *Psychology Today* 7 (May 1974):32–41, 101.

Williams, Robin M. Jr. *American Society*, 3rd ed. New York: Knopf, 1970.

Williamson, Elizabeth. "Getting Around the Rules on Lobbying." *Washington Post* (October 14, 2007a).

Williamson, Elizabeth. "Industries Paid for Top Regulators' Travel." *Washington Post* (December 2, 2007b).

Wilson, Bryan. *Religion in Sociological Perspective*. New York: Oxford University Press, 1982.

Wilson, Edward O. *On Human Nature*. Cambridge, MA: Harvard University Press, 1978.

Wilson, Edward O. *Biophilia*. Cambridge, MA: Harvard University Press, 1986.

Wilson, James Q. *The Moral Sense*. New York: Free Press, 1993.

Wilson, James Q. *Political Organizations*. Princeton, NJ: Princeton University Press, 1995.

Wilson, James Q., and Richard J. Herrnstein. *Crime and Human Nature*. New York: Simon & Schuster, 1985.

Wilson, Kenneth L., and W. Allen Martin. "Ethnic Enclaves: A Comparison of the Cuban and Black Economies in Miami." *American Journal of Sociology* 88 (July 1982):135–160.

Wilson, Stephen. *Informal Groups*. Englewood Cliffs, NJ: Prentice Hall, 1978.

Wilson, Thomas C. "Urbanism and Tolerance: A Test of Some Hypotheses Drawn from Wirth and Stouffer." *American Sociological Review* 50 (February 1985):117–123.

Wilson, Thomas C. "Urbanism, Migration, and Tolerance: A Reassessment." *American Sociological Review* 56 (February 1991):117–123.

Wilson, William Julius. *Power, Racism, and Privilege*. New York: Macmillan, 1973.

Wilson, William Julius. *The Declining Significance of Race*, 2nd ed. Chicago: University of Chicago Press, 1980.

Wilson, William Julius. "The Urban Underclass." In Leslie W Dunbar (Ed.), *Minority Report*. New York: Pantheon, 1984, pp. 75–117.

Wilson, William Julius. *The Truly Disadvantaged*. Chicago, IL: University of Chicago Press, 1990.

Wilson, William Julius. "Studying Inner-City Social Dislocations: The Challenge of Public Agenda Research." *American Sociological Review* 56 (February 1991):1–14.

Wilson, William Julius. (Ed.). *The Ghetto Underclass*. Newbury Park, CA: Sage, 1993.

Wilson, William Julius. *When Work Disappears: The World of the New Urban Poor*. New York: Knopf, 1997.

Wilson, William Julius. *Visions of Social Inequality: Race, Class, and Poverty in Urban America*. Lanham, MD: Rowman & Littlefield, 2002.

Wilson, William Julius, et al. "The Ghetto Underclass and the Changing Structure of Urban Poverty." In Fred R. Harris and Roger W. Wilkins (Eds.), *Quiet Riots*. New York: Pantheon, 1988, pp. 123–154.

Wimberley, Ronald C., and James A. Christenson. "Civil Religion and Church and State." *Sociological Quarterly* 21 (Spring 1980):35–40.

Wimberley, Ronald C., Donald A. Clelland, Thomas C. Hood, and C. M. Lipsey. "The Civil Religious Dimension: Is It There?" *Social Forces* 54 (June 1976):890–900.

Wind, James P., and James W. Lewis. (Eds.). *American Congregations*, vol. 2. Chicago, IL: University of Chicago Press, 1994.

Wingert, Pat. "The Sum of Mediocrity." *Newsweek* (December 2, 1996):96.

Wingert, Pat. "The Report Card on Charter Schools." *Newsweek* (July 22, 2002):7.

Winship, Christopher, and Robert D. Mare. "Models for Sample Selection Bias." *Annual Review of Sociology* 18 (1992):327–350.

Wirth, Louis. "Clinical Sociology." *American Journal of Sociology* 37 (July 1931):49–66.

Wirth, Louis. "Urbanism as a Way of Life." *American Journal of Sociology* 44 (July 1938):1–24.

Wirth, Louis. "The Problem of Minority Groups." In Ralph Linton (Ed.), *The Science of Man in the World Crisis*. New York: Columbia University Press, 1945, pp. 347–372.

Wisensale, Steven K. *Family Leave Policy: The Political Economy of Work and Family in America*. Armonk, NY: M. E. Sharpe, 2001.

Witte, John F. *The Market Approach to Education: An Analysis of America's First Voucher Program*. Princeton, NJ: Princeton University Press, 2000.

Wodak, Ruth. (Ed.). *Gender and Discourse*. Thousand Oaks, CA: Sage, 1997.

Wolfe, Alan. "The Moral Meanings of Work." *The American Prospect* (September/October 1997):82–90.

Wolfe, Alan. *One Nation, After All*. New York: Penguin Books, 1999.

Wolfe, Alan. "And the Winners Is. . . ." *The Atlantic* (March 2008):56–63.

Wolraich, Michael. *Blowing Smoke*. Cambridge, MA: Da Capo Press, 2010.

"Women in Elective Office 2010." Center for American Women and Politics. New Brunswick, NJ: Rutgers, 2010.

Wood, Gordon S. *The American Revolution: A History*. New York: The Modern Library, 2003

Wood, James R. *Leadership in Voluntary Organizations*. New Brunswick, NJ: Rutgers University Press, 1981.

Wooden, Wayne S. *Renegade Kids, Suburban Outlaws: From Youth Culture to Delinquency*. Belmont, CA: Wadsworth, 1995.

Woods, Andrew K. "These Revolutions Are Not All Twitter." *New York Times* (February 1, 2011).

World Almanac and Book of Facts 2011, The. New York: World Almanac Education Group Inc, 2011.

World Development Report 1994. New York: Oxford University Press, 1994.

World Development Report 2000/2001: Attacking Poverty. New York: World Bank Publishers, 2000.

World Development Report 2000–2001. New York: Oxford University Press, 2001.

World Development Report 2003: Sustainable Development in a Dynamic World: Transforming Institutions, Growth, and Quality of Life/Edition 1. New York: World Bank Publications, 2002.

World Development Report 2006: Equity and Development/Edition 2006. New York: World Bank Publishers, 2005.

World Development Report: Reshaping Economic Geography/Edition 9 New York: World Bank Publishers 2008.

World of Work Report 2008 — Global Income Inequality Gap Growing" Geneva: International Labour Organization, 2008.

World Population Data Sheet 2010. Washington, DC: Population Reference Bureau, 2010.

World's Women 2010, Trends and Statistics. New York: United Nations Publications, 2010.

"World Without Work." In Robert Staples (Ed.), *The Black Family*. Belmont, CA: Wadsworth, 1999, pp. 291–311.

Wortzel, Larry M. *Class in China*. Westport, CT: Greenwood Press, 1987.

Wray, Herbert. "When Strangers Become Family." *U.S. News and World Report* (November 29, 1999):58–67.

Wright, Charles R. "Functional Analysis and Mass Communication." *Public Opinion Quarterly* 24 (Winter 1960):606–620.

Wright, Erik Olin. *Class Counts*. Cambridge, UK: Cambridge University Press, 2000.

Wright, Lawrence. "Double Mystery." *The New Yorker* (August 7, 1995):45–62.

Wu, Jean Y., and Min Song. (Eds.). *Asian American Studies: A Reader*. Piscataway, NJ: Rutgers University Press, 2000.

Wuthnow, Robert. "Recent Patterns of Secularization: A Problem of Generations?" *American Sociological Review* 41 (October 1976):850–867.

Wuthnow, Robert. *Experimentation in American Religion*. Berkeley, CA: University of California Press, 1978.

Wuthnow, Robert. "Review of All Faithful People." *Society* 22 (March/April 1985):87–88.

Wuthnow, Robert *The Restructuring of American Religion*. Princeton, NJ: Princeton University Press, 1990.

Yang, Fenggang, and Helen Rose Ebaugh. "Transformations in New Immigrant Religions and Their Global Implications." *American Sociological Review* 66 (April 2001):269–288.

Yap, M. T. "Singapore's 'Three or More' Policy: The First Five Years." *Asia-Pacific Population Journal* 10 (1995):39–52.

Yen, Hope. "Revised Formula Counts More Americans in Poverty." *Yahoo News* (2009). http://news.yahoo.com/slap/200909041ap_on_re_us/us_older_americ

Yinger, John. *Closed Doors, Opportunities Lost: The Continuing Costs of Housing Discrimination*. New York: Russell Sage Foundation, 1995.

Yinger, Milton J. "A Structural Examination of Religion." *Journal of the Scientific Study of Religion* 8 (Spring 1969):88–89.

Yinger, Milton J. *The Scientific Study of Religion*. New York: Macmillan, 1970.

Yinger, Milton J., and Stephen J. Cutler. "The Moral Majority Viewed Sociologically." *Sociological Focus* 15 (October 1982):289–306.

Yochelson, Samuel, and Stanton E. Samenow. *The Criminal Personality*, vols. 1 and 2. London: James Aronson, 1994.

Young, Alford A., Jr., and Donald R. Deskins, Jr. "Early Traditions of African-American Sociological Thought." *Annual Review of Sociology* 27 (2001):445–477.

Young, Iris Marion. *Justice and the Politics of Difference*. Princeton, NJ: Princeton University Press, 1990.

Young, Michael. *The Rise of the Meritocracy*. New York: Penguin, 1967.

Young, T. R. "The Sociology of Sport: Structural Marxist and Cultural Marxist Approaches." *Sociological Perspectives* 29 (January 1986):3–28.

Young, T. R. *The Drama of Social Life*. New Brunswick, NJ: Transaction Books, 1990.

Yunker, James A. "A New Statistical Analysis of Capital Punishment Incorporating U.S. Postmoratorium Data." *Social Science Quarterly* 82 (June 2001):297–311.

Zachary, G. Pascal. "Bell Labs Is Gone. Academia Steps In." *New York Times* (December 16, 2007).

Zal, H. Michael. *The Sandwich Generation*. Cambridge, MA: Da Capo Press, 2001.

Zald, Mayer N., and John D. McCarthy. "Introduction." In Mayer N. Zald and John D. McCarthy (Eds.), *Social Movements in an Organizational Society*. New Brunswick, NJ: Transaction Books, 1987.

Zamble, Edward, and Vernon L. Quinsey. *The Criminal Recidivism Process*. New York: Cambridge University Press, 1997.

Zaret, David. "Calvin, Covenant Theology and the Weber Thesis." *British Journal of Sociology* 43 (1992):369–391.

Zborowski, Mark. "Cultural Components in Response to Pain." *Journal of Social Issues* 8 (1952):16–30.

Zborowski, Mark. *People in Pain*. San Francisco, CA: Jossey-Bass, 1969.

Zelditch, Morris, Jr. "Role Differentiation in the Nuclear Family: A Comparative Study." In Talcott Parsons and Robert F. Bales (Eds.), *Family, Socialization and Interaction Process*. New York: Free Press, 1955, pp. 307–352.

Zepezauer, Mark. *Take the Rich off Welfare*, 2nd ed. Cambridge, MA: South End Press, 2004.

Zigler, Edward, and S. Muenchow. *Head Start*. New York: Basic Books, 1992.

Zigler, Edward, and Sally J. Styfco. (Eds.). *Head Start and Beyond*. New Haven, CT: Yale University Press, 1993.

Zimbardo, Philip. *The Lucifer Effect*. New York: Random House Publishing Group, 2008.

Zimbardo, Philip G., S. M. Anderson, and L. G. Kabat. "Induced Hearing Deficit Generates Experimental Paranoia." *Science* (June 26, 1981):1529–1531.

Zimmer, Ron W., Richard J. Buddin, and Derrick Chau. *Charter School Operations and Performance*. Santa Monica, CA: Rand Corporation, 2003.

Zimring, Franklin E. *Contradictions of American Capital Punishment*. New York: Oxford University Press, 2004.

Zinn, Howard. *Declarations of Independence: Cross-Examining American Ideology*. New York: Harper Perennial, 2003.

Zinn, Howard. *A People's History of the United States: 1492–Present*, Deluxe ed. New York: HarperCollins Publishers, 2010.

Zinn, Maxine Baca, D. Stanley Eitzen, and Barbara Wells. *Diversity in Families*. 8th ed. Boston: Allyn and Bacon, 2010.

Zinn, Maxine Baca, Pierrette Hondagneu-Sotelo, and Michael A. Messner. (Eds.), 4th ed. New York: Oxford University Press, 2010.

Zogby, James J. *What Arabs Think: Values, Beliefs, and Concerns*. Utica/Beirut, NY/Lebanon: Zogby International/The Arab Thought Foundation, 2002.

Zola, Irving K. "Culture and Symptoms—An Analysis of Patients Presenting Complaints." *American Sociological Review* 31 (October 1966):615–630.

Zorbaugh, Harvey. *The Gold Coast and the Slum*. Chicago, IL: University of Chicago Press, 1929.

Zucher, Louis A., and David A. Snow. "Collective Behavior: Social Movements." In Morris Rosenberg and Ralph H. Turner (Eds.), *Social Psychology*. New Brunswick, NJ: Transaction Books, 1990, pp. 447–482.

Zuo, J., and S. Tang. "Breadwinner Status and Gender Ideologies of Men and Women Regarding Family Roles." *Sociological Perspectives* 43 (2000):29–43.

Zweig, Michael. *The Working Class Majority: America's Best Kept Secret*. Ithaca, NY: Cornell University Press, 2000.

Zweigenhaft, Richard L., and G. William Domhoff. *Diversity in the Power Elite*, 2nd ed. Lanham, MD: Rowan and Littlefield, 2006.

Zwerling, Craig, and Hilary Silver. "Race and Job Dismissals in a Federal Bureaucracy." *American Sociological Review* 57 (October 1992):651–660.

Name Index

Subject Index